Fundamentals of Law and Regulation

An in-depth look at therapeutic products

■ ■ ■ ■ ■

Volume II

Edited by:
David G. Adams
Richard M. Cooper
Jonathan S. Kahan

FDLI

Contents

General Chapters

Therapeutic Products Chapters

chapter 1

Introduction to Food and Drug Law and Regulation

Richard M. Cooper*

The Focus of the Law

Food and drug law is about certain types of *physical things*. These things are put into or onto, or are used with, the bodies of humans or animals—foods, drugs, medical devices, and cosmetics. The principal requirements and prohibitions of the law are about things— they shall not be adulterated or misbranded; they shall be manufactured and tested in accordance with certain standards; on their labels and in their labeling, certain disclosures must be made, and certain kinds of claims must not be made; certain kinds of things shall not be introduced into interstate commerce until they have been approved by the regulatory agency; and so on.

The principal form of enforcement action is an *in rem* proceeding against physical objects that are in violation of the law.[1] The purpose of that type of action is to protect patients or other consumers from things that may harm or deceive them. To the extent that the food and drug law regulates people and what they do, it regulates them only in relation to the physical things that are within the jurisdiction of the law.

A product within the FDA's jurisdiction (e.g., a drug or food additive) is discovered or invented after substantial research. It undergoes a developmental process that includes testing in a laboratory and then in animals and humans, creation and validation of processes for manufacturing and quality control, and development of labeling that sets forth conditions of use; it then goes through an approval process at the Food and Drug Admdinistration (FDA), and is approved; and then, on a continuing basis, it is manufactured in packaged and labeled form, is advertised and promoted, and is shipped commercially. During its life on the market, the product is from time to time the subject of reports of

---

* Mr. Cooper is a Partner in the law firm of Williams & Connolly, Washington, D.C.

[1] Federal Food, Drug, and Cosmetic Act (FDCA) § 304, 21 U.S.C. § 334 (1994). Thus, in fiscal 1994, of the 122 judicial enforcement actions initiated under FDCA, 98 were seizures directed against things and 24 were injunctions or prosecutions against people or organizations. FOOD AND DRUG ADMIN., QUARTERLY ACTIVITIES REPORT: FOURTH QUARTER, FISCAL YEAR 1994 app. 2, 3, at 33, 34 (1995).

adverse reactions in consumers and consumer complaints are received. Food and drug law and regulation addresses most stages of this product history.

This focus on physical things sets the framework for regulation by the FDA. The agency's most labor-intensive activities are: 1) the review of data submitted in support of applications for approval or clearance of new products or ingredients for use in products, and for changes with respect to already marketed products; and 2) inspections of factories and goods offered for importation, and testing of samples obtained in such inspections.

The economic value of the products regulated by the FDA amounts to more than a trillion dollars per year,[2] twenty-five percent of American consumer spending.[3]

A Little History

Although there were antecedents in the nineteenth century in America and even earlier in England,[4] the modern history of food and drug regulation begins with the Pure Food and Drugs Act of 1906.[5] The legislation, which had long been championed by Dr. Harvey W. Wiley, Chief Chemist of the U.S. Department of Agriculture (USDA),[6] finally resulted from the sensational disclosures by the muckrakers of corruption, fraud, and improper conditions in many areas of economic activity, including food processing.[7]

The law specified conditions under which foods and drugs would be adulterated or misbranded, and authorized the Division of Chemistry to recommend enforcement actions to the U.S. Department of Justice (DOJ). The law did not provide for governmental review of products prior to their marketing, and was limited in other ways.

---

[2] *Hearings on Agriculture, Rural Development, Food and Drug Administration, and Related Agencies Appropriations for 1996 Before a Subcomm. of the House Comm. on Appropriations*, 104th Cong., 1st Sess. 380 (1995) [hereinafter *Hearing on 1996 FDA Appropriation*] (statement of David A. Kessler, Commissioner of Food and Drugs).

[3] FOOD & DRUG ADMIN., THE FDA ALMANAC: FISCAL YEAR 1994, at 2 (1994).

[4] *See, e.g.*, Peter Barton Hutt, *The Basis and Purpose of Government Regulation of Adulteration and Misbranding of Food*, 33 FOOD DRUG COSM. L.J. 505, 506-09 (1978); PETER BARTON HUTT & RICHARD A. MERRILL, FOOD & DRUG LAW, CASES AND MATERIALS 378-80 (2d ed. 1991).

[5] Pub. L. No. 59-384, 34 Stat. 768 (1906). Congress previously had enacted legislation to regulate products of biological origin. Pub. L. No. 57-244, 32 Stat. 728 (1902).

[6] Dr. Wiley is considered the father of food and drug law. He was the first administrator of the law, from its enactment in 1906 until his retirement in 1912. FDA ALMANAC, *supra* note 3, at 73.

[7] GEORGE E. MOWRY, THE ERA OF THEODORE ROOSEVELT 206-08 (1958); C.C. Regier, *The Struggle for Federal Food and Drugs Legislation*, 1 LAW & CONTEMP. PROBS. 3 (1933); COMMERCE CLEARING HOUSE, HISTORIC MEETING TO COMMEMORATE FORTIETH ANNIVERSARY OF ORIGINAL FEDERAL FOOD AND DRUGS ACT (1946).

The phenomenon of enacting food and drug legislation in response to a public health disaster (perceived as resulting from a lack of adequate regulation) was repeated in 1938, when the modern food and drug statute was enacted; in 1962, when major amendments to the drug law were enacted; and in 1976, when major amendments to the device law were enacted.

Many of the recognized defects were remedied by the Federal Food, Drug, and Cosmetic Act (FDCA), enacted in 1938.[8] This statute greatly expanded the FDA's authority by providing for premarket review of drugs under a requirement of safety, for standards of identity and quality for foods, for regulation of medical devices and cosmetics, and for inspections by the FDA employees. This statute remains the basic food and drug law, and it has been amended many, many times, in most instances in ways that expand and strengthen the regulatory scheme.

The principal amendments have been the following:

- A series of amendments providing for regulation of insulin and various antibiotics.[9]
- The Miller Act, which added section 301(k) and correspondingly amended section 304(a) to the FDCA.[10]
- The Durham-Humphrey Act, which amended section 503(b) of FDCA, putting a prescription requirement on a statutory basis.[11]
- Pub. L. No. 83-217, which strengthened the FDA's inspection authority.[12]
- The Food Additives Amendment of 1958.[13]
- The Color Additive Amendments of 1960.[14]
- The Drug Amendments of 1962.[15]
- The Animal Drug Amendments of 1968.[16]
- The Drug Listing Act of 1972.[17]
- The Medical Device Amendments of 1976.[18]
- The Vitamin and Mineral Amendments.[19]
- The Orphan Drug Act.[20]
- The Drug Price Competition and Patent Term Restoration Act of 1984 (Waxman-Hatch Act).[21]
- The Drug Export Amendments of 1986.[22]
- The Prescription Drug Marketing Act of 1987.[23]

---

[8]   Pub. L. No. 75-717, 52 Stat. 1040 (1938), as amended 21 U.S.C. §§ 301 et seq.

[9]   Pub. L. No. 77-366, 55 Stat. 851 (1941) (insulin); Pub. L. No. 79-139, 59 Stat. 463 (1945) (penicillin); Pub. L. No. 90-16, 61 Stat. 11 (1947) (streptomycin); Pub. L. No. 81-164, 63 Stat. 409 (1949) (aureomycin, chloramphenicol, bacitracin); Pub. L. No. 83-201, 67 Stat. 389 (1953) (chlortetracycline).

[10] Pub. L. No. 80-749, 62 Stat. 582 (1948).

[11] Pub. L. No. 82-215, 65 Stat. 648 (1951).

[12] 67 Stat. 476 (1953).

[13] Pub. L. No. 85-929, 72 Stat. 1784 (1958) (codified at 21 U.S.C. § 348).

[14] Pub. L. No. 86-618, 74 Stat. 397 (1960) (codified at 21 U.S.C. § 376).

[15] Pub. L. No.87-781, 76 Stat. 780 (1962).

[16] Pub. L. No. 90-399, 82 Stat. 342 (1968) (codified at 21 U.S.C. § 382).

[17] Pub. L. No. 92-387, 86 Stat. 559 (1972).

[18] Pub. L. No. 94-295, 90 Stat. 539 (1976).

[19] Pub. L. No. 94-278, 90 Stat. 401, 410-13 (1976).

[20] Pub. L. No. 97-414, 96 Stat. 2049 (1983). This legislation has been subsequently amended.

[21] Pub. L. No. 98-417, 98 Stat. 1585 (1984).

[22] Pub. L. No. 99-660, 100 Stat. 3743 (1986) (codified at 21 U.S.C. § 382 and 42 U.S.C. § 262 (1994)).

[23] Pub. L. No. 100-293, 102 Stat. 95 (1988). This legislation has been subsequently amended.

- The Food and Drug Administration Act of 1988 (statutory establishment of the FDA).[24]
- The Generic Animal Drug and Patent Term Restoration Act.[25]
- The Nutrition Labeling and Education Act of 1990.[26]
- The Safe Medical Devices Act of 1990.[27]
- The Generic Drug Enforcement Act of 1992.[28]
- The Medical Device Amendments of 1992.[29]
- The Prescription Drug User Fee Act.[30]
- The Animal Medicinal Drug Use Clarification Act of 1994.[31]
- The Dietary Supplement Health and Education Act of 1994.[32]

The FDA's Place in the Government

The FDA is, and always has been, an agency in the executive branch.[33] Therefore, its budget, legislative proposals, congressional testimony, and major regulatory proposals are subject to approval by the Office of Management and Budget (OMB) on behalf of the President.

Like other executive branch agencies, the FDA is subject to a wide variety of executive orders issued by the President.[34] It is also subject to general statutes that bear on its regulatory activities.[35]

Also like other agencies in the executive branch, the FDA has no authority to represent itself in court, but is represented by the DOJ.[36] All litigation—civil and criminal—involving the agency and including litigation brought against the agency, is supervised on behalf of the agency by the Office of Consumer Litigation in the Civil Division of the DOJ. In

---

[24] Health Omnibus Programs Extension of 1988, Pub. L. No. 100-607, tit. V, 102 Stat. 3048, 3120.

[25] Pub. L. No. 100-670, 102 Stat. 3971 (1988).

[26] Pub. L. No. 101-535, 104 Stat. 2353 (1990). This legislation has been subsequently amended.

[27] Pub. L. No. 101-629, 104 Stat. 4511 (1990).

[28] Pub. L. No. 102-282, 106 Stat. 149 (1992).

[29] Pub. L. No. 102-300, 106 Stat. 238 (1992).

[30] Pub. L. No. 102-571, 106 Stat. 4491 (1992).

[31] Pub. L. No. 103-396, 108 Stat. 4153 (1994).

[32] Pub. L. No. 103-417, 108 Stat. 4325 (1994).

[33] By contrast, the Federal Trade Commission and the Consumer Product Safety Commission, for example, are independent agencies.

[34] *See, e.g.*, Exec. Order No. 12,866, 3 C.F.R. 638 (1994) (cost-benefit analysis); Exec. Order No. 12,612, 3 C.F.R. 252 (1988) (federalism); Exec. Order No. 12,630, 3 C.F.R. 554 (1989) (obligations under the Just Compensation Clause of the Fifth Amendment).

[35] *E.g.*, Paperwork Reduction Act of 1995, Pub. L. No. 104-13, 109 Stat. 163 (1995) (to be codified at 44 U.S.C. §§ 3501-3520); Unfunded Mandates Reform Act, Pub. L. No. 104-4, 109 Stat. 48 (1995) (to be codified at 2 U.S.C. §§ 1501-1571); Regulatory Flexibility Act, Pub. L. No. 96-354, 94 Stat. 1164 (1980); National Environmental Policy Act of 1969, Pub. L. No. 91-190, 83 Stat. 852 (1969) (codified at 42 U.S.C. §§ 4321-4370d (1994)).

[36] The agency is also bound by opinions of the Attorney General.

practice, responsibility for the actual conduct of litigation on behalf of the agency is divided between the Office of Consumer Litigation and the Offices of United States Attorneys throughout the country. In general, the DOJ permits lawyers in the FDA's Office of Chief Counsel to assist in the representation of the agency in litigation.

The FDA originated as the Bureau of Chemistry in the USDA before the enactment of the Pure Food and Drugs Act of 1906.[37] The agency remained part of the USDA (under various names) until 1940, when it was transferred to the Federal Security Agency, which later became the Department of Health, Education and Welfare, and then the Department of Health and Human Services (DHHS). Within DHHS, the FDA is part of the Public Health Service, which is headed by the Assistant Secretary for Health.[38] The agency was first recognized by statute in 1988.[39]

As a part of DHHS, the FDA is subject to oversight by the Department on the same matters as to which it is subject to oversight by OMB. The FDA is subject to review by DHHS of other important actions, including certain types of regulatory actions,[40] reorganizations, and important personnel actions. From time to time, issues of integrity or efficiency with respect to the FDA have been investigated by DHHS' Office of Inspector General.

Although not legally independent, the FDA is culturally independent of DHHS. The FDA's principal offices are located in Rockville, Maryland — a substantial distance from DHHS' headquarters near the U.S. Capitol in Washington, D.C. The agency perceives its statutory and regulatory systems as complex and highly technical, and its expertise in administering them as unmatched by any group outside the agency. The FDA has a long history of deferring to superior legal authority only to the extent necessary, and of acting as independently as circumstances permit.

The FDA and Congress

Despite the movement of the FDA from the USDA to DHHS, the FDA's annual appropriation is still part of the agricultural appropriations process, and is reviewed and determined by the Agricultural Subcommittees of the House and Senate Appropriations Committees. The FDA's authorizing committees are the Senate Committee on Labor and Human Resources and the House of Representative's Committee on Energy and Commerce. Within the latter, the Subcommittee on Oversight and Investigations and the Subcommittee

---

[37] The Bureau of Chemistry began in 1862 with President Lincoln's appointment of a chemist in the Department of Agriculture. FDA ALMANAC, *supra* note 3, at 72. The name "Food and Drug Administration" first officially appeared in the Agricultural Appropriation Act of 1931, Pub. L. No. 71-272, 46 Stat. 392 (1930).

[38] The other agencies in the Public Health Service are the Centers for Disease Control, the National Institutes of Health, the Health Resources and Services Administration, the Office of the Surgeon General, the Office of Disease Prevention and Health Promotion, the Substance Abuse and Mental Health Services Administration, the Indian Health Service, the Office of International Health, the Office of Minority Health, the Agency for Health Care Policy and Research, and the Agency for Toxic Substance and Disease Registry.

[39] *See supra* note 23.

[40] *See infra* note 55 and accompanying text.

on Health and the Environment historically have taken a strong interest in the agency. From time to time, other committees also have conducted hearings relating to the FDA.

The FDA frequently has been the subject of reports issued by congressional committees and by the General Accounting Office.[41]

The FDA's Statutory Authorities

The FDA administers the Federal Food, Drug, and Cosmetic Act, certain provisions of the Public Health Service Act,[42] the Filled Milk Act,[43] the Federal Import Milk Act,[44] the Tea Importation Act,[45] the Saccharin Study and Labeling Act,[46] and certain laws relating to controlled substances and drug abuse,[47] and has important functions under the Federal Caustic Poison Act,[48] the Lead-Based Paint Poisoning Prevention Act,[49] and the Fair Packaging and Labeling Act.[50] The agency also has certain functions under statutes administered principally by the USDA.[51] The functions that the FDA performs under statutes other than the FDCA are ancillary to its functions under the FDCA.[52]

All authority exercised by the FDA is derived from congressional delegations to the Secretary of Health and Human Services, and redelegations by the Secretary to the Assistant Secretary for Health, and by the Assistant Secretary to the Commissioner of Food and Drugs.[53] The FDA has no independent statutory authority delegated directly to it by Congress.

Moreover, despite the broad delegations by the Secretary and Assistant Secretary to the Commissioner, the Secretary of DHHS in 1982[54] reserved authority to approve regulations promulgated by the FDA that:

---

[41] *See* Peter Barton Hutt, *Investigations and Reports on the Food and Drug Administration,* in SEVENTY-FIFTH ANNIVERSARY COMMEMORATIVE VOLUME OF FOOD AND DRUG LAW 27-71 (FDLI 1984).

[42] The provisions are specified in 21 C.F.R. § 5.10(a) (1996).

[43] 21 U.S.C. §§ 61-64.

[44] *Id.* §§ 141 et seq. *See also Hearing on 1996 the FDA Appropriation, supra* note 2, at 560.

[45] *Id.* §§ 41 et seq. This statute was enacted in 1897 and thus antedated the FDCA. Pub. L. No. 54-358, 29 Stat. 604 (1897).This Act was repealed in 1996.

[46] Pub. L. No. 95-203, 91 Stat. 1451 (1977). This statute subsequently has been amended.

[47] Comprehensive Drug Abuse Prevention and Control Act of 1970, Pub. L. No. 91-513, tit. I, § 4, 84 Stat. 1236, 1241 (1970); Controlled Substances Act, Pub. L. No. 91-513, tit. II, § 303(f), 84 Stat. 1236, 1255 (1970) (codified at 21 U.S.C. § 823(f)).

[48] Pub. L. No. 69-783, 44 Stat. 1406 (1927). *See also* Note to 15 U.S.C. §§ 401-411.

[49] Pub. L. No. 91-695, tit. IV, § 401, 84 Stat. 2078, 2079 (1971), *as amended by* Pub. L. No. 94-317, tit. II, 90 Stat. 695, 705 (1976) (codified at 42 U.S.C. § 4831(a) (1994)).

[50] 15 U.S.C. §§ 1451 et seq. For information on the FDA's activities under the statute, see*Hearing on 1996 FDA Appropriation, supra* note 2, at 558-60.

[51] Federal Meat Inspection Act § 409(b), 21 U.S.C. § 679(b); Poultry Products Inspection Act § 24(b), 21 U.S.C. § 467f(b); Egg Products Inspection Act, 21 U.S.C. § 1031 et seq.

[52] A complete list of the statutes administered or implemented by the FDA appears in 21 C.F.R. § 5.10.

[53] 21 C.F.R. § 5.10.

[54] 47 Fed. Reg. 16,318 (1982).

(1) [e]stablish procedural rules applicable to a general class of foods, drugs, cosmetics, medical devices, or other subjects of regulation; or

(2) [p]resent highly significant public issues involving the quality, availability, marketability, or cost of one or more foods, drugs, cosmetics, medical devices, or other subjects of regulation.[55]

This reservation of authority was not intended to create any private right or benefit,[56] although, as a practical matter, it does invite lobbying at the Department with respect to regulations to which it applies.

The FDA's Internal Organization

The head of the FDA is a single Commissioner,[57] who under a statute enacted in 1988, is appointed by the President with the advice and consent of the Senate.[58] There are four Deputy Commissioners: Operations, Management and Systems, External Affairs, and Policy.[59]

Reporting to the Deputy Commissioner for Operations are the Office of the Associate Commissioner for Regulatory Affairs (which oversees agency-wide regulatory matters, agency-wide compliance and enforcement activities, and the agency's field operations), the Office of Biotechnology, the Office of Orphan Product Development, the National Center for Toxicological Research, and the agency's five operating Centers (Food Safety and Applied Nutrition (which also regulates cosmetics), Drug Evaluation and Research, Biologics Evaluation and Research, Devices and Radiological Health, and Veterinary Medicine). This is the heart of the agency.

The Deputy Commissioner for Management and Systems oversees general agency management, planning and evaluation, and information resources.

The Deputy Commissioner for External Affairs oversees legislative, public (i.e., press), health (i.e., relations with medical groups), and consumer affairs, and offices that deal with women's health and with AIDS and special health issues.

Reporting to the Deputy Commissioner for Policy are policy development and management staffs, a policy research staff, and the international policy staff. As the FDA's involvement in international harmonization of regulatory standards increases, so, too, does the importance of this last office.

---

[55] 21 C.F.R. § 5.11(a).

[56] *Id.* § 5.11(c).

[57] There is no corresponding commission.

[58] FDCA, § 903(b), 21 U.S.C. § 393(b); s ee *supra* note 24. Previously, the Commissioner had been appointed by the Secretary of DHHS, without Senate confirmation.

[59] The current organization of the FDA was designed by Commissioner David Kessler. Prior organizational structures are described in Michael Brannon, *Organizing and Reorganizing the FDA*, in SEVENTY-FIFTH ANNIVERSARY COMMEMORATIVE VOLUME, *supra* note 41, at 135 (1984).

The FDA's Office of Chief Counsel is, technically, part of the Office of the General Counsel of the DHHS, which, in turn, is part of the Office of the Secretary of DHHS.[60]

The FDA uses thirty-two advisory committees — principally for drugs, biological products, foods, and devices.[61]

In fiscal year 1994, the FDA had approximately 9500 employees.[62] Approximately one-third of those employees worked in FDA field offices,[63] which then consisted of 6 regional offices, 21 district offices,[64] 18 laboratories,[65] and 130 resident inspection posts.[66] The FDA's headquarters are located in Rockville, Maryland; within the Washington, D.C., area, the agency has offices in more than forty buildings in over twenty locations.[67]

The agency's total appropriation for FY 1994 was approximately $929,000,000.[68] Its appropriation for FY 1995 was approximately $970,000,000.[69] Its appropriation for FY 1996 is $963,000,000.[70]

The FDA's internal delegations of authority are set forth in sections 5.20 through 5.94 of title 21 of the *Code of Federal Regulations*. The agency's internal organization is set forth in sections 5.100 through 5.105 of that same title.

An Overview of the Federal Food, Drug, and Cosmetic Act

The FDA's organic statute, the FDCA, is organized into nine chapters:

*   short title,
*   definitions,
*   prohibited acts and penalties,
*   food,
*   drugs and devices,

---

[60] *See* 21 C.F.R. § 5.105; U.S GOVERNMENT MANUAL 281 (1995/1996).

[61] *Hearing on 1996 FDA Appropriation, supra* note 2, at 511-14. On FDA advisory committees generally, *see id.* at 612-13.

[62] FOOD & DRUG ADMIN., QUARTERLY ACTIVITIES REPORT: FIRST QUARTER, FISCAL YEAR 1995, at 42 (1995).

[63] FDA ALMANAC, *supra* note 3, at 13.

[64] The district offices are located in the following metropolitan areas: New York City, Boston, and Buffalo (Northeast Region); Philadelphia, Baltimore, Cincinnati, and Newark (Mid-Atlantic Region); Atlanta, Nashville, New Orleans, Orlando, and San Juan (Southeast Region); Chicago, Detroit, and Minneapolis (Midwest region); Dallas, Denver, Kansas City, and St. Louis (Southwest Region); and San Francisco, Los Angeles, and Seattle (Pacific Region). 21 C.F.R. § 5.115.

[65] The 18 laboratories are scheduled to be reduced to 9. *Hearing on 1996 Appropriation, supra* note 2, at 423, 562-65.

[66] *Id.* at 441.

[67] *Id.* at 449.

[68] *Id.* at 788.

[69] *Id.*

[70] Agriculture, Rural Development, FDA, and Related Agencies Appropriations Act of 1996, Pub. L. No. 104-37, 109 Stat. 299 (1995).

- cosmetics,
- general administrative provisions,
- imports and exports, and
- miscellaneous.

The statute is codified in title 21 of the *United States Code*. The critical terms of the statute are defined in section 201.[71] Among the terms defined are the jurisdictional terms ("food," "drug," "device," and "cosmetic"), and other terms critical to the operation of the statute (e.g., "interstate commerce," "label" and "labeling," "new drug," "food additive," and "color additive"). Section 201(u) specifies that, for purposes of food additives, animal drugs, and color additives, the term "safe" refers to "the health of man or animal;" but the statute contains no general definition of "safe" or "safety," and consequently the definitions of those terms for particular regulatory purposes must be derived from other legal and regulatory materials.

The general strategy of the statute consists of three steps. First, the statute specifies circumstances in which an article (food, drug, device, or cosmetic) is "adulterated" or "misbranded,"[72] or lacks a required approval.[73] Second, the statute defines a set of prohibited acts with respect to such an article.[74] Third, in sections 302 through 310, the statute authorizes a set of enforcement actions in response to a prohibited act.[75] With respect to food, drugs, and devices, the adulteration and misbranding provisions use terms elaborated on in other substantive provisions of the statute, located in chapter 4 (food) and chapter 5 (drugs and devices). Under FDCA section 701(a), the FDA has exercised general authority to elaborate by regulation the statutory standards for adulteration and misbranding, and those for approvals of products.[76]

Section 301 prohibits certain acts with respect to an article that is adulterated or misbranded. For example, section 301(a) declares it a prohibited act to introduce such an article into interstate commerce.[77] Similarly, section 301(d) directly (i.e., without reference to adulteration or misbranding) prohibits the introduction into interstate commerce of any new drug violating the approval requirement of section 505 and of any food subject to section 404 that is violating a permit requirement under that section.

Under section 304, an article that was adulterated or misbranded when introduced into interstate commerce is subject to seizure. Commission of prohibited acts may be enjoined under section 302, and may be the basis for a criminal prosecution under section 303. All

---

[71] 21 U.S.C. § 321.

[72] *See* FDCA §§ 402 (adulterated food), 403 (misbranded food), 501 (adulterated drugs and devices), 502 (misbranded drugs and devices), 601 (adulterated cosmetics), 602 (misbranded cosmetics), 21 U.S.C. §§ 342, 343, 351, 352, 361, 362 (1994).

[73] *See id.* §§ 404 (emergency permit control for certain foods), 505 (new drugs for human use), 21 U.S.C. §§ 344, 355. Other requirements for approval operate through the adulteration provisions. *Id.* §§ 409 (food additives), 512 (new animal drugs), 515 (class III devices), 721 (color additives), 21 U.S.C. §§ 348, 360b, 360e, 379e.

[74] 21 U.S.C. § 331.

[75] *Id.* §§ 332-37. Certain additional, administrative enforcement actions are authorized in substantive provisions of the statute. For example, FDCA § 505(e), 21 U.S.C. § 355(e), authorizes withdrawal of approval of a new drug application on certain specified grounds.

[76] *Id.* § 371(a).

[77] *Id.* § 331(a).

of the prohibited acts with respect to food, drugs, devices, and cosmetics are collected in section 301; additional prohibited acts with respect to radiation-emitting electronic products are set forth in section 538.[78]

The FDA's Mission

The FDA has stated its mission as follows:

> The Food and Drug Administration is a team of dedicated professionals working to protect, promote and enhance the health of the American people. The FDA is responsible for ensuring that:
>
> * Foods are safe, wholesome and sanitary; human and veterinary drugs, biological products, and medical devices are safe and effective; cosmetics are safe; and electronic products that emit radiation are safe.
> * Regulated products are honestly, accurately and informatively represented.
> * These products are in compliance with the law and the FDA regulations; noncompliance is identified and corrected; and any unsafe or unlawful products are removed from the marketplace.

The FDA strives to:

* Enforce the FDA laws and regulations, using all appropriate legal means.
* Base regulatory decisions on a strong scientific and analytical base and the law; and understand, conduct and apply excellent science and research.
* Be a positive force in making safe and effective products available to the consumer, and focus special attention on rare and life-threatening diseases.
* Provide clear standards of compliance to regulated industry, and advise industry on how to meet those standards.
* Identify and effectively address critical public health problems arising from use of the FDA-regulated products.
* Increase the FDA's effectiveness through collaboration and cooperation with state and local governments; domestic, foreign and international agencies; industry; and academia.
* Assist the media, consumer groups, and health professionals in providing accurate, current information about regulated products to the public.
* Work consistently toward effective and efficient application of resources to our responsibilities.
* Provide superior public service by developing, maintaining and supporting a high-quality, diverse work force.

---

[78] *Id.* § 360oo. The FDA originally regulated radiation-emitting electronic products under the Radiation Control for Health and Safety Act, Pub. L. No. 90-602, 82 Stat. 1173 (1968), which was originally codified as part of the Public Health Service Act. These provisions were recodified as sections 531 through 542 of the FDCA, 21 U.S.C. §§ 360hh-360ss, by Pub. L. No. 101-629, § 19(3), (4), 104 Stat. 4511, 4529-30 (1990). Responsibility for administration of this statute was transferred to the FDA by 36 Fed. Reg. 12,803 (1971).

- Be honest, fair and accountable in all of our actions and decisions.[79]

During the 1990s, the FDA has emphasized strong enforcement more than it did during the 1980s.[80] Despite the FDA's explicit inclusion of promotion and enhancement, as well as protection, of health in its official statement of mission, the agency's concept and implementation of its mission are controversial. An example of the mindset that raises the concern is the FDA's statement of purpose in its budgetary submission to Congress:

> The Food and Drug Administration (the FDA) is the principal consumer protection agency of the Federal Government. The FDA's goal is to protect the public health through the prevention of injury or illness due to unsafe or ineffective products.[81]

Some trade groups have proposed that the FDA's mission be redefined by Congress so that the FDA will view itself as principally a health-promotion rather than a law-enforcement agency, so that the FDA will place relatively greater emphasis on approvals of new products and relatively less emphasis on enforcement of statutory and regulatory requirements.

The FDA's International Activities

Under chapter 8 of the FDCA, the FDA long has had responsibilities with respect to import and export of articles within its jurisdiction. In connection with imports, the FDA, in cooperation with the U.S. Customs Service, conducts inspections of foreign goods presented for entry into the United States; the agency also inspects foreign facilities that manufacture or process goods for importation into the United States.[82] In connection with exports, the agency reviews applications for export approval where required,[83] and from time-to-time monitors exports in other circumstances.[84] The agency also has active programs to achieve harmonization of its regulatory requirements with those of other countries with sophisticated regulatory systems.[85]

Food and Drug Law and Regulation, and Medicine

Although food and drug law and regulation applies to articles that affect health and to arti-

---

[79] FDA ALMANAC, *supra* note 3, at 11.

[80] *Hearing on 1996 Appropriation*, *supra* note 2, at 692-93.

[81] *Id.* at 822.

[82] *See, e.g., id.* at 412-14, 415-16, 450, 453-61, 467-68, 503, 560, 561-62, 576, 598, 600-02, 625-26, 731, 776-77, 786.

[83] *See* FDCA §§ 801(e)(2), 802; 21 U.S.C. §§ 381(e)(2), 382.

[84] *See, e.g., Hearing on 1996 Appropriation, supra* note 2, at 452.

[85] *See, e.g.,* FDA ALMANAC, *supra* note 3, at 54; *Hearing on 1996 Appropriation, supra* note 2, at 572-75, 617, 639-62.

cles that are used to protect, promote, and restore health, they do not apply directly to the practice of medicine. Thus, the FDA does not regulate physicians or other providers of health care. Such regulation is carried out by professional societies and agencies acting under state law.

Food and drug law and regulation do impinge on the practice of the healing arts. The FDA's regulation of drugs, medical devices, and medical foods determines their availability to practitioners and patients. The FDA's prescribed labeling for such products influences the ways they are used. As a matter of food and drug law and regulation, practitioners are free to use such products outside the conditions stated in their labeling,[86] but they are responsible for such use under state law. Thus, for example, the FDA regulates devices used in surgical and other medical procedures, but does not regulate the procedures themselves; and physicians are free to use such devices in ways not recommended in their FDA-approved labeling.

The FDA does regulate clinical trials conducted on unapproved drugs and devices, and clinical trials intended to be submitted to the agency in support of a product approval.[87] When practitioners participate in such trials, they subject their participation to FDA regulation.

Physicians and other health-care practitioners play significant roles in the FDA's activities. In recent decades, FDA Commissioners have been physicians or have had related academic credentials. Many senior and other officials of the FDA, particularly those responsible for reviews of new products, are physicians. The FDA's advisory committees, whose advice the agency usually accepts, consist principally of physicians, most with academic appointments. Moreover, physicians design, oversee, and conduct virtually all of the clinical research on which the FDA regulatory decisions about specific products are based.

The FDA maintains an active liaison with health professional organizations through the Office of Health Affairs, part of the Office of the Commissioner.

State Regulation of Foods and Drugs

Most states have food and drug laws that are similar to the FDCA. States regulate intrastate products and activities, and work cooperatively with the FDA on matters of mutual interest. State Attorneys General from time to time, also have taken enforcement action with respect to matters within the general area of food and drug law and regulation.

---

[86]   37 Fed. Reg. 16,503 (Aug. 15, 1972); *Use of Approved Drugs for Unlabeled Indications*, 12 FDA DRUG BULL. 4
      (1982); 48 Fed. Reg. 26,720, 26,733 (1983).

[87]   21 C.F.R. pts. 50, 56, 312, 812.

chapter 2

Administrative Procedures of the Food and Drug Administration

Joel E. Hoffman*

Introduction

The administrative procedures of the Food and Drug Administration (FDA) have undergone a fundamental transformation in the ninety years since the old Bureau of Chemistry in the Department of Agriculture was put in charge of the Pure Food and Drugs Act of 1906.[1] Beginning as a police agency devoted to detection and (through the Department of Justice) court prosecution of statutory violations, the FDA has become a direct regulator of industry through issuance of substantive rules, screening of new products for safety and effectiveness prior to marketing, and adjudication of a broad range of formal and informal proceedings subject only to limited review by the courts. The nature of this transformation and the FDA's concurrent evolution of procedural techniques for carrying out its new role are the subject of this chapter.

---

* Mr. Hoffman is a Partner is the law firm of Sutherland, Asbill & Brennan, Washington, D.C.

[1] The 1906 statute named the Secretary of Agriculture as the officer responsible for its enforcement. Pub. L. No. 59-384, 34 Stat. 768 (1906). Until 1988, the FDA's authority was solely a matter of discretionary secretarial delegation. Initially, the Secretary delegated authority to the Bureau of Chemistry in the Department of Agriculture. In 1927 the Bureau of Chemistry was renamed the Food, Drug and Insecticide Administration, which was shortened in 1930 to the Food and Drug Administration. The FDA remained in the Department of Agriculture until 1940, when it and its functions — including those deriving from the Federal Food, Drug, and Cosmetic Act of 1938 — were transferred to the Federal Security Agency (FSA). Presidential Reorganization Plan IV, § 12, 54 Stat. 1237 (1940), pursuant to 53 Stat. 561 (1939). The functions and agencies of the FSA became part of the Department of Health, Education and Welfare (HEW) in 1953. Presidential Reorganization Plan I, pursuant to 63 Stat. 203 (1949). HEW was renamed the Department of Health and Human Services (DHHS) in 1979. Pub. L. No. 96-88, § 508, 93 Stat. 692 (1979). Even today, the official who is statutorily responsible is the Cabinet-level Secretary of DHHS.

For many years, bills were introduced in Congress to put the FDA on its own statutory footing and to confer authority directly on the agency, but all failed in the face of opposition from the executive branch. In the Food and Drug Administration Act of 1988, however, the conflict was resolved by establishing the FDA as a statutory agency within DHHS, headed by a presidentially-appointed Commissioner of Food and Drugs subject to Senate confirmation, and directing the DHHS Secretary to execute the 1938 Act "through the Commissioner." Pub. L. No. 100-607, § 503(a), 102 Stat. 3121 (1988), as amended 21 U.S.C. § 393 (1994).

The 1906 Act: The FDA as Police Officer

The FDA's functions under the 1906 Act seem primitive compared to the agency's current activities. But the food and drug industry practices sought to be controlled by the Act were thought to be so blatantly abusive that a tough criminal statute was deemed both necessary and sufficient.[2]

The political pressures that gave rise to the 1906 Act resulted in large part from the nation's transition from an agricultural to an industrial society. City dwellers, unable to grow or control their own food supply, had to depend on the marketplace to assure quality and quantity. The marketplace proved to be an inadequate regulator, however, as food of poor and uneven quality and drugs of little or no therapeutic value flooded the markets. For example, a study by the Food Commissioner of North Dakota found that cans of "potted chicken" or "potted turkey" contained no chicken or turkey in determinable quantities, and that the amount of boracic acid used in sausages or hamburger was five to ten times the daily medical dose.[3]

State laws also were proving inadequate to protect the public against substandard food and drugs. Statutes at that time sought to prevent the retail sale of adulterated or misbranded drugs by making acts of adulteration criminal offenses.[4] Individual state regulation, however, created uncertainty because of differing standards from one jurisdiction to another. The most important flaw was perhaps the states' inability to control the flow of impure food or drugs in interstate commerce. Although a state could prohibit sale of impure goods within its borders, it generally was regarded as powerless against goods processed in another state and shipped in unbroken packages.[5]

Thus, the need for national legislation gradually became clear, despite troubling questions over the appropriate scope of federal regulation. The primary concern centered around the constitutional authority for federal regulation of food and drugs. Some members of Congress questioned the constitutional basis for — as they viewed it — extending federal police power into the states.[6] To avoid this problem, the 1906 Act did not seek to regulate directly the adulteration or misbranding of food and drugs, but instead prohibited the shipment or delivery in interstate commerce of adulterated or misbranded goods.[7] The Constitution aside, moreover, there was resistance on policy grounds to authorizing intrusion by the federal government into putatively local — indeed, purely "private" — activities such as food processing and drug manufacturing. In debating the proposed measure, one member of Congress characterized the statute as "sumptuary legislation for the regulation of the table menu [with the next step being] to prescribe table etiquette and dress."[8]

---

2   C.C. Regier, *The Struggle for Federal Food and Drug Legislation*, 1 LAW & CONTEMP. PROBS. 3 (1933). Illustrative of public opinion at the time are numerous muckraking articles published by *Collier's Weekly* in 1905 and 1906 exposing the practices of the food and drug industry.

3   *Id.* at 7-8.

4   Fisher, *The Proposed Food and Drug Act: A Legal Critique*, 1 LAW & CONTEMP. PROBS. 74, 76-77 (1933).

5   Regier, *supra* note 2, at 10. Regulation of these goods, it was thought, would run afoul of the constitutional prohibition against unreasonable interference by the states with interstate commerce.

6   *See, e.g.*, 40 CONG. REC. 8910-15 (1906).

7   Fisher, *supra* note 4, at 75.

8   40 CONG. REC. 8955 (1906) (remarks of Rep. Adamson).

The tension between these conflicting concerns was resolved by limiting the FDA's functions under the 1906 Act to policing statutory violations. The basic violation was the shipment or delivery in interstate commerce of adulterated or misbranded food or drugs, punishable by a fine of up to $200.[9] Offending goods were subject to seizure and condemnation in civil *in rem* proceedings.[10] The FDA was authorized to examine food and drug samples to determine whether they were adulterated or misbranded.[11] The offending party was then given an opportunity for a hearing, before the FDA certified the findings to the appropriate United States Attorney for prosecution.[12]

Administrative authority under the 1906 Act was confined to the general power to make rules and regulations for its enforcement, and the power to collect and examine food and drug specimens.[13] The rulemaking power was vested jointly in the Secretaries of three Cabinet Departments: Agriculture, Commerce and Labor, and Treasury.[14] The statute did not prescribe any standards for the regulations, nor did it require any particular procedures for their promulgation; the rulemaking power was limited only by the requirement that the rules be uniform.[15] The only administrative hearing contemplated by the statute was the the FDA's referral of a case to a United States Attorney for prosecution. Once again, however, no specific procedures were mandated, and no opportunity for judicial review was directly provided. Indirect review of the FDA's determination was available, of course, in the criminal prosecution. The relative lack of administrative authority was consonant with the very limited nature of the agency's substantive role; as the FDA was not required to do much, it did not need sophisticated administrative procedures.

The FDA's role in enforcing the 1906 Act, whether initiating a criminal prosecution or civil condemnation proceedings, was a simple one.[16] Both types of cases were begun by an FDA field inspector collecting samples of food or drugs believed to be in violation of the Act. The samples were then sent to an FDA field station for analysis. If the FDA district chief determined that a criminal prosecution was advisable, the field station chief was to give the product's manufacturer and shipper notice of a hearing to show cause why prosecution should not commence. These hearings were fairly informal; the prospective defendant was given an opportunity to explain the facts, but the rules of evidence were not controlling. In determining whether to proceed with the prosecution several factors were considered, including the seriousness and willfulness of the violation.

After review by the district chief, a summary of the findings was sent to FDA headquarters at the Department of Agriculture. If the Solicitor of the Department determined that

---

[9]   Pub. L. No. 59-384, § 2, 34 Stat. at 768. The penalties for subsequent offenses were fines not exceeding $300, imprisonment for up to one year, or both. *Id.*

[10] *Id.* § 10.

[11] *Id.* § 4.

[12] *Id.*

[13] *Id.*

[14] *Id.* § 3.

[15] *Id.*

[16] The following discussion of early FDA procedures is adapted from Lee, *The Enforcement Provisions of the Food, Drug, and Cosmetic Act*, 6 LAW & CONTEMP. PROBS. 70, 73-75 (1939).

the evidence of violation was sufficient, the case was transferred to the Department of Justice for prosecution. The United States Attorney was required to follow the Department of Agriculture's findings that prosecution should commence.

Civil condemnation procedures followed the same general pattern, with two exceptions: no administrative hearing was held, and the FDA communicated directly with the United States Attorneys. The FDA also had a direct seizure procedure, enabling it to act expeditiously in emergencies, whereby the field station chief referred cases to the United States Attorney without review by either the district chief or FDA headquarters.

Thus, the 1906 Act was designed as a law enforcement statute, the ultimate sanctions being criminal prosecution of a person or seizure of the offending goods. TheFDA's role was simply to ferret out statutory violations. Only in isolated circumstances, however, could such a scheme be effective in preventing the consumption of impure foods or unsafe drugs. The FDA was given no authority to set industry-wide requirements capable of protecting the public health on a broad scale.

Between 1912 and 1923, the Act substantively was amended four times, but none of those amendments significantly expanded the FDA's administrative authority.[17] That process did not begin until the McNary-Mapes Amendment of 1930, which vested in the FDA the power to establish standards of quality, condition, and fill of containers for canned food.[18] These standards had the force and effect of law, presaging the regulatory approach that in later years would come to characterize the FDA.[19]

Despite a high rate of success in civil forfeiture actions and criminal prosecutions,[20] the 1906 Act was regarded by many as a failure. A leading modern commentator once opined that the Act "diminished food and drug quality but left the impression and appearance of consumer protection."[21] Although both FDA officials and critics of the food and drug

---

[17] The Sherley Amendment, Pub. L. No. 62-301, 37 Stat. 416 (1912), provided that a drug would be misbranded if the package or label represented the curative or therapeutic effects of the drug in a false or fraudulent manner. Congress acted in response to the Supreme Court's decision in United States v. Johnson, 221 U.S. 488 (1911), which held that the 1906 Act did not prohibit false health claims, even those known by the maker to be false. The Gould Amendment, Pub. L. No. 62-419, 37 Stat. 732 (1913), the only one of the four to deal with FDA procedure, provided that reasonable variations in the quantity of packaged food would not render the food adulterated, and authorized the issuance of regulations creating exemptions and tolerances for small packages. The Kenyon Amendment, Pub. L. No. 66-22, 41 Stat. 234 (1919), included wrapped meats within the provisions of the Gould Amendment. A definition of "butter" was added to the Act later. Pub. L. No. 67-519, 42 Stat. 1500 (1923).

[18] Pub. L. No. 71-538, 46 Stat. 1019 (1930).

[19] As a matter of practical necessity, the FDA previously had established interpretive standards of identity for use in determining whether food was adulterated or misbranded. Because the interpretive standards did not have the force and effect of law, however, the defendant in a criminal or condemnation action could argue for a different interpretation and thereby force the government in every case to relitigate the validity of its standard.

[20] From date of passage of the 1906 Act (June 30, 1906) through June 30, 1932, 19,459 civil forfeiture actions were initiated, and judgments for the United States were entered in 17,257 of them. During the same period, 9233 criminal prosecutions were initiated, and 7354 convictions (6699 of which were guilty pleas) were obtained. Fisher, *supra* note 4, at 109-10 n.274. As that author observed, however, these statistics may mask the limited effectiveness of the Act. The high percentage of guilty pleas and the large number of repeat offenders suggest that the system of fines was regarded by many as a license fee for "business as usual." *Id.* at 109-10.

[21] JAMES T. O'REILLY, FOOD AND DRUG ADMINISTRATION 3-9 (1979).

industries repeatedly had expressed dissatisfaction with its scheme, the public was generally unaware of the Act's limitations.[22] No corrective action was initiated until the New Dealers swept into Washington in 1933.

The 1938 Act: The FDA's Emergence as Regulator

The driving force behind the movement for legislative action was Rexford G. Tugwell, one of the original "Brain Trusters" and the Undersecretary of Agriculture from 1934 to 1937. Yet enactment of the Federal Food, Drug, and Cosmetic Act (FDCA) of 1938[23] did not come until five years after Senator Royal Copeland introduced Senate Bill 1944 — the "Tugwell Bill."[24] The delay was the product of Congress' inability to reconcile the perceived necessity for direct regulation of the food and drug industries with its profound distrust of New Deal administrators, especially Dr. Tugwell. The history of that legislative struggle is still worth studying. Although the conflict often was expressed in ways that now sound dated if not downright quaint, many of the proposals advanced by the warring factions of that era are startlingly similar to ideas being propounded in the mid-1990s by advocates of legislation to "reform" and "modernize" the FDA.

■ Dr. Tugwell Versus the Industry

With President Roosevelt's approval, in 1933 Tugwell organized a task force consisting of FDA officials, Department of Agriculture attorneys, and three law professors to draft a revision of the 1906 Food and Drug Act within its existing framework.[25] More radical alternatives such as setting up "a system of licensing controls, vested in an administration with broad quasi-judicial and quasi-legislative powers," were rejected as politically unpalatable, but it rapidly became clear that the fundamental scheme of the 1906 Act would have to be modified by introducing a substantial dose of direct industry regulation.[26]

As originally drafted, the task force proposal — introduced in Congress as Senate Bill 1944 — would have greatly expanded the FDA's role in setting requirements for industry, with broad discretion vested in the agency to enforce the law by promulgating regulations. Central to the new scheme was section 23, which provided that the FDA's implementing regulations would have the force and effect of law.[27] The author-

---

[22] *Id.*

[23] Pub. L. No. 75-717, 52 Stat. 1040 (1938) (codified as amended at 21 U.S.C. §§ 301 et seq).

[24] S. 1944, 73d Cong., lst Sess. (1933), *reprinted in* 1 FOOD & DRUG ADMIN., A LEGISLATIVE HISTORY OF THE FEDERAL FOOD, DRUG, AND COSMETIC ACT AND ITS AMENDMENTS 1.

[25] David F. Cavers, *The Food, Drug, and Cosmetic Act of 1938: Its Legislative History and Its Substantive Provisions*, 6 LAW & CONTEMP. PROBS. 2, 6 (1939). Professor Cavers was one of the three law professors on the task force, and his insights into the legislative battles are particularly illuminating.

[26] *Id.* at 7.

[27] S. 1944, § 23, *supra* note 24, *reprinted in* 1 LEGISLATIVE HISTORY, *supra* note 24, at 30.

ity and discretion that this provision would have conferred on the FDA produced an uproar that was astonishing in its tone and extent.[28] During the five-year legislative battle that ensued, criticism of reform proposals usually focused on their procedural provisions.

Contributing to this phenomenon was the fact that the procedural provisions of the bill would have had an impact on all segments of the diverse food, drug, and cosmetic industries, whereas the substantive provisions mostly affected only one segment or another.[29] As one commentator noted at the time, the critics' attitudes "seemed governed chiefly by fear that the provisions in question would be maladministered, a fear ascribable to what can best be described as a severe attack of jitters into which the shock of a number of New Deal measures had plunged the affected trades."[30]

In the case of the food and drug trades, Dr. Tugwell was regarded with particular disdain. Senate Bill 1944 infamously became known as the "Tugwell Bill," and repeatedly was referred to in committee hearings and floor debates as the embodiment of bureaucratic overreaching. Dr. Tugwell himself was a favorite personal target of the critics. In one well-known example, Representative Reece challenged his colleagues:

> If you want to place the advertising [of food and drugs] under Dr. Tugwell and give him a whip lash not only over business, but over the press of this country, vote for the motion made; but if you want to give it to the Federal Trade Commission, a quasi-judicial body, vote against it. [Applause.][31]

Representative McReynolds continued in the same vein:

> Now, Members of the House, what are you going to do about it? Are you going to turn this over to Tugwell for enforcement or are you going to leave it with the Federal Trade Commission with such men as Judge Davis and other men from this House on that Commission? [Applause.][32]

---

[28] The purposes of the Tugwell group were much feared. Its draft bill was dismissed by some critics as the work of naive academics, and denounced by others as the product of Communist subversives. Cavers, *supra* note 25, at 7 n.22. *See generally Food, Drugs, and Cosmetics: Hearings on S. 1944 Before a Subcomm. of the Senate Comm. on Commerce*, 73d Cong., 2d Sess. 18-24 (1933), *reprinted in* 1 LEGISLATIVE HISTORY, *supra* note 24, at 110-16.

[29] Cavers, *supra* note 25, at 5.

[30] *Id.* at 5 n.13.

[31] 80 CONG. REC. 10,677 (1936).

[32] *Id.* at 10,678. Attacks on Dr. Tugwell often brought applause. In debate concerning judicial review of FDA decisions, Rep. Robertson remarked that

> Dr. Tugwell, Acting Secretary in the absence of the Secretary of Agriculture, in misguided enthusiasm to protect the public health, well meaning but ignorant of what was involved, promulgated a tolerance as to lead residue that was nearly 100 percent below the then existing tolerance .... It was so capricious and so unreasonable that as soon as the Secretary got back and considered the matter he reversed it .... [Applause.]

83 CONG. REC. 7893 (1938). Ironically, the animosity directed at Dr. Tugwell was very similar to that inflicted on Dr. Harvey Wiley, the father of the 1906 Act, during consideration of that law. *See, e.g.,* Regier, *supra* note 2, at 12 (quoting remarks of Representative Adamson) ("I believe there are millions of old women, white and black, all over my country, who know more about victuals and good eating than my friend Doctor Wiley and all of his apothecary shop.").

Throughout the five-year congressional battle, supporters of new legislation insisted they merely were attempting "to prevent the passage of a law stripped of those provisions which they regarded as essential to consumer protection."[33] The result, nonetheless, was a statute that greatly expanded the FDA's procedural as well as substantive authority and that began the FDA's evolution into its modern role as a full-fledged rulemaking and adjudicatory agency.

■ Constraining the FDA Through Procedure: The Legislative Struggle of 1933-1938

As finally enacted, the Federal Food, Drug, and Cosmetic Act of 1938[34] authorized the FDA to establish rules setting various requirements that industry would be obligated to meet, and imposed a premarket approval requirement for new drugs. In contrast to the FDA's former authority merely to police violations of the law, the agency now was charged — to a limited but substantial extent — with direct regulation of the industries within its jurisdiction.

The 1938 Act, however, did specify closely the procedure for promulgating the rules that the FDA expressly was directed to issue.[35] The principal areas of rulemaking subject to the specific procedural requirements of the Act were the establishment of standards of identity, quality, and fill of containers for food;[36] tolerances for poisonous and deleterious substances in food;[37] lists of harmless coal-tar colors for use in food, drugs, and cosmetics;[38] and standards of drug strength, quality, and purity.[39] The FDA's exercise of premarket review authority over new drugs was subject to a separate set of procedural requirements.[40]

The original Tugwell bill, Senate Bill 1944, had offered very little procedural protection to regulated firms. For example, various provisions of Senate Bill 1944 authorized the FDA to promulgate regulations after notice and a hearing. The nature of these hearings was left unwritten. The bill spoke to this issue in general terms only, providing that the FDA would conduct the hearings and that findings of fact would be conclusive if in accordance with law.[41]

Not surprisingly, the lack of procedural safeguards drew heavy criticism, even from the sponsor of the bill, Senator Copeland.[42] As a result, the Tugwell bill went back to the orig-

---

[33] Cavers, *supra* note 25, at 2.

[34] Pub. L. No. 75-717, 52 Stat. 1040 (codified as amended at 21 U.S.C. § 301 et seq).

[35] *Id.* § 701(e), 52 Stat. at 1055 (codified as amended at 21 U.S.C. § 371(e)).

[36] *Id.* § 401, 52 Stat. at 1046 (1938) (codified as amended at 21 U.S.C. § 341).

[37] *Id.* § 406(a), 52 Stat. at 1049 (codified as amended at 21 U.S.C. § 346(a)).

[38] *Id.* § 406(b), 52 Stat. at 1049 (food); *id.* § 504, 52 Stat. at 1052 (drugs); *id.* § 604, 52 Stat. at 1055 (cosmetics). All three subsections have been repealed. Color Additive Amendments, Pub. L. No. 86-618, 74 Stat. 398 (1960).

[39] Pub. L. No. 75-717, § 501(b), 52 Stat. at 1049 (codified as amended at 21 U.S.C. § 351(b)).

[40] *Id.* § 505, 52 Stat. at 1052 (codified as amended at 21 U.S.C. § 355).

[41] S. 1944, § 23(c), *supra* note 24, *reprinted in* 1 LEGISLATIVE HISTORY, *supra* note 24, at 30-31.

[42] *See, e.g., Food, Drugs, and Cosmetics: Hearings on S. 1944 Before a Subcomm. of the Senate Comm. on Commerce,* 73d Cong., 2d Sess. 179 (1933) (statement of H.B. Thompson, General Counsel for The Proprietary Association), *reprinted in* 1 LESGISLATIVE HISTORY, *supra* note 24, at 270; 78 CONG. REC. 2728 (1934) (remarks of Sen. Copeland).

inal drafting group for revision.[43] The revised bill, reintroduced as Senate Bill 2000, would have established a Committee on Public Health "[t]o aid and advise [the FDA] in promulgating regulations for the protection of public health,"[44] and a Committee on Food "to aid and advise [the FDA] in the promulgation of regulations with respect to food."[45] Whenever the FDA determined that a regulation should be established, it was required to notify the appropriate committee. If at least three of five members of the committee approved the proposed regulation, the FDA was to give notice and hold a hearing on the proposal. After the hearing, and upon another approval by a three-fifths vote of the appropriate committee, the regulation would be promulgated.[46] Carried forward from the original Tugwell bill was the provision that all findings of fact were conclusive if in accordance with law.[47]

In the Senate hearings on the revised measure, the leading spokesman for industry strenuously objected to the provision making findings of fact conclusive, because its practical effect was "to place these regulations beyond successful court challenge." The gist of industry's objection was that the conclusiveness rule restricted a defendant's rights in fighting a criminal prosecution by shifting the burden of proof from the government to the defendant, in that the defendant would have to prove the invalidity of the regulation to establish a good defense.[48]

Fear of unbridled administrative discretion underlay not only opposition to the conclusiveness rule, but a host of proposals designed to protect industry against arbitrary FDA action.[49] Significant among these was the independent advisory committee proposal described above, which some Senators wished to extend even further. For example, an amendment offered by Senator Goldsborough[50] would have created an administrative board to review FDA determinations, made after a hearing, to seek criminal prosecution. The amendment would have made the review board's decision on whether to prosecute binding on the FDA. The asserted purposes of this additional level of review were to have

---

[43] Although some of the changes resulted from deficiencies and oversights brought to light during the hearings, Professor Cavers candidly admitted that the major force behind the changes was the need to placate industry critics. Cavers, *supra* note 25, at 10-11. Ironically, the revision did little to soothe industry, while managing to produce sweeping denunciations from consumer groups. *Id.* at 11. It is little wonder that Senator Copeland was moved to remark: "Mr. President, I desire to say for myself that I thought I had all the troubles one could have in this life; but in all my experience I have never had so many worries and so much trouble as I have had in connection with this bill." 78 CONG. REC. 2728 (1934).

[44] S. 2000, 73d Cong. 2d Sess. § 22(b) (1934), *reprinted in* 1 LEGISLATIVE HISTORY, *supra* note 24, at 628.

[45] *Id.* § 22(c). Members of the Committees were to be appointed by the President on the basis of scientific achievement and without regard to political affiliation. Officials of the Department of Agriculture and persons with a financial interest in the food, drug, or cosmetic industries were ineligible for committee membership. *Id.* § 22(e).

[46] *Id.* § 22(g). Senate Bill 2000 also authorized judicial review of FDA regulations. *Id.* § 23. Upon a showing of damage to the petitioner, U..S. district courts were given jurisdiction to restrain the enforcement of any regulation that was unreasonable, arbitrary or capricious, or not in accordance with law.

[47] *Id.*

[48] *Foods, Drugs, and Cosmetics: Hearings on S. 2000 Before the Senate Comm. on Commerce*, 73d Cong., 2d Sess. 41 (1934) (statement of Charles Wesley Dunn), *reprinted in* 2 LEGISLATIVE HISTORY, *supra* note 24, at 46; Cavers, *supra* note 25, at 10-11.

[49] The existence of substitute bills operated as a moderating influence on the Tugwell drafting group. Professor Cavers noted the group's concern that "competing bills drafted by industry counsel would be introduced and [there] was a risk that one of these, which were far from satisfactory, would be enacted . . . ." Cavers, *supra* note 25, at 10.

[50] 78 CONG. REC. 7447 (1934).

the prosecutorial decision made by an impartial body, and to protect food, drug, and cosmetic manufacturers from "erroneous" criminal prosecutions.[51] The flood of amendments providing for independent administrative review of the FDA led even the conciliatory Senator Copeland to assert that such an approach would materially weaken the bill.[52]

In the next Congress, the revised Tugwell bill was reintroduced as Senate Bill 5 without significant change,[53] but the substance of the debate shifted significantly. Opponents of the bill now objected broadly to *any* substantial delegation of legislative authority to an administrative agency, preferring instead to impose specific statutory obligations and prohibitions, and leave very little to FDA regulations.[54] These critics were not appeased by the provisions for administrative review committees, because such committees would remove the decisionmaking authority even further from the political process.

Reflecting its inherent distrust of the FDA's ability to act responsibly, the Senate opted for independent review boards as a prophylactic measure to prevent the issuance of arbitrary regulations.[55] The House of Representatives took a less hostile tack, merely requiring the FDA to follow specified procedures in promulgating its regulations.[56] These mandated procedures were designed to force the agency to compile a record in support of its regulatory decrees[57] — a development conducive to judicial review, although no explicit provision was made for judicial review, on the ground that common law remedies against administrative action in excess of statutory authority were adequate.[58] The bill foundered, however, on the more basic issue of whether Dr. Tugwell or the Federal Trade Commission was the better choice to administer the advertising provisions.

Reintroduced yet again as Senate Bill 5 when the next Congress convened, the bill languished until the elixir sulfanilamide disaster of 1937.[59] This time the effort to obtain enactment was successful. The dispute over appropriate FDA procedures was resolved along the lines favored by the House. As finally enacted, the bill provided in section 701(e) that, in promulgating regulations under specified sections of the Act, the FDA was to hold "a public hearing," at which "any interested person may be heard." A rulemaking proposal, including a proposal to amend or repeal previously issued regulations, could be

---

[51] *Id.* at 7448.

[52] *Id.* at 4572.

[53] S. 5, 74th Cong., lst Sess. (1935), *reprinted in* 3 LEGISLATIVE HISTORY, *supra* note 24, at 1.

[54] S. REP. NO. 361, Minority Views, pt. 2, 74th Cong., lst Sess. 7 (1935), *reprinted in* 4 LEGISLATIVE HISTORY, *supra* note 24, at 43.

[55] S. REP. NO. 46, 74th Cong., lst Sess. 11 (1935), *reprinted in* 4 LEGISLATIVE HISTORY, *supra* note 24, at 103.

[56] H.R. REP. NO. 2755, 74th Cong., 2d Sess. (1936), *reprinted in* 5 LEGISLATIVE HISTORY, *supra* note 24, at 144.

[57] *Id.* at 3, *reprinted in* 5 LEGISLATIVE HISTORY, *supra* note 24, at 144, 146

[58] *Id.* at 8, *reprinted in* 5 LEGISLATIVE HISTORY, *supra* note 24, at 151.

[59] The basic facts of the tragedy are well known. Sulfa compounds formed the basis of one of the early "wonder drugs." Because these compounds were insoluble in ethyl alcohol, drug manufacturers attempted to find a solvent that would allow the drug to be taken in liquid form. Diethylene glycol was used as a solvent by one drug manufacturer. It apparently had been tested for such things as appearance and flavor, but not for safety. Almost 100 people died from ingesting the drug. The FDA's immediate attempt to recover the product from the market was successful but only because of a technicality. The product was misbranded under the 1906 Act because it was labeled an "elixir," a term that could be applied properly only to an alcoholic solution. The label of the drug did not — and was not required to — list the fatal ingredient. If not labeled an elixir, it would not have violated the 1906 Act. *See generally* REPORT OF THE SECRETARY OF AGRICULTURE ON DEATHS DUE TO ELIXIR SULFANILAMIDE-MASSENGILL, S. DOC. NO. 124, 75th Cong., 2d Sess. (1937), *reprinted in* 5 LEGISLATIVE HISTORY, *supra* note 24, at 883-921.

made either by the Secretary or "any interested industry or substantial portion thereof stating reasonable grounds therefor . . . ." Unlike the earlier proposals, moreover, the bill as finally enacted required FDA regulations to be supported by "substantial evidence of record" adduced at the hearing and to be accompanied by "detailed findings of fact."[60]

The requirements of substantial evidence and detailed findings of fact were intended to ensure that FDA hearings complied with the Supreme Court's then-recent decisions in *Ohio Bell Telephone Co. v. Public Utilities Commission of Ohio*[61] and *Morgan v. United States*,[62] which were understood to establish the principle that "the right to a hearing embraces not only the right to present evidence, but also a reasonable opportunity to know the claims of the opposing party and to meet them."[63] As to judicial review, however, the dispute was not easily resolved. Both the Senate and the House bills would have allowed any person adversely affected by an FDA regulation to file a complaint in a United States district court seeking to enjoin the action. The court's decision was to be based on the administrative record, but new evidence could be presented to the court if the complainant could show reasonable grounds for doing so.[64] Both in committee consideration of Senate Bill 5 and during floor debate on the measure, this provision — which with some changes became section 701(f) of the bill as enacted[65] — was a major source of contention.

A sharply divided House Commerce Committee explained in its report that district court review of FDA regulations was designed to facilitate early determinations of the validity of agency actions and to promote certainty of legal rights.[66] According to the dissenters, however, "it would be better to continue the old law in effect than to enact Senate Bill 5 with this provision."[67] The minority objected to vesting review authority in district courts because they feared that any single district judge could enjoin the enforcement of a regulation throughout the country even if every other district judge had refused to issue an injunction.[68] Great emphasis was placed on a letter from the Secretary of Agriculture opining that section 701(f) would hamstring the FDA's administration of the law, and that it amounted to an invitation to obstruct enforcement.[69] Newspaper editorials and articles in magazines such as *Consumer Reports* attacked the "judicial review joker."[70]

To counter the critics, Representative Mapes offered an amendment providing for review of section 701(e) regulations not in the district courts but in the courts of appeals, and making the FDA's findings of fact conclusive "if supported by substantial evidence."[71] Although the Mapes amendment was defeated in the House by almost two-to-one (albeit

---

[60]   S. 5, § 701(e), 75th Cong., 3d Sess. 82-83, *reprinted in* 6 LEGISLATIVE HISTORY, *supra* note 24, at 286-87.

[61]   310 U.S. 292 (1937).

[62]   304 U.S. 1 (1938).

[63]   *Id.* at 18.

[64]   S. 5, § 701(f), *supra* note 60, at 83-85 (1938), *reprinted in* 6 LEGISLATIVE HISTORY, *supra* note 24, at 287-89.

[65]   Pub. L. No. 75-717, § 701(f), 52 Stat. at 1056 (codified as amended at 21 U.S.C. § 371(f)).

[66]   H.R. REP. No. 2139, 75th Cong., 3d Sess. 11 (1938), *reprinted in* 6 LEGISLATIVE HISTORY, *supra* note 24, at 310.

[67]   H.R. REP. No. 2139, Minority Views, pt. 2, 75th Cong., 3d Sess. 3 (1938), *reprinted in* 6 LEGISLATIVE HISTORY, *supra* note 24, at 320.

[68]   *Id.* at 2, *reprinted in* 6 LEGISLATIVE HISTORY, *supra* note 24, at 319.

[69]   *Id.* at 3, *reprinted in* 6 LEGISLATIVE HISTORY, *supra* note 24, at 319.

[70]   Examples are reported at 83 CONG. REC. 7785-86 (1938).

[71]   *Id.* at 7891.

with only ninety members voting), the House-Senate conference produced a judicial review provision that was, in one respect, even more restrictive than the Mapes amendment.

Similar to the Mapes amendment, the conference version opted for court of appeals review of section 701(e) regulations and held that the FDA's findings of fact were to be conclusive only if supported by "substantial evidence."[72] Both the original district court review provision and the Mapes amendment, however, had authorized the reviewing court to take additional evidence on a showing of reasonable grounds. The conference version allowed the reviewing court to order the taking of additional evidence, but required that it be taken before the FDA.[73] A potential technique for effectively bypassing the FDA and undermining its regulatory authority through judicial second-guessing of the facts was thereby foreclosed.

In contrast to the controversy that surrounded its rulemaking and judicial review provisions, the 1938 Act's premarketing review requirement for new drugs received virtually no debate. Indeed, the only mention of this significant new authority was Representative Coffee's complaint that the provision was too limited.[74] As emphasized by its sponsors, the new drug provision contemplated minimal governmental intrusion into drug development. Section 505 was explained as merely a mechanism for administrative review of a drug manufacturer's safety tests, not a licensing provision.[75] Nor was affirmative FDA approval required; a new drug application (NDA) would become effective unless disapproved by the FDA within a limited period after filing.[76] Orders of disapproval were to be reviewable in the district courts, with the FDA's findings of fact conclusive only if supported by substantial evidence.[77] Yet with all its limitations, the premarket review authority contained the seed of an important component of the FDA's modern role.

The legislative struggle to give the FDA direct regulatory authority over the food, drug, and cosmetic industries thus fundamentally transformed the relationship between them. Because of the significant expansion of substantive authority vested in the FDA, the provisions governing the FDA's procedures in exercising its new powers were the subject of important debate. Even more concentrated attention would be paid to FDA procedure in the years following the passage of the 1938 Act, as a series of statutory changes accelerated the FDA's transformation into a direct regulator of industry and as the agency developed new techniques for carrying out its growing responsibilities. Principal among these agency-created procedural innovations were the emergence of notice-and-comment rulemaking as a major regulatory tool, the development of an administrative summary judgment procedure to avoid evidentiary hearings, the standardization of the agency's

---

[72] H.R. REP. No. 2716, 75th Cong., 3d Sess. 25 (1938), *reprinted in* 6 LEGISLATIVE HISTORY, *supra* note 24, at 426.

[73] *Id.*

[74] 83 CONG. REC. A2075 (1938).

[75] H.R. REP. No. 2139, 75th Cong., 3d Sess. 9 (1938), *reprinted in* 6 LEGISLATIVE HISTORY, *supra* note 24, at 308. The provision applied not only to human drugs, but also to drugs for "other animals." The latter were removed from section 505 and made subject to a parallel but somewhat differing regulatory scheme by the Animal Drug Amendments of 1968, Pub. L. No. 90-399, 82 Stat. 343 (1968) (codified at 21 U.S.C. § 360b).

[76] S. 5, § 505(c), *supra* note 60, *reprinted in* 6 LEGISLATIVE HISTORY, *supra* note 24, at 279.

[77] *Id.* § 505(h), *reprinted in* 6 LEGISLATIVE HISTORY, *supra* note 24, at 281-82.

decisionmaking process, and the extensive use of advisory committees to backstop the FDA's scientific judgments. The next section of this chapter describes these developments.

Post-1938 Developments: Legislative and Administrative Expansion of the FDA's Regulatory Role

As the FDA proceeded to implement its new direct regulatory authority, deficiencies in the 1938 Act soon became apparent. In some instances, the agency obtained additional regulatory authority from Congress via substantive statutory amendments, usually subject to procedural constraints on the agency's exercise of broad discretion.[78] Even without benefit of statute, however, the FDA achieved significant expansions of authority by applying innovative procedural techniques to the administration of the law as enacted.

■ Expanding the FDA's Authority by Statute

Prescription Drugs

The Durham-Humphrey Amendment of 1951[79] was the first significant legislative change in the 1938 Act. Prior to the Amendment, the statute gave no guidance for distinguishing between prescription drugs and those suitable for use without the authorization and supervision of a physician. Nevertheless, prescription drugs were required to contain a cautionary label identifying them as such and an improperly categorized drug was deemed misbranded in violation of the Act.[80]

As with other important issues arising under the Act, the manufacturer was charged with making the initial decision as to whether a drug could be sold over-the-counter (OTC) on

---

[78]   In other instances, the FDA sought its own solutions by reinterpreting the existing statutes — more broadly, on occasion, than contemplated by Congress and unencumbered by new (or sometimes even old) procedural controls. *See, e.g.*, AMP, Inc. v. Gardner, 389 F.2d 825 (2d Cir.), *cert. denied*, 393 U.S. 825 (1968) (mechanical suturing device deemed a "drug"); USV Pharmaceutical Corp. v. Weinberger, 412 U.S. 655 (1973) (recharacterizing NDA as covering entire class of drugs, rather than specific products, for purposes of applying 1962 Drug Amendments effectiveness requirement to pre-enactment products not previously needing premarket approval); American Frozen Food Inst. v. Califano, 555 F.2d 1059 (D.C. Cir. 1977) (use of notice-and-comment rulemaking power to prescribe mandatory composition of foods entitled to bear a given "common and usual name" notwithstanding statutory requirement of formal rulemaking to establish standards of identity).

Some FDA reinterpretations, however, have proven to be too much for the courts to accept. *See, e.g.*, United States v. Two Plastic Drums . . . Viponte Ltd. Black Currant Oil, 984 F.2d 814 (7th Cir. 1993) *and* United States v. 29 Cartons, 987 F.2d 33 (1st Cir. 1993) (the FDA "defies common sense" in attempting to regulate a single-ingredient dietary supplement as a "food additive"); Public Citizen v. Young, 831 F.2d 1108 (D.C. Cir. 1987), *cert. denied*, 485 U.S. 1006 (1988) (the FDA cannot create *de minimis* exception to Delaney Anti-Cancer Clause in Color Additive Amendments); American Pharmaceutical Ass'n v. Mathews, 530 F.2d 1054 (D.C. Cir. 1976) (the FDA cannot create its own scheme to regulate substance abuse independent of Controlled Substances Act); Sixty-Two Cases of Jam v. United States, 340 U.S. 593 (1951) (the FDA cannot prohibit products expressly authorized by statute).

[79]   Pub. L. No. 82-215, 65 Stat. 648 (1951).

[80]   Pub. L. No. 75-717, § 502(f), 52 Stat. at 1050 (codified as amended at 21 U.S.C. § 352(f)).

the basis of adequate directions for use or only by prescription. If the FDA disagreed with the manufacturer's classification, it could initiate only a criminal prosecution, a seizure action, or an injunction action. Until the question was resolved, however, retail druggists could not be certain whether a given drug was misbranded. Retail sale of a drug subsequently found to be misbranded in that respect exposed the pharmacist or other retailer to prosecution.[81]

The Durham-Humphrey legislation sought to remedy this uncertainty. As reported by the House Commerce Committee, the bill would have authorized the FDA, subject to judicial review, to classify drugs as OTC or prescription on the basis of a statutory standard.[82] The Committee expressly rejected the option of directly classifying specific drugs by statute, because informed determinations would require extensive congressional hearings and could not easily be changed in response to new scientific or medical developments.[83] The Committee proposed authorizing the FDA to classify drugs on the basis of expert evidence adduced at a formal administrative hearing on the question whether a given drug would be safe and efficacious if not used under the direction of a physician.[84]

During floor debate, however, the FDA's administrative authority to classify drugs was removed, apparently for fear that the agency would make unreasonable and arbitrary determinations.[85] Application of the new statutory standard was left to the courts in traditional enforcement proceedings. In a choice characterized by some in the House as one between "administrative absolutism" and "the American way,"[86] the "American way" prevailed by a vote of 141 to 85.[87]

Although Congress thus seemingly chose to withhold direct regulatory authority in this area, the FDA has found ways to achieve similar results. The Senate Labor and Public Welfare Committee noted in reporting the Durham-Humphrey bill that, despite the deletion of specific authority to classify drugs as prescription or OTC, the agency still had authority under section 701(a) of the Act to issue regulations for the efficient enforcement of the Act.[88] The agency successfully has invoked section 701(a) as authority for regulations classifying particular drugs as requiring a prescription.[89] Although section 701(a) regulations were viewed by the 1951 Senate Committee as interpretive, they since have

---

[81]   H.R. REP. NO. 700, 82d Cong., 1st Sess. 4-5 (1951), *reprinted in* 11 LEGISLATIVE HISTORY, *supra* note 24, at 278-79. *See* United States v. Sullivan, 332 U.S. 689 (1948).

[82]   H.R. REP. NO. 700, *supra* note 81, at 7, *reprinted in* 11 LEGISLATIVE HISTORY, *supra* note 24, at 281.

[83]   *Id.* at 9, *reprinted in* 11 LEGISLATIVE HISTORY, *supra* note 24, at 283. In 1970, by contrast, when Congress addressed the problem of drug abuse, it did not shrink from just such an effort. The Controlled Substances Act directly classifies numerous specifically named compounds into five schedules subject to graduated levels of regulation and authorizes the Attorney General to make additions to and deletions from the schedules. Pub. L. No. 91-513, 82 Stat. 1242 (1970), (codified at 21 U.S.C. §§ 801 et seq).

[84]   H.R. REP. NO. 700, *supra* note 81, at 2, *reprinted in* 11 LEGISLATIVE HISTORY, *supra* note 24, at 276. The Committee judged the task of determining OTC versus prescription status to be essentially legislative and unsuited for judicial procedures. Furthermore, an administrative decisionmaking process would involve only drug manufacturers, the parties who were primarily interested. Enforcement litigation usually involved drug retailers, who were interested only in certainty.

[85]   *See, e.g.,* 97 CONG. REC. 9337-38 (1951) (remarks of Rep. Hoffman).

[86]   *Id.* at 9341 (remarks of Rep. O'Hara).

[87]   *Id.* at 9349.

[88]   S. REP. NO. 946, 82d Cong., 1st Sess. 4 (1951), *reprinted in* 11 LEGISLATIVE HISTORY, *supra* note 24, at 667.

[89]   National Nutritional Foods Ass'n v. Weinberger, 512 F.2d 688 (2d Cir. 1974), *cert. denied,* 423 U.S. 827 (1975).

come to be regarded as having the force and effect of law.[90] More frequently, the agency simply has insisted on prescription status in its review of the labeling proposed in section 505 premarket approval applications for new drugs. Congress' apparent decision notwithstanding, the FDA thus has managed to create procedures that amply meet its perceived needs in this area.

Making Section 701(e) Hearings Nonmandatory

As originally enacted, section 701(e) required the FDA to hold formal evidentiary hearings on every proposal to issue, modify, or repeal regulations under the specified provisions of the Act.[91] Even if no one objected to a proposal, the FDA was obligated to hold a formal hearing and make a record of substantial evidence to support it. Not surprisingly, this requirement was criticized widely by both the agency and the regulated industry,[92] and both industry and the agency supported the same remedy.

The problem of uncontested evidentiary hearings became apparent in the context of regulations establishing food standards under section 401 of the Act.[93] To relieve both the FDA and industry of this unnecessary burden, in 1954 Congress removed these regulations from the operation of section 701(e), creating instead a special procedural subsection to the food standards provision.[94] The amendment, known as the Hale Amendment after its chief sponsor in the House, added a new preliminary notice-and-comment phase to the procedure for issuance of food standard regulations, and required formal evidentiary hearings only where a person adversely affected by the regulation issued by the FDA after the notice-and-comment phase objected and requested a hearing.[95]

The noncontroversial nature of the measure was reflected by the singular brevity of the hearings before the House Commerce Committee. Only two witnesses testified, both in support of the bill; each stated that he knew of no opposition to it.[96] The only issue concerned the provision allowing "any interested person" to petition the FDA for issuance of a regulation, in place of the former requirement that restricted standing to "any interested industry or a substantial portion thereof."[97] The Committee viewed the original language as unnecessarily limiting the right to petition to food manufacturers and processors.[98] To control against frivolous petitions for rulemaking, the bill retained the requirement of "stating reasonable grounds therefor," defined as a "substantial showing of merit for any proposed action."[99] Two years later, in the Hale Amendment of 1956, the new two-phase food standards procedure was extended to all section 701(e) proceedings.[100]

---

[90] *Id.* For a discussion of this development, see *infra* notes 221-32 and accompanying text.

[91] Pub. L. No. 75-717, § 701(e), 52 Stat. at 1050.

[92] H.R. REP. No. 934, 83d Cong., lst Sess. 2 (1953), *reprinted in* 12 LEGISLATIVE HISTORY, *supra* note 24, at 443.

[93] *Id.* at 1, *reprinted in* 12 LEGISLATIVE HISTORY, *supra* note 24, at 442.

[94] Pub. L. No. 83-336, 68 Stat. 54 (1954).

[95] *Id.* § 1, 68 Stat. at 54.

[96] *Federal Food, Drug, and Cosmetic Act (Food Standards): Hearing on H.R. 5055 Before a Subcomm. of the House Comm. on Interstate and Foreign Commerce*, 83d Cong., lst Sess. (1953), *reprinted in* 12 LEGISLATIVE HISTORY, *supra* note 24, at 412.

[97] *See* H.R. REP. No. 934, *supra* note 92, at 1, *reprinted in* 12 LEGISLATIVE HISTORY, *supra* note 24, at 442.

[98] *Id.* at 3, *reprinted in* 12 LEGISLATIVE HISTORY, *supra* note 24, at 444.

[99] *Id.*

[100] Pub. L. No. 84-905, 70 Stat. 919 (1956) (codified at 21 U.S.C. § 371(e)).

The "reasonable grounds" requirement was expected to assume great significance in view of the liberalized standing criteria.[101] The main controversies generated by the Hale Amendments, however, have arisen out of the FDA's attempts to avoid hearings not merely in uncontested cases but also in hotly disputed ones, on the ground that the objections on which a hearing is sought are "legally insufficient" to justify relief against the regulation at issue.[102] In this respect, the Amendments may have undone much of what the drafters of the 1938 Act saw as an important check on abuse of the substantial direct regulatory authority being conferred on the agency.

Food Additives

By 1958, fears of "administrative absolutism" evidently no longer dominated the legislative process. In the Food Additives Amendment of that year,[103] Congress significantly expanded the FDA's premarketing approval authority to include "food additives" — defined as all substances added to or likely to become a component of food and that have not been "generally recognized as safe" by experts or previously approved informally by the government for the use in question.[104] In lieu of the reliance in the 1938 Act on after-the-fact enforcement litigation to keep the food supply free of harmful "poisonous and deleterious substances,"[105] the Amendment prohibits the use of any food additive except as authorized by the FDA in a regulation prescribing the conditions under which the additive lawfully can be used.

To deny a petition for issuance of such a regulation, the agency must find specifically that the data in support of the additive either fail to establish that the proposed use would be safe, or show that the proposed use would promote deception of the consumer or otherwise would result in unlawful adulteration or misbranding of food.[106] Any person adversely affected by the regulation is given the opportunity for a hearing.[107] After the hearing, the FDA is to issue an order "based upon a fair evaluation of the entire record," setting forth in detail its findings and conclusions.[108] Judicial review is available in the courts of appeals on a distinctive standard of review, permitting the FDA's findings to be upheld only if based upon a "fair evaluation" of the hearing record.[109]

Thus, unlike the 1951 Congress in dealing with the OTC/prescription drug issue, the 1958 Congress was largely willing to rely on procedural requirements as a sufficient safeguard against irresponsible action (except with respect to carcinogens, discussed below). Particular importance was attached to the quantum of evidence necessary to

---

[101] H.R. REP. NO. 934, *supra* note 92, at 3, *reprinted in* 12 LEGISLATIVE HISTORY, *supra* note 24, at 444.

[102] *Compare, e.g.,* Dyestuffs & Chems., Inc. v. Flemming, 271 F.2d 281 (8th Cir. 1959), *cert. denied*, 362 U.S. 911 (1960), *with* Certified Color Indus. Comm. v. Flemming, 283 F.2d 622 (2d Cir. 1960).*Also compare* Pactra Indus., Inc. v. Consumer Prod. Safety Comm'n, 555 F.2d 677 (9th Cir. 1977) (review of Federal Hazardous Substances Act rulemaking conducted under section 701(e) pursuant to 15 U.S.C. § 1262 (1994)) *with* Pineapple Growers Ass'n v. FDA, 673 F.2d 1083, 1085-86 (9th Cir. 1982) (hearing must be held only "where 'material' issues of fact are raised 'that should not be dispelled at the outset without a hearing,' . . . objections [are] 'made in good faith' and are 'neither frivolous or inconsequential'" (quoting *Pactra*, 555 F 2d. At 684)).

[103] Pub. L. No. 85-929, 72 Stat. 1784 (1958).

[104] *Id*. § 2, 72 Stat. at 1784 (codified at 21 U.S.C. § 321(s)).

[105] S. REP. NO. 2284, 85th Cong., 2d Sess. 1-2 (1958), *reprinted in* 14 LEGISLATIVE HISTORY, *supra* note 24, at 822-23.

[106] Pub. L. No. 85-929, § 4, 72 Stat. at 1786 (codified at 21 U.S.C. § 348(c)).

[107] *Id.*, (codified at 21 U.S.C. § 348(f)(1)).

[108] *Id.*, (codified at 21 U.S.C. § 348(f)(2)).

[109] *Id.*, (codified at 21 U.S.C. § 348(g)(2)).

sustain an FDA order. The Senate Committee regarded "substantial evidence" as being too permissive a standard because it believed that the testimony of any single expert could be regarded as "substantial" despite the contradictory testimony of other experts.[110] The courts therefore were directed to ensure that the FDA had made a "fair evaluation of the entire record." In the abstract, the two standards are difficult to distinguish, but the congressional intent that reviewing courts employ closer than usual scrutiny is clear.[111]

The one exception to Congress' reliance on procedural constraints was the incorporation in the Food Additives Amendment of an anticancer clause.[112] Known as the Delaney Clause after its chief congressional sponsor, this provision generally requires the FDA to deem an additive unsafe if found to cause cancer in man or animal.[113] Congress thus again manifested its historical distrust of FDA discretion, albeit this time as potentially not restrictive enough rather than as too restrictive — a testimonial to the importance attached by Congress to the prevention of cancer, even at the price of harsh governmental intrusion into traditional industry prerogatives.

The Food Additives Amendment resulted at least in part from the inadequacy of enforcement litigation to deal with a long-standing problem — misguided "improvements" of the food supply. Subsequent expansions of the FDA's direct regulatory authority stemmed primarily from the emergence of new problem areas, largely unappreciated or unforeseen by the original drafters of the Act. In more than a dozen major amendments between 1958 and 1994, Congress assigned the FDA important new responsibilities for controlling industry practice. Other statutory changes, prompted by unforeseen public opposition to the agency's regulatory efforts, have sought to cut back authority previously granted by Congress or claimed by the FDA under color of broad language in the 1938 Act. The most significant of these enactments are discussed below.

New Drugs and Generic Drugs

The effectiveness requirement. The accelerated development of potent new pharmaceuticals in the years following World War II led to the Drug Amendments of 1962, which greatly expanded the FDA's direct regulatory authority in that area of its jurisdiction.[114] The 1938 Act had authorized the FDA to deny premarket clearance of new drugs only on grounds of safety.[115] The purpose of the 1962 Amendments was "to strengthen the laws to keep unfit drugs off the market in the first instance and speed their removal should they

---

[110] S. REP. NO. 2284, 85th Cong., 2d Sess. 6, *reprinted in* 14 LEGISLATIVE HISTORY, *supra* note 24, at 827.

[111] *Id. See Pactra,* 555 F.2d at 679-80 n.4; Continental Chemiste Corp. v. Ruckelshaus, 461 F.2d 331, 334 n.37 (7th Cir. 1972).

[112] Pub. L. No. 85-929, § 4, 72 Stat. at 1785 (codified at 21 U.S.C. § 348(c)(3)(A)).

[113] Attempts by the FDA to escape the rigors of the Delaney Clause by statutory reinterpretation have been struck down by the courts. *See* Public Citizen v. Young, 831 F.2d 1108 (under comparable clause in 1960 Color Additive Amendments, Pub. L. No. 86-618, § 103(b), 74 Stat. at 399 (codified at 21 U.S.C. § 379e(b)(5)(B))). The court reserved judgment as to whether Congress intended the same unyielding restriction to apply under the previously enacted "almost identical wording" in the Food Additives Amendment. 831 F.2d at 1122. Subsequently, however, in Les v. Reilly, 968 F.2d 985 (9th Cir. 1992), *cert. denied,* 507 U.S. 950 (1993), another court of appeals ruled that the food additives provision must be given the same literal reading.

[114] Pub. L. No. 87-781, 76 Stat. 780 (1962).

[115] *See supra* notes 74-77 and accompanying text.

reach the market."[116] "Unfit" was redefined to mean ineffective as well as unsafe.[117] Fearful that the FDA would be too restrictive in approving drugs, however, Congress sought to limit the burden on industry by creating a unique standard of proof of effectiveness, the intended purpose of which has gone largely unappreciated.

To deny approval of a new drug for lack of effectiveness, the FDA must find not merely that the applicant has failed to prove effectiveness by a preponderance of the evidence (the usual standard in administrative proceedings), but that there is indeed a lack of "substantial evidence" that the drug is effective.[118] The Senate Judiciary Committee was unusually specific in stating exactly what was meant by the standard. Therapeutic claims must be supported by reliable pharmacological and clinical studies, but when so supported are to be permitted despite the presence of equal or even preponderant evidence to the contrary based on equally reliable studies.[119] The Committee intended to allow reasonably substantiated efficacy claims to be made to the medical profession with a proper explanation of their basis, so that the individual physician could make his or her own properly informed decision.[120]

In practice the FDA has taken a far less permissive approach, preferring to read the standard as imposing an unusually strict burden on the applicant for approval rather than an unusually limited one.[121] The correctness of the agency's position in this regard has not been fully tested in the courts.[122] Whether ultimately it will be upheld is likely to depend as much on then-prevailing attitudes toward drug regulation in general as on a close parsing of the statute and its legislative history.

Abbreviated New Drug Applications for Generic Drugs. Economics, rather than public health and safety, was the primary impetus for enactment of the Drug Price Competition and Patent Term Restoration Act of 1984, usually called the Waxman-Hatch Act after its somewhat unlikely coalition of chief congressional sponsors, Representative Henry Wax-

---

[116] S. REP. No. 1744, 87th Cong., 2d Sess. 8 (1962), *reprinted in* 22 LEGISLATIVE HISTORY, *supra* note 24, at 101.

[117] *Id.* at 9-10, *reprinted in* 22 LEGISLATIVE HISTORY, *supra* note 24, at 102-03.

[118] Pub. L. No. 87-781, § 102(c), 76 Stat. at 781 (codified at 21 U.S.C. § 355(d)). "Substantial evidence" is defined by the new statute to "mea[n] evidence consisting of adequate and well-controlled investigations, including clinical investigations." *Id.*

[119] S. REP. No. 1744, *supra* note 116, at 16, *reprinted in* 22 LEGISLATIVE HISTORY, *supra* note 24, at 109. *See* Warner-Lambert Co. v. Heckler, 787 F.2d 147, 157 (3d Cir. 1986).

[120] S. REP. No. 1744, *supra* note 116, at 16, *reprinted in* 22 LEGISLATIVE HISTORY, *supra* note 24, at 109. This unique procedure was Congress' first attempt to resolve the tension inherent in the drug approval requirement.

> The committee believes that this provision strikes a balance between the need for governmental control to assure that new drugs are not placed on the market until they have passed the relevant tests and the need to insure that governmental control does not become so rigid that the flow of new drugs to the market, and the incentive to undergo the expense involved in preparing them for the market, become stifled.

Id. at 14-15, *reprinted in* 22 LEGISLATIVE HISTORY, *supra* note 24, at 107-08.

[121] For example, the FDA traditionally has relied on the statutory reference to "investigations" in the plural to require at least two such studies in most cases; the agency disregards the quantitative limitation aspect of the "substantial evidence" concept while stressing its qualitative connotation. In 1995, facing increasingly severe criticism of its "two studies" policy, the agency issued a notice attempting to rationalize the policy on scientific rather than semantic grounds, but in essence remained firm in its requirements. 60 Fed. Reg. 39,180, 39,181 (Aug. 1, 1995).

[122] In Warner-Lambert Co. v. Heckler, 787 F.2d 147 (3d Cir. 1986), and E.R. Squibb & Sons, Inc. v. Bowen, 870 F.2d 678 (D.C. Cir. 1989), the agency was successful on subsidiary aspects of the core issue, but as of this writing the basic controversy remains unresolved.

man (D-Cal.) and Senator Orrin Hatch (R-Utah).[123] In the late 1970s and early 1980s the research-based or "pioneer" segment of the pharmaceutical industry began to face increasingly fierce competition for market share from manufacturers of generic drug products, usually much smaller companies with comparatively limited (although far from insubstantial) resources committed to product development. Each side began looking for ways to change the regulatory scheme to its advantage.

Generic manufacturers devoted most of their initial efforts to persuading the FDA to change the agency regulations and policies that effectively limited them to marketing drug products containing active ingredients marketed since before 1962 and found by the FDA to be effective under its Drug Efficacy Study Implementation (DESI) program.[124] They achieved some success in 1978 when the FDA unveiled its paper NDA policy, whereby a generic manufacturer could rely on safety and effectiveness information published in the scientific literature to support the approval of generic copies of both pre-1962 and post-1962 drugs.[125]

Generic manufacturers made further progress in 1980 when the FDA initiated annual publication of a list of Approved Drug Products With Therapeutic Equivalence Evaluations, the "main purpose of [which] was to provide information to states regarding FDA's recommendation as to which generic prescription drug products were acceptable candidates for drug product selection [i.e., generic substitution]."[126] Three years later, reversing a long-standing position, the FDA took under consideration a proposal that would have permitted the agency to approve abbreviated new drug applications (ANDAs) for post-1962 drugs on the same basis as it approved ANDAs for pre-1962 drugs. The generic industry filed a lawsuit

---

[123] Pub. L. No. 98-417, 98 Stat. 1585 (1984).

[124] Although the FDA treated unpublished safety and effectiveness data as confidential and refused to allow other manufacturers to use such data to support their NDAs, *see, e.g.,* 45 Fed. Reg. 82,052, 82,058 (Dec. 12, 1980), the agency also took the legal position that active ingredients found to be safe and effective under the DESI program were not new drugs, *see* 40 Fed. Reg. 26,142, 26,177 (June 20, 1975), and established an abbreviated new drug application process for products containing them. 21 C.F.R. § 314.2 (1996); 35 Fed. Reg. 6574 (Apr. 24, 1970). On the other hand, the FDA rejected the generic manufacturers' argument that individual generic products (that is, the old active ingredient plus excipients selected by the generic manufacturer) were not new drugs either, and thus would not be subject to the premarket approval requirements of section 505. The agency's position was upheld in United States v. Generix Drug Corp., 469 U.S. 453 (1983).

[125] Set forth at first only in an unpublished internal FDA memorandum, the policy originally was attacked by the pioneer manufacturers on procedural grounds for lack of notice-and-comment rulemaking. This attack was deflected initially on the ground that the pioneer manufacturers had failed to exhaust their administrative remedies, Hoffmann-La Roche, Inc. v. Harris, 484 F. Supp. 58 (D.D.C. 1979), and ultimately was rejected as without merit, Burroughs Wellcome Co. v. Schweiker, 649 F.2d 221 (4th Cir. 1981), albeit not until after the FDA had *de facto* provided the pioneer manufacturers with the desired opportunity to be heard, *see* 45 Fed. Reg. 82,052. A subsequent challenge to the merits of the "paper NDA" policy similarly failed. *See* Upjohn Mfg. Co. v. Schweiker, 681 F.2d 480 (6th Cir. 1982). The policy later was enacted by Congress as part of the Waxman-Hatch Act. Pub. L. No. 98-417, § 103, 98 Stat. at 1593 (codified at 21 U.S.C. § 355(b)(2)).

[126] FOOD & DRUG ADMIN., APPROVED DRUG PRODUCTS WITH THERAPEUTIC EQUIVALENCE EVALUATIONS vii (16th ed. 1996). The research-based manufacturers had sought to enjoin publication of such a list on both procedural and substantive grounds; following commencement of the litigation, the FDA bowed to the procedural objections and conducted a notice-and-comment rulemaking proceeding on both "the proposed policy of making such a list available [and] the current content and form of the list itself," 44 Fed. Reg. 2932 (Jan. 12, 1979). *See* Pharmaceutical Mfrs. Ass'n v. Kennedy, 471 F. Supp. 1224 (D. Md. 1979) (subsequently dismissing suit on ground, not raised by defendants, that the mere publication of information is not reviewable agency action within the meaning of the Administrative Procedure Act, 5 U.S.C. § 551(13) (1994)).

intended to compel implementation of this proposal.[127] Before the FDA proposal was acted on or the lawsuit decided, however, the focus of attention had shifted to the legislative arena.

This shift resulted from the efforts of some pioneer manufacturers who, concerned over the shortened period of effective patent protection their products enjoyed in consequence of the long duration of the new drug approval process, were seeking legislation to restore lost patent life.[128] Although the generic industry opposed these efforts, it was slow to launch legislative proposals of its own to facilitate generic approvals.

Eventually, however, taking a cue from the proponents of patent term restoration, advocates of expanded generic drug availability turned to Congress as well. Legislation was introduced in 1983,[129] but by the time the 98th Congress convened in 1984, it seemed that neither a patent term restoration nor a generic drug bill could pass by itself. To break the impasse, generic and pioneer manufacturers agreed to support modified versions of each other's proposals. Title I of the resulting legislation[130] established an ANDA process for generic manufacturers. For pioneer manufacturers, title II extended the duration of drug patent rights to compensate for time lost in the regulatory review process.[131]

Title I provides a simple yet comprehensive scheme for the submission and approval of ANDAs, for both post-1962 and pre-1962 drugs, largely patterned on the NDA process as modified administratively by the FDA in its pre-Waxman-Hatch regulations authorizing ANDAs for pre-1962 drugs.[132] Congress added, however, a number of measures designed to ensure expeditious processing of ANDAs.

---

[127] National Ass'n of Pharmaceutical Mfrs. v. Heckler, Civ. No. 83-4817 (S.D.N.Y. filed June 24, 1983), *dismissed without prejudice* (June 15, 1985).

[128] Patent term restoration bills were introduced every year from 1978 to 1984. *See* Alan D. Lourie, *Patent Term Restoration: History, Summary, and Appraisal*, 40 FOOD DRUG COSM. L.J. 351 (1985). One such bill passed the Senate by voice vote in 1981. Patent Term Restoration Act of 1981, S. 255, 97th Cong., 1st Sess. (1981); 127 CONG. REC. 15,118 (1981). Pioneer manufacturers, however, did not abandon the battle before the FDA and the judiciary. Despite several defeats, they scored a significant victory in the judicial arena when the Federal Circuit held that generic companies could not begin testing of patented products until the patents expired. Roche Prod., Inc. v. Bolar Pharmaceutical Co., 733 F.2d 858 (Fed. Cir.), *cert. denied*, 469 U.S. 856 (1984).

[129] Drug Price Competition Act of 1983, H.R. 3605, 98th Cong., 1st Sess. (1983).

[130] Drug Price Competition and Patent Term Restoration Act of 1984, Pub. L. No. 98-417, 98 Stat. 1585.

[131] Additionally, pioneer manufacturers received "exclusivity" protection against approval of ANDAs within five years after the initial approval of "new chemical entity" pioneer drugs and within three years after approval of new uses for previously approved pioneer drugs, as well as a prohibition against ANDA approval until any patents covering the pioneer drug have expired, are successfully challenged in court by the generic applicant, or are not asserted against the applicant within a specified period. Generic manufacturers also received a provision overturning the holding in the *Bolar* case, 733 F. 2d. 858, insofar as it had prohibited pre-patent-expiration testing of patented human drugs and biologics, medical devices, and food and color additives for purposes of obtaining FDA approval. A similar provision overturning *Bolar* as to animal drugs and biologics was added by the subsequently enacted Generic Animal Drug and Patent Term Restoration Act of 1988. Pub. L. No. 100-670, § 201(i), 102 Stat. 3971, 3988 (1988).

[132] Pub. L. No. 98-417, § 101, 98 Stat. 1585 (codified at 21 U.S.C. § 355(j)). From the start, the FDA has interpreted title I as applying only to products approved under section 505 of the FDCA, codified at 21 U.S.C. § 355. *See* letter of Harry M. Meyer, Jr., M.D., Dir., Ctr. for Drugs & Biologics, Food & Drug Admin. 1 (Nov. 16, 1984); 54 Fed. Reg. 28,872, 28,874 (July 10, 1989). Antibiotics are approved not under section 505 but under section 507 of the FDCA, 21 U.S.C. § 357. The FDA's exclusion of antibiotics from title I coverage was challenged on the ground that, because the FDA now regulates antibiotics under section 505 (the same section under which it regulates approved new drugs) once they have been approved, antibiotics must be considered to be approved under section 505. The FDA's position that the statutory authority for antibiotic approvals continues to be section 507, not section 505, was upheld in Glaxo, Inc. v. Heckler, 640 F. Supp. 933 (E.D.N.C. 1986).

The FDA is prohibited explicitly from requesting any information beyond that specified in the statute.[133] The agency is required to act on an application within 180 days of its initial receipt.[134] By contrast, the 180-day clock for full NDAs does not begin to run until the FDA accepts the application for filing, an action the agency does not take until a significant portion of its review has been completed.[135] Proving that there is more than one way to extend a review period, the FDA has parried by declaring that an ANDA will be reviewed after it has been "submitted" to determine whether it is "sufficiently complete to permit a substantive review" and therefore to be deemed "received."[136]

If the FDA refuses to approve an ANDA, it must give the applicant notice of opportunity for a hearing.[137] The applicant must request a hearing within thirty days of the notice; unless the FDA and the applicant agree to a later date, the hearing must begin within 120 days of the date of the notice.[138] The hearing must be conducted on an expedited basis and a decision issued within ninety days after the date fixed for filing final briefs.[139]

Title I of the Waxman-Hatch Act also authorizes the FDA to conduct notice-and-comment rulemaking proceedings on "suitability" petitions to allow the filing of ANDAs for generic drugs based on, but also differing in one or more specified respects from, the underlying innovator drug.[140] If the FDA denies a suitability petition, an ANDA may not be filed.[141] The House Report states that "'there is no legal requirement that the hearing opportunity provided by section 505(c) be made available to ANDA applicants who disagree with an adverse agency decision.'"[142] An aggrieved petitioner's only remedy is judicial review under the "arbitrary and capricious" standard of of the Administrative Procedure Act (APA).[143]

In contrast to the detailed procedures established for ANDAs, the Waxman-Hatch Act is silent as to procedures for resolving disputes under the "non-patent exclusivity" provisions, which grant five years of exclusivity for new chemical entities and three years of exclusivity for new uses of previously approved drugs if specified criteria are met.[144] The FDA, however, has established a petition procedure to govern exclusivity controversies.[145]

The Waxman-Hatch Act only deals with human drugs. The inclusion of veterinary products within the Act's patent extension provisions (but not its abbreviated generic applica-

---

[133] FDCA § 505(j)(2)(A), 21 U.S.C. § 355(j)(2)(A).

[134] *Id.* § 505(j)(4)(B), 21 U.S.C. § 355(j)(4)(B).

[135] *Id.* § 505(c)(1), 21 U.S.C. § 355(c)(1). *See* Newport Pharmaceuticals Int'l, Inc. v. Schweiker, [1981-1982 Transfer Binder] Food Drug Cosm. L. Rep. (CCH) ¶ 38,148 (D.D.C. Dec. 2, 1981).

[136] 21 C.F.R. § 314.101(b).

[137] FDCA § 505(j)(4)(C), 21 U.S.C. § 355(j)(4)(C).

[138] *Id.*

[139] *Id.*

[140] *Id.* § 505(j)(2)(C), 21 U.S.C. § 355(j)(2)(C).

[141] *Id.*

[142] H.R. REP. No. 857, pt. I, 98th Cong., 2d Sess. 23 (Aug. 1, 1984), *quoting* 48 Fed. Reg. 2751, 2752 (Jan. 21, 1983).

[143] *Id. See* 5 U.S.C. § 706(2)(A).

[144] FDCA § 505(j)(4)(D), 21 U.S.C. § 355(j)(4)(D).

[145] *See* 51 Fed. Reg. 4991, 4992 (Feb. 10, 1986).

tion procedures) was proposed at one point,[146] but this idea was dropped before final passage of the bill. Even so, there was considerable support among animal drug and feed manufacturers (and in the FDA) for animal drug legislation similar to the Waxman-Hatch Act. Their efforts to negotiate a "consensus bill" eventually resulted in the Generic Animal Drug and Patent Term Restoration Act of 1988 (GADPTRA).[147]

GADPTRA was intended to create the same regime of abbreviated generic applications and patent term restoration for animal drugs as was created for human drugs by the Waxman-Hatch Act.[148] Thus, the two laws are closely parallel in both form and substance. Title I establishes an abbreviated application procedure for generic animal drugs very similar to that for generic human drugs; title II provides comparable patent term restoration remedies.

In title I, a potentially significant difference between Waxman-Hatch and GADPTRA is in the procedures for disapproving a generic animal drug. In the animal drug context, the FDA can refuse to approve an abbreviated application on the ground that the safety or effectiveness of the pioneer drug is under a cloud only if a notice of hearing for the pioneer drug has been published, rather than merely a notice of opportunity of hearing (NOOH) as with ANDAs for human drugs.[149] Congress thus sought to prevent the FDA from imposing on generic applicants the consequences of its often lengthy delays between publication and disposition of an NOOH.[150]

ANDA Fraud. The explosive growth of the generic drug industry made possible by title I of the Waxman-Hatch Act had its dark side. Some ANDA applicants sought to shortcut the already abbreviated approval process by paying unlawful gratuities to FDA reviewers in the hope of receiving at least expedited consideration of their ANDAs. Others, not content with buying their way to the head of the queue, shored up inadequate ANDAs with fabricated or fraudulent data. Congress responded with the Generic Drug Enforcement Act of 1992 (GDEA).[151]

GDEA authorizes the FDA to conduct two new types of proceedings involving generic drugs, and expands the agency's authority in the ANDA process itself.[152] First, it provides for debarment of firms and individuals convicted of fraud or other crimes in the course of the ANDA process.[153] Debarment is mandatory in some circumstances, discretionary with

---

[146] S. 2748, 98th Cong., 2d Sess. (1984).

[147] Pub. L. No. 100-670, 102 Stat. 3971.

[148] H.R. REP. NO. 972, pt. I, 100th Cong., 2d Sess. 2 (Sept. 23, 1988); H.R. REP. NO. 972, pt. II, 100th Cong., 2d Sess. 14 (Sept. 23, 1988). In addition, the distinction between prescription and non-prescription veterinary drugs for the first time was given an explicit statutory basis parallel to that provided by the Durham-Humphrey Amendment for human drugs. Pub. L. No. 100-670, § 105, 102 Stat. at 3983 (codified at 21 U.S.C. § 353(f)).

[149] *Compare* Pub. L. No. 100-670, § 101(c), 102 Stat. at 3976 (codified at 21 U.S.C. § 360b(c)(2)(A)(ix)) *with* 21 U.S.C. § 355(j)(2)(I).

[150] H.R. REP. NO. 972, pt. I, *supra* note 148, at 2. *Cf.* Barr Laboratories, Inc. v. Harris, 482 F. Supp. 1183 (D.D.C. 1980).

[151] Pub. L. No. 102-282, 106 Stat. 149 (1992) (codified at 21 U.S.C. §§ 335a-335c).

[152] In addition, GDEA creates new procedures for the temporary denial of ANDA approval and temporary suspension of distribution of drugs covered by previously approved ANDAs, by reason of a pending fraud investigation, FDCA § 306(f), (g), 21 U.S.C. § 335a(f), (g), and establishes ANDA fraud as a new ground for withdrawal of previously granted ANDA approvals, FDCA § 308, 21 U.S.C. § 335c. Temporary denial of approval must be preceded by an "informal hearing," not defined in the GDEA but presumably a hearing pursuant to the FDA's existing "regulatory hearing" procedure. 21 C.F.R. pt. 16; FDCA § 308(f)(3), 21 U.S.C. § 335a(f)(3).

[153] Pub. L. No. 102-282, § 2, 106 Stat. at 150 (codified at 21 U.S.C. § 335a).

the FDA (permissive) in others.[154] Debarment precludes a firm from submitting or assisting in the submission of an ANDA; debarred individuals are forbidden to render services "in any capacity" to the sponsor of any drug product application, approved or pending, abbreviated or otherwise.[155]

Debarment orders may be issued only after an opportunity for an on-the-record hearing on disputed issues of material fact.[156] Most notably, from the standpoint of agency procedure, the FDA is authorized to issue subpoenas *ad testificandum* and *duces tecum* in such proceedings.[157] This marks only the second time that Congress has given the FDA such authority,[158] which is conspicuous by its absence from the procedures that govern most FDA formal adjudicatory and rulemaking proceedings.[159] Debarment orders are judicially reviewable in the courts of appeals, except for orders based on certain grounds that Congress may have deemed especially subjective and outside the scope of the FDA's established expertise;[160] these debarment orders are reviewable *de novo* in district court civil actions.[161]

Second, the GDEA authorizes the FDA to impose civil monetary penalties for ANDA fraud, up to $250,000 against individuals and up to $1,000,000 against firms.[162] As in debarment proceedings, there must be an opportunity for an on-the-record hearing on disputed issues of material fact, as well as on the amount of the penalty, and the FDA is granted subpoena power.[163] Alternatively, the FDA may request the Attorney General to sue for civil penalties in a federal district court.[164] An unusual feature of the GDEA civil penalty provisions is the authority conferred on the FDA to reward informants with up to half the penalty "imposed and collected," up to a maximum of $250,000.[165]

Patent Term Restoration For Innovator Drugs. Title II of the Waxman-Hatch Act establishes procedures for extending the term of a patent claiming an FDA-approved product, its method of use, or its method of manufacturing.[166] Such a product may be a human or animal drug or antibiotic, a medical device, a food additive, or a color additive. In general,

---

[154] FDCA § 306(a), (b), 21 U.S.C. § 335a(a), (b).

[155] *Id.*

[156] *Id.* § 306(i), 21 U.S.C. § 335a(i).

[157] *Id.*

[158] The first such statute was the Safe Medical Devices Act of 1990, discussed *infra* notes 213-20 and accompanying text.

[159] *See, e.g.,* Pub. L. No. 75-717, § 505(e) (codified as amended at 21 U.S.C § 355(e)) (revocation of NDA approval). For a striking example of the consequences that may flow from the FDA's general lack of subpoena authority, *see* National Nutritional Foods Ass'n v. FDA, 504 F.2d 761, 793 n.45 (2d Cir. 1974).

[160] These are permissive-debarment orders against individuals, based on FDA findings of a "pattern of conduct sufficient to find that there is reason to believe" that the individual presents a risk of future violations, FDCA § 306(b)(2)(B)(iii), 21 U.S.C. § 335a(b)(2)(B)(iii), or on FDA findings that the individual was a "high managerial agent" who had actual or constructive knowledge of especially serious ANDA fraud by another debarred individual and failed to report the fraud, *id.* § 306(b)(2)(B)(iv), 21 U.S.C. § 335a(b)(2)(B)(iv).

[161] *Id.* § 306(j)(2), 21 U.S.C. § 335a(j)(2).

[162] *Id.* § 307, 21 U.S.C. § 335b.

[163] *Id.* § 307(b)(1)(A), 21 U.S.C. § 335b(b)(1)(A).

[164] *Id.* § 307(b)(1)(B), 21 U.S.C. § 335b(b)(1)(B).

[165] *Id.* § 307(e), 21 U.S.C. § 335b(e).

[166] Title II amends the patent laws, not the FDCA. Pub. L. No. 98-417, § 201(a), 98 Stat. at 1598 (codified at 35 U.S.C. § 156 (1994)).

a patent term may be extended for up to five years,[167] with credit given for a "regulatory review period" comprising half the time spent performing human clinical trials on the product, plus all of the time spent by the FDA in reviewing the product's marketing application.[168] Moreover, the length of the extension must be reduced by the amount of time during which the marketing applicant did not employ "due diligence" in seeking marketing approval.[169]

Administration of title II is split between the FDA and the Department of Commerce's Patent and Trademark Office (PTO). The statute commits the determination of eligibility for, and length of, the extension to the PTO.[170] The FDA's role is limited to determining the length of the "regulatory review period."[171]

Title II has two noteworthy procedural aspects. First, as in title I, both the FDA and the PTO are bound to a very tight timetable. The agency must make and publish its regulatory review determination within thirty days of receipt of an extension application from the PTO.[172] Following publication, interested parties have 180 days in which to petition the FDA to determine whether the applicant acted with "due diligence" during the regulatory review period.[173] The FDA must render a decision upon any due-diligence petition within ninety days of receipt and publish it in the *Federal Register*.[174] Within sixty days of the FDA's decision, any interested party may request an informal hearing, which the FDA is required to hold within thirty days (or sixty days if so requested by the party seeking a hearing).[175] The FDA either must affirm or revise its decision within thirty days of completion of the hearing.[176]

Second, the making of due-diligence determinations specifically calls on the FDA to make decisions based on nonscientific grounds, a relatively new type of authority for the agency.[177] The potential for confusion in this area can be seen in the FDA's attempt in the title II implementing regulations to provide guidance on what constitutes "due diligence." The proposed rule recited the statutory definition ("that degree of attention, continuous directed effort, and timeliness as may reasonably be expected from, and are ordinarily

---

[167] 35 U.S.C. § 156(c)(3). If the patent was issued before the date of enactment, and testing had begun before the date of enactment, the total length of extension cannot exceed two years. *Id.* § 156(g)(4)(C). Moreover, the period between the date of approval of the product and the expiration of the patent as extended must not exceed 14 years. *Id.* § 156(g)(4).

[168] *Id.* § 156(g).

[169] *Id.* § 156(c)(1). Curiously, the clinical trials, marketing application, and "due diligence" need not necessarily have been those of the patent holder. *See* 55 Fed. Reg. 65,111 (Oct. 3, 1991) (allowing "regulatory review" period based on trials conducted and NDA submitted by patent holder's competitor, with patent holder's acquiescence, while unsuccessfully seeking license under patent).

[170] 35 U.S.C. § 156(e).

[171] *Id.* § 156(d)(2)(A). Pursuant to a memorandum of understanding, 52 Fed. Reg. 17,830 (May 12, 1987), however, the FDA assists the PTO with eligibility determinations. 21 C.F.R. § 60.10.

[172] 35 U.S.C. § 156(d)(2)(A).

[173] *Id.* § 156(d)(2)(B)(i).

[174] *Id.*

[175] *Id.* § 156(d)(2)(B)(ii).

[176] *Id.* § 156(d)(2)(b)(ii).

[177] *See also infra* notes 188-89 and accompanying text (discussing the economic aspects of "orphan drug" status determinations under the Orphan Drug Act of 1983 and its amendments).

exercised" by an applicant) and then listed eight illustrative factors that the agency proposed to take into consideration when making a determination.[178] In response to adverse comments, however, the agency dropped the list of illustrative factors. Thus, the final rule adds nothing to the statutory language and the legislative history except a vague preamble reference to a "flexible approach."[179]

Whether these unique procedural aspects of title II will ever be utilized remains an open question. Thus far, no "due diligence" hearings have been requested or held.

Title II of the GADPTRA provides an opportunity for patent term restoration for animal drugs and veterinary biologicals on terms comparable to the Waxman-Hatch Act.[180] The procedural features of title II of the Waxman-Hatch Act, especially those pertaining to due diligence, generally are replicated in the GADPTRA.[181]

Orphan Drugs

Generally speaking, an orphan drug is one used for treatment of a disease or condition that affects too few persons to justify private investment of the research and development resources necessary to bring the drug to market.[182] Congress passed the Orphan Drug Act of 1983 to facilitate the development of orphan drugs.[183] The Act offers three incentives to manufacturers of orphan drugs: 1) FDA assistance in designing the necessary studies of the orphan drug;[184] 2) grants to subsidize the cost of such testing;[185] and 3) seven years of marketing exclusivity for the orphan indication, which commences on the date the NDA for a designated orphan drug is approved.[186] Little controversy surrounded the Act's original passage, as reflected by the sponsorship of 171 House members.[187] Although experience under the Act has led to the modification or refinement of certain provisions, these amendments were noncontroversial as well.[188]

Perhaps because of the Act's ostensibly noncontroversial nature, Congress established few procedures for the FDA to follow in implementing the Orphan Drug Act. The most note-

---

[178] 51 Fed. Reg. 25,338, 25,347 (July 11, 1986).

[179] 53 Fed. Reg. 7298, 7304 (Mar. 7, 1988); 21 C.F.R. § 60.36.

[180] Pub. L. No. 100-670, § 201, 102 Stat. at 3984-89 (codified at 35 U.S.C. §156).

[181] *Id.* § 201(f), 102 Stat. at 3986 (codified at 35 U.S.C. § 156(d)(2)(B)). Under the 1988 Act, however, the patent holder may choose to have the patent extension based on either the regulatory review period for the first approved commercial marketing or use of the product or, if the first approval relates to nonfood producing animals, on the regulatory review period for the first approved commercial marketing or use for food-producing animals. *Id.* § 201(a), 102 Stat. at 3984-85 (1988) (codified at 35 U.S.C. § 156(a)(5)(C)). If the patent holder elects the latter option, then the rights derived from the patent during the extension period do not apply to uses covered by earlier approvals for nonfood producing animals. *See* H.R. REP. NO. 972, pt. I, 100th Cong., 2d Sess. 8 (1988).

[182] *See* H.R. REP. NO. 840, pt. 1, 97th Cong., 1st Sess. 6, 8-9 (1982), *reprinted in* 1982 U.S.C.C.A.N. 3577, 3578.

[183] Pub. L. No. 97-414, 96 Stat. 2049 (1983).

[184] *Id.* § 525, 21 U.S.C. § 360aa.

[185] *Id.* § 5, 21 U.S.C. § 360ee.

[186] *Id.* § 527, 21 U.S.C. § 360cc.

[187] 128 CONG. REC. 25,440 (Sept. 28, 1982) (statement of Rep. Waxman).

[188] Health Promotion and Disease Prevention Amendments of 1984, Pub. L. No. 98-551, 98 Stat. 2817 (adding presumption that drugs for treatment of diseases affecting fewer than 200,000 persons annually qualify as orphan drugs); Orphan Drug Act Amendments of 1985, Pub. L. No. 99-91, 99 Stat. 387 (removing original prohibition against exclusivity for patented orphan drugs); Pub. L. No. 100-290, 102 Stat. 90 (1988) (adding requirement that request for designation as orphan drug precede submission of NDA).

worthy check on agency discretion comes into play when, during the seven-year exclusivity period of an orphan drug, the FDA proposes to approve a second sponsor's NDA. The second NDA can be approved only if the FDA finds that the original sponsor cannot assure the availability of quantities of the drug sufficient to meet the needs of persons with the disease or condition.[189] The Act requires the FDA to provide the original sponsor with notice and opportunity for the submission of views before it makes such a finding.[190]

Procedures for designation as an orphan drug, which is a prerequisite to obtaining the benefits of the Act, are left almost wholly to the FDA's discretion. Upon request, which since 1988 must be made prior to submission of an application for marketing approval, the FDA is required to designate an eligible drug as an orphan drug.[191] The only prerequisites to eligibility for orphan drug designation are that a drug "is being or will be investigated for a rare disease or condition," and that the applicant for marketing approval consents to public notice of the designation.[192]

The Act does direct the FDA to promulgate regulations to establish procedures for the designation of orphan drugs.[193] Although the Act dates from 1983, implementing regulations were not promulgated until the waning hours of 1992.[194] Some five years after the statute's enactment, with no regulations yet promulgated, the FDA's inaction was challenged as a violation of the Orphan Drug Act, the APA, and the Fifth Amendment.[195] The litigation terminated without a decision on these issues, but the court chastised the FDA for failing to establish policies implementing the Act.[196]

Medical Devices

The most rapidly changing technology sector within the FDA's regulatory jurisdiction undoubtedly has been the medical device industry. Provisions granting the FDA authority to police medical device safety and the claims made for devices were included in the 1938 Act, but these provisions were concerned mainly with ensuring truthful labeling.[197] By the mid-1970s, however, sophisticated modern devices had made careful design essential to ensuring that a device was both safe and effective.[198] Rejecting the FDA's initial approach of simply sweeping devices within the Act's drug regulatory provisions on the basis of overlaps in the statutory definitions, Congress has grappled with the problem directly, repeatedly, and in considerable detail.

---

[189] FDCA § 527(b)(1), 21 U.S.C. § 360cc(b)(1).

[190] *Id.*

[191] *Id.* § 526(a)(1), 21 U.S.C. § 360bb(a)(1).

[192] *Id.*

[193] *Id.* § 526(c), 21 U.S.C. § 360bb(c). The FDA also is required to establish regulations implementing the provisions that require it to assist sponsors in designing orphan drug studies. *Id.* § 525(b), 21 U.S.C. § 360aa(b).

[194] 57 Fed. Reg. 62,085 (Dec. 29, 1992); 21 C.F.R. pt. 316.

[195] *See, e.g.*, First Amended Complaint of Genentech, Inc. ¶¶ 33, 43, 61 (filed Mar. 10, 1987), Genentech, Inc. v. Bowen, Civ. No. 87-0605, *dismissed per stipulation* (D.D.C. Aug. 23, 1989). The litigation primarily involved a dispute over the scope of orphan drug exclusivity. Genentech, the original plaintiff, withdrew from the litigation in 1988, but similar substantive and procedural claims continued to be pressed by intervening parties for almost another year until they also abandoned the proceeding.

[196] Genentech, Inc. v. Bowen, 676 F. Supp. 301 (D.D.C. 1987).

[197] Pub. L. No. 75-717, § 502, 52 Stat. at 1050.

[198] S. Rep No. 33, 94th Cong., 2d Sess. 5 (1975), *reprinted in* 1976 U.S.C.C.A.N. 1070, 1075.

Under the Medical Device Amendments of 1976,[199] as refined and modified by subsequent enactments in 1990 and 1992,[200] the distinction between drugs and devices has been significantly (although by no means completely) clarified. For devices, misbranding and adulteration charges are no longer the agency's sole weapons for ensuring compliance with the statutory requirements. All medical devices are now subject to direct regulation of different kinds, based on their classification by the FDA into one of three escalating regulatory categories under criteria defined in the statute.

When "general controls" — the basic misbranding and adulteration provisions — are sufficient to provide reasonable assurance of safety and effectiveness, and the device is not used for supporting or sustaining life and does not otherwise present a potential unreasonable risk of illness or injury, it is to be grouped in Class I.[201] When general controls are insufficient but "special controls" such as a performance standard, postmarket surveillance, patient registries, guidelines, or recommendations will provide the necessary assurance, a device is to be grouped in Class II.[202] Class III devices, requiring premarket clearance, are those devices that are intended for use in supporting or sustaining life or otherwise presenting a potential unreasonable risk, and that cannot adequately be regulated by the application of either general or special controls.[203]

Although the FDA was made responsible for classifying every medical device into one of the three regulatory classes,[204] Congress mandated specific procedures intended to preclude arbitrary agency action.[205] In this instance, Congress was not satisfied to rely on agency expertise. Instead, the agency was directed to consult classification panels consisting of outside experts in a variety of scientific and technical disciplines.[206] Furthermore, the device provisions contain unusually specific and detailed judicial review provisions.[207]

The 1976 Amendments also gave the FDA a variety of novel powers over marketing medical devices. These include the authority to develop performance standards for particular types of devices;[208] to impose a prescription requirement or other restrictive conditions on the sale, distribution, or use of a device if specified conditions are met, similar to those long previously employed by the FDA in requiring (despite the absence of express statutory authority) certain devices to be sold only on prescription;[209] to impose an outright ban on devices the use of which presents "substantial deception or an unreasonable and sub-

---

[199] Pub. L. No. 94-295, 90 Stat. 539 (1976).

[200] Safe Medical Devices Act of 1990, Pub. L. No. 101-629, 104 Stat. 4511; Medical Device Amendments of 1992, Pub. L. No. 102-300, 106 Stat. 238.

[201] FDCA § 513(a)(1)(A), 21 U.S.C. § 360c(a)(1)(A).

[202] *Id.* § 513(a)(1)(B), 21 U.S.C. § 360c(a)(1)(B).

[203] *Id.* § 513(a)(1)(C), 21 U.S.C. § 360c(a)(1)(C).

[204] *Id.* § 513(b)(1), 21 U.S.C. § 360c(b)(1).

[205] *Id.* § 513(f), 21 U.S.C. § 360c(f).

[206] *Id.* § 513(b)(2), 21 U.S.C. § 360c(b)(2).

[207] *Id.* § 517, 21 U.S.C. § 360g.

[208] *Id.* § 514, 21 U.S.C. § 360d.

[209] *Id.* § 520(e), 21 U.S.C. § 360j(e). Section 520(e) requires this to be done "by regulation." The FDA attempted to do so merely by publishing a notice declaring that all devices previously deemed subject to the nonstatutory prescription requirement would henceforth be deemed "restricted devices," 41 Fed. Reg. 22,620 (June 4, 1976), but this was held unlawful in Becton Dickinson Co. v. FDA, 589 F.2d 1175 (2d Cir. 1978). Curiously, to this day the FDA never has conducted the requisite notice-and-comment rulemaking.

stantial risk of illness or injury," as well as to make a proposed ban effective after merely an "informal hearing" prior to completion of the required plenary proceedings;[210] to require the persons "best suited under the circumstances involved," after "consultation" therewith, to provide notification to users, health professionals, and others in the distribution chain that a device poses "an unreasonable risk of substantial harm";[211] and again after merely an "informal hearing," to require device manufacturers and others in the distribution chain to repair, replace, or provide purchase price refunds for improperly designed or manufactured devices that present "an unreasonable risk of substantial harm."[212]

The Safe Medical Devices Act of 1990 (SMDA) made substantial additions to this formidable procedural arsenal.[213] In addition to expanding the range of "special controls" beyond the performance standards authorized by the 1976 Medical Device Amendments,[214] the SMDA explicitly authorized the FDA to compel the recall of devices found reasonably probable to cause "serious, adverse health consequences or death."[215] This is the first recall authority ever to be explicitly conferred on the agency.

A recall order may be preceded, without a hearing or consultation of any kind, by a cease-and-desist order requiring the manufacturer and others in the distribution chain to cease distribution and to notify health professionals and user facilities to cease use of the device. Within ten days of issuance, however, the FDA must provide persons subject to such an order with an opportunity for an "informal hearing," at which one issue must be whether a recall should be required.[216]

Another new procedural weapon made available to the FDA by the SMDA is the agency's first-ever grant of explicit authority to impose civil penalties.[217] Penalties of up to $15,000 per violation may be imposed for "violat[ing] any requirement of [the 1938 Act, as amended] that relates to devices," up to a maximum of $1,000,000 in a single proceeding.[218] Opportunity for an on-the-record adjudicatory hearing must be afforded, in which — again for the first time — the FDA is given subpoena power.[219] Judicial review of SMDA civil penalty orders occurs in the courts of appeals.[220]

---

[210] FDCA § 516, 21 U.S.C. § 360f.

[211] *Id*. § 518(a), 21 U.S.C. § 360h(a).

[212] *Id*. § 518(b), 21 U.S.C. § 360h(b). The FDA also may require such a person to reimburse the expenses of others in the distribution chain where "required for the protection of the public health." *Id*. § 518(c), 21 U.S.C. § 360h(c).

[213] Pub. L. No. 101-629, 104 Stat. 4511.

[214] *Id*. § 5(a), 104 Stat. at 4517 (amending 21 U.S.C. § 360c(a)(1)).

[215] *Id*. § 8, 104 Stat. at 4520-21 (codified at 21 U.S.C. § 360h(e)).

[216] FDCA § 518(e)(1), 21 U.S.C. § 360h(e)(1).

[217] *Id*. § 303(f), 21 U.S.C. § 333(f). Two slightly earlier statutes administered by the FDA created civil penalty liability for violations, but without specifying whether the penalties were to be imposed in administrative proceedings before the agency or judicially in lawsuits brought by the United States. National Childhood Vaccine Injury Act of 1986, Pub. L. No. 99-660, 100 Stat. 3755 (codified at 42 U.S.C. § 262(d)(2)(B)); Prescription Drug Marketing Act of 1987, Pub. L. No. 100-293, 102 Stat. 100 (codified at 21 U.S.C. § 333(b)). In promulgating its 1995 procedural regulation governing civil penalty proceedings under all the statutes that currently confer such authority on the agency, the FDA claimed that congressional silence as to the forum "gives FDA the option." 58 Fed. Reg. 30,680, 30,681 (May 26, 1993) (preamble to proposed rule); *see* 60 Fed. Reg. 38,612, 38,613 (July 27, 1995) (preamble to final rule).

[218] FDCA § 303(f)(1)(A), 21 U.S.C. § 333(f)(1)(A).

[219] *Id*. § 303(f)(2)(A), 21 U.S.C. § 333(f)(2)(A).

[220] *Id*. § 303(f)(3), 21 U.S.C. § 303(f)(3).

■ Expanding the FDA's Authority by Procedural Innovation

To catalogue the many innovations that characterize the FDA's current administrative procedures would stretch this chapter beyond reasonable compass. Suffice it to mention a few of the most significant aspects of the agency's creativity in responding to the challenges of its role as direct regulator of industry. First, notice-and-comment rulemaking under section 701(a) of the original Act has become the FDA's principal regulatory tool. Second, the agency has centered its formal adjudicatory process around a highly structured summary judgment procedure designed to avoid evidentiary hearings in all but the most intractable cases. Third, the FDA has regularized its decisionmaking process under published standardized procedures. Fourth, the agency has come to rely heavily on outside advisory committees for assistance in making regulatory judgments.

Not all the FDA's attempted innovations have succeeded. As part of its massive reshaping and codification of agency procedures in the mid-1970s, the agency created alternative dispute resolution mechanisms employing scientists as decisionmakers rather than administrative law judges. These new techniques have never been used, although the formal evidentiary hearings they were meant to displace have proven almost equally rare.

Rulemaking

Section 701(a) of the Act states that the FDA shall have "authority to promulgate regulations for [its] efficient enforcement."[221] Until relatively recently, such grants of general rulemaking authority were regarded as conferring only the power to issue "interpretive" rules subject to *de novo* judicial review in enforcement actions.[222] Over time, however, rulemaking provisions such as section 701(a) have come to be regarded as authorizing issuance of regulations with the force and effect of law.[223] Beginning in the early 1970s, the FDA seized upon this heretofore innocuous provision in the statute and made it the fulcrum of virtually all the agency's regulatory efforts. For reasons unique to the FDA, however, the shift did not come easily.

The primary problem in the FDA's use of this section has been that Congress included in the 1938 Act two separate rulemaking provisions, one — section 701(a) — for the promulgation of "efficient enforcement" regulations, and the other — section 701(e) — for the promulgation of regulations expressly having the force and effect of law. Section 701(e) enumerates the substantive provisions of the Act expressly requiring compliance with regulations issued by the FDA, and prescribes an elaborate procedure for on-the-record evidentiary trial-type rulemaking, with specific provision for judicial review in a court of appeals.[224] Because it is clear that regulations issued under section 701(e) with

---

[221] 21 U.S.C. § 371(a).

[222] As one court candidly admitted while upholding the FDA's authority under section 701(a) to issue binding regulations:

> In the interest of historical accuracy, it should be noted that at one time it was widely understood that generalized grants of rulemaking authority conferred power only to make rules of a procedural or an interpretive nature, and not binding substantive regulations, for which a specific delegation was thought necessary.

National Ass'n of Pharmaceutical Mfrs. v. FDA, 637 F.2d 877, 880 (2d Cir. 1981).

[223] For a review of decisions to this effect, see National Petroleum Refiners Ass'n v. FTC, 482 F.2d 672 (D.C. Cir. 1973), *cert. denied*, 415 U.S. 951 (1974).

[224] 21 U.S.C. § 371(e). *See* William F. Cody, *Authoritative Effect of FDA Regulations*, 24 FOOD DRUG COSM. L.J. 195, 199 (1969).

its special procedural requirements were meant to have the force and effect of law, it has been argued that both the congressional silence about the effect of section 701(a) regulations and the absence of explicit procedural safeguards (and of any provision for judicial review) demonstrate an intention that section 701(a) regulations be merely interpretive.[225]

Traditionally, the distinction between binding and interpretive regulations was crucial because under an interpretive regulation it was not enough for the FDA to show, in an enforcement action, simply that the regulation was violated. The agency was required to establish that the violative conduct was also within the prohibition of the statute itself. Regulations having the force and effect of law, in contrast, are directly enforceable in court and if within the FDA's rulemaking authority must be complied with *ex proprio vigore*. As noted previously in this chapter, the distinction was a major issue in Congress' deliberations on the 1938 Act.

Since the Supreme Court's 1967 decision in *Abbott Laboratories v. Gardner*,[226] the FDA consistently has asserted that regulations promulgated pursuant to section 701(a) have the force and effect of law. Yet *Abbott Laboratories* is not conclusive authority for the proposition. That case dealt with the issue of whether certain drug labeling regulations promulgated pursuant to section 701(a) were ripe for pre-enforcement judicial review.[227] Because the Court held the regulations ripe for review because of their practical impact on the pharmaceutical industry, it had no occasion to decide whether they had the force and effect of law.

In 1973, however, in *Weinberger v. Hynson, Westcott & Dunning, Inc.*,[228] the Court upheld the FDA's right to deny an evidentiary hearing in a proceeding to withdraw approval of an NDA when the applicant failed to make the threshold showing required by the FDA in a regulation issued under section 701(a). The *Hynson* decision has been viewed judicially as dispelling "[w]hatever doubts might have been entertained regarding the FDA's power under section 701(a) to promulgate binding regulations."[229]

As one court has noted, a contrary interpretation at this time would create regulatory chaos in many areas of FDA jurisdiction.[230] For better or worse, rulemaking under section 701(a) rapidly became the FDA's primary regulatory tool,[231] even to the point of displacing section 701(e) rulemaking on matters expressly subject to the section 701(e) pro-

---

[225] Cody, *supra* note 224, at 199-200.

[226] 387 U.S. 136 (1967).

[227] 387 U.S. at 152-53, *see also* Cody, *supra* note 224, at 201-02.

[228] 412 U.S. 609 (1973).

[229] *National Nutritional Foods Ass'n*, 512 F.2d at 696.

[230] *National Ass'n of Pharmaceutical Mfrs.*, 637 F.2d at 888.

[231] *See, e.g.*, Upjohn Co. v. FDA, 811 F.2d 1583 (D.C. Cir. 1987). Because of the high degree of deference accorded by the courts to administrative agency interpretations, *see* Young v. Community Nutrition Inst., 476 U.S. 974 (1986), today the practical distinction between substantive and interpretive rulemaking is less than clear. *See* Vietnam Veterans of Am. v. Secretary of the Navy, 843 F.2d 528, 536-38 (D.C. Cir. 1988). Some courts, however, have forced the FDA to comply with notice-and-comment procedures in taking regulatory actions that traditionally had been viewed as subject to no procedural requirements whatsoever. *See, e.g.*, Bellarno Int'l Ltd. v. FDA, 678 F. Supp. 410 (E.D.N.Y. 1988) (issuance of Import Alerts); Community Nutrition Inst. v. Young, 818 F.2d 943 (D.C. Cir. 1987).

cedure when the same functional regulatory objective can be achieved in a superficially different way.[232]

Perhaps the most notable use of section 701(a) has been the OTC Drug Review, a monumental effort to apply the effectiveness requirements of the 1962 Drug Amendments to the multitude of OTC medicines on the market. The regulations creating the review provide for the making of effectiveness (and also safety) determinations by the FDA on an ingredient-by-ingredient basis in notice-and-comment rulemakings that cover whole therapeutic categories, in lieu of product-by-product or even ingredient-by-ingredient adjudications.[233] Although the lawfulness of making these ingredient-oriented determinations through rulemaking never has been sanctioned expressly by the Supreme Court,[234] the program has come to have the full support of industry and at this late date is unlikely to face serious challenge.

One of the hallmarks of the FDA's notice-and-comment rulemaking process, enshrined in its procedural regulations,[235] has been the publication of extensive preambles to accompany notices of proposed rulemaking and the promulgation of final rules. Growing out of the APA's requirement that all rules "incorporate . . . a concise general statement of their basis and purpose,"[236] these lengthy explanatory essays typically present an elaborate factual and policy justification for the agency action involved. Preambles accompanying final regulations typically summarize and respond to virtually all comments submitted to the agency during the rulemaking. Importantly, the FDA's procedural regulations confer on preambles the status of "advisory opinions,"[237] which the regulations make binding on the agency.[238]

The FDA's commitment to this important but resource-intensive practice, while admirable in many ways, paradoxically has led to a growing reluctance by the agency to use the notice-and-comment process at all. As originally promulgated, the FDA's comprehensive procedural regulations required the agency to use notice-and-comment rulemaking procedures when issuing interpretive rules and rules of agency practice and procedure, even though the APA exempts those types of rules from the notice-and-comment requirement.[239] In 1991 the procedural regulations were amended to make notice-and-comment proceedings in such cases discretionary with the agency.[240] The FDA argued that the change was necessary because court decisions had expanded the definition of "rules" to

---

[232] *See American Frozen Food Inst.*, 555 F.2d 1059. *See also* Young v.Community Nutrition Inst., 476 U.S. 974 (1986) ("action levels" for contamination in food can be established informally rather than in formal rulemaking to set tolerances as provided in section 406 of the 1938 Act, 21 U.S.C. § 346), *on remand*, 818 F.2d 943 (D.C. Cir. 1987) (section 701(a) notice-and-comment rulemaking on action levels required).

[233] 21 C.F.R. pt. 330.

[234] *But see, e.g.*, Weinberger v. Bentex Pharmaceuticals, Inc., 412 U.S. 645, 650 (1973).

[235] 21 C.F.R. §§ 10.40(b)(1)(vii), 10.40(c)(3).

[236] 5 U.S.C. § 553(c).

[237] 21 C.F.R. § 10.85(d)(1).

[238] *Id.* § 10.85(e). In 1992 the agency proposed to repeal this provision, on grounds of inconsistency with the principle that the government cannot be estopped and with the requirement of notice-and-comment proceedings before binding rules may be promulgated. 57 Fed. Reg. 47,314 (Oct. 15, 1992). The proposal was denounced widely, and almost four years later remains pending. *See* 61 Fed. Reg. 9181, 9183 n.1 (Mar. 7, 1996) ("the agency plans to make final decisions").

[239] 5 U.S.C. § 553(b).

[240] 56 Fed. Reg. 13,757 (Apr. 4, 1991), 21 C.F.R. § 10.40(d).

encompass "a great number of other agency pronouncements that FDA does not consider rules but that reviewing courts may consider rules within the meaning of the . . . [APA]" and such widespread use of notice-and-comment procedure was "not feasible."[241]

Even with this change, the FDA has found the notice-and-comment requirement increasingly onerous. More and more, the agency has resorted to issuing important pronouncements with no public process whatsoever, by labeling them as "guidance" documents that ostensibly are not binding but merely provide assistance to those concerned. The practice has become so extensive, and so controversial, that the FDA has undertaken to develop procedures for public participation in the development and formulation of "guidance" without the "burden and inherent delay" of APA notice-and-comment procedures.[242] It remains to be seen whether the resulting scheme, no matter how complex, will be any less burdensome or time-consuming.

Summary Judgment

Although the Act seems to contemplate that much of the FDA's business be conducted in the form of trial-type evidentiary hearings, particularly with respect to new drugs,[243] in fact such hearings are rare. The agency has pioneered the use of summary judgment procedures to cut off requests for hearings at the threshold by establishing, through notice-and-comment rulemaking, strict burdens of proof for ultimate success on the merits and requiring applicants for a hearing to show at the outset that those criteria potentially are satisfied by the data they would present. The scheme has been so successful that only a single administrative law judge is needed to handle the entirety of the agency's evidentiary hearing obligations, including those arising under the food and color additive provisions of the Act and the formal rulemaking provisions of section 701(e), as well as under the new drug approval provisions.

The use of summary judgment principles by the FDA was upheld by the Supreme Court in *Weinberger v. Hynson, Westcott & Dunning, Inc.,*[244] a case growing out of the agency's program for applying the effectiveness requirements of the 1962 Drug Amendments to previously approved prescription drugs.[245] The Court noted the magnitude of the FDA's task, in light of the thousands of pre-1962 drugs still on the market, and the difficulty, if not impossibility, of accomplishing the statutory objective "[i]f FDA were required automatically to hold a hearing for each product whose efficacy was questioned."[246] The FDA's particularization of the statutory "substantial evidence" standard (defined in the Act to mean "adequate and well controlled investigations")[247] in regulations "reduc[ing] . . . that standard to detailed guidelines" was found to make "appropriate" the summary disposition of cases without a hearing "where it is apparent at the threshold that the applicant has not tendered *any* evidence which *on its face* meets the statutory standards as particularized by the regulations," and it thus "appears conclusively from the applicant's 'pleadings' that the

---

[241] 59 Fed. Reg. 31,080 (July 31, 1990) (citing 5 U.S.C. § 551(4)) (preamble to notice of proposed rulemaking). *See also* 60 Fed. Reg. 13,757 (Apr. 3, 1990) (preamble to final rule).

[242] 61 Fed. Reg. 9181, 9183 (Mar. 7, 1996).

[243] FDCA § 505(d), (e), 21 U.S.C. § 355(d), (e).

[244] 412 U.S. 609.

[245] *See also* American Public Health Ass'n v. Veneman, 349 F. Supp. 1311 (D.D.C. 1972).

[246] 412 U.S. at 621.

[247] FDCA § 505(d), 21 U.S.C. § 355(d).

application cannot succeed."[248] The principle has been applied since to sanction summary judgment even when the statutory standards have not been particularized through regulations but the factual issues thus raised can be deemed not "material."[249]

Despite the Court's emphasis on the limited circumstances in which summary disposition without a hearing would be appropriate, the FDA came close to taking the decision as carte blanche for reading the evidentiary hearing requirement almost entirely out of the Act. In case after case, the withdrawal of a new drug approval was reversed on appeal because the FDA had improperly substituted summary judgment practice for evidentiary hearings as the vehicle for deciding genuinely disputed issues of fact even in the absence of a dispositive and appropriately "precise" regulation.[250] The FDA's enthusiasm for summary disposition was at one time so great that the District of Columbia Circuit was driven to question the agency's "good faith" in administering its summary judgment regulations.[251] Although a handful of hearing requests subsequently have been granted, and a few hearings actually have been held,[252] summary judgment remains by and large the mainstay of the FDA's formal adjudicatory process.

Recently, the FDA has extended its use of summary judgment procedure to informal regulatory hearings.[253] An opportunity for this type of hearing is mandated by several provisions of the Act relating to medical devices,[254] and is available under numerous FDA regulations as a less time-consuming and resource-intensive "due process" alternative to the traditional on-the-record adjudicatory hearing before an administrative law judge.[255]

Publication of Standardized Agency Procedures

In 1975 the FDA could describe accurately the state of its procedures as follows:

> The present administrative practices and procedures of the Food and Drug Administration are largely uncodified and, to the extent that they are included in

---

[248] 412 U.S. at 617, 620-21.

[249] John D. Copanos & Sons, Inc. v. FDA, 854 F.2d 510 (D.C. Cir. 1988); Community Nutrition Inst. v. Novitch, 773 F.2d 1356 (D.C. Cir. 1985), *cert. denied*, 475 U.S. 1123 (1986).

[250] E.R. Squibb & Sons, Inc. v. Weinberger, 483 F.2d 1382 (3d Cir. 1973); Edison Pharmaceutical Co. v. FDA, 513 F.2d 1063 (D.C. Cir. 1975); SmithKline Corp. v. FDA, 587 F.2d 1107 (D.C. Cir. 1978); American Cyanamid Co. v. FDA, 606 F.2d 1307 (D.C. Cir. 1979). *See* USV Pharmaceutical Corp. v. Secretary of HEW, 466 F.2d 455 (D.C. Cir. 1972) (pre-*Hynson*). *Cf.* Marshall Minerals, Inc. v. FDA, 661 F.2d 409 (5th Cir. 1981) (reversing denial of hearing on petition for issuance of food additive regulation).

[251] *Edison Pharmaceutical Co.*, 513 F.2d at 1072.

[252] The number of hearings held has been so few that the courts have had only limited opportunity to review the resulting adjudicatory orders. It appears, however, that the "substantial evidence" standard of review in its familiar sense is likely to give the FDA great leeway in resolving drug safety and effectiveness issues on the merits, once it has employed necessary and appropriate adjudicatory procedures. *See* E.R. Squibb & Sons, Inc. v. Bowen, 870 F.2d 678 (D.C. Cir. 1989); Edison Pharmaceutical Co. v. FDA, 600 F.2d 831 (D.C. Cir. 1979); American Cyanamid Co. v. Young, 770 F.2d 1213 (D.C. Cir. 1985).

[253] 21 C.F.R. § 16.26.

[254] *See, e.g.,* FDCA § 515(e)(1), 21 U.S.C. § 360e(e)(1) (proposed withdrawal of approval of a device premarket approval application).

[255] *See, e.g.,* 21 C.F.R. § 292.1(j)(5) (approval of prescription drug advertisements); *id.* § 56.121(a) (disqualification of a clinical research institutional review board). Twenty-six other regulations providing for informal regulatory hearings are listed in title 21 of the *Code of Federal Regulations*, section 16.1(b)(2).

existing regulations, are spread throughout numerous sections in the Code of Federal Regulations and in agency manuals. Many of these practices and procedures have been developed over the years on an ad hoc basis, to meet immediate needs, without systematically integrating them into the agency's overall practices and procedures. Many of the agency's practices and procedures have not been written down in any manual or regulation.[256]

To remedy the situation, in the mid-1970s the agency undertook a comprehensive review and codification of all its practices and procedures for the purpose of integrating them into a comprehensive and coherent whole. The extent of this project is probably unique in the history of administrative agencies and was so broad that, as the preamble to the codification noted,[257] many of the agency activities covered by the regulations are not explicitly authorized in any of the laws administered by the FDA.

Ironically perhaps, the FDA's epic procedural reform was flawed by its own procedural lapse. Rather than following the usual APA notice-and-comment sequence of publishing a proposed rule, receiving comments from affected interests, and then publishing a final rule reflecting consideration of the comments received,[258] The FDA opted to publish final regulations subject to subsequent modification on receipt of public comments.[259] This course was justified, the agency asserted, by the necessity of establishing operating procedures for ongoing agency activities with no uncertainty about which set of rules governed the agency's processes in the interim.[260]

A reviewing court did not agree. Despite the exemption in the APA from normal notice-and-comment procedure for rules of practice and procedure[261] and for situations when compliance would be impracticable, unnecessary, or contrary to the public interest,[262] adherence to the notice-and-comment scheme was held to be required.[263] The pervasiveness and complexity of the codification were found to preclude its treatment as a mere rule of practice or procedure.[264] The opportunity to submit *post hoc* views on final regulations was held no substitute for the right to comment on proposed regulations prior to final promulgation.[265] Only after republishing its work in the form of proposed regulations[266] and

---

[256] 40 Fed. Reg. 22,950 (May 27, 1975).

[257] *Id.*

[258] 5 U.S.C. § 553(b).

[259] 40 Fed. Reg. 22,950.

[260] *Id.*

[261] 5 U.S.C. § 553(b).

[262] *Id.*

[263] American College of Neuropsychopharmacology v. Weinberger, [1975 Transfer Binder] Food Drug Cosm. L. Rep. (CCH) ¶ 38,025 (D.D.C. July 31, 1975).

[264] *Id.* at 38,083.

[265] *Id.* The court's sternness was vindicated by the FDA's response to its order. In the preamble accompanying the republication of the regulations as proposed rules, the FDA noted its intention to continue following procedures it previously observed "or could have observed" even without the regulations, 40 Fed. Reg. 40,682 (Sept. 3, 1975) (emphasis added). Thus, the agency's original rationale for promulgating final regulations — the purported need immediately to change outmoded practices — was undercut by its subsequently demonstrated ability to change those practices when necessary while still employing notice-and-comment procedure.

[266] 40 Fed. Reg. at 40,682.

modifying them before final adoption in light of comments received[267] was the FDA able to implement its comprehensive procedural reform.

The result was a set of uniform and consistent rules of practice covering all the FDA's varied functions, with special provisions to govern formal evidentiary hearings[268] and with a wholly novel set of provisions for alternative forms of hearings — the public board of inquiry[269] and the public advisory committee[270] — in lieu of the traditional adjudicatory or quasi-adjudicatory proceeding before an administrative law judge. In general, the regulations embody a policy of free public participation in agency proceedings subject to a scheme of strict formal requirements to which submissions by public participants purportedly must conform. The entire procedural structure is designed to give maximum scope to the doctrine of primary jurisdiction.

The rule of standing adopted by the FDA for participation in its proceedings is simply stated — any member of the public who wishes to participate in any FDA proceeding is deemed to be an "interested person adversely affected,"[271] although the extent of participation permitted may vary depending on the type of proceeding involved.[272] To prevent uncontrolled public participation from overwhelming the FDA's ability to manage its business, the regulations require rigid adherence to the prescribed form of written submissions.[273] Failure to comply with the regulations may result in rejection of the submission or refusal to consider the noncomplying portions.[274]

Except as otherwise provided by statute, every submission seeking agency action for which no particular procedure is established by regulation must be in the form of a "citizen petition."[275] The petition must be organized in a specified way,[276] and must include representative unfavorable information known to the petitioner as well as all favorable information on which the petition relies.[277] The citizen petition procedure enables anyone to ask the FDA to do anything.

The regulations promise a response to every citizen petition within 180 days of receipt.[278] The response, however, may be simply, that the agency is working on petition or even that the agency does not have time to work on it.[279]

---

[267] *See, e.g.*, 42 Fed. Reg. 4680 (Jan. 25, 1977) (abandoning requirement that submissions to the FDA signed by attorneys be accompanied by signed statements of authorization); 41 Fed. Reg. 51,706, 51,719 (Nov. 23, 1976) (deleting recommended decision procedure from provisions governing presiding officers' decisions after hearing).

[268] 21 C.F.R. pt. 12.

[269] *Id.* pt. 13.

[270] *Id.* pt. 14.

[271] 40 Fed. Reg. 40,520 (Sept. 3, 1975); *id.* at 40,683.

[272] The regulations, however, do distinguish between "parties" and "participants." The former receive full rights of participation, whereas the latter's rights are to some extent restricted. *See* 21 C.F.R. § 10.3 (defining "participant" and "party"); *id.* § 12.89 (defining rights of nonparty participants).

[273] *Id.* § 10.20.

[274] *Id.* § 10.20(c)(6).

[275] *Id.* § 10.30(a).

[276] *Id.* § 10.30(b).

[277] *Id.*

[278] *Id.* § 10.30(e)(2).

[279] *Id.* § 10.30(e)(2)(iii).

The requirement that unfavorable as well as favorable data be submitted with every request for agency action reflects the FDA's policy of compiling as complete a factual record as possible for each decision. Underlying this policy is the FDA's determination to maximize its ability to assert the doctrine of primary jurisdiction when its factual determinations are challenged. The primary jurisdiction doctrine makes the FDA the primary arbiter of factual matters within its jurisdiction, subject only to judicial review of limited scope.[280] The independent fact-finding role of the courts is reduced — perhaps even eliminated — under the primary jurisdiction doctrine, thus giving the agency the greatest possible leeway in setting regulatory policy and applying it in particular cases.

Other provisions of the regulations similarly undergird the FDA's role as primary arbiter of the facts. The regulations provide that new information allegedly calling an agency decision into question will be received and considered by the agency via a petition for reconsideration.[281] If the administrative record is found inadequate by a court, the FDA promises to take steps to supplement the record, thus making evidentiary hearings by the court unnecessary.[282] By such means, the agency's procedural regulations encourage judicial deference to FDA expertise; perhaps for this reason, the agency has declared it will refrain from interposing "technical objections, such as a lack of standing," to judicial review.[283]

Advisory Committees

Another distinctive characteristic of the FDA's administrative procedures is the agency's extensive use of advisory committees composed of experts from outside of government. Under the FDA's regulations, "[a]n advisory committee ordinarily has . . . a defined purpose of providing advice to the agency on a particular subject, . . . and serves as a source of independent expertise and advice rather than as a representative of or advocate for any particular interest."[284] The regulations contemplate the establishment of two types of committees: policy committees to advise on broad and general matters, and technical committees to advise on specific technical or scientific issues relating to regulatory decisions before the agency.[285]

An advisory committee must be constituted and conduct its affairs as provided in the regulations[286] and in the Federal Advisory Committee Act,[287] both of which contain extensive

---

[280] *See Bentex Pharmaceuticals, Inc.*, 412 U.S. 645.

[281] 21 C.F.R. § 10.33.

[282] *Id.* § 10.45(h)(1).

[283] 40 Fed. Reg. at 40,689. This benign view, however, is not shared by the Department of Justice, which controls the conduct of all litigation involving the FDA. 1 DEPARTMENT OF JUSTICE MANUAL §§ 2-1.202(D), 4-1.216 (Prentice Hall Law & Business 1989); *id.* § 4-1.440 ("Pleadings and papers prepared by agency counsel should be critically examined, and rewritten as necessary, to assert the proper litigating position for the government."). *See* Health Research Group v. Kennedy, 82 F.R.D. 21, 23 n.3 (D.D.C. 1979) (describing one such struggle over a defense of lack of standing). Although one court questioned the propriety of a Justice Department challenge to judicial review of plaintiffs' standing "notwithstanding an explicit concession of standing by the specialized agency charged with interpretation and enforcement of the relevant statute," Bradley v. Weinberger, 483 F.2d 410, 414 n.1 (1st Cir. 1973), such challenges are not infrequently advanced. Moreover, private parties intervening in support of a challenged FDA action may raise the "technical objections" foresworn by the FDA. *See Health Research Group*, 82 F.R.D. at 22.

[284] 21 C.F.R. § 14.1(b)(5).

[285] *Id.* § 14.1(b)(2).

[286] *Id.* §§ 14.20-.39.

[287] Pub. L. No. 92-463, 86 Stat. 776 (codified as amended at 5 U.S.C. app). Whether the composition of an advisory committee meets the balance requirements of the Federal Advisory Committee Act, however, is not judicially reviewable. Public Citizen v. HHS, 795 F. Supp. 1212 (D.D.C. 1992).

requirements designed to ensure the maximum possible public scrutiny of advisory committee deliberations and recommendations.[288] Whether a particular group of individuals consulted by the FDA is an advisory committee therefore is important, because a regulation arguably is subject to challenge if the agency consulted with an advisory committee during its promulgation without observing the required procedures.[289]

The involvement of advisory committees in the FDA's decisional processes is substantial. The OTC Drug Review, for example, is bottomed on the work of seventeen advisory committees, which draft proposed monographs for each therapeutic category of OTC medicines. Each proposed monograph has been published by the FDA for public comment prior to the agency's formulation of a proposed rule.[290] In some respects the agency has come close to delegating its power of decision to such committees, raising potentially serious questions of legality as well as judgment.[291] Thus, for example, the OTC Drug Review regulations permit the marketing of new OTC products on the basis of an advisory committee recommendation in a proposed monograph as long as the agency itself has not noted disagreement with the recommendations.[292] The presentation of data at advisory committee meetings has become an important aspect of practice before the FDA by representatives of the regulated industries.

The FDA has justified its wide-ranging involvement of advisory committees in the agency's decisionmaking process on the ground that they improve the quality of decisions by bringing "the best scientific talent" to bear on the difficult questions of science and medicine that so often are at issue.[293] In many cases this is doubtless true. Advisory committees, however, also may play a different, more pragmatic role — sharing and diffusing the responsibility for controversial or unpopular agency decisions. The part-time nature of advisory committee service, the plethora of demands on the attention of the distinguished experts who serve on these committees, and their dependence on the agency to define the issues and present the data on which committee judgment is sought, mean that agency staff often are in a position to guide the committees into agreement with conclusions previously reached within the agency and to obtain their imprimatur as protection against industry or public criticism.

The relationship between the FDA and its advisory committees thus is not just a matter of supplementing FDA's scientific resources; in a real sense, the committee members provide the FDA not merely with their advice but with credibility.

Alternative Forms of Hearing

The FDA's mid-1970s reform of its administrative practices introduced two procedurally innovative hearing forms: the public board of inquiry and the public advisory committee.

---

[288] *See* 5 U.S.C. app. 2, § 10; 21 C.F.R. §§ 14.20-.39. *See also* Food Chem. News v. HHS, 980 F.2d 1468 (D.C. Cir. 1993) (except for documents claimed by the agency to be covered by a Freedom of Information Act exemption from mandatory disclosure, all materials prepared by or for an advisory committee must be made publicly available, without requiring resort to Freedom of Information Act procedures and consequent delays, before or at the committee meeting to which the materials relate).

[289] *See* Food Chem. News v. Young, 900 F.2d 328 (D.C. Cir.), *cert. denied*, 498 U.S. 846 (1990). *Compare* Nat'l Nutritional Foods Ass'n v. Califano, 603 F.2d 327, 336 (2d Cir. 1979)*with Public Citizen*, 795 F. Supp. 1212.

[290] 21 C.F.R. § 330.10(a)(6).

[291] *See* A.L.A. Schecter Poultry Corp. v. United States, 295 U.S. 495, 537 (1935); Fashion Originators' Guild of Am., Inc. v. FTC, 312 U.S. 457, 465 (1941).

[292] 21 C.F.R. § 330.13(b)(2).

[293] FOOD & DRUG ADMIN., ANNUAL REPORT 3 (1975).

Prior to their introduction, all statutorily-required FDA hearings were held before an administrative law judge. Dissatisfaction with the length of these hearings and a perception that the adversarial process sometimes obscured scientific issues led to support for the concept of decisionmaking by a scientific tribunal. Thus, both of these new forms were intended to de-emphasize the role of lawyers and the adversarial process, and to substitute a scientific forum for a legalistic forum.

Public Board of Inquiry. Parties entitled to formal evidentiary hearings may waive that right and instead request a Public Board of Inquiry (PBOI).[294] A PBOI is composed of three scientists chosen by the Commissioner.[295] The procedures employed by a PBOI reflect the intent to de-emphasize the adversarial process.[296] Prior to the hearing, all parties are afforded the opportunity to make submissions to the Board.[297] At the hearing, participants may make oral presentations, which only members of the PBOI may interrupt for the purpose of asking questions.[298] When the oral presentations are finished, other participants may comment on presentations and may request that the Board conduct further questioning.[299] The PBOI also may have its own consultants make presentations.[300]

After the hearing, participants may submit statements of their position, proposed findings and conclusions, and rebuttals of other parties' presentations.[301] The Board is required to issue a decision on all issues before it, including specific findings and a detailed statement of the reasoning upon which its conclusions are based.[302] The Board's decision is accorded the same status as the initial decision of an administrative law judge.[303]

PBOIs have been convened only twice: to review the FDA's proposed approval of a food additive petition for aspartame[304] and to review FDA's refusal to approve the injectable contraceptive Depo-Provera.[305] In each instance, the PBOI eventually upheld the agency's original determination. Reaction to the PBOI has been mixed. Although there has been satisfaction with the fairness of the results, the PBOI alternative has turned out to be a lengthier and more costly process than originally contemplated.[306]

---

[294] 21 C.F.R. § 12.32(a).

[295] *Id.* § 13.10. One member must be chosen from a list of nominees compiled by FDA staff or from a list compiled by the person requesting the PBOI, one from a list of nominees chosen by other participants in the hearing, and one from the Commissioner's list of nominees, who serves as the chairman. *Id.* § 13.10(b). An alternative method of selecting the PBOI may be used if the participants so agree. *Id.* § 13.10(d).

[296] The Board's procedures retain two significant procedures used in formal evidentiary hearings: separation of functions and prohibition of *ex parte* contacts. *Id.* § 13.15.

[297] *Id.* § 13.30.

[298] *Id.* § 13.20(c).

[299] *Id.*

[300] *Id.* § 13.30(f).

[301] *Id.* § 13.30(e), (i).

[302] *Id.* § 13.30(j).

[303] *Id.* § 12.32(f)(1).

[304] *See* Aspartame, 46 Fed. Reg. 38,285 (July 24, 1981).

[305] *See* Depo-Provera, [1984-1985 Transfer Binder] Food Drug Cosm. L. Rep. (CCH) ¶ 38,291 (FDA Public Bd. of Inquiry Oct. 17, 1984).

[306] *See* S. Schapiro, *Scientific Issues and the Function of Hearing Procedures: An Evaluation of FDA's Public Board of Inquiry*, 1986 DUKE L.J. 288 (1986) (report for Administrative Conference of the United States).

Public Advisory Committee. The second new procedural form, the public hearing before an *ad hoc* Public Advisory Committee (PAC), has been used only once to reconsider the FDA's denial of a premarket approval application under the Medical Device Amendments for an antibiotic-bearing bone cement. As with the two PBOIs, the scientific tribunal upheld the agency.[307]

The procedures prescribed for *ad hoc* PACs are largely the same as those for standing technical or policy advisory committees.[308] Unlike the recomendations of those advisory committees, however, the decision of an *ad hoc* PAC is binding on the parties.[309] It remains to be seen whether PACs will become a popular alternative method of decision-making.

Newton's Law Revisited: Reversing the Expansion of FDA Discretion

A basic principle of science is that to every action there is always opposed an equal reaction.[310] The FDA is nothing if not a scientific regulatory agency, and its most recent experiences with Congress have given it ample opportunity to ponder that scientific principle. Even before the "Republican Revolution" of 1994 made anti-regulatory sentiment a driving force behind Congress' agenda, the FDA had begun to encounter legislative dissatisfaction with the extent of the policy discretion the agency has come to possess, or at least dissatisfaction with a perceived unaccountability in its exercise. As always, Congress' changing attitude toward the FDA resulted in renewed attention to matters of agency procedure as well as to substantive issues.

In retrospect, the Nutrition Labeling and Education Act of 1990 (NLEA)[311] and the SMDA,[312] while adding significantly to the FDA's regulatory authority, were harbingers of this development as well.

Characterized by the FDA as "the most important piece of legislation about food and the way it is labeled since the Federal Food, Drug, and Cosmetic Act was passed in 1938,"[313] the NLEA is to food regulation what the Medical Device Amendments of 1976 were to device regulation. Congress endorsed and legitimized the FDA's initiatives to require standardized nutrition labeling on most food sold in the United States and to regulate health claims in food labeling.

---

[307] *See* 53 Fed. Reg. 1171 (Apr. 8, 1988).

[308] 21 C.F.R. pt. 14.

[309] *Id.* § 14.7.

[310] *See* Sir Isaac Newton's Mathematical Principles of Natural Philosophy and His System of the World 13 (Andrew Motte trans., 1729 & Florian Cajori ed., Univ. of Cal. Press 1946).

[311] Pub. L. No. 101-535, 104 Stat. 2353.

[312] Pub. L. No. 101-629, 104 Stat. 4511.

[313] Fred R. Shank, *The Nutrition Labeling and Education Act of 1990*, 47 Food & Drug L.J. 247 (1992).

In doing so, however, Congress bluntly expressed its impatience with the slowness of the FDA's regulatory process,[314] and for the first time put teeth in the often-imposed but typically ignored statutory deadlines for the issuance of implementing regulations. The FDA was required to propose nutrition labeling regulations within twelve months after enactment of the NLEA and to promulgate final regulations within twenty-four months after enactment.[315] If the FDA failed to meet those deadlines, Congress directed that the proposed regulations would become final by operation of law and the FDA would be required to publish a *Federal Register* notice to that effect.[316] Similar "hammers" were enacted for other regulations mandated by the NLEA.[317]

The SMDA, passed by Congress contemporaneously with the NLEA, contained similar expediting mechanisms. FDA regulations required to be promulgated under the SMDA's medical device reporting and device tracking provisions were made subject to a "hammer."[318] An "approval by default" provision was incorporated into the SMDA directive that the FDA consider removing the premarket approval requirement for contact lenses.[319]

The FDA's enforcement discretion was further restricted by both the Animal Medicinal Drug Use Clarification Act of 1994 (AMDUCA)[320] and the Dietary Supplement Health and Education Act of 1994 (DSHEA).[321] AMDUCA sharply limits the FDA's authority to proceed against the use of approved animal drugs outside the scope of the approved labeling. Although the FDA retains a significant regulatory role with respect to such off-label uses, it is no longer authorized to treat them as *per se* violations of the new animal drug approval requirement.[322] Even more dramatically, DSHEA was inspired by Congress' belief that "the Food and Drug Administration has pursued a heavy-handed enforcement agenda against dietary supplements for over 30 years," and that "congressional action [was needed] to assure citizens have continued access to dietary supplements and information about their benefits."[323] The new statute "clarif[ies] that dietary supplements are not

---

[314]   Since the FDA has been extremely slow in issuing comprehensive nutrition regulations, legislation with a mandatory timetable is necessary to ensure that the program is implemented within a reasonable period of time . . . . [HHS] Secretary Sullivan acknowledged that "unfounded health claims are being made in the marketplace." Yet the FDA has been unable to issue final regulations that establish clear, enforceable rules regarding claims that may be made on food.

   H. REP. NO. 101-538, at 9.

[315]   Pub. L. No. 101-535, § 2(b)(1), 104 Stat. at 2356-57 (codified at 21 U.S.C. § 343 note).

[316]   *Id.* § 2(b)(2), 104 Stat. at 2357 (codified at 21 U.S.C. § 343 note).

[317]   *See, e.g., id.* § 3(b)(2), 104 Stat. at 2361-62 (codified at 21 U.S.C. § 343 note) (health claims). Other expediting mechanisms enacted in the NLEA were provisions for automatic approval of a petition for permission to use a brand name making implied nutrient claims unless the FDA acts on the petition within 100 days after it is submitted, *id.* § 403(r)(4)(A)(iii), 21 U.S.C. § 343(r)(4)(A)(iii), and provisions placing the burden of proof on the FDA to rebut proposed health claims that are based "on a report from an authoritative scientific body of the United States," *id.* § 403(r)(4)(C), 21 U.S.C. § 343(r)(4)(C).

[318]   Pub. L. No. 101-629, § 3(c), 104 Stat. at 4514-15 (codified at 21 U.S.C. § 360i note).

[319]   *Id.* § 4(b)(3)(D), 104 Stat. at 4517 (codified at 21 U.S.C. § 360c note).

[320]   Pub. L. No. 103-396, 108 Stat. 4153 (1994).

[321]   Pub. L. No. 103-417, 108 Stat. 4325 (1994).

[322]   FDCA § 512(a)(4)-(5), 21 U.S.C. § 360b(a)(4)-(5).

[323]   S. REP. NO. 103-410, 103rd Cong., 2d Sess. 16-17 (1994). The Senate report is instructive, notwithstanding the attempt of the bill's sponsors to foreclose reliance on any of its legislative history save for a single five-paragraph *post hoc* "statement of agreement" inserted by them into the *Congressional Record* without objection immediately after its passage in each House. 140 CONG. REC. H11,179 (daily ed. Oct. 6, 1994); 140 CONG. REC. S14,801 (daily ed. Oct. 7, 1994).

drugs or food additives, that dietary supplements should not be regulated as drugs, and that burden of proof is on the Food and Drug Administration . . . to prove that a product is unsafe before it can be removed from the marketplace."[324]

Insofar as the FDA's administrative procedures with respect to dietary supplements are concerned, DSHEA abolishes the premarket approval requirement for new dietary ingredients that the FDA effectively had imposed by invoking the new drug and food additive approval laws, in favor of a novel optional scheme. Manufacturers may proceed in either of two ways: simply notifying the FDA seventy-five days in advance of marketing, in a submission that discloses a historical or other evidentiary basis for concluding that the use of the ingredient "will reasonably be expected to be safe,"[325] or submitting a petition for issuance of a regulation approving specified uses of the ingredient.[326] If the petition route is chosen, the FDA is instructed to act within 180 days; there is, however, no "hammer" or automatic approval provision.[327]

At this writing, the 104th Congress has before it numerous proposals that radically would alter both the substantive scope of the FDA's regulatory authority and the procedures it employs, including an array of provisions for automatic approvals, referrals to private bodies for decision, and other mechanisms intended to expedite administrative action.[328] It is too early to tell what, if any, statutory changes will be enacted.

If nothing else, however, the threat of drastic legislation has spurred the FDA to undertake its own comprehensive reform program under the aegis of President Clinton's "Reinventing Government" initiative. The agency's administrative practices and procedures generally, as well as specific areas of perceived concern, are being reexamined with a view to "eliminat[ing] or revis[ing] those that are outdated or otherwise in need of reform."[329] Again, however, at this writing it is too early to tell what changes will result.

Conclusion

Today's FDA is a far cry procedurally from the police authority created by the Pure Food and Drugs Act of 1906. No longer confined to the basic law enforcement functions of inspection, seizure, and prosecution — although these remain a vital part of its mission — the FDA now functions primarily as a direct regulator of the industries subject to its jurisdiction, through a variety of formal and informal administrative proceedings. Its proce-

---

[324] S. REP. NO. 103-410, *supra* note 323 at 2.

[325] FDCA § 413(a)(2), 21 U.S.C. § 350b(a)(2).

[326] *Id.* § 413(c), 21 U.S.C. § 350b(c).

[327] *Id.*

[328] *See, e.g.,* H.R. 3199, 104th Cong., 2d Sess. (1996) (drugs); H.R. 3200, 104th Cong., 2d Sess. (1996) (food); H.R. 3201, 104th Cong., 2d Sess. (1996) (medical devices); S. 1477, 104th Cong., 2d Sess. (1996) (omnibus).

[329] *See, e.g.,* 61 Fed. Reg. 28,816 (June 4, 1996) (advance notice of proposed rulemaking on "Reinvention of Administrative Procedures Regulations").

dures therefore have an enormous impact on the practical effect of the regulatory statutes it administers.

Many of the FDA's most important and distinctive procedural tools were provided not by its basic modern charter, the Federal Food, Drug, and Cosmetic Act of 1938, but were constructed piecemeal over almost sixty years of subsequent legislation or have been devised by the agency itself in response to changing circumstances and responsibilities. The evolution of the FDA's administrative procedures thus reflects and illuminates the substantive development of modern food and drug law. The current debate in and out of Congress over what the FDA's role should be and how it should be performed illustrates once more that the evolutionary process is not — and likely never will be — complete.

chapter 3

Enforcement Powers of the Food and Drug Administration: Drugs and Devices

I. Scott Bass*

An Introduction to the Food and Drug Administration's Powers of Enforcement

With the dizzying speed at which technology has driven pharmaceutical and medical device innovation, the time-consuming regulatory process has not been able to serve as a practical means to exact industry compliance. As a result, the Food and Drug Administration (FDA) has of necessity looked toward increased enforcement, rather than increased regulation, for greater protection of the public.[1] The extensive time and technological knowledge required to craft meaningful and current manufacturing regulations have left a systems focus the only viable means by which to exact widespread compliance. The integrity of good manufacturing practices systems and manufacturing fraud have been the major targets of enforcement in recent years, and Congress has assisted by adding to the arsenal of civil and criminal sanctions to fortify the FDA's message.

This chapter will examine the statutory powers that Congress has conferred on the FDA, their regulatory expansion by the FDA, and subsequent judicially-imposed limitations on the exercise of those powers.

---

*   Mr. Bass is a Partner in the law firm of Sidley & Austin, Washington, D.C.

[1]   *See, e.g.,* David A. Kessler, M.D., Comm'r of Food and Drugs, Statement Before the Subcomm. on Health and the Env't of the House Comm. on Energy and Commerce, 102d Cong., 1st Sess. (Mar. 13, 1991); Ronald G. Chesemore, Assoc. Comm'r for Reg. Aff., Statement Before the Subcomm. on Oversight and Investigation of the House Comm. on Energy and Commerce, 102d Cong., 1st Sess. (Mar. 7, 1991); Margaret J. Porter, Chief Counsel, Food & Drug Admin., Address at FDLI's Annual Educational Conference, Washington, D.C. (Dec. 12, 1989), *quoted in* F-D-C REP. ("The Pink Sheet"), Dec. 18, 1989, at 8.

■ The Historical Development of the FDA's Enforcement Authority[2]

Laws relating to the adulteration of drugs were enacted in a large number of states and territories in the late nineteenth century.[3] The proliferation of fraudulent patent medicines led to federal legislation proscribing poor-quality imported drugs.[4] Import interception was an early tool of food and drug enforcement.

The Pure Food and Drugs Act of 1906,[5] the first wide-scale federal effort at drug regulation, granted to the FDA's precursor agency the power to seize drugs and foods.[6] There were, however, a number of enforcement limitations under the Pure Food and Drugs Act. A product was "misbranded," for example, only if its label contained false statements about its ingredients. False claims as such were not proscribed.[7] The 1912 Sherley amendment[8] added fraudulent therapeutic claims to the misbranding definition.

The 1912 amendment did not close a number of other gaping enforcement loopholes in the 1906 Act. In 1938, the Federal Food, Drug, and Cosmetic Act (FDCA), the law under which the FDA currently operates, was passed.[9] The law expanded the FDA's jurisdiction to cover medical devices and cosmetics; provided explicit authority for establishment inspections; and imposed criminal penalties for a host of additional acts, including the distribution or sale of unsafe drug products.

In the early years following passage of the 1938 Act, FDA litigation consisted almost entirely of seizures and criminal prosecutions.[10] Injunctions were not widely used, in part because of the administrative burdens attendant to their approval within the FDA.[11] As the modern era of enforcement evolved, the FDA also began to rely more heavily on administrative pronouncements, rather than solely on court tests, to achieve wide-ranging compliance results.[12]

As its jurisdictional umbrella expanded, the FDA increasingly turned to warning letters (*see* section on warning notices later in this chapter) as a means of communicating its enforcement intentions. Voluntary compliance was thereby encouraged without protracted litigation. Recalls represented an additional FDA effort to secure compliance (*see* section on "voluntary" recalls later in this chapter).[13]

---

[2]   For an examination of the historical roots of modern food and drug regulation, see I. Scott Bass, *The Enforcement Powers of the Food and Drug Administration: Foods and Cosmetics, in* 1 Fundamentals of Law and Regulation ch. 3 (FDLI 1997).

[3]   Wallace F. Janssen, *America's First Food and Drug Laws,* 30 Food Drug Cosm. L.J. 665 (1975).

[4]   The Import Drugs Act of 1848, 9 Stat. 237 (1848).

[5]   Pub. L. No. 59-384, 34 Stat. 768 (1906).

[6]   By 1907, the FDA already had collected more than 13,000 samples for possible seizure recommendations. Food Law Inst., Federal Food, Drug, and Cosmetic Law Administrative Reports 1907-1949 (1951), *cited in* Eugene M. Pfeifer, *Enforcement, in* Seventy-Fifth Anniversary Commemorative Volume of Food and Drug Law 72, 78 (1983).

[7]   United States v. Johnson, 221 U.S. 488 (1911).

[8]   Pub. L. No. 62-301, 37 Stat. 416 (1912).

[9]   Pub. L. No. 75-717, 52 Stat. 1040 (1938) (codified as amended 21 U.S.C. §§ 301 et seq. (1994)).

[10] *See* Federal Food, Drug, and Cosmetic Law Administrative Reports 1907-1949, *supra* note 6, at 84.

[11] *See id.*

[12] *Id.* at 86.

[13] Both enforcement tools were made the subject of *Federal Register* announcements. 43 Fed. Reg. 27,498 (1978) (warning letters); 43 Fed. Reg. 26,202 (1978) (recalls).

In the 1970s, the FDA sought and obtained legislation to clarify and expand its authority over all aspects of the marketing of medical devices.[14] Even in that field, however, enforcement lagged, and Congress responded with the Safe Medical Devices Act of 1990 to strengthen the FDA's hand.[15] For the first time, Congress authorized the FDA and the courts to require recalls with respect to an entire class of products, an enforcement power previously available only on a "voluntary" basis (except for infant formulas).[16] In addition, provisions authorizing temporary suspensions of approvals and civil penalties were enacted.[17]

The use of draconian penalties as an enforcement tool had been ushered in by passage of the Prescription Drug Marketing Act of 1987 (PDMA).[18] In that Act, for the first time, Congress regulated what it considered outrageous practices in the secondary pharmaceutical sales market and the handling of pharmaceutical samples by pharmaceutical company sales representatives (known as "detailmen").[19] Large civil penalties, increased criminal penalties, and whistleblower provisions were added to the law.[20] The Safe Medical Devices Act of 1990 extended the civil penalty concept with a $1 million ceiling,[21] and further extensions have been proposed.[22]

Similarly, pervasive fraud uncovered in the manufacture and approval of generic pharmaceutical products led to passage of the Generic Drug Enforcement Act of 1992.[23] Lifetime debarment of individuals convicted of fraud in the generic drug approval process;[24] FDA suspensions of approvals for generic drugs;[25] mandatory and temporary debarment of corporations;[26] temporary denial of approval of applications;[27] civil penalties;[28] and withdrawals of generic drug approvals[29] are among the enforcement arsenal now provided to the FDA.

■ Drug and Device Enforcement by Other Agencies

Enforcement of the FDCA is not limited to the FDA.[30] Seizure, injunction, and misdemeanor or felony proceedings are instituted by the U.S. Attorney in the district in which

---

[14] Medical Device Amendments of 1976, Pub. L. No. 94-295, 90 Stat. 539 (codified in scattered sections of 21 U.S.C.).

[15] Safe Medical Devices Act of 1990, Pub. L. No. 101-629, 104 Stat. 4511 (codified in scattered sections of 21 U.S.C.).

[16] FDCA § 412(e)(1), 21 U.S.C. § 350a(e)(1).

[17] Pub. L. No. 101-629, §§ 9, 17, 104 Stat. at 4521, 4526-28 (codified at 21 U.S.C. §§ 351(f)(1), 360(e), 333(f)).

[18] Pub. L. No. 100-293, 102 Stat. 95 (1988) (codified at 21 U.S.C. §§ 331, 333, 353, 381).

[19] STAFF OF THE SUBCOMM. ON OVERSIGHT AND INVESTIGATIONS OF THE COMM. ON ENERGY AND COMMERCE, 99TH CONG., 1ST SESS., PRESCRIPTION DRUG DIVERSION AND THE AMERICAN CONSUMER: WHAT YOU THINK YOU SEE MAY NOT BE WHAT YOU GET (Comm. Print 99-R 1985).

[20] 21 U.S.C. § 333(a), (b).

[21] Id. § 333(f).

[22] See, e.g., H.R. 2597, 102d Cong. 1st Sess. (1991); H.R. 3562 and H.R. REP. No. 4610, 102d Cong., 1st Sess. (1991); Medical Device Amendments of 1992, Pub. L. No. 102-300, 106 Stat. 238 (codified at 21 U.S.C. §§ 360d, 360i note); Nutrition Labeling and Education Act Amendments of 1993, Pub. L. No. 103-80, 107 Stat. 773 (codified at 21 U.S.C. §§ 321, 360d, 360nn, 371, 42 U.S.C. § 263b note 1994).

[23] Pub. L. 102-282, 106 Stat. 149; see 21 U.S.C. § 301 note.

[24] 21 U.S.C. § 335a(c)(2)(A)(ii).

[25] Id. § 335a(g).

[26] Id. § 335a(a).

[27] Id. § 335a(f).

[28] Id. § 335b.

[29] Id. § 335c.

[30] There is no private right of action under the FDCA. See, e.g., Bailey v. Johnson, 48 F.3d 965, 968 (6th Cir. 1995).

the case is brought.[31] In addition, the U.S. Department of Health and Human Services (DHHS) Inspector General has been given the responsibility for investigating felony violations of the FDCA,[32] except for matters "that should remain a function of the Food and Drug Administration."[33] The FDA also shares jurisdiction with the Federal Trade Commission (FTC) with respect to the advertising of over-the-counter drugs and devices. Under section 707 of the FDCA,[34] the FTC has been given primary jurisdiction over enforcement with respect to such advertising.

An increasing share of drug and device enforcement is borne by state agencies. FDA has long worked cooperatively with such agencies. In the 1980s, as a deregulatory philosophy and budgetary limitations contracted federal enforcement efforts, states increased enforcement of their own food and drug laws. Recognition of this increased state activity was reflected in the Nutrition Labeling and Education Act of 1990,[35] in which specific authority was provided for states to institute civil proceedings if the FDA fails to act against a food misbranding violation after thirty-days' notice.

From 1991 to 1993, numerous memoranda of understanding (MOUs) were entered into between the FDA and various states providing for joint enforcement efforts.[36] These include inspection of food and medicated feed firms; investigation of fraud and deception involving foods, drugs, devices and cosmetics; investigation and control of violative lev-

---

[31] 28 U.S.C. § 547 (1994).

[32] Letter from Dr. Louis Sullivan, Sec'y of the Dept. of Health and Human Servs., to Richard Kusserow, Inspector Gen. of the Dept. of Health and Human Servs. (July 24, 1989).

[33] *Id.* The Nuclear Regulatory Commission has assumed joint regulatory responsibility over certain medical devices as well. CPG 7155p.01 (Aug. 26, 1993) (FDA-225-93-4007).

[34] 21 U.S.C. § 378.

[35] Pub. L. No. 101-535, § 4, 104 Stat. 2353, 2362 (codified at 21 U.S.C. § 337(b)).

[36] *See, e.g.*, MOU with Wyoming Department of Agriculture Regarding the Inspection of Food, Drugs and Medical Device Firms, CPG 7157.45 (FDA-225-92-4001) (Mar. 20, 1992); MOU with Utah Department of Agriculture Regarding the Inspection of Food, Drugs, and Medical Device Firms, CPG 7157.46 (FDA-225-92-4006) (Apr. 16, 1992); MOU with State of Arkansas Attorney General and Arkansas Department of Health Regarding the Inspection of Foods, Drugs, Devices, and Cosmetics, CPG 7157.47 (FDA-225-92-4004) (Apr. 17, 1992). MOU with Alabama Department of Agriculture and Industries Regarding Regulation of Wholesale Food Storage Warehouses, Disasters, Recalls, and Exchange of Information, CPG 7157.26; MOU with California Department of Health Services Regarding Inspections, Investigations, Recalls and Emergencies, CPG 7157.20; MOU with Colorado Department of Health and Department of Law Regarding Inspections of Food, Drug, Cosmetic and Medical Device Firms, CPG 7157.48; MOU with Connecticut Department of Consumer Protection Regarding the Coordination of Joint Efforts in Monitoring Pesticide and Industrial Chemical Residues in Foods, CPG 7157.37; MOU with Delaware Board of Pharmacy Concerning Regulatory Activities Relating to the Inspection of Drug Manufacturers, Wholesalers and Distributors, CPG 7157.24; MOU with Florida Department of Agriculture and Consumer Services Delineates Activities Relating to the Regulation of Milk, Foods, Medicated Feeds, and Pesticides, CPG 7157.18; MOU with Georgia Department of Agriculture and USDA/FSIS Regarding Regulatory Investigations Involving Drug, Pesticide, and Toxic Chemical Residues in Animal Feeds and in Meat Tissues, CPG 7147.41; MOU with Illinois Attorney General Regarding Development and Implementation of Appropriate Sanctions Concerning Fraud and Deception Involving Foods, Drugs, Devices, and Cosmetics, CPG 7157.04; MOU with Kansas Department of Health and Environment Concerning Inspection, Investigation, and Analytical Findings Related to Food and Drug Firms, CPG 7157.21; CPG 7157.13 with Maryland Department of Health and Mental Hygiene Concerning the Inspection of Food Processing and Storage Industries; MOU with Michigan Department of Agriculture Regarding Inspections, Investigations, and Analytical Findings Related to Food Firms, CPG 7157.49; MOU with Minnesota Department of Agriculture Regarding the Inspection of Food and Medicated Feed Firms, CPG 7157.50; MOU with Virginia Department of Health Concerning the Inspection of the Crabmeat Industry, CPG 7157.15.

els of drugs, pesticides and toxic chemical residues in edible tissues derived from food animals; and other related regulatory activities.[37]

Jurisdictional Definitions

Section 201 of the FDCA contains the definitions utilized in the Act. The most important for purposes of drug and device enforcement are: "interstate commerce,"[38] "new drug,"[39] "labeling,"[40] "new animal drug,"[41] "counterfeit drug,"[42] "device,"[43] "knowingly or knew,"[44] and "high managerial agent."[45]

The interstate commerce definition is read in conjunction with section 301, which prohibits, *inter alia*, "the introduction or delivery for introduction into interstate commerce" of violative articles,[46] their "receipt in interstate commerce,"[47] or their "delivery or proffered delivery" in interstate commerce.[48] In enforcement litigation, the FDA generally must prove the required nexus with interstate commerce. Only under the Medical Device Amendments of 1976 did the FDA obtain a presumption of interstate commerce.[49] Moreover, violative devices can be seized and condemned without evidence of having moved in interstate commerce.[50]

The interstate commerce requirement of the FDCA thus confers a more limited grant of jurisdictional authority than that provided to the federal government in other statutes or permitted by the U.S. Constitution. Notwithstanding that limitation, the courts increasingly have read the FDCA to reach activities that were conducted almost completely intrastate.[51] In *United States v. Sullivan*,[52] for example, the language "held for sale after shipment in interstate commerce" was held to include a resale six months after the defendant had received the goods in question in interstate commerce. Sixteen years later, in *United States v. Wiesenfeld Warehouse Co.*,[53] the Supreme Court affirmed that the word "holding" was sufficient to impose liability on a defendant who is merely a bailee, not a seller, of the food in question. The title to the goods, Justice Stewart wrote for the major-

---

[37]　*See supra* note 36.

[38]　FDCA § 201(b), 21 U.S.C. § 321(b).

[39]　*Id.* § 201(p), 21 U.S.C. § 321(p).

[40]　*Id.* § 201(m), 21 U.S.C. § 321(m).

[41]　*Id.* § 201(v), 21 U.S.C. § 321(v).

[42]　*Id.* § 201(g)(2), 21 U.S.C. § 321(g)(2).

[43]　*Id.* § 201(h), 21 U.S.C. § 321(h).

[44]　*Id.* § 201(bb), 21 U.S. C. § 321(bb).

[45]　*Id.* § 201(cc), 21 U.S.C. § 321(cc).

[46]　*Id.* § 301(a), (d), 21 U.S.C. § 331(a), (d).

[47]　*Id.* § 301(c), 21 U.S.C. § 331(c).

[48]　*Id.*

[49]　*Id.* § 709, 21 U.S.C. § 379a.

[50]　*Id.* § 304(a)(2)(D), 21 U.S.C. § 334 (a)(2)(D).

[51]　Venue determinations have not always followed suit. *See, e.g.*, United States v. Beech-Nut Corp., 871 F.2d 1181, 1188-91 (2d Cir.), *cert. denied sub nom.*, Lavery v. United States, 493 U.S. 933 (1989).

[52]　332 U.S. 689, 696 (1948).

[53]　376 U.S. 86, 92 (1964).

ity, is not a prerequisite to imposing the FDCA's public protection mechanisms on those who may happen to handle violative products within the Act's scope.[54]

Once a product has entered the stream of interstate commerce, whether through domestic origin or by passage through Customs,[55] the statutory prohibitions and penalties will apply. Moreover, as long as any constituent — no matter how small — of a domestically produced product derives from interstate commerce, the courts will view that product as within the reach of the FDCA's definition of "interstate commerce." In a case where a blend of oils was manufactured completely in New York, sold in New York, and stored there as well, the Second Circuit held that the foreign origin of a small proportion of the oil rendered the finished food product subject to the FDCA.[56] Similarly, where soft drink beverages were manufactured and consumed within the Commonwealth of Puerto Rico, the inclusion of potassium nitrate, a minor ingredient that had been shipped previously in interstate commerce, rendered the beverages subject to the Act.[57]

The scienter definition in section 201(bb) was added to the FDCA by the Generic Drug Enforcement Act to establish that "knowledge" means, "with respect to information" (e.g., in a pre-approval application), both "actual knowledge" and "acts in deliberate ignorance or reckless disregard of the truth or falsity of the information."[58] Subsection (cc), added by the same statute, assigns responsibility for violations to those persons in a corporation, association, or partnership who "may fairly be assumed to represent the policy" of that entity, including those with "management responsibility" for FDA submissions, quality control, and research and development.[59]

■ An Overview of Statutory Offenses

Chapter 3 of the FDCA enumerates the prohibited acts under the statute, specifies most of the enforcement powers that are available to FDA, and prescribes the penalties attendant thereto.[60]

Both specific "acts" and "the causing thereof" are prohibited. The latter standard has been utilized for the prosecution, for example, of laboratories that have been involved either in the formulation or testing of products that were later found to be adulterated or misbranded.[61]

---

[54] *Id.*

[55] 230 Boxes, More or Less, of Fish . . . v. United States, 168 F.2d 361 (6th Cir. 1948). *See also* United States v. First Phoenix Group, 64 F.3d 984 (5th Cir. 1995) (plain language of Section 334 permits the FDA to initiate a seizure and condemnation action when goods are seized at the port of entry and not just when released by Customs).

[56] United States v. 40 Cases . . . "Pinocchio Brand . . . Oil," 289 F.2d 343 (2d Cir.), *cert. denied*, 368 U.S. 831 (1961).

[57] United States v. An Article of Food . . . CoCo Rico, 752 F.2d 11, 14 (1st Cir. 1985).

[58] 21 U.S.C. § 321(bb).

[59] *Id.* § 321(cc); *see also* Arthur Pew Constr. Co. v. Lipscomb, 965 F.2d 1559, 1576 (11th Cir. 1992) (under 18 U.S.C. § 1001 (1994), misrepresentation "must have been deliberate, knowing and willful, or at least with a reckless disregard of the truth"); United States v. Joan Mitcheltree, 940 F.2d 1329 (10th Cir. 1991) ("knowledge of the essential nature of the alleged fraud is a component of the intent to defraud," and this knowledge was not established beyond a reasonable doubt) (*quoting* United States v. Hiland, 909 F.2d 1114, 1128 (8th Cir. 1990)).

[60] The limits on fines set forth by section 303 are superseded by 18 U.S.C. § 3571.

[61] *See, e.g.*, United States v. Industrial Testing Labs. Co., 456 F.2d 908 (10th Cir. 1972).

The two major types of violations specific to the FDCA relate to "adulteration" and "misbranding." These terms underlie the majority of enforcement actions instituted under the Act. The definition of adulterated drugs and devices is found in section 501,[62] Most of the adulteration offenses incorporate the common meaning of the term, that is, they encompass filthy or putrid foods, poisons added to food, unapproved color additives,[63] and drugs or devices that fail to meet compendial standards or that diverge from the rigorous requirements of good manufacturing practices.[64]

The concept of misbranding derives from historical notions of economic fraud, but has been extended to other types of misstatements and violations such as devices that are unlisted or are from an unregistered facility. Misbranded foods are described in section 403 of the Act,[65] misbranded drugs and devices in section 502,[66] and misbranded cosmetics in section 602.[67] In determining whether an article is misbranded, the statute specifically relies not only on words and visual representations, but also on a failure to reveal "material facts" relevant to claims or representations actually made.[68]

Section 301 enumerates twenty-two statutory offenses. They primarily prohibit the manufacture, sale, delivery, receipt, or holding for delivery or sale of adulterated or misbranded products.[69] Parallel provisions also bar the introduction or delivery into interstate commerce of unapproved new drugs; unapproved medical devices categorized under Class III; and unapproved new animal drugs, food additives, or antibiotics.[70]

Section 301 also encompasses offenses relating to counterfeit products,[71] furnishing a false guarantee to a customer that a product is not adulterated or misbranded,[72] misuse by FDA personnel of certain types of trade secret information submitted to the agency,[73] the use in advertising or labeling of any statement that a product is "FDA approved;"[74] failure of manufacturers or importers to register with the agency;[75] and, *inter alia,* the sale or importation of drugs in violation of the PDMA.[76] The PDMA proscribes the import of American goods returned, the sale or trade of drug samples, the failure to supply "a paper trail" in connection with sales of prescription drugs by unauthorized wholesalers to other wholesalers, and the resale or distribution of prescription drugs by health care entities.[77]

---

[62] 21 U.S.C. § 351.

[63] FDCA § 402(a)-(c), 21 U.S.C. § 342(a)-(c).

[64] *Id.* § 501(b)-(e), 21 U.S.C. § 351(b)-(e).

[65] 21 U.S.C. § 343.

[66] *Id.* § 352.

[67] *Id.* § 362.

[68] FDCA § 201(n), 21 U.S.C. § 321(n).

[69] *Id.* § 301(a)-(d), (g), (k), 21 U.S.C. § 331(a)-(d), (g), (k).

[70] *Id.* § 301(a), (d), (p), 21 U.S.C. § 331(a), (d), (p); *id.* § 409, 21 U.S.C. § 348.

[71] *Id.* § 301(i), 21 U.S.C. § 331(i).

[72] *Id.* § 301(h), 21 U.S.C. § 331(h).

[73] *Id.* § 301(j), 21 U.S.C. § 331(j).

[74] *Id.* § 301(l), 21 U.S.C. § 331(l).

[75] *Id.* § 301(o), (p), 21 U.S.C. § 331(o), (p).

[76] *Id.* § 301(t), 21 U.S.C. § 331(t).

[77] Pub. L. No. 100-293, 102 Stat. at 95 (codified at 21 U.S.C. §§ 333(b), 353(c)-(e)).

The FDCA is unusual in that it authorized both civil and criminal remedies for the same violations. First-time criminal acts are misdemeanors, except where there is intent to defraud or mislead.[78] Repeat offenses and those with the requisite criminal intent are felonies.[79] Civil penalties also may be imposed for certain offenses relating to medical devices and radiation-emitting products, and for violation of the PDMA.[80]

The various enforcement means available to the FDA, most of which are set forth in chapter 3 of the Act, are the subject of the remaining sections of this chapter. Briefly, section 302[81] provides for injunctions and for jury trials in the case of a violation of an injunction. Section 303[82] contains the FDCA penalty provisions and a delineation of the PDMA offenses. Seizures of drugs and devices are authorized by section 304.[83] This section further provides for detentions in the case of medical devices,[84] and for multiple seizures of adulterated products and, in certain cases, misbranded products.[85]

FDA inspections of common carriers, factories, warehouses, and other establishments are authorized expressly by sections 703 and 704 of the FDCA.[86] The agency's powers over imports and exports are delineated in sections 801 and 802,[87] which grant to the FDA substantial sampling powers that are performed in conjunction with the U.S. Customs Service. Section 705 provides a broad publicity power, which has been utilized very effectively by the FDA.[88]

The Generic Drug Enforcement Act added the powers set forth in sections 306,[89] 307,[90] and 308,[91] dealing with debarment,[92] temporary denial of approval and suspension, civil penalties, and withdrawal of abbreviated new drug approvals.

Other enforcement provisions of note are section 309,[93] which confirms the FDA's prosecutorial discretion by providing that minor violations may be dealt with by written notice or warning rather than by prosecution, injunction, or seizure, and section 305, a critical pre-

---

[78]　FDCA § 303(a)(1), 21 U.S.C. § 333(a)(1).

[79]　*Id.* § 303 (a)(2), 21 U.S.C. § 333(a)(2).

[80]　21 U.S.C. § 333(b)(2)(B), (f)(1)(A). *See also* Radiation Control for Health and Safety Act of 1968, 42 U.S.C. § 263B (enforced by the FDA).

[81]　21 U.S.C. § 332.

[82]　*Id.* § 333.

[83]　*Id.* § 334.

[84]　*Id.* § 334(g).

[85]　*Id.* § 334(a)(1).

[86]　*Id.* §§ 373, 374.

[87]　*Id.* §§ 381, 382.

[88]　*Id.* § 375. *See also infra* notes 179-189 and accompanying text.

[89]　*Id.* § 335a.

[90]　*Id.* § 335b.

[91]　*Id.* § 335c.

[92]　Bae v. Shalala, 44 F.3d 489, 496 (7th Cir. 1995) held that the Generic Drug Enforcement Act, designed to "safeguard the integrity of the generic drug industry," does not violate the Constitutional prohibition against *ex post facto* laws in permitting permanent debarment of convicted individuals.

[93]　21 U.S.C. § 336. The FDA also was granted new emergency powers under the Dietary Supplement Health and Education Act, discussed in I. Scott Bass, *Enforcement Powers of the Food and Drug Administration: Foods, Dietary Supplements, and Cosmetics, supra* note 2.

indictment hearing procedure that provides an informal opportunity to discuss with the FDA potential criminal charges prior to the FDA's referral of the charges to the Department of Justice.[94]

Finally, the FDA derives its enforcement authority indirectly by virtue of delegation from the Secretary of DHHS to the Commissioner of Food and Drugs.[95] The FDA exercises these enforcement powers pursuant to specific delegations of authority contained in the *Code of Federal Regulations*.[96] The regulations empower the FDA to enforce not only the FDCA, but certain other statutes as well. The Commissioner of Food and Drugs, in turn, has redelegated his authority to permit the Deputy Commissioner and the Associate Commissioner for Regulatory Affairs to perform the enforcement functions of the Commissioner.[97] It is extremely rare for the Commissioner to become personally involved in individual enforcement cases.

Civil Enforcement of the Federal Food, Drug, and Cosmetic Act

The primary enforcement powers available to the FDA for drug and device violations are:[98]

- establishment inspections;
- warning letters and other regulatory correspondence;
- recalls;
- publicity;
- product seizures and reconditionings or destructions;
- injunctions;
- import inspections, detentions and refusals, and re-export refusals;
- product approval or license withdrawals and suspensions and "alert/reference" lists;

---

[94] 21 U.S.C. § 335. *See also* 21 C.F.R. § 7.84-.87 (1997).

[95] FDCA § 903(b)(2), 21 U.S.C. § 393(b)(2); 21 C.F.R. § 5.10.

[96] 21 C.F.R. § 5.10(a).

[97] *Id.* § 5.20(b) (1995).

[98] Sources of FDA enforcement information are:
  - the statute: 21 U.S.C. §§ 301 et seq.;
  - the regulations: primarily title 21 of the *Code of Federal Regulations*, as well as other titles that may be relevant to specific products, such as dairy and meat;
  - the *Federal Register* (containing proposed regulations, interpretative rules, and policy announcements);
  - the *FDA Compliance Policy Guides Manual* (an internal but publicly available document utilized by the FDA field offices in interpreting regulatory policies and in communicating various enforcement actions such as import alerts);
  - the *FDA Regulatory Procedures Manual* (an internal but publicly available FDA document that sets forth agency policy on various enforcement matters);
  - the *FDA Investigations Operations Manual* (an internal but publicly available FDA guide for field inspectors); and
  - the *FDA Compliance Program Guidance Manual* (a publicly available supplement to the FDA's *Inspection Operations Manual* that provides details on certain types of inspections).

- application integrity policy (deferral or review of applications);
- civil penalty proceedings;
- debarment;
- misdemeanor prosecutions; and
- felony prosecutions.

■ The First Interface: Inspections

Since the FDA does not have general civil subpoena powers,[99] it must rely principally on inspections for the acquisition of documentary and other information. Under sections 703 and 704 of the FDCA,[100] the agency is permitted access to, respectively, interstate shipment records held by a common carrier, and to most records held in a facility that manufactures, ships, or holds "food, drugs, devices, or cosmetics" as long as they are manufactured, processed, packed, or held for introduction into interstate commerce (including vehicles used therefor). Section 704 provides for much broader inspection powers in the case of plants that manufacture prescription drugs or restricted devices.

Although a search warrant normally is required by the Fourth Amendment for inspections of premises, an exception to this protection has been carved out by the Supreme Court for industries "long subject to close supervision and inspection." This exception was articulated in *Colonnade Catering Corp. v. United States*,[101] and re-articulated for "pervasively regulated business[es]" in *United States v. Biswell* in 1972.[102] *Colonnade* involved inspections pursuant to the authority of the Bureau of Alcohol, Tobacco and Firearms (BATF) to regulate liquor; *Biswell* involved a BATF inspection of firearms.

In 1981, the Eighth Circuit put to rest the question whether the *Colonnade-Biswell* exception applies to inspections under the FDCA:

> We think the drug-manufacturing industry is properly within the *Colonnade-Biswell* exception to the warrant requirement. The drug-manufacturing industry has a long history of supervision and inspection . . . . That Act was an attempt by Congress "to exclude from interstate commerce impure and adulterated foods and drugs . . ." and to prevent the transport of such articles "from their place of manufacture."[103]

---

[99] The Safe Medical Devices Act of 1990, Pub. L. No. 101-629, § 17, 104 Stat. at 4526-28 (21 U.S.C. § 333(f), did provide the FDA with limited subpoena authority with respect to medical devices. *See also* H.R. 2597, 102d Cong., 1st Sess. § 5 (1991).

[100] 21 U.S.C. §§ 373, 374.

[101] 397 U.S. 72, 77 (1970).

[102] 406 U.S. 311, 316 (1972). *But cf.* Marshall v. Barlows, Inc., 436 U.S. 307 (1978) (OSHA); Camara v. Municipal Court, 387 U.S. 523 (1967).

[103] United States v. Jamieson-McKames Pharmaceuticals, Inc., 651 F.2d 532, 537 (8th Cir. 1981), *cert. denied*, 455 U.S. 1016 (1982) (quoting McDermott v. Wisconsin, 228 U.S. 115, 128 (1913)). The holding applies to intrusions "limited to the purposes specified in the statute." 651 F.2d at 542. It has been held that the Fourth Amendment exclusionary rule does not apply to condemnation proceedings pursuant to FDCA § 304. United States v. An Article of Food . . . Lumpfish Roe, 477 F. Supp. 1185, 1191 (S.D.N.Y. 1979). *But see*, Unites States v. Various Articles of Drug, No. C94-112OC (W.D. Wash. 1994) (holding that the Fourth Amendment's warrant requirement applies to seizures under FDCA § 304, in contrast to inspections under FDCA § 704).

This reasoning almost certainly extends to the other types of products regulated by the FDA.[104]

Conceptually, in the absence of a warrant, the FDA can inspect an establishment only with the consent of those in charge of it. A refusal to permit an inspection by an FDA inspector who presents proper identification and a valid inspection notice (Form FD482), however, is a violation of FDCA section 301(f).[105] A refusal constituting a violation of 301(f) can be total or partial. A partial refusal can include denying an inspector access to certain records or to particular parts of a facility, or refusing to agree to certain sampling requests. Evidence obtained by the FDA in a warrantless inspection where a company representative has refused access may be excluded under the Fourth Amendment in a criminal trial on the ground that the company did not "consent" to the inspection.[106]

When consent to an inspection is refused, the FDA generally seeks an inspection warrant from a district court.[107] Once that step has been taken, further enforcement action usually follows. For example, in a case in which a laboratory accused the FDA of harassment by excessive searches and requests for too many expensive samples, the district court not only upheld the FDA's inspection authority but found the corporation in civil contempt of the warrant that was issued following the refusal of inspection.[108] Seizures, injunction actions, or criminal prosecution can thus be the result of a refusal of inspection.[109]

Sometimes, the inspection may be conducted as part of a criminal investigation. In the wake of the generic drug scandal, the FDA created the Office of Criminal Investigations (OCI), which directs criminal investigations activities in coordination with other federal and local authorities. OCI personnel may be involved in FDA inspections as part of an ongoing criminal investigation. OCI helps implement criminal investigations, policy, and training, and participates in Grand Jury proceedings as requested.[110]

Inspections normally are carried out in a fairly cooperative fashion. An inspector must first present credentials and an FD482 Notice of Inspection. On request, the inspector will inform the company whether a directed or general inspection is involved, i.e., whether the inspector is there solely to obtain specific products or literature, or to conduct a full premises inspection. It is incumbent upon the inspected company to provide access to the inspector to all areas where foods, drugs, cosmetics, biologics, or devices are held or are being manufactured (including labeling).

---

[104] Although arguments can be made that the devices industry has been regulated for only the last 20 years, most devices were in fact regulated as drugs before 1976.

[105] 21 U.S.C. § 331(f).

[106] *Jamieson-McKames*, 651 F.2d at 540. *Cf. infra* note 94.

[107] The showing needed for the issuance of an inspection warrant is less than the probable cause needed for a criminal search warrant. *See, e.g., In re* Establishment Inspection of Medtronic, Inc., 500 F. Supp. 536 (D. Minn. 1980); *cf.* United States v. Roux Labs., Inc., 456 F. Supp. 973, 976-78 (M.D. Fla. 1978).

[108] *Roux Labs., Inc.*, 456 F. Supp. at 975-78.

[109] The question also has arisen as to whether *Miranda* warnings (*see* Miranda v. Arizona, 384 U.S. 436 (1966)) are required in FDA inspections where a criminal investigation is under way. In the Eighth Circuit's *Jamieson-McKames* decision, such warnings were held inapplicable because FDA inspectors have no authority to make arrests. 651 F.2d at 543.

[110] FDA Investigations Operations Manual § 217.4 (1995) (ORA Headquarters Organization).

FDA maintains an *Investigations Operations Manual*,[111] which contains descriptions of the procedures and the training materials utilized by field office personnel. Most inspection issues are dealt with in this volume. The *Manual* is supplemented by the *Compliance Policy Guides Manual*,[112] the *Compliance Program Guidance Manual*, and the *Regulatory Procedures Manual*.[113]

A great deal has been written about the powers of the FDA and the tactics to be used in inspections.[114] Accordingly, most larger companies under the jurisdiction of the FDA have developed inspection procedures (as have trade associations for their FDA-regulated members) and are well aware of the FDA's powers.

Nonetheless, certain issues with respect to the scope of inspections occasionally are contested. Section 704 of the Act states that inspections must be conducted during "reasonable times," "within reasonable limits," and in a "reasonable manner."[115] These standards rarely are litigated and, when they are, the determination of reasonableness usually favors the agency.[116] On a practical basis, however, the agency often compromises with a company if the matter is resolved without resort to inspectional warrants or litigation.

Another issue is the applicability of the immunity provision of section 703, which states that "evidence obtained under this section, or any evidence which is directly or indirectly derived from such evidence, shall not be used in a criminal prosecution of the person from whom obtained."[117] Although many defendants seek this criminal immunity, few obtain it. Section 703 has been interpreted quite strictly to cover only inspections of common carriers and a few limited categories of persons receiving regulated products, thereby eliminating the vast majority of inspections that are conducted pursuant to section 704. In a recent criminal case in which the inspection issues were heavily litigated, the court fairly easily found that the FDA did not invoke section 703 in order to obtain the documents relied upon by the prosecution.[118]

Many inspectors request permission to take photographs. There has been traditional reluctance on the part of inspected companies to permit such photographs because of the possibility of distortion of conditions, particularly in a food sanitation dispute. There has been no case law explicitly permitting the FDA to take photographs. In *United States v. Gel Spice*, a motion to suppress the admission of photographs was denied on the grounds that the photographs were not "unfairly prejudicial" and that "FDA personnel followed all

---

[111] FDA INVESTIGATIONS OPERATIONS MANUAL (1995).

[112] FDA COMPLIANCE POLICY GUIDES MANUAL ch. 3, § 300.100 (1993).

[113] FDA REGULATORY PROCEDURES MANUAL ch. 6 (1995).

[114] *See, e.g.*, Linda R. Horton, *Warrantless Inspections Under the Federal Food, Drug and Cosmetic Act*, 42 GEO. WASH. L. REV. 1089 (1974); Peter B. Hutt, *Factory Inspection Authority — The Statutory Viewpoint*, 22 FOOD DRUG COSM. L.J. 667 (1967); Richard A. Shupack, *The Inspectional Process — A Statutory Overview*, 33 FOOD DRUG COSM. L.J. 697 (1978).

[115] FDCA § 704(a)(1), 21 U.S.C. 374(a)(1).

[116] *See, e.g.*, United States v. Gel Spice Co., Crim. No. 80 CR 650 (E.D.N.Y. 1983), *reprinted in* FEDERAL FOOD, DRUG, AND COSMETIC ACT JUDICIAL RECORD 1983-1984, at 90, 91 (FDLI 1988); *Roux Labs., Inc.*, 456 F. Supp. at 973, 976.

[117] 21 U.S.C. § 373.

[118] *Gel Spice Co.*, Crim. No. 80 CR 650, *reprinted* in FEDERAL FOOD, DRUG, AND COSMETIC ACT JUDICIAL RECORD 1983-1984, *supra* note 116, at 92-93.

applicable procedural requirements."[119] The evidence was thus admitted under rule 403 of the Federal Rules of Evidence, without any discussion of whether the FDA had the power to take such photographs without consent.

The *FDA Investigations Operations Manual* informs its inspectors that they are not to request permission from management to take photographs.[120] The *Manual* cites two decisions in support of the FDA's rights: *Dow Chemical Co. v. United States*[121] and *United States v. Acri Wholesale Grocery Co.*[122] In *Dow Chemical*, the taking of an aerial photograph by the Environmental Protection Agency (EPA) pursuant to the Clean Air Act was upheld as a valid exercise of the EPA's inspectional powers and not a violation of Dow's privacy rights. The *Dow* decision does not address directly the issues concerning photographs under the FDCA, nor does it deal with the taking of photographs inside a plant. In *Acri Wholesale*, the court upheld the admission into evidence of photographs taken by FDA inspectors inside a warehouse. Whether FDA had the right to take the photographs was not an issue decided in that case. No objection was raised at the time of inspection to the taking of photographs; the court accordingly found that there had been full consent by the company.

Section 704 also permits the FDA to take samples of drugs or devices and labeling. Although manufacturing records and quality control procedures are not specifically within the purview of section 704 for over-the-counter drugs and nonrestricted devices, the FDA demands access to these documents and normally obtains them. For restricted devices and prescription drugs, the statute explicitly permits inspection and copying.[123]

Under section 704, confidential pricing, sales, and personnel records are not to be part of the inspection of documents. In reality, however, much confidential information is contained in documents that are part of the permissible inspection, and that information can be reported in internal FDA inspectional reports. In such circumstances, companies often seek and obtain FDA's agreement to expunge the confidential information from records released under the Freedom of Information Act.[124]

In the course of an inspection, FDA investigators frequently request that an individual at the inspected company sign an affidavit confirming particular results of the inspection. The affidavit usually lists the documents taken and records answers provided by company personnel during the course of the inspection. Company personnel are under no statutory duty to sign or even review such affidavits.

At the conclusion of an inspection, the inspector provides the Form FD483, or the list of "observations," made during the tour of the facility. An exit interview is provided when requested by the inspected company. FD483 observations do not constitute formal FDA

---

[119] *Id.* at 93. *See also* United States v. Agnew, 931 F.2d 1397, 1409-10 (10th Cir.), *cert. denied*, 502 U.S. 884 (1991) (finding proper chain of custody established for admission of photographs).

[120] FDA INVESTIGATIONS OPERATIONS MANUAL, *supra* note 110, § 523.1.

[121] 476 U.S. 227 (1986).

[122] 409 F. Supp. 529, 533 (S.D. Iowa 1976).

[123] 21 U.S.C. § 374.

[124] *See* Pub. L. No. 89-487, 80 Stat. 250 (1966) (codified as amended 5 U.S.C. § 552 (1994)). The FDA generally is cooperative in deleting confidential information from publicly released documents, although the agency is less so when a company seeks overbroad protection of information.

notices of violations, but rather the opinion of the inspector as to possible violations. It is expected that an inspected firm will respond in writing to each observation reported on the form. The FDA evaluates the responses when deciding what further action, if any, to take. FD483 reports are available for public disclosure.[125]

After the investigator returns to the district office, a draft is prepared of an establishment inspection report (EIR), which is then put into final form by the supervisory investigator and sent to FDA headquarters in Rockville, Maryland. If particularly egregious conduct is found, an official action indicated (OAI) alert will be communicated to agency headquarters, in which case further enforcement action may be taken against the inspected company. These reports also are subject to Freedom of Information Act disclosure, except during an ongoing investigation.

Depending on the complexity of the subject matter and the interest of the FDA district office in obtaining evidence of suspected violations, an inspection can take anywhere from a matter of minutes to a number of weeks or months. Drug manufacturing facilities are inspected at least once every two years, while food plants are inspected by the FDA at varying intervals. A representative example of how an inspection is conducted and the manner in which an inspection may lead to enforcement action appears in *United States v. General Foods Corporation.*[126]

■ Warning Notices: Letters and Other Regulatory Correspondence

Following an inspection or the discovery of an alleged violation in the field, either FDA headquarters or the district office may communicate to a company the findings of alleged violations. These communications constitute an official enforcement mode known as "warning letters." The letters are authorized generally by section 309 of the FDCA,[127] which permits the use of a "written notice or warning" in lieu of the institution of seizures or injunctions for minor violations of the Act.

Until May 1991, there were two officially designated letters, "notices of adverse findings" and "regulatory letters," both discussed in an FDA *Federal Register* announcement in 1978.[128] The notice of adverse finding, previously known as an "information letter," requested voluntary action by a party with a response to the FDA within thirty days. When a notice of adverse finding was issued, it stated that, although the FDA believed that violations existed, no decision had been made by the agency as to whether further enforcement action would be taken.[129] A regulatory letter, however, was a threat to sue if corrective action was not taken.[130] A response was demanded within ten days, and enforcement action very often did follow a refusal to reply in an acceptable manner.[131]

---

[125] 21 C.F.R. § 20.20.

[126] 446 F. Supp. 740 (N.D.N.Y.), *aff'd*, 591 F.2d 1332 (2d Cir. 1978). In that case, the FDA was denied an injunction despite the presence of green, slimy material on green bean processing machinery. *Id.* at 754.

[127] 21 U.S.C. § 336.

[128] 43 Fed. Reg. 27,498 (1978).

[129] REGULATORY PROCEDURES MANUAL, *supra* note 113, chs. 8-10.

[130] *Id.*

[131] *See, e.g., In re* Highland Labs., Inc., Dkt. No. 90-604(a) (D. Ore. 1990).

In May 1991, FDA Commissioner David Kessler issued a memorandum announcing the revocation of the regulatory letter and a notice of adverse findings warning system.[132] Explaining that "[t]he FDA cannot afford to be perceived as a 'paper tiger' that inspects a firm, writes a letter, waits, then writes another letter . . . ," Commissioner Kessler introduced the new warning letter system (along with a streamlined review procedure for injunctions and criminal fraud cases).[133]

Reiterating that "responsible individuals should not assume that they will receive a Warning Letter, or other prior notice, before FDA initiates an enforcement action"[134] (especially when there have been repeated or intentional violations, or when death or injury may result[135]), the FDA's guidelines nonetheless characterize the warning letter as "the principal means for notifying regulated industry of violations (prior notice) and of achieving prompt voluntary correction."[136]

Warning letters may be issued by District Directors without FDA headquarters' concurrence, except when the letters raise one of twenty-six enumerated subject matter areas.[137] In the latter case, the letters will be issued directly by one of the FDA's Centers or by the District after referral to the appropriate Center.

A firm usually must respond to a warning letter within fifteen working days after receipt of the letter.[138] When drugs or devices are involved, the letter often states that the FDA is advising federal agencies of the issuance of the letter, so that those agencies may consider that information in the award of applicable government contracts for the affected products.[139] The warning letter may further place a hold on pending product or export approvals.[140]

One of the most critical questions that arises with respect to Warning Letters is whether they constitute "final agency action" that is reviewable by the judiciary. The first answer, by the U.S. District Court for the District of Columbia when dealing with the analogous regulatory letter, was in the negative. In *Estee Lauder, Inc. v. FDA*,[141] a cosmetic company sought a declaration that anti-aging claims for face creams did not render the products unapproved new drugs. The FDA had sent more than twenty manufacturers regulatory letters taking the position that such claims were illegal.[142] The FDA nonetheless moved to dismiss on the ground that the action was not ripe for adjudication and that the plaintiff had failed to exhaust its administrative remedies.[143]

---

[132] FDA Memorandum from Commissioner David Kessler to all FDA enforcement and field offices (May 23, 1991).

[133] *Id.*

[134] REGULATORY PROCEDURES MANUAL, *supra* note 113, ch. 4, subch. "Warning Letters," sec. "Purpose."

[135] *Id.*

[136] *Id.* sec. "Issuance."

[137] *Id.* sec. "Center Concurrence."

[138] *Id.* sec. "Time Frames."

[139] *Id.* sec. "Format."

[140] *Id.* exhibits 4-6, 4-7.

[141] 727 F. Supp. 1 (D.D.C. 1989). *See also* Dietary Supplemental Coalition, Inc. v. Sullivan et al., 978 F.2d 560, 561 (9th Cir. 1992).

[142] 727 F. Supp. at 2-3.

[143] *Id.* at 2.

Estee Lauder argued that FDA *had* taken final action by sending the regulatory letters, and that the next step was merely the procedural nicety of an action for seizure (or some other enforcement mode) against the products.[144] The court accepted the FDA's position that its regulatory letters were not final agency action because they were an equivocal, not final, enforcement threat.

Six years later, however, the same court took a different position.[145] The Washington Legal Foundation filed suit for a declaratory judgment challenging the FDA's policy prohibiting doctor members of the organization from receiving information regarding "off-label" uses of drugs and medical devices. Warning letters and policy pronouncements had been issued by the FDA threatening further enforcement against the distribution of scholarly articles and speeches. Despite the FDA's assertion, in a motion to dismiss, that no final agency position had been adopted, the court held that the question of finality of conduct turned not on theFDA's view of whether a final policy existed, but rather on the effect of the conduct on the industry.[146] The case was deemed ripe for review.[147]

Washington Legal Foundation guides future judicial determinations, but it does not settle the law, as illustrated by other, contrary decisions.[148] Clearly, the publicity given to a warning letter within the trade can create overwhelming pressure to comply with the FDA's position,[149] even absent the right to a legal challenge. Warning letters thus significantly expand the FDA's effective enforcement powers regardless of the ripeness of a later court challenge.

■ "Voluntary" Recalls

Except for infant formulas,[150] and medical devices since 1990,[151] the FDA has no authority to require a recall of products. Yet, the recall is one of the FDA's most potent enforcement tools and provides the greatest measure of publicity for the agency.

---

[144] *Id.* at 4-5.

[145] Washington Legal Foundation v. Kessler, 880 F. Supp. 26 (D.D.C. 1995). *But see* Summit Tech v. High-Line Med. Instruments, Co., 1996 U.S. Dist. LEXIS 10,562 note 9 (C.D. Cal. July 16, 1996); Professionals and Patients for Customized Care, 847 F. Supp. 1359, 1365 (S.D. Tex. 1994).

[146] *Id.* at 34.

[147] *Id.* at 36. *See also* Den-Mat Corp. v. United States, 1992 U.S. Dist. LEXIS 9255 (D. Md. Apr. 24, 1992) [the FDA might have gone beyond a statement of its position and taken "affirmative action" to enforce its decision. Den-Mat's subsequent motion to dismiss the FDA's enforcement was denied. Den-Mat Corp. v. United States, 1992 U.S. Dist. LEXIS 12,233 (D. Md. Aug. 17, 1992).]

[148] *See supra* note 145.

[149] Antiplaque dental rinses provide an example of an industry reaction to trade press sparked by regulatory letters. The FDA issued regulatory letters threatening action against claims that the "special ingredients" destroyed bacteria that caused plaque and/or gingivitis in the mouth. Some companies who received the letters declined to accept the FDA's position. In the meantime, the FDA announced a plan to "begin an Advisory Panel review of OTC oral health care drug products bearing antiplaque and antiplaque-related claims." F-D-C REP. ("The Pink Sheet"), June 19, 1989, at T&G 12-13. The FDA later issued a public notice requesting comments on these claims. 55 Fed. Reg. 38,560 (1990).

[150] FDCA § 412(e)(1), 21 U.S.C. § 350a(e)(1).

[151] Safe Medical Devices Act of 1990, Pub. L. No. 101-629, § 8, 104 Stat. at 4501 (codified at 21 U.S.C. § 360(h)(e)).

In the FDA's terms, a "recall" is a withdrawal or correction of a product that is in violation of the FDCA or another statute administered by the agency.[152] Thus, the FDA views a recall as an alternative to seizure, injunction, or other enforcement action by the agency. An implicit or explicit threat of such enforcement action, together with the risk that the agency will initiate adverse publicity, generally brings about any recall desired by the agency and does so without time-consuming procedures.

The increasing use of recalls by the FDA supports the notion that the agency has recognized it as a valuable enforcement tool. In 1939, the FDA listed no recalls in its enforcement report, followed by only 54 in 1951, 101 in 1963, 837 in 1972,[153] and 3,236 reported in 1994.[154] As the FDA recognizes in its *Regulatory Procedures Manual*, recalls are "generally more efficient and afford equal and more timely consumer protection than formal administrative or civil actions, especially when the product has been widely distributed."[155]

The FDA induces a recall after it determines that a product is violative of one of the laws it administers.[156] By characterizing a withdrawal or correction of a product as a "recall," the FDA takes a position on the compliance status of the product. Thus, although recalls technically are voluntary for most products under the FDA's jurisdiction, in reality, the FDA is informing the company involved that other enforcement action will be taken if a recall is not commenced. The FDA often has sought recalls as part of the injunctive relief granted in successfully-concluded lawsuits. Most courts have, however, declined to include such provisions in injunctions.[157]

In detailed regulations governing the agency's recall policy,[158] the FDA has divided product recalls into four categories.[159] The categorization within one of the four groups is dependent on a health hazard evaluation.[160] When products subject to a recall pose a minor health risk or involve a "minor violation for which FDA would not initiate legal action,"[161] the manufacturer may term the action a "market withdrawal" rather than a recall.[162]

A Class I recall is the most serious. It occurs when there is a "strong likelihood that the use of, or exposure to, a violative product will cause serious, adverse health consequences or death."[163] Such recalls are generally required at the consumer or user level, including

---

[152] *See* 21 C.F.R. §§ 7.3(g)-(k), 7.40. Under these regulations, not every product withdrawal or upgrade is technically a "recall." For an action to be a recall, it must be carried out to remove a condition that the FDA considers violative. *Id* § 7.3(g)-(k).

[153] PETER B. HUTT & RICHARD A. MERRILL, FOOD AND DRUG LAW, CASES AND MATERIALS 1205 (2d ed. 1991).

[154] Off. of Enforcement, Off. of Reg. Affrs., FDA (1995).

[155] REGULATORY PROCEDURES MANUAL, *supra* note 113, ch. 7, subch. "Policy."

[156] *Id.* at ch. 7, subch. "Policy," sec. "General."

[157] *See, e.g.*, United States v. Generix Drugs Corp., 498 F. Supp. 288, 294 (S.D. Fla. 1980), *vacated and remanded on other grounds*, 654 F.2d 1114 (5th Cir. Unit B 1981), *rev'd*, 460 U.S. 453 (1983); United States v. C.E.B. Prods., Inc., 380 F. Supp. 664 (N.D. Ill. 1974). *But cf.* United States v. K-N Enter., Inc., 461 F. Supp. 988 (N.D. Ill. 1978).

[158] 21 C.F.R. §§ 7.40-.59.

[159] *Id.* § 7.3(m).

[160] *Id.* § 7.41.

[161] REGULATORY PROCEDURES MANUAL, *supra* note 113, ch. 11 (definition of market withdrawal).

[162] 21 C.F.R. § 7.3(j).

[163] REGULATORY PROCEDURES MANUAL *supra* note 113, ch. 7.

intervening wholesalers or retailers.[164] Public warnings also are utilized in Class I recalls.[165]

A Class II recall is one in which the product may "cause temporary or medically reversible adverse health consequences or where the probability of serious adverse health consequences is remote."[166] A Class II recall may reach only to the retail level.[167]

A Class III recall is one in which the violative product "is not likely to cause adverse health consequences."[168] Wholesale level recalls generally are utilized.[169]

From the perspective of a manufacturer or distributor, a "market withdrawal" is preferable to a "recall" because of the publicity accorded the latter. A market withdrawal does not require the publicity or the listing in the *FDA Enforcement Reports* that a recall requires.[170] The FDA may, however, unilaterally classify a product correction or removal as a recall, rather than as a market withdrawal.

Once a recall situation has been identified, the FDA works with the recalling company to determine the scope (product lots) and depth (distribution levels) of the recall, the means to be utilized to conduct an effectiveness check, and the type of notices and publicity that will be required for the recall.[171] The FDA's participation is the same whether the recall is initiated by the firm or by the agency.[172]

Effectiveness checks range from level A, constituting 100% of the total number of consignees to be contacted, to level E, which requires no effectiveness check.[173] The FDA permits the use of personal visits, telephone calls, letters, or a combination of these methods, and ordinarily permits the recalling firm itself to do the effectiveness checks.[174] The FDA comments on a firm's proposed effectiveness check level, and responds if it believes that the scope of the effectiveness checks is inadequate.

Much of the recall procedure is a matter of negotiation. Companies that voluntarily notify the FDA stand in a better position to obtain a more favorable recall classification or a less onerous effectiveness check. Consequently, although there is no legal requirement to inform the FDA of a defect-related market withdrawal (except as to medical devices),[175] it is considered good practice to notify the agency in any event.

---

[164] *See* 21 C.F.R. § 7.42(b)(1).

[165] *See id.* § 7.42(b)(2).

[166] REGULATORY PROCEDURES MANUAL, *supra* note 113, ch. 11 (definition of recall classification).

[167] *See* 21 C.F.R. § 7.42(b)(1).

[168] REGULATORY PROCEDURES MANUAL, *supra* note 113, ch. 11.

[169] *See* 21 C.F.R. § 7.42(b)(1).

[170] *Id.* §§ 7.46(b), 7.50.

[171] REGULATORY PROCEDURES MANUAL, *supra* note at 113, ch. 7, subch. "Policy," sec. "Recall Strategy"; 21 C.F.R. §§ 7.41-.45.

[172] 21 C.F.R. § 7.46. The FDA expects firms to notify the agency of any firm-initiated recall; such notice is now mandated for medical devices after the passage of the Safe Medical Devices Act of 1990, Pub. L. No. 101-629, § 7, 104 Stat. at 4501 (codified at 21 U.S.C. §§ 360i(f)(1).

[173] 21 C.F.R. § 7.42(b)(3)(i)(v).

[174] *Id.* § 7.42(b)(3).

[175] 21 U.S.C. § 360i(f).

In any recall situation, the FDA takes an active role in reviewing the notices utilized by a company, inspecting the effectiveness check response (often in the form of return post-cards), and monitoring the publicity that has been issued by the recalling firm. In addition, the FDA, pursuant to regulation, promptly makes available in its weekly *FDA Enforcement Reports* a listing of all recalls, and utilizes public media when the agency believes that a critical health hazard requires such recourse.[176]

Finally, as noted earlier, the Safe Medical Devices Act of 1990, by amending section 518 of the FDCA, confers recall authority where "there is a reasonable probability that a device intended for human use would cause serious, adverse health consequences or death."[177] The recall procedure is instituted after an informal hearing procedure. No recall order is issued until the FDA first has notified companies to cease distribution of the device, and instructed the manufacturer to notify health professionals and device users to cease use of the device. Once a recall order is issued, it does not apply to devices held by individuals or to devices in the possession of facilities where the risk of recalling presents a greater risk than a recall would entail.[178] It remains to be seen whether the FDA will find it beneficial to rely on this new statutory authority rather than on its ability to induce recalls informally.

■ The Power of Publicity

The publicity provisions in the recall regulations are only a small portion of the FDA's powers under section 705 of the Act,[179] which affords the FDA various publicity options. The FDA not only issues public notices of health hazards associated with violative products during a recall; it also regularly issues press releases and *FDA Enforcement Reports*, holds press conferences, testifies at congressional hearings, and sends representatives to comment before the national media on current issues.

Section 705 provides that the FDA shall cause "to be published from time to time reports summarizing all judgments, decrees, and court orders,"[180] and that the agency shall disseminate "information regarding food, drugs, devices, or cosmetics in situations involving, in the opinion of the Secretary, imminent danger to health, or gross deception of the consumer."[181] The FDA has been quick to issue press releases or to televise warnings when imminent death has been presented as a probable consequence of food ingestion. On November 9, 1977, FDA Commissioner Donald Kennedy issued warnings about the deleterious effects of liquid protein diets; the warning was followed by a proposed regulation to require a death warning on the products.[182] Similarly, when a large number of L-tryptophan-induced cases of *eosinophilia myalgia* surfaced, the FDA was most effective not only in instigating recalls,[183] but also in stopping sales of the product almost immediately through the use of widespread national publicity in print and the television media.

---

[176] 21 C.F.R. §§ 7.42(b)(2), 7.50.

[177] Pub. L. No. 101-629, § 8, 104 Stat. at 4501 (codified at 21 U.S.C. § 360h(e)).

[178] 21 U.S.C. § 360h(e)(2)).

[179] *Id.* § 375.

[180] FDCA § 705(a), 21 U.S.C. § 375(a).

[181] *Id.* § 705(b), 21 U.S.C. § 375(b).

[182] 21 C.F.R. § 101.17(d).

[183] Malcolm Gladwell, *FDA Recalls Products Based on L-Tryptophan*, WASH. POST, Mar. 23, 1990, at A8.

In the case of a batch of Chilean grapes that allegedly had been found to contain cyanide, the FDA mounted a major consumer publicity campaign and virtually stopped the importation of Chilean fruit for a period long enough for the agency to establish a meaningful sampling procedure.[184]

Even where public health is not an issue *per se*, the FDA may use widespread publicity to signal a new enforcement posture in order to exact voluntary industry compliance. A classic example was the FDA's seizure of Citrus Hill Orange Juice on the ground that its use of the term "fresh" rendered the pasteurized juice misbranded.[185]

The means of publicity, as well as the publicity itself, can sometimes be negotiated with the FDA. If the agency determines that there is an imminent risk of a public health disaster, however, it may not consult with industry beforehand. The FDA also has participated in joint publicity efforts, such as that involving the manufacturer of Tylenol®.[186] Many larger pharmaceutical manufacturers have prepared emergency publicity procedures to be implemented in conjunction with the FDA in the event of a tampering-type incident.

The FDA's power to conduct long-term publicity campaigns through press releases, seminars, and public announcements has been challenged as an "unlawful interference" with the business rights of regulated firms. In *Ajay Nutrition Foods, Inc. v. FDA*,[187] this challenge, premised on the FDA's characterization of health food industry participants as "quacks" and "faddists," was dismissed.[188] The court adverted, *inter alia*, to the FDA's duty under section 705 to disseminate information to the public.[189]

■ Enforcement Against the Product: Seizures

The Seizure Remedy in General

The civil remedy provided in section 304 of the FDCA[190] is a powerful one. The outcome of a successful seizure action is a judicial condemnation and either the destruction of the goods at issue or a reconditioning procedure supervised by the FDA pursuant to a court order.[191] A company that seeks to recondition its condemned goods must post a bond, and subject itself to judicial and FDA discretion as to whether the company's reconditioning proposal is a reasonable one.[192]

---

[184] A later evaluation of the episode in the wake of industry complaints stated that the FDA had acted responsibly and promptly. U.S. GEN. ACCT. OFFICE, FOOD TAMPERING: FDA'S ACTIONS ON CHILEAN FRUIT BASED ON SOUND EVIDENCE (1990).

[185] Warren Leary, *Citing Labels, U.S. Seizes Orange Juice*, N.Y. TIMES, Apr. 25, 1991, at 18, col. 1.

[186] Michael Waldholz, *Tainted Tylenol Found in 2 More Bottles in New York; Nationwide Alert Issued*, WALL ST. J., Feb. 14, 1986; *see also* Robert D. McFadden, *Poison Deaths Bring U.S. Warning on Tylenol Use*, N.Y. TIMES, Oct. 2, 1982, at 1.

[187] 378 F. Supp. 210 (D.N.J.), *aff'd*, 513 F.2d 625 (3d Cir. 1975).

[188] *Id.* at 218-19.

[189] *Id.* at 217-18.

[190] 21 U.S.C. § 334.

[191] FDCA § 304(d)(1), 21 U.S.C. § 334(d)(1).

[192] United States v. . . . Among Others, an Article of Drug [Copanos], Food Drug Cosm. L. Rep. (CCH) ¶ 38,112 (W.D. Mo. 1989). The FDA can require destruction of imported violative goods, even if they were never released by Customs. Unites States v. 2,988 Cases . . . , 64 U.S. L.W. 2216 (5th Cir. 1995).

The FDA, acting through the Department of Justice, has authority under section 304 to have U.S. marshals or other employees of the U.S. government seize any drug that meets the FDCA test for interstate commerce, and to seize any medical device.[193] Section 304(g)[194] also permits the detention of medical devices for twenty to thirty days by the FDA (prior to a seizure pursuant to judicial process). That section does not provide for preseizure detention of drugs. Most states, however, provide for an embargo without resort to court action in the case of potentially adulterated products. Thus, the FDA often seeks the cooperation of state agencies in imposing an embargo while it pursues judicial seizure remedy.

The FDA's *Regulatory Procedures Manual* sets forth in detail the procedural requirements for the issuance of an FDA referral for a seizure action to the Department of Justice.[195] Seizures usually are instituted by means of a recommendation letter sent by the FDA district office to the local U.S. attorney,[196] and generally are not brought against out-of-compliance articles that "apparently could have been easily corrected by the owner without litigation."[197]

A seizure action is filed against the goods that are claimed to be violative rather than against a company or person. Thus, the title of a case will be of the form *"United States v. 200 Cases . . . -[Brand]."* Because the seizure action is filed against property, it is an *in rem* action. *In rem* cases are subject to the Federal Rules of Admiralty, found as the "Supplemental Rules for Certain Admiralty and Maritime Claims" appended to the *Federal Rules of Civil Procedure.*[198]

The procedure for the institution and prosecution of a seizure case differs slightly from that for other federal civil cases.[199] The government must file a Verified Complaint and seek an order from the court authorizing the process of attachment[200] (i.e., an order for arrest of the *res*, or property).[201] Once a court issues the order, it is delivered to the clerk, who prepares a warrant for delivery to the U.S. marshal or other U.S. government employee. The marshal, in turn, executes the order by affixing a copy of it to the property in a conspicuous place and leaving a copy of the Complaint with the person having possession of the *res*.[202] It is not uncommon for companies to be confronted with more than one U.S. and an FDA district compliance officer who arrive to execute the seizure warrant. Efforts to hide the goods subject to the seizure may be met with personal arrest by the U.S. marshal for obstruction of justice.

---

[193] Pursuant to amendments to the supplemental rules effective December 1, 1991, any U.S. officer or employee authorized to enforce the warrant, not just a marshal, will be permitted to execute the order of attachment. FED. R. CIV. P. SUPP. R. FOR CERTAIN ADM. AND MARITIME CLAIMS C(3).

[194] 21 U.S.C. § 334(g).

[195] REGULATORY PROCEDURES MANUAL, *supra* note 113, ch. 6, subch. "Seizures."

[196] *Id.* sec. "Types of Seizure Recommendations."

[197] *Id.* sec. "General Guidelines for Seizures."

[198] FED. R. CIV. P. SUPP. R. A; FDCA § 304(b), 21 U.S.C. § 334(b).

[199] FED. R. CIV. P. SUPP. R. C.

[200] *Id.* E.

[201] *Id.* E(4).

[202] *Id.* E(4).

Once a product has been seized, public notice is required to alert persons who might have an interest in the property of the need to file a Notice of Claim.[203] Normally, this Notice is published in local newspapers with "general circulation in the district."[204] The costs of such Notice are borne ultimately by an unsuccessful claimant.[205] If no person claims the property, or if a seizure action is contested and lost by the claimant, then the FDA is authorized, pursuant to instructions of the court, to destroy or sell the property at issue.[206]

Those wishing to challenge a seizure must file a Notice of Claim.[207] The Notice must be filed within ten days after process was executed by the marshal. A Verified Answer must be served within twenty days after the filing of the Claim.[208] If interrogatories were served by the government, answers to those interrogatories must be served at the time of filing the Answer.[209] A failure to file a timely Notice of Claim or Answer can, and often does, lead to a default.[210]

Some parties have attempted to withdraw their Notice of Claim after the case has proceeded past the joinder of issue, either to avoid imposition of costs or to prevent entry of an injunction if the FDA amends its Complaint to add an *in personem* claim for injunction. Case law supports the FDA's position that the agency is entitled to a full adjudication once a Notice of Claim has been filed, and that no withdrawal is permitted.[211]

Once an Answer has been filed, the *Federal Rules of Civil Procedure* apply, and the seizure action is treated as if it were an injunction proceeding.[212] The FDA usually seeks an injunction against the claimant in contested seizure cases. For this reason, some companies decide not to contest certain seizure actions. The judgment entered in an uncontested seizure action is against the seized *res*, and not against other units of the product or against the company. A potential claimant can thus avoid a *res judicata* determination that might affect it in other jurisdictions, or it may choose to default in one jurisdiction merely to await litigation of the issue in a more favorable forum.

Where a seizure is contested, even if the FDA does not seek an injunction in the seizure case itself, the agency takes the position that a successfully litigated seizure action oper-

---

[203] *Id*. C. In order to find a claimant, the government is required to publish a notice of the seizure in "reasonable" publications. Litigants may dispute whether the government has exceeded its mandate and incurred excessive costs by placing notices in expensive daily newspapers when a trade press listing, or even a telephone call, would have sufficed.

[204] *Id*. C(4).

[205] 28 U.S.C. § 1921 (1994).

[206] FDCA § 304(d)(1), 21 U.S.C. § 334(d)(1).

[207] FED. R. CIV. P. SUPP. R. C(6). Generally, there is no release of the seized goods *pendente lite* under bond. United States v. 893 One-Gallon Cans . . . Labeled Brown's Inhalant, 45 F. Supp. 467 (D. Del. 1942).

[208] FED. R. CIV. P. SUPP. R. C(6).

[209] *Id*.

[210] *See, e.g.*, United States v. An Article of Drug . . . "Wilfley's Bio Water," 1989 U.S. Dist. LEXIS 12833, at *4 (D. Or. Oct. 20, 1989).

[211] *See, e.g.*, United States v. Articles of Drug . . . Penapar VK, 458 F. Supp. 687 (D. Md. 1978); United States v. 4 Cases of 12 Packages, More or Less, Etc., Notices of Judgment Under the Federal Food, Drug and Cosmetic Act, FDA Papers No. 33 (Feb. 1968) *reprinted in* FEDERAL FOOD, DRUG, AND COSMETIC ACT JUDICIAL RECORD 1965-1968, at 45 (FDLI 1973).

[212] United States v. Nysco Labs., Inc., 215 F. Supp. 87, 89 (E.D.N.Y.),*aff'd*, 318 F.2d 817 (2d Cir. 1963); United States v. An Article . . . Sudden Change, 36 F.R.D. 695, 698-99 (E.D.N.Y. 1965).

ates as *res judicata* in any subsequent proceeding for an injunction against the company that filed the Notice of Claim. The Fifth Circuit has held that the *res judicata* determination runs both ways, benefiting a claimant that wins the seizure proceeding as well.[213] Because the proceeding is *in rem*, the destruction of the seized *res* renders any further proceedings (including appellate proceedings) moot.[214]

Multiple and Mass Seizures

The statute permits the FDA, through the Department of Justice, to file seizures simultaneously in a number of jurisdictions against different lots of the same product.[215] These "multiple seizures" are available to the FDA for products that the agency alleges are adulterated or are unlawfully distributed because they lack a statutorily required approval.[216] Multiple seizures are also available against an allegedly misbranded product, but only if it: a) has been the subject of a prior court judgment, b) poses a danger to health or c) bears labeling that is "fraudulent, or would be in a material respect misleading to the injury or damage of the purchaser."[217]

If the FDA chooses to file multiple seizures, then section 304(b) of the Act permits the claimant to choose, from among the jurisdictions in which seizure actions have been filed, the jurisdiction where the proceedings will be consolidated.[218] No matter what convenience factors militate in favor of the government's retention of the case in another jurisdiction, venue is placed in a district chosen by the claimant that is within "reasonable proximity to claimant's principal place of business."[219]

The multiple seizure remedy is a powerful tool for FDA, and is utilized when an effective nationwide cessation of sales is required in a short period of time. Because of the devastating impact of multiple seizures, a number of constitutional challenges were made to the statutory scheme, culminating in the Supreme Court's decision in *Ewing v. Mytinger & Casselberry, Inc.*[220] Units of a dietary supplement were seized in a number of jurisdictions throughout the country due to misbranding caused by health claims for the supplement. Justice Douglas, writing for the Court, held that the opportunity afforded a claimant to appear and have a full judicial hearing *after* the seizures satisfies the due process clause of the Fifth Amendment.[221] As long as "there is at some stage an opportunity for a hearing and a judicial determination," an individual's property rights are protected under the Constitution.[222] The Court held that the devastating impact of this multiple seizure procedure was weighed properly by Congress against the potential injury to the public from misbranded or adulterated articles.[223]

---

[213] United States v. An Article of Drug . . . [Neoterramycin], 725 F.2d 976, 984 (5th Cir. 1984).

[214] United States v. 3 Unlabeled 25-Pound Bags Dried Mushrooms, 157 F.2d 722 (7th Cir. 1946).

[215] FDCA § 304(a), 21 U.S.C. § 334(a).

[216] *Id.*

[217] *Id.*

[218] *Id.* § 304(b), 21 U.S.C. § 334(b).

[219] *Id.* § 304(a), 21 U.S.C. § 334(a).

[220] 339 U.S. 594 (1950).

[221] *Id.* at 599.

[222] *Id.*

[223] *Id.* at 601.

Section 304(d)(1) of the FDCA[224] permits the entry of a reconditioning decree for seized and condemned goods. That provision also permits re-exportation if the product became adulterated or misbranded *before* it was imported, was imported in good faith by the claimant, and meets the general conditions of section 801(d) of the Act for export.[225]

Procedural Limitations of the Seizure Remedy

Although seizures continue to be a very effective enforcement tool for the FDA, the inherent problem with this procedure is that a company is free to sell its products in other jurisdictions even after a condemnation of the seized *res* occurs in the district where the FDA brought the case. In addition, there have been instances where companies have obtained stays of enforcement of a judgment for condemnation pending appeal,[226] thus permitting the continued sale of an allegedly misbranded or adulterated product for years without penalty.

Another limitation of the seizure remedy is that the products condemned under a final judgment must be reasonably within the scope of the initial seizure order. In a case where the government seized approximately $680,000 worth of pharmaceuticals, the claimant sought release of two-thirds of the drugs (intermediates) on the ground that they were not intended for use in the manufacture of the finished drug products that were the subject of the seizure order.[227] The district court held that the intermediate drug products at issue were both perishable and capable of being utilized in other, lawfully-marketed drugs. Accordingly, it released those products from the seizure order.[228] After the FDA filed a follow-up injunction action, the Seventh Circuit enjoined the sale of the intermediate products.[229]

■ Civil Enforcement Against the Company: Injunctions

"Injunctions with TRO's [temporary restraining orders] have the highest priority ranking of all legal actions."[230] Injunctions are authorized by section 302 of the FDCA [231] and are utilized to enjoin conduct where there is a likelihood that violations will continue or recur.[232] The FDA need not prove in an injunction action that there will be "irreparable injury,"[233] but merely that the violative conduct is likely to continue.[234]

---

[224] 21 U.S.C. § 334(d)(1).

[225] *Id.*; section 801 is discussed *infra* notes 246-71 and accompanying text. *See also* REGULATORY PROCEDURES MANUAL, *supra* note 113, ch. 9, subch. "Priority Enforcement Strategy for Problem Importers," sec. "Approach."

[226] *See, e.g.,* United States v. Sandoz Pharmaceutical Corp., 894 F.2d 825, 826 (6th Cir.), *cert. denied,* 498 U.S. 810 (1990); United States v. 225 Cartons . . . "Fiorinal with Codeine," 687 F. Supp. 946 (D.N.J. 1988), *aff'd,* 871 F.2d 409 (3d Cir. 1989).

[227] United States v. Undetermined Quantities of Drugs . . . [Travenol Labs.], 675 F. Supp. 1113 (N.D. Ill. 1987).

[228] *Id.* at 1117.

[229] United States v. Baxter Healthcare Corp., 901 F.2d 1401 (7th Cir. 1990).

[230] REGULATORY PROCEDURES MANUAL, *supra* note 113, ch. 6, subch. "Injunctions," sec. "General Guidelines."

[231] 21 U.S.C. § 332.

[232] REGULATORY PROCEDURES MANUAL, *supra* note 113, ch. 6, subch. "Injunctions," sec. "General Guidelines."

[233] United States v. Diapulse Corp., 457 F.2d 25, 28 (2d Cir. 1972).

[234] United States v. W.T. Grant Co., 345 U.S. 629, 633 (1953). *But see, e.g.,* Unites States v. Nutri-Cology, Inc., Food & Drug Dec. (CCH) 38,235 (N.D. Cal. July 19, 1991).

Injunctions under the FDCA may be entered against both corporations and individuals, and they can range from a prohibition on the introduction of new products with specified ingredients[235] to the virtual shut-down of a business during the pendency of the injunction.[236]

The injunction remedy generally is utilized by the FDA where: a) "[t]here is a current and definite health hazard or a gross consumer deception, requiring immediate action," b) "[t]here are significant amounts of violative products owned by the same person in many locations . . . and multiple seizures are impractical or uneconomical," or c) there have been chronic violations that have not been corrected voluntarily by the company.[237] In part because, until recently, injunctions had to be authorized through a rather lengthy approval process at the FDA,[238] and in part because injunction proceedings inevitably take far longer to resolve than seizure cases (which often result in defaults), the FDA has not initiated injunction actions nearly as frequently as seizure actions. Many injunction actions emanate from seizures that have ripened into full-scale judicial proceedings.

The only practical limitation on the scope of an injunction is that it must properly delimit the acts enjoined. Thus, for example, an injunction issued against the sale of "drug products identical or similar to those described in [the complaint]" was remanded for greater specificity so as not to preclude the defendant from improperly marketing other products that might be subject to a shifting interpretation by the FDA of the word "similar."[239]

In an injunction case involving violations of the FDA's good manufacturing practice (GMP) regulations, a company's operations typically will be shut down pending rehabilitation procedures supervised by the FDA.[240] The company is required to bring its procedures into compliance, to relabel improperly labeled products, to destroy adulterated or outdated ingredients or products, to revise standard operating procedures, to remedy unsanitary conditions, and to produce for introduction into interstate commerce products that are assayed by the FDA pursuant to the terms of the injunction or consent decree.[241] Commonly, an injunction will require certification by an independent expert that the defendant is in compliance before the FDA will conduct an inspection to confirm compliance.

---

[235] *See, e.g.,* United States v. Articles of Drug . . . Midwest Pharmaceuticals, Inc., 825 F.2d 1238, 1247-48 (8th Cir. 1987).

[236] *See, e.g.,* United States v. Lit Drug Co., 333 F. Supp. 990 (D.N.J. 1971). The FDA has, on occasion, been denied requests for injunctive relief where a company has demonstrated adequate safeguards to prevent future violations. *See, e.g.,* United States v. Flea-Tabs, Inc., Food Drug Cosm. L. Rep. (CCH) ¶ 38,123 (C.D. Cal. 1981); United States v. Sars of Louisiana, Inc., 324 F. Supp. 307 (E.D. La. 1971).

[237] REGULATORY PROCEDURES MANUAL, *supra* note 113, ch. 6 "Injunctions," sec. "General Considerations."

[238] *See id.* ch. 6, subch. "Injunctions." The FDA revised its internal review procedures for injunction and seizures. *See* FDA Memorandum from Assoc. Comm'r Ronald G. Chesemore to enforcement personnel (May 23, 1991).

[239] *Midwest Pharmaceuticals, Inc.,* 825 F.2d at 1247.

[240] *See, e.g., Lit Drug Co.,* 333 F. Supp. at 990.

[241] *See, e.g., id.* at 997-99. The *Regulatory Procedures Manual* contains a number of model injunction provisions that provide not only for assay and supervision methodology, but also specify that all costs for the supervision will be borne by the defendant pursuant to preset schedules of charges. REGULATORY PROCEDURES MANUAL *supra* note 113, ch. 6, subch. "Injunctions."

In the past decade, the FDA has turned to draconian injunctive consent decrees to clean up many of the pharmaceutical manufacturing deficiencies that were uncovered in the wake of the generic drug criminal investigations. *Barr Laboratories*[242] is the most exhaustive judicial decision analyzing the GMP authority of the FDA. While the decision's underlying premise — that a judge is a qualified party to make extrastatutorial manufacturing standards determinations — is questionable, the FDA has utilized this decision in extracting strong decree language in subsequent enforcement actions. Two of the more prominent decrees were entered thereafter against reputable pioneer drug and device companies. Six Warner-Lambert[243] facilities were closed until compliance with GMPs was demonstrated; product certifications were required by outside consultants; and $25,000 was assessed in contempt penalties for noncompliance by the company or responsible individuals. In the *Seimens*[244] medical device decree, three plants were shut down until GMP compliance was demonstrated; the company also had to certify the GMP compliance of foreign component manufacturing sources.

■ Import/Export Powers

The Herculean task of protecting U.S. citizens from the importation of unapproved, adulterated, or misbranded drugs, medical devices, biologics, foods, and cosmetics is placed upon the FDA through the enforcement powers conferred in sections 801[245] and 802[246] of the FDCA. Section 801 covers both imports and exports, and provides to the FDA and the U.S. Customs Service in the U.S. Department of the Treasury the power to sample, detain, refuse admission to, or ultimately destroy, products pending their importation into domestic commerce. Section 802 was enacted to regulate the export of unapproved products manufactured or held in U.S. commerce. Unapproved drugs and biologics must meet a number of stringent conditions for the FDA to permit them to be exported.

Products regulated by the FDA legally enter this country only after they are released by the FDA. Pursuant to a Memorandum of Understanding (MOU) with Customs,[247] FDA district offices handle most of the procedural aspects of such imports. When a product appears at a U.S. port, the importer files an Entry Notice.[248] If the product appears acceptable to the FDA, a "may proceed notice"[249] or "white sheet" is issued. The "may proceed notice" permits a company to take the goods out of import jurisdiction and place them in a warehouse pending the issuance of a "Notice of Release."[250] In situations where the FDA wishes to take a sample of a product, it issues a "Notice of Sampling."[251] Although the law confers the responsibility for this issuance on Customs, pursuant to the MOU the FDA

---

[242] United States v. Barr Labs., Inc., 812 F. Supp. 458 (D.N.J. 1993).

[243] United States v. Warner-Lambert Co., Civ. No. 93-3525 (D.N.J. 1993).

[244] United States v. Siemens Med. Sys., Inc., Civ. No. 940-912 (D.N.J. 1994).

[245] 21 U.S.C. § 381.

[246] *Id.* § 382.

[247] 44 Fed. Reg. 53,577 (1979).

[248] FDA Form FD700.

[249] FDA Form FD702. Since 1990, a number of FDA district offices utilize a standard, computerized form for all Notices. It is predicted that this standard form will replace the various FDA forms used previously.

[250] FDA Form FD717.

[251] FDA Form FD712.

field offices sign the document over the facsimile signature of the Regional or District Director of Customs.[252] After a company has received a Notice of Sampling, it may not ship the goods until a Notice of Release is received.

Pursuant to a recent MOU entered into with the Customs Service, the FDA began a pilot program for low-risk imported products that eliminates all paper in favor of on-line computer entries accessed by the importer of record.[253] This system merges the two agencies' existing computer networks, and should be in full operation by 1997.[254]

If the FDA finds that a product is in violation of the FDCA or any other law under its jurisdiction, it makes charges in the form of a Notice of Detention and Hearing.[255] A Notice of Detention provides for a hearing within ten days, or such other time as agreed by the agency. The "hearing" often takes the form of telephone calls or letters of protest, which are then considered by the FDA before further action is taken. If the FDA agrees with the response of the importer, the goods will be released pursuant to a Notice of Release marked as "originally detained and now released."[256]

If the FDA decides that the product may not be imported, it issues a "Notice of Refusal,"[257] once again through agreement with the local District Director of Customs, because the responsibility technically is vested in Customs.[258]

If a product has been refused entry, minor reconditioning may be accomplished under section 801 to bring it into compliance for import purposes. An example is labeling that has relatively insignificant omissions that can be remedied by the addition of a sticker with the requisite information. The FDA, however, generally will not permit the relabeling of a product that, by virtue of its original label claims, is an unapproved new drug.[259] An importer whose products were refused entry must file a form[260] specifying the timetable and type of steps that will be taken to bring the products into compliance. A bond is posted as a guarantee. Notice-and-comment rulemaking is not required for the FDA's issuance of a refusal based on an adulteration or misbranding determination, or for its refusal to approve a reconditioning proposal.[261]

If the FDA refuses entry to a product, it may be exported under the conditions set forth in sections 801(a)[262] and 802.[263] The FDA normally grants transportation and exportation

---

[252] REGULATORY PROCEDURES MANUAL, *supra* note 113, ch. 9, subch. "Import Procedures," sec. "Notice of Sampling."

[253] 56 Fed. Reg. 47,755 (1991).

[254] The FDA's original "green sheet" procedure still exists; the paperless system is not mandatory. Currently, the filer has the choice of submitting either electronically or on paper. Paper procedures may be required if the FDA determines that an examination of cargo is necessary.

[255] FDA Form FD718.

[256] REGULATORY PROCEDURES MANUAL, *supra* note 113, ch. 9, subch. "Releases," sec. "Release After Detention."

[257] FDA Form FD772.

[258] *See* REGULATORY PROCEDURES MANUAL, *supra* note 113, ch. 9, subch. "Notice of Refusal of Admission," sec. "Guidance."

[259] *Id.* ch. 9, subch. "Reconditioning," sec. "Reconditioning Operations." The reason for this policy, presumably, is to deter attempts to import products improperly labeled in that way.

[260] FDA Form FD766.

[261] Sugarman v. Forbragd, 405 F.2d 1189 (9th Cir. 1968), *cert. denied*, 395 U.S. 960 (1969).

[262] 21 U.S.C. § 381(a).

[263] *Id.* § 382.

entry permits[264] to allow companies to move refused merchandise from one port to another for exportation. Nonetheless, such permits are refused if the article presents a hazard to consumers or if there is evidence that there was an abuse by the importer of similar permits in the past.[265] the FDA has the right to prohibit an export if it believes that there is a danger of re-importation of all or part of the refused shipment.[266]

The FDA often issues Import Alerts in order to notify Customs and FDA district offices of categories of products that it considers adulterated or misbranded and not appropriate for importation into the United States.[267] These products are detained automatically when they enter the jurisdiction of Customs, the list serving as an effective first-line screening method. In reality, the Import Alert system guarantees that the specified categories of imports are examined more stringently than domestic goods of the same type. Issuance of Import Alerts must be made pursuant to notice-and-comment rulemaking.[268]

Even with its broad powers to sample, detain, or refuse import, the import burden on the FDA is an overwhelming one. In one year, the FDA administered 25,740 import product detentions and 44,936 import sample examinations.[269] Despite these impressive numbers, a large majority of foods imported into the United States are never sampled by the FDA.[270]

■ The "Other" Civil Powers

Beginning with the enactment of the PDMA,[271] Congress embarked on a new phase of enforcement strategy. Since then, in addition to retaining the basic enforcement tools discussed above, various congressional proposals and enactments have contained civil penalty provisions intended for both their retributive consequences and their deterrence value.

Persons who violate prohibitions in the PDMA against the sale or trade of drug samples face civil penalties of up to $50,000 for each of the first two violations, and up to

---

[264] *See* REGULATORY PROCEDURES MANUAL, *supra* note 113, ch. 9, subch. "Import Procedures," secs. "Exportation of Merchandise Refused Admission" and "Shipment to Other Ports."

[265] *See id.*

[266] United States v. 76,552 Pounds of Frog Legs, 423 F. Supp. 329 (S.D. Tex. 1976).

[267] REGULATORY PROCEDURES MANUAL, *supra* note 113, ch. 9, subch. "Import Information Directives," sec. "Import Alerts." *See also id.* subch. "Priority Enforcement Strategy for Problem Importers." The FDA addresses importers who regularly evade the lawful import regulations.

[268] Bellarno Int'l, Ltd. v. FDA, 678 F. Supp. 410 (E.D.N.Y. 1988).

[269] FDA Talk Paper (Jan. 8, 1990).

[270] F-D-C REP. ("The Pink Sheet"), May 29, 1989. Approximately nine percent of food imports are sampled *Id.* Two recent attempts to deal with this burden are found in FDA COMPLIANCE POLICY GUIDES MANUAL, *supra* note 99, ch. 21, Program No. 7321.004 (Imported Foods — Labeling and Economics (FY 94)) and REGULATORY PROCEDURES MANUAL, *supra* note 113, ch. 9, subch. "Priority Enforcement Strategy for Problem Importers," sec. "Approach."

[271] Pub. L. No. 100-293, § 7, 102 Stat. 95 (1988) (codified at 21 U.S.C. §§ 331(t), 333).

$1,000,000 thereafter.[272] Companies that fail to issue drug sample reports are subject to $100,000 in civil penalties.[273]

Under the Safe Medical Devices Act of 1990[274] civil penalties up to $15,000 for each violation, with a ceiling of $1,000,000 for all violations combined, are provided for in section 303(f)(1)(A) of the FDCA.[275] In addition to these civil penalty provisions, Congress also has enacted whistleblower provisions.[276]

Another civil remedy provided by the Safe Medical Devices Act is the temporary suspension of approvals of applications.[277] In addition to this explicit statutory authority, the FDA also has looked to the GMP regulations[278] as the grounds for withdrawal of approval of applications for new drug products.[279]

A related regulatory remedy available to the FDA where medical devices present substantial deception or an unreasonable risk of illness or injury is formal banning, a power conferred by section 516 of the FDCA.[280] The FDA may, by regulation, eliminate a "generic type of device . . . [rather than proceed] against an individual device."[281] Although this remedy is "essentially a last resort action,"[282] it can be applied to "a quack but relatively harmless product that is resource intensive to control."[283]

Finally, debarment of corporations from the pharmaceutical approval process;[284] debarment of individuals from the pharmaceutical industry;[285] withdrawal and suspension of product approvals,[286] and civil penalties of up to $250,000 for individuals and $1,000,000 for corporations[287] are the sanctions imposed under the Generic Drug Enforcement Act, along with whistleblower awards of up to $250,000.[288]

---

[272] FDCA § 303(b)(2)(A)-(B), 21 U.S.C. § 333(b)(2)(A)-(B).

[273] *Id.* § 303(b)(3), 21 U.S.C. § 333(b)(3).

[274] Pub. L. No. 101-629, § 17, 104 Stat. at 4511 (codified at 21 U.S.C. § 333(f)(1)).

[275] 21 U.S.C. § 333(f)(1)(A).

[276] *See, e.g.*, FDCA § 303(b)(5), 21 U.S.C. § 333(b)(5).

[277] 21 U.S.C. § 360e(e)(3).

[278] 21 C.F.R. § 210. *See, e.g., Copanos*, Food Drug Cosm. L. Rep. (CCH) ¶ 38,112.

[279] *See* F-D-C REP. ("The Pink Sheet"), Jan. 1, 1990 at T&G 3-4. The FDA also has recourse to several additional enforcement means of a purely administrative nature. The FDA may withdraw product approvals because of false statements in applications or for failure to file annual reports (21 C.F.R. § 314.150(a)(2)(v),(b)(1)). In the investigational phase of the drug or device approval procedure, the FDA may disqualify investigators, institutional review boards, laboratories, or sponsors, or may terminate INDs or IDEs for noncompliance (*Id.* § 312.44). In addition, the FDA announced a final policy under which it intends to withdraw approvals or refuse to approve applications, and to seek recalls where fraud, bribery, or material false statements are discovered. 55 Fed. Reg. 46,191 (1991). The FDA also may revoke biologic product and establishment licenses. 21 C.F.R. § 601.5.

[280] 21 U.S.C. § 360f.

[281] REGULATORY PROCEDURES MANUAL, *supra* note 113, ch. 8-97, § 8-97-20-(B).

[282] *Id.* ch. 8-97, § 8-97-20-(A).

[283] *Id.* ch. 8-97, § 8-97-20-(C).

[284] 21 U.S.C. § 335a(a)(1).

[285] *Id.* § 335a(c)(1)(B).

[286] *Id.* § 335a(g)(1).

[287] *Id.* § 335b(a).

[288] *Id.* § 335b(e).

When the FDA Decides to Set an Example: Criminal Proceedings

■ The FDA's Criminal Powers

Although the number of criminal cases filed by the FDA declined in the decade prior to 1991,[289] the fear of criminal prosecution has remained a serious deterrent to those involved in the industries regulated by the FDA. All violations of the FDCA are subject to civil or criminal enforcement — or both — based on the FDA's discretion.

The FDA generally decides to recommend a criminal prosecution in cases where there are: a) gross violations that evidence management's disregard for unsafe conditions; b) obvious and continuing violations where management has not exercised normal care; c) life threatening violations or those where injuries already have occurred; and d) "deliberate attempts to circumvent the law," such as the submission of false data to the agency.[290]

The numerous prohibitions set forth in section 301 of the FDCA are subject to the criminal penalties set forth in section 303.[291] Section 303(a)(1)[292] authorizes a fine of up to $1000, and imprisonment for up to one year, for any misdemeanor violation. The misdemeanor provision applies to a first offense unless it was committed with "the intent to defraud or mislead."[293]

For repeat offenders, or for those who are found to have intentionally defrauded or misled the agency or consumers, section 303(a)(2) provides for felony prosecution, with a penalty of up to three years' imprisonment and up to $10,000 in fines.[294] Penalties of up to ten years' imprisonment and fines of not more than $250,000 are authorized by the PDMA,[295] and a five-year maximum sentence was added under section 303(e)[296] for the intentional unlawful distribution of anabolic steroid products.

Once the FDA has decided to seek criminal prosecution against a corporation and/or an individual, it proceeds through the Department of Justice to obtain an information or indictment, depending on whether a misdemeanor or felony charge is involved. If serious

---

[289] Eight criminal cases were filed in 1994, 26 in 1993, and 52 in 1992, principally as part of the generic drug fraud investigations. Food & Drug Admin., Off. of Reg. Aff., Off. of Reg. Resource Mgmt. & Regional Operations. In 1991, 37 criminal cases were referred to the Department of Justice by Sept. 1, 1991. F-D-C REP. ("The Pink Sheet"), Sept. 16, 1991, at 9-11. Twenty-four criminal cases were filed in 1988, 42 in 1970, and 248 in 1960. FDA Talk Paper (Jan. 8, 1990) and FDA ANN. REP. (1950-1974).

[290] Sam D. Fine, *The Philosophy of Enforcement*, 31 FOOD DRUG COSM. L.J. 324 (1976).

[291] 21 U.S.C. § 333.

[292] *Id.* § 333(a)(1).

[293] *Id.* § 333(a)(2).

[294] In addition, for criminal offenses committed after November 1, 1987, the Criminal Fine Improvement Act of 1987, Pub. L. No. 100-185, § 6, 101 Stat. 1280 (18 U.S.C. § 3751), adds penalties for convicted individuals of up to $100,000 (misdemeanors not resulting in death) and $250,000 (felonies and misdemeanors resulting in death), and for corporations of up to $200,000 (misdemeanors) and $500,000 (felonies). In addition, fines can be based on the gain or loss resulting from the offense. 18 U.S.C. § 3571(d).

[295] FDCA § 303(b)(1), 21 U.S.C. § 333(b)(1).

[296] 21 U.S.C. § 333(e).

criminal conduct has been widespread, as in the case of the generic drug scandal of the past decade, the government may seek to prosecute a large number of companies and individuals, rather than attempt to make an example by one prosecution.[297]

The FDA rarely obtains a criminal search warrant as part of its criminal investigations. This enforcement tool is utilized, however, where the FDA believes that a company under investigation is being recalcitrant. In such instances, the Associate Commissioner for Regulatory Affairs and the Deputy Chief Counsel for Litigation must personally approve the use of the warrant.[298]

■ When Individuals Are Named

FDA names individual corporate officers or employees in all of its criminal cases. The FDCA imposes on responsible corporate officials strict vicarious misdemeanor liability. The fact that a corporate officer has no direct involvement in the conditions that give rise to a criminal violation does not excuse that officer from liability.

The seminal case of *United States v. Dotterweich*[299] involved the prosecution of a chief executive of a company with twenty-six employees located in one facility. Dotterweich was found guilty of distributing misbranded and adulterated drugs in interstate commerce.[300] He argued that his lack of involvement with the distribution at issue was a bar to an individual conviction. The Supreme Court strongly held otherwise:

> [U]nder § 301 a corporation may commit an offense and all persons who aid and abet its commission are equally guilty. Whether an accused shares responsibility in the business process resulting in unlawful distribution depends on the evidence . . . . Balancing relative hardships, Congress has preferred to place it upon those who have at least the opportunity of informing themselves of the existence of conditions imposed for the protection of consumers . . . rather than to throw the hazard on the innocent public who are wholly helpless.[301]

Taking *Dotterweich* a significant step further was the Court's decision in *United States v. Park*,[302] which involved a chain of retail food markets with 36,000 employees, 874 retail outlets, and 16 warehouses. Park, whose office was in Pennsylvania, was the chief executive of that corporation and was named in an information based on a rodent-infested warehouse in Baltimore, Maryland. There was no dispute that Park had employees who were in charge of legal affairs and regulatory matters, and who oversaw the sanitary conditions at the company's facilities, and that all phases of the warehouse operation were assigned to "dependable subordinates." Nonetheless, the Court found that the bylaws of the corporation prescribing the duties of the chief executive officer placed ultimate responsibility for all of the relevant functions on him.

---

[297] *See* F-D-C Rep. ("The Pink Sheet"), Dec. 3, 1990, at 9.

[298] Regulatory Procedures Manual, *supra* note 113, ch. 6, subch. "Search Warrants."

[299] 320 U.S. 277 (1943).

[300] *Id.* at 278. The jury hung as to the guilt of the corporation.

[301] *Id.* at 284-85.

[302] 421 U.S. 658 (1975).

The Court, in a majority opinion by Chief Justice Burger, applied the *Dotterweich* doctrine and explained the FDCA's governing concept of responsibility:

> [T]he Act imposes not only a positive duty to seek out and remedy violations when they occur but also, and primarily, a duty to implement measures that will ensure that violations will not occur.
>
> * * *
>
> [I]t is equally clear that the Government establishes a prima facie case when it introduces evidence sufficient to warrant a finding by the trier of the facts that the defendant had, by reason of his position in the corporation, responsibility and authority either to prevent in the first instance, or promptly to correct, the violation complained of, and that he failed to do so.[303]

In a number of cases where individual defendants have been named,[304] the individuals have attempted to rely on an "objective impossibility" defense derived from *dictum* in *United States v. Park*. The *Park* Court stated that an instruction on the defendant's lack of power or capacity to prevent a violation ("objective impossibility") should be given if the defendant comes forward with sufficient evidence to put such a defense at issue.[305] This *dictum* derived from a 1964 Supreme Court decision that affirmed the issue as a factual, rather than a legal, issue that must first be raised defensively at trial.[306]

Subsequent to the *Park* decision, the Ninth Circuit handed down two decisions treating the "objective impossibility" defense in food warehouse infestation cases. In *United States v. Y. Hata & Co., Ltd.*,[307] the court declined to rule on whether the objective impossibility defense was available to corporations as opposed to individuals. Instead, it found that the absence of proof that the responsible officers were unable to install a sufficient protective mechanism to prevent continuing aviary infestation in a warehouse rendered the impossibility defense inapplicable. In *United States v. Starr*,[308] the objective impossibility argument was rejected on the merits. Starr, the defendant corporate officer, was held to a standard of reasonable foresight that the plowing of a nearby field would cause mice to flee to the adjacent warehouse. In addition, the court ruled that the refusal of a janitor to comply with clean-up instructions was not only not "impossible" to prevent, but was, in the court's view, foreseeable.[309]

In *United States v. New England Grocers Supply*,[310] a magistrate's finding of strict liability under *Park* for three corporate officers was reversed and remanded. The court held

---

[303] *Id.* at 672, 673-74. *See also Gel Spice Co.*, Crim. No. 80 CR 650, *reprinted in* Federal Food, Drug, and Cosmetic Act Judicial Record 1983-1984, *supra* note 116, at 115.

[304] For a discussion of *Park* and *Dotterweich*, see Stephen C. Jones, *Individual Liability Under the Federal Food, Drug, and Cosmetic Act: The Defenses Find a Defendant*, 39 Food Drug Cosm. L.J. 385 (1984); Daniel F. O'Keefe, *Criminal Liability; Park Update*, 32 Food Drug Cosm. L.J. 392 (1977); Richard A. Merrill, *The Park Case*, 30 Food Drug Cosm. L.J. 683 (1975).

[305] 421 U.S. at 676-78.

[306] *Wiesenfeld Warehouse Co.*, 376 U.S. at 86.

[307] 535 F.2d 508 (9th Cir.), *cert. denied*, 429 U.S. 828 (1976).

[308] 535 F.2d 512 (9th Cir. 1976).

[309] *Id.* at 515-16.

[310] 488 F. Supp. 230 (D. Mass. 1980).

that there had been no explicit finding that these officers were "not powerless to prevent" the violations.[311] On remand, the magistrate found the defendants not guilty.[312] The defendants having established the affirmative defense, the magistrate held that the government had then to present evidence to support a finding beyond a reasonable doubt that the defendants "could by the use of extraordinary care correct or prevent the violations."[313]

■ The Role of Guaranties

Section 303(c)(2) and (3) of the FDCA[314] provide a safe harbor from criminal liability under the general criminal penalty provisions of section 303(a) and the food misbranding penalty provisions of section 303(d).[315] A guaranty received by a corporation, individual, or employee of a corporation should state that the articles delivered by the guarantor are not adulterated or misbranded within the meaning of the FDCA, and (as applicable) that they are not unapproved food additives, color additives, drugs, or Class III devices subject to an approval requirement. Guaranties may be limited to a specific shipment or may be general and continuing.[316] A guaranty covering color additives under section 303(c)(3)[317] must be signed by a manufacturer of the colors, and, if from a foreign source, must be signed by both the foreign manufacturer and an agent of that manufacturer who resides in the United States.[318]

In its enforcement regulations covering guaranties,[319] the FDA provides that "[t]he application of a guaranty . . . shall expire when" after the covered products are shipped or delivered by the guarantor, the products become adulterated or misbranded, or become unapproved products under sections 404, 505, or 512 of the Act.[320] The original guarantor's guaranty is not operative, therefore, if the product subsequently is adulterated, misbranded, or caused to become a violative unapproved product.

Furnishing a false guaranty is a prohibited act under section 301(h) that can give rise to criminal liability.[321] Under section 301(h), however, a company that receives a guaranty and then, in good faith, provides a subsequent guaranty premised on the original guarantor's representations is not guilty of a prohibited act.[322]

---

[311] *Id.* at 234-36.

[312] FEDERAL FOOD, DRUG, AND COSMETIC ACT JUDICIAL RECORD 1978-80, at 233 (FDLI 1983).

[313] *Id.* at 234. The *Park* standard also has been utilized in a civil context. *See* United States v. Hodges X-Ray, Inc., 759 F.2d 557 (6th Cir. 1985) (Radiation Control for Health and Safety Act violation). *See also* United States v. Able Lab., Inc., Civ. No. 91-4916 (filed D.N.J. May 2, 1992); United States v. Physio-Control Corp., Civ. No. C-92-1163CC (filed W.D. Wash. July 21, 1992).

[314] 21 U.S.C. § 333(c)(2), (3).

[315] Prescription Drug Marketing Act violations are not included in section 303(b).

[316] 21 C.F.R. § 7.13(a)(2).

[317] 21 U.S.C. § 333(c)(3).

[318] 21 C.F.R. § 7.13(d).

[319] *Id.* § 7.12-.13.

[320] *Id.* § 7.13(c).

[321] 21 U.S.C. § 331(h).

[322] *Id. See, e.g.,* United States v. Crown Rubber Sundries Co., 67 F. Supp. 92 (N.D. Ohio 1946).

The guaranty provisions are contained in the criminal penalties section of the FDCA. The recipient of a guaranty is not protected against the imposition of civil remedies such as injunctions, seizures, or recalls. In the civil setting, fairness to the recipient is outweighed by the interest in protecting the public.

■ Section 305 Hearing

In most instances where a criminal case will be brought, the FDA is instructed by section 305 of the FDCA[323] to hold a "hearing" to provide the target company and individuals an opportunity to present views orally or in writing. Section 305 on its face requires such an opportunity "[b]efore any violation of this Act is reported by the Secretary to any United States attorney for institution of a criminal proceeding." A section 305 "hearing" will not be provided, however, "if the Commissioner has reason to believe that [the opportunity for a hearing] may result in the alteration or destruction of evidence or in the prospective defendant's fleeing to avoid prosecution," or if a grand jury investigation is planned.[324]

The hearing is held pursuant to a formal notice (known as a "Section 305 Notice"). It actually is a meeting, and is referred to as such in the *Regulatory Procedures Manual*.[325] The meeting is informal, often held in a district office, and is designed to give a party an opportunity to convince the FDA not to make a criminal referral to the Department of Justice. There are many strategic considerations involved for a company or individual invited to a section 305 hearing because participation in the procedure is completely voluntary and can be accomplished either through a written or oral presentation. The FDA usually is involved alone when a section 305 notice initially is sent to a company, but there are times following the entry of consent orders in civil cases when the U.S. Attorney's Office also is involved in the recommendation to consider instituting criminal proceedings.

If a party avails itself of the opportunity to present oral testimony, it is the FDA's position that no *Miranda* warning is necessary because section 305 meetings do not involve a person being "taken into custody or otherwise deprived of his freedom." [326] Statements made at a section 305 meeting can be utilized against a defendant in a later criminal proceeding. At the section 305 meeting, a party claiming the protection of a guaranty under section 303(c) should provide the FDA with a verified copy of the guaranty.

The section 305 proceeding may be transcribed at the expense of the respondent.[327] If there is no transcript, an FDA employee dictates a summary of the presentation, which thereafter is available to the respondent.[328] The respondent has a later opportunity to submit supplemental information before the summary is passed on to FDA headquarters.[329]

---

[323] 21 U.S.C. § 335. Failure to provide the "hearing," however, does not preclude prosecution. *See Dotterweich*, 320 U.S. at 277.

[324] 21 C.F.R. § 7.84(a)(2).

[325] REGULATORY PROCEDURES MANUAL, *supra* note 113, ch. 5, subch. "Section 305 Meeting."

[326] *Id*. sec. "Conducting the 305 Meeting," subsec. "Miranda Warning."

[327] 21 C.F.R. § 7.85(e).

[328] *Id*. § 7.85(f).

[329] *Id*. § 7.85(g).

Enforcement Strategies of the FDA

■ Enforcement Discretion

Apart from the language of section 309 of the FDCA,[330] which states that the FDA will not be required to pursue minor violations when it believes "that the public interest will be adequately served by a suitable written notice or warning," there is no statutory provision dictating how the FDA is to use its limited resources to remedy all the violations that are reported to, or discovered by, the agency.

In 1985, the Supreme Court addressed a major challenge to the FDA's decision not to take action against a drug that was used for execution by lethal injection, a use outside the drug's labeled indications. The Court in *Heckler v. Chaney* upheld, as an exercise of unreviewable enforcement discretion, the FDA's decision not to pursue the unapproved use of this drug.[331]

Moreover, in *National Milk Producers Federation v. Harris*,[332] the Eighth Circuit found no basis for a mandamus action against the FDA for the agency's failure to take enforcement action against allegedly misbranded cheese substitutes. Enforcement proceedings were, according to the court, committed to the FDA's discretion by law.

Notwithstanding these decisions, in addition to the plain language of section 309 of the Act, there have been several cases in which the FDA has been required to account for its decision to proceed against some parties but not others. In *United States v. Undetermined Quantities of an Article of Drug Labeled as "Exachol,"*[333] the FDA had seized, and subsequently sought an injunction against the marketing of, a dietary supplement that made claims for the prevention of cardiovascular disease. The claims were similar to those made for cereal products and other low-fat or low-cholesterol foods. Because the FDA had issued a proposed "health messages" regulation[334] under which it had permitted the marketing of a bran cereal with colon cancer claims and of vegetable oils with heart disease claims, the court denied a summary judgment motion by the government on the ground that an examination had to be made as to whether the claims at issue fell within the same proposed regulatory policy.

In *United States v. Diapulse Corp.*,[335] the Second Circuit reviewed FDA decisions to take enforcement action against one medical device that failed to meet certain internal FDA scientific standards and not to proceed against a similar device that had the same compliance problems. The court chastised the FDA's failure to "apply its scientific conclusions even-handedly" and held that: "[d]eference to administrative discretion or expertise is not a license to a regulatory agency to treat like cases differently."[336] Similarly, the FDA's fail-

---

[330] 21 U.S.C. § 336.

[331] 470 U.S. 821 (1985).

[332] 653 F.2d 339 (8th Cir. 1981). *See also* Pan Am. Pharmaceuticals, Inc. v. Kessler, Food Drug Cosm. L. Rep. (CCH) ¶ 38,212 (W.D. Mich. 1991).

[333] 716 F. Supp. 787 (S.D.N.Y. 1989).

[334] 52 Fed. Reg. 28,843 (1987).

[335] 748 F.2d 56 (2d Cir. 1984).

[336] *Id.* at 62.

ure to take enforcement action against one of two companies that received warning letters and failed to alter its allegedly illegal conduct, led the D.C. District Court to require the FDA to "treat similarly situated entities" in a "fair and even-handed manner."[337]

The reasoning of *Heckler* survives, however, with the FDA often choosing to pursue one enforcement strategy against a principal target and varying strategies against subsequent violators.[338]

■ **How FDA Chooses to Employ Its Enforcement Powers**

FDA Enforcement Activities[339]

Fiscal Year	1990	1991	1992	1993	1994	1995 (1st ¼)
Inspections	16,811	18,609	17,064	17,315	15,179	2,107
Import Product Detentions	26,392	27,298	41,155	33,088	28,479	n/a
Import Sample Examinations	41,108	42,200	50,382	42,758	36,586	7,287
Recalls	2,352	2,858	2,922	2,375	3,236	586
Warning/ Regulatory Letters	498	832	1564	1,785	1,595	312
Seizures	144	168	183	117	98	23
Injunction Requests	9	21	31	23	16	11
Criminal Actions	19	43	52	26	8	1

The seeming rise in criminal enforcement activities in 1991-1993 can be linked directly to the other generic drug investigations begun in 1988 and concluded in 1995. To assess the criminal action statistics, it also should be noted that the number of criminal actions does not reflect the number of proposed criminal referrals, some of which are resolved through the section 305 hearing process or are declined by the Department of Justice. Criminal jurisdiction with respect to controlled drug substances also lies with the Drug Enforce-

---

[337] Allergan, Inc. v. Shalala, Civ. No. 94-1223 (D.D.C. filed Nov. 10, 1994) (finding that once the FDA began industry-wide enforcement by means of a Drug Efficacy Study Implementation (DESI) notice and warning letters, "it must do so in a fair and even-handed manner").

[338] One example involved the FDA's two seizure actions against the manufacturer of a combination drug composed of pre-1983 "old drugs." The manufacturer lost both cases, appealed, obtained stays, and continued to sell millions of dollars worth of the product. United States v. Sandoz Pharmaceutical Corp., 894 F.2d 825 (6th Cir. 1990); United States v. 225 Cartons . . . "Fiorinal with Codeine," 687 F. Supp. 946 (D.N.J. 1988), aff'd, 871 F.2d 409 (3d Cir. 1989). In the meantime, the FDA threatened criminal prosecutions against any other company marketing the product. Ostensibly, neither *Exachol* nor *Diapulse* would have assisted a subsequently-indicted manufacturer.

[339] Source: Food & Drug Admin., Off. of Reg. Aff., Off. of Reg. Resource Mgmt. and Regional Operations.

ment Administration in the Department of Justice, which actively monitors the distribution of such pharmaceuticals and their predicate substances.

The figures also do not take into account the large number of informal agency letters that lead firms to alter their practices, or the numerous FD483 exit interviews and exchanges of correspondence, that frequently make further enforcement action unnecessary. The number of inspections is not always an accurate indicator of enforcement prominence. Inspections have played an effective and considered role in manufacturing standards enforcement. New pre-approval inspection procedures serve as a powerful enforcement tool; the FDA has used these effectively to defer approvals until GMP compliance is achieved in the plant where a new drug or device is to be manufactured. The FDA also initiated a strict detailed Compliance Program for Medical Devices in 1995 that has set new standards for industry inspections.[340]

Penalties recovered by the FDA are another factor not fully explained by the chart above. In addition to the powerful injunctive remedies outlined in the immediately preceding section of this chapter, the FDA negotiated, for example, a $30,000,000 civil penalty as part of the *United States v. C.R. Bard, Inc.* litigation.[341]

Also not demonstrated by the chart is the increase in enforcement activities by state authorities in the food and drug field. The FDA meets regularly with organizations such as the National Association of Attorneys General and the Association of Food and Drug Officials to discuss the institution of test cases or the development of new regulatory policies.

Budgetary limitations have led to even greater cooperation between the FDA and the FTC, the U.S. Postal Service, the U.S. Department of Agriculture, the Drug Enforcement Administration, and state agencies. The FDA, however, will continue to take the lead in enforcement decisions that ensure the continued safety, efficacy, and regulatory compliance of the products under its jurisdiction.

---

[340] COMPLIANCE PROGRAM GUIDANCE MANUAL ch. 82, § 7382.830 (May 4, 1995).
[341] 848 F. Supp. 287 (D. Mass. 1994).

chapter 4

Overview of the Federal Trade Commission

Caswell O. Hobbs*

Introduction

The Federal Trade Commission (FTC) and the Food and Drug Administration (FDA) exercise concurrent jurisdiction over the labeling and advertising of drugs, medical devices, and other therapeutical products.[1] Pursuant to a liaison agreement between the two agencies, the FTC has assumed primary responsibility with respect to deceptive or unfair "advertising" of such products, other than prescription drugs, and the FDA has assumed primary responsibility for matters relating to false or misleading "labeling," as well as advertising for prescription drugs.[2] This chapter provides an overview of the structure, powers, and procedures of the FTC, reviews generally the Commission's regulatory approach to false, misleading, or unfair advertising; and focuses specifically on theFTC's regulation of advertising for drugs and medical devices, including biological products regulated as drugs and devices. The interaction between the FTC and the FDA in these matters is specifically discussed.

Overview of the Federal Trade Commission

■ Organization of the Commission

In 1914, the Federal Trade Commission Act established the FTC as an independent administrative agency.[3] The Commission is composed of five Commissioners, each

---

*   Mr. Hobbs is a Partner in the law firm of Morgan, Lewis & Bockius, L.L.P., Washington, D.C.

1   *See* 15 U.S.C. §§ 41-77 (1994), and 21 U.S.C. §§ 321-392 (1994). *See generally*, Kordell v. United States, 335 U.S. 345 (1948); Thompson Medical Co. v. FTC, 791 F.2d 189 (D.C. Cir. 1986), *cert denied*, 479 U.S. 1086 (1987) United States v. Research Laboratories, Inc., 126 F.2d 42 (9th Cir.), *cert denied*, 317 U.S. 656 (1942).

2   *See* 36 Fed. Reg. 18,539 (1971) (memorandum of understanding between the FTC and the FDA). *See generally*, United States v. Paddock, 67 F. Supp. 819 (W.D. Mo. 1946).

3   Act of Sept. 26, 1914, ch. 311, 38 Stat. 717 (1914) (as amended 15 U.S.C. §§ 41-64 (1994)).

appointed by the President and confirmed by the Senate, one of whom is designated by the President as Chairman. The Commissioners serve for staggered seven-year terms, and no more than three may be of the same political party. All official actions and statements of the Commission require a majority vote of the Commissioners. The Chairman, who is the executive and administrative head of the agency, is selected by and serves at the pleasure of the President. Each Commissioner has a small personal staff of lawyers and economists. The remaining staff of the FTC is organized into operating bureaus, regional offices, and support offices, and consists of several hundred lawyers, economists, and support personnel.

The principal investigative and adjudicative work of the FTC is carried out by two operating bureaus: the Bureau of Competition and the Bureau of Consumer Protection. These Bureaus are supported and assisted by the Bureau of Economics, the Office of Executive Director, the Office of the General Counsel, and the Office of the Secretary. The Office of Administrative Law Judges consists of administrative law judges (ALJs) who conduct FTC adjudicative and rule-making proceedings.[4] Although most FTC attorneys are located in Washington, D.C., the FTC does have attorneys in Regional Offices in ten other cities.[5] The Bureau Directors, and Regional Office Directors are appointed by the Chairman, subject to the approval of the other Commissioners, while appointment of most other staff officials is the prerogative of the Chairman.

■ Jurisdiction and Powers of the Commission

The Federal Trade Commission is responsible for investigating and prosecuting "unfair methods of competition . . . and unfair or deceptive practices or acts in or affecting commerce."[6] Under this statutory mandate, the FTC focuses on two areas:

(1) antitrust — prohibiting "unfair methods of competition" that adversely affect competitive markets and business relationships; and

(2) consumer protection — protecting consumers from "unfair or deceptive" advertising or marketing practices.

The FTC's investigative, adjudicatory, and other powers and procedures are defined with specificity in the FTC Act. The Commission is also governed by the more general provisions of the Administrative Procedure Act,[7] which contains statutory requirements that

---

[4]   *See* 16 C.F.R. §§ .9-.18 (1997) for a description of the responsibilities of the FTC's Bureaus and Offices.

[5]   For a listing of the locations of Regional Offices, see 16 C.F.R. § .19.

[6]   15 U.S.C. §§ 45(a)(1). The FTC Act, as passed in 1914, proscribed only "unfair methods of competition." In order to enhance the effectiveness of the FTC's consumer protection powers, Congress expanded the Act in 1938 to prohibit "unfair or deceptive acts or practices." Wheeler-Lea Amendments of 1938, ch. 49, 52 Stat. 111 (1938) (codified at 15 U.S.C. § 45(a)(1)). For an appreciation of why this legislation was necessary, see FTC v. Raladem Co., 238 U.S. 643 (1931). Additional amendments of significance were made to the FTC Act in 1973, 1980, and 1994. *See* Magnuson-Moss Warranty — Federal Trade Commission Improvement Act, Pub. L. No. 93-637, 88 Stat. 2183 (1975) (codified at various sections of 15 U.S.C.); Federal Trade Commission Improvements Act of 1980 Pub. L. No. 96-252, 94 Stat. 374 (1980) (codified as amended at various sections of 15 U.S.C.); Federal Trade Commission Act Amendments of 1994, Pub. L. No. 103-312, 108 Stat. 1691 (1994) (codified at various sections of 15 U.S.C.).

[7]   Pub. L. No. 79-404, 60 Stat. 237 (1946) (codifed at 5 U.S.C. §§ 551 et seq.).

specify how agencies such as the FTC conduct adjudicative, rulemaking, disclosure of information, and other administrative activities.

The jurisdiction of the Federal Trade Commission generally encompasses all persons, partnerships, or corporations, and extends to matters "affecting commerce" in which a proceeding by the FTC would be in the "interest of the public." [8] Thus, the FTC possesses very broad jurisdiction that extends to almost all businesses and business practices in the country. [9]

The Commission also is endowed with extensive investigatory powers. FTC investigations may be commenced on the request of practically anyone, including disgruntled consumers, consumer organizations, competitors, members of Congress, state officials, or by the Commission on its own initiative. [10] The FTC initiates an investigation if it believes there is a general public interest in the matter, and does not become involved if only a "private controversy" is at issue. [11] Because of limited financial and staff resources, moreover, the Commission exercises considerable discretion and selectivity as to the investigations it opens.

During an FTC investigation the Commission has broad powers to require submission of documents, testimony, and special reports concerning the business practices in question. [12] The FTC's investigative powers extend to third parties who may possess relevant evidence or information, [13] as well as to the specific companies being investigated. Based on the findings of the investigation, the Commission may regulate business practices through administratively adjudicated cease-and-desist orders entered against specific companies; [14] may promulgate industry-wide "trade regulation rules," [15] may issue guidelines or policy statements to advise business conduct, [16] or may prepare reports regarding enforcement activities or demonstrating the need for new legislation. [17]

If its investigation leads the Commission to believe that a violation of the FTC Act may exist, the FTC customarily commences an administrative hearing to adjudicate the legality

---

[8] 15 U.S.C. § 45.

[9] *Id.* There do exist, however, various narrowly defined exemptions from the FTC Act. *See* 7 U.S.C. §§ 181-229 (1994) (businesses subject to the Packers & Stockyards Act); 49 U.S.C. § 40., 101 et seq. (1994) (common carriers subject to Federal Aviation Act). Further, the FTC's jurisdiction over nonprofit entities is dependent upon the factual circumstances. *See, e.g.,* College Football Ass'n, 5 Trade Reg. Rep. (CCH) ¶ 23,631 (1994) (final opinion).

[10] FTC investigations are governed by sections 2.1 through 2.16 of the Commission Rules. *See* 16 C.F.R. §§ 2.1-2.16.

[11] *Id.* § 2.1.

[12] *See* FTC Act §§ 6(b), 9, 15 U.S.C. §§ 46(b), 49. *See, e.g.,* FTC v. Invention Submission Corp., 965 F.2d 1086 (D.C. Cir. 1992), *cert. denied,* 507 U.S. 910 (1993); FTC v. O'Connell Associates, Inc., 1993-2 Trade Cas. (CCH) ¶¶ 70,312 (E.D.N.Y. 1993).

[13] For cases affirming the FTC's power to subpoena documents and testimony from "third party" sources, see, e.g., FTC v. Winters Nat'l Bank & Trust, 601 F.2d 395 (6th Cir. 1979); FTC v. Harrell, 313 F.2d 854 (7th Cir. 1963); FTC v. Tuttle, 244 F.2d 605 (2d Cir.), *cert. denied,* 354 U.S. 925 (1957); FTC v. Metropolitan Communications Corp., 1995-2 Trade Cas. (CCH) ¶ 71,183 (S.D.N.Y. 1995); Freeman v. Brown Bros. Harriman & Co., 250 F. Supp. 32 (S.D.N.Y.), *aff'd,* 357 F.2d 741 (2d Cir.), *cert. denied,* 384 U.S. 933 (1966).

[14] 16 C.F.R. §§ 2.31-2.34.

[15] *Id.* § 1.8.

[16] *Id.* §§ 1.5-1.6. *See, e.g.,* Guides for the Use of Environmental Marketing Claims, *id.* § 260.1-.8; Guides Concerning the Use of Endorsements and Testimonials in Advertising, *id.* § 255.1-.5.

[17] *Id.* § 1.9.

of the company's practices. Increasingly, however, where the situation warrants, the FTC may file a complaint in federal court seeking preliminary or permanent injunctive relief against ongoing or potential violations of the FTC Act. [18]

The FTC's administrative adjudication is instituted by the issuance of a formal FTC complaint, which states the factual allegations upon which the Commission's proceeding is based, the law alleged to have been violated, and the form of relief being sought. [19] The complaint is the predicate for public administrative trial, held before an impartial ALJ, who is employed by the FTC solely to conduct administrative hearings. [20] In the adjudicative proceeding, the FTC staff from the relevant operating bureau (complaint counsel) will present documentary evidence and facts, and expert witnesses, and will argue that the company against which the complaint has been issued (the respondent) has violated the FTC Act; the respondent, in turn, will offer evidence, witnesses, and arguments, in its defense. [21] The opinion of the ALJ is known as the "initial decision" and includes, if a violation is found to exist, a proposed cease-and-desist order to be issued against the respondent.

The opinion of the ALJ can be appealed by the respondent or complaint counsel to the five Commissioners, who, for this purpose, sit in an adjudicatory capacity and act as an appellate body. [22] If neither side appeals the initial decision, the ALJ's opinion and recommended order automatically become the decision of the Commission [23] unless the

---

[18] *See* FTC Act § 13, 15 U.S.C. § 53 (a-b); 16 C.F.R. § 1.61. *See, e.g.,* FTC v. Security Rare Coin & Bullion Corp., 931 F.2d 1312 (8th Cir. 1991); FTC v. Southwest Sunsites, Inc., 665 F.2d 711, 718 (5th Cir.),*cert. denied,* 456 U.S. 973 (1982) (in an FTC action for an injunction under the FTC Act, a district court is empowered "to exercise the full range of equitable remedies traditionally available to it"); FTC v. Nat'l Comm'n on Egg Nutrition, 517 F.2d 485 (7th Cir. 1975), *cert. denied,* 439 U.S. 281 (1978) (enjoining the dissemination of food advertising alleged to be false); FTC v. Rhodes Pharmaceutical Co., 191 F.2d 744 (7th Cir. 1951) (defining legal standards governing FTC injunctive proceedings against false advertising of foods and drugs pursuant to section 12 of the FTC Act); FTC v. NCH, Inc. 1995-2 Trade Cas. (CCH) ¶ 71,114 (D. Nev. 1995) (issuing permanent injunction); FTC v. Silueta Distribution, Inc., 1995-1 Trade Cas. (CCH) ¶ 70,918 (N.D. Cal. 1995) (enjoining false advertising for purported cellulite reduction products); FTC v. California Pacific Research, Inc., 1991-2 Trade Cas. ¶ 69,564 (D. Nev. 1991) (permanent injunction against hair growth product claims that were unsubstantiated and contrary to FDA final rule). For a discussion of the nature of the evidence of "deception" that the FTC must present to a federal court in an injunction proceeding designed to enjoin deceptive advertising, see FTC v. Pantron I Corp., 33 F.3d 1088 (9th Cir. 1994), *cert. denied,* 115 S. Ct. 1794 (1995); FTC v. Brown & Williamson Tobacco Corp., 778 F.2d 35 (D.C. Cir. 1985).

[19] 16 C.F.R. § 3.11.

[20] *Id.* § 3.42.

[21] *See* Commission Rule 3.43, 16 C.F.R. § 3.43 (relating to evidentiary standards and burden of proof).*See generally* 16 C.F.R. §§ 3.1-3.83 (the Commission's rules governing adjudicatory proceedings).

[22] Constitutional challenges to the FTC Act, based on the argument that the combination of powers vested in the Commissioners violates the constitutional principle of separation of powers, have been unsuccessful to date. *See, e.g.,* FTC v. American Nat'l Cellular, Inc., 810 F.2d 1511 (9th Cir. 1987); Ticor Title Insurance Co. v. FTC, 625 F. Supp. 747 (D.D.C. 1986), *aff'd in part, and vacated in part,* 814 F.2d 731 (D.C. Cir. 1987). *See generally* Humphrey's Ex'r v. United States, 295 U.S. 602 (1935); *compare* Bowsher v. Synar, 478 U.S. 714 (1986). Such constitutional challenges have undoubtedly been discouraged by a 1988 Supreme Court decision upholding the constitutionality of the independent counsel provisions of the Ethics in Government Act of 1978, and holding that the power of the Executive Branch to remove an independent counsel for "good cause" provided sufficient supervisory control by the Executive to support the separation of powers between the Executive and Legislative Branches. *See* Morrison v. Olson, 487 U.S. 654 (1988). In so holding, the court noted that the Executive Branch exercised similar "good cause" removal authority over various federal agencies, including the FTC, and analogized the civil enforcement powers of the FTC to the prosecutorial powers of the independent counsel.*Id.* at 691 n. 31.

[23] 16 C.F.R. § 3.51(a).

Commission decides to review the initial decision on its own initiative.[24] If the five Commissioners decide adversely to the respondent, an appeal from the Commission's decision can be taken to one of the federal courts of appeal.[25] The cease-and-desist order entered by the ALJ or the Commission upon completion of the administrative adjudication will mandate that the company halt any practices found to violate the FTC Act. Most FTC proceedings, however, are resolved by a pre-adjudication settlement and entry of a consent order,[26] or by a consent order agreed to during the course of the adjudicatory proceeding.[27] Cease-an-desist orders, whether adjudicated or entered by consent, can prohibit not only past unlawful practices, but also can (and usually do) proscribe related practices not previously engaged in by the company.[28] Final FTC orders are enforceable by injunctive, civil penalty, and criminal contempt proceedings initiated by the FTC in U.S. district courts.[29] Penalties of up to $10,000 per day per violation can be assessed by the court, [30] as well as the imposition of prison sentences.[31] The FTC also has the power to order the payment of monetary consumer redress;[32] generally the appropriate amount of restitution in consumer redress cases is the full purchase price of the product less any refunds paid.[33]

While the FTC's customary law enforcement approach involves adjudication against a single company, the Commission does have the power to engage in industry-wide rule-

---

[24]   *Id.* § 3.53.

[25]   FTC Act § 5(c), 15 U.S.C. § 45(c); 5 U.S.C. §§ 702, 704, 706. The courts of appeal give substantial deference to FTC decisions, and require only that they be supported by substantial evidence. *See, e.g.,* Kraft, Inc. v. FTC, 970 F.2d 311 (7th Cir. 1992), *cert. denied,* 507 U.S. 909 (1993). Except while pending in a U.S. court of appeals on a petition for review or in the U.S. Supreme Court, a proceeding may be reopened by the Commission at any time in accordance with title 16 of the *Code of Federal Regulations,* section 3.72. *See* 16 C.F.R. § 3.71.

[26]   16 C.F.R. §§ 2.31-2.34.

[27]   *Id.* § 3.25.

[28]   *See* Caswell O. Hobbs, *Advertising for Therapeutic Products, in* 2 FUNDAMENTALS OF LAW AND REGULATION 13, notes 71-86 and accompanying text (FDLI 1997).

[29]   *See, e.g.,* James Norman Wells v. United States, 1995-2 Trade Cas. (CCH) ¶ 71,171 (S.D. Cal. 1995) (civil contempt for order violation; criminal contempt for violating asset freeze).

[30]   15 U.S.C. § 45(1). *See, e.g.,* United States v. ITT Continental Baking Co., 420 U.S. 223 (1975); United States v. Louisiana Pacific Corp., 967 F.2d 1372 (9th Cir. 1992) ($4,000,000 civil penalty for failure to comply with a merger divestiture decree); United States v. Readers Digest Ass'n, 662 F.2d 955 (3d Cir. 1981), *cert. denied,* 455 U.S. 908 (1982) (assessing civil penalties of $1,750,000 for violations of FTC consumer protection consent order); Dahlberg, 5 Trade Reg. Rep. (CCH) ¶ 23,928 (1995) (proposed consent decree recommending a record $2,750,000 civil penalty for violation of order regarding performance claims for hearing aids); General Nutrition, Inc., 5 Trade Reg. Rep. (CCH) ¶ 23,600 (1994) (proposed consent order) (civil penalty of $2,400,000 for violation of FTC order proscribing false claims for hair-growing products).

[31]   *See, e.g.,* United States v. Vlahos, 1995-1 Trade Cas. (CCH) ¶ 70,925 (N.D. Ill. 1995); James Norman Wells, 5 Trade Reg. Rep. (CCH) ¶ 23,557 (1994) (order to show cause why defendant in an FTC weight-loss fraud case should not be charged with criminal contempt).

[32]   *See, e.g.,* FTC v. Pantron I Corp., 33 F.3d 1088 (9th Cir. 1994), *cert. denied,* 115 S. Ct. 1794 (1995); FTC v. Figgie Int'l, Inc., 994 F.2d 595 (9th Cir. 1993), *cert. denied,* 114 S. Ct. 1051 (1994); FTC v. Security Rare Coin & Bullion Corp., 931 F.2d 1312 (8th Cir. 1991); FTC v. Silueta Distributors, Inc., 1995-1 Trade Cas. (CCH) ¶ 70,918 (N.D. Cal. 1995); FTC v. California Pacific Research, Inc., 1991-2 Trade Cas. (CCH) ¶ 69,564 (D. Nev. 1991) ($2,000,000 equitable restitution); L&S Research Corp., 5 Trade Reg. Rep. (CCH) ¶ 23,633 (1994) (consent order) (payment of $1,450,000 for misrepresentation of efficacy of body-building and weight-loss claims); *see also* FTC v. Abbott Labs., 1992-2 Trade Cas. (CCH) ¶ 69,996 (D.D.C. 1992) (affirming FTC authority to obtain restitution under section 13(b) for "unfair methods of competition"); *In re* Austin, 1992-1 Trade Cas. (CCH) ¶ 69,779 (N.D. Ill. 1992) (FTC consumer redress judgment based on a finding of deceptive practices was not dischargeable in bankruptcy court).

[33]   *See, e.g.,* FTC v. Renaissance Fine Arts, Ltd., 1995-2 Trade Cas. ¶ 71,068 (N.D. Ohio 1995).

making.[34] During the 1970s, the FTC considered numerous "trade regulation rules," many involving food and drug products, but most of these proceedings were terminated with the FTC concluding that case-by-case enforcement was the more appropriate regulatory approach.[35] On occasion, the Commission or its staff will make its law enforcement views known through the issuance of an advisory opinion or enforcement policy statement.[36]

Despite one District Court decision to the contrary, the overwhelming judicial authority is that no private right of action was created by the FTC Act.[37] The vast majority of states, however, authorize private actions for violations of state "Little FTC Acts"[38] or comparable statutes. An FTC proceeding does not necessarily preempt state action arising out of the same facts.[39] Similarly, "Congress, has not, in the FTC Act, or elsewhere, expressly preempted state laws regulating false, misleading or deceptive advertising by companies."[40]

■ The FTC-FDA Relationship

The FTC and the FDA have overlapping and concurrent jurisdiction over the labeling of foods, drugs, medical devices, and cosmetics and over advertising of prescription drugs and restricted devices.[41] Section 5 of the FTC Act authorizes the Commission to monitor and proceed against advertising, sales, and marketing practices that deceive consumers or

---

[34] 15 U.S.C. § 57a(1). *See also* Beltone Electronics Corp. v. FTC, 402 F. Supp. 590 (D.C. Ill. 1975). For confirmation of the FTC's pre-Magnuson-Moss Act rulemaking powers (implied from the general provisions of the FTC Act), see Nat'l Petroleum Refiners Ass'n v. FTC, 340 F. Supp. 1343 (D.D.C. 1972), *rev'd*, 482 F.2d 672 (D.C. Cir. 1973), *cert. denied*, 415 U.S. 951 (1974). For limitations on the FTC's rulemaking authority based on "unfairness," see Federal Trade Commission Act Amendments of 1994, Pub. L. No. 103-312, 108 Stat. 1691 (1994). For a discussion of the circumstances in which the FTC will undertake an industry-wide rulemaking proceeding, as opposed to proceeding on a case-by-case basis, see Diet Center, Inc., 5 Trade Reg. Rep (CCH) ¶ 23,357 (1993) (ruling denying petition to engage in a rulemaking).

[35] *See, e.g.,* 48 Fed. Reg. 23,270 (1983) (FTC termination of proposed food advertising trade regulation rule); 46 Fed. Reg. 24,584 (1981) (FTC termination of proposed OTC drug advertising rule). For a case that provides a flavor of the "tumultuous history" of an FTC rulemaking proceeding, see Consumers Union of U.S., Inc. v. FTC, 801 F.2d 417 (D.C. Cir. 1986) (pertaining to the FTC's "used car rule"). For a case unsuccessfully challenging FTC case-by-case approach to enforcement and arguing that the FTC was obligated to initiate a rulemaking proceeding, see Weight-Watchers Int'l, Inc. v. FTC, 1995-1 Trade Cas. (CCH) ¶ 70,892 (9th Cir. 1995).

[36] *See generally* 16 C.F.R. pt. 15 (codified FTC Advisory Opinions); Finding Lists, 1 Trade Reg. Rep. (CCH) ¶¶ 50 (advisory opinions), 60 (other departmental rulings, decisions, releases).

[37] *Compare* Guernsey v. Rich Plan, 408 F. Supp. 582 (D. Ind. 1976), *with, e.g.,* Dreisbach v. Murphy, 658 F.2d 720 (9th Cir. 1981); Fulton v. Hecht, 580 F.2d 1243 (5th Cir. 1978), *cert. denied,* 440 U.S. 981 (1979); Alfred Dunhill Ltd. v. Interstate Cigar Co., 499 F.2d 232 (2d Cir. 1974); Action on Safety and Health v. FTC, 498 F.2d 757 (D.C. Cir. 1974); Holloway v. Bristol-Meyers Corp. 485 F.2d 986 (D.C. Cir. 1973); Tacker v. Wilson, 830 F. Supp. 422 (W.D. Tenn. 1993).

[38] *See generally* 2 George E. Rosden & Peter E. Rosden, The Law of Advertising, §§ 13.03(5), 14.01(5) (1990 and Supp. 1992); Kenneth A. Plevan & Miriam L. Siroky, Advertising Compliance Handbook 293-94 (Practicing Law Inst. 1991); Marshall A. Leaffer & Michael E. Lipson, *Consumer Actions Against Unfair or Deceptive Acts or Practices: The Private Uses of Federal Trade Commission Jurisprudence,* 48 Geo. Wash. L. Rev. 521 (1980).

[39] *See* Louisiana *ex rel.* Guste v. Fedders Corp., 543 F. Supp. 1022 (M.D. La. 1982).

[40] Kellogg Co. v. Mattox, 763 F. Supp. 1369, 1380 (N.D. Tex. 1991), *aff'd without opinion*, Kellogg Co. v. Morales, 940 F.2d 1530 (5th Cir. 1991) (citing Patterson Drug Company v. Kingery, 305 F. Supp. 821, 825 (W.D. Va. 1969)).

[41] See *supra* note 2. The FDA's jurisdiction over advertising is limited to prescription drugs, 21 U.S.C. § 852(m), and restricted devices, 21 U.S.C. § 352(r).

treat consumers unfairly.[42] The FTC's jurisdiction thereby extends to all forms of promotional claims for consumer products, regardless of whether such claims are found on package labeling or in media advertising. Thus, the FTC's jurisdiction overlaps the FDA's jurisdiction over the misbranding of drugs (human and animal) and human medical devices, and human biologicals regulated as drugs or devices. [43] The courts have held that an FDA proceeding does not preclude, or necessarily obviate, anFTC proceeding on the same subject.[44] It is also noteworthy that the remedies available to the FTC and the FDA are cumulative rather than exclusive.[45]

In a 1995 FTC proceeding involving hearing aids,[46] for example, the court affirmed that the FDA's jurisdiction over "intended use claims" for medical devices does not bar FTC regulation of advertising for such products. To avoid duplication or inconsistency of their efforts, the two agencies have entered into a "liaison agreement" pursuant to which the FTC exercises primary responsibility for the regulation of false or deceptive *advertising* claims for jointly FTC/FDA-regulated products other than prescription drugs, e.g., over-the-counter drugs and medical devices and the FDA exercises primary jurisdiction over false and misleading *labeling* of all jointly regulated products and over advertisements of prescription drugs.[47] This liaison agreement, signed in 1971, facilitates the exchange of information and coordination of action by the two agencies, with the result that the initiation of proceedings involving the same parties by both agencies is restricted to "highly unusual situations where public interest requires two separate proceedings.[48]

An interesting example of simultaneous but coordinated enforcement initiatives occurred in a 1991 matter involving Sporicidin Co., a marketer of chemical germicide for sterilizing medical instruments.[49] In that matter, the FTC charged Sporicidin with falsely advertising the effectiveness of the product, alleging that the company falsely claimed that the product

---

[42] 15 U.S.C. §§ 45, 52, 55(a).

[43] *See generally* 21 U.S.C. §§ 301-392. The definition of "misleading advertising" in section 15(a)(1) of the FTC Act, 15 U.S.C. § 55(a)(1), is nearly identical to the definition of "misleading labeling" in section 201(n) of the Federal Food, Drug, and Cosmetic Act (FDCA), 21 U.S.C. § 321(n). The conference report on the final version of the FDCA confirms that the two sections were intended to have the same meaning. H.R. Rep. No. 2139, 75th Cong., 3d Sess. 3 (1938); 83 Cong. Rec. 3255 (daily ed. Mar. 11, 1938) (statement of Sen. Wheeler).

[44] "[C]oncurrent FDA-FTC proceedings involving the same or similar matters are proper, and . . . the statutory remedies of the two agencies are cumulative and not mutually exclusive." Warner-Lambert Co. v. FTC, 361 F. Supp. 948 (D.D.C. 1973); *accord* Fresh Grown Preserve Corp. v. FTC, 125 F.2d 917 (2d Cir. 1942); *see also In re* Children's Advertising, 92 F.T.C. 258 (1978) (interlocutory order denying petition); *In re* Dollar Vitamin Plan, Inc., 69 F.T.C. 933 (1966) (order); *In re* Life Nutrition, 69 F.T.C. 985 (1966) (order); *cf.* Thompson Medical Co., Inc. v. FTC, 791 F.2d 189, 192-93, (D.C. Cir. 1986), *cert. denied*, 479 U.S. 1086 (1987) (FTC proceeding against maker of an over-the-counter drug was proper even though the FDA was conducting a general, long-term review of such drugs).

[45] Warner-Lambert Co. v. FTC, 361 F. Supp. 948 (D.D.C. 1973);*see also* United States v. Five Cases of Capon Spring Water, 156 F.2d 493 (2d Cir. 1946); United States v. Research Laboratories, 126 F.2d 42 (9th Cir.), *cert. denied*, 317 U.S. 656 (1942); *In re* Dahlberg and the Federal Trade Commission, 1995-1 Trade Cas. (CCH) ¶ 70,963 (D. Minn. 1995). Printed material indirectly accompanying distribution of a product can be deemed both advertising and labeling, and thus be subject to the dual jurisdiction of the FTC and the FDA. Kordell v. United States, 335 U.S. 345 (1948).

[46] *In re* Dahlberg and the Federal Trade Commission, 1995-1 Trade Cas. (CCH) ¶ 70,963.

[47] *See* Memorandum of Understanding Between FTC and FDA, 36 Fed. Reg. 18,539 (1971).

[48] *Id. See also supra* note 43, regarding similarity of definitions of "misleading advertising" and "misleading labeling" in the FTC Act and the FDCA.

[49] Federal Trade Commission Press Release (Dec. 13, 1991).

was a sterilant and a high-level disinfectant.[50] The FTC asked the federal district court in Baltimore to order a preliminary injunction halting misrepresentations concerning the effectiveness of any dilution of Sporicidin.[51]

At the time the FTC took its action, the Environmental Protection Agency (EPA) and the FDA also initiated law enforcement actions against Sporicidin.[52] The EPA issued a stop sale and seizure order on all sales of the cold sterilizing solution, and the FDA filed a seizure and condemnation action in the same federal court as the FTC. As a result of these combined actions, all sales of disinfectant products manufactured by the defendants — including any sprays and wipes, as well as the cold sterilizing solution — were halted.[53] The defendants ultimately reached a settlement with both the FTC and the FDA.

---

[50] *Id.*

[51] United States v. Various Articles of Device . . . which include Sporicidin, 1992-1 Trade Cas. (CCH) ¶ 69,768 (D. Md. 1992).

[52] Federal Trade Commission Press Release *supra* note 49.

[53] *Id. See also* Sporicidin Cold Sterilizing Solution, 58 Fed. Reg. 37,931 (1993) (EPA notice of settlement).

chapter 5

The Food and Drug Administration's International Harmonization, Enforcement, and Trade Policy Activities

Linda R. Horton*

Introduction

This chapter describes the Food and Drug Administration (FDA's) international harmonization policy and strategy; relevant legal authority (national and international) bearing on harmonization, enforcement, and trade; the FDA's approaches for imports and other international enforcement matters; exports; the FDA's involvement in trade-related activities; and a brief overiview of FDA's international activities over the years. Separate chapters in this book cover international harmonization of pharmaceuticals regulation,[1] and international harmonization of medical device regulation.[2]

The FDA's International Harmonization Policy Landmarks

The FDA's international harmonization activities comprise a wide variety of efforts to maintain and strengthen public health safeguards while striving toward common ground

---

* Ms. Horton is the Director of International Policy, Food and Drug Administration. The views expressed are the author's and do not necessarily represent those of the FDA.

[1] Linda R. Horton, et al., *International Harmonization of the Regulation of Drugs and Biologics, in* 2 FUNDAMENTALS OF LAW & REGULATION ch. 16 (FDLI 1997).

[2] Linda R. Horton, et al., *International Harmonization of Medical Device Regulations, in* 2 FUNDAMENTALS OF LAW & REGULATION ch. 17 (FDLI 1997).

internationally on product standards, criteria for the assessment of test data, and enforcement procedures.

The landmarks of these harmonization activities include 1) the 1992 report of the FDA's Task Force on International Harmonization; 2) the agency's strategic plan, with its vision statement for the agency's international activities; 3) the FDA's international harmonization policy on standards, proposed in 1994 and made final in 1995; 4) the placement of harmonization as an FDA priority in the Clinton-Gore National Performance Review Initiative ("Reinventing Government") in 1995 and 1996; and 5) the agency's progressive elimination of barriers to sharing information with foreign counterparts, through a series of actions between 1992 and 1995. The history section in the product-oriented book chapters on international harmonization, describe other harmonization landmarks such as the creation of the International Conference for the Harmonization of Technical Requirements for the Registration of Pharmaceuticals for Human Use (ICH).

■ Task Force on International Harmonization

A 1992 FDA Task Force report[3] documented the breadth and depth of the FDA's international activities and the results of a comprehensive survey of the views of many groups inside and outside government on the FDA's international programs. Importantly, the report cited three broad trends that had compelled the agency to rethink its international strategy: economic globalization (as evidenced by the growth of U.S. imports and exports,[4] the increasingly international character of the products and industries that the FDA regulates, and new world trade agreements); public health globalization, particularly the risk of the cross-border spread of communicable diseases; and the absolute certainty that agency resources would not keep pace with the challenges presented by these trends.

The report recommended that the FDA refocus its efforts, especially to emphasize harmonization, and set forth the agency's international goals as:

*   safeguarding U.S. public health,
*   ensuring that consumer protection requirements are met,
*   facilitating availability of safe and effective products,
*   developing and using product standards and requirements more effectively, and
*   minimizing inconsistent standards internationally.

Several principles would guide the FDA's participation in international harmonization efforts:

*   The harmonization activity should be consistent with U.S. government policies and procedures, and should promote U.S. interests with foreign countries.
*   The harmonization activity should further the FDA's mission.
*   The FDA's involvement in international standard-setting activities should be open to pub-

---

3   FOOD & DRUG ADMIN., REPORT OF THE FDA TASK FORCE ON INTERNATIONAL HARMONIZATION (Dec. 1992). *See* Notice of Availability of Report, 58 Fed. Reg. 7791 (Feb. 9, 1993). The report is available from the National Technical Information Service, 5285 Port Royal Road, Springfield, VA 22161 (tel. no. 703-487-4650).

4   Even today, with U.S. imports and exports of goods in general occupying an increasing share of the U.S. gross domestic product — about 25% — this share is small compared to the trade dependency of other countries.

lic scrutiny and should provide the opportunity for consideration of all parties' views.
- The FDA should accept, where legally permissible, the equivalent standards, compliance activities, and enforcement programs of other countries, provided that the FDA is satisfied that its level of public health protection is met.
- Scientific and regulatory information and knowledge should be exchanged with foreign government officials, to the extent possible within legal constraints, to expedite the approval of products and protect public health.

■ The FDA's Strategic Plan

To give focus to the many international activities catalogued in the report of the FDA Task Force on International Harmonization, the FDA's 1994 strategic plan included the following:

> FDA envisions the development of consistent, harmonized and scientifically-based international standards, which will keep abreast of the complexity of international health, safety, and commerce issues. As a result, consumers worldwide will have access to safe and effective products without being exposed to unnecessary risks. Unnecessary multiple regulatory burdens on industry will be eliminated and industry will be assured that policies affecting international markets will be based on scientifically sound decisions.

> FDA will strive to achieve internationally recognized and enforced product safety standards, good manufacturing practices, and inspection protocols. Inspection information will be shared among regulatory authorities. Adverse event information will be reported in a timely fashion and foreign regulatory authorities will collaborate in addressing product safety issues.

> FDA will foster internationally harmonized product testing and reporting procedures so that regulatory burdens associated with pre-market approval might be reduced (even if different countries maintain different safety and effectiveness standards for approval). FDA also envisions much progress on bilateral and multilateral product reviews.

> FDA will cooperate with the international regulatory community, with the goal of assuring a more thorough and consistent adherence to FDA-endorsed regulatory requirements and practices, thereby enhancing public health and safety worldwide. This will be achieved both through regular and effective participation in trade policy development, and through a coordinated program of technical assistance, education, and information exchange.[5]

Agency reorganizations in support of the enhanced emphasis on globalization are discussed further in this chapter.

■ Standards Policy

On October 11, 1995, the FDA published a policy on its development and use of standards with respect to international harmonization of regulatory requirements and guidelines.[6]

---

[5]   Food & Drug Admin., *International Vision for the Year 2000, in* FDA 2000: BUILDING FOR THE FUTURE 53 (Exec. Ed. 1994).

This publication coincided with World Standards Day 1995, which marked the forty-ninth anniversary of the founding of the International Organization for Standardization (ISO).[7] In an earlier notice published in 1994,[8] the FDA had published a draft of its standards policy for public comment.

Specifically, the FDA's standards policy addresses the conditions under which the FDA will participate with standards bodies outside of the FDA, whether domestic or international, in the development of standards applicable to products regulated by the FDA. It also covers the conditions under which the FDA intends to use the resultant standards, or other available domestic or international standards, in fulfilling its statutory mandates for safeguarding the public health.[9]

After stating that the policy is intended to help safeguard the public health, harmonize regulatory requirements, and comply with laws and policies that support the use of international standards[10] the policy details the agency's requirements concerning the development and use of standards:

A. FDA participation in standards development will be based on the extent to which the development activity and expected standard conform to certain factors, with consideration also being given to the resources available in FDA to devote to the effort and expected efficiencies to be gained as a result of the effort; the factors are as follows:

1. The standard stresses product safety and effectiveness and therefore contributes to safe, effective, and high quality products; when necessary, the standard also covers all factors required to ensure safety and effectiveness, including product and process design, and process performance;

2. The standard is based on sound scientific and technical information and permits revision on the basis of new information;

3. The development process for the standard is transparent (i.e., open to public scrutiny), complies with applicable statutes, regulations, and policies, specifically including [21 CFR] § 10.95 and OMB Circular A-119, and is consistent with the codes of ethics that must be followed by FDA employees;

4. The development of an international standard that achieves the agency's public health objectives is generally, but not always, given a higher priority than the development of a domestic standard; and

---

6   60 Fed. Reg. 53,078 (Oct. 11, 1995).

7   ISO is a nongovernmental worldwide federation of national standard-setting bodies based in Switzerland that encourages international development, unification, and publication of industrial standards. ISO covers all fields except electrical and electronic engineering. Those fields are covered by the International Electrotechnical Commission and International Telecommunications Union. Currently, more than 100 countries are represented in ISO. Each country is allowed one member. The U.S. representative is the American National Standards Institute (ANSI); The FDA's Director, International Policy, is a government member of the ANSI Board of Directors.

8   59 Fed. Reg. 60,870 (Nov. 28, 1994).

9   A footnote to the policy document explains that it does not create or confer any rights, privileges, or benefits, for or on any person, nor does it operate to bind the FDA in any way. 60 Fed. Reg. at 53,084 n.1.

10   *Id.* at 53, 078.

5. The development of a horizontal standard which applies to multiple types of products is generally, but not always, given higher priority than the development of a vertical standard which applies to a limited range of types of products.

B. FDA is not bound to use standards developed with FDA participation. For example, the agency will not use a standard when, in the judgment of FDA, doing so will compromise the public health.

C. The uses of final (and selected draft or proposed) standards, or selected relevant parts, will include, where appropriate:

(1)Incorporating such standards into guidance documents for nonclinical testing, applications for conducting clinical trials with investigational products, and applications for permitting products to be marketed;

(2)conducting reviews of such applications;

(3)incorporating such standards into compliance policy guides;

(4)conducting reviews of test protocols used by firms as part of good manufacturing practices;

(5)conducting reviews of study protocols submitted by firms as required for postmarket surveillance studies or programs;

(6)serving as the basis for mandatory standards or other regulations promulgated by FDA; and

(7)serving as the basis for reference (e.g., evaluation criteria) in a memorandum of understanding with other government agencies.

D. The use of a standard in the regulatory programs of FDA is dependent upon the following factors:

1. The standard stresses product safety and effectiveness and therefore, if adhered to, would help ensure the safety, effectiveness, or quality of products; when necessary, the standard also covers all factors required to ensure safety and effectiveness, including product and process design, and process performance;

2. The standard is based on sound scientific and technical information and is current;

3. The development process for the standard was transparent (i.e., open to public scrutiny), was consistent with the codes of ethics that must be followed by FDA employees, and the standard is not in conflict with any statute, regulation, or policy under which FDA operates;

4. Where a relevant international standard exists or completion is imminent, it will generally be used in preference to a domestic standard, except when the international standard would be, in FDA's judgment, insufficiently protective, ineffective, or otherwise inappropriate; and

5. Where a relevant horizontal standard which applies to multiple types of products exists or its completion is imminent, it will generally be used in

preference to a vertical standard, which applies to a limited range of types of products, except when such horizontal standard would be insufficiently protective, ineffective or otherwise inappropriate.

E. FDA employees will comply with agency regulations ([21 C.F.R.] § 10.95) covering participation in standard setting activities outside the agency.[11]

The FDA's standards policy thus describes the agency's approach to development and use of standards related to international harmonization of regulatory requirements and guidelines. It also announces the FDA's plan to uphold protective standards and to refrain from least common denominator standards.[12]

In the preamble to the policy,[13] the FDA emphasized that there are three routes to development of a harmonized international standard, all of which are favored under FDA policy: the U.S. voluntary standards community or an agency, such as the FDA, develops a U.S. standard and takes it to an international forum so it can be made an international standard; a standard already developed in an international forum (or by another country or a regional standards body) is adopted as a U.S. voluntary or regulatory standard; or a new international standard is developed in an international forum. Which of these routes is followed in a particular case will vary with the facts of that case. Although starting a standards activity in an international forum offers many efficiencies in avoiding duplication of effort, in many cases it makes sense first to develop a domestic standard (voluntary or regulatory) and then to take it, as appropriate, to an international forum.

The FDA recognizes that standards often serve as useful adjuncts to agency regulatory controls, and that economies of time and human resources often are realized in solving problems when consensus-building activities are undertaken and conducted in open, public arenas. The process of FDA staff working with other professionals outside the agency in standards bodies effectively multiplies the technical resources available to the FDA. Further, the procedures used by standards bodies for reviewing and updating standards extend the resource multiplier effect and help keep the solutions current with the state of knowledge. The economy of effort translates into monetary savings to the agency, regulated industries, and ultimately consumers. Further, using standards, especially international ones, is a means to facilitate the harmonization of FDA regulatory requirements with those of foreign governments, to better serve domestic and global public health.

Another benefit of standards participation is that FDA representatives have opportunities to learn other views on an issue and better ways of doing things, to serve as scientific leaders in their areas of training or official responsibility, and to stay informed of state-of-the-art science and technology.

The FDA has been involved in standards activities for many years; since 1977 an FDA regulation has covered the participation by FDA employees in standards-setting activities

---

[11] *Id.* at 53,080.

[12] *Id.* at 53,082.

[13] *Id.* at 53,083.

outside the agency.[14] This regulation encourages FDA participation in standards-setting activities that are in the public interest and specifies the circumstances in which FDA employees can participate in various types of standards bodies.

For a number of reasons, standards must be screened rather than accepted unequivocally by regulatory agencies. Standards can take a long time to create, be used for anticompetitive or anti-import reasons, be used by countries to generate testing agency fees for products that have already been tested, overemphasize the composition or design features rather than clinical trial aspects of a product, and tend "to memorialize already superseded scientific knowledge."[15] Despite these potential disadvantages, the advantages of standards mean that they will continue to play an important part in the marketplace and in regulation.

■ Harmonization as Part of Reinventing Government

Harmonization of the FDA's regulatory requirements and guidelines with those of other countries was embraced as a pillar of President Clinton's and Vice President Gore's National Performance Review. Both *Reinventing Drug & Medical Device Regulations,*[16] issued in April 1995, and *Reinventing Food Regulations,*[17] which followed in January 1996, included several international initiatives. These are discussed in the product-related chapters of this book.[18]

■ Elimination of Barriers to the Sharing of Information

The FDA's regulations on sharing information with officials in other countries are found in section 20.89 of title 21 of the *Code of Federal Regulations*. These regulations have undergone several revisions in the interest of enhanced regulatory cooperation and harmonization.

The FDA's historical position was reflected in the agency's public information rules in 1974.[19] Essentially, the FDA's communications with foreign government officials had, in general, the same status as communications with any member of the public. In almost all circumstances, the major exception being particular law enforcement matters, the disclosure of agency records by the FDA to foreign officials constituted disclosure to the public and obligated the FDA to make the same records available on request to the public.

Under the 1974 approach, the FDA was not able to share essential nonpublic information with foreign governments — and the FDA's counterparts in other countries, in turn, were wary of sharing information with the FDA when the agency could not guarantee continued confidentiality.

---

[14] 21 C.F.R. § 10.95 (1997).

[15] Joel J. Nobel, *The Universe of Medical Devices, in* MEDICAL DEVICES: INTERNATIONAL PERSPECTIVES ON HEALTH AND SAFETY (C.W.D. Van Gruting ed. 1994).

[16] REINVENTING DRUG AND MEDICAL DEVICE REGULATIONS, NATIONAL PERFORMANCE REVIEW (1996).

[17] REINVENTING FOOD REGULATIONS, NATIONAL PERFORMANCE REVIEW (1996).

[18] *See supra* notes 1, 2.

[19] 39 Fed. Reg. 44,602, 44,636 (Dec. 24, 1974).

Over the next two decades, globalization made section 20.89 obsolete and this change caused the FDA to re-evaluate its interpretation of how the Freedom of Information Act[20] and related laws apply to the FDA's dealings with other countries:

> Since 1974, significant changes in the world economy and in the activities of the regulatory agencies of the world's governments have caused FDA to work more closely with other government officials (i.e., local, State, and foreign officials, as well as fellow Federal officials) as professional colleagues in the attempt to find solutions to public health and consumer protection problems.
>
> Increased international commerce and diminished resources for regulation have resulted in efforts by public health regulatory agencies around the globe to enhance the effectiveness and efficiency of their operations. Public health regulatory agencies are protecting the public by harmonizing regulatory requirements; minimizing duplicative regulations; and cooperating in scientific, regulatory and enforcement activities.[21]

By taking four steps between 1992 and 1995, the FDA progressively eliminated its barriers to sharing with foreign counterparts the kind of information needed for effective cooperation, particularly joint reviews and harmonization:

- In 1992, the FDA published a notice of proposed rulemaking to remove restrictions on sharing confidential commercial information, when sharing this information was important to joint reviews or other forms of regulatory cooperation (e.g., joint enforcement efforts when key information is proprietary).[22]
- In 1993, the FDA issued a final rule on this proposal, followed soon after by internal procedures and model confidentiality agreements to ensure confidentiality.[23]
- In January 1995, the FDA published a notice of proposed rulemaking to permit the agency to disclose remaining categories of nonpublic documents, notably draft rules, to regulatory officials in other countries and to receive similar documents from foreign counterparts without being compelled to disclose the documents in response to a Freedom of Information Act request.[24]
- In December 1995, the FDA issued a final rule[25] based on the January 1995 proposal.[26]

Under these regulations, confidentiality is safeguarded through signed commitments by foreign regulatory officials. Officials of international organizations also are covered.

The FDA views its ability to share predecisional documents with officials of other countries as a critical part of global harmonization. The ability to communicate about draft standards and preliminary regulatory findings with officials in other countries confronting similar public health problems is considered essential to regulatory partnerships and to

---

[20]　Pub. L. No. 89-487, 80 Stat. 250 (1996) (codified at 5 U.S.C.§ 552 (1994)).

[21]　60 Fed. Reg. 5530 (Jan. 27, 1995).

[22]　57 Fed. Reg. 28,648 (June 26, 1992).

[23]　58 Fed. Reg. 61,598 (Nov. 19, 1993).

[24]　60 Fed. Reg. at 5530.

[25]　60 Fed. Reg. 63,372 (Dec. 8, 1995).

[26]　60 Fed. Reg. at 5530.

global harmonization. Uniformity also may give U.S. firms a fair opportunity to compete in overseas markets.

Legal Authority Relevant to International Harmonization

The categories of legal authority discussed in this section are: 1) relevant provisions in the U.S. Constitution; 2) provisions in the Federal Food, Drug, and Cosmetic Act (FDCA) and other statutes administered by the FDA that apply to international matters; 3) export controls in the country of origin; 4) agreements between the FDA and foreign regulatory counterparts; 5) provisions in trade agreements, implementing legislation, and related Presidential proclamations and executive orders; and 6) international law. Although beyond the scope of this chapter, private measures such as contractual provisions between a U.S. importer and an overseas supplier have been useful in securing compliance with U.S. requirements.

■ U.S. Constitution

The constitutional basis for the FDCA is the interstate commerce clause of the U.S. Constitution[27] vesting in the U.S. Congress sweeping plenary powers over interstate and foreign commerce. Also, Congress is empowered to "provide for the . . . general Welfare of the United States"[28] and "[t]o promote the Progress of Science and useful Arts . . . ."[29]

A catch-all "necessary and proper" clause empowered Congress to "make all laws which shall be necessary and proper for carrying into execution the foregoing powers, and all other powers vested by this Constitution in the government of the United States, or in any department or office thereof."[30]

The founders were quite clear that, with respect to foreign affairs, and particularly imports and exports, the responsibility is vested in the President[31] and Congress.[32] Individual U.S. states are to play no role. This was no accident. Experiences under the Articles of Confederation — when the newly independent U.S. states were behaving like "states" (nations) in the international law sense of the term — persuaded the authors of the Constitution that only the national government of the United States should conduct foreign affairs, regulate foreign commerce, and sign agreements with other countries.[33]

---

[27] U.S. CONST. art. I, § 8. *See generally* Wallace F. Janssen, *The Constitution and the Consumer: Discovering the Connections*, 42 FOOD DRUG COSM. L.J. 588, 593 (1987).

[28] U.S. CONST. art. I, § 8, cl. 1.

[29] *Id.* art. I, § 8, cl. 8.

[30] *Id.* art. I, § 8, cl. 18.

[31] *Id.* art. 2, § 1. "The executive power shall be vested in a President . . . . Sec. 2. The President shall be commander in chief . . . . He shall have the power, with the advice and consent of the Senate, to make treaties [and] appoint ambassadors . . . . Sec. 3 [h]e shall receive ambassadors . . . ."

[32] *See supra* discussion at note 31 and accompanying text.

[33] U.S. CONST. art. I, § 10.

In particular, two constitutional provisions[34] bar states from entering into treaties or compacts with foreign governments and, in an odd surfeit of detail, states are told that any inspection charges for imports and exports (other than small fees) are to be turned over to the U.S. Treasury unless Congress directs otherwise.[35] This provision is relevant to the discussion later in this chapter of user fees for export certificates in that several states are charging user fees for export certificates, but are not turning the proceeds over to the U.S. Treasury.

Finally, and importantly, international law was incorporated into U.S. law by the Supremacy Clause's treatment of treaties, as well as the Constitution and the laws of the United States, as "the supreme Law of the Land."[36] Further, Congress was empowered to "define and punish . . . offenses against the law of nations."[37] Under long-standing case law, international law is considered a part of the law of the United States.[38]

■ Statutes Administered by the FDA[39]

The Federal Food, Drug, and Cosmetic Act[40]

International harmonization is not mentioned in the FDCA, except with regard to medical devices.[41] In a sense, however, the entire Act is an international authorization in that it applies evenhandedly to food, drugs, medical devices, and cosmetics, whether domestically produced, imported, or (with exceptions) exported. As was discussed in the preceding section, this statute was enacted under the authority of Congress' broad power over interstate and foreign commerce.

International activities that are consistent with the Act and support its purposes may be undertaken by the FDA, not only under the product-specific provisions but also under the cross-cutting, general authority. For example, the FDA has employed its authority "to promulgate regulations for the efficient enforcement of [the] Act"[42] as well as the import pro-

---

[34]   *Id.* art. I, § 10, cl. 1,3.

[35]   *Id.* art. I, § 10, cl. 2.

[36]   *Id.* art. VI.

[37]   *Id.* art. III, § 8, cl.10.

[38]   The U.S. Supreme Court has stated:

> International law is part of our law, and must be ascertained and administered by the courts of justice of appropriate jurisdiction as often as questions of right depending upon it are duly presented for their determination. For this purpose, where there are no treaty and no controlling executive or legislative act or judicial decision, resort must be had to the customs and usages of civilized nations, and, as evidence of these, to the works of jurists and commentators who by years of labor, research and experience have made themselves peculiarly well acquainted with the subjects of which they treat.

> The Paquete Habana, 175 U.S. 677, 700 (1900).

[39]   Other important laws applicable to food that are administered, in part, by the FDA include the Fair Packaging and Labeling Act, Pub. L. No. 89-755, 80 Stat. 1296 (codified at 15 U.S.C. §§ 1451-1461 (1994)), and the communicable disease provisions of the Public Health Service Act, Ch. 288, 37 Stat. 309 (1912) (codified at 42 U.S.C. § 264 (1994)). A complete listing of FDA authority is found at 21 C.F.R. § 5.10.

[40]   Pub. L. No. 75-717, 52 Stat. 1040 (1938) (codified as amended 21 U.S.C. §§ 301 et seq. (1994)).

[41]   *See* FDCA §§ 514, 803, 21 U.S.C. §§ 360d, 383.

[42]   *Id.* § 701(a), 21 U.S.C. § 371(a).

visions,[43] to issue import control regulations.[44] The FDA could expand its present use of rulemaking to deal with international enforcement problems. For example, just as the FDA can issue requirements that anticipate and seek to prevent violations and protect both consumers and the stream of commerce from bad products — a good example of which is the FDA's 1982 rule[45] requiring tamper-evident packaging for over-the-counter drugs under the drug adulteration[46] and general rulemaking provisions[47] — the FDA might be able, under similar legal analysis, to strengthen its regulations for imports.

Fair applicability is required. The Act applies to domestically produced food, drugs, and devices, and to imports and, with certain exceptions, exports. Requirements apply not only to the products but also to the conditions under which they were processed or stored. Thus, foreign producers that ship to the United States, like domestic ones, need to avoid running afoul of the provision deeming a food or drug adulterated "if it consists in whole or in part of any filthy, putrid, or decomposed substance," [48] and also the provision that bars from U.S. commerce a food or drug that was "prepared, packed or held under insanitary conditions whereby it may have become contaminated with filth, or it may have been rendered injurious to health . . . ."[49] This requirement is mentioned not only in the Act's adulteration provisions[50] but also in its import provisions[51] — thus affording equal protection to U.S. consumers with respect to the conditions under which an article is processed or held, whether domestically produced or imported. Protection of U.S. consumers from products produced under conditions that do not meet FDA requirements applies regardless of where the violative conditions occurred (in the United States, in a processing facility in another country preparing a product for export to the United States, or in transit[52] from there to here).

In general, the statute and its legislative history are silent as to what Congress intended with respect to the international ramifications of statutory provisions. For example, the issue of whether a substance used in food is a "food additive" or is "generally recognized as safe" (GRAS) under section 201(s)[53] turns on the substance's history of use, yet Congress did not specify whether use in other countries would qualify. In *Fmali Herb, Inc. v. Heckler*,[54] the court struck down — as inconsistent with its interpretation of the Act — an FDA regulation that stated that only substances commonly used in food *in the United States* were eligible for the GRAS exemption from the food additive definition and approval procedure. The court found that, because the regulation

---

[43]   *Id.* § 801(a), 21 U.S.C. § 381(a).

[44]   *See* 21 C.F.R. pt. 1.

[45]   47 Fed. Reg. 50,442 (Nov. 5, 1982).

[46]   FDCA § 501, 21 U.S.C. § 351.

[47]   *Id.* § 701(a), 21 U.S.C. § 371.

[48]   *Id.* § 402(a)(3), 21 U.S.C. § 342(a)(3).

[49]   *Id.* § 402(a)(4), 21 U.S.C. § 342(a)(4).

[50]   *Id.* §§ 402(a)(4), 501(a)(1), 21 U.S.C. §§ 342(a)(4), 351(a)(1)).

[51]   *Id.* § 801(a), 21 U.S.C. § 381(a).

[52]   *Id.* § 801, 21 U.S.C. § 381. *Cf.* United States v. 2,998 Cases Canned Chinese Mushrooms, 64 F.3d 984, 988-89 (5th Cir. 1995).

[53]   21 U.S.C. § 321(s).

[54]   715 F.2d 1385 (9th Cir. 1983).

operates as a blanket exclusion of evidence of safety based on use of food outside
the United States . . . it fails to comport either with the express terms of the statute
that contain no such restriction, or with the purpose of the "common use" exception
as articulated by legislators, that was to allow use of "any substances which over
the years have been clearly demonstrated by long use to be completely safe." [55]

The *Fmali* decision is based upon statutory interpretation, not international legal principles. Nevertheless, one may draw the inference that, despite the body of case law to the
effect that the FDCA should be liberally construed in a manner consistent with its public
health purposes,[56] a reviewing court may nevertheless strictly scrutinize an agency interpretation that rejects evidence of foreign experience while accepting evidence of domestic
experience. The decision has implications for what is a "new drug" as well as for what is a
food additive: both terms' definitions exempt articles from approval due to experience
information, supporting general recognition of safety in the case of food substances and
general recognition of safety and effectiveness for drugs. The *Fmali* case has been cited in
support of industry petitions requesting the FDA to treat various drug substances as
exempt from the new drug approval provisions.[57]

The requirement of similar treatment of like domestic goods and imports is, as this chapter
discusses later, a cardinal principle in trade law, referred to as "national treatment."[58] The
FDA has authority to detain imports that "appear" to be adulterated or misbranded, but the
agency does not have identical detention authority for domestically produced goods of
such appearance. These FDA import controls do comply, however, with the national treatment principle because the agency's greater authority over "apparent" import violations
reflects the greater difficulty in ascertaining compliance of imported products and their
conditions of manufacture in comparison to compliance of domestic goods. Detention of
imported products that do not meet FDA requirements is analogous to seizure of domestic
products or to injunctions against domestic producers for the same violations.

imports and exports are subject to the Act.[59] As discussed above, the sale and distribution
of food, drugs, devices, and other FDA-regulated products are considered to be in interstate and foreign commerce.[60] Imports and exports are subject to special procedures.[61]

The Public Health Service Act

Several sections of the Public Health Service (PHS) Act that authorize international activities have been delegated to the FDA.[62]

---

[55]   *Id.* at 1391.

[56]   United States v. Dotterweich, 320 U.S. 277, 284-85 (1943).

[57]   Citizen Petition from European American Phytomedicines Coalition to the FDA (1992).

[58]   General Agreement on Tariffs and Trade, Art. III, para. 4, Oct. 30, 1947, 61 Stat. A-11, T.I.A.S. 1700, 55 U.N.T.S.
       194, *in* III COMPILATION OF INTERNATIONAL LAWS 201 (FDLI 1996) [hereinafter GATT].

[59]   FDCA §§ 801, 802, 21 U.S.C. §§ 381, 382).

[60]   "The term 'interstate commerce' means . . . commerce between any State or Territory and any place outside thereof
       . . . ." *Id.* § 201(b), 21 U.S.C. § 321(b). Among acts that are prohibited is: the introduction or delivery for introduc-
       tion into interstate commerce of any food, drug, device, or cosmetic that is adulterated or misbranded. *Id.* §301(a),
       21 U.S.C. § 331(a).

[61]   *See infra* notes 179-235 and accompanying text

[62]   21 C.F.R. § 5.10(a)(2)-(7).

Section 301 of the PHS Act allows the FDA to:

> conduct . . . and encourage, cooperate with, and render assistance to other appropriate public authorities, scientific institutions, and scientists in the conduct of, and promote the coordination of, research, investigations, experiments, demonstrations, and studies relating to the causes, diagnosis, treatment, control, and prevention of physical and mental diseases and impairments of man, including water purification, sewage treatment, and pollution of lakes and streams.[63]

Information sharing, research, grants, contracts, and technical advice and assistance are mentioned specifically in this broad grant of authority shared by the FDA and other PHS agencies. Also, several provisions in section 301 are explicitly international: an authorization to secure the assistance and advice of experts, scholars, and consultants from the United States "or abroad,"[64] and permission to conduct or fund biomedical research on diseases that do not occur to a significant extent in the United States.[65]

Section 307 of the PHS Act, captioned "International Cooperation," states:

> For the purpose of advancing the status of the health sciences in the United States (and thereby the health of the American people), the Secretary [and, by delegation,[66] the Commissioner] may participate with other countries in cooperative endeavors in biomedical research, health care technology, and the health services research and statistical activities . . . [67]

This language has been interpreted to mean that, for an activity to be authorized under this section, it must bestow a benefit to U.S. public health or health sciences.

In connection with these cooperative endeavors, section 307 states that the Secretary and therefore, by delegation, the FDA may:

(1) make such use of resources offered by participating foreign countries as [the Commissioner] may find necessary and appropriate;

(2) establish and maintain fellowships in the United States and in participating foreign countries;

(3) make grants to public institutions or agencies and to non-profit private institutions or agencies in the United States and in participating foreign countries for the purpose of establishing and maintaining the fellowships authorized by paragraph (2);

(4) make grants or loans of equipment and materials, for use by public or nonprofit private institutions or agencies, or by individuals, in participating foreign countries;

---

[63]   42 U.S.C. § 241.

[64]   *Id.* § 241(a)(4).

[65]   *Id.* § 241(c). This provision was added to the PHS Act by the Drug Export Amendments Act of 1986, Pub. L. No. 99-660, 100 Stat. 3743 (codified at 21 U.S.C. § 382, 42 U.S.C. §§ 241, 262).

[66]   *See* 21 C.F.R. § 5.10(a)(2).

[67]   42 U.S.C. § 242l.

(5) participate and otherwise cooperate in any international meetings, conferences, or other activities concerned with biomedical research, health services research, health statistics, or health care technology;

(6) facilitate the interchange between the United States and participating foreign countries, and among participating foreign countries, of research scientists and experts . . . and in carrying out such purpose may pay per diem compensation, subsistence, and travel . . . ; and

(7) procure, in accordance with section 3109 of title 5, United States Code, the temporary or intermittent services of experts or consultants.[68]

Section 307 does not authorize the Commissioner to provide financial assistance for the construction of any facility in any foreign country.[69] Calling conferences and issuing health information are authorized by section 310 of the PHS Act.[70] The biologics provisions of sections 351 and 352 of the Public Health Service Act [71] apply to imports as well as domestic products.

Section 361 of the PHS Act[72] authorizes the FDA to issue regulations, including quarantine regulations, to control the spread of communicable disease in interstate or foreign commerce. To draw a line between the FDA's responsibilities and those of the Centers for Disease Control, the delegation of authority[73] limits the functions delegated to the FDA to those "which relate to the law enforcement functions of the Food and Drug Administration" concerning "food (including milk and food service and shellfish sanitation)" and other FDA-regulated products.

■ Authority for Agreements with Regulatory Counterparts in Other Countries

The FDA has a number of agreements with its counterparts in other countries. These agreements are called memoranda of understanding or, if needed by the foreign counterpart, memoranda of cooperation (MOCs). These FDA agreements bond the participants in a joint venture toward mutually beneficial goals. This is their value; none of the agency's agreements prior to 1997 had been binding or "enforceable." A mutal recognition agreement covering pharmaceuticals and medical devices with the European Union, initialled in 1997, includes binding elements. (This agreement is discussed further in later chapters of this book.[74]) The discussion that refers to FDA agreements as either "MOUs" or "agreements with regulatory counterparts" rather than "international agreements," because the latter term, as defined in the Vienna Convention on the Law of Treaties, is reserved for binding agreements.[75]

---

[68] *Id.*

[69] *Id.*

[70] *Id.* § 242n.

[71] *Id.* §§ 262-63.

[72] *Id.* § 264.

[73] 21 C.F.R. § 5.10(a)(4).

[74] *See* Horton, et al., *supra* note 1. *See also* Horton, et al., *supra* note 2.

[75] Because of the popularity of nonbinding as well as binding agreements in the world of diplomacy, and there is need for international norms as to both types of agreements, the Vienna Convention is frequently resorted to for guidance on the interpretation of nonbinding agreements as well as binding ones. The treaty is not in force in the United States.

The FDA's agreements with regulatory counterparts are not treaties as that phrase is used in the U.S. Constitution,[76] so they do not need ratification by the U.S. Senate. Rather, FDA agreements are executive branch agreements, the authority for which derives from the statutes it administers, principally the FDCA and the PHS Act. The FDA's typical agreements with regulatory counterparts are examples of the nonbinding, agency-to-agency agreements that are dominant in the world of "technical agency diplomacy."

The FDA clears its MOUs with the U.S. Department of State under procedures governing clearance of agency agreements.[77] The State Department, in turn, is required to inform the Congress of executive branch agreements with other countries that were not submitted to the Congress as treaties.[78] In addition to treaties and executive branch agreements, under U.S. law there is a third, hybrid category of executive-legislative international agreements, typified by the trade agreements discussed below.

The FDA's general authority to enter MOUs derives from a broad reading of the FDCA, particularly whatever substantive provisions, such as those on adulteration and misbranding, apply to the affected products: section 801 on imports (allowing decisions on imports to be made on the basis of examination of samples "or otherwise"), and, for drugs and devices, sections 510(i) (conditioning registration on measures to ensure compliance).[79] To the extent that an MOU with another country helps the FDA to protect the channels of commerce from violative products, the agency's general authority to prevent violations also comes into play.[80]

Furthermore, the FDA possesses broad authority under several sections of the PHS Act that authorize agreements with other countries: sections 301 (granting broad authority for public health cooperation); 307 (authorizing international cooperation); 351 (controlling biological products, some of which are medical devices, e.g., certain *in vitro* diagnostic products and tissue-derived devices); and 361 (authorizing regulations to control communicable disease.)[81] The FDA has additional, product-specific authority to enter MOUs on food, drugs, and devices.

First, with respect to food, the Pesticide Monitoring Improvements Act of 1988[82] directs the FDA to enter into cooperative agreements with the governments of the countries that are the major sources of food imports into the United States, subject to pesticide residue monitoring by the agency for the purpose of ensuring compliance of imported food with the pesticide tolerance requirements of the FDCA.[83] The FDA has entered into broad cooperative agreements with its counterpart agencies in Mexico and Canada that include activities on foods as well as drugs and devices.[84] Second, with respect to drugs and

---

[76] U.S. Const. art. II, § 2, cl. 2.

[77] Circular 175 Procedure of the Department of State, 39 Fed. Reg. 29, 604 (Aug. 16, 1974).

[78] 1 U.S.C. § 1126 (the Case-Zablocki Act).

[79] FDCA §§ 801, 510(i), 21 U.S.C. §§ 381, 360(i).

[80] *See, e.g., 2998 Cases Canned Chinese Mushrooms*, 64 F.3d 984. *Cf.* United States v. Park, 421 U.S. 658 (1975).

[81] 42 U.S.C. §§ 241, 2421, 262, 264.

[82] 21 U.S.C. §§ 1401-1403.

[83] *Id.* § 1402.

[84] *See* Memorandum of Cooperation Between the Food and Drug Administration, Mexico, and Canada, 61 Fed. Reg. 11, 645 (Mar. 21, 1996).

devices, section 510(i) of the FDCA, which permits foreign firms to register and requires them to list their products with the FDA, states that:

> [The FDA's implementing regulations] shall include provisions for registration of any such establishment upon condition that adequate and effective means are available, by *arrangement with the government of the foreign country* or otherwise, to enable the Secretary to determine from time to time whether drugs or devices manufactured, prepared, propagated, compounded, or processed in such establishment, if imported or offered for import into the United States shall be refused admission on any of the grounds set forth in section 801(a) of this Act [on imports].

Third, with respect to devices, the FDA may "enter into agreements with foreign countries to facilitate commerce in devices between the United States and such countries consistent with the requirements of this," and in such agreements the FDA "shall encourage the mutual recognition of . . . good manufacturing practice regulations . . . and other regulations and testing protocols as the [Commissioner] determines to be appropriate."[85]

While the FDA's authority under its statutes to enter into nonbinding agreements is long-established, its authority to enter into binding agreements is a relatively new issue. The issue has arisen in the context of several negotiations with the Commission for the European Communities resulting in MRAs in drugs and devices that were intitialled by Lead Deputy Commissioner Michael Friedman, M.D., in 1997. The same authority that empowers the FDA to enter nonbinding agreements with regulatory counterparts would seem also to authorize binding ones, under a liberal construction applied to the FDCA[86] and as seen in case law upholding the FDA's authority to promulgate a wide range of regulations for the efficient enforcement of the Act.[87]

Assuming that the FDA has the authority to enter binding agreements, the next question is, what procedure must be followed to make such agreements binding? FDA's view is that the FDA has the authority to enter into binding agreements with regulatory counterparts in other countries, provided that the agency goes through notice-and-comment rulemaking on the aspects of the agreement that constitute "binding norms" with respect to the FDA.[88] An alternative theory is that international agreements, even executive branch agreements under agency statutory authority, are a species of decisions separate from rules, orders, or other products of U.S. administrative procedure. There is some support for this view in *International Brotherhood of Teamsters v. Pena*,[89] in which the Teamster group challenged a Department of Transportation finding that Mexican truck drivers' licenses are equivalent to U.S. licenses.

---

[85] FDCA § 803, 21 U.S.C. § 383, as amended by the Safe Medical Devices Act, Pub. L. No. 101-629, 104 Stat. 4511 (1990).

[86] *Dotterweich*, 320 U.S. at 284-85.

[87] *See* Joel E. Hoffman, *Administrative Procedures of the Food and Drug Administration*, *in* 1 FUNDAMENTALS OF LAW AND REGULATION ch. 2 (FDLI 1997).

[88] Community Nutrition Institute v. Young, 818 F.2d 943 (D.C. Cir. 1987).

[89] 17 F.3d 14778 (D.C. Cir. 1994)

An interesting development in this debate is a provision in the Uruguay Round Agreements Act,[90] the implementing legislation for the WTO agreements. The provision says:

Equivalence determinations

(a) In general

An agency may not determine that a sanitary or phytosanitary measure of a foreign country is equivalent to a sanitary or phytosanitary measure established under the authority of Federal law unless the agency determines that the sanitary or phytosanitary measure of the foreign country provides at least the same level of sanitary or phytosanitary protection as the comparable sanitary or phytosanitary measure established under the authority of Federal law.

(b) FDA Determination

If the Commissioner proposes to issue a determination of the equivalency of a sanitary or phytosanitary measure of a foreign country to a measure that is required to be promulgated as a rule under the Federal Food, Drug, and Cosmetic Act (21 U.S.C. 301 et seq.) or other statute administered by the Food and Drug Administration, the Commissioner shall issue a proposed regulation to incorporate such determination and shall include in the notice of proposed rulemaking the basis for the determination that the sanitary or phytosanitary measure of a foreign country provides at least the same level of sanitary or phytosanitary protection as the comparable Federal sanitary or phytosanitary measure. The Commissioner shall provide opportunity for interested persons to comment on the proposed regulation. The Commissioner shall not issue a final regulation based on the proposal without taking into account the comments received.

(c) Notice

If the Commissioner proposes to issue a determination of the equivalency of a sanitary or phytosanitary measure of a foreign country to a sanitary or phytosanitary measure of the Food and Drug Administration that is not required to be promulgated as a rule under the Federal Food, Drug, and Cosmetic Act [21 U.S.C.A. § 301 et seq.] or other statute administered by the Food and Drug Administration, the Commissioner shall publish a notice in the Federal Register that identifies the basis for the determination that the measure provides at least the same level of sanitary or phytosanitary protection as the comparable Federal sanitary or phytosanitary measure. The Commissioner shall provide opportunity for interested persons to comment on the notice. The Commissioner shall not issue a final determination on the issue of equivalency without taking into account the comments received.[91]

---

[90] Pub. L. No. 103-465, 108 Stat. 4809 (1994) (codified at 19 U.S.C. §§ 2252 et seq. (1994)).

[91] *Id*. tit. IV, § 432, 108 Stat. at 4971 (codified at 19 U.S.C. § 2578a).

In a nutshell, this new law compels the FDA to undertake a notice-and-comment process (either rulemaking or a *Federal Register* notice) whenever the agency makes a finding that another country has an equivalent "sanitary or phytosanitary measure"[92] (e.g., a country's seafood safety inspection system). If the FDA already was obliged by the Administrative Procedure Act (APA)[93] to undertake notice-and-comment rulemaking before finding another country's food law to be equivalent, why was it necessary for Congress to include this requirement in the Uruguay Round Agreements Act? Or did Congress believe it was merely codifying an existing APA requirement? In enacting this provision, Congress most likely was addressing what it thought to be the right policy outcome, i.e., that the public should have the opportunity to participate in decisions affecting its food supply, without focusing on whether the requirement was a new one or a restatement of prior law.

The FDA's view is that the notice-and-comment rulemaking requirement does not apply when an MOU merely records an understanding between the FDA and a foreign counterpart that producers in each country intend to comply with the other country's requirements. With this mindset, the FDA signed a nonbinding cooperative arrangement with the New Zealand seafood authorities[94] that was not a determination of equivalence between the two countries' food laws, but consisted of reciprocal statements as to compliance.[95]

The FDA would not need to submit for notice-and-comment its finding that another country's system is *not* equivalent, any more than the agency would use rulemaking when it declines to initiate any decisionmaking process when the decision is not required. There is little case law in this area, and the few decisions reported are not clearly helpful.

■ FDA Policy

The FDA sees value in entering into agreements with other countries to enhance public health protection and facilitate commerce in safe and quality foods, drugs, and medical devices consistent with public health objectives and the requirements of the law. The FDA's overall policy for initiating, developing, and monitoring MOUs was set forth in a 1995 Compliance Policy Guide:

> It is the policy of FDA to pursue the development of MOUs that will further the agency's public health mission [and are] designed to meet the following goals:
>
> (1) To enhance FDA's ability to ensure that regulated products are safe, effective, of good quality, and properly labeled;
>
> (2) To allow FDA to utilize its resources more effectively or efficiently, without compromising its ability to carry out its responsibilities; and

---

[92] See *infra* for a discussion of this term.

[93] Pub. L. No. 79-404, 60 Stat. 237 (1946) (codified at scattered sections of 5 U.S.C.).

[94] The two agencies with authority over seafood in New Zealand are the Ministry of Agriculture and the Ministry of Health. Cooperative Agreement Between the U.S. Food and Drug Administration and the New Zealand Ministry of Agriculture and Ministry of Health to Ensure the Safety of Imported Fish and Fishery Products, FDA Agreement No. 225-96-2004 (Dec. 20, 1995), *reprinted in* INTERNATIONAL COOPERATIVE AGREEMENTS MANUAL, *supra* note 96, at 225. *See also* Cooperative Arrangement Between the Food and Drug Administration and New Zealand Covering Seafood, 61 Fed. Reg. 7112 (Feb. 26, 1995).

[95] 61 Fed. Reg. at 7112.

(3)To improve communications between FDA and foreign officials concerning FDA regulated products.[96]

The Guide described three categories of MOUs as examples: reciprocal agreements with countries having the same or similar systems, agreements dealing with certification of imports or exports, and agreements to formalize cooperation in the interest of harmonization, improved FDA decisionmaking, and reduced expenditures on import control.[97]

■ Mutual Recognition Agreements

Under FDA usage, mutual recognition agreements (MRAs) might be viewed as a kind of superlative MOU, a reciprocal agreement reached after a finding that the MOU partner's system is sufficiently trustworthy that the FDA can safely reduce its coverage of a product from that country.

The phrase "mutual recognition agreements" has several meanings, but generally refers either to reliance upon one another's conformity assessment system or, where such reliance is not practicable, to the exchange of results of conformity assessments.

The European Definition

Europe's use of MRAs has been influenced heavily by its internal market harmonization activities, aided by the European Court of Justice's interpretation of the Treaty of Rome.[98] Mutual exchange of conformity assessment results was a key part of the 1985 European Council Resolution on the New Approach.[99] Reference is made in that resolution to "the mutual recognition of the results of tests." More recent interpretive documents elaborate: "To further promote international trade in regulated products, mutual recognition agreements for test reports or conformity certificates may be concluded on a case by case basis between the Community and the non-Community partners concerned."[100]

Agreement on Technical Barriers to Trade[101]

The Agreement on Technical Barriers to Trade (TBT) states, "Members of the WTO are encouraged, at the request of other Members, to be willing to enter into negotiations for the conclusion of agreements for the mutual recognition of results of each other's conformity assessment procedures."[102]

---

[96] 60 Fed. Reg. 31,485 (June 15, 1995).

[97] *Id.* at 31,485.

[98] Treaty Establishing the European Economic Community, Jan. 1, 1958, 290 U.N.T.S. 11, 15 [hereinafter Treaty of Rome]. See also the discussion of the European Union at the end of this chapter for further explanation.

[99] Council Resolution of 7 May 1985 on a new approach to technical harmonization and standards, 1985 O.J. (C136)1.

[100] E. Jongen, The Creation of an Internal Market for Industrial Goods in Europe Through Technical Harmonization, Standardization, Certification and Mutual Recognition (1991)

[101] Agreement on Technical Barriers to Trade, Apr. 15, 1994, in Final Act Embodying the Results of the Uruguay Round of Multilateral Trade Negotiations, Apr. 15, 1994, 33 I.L.M. 1125, 1427, *reprinted in* III Compilation of International Laws 281 (FDLI 1996) [hereinafter TBT Agreement].

[102] *Id.* art. 6.3. This provision goes on to refer to the provision in article 6.1 that each Member be assured of the equivalence of the other's systems.

The Trade Agreements Act[103]

This law provides that:

> The Trade Representative has responsibility for coordinating United States discussions and negotiations with foreign countries for the purpose of establishing mutual arrangements with respect to standard-related activities. In carrying out this responsibility, the Trade Representative shall inform and consult with any Federal agency having expertise in the matters under discussion and negotiation.[104]

The FDA's Authority

As described above, the FDA has broad agreement authority. A "mutual recognition" agreement provision in the FDCA applies to device agreements, and several long-standing agreements concerning exchange of inspection reports have mutual recognition aspects, as is discussed in greater detail below.

Mutual Recognition Agreements Among Conformity Assessment Bodies

Many public and private sector entities such as accreditation bodies enter MRAs with one another on conformity assessment practices, particularly relating to either the recognition of the results of product testing and quality system audits or the exchange of reports from such testing or audits. These MRAs might have a binding or influential effect upon regulatory agencies in other countries (particularly with the increased use of private sector conformity assessment activities discussed earlier) but, unless the FDA is a party to the agreement, these MRAs have no impact on the FDA.

The term "MRA" has become popular among those involved in regulations, trade, standards, and conformity assessment discussions, and yet those who use it do not ensure that it is understood through a common definition. A fundamental question remains, whose requirements are being met? Private testing bodies such as Underwriters Laboratories, for example, test to the requirements of the customer. The international analogue is that the conformity assessment is done in accordance with the laws of the *importing country*, and this certainly is what trade agreements contemplate. A different model calls for the laws of the *exporting country* to be the operative standard.

The Transatlantic Business Dialogue has embraced the concept of "tested once, accepted everywhere."[105] Of necessity, there must be considerable harmonization for this view to prevail, for a country like the United States is not going to change its laws on foods, drugs, and medical devices so that *whatever* testing occurred in the country of origin will be *per se* acceptable here. There also is the possibility of an uneven playing field to the disadvantage of domestic producers, if they continue to be held to domestic requirements while for-

---

[103] Trade Agreements Act of 1979, Pub. L. No. 96-39, 93 Stat. 144 (codified at 19 U.S.C. §§ 2501 et. seq.).

[104] *Id.* (codified at 19 U.S.C. § 2541) (as amended by the Uruguay Round Agreements Act, Pub. L. No. 103-465, 108 Stat. at 4809).

[105] Transatlantic Business Dialogue, Executive Summary Draft 2 (1996). The Transatlantic Business Dialogue, launched by Ronald Brown, the late Secretary of the U.S. Department of Commerce, was initiated through a meeting in Seville in November 1995. Meetings continue among U.S. and European business leaders and government officials.

eign competitors, in countries whose laws and enforcement may be laxer, can enter the U.S. market based solely on compliance with their own laws.

■ FDA Policy

The 1995 FDA Compliance Policy Guide[106] shows that the FDA will seek MOUs when they support the agency's mission and will help it make better use of its resources.

A variety of MOUs is possible:

- A cooperation MOU, exemplified by an agreement signed by the FDA and its counterparts in Canada and Mexico,[107] contemplates mutual cooperation and information-sharing activities. What FDA wishes to put in place is a joint work program, joint training, and joint inspections.
- A compliance MOU, which may be reciprocal or one-way, contemplates compliance by the exporting country with the requirements of the importing country.
- An equivalence MOU contemplates a finding that the other country has a regulatory system equivalent to the FDA's; as discussed previously, APA notice-and-comment requirements may come into play when the FDA makes a determination that another country's regulatory food system is equivalent.
- An MRA often is viewed as obviating a finding of equivalence, i.e., two countries decide to accord each other's system mutual recognition despite lack of harmonization or equivalence. Some confusion results from the lack of consistency, in discussions of MRAs, as to whose requirements are being met: the exporting country's or the importing country's. The FDA's policy insists on equivalence as a prerequisite to mutual recognition.

A few FDA MOUs contain mutual recognition features, including several agreements on good laboratory practices (GLPs). Also, the FDA has MOUs with regulatory counterparts in Canada and Sweden that include mutual acceptance of results from inspections for compliance with current good manufacturing practices (GMPs). Likewise, the FDA and its counterpart in the United Kingdom have a similar agreement under which reports are exchanged on device GMP inspections.

The agency plans to follow-up on its 1995 Compliance Policy Guide with additional documents on MOUs, publication of which is expected in 1997. To articulate what is meant by "equivalence," the FDA can draw upon several efforts:

- a draft guideline that the agency prepared for the 1996 meeting of the Codex Alimentarius Committee on Import and Export Food Inspection and Certification Systems;[108]

---

[106] 60 Fed. Reg. at 31,485.

[107] 61 Fed. Reg. at 11,645.

[108] Codex Alimentarius Commission, Codex Committee on Import and Export Food Inspection and Certification Systems, Fourth Sess. CX/FICS 96/7 (agenda item 8), Sydney, Australia (Feb. 19-23, 1996). Naomi Kawin, an FDA Internat'l Policy official, was principal author of this guideline.

- for drugs, a similar document that the FDA developed to serve as an annex to a draft agreement with the European Commission on equivalence of inspection systems for drug GMP compliance;
- for devices, documents produced by Working Group 4 of the Global Harmonization task force;
- International Standards Organization (ISO) guidelines and standards.[109]

These efforts demonstrate how essential close cooperation is: without it, there is no assurance of similarity in what inspectors look for or in what corrective actions are to be taken.

■ Trade Agreements, Implementing Laws, and Presidential Documents

The General Agreement on Tariffs and Trade, the Uruguay Round, and the WTO

The principal international trade agreement is the General Agreement on Tariffs and Trade (GATT), which entered into force on January 1, 1948.[110] GATT has been amended several times, following negotiation sessions known as "rounds." The most recent GATT round, the Uruguay Round, was concluded on December 15, 1993, and was formally signed at the Marrakesh Ministerial Meeting on April 15, 1994.[111] On December 8, 1994, President Clinton signed into law the Uruguay Round Agreements Act,[112] thereby approving the U.S. obligations under the WTO agreements.

The Uruguay Round included an agreement to establish the WTO to administer the new GATT and other Uruguay Round agreements, and every country that is a member of the WTO will be required to adhere to all the agreements.

Due to the problem of trade barriers instituted as health and consumer protection measures, these agreements contain not only "sovereignty protection provisions" that explicitly recognize the sovereign right of countries to establish their chosen levels of consumer protection,[113] but also provisions that enable an exporting country to challenge an importing country's requirement as more trade restrictive than necessary to fulfill the objective.[114] Exporting countries also may request that their technical regulations or inspection systems be considered equivalent.[115]

---

[109] *See generally* GLOBAL BUSINESS RELATIONS, INC., THE INTERNATIONAL BUSINESS ISSUES MONITOR, THE INTERNATIONAL ORGANIZATIONS REGULATORY GUIDEBOOK: A REVIEW AND OUTLOOK REPORT ON INTERNATIONAL ORGANIZATION ACTIVITIES IMPACTING INTERNATIONAL BUSINESS (updated annually).

[110] General Agreement on Tariffs and Trade, Oct. 30, 1947, 61 Stat. A-11, T.I.A.S. 1700, 55 U.N.T.S. 194.

[111] *See* Final Act Embodying the Results of the Uruguay Round of Multilateral Trade Negotiations, Apr. 15, 1994, 33 I.L.M. 1125, *reprinted in* III COMPILATION OF INTERNATIONAL LAWS 241 (FDLI 1996) [hereinafter Final Act].

[112] 19 U.S.C. §§ 2252 et seq.

[113] Agreement on the Application of Sanitary and Phytosanitary Measures, Apr. 15, 1994 preamble, Art. 2.1, 3.3, in Final Act, *supra* note 125, 33 I.L.M. at 1381, *reprinted in* III COMPILATION OF INTERNATIONAL LAWS 273 (FDLI 1996) [hereinafter SPS Agreement]. TBT Agreement, *supra* note 114, preamble. Similar safeguards are found in the North American Free Trade Agreement (NAFTA), which entered into force on January 1, 1994. North American Free Trade Agreement, Oct. 7, 1992, U.S.-Can.-Mex., 32 I.L.M. 289 (1993) & 32 I.L.M. 605 (1993); *see also* NAFTA Implementation Act, Pub. L. No. 103-182, 107 Stat. 2057 (1993).

[114] SPS Agreement, *supra* note 125, art. 2.1, 4.1, 5.6, 5.8, 11; TBT Agreement, *supra* note 113, art. 2.2, 2.3.

[115] TBT Agreement, *supra* note 113, art. 2.7; SPS Agreement, *supra* note 125, art. 4.1.

During consideration of the agreements that became the WTO and the North American Free Trade Agreement (NAFTA), and during congressional consideration of the implementing legislation for each, there was intense controversy as to whether these agreements would allow another country, on behalf of its food manufacturers, to secure a decision by an international trade panel under the WTO Agreement or NAFTA that an importing country's food safety law violates a trade agreement.[116] The answer is that such a decision is possible, but unlikely. Although no country can be compelled to change any law, a country that loses a case (after an elaborate procedure) under the WTO or NAFTA — and refuses to change the offending measure — could be required, by the terms of the WTO Dispute Resolution Understanding,[117] to pay reparations to the prevailing country. This outcome is unlikely, due to safeguards in the trade agreements that protect the ability of a sovereign country to establish and maintain requirements that fulfill a legitimate objective, that are based on science and that achieve the level of protection chosen by that country.

In 1997, a WTO panel ruled in favor of the United States in a longstanding controversy with the EU concerning the EU's refusal to allow imports of beef from cattle that had been treated with hormones for growth promotion. The decision aroused new concerns among consumer groups concerned about national consumer protection laws.

The Technical Barriers to Trade Agreement, Implementing Laws, and Office of Management and Budget Circular

The current TBT Agreement,[118] popularly known as the "Standards Code," was negotiated as part of the Uruguay Round and replaced an agreement that had been part of the last GATT Round (the Tokyo Round) that had entered into force on January 1, 1980.

The new TBT Agreement is similar in many respects to the 1980 TBT Agreement. As before, the purpose of the new Agreement is to ensure that product standards, technical regulations, and related procedures do not create unnecessary obstacles to trade. The new TBT agreement ensures, and clearly states, that each country has the right to establish and maintain technical regulations for the protection of human, animal, and plant life and health and the environment, and for prevention against deceptive practices.[119]

In the new TBT Agreement,[120] the term "standard" is defined as a:

> Document approved by a recognized body, that provides, for common and repeated use, rules, guidelines or characteristics for products or related processes and production methods, *with which compliance is not mandatory* [emphasis added]. It may also include or deal exclusively with terminology, symbols,

---

[116] *See, e.g.*, Public Citizen, Environmental Working Group, Trading Away Food Safety (1993).

[117] Understanding on Rules and Procedures Governing the Settlement of Disputes, in Final Act, *supra* note 123, *reprinted in* III Compilation of International Laws 311 (FDLI 1996) [hereinafter DSU].

[118] TBT Agreement, *supra* note 113.

[119] *Id.*, preamble, para. 4.

[120] Annex 1 in the TBT Agreement sets forth terms and their definitions for the purpose of the agreement. Otherwise, terms used in the TBT Agreement shall, according to Annex I, have the same meaning as given in the definitions of the sixth edition of the ISO/IEC Guide 2-1991, General Terms and Their Definitions Concerning Standardization Related Activities.

packaging, marking or labeling (sic)[121] requirements as they apply to a product, process or production method.[122]

For example, a voluntary standard of the Association for the Advancement of Medical Instrumentation and the American National Standards Institute would meet this definition. Furthermore, the FDA's many guidance documents[123] are "standards" if they otherwise meet the above definition.

"[T]echnical regulation" is defined as a:

> Document which lays down product characteristics or their related processes and production methods, including the applicable administrative provisions, *with which compliance is mandatory*. It may also include or deal exclusively with terminology, symbols, packaging, marking or labeling requirements as they apply to a product, process or production method.[124]

In the United States, a product- or process-related requirement in a requirements statute such as the FDCA — or a mandatory regulation such as drug or device GMP regulation — would be a technical regulation.

Finally, "conformity assessment procedure" is defined as "[a]ny procedure used, directly or indirectly, to determine that relevant requirements in technical regulations or standards are fulfilled."[125] An explanatory note states that "[c]onformity assessment procedures include, *inter alia*, procedures for sampling, testing, and inspection; evaluation, verification and assurance of conformity; registration, accreditation, and approval as well as their combinations."[126]

For the FDA, the definition of "conformity assessment procedure" includes inspections, laboratory testing, and validation.

Thus, when a government accepts a voluntary *standard* and makes it mandatory, the resulting document is a *technical regulation*. A measure used to ascertain compliance with either a standard or a technical regulation is a *conformity assessment procedure*.[127] A good example of this is the FDA's new device GMP rule. The FDA adapted a voluntary standard, the ISO-9001 quality systems standard,[128] applied the standard in a technical regulation,[129] and inspections will serve as conformity assessment procedures.

---

[121] Commonly labeling is spelled "labelling" in international texts, e.g., those of Codex Alimentarius, reflecting the preferred European spelling.

[122] TBT Agreement, *supra* note 113, annex 1 (emphasis added).

[123] *See, e.g.,* 61 Fed. Reg. 9181 (Mar. 7, 1996).

[124] TBT Agreement, *supra* note 113, annex 1 (emphasis added).

[125] *Id.*

[126] *Id. See also* INTERNATIONAL ORGANIZATION FOR STANDARDIZATION AND INTERNATIONAL ELECTROTECHNICAL COMMISSION, ISO/IEC GUIDES COMPENDIUM: CONFORMITY ASSESSMENT (3d ed. 1995).

[127] *See* OFFICE OF U.S. TRADE REPRESENTATIVE, STATEMENT OF ADMINISTRATIVE ACTION, URUGUAY ROUND AGREEMENT ACT 120-22 (1994).

[128] INTERNATIONAL STANDARDS ORGANIZATION, ISO 9001: QUALITY SYSTEMS — MODEL FOR QUALITY ASSURANCE IN DESIGN, DEVELOPMENT, PRODUCTION, INSTALLATION, AND SERVICING (1994).

[129] *See* 61 Fed. Reg. 52,602 (Oct. 7, 1996).

The new TBT Agreement continues and strengthens the reference to international standards found in the 1980 TBT Agreement. Specifically, the new Agreement provides that, where a technical regulation is "required" (either "needed" as a technical matter or "legally compelled"), and a relevant international standard exists or its completion is imminent, WTO-member countries shall use the standard, or the relevant parts of it, as a basis for their technical regulations; an exception is provided when the international standards or relevant part would be an ineffective or inappropriate means for the fulfillment of the legitimate objectives pursued.[130] For example, if ISO issued a standard on aspects of pharmaceutical manufacturing that was an ineffective or inappropriate means for the fulfillment of the FDA's objectives, the FDA would be under no obligation to use the standard as the basis for its technical regulation.

Further, the Agreement states that, with a view toward harmonizing technical regulations on as wide a basis as possible, WTO-member countries shall play a full part within the limits of their resources in the preparation by appropriate international standards bodies of international standards for products for which they either have adopted or expect to adopt technical regulations.[131] The FDA believes it already meets this obligation, so that the principal impact of this provision may be merely to support the importance of its existing standards efforts.

Due to the APA, U.S. agencies such as the FDA have no difficulty complying with the procedural safeguards of the TBT Agreement. When the FDA wishes to accept an international standard in a regulation, the APA requires the agency to publish a proposed rule and otherwise act in an open manner, give adequate time for interested persons to submit comments, and consider the comments before promulgating a final regulation. The FDA's procedure for promulgating regulations[132] is explicit with respect to the need for transparency of the process and the opportunity for participation by interested persons. Other FDA procedural regulations govern guidelines and similar documents;[133] and interested persons may use correspondence, meetings,[134] petitions,[135] or reviews by supervisors[136] to raise issues and present views about other nonbinding guidance documents, which provides industry with useful information about recommended or alternative ways to comply with requirements. The FDA increasingly has used public meetings to elicit and share information, and the agency has developed procedures for guidance documents to ensure sufficient transparency in the process.[137]

As part of a general effort to reduce unnecessary nontariff barriers to trade, the old and the new versions of the TBT Agreement promote use by countries of standards, technical regulations, and conformity assessment procedures that are based on work done by international standards bodies.

---

[130] TBT Agreement, *supra* note 113, art. 2.4.

[131] *Id.* art. 2.6.

[132] 21 C.F.R. § 10.40.

[133] *Id.* § 10.90.

[134] *Id.* § 10.65.

[135] *Id.* § 10.30.

[136] *Id.* § 10.75.

[137] 61 Fed. Reg. 9181 (Mar. 7, 1996); 62 Fed. Reg. 8961 (Feb. 27, 1997).

The technical barriers to trade provisions of the 1994 Uruguay Round Agreements Act,[138] like the 1979 implementing legislation for the Tokyo Round agreements[139] that they amend, may be viewed as providing additional authority for the FDA's international standards activities. To ensure that harmonization does not result in lowering safety or quality standards for U.S. consumers, this law provides that U.S. statutes prevail over trade agreements when in conflict[140] and that

> [n]o standard-related activity of any private person, Federal agency, or State agency shall be deemed to constitute an unnecessary obstacle to the foreign commerce of the United States if the demonstrable purpose of the standards-related activity is to achieve a legitimate domestic objective including, but not limited to, the protection of legitimate health or safety, essential security, environmental, or consumer interests and if such activity does not operate to exclude imported products which fully meet the objectives of such activity.[141]

The TBT provisions of the Uruguay Round Agreements Act do not create a private right of action.[142] Also, no standards-related activity in the United States may be stayed in any judicial or administrative forum on the basis that there is a WTO proceeding involving the activity.[143]

The National Technology Transfer and Advancement Act of 1996[144] codifies certain long-standing guidances to federal agencies concerning the use of standards, as had been issued by the U.S. Office of Management and Budget (OMB) in 1993.[145]

Section 12(d) of this law provides as follows:

> (d) Utilization of Consensus Technical Standards by Federal Agencies; Reports.
>
> (1) In general. — Except as provided in paragraph (3) of this subsection, all Federal agencies and departments shall use technical standards that are developed or adopted by voluntary consensus standards bodies, using such technical standards as a means to carry out policy objectives or activities determined by the agencies and departments.
>
> (2) Consultation; participation. — In carrying out paragraph (1) of this subsection, Federal agencies and departments shall consult with voluntary, private sector, consensus standards bodies and shall, when such participation is in the public interest and is compatible with agency and departmental missions, authorities, priorities, and budget resources, participate with such bodies in the development of technical standards.

---

[138] *See* 19 U.S.C. §§ 2531-2582.

[139] The Trade Agreements Act of 1979, Pub. L. No. 96-39, 93 Stat. 144.

[140] 19 U.S.C. § 2504.

[141] *Id.* § 2531.

[142] *Id.* § 2551.

[143] *Id.* § 2562.

[144] Pub. L. No. 104-113, 110 Stat. 775.

[145] OMB Circular No. A-119, 58 Fed. Reg. 57,643 (Oct. 26, 1993).

(3) Exception. — If compliance with paragraph (1) of this subsection is inconsistent with applicable law or otherwise impractical, a Federal agency or department may elect to use technical standards that are not developed or adopted by voluntary consensus standards bodies if the head of each such agency or department transmits to the Office of Management and Budget an explanation of the reasons for using such standards. Each year, beginning with fiscal year 1997, the Office of Management and Budget shall transmit to Congress and its committees a report summarizing all explanations received in the preceding year under this paragraph.

(4) Definition of technical standards. — As used in this subsection, the term "technical standards" means performance-based or design-specific technical specifications and related management systems practices.[146]

This new law supplements OMB guidance, known as Circular A-119, the 1993 version of which stated that:

It is the policy of the Federal Government in its procurement and regulatory activities to:

a. Rely on voluntary standards, both domestic and international, whenever feasible and consistent with the law and regulation pursuant to law;

b. Participate in voluntary standards bodies when such participation is in the public interest and is compatible with agencies' missions, authorities, priorities, and budget resources; and

c. Coordinate agency participation in voluntary standards bodies so that: (1) The most effective use is made of agency resources and representatives; and (2) the views expressed by such representatives are in the public interest and, as a minimum, do not conflict with the interests and established views of the agencies.[147]

OMB Circular No. A-119 provides policy guidance for U.S. government agencies concerning domestic and international voluntary standards activities, but not standards activities under treaties and international agreements. Thus, Circular A-119 (and presumably the 1996 Technology Act) would have no applicability to Codex Alimentarius standards activities, as its parent United Nations (U.N.) bodies, the Food and Agricultural Organization (FAO) and the World Health Organization (WHO) are treaty-based organizations.

The term "standard," as defined in the 1993 version of OMB Circular No. A-119, means "a prescribed set of rules, conditions, or requirements concerned with the definition of terms; classification of components; delineation of procedures; specification of dimensions, materials, performance, design, or operations; measurement of quality and quantity in describing materials, products, systems, services, or practices; or descriptions of fit and measurement of size."[148] The Circular defines "voluntary standards" as "established gen-

---

[146] Pub. Law 104-113, § 12(d)(4), 110 Stat. at 783 (codified at 15 U.S.C. § 272 note).

[147] 58 Fed. Reg. at 57,645.

[148] *Id.*

erally by private sector bodies, both domestic and international, and . . . available for use by any person or organization, private or governmental."[149] The term "voluntary standard" includes what are commonly referred to as "industry standards" as well as "consensus standards," but does not include professional standards of personal conduct, institutional codes of ethics, private standards of individual firms, or standards mandated by law, such as those contained in the *U.S. Pharmacopeia* and the *National Formulary*, as referenced in title 21 of the *United States Code*, section 351.[150]

The 1993 OMB Circular's definition of standards is inconsistent with that in the TBT Agreement. The TBT Agreement definition is narrower in that it considers "standards" to be voluntary measures, and that it covers treaty organizations' standards. This inconsistency promotes confusion in an area where confusion already is rampant. In its standards policy, the FDA described both definitions in the interest of promoting familiarity in the FDA community with both usages.

In late 1996, the Office of Management and Budget published for public comment a revised draft of Circular A-119 to take into account the 1996 Technology Transfer Act discussed above.[151]

SPS Agreement; WTO Implementing Law; Presidential Proclamation

Another agreement of the Uruguay Round administered by the WTO is the Agreement on the Application of Sanitary and Phytosanitary Measures (SPS Agreement).[152] This agreement pertains to those measures intended: 1) to protect animal or plant life or health within a territory from risks arising from the entry, establishment, or spread of pests, diseases, disease-carrying organisms, or disease-causing organisms; 2) to protect human or animal life or health within a territory from risks arising from additives, contaminants, toxins, or disease-causing organisms in foods, beverages, or feedstuffs; 3) to protect human life or health within a territory from risks arising from diseases carried by animals, plants, or products thereof, or from entry, establishment, or spread of pests; or 4) to prevent or limit other damage within a territory from the entry, establishment, or spread of pests.[153] Thus, "sanitary" refers to the protection of people and animals; "phytosanitary" refers to the protection of plants. Although the SPS Agreement is much more significant for food regulation than for drug and device regulation, it has applicability to drugs and devices of animal origin.

SPS measures include measures "to protect human or animal life or health within the territory of the Member from risks arising from additives, contaminants, toxins, or disease-causing organisms in foods, beverages or feedstuffs . . . ."[154] SPS measures include "all relevant laws, decrees, regulations, requirements and procedures including, *inter alia*, end product criteria; processes and production methods; testing, inspection, certification and approval procedures . . . provisions on relevant statistical methods, sampling procedures

---

[149] *Id.*

[150] *Id. See* 21 U.S.C. § 351.

[151] 61 Fed. Reg. 68,312 (Dec. 27, 1996).

[152] SPS Agreement , *supra* note 125.

[153] *Id.* annex A.

[154] *Id.*

and methods of risk assessment; and packaging and labeling requirements directly related to food safety."[155] Examples of SPS measures are FDA safety requirements for additives, contaminants, and microbial adulteration.

To harmonize SPS measures on as wide a basis as possible, the SPS Agreement encourages Members to base their SPS measures on international standards, guidelines, or recommendations.[156] Like the TBT Agreement,[157] the SPS Agreement encourages "harmonization" (the "establishment, recognition and application of common sanitary and phytosanitary measures by different members"[158]) and the use of international standards therefor. There are important exceptions to harmonization, however, that are crucial for the FDA. A member may set higher standards if there is a scientific justification, or as a consequence of the level of protection the importing country determines to be appropriate.[159]

SPS measures must be based on scientific principles, may not be maintained without sufficient scientific evidence, and must be based on an assessment of the risk to health that is appropriate to the circumstances.[160]

Furthermore, countries are strongly encouraged to use standards set by certain international bodies, including the food safety-related standards of the Codex Alimentarius Commission.[161] The effect is to give countries an incentive to accept Codex standards. Members who do so need not justify their sanitary measures. Members who do not base their requirements on Codex may need to justify them, either as scientifically based or as a consequence of the country's desired level of protection.

Because the SPS Agreement contains provisions both to induce countries to follow Codex standards, and to excuse a country from doing so as a result of a scientific rationale or its chosen level of protection, the outcome of WTO disputes based on a country's choice to enforce requirements stricter than Codex cannot be predetermined but will be handled on a case-by-case basis under the WTO Dispute Resolution Understanding.[162] While a detailed treatment of this topic is not included in this chapter, a few basics are in order:

- only governments can bring cases in the WTO, and government attorneys, generally trade specialists, handle these matters;
- a dispute about a trade agreement must be handled under the procedures provided; a trade agreement or its implementing legislation does not create a cause of action in U.S. courts;
- as is the case in other international law situations, a business can take its complaint about another country's laws to its government and that government may "take up" the case on behalf of that business;

---

[155] *Id.*

[156] *Id.* art. 3.1.

[157] TBT Agreement, *supra* note 113, arts. 2.4, 2.6, 5.5, 9.1.

[158] SPS Agreement, *supra* note 125, arts. 3, 12.4; annex A.2.

[159] *Id.* art. 3.3.

[160] *Id.* art. 2.2, 3.3, 5.

[161] *Id.* art. 3.2, 3.4. TBT Agreement, *supra* note 113, art. 2.5.

[162] DSU, *supra* note 129.

- U.S. trade agencies attempt to resolve the matter with the other country through communication, negotiations, and, on occasion, scientific critiques prepared by the appropriate agency, e.g., the FDA;
- if these attempts fail, the WTO process encourages settlements through a range of alternative dispute resolution options (informal consultations, mediation, and arbitration);
- the WTO procedure is not transparent; hearings are closed and the parties' briefs generally are not made public (although the United States discloses parts of its briefs); and
- the WTO procedure was strengthened as part of the Uruguay Round, to ensure enforceability of its judgments.

North America Free Trade Agreement

NAFTA also contains TBT and SPS agreements similar to those in the new WTO agreements. An Appendix to this chapter provides additional details about the WTO and NAFTA agreements on TBT and SPS.

■ International Law

The Charter of the U.N. identified harmonization as one of the organization's four core purposes: 1) to maintain international peace and security, 2) to develop friendly relations among nations, 3) to achieve international cooperation in solving international problems of an economic, social, cultural, or humanitarian character, and 4) to be "a centre for *harmonizing the actions of nations in the attainment of these common ends.*"[163] For the FDA, the principal U.N. bodies are the WHO and the FAO.

International Compliance

■ Approaches and Trends

Through its Office of Regulatory Affairs (ORA), the FDA attempts to ensure that imports of food, drugs, and devices meet its requirements by means of point-of-entry inspections, sampling and testing, foreign inspections and audits of the exporting countries' inspection systems, and checking any certificates for authenticity and accuracy.

MOUs with other countries help to ensure that their products meet the FDA's requirements, and the agency sometimes provides technical assistance to address deficiencies in other countries' control systems. Point-of-entry controls by themselves have only limited effect on product safety[164] and quality. The way goods are produced and regulated in other countries is increasingly important to public health protection in the United States, as discussed below.

---

[163] U.N. CHARTER art. 1.

[164] FDA TASK FORCE REPORT, *supra* note 4, at 16.

One-third of the imports into the United States are FDA-regulated products,[165] and food imports make up seventy-six percent of the entries of these FDA-regulated products.[166] The sheer number of formal import entries that the FDA must review is climbing toward 3,000,000. Equally important is the changing nature of those imports — for example, there is a shift toward foods that are ready for sale without further U.S. processing.[167] Increasing imports of foods, bulk pharmaceutical chemicals, and medical devices challenge the FDA's ability to handle these imports effectively.

■ The Importance (and Difficulty) of Ensuring Adequate Processing Controls

The FDA has initiated activities that address various issues including: conditions in the country of origin by production-related requirements, such as those involving good manufacturing practices (GMPs) for drugs and quality systems requirements for medical devices; strict enforcement, including automatic detention; and cooperative approaches such as international standards, training and information sharing, MOUs with other governments, technical assistance, inspections of foreign processors, and audits of foreign systems.[168]

■ Import Law and Procedures

Section 801 of the FDCA[169] prescribes the procedure for handling imports of food, drugs, devices, and cosmetics imported or offered for import into the United States. Import control for these products is a cooperative responsibility of two agencies: the U.S. Customs Service and the FDA. An article shall be refused admission "[i]f it appears from the examination of such samples or otherwise" that it:

- has been manufactured, processed, or packed under insanitary conditions or, in the case of a device, the methods used in, or the facilities or controls used for, the manufacture, packing, storage, or installation of the device, do not conform to the FDA's GMP regulations;

- is forbidden or restricted in sale in the country in which it was produced or from which it is being exported;[170] or

- is adulterated, misbranded, or in violation of the new drug provisions.

---

[165] David A. Kessler, *Remarks by the Commissioner of Food and Drugs*, 50 FOOD & DRUG L.J. 327 (1995) (speech by Commissioner of Food and Drugs, Dr. David A. Kessler at Annual Educational Conference of FDLI (Dec. 12, 1994)).

[166] An entry is a line-item in U.S. Customs recordkeeping. The FDA's statistics on imports are based on Customs data. The breakdown is as follows: of entries of FDA-regulated imported products, 76% are food, 14% are drugs or cosmetics, 7% are devices, 2% are veterinary products, and 1% are biologic products (vaccines and blood products). Thomas Gardine, FDA, Presentation at FDLI seminar on Import and Export of FDA-Regulated Products, Washington, D.C. (May 18, 1994).

[167] FDA TASK FORCE REPORT, *supra* note 4, at 8.

[168] E.g., the FDA's 1974 *Annual Report* described plans to begin inspecting foreign canners of low-acid canned foods; over 800 foreign canners had registered to participate.

[169] FDCA § 801, 21 U.S.C. § 381.

[170] This provision was found in the Pure Food and Drugs Act, Pub. L. No. 59-384, § 11, 34 Stat. 768 (1906), as well as antecedent laws. It shows the unwillingness of the United States to receive articles that fail to meet the requirements of the country of origin.

The FDA Export Reform and Enhancement Act of 1996[171] provides for importation of ingredients or components, not otherwise allowed in the United States, for inclusion in an article for export only. Recordkeeping is required.

Screening of entries to determine which products are entitled to admission is done by Customs, which notifies the FDA of FDA-regulated products offered for entry. The FDA determines what action to take regarding the entry. For example, the FDA may decide to conduct a wharf examination, sample the product, or permit the product to proceed without agency review.[172]

With Customs, the FDA screens entry documents, either electronically or manually, at nearly a one hundred percent level, to determine its degree of regulatory interest based on compliance history, policies, priorities, and information from various sources.[173] Approximately three to four percent of entries are sampled, and approximately three to four percent of entries are wharf-examined.[174] The FDA targets high-risk products or products with high violation rates. If it "appears from the examination of such samples or otherwise" that an article is adulterated or misbranded, or there is reason to believe it was processed under insanitary conditions, the article may be rejected.

The FDA's actions on import detentions, including automatic detentions, are public and are available on the Internet.[175] Thus, foreign countries, exporters, and importers easily can learn about which products have had problems meeting FDA requirements and why.

When detained imported products are found not to comply with the FDCA, they are subject to re-exportation or destruction.[176] The owner or consignee "may appear before the [FDA] and have the right to introduce testimony."[177] This proceeding is referred to as a hearing in the FDA regulations,[178] but it is not a full-blown, trial-type administrative hearing.

The hearing on rejected imports is not adversarial. The importer can introduce testimony orally or in writing. FDA officials do not offer evidence, but listen to the importer's presentation. It is an opportunity for the importer to try to convince the FDA that its proposed action concerning the shipment is in error. The importer may submit views by letter instead. There is no cross-examination, and often no recording or transcript made of the proceeding. Courts have agreed with the FDA that there is no constitutional right to a more formal hearing.[179] One court held that a series of phone calls and correspondence satisfied the right to provide testimony.[180]

---

[171] Pub. L. No. 104-134, 110 Stat.1321 (codified at 21 U.S.C. §§ 334, 381, 382; 42 U.S.C. § 262).

[172] 21 C.F.R. § 1.90.

[173] Thomas Gardine, *supra* note 177.

[174] *Id.*

[175] *See* FDA Internet homepage <http://www.fda.gov>.

[176] FDCA § 801(a), 21 U.S.C. § 381(a).

[177] *Id.*

[178] 21 C.F.R. § 1.94(a).

[179] *See, e.g.*, Bowman v. Retzlaff, 65 F. Supp. 265 (D. Md. 1946); Sugarman v. Forbragd, 405 F.2d 1189 (9th Cir. 1968), *cert denied*, 395 U.S. 960 (1969). *See also* Paul M. Hyman, *Legal Overview of FDA Authority Over Imports*, 49 FOOD & DRUG L.J. 525 (1994).

[180] Meserey v. United States, 447 F. Supp. 548 (D. Nev. 1977).

As an alternative to re-exportation or destruction, an importer may be permitted, at the discretion of the FDA, to try to bring the illegal product into compliance with the law through reconditioning, before a final decision is made as to whether it may be admitted. Conditional release of a product for reconditioning is regarded as a privilege rather than a right, and repetitious shipments of the same illegal product may result in automatic detention and re-exportation.

The option of seizure and destruction is available. Section 801 of the FDCA appears to give the importer of a violative article the option to re-export (or recondition) — rather than destroy — articles offered for importation that does not comply. Section 304 of the FDCA, the source of the FDA's seizure authority, provides another option. The FDA can admit an imported product into interstate commerce, and then seize it and seek its court-ordered destruction. This seizure authority thus applies to both domestic and imported products, and is a particularly important tool to compel destruction of a product that presents a risk to health.

The FDA interprets the FDCA as providing the agency with the alternative, under section 304 rather than the import provisions of section 801, to seize and order the destruction of food that may be dangerous due to inadequate processing procedures. The agency's usual remedy for imports that appear to be adulterated or misbranded is the detention of articles offered for importation. This course of action is administrative and thus generally more efficient than FDA's judicial remedies, namely seizure, injunction, and criminal prosecution, under sections 304, 302, and 303, respectively, of the FDCA.[181] A disadvantage of import detention under section 801 is that it has been interpreted to give the importer the option in all cases of exportation in lieu of destruction, even as to products so hazardous — or incapable of being reconditioned — that the FDA believed they should be destroyed to deter efforts to re-enter them at another U.S. port, or ship them to Canada, Mexico, or another country.

In an effort to deal more effectively with imports of this type, in May 1992 the FDA devised a strategy to use its seizure authority in section 304 to ensure destruction of such imports. Under section 304, unlike section 801, the FDA can obtain a court order to have food destroyed. In *United States v. 2,998 Cases . . . Canned Chinese Mushrooms,*[182] the U.S. Court of Appeals for the Fifth Circuit upheld this approach, in a decision that is potentially applicable as well to drugs and devices. That court held that the FDA could properly use its section 304 authority to seize imported products, and that section 801 was not the agency's exclusive authority over imports.[183] Thus, a court could then order destruction of the seized product, and the importer in this case was not entitled under section 802 to re-export the dangerous product. The Fifth Circuit overruled the district court in this matter[184] and agreed with the FDA's interpretation. Intriguingly, in reaching this result, the court described the FDA's jurisdiction over the products in question as beginning at the place where the intent was formed to ship the products to the United States: "If . . . goods are destined for sale in a state other than the place from which they are shipped,

---

[181] 21 U.S.C. §§ 334, 332, 333.

[182] 64 F.3d 984.

[183] *Id.* at 992.

[184] United States v. 2,998 Cases . . . Canned Mushrooms, Civ. No. 93-3623, 1994 U.S. Dist. LEXIS 5141 (E.D. La. filed Apr. 18, 1994).

then goods are in 'interstate commerce' without the necessity of physically crossing a state boundary."[185]

Automatic detention is an FDA program that was developed to deal with recurrent violations.[186] An automatic detention is the administrative act of detaining an entry of a specified article without physical examination, solely on the basis of information regarding its past violative history and/or other information indicating that the product may be violative.

Given the huge volume of imported products, and the practical impossibility of sampling every product offered for import or inspecting every foreign firm, the FDCA provides that the FDA may refuse admission of any product that "appears" from examination, or otherwise, to be violative.[187] This provision permits efficient regulation of imports, because, for example, products that have a history of being violative when offered for entry may be detained until their compliance with the law is established. Based on this provision, when the FDA has established that future shipments of products will appear violative, the products may be "automatically detained," i.e., detained subject to refusal, until the products are established to comply with the Act.

Automatic detention actions are implemented through FDA documents known as Import Alerts. FDA headquarters issues to its investigators, and to Customs, an Import Alert stating that all shipments of a certain product or class of products from a certain supplier, or from a certain country, are subject to automatic detention. In some cases, goods subject to automatic detention may be permitted into the country only if the importer produces a certificate from the foreign government, or an acceptable private laboratory test result that the FDA accepts as assurance that the product is in compliance with the requirements of the Act.

Certificates or laboratory test results often are accepted by the FDA in cases where the violation involved an impermissible contaminant such as pesticide residues, and the agency may conduct audits or spot checks of "certified" shipments to ensure that the products covered by the certificates comply with the law. In other cases, test results do not satisfy the agency's need for assurance that the problem was remedied, e.g., such problems as underprocessed canned foods, most drug GMP violations, and GMP problems with defective steel surgical devices.

Automatic detention thus amounts to a lot-by-lot release program in which the importer must prove the eligibility of the product to be sold in the United States.[188] As discussed more below, if the FDA determines that an entry appears violative, it may refuse entry of the article unless it can be brought into compliance with the Act. If the article cannot be brought into compliance, it must be re-exported or destroyed.

---

[185] 64 F.3d at 988 (citing Merchants Fast Motor Lines, Inc. v. Interstate Commerce Comm'n, 528 F.2d 1042, 1044 (5th Cir. 1976); Texas v. United States, 866 F.2d 1546, 1556 (5th Cir. 1989)).

[186] *Automatic Detention, in* FDA Regulatory Procedures Manual ch. 9-25 (1988).

[187] FDCA § 801(a), 21 U.S.C. § 381(a).

[188] Some firms view their automatic detention status not as a liability, but as a way to prove their legitimacy. For example, three of the five Hong Kong mushroom canners are on automatic detention and want to stay there, to aid efforts to distinguish their mushrooms from Chinese mushrooms. Interview with Fred Phillips, Div. of Enforcement, Off. of Field Programs, CFSAN, FDA, Washington, D.C. (Mar. 25, 1994).

Creative import compliance strategies are needed because import surveillance is not keeping pace with increased entries,[189] and fiscal reality makes it improbable that regulatory resources will ever match this increase. Accordingly, the agency's ability to ensure the compliance of imported drugs and devices depends on how well it targets its resources to the most pressing problems. The agency is therefore developing an automated entry system,[190] seeking user fees to help support that system,[191] focusing its sampling and testing on products expected to be problematic (based on characteristics of the product or history of the firm or country), and developing effective enforcement techniques that will help the agency cope with increased imports.[192]

■ Foreign Inspections

Foreign inspections by the FDA were initiated in 1995 for antibiotics; they have occurred since the 1960s for other drugs.[193] These inspections have risen from about 330 per year in 1990 and 1991, to 1805 for fiscal year 1994. Most foreign inspections involve drug (including biologic), or medical device producers. In 1997, FDA issued a report of an agency task group that reviewed FDA's foreign inspection programs.

■ Technical Assistance

The FDA provides technical assistance to foreign countries on a broad front, ranging from work through the Pan American Health Organization on deaths of children in Haiti in 1997 due to a cough syrup with a hazardous ingredient to activities with the Russian Federation in the area of technical cooperation and information exchange involving pharmaceuticals.

In particular, the FDA is intensifying its efforts to work with developing countries that have a large number of entries detained. The objective of such efforts is to identify and deal with a problem at the source, before it is passed into the United States. Traditionally, the FDA has not offered other countries unsolicited technical assistance; a country usually asks for the FDA's help because it wants to strengthen its program for consumer protection or because it has a problem with import rejections by the FDA.[194] The FDA targets technical assistance, just as it targets enforcement attention, to those products and countries who present the greatest problem.[195]

---

[189] Food and Drug Admin., International Harmonization Report, at 5. The FDA examines only about 7% of import entries, and conducts sample analysis of only about 3% of these. The agency uses about 40% of its total field food resources for coverage of imported foods. *Id.*

[190] Gary J. Dykstra, *Electronic Processing of Import Entries,* 49 FOOD & DRUG L.J. 425 (1993).

[191] Vice President Gore's recommendation that the FDA be given user fees for imports and export certificate, *see* REPORT OF THE NATIONAL PERFORMANCE REVIEW: CREATING A GOVERNMENT THAT WORKS BETTER AND COSTS LESS (1993) was partially implemented in the FDA Export Reform and Enhancement Act of 1996, Pub. L. No. 104-134, 110 Stat. at 1321.

[192] *FDA's Regulation of Food Imports: Hearings Before the Subcomm. on Oversight and Investigations of the House Comm. on Energy and Commerce,* 103d Cong., 1st Sess. (1993) (statement of Edward Warner, FDA).

[193] FDA TASK FORCE REPORT, *supra* note 4, at 1, app. E.

[194] Interview with Thomas R. Mulvaney, Ph.D., Sci. Advisor, Off. of Plant and Dairy Foods and Beverage, CFSAN, FDA, Washington, D.C. (Mar. 25, 1994).

[195] Interview with Maritza Colon-Pullano, Int'l Reg. Affrs. Staff, Off. of Reg. Affrs., FDA, Rockville, MD (Mar. 17, 1994).

A widespread problem is the relative ease with which strong laws and regulations can be adopted — and the concomitant challenge of making the reality match the written requirements, through implementation and enforcement.[196]

An FDA seminar in Moscow in 1993 was followed by a series of training programs, visits, and MOUs to strengthen cooperation between the FDA and its counterparts in the Russian Federation, to streamline Russian procedures for vitally-needed imports of U.S. products, and to establish a reliable system to ensure production of safe and effective vaccines. In this instance and others, particularly in the Middle East (with Israel, Egypt, and Saudi Arabia) and in Eastern Europe (Russia and Ukraine), the FDA's technical assistance activities were stimulated not by violative imports, but by foreign policy priorities of the U.S. presidential administration.

Many of these activities are funded by the U.S. Agency for International Development (AID) and other national or international development assistance agencies,[197] because it would be difficult for the FDA — a domestic consumer protection agency — to justify the expenditure of appropriations in this manner, except under a most generous reading of the PHS Act and the FDCA. The FDA is trying to strengthen its review of technical assistance in developing countries, because the agency in the past has contributed resources (personnel, if not actual funding) to assistance activities that did not have a clear value to the agency.[198]

■ Private Sector Conformity Assessment

Although food and drug regulation has been a governmental function for many centuries, in the last several years the issue of whether the private sector can play a useful role in inspection and certification has received increased attention. Independent of the "regulatory privatization" debates in the U.S. Congress in 1995 and 1996, related concepts were provoking spirited debates in international fora such as the Codex Alimentarius Commission.[199] The concepts are receiving attention for several reasons: shortages of governmental resources in countries generally, the weakness of governmental infrastructure in developing countries particularly, and the increasing marketplace demands for suppliers to obtain ISO-9001 quality systems registration.[200] In Codex meetings, the U.S. government and others have expressed skepticism about whether the already-thin governmental oversight for GMP compliance or Hazard Analysis Critical Control Point (HACCP) compliance could be displaced by private sector bodies. Less controversial is the notion that, when the marketplace demands third-party testing above and beyond governmental requirements, either fee-for-service governmental programs such as those of the Agricultural Marketing Service or private sector certification schemes (for compliance with prod-

---

[196] FDA TASK FORCE REPORT, *supra* note 4, at 12.

[197] Sources of funding include AID, WHO, FAO, foreign governments, and academic institutions. FDA TASK FORCE REPORT, *supra* note 4, at 25.

[198] *Id.* app. E (Feb. 28, 1992) (Memorandum of Meeting, Center for Drug Evaluation and Research.

[199] Reports of the Codex Committee on Import and Export Food Inspection and Certification Systems, 3d Sess. (Feb. 1995) and 4th Sess. (Feb. 1996).

[200] *See* Catherine E. Adams, *ISO 9000 and HACCP Systems*, 49 FOOD & DRUG L. J. 603 (1993). *See also* interview with Frank E. Samuel, Jr., former member of Advisory Committee on the FDA (Mar. 13, 1992) *in* FDA TASK FORCE REPORT, *supra* note 4, App. I.

uct standards or quality systems standards) may be useful. For example, some supermarket chains or the U.S. Department of Agriculture school lunch program might require that food suppliers pay for either governmental quality grading services or private sector certification. Sometimes these programs play an international role as well, such as the participation of the U.S. Department of Commerce's National Marine Fisheries Service in the FDA's program for issuing seafood hygiene certificates to the European Union (EU).

Those who favor use of private sector bodies in food or device inspection, testing, and certification (a private sector role with respect to pharmaceuticals is less discussed) would have the certifying body, such as a private laboratory or a firm registered to perform ISO-9000 audits, check the product or the manufacturing establishment to verify the information presented on the certificate issued by that body.

Exporting countries are expected to oversee the work of certifying bodies through validation measures to justify confidence in the bodies' certificates, i.e., confidence that the product or process referred to in the certificate conforms to applicable requirements.

In the 1990s, there has been increased interest in the applicability to the FDA-regulated industry of the ISO-9000 quality system standards. Clearly, ISO-9000 supports the FDA's view that in-process quality control is critical — that end-product testing cannot make up for insanitary practices on a production line.

Exports

■ Federal Food, Drug, and Cosmetic Act

A food, drug, device, or cosmetic that is in compliance with the FDCA so that it may be commercially distributed within the United States may be exported without any FDA approval or involvement.

A food, drug, device, or cosmetic intended for export that could not be commercially distributed within the United States because it would be considered either adulterated or misbranded may be exported if it:

- accords to the specifications of the foreign purchaser,
- is not in conflict with the laws of the country of destination,
- is labeled on the outside of the shipping package that it is intended for export, and
- is not sold or offered for sale in domestic commerce.[201]

---

[201] FDCA § 801(e)(1), 21 U.S.C. § 381(e)(1). This statutory provision does not apply to food that fails to meet the emergency permit control provisions of 21 U.S.C. § 344 and regulations thereunder. That is because a violation of section 344 is a separate prohibited act (21 U.S.C. § 331(d)) and a separate ground for seizing the food (*id.* § 334(a)(1)). Seized food that is in violation of such controls is ineligible for reconditioning or exportation but "shall be disposed of by destruction." FDCA § 404, 21 U.S.C. § 344.

Thus, an exporter shipping articles from the United States must comply either with the FDA's requirements or with the laws of the importing country. This section describes general provisions, while specific provisions for exports of drugs and devices are discussed in the later chapters of this book on international harmonization of drugs and biologics[202] and medical devices.[203]

■ Export Controls in the Country of Origin

There is strong international interest in holding exporting countries responsible for the safety of their products and concurrently reducing controls by importing countries. Arguments in favor of this approach are that inspections are more efficiently conducted of producers within one's own borders than of producers in a foreign country, and reliance on border checks can result in delays that undermine the quality of products and can add otherwise avoidable storage costs.

Arguments against reliance on the exporting country's controls are that, whatever the regulatory system, the quality of a product such as bult active ingredients may diminish due to conditions of transport and handling. There also is a risk that, due to domestic politics, an exporting country's inspections may be less reliable than an importing country's. The FDA wants to be able to increase its reliance on other countries' systems and is actively seeking agreements with foreign counterparts to that end.

■ Export Certificates

In administering their import controls, many countries demand or request export certificates as a way for a supplier to show that a product meets 1) the requirements of the country of origin, 2) the requirements of the country of destination, 3) international standards set by the World Health Organization, e.g., GMPs or vaccine standards, or 4) the specifications agreed to by the buyer and the seller.[204] Certificates are issued either by governmental authorities or by officially recognized nongovernmental organizations (including cooperative and private organizations). For example, some foreign countries have been satisfied with an export certificate prepared by a state agency.

As international trade in food, drugs, and devices has increased, the numbers of certificates requested have grown, and the nature of the certification provided to importing countries has changed (for example, the seafood certificates required by the EU).

If the importing country requires some attestation that a drug or device complies with U.S. law, the exporter may request the FDA[205] to provide an export certificate. In 1994, the FDA issued a revised Compliance Policy Guide on export certificates following a review by the agency of its export certificate program, resulting in several recommended

---

[202] *Id.*

[203] Horton, et al., *supra* note 2.

[204] Joint FAO/WHO Food Standards Programme, Codex Alimentarius Commission, Report of the 2d Sess. of the Codex Committee on Import and Export Food Inspection and Certification Systems 8 (ALINORM 95/30) (1993) (session held in Canberra, Australia (Nov. 29-Dec. 3, 1993)).

[205] Certification for Exports; Revised Compliance Policy Guide 7150.01; 59 Fed. Reg. 46,257 (Sept. 7, 1994).

improvements.[206] In late 1996, the FDA published a revision of this Guide to take into account the provisions of the FDA Export Reform Act of 1996 with respect to deadlines and user fees for export certificates.[207]

The FDA issued 12,000 export certificates in 1993 to U.S. exporters of foods, drugs, biologics, and medical devices; this is double the number issued in 1992. In addition to attesting the free sale of the product in this country, the requester often asks that the certification include a statement that the processor is in compliance with GMPs.[208]

The FDA hopes to persuade other countries of the value of alternatives to export certificates that can build confidence in a country's products in a more meaningful, and perhaps less costly, way. The agency seeks MOUs that forego certificates with trading partners. One way to replace export certificates would be for the FDA to allow foreign countries' governments access to information that would relay to them immediately the compliance status of U.S. firms.[209]

The FDA has a database on the compliance status of drug and device firms, known as COMSTAT.[210] Canada, Denmark, and Australia already have access to this system with respect to information in it that is publicly available. Enhanced availability to other countries of a firm's compliance status information would save regulatory resources and exporters' costs. At the same time, widespread availability of information that a firm, when last inspected, was categorized as "Official Action Indicated," or even "Voluntary Action Indicated," would present some of the same difficulties as the agency's Reference List did for device compliance. That list became a contentious issue between the FDA and the medical device industry, and eventually was discontinued.

Regulatory agencies like the FDA — whose focus is on domestic consumer protection — traditionally have viewed preparation of export certificates[211] as a service to industry outside the scope of normal regulatory duties and, therefore, suitable for user fees. Although export certificates are a legitimate international activity, their only value in advancing the FDA's consumer protection mission is when the agency secures reciprocal commitments concerning the compliance of products from other countries.

User fees for FDA export certificates, a feature of the 1996 export reform legislation, are not new; several FDA Centers have long charged for these documents. Because the true cost of this service averages nearly $200, and all sums collected go to the general Treasury rather than to the FDA, Vice President Gore's and President Clinton's 1993 report on reinventing government recommended user fees for export certificates. The FDA Export

---

[206] Report of the FDA Task Force on Export Certificates (1994). In response to the recommendations described in this text, CFSAN issued new standard operating procedures on export certificates.

[207] 61 Fed. Reg. 57,444 (Nov. 6, 1996)

[208] Murphy, *supra* note 215, at 583.

[209] *See id.* at 581.

[210] COMSTAT is an abbreviation for Compliance Status Information System. It was formerly known as GWQAP, the Government-Wide Quality Assurance System, that the FDA developed when the agency assumed responsibility (previously held by the Department of Defense and other procurement agencies) of ensuring the quality of drugs and devices purchased under federal government programs.

[211] The FDA called these certificates "Certificates of Free Sale" prior to a nomenclature change announced on September 7, 1994. *See* 59 Fed. Reg. 46,257; 54 Fed. Reg. 25, 497 (June 15, 1989).

Reform and Enhancement Act of 1996 addressed this goal by providing for the sale of export certificates for drugs and devices (at a cost of up to $175) that the FDA issues within twenty days after request.[212]

In exceptional circumstances the FDA has demanded that certain imports to the United States be accompanied by export certificates from the country of origin, usually pursuant to an MOU with the exporting country. For example, for some years the FDA has had MOUs with several countries regarding dried milk products, in which the exporting countries commit to specific inspection and testing procedures.

FDA Activities with Canada and Mexico

■ Trilateral

Officials of the FDA, Canada's Health Protection Branch (HPB), and Mexico's Subsecretariat de Salud (SSA) come together annually in a meeting called the "Trilateral." Before 1993, the meeting was an FDA-SSA bilateral, but the meeting became trilateral with the conclusion of NAFTA.

FDA, HPB, and SSA officials signed a new MOC in October 1995 that puts in place the framework for what might be called a North American health protection agenda.[213] This activity builds upon many years of cooperation between the United States and its coterminous neighbors regarding food and drug control.

■ Canada-U.S.-Mexico Compliance Information Group

The Canada-U.S.-Mexico Compliance Information Group (CUMCIG) is comprised of compliance and policy officials in the FDA, SSA, HPB, and two other Canadian food agencies (Agriculture and Fisheries). This group meets twice a year and stays in regular contact to strengthen coordination, improve mechanisms for sharing information, and reduce overlap.

Europe

■ The European Union, the European Free Trade Association, and the European Economic Area

FDA regulatory officials, U.S. food and drug law specialists, and industry need to have a basic understanding of today's Europe; its principal treaty groupings; and its basic regula-

---

[212] Pub. L. No. 104-134, § 2102, 110 Stat. 1321 (1996) (codified at 21 U.S.C. § 381(e)(4)(B)).

[213] *See* 61 Fed. Reg. 11,645.

tory approaches to food, drugs, and devices. Although this chapter cannot address all issues to this topic, the following summary may be a helpful primer. Also, the product-specific chapters in these volumes refer to various European regulatory approaches.

The EU was formerly known as the European Community or the European Economic Community, and had its origin in the 1957 Treaty of Rome, signed by the original six members: France, Germany, Italy, and the three Benelux countries (Belgium, Netherlands, and Luxembourg).

The directives, regulations, and laws enacted by EU institutions must be based on this treaty or others entered into by the member states; it is regularly referred to in EU directives. A directive is a requirement directed to the EU member states to incorporate ("transpose") the substance of the directive into their national laws, through legislation or binding administrative rules.

The formation of the EU allowed for free movement of goods, services, capital, and people ("the four freedoms") and, not incidentally, helped ensure permanent peace in Western Europe.[214] The EU originally consisted of six countries but, as of 1997, it has fifteen members — Austria, Belgium, Denmark, Finland, France, Germany, Greece, Ireland, Italy, Luxembourg, the Netherlands, Portugal, Spain, Sweden, and the United Kingdom. Other countries are expected to join by the end of the century (i.e., Bulgaria, the Czech Republic, Estonia, Hungary, Latvia, Lithuania, Poland, Slovakia, Slovenia, and Romania). Turkey has an application for membership pending and has signed an "association agreement" as a building block toward possible future membership.

Other important milestones leading toward alignment of EU laws were the Single European Act of 1986 — setting the stage for the remarkable success of the Community in achieving a single market in 1992 — and the Maastricht Treaty on the European Union, which entered into force on November 1, 1993,[215] and calls for common security and foreign policy as well as an economic and monetary union.

The European Free Trade Association (EFTA) was formed in 1960 to promote closer trade throughout Europe. Originally made up of a larger group, to accommodate original Community hold-outs (such as the United Kingdom, which eventually relented and joined the Community, and Norway, which has not), EFTA, as of 1996, includes Iceland, Norway, Switzerland, and Liechtenstein.

The European Economic Area (EEA) is the result of a treaty that entered into force in January 1, 1993, and includes all fifteen EU countries and three of the four EFTA countries. Switzerland is not in the EEA due to constitutional limits that bar an agreement of this sort because Switzerland is a confederation of quasi-autonomous cantons. As a result, Liechtenstein at one time could not be part of the EEA because its monetary and foreign policy are linked to Switzerland's. The effect of the EEA is to bind EFTA, as well as EU, countries to adopt EU directives in certain areas, notably trade in goods. Although not a signer

---

[214] *See* F. Duchene, Jean Monnet: The First Statesman of Interdependence 224, 292 (W.W. Norton & Co. 1994).

[215] The Treaty on European Union was signed in Maastricht on February 7, 1992. *See* Office for Official Publications of the European Communities, Treaty on European Union: Treaty Establishing the European Community 11-89 (1993).

of the EEA treaty, Switzerland has decided unilaterally to follow EU requirements for goods; consequently their omission from the EEA is a technicality for food, drug, and medical device regulation.

In sum, EU requirements for these products apply directly to nineteen countries, the largest trading bloc in the world. Through bilateral "Europe agreements," another ten or more countries at various stages of accession to the EU are aligning their regulatory requirements to those of the EU.

"Old" and "New" Regulatory Approaches

EU regulatory discussions on foods, drugs, and devices include frequent references to "old approach directives" (exemplified by those on food and drugs) and "new approach directives (exemplified by those on medical devices). The "old approach" refers to the original intent of the EU to write harmonizing directives in all areas involving safety or environment, with enforcement by member state ministries. During the 1960s, 1970s, and early 1980s, substantial progress was made in developing directives for such FDA-regulated products as processed foods, certain chemicals, pharmaceuticals, and cosmetics because the member states already had similar requirements. The distinguishing feature of these "old approach" EU directives for regulated products is their level of detail. Many attempt to define virtually all the characteristics of a product.

For some product categories, the old approach resulted in little progress due to very diverse member state requirements. Two factors — European court rulings striking down diverse member state requirements and frustration with the continued proliferation — led to a "new approach." Under the 1979 *Cassis de Dijon* decision[216] by the European Court of Justice, it is extremely difficult for member countries to impose requirements beyond EU directives. Adopted by the EU Council on May 7, 1985, the new approach departed from the old approach in that harmonization was limited to essential requirements, voluntary standards would supplement requirements, and conformity assessment would be carried out by conformity assessment bodies ("notified bodies") operating under the oversight of member states in accordance with uniform directives.[217]

Medical devices are the only FDA-regulated products falling under the new approach. When EU directives require the use of a third party for conformity assessment, each member country government must ensure that the party is competent to declare that a regulated product is in conformance with the "essential requirements" of a particular "new approach" directive.

Although new approach directives lay down the essential requirements for safety, health, and environment, the specifics are not included in the directive. Rather, the essential requirements serve as general requirements that guide the EU regional standards bodies (CEN and CENELEC) who are responsible for developing Europe-wide standards. The standards developed under the new approach system are voluntary in the sense that manufacturers may refer to other standards when certifying compliance with the directive.

---

[216] Case 120/78, Rewe-Zentral AG v. Burdesmonopolverwaltung .fur Brantwein, 1979-2 E.C.R. 649 (1979)

[217] Council Resolution of 7 May 1985 on a new approach to technical harmonization and standards, 1985 O.J. (C136) 1.

The EU intends to rely on international standards as much as possible for adoption by European standards bodies. Agreements among CEN, CENELEC, ISO, and International Electrotechnical Commission will help achieve this EU objective.

Each member country government provides the EU with a list of "notified bodies"[218] that have been confirmed to be competent under one or more directives. Originally, notified bodies were expected to be located solely in the EU. Subcontracting with bodies outside the EU can be done, however, at the discretion of the notified body, but the main office of the body, rather than any contractor, would be responsible for final assessment. (When the EU enters an MRA with a country such as the United States, these restrictions are related as to that country).[219]

On completion of an acceptable assessment, a certificate, valid for a specific period of time, is issued. Each EU country must accept the results of conformity assessments by notified bodies in all other EU countries unless that country provides extremely compelling reasons to the contrary, under a provision known as the safeguard clause. Each country's government is expected to retain responsibility for enforcement of pertinent directives. The expectation is that market forces would augment governmental efforts by stimulating demand for private third-party assessment, in addition to government inspectional oversight, to effect conformance with requirements and standards. For example, the subject of MRAs between EU countries and accrediting bodies reportedly is being explored; the effect of these agreements could be virtual relinquishment of governmental functions in the EU to nongovernment entities, if the accrediting bodies rather than member state regulators are tasked with oversight of the notified bodies.

Underlying each EU directive is the principle of mutual recognition of member state controls. If a product is deemed to meet essential requirements for acceptability for marketing in one member state, then it may be marketed throughout the EU. No EU country can retain, in principle, national legislation that deviates from an EU directive unless it can prove this retention is necessary to protect the health and safety of its citizens, the environment, or the like.[220]

The FDA's Dealings with the European Union

Since 1989, the FDA has held annual bilateral meetings with European Commission officials in Directorate-General-III (DG-III), Industry, who are responsible for harmonized directives on food, drugs, and devices. A Directorate-General (DG) is an administrative unit in the Commission of the European Communities, more commonly known as the European Commission. The European Commission is not only the executive body of the EU institutions, but also is the only institution that can initiate legislation.

At present, the most intense and productive FDA-EU activities are those carried out in bilateral or multilateral, but manageably sized, harmonization groups. Examples of such groups include working groups of the Codex Alimentarius Committee on Food Additives,

---

[218] A "Notified Body" is a conformity assessment that tests or evaluates products and designs/certifies (may or may not perform the audit) quality systems. The term derives from EC policy that member states notify the Commission as to which bodies on their territory can perform specific evaluations in each directive.

[219] *See* Horton, et al., *supra* note 2.

[220] TREATY OF ROME, *supra* note 110, art. 36.

the International Conference on Harmonization, the Veterinary International Conference on Harmonization, and the Global Harmonization Task Force.

More challenging were activities led by U.S. trade officials (with FDA participation) and EU trade officials in DG-I, External Affairs, to reach an MOU on GLPs, MRAs on drug GMPs and devices, and equivalence agreements on veterinary (animal-derived) food (e.g., meat, poultry, eggs, seafood, dairy products, game meat, and pet food). In discussions driven by a trade liberalization agenda, the FDA has insisted on information about the adequacy of member states' systems, exchange of inspection reports rather than certificates, and the importing country's right of inspection when that country deems it necessary. In 1997, the FDA completed negotiating the texts of MRAs with the EU on drugs and devices as well as the veterinary equivalence agreement.

During the 1970s and 1980s, the FDA entered into bilateral GLP MOU's with regulatory counterparts in six EU member states (France, Germany, Italy, the Netherlands, Sweden, and the United Kingdom). Because the advent of an EU-wide GLP program meant that only the European Commission can negotiate new MOUs starting in 1993, the FDA, EPA, and representatives of the European Commission began discussions toward a U.S.-EU GLP agreement. Although several drafts were exchanged in the 1994-1995 period, discussions broke down due to differences on the subject of whether, once the agreement was signed, a regulatory authority such as the FDA could continue to schedule foreign inspections when it deemed it necessary and could continue to receive inspection results.

Trade Issues

The FDA was an active participant in developing NAFTA and GATT. By doing so, the agency played a part in strengthening the basic principles that a country can set the level of protection its citizenry wants, as expressed through the laws it enforces, and that harmonization does not mean harmonizing downward.

Some observers have been concerned that harmonization could result in lowered standards, with potential adverse effects on public health protection.[221] This concern was expressed in comments on the FDA's proposed standards policy.[222] The Clinton Administration issued a paper intended to allay these concerns. Also, the FDA's final standards policy[223] offered reassurance that the FDA's participation in international harmonization activities is intended to safeguard the U.S. public health and to ensure that consumer protection standards and requirements are met.

By continuing to stay involved in the implementation phase, the FDA can make sure that its mandates, values, and expertise are factored into international decisions. Since 1994, the FDA and EPA have had seats on two key committees under the Office of the U.S.

---

[221] *See* PUBLIC CITIZEN, *supra* note 128.

[222] *See generally* 59 Fed. Reg. at 60,870.

[223] 60 Fed. Reg. at 53,078.

Trade Representative — the Trade Policy Staff Committee and the Trade Policy Review Group. These memberships are crucial to improved communication and understanding between the regulatory agencies and trade agencies: the FDA can inject consumer protection interests into discussions with other countries; the FDA can help the U.S. government refrain from criticizing other countries that enforce regulatory systems similar to the FDA's; the FDA can more effectively deflect pressure to engage in unwarranted restrictions of imports from countries that are unfairly shutting out U.S. products; the FDA learns of deficiencies in other countries' intellectual property protection laws that may call for heightened scrutiny of those countries' requests for nonpublic information or technical assistance; and the FDA obtains useful information about developments in countries' economic relations with the United States that have implications for the levels of imports or their compliance status (for example, exchange rate changes, antidumping cases, or tariff or quota preferences given developing countries).

The FDA also is active in several aspects of WTO and NAFTA implementation, particularly the NAFTA Committee on Standards-Related Measures, the NAFTA Committee on SPS Measures, and the WTO SPS Committee.

Progress toward trade agreements continues, with active discussions underway since 1989 in the Asia Pacific Economic Cooperation forum, since 1994 in a Free Trade Area of the Americas (FTAA), and since late 1995 regarding a free trade relationship with the EU called the Transatlantic Marketplace. The goal of a Transatlantic Marketplace would be in lieu of a formal U.S.-EU free trade agreement, which is considered both unnecessary — in light of already-high levels of trade — and possibly detrimental to the nascent WTO. MRAs generally, as well as a harmonized core technical data set in the studies supporting pharmaceutical marketing approvals, have been adopted as objectives in the Transatlantic Marketplace. FDA participates in these discussions because standards regarding FDA-regulated products can operate as "technical barriers to trade."

Relevant to the FTAA is that on January 1, 1995, the Mercado Comun del Sur (MERCOSUR),[224] or common market of the south, came into being. With NAFTA countries, the Andean pact countries, and the Caribbean trade area countries, MERCOSUR is a major building block toward the achievement of FTAA objectives. Encompassing Argentina, Brazil, Paraguay, and Uruguay, with possible expansion to Bolivia and Chile, MERCOSUR is worthy of attention by U.S. regulatory officials and industry for several reasons. First, regulators from the four MERCOSUR countries are writing standards that in some instances try to achieve harmony between U.S. and EU requirements. Second, these countries collectively comprise the fourth largest economic bloc in the world — after the NAFTA countries, the EU, and Japan — and are therefore "big emerging markets" (a U.S. Commerce Department term) for U.S. exports. Third, they are major producers of imports into the United States, particularly foods, and the FDA and U.S. consumers have an interest in the MERCOSUR countries having strong, effective laws that ensure the safety of these products. Fourth, trade liberalization and the elimination of internal borders among these countries has implications for international narcotics control in that there would be fewer checkpoints on what is crossing international borders.

---

[224] MERCOSUR is the Spanish name; MERCOSUL is the Portuguese name

The FDA's Budget and Administrative Structures for International Activities

■ Budget

All resources for international harmonization derive from the FDA's basic operating budget, because the agency has not been appropriated any money earmarked for international harmonization.[225]

In 1994, work specifically identified as international — including foreign inspections, technical assistance, harmonization activities such as standards, and administrative costs — was estimated to comprise five to six percent of FDA's budget.[226] This sum included foreign inspections, technical aid, and the costs associated with implementing and defining International Conference on Harmonization (ICH) and other standards. This figure does not take into account the extent to which almost every decision made or activity undertaken by the FDA has an international aspect. A factor that compels refocusing of the FDA's international activities and a new emphasis on harmonization is the almost certain prospect that the agency's budget will not grow in corresponding proportion to the expanding demands on its resources. Therefore, in all of its activities — domestic and international — the FDA must set priorities and make more efficient use of its resources.

■ Organizing the FDA's International Programs

Evolution of FDA's International Organizational Structures

FDA Field offices took responsibility for the agency's early international activities through their efforts to screen and detain violative imports. The FDA has been an international agency since its origins.

In the 1960s, the agency began to look for preventive approaches. For example, the New York District met with foreign consulate officials on import detentions,[227] and the Dallas District inaugurated bilateral meetings with Mexico on recurrent import problems with products such as cantaloupes, strawberries, and shellfish.[228] In 1974, that office established a Mexican liaison staff and, under a new agreement with Mexico, trained Mexican chemists in techniques of pesticide analysis so that Mexican labs could examine fruits and vegetables intended for the U.S. market and certify that legal residue tolerances have not been exceeded.[229]

The Office of Legislative and Governmental Services handled international relations as well as congressional and state relations from 1966 to 1970.[230] Under Commissioner Charles Edwards' 1970 reorganization, international activities were split between the

---

[225] FDA TASK FORCE REPORT, *supra* note 4, at 36.

[226] Naomi Kawin, FDA, Estimate (1994).

[227] Interview with John Zaic, FDA Oral History Project 19 (Dec. 4, 1986).

[228] Interview with Kenneth A. Hansen, FDA Oral History Project 31-35 (June 13, 1990).

[229] FOOD AND DRUG ADMIN., ANNUAL REPORT 1974, at 1015-16.

[230] Telephone interview with Paul Pumpian, Dir., Off. of Legislative and Gov't. Servs., 1966-1970 (Apr. 11, 1996).

Offices of the Associate Commissioner for Regulatory Affairs and the Associate Commissioner for Science.

ORA enforcement leaders such as the Associate Commissioner for Regulatory Affairs and the Executive Director, Regional Operations, began to seek out cooperative and preventive approaches to import problems, carried out by an ORA International Affairs Office.[231] In 1968, a program of briefings was conducted in Washington, D.C. for the commercial, agricultural, and economic attachés for foreign governments to acquaint them with FDA requirements, in hopes of reducing the incidence of rejected imports.[232]

In 1971, an import strategy was developed.[233] An Assistant for Import Operations provided central direction of imports activities, and a number of innovative approaches to imports were initiated (ship-to-ship inspections in major ports, circuit-rider coverage of smaller ports, use of mobile laboratories, use of a new Report of Import Entry form, voluntary cooperation by the spice trade, overseas inspections, technical advice to producers and officials in other countries, and cooperative agreements with other governments).[234]

The scientific offices of the FDA — the Bureau of Science during the 1960s, the Office of the Associate Commissioner for Science during the 1970s, and the FDA Bureaus/Centers during the last three decades — have assumed leadership positions in various international organizations. These include WHO and later ICH.

The demise of the FDA's Office of Science resulted in the movement of its nonregulatory international activities first to a free-standing Office of International Affairs, then to the Office of the Associate Commissioner for Health Affairs.

Led by the FDA's Associate Commissioner for Health Affairs, Dr. Stuart Nightingale, the Office of Health Affairs established important relationships with the FDA's counterparts in other countries, particularly pharmaceutical regulators. It also played a leadership role in strengthening bonds with the Commission of the European Communities during its successful drive to a harmonized internal market. The many U.S.-like features of EU legislation are a credit to the cooperation of this era. As was mentioned earlier, the FDA began holding regular bilaterals with the Commission in 1989.

Agency Organizational Changes Under Commissioner Kessler

When David A. Kessler, M.D., became Commissioner of Food and Drugs in 1990, he reorganized the Office of the Commissioner, and with respect to international activities:

- created an Office of Policy, headed by a Deputy Commissioner for Policy, to be responsible for domestic policy and for international harmonization, including standards and bilateral inspection agreements;
- combined under a Deputy Commissioner for External Affairs several of the Associate Commissioner offices that previously had reported directly to the Commissioner; among these was the Office of Health Affairs and, under it at the time, the International

---

[231] Interview with John Zaic, *supra* note 238, at 20-21, 38-42.

[232] FOOD AND DRUG ADMIN., ANNUAL REPORTS 1968, at 625.

[233] Interview with John Zaic, *supra* note 238, at 20.

[234] FOOD AND DRUG ADMIN., ANNUAL REPORTS 1971, at 803-04.

Affairs Staff;

- established a new position of Deputy Commissioner for Operations to oversee the Centers and ORA, all of which have vital international responsibilities;
- named a Deputy Commissioner/Senior Advisor, who met the need for high-level FDA leadership when, after the collapse of the U.S.S.R. in 1990, the Russian Federation and new independent states requested U.S. technical assistance to strengthen their regulatory capabilities in the areas of vaccines, other drugs, foods, and medical devices; and
- established a new position and appointed a Deputy Commissioner for Management and Operations, who personally led several important information technology initiatives to improve safety data management, and whose Office of Planning and Operations developed a strategic plan with international vision, described earlier in this chapter.

International Focal Points

In response to a recommendation of the FDA Harmonization Task Force,[235] each FDA Center and Office established a contact point for international activities, suitable to its structure and activities. In particular, the Office of Regulatory Affairs has strengthened its leadership on international enforcement issues, through an International Regulatory Issues Office, established in 1995.

To give focus to the agency's international harmonization, standards, trade, and agreements activity, in late 1993 Dr. Kessler created an Office of International Policy within the Office of Policy, headed by the author, and provided it with agency-wide leadership responsibility.[236] This office:

- plans, directs, and coordinates a comprehensive international policy program for the FDA; serves as the agency focal point on international policy, including harmonization, trade negotiations, and international standard-setting, to facilitate communication and decisionmaking within the agency on international policy, and to enhance FDA representation in international policy activities;
- plays a leadership role in the FDA's formulation of international policy, particularly when issues involve more than one component of the agency, through coordination and negotiations with other affected components;
- advises the Commissioner, Deputy Commissioner for Policy, and other Deputy Commissioners and senior agency officials on the formulation of broad agency international regulatory policy; and, in cooperation with the International Affairs Office, keeps them informed of international developments that may affect current or proposed FDA policies; and
- represents the agency on international policy matters with other federal agencies, at international meetings, and before international groups, in cooperation with the International Affairs Office. (The other federal agencies include the U.S. Trade Representative, the Department of State, and the Department of Commerce).

Placement of the FDA's international policy leadership in the Office of Policy recognizes the considerable synergy between the FDA's domestic policy and its international policy

---

[235] FDA TASK FORCE REPORT, *supra* note 4, at ix.

[236] 58 Fed. Reg. 58,699 (Nov. 3, 1993).

priorities, particularly given the increasingly global focus of various executive branch and congressional reform proposals, as discussed in the beginning of this chapter.

The appointment of Sharon Smith Holston as Deputy Commissioner for External Affairs in late 1994 launched a new era of international leadership in the FDA, particularly concerning ICH and MRAs. To give more prominence to the FDA's burgeoning international activities, the office of International Affairs was removed from the Office of Health Affairs and elevated to a separate unit under the Office of External Affairs in 1995. The Office of Health Affairs continues to coordinate ICH and WHO matters, as well as drug abuse scheduling activities. The Office of International Affairs, headed by Walter Batts, coordinates a wide range of international activities other than those coordinated by the Office of Policy, as discussed above, or the Office of Health Affairs. For example, the Office of International Affairs:

- provides leadership and direction as the agency focal point for developing and maintaining international communications and programs;
- establishes and provides an agency liason on international activities with the Department of Health and Human Services, other federal agencies, foreign governments, including foreign embassies, and international organizations;
- represents the agency at meetings, conferences, and symposia relating to the FDA's international activities; plans and implements bilateral or multilateral meetings with foreign counterparts' officials to address common issues;
- establishes and maintains an international information exchange program conerning agency policies and programs to provide interchange between the FDA and counterpart agencies in foreign countries and international organizations;[237]
- assists in the development, negotiation, and monitoring of agreements with foreign governments and international organizations in cooperation with other agency components;
- negotiates the preparation and implementation of technical assistance programs (including formal training programs and surveys) with foreign governments and international organizations in areas relating to the agency mission; and
- directs the agency's International Visitors Program, providing participants with policy briefings, technical training, and/or assistance in response to specific needs.

The office of Health Affairs retained responsibility for WHO, ICH coordination, and international drug abuse control matters.

If there is a single lesson the FDA would draw from this decade, it is that international issues are no longer isolated from domestic issues; virtually every FDA program engenders and encounters international issues in its everyday operations.

---

[237] *See, e.g.*, FOOD AND DRUG ADMIN., INFORMATION GUIDE FOR THE INTERNATIONAL COMMUNITY (1995) (available from Off. of Int'l Affrs, FDA, Rockville, MD).

Conclusion

The FDA has formulated a strong and coherent approach to harmonization, one that underlines the importance of participation in this work, as long as it contributes to the agency's mission by enhancing consumer protection. This goal has a substantive aspect — upholding protective standards and refraining from least-common-denominator standards. This goal has a fiscal aspect — avoiding activities that consume scarce resources without corresponding gains, and seeking innovative funding sources for necessary activities. This goal also has a procedural aspect — deciding how the FDA can incorporate preferred international or voluntary domestic standards into enforceable food and drug laws. The procedural answer lies in U.S. domestic administrative law and food and drug law, namely the issuance of FDA regulations under section 701(a) of the FDCA.

Just over fifty years ago, President Franklin Delano Roosevelt made the observation, as true today as then, "We have learned that we cannot live alone, at peace; that our own well-being is dependent on the well-being of other nations, far away . . . . We have learned to be citizens of the world, members of the human community."

Appendix: Trade Agreements

The principal trade agreements of interest to the FDA are those on the Application of Sanitary and Phytosanitary Measures[238] and on Technical Barriers to Trade in both the WTO Agreement (the Uruguay Round of the GATT) and the earlier NAFTA. This appendix summarizes the provisions in WTO and NAFTA that would be relevant in challenges to food laws, for readers interested in this degree of technical legal detail.

■ GATT

The GATT is a global trade agreement that entered into force on January 1, 1948, and has been amended several times following negotiations known as "rounds." The term "GATT" also was used for many years to describe the institutional body in Geneva that administered the agreement. As of January 1, 1995, this body became a new international organization known as the WTO.

■ The WTO and the Uruguay Round Agreements

The most recent GATT round, the Uruguay Round, was so-named because it began in Punta del Este, Uruguay in 1986. It was concluded in Geneva on December 15, 1993, and

---

[238] SPS measures include measures "to protect human or animal life or health within the territory of the Member from risks arising from additives, contaminants, toxins, or disease-causing organisms in foods, beverages or feedstuffs . . . ." SPS measures include "all relevant laws, decrees, regulations, requirements and procedures including,*inter alia*, end product criteria; processes and production methods; testing, inspection, certification and approval procedures . . . provisions on relevant statistical methods, sampling procedures and methods of risk assessment; and packaging and labeling requirements directly related to food safety." SPS Agreement, annex A.

formally signed by the contracting parties at the Marrakech Ministerial Meeting on April 15, 1994.

Under U.S. law, the formally signed trade agreement enters into force only after both Houses of Congress have passed implementing legislation and the President has signed this legislation. The domestic ratification process for a trade agreement is thus somewhat different from that applicable to a treaty, which is ratified by a two-thirds vote of the Senate without need for House action or legislation presented to the President.

Congressional consideration of the legislation to implement the Uruguay Round WTO agreement occurred in late 1994 and was signed by the President on December 8, 1994.[239]

As with other recent trade agreements, including its 1993 ratification of NAFTA, Congress committed itself to use of a fast-track procedure during its consideration of the legislation to implement the Uruguay Round.[240] This procedure limits debate, forbids amendment, includes expedited deadlines, and forces each member to vote on the agreement as a whole. The purpose of the procedure is to protect the credibility of the President and his ambassador on these matters, the United States Trade Representative (USTR). Without an advance commitment by Congress to refrain from tampering with the carefully negotiated terms of trade agreements, the leaders of other countries would have no confidence in the ability of the President and the USTR to make good faith agreements in trade negotiations.

At the time this chapter was written, the fast-track authority had expired, and Chile's accession to NAFTA was stalled due to congressional failure to re-enact such legislation.

Before discussing provisions in the WTO Agreement added by the Uruguay Round, a general review of long-standing WTO principles that remain relevant to the issue of whether a country can maintain its own unique food and drug laws would be in order.

Article III on National Treatment

Article III, paragraph 4 of the WTO agreement has long required that "[t]he products of the territory of any contracting party imported into the territory of any other contracting party shall be accorded treatment no less favorable than that accorded to like products of national origin in respect of all laws, regulations, and requirements affecting their internal sale, offering for sale, purchase, transportation, distribution, or use."

Equality of treatment of domestic and imported goods is the key principle, and is closely related to Article I's assurance of "most favored nation" treatment among WTO contracting parties: "With respect to . . . all rules and formalities in connection with importation and exportation, . . . any advantage, favour, privilege or immunity granted by any contracting party to any product originating in or destined for any other country shall be accorded immediately and unconditionally to the like product originating in or destined for the territories of all other contracting parties."

Article XX sets forth general exceptions to such general GATT principles as the national treatment test:

---

[239] Pub. L. No. 103-465, 108 Stat. 4809 (codified at 19 U.S.C. §§ 2531-2582).
[240] 19 U.S.C. § 2191.

Subject to the requirement that such measures are not applied in a manner which would constitute a means of arbitrary or unjustifiable discrimination between countries where the same conditions prevail, or a disguised restriction on international trade, nothing in this Agreement shall be construed to prevent the adoption or enforcement by any contracting parties of measures. . . necessary to protect human, animal or plant life or health [or] . . . necessary to secure compliance with laws or regulations which are not inconsistent with the provisions of this Agreement, including those relating to . . . prevention of deceptive practices . . . .

FDA's statutes and implementing regulations clearly meet the national-treatment and most-favored-nation tests. These U.S. requirements are "trade blind" in that they give equal treatment to all foods, whatever their origin. Because FDA regulations thus create a level playing field, it should not be necessary for the United States, if called upon to defend the regulations, to invoke Article XX of the WTO agreement.

FDA's regulations are necessary both to protect human health and to prevent deceptive practices, and therefore should meet these criteria. In the unlikely event of a WTO dispute about these requirements, the case should not reach the issue of the applicability of an exception, since the case will be resolved under the national treatment standard and other disciplines discussed below, as a valid exercise of a sovereign's right to establish a reasonable program to fulfill a legitimate objective. No FDA regulation has ever been the subject of a GATT case. The agency is hopeful that this will continue with the WTO.

Only member countries of WTO can bring cases under the WTO agreements. To understand how a WTO challenge to FDA requirements would need to be framed, it is necessary to turn to a discussion of the three relevant agreements: the Agreement on Technical Barriers to Trade, the Agreement on the Application of Sanitary and Phytosanitary Measures, and the Agreement on Dispute Resolution.

The SPS Agreement applies to measures directly related to food safety and those otherwise pertaining to protection of human life or health from risks arising from additives, contaminants, toxins or disease-causing organisms in foods, beverages, or feedstuffs.

The Previous Agreement on Technical Barriers to Trade

This agreement entered into force on January 1, 1980, as part of the Tokyo Round of the GATT concluded the preceding year. It was replaced by the TBT Agreement on January 1, 1995, when the new WTO agreements entered into force. The TBT Agreement was developed to address the fact that, as tariffs and other economic trade barriers fell as a result of earlier GATT rounds, trade continued to be hindered by national technical regulations and standards that had either the intent or the effect of excluding imports.

Although the original TBT Agreement has been replaced, its provisions are worth a brief summary, even if only as a reminder that the new WTO agreements are not the first to target countries' use of regulations that have the intent or effect of unduly encumbering trade. In the fifteen years that the TBT code was in effect, there were no disputes under it. Thus, there has been no jurisprudence under the old TBT that can be used to address how issues will be resolved under the present TBT code. National regulatory bodies hope that the new TBT code will achieve success more as process-oriented transparency measure as an "International APA (Administrative Procedure Act)," than as a license to litigate.

In any event, the TBT Agreement is, first and foremost, a transparency code designed to open up the rulemaking processes of trading partners with respect to mandatory technical regulations and voluntary standards. As discussed below, it also encourages adoption of international standards, and requires contracting parties to notify each other of new technical regulations.

The TBT Agreement contains several provisions — notably the prohibition against unnecessary obstacles to international trade in article 2.1, paragraph 1 — that are pertinent to the present discussion:

> 2.1 Members were required to ensure that technical regulations and standards are not prepared, adopted or applied with a view to creating obstacles to international trade. Furthermore, products imported from the territory of any Party were required to be accorded treatment no less favorable than that accorded to like products of national origin and to like products originating in any other country in relation to such technical regulations or standards. They likewise were required to ensure that neither technical regulations nor standards themselves nor their application have the effect of creating unnecessary obstacles to international trade.

The U.S. implementing legislation clarified that "no standards-related activity of any private person, Federal agency, or State agency shall be deemed to constitute an unnecessary obstacle to the foreign commerce of the United States if the demonstrable purpose of the standards-related activity is to achieve a legitimate domestic objective including, but not limited to, the protection of legitimate health or safety, environmental, or consumer interests and if such activity does not operate to exclude imported products which fully meet the objectives of such activity."

Present Agreement on Technical Barriers to Trade

The present Agreement largely carries over the provisions of the earlier TBT Agreement, and extends the Agreement beyond product-related technical regulations and voluntary standards to also cover conformity assessment procedures, product-related process, and production methods.

Of relevance to this chapter is the strengthening of the language in the preamble recognizing a country's right to enact consumer protection laws and of the anti-trade-barrier disciplines in articles 2.1 and 2.2.

The language that follows shows how the new TBT Agreement adds a new phrase in the preamble to clarify the ability of countries to take measures at the levels of protection it considers appropriate:

> [N]o country should be prevented from taking measures necessary to ensure the quality of its exports, or for the protection of human, animal or plant health, of the environment, or for the prevention of deceptive practices, *at the levels it considers appropriate*, subject to the requirement that they are not applied in a

manner which would constitute a means of arbitrary or unjustifiable discrimination between countries where the same conditions prevail or a disguised restriction on international trade . . . .

Part of the negotiating history of this language is a discussion in a letter dated December 15, 1993, from Peter D. Sutherland, the Director-General of the GATT, to Ambassador John Schmidt, the Chief U.S. Negotiator:

> Representatives of the participants involved in the discussions agreed that each government is free to choose the levels it considers appropriate for the protection of human animal or plant life or health and of the environment and that no country should be prevented from taking measures necessary to achieve those levels subject to the requirement, *inter alia*, that the measures are in accordance with the provisions of the Agreement. This has been reflected in the fifth clause of the Preamble to the Agreement. It was clear from our consultations also that participants felt the Agreement could not be read, most particularly because of this preambular clause, to require the upward or downward harmonization of technical regulations or standards as a result of international harmonization activities.

New article 2.1 merely carries over the national treatment and most-favored-nation clauses found in the second sentence of the old article 2.1.

New article 2.2 sets forth the central (and, arguably, the only) discipline in the new TBT Agreement, with its "no more trade-restrictive than necessary" test underlined in this excerpt:

> 2.2 Members shall ensure that technical regulations are not prepared, adopted or applied with a view to or with the effect of creating unnecessary obstacles to international trade. *For this purpose, technical regulations shall not be more trade-restrictive than necessary to fulfil a legitimate objective taking account of the risks non-fulfillment would create. Such legitimate objectives are inter alia* . . . the prevention or deceptive practices [or] protection of human health or safety . . .

In the final days of the Uruguay Round negotiations, U.S. negotiators succeeded in securing the deletion of a footnote to 2.2 that might have proved problematic for countries defending regulations attacked as unduly trade-restrictive. This footnote originally had been favored by the United States as possibly helpful in shielding legitimate regulations, but its "proportionality approach" turned out to have some unwanted jurisprudential issues — particularly from European environmental law perspective — that could have been read to compel an economic balancing test even where it would have been inappropriate to the underlying legitimate objective at stake.

In the closing days of the Uruguay Round, the U.S. negotiators on the TBT Agreement sought unsuccessfully to replace the proportionality footnote to article 2.2 with a new footnote designed to clarify how article 2.2 would operate. This effort was unsuccessful because other countries' negotiators thought it inappropriate to reopen the TBT text to include an explanation considered unnecessary.

A footnote of the type sought for the TBT Agreement, by a separate multilateral technical group in the final Uruguay Round discussions, already had been added to the draft text of the new SPS Agreement. At the same time, its language was revised to eliminate a phrase compelling measures that were not the "least restrictive to trade," in favor of the following, which is more consistent with the test in article 2.2 of TBT Agreement:

> 21. Without prejudice to paragraph 10 [according presumptive validity to SPS measures which conform to international standards], when establishing or maintaining sanitary or phytosanitary measures to achieve the appropriate level of sanitary or phytosanitary protection, Members shall ensure that such measures are not more trade restrictive than required to achieve their appropriate level of protection, taking into account technical and economic feasibility.

The footnote accompanying paragraph 21 reads:

> For purposes of paragraph 21, a measure is not more trade restrictive than required unless there is another measure, reasonably available taking into account technical and economic feasibility, that achieves the appropriate level of protection and is significantly less restrictive to trade.

It had been a U.S. negotiating objective in the concluding GATT negotiations to attach a footnote of this type not only to paragraph 21 of the SPS Agreement, but also to article 2.2 of the TBT Agreement. Although this objective was achieved for SPS but not TBT, the December 15, 1993, letter from Peter Sutherland to John Schmidt included the following helpful discussion of the TBT negotiations:

> Representatives of the participants involved in the discussions also agreed that the removal of the existing footnote to Article 2.2 of the Agreement was an improvement to the text.

> It was not possible to achieve the necessary level of support for the U.S. proposal to add a new footnote to article 2.2 and 2.3 of the new TBT Agreement. The U.S. proposal for such a footnote was:

>> For purposes of paragraphs 2 and 3 of Article 2, a technical regulation to protect human health or safety, animal or plant life or health, or the environment, or to prevent deceptive practices, is not more trade-restrictive than necessary, and the changed circumstances or objectives cannot be addressed in a less trade-restrictive manner, unless there is another technical regulation, including alternative versions of the technical regulation, reasonably available taking into account technical and economic feasibility, that fulfills the legitimate objective and is significantly less restrictive to trade.

> Nevertheless, it was clear from our consultations at the expert level that participants felt it was obvious from other provisions of the [new TBT] Agreement that the Agreement does not concern itself with insignificant trade effects nor could a measure be considered more trade-restrictive than necessary in the absence of a reasonably available alternative.

This negotiating history is also relevant to article 2.3 of the new TBT Agreement, a new provision that "[t]echnical regulations shall not be maintained if the circumstances or objectives can be addressed in a less trade-restrictive manner." This provision describes how regulations already in place will be judged under the new TBT.

Article 2.4 of the new TBT Agreement continues and strengthens the duty under article 2.2 of the old TBT Agreement to consider international standards, as a basis for national voluntary standards as well as mandatory technical regulations (new language is italicized and deleted language is struck out):

> 2.4 Where technical regulations *or standards* are required and relevant international standards exist or their completion is imminent, Members shall use them, or the relevant parts of them, as a basis for their technical regulations or standards except where, ~~as duly explained upon request,~~ such international standards or relevant parts ~~are inappropriate for the Parties concerned, for~~ *inter alia* ~~such reasons as . . . the prevention of deceptive practices [or] protection for human health or safety...~~ *would be an ineffective or inappropriate means for the fulfillment of the legitimate objectives pursued, for instance because of fundamental climatic or geographical factors or fundamental technological problems.*

FDA believes that the its regulations have neither the intent nor the effect of creating unnecessary obstacles to international trade and are not more trade-restrictive than necessary to fulfill their legitimate objective. The TBT Agreement preamble states the right of a country to take measures necessary to protect human health and to prevent deceptive practices, *at the levels it considers appropriate*.

Agreement on the Application of Sanitary and Phytosanitary Measures

The food measures that are subject to the SPS Agreement are those measures directly related to food safety and those otherwise pertaining to protection of human life or health from risks arising from additives, contaminants, toxins or disease-causing organisms in foods, beverages, or feedstuffs.

The provisions of the SPS Agreement that would be relevant in a trade challenge to a food law are:

- Countries have a right to adopt and enforce measures necessary to protect human health that are nondiscriminatory (preamble and article 2).
- Countries shall ensure that any SPS measure is applied only to the extent necessary to protect human health, is based on scientific principles, and is not maintained without sufficient scientific evidence (article 2).
- Countries shall base their SPS measures on international standards, except that they may introduce or maintain SPS measures that result in a higher level of SPS protection if there is a scientific justification, or as a consequence of the level of protection a country determines to be appropriate (article 3).
- There is a scientific justification to deviate from an international standard if, on the basis of an examination and evaluation of available scientific information in conformity with the relevant provisions of the SPS agreement, a country determines that the rele-

vant international standards is not sufficient to achieve its appropriate level of protection (footnote to article 3).

- Countries are required to accept the SPS measures of other countries as equivalent only if the exporting country objectively demonstrates to the importing country that its measures achieve the importing country's appropriate level of SPS protection (article 4).

FDA believes that its regulations would satisfy the standards in the TBT and SPS agreements. The regulations are nondiscriminatory, solidly grounded in science, and based on what the United States has chosen as the appropriate level of protection.

WTO Dispute Settlement

A detailed discussion of the new WTO dispute procedures is beyond the scope of this chapter. In sum, if a trade challenge were to be brought against an FDA regulation or any other nation's food and drug law under the new WTO and were to result in a final decision that the law being challenged is inconsistent with the WTO agreements, e.g., is more trade-restrictive than necessary to fulfil the public health objective at stake under the new TBT Agreement, the country should re-examine the law. Pressure to do so would be much greater than occurred under the old WTO procedure.

Although no country is ever compelled to change a law in response to an adverse WTO ruling, under the old or new procedures trade sanctions in the form of compensation and the suspension of concessions or other obligations are available, in the event that a country does not implement a WTO ruling within a reasonable time.

The new WTO places increased pressure on countries to accept rulings, through a strengthened dispute-resolution procedure. Whereas, in the old WTO, a single member (even the losing party) could block adoption of a WTO decision, the new WTO procedure requires that a WTO appellate report be adopted and unconditionally accepted by the parties to the dispute unless there is a consensus decision by the Dispute Settlement Body not to adopt the report within thirty days after its issuance to WTO members. It also has deadlines and procedures for automatic appeals, designed to expedite resolution of trade disputes and prevent them from languishing.

Informal conciliatory processes precede dispute settlement. These steps include informal communications, consultations, conciliation, mediation, and arbitration. When a dispute goes to a panel for resolution, each party has the option of requesting the establishment of a technical expert group to assist in questions of a technical nature.

■ NAFTA

SRM and SPS

NAFTA's relevant provisions on Standards-Related Measures (SRMs corresponding to the TBT agreement) and on SPS measures provide as follows:

- Each party may adopt, maintain, or apply any standards-related measure, including any such measure relating to safety; the protection of human, animal, or plant life or health; the environment or consumers; and any measure to ensure its enforcement or implementation (SRM article 904.1, SPS article 712.1).

- Each party may establish the levels of protection it considers appropriate (SRM Article 904.2, SPS article 712.2).
- Measures must be nondiscriminatory (SRM article 904.3, 907.2; SPS article 712.4).
- Measures may not have the intent or effect of creating an unnecessary obstacle to trade. An unnecessary obstacle to trade is not created by a legal provision whose purpose is to achieve a legitimate objective and that does not exclude a party's goods that meet that objective (SRM article 904.4).
- International standards are to be used as the basis for national standards and are presumed to be consistent with NAFTA. Parties can apply any standards-related measure, however, that results in a higher level of protection. (SRM article 905, SPS article 713).
- Parties shall work toward compatibility of measures and treat as equivalent a measure that an exporting party demonstrates to the satisfaction of the importing party that will adequately fulfill the importing party's legitimate objectives (SRM article 906, SPS article 714).
- Each party may conduct risk assessment (TBT 907.1, SPS article 715). Each party shall ensure that its SPS measures are science-based (SPS article 712.3).
- SPS measures shall be applied only to the extent necessary to achieve the appropriate level of protection, taking into account technical and economic feasibility (SPS article 712.5).
- There is no language similar to that in article 2.2 of the new WTO-TBT Agreement to the effect that regulations be no more trade restrictive than necessary.

NAFTA Dispute Resolution

As a general rule, disputes arising under both WTO and NAFTA may be settled in either forum "at the discretion of the complaining party." In any dispute arising under NAFTA-TBT or NAFTA-SPS, however, the responding party may request that the dispute be considered under NAFTA dispute resolution procedures. If the responding party so requests, the dispute is resolved under NAFTA. Thus, although NAFTA would not preclude Canada or Mexico from bringing a trade dispute against the United States under the WTO, if the matter concerns a standard or an SPS measure the United States has the option of having the matter resolved through NAFTA dispute resolution.

chapter 6

Human Drug Regulation

Geoffrey M. Levitt*
James N. Czaban**
Andrea S. Paterson***

Introduction: The Continuing Evolution of FDA Drug Review

From the moment a new drug compound enters preclinical testing, it is comprehensively regulated by the Food and Drug Administration (FDA) at every step of the way. The agency not only decides when and whether the drug has met the substantive standards required for marketing approval, but also establishes and enforces the rules governing how it must be investigated to determine its safety and efficacy, how it must be manufactured, how its use must be monitored following approval, and many other aspects of its existence.

In short, the FDA literally holds life-and-death power over a new drug. That power is exercised in an arena populated by influential players with vital interests at stake — drug companies, patient groups, doctors, pharmacists, managed care organizations, health care payers, and others. It is understandable that the FDA's regulation of human drugs is a perennial target of criticism and proposals for reform.

In recent years, the debate increasingly has centered on the issue of speeding up the drug review process. The result, as discussed below, has been a series of regulatory and legislative initiatives ranging from user fees to accelerated approval. Beyond these specific changes, there unquestionably has been a broadening of the drug review process, with increased participation by advisory committees and others outside the FDA.

As of this writing, more fundamental reform of the drug review process has proven elusive, with the notable exception of drug exports. Even those steps that have produced con-

* Mr. Levitt is a Partner and Head of the Food and Drug Law Practice in the law firm of Venable, Baetjer, Howard & Civiletti, Washington, D.C.

** Mr. Czaban is a Senior Associate in the law firm of Venable, Baetjer, Howard & Civiletti, Washington, D.C.

*** Ms. Paterson is a Senior Associate in the law firm of Venable, Baetjer, Howard & Civiletti, Washington, D.C.

The authors would like to express their appreciation to Adrianne G. Threatt for her diligence and perseverance in the preparation of this chapter.

crete results, like user fees, have only partially smoothed out the inherent uncertainties and complexities of the new drug review process. Meanwhile, the area in which the FDA's powers are in some ways at their strongest — namely, the regulation of drug manufacturing — has thus far received relatively little attention as a subject of reform efforts.

This chapter should therefore be likened to a snapshot of a regulatory system in a state of continuing evolution. Its emphasis is on both the fundamental constants of the FDA regulatory process, and on the more important and enduring of the recent changes to that process. The first half of the chapter is devoted to a description of the key regulatory phases through which the typical new drug must pass, from preclinical testing to clinical investigation to new drug application (NDA) review to postmarketing oversight. Its second half concentrates on "special cases" such as generic drugs, antibiotics, over-the-counter drugs, combination drugs, and exports. Finally, a short reference section is included for readers in search of more detailed knowledge of any of the topics covered herein.

FDA Drug Review: The Standard Model

The Federal Food, Drug, and Cosmetic Act (FDCA) defines the term "drug" to include 1) articles recognized in the U.S. Pharmacopeia, the U.S. Homeopathic Pharmacopeia, or the National Formulary; 2) articles "intended for use in the diagnosis, cure, mitigation, treatment, or prevention of disease;" 3) articles (other than food) "intended to affect the structure or any function of the body;" and 4) articles intended for use as a component of any of the above.[1] With two exceptions — drugs that are "generally recognized as safe and effective" (a category whose main practical importance is in the context of over-the-counter drugs, discussed below), and the peripheral category of "grandfathered" drugs — most drugs are regulated as "new drugs" that require an approved NDA to be marketed lawfully in the United States.

Although the specifics of product development, FDA review, and marketing may differ for each new drug product, the process of bringing a new compound onto the market generally follows a series of defined phases: preclinical investigation; clinical trials; NDA submission and review; and postmarketing. Each of these phases is discussed in turn below.

■ Preclinical Investigation

The first stage in a drug's regulatory lifecycle is preclinical investigation. The basic goals of preclinical investigation are to identify the potential *in vivo* effects of the chemical substance being investigated, through the use of both *in vitro* experimentation and animal testing, and to gather sufficient evidence on the potential new drug to determine if it is reasonably safe to begin preliminary trials in humans.[2]

---

[1]   Pub. L. No. 75-717, § 201(g), 52 Stat. 1040, 1041 (1938) (codified as amended at 21 U.S.C. § 321 (g)(1) (1994)). This definition explicitly excludes foods and dietary supplements for which certain kinds of health-related claims are made. 21 U.S.C. § 321(g)(1)(D).

[2]   21 C.F.R. § 312.23(a)(8) (1997).

The FDA's regulatory interest in preclinical investigations is largely after-the-fact. No FDA approval is required to commence a preclinical investigation, and unapproved drugs shipped interstate as part of such an investigation are exempted from the FDCA's blanket prohibition barring such shipment, as long as the drugs are labeled appropriately and adequate records of shipment and receipt are maintained.[3] The FDA may terminate a preclinical investigator's ability to ship unapproved drugs, however, if the agency determines that continuing the investigation is "unsafe or otherwise contrary to the public interest" or that the drugs are being used for purposes other than "bona fide scientific investigation."[4]

FDA involvement in preclinical investigations ordinarily comes only after the investigation is finished, when the agency reviews the investigational new drug application that a drug sponsor must submit before beginning human clinical trials.[5] At that point, the FDA evaluates the soundness and integrity of the relevant preclinical data and practices, as well as the investigational methodologies used. This evaluation focuses on the preclinical pharmacological and toxicological data that the sponsor relied on to reach the required conclusion that it was "reasonably safe to conduct the proposed clinical investigations."[6] The sponsor also must provide information on the identity and qualifications of the individuals who evaluated the studies and determined that clinical trials could reasonably commence.[7]

Good Laboratory Practices

FDA regulations on preclinical testing are commonly referred to as the good laboratory practices (GLP) regulations.[8] The GLP regulations govern the labwork and facilities associated with any nonclinical study intended to support a marketing application for an FDA-regulated product, including all human and animal drugs, medical devices, and biologics.[9] These regulations establish certain minimum requirements for different aspects of a testing laboratory's practices, subject the testing laboratory to FDA inspectional oversight, and provide penalties for noncompliance.

In general, the GLP regulations operate by specifying minimum standards in such areas as personnel, facilities, equipment, and operations. As with the regulations pertaining to current good manufacturing practices (CGMPs) (discussed elsewhere in this treatise), the GLP regulations typically set these standards through procedural and structural safeguards, rather than through specific substantive requirements.

For example, in the area of personnel, the GLP regulations require that individuals involved in preclinical studies be sufficiently trained to conduct the study appropriately, but do not specify what such training must encompass.[10] The personnel controls also require the designation of a study director to oversee, monitor, and certify the study,[11] and the establishment of a separate quality assurance unit charged with independently moni-

---

[3]   *Id.* §§ 312.160, 312.2(b)(3).

[4]   *Id.* § 312.160 (b)(2).

[5]   FDA regulation of clinical trials is discussed in detail below. *See infra.*

[6]   21 C.F.R § 312.23(a)(8).

[7]   *Id.*

[8]   *Id.* pt. 58.

[9]   *Id.* § 58.1.

[10]   *Id.* § 58.29.

[11]   *Id.* § 58.33.

toring the progress and scientific soundness of any study being conducted.[12] This quality assurance unit must, among other tasks, maintain copies of study schedules and written protocols, conduct periodic inspections to ensure compliance with all regulations and specifications, submit regular status reports to the management of the testing facility, and prepare and sign a written statement outlining quality assurance efforts, to be included in the final study report.[13]

The GLP regulations also require facilities of suitable size and construction, the appropriate separation of various types of materials, and proper animal care facilities, as applicable.[14] Under the GLP regimen, any study to be submitted to the FDA must proceed by way of a detailed protocol specifying the study's objectives and methodologies,[15] and all relevant records and data from the study must be retained for various specified periods.[16] In addition, the FDA may inspect any GLP-covered facility to determine that facility's compliance with applicable standards.[17] The regulations give the FDA inspector authority to inspect the records and facilities of the laboratory itself, and to review the inspection procedures that the institution's quality assurance unit is required to maintain.[18]

A testing facility's failure to conform with applicable GLP requirements can result in its disqualification, if the nonconformance "adversely affected the validity of the nonclinical laboratory studies" and "[o]ther lesser regulatory actions" are inadequate.[19] Any studies undertaken at a disqualified testing facility that are submitted in support of a subsequent FDA application may be excluded from consideration in the evaluation of that application.[20] Indeed, the FDA may disregard a nonclinical laboratory study from a nonconforming facility even if the facility's nonconformance with GLP regulations would not warrant a formal disqualification.[21] In addition, if studies performed at a particular facility were submitted as part of a marketing application, and that facility later becomes disqualified, the corresponding study data must be eliminated from consideration (unless the data are determined to be either not essential to the application or otherwise acceptable). This may lead to the termination or withdrawal of approval of the application in question.[22]

In sum, the direct burden of GLP compliance is on the testing facility itself,[23] but the GLP regulations create strong incentives for sponsors who plan to rely on nonclinical studies in subsequent FDA applications to take an active role in ensuring their proper execution.

---

[12]   *Id.* § 58.35.

[13]   *Id.*

[14]   *Id.* § 58.41-.51.

[15]   *Id.* § 58.120-.130.

[16]   *Id.* §§ 58.185-.195.

[17]   *Id.* § 58.15.

[18]   *Id.* § 58.35(d).

[19]   *Id.* § 58.202.

[20]   *Id.* § 58.200.

[21]   *Id.* § 58.215(b).

[22]   *Id.* § 58.210(a).

[23]   *Id.* § 58.219.

■ Clinical Investigation

As discussed above, a primary purpose of the preclinical investigation is to gather sufficient evidence about the proposed new drug to proceed to the next regulatory stage, i.e., clinical investigation. The primary goal of the clinical investigation, in turn, is to gather sufficient information about the safety and efficacy of the drug to support an NDA. In contrast to the preclinical stage, clinical trials involve significant contemporaneous FDA oversight, designed both to protect the health and safety of the human test subjects and to ensure the integrity and usefulness of the data derived.

The Investigational New Drug Application

Unlike the preclinical stage, commencement of clinical trials requires formal notification to the FDA. At least thirty days before the drug's sponsor wishes to begin such trials, the sponsor must submit an investigational new drug (IND) application to the agency.[24] If the FDA does not object to the IND within thirty days, the IND becomes effective and clinical trials may begin.[25] If the FDA finds a problem with the IND, however, it may impose a "clinical hold," barring commencement of the investigational studies proposed in the IND until the problem is resolved to the agency's satisfaction.[26]

The specific contents of an IND depend on the nature of the drug and on the scope of the proposed trials. All INDs must include the following basic elements: 1) a detailed cover sheet; 2) a table of contents; 3) an introductory statement and general investigative plan; 4) an investigator's brochure (except in the case of sponsor-investigator INDs, i.e., where the investigator also is the sponsor); 5) a set of comprehensive investigative protocols; 6) information on the proposed drug's chemistry, manufacturing, and controls; 7) pharmacology and toxicology information; 8) a summary of previous human experience with the drug; and 9) such additional information as the FDA deems necessary.[27]

Thus, the IND covers two basic categories of information; that is, information on the study drug itself and on the proposed clinical investigation. As to the drug itself, the sponsor must provide the pharmacological and toxicological data from which the sponsor concluded it was reasonably safe to propose clinical trials involving humans.[28] The IND also must include information describing the manufacturing and control of the study drug,[29] as well as comprehensive details on the drug's chemical composition, structural formula, proposed dosage form, and proposed route of administration. Information on any prior human experience with the drug is required, including any relevant foreign experience,[30] as well as any prior history of the drug having been withdrawn from investigation or marketing.

As to the information on the proposed investigation, the IND must include proposed study protocols with varying levels of detail depending on the phase of the clinical trial con-

---

[24] *Id.* § 312.40.

[25] *Id.* In practice, the FDA often communicates informally with the sponsor to indicate that clinical trials may proceed.

[26] *Id.* § 312.42. Clinical holds are discussed in more detail below. *See infra* notes 66-71 and accompanying text.

[27] 21 C.F.R. § 312.23.

[28] *Id.* § 312.23(a)(8).

[29] *Id.* § 312.23(a)(7).

[30] Id. § 312.23(a)(9).

cerned.[31] Generally, protocols must identify the objectives and purpose of the study, names and qualifications of investigators, patient selection criteria, study design and methodologies, and the study's measurement criteria, including clinical or laboratory monitoring.[32] The IND also must identify the person(s) with overall responsibility for monitoring the study, as well as any participating contract research organizations.[33]

In addition, the IND must include an "investigative plan" containing, among other things, a detailed plan for the drug's investigation, including the rationale behind the research, an outline of the proposed approach, the types of clinical trials to be conducted, an estimate as to the number of patients involved, and a discussion of any significant anticipated patient risks, based on prior toxicological data.[34] Further, the IND must contain a commitment from the sponsor to conduct clinical trials under the supervision of an Institutional Review Board (IRB), and to follow all applicable rules and regulations, including those pertaining to informed consent.

Informed Consent and Institutional Review Boards

A fundamental goal of FDA regulations on informed consent [35] and IRBs [36] is to ensure the protection of the rights and welfare of human subjects.[37] FDA investigators regularly check for compliance with these regulations, and an institution's or sponsor's noncompliance can result in the temporary suspension or formal termination of a clinical study, as well as other administrative sanctions or legal proceedings.

The thrust of the informed consent regulations is to ensure that patient participation in clinical trials is entirely voluntary and knowing. Potential participants in clinical trials must be adequately informed about risks, possible benefits, alternative courses of treatment, and the like, before making the decision to participate in the experimental research.[38] Such consent must be documented,[39] and research subjects cannot be forced to waive any potential future claims for negligence against the study's investigator, sponsor, or institution.[40] Furthermore, in the case of prisoners used as research subjects, additional restrictions and requirements exist to ensure truly voluntary participation in light of the inherently coercive penal environment.[41]

---

[31]   *Id.* § 312.23(a)(6); the phases of a clinical investigation are discussed below.

[32]   *Id.* § 312.23(a)(6)(iii). In late 1994, in response to a series of deaths in clinical trials for the hepatitis drug FIAU, the FDA proposed a number of safety-related changes to the required IND protocol. *See* Adverse Experience Reporting Requirements for Human Drug and Licensed Biological Products, Proposed Rule, 59 Fed. Reg. 54,046 (1994). As of early 1997, however, these proposed changes had not been finalized.

[33]   21 C.F.R. § 312.23(a)(1).

[34]   *Id.* § 312.23(a)(3).

[35]   *Id.* pt. 50.

[36]   *Id.* pt. 56.

[37]   *See id.* § 56.102(g).

[38]   *Id.* § 50.25. Recent amendments to the regulations, however, provide a narrow exception to the informed consent requirement for research activities involving human subjects who require immediate medical intervention, who cannot provide effective consent due to their medical condition, and who lack a suitable representative to provide such consent on their behalf. *See* Protection of Human Subjects; Informed Consent, Final Rule, 61 Fed. Reg. 51,498, 51,528-29 (1996) (adding 21 C.F.R. § 50.24).

[39]   21 C.F.R. § 50.27.

[40]   *Id.* § 50.20.

[41]   *Id.* pt. 50, subpt. C.

The regulations pertaining to IRBs obligate the institution under whose auspices a clinical study is conducted to take a sufficiently active role in the conduct of that study to ensure that the rights of the human test subjects are adequately protected, while rigorous scientific and medical standards are maintained.[42] The IRB essentially is a committee designated by the respective institution to review biomedical research involving human subjects.[43] The responsible IRB must review and approve any proposed clinical study before the study commences, and must continue to monitor the research as it progresses.[44] An IRB may approve a proposed clinical study only after determining that certain conditions are met, including that the proposed research appropriately minimizes patient risks, and that such risks are reasonable in relation to anticipated benefits.[45]

The regulations also set up relatively detailed requirements for an IRB's internal "housekeeping." Thus, the IRB must establish written procedures detailing, among other things, its review processes and criteria and its procedures designed to ensure the prompt reporting of changes in ongoing clinical research or in informed consent documents.[46] Moreover, the IRB members must come from sufficiently diverse disciplines to enable the board to review the study not only in terms of specific research issues, but also in terms of the study's acceptability under existing community and legal standards, as well as professional conduct and practice norms.[47] The IRB also must keep detailed records of its activities, which are subject to FDA inspection.[48]

The Phases of a Clinical Investigation

Clinical investigations typically are divided into three phases.[49] Although these phases are analytically distinct, in practice they often overlap, with significant FDA involvement throughout.

Phase 1 studies involve the initial administration of the drug to a small number (typically twenty to eighty) of healthy test subjects. Such studies are designed "to determine the metabolism and pharmacologic actions of the drug in humans, the side effects associated with increasing doses, and, if possible, to gain early evidence on effectiveness."[50] The drug's sponsor must derive sufficient pharmacokinetic and general pharmacological data from phase 1 trials to devise appropriate phase 2 studies.

Phase 2 investigations involve an expanded patient group (up to several hundred patients) afflicted with the disease or condition being studied. The thrust of phase 2 trials is to obtain evidence of the drug's effectiveness against the targeted disease, to explore further risk and side effect issues, and to confirm preliminary data regarding optimal dosage ranges.[51] At the end of phase 2 trials, the sponsor typically meets with appropriate FDA

---

[42] *Id.* pt. 56.

[43] *Id.* § 56.102(g).

[44] *Id.* pt. 56, subpt. C.

[45] *Id.* § 56.111.

[46] *Id.* pt. 56, subpt. C.

[47] *Id.* § 56.107.

[48] *Id.* § 56.115.

[49] *Id.* § 312.21.

[50] *Id.* § 312.21(a)(1).

[51] *Id.* § 312.21(b).

officials to discuss specific regulatory or scientific concerns the sponsor must address in designing and conducting its phase 3 studies. While such conferences technically are optional, they almost always are advisable, as they can provide an invaluable opportunity to address agency concerns that might otherwise impede review of the application.

Phase 3 clinical trials may commence, with FDA clearance, once the drug's sponsor has gathered "preliminary evidence suggesting effectiveness of the drug."[52] Such studies may involve up to several thousand patients.[53] They frequently take place at multiple locations and involve more clinical investigators than in earlier phases. The primary goal of a phase 3 clinical trial is to collect the data necessary to meet the safety and efficacy standards required for FDA approval.

Obligations of Clinical Sponsors and Investigators

Throughout all phases of a clinical investigation, both the sponsor of the study and the individual investigators have responsibilities and duties designed to ensure patient safety as well as the integrity and soundness of the data derived from the investigation. Noncompliance with these requirements may provoke FDA regulatory actions including warning letters, exclusion of a disqualified individual investigator's study results, suspension of an IND or new drug approval predicated on discredited study data, or, in the case of serious violations, civil or criminal proceedings.

The study sponsor is responsible for ensuring patient safety and appropriate scientific conduct, and has the primary responsibility to keep the FDA informed of the progress of the study and of any significant safety-related events.[54] The sponsor also has numerous specific obligations regarding such matters as selecting appropriate investigators,[55] adherence to proper protocols and practices, recordkeeping, and shipping and handling of investigational product.[56] In addition, sponsors are responsible for compliance with applicable regulations on informed consent and IRBs.[57]

The sponsor also bears responsibility for reporting to the FDA and to clinical investigators any adverse safety events that occur during clinical trials.[58] If the adverse event is serious and unexpected, e.g., it suggests a significant life-threatening hazard or side effect that is not sufficiently identified in the written investigative materials accompanying the study, the sponsor must make such a report within ten days of receiving the information.[59] A telephone report to the agency within three days is required if an unexpectedly life-threat-

---

[52] *Id.* § 312.21(c).

[53] *Id.*

[54] *Id.* §§ 312.32, 312.50-.70. Under the regulations, a sponsor may have either an investigating or noninvestigating role, in addition to its role of shouldering primary responsibility for and initiating the clinical investigation. *Id.* § 312.3(b).

[55] Under a 1994 proposed amendment to the regulations, study sponsors would be required to obtain financial information on clinical investigators, as part of an overall effort to uncover possible bias on the part of investigators with a financial interest in certain study outcomes. Sponsors also would be required to maintain records detailing investigator compensation agreements and other relevant financial interests. As of early 1997, the proposed rule has not been adopted. Financial Disclosure by Clinical Investigators, Proposed Rule, 59 Fed. Reg. 48,708 (1994).

[56] 21 C.F.R. § 312.50-.70.

[57] *Id.*

[58] *Id.* § 312.32.

[59] *Id.* § 312.32(a), (c)(i).

ening or fatal event has occurred, i.e., the patient was, "in the view of the investigator, at *immediate* risk of death from the reaction as it occurred."[60]

For their part, investigators are required, among other things, to obtain valid informed consent from any participating subjects,[61] to follow study protocols, to ensure that other study personnel follow the required protocols, and to report significant adverse events.[62] An investigator may be disqualified from participation in a study for repeated violations of the regulations or be subject to further administrative, civil, or criminal proceedings.[63] If an investigator disqualification occurs, the study's sponsor will be required to establish that the study's overall viability is not threatened by the investigator's misconduct.[64] Investigator misconduct may also result in an FDA determination that the IND can no longer remain in effect, or that a new drug approval predicated on the data must be withdrawn.[65]

FDA Oversight: Clinical Holds

Through the imposition of a "clinical hold," the FDA may delay a proposed clinical investigation or suspend an existing one.[66] A clinical hold can be imposed for a number of reasons, including an unreasonable and significant risk to patients, the use of improperly qualified investigators, a deficient or disregarded investigative protocol, or any other serious deficiency in the IND or a particular clinical trial.[67] The FDA must communicate the imposition of a clinical hold by telephone or other form of rapid communication, and must provide the drug sponsor, within thirty days, with a written explanation of the basis for the clinical hold.[68] As a general rule, until the agency's consent to lift a clinical hold is obtained, any clinical trial or trials subject to the hold cannot commence or resume.

Starting in the early 1990s, the FDA undertook various initiatives to evaluate whether clinical holds traditionally had been imposed in a consistent and fair manner, ultimately concluding that the regulations generally had been followed.[69] A committee also was established within the Center for Drug Evaluation and Research (CDER) "to review selected clinical holds for scientific and procedural quality."[70] This committee meets semi-annually to review randomly chosen clinical hold orders and those orders forwarded by drug sponsors who disagree with the agency's grounds for imposing the hold.[71]

---

[60] *Id.* § 312.32(c)(2) (emphasis in original). As noted above, *supra* note 32, in response to the FIAU situation in 1994, the FDA proposed various safety-related changes in the IND regulations. The proposal would, among other changes, significantly increase the obligations placed on sponsors to report adverse safety incidents to both the FDA and to clinical investigators. 59 Fed. Reg. at 54,046.

[61] 21 C.F.R. § 312.60.

[62] *Id.*

[63] *Id.* § 312.70.

[64] *Id.*

[65] *Id.*

[66] *Id.* § 312.42.

[67] *Id.*

[68] *Id.* § 312.42(d).

[69] *See* Investigational New Drugs; Procedure to Monitor Clinical Hold Process; Meeting of Review Committee and Request for Submissions, Notice, 60 Fed. Reg. 43,804 (1995).

[70] *Id.* at 43,805.

[71] Investigational Biological Product Trials; Procedure to Monitor Clinical Hold Process; Meeting of Review Committee and Request for Submissions, Notice, 61 Fed. Reg. 1032 (1996).

IND Withdrawal

As with the imposition of a clinical hold, the FDA can halt further use or distribution of an investigational drug through withdrawal or suspension of an IND.[72] Similar concerns, such as undue patient risk or serious deficiencies in the IND or the clinical protocol, trigger both types of agency action, with IND withdrawal reserved for the more serious cases.

Where the continuation of a clinical study poses, in the FDA's judgment, an immediate and substantial danger to human subjects, the agency may order immediate termination of an IND, subject to possible reinstatement.[73] Where no such immediate risk is present, if the FDA proposes to withdraw an IND, the agency will notify the sponsor in writing and "invite correction or explanation within a period of 30 days."[74] The sponsor's failure to respond within the specified timeframe results in the termination of the IND.[75] The sponsor may, however, request a formal hearing if the FDA refuses to accept the submitted correction or explanation.[76]

■ The New Drug Application: Standards and Procedures

Once phase 3 clinical trials are completed, the applicant prepares to submit its NDA.[77] This preparation ordinarily includes a pre-NDA meeting with appropriate FDA staff, with the goal of helping to ensure that the NDA will be submitted in the proper format and will contain all required data. After this consultation, the applicant formally submits its NDA.

Contents of the NDA

The regulatory requirements that govern the contents of an NDA are intended to give the FDA sufficient information to meaningfully evaluate the drug for which the applicant seeks approval.[78] Although the specific data requirements are lengthy and detailed, there are seven broad categories into which the required data fall: 1) preclinical data, such as animal and *in vitro* studies, evaluating the drug's pharmacology and toxicology;[79] 2) human pharmacokinetic and bioavailability data;[80] 3) clinical data, i.e., data obtained from administering the drug to humans,[81] which must include "adequate tests" to demonstrate that the drug is safe for use under the proposed conditions of use,[82] as well as "substantial evidence" that the drug is effective under the proposed conditions;[83] 4) a description of proposed methods by which the drug will be manufactured, processed, and packed;[84] 5) a

---

[72] 21 C.F.R. § 312.44.

[73] *Id.* § 312.44(d).

[74] *Id.* § 312.44(c)(1).

[75] *Id.* § 312.44(c)(2).

[76] *Id.* § 312.44(c)(3).

[77] In some cases, phase 3 trials may continue after submission of the NDA (the "Phase 3B" trial).

[78] 21 U.S.C. § 355(b); 21 C.F.R. § 314.50.

[79] 21 U.S.C. § 355(b)(1)(A); 21 C.F.R. § 314.50(d)(2)

[80] 21 C.F.R. § 314.50(d)(3).

[81] *Id.* § 314.50(d)(5).

[82] 21 U.S.C. § 355(d)(1).

[83] *Id.* § 355(d)(5); 21 C.F.R. § 314.50(d)(5)(iv).

[84] 21 U.S.C. § 355(b)(1)(D); 21 C.F.R. § 314.50(d)(1)(i)-(ii).

description of the drug product and drug substance;[85] 6) a list of each patent claiming the drug, drug product, or method of use, or a statement that there are no relevant patents making such claims;[86] and 7) the drug's proposed labeling.[87]

In addition to these requirements, the applicant also must provide a summary of the application "in enough detail that the reader may gain a good general understanding of the data and information in the application, including an understanding of the quantitative aspects of the data."[88] The summary must conclude with a presentation of both the risks and benefits of the new drug.[89]

Unless an application is publicly disclosed or acknowledged, the FDA will keep the application's existence a secret until the agency sends an approvable letter.[90] Similarly, the contents of an application are generally kept secret until an approval letter is sent, if the existence of the application is known.[91]

Filing of the NDA

When an NDA arrives at the FDA, the agency considers it to be "received," not "filed." The application is considered "filed" when the FDA formally accepts it for filing. The FDA must determine whether or not to file an application within sixty days of its receipt.[92] If no grounds for refusing to file the application exist, the FDA must file it; the filing date will be sixty days after the date of receipt.[93]

The FDA will accept an application for filing only if the application is "sufficiently complete to permit a substantive review."[94] The FDA has the authority to refuse to file an application on several grounds, such as 1) if the application is incomplete or in improper form or omits data critical to assessing safety, efficacy, or adequate directions for use;[95] 2) if the application fails to make required certifications regarding how the preclinical and clinical trials were conducted;[96] or 3) if the application covers a drug product that is already covered by another application.[97]

---

[85] 21 U.S.C. § 355(b)(1)(B)-(C); 21 C.F.R. § 314.50(d)(1)(i)-(ii).

[86] 21 C.F.R. § 314.50(h)-(i).

[87] 21 U.S.C. § 355(b)(1)(F); 21 C.F.R. § 314.50(e). NDA applications also must contain a certification that the applicant has not and will not use the services of any person who has been debarred by the Secretary of the Department of Health and Human Services (DHHS) due to a conviction for conduct related to drug approval, or for conspiring, aiding, or abetting with respect to such an offense. 21 U.S.C. § 335a(k).

[88] 21 C.F.R. § 314.50(c).

[89] *Id.* § 314.50(c)(2)(ix).

[90] 21 C.F.R. § 314.430(b).

[91] *Id.* § 314.430(d). However, if an application has been publicly acknowledged, the FDA may, in its discretion, disclose a summary of selected portions of safety and efficacy data that are appropriate for public consideration. For instance, data to be considered at an open session of an advisory committee that is evaluating the drug could be released in summary form.

[92] *Id.* § 314.101(a)(1).

[93] *Id.* § 314.101(a)(2).

[94] *Id.* § 314.101(a)(1).

[95] *Id.* § 314.101(d)(1)-(2).

[96] *Id.* § 314.101(d)(6)-(7). For instance, an application that fails to state that preclinical studies were conducted in conformity with GLPs can be refused. Similarly, the FDA may refuse to file an application that does not state that clinical studies were conducted in accordance with informed consent and IRB requirements.

[97] *Id.* § 314.101(d)(8).

Although its refusal to file (RTF) authority sounds quite broad, the FDA typically uses that authority only for obvious deficiencies in the application, not in cases that involve "matters of subtle judgment."[98] As the agency's 1993 RTF guideline states: "It is important . . . that [RTF] be reserved for applications . . . plainly inadequate, non-reviewable without major repair, or that make review unreasonably difficult."[99] Applications that contain deficiencies this severe will be subject to refusal, because the FDA believes that accepting applications in need of extensive repair is unfair to new drug sponsors whose submissions were complete and properly formatted.[100]

There are three circumstances in particular where the FDA is especially likely to use its RTF power: 1) omission of a required section of the NDA, or presentation of a section in so haphazard a manner as to render it incomplete on its face; 2) clear failure to include evidence of effectiveness that can meet the statutory and regulatory standards; and 3) omission of critical data, information, or analyses needed to evaluate safety and effectiveness, or to provide adequate directions for use.[101] Because the agency's RTF power is discretionary, however, the FDA can choose not to use the RTF procedure for particularly critical drugs even if specific grounds for invoking it are present.[102] In practice, potential RTF issues usually are addressed and resolved before the NDA is submitted. The pre-NDA meeting often provides a forum for this process.

If the FDA chooses to use its RTF authority, it will notify the applicant, which can then request an informal conference on the issue of whether its application should be filed.[103] After the conference, the applicant can request that the FDA file the application, with or without amendments to correct the deficiencies. The agency will then file the application "over protest."[104] As a practical matter, however, an applicant has little or no incentive to ask the agency to do this. If the FDA believes the application contains deficiencies egregious enough to warrant an RTF response, there is little chance of subsequent favorable FDA action on the application.[105] Therefore, requests to file an application "over protest" are a rarity.[106]

---

[98] CENTER FOR DRUG EVALUATION AND RESEARCH, FOOD & DRUG ADMIN., NEW DRUG EVALUATION GUIDANCE DOCUMENT: REFUSAL TO FILE 3 (July 12, 1993).

[99] *Id.*

[100] *Id.* at 1.

[101] *Id.* at 4-5.

[102] *Id.* at 3.

[103] 21 C.F.R. § 314.101(a)(3). Such a meeting must be requested within 30 days of the FDA's notification.

[104] *Id.*

[105] In one instance, after the FDA determined that Discovery Experimental and Development, Inc.'s application for the drug deprenyl was incomplete for substantive review, the applicant requested that the FDA file the application over protest. The FDA reviewed the application as filed and then proposed to disapprove it because it had numerous problems and deficiencies. *See* Discovery Experimental and Development, Inc.; Deprenyl Gelatin Capsules and Liquid (Deprenyl Citrate); Proposal to Refuse to Approve a New Drug Application; Opportunity for a Hearing, Notice, 59 Fed. Reg. 26,239 (1994).

[106] In the event that an application is filed over protest, the review clock will begin on the date the applicant requested the conference rather than on the day the application was received (New Drug and Antibiotic Regulations, Final Rule, 50 Fed. Reg. 7452, 7479 (1985)), and the filing clock will begin 60 days after the applicant's conference request (21 C.F.R. § 314.101(a)(3)). The triggering dates are moved back in this fashion because the hearing on whether the application should be filed consumes part of the review and filing periods. Review and filing clocks are discussed in more detail below.

Substantive Standards for Review

FDA reviewers must find that an application meets several substantive requirements before the agency will approve the NDA. The most basic requirement is that the drug be both "safe" and "effective." These words have specialized meanings in the new drug approval context.

The FDCA, as enacted in 1938, did not require a showing of efficacy as a condition for marketing a new drug — only proof of safety. The Drug Amendments of 1962[107] added the requirement that a new drug must be supported by "substantial evidence" that the drug will have the effect it purports to have under the indicated conditions of use.[108] "Substantial evidence" means evidence from adequate and well-controlled clinical studies.[109] Normally, the FDA requires two independent studies to demonstrate efficacy.[110] In 1995, however, the agency issued a statement memorializing a practice it had begun to follow, namely, that if it is possible to replicate efficacy results within one large, well-designed, multicenter study, and those study results are strong,[111] a single study may suffice for approval.[112] This policy clearly remains the exception rather than the rule, however.

In addition, a drug may not be approved unless there are "adequate tests by all methods reasonably applicable to show whether or not such drug is safe for use under the conditions prescribed, recommended, or suggested in the proposed labeling thereof."[113] In applying this statutory standard, the FDA recognizes that there is no such thing as an absolutely safe drug; in addition to the benefits it provides, every drug will present some risks. Therefore, the FDA's safety assessment requires consideration of a producer's efficacy. As the agency stated, "[The] FDA weighs the product's demonstrated effectiveness against its risks to determine whether the benefits outweigh the risks."[114] This risk/benefit analysis takes account of information such as the seriousness of the disease, the presence and adequacy of existing remedies, and adverse reaction and any other safety data.[115]

In addition to evidence of safety and effectiveness, there also must be adequate manufacturing controls in place before the FDA will approve a drug.[116] In particular, the methods used in, and the controls and facilities used for, manufacturing, processing, packing, and holding the drug substance and finished product must comply with the FDA's CGMPs, and must be adequate to maintain the drug's purity, quality, strength, identity, and bioavailability.[117] A pre-approval inspection of the applicant's facilities typically will be conducted to verify compliance with these requirements.[118]

---

[107] Pub. L. No. 87-781, 76 Stat. 780.

[108] 21 U.S.C. § 355(d); 21 C.F.R. § 314.105(c).

[109] 21 U.S.C. § 355(d).

[110] Statement Regarding the Demonstrations of Effectiveness of Human Drug Products and Devices, Notice, 60 Fed. Reg. 39,180, 39,181 (1995).

[111] "Strong" results are those that are not "statistically marginal." *Id.*

[112] *Id.*

[113] 21 U.S.C. § 355(d)(1).

[114] 60 Fed. Reg. at 39,180.

[115] *Id.*

[116] 21 U.S.C. § 355(d)(3).

[117] 21 C.F.R. § 314.125(b)(1).

[118] *Id.* § 314.125(b)(12).

An additional prerequisite to approval is that the drug's labeling meet applicable statutory and regulatory requirements. The labeling cannot be false or misleading in any particular,[119] and must comply with general requirements concerning both the content and form of the information that must accompany a drug, such as clinical data, warnings, and dosage and administration information.[120]

Advisory Committee Review

Although the primary review of an NDA is carried out by the appropriate division within CDER, the FDA refers many applications to outside advisory committees for their comments and recommendations.[121] These advisory committees, which are composed primarily of prominent research and clinical specialists, review certain critical studies regarding drug products under consideration, as well as proposed labeling.[122] Advisory committees respond to specific questions posed by the agency regarding safety and efficacy, and evaluate whether additional studies are needed to support approval.[123] The FDA is likely to use advisory committee review if the new drug being studied is particularly significant, or if review of the drug involves evaluation of complex scientific data. In addition to advisory committees, the FDA also has discretion to consult outside expert reviewers from the scientific community for their views.[124] Advisory committee and outside review recommendations, however, are not binding on the agency.

■ The New Drug Application: FDA Action and Timeframes

The length of FDA review times on NDAs has been a major source of frustration over the years for both the agency and the drug industry. In response to this chronic problem, Congress enacted the Prescription Drug User Fee Act of 1992 (PDUFA).[125] This legislation is one of the most important recent developments for new drug approvals. It has altered significantly the way the FDA and drug sponsors approach the NDA process, and generally has decreased formal review times for new drugs.

Timeframes for Agency Action: The Statutory and Regulatory Model

To appreciate the changes wrought by PDUFA, it is helpful first to review the standard (pre-PDUFA) model for FDA response times on NDAs. Under that model, both the date of receipt and the date of filing of the NDA are figured into setting timeliness for future FDA action with respect to the application. The period of time triggered by the receipt of the application is called the "review clock."[126] Under the review clock, the agency has 180 days from the date of receipt to send an "action letter," which can be either an approval letter, an "approvable" letter, or a "not approvable" letter.[127] The period of time triggered

---

[119] 21 U.S.C. § 355(d)(7); 21 C.F.R. § 314.125(b)(6).

[120] 21 C.F.R. § 314.125(b)(8). *See* 21 C.F.R. pt. 201 for a detailed description of labeling requirements.

[121] *See* Final Rule on New Drug and Antibiotic Regulations, 50 Fed. Reg. 7452, 7482 (1985).

[122] *Id.*

[123] *Id.*

[124] *Id.*

[125] Pub. L. No. 102-571, 106 Stat. 4491 (codified at 21 U.S.C. §§ 379g-379h).

[126] 21 C.F.R. § 314.100(a).

[127] *Id.*

by filing is called the "filing clock."[128] Under the filing clock, the FDA has 180 days from the filing date to either approve the application or give the applicant notice and the opportunity for a hearing on the issue of whether the application is approvable.[129]

The FDA's choice of which type of action letter to send under the review clock is governed by the agency's judgment of the extent to which the application meets the substantive requirements for approval, discussed above. If the requirements for approval are met, the FDA will approve the application and send the applicant an approval letter.[130] The approval becomes effective on the date the approval letter is issued.[131]

If the application contains only minor deficiencies, the FDA will send the applicant an approvable letter, which indicates that the application basically is approvable provided the deficiencies are resolved.[132] To qualify for this type of action letter, the application must "substantially comply" with the approval requirements.[133] Upon receipt of an approvable letter, the applicant has ten days to submit a response, which may take one of several forms. First, the applicant can either amend the application or indicate that it intends to amend the application, to address the FDA's concerns.[134] Under the regulations, this action constitutes an agreement by the applicant to extend the review period by forty-five days from the date the agency receives the amendment.[135] Second, the applicant can withdraw its application. Failure to enter any response within the ten-day period will be treated as a request by the applicant to withdraw the NDA.[136] Third, the applicant can ask the agency for a hearing on whether there are grounds for denying approval of the NDA.[137] If the applicant chooses the hearing option, within sixty days of the date the approvable letter was sent the FDA either will approve the application or issue a notice of an opportunity for a hearing on the question of whether the application is approvable.[138]

If the FDA believes the application is not approvable because the applicable substantive requirements are not satisfied, the agency will send a not approvable letter.[139] The responsive actions available to the applicant with respect to a not approvable letter mirror those for approvable letters, i.e., the applicant has ten days to amend or indicate intent to amend,

---

[128] *Id.* § 314.101(a)(2).

[129] 21 U.S.C. § 355(c)(1). In practical terms, the review clock is far more important than the filing clock. As the agency stated in the preamble to the 1985 NDA Rewrite, "[e]xcept in those rare cases that may culminate in a formal evidentiary hearing [*see* discussion *infra*], the 180-day 'filing clock' has no practical significance." 50 Fed. Reg. at 7479.

[130] 21 C.F.R. § 314.105(a).

[131] *Id.* This interpretation of the date of "approval" was upheld in Mead Johnson Pharmaceutical Group v. Bowen, 838 F.2d 1332 (D.C. Cir. 1988) (approval for a conditionally approved drug became effective on date approval letter was sent, even though conditions of approval were not fulfilled until a later date). There is an exception to this rule in the case of some 505(b)(2) and ANDA applications, discussed in the text below. Some such applications will have a delayed effective date, and in those cases the FDA will consider the application's approval tentative until the specified effective date.

[132] 21 C.F.R. § 314.110(a).

[133] *Id.* § 314.110(b).

[134] *Id.* § 314.110(a).

[135] *Id.*

[136] *Id.* § 314.110(a)(2).

[137] *Id.* § 314.110(a)(3).

[138] *Id.*

[139] *Id.* § 314.120.

withdraw the application, or request a hearing.[140] The hearing option is the same as in the case of an approvable letter, with the agency either approving the application or issuing a notice of opportunity for a hearing within sixty days of the date the letter was sent.[141]

If the applicant receives notice of an opportunity for a hearing pursuant to an approvable or not approvable letter, it has thirty days after receipt of the notice to accept the opportunity for a hearing.[142] The FDA then has ninety days to schedule the hearing; the agency's decision is due within ninety days after the date fixed for filing final briefs in connection with the hearing.[143] If, after the hearing, the agency finds that the statutory and regulatory requirements have not been met, the agency will refuse to approve the application.[144] In practice, applicants rarely request the hearing, because it is extremely unlikely to result in approval.

Applicants can take action that will extend the review and/or filing clocks. If the applicant submits a "major amendment" while the NDA is pending, the review period will be extended by the time necessary to review the amendment, but not by more than 180 days.[145] The term "major amendment" is described in the FDA's regulation as an amendment containing either significant new data or detailed new analysis of previously submitted data.[146] Moreover, both the review and filing clocks can be extended by mutual agreement between the applicant and the agency.[147]

Reality of FDA Timeframes and the PDUFA Response

Although the FDCA contemplates a final FDA decision 180 days after receipt of an NDA, the FDA generally has taken much longer to reach decisions than either the statute or its own regulations permit. Drug sponsors historically have acquiesced in this situation, for a variety of practical reasons. Although NDA applicants could attempt to challenge the agency in court for failing to meet the statutory deadline, the general perception is that there is much more to be gained by cooperation. Moreover, the litigation itself could be quite time-consuming, and therefore self-defeating, and the courts in any case are unlikely to force the agency that has the technical expertise to evaluate a drug, and that is charged by statute with the responsibility for that evaluation, to take action with respect to the drug before it is ready to do so.[148]

The legislative response to the problem of slow review times came in the form of the PDUFA legislation, which allows the FDA to collect a substantial user fee for each new

---

[140] *Id.* § 314.120(a)(1)-(a)(3).

[141] *Id.* § 314.120(a)(3).

[142] *Id.* § 355(c)(1)(B).

[143] *Id.*

[144] *See id.* § 355(d); 21 C.F.R. § 314.125(a).

[145] 21 C.F.R. § 314.60(a).

[146] *Id.*

[147] *Id.* § 314.100(c); 50 Fed. Reg. at 7479. Such extension may, for instance, be necessitated by the time required for outside advisory committee review. *See id.*

[148] In one case where a disgruntled drug company did sue the FDA for not reviewing its drug applications within the 180-day deadline, the court agreed that the FDA's delay violated the statute, but refused to do anything about it on the ground that it was up to the agency, not the court, to set drug review priorities, and that to order the FDA to meet the deadline on the plaintiff's applications would disadvantage other, equally worthy, applicants. *In re* Barr Lab., Inc., 930 F.2d 72 (D.C. Cir.), *cert. denied*, 502 U.S. 906 (1991).

drug application it receives.[149] In return, the agency is expected to use the fee money to decrease its NDA response time.[150] This legislation applies only to prescription drug NDAs, biologic product and establishment licenses, and their supplements,[151] not to generic drugs or medical devices. [152]

PDUFA provides two means of improving review times. First, the high fee per application discourages companies from submitting applications until the applications are strong enough to have a good probability of success with minimal mid-review amendment.[153] Second, and most significantly, the revenue generated through the user fee mechanism gives the agency additional funding for its NDA review effort, enabling it to respond to applicants more quickly.

In conjunction with the PDUFA legislation, the FDA set its own goals for expediting the review process. Specifically, Commissioner Kessler stated in a 1992 letter to Congress that the agency's PDUFA goal was to provide a final response within one year of receipt of the application, and within six months for priority applications.[154] The Kessler letter also stated that if a major amendment is filed within three months prior to the decision due date, the review clock will be extended by an additional three months.[155] The target date for meeting the PDUFA response time goals was set for September 1997, with these ultimate goals being phased in gradually over the intervening five-year period.[156]

PDUFA also requires the FDA to submit an annual "report card" to Congress detailing the agency's progress toward meeting its response time goals.[157] In addition, PDUFA was enacted as "sunset" legislation set to expire in October 1997, subject to reauthorization.[158]

To most observers, PDUFA has been a success. User fees have enabled the FDA to hire more than 200 new personnel for the drug review process, and the agency appears to have met or surpassed most of its user fee goals.[159] The rate of on-time actions under PDUFA goals was ninety-five percent for 1995 applications, and the median approval time

---

[149] In FY 1996 the fee was $217,000 per application; in FY 1997 it is $233,000 per application. 21 U.S.C. § 379h(b)(1). These amounts can be adjusted downward for small businesses, or waived entirely under specified circumstances. *Id.* § 379h(b)(2), (c)-(d). Fifty percent of the applicable fee is due when the application is submitted; the remaining fifty percent is due upon the expiration of thirty days from the date an action letter is sent, or upon the withdrawal of the application or supplement after it is filed, unless the FDA waives the fee (or a portion of the fee) because no substantial work was done on the application after filing. *Id.* § 379h(a)(1)(B).

[150] *See* Pub. L. No. 102-571, §§ 102(2)-(3), 106 Stat. at 4491.

[151] Including supplements seeking a prescription to over-the-counter switch, as described in the text below.

[152] 21 U.S.C. § 379(g).

[153] PDUFA also contains a monetary incentive not to submit applications vulnerable to refusal. The statute provides that only half of the first user fee installment payment (this installment is 50% of the overall fee amount), which is paid upon submission of the application, will be returned if the application is not accepted for filing. 21 U.S.C. § 379h(a)(1)(D). Under the FY 1996 fee schedule, the amount lost due to an RTF response would be $54,250.

[154] Letter from David Kessler, Comm'r of Food and Drugs, to Reps. John Dingell (D-MI) and Norman Lent (R-NY), *reprinted in* 138 CONG. REC. H9099-9100 (daily ed. Sept. 22, 1992).

[155] *Id.* Note that the regulations would allow up to a six-month extension under these circumstances. *See* discussion in the text above.

[156] *Id.*

[157] Pub. L. No. 102-571, § 104, 106 Stat. at 4498.

[158] Pub. L. No. 102-571, § 105, 106 Stat. at 4498.

[159] *New Shot at FDA Reform Via PDUFA Reauthorization*, DICKINSON'S FDA REV., Nov. 1996, at 21.

dropped from twenty-three months pre-PDUFA to fifteen months for fiscal 1995.[160] Indications are that the quality of applications has improved, as reflected by a decrease in the RTF rate over the life of the PDUFA legislation.[161] Approval rates also have increased under PDUFA, from historical levels of fifty to sixty percent to almost eighty percent,[162] and in 1995 the FDA approved roughly twice as many NMEs as it has ever approved in a one-year period.[163]

A frequently-mentioned "loophole" in PDUFA, however, is the fact that its timing goals apply to the date by which an action letter is due, rather than the date by which a final decision is due. This can cause delays when the FDA's initial "on-time" response is an approvable letter, because no response time goal applies to the period between an approvable letter and final approval.[164]

■ The Postmarketing Period

An applicant's responsibilities with respect to its new drug application do not cease upon the application's approval. The postapproval stage brings with it its own set of obligations for the NDA holder.

Changes Affecting an Approved Application

To makes changes affecting an approved drug that go beyond the conditions established in the NDA, an applicant must reckon with the requirements of the supplemental NDA process. Changes affecting an approved drug are grouped into three categories, each of which carries different procedural requirements. For some changes, the sponsor must submit a supplement to its NDA, and the FDA must approve that supplement, before the sponsor can implement the desired changes — the so-called "prior approval" supplement. A second group of changes also requires supplementing the NDA, but the sponsor can implement the changes before the FDA approves the supplement. These supplements are commonly referred to as "changes being effected" supplements. A third category of changes need only be listed in the annual report that the sponsor must file with respect to the drug covered by the NDA.

Under the FDA's regulation on supplements, prior approval supplements are required for such matters as changes in the synthesis of the drug substance [165] or changes in the facility that manufactures the drug substance, if the manufacturing process at the new facility is materially different than the current one, or if the new facility has not received a satisfactory CGMP inspection covering that manufacturing process.[166] Changing the facility that manufactures the finished drug product requires a prior approval supplement regardless of

---

[160] *FDA Fiscal 1995 NDA/PLA Class Will Achieve Approval Rate of Approximately 80%*, Health News Daily, Dec. 10, 1996, at 2.

[161] *Id.* at 1-2.

[162] *Id.* at 2; *see also FDA Clears 53 NMEs in 1996 — Average Approval Time is 20.5*, F-D-C Rep. ("The Pink Sheet"), Jan. 6, 1997, at 19.

[163] *FDA Clears 53 NMEs in 1996*, F-D-C Rep. ("The Pink Sheet"), Jan. 6, 1997, at 19.

[164] *The FDA's User-Fee Review Commitments and the Final Stages of Drug Approval*, U.S. Reg. Rep., Apr. 1994, at 1. In 1993, for example, the approvable letter/drug approval interval ranged from nine days to 181 days. *Id.* at 3.

[165] 21 C.F.R. § 314.70(b)(1)(iv).

[166] *Id.* § 314.70(b)(1)(v).

whether the new facility materially differs from the current facility.[167] And all changes in labeling require a prior approval supplement, with three exceptions that will be discussed below.[168]

The regulation contemplates a "changes being effected" supplement for alterations in labeling that strengthen warnings or dosage and administration information, or that delete false or misleading information;[169] the addition of new specifications or tests that provide increased assurance that the drug will have the characteristics it purports or is represented to possess, or changes in methods, facilities, and controls that increase such assurances;[170] or a change in a facility that manufactures the drug substance if the new facility does not materially differ from the current facility, or the new facility has received a satisfactory CGMP inspection.[171]

Finally, according to the regulation, changes in conditions not requiring either type of supplement only need to be described in the annual report submitted by the applicant.[172] Examples of changes affecting the application that must be listed in the annual report include editorial or minor changes in labeling, deletion of an ingredient that affects only the product's color, and changes in the container's size without changes in the closure system.[173]

Many NDA holders have criticized the literal requirements of the FDA's supplements regulation as ambiguous, too onerous, or both. In response, the FDA issued additional notices in 1994 and 1995.[174] The first notice clarified the regulatory scheme, detailing which procedures applied to which types of changes.[175] The second notice decreased the number of changes requiring prior approval supplements,[176] confining the prior approval requirement to those changes in facility, manufacturing process, or composition that could have, or are likely to have, a significant impact on the drug's formulation, quality,

---

[167] *Id.* § 314.70(b)(2)(vi).

[168] *Id.* § 314.70(b)(3), (c)(2).

[169] *Id.* § 314.70(c)(2), 3

[170] *Id.* § 314.70(c)(1).

[171] *Id.* § 314.70(c)(3).

[172] *Id.* § 314.70(d). The annual report is a document the applicant must submit each year within 60 days of the anniversary date of the NDA's approval date. *Id.* § 314.81(b)(2). This annual report contains various current data about the drug, including a summary of significant new information that might affect the safety, labeling, or effectiveness of the drug product; information about the quantity of the drug distributed; the currently used labeling that accompanies the drug; and changes in chemistry, manufacturing, and controls. *Id.*

[173] *Id.* § 314.70(d).

[174] *See* Supplements to New Drug Applications, Abbreviated New Drug Applications, or Abbreviated Antibiotic Applications for Nonsterile Drug Products, Draft Guideline, 59 Fed. Reg. 64,094 (1994); and Immediate Release Solid Oral Dosage Forms; Scale-up and Postapproval Changes: Chemistry, Manufacturing, and Controls; In Vitro Dissolution Testing; In Vivo Bioequivalence Documentation, Guidance, 60 Fed. Reg. 61,638 (1995).

[175] 59 Fed. Reg. at 64,094. For example, the notice made clear that using a different facility or materially different manufacturing process for manufacturing the drug substance would require prior approval, but relocating processing areas or equipment within a plant would only need listing in the annual report. *Id.* at 64,096. In addition, the notice specified that changing to equipment of a different design would require prior approval, while changing to different equipment of the same design would only need listing in the annual report. *Id.* at 64,095.

[176] 60 Fed. Reg. at 61,638. The agency was able to effect these changes by issuing a notice rather than engaging in full notice and comment rulemaking because of the section in 21 C.F.R. § 314.70 that allows NDA holders to comply with less burdensome notice requirements that have been published by the agency in the *Federal Register*, in lieu of complying with the requirements in the regulation itself.

or performance.[177] The notice also clarified the documentation that should support each type of change.[178]

Adverse Reaction Reporting

"Adverse drug experiences" are somewhat circularly defined under the FDA's regulations as any adverse events associated with the use of a drug in humans.[179] An applicant holding an approved NDA must promptly review reports of adverse drug experiences associated with its drug, regardless of the source from which such reports were obtained.[180] If a reaction is both serious (e.g., fatal, life-threatening, or permanently disabling) and unexpected (not listed in labeling, or differing from reactions listed in the labeling due to greater severity or specificity), it must be reported in an "alert report" within fifteen working days of the applicant's receipt of the information.[181] Finally, all adverse reactions that are not serious and unexpected must be reported at quarterly intervals for three years after an application is approved, and annually thereafter.[182]

NDA Withdrawal

Although the FDA rarely invokes its authority to withdraw NDAs under section 505(e) of the FDCA, there are several circumstances under which the agency can take such action.[183] As might be expected, the conditions for NDA withdrawal generally relate to serious problems with the drug or the application. For instance, the FDA can withdraw an NDA if the drug is unsafe for use under the conditions of use for which the application was approved.[184] Similarly, the FDA can use its withdrawal authority if new clinical evidence shows that the drug is not safe under approved conditions, or if the drug is not effective.[185] Additionally, the FDA can seek withdrawal of an application if the drug's labeling is false or misleading, or if there are inadequate assurances that the drug's quality, strength, and purity are as claimed.[186] The agency also can withdraw an NDA if the sponsor fails to file required patent information in a timely manner, or if the NDA contains false statements of material fact.[187]

If the FDA seeks to withdraw an NDA, normally it must give the applicant notice and the opportunity for a hearing.[188] If the drug in question presents an "imminent hazard," however, the Secretary of DHHS can summarily suspend approval of the application and give

---

[177]   60 Fed. Reg. at 61,640-41.

[178]   *Id.* at 61,639.

[179]   21 C.F.R. § 314.80(a).

[180]   *Id.* § 314.80(b).

[181]   *Id.* § 314.80(c)(1)(i). In June 1997 the FDA revoked a previous requirement that significant increases in the frequency of adverse event reports be reported to the agency within 15 days of the determination of increased frequency. Postmarketing Expedited Adverse Experience Reporting for Human Drug and Licensed Biological Products; Increased Frequency Reports, Final Rule, 62 Fed. Reg. 34,166 (1997).

[182]   21 C.F.R. § 314.80(c)(2).

[183]   21 U.S.C. § 355(e); 21 C.F.R. § 314.150.

[184]   21 U.S.C. § 355(e)(1); 21 C.F.R. § 314.150(a)(2)(i).

[185]   21 U.S.C. § 355(e)(2)-(3); 21 C.F.R. § 314.150(a)(2)(ii)-(iii).

[186]   21 C.F.R. § 314.150(b)(2)-(3).

[187]   21 U.S.C. § 355(e)(4)-(5). A complete list of grounds for NDA withdrawal is set forth in 21 C.F.R. § 314.150.

[188]   21 U.S.C. § 355(e); 21 C.F.R. § 314.150(a).

the applicant the opportunity for an expedited hearing.[189] The Secretary cannot delegate the authority to summarily suspend NDAs in this fashion, but she has delegated to the FDA the authority to hold the expedited hearing.[190] In practice, the FDA rarely invokes its authority to withdraw or summarily suspend approval of NDAs.[191]

Phase IV Studies

Although clinical studies generally are thought of as a prerequisite to approval, there are also clinical studies that take place after approval — the so-called "phase IV" studies. Such studies can be designed to: 1) obtain additional safety data; 2) obtain additional efficacy data; 3) detect new uses for or abuses of a drug; or 4) determine effectiveness for labeled indications under conditions of widespread usage. [192]

There are at least two reasons the FDA may be interested in phase IV studies. First, such studies allow the FDA to grant approval of a new drug on the condition that the applicant complete studies that resolve remaining questions about the drug's safety and efficacy. Using phase IV studies to implement a conditional approval of this sort avoids delaying approval of drugs with apparent therapeutic importance. Phase IV studies can also be used to facilitate the FDA's postapproval monitoring of an approved drug when concerns about its safety or efficacy arise.

Phase IV studies originally were a creature of practice, not regulation. Although the FDA historically had no specific authority to require postmarketing studies as a condition of approval, the agency cited sections 505(k) and 701(a) of the FDCA in support of this practice.[193] Section 505(k) grants the FDA authority over the establishment and maintenance of records and reports necessary to determine whether there are grounds for withdrawing an NDA, while section 701(a) gives the agency the authority to promulgate regulations for the efficient enforcement of the FDCA. Taken together, these sections have been interpreted by the FDA as giving the agency the right to compel a sponsor to gather and report new clinical data in the postmarketing period as a condition of NDA approval.[194] In 1992, however, the concept of the phase IV study was enshrined in the FDA's final rule on accelerated approval, discussed below.

---

[189] 21 U.S.C. § 355(e)(5).

[190] *Id.*; *see also* 21 C.F.R. § 314.150(a)(1).

[191] A noteworthy recent case of the agency's exercise of this authority is the proposal to withdraw the NDAs for terfenadine (Seldane®) and a combination terfenadine/pseudoephedrine product (Seldane-D®), Hoechst Marion Roussel, Inc., and Baker Norton Pharmaceuticals, Inc.; Terfenadine, Proposal To Withdraw Approval of Two New Drug Applications and One Abbreviated New Drug Application; Opportunity for a Hearing, Notice, 62 Fed. Reg. 1889 (1997). These NDAs were approved in 1985 and 1991, respectively. Since that time, these products have been used to treat allergy symptoms, but there have been reports of serious, potentially fatal cardiac reactions in some patient subpopulations. In 1996, the FDA approved fexofenadine hydrochloride (Allegra®). This drug has the same therapeutic effects as terfenadine, but as of five months postapproval there had been no reports of serious cardiac arrhythmias associated with its use. Because fexofenadine can provide therapeutic benefits identical to terfenadine without the serious and potentially fatal cardiovascular side effects, the FDA concluded that the terfenadine products are no longer safe for use under the conditions of use for which the NDA was approved, and proposed to withdraw them.

[192] *See* Marion J. Finkel, *Phase IV Testing: FDA Viewpoint and Expectations*, 33 FOOD DRUG COSM. L.J. 181 (1978).

[193] 21 U.S.C. §§ 355(k), 371(a).

[194] Finkel, *supra* note 195, at 183.

■ Marketing Protection

An issue that virtually all drug applicants must face is whether, and what kind of, market protection is available for their product — or, conversely, what kind of marketing exclusivity for other will have to be overcome for the drug applicant to enter the market. There are three main statutory routes to marketing protection for qualifying new drug products outside of, or in addition to, standard patent protection: 1) the patent term extension provisions; 2) nonpatent statutory exclusivity provisions for new chemical entities and approvals requiring new clinical studies; and 3) nonpatent exclusivity for orphan drugs. These three mechanisms operate in different ways, but all are potentially important from the perspective of the NDA applicant.

Patent Term Extension

The statutory patent term extension provision[195] recognizes the reality that many pharmaceutical products receive patents long before they are approved for marketing because the products must go through a lengthy premarketing regulatory review. Because this review period may last for a large portion of the product's patent life, Congress amended the patent law as part of the 1984 amendments to the FDCA[196] to allow extensions of a product's patent term in certain situations.

In brief, a drug is eligible for a patent term extension if its patent has not expired and has not been extended previously, and if the drug has been subject to a "regulatory review period" prior to commercial marketing or use.[197] Only one patent per product is eligible for extension.[198]

Computation of the length of the extension is based in the first instance on the length of the regulatory review period. The regulatory review period in turn includes a "testing period," which begins on the date the IND exemption became effective and ends on the date the NDA was submitted,[199] and an "approval period," which covers the time from the submission of the NDA to its approval.[200] In determining the patent extension, each of these two periods will be reduced by: 1) any portion of the period that took place prior to the patent's issuance;[201] and 2) any amount of time during which the applicant did not act with due diligence in pursuing regulatory review.[202] After each component of the review period has been calculated and adjusted, the patent will be extended for one-half of the "testing" period and all of the "approval" period.[203]

---

[195] 35 U.S.C. § 156 (1994).

[196] Drug Price Competition and Patent Term Restoration Act of 1984, Pub. L. No. 98-417, 98 Stat. 1585. The 1984 amendments are discussed in detail below.

[197] 35 U.S.C. § 156(a).

[198] *Id.* § 156(c)(4).

[199] *Id.* §156(g)(1)(B)(i).

[200] *Id.* § 156(g)(1)(B)(ii).

[201] *Id.* § 156(c).

[202] *Id.* §§ 156(c)(1), (d)(3).

[203] *Id.* § 156(c)(2); but note that, depending on the date of the patent's issuance, the length of the extension can be capped at either two or five years, regardless of the length of the review period. *Id.* § 156(g)(6). In no case can an extension exceed fourteen years. *Id.* § 156(c)(3).

A drug patent owner seeking an extension must submit an application to the Commissioner of Patents and Trademarks within sixty days of receiving NDA approval.[204] The FDA assists the Patent and Trademark Office (PTO) in reviewing the application, because the FDA has the information necessary to calculate the regulatory review period and make the due diligence determination. At the end of the review process, the PTO issues or denies the extension.[205]

A recent complication regarding patent extensions is the 1994 Uruguay Round of the General Agreements on Tariffs and Trade (GATT). The Uruguay Round Agreements Act (URAA), which Congress enacted to implement this international agreement, changed the terms of U.S. patents from seventeen years from the date of the patent's issuance to twenty years from the date the patent application was filed.[206] Patents in effect on the effective date of the URAA, June 8, 1995, were awarded terms of either twenty years from the application date or seventeen years from the date of issuance, whichever was greater.[207]

Statutory Exclusivity for New Chemical Entities and Approvals Based on New Studies

In addition to patent term extension, the FDCA contains provisions that authorize various periods of marketing exclusivity independent of a product's patent status.[208] The goal of these exclusivity provisions is to give pioneer drug companies a monetary incentive to invest in the research and testing needed to develop new products, while affording consumers broader access to drug products by making available nonpioneer products that rely on studies conducted by a pioneer company.

Under the exclusivity provisions, if an NDA is approved for a drug containing a new chemical entity,[209] then no application under sections 505(j) (i.e., an ANDA) or 505(b)(2) of the Act [210] that references the drug may be submitted until the expiration of five years from the date of approval of the drug.[211] Thus, the NDA holder in that situation effectively delays generic competition for five years plus the time it takes the FDA to review and approve the first generic application. An exception to the five-year rule allows a generic applicant who is relying on the pioneer's studies to submit its application after four years from the date of approval, provided the generic application contains a certification of patent invalidity or noninfringement that may result in the filing of a patent suit that can further delay marketing of the generic drug.[212] A manufacturer will get three years of exclusivity for a previously-approved active ingredient if its application (either a

---

[204] *Id.* § 156(d)(1).

[205] *Id.* § 156(e)(1).

[206] Uruguay Round Agreements Act (URAA), Pub. L. No. 103-465, 108 Stat. 4809 (1994) (codified at 19 U.S.C. §§ 2252 et seq. (1994)) *See* § 532 of the URAA.

[207] *See* 35 U.S.C. § 154(c)(1). For a discussion of the transitional provisions under this law, see Bristol-Myers Squibb Co. v. Royce Labs., Inc., 698 F.3d 1130 (Fed. Cir. 1995), *cert. denied*, 116 S. Ct. 754 (1996).

[208] 21 U.S.C. § 355(c)(3); 21 C.F.R. § 314.108.

[209] "New chemical entity" is defined as a drug that contains no active moiety that has been approved by the FDA in any other application submitted under section 505(b) of the Act. 21 C.F.R. § 314.108(a).

[210] ANDAs and section 505(b)(2) applications are discussed below.

[211] 21 U.S.C. § 355(c)(3)(D)(ii); 21 C.F.R. § 314.108(b)(2).

[212] 21 U.S.C. § 355(c)(3)(D)(ii); 21 C.F.R. § 314.108(b)(2). See the text below for a discussion of such certifications.

new NDA or an NDA supplement) contains reports of new clinical studies essential to approval of the application.[213]

A nonpioneer applicant who wishes to market its drug sooner than the exclusivity provisions allow can avoid those provisions by doing its own studies and submitting a full NDA for its version of the product, although in practice few companies choose this route because of the cost involved. The exclusivity protections also will not apply if the party using the studies of the first applicant has obtained a right of reference or use from the party who conducted the studies.[214]

Orphan Drug Exclusivity

The goal of the Orphan Drug Act of 1983,[215] as amended, was to motivate pharmaceutical manufacturers to develop and bring to market drugs for orphan diseases — that is, diseases thought to be too rare to attract the commercial interest of pharmaceutical manufacturers in the ordinary course of business. A "rare" disease is defined in the statute as any disease that affects fewer than 200,000 persons in the United States, or that affects more than 200,000 persons and for which there is no reasonable expectation that the manufacturer will recover from U.S. sales the cost of developing and making the drug available in the United States.[216]

Although the Orphan Drug Act created a series of incentives for manufacturers to develop drugs for these rare diseases — including FDA assistance with clinical protocols, available grant assistance for clinical development, and a tax credit for a portion of research and development expenses[217] — by far the most important incentive under this Act is the seven-year market exclusivity awarded to the first applicant to obtain marketing approval of a designated orphan drug for a particular disease or condition. For this exclusivity to attach, the applicant must request orphan drug designation for the drug in question[218] prior to the submission of the marketing application,[219] and the drug must be so designated prior to approval of the application.[220] If these conditions are met and the drug was approved, the FDA will not approve another applicant's application for the same drug for the same disease or condition until seven years from the date of the first applicant's approval, unless 1) the drug's orphan designation is revoked;[221] 2) its marketing approval is withdrawn; 3) the orphan exclusivity holder consents to the approval of another applicant's product; or 4)

---

[213] 21 U.S.C. § 355(c)(3)(D)(iii); 21 C.F.R. § 314.108(b)(4).

[214] 21 U.S.C. § 355(c)(3)(D)(ii), (iii).

[215] Pub. L. No. 97-414, 96 Stat. 2049 (1983).

[216] 21 U.S.C. § 360bb(a)(2).

[217] The orphan tax credit, codified at 26 U.S.C. § 28 (1994), is not a permanent provision but must be re-extended annually or biennially (depending on the expiration date set in any particular re-extension).

[218] Orphan exclusivity may apply not only to new drugs approved under section 505 of the FDCA, 21 U.S.C. § 355, but also to biologics licensed under section 351 of the Public Health Service Act, ch. 288, 37 Stat. 309 (1912) (codified at 42 U.S.C. § 262 (1994)), and to antibiotics certified under section 507 of the FDCA, 21 U.S.C. § 357.

[219] 21 C.F.R. § 316.23(a).

[220] *Id.* § 316.31(a).

[221] Revocation of orphan drug status can occur if the request for designation contained an untrue statement of material fact or omitted required material information, or if the FDA subsequently finds that the drug was in fact not eligible for orphan designation at the time it was granted. *Id.* § 316.29(a).

the orphan exclusivity holder is unable to ensure the production of sufficient quantity of the drug.[222]

The Orphan Drug Act has been both successful and controversial. Its success can be measured not only by the sharp increase in the number of drugs for orphan diseases that have been developed since its passage — a phenomenon that may owe as much to underlying advances in biomedical technology as to the incentives provided by the Act — but also by the fact that orphan exclusivity has become a built-in consideration in the development of new products for disease categories such as cancer and autoimmune diseases. That very success, however, has sown the seeds of controversy. Significant financial rewards reaped by some firms under the mantle of orphan exclusivity led to legislative efforts in the late 1980s aimed at limiting that exclusivity. Those efforts culminated in a 1990 bill that would have allowed different firms that developed an orphan product simultaneously to share exclusivity, and would have provided for FDA withdrawal of orphan exclusivity when a relevant patient population exceeded the 200,000 mark.[223] The bill was vetoed by President Bush on the ground that it would undermine the incentives of the Orphan Drug Act.[224]

Although the basic incentive structure of the Orphan Drug Act has survived legislative challenge thus far, the application of that structure to specific products has on occasion been the subject of fierce dispute. Not long after the passage of the Act, the FDA's designation of a recombinant human growth hormone (rHGH) product as an orphan drug was challenged by the holder of an orphan marketing approval for a different rHGH product.[225] The challenge was based on the argument that the newly designated rHGH product was structurally identical to a previously-approved human-derived (i.e., nonrecombinant) HGH product, and therefore was ineligible for orphan designation because an NDA already had been granted for the "same" drug. In a decision that would establish important guidance for the FDA's interpretation of the Orphan Drug Act, the court held that even though the newly-designated rHGH product was structurally identical to the previously-approved human-derived HGH, it was not the "same drug" for orphan purposes because it was demonstrably safer than the human-derived version, which had been taken off the market for safety reasons. The court held, in effect, that Congress could not have intended the Orphan Drug Act to block the development and availability of safer versions of existing drugs.[226]

This conclusion emerged, in somewhat expanded form, in the FDA's 1992 regulations implementing the Orphan Drug Act. Those regulations provide that a sponsor's drug will not be blocked by a previous sponsor's orphan exclusivity, even if the two sponsors' drugs otherwise would be considered structurally the same, if the second sponsor's drug is "clinically superior" to the first sponsor's drug.[227] Clinical superiority, in turn, may include greater effectiveness, greater safety, or "in unusual cases," a "major contribution to patient

---

[222] *Id.* § 316.31(a); 21 U.S.C. § 360cc(b).

[223] Orphan Drug Amendments of 1990, H.R. 4638, 101st Cong., 2d Sess. (1990).

[224] Memorandum of Disapproval for the Orphan Drug Amendments of 1990, 26 WEEKLY COMP. PRES. DOC. 1796 (Nov. 8, 1990).

[225] Genentech, Inc. v. Bowen, 676 F. Supp. 301 (D.D.C. 1987).

[226] *Id.* at 312.

[227] 21 C.F.R. § 316.3(b)(13).

care."[228] The courts have upheld the FDA's authority under these regulations to override one drug's orphan exclusivity on the basis of a second drug's greater safety.[229]

FDA Regulation of Drugs: Variations on the Standard Model

■ Non-NDA Routes to Market: Historical Development

As is evident from the discussion above, meeting the safety and efficacy standards required to obtain approval of an NDA entails substantial expense, effort, and expertise. These factors create significant barriers to market entry, a situation that — as in any area of economic activity — can lead to higher prices for consumers. This situation sets up an inherent tension between maintaining the regulatory standards needed to protect public health and safety, on one hand, and mitigating the economic burdens imposed by drug prices, on the other. When one adds into this mixture the need to offer adequate financial incentives to encourage companies to undertake the formidable task of new drug development, the policy equation becomes complex indeed.

Since the passage of the FDCA in 1938, Congress and the FDA have made periodic efforts to readjust the balance between these goals. As discussed in the following sections, each such effort was followed by moves to re-level the economic playing field.

"Not New" Drugs

Prior to the enactment of the FDCA in 1938, there were no significant regulatory barriers to generic competition in the drug market. With the statutory establishment of the "new drug" category, however, a drug could not be marketed unless it was either "generally recognized as safe" or its NDA was allowed to become effective absent affirmative FDA disapproval, which was the standard approval process under the 1938 version of the FDCA.[230] This process was minimal by today's standards, but it was not cost-free, and it did impose certain barriers to entry.

Thus, to facilitate generic competition for post-1938 drugs, the FDA established an informal practice whereby, on request, the agency would inform an interested party whether a particular drug was generally recognized as safe, and consequently not a "new drug" subject to a premarket application.[231] The factual basis for a positive "general recognition" decision typically was a history of safe marketing of the pioneer version of the drug in the United States. This policy continued under the 1962 amendments (modified to consider general recognition of both safety and efficacy), but at a slower pace, until the practice

---

[228] *Id.* § 316.3(b)(3).

[229] Berlex Labs, Inc. v. FDA, 942 F. Supp. 19 (D.D.C. 1996).

[230] The current requirement for affirmative FDA approval of an NDA was added by the 1962 Drug Amendments. *See supra* notes 107-10.

[231] *See* New-Drug Status Opinions; Statement of Policy, 33 Fed. Reg. 7758 (Jan. 23, 1968).

was discontinued in 1968, and all such "not new drug" letters were formally revoked by the agency.[232]

The DESI Review

The 1962 Drug Amendments included a provision for the retroactive evaluation of the efficacy of drugs approved as safe (or which had been subject to a "not new drug" letter) between 1938 and 1962. The Drug Efficacy Study Implementation (DESI) Review, established in 1968, directed the National Academy of Sciences to establish expert panels to review available data on all marketed post-1938 drugs, and to make recommendations as to their efficacy. The FDA was then to act on those recommendations by withdrawing drugs found ineffective and by notifying potential generic manufacturers as to what information would be required for approval of a generic version (other than proof of safety and efficacy, which were deemed to have been established by the DESI Review panel). In response, the agency created a new form of NDA, known as an abbreviated new drug application (ANDA), for which approval was based on sameness of active ingredients and on bioequivalence rather than on safety and efficacy data. This ANDA process for DESI drugs later was codified by statute in the 1984 amendments.[233] The DESI Review was supposed to have been completed in only two years, but notwithstanding two court-ordered completion deadlines,[234] as of 1997 it remains unfinished (and essentially inactive).

The "Paper NDA" Policy

As the patent terms on post-1962 drugs began to expire in the 1970s and early 1980s, it became evident that under existing laws there were no feasible means for competing versions of approved drugs to enter the market without costly and repetitive testing for safety and efficacy. Because such repeat testing would put more human test subjects at risk unnecessarily, and would waste scarce clinical and agency resources, the FDA sought expansion of the concept of the DESI Review and ANDA policy to generic versions of certain post-1962 drugs. The result was the "paper NDA" policy, which, although short-lived, provides a historical and conceptual bridge between the "old drug"/"general recognition" bases for generic drug marketing and the modern statutory ANDA approval process.

The paper NDA policy permitted competing versions of approved new drugs to be approved based on the submission of publicly-available reports of well-controlled studies demonstrating the drug's safety and efficacy. The policy was challenged and ultimately upheld in court.[235] Because adequate published studies documenting safety and efficacy were available for only a very few post-1962 drugs, however, and because FDA review of such paper NDAs was not significantly easier than for full NDAs, the policy only marginally contributed to fostering generic competition.[236]

---

[232] *Id.*

[233] *See infra* notes 245-311 and accompanying text.

[234] American Pub. Health Ass'n v. Veneman, 349 F. Supp. 1311 (D.D.C. 1972); American Public Health Ass'n v. Harris, [1980-81 Transfer Binder] Food Drug Cosm. L. Rep. (CCH) ¶ 38,068 (D.D.C. Sept. 24, 1980).

[235] *See* Burroughs Wellcome Co. v. Schweiker, 649 F.2d 221 (4th Cir. 1981).

[236] *See* Proposed Rule on Abbreviated New Drug Application Regulations, 54 Fed. Reg. 28,872, 28,873-74 (1989).

■ Generic Drugs and the Abbreviated New Drug Application Process

Legislative Background

In response to the lack of a viable generic drug approval process for post-1962 drugs, in the late 1970s and early 1980s Congress began to consider legislative options to address the problem.[237] During that time, other legislative efforts were underway to restore the part of drug patents' effective life lost due to increasingly lengthy FDA review times. In 1983, a patent term restoration bill was defeated narrowly in the House of Representatives, but it soon became apparent that neither an ANDA bill nor a patent term restoration bill could pass Congress independently.[238] As a result, leaders of the generic and innovator sides of the pharmaceutical industry cooperated in crafting a bill incorporating both an ANDA mechanism for all generic drugs and patent restoration for research-based companies. The resulting legislation was enacted in 1984.[239]

The dual purpose of this legislation was to expedite the availability of safe, effective, but less expensive generic versions of approved drugs, while simultaneously encouraging the costly research and development efforts that lead to the discovery of therapeutically important new drugs.[240] Briefly stated, the amendments created an abbreviated approval process whereby generic companies could gain approval of their drugs without repeating the expensive and lengthy clinical trials already performed for the drug, and innovator companies were given restoration of patent rights to compensate for the time expended in the FDA review process, as well as nonpatent marketing exclusivity for qualifying drug products.[241]

The amendments also provided protection for the generic drug industry in the form of a provision establishing that it is not an act of patent infringement for a nonpatentholder to make, use, or sell a patented drug during the term of the patent, so long as such activity reasonably is related to the contemplated submission of an application to the FDA.[242] This provision, which specifically overruled the early 1984 decision of the newly created Court of Appeals for the Federal Circuit in *Roche Prods., Inc. v. Bolar Pharmaceutical Co.*,[243] was necessary to allow generic applicants to have their ANDAs submitted and approved in time to begin marketing on the date of patent expiration. If the court's ruling had stood, development of ANDAs could not have begun until patent expiration. As a result, *de facto* market exclusivity would have extended well beyond the term of the patent. The protection provided by the statutory provision overruling the *Roche* decision was counterbal-

---

[237] *See* H.R. Rep. No. 857, 98th Cong., 2d Sess. at 14-17 (1984), *reprinted in* 1984 U.S.C.C.A.N. 2647-50.

[238] *See* Allan M. Fox & Alan R. Bennett, The Legislative History of the Drug Price Competition and Patent Term Restoration Act of 1984 iv (1986).

[239] Drug Price Competition and Patent Term Restoration Act of 1984, Pub. L. No. 98-417, 98 Stat. 1585.

[240] In reference to the 1984 Act's main congressional sponsors, Senator Orrin G. Hatch (R-UT) and Representative Henry A. Waxman (D-CA), the law typically is referred to either as "Hatch-Waxman" or "Waxman-Hatch." In the interest of neutrality, "1984 Amendments" will be used here throughout.

[241] See the discussion above regarding patent term restoration.

[242] *See* 35 U.S.C. § 271(e)(1). The Supreme Court has held that this exemption from the infringement definition applies to making or using a patented product in connection with any submission to the FDA, including specifically device premarket submissions. Eli Lilly & Co. v. Medtronic, Inc., 496 U.S. 661 (1990).

[243] 733 F.2d 858 (Fed. Cir. 1984).

anced by a provision allowing an innovator to sue an ANDA applicant upon submission of an ANDA claiming not to violate the innovator's patent.[244]

The Statutory ANDA Requirements

The required contents of an ANDA are set forth in section 505(j) of the FDCA[245/] and in agency regulations.[246] Simply summarized, the statute requires that ANDAs contain the following:

(a) information showing that the proposed conditions of use for the drug have previously been approved for a drug that is listed by the FDA as approved for safety and efficacy;[247]

(b) proof that the active ingredient(s) are the same as in the listed drug;[248]

(c) proof that the generic drug will use the same route of administration, dosage form, and strength as the listed drug;[249]

(d) proof that the generic drug is bioequivalent to the listed reference drug;[250]

(e) information showing that the proposed generic labeling is the same as the labeling approved for the listed drug, except for differences related to an approved suitability petition;[251]

(f) the basic technical information required of a full NDA, including a list of components, statement of the composition of the drug, and description of the methods and facilities used in the production of the drug;[252]

(g) samples of the generic product and proposed labeling; and

(h) a patent certification informing the FDA of the patent status of the listed reference drug relied upon by the ANDA.[253]

Although the statutory requirements for an ANDA appear relatively straightforward on their face, many of these requirements have been the bases of contentious administrative and judicial battles. The following sections discuss the ANDA requirements in the context of the relevant cases and disputes.

The Prior Approval and Current Listing Requirements. Two threshold requirements for a drug to be ANDA-eligible are 1) that the drug's active ingredient already has been approved by the FDA for the conditions of use proposed in the ANDA, and 2) that nothing has changed to call into question the basis of approval of the original drug's NDA. The second of these requirements has given rise to some complex issues, as illustrated below.

---

[244] 21 U.S.C. § 355(j)(4)(B)(iii).

[245] *Id.* § 355(j).

[246] 21 C.F.R. § 314.94.

[247] 21 U.S.C. § 355(j)(2)(A)(i).

[248] *Id.* § 355(j)(2)(A)(ii). There also are provisions allowing the use of a different active ingredient as part of an ANDA for a multiple-active ingredient drug product when subject to an approved "suitability petition" under section 505(j)(2)(C), as discussed in the text below.

[249] *Id.* § 355(j)(2)(A)(iii). These requirements also may be modified pursuant to an approved suitability petition.

[250] *Id.* § 355(j)(2)(A)(iv).

[251] *Id.* § 355(j)(2)(A)(v).

[252] *Id.* § 355(j)(2)(A)(vi), incorporating by reference 21 U.S.C. § 355(b)(1)(B)-(F).

[253] *Id.* § 355(j)(2)(A)(vii).

The 1984 amendments require the FDA to publish a monthly list of all approved drugs.[254] That publication, commonly known as the "Orange Book,"[255] serves as the crucial point of reference for many aspects of the ANDA process. In particular, an ANDA may be submitted only if the drug it copies is currently listed in the Orange Book as a "reference" listed drug.[256] Such a listing signifies that the drug has been approved, and that as of the date of the Orange Book edition consulted, the drug has not been withdrawn from the market over issues of safety or efficacy.[257] Although it is rare for approved drugs later to be found unsafe, an approved drug occasionally is withdrawn from the market voluntarily by the manufacturer. In such cases the FDA must make a determination of whether the drug was withdrawn for safety or effectiveness reasons 1) before approving any ANDA that refers to the listed drug, 2) if any ANDAs that reference the drug already have been approved, or 3) if an interested person petitions the FDA to make such a determination.[258]

An example of this situation occurred in 1996, when the FDA made such a determination with respect to the drug ibuprofen in 200 mg capsules. Although an NDA was approved for the drug in 1987, the sponsor never actually marketed the product. After a generic company sought the FDA's ruling on whether the drug was "withdrawn" for safety or efficacy reasons, the FDA determined that it had not been withdrawn for such reasons, and that ANDAs could therefore be filed and approved for that product.[259]

The other situation in which current listing in the Orange Book is significant is when the FDA withdraws approval of an NDA pursuant to FDCA section 505(e).[260] This rare occurrence will prevent approval of any pending ANDA for the product and also will serve to withdraw approval of any existing approved ANDAs.[261]

"Suitability Petitions" for Different Active Ingredient(s), Routes of Administration, Dosage Forms, and Strengths. Although a product approved under an ANDA must have the same active ingredient(s), route of administration, dosage form, and strength as the listed drug it seeks to copy,[262] the Act also permits generic products to incorporate differences from each of those requirements where such differences ultimately will not affect the safety and efficacy of the generic product.[263]

To market a generic product with any of these differences, however, the generic applicant must first submit, and the FDA must approve, a so-called "suitability petition" under section 505(j)(2)(c). The Act requires the FDA to approve any such petition unless the agency finds: 1) that investigations must be conducted to demonstrate the safety and efficacy of

---

[254] *Id.* § 355(j)(6).

[255] Food & Drug Admin., Approved Drug Products with Therapeutic Equivalence Evaluations (17th ed. 1997) (the "Orange Book").

[256] *Id.* § 355(j)(2)(A)(i).

[257] *See* 21 U.S.C. §§ 355(j)(6)(C), 355(e).

[258] 21 C.F.R. § 314.161(a).

[259] Determination That Ibuprofen 200-Milligram Capsule Was Not Withdrawn From Sale for Reasons of Safety or Effectiveness, 61 Fed. Reg. 58,565 (1996).

[260] 21 U.S.C. § 355(e).

[261] *Id.* § 355(j)(5). See the discussion of NDA withdrawal in the text above.

[262] *Id.* § 355(j)(2)(A).

[263] *Id.* § 355(j)(2)(C).

the generic drug proposed to be marketed with different active ingredients, route of administration, dosage form, or strength; or 2) that any proposed generic drug with a different active ingredient cannot be adequately evaluated for safety and effectiveness based on the information required to be submitted in an ANDA.[264]

Bioequivalence. The primary substantive requirement for approval of an ANDA is that the proposed generic drug be shown to be "bioequivalent" to the innovator drug it purports to copy.[265] For generic products that meet the bioequivalence requirement, the FDCA allows the presumption that the generic version of the drug will be as safe and effective as the original version.

The definition of "bioequivalence" in the Act is lengthy and complex.[266] The core of the bioequivalence concept, as interpreted by the FDA in regulations, is an "absence of a significant difference" in the extent to which, and the rate at which, two different drug products' active ingredients "become[ ] available at the site of drug action when administered at the same molar dose under similar conditions in an appropriately designed study."[267] For the typical solid oral dosage form drug, this concept means that one version of the drug provides the same blood concentration of the active ingredient, at the same rate, as another version. In reality, however, bioequivalence determinations are not always that simple, as described in more detail below.

FDA regulations require ANDAs to contain either 1) "evidence" of bioequivalence of the ANDA product to the listed reference drug,[268] or 2) "information" showing bioequivalence that is sufficient to allow the FDA to waive the "evidence" requirement.[269] In practice, this means that an ANDA must contain either results of human studies showing

---

[264] *Id.* § 355(j)(2)(C)(i), (ii). Inclusion of a different active ingredient from the listed drug is allowed only for combination drugs in which at least one active ingredient is identical to the listed drug and the second active ingredient is approved in a similar drug.

[265] *Id.* § 355(j)(2)(A)(iv).

[266] The statute requires a finding of bioequivalence if:

(i) the rate and extent of absorption of the drug do not show a significant difference from the rate and extent of absorption of the listed drug when administered at the same molar dose of the therapeutic ingredient under similar experimental conditions in either a single dose or multiple doses; or

(ii) the extent of absorption of the drug does not show a significant difference from the extent of absorption of the listed drug when administered at the same molar dose of the therapeutic ingredient under similar experimental conditions in either a single dose or multiple doses and the difference from the listed drug in the rate of absorption of the drug is intentional, is reflected in its proposed labeling, is not essential to the attainment of effective body drug concentrations on chronic use, and is considered medically insignificant for the drug.

Id. § 355(j)(7)(B).

[267] 21 C.F.R. § 320.1(e). The bioequivalence regulation also provides:

Where there is an intentional difference in rate (e.g., in certain controlled release dosage forms), certain pharmaceutical equivalents or alternatives may be considered bioequivalent if there is no significant difference in the extent to which the active ingredient or moiety from each product becomes available at the site of drug action. This applies only if the difference in the rate at which the active ingredient or moiety becomes available at the site of drug action is intentional and is reflected in the proposed labeling, is not essential to the attainment of effective body drug concentrations on chronic use, and is considered medically insignificant for the drug.

Id.

[268] *Id.* § 320.21(b)(1).

[269] *Id.* § 320.21(b)(2).

bioequivalence, or other facts upon which the FDA can conclude that the ANDA product will be bioequivalent to its reference listed drug.

The regulations regarding "evidence" of bioequivalence specifically state that the FDA may accept such evidence based on *in vivo* or *in vitro* testing, or both.[270] Those regulations also set out, in rank order of acceptability, types of *in vivo* and *in vitro* tests that may be used to establish bioequivalence. Those tests include blood concentration tests, or *in vitro* tests that have been correlated to such *in vivo* blood tests, urinary excretion tests, measurement of observable pharmacological effects over time, comparative clinical trials of safety and efficacy, FDA-accepted *in vitro* dissolution tests, or the catch-all "any other approach deemed adequate by FDA" to establish bioequivalence.[271] Consistent with these options, the regulations state: "FDA, for good cause, may waive a requirement for the submission of evidence of *in vivo* bioavailability if waiver is compatible with the public health."[272]

Bioequivalence issues associated with generic versions of innovator drugs have spawned considerable debate and litigation between and amongst innovator and generic drug companies and the FDA. This debate has been sharply focused with respect to drugs that are not "systemically effective" — that is, their active moiety is not delivered to the site of drug action by systemic blood flow.

The most prominent specific example of conflict in this area involved the bronchodilator albuterol administered by metered dose inhaler. The NDA holder for the drug filed a citizen petition arguing that the statutory bioequivalence requirement, which specifies only measurements of "rate and extent of absorption," categorically precluded the FDA from approving any ANDAs for nonsystemically-absorbed drugs. The petition requested the FDA to "deny all applications for abbreviated approval of nonsystemic drugs."[273] The FDA denied the petition on the basis that the statute specifically contemplates determinations of bioequivalency based on evidence other than rate and extent of absorption. The company then sued the FDA in federal district court, but the court agreed with the FDA's interpretation and dismissed the complaint.[274] During the pendency of the subsequent appeal, the FDA finalized its ANDA regulations, including the bioequivalency requirements of 21 C.F.R. part 320, which directly addressed the legal issue involved in the citizen petition.[275] Consequently, the appellate court dismissed the appeal as moot.[276] The company sued the FDA again, seeking to overturn the final regulations. In that suit, the district court specifically adopted the reasoning of the first district court, and dismissed the complaint.[277] On appeal, the holding was affirmed; the appellate court stated that "section 355(j)(7)(B) is ambiguous but . . . the FDA interpretation of that provision embodied in its regulation at 21 C.F.R. § 320.1(e) is reasonable."[278] In subsequent cases involving similar

---

[270] *Id.* § 320.24.

[271] *Id.* § 320.24(b)(1)-(6).

[272] *Id.* § 320.22(e).

[273] *See* Schering Corp. v. Sullivan, 782 F. Supp. 645, 647 (D.D.C. 1992), *vacated*, 995 F.2d 1103 (D.C. Cir. 1993).

[274] *Id.*

[275] Abbreviated New Drug Application Regulations, Final Rule, 57 Fed. Reg. 17,950, 17,975 (1992).

[276] Schering v. Shalala, 995 F.2d 1103 (D.C. Cir. 1993).

[277] Schering Corp. v. FDA, 866 F. Supp. 821, 826 (D.N.J. 1994), *aff'd*, 51 F.3d 390 (3d Cir. 1995), *cert. denied*, 116 S. Ct. 274 (1995).

[278] Schering Corp. v. FDA, 51 F.3d 390, 400 (3d Cir.), *cert. denied*, 116 S. Ct. 274 (1995).

issues of bioequivalence testing of ANDA products, the courts have also upheld the FDA's discretion on such issues.[279]

The "Same Labeling" Requirement. The statutory requirement that a generic version of a new drug contain the "same labeling" as the listed reference drug[280] has been construed by the FDA to require that the "labeling (including the container label and package insert) proposed for the drug must be the same as the labeling approved for the reference listed drug, except for [differences approved under a suitability petition, or relating to the difference in manufacturers] . . . or omission of an indication or other aspect of labeling protected by patent or accorded exclusivity under section 505(j)(4)(D) of the [A]ct."[281]

In 1994, Bristol-Myers Squibb sued the FDA over the interpretation of the "same labeling" requirement with regard to the drug Capoten® (captopril),[282] for which Bristol recently had received approval of a supplemental NDA for new indications. Bristol argued that no generic captopril products could be approved for any uses until the three-year exclusivity it had received for the newly-approved indications had expired because the proposed generic labeling could not be "the same as" Bristol's approved labeling for the drug, inasmuch as that generic labeling could not include the new indications.[283] Bristol's complaint was dismissed on appeal by the D.C. Circuit,[284] which held that the statutory exception to the "same labeling" requirement for differences required because the generic drug and the listed drug are made by different manufacturers[285] "does 'accommodate the situation in which the generic drug manufacturer has sought approval for fewer than all of the indications of the pioneer manufacturer's drug'" and is the only interpretation that "works in harmony" with the other relevant provisions of the Act.[286]

Patent Certification. The final procedural requirement for an ANDA is a patent certification "with respect to each patent which claims the listed drug . . . or which claims a use for such listed drug for which" the ANDA is filed.[287] This provision relates to the requirement that an NDA must include the number and expiration date of "any patent which claims the drug" and "with respect to which a claim of patent infringement could reasonably be asserted" if an unlicensed person were to make, use, or sell the drug.[288] All patents thus submitted to the FDA will be listed in the Orange Book. Such listing is intended to give public notice of patents that could be enforced against potential competitors.

---

[279] *See, e.g.,* Bristol-Myers Squibb v. Shalala, 923 F. Supp 212, 218 (D.D.C. 1996).

[280] 21 U.S.C. § 355(j)(2)(A)(v).

[281] 21 C.F.R. § 314.94(a)(8)(iv).

[282] Bristol-Myers Squibb Co. v. Shalala, [1995 Transfer Binder] Food Drug Cosm. L. Rep. (CCH) ¶ 38,433, 39,497 (D.D.C. Nov. 7, 1995); *rev'd*, 91 F.3d 1493 (D.C. Cir. 1996).

[283] *Id.*

[284] Bristol-Myers Squibb Co. v. Shalala, 91 F.3d 1493 (D.C. Cir. 1996).

[285] 21 U.S.C. § 355(j)(2)(A)(v).

[286] 91 F.3d at 1500. The court also noted that there was direct legislative history refuting Bristol's contention, in H.R. REP. No. 98-857, pt.1, at 21-22 (1984), *reprinted in* 1984 U.S.C.C.A.N. 2647, 2654-55 (noting that the bill "permits an ANDA to be approved for less than all of the indications for which the listed drug has been approved").

[287] 21 U.S.C. § 355 (j)(2)(A)(vii).

[288] *Id.* § 355(b)(1)(F).

There are four types of patent certifications that can be made and, where multiple patents claim the drug at issue, different types of certifications can be made for each patent. The four certifications are:

(1) that information on the patent has not been filed with the FDA by the patent owner;
(2) that the patent already has expired;
(3) a statement of the date on which the patent will expire; or
(4) "that such patent is invalid or will not be infringed by the manufacture, use, or sale of the new drug for which the application is submitted."[289]

If a paragraph I or II certification is filed, the FDA may make approval of the ANDA effective immediately.[290] If a paragraph III certification is filed, the approval may be made effective on the patent expiration date specified in the ANDA, although a tentative approval may be issued before that time.[291] If the ANDA contains a paragraph IV certification, however, a series of events will be triggered, the outcome of which will determine the effective date of approval of the ANDA.

As an initial step, generic companies seeking to market their own versions of patented drugs will refer to the Orange Book 1) to determine the latest date of patent expiration, and/or 2) to investigate whether any listed patents are invalid, unenforceable, or would not be infringed by a generic version of the drug. If it appears that the patent would not preclude marketing of the generic drug, the generic company may decide to file a paragraph IV certification. That certification initiates a formal process whereby the generic drug company's challenge to the patent can be resolved by the courts before the generic drug is granted a final, effective approval. As the agency itself has explained:

> In matters related to patents, the agency does not claim expertise. We believe that Congress intended to leave the ultimate resolution of patent issues to the U.S. Patent and Trademark Office and to the courts. Therefore, we are interpreting the statute and establishing procedures so that disputes between new drug applicants involving patents will be resolved by the notification and litigation process that is contained in the statute.[292]

This process begins when a generic company submits an ANDA containing a paragraph IV certification and, as required, notifies the patent owner of the fact that it has filed such a certification.[293] That notification must set forth in detail the factual and legal bases for the ANDA applicant's belief that the listed patent is invalid, will not be infringed,[294] or is unenforceable.[295]

---

[289] *Id.* § 355(j)(2)(A)(vii).

[290] *Id.* § 355(j)(4)(B)(i).

[291] *Id.* § 355(j)(4)(B)(ii).

[292] Letter from Paul D. Parkman, M.D., Dep. Dir., Center for Drugs and Biologics, Food & Drug Admin., to All NDA and ANDA Holders and Applicants (Oct. 31, 1986).

[293] 21 U.S.C. § 355(j)(2)(B)(i).

[294] *Id.* § 355(j)(2)(B)(ii).

[295] Based on a ruling by the Federal Circuit, the FDA has administratively added unenforceability of a patent as a basis for attempting a paragraph IV challenge. *See* Abbreviated New Drug Application Regulations; Patent and Exclusivity Provisions, Final Rule, 59 Fed. Reg. 50,338, 50,339 (1994) and Merck & Co. v. Danbury Pharmacal, Inc., 694 F. Supp. 1 (D. Del. 1988), *aff'd*, 873 F.2d 1418 (Fed. Cir. 1989).

After receiving the paragraph IV notification, the patent holder must evaluate the legal and factual arguments asserted by the ANDA applicant. If the patent holder disagrees, it may file a lawsuit against the applicant for patent infringement.[296] Such a lawsuit must be filed within forty-five days of receipt of the paragraph IV notification, or the FDA may make approval of the ANDA effective immediately.[297] If such a case is brought, however, an automatic statutory injunction prohibits the FDA from making approval of the ANDA effective for thirty months, unless the court rules in favor of the generic company.[298] FDA regulations state that only a "final" judgment from which no appeal lies satisfies the "court ruling" requirement for FDA approval before the thirty-month period expires.[299] During the litigation, however, the thirty-month injunction may be shortened or lengthened by the district court in response to undue delay by either party to the litigation.[300]

The filing of a paragraph IV certification is an "artificial act" of patent infringement[301] created by the 1984 amendments to allow the courts to decide whether the patent is valid, or if the proposed future manufacture and sale of the generic version would infringe the patent. Without making the paragraph IV certification itself an "act" of infringement, it was believed that the courts would be barred under the Constitution from issuing what would otherwise amount to an advisory opinion about potential future infringement by the generic competitor. Thus, even though the paragraph IV filing is the "act" upon which a patent holder may sue the generic applicant, once such a suit is filed, the only issues to be decided are whether the proposed generic marketing of the drug will infringe the patent or whether the patent is otherwise invalid under traditional patent jurisprudence.[302]

The paragraph IV challenge procedure has been used to challenge patents on a wide variety of bases, including invalidity,[303] unenforceability due to inequitable conduct by the patentee in procuring the patent,[304] noninfringement based on a claim that the challenged patent does not cover the overall composition of the generic drug product,[305] noninfringement based on differences in the chemical form of the active drug ingredient used in the generic product,[306] and that the patent extensions granted pursuant to the GATT treaty did not bar generic versions of drugs affected by the extension.[307]

---

[296] 21 U.S.C. § 355(j)(4)(B)(iii).

[297] *Id.*

[298] *Id.*

[299] 21 C.F.R. § 314.107(e).

[300] 21 U.S.C. § 355(j)(4)(B)(iii).

[301] *See* Bristol-Myers Squibb Co. v. Royce Labs., Inc., 69 F.3d. 1130, 1131 (Fed. Cir.), *cert. denied*, 116 S. Ct. 754 (1995); Eli Lilly & Co. v. Medtronic, Inc., 496 U.S. 661, 676, 678 (1990).

[302] *See* Bristol-Myers Squibb Co. v. Royce Labs, Inc., 36 U.S.P.Q. 1637, 1640 (S.D. Fla. 1995), *rev'd*, 69 F.3d at 1130, *cert. denied*, 116 S. Ct. at 670; Eli Lilly Co. v. Medtronic, 496 U.S. at 678.

[303] *See, e.g.,* Marion Merrell Dow, Inc. v. Geneva Pharmaceuticals, 877 F. Supp. 531 (D. Colo. 1994).

[304] *See, e.g.,* Merck v. Danbury, 694 F. Supp. at 1, *aff'd*, 873 F.2d at 1418.

[305] *See, e.g.,* Upjohn Co. v. Mova Pharm. Corp., 936 F. Supp. 55, 56 (D.P.R. 1996), *summ. judgment granted in part*, 951 F. Supp. 333 (D.P.R. 1997).

[306] *See, e.g.,* Marion Merrell Dow Inc. v. Baker Norton Pharmaceuticals, Inc., 948 F. Supp. 1050 (S.D. Fla. 1996); Glaxo, Inc. v. Novopharm Ltd., 931 F. Supp. 1280 (E.D.N.C. 1996), *aff'd*, 110 F.3d 1562 (Fed. Cir. 1997).

[307] *See, e.g.,* Bristol-Myers Squibb v. Royce, 69 F.3d at 1130, *cert. denied*, 116 S. Ct. at 754. Patent extensions under the Uruguay Round of GATT are discussed *infra.*

Although a paragraph IV challenge often is costly and difficult, the 1984 amendments included incentives for generic companies to bring such challenges by providing for the possibility of a six-month delay in FDA approval of subsequent ANDAs, to benefit generic companies that successfully challenge a listed drug patent. This incentive for qualifying paragraph IV filers, codified at section 505(j)(4)(B)(iv),[308] provides for delayed ANDA approval dates for subsequent paragraph IV challengers under certain circumstances. The delayed effective date provisions for subsequent paragraph IV ANDAs are complex, and as of this writing were the subject of ongoing litigation between generic companies and the FDA.[309] The FDA's regulatory interpretation of the provision provided the 180-day exclusivity to a generic company that 1) was first to submit a substantially complete ANDA (containing bioequivalence data) that also contained a paragraph IV certification, and 2) successfully defended against a patent infringement suit brought by the patent owner within forty-five days of the paragraph IV notification.[310] One district court has held recently that the latter criterion is not required under the Act.[311]

■ The New "Paper NDA" — Section 505(b)(2) Applications

In addition to codifying procedures for ANDAs, the 1984 amendments also modified the new drug application provisions of section 505(b) of the FDCA to establish a new category of NDA — the "505(b)(2) application." This type of application, like the earlier paper NDA, provides for new drug applications submitted by an applicant that did not conduct its own clinical safety and/or efficacy work. Section 505(b)(2) applicants typically rely on data from clinical safety and efficacy trials conducted by a previous applicant, which are already in the FDA's files, but to which the 505(b)(2) applicant has no right of reference. Section 505(b)(2) applicants may still rely on published reports, as was the case under the old paper NDA policy.[312]

There are several scenarios where a 505(b)(2) application comes into play. One scenario involves an applicant who seeks to market an established drug for a new therapeutic indication or with some other modification requiring new clinical studies, and relies on relevant safety reports about the drug in a previously-approved NDA. Another scenario is where an ANDA suitability petition for a significantly different version of an approved drug is inappropriate because clinical studies are required, but prior studies on the original drug product are still relevant to showing the overall safety and efficacy of the new version of the drug.

---

[308] Subsection (B)(iv) states:

If the application contains a certification described in subclause (IV) of paragraph (2)(A)(vii) and is for a drug for which a previous application has been submitted under this subsection continuing such a certification, the application shall be made effective not earlier than one hundred and eighty days after –

(I) the date the Secretary receives notice from the applicant under the previous application of the first commercial marketing of the drug under the previous application, or

(II) the date of a decision of a court in an action described in clause (iii) holding the patent which is the subject of the certification to be invalid or not infringed, whichever is earlier.

[309] Mova Pharm. Corp. v. Shalala, 955 F. Supp. 128 (D.D.C. 1997).

[310] 21 C.F.R. § 314.107(c).

[311] *Mova*, 955 F. Supp. at 128.

[312] *See* 57 Fed. Reg. at 17,592.

The 505(b)(2) application also is similar to an ANDA in that the applicant is required to certify to the patent status of the drug for which the referenced investigations were conducted, by stating: that the relevant patent information has not been filed by the original applicant (as evidenced by the lack of a listing in the Orange Book); that such patent has expired; the date on which the patent will expire; or that the patent is invalid or will not be infringed by the manufacture, use, or sale of the proposed 505(b)(2) drug.[313] Also, as with ANDAs, the 505(b)(2) applicant who files a "paragraph IV" patent certification of invalidity or noninfringement must notify the patent holder,[314] who then has forty-five days to decide whether to sue the applicant for patent infringement and trigger an automatic thirty-month statutory injunction while the courts decide the substantive patent issues involved.[315]

■ Antibiotics

Antibiotics are regulated both as new drugs under section 505 of the FDCA[316] and under their own special provision, section 507.[317] Section 507 originally was enacted in response to concerns about the special manufacturing processes — in particular, fermentation — involved in producing antibiotics. It authorizes the FDA to establish standards of identity, strength, quality, and purity for antibiotic drugs, and requires that each batch of an antibiotic be certified by the FDA as conforming to the applicable standards set forth in the relevant antibiotic monograph before the antibiotic may be lawfully marketed, unless it has been exempted from the batch certification requirement.[318] In addition to the special requirements of section 507, antibiotic drugs are approved as part of the general new drug approval process under section 505 of the FDCA, and must meet all requirements applicable to new drugs under that section, including proof of effectiveness by adequate and well-controlled clinical investigations.[319]

In 1982, however, the FDA adopted a blanket waiver of the requirement for batch-by-batch certification of antibiotics and declared that all approved antibiotics would be exempt from certification and would, after approval, be regulated as new drugs. This action was based on section 507(e) of the FDCA, and its implementing regulation, 21 C.F.R. section 433.1, which state that approved antibiotics that are also new drugs and are exempted from certification are deemed to be the subject of an approved NDA under section 505(b) of the FDCA.[320] Because antibiotics are approved under section 507 rather than section 505, however, they are not subject to the exclusivity and patent certification provisions of section 505.[321]

---

[313] 21 U.S.C. § 355(b)(2)(A).

[314] *Id.* § 355(b)(3).

[315] *Id.* § 355(c)(3)(C).

[316] *Id.* § 355.

[317] *Id.* § 357.

[318] *Id.*

[319] 21 C.F.R. § 431.17.

[320] Exemption of Antibiotic Drugs and Antibiotic Susceptibility Medical Devices from Certification, Final Rule, 47 Fed. Reg. 39,155 (1982).

[321] Glaxo, Inc. v. Heckler, 623 F. Supp. 69 (E.D.N.C. 1985).

■ OTC Drugs

The OTC Review

As noted above to avoid regulation as a new drug, a drug (unless it is grandfathered) must be deemed generally recognized as safe and effective (GRAS/E). The test for general recognition of safety and effectiveness, as it has been applied by the FDA and the courts, is a stringent one. In brief, it requires 1) that the drug be "generally recognized, among experts qualified by scientific training and experience to evaluate the safety and effectiveness of drugs, as safe and effective for use under the conditions prescribed, recommended, or suggested in the labeling thereof;"[322] 2) that such general recognition be based on adequate published data demonstrating the drug's safety and efficacy;[323] and 3) that the drug has been used "to a material extent" and "for a material time" under the labeled conditions.[324] The courts have stipulated that general recognition of effectiveness for an individual drug product must be supported by the same level of evidence as required for an NDA, including adequate and well-controlled investigations demonstrating efficacy.[325]

Although it is therefore exceedingly difficult for a drug product to qualify as GRAS/E on an individual basis, the GRAS/E concept has provided the FDA with a key legal tool to regulate over-the-counter (OTC) drugs, namely the OTC review. Starting in 1972, the FDA instituted a system to review the safety and efficacy of active ingredients (as opposed to individual drug products) in each category of OTC drugs. For each category, the FDA issued a call-for-data notice that was published in the *Federal Register*. These notices asked manufacturers to submit clinical/marketing data for the individual active ingredients contained in their products. The agency then convened expert advisory panels that were responsible for reviewing the data submissions for the active ingredients in each category.

Once each panel was finished with its review of the active ingredients and the submitted data, it was responsible for providing a final report to the FDA. This report reviews each ingredient and places it into one of three categories: category I ingredients are those that are deemed GRAS/E; category II ingredients are considered neither safe nor effective; and category III ingredients are viewed as having insufficient data to determine safety and/or efficacy. The report is then published by the FDA in the *Federal Register* as an advanced notice of proposed rulemaking with an opportunity for public comment. The FDA then reviews the report, taking into account any public comments, and publishes in the *Federal Register* the agency's interpretation of the report, sometimes disagreeing with the panel's interpretations and making changes as necessary. This action, which also is open for public comment, is called a notice of proposed rulemaking and is sometimes referred to as the tentative final monograph.

The FDA undertakes a final review of the ingredients, again taking public comments into account and including any new or additional data. The agency then publishes in the *Fed-*

---

[322] 21 U.S.C. § 321(p)(1).

[323] *See* Weinberger v. Hynson, Westcott & Dunning, Inc., 412 U.S. 609, 629-32 (1973); Weinberger v. Bentex Pharm., Inc., 412 U.S. 645, 652 (1973).

[324] 21 U.S.C. § 321(p)(2).

[325] *Hynson, Westcott & Dunning*, 412 U.S. at 609.

eral Register a rule establishing a final monograph, which categorizes each reviewed ingredient in that particular category based on its safety and efficacy. Following the effective date of the final monograph (usually a year after publication), only drug products that contain active ingredients, labeling claims, dosage strengths, and other specified conditions included in the final monograph are allowed to continue marketing.

Occasionally, companies petition the FDA to re-open or amend an OTC monograph, or the FDA sees a need to re-open the review of a particular category of drugs; the agency publishes a notice in the *Federal Register* to that effect. This action is considered a proposed monograph amendment. Referred to as a notice of proposed rulemaking, the process is opened again for public comment. The review process then proceeds as explained above.[326]

While many OTC drug categories have been finalized by the FDA, the OTC Drug Review process remains quite active, with many categories of drugs still being reviewed. Until a final monograph is published in the *Federal Register*, and takes effect, all products that contain active ingredients under review in a particular category, and that meet certain other conditions regarding labeling claims and other product attributes, are allowed to continue marketing unless the FDA specifically takes action against an individual ingredient for safety concerns or substantial lack of data for efficacy.

Rx-to-OTC Switches

A rapidly increasing proportion of the OTC market is made up of products that originally were approved as prescription drugs and subsequently were switched to OTC status, a transition commonly referred to as an "Rx-to-OTC switch." There are three ways to accomplish such a switch; a drug manufacturer can supplement the drug's existing NDA,[327] the FDA may create or amend an OTC monograph,[328] or the manufacturer may petition the FDA to make the switch.[329]

Currently, the most common way to accomplish the Rx-to-OTC switch is by supplementing the drug's NDA, due in large part to the opportunity this route affords the drug's sponsor to obtain marketing exclusivity for the switched product. In particular, if the Rx-to-OTC switch supplement involves a change to the drug that is supported by "new clinical investigtations" that are "conducted or sponsored by [the applicant]" and are "essential to the [supplement's] approval," the applicant will gain three additional years of marketing exclusivity for the OTC product.[330] There is no set formula for determining what kinds of changes will meet the exclusivity requirements; according to a list prepared by the FDA, such changes can relate to such matters as active ingredient, dosage form, route of administration, conditions of use, or dosing regimen.[331]

---

[326] The FDA recently published an advance notice of proposed rulemaking to expand eligibility criteria for inclusion in the OTC review. Eligibility Criteria for Considering Additional Conditions in the Over-the-Counter Drug Monograph System; Request for Information and Comments, Advance Notice of Proposed Rulemaking, 61 Fed. Reg. 51,625 (1996).

[327] 21 C.F.R. § 314.70-.71.

[328] *Id.* pt. 330.

[329] *Id.* § 310.200(6).

[330] 21 U.S.C. § 355(c)(3)(D)(iv); 21 C.F.R. § 314.108.

[331] *See* Proposed ANDA Regulations, 54 Fed. Reg. 28,872, 28,892 (1989); 59 Fed. Reg. 50,338, 50,357 (1994). *See also Three-Year Exclusivity Can Be Granted for Dosage Changes, Waxman/Hatch Title I Rule Clarifies, ANDA 180-Day Exclusivity Start with Final Court Ruling,* F-D-C Rep. ("The Pink Sheet"), Oct. 10, 1994, at 10-12.

Procedurally, an applicant seeking to switch a product must first file a prior approval supplement to the drug's NDA.[332] A supplement by itself will not result in exclusivity, however. When filing its supplement, the manufacturer must include a statement explaining why its studies regarding the switched product meet the requirements that will entitle the drug to exclusivity.[333] Thus, the applicant must convince the FDA that the studies in support of the switch are "new," "clinical," "conducted or sponsored by [the applicant]," and "essential to the approval."[334] The FDA first will decide whether to approve the switch and subsequently will make the exclusivity determination.[335] That determination may be contested. For instance, generic manufacturers of the switched product may file citizen petitions to encourage the FDA to deny exclusivity. Conversely, a manufacturer who is unhappy with an agency denial of exclusivity may challenge that determination in court.

The FDA's decision on whether to grant exclusivity turns on whether the applicant's studies meet the statutory requirements, as amplified by the regulation governing exclusivity and other FDA policy statements, discussed above.[336] In recent years, there has been some controversy over how these requirements apply to Rx-to-OTC switches, particularly with respect to what types of studies qualify as "essential to approval" and as "clinical studies." In *Upjohn v. Kessler*,[337] the first litigated case on the "essential" requirement, Upjohn challenged the FDA's denial of exclusivity for its minoxidil (Rogaine®) product. The FDA had denied exclusivity in part because the studies on which Upjohn relied had evaluated a product with a different strength than the switched product, and thus were not "essential" to approving the switch. Notwithstanding its concerns over the gaps in the FDA's administrative record, the court refused to grant relief to Upjohn, deferring to the FDA's determination of which studies were essential.[338]

In the agency's letter granting exclusivity to OTC Nicorette® gum,[339] the FDA confirmed that studies evaluating patients' label comprehension and actual use patterns were "clinical," because they involved administering the drug to humans. The agency noted that studies do not need to be adequate and well-controlled, or meet the substantial evidence standard, in order to qualify as clinical.[340] The Nicorette® case also shed further light on what kind of study is "essential." In the FDA's view, the actual use and labeling compre-

---

[332] 21 C.F.R. § 314.70. For a full discussion of prior approval supplements, *see* text *supra*.

[333] 21 C.F.R. §§ 314.50(j), 314.54, 314.70-.71.

[334] 21 U.S.C. § 355(c)(3)(D)(iv); 21 C.F.R. § 314.108.

[335] According to a recently published FDA guidance document, as part of the determination of whether to grant the switch, an application for initial OTC marketing of a drug product usually should be presented to a joint meeting of the Non-prescription Drugs Advisory Committee and the advisory committee with clinical expertise. Such advisory committee review is not necessary if the product in question is another in a line of similar products already switched, the first such product was presented for advisory committee review, and no new or outstanding issues are present. FOOD & DRUG ADMIN., CENTER FOR DRUG EVALUATION AND RESEARCH, MANUAL OF POLICIES AND PROCEDURES NO. 6020.5, Review Management at 14 (1997) [hereinafter OTC GUIDE].

[336] *See* 54 Fed. Reg. at 28,872 (listing the types of changes that likely would warrant exclusivity); 59 Fed. Reg. at 50,357 (stating the FDA's views about what kinds of studies are "essential").

[337] 938 F. Supp. 439 (W.D. Mich. 1996).

[338] *Id.* at 442-43.

[339] Letter from Janet Woodcock, M.D., Dir., FDA Center for Drug Evaluation and Research, to Gary L. Yingling, McKenna & Cuneo (Oct. 31, 1996) (on file with the Food & Drug Admin., Dkt. No. 95P-0366).

[340] The FDA recently defined "clinical investigations" to include OTC actual use studies, but not OTC label comprehension studies. OTC GUIDE, *supra* note 335, at 3.

hension studies were essential because they demonstrated both the comparative efficacy of the prescription and OTC products, and the ability of patients to effectively choose between self-treatment and a physician-monitored program.

The Rx-to-OTC switch will continue to be important in future years. As more drugs are switched from prescription to OTC status, this area is likely to see further battles over exclusivity, as generic companies try to get the FDA to deny exclusivity for switched products and innovator companies defend their interests in response.

■ Expedited Availability

In response to increasingly vociferous complaints about drug approval delays from various quarters, including patient groups — particularly, but not exclusively, AIDS patient groups — throughout the late 1980s and early 1990s, the FDA and sister agencies within HHS took a series of initiatives aimed at getting drugs to critically ill patients sooner. The three chief efforts along these lines were treatment INDs, parallel track, and accelerated approval.

Treatment INDs

The treatment IND mechanism, established in 1987, allows an investigational drug to be provided outside controlled clinical trials in order to treat patients with serious or immediately life-threatening diseases for which no comparable or satisfactory alternative therapy is available.[341] The standard for FDA clearance of a treatment IND for a "life-threatening disease" is whether the "available scientific evidence, taken as a whole" provides a "reasonable basis" for concluding that the drug "[m]ay be effective for its intended use in the intended patient population," and would not expose patients to an "unreasonable and significant additional risk of illness or injury."[342] For a "serious" disease, the standard is whether there is "sufficient evidence of safety and effectiveness" to support treatment use.[343] Most IND procedural requirements apply to treatment INDs, including informed consent requirements and prohibitions on preapproval promotion or other commercialization of experimental treatments (although companies may charge patients enough to cover costs).[344] In addition, the drug sponsor is expected to continue conventional clinical trials and to pursue marketing approval of the drug with "due diligence."[345]

Parallel Track

The parallel track mechanism was designed specifically for AIDS patients. Under this mechanism, which was set forth in its final form in an April 1992 Public Health Service (PHS) notice, "promising" investigational agents may be provided to AIDS patients who are not able to take standard therapy or for whom standard therapy is no longer effective, and who are not able to participate in ongoing clinical trials.[346] Parallel track drugs are dis-

---

[341] 21 C.F.R. § 312.34.

[342] *Id.*

[343] *Id.*

[344] *Id.* § 312.7(d)(2).

[345] *Id.* § 312.34(b).

[346] Expanded Availability of Investigational New Drugs Through a Parallel Track Mechanism for People with AIDS and Other HIV-Related Diseases, Notice, Final Policy Statement, 57 Fed. Reg. 13,250 (1992).

tributed entirely outside the controlled clinical trial framework, although they must be under a study protocol, and data on safety and side effects are still supposed to be collected.[347] For a drug to qualify for parallel track, there must be "promising evidence of efficacy," combined with evidence that the drug is "reasonably safe."[348] In reviewing a parallel track proposal, the FDA also will look at factors such as evidence of a lack of satisfactory alternative therapy, and what the impact of the parallel track study may be on the controlled trials that will be the primary source of evidence of the drug's efficacy. In addition, certain formal IND requirements do not apply, most notably supervision by an IRB.[349] Individual patients seeking access to parallel track treatments, however, are supposed to satisfy a fairly detailed and stringent set of entry criteria designed to exclude patients who could participate in controlled clinical trials or who could take standard approved treatments.[350]

Accelerated Approval

Unlike treatment INDs and the parallel track, which are intended to expand access to experimental treatments before they are approved, the accelerated approval program is aimed at abbreviating the approval process itself. This procedure, which was adopted in its final form in December 1992, is available only for drugs or biologics that offer "meaningful therapeutic benefit compared to existing treatment [for serious or life-threatening illnesses.]"[351] There are two different routes to accelerated approval. Under the first route, the FDA may approve a treatment subject to special distribution or use restrictions that address outstanding safety issues. The second route, which is much more significant, provides for approval based on evidence of the drug's effect "on a surrogate endpoint that reasonably suggests clinical benefit or . . . on a clinical endpoint other than survival or irreversible morbidity."[352] Such approval is conditioned on the completion of postmarketing clinical studies to "verify and describe the drug's clinical benefit and to resolve remaining uncertainty" about the relationship of the surrogate endpoint to clinical benefit.[353] Drugs and biologics approved under the accelerated procedure also are subject to predissemination review requirements for promotional labeling and advertising and to a streamlined procedure for withdrawal of approval if, among other reasons, a postmarketing clinical study fails to verify clinical benefit.[354]

■ The Combination Drug Policy

The FDA's Combination Drug Policy provides that:

> Two or more drugs may be combined in a single dosage form when each component makes a contribution to the claimed effects and the dosage of each

---

[347] *Id.* at 13,256.

[348] *Id.* at 13,257.

[349] *Id.* at 13,258-59.

[350] *Id.* at 13,257-58.

[351] New Drug, Antibiotic, and Biological Drug Product Regulations; Accelerated Approval, Final Rule, 57 Fed. Reg. 58,942 (1992).

[352] *Id.*

[353] *Id.*

[354] *Id.* at 58,943.

component (amount, frequency, duration) is such that the combination is safe and effective for a significant patient population requiring such concurrent therapy as defined in the labeling for the drug. Special cases of this general rule are where a component is added:

(1) To enhance the safety or effectiveness of the principal active component; and

(2) To minimize the potential for abuse of the principal active component.[355]

Although this regulation on its face reads as a permissive policy, it actually was promulgated to require additional evidence of efficacy for many fixed combination drug products already on the market.[356] For an NDA for a combination drug containing two (or more) active ingredients, the combination policy means that evidence of safety and efficacy would be required not only for the drug as a whole, but also for each of the components. In other words, each component must be shown to contribute individually to the claimed overall effects of the product. This contribution, however, need not relate to efficacy — a component also may be added if it is shown to increase the safety of the other component or components. Of key importance under the combination drug policy is the principle that prior efficacy (or safety) results on individual active components cannot be extrapolated to a proposed combination drug — rather, that combination drug must undergo its own clinical investigations to demonstrate safety, efficacy, and the contribution of the active components.[357] Like many such principles in the drug approval setting, however, this one is not necessarily absolute, and the FDA may exhibit more or less flexibility in individual cases.

■ Exports

Export Law Prior to 1996

Under the FDCA as originally enacted (and its counterpart for biologics, section 351 of the Act) new drugs and biologics had to be approved or licensed, respectively, for marketing before they could lawfully be shipped in "interstate commerce" (in the case of drugs) or sold "from any State or possession into any other State or possession or into any foreign country" (in the case of biologics). Because those provisions, by their terms, cover exports as well as domestic sales, unapproved new drugs and unlicensed biologics could not be exported lawfully any more than they could lawfully be sold in the United States.[358]

Although this situation may have been more of a congressional oversight than an intentional policy decision,[359] the prohibition on the export of most unapproved new drugs and biologics stood unchanged for decades. In 1986, however, responding to pleas from phar-

---

[355] 21 C.F.R. § 300.50.

[356] *See* Combination Drugs for Human Use: Proposed Statement Amplifying Policy on Drugs in Fixed Combinations, 36 Fed. Reg. 3126 (1971).

[357] *See, e.g.*, U.S. v. Articles of Drug . . . Promise Toothpaste, 826 F.2d 564 (7th Cir. 1987).

[358] Unapproved new drugs and unlicensed biologics, in the FDA's view, meant not just products whose active ingredients had not been approved, but products whose dosage form, strength, route of administration, packaging, or labeling fell outside the terms of any existing FDA approval.

[359] *See* Sheila R. Shulman et al., *The Drug Export Amendments Act of 1986: Is It All It Was Intended To Be?*, 49 Food & Drug L.J. 367, 368 n.6 (1994).

maceutical companies increasingly frustrated by this prohibition as the industry became more and more internationalized, Congress provided partial relief in the form of the Drug Exports Amendments Act of 1986 (DEAA).[360]

The DEAA provided three "tracks" under which new drugs or biologics that were not approved in the United States could be exported for commercial sale abroad. Under track 1, an unapproved new drug or biologic could be exported for sale to any of twenty-one specified countries upon FDA approval of an export application. To be approved for export, there had to be "active pursuit" of full approval of the drug in the United States, among other requirements.

Track 2 of the DEAA allowed an unapproved drug or biologic to be exported from the United States upon a finding by the FDA, based on "credible scientific evidence" including clinical investigations, that the product was safe and effective in an importing country for the treatment or prevention of a tropical disease.[361] Although its humanitarian goals were laudable, this provision turned out to be of little practical importance.

Track 3 of the DEAA covered exports of unlicensed "partially processed biologics," defined as biological products not in a form applicable to the prevention, treatment, or cure of disease, and intended for further manufacture into final dosage form outside the United States.[362] Track 3 exports could take place only to the same twenty-one countries for which track 1 exports could be authorized, but no "active pursuit" requirement applied to track 3.

From the viewpoint of an exporter interested in marketing an unapproved drug or unlicensed biologic abroad, the DEAA certainly was better than nothing, but the amendments still left a great deal to be desired. The conditions and procedures required to export a product under track 1 of the DEAA, although far short of full-scale NDA or PLA requirements, were still burdensome. The "active pursuit" requirement precluded the potentially profitable and convenient business of manufacture for export only — unless the manufacturer (or another company) was pursuing product approval in the United States, it could not avail itself of DEAA's track 1 at all. Even if a manufacturer could get past the procedural hurdles of track 1, its products could be exported only to the twenty-one specified countries.

Understandably there was strong support in the pharmaceutical industry and Congress for a revamping of the export structure under the FDCA.[363] The combination of that sentiment and the broader FDA reform movement sparked a series of legislative initiatives that led to fundamental export reform.

---

[360] Pub. L. No. 99-660, 100 Stat. 3743.

[361] FOOD & DRUG ADMIN., A REVIEW OF FDA's IMPLEMENTATION OF THE DRUG EXPORT AMENDMENTS OF 1986, at 6 (1990).

[362] The FDA's interpretation of this requirement was that the product in question had to require further purification, inactivation, fractionation, or significant chemical modification before it could be used. Finished bulk products capable of being formulated into final dosage form through manufacturing steps other than these were not eligible for track 3 export, although they might qualify for export under track 1. *Id.* at 7.

[363] *See, e.g., Device/Drug Export Bill Should Be Passed and Put in Rescission Bill*, MDDI REP. ("The Gray Sheet"), June 19, 1995, at 6-7 (quoting House Speaker Gingrich as calling the then-existing FDA export regime "the dumbest single law . . . we have").

The 1996 Export Reform Act

The FDA Export Reform and Enhancement Act of 1996[364] has dramatically widened the path for export of unapproved pharmaceutical products. The pre-approval and reporting restrictions of the 1986 DEAA have been replaced in most cases by a requirement for mere notification to the FDA upon exportation. On the whole, the Export Reform Act makes it much easier for U.S. manufacturers to send new drugs and biologics abroad without first having to obtain FDA approval.

The Export Reform Act is organized into three tiers. In the first tier, an unapproved new drug or unlicensed biologic that has valid marketing authorization from the "appropriate authority" in any one of twenty-five listed countries[365] may be exported to any country in the world as long as it complies with the laws of that country.[366]

The only procedural requirement attached to the export of a drug under this authority is that the exporter must provide "simple notification" to the FDA identifying the drug when the exporter first begins to export the drug to a listed country;[367] if the drug is being exported to a nonlisted country, the exporter must notify the FDA as to the country of destination as well as identifying the drug.[368] The law requires that exporters maintain records of exported drugs and destination countries, but does not mandate reporting to the FDA.[369]

The second tier under the Export Reform Act is for exports of unapproved products that do not have valid marketing authorization from a listed country, but do comply with the laws of the country of destination and have valid marketing authorization from the responsible authority within that country. Such products may be exported to the country in question if the FDA determines that that country meets a set of requirements intended to ensure that its regulatory system is commensurate with those of the countries specifically listed in the law.[370]

Under the third tier of the Export Reform Act, a product that does not meet the requirements of either the first or second tiers still may be exported if the would-be exporter provides the FDA with "credible scientific evidence" that satisfies the agency as to the safety and effectiveness of the drug under the conditions of use in the destination country and meets certain other procedural conditions.[371]

---

[364] Incorporated as Chapter 1A of the Omnibus Appropriations Act, Pub. L. No. 104-134, 110 Stat. 1321-313 (codified at 21 U.S.C. §§ 334, 381, 382).

[365] Listed countries are members of the European Union (Belgium, Denmark, France, Germany, Greece, Ireland, Italy, Luxembourg, The Netherlands, Portugal, Spain, and the United Kingdom) and the European Free Trade Association (Austria, Finland, Iceland, Liechtenstein, Norway, Sweden, and Switzerland), Australia, Canada, Israel, Japan, New Zealand, Switzerland (already covered as an EFTA member but listed separately in the statute), and South Africa.

[366] 21 U.S.C. § 382(b)(1)(A). In addition, the Secretary of DHHS has the nondelegable discretion to add countries to the list of those whose marketing authorization can be used as a basis for drug exportation. *Id.* § 382(b)(1)(B). All unapproved products exported under the new law also must meet a set of general conditions concerning such matters as compliance with GMP requirements.

[367] *Id.* § 382(g).

[368] *Id.*

[369] *Id.*

[370] *Id.* § 382(b)(2).

[371] *Id.* § 382(b)(3).

Investigational Exports. In addition to these three tiers for commercial exports described above, the Export Reform Act contains a number of other avenues for unapproved products to be exported for specified uses. The first of these is a provision allowing an unapproved new drug or unlicensed biologic to be exported to a listed country if it is intended for investigational use and is exported in accordance with the laws of such country. A drug exported in this manner is exempt from IND requirements.[372]

Pipeline Products. The Export Reform Act specifically allows export of an unapproved product to a listed country, in accordance with that country's laws, if the drug is intended for formulation, filling, packaging, labeling, or further processing in anticipation of valid marketing authorization.[373]

Partially Processed Biologicals. The Export Reform Act expanded the track 3 provisions of the 1986 DEAA to allow the export of partially processed biological products to any country — not just listed countries — provided the same basic requirements were met as under the DEAA, and provided that the partially processed biological also meets the four general export requirements of FDCA section 801(e).[374]

Imports for Export. The Export Reform Act provides that no component of a drug can be excluded from importation into the United States if the importer of the drug certifies to the FDA that the article will be incorporated into a drug, device, food, food additive, color additive, dietary supplement, or biological product that will be exported in accordance with applicable law;[375] the responsible owner or consignee maintains records detailing the use of the imported article and, upon request by the FDA, submits a report detailing the use and disposition of the drug;[376] and any imported drug or component that is not incorporated into an exported product is destroyed or re-exported by the owner or consignee.[377]

---

[372] *Id.* § 382(c).

[373] *Id.* § 382(d).

[374] PHS Act, ch. 288, § 351(h), 37 Stat. 309 (1912) (codified at 42 U.S.C. §262).

[375] 21 U.S.C. § 381(a)(3)(A).

[376] *Id.* § 381(a)(3)(B).

[377] *Id.* § 381(a)(3)(C).

chapter 7

Adulteration and Misbranding of Drugs

Jeffrey N. Gibbs*
Judith E. Beach**

Introduction

One of Congress' primary purposes in enacting the Federal Food, Drug, and Cosmetic Act (FDCA) was to ensure the quality, purity, safety, and appropriate labeling of drugs in the United States.[1] To achieve these objectives, Congress set forth broad standards in the FDCA for determining whether drugs are adulterated or misbranded.[2] These standards have been refined over time through regulations, policy statements, agency and industry practice, judicial rulings, and other means.

The adulteration and misbranding provisions of the FDCA are enforced through other provisions defining prohibited acts involving interstate commerce[3] and seizures.[4] More specifically, the FDCA prohibits the 1) introduction of any adulteration or misbranded drug into interstate commerce;[5] 2) adulteration or misbranding of an article in interstate commerce;[6] 3) receipt of delivery of an adulterated or misbranded drug;[7] and 4) adulteration or misbranding of a drug while it is held for sale (excluding articles held for personal consumption[8]) after interstate shipment.[9] The latter provision, 21 U.S.C. § 331(k), was

---

* Mr. Gibbs is a Partner with the law firm of Hyman, Phelps & McNamara, P.C., Washington, D.C.

** Ms. Beach is an Associate with the law firm of Hyman, Phelps & McNamara, P.C., Washington, D.C.

1 United States v. Wiesenfeld Warehouse Co., 376 U.S. 86 (1964).

2 FDCA §§ 501, 502; 21 U.S.C. §§ 351, 352 (1994).

3 The term "interstate commerce" is defined as "1) commerce between any state or territory and any place outside thereof, and 2) commerce within the District of Columbia or within any other territory not organized with a legislative body." *Id.* § 201(b), 21 U.S.C. § 321(b).

4 *Id.* § 304, 21 U.S.C. § 321 (b).

5 *Id.* § 301(a), 21 U.S.C. § 331 (a).

6 *Id.* § 301(b), 21 U.S.C. § 331 (b).

7 *Id.* § 301(c), 21 U.S.C. § 331 (c).

8 United States v. Bronson Farms, Inc., [1985-1986, Transfer Binder] Food Drug Cosm. L. Rep. (CCH) ¶ 38,354.

9 FDCA § 301(k), 21 U.S.C. § 331(k).

designed to fill the gap created when a drug that has already been transported in interstate commerce is misbranded by a person who neither ships nor receives the drug in interstate commerce.[10]

The Food and Drug Administration's (FDA's) broad authority over drugs applies to articles defined as drugs under the FDCA.[11] The term "drug" includes four types of articles:[12] 1) articles recognized in official compendia, i.e., the *United States Pharmacopeia* (*USP*),[13] the *National Formulary* (*NF*, now combined with the *USP*), or the *Homeopathic Pharmacopeia of the United States*;[14] 2) articles *intended* for use in the diagnosis, cure, mitigation, treatment, or prevention of disease; 3) articles *intended* to affect the structure or function of the body; or 4) articles *intended* for use as a component of any of these articles.[15] Courts have followed the "intended use" principle for determining whether an article is a drug.[16] Thus, a product that is ordinarily not considered to be a drug can become one because of the promotional claims.[17] The intended use is determined by the objective intent of the persons legally responsible for the labeling of drugs, i.e., such persons' expressions or the surrounding circumstances.[18] In determining the intended use, the FDA — and a court — may rely upon objective evidence, including current and previous packaging, labeling, instructions for use,[19] and oral and written promotional statements from *any source*.[20] Moreover, the court in *Coyne Beahm, Inc. et al. v. FDA*[21] went further and ruled that objective evidence *other than* the manufacturer's claims can be material to a determination of intended use under the statutory definition so that the intended uses of an article may change after it has been introduced into interstate commerce by its manufacturer.

---

[10] United States v. Evers, 643 F.2d 1043 (5th Cir. 1981).

[11] The FDA also has the authority to regulate biologicals. Generally, the adulteration and misbranding provisions for drugs also apply to biologicals.

[12] United States v. Generix Drug Corp., 460 U.S. 453, 457-59 (1983).

[13] Despite the literal wording of the statute, neither the FDA nor courts contend that every substance listed in the *USP* is regulated as a drug. United States v. Ova II, 414 F. Supp. 660, *aff'd without opinion*, 535 F.2d 1248; National Nutritional Foods Ass'n v. Mathews, 557 F.2d 325 (2d Cir. 1977). For example, the *USP/NF* includes monographs for nutritional supplements, such as vitamins, sutures, foods, and peanut oil, which are not regulated as drugs.

[14] Drugs labeled and offered for sale as a homeopathic drug are subject to the provisions of the *Homeopathic Pharmacopeia* of the United States instead of the *USP* FDCA 21 § 501(b), U.S.C. § 351(b). The FDA regards over-the-counter homeopathic drugs as those for treatment of nonserious diseases, which are self-limiting and amenable to self-diagnosis and treatment by the laity. Otherwise, the FDA treats homeopathic drugs offered for treatment of serious diseases as *prescription* homeopathic drugs. *See* Warning Letter Reference Guide, Prescription Homeopathic Products Marketed Over-the-Counter, Health Fraud Bulletin #17 (Oct. 1994). Homeopathic drug products are specifically exempted from expiration dating requirements. 21 C.F.R. § 211.142(e) (1997). Also, for homeopathic drugs, the FDA is not enforcing the requirement under 21 C.F.R. § 211.154 for laboratory determination of identity and strength of each active ingredient prior to release for distribution.

[15] FDCA § 201 (g)(1), 21 U.S.C. § 321(g)(1) (emphasis added).

[16] United States v. Articles of Drug Labeled No. 26 Formula GM, 132 F. Supp. 569 (S.D. Cal. 1952).

[17] United States v. 500 Plastic Bottles, More or Less . . . Wilfley's Bio water, 1990-1993 Food Drug Cosm. Rep. (CCH) 30 (Wilfley's "Bio water" was deemed a drug).

[18] 21 C.F.R. § 201.128 (1997).

[19] *See, e.g.,* Nutrilab Inc. v. Schweiker, 547 F. Supp. 880 (N.D. Ill. 1982), *aff'd on other grounds,* 713 F.2d 335 (7th Cir. 1983) (labeling and promotional claims regarding testing, approval, effectiveness, and the prevention of degenerative diseases all showed intended uses that brought the product within the statutory definition of a "drug").

[20] *See, e.g.,* V.E. Irons Inc. v. United States, 244 F.2d 34 (1st Cir. 1957); United States v. Article of Drug . . . B-Complex Cholinos Capsules, 362 F.2d 923 (3d Cir. 1966).

[21] Memorandum Opinion Civ. No. 2:95CV00591 (M.D. N.C. Apr. 5, 1997) at n.31. Class appeals have been filed by the parties in this case.

The definition excludes dietary supplements.[22] In addition, a therapeutic product sometimes consists of both a drug and device, and these products are regulated based on their primary mechanism of action.[23]

Adulteration

Under the FDCA, a drug can be deemed adulterated for a variety of reasons. These include general standards for strength, quality, and purity; the requirements that drugs meet specific standards for strength, quality, and purity set forth in applicable compendia; that the drug be manufactured in accordance with current good manufacturing practice; and a number of other grounds.

The term "adulteration," at least originally, applied primarily to drugs that were adulterated in the ordinary meaning of the word. For example, a drug was adulterated if it consisted of any filthy, putrid, or decomposed substance. A drug was also adulterated if it was prepared, packed, or held under insanitary conditions, regardless of the presence of a filthy, putrid or decomposed substance.[24] The definition is no longer so limited. A drug can meet all of its specifications, and still be "adulterated" because of recordkeeping violations. Thus, not every drug deemed to be "adulterated" under the FDCA is adulterated in the customary sense of the word.

■ Acceptability of Drug Production Practices — Current Good Manufacturing Practices

The most important adulteration provision is one declaring a drug to be adulterated if the facilities, controls, and the manufacturing, processing, packing, and storage methods[25] under which it is produced do not conform to "current good manufacturing practice[s]" (cGMPs).[26] The FDA relies on this provision more often than the other adulteration provisions.

The purpose of the cGMP provision of the FDCA is to ensure that a drug meets applicable statutory standards of safety,[27] has the requisite identity and strength, and meets the quality and purity characteristics required by law.[28] It is not a defense to an enforcement pro-

---

[22] FDCA § 403, 21 U.S.C. § 343.

[23] *Id.* § 503(g)(1), 21 U.S.C. § 353(g)(1). The FDA has established a procedure whereby companies can request that a combination article be designated as a drug or device. 21 C.F.R. pt. 3. The designation procedure also can be used for a single entity product where its status is unclear, e.g., whether it is a drug, biologic or device. *See Coyne Beahm,* Memorandum Opinion Civ. No. 2:95CV00591 (court held that the FDA had the discretion to regulate tobacco products as drugs, devices or combination products).

[24] FDCA § 501(a)(2)(A), 21 U.S.C. § 351(a)(2)(A).

[25] United States v. Dino, 919 F.2d 72, 75 (8th Cir. 1990), *cert. denied,* 502 U.S. 808 (1991)(unlike original specially-designed containers, the jugs that the defendant used to store samples of cough syrup were intended for short-term contact and may have leaked into product causing its adulteration).

[26] FDCA § 501(a)(2)(B), 21 U.S.C. § 351(a)(2)(B).

[27] *Id.* Under the FDCA, a drug can be safe and yet cause adverse reactions in some patients.

[28] *Id.*

ceeding that the drug is actually safe and effective or even that the drug actually meets applicable standards of strength, quality, and purity. The violation of the cGMP standard itself renders a drug adulterated.

One of the key features of the cGMPs is that a company must document the legally required operations. It is not enough that the operations were properly performed; the company must be able to demonstrate that it was performed. Thus, a company can manufacture a safe, effective drug that meets specifications and yet violate cGMPs because of lack of documentation.

cGMP violations are a primary source of enforcement actions. For example, in fiscal year 1996 the FDA issued fifty-nine cGMP warning letters to drug manufacturers, repackers, and testing laboratories; over 100 had been issued in each of the two previous fiscal years.[29]

Constitutional Validity of Current Good Manufacturing Practices

The phrase "Current Good Manufacturing Practices" is undefined in the statute and in the implementing regulations. Nevertheless, courts have consistently rejected the claims that the cGMPs are unconstitutionally vague. Rather, courts, in upholding the statutory provisions and the regulations promulgated by the FDA,[30] have stated that the cGMP standards are as definite as standards in other sections of the FDCA.[31]

The courts have also noted that the pharmaceutical industry participated in the congressional hearings from which the term arose and, according to the courts, the industry now customarily refers to the term cGMPs.[32] Also, the word "current" fixes the point in time when the acceptability of the production practices can be determined,[33] and the term "good" likewise acquires adequate meaning when read with respect to objective criteria and is not "unduly subjective."[34] In addition, requirements for cGMPs have been covered widely in printed publications, educational courses, and trade association seminars.[35] The courts have also said that the regulations are worded to provide some flexibility to manufacturers in complying with them,[36] but are sufficiently definite to assure that a particular drug is safe and reliable,[37] to give notice of the required conduct to one seeking to avoid penalties, and to guide a judge in application of cGMPs and a lawyer in defending one charged with violating cGMPs.[38]

---

[29]　*FDA Issues Fewer Warning Letters in FY 1996*, QUALITY CONTROL REP., ("The Gold Sheet"), Feb. 1997, at 1. It is not unusual for the number of enforcement actions to fluctuate from year to year.

[30]　21 C.F.R. pts. 210, 211.

[31]　United States v. Bel-Mar Laboratories, Inc., 284 F. Supp. 875, 882 (E.D.N.Y. 1968); United States v. An Article of Drug . . . White Quadrisect, 484 F.2d 748 (7th Cir. 1973) (per curiam) (given the ambiguity elsewhere in the FDCA, it is not clear that this is an adequate justification.)

[32]　*Bel-Mar Laboratories, Inc.*, 284 F. Supp. at 883, citing H.R. REP. No. 2464, 87th Cong., 2d Sess. 2 (1962).

[33]　*White Quadrisect*, 484 F.2d at 749.

[34]　*Id.* at 750.

[35]　United States v. Morton Norwich Products, Inc., 461 F. Supp. 760 (N.D.N.Y. 1978). Unfortunately, these various sources do not always agree on the interpretation of the cGMPs.

[36]　*Id.* at 760; National Ass'n of Pharmaceutical Manufacturers v. HHS, 586 F. Supp. 740 (S.D.N.Y. 1984).

[37]　*Bel-Mar Laboratories, Inc.*, 284 F. Supp. at 875.

[38]　*National Ass'n. of Pharmaceutical Manufacturers,* 586 F. Supp. at 740.

On the other hand, one of the few courts called on to interpret and apply the cGMP regulations in detail, *United States v. Barr Laboratories, Inc.*,[39] complained that "[i]ronically, the regulations . . . whose broad and sometimes vague instructions allow conflicting, but plausible, views of the precise requirements transform what might be a routine evaluation into an arduous task." The court noted that, to the extent that the regulations create ambiguities, the industry "can turn for guidance to literature from seminars and pharmaceutical firms, textbooks, reference books and FDA letters to manufacturers . . . or employ scientific judgement where appropriate."[40] The court cautioned, however, that it "cannot rely on industry practice alone to determine whether an individual firm meets the statutory requirements, because industry standards themselves must be reasonable and consistent with the spirit and intent of the cGMP regulations."[41]

Current Good Manufacturing Practices Regulations

The FDA has issued binding cGMP regulations[42] for finished pharmaceuticals that contain minimum requirements for the methods to be used in, and the facilities or controls to be used for, the manufacture, processing, packing, or holding of a drug product.[43] The FDA intends the cGMP regulations to function as prophylactic quality control measures to ensure that the product is safe for use, and that it has the identity and strength and meets the quality and purity characteristics it purports to possess. The regulations are designed to prevent problems such as super- and sub-potency, product mix-ups, contamination, and mislabeling of drugs. Accordingly, they provide a regulatory framework for virtually all aspects of drug manufacture, including personnel, buildings and facilities, equipment, control of components and drug product containers and closures, production, packaging and labeling, warehousing and distribution procedures, laboratory controls, records, reports, complaint handling, and returned and salvaged drug products.[44]

As the word "current" implies, the cGMPs are an evolving concept. The FDA periodically amends and revises the cGMP regulations. For instance, in 1995 the FDA amended 21 C.F.R. § 211.42(c) to clarify the degree of discretion provided to manufacturers to determine whether separate or defined areas of production and storage of drug products and their ingredients are necessary.[45] In addition, the FDA's interpretation can change over time, even if the wording of the regulations remains static.

For example, the Scale-Up and Post-Approval changes (SUPAC) Task Force was established by the Center for Drug Evaluation and Research's Chemistry, Manufacturing and Controls Coordinating Committee to develop guidance on scale-up and other post-approval changes for different dosage-form categories of drug products. A guidance has been issued to provide recommendations to sponsors of new drug applications (NDAs) and abbreviated new drug applications who intend to change, during the post-approval period, the components or composition; the site of manufacture; the scale-up/scale-down

---

[39]   812 F. Supp. 458, 465 (D. N.J. 1993).

[40]   *Id.*

[41]   *Id.*

[42]   National Ass'n of Pharmaceutical Manufacturers v. FDA, 637 F.2d 877, 878 (2d Cir. 1981) (the cGMP regulations are binding, not merely interpretive).

[43]   21 C.F.R. pts. 210, 211.

[44]   *Id.*

[45]   60 Fed. Reg. 4087 (Jan. 20, 1995).

of manufacture; and/or the manufacturing of an immediate release oral dosage formulation.[46]

A controversial issue has been the extent to which cGMPs apply to what were initially called bulk pharmaceutical chemicals and are now known as active pharmaceutical ingredients (APIs). APIs differ in several respects from dosage form drugs, including the processes used for the production of APIs and those for the finished products. During the production of APIs, the starting materials, or derivatives of the starting materials, undergo some significant chemical change. Impurities, contaminants, carriers, vehicles, inerts, diluents, and/or unwanted crystalline or molecular forms, which may be present in the raw materials, are largely removed by various treatments in the production process, and must be confirmed by various chemical, biological and/or physical tests. Finished drug products, however, are the result of a formulation from bulk materials whose quality can be measured against fixed specifications. For the finished drug product production, purification steps typically are not involved. Although the cGMP regulations apply only to finished drugs and not bulk drugs, according to the FDA the FDCA does not make this distinction. Thus the failure of an API manufacturer to comply with cGMPs renders the product adulterated. In determining whether there is cGMP compliance, the FDA relies upon the cGMP regulations.[47]

The FDA has issued warning letters to API manufacturers for non-compliance with good manufacturing practice[s] (GMPs). For example, in a warning letter issued on February 17, 1995, the FDA charged a bulk drug manufacturer with GMP violations including failure to maintain adequate batch records, failure to validate processes, failure to assure equipment maintenance and cleanliness, and failure to establish and follow written procedures.

Judicial Enforcement

The FDA frequently finds one or more cGMP violations during an inspection of a drug facility. Although most allegations of cGMP violations are resolved without litigation, some disputes wind up in court.

In the cases that have been litigated, the courts have generally agreed with the FDA that the drugs in question were adulterated based on failure to comply with cGMPS, especially where the manufacturer had committed numerous violations of cGMPs. For example, in separate cases, the following combined violations of cGMP regulations supported findings that the respective drug products were adulterated: 1) lack of quality testing of the final product, inadequate controls to assure batch-to-batch consistency of product quality, and failure to evaluate the quality of raw materials;[48] 2) the presence of as few as one bacterial colony in the drug production area, unexplained changes in amounts of chemicals from that of the master formula, inadequate sterility procedures of sterile drug product, inadequate records comparing theoretical and actual batch yields, and inadequate controls for pH;[49] 3) inadequate quality controls for verifying specifications, identity and strength, and

---

[46]   60 Fed. Reg. 61,637 (Nov. 30, 1995).

[47]   *See* GUIDE TO INSPECTION OF BULK PHARMACEUTICAL CHEMICALS (May 1, 1994) (D.C. E.D. Mich. 1990).

[48]   United States v. Sopcak [1989-1992 Transfer Binder] Food Drug Cosm. L. Rep. (CCH) ¶ 18,162 (D.C. E.D. Mich. 1990).

[49]   United States v. Dianovin Pharmaceuticals, Inc., 342 F. Supp. 724 (D.P.R. 1972), *aff'd*, 475 F.2d 100 (1st Cir. 1973), *cert. denied*, 414 U.S. 830 (1973).

stability of the drug, lack of sample retention and laboratory data, lack of verification of adherence to standard operating procedures, and improper labeling and packaging of product;[50] and 4) "dusty conditions, overhanging pipes, loose or missing ceiling tiles," inadequate humidity control, no written standard operating procedures for cleaning the manufacturing facilities and equipment or for weighing drug components.[51]

The Barr Decision. Although most courts have decided cGMP cases with little analysis or detail, one recent case broke that pattern. Hearing sharply conflicting expert testimony regarding the cGMP regulations, the court in *United States v. Barr Laboratories*[52] refused to accept all aspects of the FDA's interpretation of its cGMP regulations and discussed various aspects of the cGMPs at some length.

For example, in addressing "out-of-specification" test results, the court disagreed with the FDA's view that each individual test result falling outside of specifications outlined in the *USP* or the firm's predetermined testing procedures, constituted a "batch failure," requiring a full investigation. The court adopted instead a "sliding-scale approach," proposed by the manufacturer, where the nature of the failure governed the intensity of the "failure investigation" under the cGMP regulations, 21 C.F.R. § 211.192.

On the other hand, the court agreed with the FDA that if manufacturing firms either adopt methods that the *USP* does not recognize or modify *USP* procedures, they must validate these methods and provide the FDA with the raw data used to prepare the validation studies.[53] The court also held that 2 1C.F.R. §211.67 requires "description in sufficient detail" of the methods and materials used for cleaning; therefore Barr needed to identify the cleaning agents involved.[54]

Although the court's ruling was not uniformly favorable to the FDA and was fact specific, the agency has apparently embraced the court's opinion and attempted to translate the elements of the opinion that were favorable to the FDA into "rules of general pharmaceutical industry applicability."[55] One industry commentator, however, has suggested that the FDA's reliance on the *Barr* decision is overstated because the case "was not a review of cGMP regulations," but instead "was an attempt to apply those regulations to one defendant, based on one set of facts."[56]

Consent Decree of Injunction. While some cGMP cases are litigated to a judgment, most cGMP court cases are resolved through agreements between the government and the corporate and individual defendants in the form of a consent decree of permanent injunction.[57] The consent decree generally imposes both prohibitory and mandatory requirements on the

---

[50] United States v. Articles of Drug . . . Colchicine, 442 F. Supp. 1236 (S.D.N.Y. 1978), *aff'd without op.,* 603 F.2d 214 (2d Cir. 1979).

[51] United States v. Richlyn Laboratories, Inc., 822 F. Supp. 268, 272-73 (E.D. Pa. 1993).

[52] 812 F. Supp. 458 (D.N.J. 1993).

[53] *Id.* at 482.

[54] *Id.* at 483.

[55] Michael P. Peskoe, *Lessons Learned from Good Manufacturing Practice Compliance* , 50 FOOD DRUG L.J. 65, 66 (1995).

[56] *Id.* at 70.

[57] See discussion of injunction actions *infra.*

company. Usually, the prohibitory requirements enjoin the defendants from continuing their operations "unless and until" they meet certain enumerated requirements in the consent decree. Violation of a consent decree may result in being held in contempt of court.

Consent decrees can be useful sources of information regarding the elements that the FDA believes are part of the cGMPs (or at least are desirable for companies with cGMP difficulties). For example, mandatory injunctive requirements have included the retaining of a qualified consultant by the defendant to inspect the facility and certify the production of certain lots of product prior to shipment, the development of an adequate quality assurance/quality control program, and future compliance with cGMP practices.

In *United States v. Warner-Lambert Company*,[58] the company entered into a consent decree with the FDA governing Warner-Lambert's production of certain drug products and drug substances at six named facilities. The decree addressed several specific cGMP requirements and imposed explicit obligations on Warner-Lambert. For instance, FDA required Warner-Lambert to submit a remedial action plan for each drug product for validation of in-process, finished product and stability-test methods, and reformulation and revalidation of the manufacturing process. The named facilities had to undergo inspection for cGMP compliance and to have expert certification of the manufacturing process, testing procedures, and cGMP compliance prior to manufacturing or distributing drug products from these facilities.

Also, the court-ordered consent decree with Eli Lilly and Company (Lilly), entered into between the FDA and the company in July 1995, was designed to address the FDA's concerns about the company's practices for controlling and reporting manufacturing changes made to prevent product failure.[59] The complaint alleged that Lilly did not obtain prior approval from the FDA before changing manufacturing conditions for an antibiotic after indications that the product might not meet stability standards. The consent decree requires, among other things, that process or formulation changes undertaken to address potential product quality problems need to be evaluated for regulatory compliance.

■ Compendial Standards

All drug products marketed in the United States must meet standards of strength, quality and purity, or state otherwise on their labels, or be considered adulterated.[60] Drug monographs in the official compendia provide many of these standards. A monograph is a document that establishes titles, definitions, descriptions, and standards for the identity, quality, strength, purity, packaging, and labeling for a drug. The United States Pharmacopeia (USP) is a nonprofit organization that develops drug product standards with the cooperation of professionals from academia, the medical community, the pharmaceutical industry, and the FDA.

The FDA can participate in the process in various ways, such as by performing research on testing methods, and by taking part in the USP Reference Standards collaborative study

---

[58]   Civ. No. 93-325, D. N.J. (Aug. 17, 1993) (consent decree of permanent injunction).

[59]   Civ. No. 95-2219, D. Md. (July 31, 1995) (consent decree of permanent injunction).

[60]   United States v. Lanpar Co., 293 F. Supp. 147 (N.D. Tex. 1968).

program. The USP/NF establishes and improves standards through a review and comment procedure for all proposed new monographs and monograph changes. Industry and other interested parties have the opportunity to participate in the development of USP/NF monographs.

The FDA conducts periodic surveillance of marketed drug products to verify that they meet monograph standards. If the manufacturer knows that a drug product's strength, quality, or purity differs from the monograph standards, it must state any differences plainly on the drug's label.[61]

In one case, a pharmaceutical company purchased potassium penicillin G, ground the pills in a coffee grinder, and packed the material into capsules labeled "Ampicillin."[62] Both penicillin G and ampicillin are recognized by the *USP* and are related drugs, but they are different from each other and have different pharmacological effects. The court determined that a product containing penicillin G cannot meet the standard for ampicillin; thus, the strength of the drugs differed from the standard set out in the *USP* Accordingly, the court held that the drugs were adulterated under 21 U.S.C. § 351(b).

Further, for determinations of strength, purity and quality, the *USP* sets forth minimum testing requirements for drug products.[63] However, a manufacturer need not use a USP or NF method to analyze a compendial product, even though one exists in the monograph for the product. The manufacturer may use another method provided that it is of equivalent or higher accuracy and the product meets compendial requirements when tested by the FDA using the USP or NF method. The product's conformance to the monograph standard must be assured by suitable means, including validation and control. On the other hand, compendial methods must be adhered to for a compendial drug product when a firm has made specific commitments to do so (as in a new drug application or other submission), or where the official method is the only appropriate test.[64]

Scientifically sound, alternative methods may be acceptable for the purpose of "batch release testing" of an official drug. However, in the event of a dispute as to whether or not a drug product meets the standard, the compendial method will be applied as the "referee test."[65]

■ Other Types of Adulteration

In contrast to the requirements for "official drugs," the FDCA is silent as to the method required for determining strength, purity, or quality of drugs not recognized in an official compendium at the time of interstate shipment, i.e., "nonofficial drugs."[66] If such a drug does not conform to the strength, purity, or quality it is represented or purported to pos-

---

[61] FDCA § 501(b), 21 U.S.C. § 351(b).

[62] United States v. Jamieson-McKames Pharmaceuticals, Inc., 651 F.2d 532, 548 (8th Cir. 1981), *cert. denied*, 455 U.S. 1016 (1981).

[63] FDCA § 501(b), 21 U.S.C. 351(b).

[64] Compliance Policy Guide 7132.05.

[65] *Id.*

[66] Woodard Laboratories, Inc. v. United States, 198 F.2d 995, 999 (9th Cir. 1952).

sess, then it is adulterated.[67] Nevertheless, if a *USP* assay method is adopted by the manufacturer for determining the strength, purity, or quality of a "nonofficial drug," the method is "entitled to great weight."[68]

A drug shall be deemed adulterated if any substance has been mixed or packed with the drug so as to reduce its quality or strength or if any substance has been substituted in whole or in part.[69] This is true whether or not the substituted substance is better or worse than the original or normal ingredient, or whether the drug is "official" or "nonofficial."

A drug is also adulterated if its container is composed, in whole or in part, of any poisonous or deleterious substance that may render the contents injurious to health.[70] There need not be any definite proof that the substance actually has contaminated the drug, only that it "may" render the contents injurious to health. The FDA may also consider a drug adulterated if it contains, for purposes of coloring only, an unsafe color additive.[71] As is the case with a number of the adulteration provisions, this provision is rarely invoked.

Misbranding of Drugs

The FDCA prohibits the introduction into interstate commerce of any drug that is misbranded and the holding for sale of a misbranded drug after shipment.[72] As in the case of adulteration, a product may be deemed misbranded in a variety of ways. In some instances, the term "misbranding" seems like a misnomer in that it is not related to the product's labeling in any way. Misbranding, though, is a catch-all phrase that can encompass many different activities that Congress or the FDA has decided to regulate.[73]

■ Labels and Labeling

Most misbranding cases involve product labels and labeling. First, it is important to understand that the terms "label" and "labeling" are not synonymous.[74] "Label" means a "display of written, printed, or graphic matter upon the immediate container of any article."[75] The term "labeling," however, is much broader, because it includes all labels and other "written, printed, or graphic material 1) upon any article or any of its containers or wrap-

---

[67]   FDCA § 501(c), 21 U.S.C. § 351(c); *see* United States v. Lanpar Co., 293 F. Supp. 147, at 153 (N.D. Tex. 1968) (drug tablets which failed to meet standards set forth in the *USP* for tablet disintegration were adulterated).

[68]   *Id.* at 153.

[69]   FDCA § 501(d), 21 U.S.C. § 351(d).

[70]   *Id.* § 501(a)(3), 21 U.S.C. § 351(a)(3).

[71]   *Id.* § 501(a)(4), 21 U.S.C. § 351(a)(4).

[72]   *Id.* § 301(a), 21 U.S.C. § 331(a).

[73]   For example, a drug can be misbranded because it was manufactured at a facility that was not registered with the FDA. *Id.* § 502(o), 21 U.S.C. § 352(o).

[74]   *Id.* § 201(k), (m), 21 U.S.C. § 321(k), (m).

[75]   *Id.* § 201(k), 21 U.S.C. § 321(k).

pers, or 2) accompanying such article."[76] Any type of written materials, including bro-chures, reprints of scientific articles and pamphlets that provides supplemental informa-tion relating to the use of the drug, can be considered labeling.[77]

Frequently, the key issue regarding labeling is whether the materials "accompany" the drug. The courts have adopted a very expansive interpretation: that information "accom-panies" the drug, even if sold or delivered separately from the drug product, so long as the drugs and the information had "a common origin and a common destination."[78] If the manufacturer makes such material part of an "integrated distribution program" for its product, the materials could be regarded as labeling.[79] While courts have often found materials and products to be labeling even though distributed at different times and in dif-ferent ways, that has not always been the case.[80]

The FDA has broadly defined labeling to include:

> [b]rochures, booklets, mailing pieces, detailing pieces, file cards, bulletins, calendars, price lists, catalogs, house organs, letters, motion picture films, film strips, lantern slides, sound recordings, exhibits, literature, and reprints and similar pieces of printed, audio, or visual matter descriptive of a drug and references published (for example, the "Physicians Desk Reference") for use by medical practitioners, pharmacists, or nurses, containing drug information supplied by the manufacturer, packer, or distributor of the drug and which are disseminated by or on behalf of its manufacturer, packer, or distributor . . . .[81]

As technology has developed, the FDA has expanded the definition even further to include videotapes, software, and new forms of communication. The statutory definition refers to "written, printed, or graphic materials." Nevertheless, a number of courts have held oral statements to be labeling.[82] An FDA draft guidance states that independent scientific and educational activities, including oral presentations at continuing medical education pro-grams, are subject to regulation as labeling or advertisements, but that the FDA will not regulate the activity if certain criteria are met.[83]

---

[76] *Id.* § 201(m), 21 U.S.C. § 321(m).

[77] Kordel v. United States, 335 U.S. 345, 348 (1948).

[78] *Id.*; United States v. 47 Bottles More or Less, Jenasol RJ Formula "60", 320 F.2d 564 (3d Cir. 1963).

[79] *Kordel,* 335 U.S. at 350; United States v. Vital Health Products, Ltd., 786 F. Supp. 761, 775-76 (E.D. Wis. 1992); *but see,* United States v. Guardian Chemical Corp., 410 F.2d 157, 161 (2d Cir. 1969) (as for an article handed out at the American Medical Association convention about the drug, the court stated there was "more doubt" whether the article "accompanied" the distribution of the drug); *see, e.g.,* United States v. Articles of Drug . . . 5,906 Boxes, 745 F.2d 105 (1st Cir. 1984), *cert. denied,* 470 U.S. 1004 (1985) (index file cards delivered to physicians are label-ing because the cards supplemented and/or explained the drug).

[80] United States v. Sterling Vinegar and Honey . . . and an Undetermined Number of Copies of . . . Books, 333 F.2d 157 (2d Cir. 1964) (a health food store could properly sell both a honey-vinegar product and, separately, books about the purported health- and disease-related benefits of the honey-vinegar combination, without having the books deemed labeling).

[81] 21 C.F.R. § 202.1(l)(2).

[82] *See, e.g.,* United States v. Hohensee, 243 F.2d 367, 370 (3d Cir. 1957); *V.E. Irons, Inc.,* 244 F.2d at 34.

[83] 57 Fed. Reg. 56,412, 56,413 (Nov. 27, 1992) (the FDA set forth several factors as indicia of independence that may demonstrate whether industry-supported scientific and educational activities are independent of the influence of the supporting company). The FDA's policy has been challenged in court. *See* Washington Legal Foundation v. Kessler, 880 F. Supp. 26 (D.D.C. 1995) (denying the FDA's motion to dismiss).

Reprints of scientific articles and textbooks that are distributed by drug companies that relate to marketed drugs are also considered to be labeling, even when not written by company employees. These sources often discuss "off-label" use of approved drugs. The FDA's regulation of reprints and textbooks has become a source of controversy. The FDA has adopted a policy that allows, albeit under narrowly circumscribed circumstances, certain textbooks and reprints to be actively disseminated even though they refer to off-label uses.[84]

Exhibits may also constitute labeling. For example, "unapproved" drugs may not be promoted prior to approval through commercial exhibits at meetings or trade shows. However, information about unapproved drugs may be displayed at scientific and educational exhibits.[85]

False or Misleading Labeling

A drug is misbranded under the FDCA if its label fails to bear the statements required by the FDCA or its labeling is false or misleading "in any particular."[86] Courts have upheld the constitutionality of the provision, finding it neither "vague nor indefinite." [87] The burden on the government is to establish that the labeling is in some respect false or misleading;[88] it need not demonstrate that the labeling reflects "conscious fraud."[89] Nor need the government demonstrate that the entire labeling is false or misleading. It need only be false or misleading "in any particular." Thus, a lengthy piece of labeling can be misbranded because it contains a single false or misleading statement.

Somewhat surprisingly, there has been relatively little discussion by the courts regarding the quantum of evidence needed to substantiate a claim so that a statement is not considered false or misleading. A statement can be deemed misleading, though, if it lacks any evidentiary support; evidentiary support may include testimony by experts based on 1) tests made on the product itself; 2) the consensus of medical opinion about the product; and 3) personal opinions.[90]

Furthermore, the FDCA prohibits false or misleading labeling or advertising of drugs by representations made or by failure to reveal material facts relating to potential consequences under customary conditions of use.[91] Accordingly, promotional materials for prescription drugs must present a "fair balance" both in the content of the materials and the format or manner in which risks and benefit information are presented.[92]

---

[84] 61 Fed. Reg. 52,800 (Oct. 8, 1996).

[85] Division of Drug Marketing, Advertising & Communications, Center for Drug Evaluation & Research, Food & Drug Admin., Pre-Approval Promotion Guidance (1994).

[86] FDCA § 502(a), 21 U.S.C. § 352(a).

[87] See, e.g., United States v. Dr. Salsbury's Rakos, 53 F. Supp. 746 (D.C. Minn. 1944); United States v. Marmola Prescription Tablets, 48 F. Supp. 878 (W.D. Wis. 1943), aff'd, 142 F.2d 107 (7th Cir. 1944), cert. denied, 323 U.S. 731.

[88] United States v. Articles of Drug..... Colchicine, 442 F. Supp. 1236, 1241 (S.D.N.X. 1978), aff'd without op., 603 F.2d 214 (2d Cir. 1979).

[89] Id.

[90] Research Laboratories, Inc. v. United States, 167 F.2d 410 (9th Cir. 1948).

[91] FDCA § 201(n), 21 U.S.C. § 321(n).

[92] Division of Drug Marketing, Advertising & Communications, Center for Drug Evaluation & Research, Food & Drug Admin., Current Issues and Procedures, (1994); 21 C.F.R. § 202.1(e)(6), (7) (regulations describe ways in which promotional materials may be misleading because they lack fair balance).

The question of whether labeling is misleading is a question of fact.[93] In determining whether the drug is misbranded, the fact finder may take into account statements or representations made about the drug, as well as the seller's failure to reveal material facts about the drug.[94] The FDA describes "material fact" as including those facts that concern "consequences which may result from use of the product under the labeled conditions of use or under customary or usual conditions for use."[95] "[S]cientific half-truths in the labeling alone make out a case of actionable misbranding."[96] In one case, a company quoted verbatim from official compendia and textbooks regarding its "Analysis of Ingredients," but the labeling omitted unfavorable comments from these sources regarding the ingredients.[97] The court ruled that the jury "shall" take into account omissions or suppressions in its deliberations.[98]

The FDA considers labeling to be inadequate if it fails to reveal facts concerning possible side effects that could result from customary or usual conditions of use.

Omission of Identifying Information

A drug in package form[99] is misbranded unless it bears the name and address of the manufacturer, packer, or distributor and an accurate statement of the quantity of the contents.[100] (The FDCA, however, does not require pharmacists or other licensed dispensers to include the information on prescription drug product labels if other requirements are met.[101]) The failure to bear the established name of the drug and each active ingredient, the amount and identity of any alcohol, and the quantity of certain ingredients in prescription drugs also constitutes misbranding.[102] Furthermore, the label must bear required information prominently and conspicuously enough for an ordinary individual to read and understand.[103]

Established Name of the Drug. The established name refers to the official name for a drug designated by the FDA. Otherwise, for the established name, the FDA deems the nonproprietary name adopted by U.S. Adopted Name Council (USAN) and published in the USAN and the *USP Dictionary* of drug names as preferable to a drug's compendia name.[104]

---

[93] United States v. Vital Health Products, Ltd., 786 F. Supp. 761, 767 (E.D. Wis. 1992); *see also* United States v. Dino (8th Cir. 1990), 919 F.2d 72, 75 (the court agreed that while "marketing of sample drugs is not *per se* misbranding . . . the language 'false or misleading in any particular' includes drugs received without lot numbers or expiration dates.").

[94] FDCA § 201(n), 21 U.S.C. § 321(n); *see Vital Health Products, Ltd.,* 786 F. Supp. at 767.

[95] 59 Fed. Reg. 64,240 (Dec. 13, 1994).

[96] *Research Laboratories, Inc.,* 167 F.2d at 418, 421-22; Pasadena Research Laboratories, Inc. v. United States, 169 F.2d 375 (9th Cir. 1948).

[97] *Research Laboratories, Inc.,* 167 F.2d at 422.

[98] *Id.*

[99] Package is defined in the Fair Packaging and Labeling Act (FPL Act), Pub. L. No. 89-755, 80 Stat. 1296 (1966), as amended 15 U.S.C. § 1459 (1994), as any container or wrapping in which a product is enclosed for delivery or display to the retail purchaser, not including shipping containers or outer wrappers. The FPL Act does not apply to prescription drugs. 15 U.S.C. § 1459(a).

[100] FDCA § 502(b), 21 U.S.C. § 352(b); 21 C.F.R. §§ 201.1, 201.62, 201.100(b)(4); United States v. Bel-Mar Laboratories, Inc., 284 F. Supp. 875, 879 (E.D.N.Y. 1968).

[101] FDCA § 503(b)(2), 21 U.S.C. § 353(b)(2).

[102] *Id.* § 502(e), 21 U.S.C. § 352(e); 21 C.F.R. §§ 201.10, 201.50, 201.61.

[103] FDCA § 502(c), 21 U.S.C. § 352(c); 21 C.F.R. § 201.15.

[104] 49 Fed. Reg. 37,574 (Sept. 17, 1984) (preamble).

In *Abbott Laboratories v. Gardner*,[105] the court held that Congress did not intend that a drug's established name would have to accompany *each* appearance of the proprietary name on the drug's labeling and advertising materials. Under the FDA's current regulations, the established (or generic) name must be cited every time the brand name is "featured," i.e., displayed in a way that creates an impression of importance.[106] Also, if the brand name appears only in running text on a page of the advertisement, but is not "featured," the generic name must appear at least once in the running text. [107]

Name and Place of Business of the Manufacturer, Packer, or Distributor. The drug's label must bear the name and place of the manufacturer, packer, or distributor.[108] If the manufacturer is identified on the label, the FDA does not have the authority to require that the distributor or packer also be identified on the label. [109]

A company can identify itself as a manufacturer only if it is, in fact, the manufacturer of the drug. The FDA defines a "manufacturer" as a firm that performs more than half of ten operations designated in the FDA's regulations as functions of the manufacturing process. The ten operations are "1) [m]ixing, 2) granulating, 3) milling, 4) molding, 5) lyophilizing, 6) tableting, 7) encapsulating, 8) coating, 9) sterilizing, and 10) filling sterile, aerosol, or gaseous drugs into dispensing containers."[110] The manufacturer must also identify other companies performing any one of the remaining applicable operations as "joint manufacturers" or state that "[c]ertain manufacturing operations have been performed by other firms."[111] If a company is simply a distributor, then its label may say "distributed by" or contain a similar phrase.[112]

For prescription drugs, the street address, city, state and zip code of the manufacturer, packer, or distributor must be included on both the label and labeling.[113] The street address, however, may be omitted if it is shown in a current drug directory or telephone directory.[114] For nonprescription drugs, this information must be included only on the label, not the labeling.[115]

Ingredients. If a drug is prepared from two or more ingredients, its label must bear the established name and quantity of each active ingredient, or it will be deemed mis-

---

[105] 387 U.S. 136, 137-39 (1967).

[106] 21 C.F.R. § 201.10(g).

[107] *Id.*

[108] FDCA § 502(b), 21 U.S.C. § 352(b).

[109] If a company both packs and distributes a drug product, it may identify itself as a packer or distributor, or both. 45 Fed. Reg. 25,768 (Apr. 15, 1980)(preamble). *See also* 21 C.F.R. § 201.1(h)(5) for manner in which the name of the distributor or packer is to appear on the label.

[110] 21 C.F.R. § 201.1(b),(c).

[111] *Id.* § 201.1(c)(1), (3).

[112] *Id.* § 201.1(h)(5).

[113] *Id.* § 201.1(i).

[114] *Id.*

[115] *Id.* § 201.1(l); *see also* 45 Fed. Reg. at 25,765. In United States v. An Article of Drug (Biflav-C-2), 292 F. Supp. 346, 347 (C.D. Cal. 1968), the court held that a drug was misbranded because the name and place of business of the drug manufacturer were not included on the drug's label, that is, on the immediate container which, in this case, was plastic packets containing the drug.

branded.[116] The term "ingredient" applies to any substance in the drug, whether it is added to the formulation as a single substance or in the drug mixture with other substances.[117]

In determining which of the ingredients in a drug product are active, the manufacturer should consider the purpose for which the ingredient is used and its physiological effects, if any. The FDA suggests that the active ingredients of a prescription drug be listed in order of their significance to the product's efficacy, but the FDA does not require, or, for that matter, prohibit, the listing of the inactive ingredients (except for those specified in section 502(e)(1)(A)(ii) of the FDCA, including, for example, bromides, ether, atropine, digitalis, strychnine, and thyroid.

Any statement regarding the quantity of an ingredient in a drug product that is in a unit dosage form, such as a tablet or capsule, must express the amount of the ingredient in each unit. If the drug is not in a unit dosage form, the amount of the ingredient must be specified as a particular unit of weight or measure or as a percentage of the ingredient in the drug. For prescription drugs, the statement must be informative to a licensed practitioner. For nonprescription drugs, the statement must be adequate to enlighten a layperson.[118]

Further, a drug in package form is misbranded unless it bears a label containing "an accurate statement of the quantity of the contents in terms of weight, measure, or numerical count."[119] For example, in *United States v. Articles of Drug . . . Colchicine*,[120] where a drug label stated "100 capsules," but contained only six capsules in each packet, the court held that the drug was misbranded, in violation of 21 U.S.C. § 352(b)(2). The court also found that the labeling violated section 502(a) of the FDCA because it was "false or misleading *in any particular.*"[121]

Failure to Provide Adequate Directions and Required Warnings

A drug is also misbranded if it lacks "adequate directions for use."[122] This has been an important enforcement provision for the FDA over the years.[123] "Adequate directions for use" means directions under which a layperson can use a drug safely and effectively.[124] The adequacy of such directions necessarily depends upon the indications for which the drug is intended.[125] The requirement of "adequate directions for use" has been upheld by the courts as a standard that it is not unconstitutionally vague, indefinite, or uncertain.[126]

---

[116] FDCA § 502(e), 21 U.S.C. § 352(e).

[117] 21 C.F.R. § 201.10(b).

[118] *Id.* § 201.10(d).

[119] FDCA § 502(b)(2), 21 U.S.C. § 352(b)(2); 21 C.F.R. § 201.62.

[120] 442 F. Supp. at 1236.

[121] 21 U.S.C. § 352(a) (emphasis added).

[122] FDCA § 502(f)(1), 21 U.S.C. § 352(f)(1).

[123] The FDA has, in effect, used this provision to take action against products where the FDA believes the claims are not properly substantiated. *See, e.g.,* United States v. Miami Serpentarium Laboratories, [1981-1982 Transfer Binder] Food Drug Cosm. L. Rep. (CCH) ¶ 38,164 (D.C. S.C. Fla 1982).

[124] Alberty Food Products Co. v. United States, 185 F.2d 321 (9th Cir. 1950).

[125] 21 C.F.R. § 201.5; United States v. Articles of Drug ... B-Complex Cholinos Capsules, 362 F.2d 923, 923 (3d Cir. 1966).

[126] United States v. Hohensee, 243 F.2d 367, 370, citing Kordel v. United States, 335 U.S. 345, 345 (1948).

A twofold scheme emerges from the statute, 21 U.S.C. § 352(f)(1), when it is read in context of the FDA's interpretation of the "adequate directions for use" requirement and of the regulatory and statutory exceptions to that requirement, section 503 (b)(2). This means that the distributor himself must provide adequate directions in lay terms for the patient.[127] While this can be done for a nonprescription drug, it cannot be done for a prescription drug. For a prescription drug, the distributor must provide the information that is necessary[128] to health-care professionals who will prescribe and use the drug. The burden of providing information to the customer is shifted from the manufacturer to the health professional.[129] This has been done because it is considered largely impossible for laypeople to understand and assimilate all the information needed to use a prescription medication safely and effectively. Consequently, drug companies provide information to the licensed practitioner, who must then make the decision whether or not to prescribe the medicine, knowing the risks and benefits associated with it.[130]

Recently, however, there has been a trend toward providing more information to patients about prescribed drugs. The FDA has attempted to transform this voluntary effort into a mandatory "Medication Guide" program, which met with significant opposition from various sources.[131]

The FDA exempts prescription drugs from the general requirement in section 502 (f)(1) of adequate directions for drug use if certain conditions are met. The purpose of this regulatory scheme is to ensure that adequate information is provided to the person who must decide whether and how to administer the drug. It is the FDA's view that "the primary objective of prescription drug labeling is to provide the essential information the *practitioner* needs to use the drug safely and effectively in the care of patients"[132] such as "the directions for use and cautionary statements, if any. . . ."[133] By contrast, for nonprescription drugs, the rule is supposed to result in full, adequate disclosure to laypeople purchasing the drugs.

This regulatory scheme provides the FDA with an indirect but still potent means by which to enforce the prohibition against the distribution of "off-label" information. Drugs must bear adequate directions for use. As noted above, the directions must be adequate for a layperson. For a prescription drug, this is not achievable. Prescription drug products are exempt from the adequate directions for use requirement if they comply with the labeling in the approved new drug application.[134] However, if the product is promoted for unapproved uses, it no longer qualifies for this exemption and is therefore misbranded under section 502(f)(1).

---

127 *Alberty*, 185 F.2d at 325.

128 FDCA § 503(b)(2), 21 U.S.C. § 353(b)(2).

129 *Vital Health Products, Ltd.*, 786 F. Supp. at 768.

130 United States v. Evers, 643 F.2d 1043, 1052 (5th Cir. 1981). This rationale has its parallels in the product liability field. Physicians are considered the "learned intermediaries." Typically, the adequacy of the labeling is evaluated by whether it gives sufficient information to the learned intermediary.

131 *See infra* notes 174-75 and accompanying text.

132 40 Fed. Reg. 15,392 (1975)(emphasis added).

133 FDCA § 503 (b)(2), 21 U.S.C. § 353(b)(2).

134 21 C.F.R. § 201.100(d).

The FDA has adopted, by regulation, other exemptions from the adequate directions for use requirement. These include, with limitations, bulk drugs intended for use in compounding,[135] manufacturing, processing, or repacking,[136] drugs for use in teaching, law enforcement, research, and analysis,[137] and radioactive drugs for research use.[138]

OTC Labeling

Since 1974, the FDA has conducted extensive rulemaking for over-the-counter (OTC) drugs, resulting in detailed, painstakingly drafted labeling. The objective is to provide the information consumers need to use OTC drugs properly.

To advance this goal, a "7-point label" containing the following is required for the legal marketing of OTC drugs:

1. The name of the product;
2. The name and address of the manufacturer, packer, or distributor;
3. The net contents of the package;
4. The established name of all active ingredients and the quantity of certain other ingredients, whether active or not;
5. The name of any habit-forming drug contained in the preparation;
6. Cautions and warnings needed for the protection of the user; and
7. Adequate directions for safe and effective use.

The FDA's rules, also known as monographs, specify the labeling that a particular type of OTC drug must bear. For example, the regulation will specify any warnings that may be required, such as appropriate dosing requirements or symptoms that may warrant discontinuance of the drug. OTC drug products that are subject to a final monograph must essentially follow the prescribed language or be misbranded. However, the OTC regulations do allow some flexibility with respect to the specific wording of label indications.

Certain directions for use may not be required when they are commonly known to the ordinary individual.[139] Similarly, harmless inactive ingredients such as a coloring, emulsifier, excipient, flavoring, lubricant, preservative, or solvent, are also exempt from these OTC labeling requirements.[140]

■ Dispensing Prescription Drugs

A prescription drug is misbranded unless dispensed only 1) "upon a written prescription of a practitioner licensed by law to administer such drug[s],"[141] 2) "upon an oral prescription

---

[135] *Id.* § 201.120. The FDA has said that this exemption applies only if the compounded drug is not a "new drug." *Id.* § 201.120(c).

[136] *Id.* § 201.122.

[137] *Id.* § 201.125.

[138] *Id.* § 201.129.

[139] *Id.* § 201.116.

[140] *Id.* § 201.117.

[141] FDCA § 503(b)(1)(C)(i), 21 U.S.C. § 353(b)(1)(C)(i).

of such practitioner which is reduced promptly to writing and filed by the pharmacist," [142] or 3) "by refilling any such written or oral prescription if such refilling is authorized by the prescriber either in the original prescription or by oral order. . . ."[143]

The statute describes three categories of "prescription drugs"[144] 1) habit-forming drugs and their derivatives,[145] 2) drugs unsafe for use without supervision,[146] and 3) drugs limited by an approved new drug application (NDA)[147] to use under the supervision of a licensed practitioner.[148]

Generally, only practitioners licensed by the respective states are authorized to issue prescriptions for prescription drugs.[149] However, the categories of professions deemed to be practitioners vary from state to state. For example, all states require licenses for physicians, surgeons, osteopathic physicians and surgeons, dentists, and dental surgeons; therefore, the FDCA permits these "licensed practitioners" to prescribe prescription drugs. Most states also license podiatrists and optometrists so that, in those states, individuals in those professions may also write prescriptions. Some states license other medical professionals or paraprofessionals to prescribe drugs.

■ Labeling of Prescription Drugs for Health Care Professionals

Labels of prescription drugs must bear the statement: "Caution: Federal law prohibits dispensing without prescription."[150] Conversely, drugs that are not required to be dispensed by prescription are misbranded if they bear the prescription caution.[151]

Because a prescription drug, by definition, can be used only under a physician's supervision,[152] it cannot meet the requirement of section 502(f)(1) for "adequate directions for use" to a layperson.[153] The FDA has accordingly issued detailed regulations exempting prescription drugs from this requirement so long as the labeling is not necessary for the protection of the public health.[154] If these extensive requirements are met, the drug is exempt from § 502(f)(1), and the distributor of the drug need not provide "adequate directions for use" to the layperson. This regulatory exemption protects any person who holds the drug for sale at any point in the distribution process. The exempting regulation requires, however, that the

---

[142] *Id.* § 503(b)(1)(C)(ii), 21 U.S.C. § 353(b)(1)(C)(ii).

[143] *Id.* § 503(b)(1)(C)(iii) 21 U.S.C. § 353(b)(1)(C)(iii). If by verbal order, it must be "reduced promptly to writing and filed by the pharmacist." *Id.*

[144] *Id.* § 503(b)(1)(A), (B), (C), 21 U.S.C. § 353(b)(1)(A), (B), (C); *see generally* Alan H. Kaplan, *Over-the-Counter and Prescription Drugs: The Legal Distinction under Federal Law*, 37 FOOD DRUG COSM. L. J. 441 (1982).

[145] FDCA § 502(d), 21 U.S.C. § 352(d). Habit-forming drugs that are controlled substances are also subject to the provisions of the Controlled Substances Act, Public L. No. 91-513, 84 Stat. 1242 (1970) (codified at 21 U.S.C. §§ 801 et seq. (1994), which is administered by the Drug Enforcement Administration (DEA).

[146] FDCA § 503(b)(1)(B), 21 U.S.C. § 353(b)(1)(B).

[147] *Id.* § 505, 21 U.S.C. § 355.

[148] *Id.* § 503(b)(1)(C), 21 U.S.C. § 353(b)(1)(C).

[149] *Id.* § 503(b)(1)(C)(i), 21 U.S.C. § 353(b)(1)(C)(i).

[150] *Id.* § 503(b)(4), 21 U.S.C. § 353(b)(4).

[151] *Id.*

[152] *Id.* § 503(b)(1), 21 U.S.C. § 352(b)(1).

[153] *Id.*

[154] *Id.* § 502(f), 21 U.S.C. § 352(f).

prescription drug's labeling must meet numerous labeling requirements designed to allow the health care professionals to prescribe "the drug safely and for the purpose for which it is intended, including all purposes for which the drug is advertised or represented."[155]

This labeling, called "full disclosure" labeling, must include indications, effects, dosages, routes, methods, and frequency of and duration of administration, and any relevant hazards, contraindications, side effects, and precautions. Furthermore, the labeling must include, for example, certain information regarding dosage, administration, and the drug's active ingredients; a warning that the drug cannot lawfully be dispensed without a prescription;[156] an identifying number from which one may determine the manufacturing history of the particular package of the drug; a statement directed to the pharmacist specifying the type of container to be used in dispensing the drug; and, with certain exceptions, the names of all inactive ingredients of drugs that are not taken orally.[157] The regulations also provide that the labeling, like the label,[158] must, among other things, bear "conspicuously the name and place of business of the manufacturer, packer or distributor."[159] If the name of the individual or company appears on the product without qualification, FDA assumes that the name is that of the manufacturer.[160]

■ Labeling of Prescription Drugs for Consumers

The statute states that if certain basic information is provided on the label[161], drugs prescribed and dispensed by a licensed physician[162] are exempt from a number of misbranding provisions of the FDCA, including § 502(f)(1).[163]

The exemption, though, does not extend to all misbranding provisions of the FDCA. The labeling still must be adequate for practitioners licensed by law to be able to administer or dispense the drug safely and for the purposes for which it was intended.[164] It must not bear any false or misleading labeling. Representations about therapeutic claims, if false or misleading, can lead to a charge of misbranding.[165] Likewise, the exemption does not extend to the following misbranding provisions of the FDCA:[166] 1) packaging of drugs as pre-

---

[155] 21 C.F.R. § 201.100(c); United States v. Evers, 643 F.2d 1043, 1051 (5th Cir. 1981).

[156] Prescription drugs must bear the statement, "Caution: Federal law prohibits dispensing without prescription." FDCA § 503(b)(4), 21 U.S.C. § 353(b)(4); 21 C.F.R. § 201.100(b)(1); *see* United States v. Guardian Chemical Corp., 410 F.2d 157, 160 (2d Cir. 1969).

[157] 21 C.F.R. § 201.100(b).

[158] *Id.* § 201.1.

[159] *Id.* § 201.100(e).

[160] *Id.* § 201.1(h)(2).

[161] FDCA § 503(b)(2), 21 U.S.C. § 353(b)(2). The dispenser label must bear the name and address of the dispenser, the serial number and date of prescription or its filling, the name of the prescriber, and, if stated on the prescription, the name of the patient, directions for use, and any cautionary statements.

[162] United States v. Evers, 643 F.2d 1043, 1051 (5th Cir. 1981).

[163] FDCA § 503(b)(2), 21 U.S.C. § 353(b)(2).

[164] 21 C.F.R. § 201.100.

[165] John Agar, *Labeling of Prescription Devices for the Food and Drug Administration and Product Liability: A Primer — Part I*, 45 FOOD DRUG COSM. L.J. 447, 453 (1990).

[166] The exemption assumes that the drug has an approved NDA. United States v. Amodril Spancap, [Tranfer Binder] Food Drug Cosm. L. Rep. ¶ 38,009 (S.D. Fla. 1974).

scribed in the official compendia;[167] 2) packaging of drug liable to deteriorate;[168] 3) imitation of another drug or the sale under the name of another drug;[169] 4) certification and release of insulin or antibiotics;[170] or 5) poison prevention packaging.

Also, for some prescription drugs with special considerations, the FDA has issued regulations requiring patient package inserts for the individuals for whom the drug is prescribed. For example, oral contraceptives must include a patient package insert which clearly defines their side effects.[171] This information allows the patient to make her own risk-benefit determination as a personal life decision.

In order to avoid issuing regulations to require patient package inserts for certain drugs on a case-by-case basis, the FDA issued a proposed rule setting forth a Comprehensive Medication Guide (MedGuide) program for *all* prescription drugs.[172] This proposed rule met with considerable opposition due to the government involvement, allegedly burdensome requirements, and mandatory nature. In response, Congress passed a "MedGuide" provision, which blocked the FDA from acting until it had evaluated a private sector MedGuide proposal.[173] The final draft of the private sector MedGuide Action plan was submitted to the Secretary of the Department of Health and Human Services (DHHS) on December 13, 1996, and was accepted by the Secretary on January 13, 1997. This DHHS-endorsed MedGuide Plan will not include government oversight of implementation until the year 2000.

■ Warnings

"Habit-Forming" Warning

If a human drug contains any quantity of certain designated narcotic or hypnotic substances,[174] it is deemed habit-forming.[175] The FDA has also, by regulation, designated chemical derivatives of these substances as habit-forming.[176] Habit-forming drugs are misbranded unless their label bears the name, and quantity or proportion of the substance or its derivative. The label must also state: "Warning - may be habit-forming."[177]

The FDA can exempt certain habit-forming drugs from the prescription requirements when it determines that the labeling is not necessary for the protection of the public health.[178] For

---

[167] FDCA § 502(g), 21 U.S.C. § 352(g).

[168] *Id.* § 502(h), 21 U.S.C. § 352(h).

[169] *Id.* § 502(i), 21 U.S.C. § 352(i).

[170] *Id.* § 502(k),(l), 21 U.S.C. § 352(k), (1).

[171] 21 C.F.R. § 310.501.

[172] 60 Fed. Reg. 44,182 (Aug. 24, 1995).

[173] H.R. REP. No. 109-3603, 104th Cong., 2d. Sess. (1996).

[174] The drugs designated in the FDCA are as follows: *alpha*-eucaine, barbituric acid, *beta*-eucaine, bromal, cannabis, carbromal, chloral, coca, cocaine, codeine, heroin, marijuana, morphine, opium, paraldehyde, peyote, or sulfonmethane.

[175] FDCA § 502(d), 21 U.S.C. § 352(d); 21 C.F.R. § 329.1.

[176] 21 C.F.R. § 329.1.

[177] FDCA § 502(d), 21 U.S.C. § 352(d).

[178] 21 C.F.R. § 329.20.

example, the FDA has exempted, by regulation, a few preparations that contain precisely limited amounts of opium, morphine, codeine, dihydrocodeine, and ethylmorphine.[179]

When a drug is designated exempt or habit forming by regulation, "it must be considered 'habit-forming' as a matter of law and no further proof is necessary."[180]

Adequate Warnings Against Unsafe Use

A drug—whether prescription or OTC—is misbranded unless its labeling bears adequate warnings against uses that may be dangerous to health or against unsafe dosage.[181]

Furthermore, a prescription drug loses its exemption from the "adequate directions for use" requirement if its labeling fails to inform physician users about side effects, contraindications, or potential hazards that can reasonably be expected to be associated with the use of the drug.[182] For example, a court found that the labeling of defendants' prescription drugs for treatment of obesity did not furnish adequate directions to inform physician users about potential problems that could reasonably be expected to occur during the treatment program.[183]

■ Promotional Activity for Prescription Drugs

A prescription drug may be considered misbranded if the manufacturer, packer, or distributor does not include, in all advertisements and other descriptive matter, a "true statement" of the established name and formula, with the quantities of ingredients as required by the FDCA. The advertisement must also contain a brief summary of side effects, contraindications, and effectiveness, as required by regulation.[184] While the statutory standard for prescription drug advertisements is quite general, the FDA's regulations implementing this standard are lengthy and detailed.

Regulations

Although the FDCA uses the term "advertising," it never defines that term. The FDA has, by regulation, given examples of what it believes to constitute advertising.

The types of advertisements subject to the prescription drug advertisement provisions include those in journals, magazines, other periodicals, newspapers, and in broadcasts communicated through radio, television, and telephone media. In general, advertisements involve communications through the mass media, rather than communications targeted to individuals.

---

[179] *Id.*

[180] Archambault v. United States, 224 F.2d 925, 928 (10th Cir. 1955) (pharmacist sold, in an unlabeled container and without a prescription, sodium pentobarbital tablets, a habit-forming drug, to an undercover the FDA investigator).

[181] FDCA § 502(f)(2), 21 U.S.C. § 352(f)(2).

[182] United States v. Lanpar Co., 293 F. Supp. 147, 154 (N.D. Tex. 1968).

[183] *Id.; see also* United States v. Sullivan, 332 U.S. 689, 695 (1948) (a court deemed a drug misbranded when a pharmacist transferred a drug from a properly labeled bottle into pillboxes with only the drug's name on the label).

[184] FDCA § 502(n), 21 U.S.C. § 352(n).

On the other hand, the following printed matter are examples of printed matter not regarded as advertising but as labeling: brochures, mailing pieces, detailing pieces, bulletins, price lists, catalogues, in-house publications, and literature reprints.[185]

A newly developing issue, which could not have been anticipated when the FDA wrote its regulations many years ago, is the regulatory characterization of the Internet. There has already been considerable debate over whether the Internet should be deemed advertising or labeling. The FDA, though, is not waiting for resolution of this jurisdictional issue to regulate promotional material on the Internet.[186] The agency has made it clear in speeches and through issuing warning letters that it *will* regulate promotional information that companies place on the Internet. The FDA's Division of Drug Marketing, Advertising and Communications (DDMAC) is in the process of developing Internet guidelines.

The FDA's stated objective is to ensure that promotional materials are fairly balanced, informative, and not false or misleading. Some of these regulations are described below.

Any advertisement that includes both the name of the drugs and its uses also must contain a brief summary of the package insert.[187] Information relating to effectiveness may be limited to a statement of the effectiveness of the drug for the selected purposes for which the drug is recommended or suggested.[188] Information relating to side effects and contraindications, including warnings, precautions, and special considerations, must be specific.[189] There must also be fair balance between claims of efficacy and adverse effects. Misleading or false information in one part of the advertisement cannot be corrected by the inclusion of true information elsewhere.[190] Although the regulation addressing ingredient information is similar to that specified for drug labeling, it also prohibits use of a fanciful proprietary name implying that a common drug or composition is somehow unique, featuring inert or inactive ingredients in a manner that implies greater value, or designating a proprietary name that may be confused with the established name of a different drug or ingredient.[191]

The FDCA provides that except in "extraordinary circumstances," the FDA is not to require routine submission of advertising in advance of its being used.[192] The regulations specify one circumstance when prior approval of an advertisement is required, namely, when there is information not widely known that the drug may cause fatalities or serious danger.[193]

---

[185] 21 C.F.R. § 202.1(k).

[186] 61 Fed. Reg. 48,707 (Sept. 16, 1996) (notice of public meeting on "promotion of FDA-regulated medical products on the Internet").

[187] 21 C.F.R. § 202.1(e)(4).

[188] *Id.* § 202.1(e)(6)(i).

[189] *Id.* § 202.1(e)(6).

[190] *Id.* § 202.1(e)(3)(i).

[191] *Id.*

[192] FDCA § 502(n), 21 U.S.C. § 352(n).

[193] 21 C.F.R. § 202.1(j). In addition, 21 C.F.R. § 314.550 provides that for drugs being considered for accelerated approval for serious or life-threatening conditions, applicants must submit to the FDA during the preapproval review period all promotional materials. For the first 120 days after approval, new promotional materials must be submitted at least thirty days in advance.

Though not required in the regulations, the FDA may request submission of advertising and promotional materials for approval when it believes that there has been a serious or repeated violation of the regulations. Also, when a major new product is being approved, the FDA generally requests that the initial advertising and promotional materials be submitted prior to approval. Although the FDA has no clear authority to require it. The FDA has strongly encouraged this practice and as a practical matter, companies generally do submit many new materials for clearance by the agency before launching a new drug product.[194]

Exemptions for Certain Forms of Advertisements

The FDA's regulations provide for three types of exemptions from the "full-disclosure" prescription drug advertisement requirements:[195] 1) reminder advertisements;[196] 2) advertisements of bulk-sale drugs;[197] and 3) advertisements of prescription-compounding drugs.[198]

Reminder advertisements are those that "call attention to the name of the drug product but do not include indications or dosage recommendations for use of the drug product."[199] Under the regulations, these reminder advertisements may contain only the following kinds of information: 1) the proprietary name or established names of the drug product, if any; 2) the established name of each active ingredient in the drug product; and 3) optionally, the amount of each ingredient, the dosage form, the quantity in a package, the price, and the name and address of the manufacturer, packer or distributor, or other written, printed, or graphic matter that does not represent or suggest any relation to the advertised drug product.

Advertisements intended to provide consumers with information concerning the price charged for a drug prescription are also considered reminder advertisements. However, to qualify for this exemption, the advertisement still must satisfy all the conditions contained in the regulations for consumer price listing of prescription drugs, e.g., it can contain no representation or suggestion concerning the drug product's safety, effectiveness, or indications for use.[200]

The DDMAC considers a representation of bioequivalence or therapeutic equivalence ("AB-rating") to be outside the scope of information allowed under the reminder advertisement exemption.[201] Thus, any such representation or suggestion about the generic product being equivalent to the brand name drug requires full disclosure (labeling) or a brief summary (advertising).[202]

---

[194] DIVISION OF DRUG MARKETING, ADVERTISING & COMMUNICATION, CENTER FOR DRUG EVALUATION & RESEARCH, FOOD & DRUG ADMIN., GUIDANCE TO EXPEDITE THE REVIEW OF LAUNCH CAMPAIGN SUBMISSIONS (1994). On Mar. 5, 1997, the Center for Biologics Evaluation and Research deleted its requirement for prior approval of promotional material. 62 Fed. Reg. 10,062 (Mar. 5, 1997).

[195] 21 C.F.R. § 202.1(e)(2).

[196] *Id.* § 202.1(e)(2)(i).

[197] *Id.* § 202.1(e)(2)(ii).

[198] *Id.* § 202.1(e)(2)(iii).

[199] *Id.* § 202.1(e)(2)(i).

[200] *Id.* § 200.200.

[201] DIVISION OF DRUG MARKETING, ADVERTISING & COMMUNICATION, CENTER FOR DRUG EVALUATION & RESEARCH, FOOD & DRUG ADMIN., CURRENT ISSUES AND PROCEDURES, *supra* note 92 (FDA industry-wide letter).

[202] *Id.* (generally, this does not apply to a price catalog).

Bulk-sale drugs that promote the sale of the drug in bulk packages to be processed, manufactured, labeled, or repackaged in substantial quantities are exempt from the requirements for providing information pertaining to side effects, contraindications, and effectiveness.[203] As in the case of reminder advertisements, such bulk-sale advertisements may not contain claims for the therapeutic safety or effectiveness of the drug.[204]

The regulations contain a similar exemption for advertisement for drugs sold to pharmacists for the purpose of compounding.[205]

Over the years, DDMAC has issued many letters, guidance documents, and other communications stating its views on various promotional issues. Many of those policies are now undergoing active review.[206] Some policy communications will be consolidated, others deleted, and some substantially revised.

■ Packaged and Labeled as Required by Official Compendia

If a drug is recognized in official compendia such as the *USP/NF,* it is misbranded unless it is packaged and labeled in accordance with compendia specifications.[207] For example, vitamin K for injection was listed in the *National Formulary,* which required that sterile ampules for injection be packed in such a manner as to prevent contamination or loss of contents. The court in *Dianovin Pharmaceuticals, Inc.*[208] ruled that ampules of vitamin K for injection were misbranded because they were not completely sealed and, therefore, failed to comply with the compendial standard of packaging for sterile drugs for injection.

■ Imitations and Counterfeits

A drug is misbranded if it is an imitation of another drug or offered for sale under the name of another drug.[209] The agency has relied on this provision to challenge the marketing and distribution of imitation or "look-alike drugs" that, because of their appearance, were susceptible to being "passed off" to the ultimate consumer as controlled substances.[210]

In one case brought by the agency, a pharmaceutical company placed inert brown beads similar in appearance to those used in amphetamine capsules and included markings and imprints on its tablets and capsules similar to imprints on controlled substances. The court concluded that for a drug to meet the statutory definition of "imitation" (21 U.S.C.

---

[203] 21 C.F.R. § 202.1(e)(2)(ii).

[204] *Id.*

[205] *Id.* § 202.1(e)(2)(iii).

[206] *See* 62 Fed. Reg. 8961 (Feb. 27, 1997).

[207] FDCA § 502(g), 21 U.S.C. § 352(g).

[208] 342 F. Supp. at 724.

[209] FDCA § 502(i)(2),(3), 21 U.S.C. § 352(i)(2), (3); *see* United States v. Jamieson-McKames Pharmaceuticals, Inc., 651 F.2d 532, 543 (8th Cir. 1981) *cert. denied,* 455 U.S. 1016 (1981) (company falsely purported or represented its drugs to be the product of other drug manufacturers).

[210] United States v. Articles of Drug, 633 F. Supp. 316 (D. Neb. 1986), *aff'd in part, rev'd in part, remanded,* 825 F.2d 1238 (8th Cir. 1987), 601 F. Supp. 392 (D. Neb. 1988), *aff'd,* 890 F.2d 1004 (8t hCir. 1989).

§ 352(i)(2)), the government must show more than similarity to other drugs[211] or "resemblance."[212] The "imitation" drug must be identical or similar in general appearance, color, shape, size, or other physical properties and similar in effect to the "real" product.[213] Although the FDA succeeded in this case, in practice, this is a difficult standard for the FDA to meet.

The FDC Act also prohibits the sale of counterfeit drugs.[214] The FDA is authorized to seize counterfeit drugs, their containers, and their dies and punches.[215] The term "counterfeit" is not defined and the FDA has rarely relied on this provision.

■ Dangerous to Health When Used as Labeled

When the drug is dangerous to the health of the user even when used as recommended on the label, it is misbranded. Although most cases involve toxicity or other direct harm (and there are not many cases involving this provision),[216] an absence of efficacy may also give rise to a charge under this provision. For example, penicillin G and ampicillin are, in fact, effective against different types of infections caused by different types of bacteria.[217] Also, the absorption rates of the two drugs are different so that different doses of each are required. Thus, even in instances when both drugs are generally effective, substitution of penicillin G for ampicillin could result in ineffective treatment. Accordingly, when a pharmaceutical company labeled penicillin G as ampicillin, the court held that the drug was misbranded under section 502(j) because it was dangerous to health when used in the manner or dosage prescribed.[218]

■ Drug Establishment Registration and Listing of Drugs with FDA

"Manufacturers" of drugs are required to register their drug establishments with the FDA and to provide the FDA with a list of all drugs they introduce for commercial distribution in the United States.[219] The term "manufacturer" is broadly defined. It includes companies that actually make the drug, as well as repackers, relabelers, or own-label distributors. Certain classes of persons, such as pharmacies and licensed practitioners, are exempted from registration and drug listing if they meet other requirements.[220] Unless otherwise exempted, a drug manufactured, prepared, propagated, compounded, or processed in an establishment in the United States not registered with the FDA, would be deemed mis-

---

[211] 825 F.2d at 1245.

[212] *Id.* at 1244.

[213] *Id.* at 1245.

[214] FDCA § 301(i)(2), 21 U.S.C. § 331 (i)(2).

[215] *Id.* § 304(a)(2), 21 U.S.C. § 334(a)(2).

[216] *Id.* § 502(j), 21 U.S.C. § 352 (j); United States v. 62 Packages Marmola Prescription Tablets, 48 F. Supp. 878, 887 (W.D. Wis. 1943), *aff'd* 142 F.2d 107 (7th Cir.), *cert. denied,* 323 U.S. 731 (1944) (when tablets for treatment of obesity were used in the dosage, frequency, and for the duration suggested by their labels, the drugs were dangerous to health and, therefore, misbranded); United States v. EL-O-Pathic Pharmacy, 192 F.2d 62 (9th Cir. 1951).

[217] United States v. Jamieson-McKames Pharmaceuticals, 651 F.2d 532, 548-49 (8th Cir. 1981), *cert. denied,* 455 U.S. 1016 (1981).

[218] *Id.*

[219] FDCA § 510, 21 U.S.C. § 360.

[220] *Id.* § 510(g), 21 U.S.C. § 360(g); 21 C.F.R. § 207.10.

branded.[221] Although the registration requirement does not apply to foreign manufacturers, many overseas manufacturers voluntarily register.

Each registered pharmaceutical company[222] must provide the FDA with a list of drugs marketed commercially in the United States. The failure to include such a drug on the list will result in the product being misbranded.[223]

Upon receipt of the list, the FDA assigns a drug listing number, a unique code, to each drug or class of drug products.[224] This code is a ten-digit, three segment number, called the National Drug Code (NDC) Labeler Code.[225] The NDC number permits automated processing of drug data by a wide variety of entities, including government agencies, law enforcement agencies, drug manufacturers and distributors, hospitals, poison control centers, and insurance companies.

"FDA requests but does not require that the NDC number appear on all drug labels and in other drug labeling, including the label of any prescription drug container furnished to a consumer."[226] If, however, the NDC number is shown on the drug label, the FDA has issued regulations as to how and where the number should appear.[227] Further, the FDA warns that the listing of a drug establishment's products in no way implies that its listed drugs have been approved for marketing in the United States.[228] If a pharmaceutical company represents or creates an impression of official approval because of its registration or possession of a registration number or NDC number, the product may be deemed misbranded under the FDA's regulations.[229]

■ Imprinting of Solid Oral Dosage Form Drug Products for Human Use

The FDA has issued regulations concerning solid oral dosage form drug products for human use that are marketed in interstate commerce.[230] Solid oral dosage form refers to "capsules, tablets, or similar drug products intended for oral use."[231] These regulations require, unless specifically exempted,[232] that solid oral dosage forms be clearly marked or imprinted with a code imprint.[233] A code imprint means:

> any single letter or number or any combination of letters and numbers, including, e.g., words, company name, and National Drug Code, or a mark symbol, logo, or

---

[221] FDCA § 502(o), 21 U.S.C. § 352(o).

[222] The FDA provides the drug establishment registrant with a validated copy of the registration form. 21 C.F.R. §207.35.

[223] FDCA § 510(j), 21 U.S.C. § 360(j).

[224] 21 C.F.R. § 207.35.

[225] *Id.*

[226] *Id.* § 207.35(b)(3).

[227] *Id.*

[228] Food and Drug Admin., Drug Listing Act Information Bull.

[229] 21 C.F.R. § 207.39.

[230] *Id.* pt. 206. Moreover, the FDCA specifically prohibits companies from saying that their drugs have been approved. FDCA § 301(1), 21 U.S.C. § 331(1).

[231] 21 C.F.R. § 206.3.

[232] *See id.* § 206.7.

[233] *Id.* § 206.10(a).

monogram or a combination of letters, numbers, and marks or symbols, assigned by a drug firm to a specific drug product.[234]

The FDA intends that, "with the product's size, shape, and color," the code imprint would permit the "unique identification of the drug product and the manufacturer or distributor of the product."[235] The classes of drugs that may be exempted from imprinting include drugs under clinical investigation (not including drugs under a treatment investigational new drug exemption),[236] drugs "extemporaneously compounded by licensed pharmacists" pursuant to a valid prescription, and drugs having unique physical characteristics that do not lend themselves to imprinting.[237]

In justifying these new regulations, the FDA explained that drug identification by imprinting serves a number of public health purposes related to the FDA's responsibilities under the FDCA. Imprinted drug codes, the FDA said,

> are used by poison control centers and others to identify drug products in drug overdose emergencies, . . . assist[] patients and health professionals in determining when different manufacturers' products are dispensed, help[] patients identify prescriptions that are incorrectly filled, aid[] in the battle against drug abuse, help[] drug regulatory officials trace counterfeit and defective drug products, and help[] hospitals, nursing homes, and community pharmacies operate their drug distribution accounting systems.[238]

Imported Drugs

Virtually all of the misbranding and adulteration provisions applicable to drugs manufactured in the United States apply to imported drugs. The FDA has the power to refuse to allow an imported drug into the United States if the agency believes that the product violates the FDCA.

The FDCA allows the FDA to act against an imported product on a standard that is highly deferential to the agency. The FDA does not need to prove that the product is actually violative. Rather, the agency must only decide that it "appears" that the drug is misbranded or adulterated.[239] A court will overturn FDA's decision only if it is arbitrary and capricious.

If the FDA determines that an imported drug appears to be adulterated or misbranded, it will issue a Notice of Detention and Hearing.[240] The company may then respond by trying to

---

[234] *Id.* § 206.10(d).

[235] *Id.* § 206.10(a).

[236] 21 U.S.C. § 312.

[237] 21 C.F.R. § 206.7; 58 Fed. Reg. 47,948 (Sept. 13, 1993) (preamble).

[238] 58 Fed. Reg. 47,948.

[239] FDCA § 704(a), 21 U.S.C. § 374(a).

[240] *Id.* § 801(a), 21 U.S.C.§ 381(a); 21 C.F.R. § 1.94; FOOD AND DRUG ADMIN., REGULATORY PROCEDURES MANUAL §§ 9-25-10, 9-20-20.

provide evidence, orally or in writing, that the product is in compliance.[241] Should the FDA agree, which, based on experience, does not often appear to be the case, the product will be admitted; if the FDA disagrees, the agency will issue a Notice of Refusal of Admission.

Alternatively, the company can try to recondition the goods (i.e., bring the goods into compliance with U.S. law) or re-export the goods.[242] The ability to recondition is largely determined by the nature of the purported violation. Technical labeling violations can be corrected through new labeling, 21 U.S.C. § 381(b); there is no easy fix to the lack of an NDA. If re-exported, the goods can only be reimported by the manufacturer (unless the drug is required for emergency medical care) or the Prescription Drug Marketing Act [243] would be violated.[244] If the company fails to exercise its option to re-export within ninety days after issuance of the Notice of Refusal of Admission the goods will be destroyed at the expense of the owner or consignee.[245]

The FDA can refuse to allow product on a shipment-by-shipment basis. The agency can also determine that all products from a facility, or a particular type of drug from any facility, is unlawful and refuse to allow it entry. The FDA implements this decision by issuing an Import Alert. Products subject to an Import Alert will not be allowed into the country. The FDA will issue an Import Alert without prior notice to affected parties.

---

[241] 21 C.F.R. § 1.94.

[242] *Id.* §§ 1.95, 1.96. This may be readily accomplished with certain technical labeling violations, but very difficult with cGMP or other violations; FDCA § 801(a), 21 U.S.C. § 381(a).

[243] Pub. L. No. 100-293, 102 Stat. 95 (codified at 21 U.S.C. §§ 301 note, 331,333,353,353 notes (1994)).

[244] FDCA § 801(d), 21 U.S.C. § 381(d).

[245] *Id.* § 801(a),(c), 21 U.S.C. § 381(a), (c).

chapter 8

Over-the-Counter Drugs

Alan H. Kaplan*
Kinsey S. Reagan**
Bonnie A. Beavers***
Daniel R. Dwyer****
Prescott M. Lassman*****

Introduction

■ Prescription/Over-the-Counter Distinctions

The Federal Food, Drug, and Cosmetic Act[1] (FDCA) sets forth three criteria that justify the classification of a drug for prescription use only: habit-forming characteristics; the need for a physician's supervision; or limitations set by an effective new drug application (NDA) for the drug.[2] A drug that does not meet these criteria for prescription-only dispensing would be an over-the-counter (OTC) drug. The FDCA gives the Food and Drug Administration (FDA) greater inspection authority with respect to prescription drugs,[3] and FDA regulations impose additional record-keeping requirements for prescription drugs that do not apply to non-NDA'd OTC drugs.[4] Section 505 of the FDCA, the "new drug" section, does not distinguish between OTC and prescription drugs,[5] but there are important differences in approval and enforcement schemes applicable to the two types of drugs.

---

*   Mr. Kaplan is a Partner in the law firm of Kleinfeld Kaplan and Becker, Washington, D.C.

**   Mr. Reagan is a Partner in the law firm of Kleinfeld Kaplan and Becker, Washington, D.C.

***   Ms. Beavers is a Partner in the law firm of Kleinfeld Kaplan and Becker, Washington, D.C.

****   Mr. Dwyer is a Partner in the law firm of Kleinfeld Kaplan and Becker, Washington, D.C.

*****   Mr. Lassman is an Associate in the law firm of Kleinfeld Kaplan and Becker, Washington, D.C.

1.   Pub. L. No. 75-717, 52 Stat. 1040 (1938) (codified at 21 U.S.C. §§ 301 *et seq.* (1994)).

2.   FDCA § 503(b)(1)(A)-(C), 21 U.S.C. § 353(b)(1)(A)-(C). *See* discussion *infra.*

3.   *Id.* § 704(a)(1); 21 U.S.C. § 374(a)(1).

4.   21 C.F.R. § 310.305 (1997).

5.   21 U.S.C. § 355(d).

As a result, the status of a drug as available OTC has major implications because the FDA's administration of the FDCA subjects OTC drugs to a different regulatory scheme.

Market entry for OTC drugs in general is significantly less restrictive than for prescription drugs. To a great extent, the FDA regulates OTC drugs as "old drugs" not requiring pre-market clearance, whereas prescription drugs almost always require an NDA or abbreviated new drug application (ANDA). Further, the amount and quality of scientific data the FDA requires to support the marketing of an OTC drug is different from, and often considerably less than, for a prescription drug. Also, many OTC drugs that do not meet the FDA's promulgated criteria for marketing currently enjoy a regulatory "moratorium" on enforcement until the effective date of a final monograph, unless they pose a safety hazard or contain fraudulent representations.[6]

The FDA's reduced scrutiny of OTC drug products stems from pragmatic considerations, such as the agency's limited resources to examine each and every drug on the market. An individualized product review would have increased the cost of such drugs to the consumer. Most importantly, OTC drugs generally pose fewer safety hazards, in part because most OTC drugs are intended to alleviate symptoms rather than to treat disease. The benefits of easier consumer access to these products facilitated by a generalized review presumably outweighs the risk of side effects, which can be addressed in labeled warnings. These practical considerations led the agency to distinguish between OTC and prescription drugs in implementing the efficacy requirements of the Drug Amendments of 1962,[7] and the resulting Drug Efficacy Study Implementation (DESI) review begun in 1964.

Under the DESI review, the FDA, with the assistance of the National Academy of Science[s]/National Research Council, evaluated the efficacy of all drug products marketed between 1938 and 1962 that were the subject of effective NDAs. Although most of the drug products the FDA reviewed under the DESI program were prescription drugs, there were also some four hundred OTC drug products covered by approved NDAs. A systematic agency review of these OTC drugs did not get underway until almost ten years after enactment of the 1962 Amendments, at which time the FDA was confronted with the realization that thousands of OTC products were on the market without NDAs. The FDA was forced to acknowledge that while an individualized, case-by-case product review was possible for the limited number of NDA prescription products subject to the DESI program (approximately 3500), it was not feasible to conduct such a review of the many thousands of OTC products that had never been the subject of individual agency assessment.

On January 5, 1972, the FDA published proposed regulations outlining the scope and procedures of a planned review of OTC drug products.[8] For each therapeutic category of OTC drug, an advisory panel would be convened to help create and review data. In a substantial departure from the DESI program's evaluation of individual drug products, the OTC Review proposed to focus only upon *active ingredients* for each category. The FDA

---

6   Compliance Policy Guide 7132b.15 (Oct. 1, 1980); 45 Fed. Reg. 31,422 (May 13, 1980). The proposed rule followed a challenge to the FDA's policy in Cutler v. Kennedy, 475 F. Supp. 838 (D.D.C. 1979).

7   Pub. L. No. 87-781, 76 Stat. 780 (1962) (codified at 21 U.S.C. § 357).

8   37 Fed. Reg. 85 (Jan. 5, 1972).

anticipated its review would be limited to approximately 200 active ingredients used in existing OTC preparations. As for the inactive ingredients, the OTC review contemplated only general limitations: inactives were to be suitable and safe in the amounts administered, and must not interfere with the product's effectiveness or with tests used to determine the product's quality.[9] The review of active ingredients would result in the promulgation of a regulation that would be a "monograph" of requirements applicable to the therapeutic category of OTC drugs covered by the particular monograph.

In establishing OTC monographs of general applicability, the FDA acknowledged that the safety and efficacy of OTC drugs might be achieved without the showing required for prescription drugs in section 505(d) of the FDCA.[10] The FDA requires sound scientific justification to show "general recognition" of the safety and effectiveness of the active ingredients. Proof of effectiveness necessitates controlled clinical investigations "unless this requirement is waived on the basis of a showing that it is not reasonably applicable to the drug...."[11] The preamble to the FDA's proposed regulations specified that "[e]xceptions [to the otherwise stringent standards] are permitted where they can be justified."[12] For example, the panel could consider unpublished data "if in its expert opinion there is a sound scientific basis for such a decision which is sufficiently widespread to establish general recognition."[13] In general, evidence of general recognition of safety and effectiveness may consist of "[o]bjective or subjective clinical studies; bioavailability of ingredients; documented clinical experience or uncontrolled clinical studies; market research studies; animal studies; general medical and scientific literature, published and unpublished; any use by the professional and the consumer; and common medical knowledge."[14] Further, the FDA designed the monographs to permit certain combinations of active ingredients, without a specific showing that the combination is effective in a particular product. This result, much less stringent than the "combination drug policy" applicable to FDA approval of prescription drugs,[15] is another example of different standards for OTC products.

Under the OTC Review as it has evolved, an OTC drug is excluded from "new drug" status if the agency finds the product meets certain requirements. The active ingredient or combination of active ingredients must be deemed generally recognized as safe and effective (GRASE) in a final OTC monograph regulation, and the labeling of the product must conform to the regulations.[16] Drugs in the OTC Review need not comply with tentative or proposed monographs, or even with final monographs, until the regulations become final and effective. Such drugs may continue to be marketed without regulatory action unless they present a significant health hazard or are likely to defraud consumers.[17]

---

[9] 21 C.F.R. § 330.1(e).

[10] *Id.*

[11] *Id.* § 330.10(a)(4)(ii).

[12] 37 Fed. Reg. 9464, 9468 (1972).

[13] *Id.* at 9469.

[14] *Id.*

[15] 21 C.F.R. § 300.50.

[16] *Id.* § 330.1.

[17] *See supra* note 7.

■ OTC Monograph System

The FDA's proposed regulations establishing the OTC Review were finalized on May 11, 1972. The regulations set forth a complex, four-step process for the development of final monographs for twenty-six broad therapeutic classes of OTC drugs (antacids, cough and cold preparations, etc.).[18] Each step is designed to provide ample opportunity for public participation and comment.

In the first phase of the monograph development process, an expert panel reviewed the available data relating to marketed OTC drug products within a particular therapeutic class and provided the FDA with its recommendations regarding the safety, effectiveness, and labeling for particular active ingredients within that class. Beginning in 1972, the FDA convened seventeen panels of qualified experts to review data relating to the twenty-six therapeutic classes of OTC drugs. During the next ten years, the panels reviewed data, conducted hearings, and heard testimony concerning 722 active ingredients and 1454 active ingredient uses (as some active ingredients have more than one use).

In the second phase of the OTC Review, the FDA published each panel recommendation in the *Federal Register*, along with a proposed monograph, as an Advance Notice of Proposed Rulemaking (ANPR). The ANPR sets out the conditions under which the panel believes OTC drug products in particular therapeutic classes will be deemed GRASE and not misbranded. In practice, the ANPR often provided FDA commentary on the panel's views, particularly when the agency disagreed with a specific panel recommendation, and requested comments by interested parties and the general public.[19]

In the third phase of the monograph development process, the agency publishes a Tentative Final Monograph (TFM) in the *Federal Register*, which has the regulatory status of a proposed rule. The TFM announces the FDA's preliminary position regarding the safety and effectiveness of particular active ingredients within a therapeutic class as well as acceptable labeling for indications, warnings and directions for use. In addition, the preamble to the TFM contains a detailed discussion of and response to each comment submitted by interested parties in response to the ANPR. As of the date of this publication, this third phase of the FDA's review of OTC drugs is substantially complete.

In the fourth and final phase, the FDA publishes a final monograph having the status of a binding, substantive regulation. Before issuing a final monograph, the agency must evaluate and address all comments received in response to the publication of a TFM, as well as all requests for a public hearing. The agency usually addresses these issues in the preamble to its final rule. Once finalized, a monograph conclusively establishes the conditions under which a drug product within a particular therapeutic class will be considered GRASE and not misbranded. The final monograph is codified in FDA regulations and typically provides an effective date one year after publication in the *Federal Register*.

Following the effective date of a final monograph, all covered drug products that fail to conform to its requirements are subject to misbranding charges or to charges of being an

---

[18] 21 C.F.R. pt. 330.

[19] Some monographs have been reopened to include additional ingredients or claims. *See, e.g.,* 55 Fed. Reg. 38,560 (Sept. 19, 1990) (plaque and gingivitis claims).

unapproved new drug, in the absence of an approved NDA. At this writing, the FDA has issued final monographs that apply, either partially or completely, to fifteen of the twenty-six originally-identified therapeutic classes. In addition, the agency has issued over twenty final regulations determining that certain types of OTC drug products (such as aphrodisiac drug products) are *not* GRASE and are new drugs.

The OTC Review has proved a much more burdensome and protracted process than anyone expected at its outset in 1972. The Review was expected to be complete in two to four years, but after almost twenty-five years and litigation over its pace,[20] it is still several years from completion. Many monographs have been reopened to accept new data and comments as new information about ingredients comes to light, further slowing the review process.[21] However, despite the procedural delays and the lack of final, effective monographs for many categories of drugs, few would dispute that the Review has been a useful and successful regulatory effort. Though ingredients in most available OTC products were first discovered and marketed long before the proliferation of today's potent prescription drugs, industry has collected a vast quantity of data under the OTC Review in an attempt to meet the FDA's new standards. In addition, products have been and are being reformulated to meet the requirements even of those monographs that are not yet final. In cases in which manufacturers have disagreed about the need for further evidence or reformulation of products, it appears that most have worked towards maximizing voluntary compliance with the objectives of the program, or have formed a coalition of similarly-affected product manufacturers to address or supplement the scientific evidence and seek a compromise with the FDA.[22]

OTC monographs have served as a mechanism for addressing both adulteration and misbranding requirements. OTC drugs must be manufactured in compliance with current good manufacturing practices as established by regulation.[23] The label and labeling of the product must be in accordance with the monograph and other applicable regulations, such as the required warnings.[24] The FDA initially took the position that the "indications" section of OTC drug labeling must use the exact terminology set forth in the monograph. In 1986 the agency adopted the "flexibility policy," which permitted other truthful, nonmisleading statements to describe the indications established for the product.[25] The manufacturer has the option of placing the exact monograph indications within a boxed area on the label or labeling, marked "FDA APPROVED USES" or similar wording. Aspects of the label or labeling other than the indications must still follow the monograph precisely, and may also appear within a boxed area marked "FDA APPROVED INFORMATION."[26] In this respect, OTC products differ from almost all other medical products, which may not suggest in labeling that they are FDA-approved.[27]

---

[20] *See* Cutler v. Hayes, 818 F.2d 879 (D.C. Cir. 1987).

[21] *See, e.g.,* proposed monographs for OTC internal analgesic (59 Fed. Reg. 18,507 (Apr. 19, 1994)) and sunscreen (59 Fed. Reg. 29,706 (June 8, 1994)) products.

[22] *See, e.g.,* hydroquinone-containing skin bleaching drug products.

[23] 21 C.F.R. § 330.1(a) (1995).

[24] *See, e.g., id.* § 330.1(g) (general warnings for OTC products); *id.* § 330.2 (pregnancy-nursing warning).

[25] *Id.* § 330.1(c)(2); 51 Fed. Reg. 16,266 (May 1, 1986).

[26] 21 C.F.R. § 330.1(c)(2)(i).

[27] FDCA § 301(l), 21 U.S.C. § 331(l); the other exception is antibiotics for human use.

Once a monograph becomes final, new ingredients or indications may be added only through the administrative rulemaking process. Alternatively, such ingredients or uses may be the subject of a new drug application which would be reviewed by the FDA under the same standards as any other NDA. Additionally, prescription products that are the subject of approved NDAs may be changed to OTC status through new or supplemental NDAs. Thus, it is likely that in the years ahead, the existing OTC monographs will essentially become frozen with regard to claims and active ingredients and most new OTC products will enter the market through the NDA switch routes.

There is also evidence that the FDA may be focusing more on product characteristics other than "active ingredients" and labeled claims. The agency announced new restrictions on market eligibility for certain categories of products that had been deemed GRASE under a proposed or final regulation.[28] Perhaps the agency is now concerned that the standards of the OTC Review may not always be adequate for certain classes of products. In some cases, the agency has required final product testing to provide the degree of comfort to assure market safety, even though no specific problem has arisen.[29] Whether this change in focus from active ingredient to product review is an anomaly or trend remains for future determination.

Regulatory Developments and Distinctions

■ OTC Switches

Background and Definitions

The concept of an OTC "switch" generally refers to moving a drug product that can be lawfully obtained only by prescription to a status that permits purchase directly by laypersons, without the need for a physician's involvement. There is no formal definition of a "switch" and no single way it can occur. A switch may involve variations in the drug's dosage, indications, or combination of ingredients.

Prior to 1951, the dispensing status of a drug was governed solely by the FDA regulations under section 502(f) of the 1938 Act,[30] requiring adequate directions for use. The FDA took the position that any drug that could not be used safely by a layman was not capable of bearing adequate directions for use. Such drug could be distributed only if labeled with a prescription legend. Manufacturers of drugs largely exercised their own judgment in drawing distinctions. Thus, one manufacturer might label a particular drug with the prescription legend in the belief that adequate directions could not be provided by lay use,

---

[28] *See, e.g.,* Cough/Cold Drug Products — Metered-Dose Inhalants (Proposed Rule), 60 Fed. Reg. 13,014 (Mar. 9, 1995); Vaginal Contraceptive Drug Products (Proposed Rule), 60 Fed. Reg. 6892 (Feb. 3, 1995).

[29] *See* discussion *infra.*

[30] *See* United States v. Sullivan, 332 U.S. 689 (1947), citing 21 C.F.R. § 2.106(b); FDCA § 502(f), 21 U.S.C. § 352(f).

while another manufacturer of the same drug would provide what it considered to be adequate directions.

Congress in 1951 passed the Durham-Humphrey Amendments[31] to clarify drug dispensing status. The new statute set forth three classifications of drugs that must be limited to prescription use: 1) certain habit-forming drugs listed in section 502(d) of the FDCA; 2) drugs not safe for use except under the supervision of a licensed practitioner because of toxicity or other potentiality for harmful effect, method of use, or the collateral measures necessary for use; and 3) drugs limited to prescription under an approved NDA under section 505.[32] The FDA may remove by regulation a drug subject to section 502 or 505 from prescription status "when such requirements are not necessary for the public health."[33]

For drugs initially limited to prescription use under an approved NDA, the FDA has switched some by regulation and has provided a standard for switching others by petition or supplement. A prescription drug may be switched to OTC status when the FDA finds that the prescription requirements are not necessary for the protection of public health and that the drug is safe and effective for use in self-medication as directed in the proposed OTC product labeling.[34] This is generally accomplished by the NDA owner's petitioning the FDA for the switch. The petitioner bears the burden of proof to establish that prescription status is not needed for the safe and effective use of the drug.

The FDA may decide on its own initiative to switch a product from prescription to OTC. The FDA published the first "switch" regulation in July 1956.[35] That regulation applied to acetaminophen (at that time, exclusively Tylenol) and spelled out the conditions under which acetaminophen could be marketed OTC "if the preparation is a new drug [and] an application pursuant to the [new drug provisions] is effective for it."[36] Implicit in the word "if" as used in that regulation is the recognition that a drug that has been switched from prescription to OTC might lose its new drug status and therefore need not have any effective NDA. This result appears to have been the FDA's intent because after a period of time, other versions of acetaminophen (and other former prescription new drugs) were able to be marketed without an NDA or ANDA, as long as they followed the standards of the "switch" regulation. The FDA did not interfere with their marketing as OTC as long as the products were labeled appropriately.

Between 1956 and today, more than twenty new drugs that had originally been marketed as prescription new drugs have been switched to OTC status. These switches have either been done under the FDA's own initiative, through development of an OTC monograph, or as a result of a manufacturer's petition to modify an existing OTC monograph to include the prescription drug.

---

[31] Pub. L. No. 82-215, 65 Stat. 648 (1951), as amended, FDCA § 503, 21 U.S.C. § 353.

[32] FDCA § 503(b)(1)(A)-(C), 21 U.S.C. § 353(b)(1)(A)-(C). Section 502(d) lists seventeen narcotic or hypnotic substances, thus categorized as prescription drugs under section 503(b)(1)(A), including derivatives of such drugs designated by regulation as habit-forming.

[33] FDCA § 403(b)(3), 21 U.S.C. § 353(b)(3).

[34] 21 C.F.R. § 310.200(b).

[35] *Id.* § 130.102(a)(1)(iii).

[36] *Id.*

The FDA's decisions as to whether drugs were safe for lay use have been made in the context of each of the legal procedures by which a drug may be switched from prescription to OTC status: 1) "switch" regulations applicable to new drugs pursuant to section 353(b)(3) of the FDCA and section 310.201 of the FDA's regulations; 2) supplemental NDAs or ANDAs; or 3) inclusion in the FDA's OTC drug monographs of drugs previously available only be prescription.

The switch regulation procedures have been used successfully in a number of recent approvals requiring warnings. For example, the switch regulations for triaminoheptane sulfate and methoxyphenamine hydrochloride require warnings against use by individuals with high blood pressure, heart disease, diabetes, or thyroid disease unless directed by a physician.[37] Similarly, the FDA has recommended warnings for OTC drugs containing phenylpropanolamine hydrochloride that persons with high blood pressure, heart disease, diabetes or thyroid disease should use them only as directed by a physician.[38] Thus, generic versions of these drugs existed long before the Hatch-Waxman Amendments[39] or the FDA's original administrative creation of ANDAs. In addition, several prescription new drugs have been approved as OTC drugs under their own NDAs in somewhat different strengths than the prescription versions, rather than relying on the switch regulation route.

For the purposes of switching, the criterion specified in the Durham-Humphrey Amendment that a drug be deemed a prescription drug unless it is "safe" for use without supervision of a physician is the most important. The meaning of this legal standard has been considered by the courts in cases in which the FDA has challenged a manufacturer's failure to place a drug in prescription status. The most carefully reasoned court decision on this issue is *United States v. An Article of Drug . . . Decholin*.[40] The court in that case emphasized that the test was a practical one based on benefits as well as specific and significant concerns of actual danger to users. The court also suggested that the adequacy of labeling to guide lay use was an important factor in whether OTC status was appropriate for a particular drug. It has also been interpreted by the FDA in making "new drug approval" determinations whether a drug should be approved as prescription or whether an approved drug should be switched from prescription to OTC status.

The established warnings recommended or required by the FDA pursuant to existing OTC monographs or final regulations demonstrate the adequacy of label warnings to alert consumers to certain conditions that they can recognize. Thus the FDA recognizes that even serious disease conditions that may be of concern in connection with certain OTC switches can be addressed by labeling. As a result, it is generally expeditious to file a section 505(b)(2) NDA to accomplish appropriate changes to an approved prescription prod-

---

[37]   21 C.F.R. §§ 310.201(a)(16)(viii)(b), (26)(vii)(b).

[38]   *Id.* § 369.20. Other examples include antacids containing more than 50 mEq. of magnesium, which must bear a warning that they are not to be used except under a physician's advice by persons having kidney disease (*id.* § 331.30(c)(4)). In the cough/cold monograph, bronchodilator drugs must warn that they are not for use if an individual has heart disease, high blood pressure, thyroid disease, or diabetes unless directed by a doctor (*id.* § 314.76(c)(2)). Likewise, vasoconstrictors in the anorectal drug products monograph must bear a similar warning statement (*id.* § 346.50(c)(7)). The anthelmintic drug product monograph requires a warning regarding pregnancy or liver disease (*id.* § 357.150(c)(2)).

[39]   Drug Price Competition and Paten Term Restoration Act of 1984, Pub. L. No. 98-417, 98 Stat. 1585.

[40]   264 F. Supp. 273 (D. Mich. 1967).

uct, rather than to seek to amend an existing OTC monograph to include a prescription product. Also, for prescription NDA products that are switched, ANDAs or supplements can be approved for OTC versions of the generics when the applicable periods of exclusivity expire. The option of filing ANDAs will ensure that generic drugs can also be marketed OTC.

Exclusivity Issues

Particularly in new product categories, there are significant economic rewards associated with newly switched products for the OTC marketplace. Manufacturers are interested in establishing pioneer brand OTC drugs prior to the availability of competing generic brands or branded products licensed from generic applicants. Thus, through the mechanism of an OTC switch via an NDA supplement, the provisions of section 505(j) for three-year non-patent exclusivity for those supplements requiring new clinical studies is a critical component of any OTC switch strategy. If the application contains reports of new clinical investigations (other than bioavailability studies) essential to the approval of the application and conducted or sponsored by the applicant, that supplement is entitled to three years non-patent exclusivity.[41]

Over the years, there has been litigation on what constitutes studies "essential" for purposes of granting exclusivity as part of OTC switches. There is little debate that when an OTC product is to be marketed at a lower strength than the prescription version, studies must be conducted to demonstrate efficacy, and those studies qualify for exclusivity.[42] But where the product being switched is *identical* in dose and strength to the formerly prescription product, much of the data on which the agency and the applicant focus are the marketing history of the product and the safety profile, as well as OTC labeling comprehension studies. In these instances, the data package often may not consist of any "clinical" studies, and the drug may not even have been administered to patients in an OTC setting.[43] In such instances, three-year exclusivity may not be available.

However, the issue is not whether switch candidates are identical to prescription products, but whether the particular course of approval and studies in support of approval meet the statutory criteria for exclusivity. In one OTC switch, Femstat, an antifungal switched in the identical dosage as its prescription version, received three-year exclusivity based on a clinical trial establishing that it was at least as effective as other OTC products on the market. Where the OTC switch requires study under conditions of OTC use in order to establish either the safety or efficacy in an OTC setting, or the FDA demands additional safety or effectiveness information to support the application, then there is a strong argument that the statutory requirement for clinical studies "essential" to approval has been met. Even in this situation, the agency must agree with the drug manufacturer on what data are "essential" before exclusivity will be granted.[44]

---

[41] FDCA § 505(j)(4)(D)(iii), 21 U.S.C. § 355 (j)(4)(D)(iii).

[42] There has been relatively little controversy regarding three-year exclusivity for switches of lower strength versions of prescription drug products. Examples include ibuprofen 200 mg (Advil), Naproxen 100 mg (Aleve), Cimetidine 100 mg (Tagamet HB). In each of these cases, there was no question that new clinical studies had to demonstrate that the products were effective at lower doses than were previously available on prescription.

[43] OTC clotrimazole is an example.

[44] *See, e.g.,* Upjohn Co. v. Kessler (W.D. Mich. 1996).

■ Final Formulation Testing

The FDA's OTC monographs generally reflect an agency determination that the active ingredient or combination of active ingredients can be considered to be generally recognized as safe and effective at the strength(s) used and for the intended use(s). However, under certain circumstances, the FDA monograph requirements will exclude a drug product which contains ingredients or combination of active ingredients that the FDA itself recognizes as being generally recognized as safe and effective. This occurs where the FDA has concerns that the final product formulation or dosage presentation could have a negative impact on the safety or effectiveness of the product. Where there is a standard *in vitro* or *in vivo* test for assessing the safety or effectiveness of the final product formulation, the FDA will include the test in the monograph. Examples of such standard tests are the *in vitro* acid neutralizing capacity test for antacids,[45] the *in vitro* USP dissolution tests for enteric coated and delayed release aspirin preparations,[46] and the proposed *in vivo* sun protection factor and water resistant tests for sunscreen preparations.[47]

Where there is no standardized test, or where the FDA deems a standardized test to be inadequate, the FDA may deny monograph status and require an NDA. For example, the FDA has recently proposed to deny monograph status for vaginal contraceptive drug products, even though they may contain active ingredients (e.g., nonoxynol 9 and octoxynol 9) that are generally recognized as safe and effective under OTC vaginal contraceptives monograph. The FDA's rationale was that the final product formulation of such products could have a negative impact upon their effectiveness, and there is no current *in vitro* or *in vivo* standard for assessing this impact.[48] Some have argued that this rationale could be extended to apply to most OTC drugs, and thereby defeat or significantly weaken the FDA's ability to use general rulemaking (i.e., monographs), rather than product-by-product clearance (i.e., NDAs), as a means of regulating OTC drugs. It is more likely that this rationale will be limited to situations where differences in final formulations could result in significant public health or public policy concerns, such as an unwanted pregnancy or failure to protect against the HIV virus or other sexually transmitted diseases.

■ Homeopathic Drugs

A growing class of OTC drugs that generally fall outside the OTC monograph process are known as homeopathic drugs. The practice of homeopathy is based on the belief that disease symptoms can be cured by small doses of substances that produce similar symptoms in healthy people. The FDCA recognizes as drug products substances listed in the *Homeopathic Pharmacopeia of the United States (HPUS)* and its supplements.[49] The FDCA also specifies that homeopathic drugs generally must meet the standards for strength, quality, and purity set forth in the HPUS.[50] Since 1988, the FDA has provided guidance on the

---

45 *See* 21 C.F.R. §331.26

46 *See* proposed 21 C.F.R. § 343.90, 53 Fed. Reg. 46,360 (Nov. 16, 1988).

47 *See* proposed 21 C.F.R. pt. 352, subpt. D, 58 Fed. Reg. 28,298 (May 12, 1993).

48 60 Fed. Reg. 6892 (Feb. 3, 1995).

49 FDCA § 201(g)(1), 21 U.S.C. § 321(g)(1). The fact that the act passed by Congress in 1938 contains a section recognizing homeopathic drugs was largely due to the efforts of Senator Royal Copeland, one of the foremost homeopathic physicians of his day. *See* Pub. L. No. 75-717, 52 Stat. at 1041, as amended.

50 FDCA § 501(b), 21 U.S.C. § 351(b).

regulation of OTC, as well as prescription, homeopathic drugs, and delineated those conditions under which homeopathic drugs may ordinarily be marketed in the United States.[51] The FDA appears to take the position that its regulations do apply to homeopathic drugs, but that the agency exercises its discretion not to enforce them, or apply only certain ones, against homeopathic drugs.

Allopathic Versus Homeopathic Drugs

The nature of homeopathic drugs, and the fact that the FDCA recognizes the drugs and standards in the *HPUS*, present a dichotomy in new drug development processes. This bias resulted in significant differences between regulatory requirements for introduction of new allopathic and new homeopathic drugs into the marketplace in the United States. In contrast to allopathic drugs, the FDCA exempted homeopathic products from safety review. The 1962 Kefauver-Harris Drug Amendments[52] left the homeopathic exemption intact so that while allopathic drugs are scientifically tested and reviewed for safety and effectiveness, homeopathic products are checked for neither.[53] Thus, homeopathic drugs have not been proven effective against disease by scientific means such as randomized, controlled double-blind trials.

Definition

The FDA's Center for Drug Evaluation and Research has issued a Compliance Policy Guide (CPG) that provides a definition of "homeopathic drugs."[54] First, the drug must contain active ingredients listed in the *HPUS*, an addendum to it, or its supplement. Second, the potencies of homeopathic drugs must be specified in terms of dilution (i.e., 1X (1/10 dilution), 2X (1/100 dilution), etc.). Third, homeopathic drug products must contain diluents commonly used in homeopathic pharmaceutics, such as water or alcohol.[55] With regard to alcohol, under the FDA's final rule establishing maximum alcohol concentration limits for orally ingested OTC drugs,[56] the FDA declared that orally ingested homeopathic drugs are exempt from the FDA alcohol content limits, but as an interim measure, will have to be relabeled to disclose their alcohol content, and in certain circumstances, to advise consumers to consult a physician for use in children of particular age levels.

Drug products containing homeopathic ingredients in combination with nonhomeopathic ingredients are *not* considered homeopathic drugs.[57] The FDA has issued warning letters to about a half-dozen companies over the past two to three years based on determinations that ostensibly homeopathic drugs failed to meet this standard.[58]

---

[51] Conditions Under Which Homeopathic Drugs May be Marketed Compliance Policy Guide 7132.15 (May 31, 1988, as revised in Mar., 1995).

[52] Pub. L. No. 87-781, 76 Stat. 780 (1962).

[53] FDA Talk Paper No. T-88-68 (Sept. 15, 1988).

[54] See *supra* note 51.

[55] Most medicines used in homeopathic practice can be prepared in the form of "tinctures" (as well as in the form of "attenuation"). Tinctures are made from a variety of zoological or botanical substances which are wholly or partially soluble in alcohol of various strengths. HPUS, General Pharmacy, at 21.

[56] 59 Fed. Reg. 51,030 (Oct. 6, 1994).

[57] *See* Compliance Policy Guide. *supra* note 51.

[58] *See, e.g.,* Warning letters to Professional Health Products, Ltd. (June 19, 1995), Botanical Laboratories Inc. (June 10, 1994); Consolidated Health Products/Nu-Leaf Products (Aug. 21, 1993).

Prescription Versus OTC Status

The statutory criteria specified in section 503(b) of the FDCA for the determination of prescription status apply to homeopathic drug products.[59] However, if the *HPUS* declares a homeopathic drug to be a prescription drug based on strength (e.g., 20X), the FDA will regard the drug as a prescription drug even if it fails to meet the criteria of section 503(b) of the FDCA. In practice, the FDA has only permitted homeopathic products intended solely for "self-limiting disease conditions amenable to self-diagnosis (of symptoms) and treatment" to be marketed OTC. Homeopathic drug products that do not meet this standard must be marketed as a prescription drug bearing the prescription legend, "Caution: Federal law prohibits dispensing without prescription."[60]

In 1992, in its first action against a homeopathic drug based on prescription drug status, the FDA issued a warning letter based on its *Health Fraud Bulletin* Number 17, "Prescription Homeopathic Products Marketed Over-the-Counter."[61] The action is noteworthy because the agency stated that the diseases or conditions for which a homeopathic product is indicated determine the product's prescription or OTC status, rather than the homeopathic compendial standard that is based solely on strength. The FDA's primary enforcement concern with respect to homeopathic drug products continues to be the OTC marketing of homeopathics for indications that should require a prescription.

Labeling

Homeopathic drug product labeling must comply with the labeling provisions of sections 502 and 503 of the FDCA,[62] and 21 C.F.R. part 201. Regardless of container size, each product, at a minimum, must bear a label containing statement of identity, potency, and the name and place of business of the manufacturer, packer, or distributor.[63] With regard to potency, labeling must bear a statement of quantity and amount of ingredients in the product expressed in homeopathic terms.[64] Each drug product offered for retail sale must also bear adequate directions for use,[65] and an established name.[66] All labeling must be in english although it is permissible to include in the labeling both english and latin names of the homeopathic ingredients.[67]

OTC homeopathic drug products must additionally comply with the principal display panel and the declaration of net quantity of contents provisions,[68] and contain a statement of identity,[69] which must include the established name of the drug, if any there be, and a minimum of one indication for use. Homeopathic products offered for OTC retail must bear "at least one major OTC indication or use, stated in terms likely to be understood by

---

[59] 21 U.S.C. § 353(b).

[60] FDCA § 501(b)(1), 21 § 351(b)(1).

[61] Warning letter to King Bio Pharmaceuticals, Inc. (Oct. 8, 1992). *See also* Warning letter to Dolisos (Mar. 23, 1995) and L.B.L.-Bot. Bio. Hom. Corp. (Apr. 29, 1994).

[62] 21 U.S.C. §§ 352, 353.

[63] 21 C.F.R. § 201.1.

[64] FDCA § 502(b), 21 U.S.C. § 352(b); 21 C.F.R. § 201.10.

[65] 21 C.F.R. § 201.5.

[66] FDCA § 502(e)(1)(3), 21 U.S.C. § 352(e)(1), (3); 21 C.F.R. § 201.10.

[67] FDCA § 502(c), 21 U.S.C. § 352(c); 21 C.F.R. § 201.15(c)(1).

[68] 21 C.F.R. § 201.62.

[69] *Id.* § 201.61.

lay persons." However, unlike other OTC drugs, an indication need not be listed in one of the proposed or final OTC monographs, although OTC homeopathic drug products, like monograph products, must bear adequate warnings.[70]

Other Requirements

All firms that manufacture, prepare, propagate, compound, or otherwise process homeopathic drugs must register as drug establishments,[71] and all homeopathic drug products must be listed with the FDA.[72] Homeopathic drug products must also be packaged in accordance with the FDCA,[73] and be manufactured in conformance with good manufacturing practices.[74] Due to the unique nature of these drug products, however, some good manufacturing practices requirements are currently not applicable. Namely, homeopathic drugs are exempt from expiration dating requirements,[75] and the requirement for laboratory determination of identity and strength of each active ingredient prior to release for distribution.[76] Also, effective September 15, 1995, homeopathic drug products in solid oral dosage form are required to bear a code imprint that identifies the manufacturer and their homeopathic nature, but not the specific product.[77]

Recent Developments

An August 31, 1994 Citizen Petition to the FDA requested the agency to require that all OTC homeopathic drugs meet the same standards of safety and effectiveness as nonhomeopathic OTC drugs. In a letter dated December 29, 1994, the American Homeopathic Pharmaceutical Association (AHPhA) responded to the Citizen Petition. AHPhA maintained that using agency resources to enforce the existing CPG would provide greater benefits than to begin an OTC-type review of homeopathics. AHPhA also asserted that the petition's suggestion was ill-timed because the National Institutes of Health was currently examining alternative medicines, including homeopathy.[78]

Nearly twenty-two centuries have passed since Hippocrates described his "like cures like" theory of homeopathy. While the regulation of allopathic drugs is based on the full framework of federal laws and regulations, most homeopathic remedies have not been subjected to regulation under the new drug provisions of the FDCA. The *HPUS* is the sole authority in the United States for determining whether homeopathic remedies are "proven." Until recently, homeopathic drugs were marketed on a limited scale by a few manufacturers who have predominantly served the needs of licensed practitioners. As this has changed, so has the degree of interest in homeopathic drug products. It remains to be seen how the FDA will respond to the recently proposed changes in the manner in which homeopathic drugs are regulated, and how the industry, in turn, will respond.

---

[70] *Id.* § 201.63.

[71] FDCA § 510, 21 U.S.C. § 360; 21 C.F.R. § 207.

[72] 21 C.F.R. § 207.

[73] FDCA § 501(g), 21 U.S.C. § 351(g).

[74] *Id.* § 501(a)(2)(B), 21 U.S.C. § 351(a)(2)(B); 21 C.F.R. § 211.

[75] 21 C.F.R. § 211.137.

[76] *Id.* § 211.165. In the *Federal Register* of Apr. 1, 1983 (48 Fed. Reg. 14,003), the agency proposed to amend 21 C.F.R. § 211.165 to exempt homeopathic drug products from this testing requirement. According to the CPG, the testing requirement will not be enforced for homeopathic drugs, pending a final rule on the exemption.

[77] 21 C.F.R. § 206.10. *See* 58 Fed. Reg. 47,948 (Sept. 13, 1993).

[78] *Id.*

Labeling and Advertising

Labeling of OTC drugs has been primarily governed by the OTC Review. Scrutiny of drug labeling is a regular part of the Review, and each OTC monograph must specify the label that is justified for each OTC drug product.

OTC drug labels have historically been subject to only very limited controls on the design and format of labels, e.g., placement of the net contents statement. The OTC monograph system imposes more significant uniformity on the textual content of OTC labels, requiring use of specified language to describe directions for use and warnings. In response to industry demands for more flexibility in label wording, the FDA in 1986 modified its so-called exclusivity policy to permit deviations from the previously exclusive indications language established in OTC monographs.[79]

■ Reform Efforts

Uniformity of OTC Labeling

Today, the pendulum is swinging away from flexibility in the direction of more uniform standards for OTC labeling. With concern over health care costs leading to greater emphasis on self-medication and with more sophisticated drugs being considered for switching from prescription to OTC status, the FDA is increasingly concerned that consumers actually read, comprehend and act in accordance with the information provided in OTC drug labeling.

In an August 1995 *Federal Register* notice, the agency issued a call for comments and announced the holding of a public hearing to receive input on the benefits, costs, and methods for improving the communication of OTC drug information.[80] The FDA identified a number of issues that would be involved in this process, including:

- Identifying the sources of consumer information about OTC drugs.
- Evaluating the comprehensibility of OTC drug information.
- Considering improvements in the terms and text used in OTC drug labeling
- Proposing minimum standards of type size, legibility, contrast, spacing and other label design features.
- Considering the possibility of uniform format requirements for OTC drugs.
- Considering whether the standardized food label established under the Nutrition Labeling and Education Act of 1990[81] is an appropriate model for OTC drugs.[82]

The potential for the FDA to expand regulatory standards in these areas runs counter to the current deregulatory political climate. The FDA recognizes that standardization may inhibit flexibility in label content and design. Nevertheless, the indications are that at least some the FDA officials believe that enhanced regulatory requirements will produce a net public benefit. As additional prescription drugs are considered for OTC switches,

---

[79] *See* 21 C.F.R. § 330.1(c)(2).

[80] 60 Fed. Reg. 42,578 (Aug. 16, 1995).

[81] Pub. L. No. 101-535, 104 Stat. 2353 (codified at 21 U.S.C.§§ 301 note, 321, 337, 343, 343 notes, 343-1, 343-1 note, 345, 371(1994)).

[82] 60 Fed. Reg. at 52,474 (Oct. 6, 1995).

what may be most important in resolving this issue is determining, through studies or other evidence, the actual link between regulatory standards for drug labeling and the safe and effective use of these products by consumers. Although the possible issuance of new regulations lies in the hazy future, it is clear today that the FDA views the improvement and potential standardization of OTC drug labeling as an important public health mission.

Metric Labeling

In an early effort toward international harmonization, Congress in 1992 amended the Fair Packaging and Labeling Act[83] to make metric labeling mandatory on consumer commodities, including OTC drugs, effective for labels printed on or after February 14, 1994. Specifically, the legislation required the appropriate federal agency (the FDA for OTC drugs) to promulgate regulations to require use of both the customary inch/pound system and the metric system in net quantity statements on most OTC drug labels. The FDA issued proposed regulations in December 1993.[84] While the FDA had previously issued policy guidelines permitting use of metric labeling, the need to implement mandatory standards required the Agency to address a variety of technical issues, including standardization of conversion factors, use of abbreviations and punctuation, and rules for rounding off and significant figures. As of this writing, the FDA has not issued final rules to implement the 1992 legislation. While many OTC drugs already employ both inch/pound and metric labeling, the evident difficulties in deciding on appropriate regulations for this relatively simple issue foreshadow the problems that may lie ahead in resolving more contentious harmonization matters.

■ FTC and Self-Regulation of OTC Advertising

Federal Trade Commission

The FDCA does not give the FDA authority to regulate advertising of OTC drugs. Instead, this statutory responsibility falls to the Federal Trade Commission (FTC).[85] The FDA can use its authority to ensure that drugs bear "adequate directions for use"[86] as a means to object to OTC drugs that it believes are improperly advertised for off-label uses. The agency argues that the advertising suggests uses that are not adequately labeled, so that laypersons cannot use the product safely and effectively for its intended purposes. This particular the FDA strategy is known as the "squeeze play."[87] The FDA has also used its new drug approval authority in the context of the ibuprofen "switch" to determine whether advertising for an OTC drug might undercut the required warnings, and to condition acceptance of the supplemental NDA on assurances regarding advertising.[88]

---

[83] Pub. L. No. 89-755, 80 Stat. 1296 (1966) (codified at 15 U.S.C. §§ 1451 et seq. (1994)).

[84] 58 Fed. Reg. 67,444 (Dec. 21, 1993).

[85] Federal Trade Commission Act §§ 5, 12, 15(a), 15 U.S.C. §§ 45, 52, 55(a).

[86] FDCA § 502(f)(1), 21 U.S.C. § 352(f)(1).

[87] See, e.g., United States v. An Article of Drug . . . B-Complex Cholinos Capsules, 362 F.2d 923, 925-26 (3d Cir. 1966).

[88] See McNeilab, Inc. v. Heckler, No. 84-1617 (D.D.C. June 5, 1985).

The FDA and the FTC have a Memorandum of Understanding that provides for cooperation in exercising their responsibilities.[89] Prior to its announcement of the "exclusivity policy" requiring that OTC drug labeling of indications for use conform to the exact wording of the applicable monograph, the FDA sought an FTC rulemaking that would similarly limit OTC drug advertising claims to the exact wording of the monographs. The FTC concluded in 1981 that OTC drug advertising should not always be limited to labeling language approved by the FDA.[90] Subsequently, the FDA abandoned its exclusivity policy.[91] The FTC has taken no further official action with respect to OTC drug advertising, but as a practical matter, the FTC will consider and cite the monograph requirements in an enforcement proceeding regarding an OTC drug.

Private Regulation

The OTC drug industry and allied bodies engage in extensive private regulation of labeling and advertising claims. Concerns about the extent to which an advertiser has substantiation for claims about its own products or those of a competitor are frequently resolved in a forum other than the courtroom.

When an advertisement is being developed for broadcast over national networks, the networks will apply their own standards for ensuring that advertising is adequately substantiated. In general, the ABC, CBS, and NBC networks require that adequate testing to support advertising claims be done before the advertisements are approved for airing. In addition, the networks have procedures under which a competitor may challenge a company's advertising. In general, the process involves the submission of a challenge by a competitor and the submission of substantiating data by the advertiser. A network will discontinue a challenged advertisement at the request of the advertiser or if the dispute is resolved against the advertiser.

Challenging an advertisement in the forum in which it is run (i.e., on the broadcast networks, or even at a newspaper, magazine, or non-network broadcast station) is attractive because, if successful, the outcome is guaranteed: the advertisement will not be run in that forum. However, it is also inefficient because of the many available forums for advertising. The National Advertising Division (NAD) of the Council of Better Business Bureaus, Inc. offers a central, non-judicial forum for resolving disputes about national advertising in different forums.

The NAD, which began in 1971, is funded by member companies and provides impartial opinions about whether advertising claims are adequately substantiated. The organization acts in response to challenges by competitors, individual consumers, local Better Business Bureaus (BBBs), trade associations, and other groups who file queries or complaints about national ads. In addition, the NAD conducts systematic monitoring of national broadcast and cable television and print advertising, and initiates certain cases on its own initiative. In recent years, approximately 20 percent of cases have originated from consumers and

---

[89] FDA-FTC Memorandum of Understanding, 36 Fed. Reg. 18,539 (Sept. 16, 1971).

[90] 46 Fed. Reg. 24,584 (May 1, 1981) (terminating the rulemaking proceeding to make it a violation of the FTC act to make a claim in advertising in wording other than that required by the final monograph established for that drug category).

[91] *See* discussion of the "flexibility policy," *supra*.

BBBs, 50 percent from competing advertisers, and 30 percent from the NAD's monitoring program.

The NAD process has been widely used by OTC drug manufacturers for a variety of reasons. Perhaps the most important are: 1) The proceedings follow a strict, and relatively prompt, time schedule and are conducted in confidence until the final decision is released; 2) NAD review provides a useful test of both the challenger's and advertiser's data, to which a court may later give substantial weight in the event that a court challenge is later necessary; and 3) the proceedings are less expensive than litigation. The principal drawback of the NAD process is that the decision cannot be enforced in the event that unsubstantiated advertising is continued in contravention of the NAD's recommendation— although, of course, judicial relief can later be sought, if necessary.

Conclusion

What does the future hold for OTC drugs? It is likely that all of the currently proposed monographs will become final and effective in the next ten years, and OTC labeling will be streamlined and more uniform from product to product. It is unlikely that the FDA will extend the OTC review beyond those ingredients it has already considered; rather, the FDA will probably continue to take the position that any product containing an active ingredient not in a final monograph and labeled in conformity with the standards of that monograph is an unapproved new drug. This position subjects new OTC drug products to the new drug approval standards, and to a separate approval application for each product. Under these new drug provisions, including the Hatch/Waxman standards for ANDAs, the FDA will continue to "switch" appropriate prescription drugs to an OTC status and, where science and the law justify it, may approve new products initially as OTC drugs. Because of the potential for three-year exclusivity for OTC switches, and the relative ease of ANDA approval for marketing when the OTC reference drug's three-year exclusivity expires, more and more drugs will follow these routes to OTC marketing rather than the old monograph system.[92]

Particularly as a result of increased new drug submissions, there may be an increase in the FDA scrutiny of OTC drugs. Currently, the only submissions required of OTC manufacturers are registration and drug listing obligations. Other than current good manufacturing practice inspections, the only means by which the agency can systematically enforce the monograph requirements is through its review of labeling for OTC products submitted for export certification. While competitors often assist the agency in its "seek and destroy" regulatory enforcement endeavors, the process remains uneven and inefficient. With more drug approvals and OTC switches, the FDA will have a much better awareness of the status of the OTC market without having to police the field somewhat randomly.

---

[92] *See* FDCA § 505(j)(4)(D, 21 U.S.C. § 355(j)(4)(D).

chapter 9

Combination Products and Other Jurisdictional Conundrums

Nancy L. Buc*
Kate C. Beardsley**

Combination Products and the FDA

Combination products are the Flubadubs[1] of products regulated by the Food and Drug Administration (FDA). If a product is part drug and part device, for example, should its sponsor submit a new drug application (NDA), a premarket approval application (PMA), or both? Which FDA Center will review the application(s)? The Center for Drug Evaluation and Research (CDER), the Center for Devices and Radiological Health (CDRH), or both? The answers to these questions can have significant effects on the time it takes to bring a product to market and how much it will cost.[2]

Traditionally, the FDA responded to such questions on an ad hoc basis. Prophylaxis pastes containing fluoride are regulated as drugs, although prophylaxis pastes without fluoride are considered medical devices.[3] Bone cement, however, is treated as a device, regardless of whether it is combined with an antibiotic drug.[4]

Although both extracorporeal and peritoneal dialysis systems are regulated as devices,[5] dialysate concentrate for use with the former is a device but prepackaged dialysate for use

---

[*]   Ms. Buc is a Partner in the law firm of Buc & Beardsley, Washington, D.C.

[**] Ms. Beardsley is a Partner in the law firm of Buc & Beardsley, Washington, D.C.

[1]   A puppet on the Howdy Doody show, Flubadub was an amalgamation of eight different animals. STEPHEN DAVIS, SAY KIDS! WHAT TIME IS IT? 72 (1987).

[2]   For example, the sponsor of a product designated a drug is subject to user fees and the FDA must bear in mind user fee review deadlines in processing an NDA; if the same product were designated a device, no user fee would be due to the FDA and no corresponding FDA deadlines would be imposed.

[3]   Letter from William F. Randolph, Dep. Assoc. Comm'r for Reg. Affairs, Food & Drug Admin., to Robert A. Abodeely, Dir., Reg. Affairs and Quality Assurance, Johnson & Johnson Dental Prods. Co. (Sept. 18, 1981).

[4]   Letter from William F. Randolph, Dep. Assoc. Comm'r for Reg. Affairs, to Timothy M. Wendt, Vice Pres., Div. Counsel, Zimmer (Jan. 17, 1983) (re: bone cement containing an antibiotic); 21 C.F.R. § 888.3027 (1997) (re: bone cement itself).

[5]   See 21 C.F.R. § 876.5820 (hemodialysis system with extracorporeal blood system); id. § 876.5630 (peritoneal dialysis system).

with the latter is a drug.[6] Sometimes consistency was elusive even when there was no combination, but just a single product. For example, *in vitro* diagnostics for detecting antibodies to HIV are regulated as biologics when they are used for screening the blood supply, but as medical devices when used for diagnostic or other screening purposes.[7] When the FDA decided quickly and unequivocally on the regulatory status of a product, whether it was deemed a single product or was in combination with another product, there was relatively little objection to the agency's decisions about how to regulate combination products and products whose status was uncertain.

In two situations, however, the agency's decisions were troublesome to sponsors. When the FDA required two separate approvals, one for the device and one for the drug element of the product, as it did with the drug ursodiol for use with lithotripters, the agency created difficulty and delay in getting the products licensed so they could be used together.[8] Similarly, the FDA's indecisiveness in this area made it particularly difficult for companies such as Robertson Resources. Robertson marketed Revital, a medical protein hydrolysate that came in both powder and gel forms; it was used for wound exudate removal. In 1978, the company received a letter from the Bureau of Medical Devices stating that its product was substantially equivalent to another device on the market prior to May 20, 1976. In 1981, however, the FDA told Robertson the product was not a device but was an unapproved new drug. A year later, the FDA decided that the product was a medical device again and reinstated its 510(k).[9] In the meantime, of course, Robertson had been the subject of intense enforcement attention.[10]

In the Safe Medical Devices Act of 1990 (SMDA),[11] Congress took these issues in hand and amended the Federal Food, Drug, and Cosmetic Act (FDCA)[12] to make it easier for the FDA to regulate combination products in a rational fashion. The new provisions altered the substantive provisions of the FDCA only in minor respects.[13] The main thrust of the new law was managerial, directing the FDA to make decisions about which Center would have "primary jurisdiction" over a combination product, based on the agency's

---

[6]   *Id.* §§ 876.5820(a)(3) (extracorporeal), 876.5630(a)(4) (peritoneal). Even the FDA was confused on this categorization. *See* Letter from William V. Purvis, Asst. to the Dir., Div. of Drug Advertising and Labeling, Off. of Drug Standards, Food & Drug Admin., to Bicarbolyte Corp. (Mar. 13, 1985), alleging that dialysate failed to comply with the drug labeling requirements. The dialysate in question was a medical device.

[7]   Intercenter Agreement Between the Center for Biologics Evaluation and Research and the Center for Devices and Radiological Health 5 (Oct. 25, 1991); *Update on AIDS Test Kits*, FDA Talk Paper (Oct. 26, 1987).

[8]   M-D-D-I REP. ("The Gray Sheet"), Jan. 8, 1996, at 9-10; M-D-D-I REP. ("The Gray Sheet"), Sept. 24, 1990, at 4-5.

[9]   *See* Medical Device Amendments, Pub. L. No. 94-295, § 4(a)(9), 90 Stat. 540, 580 (1976) (codified at 21 U.S.C. § 360(k) (1994)) (amending FDCA § 510(k)). 510(k) refers to a relatively quick route to market products that involves premarket notification to the FDA.

[10] *See* Letter from Joseph P. Hile, Assoc. Comm'r for Reg. Affairs, Food & Drug Admin., to Vance Hartke, Esq., Hartke & Hartke (May 6, 1982), and Memorandum of Meeting (May 10, 1982). The costs of dual approvals and uncertainty were not borne only by sponsors. Without a strong internal process, the FDA also spent much time and energy deciding how to handle individual products.

[11] Pub. L. No. 101-629, 104 Stat. 4511.

[12] Pub. L. No. 75-717, 52 Stat. 1040 (1938) (codified at 21 U.S.C. §§ 301 et seq.).

[13] Specifically, Congress deleted from the definition of "drug" the phrase "but does not include devices or their components," thus allowing the FDA to approve a combination product as a drug. S. REP. NO. 513, 101st Cong., 2d Sess. 30 (1990). Congress also changed the definition of "device." Pre-SMDA, a product could not be a device if it "achieve[d] any of its principal purposes through chemical action" . . . , etc. The SMDA deleted "any of" and substituted "primary" for "principal." *Id.*

decision about the "primary mode of action" of the product.[14] The SMDA provisions also explicitly stated that nothing in the new amendment prevented the FDA from using any of its resources necessary to ensure adequate review of the safety, effectiveness, or substantial equivalence of an article.[15]

The SMDA also ordered the FDA to issue regulations implementing market clearance procedures in accordance with the new section 503(g) within one year.[16] The FDA did so, and published its new regulations on November 21, 1991.[17]

The regulations implemented the new statutory provisions governing combination products, and also provided a means of resolving questions about which Center will have primary jurisdiction for any drug, device, or biological product, whether a combination product or not, where such jurisdiction is unclear or in dispute.[18]

Although the statute does not define "combination products," the regulations define them to include:[19]

- A product comprised of two or more regulated components, i.e., drug/device, biologic/device, or drug/biologic that are physically, chemically, or otherwise combined or mixed and produced as a single entity;
- Two or more separate products packaged together in a single package or as a unit and comprised of drug or device products, device and biological products, or biological and drug products;
- A drug, device, or biological product packaged separately that according to its investigational plan or proposed labeling is intended for use only with an approved individually specified drug, device, or biological product where both are required to achieve the intended use, indication, or effect and where upon approval of the proposed product the labeling of the approved product would need to be changed, e.g., to reflect a change in intended use, dosage form, strength, route of administration, or significant change in dose; or
- Any investigational drug, device, or biological product packaged separately that according to its proposed labeling is for use only with another individually specified investigational drug, device, or biological product where both are required to achieve the intended use, indication, or effect.[20]

---

[14] FDCA § 503(g)(1), 21 U.S.C. §353(g)(1). Because the FDA considered the new statute to govern administration and management rather than substance, it decided that its procedures for issuing implementing regulations were exempt from notice and comment under the Administrative Procedure Act. Preamble to Final Rule, 56 Fed. Reg. 58,754, 58,755 (Nov. 21, 1991).

[15] FDCA § 503(g)(2), 21 U.S.C. § 353(g)(2). Presumably the FDA already had this authority, for nothing in the FDCA or the Public Health Service Act otherwise requires or prevents the Commissioner of Food and Drugs' delegation of authority (as delegated to him or her by the Secretary of the Department of Health and Human Services (DHHS)) to any of the agency's employees.

[16] Id. § 503(g)(3), 21 U.S.C. §353(g)(3).

[17] Assignment of Agency Component for Review of Premarket Applications, Final Rule, 56 Fed. Reg. 58,754 (Nov. 21, 1991) (hereinafter Final Rule).

[18] Id. at 58,756.

[19] Use of the word "include" suggests the possibility that additional products also fit the definition.

[20] 21 C.F.R. § 3.2(e).

For these products, Center jurisdiction turns on the primary mode of action. If the primary mode of action is that of a drug, then CDER has primary jurisdiction; if it is that of a device, jurisdiction is with CDRH; if that of a biological product, the Center for Biologics Evaluation and Research (CBER) has this jurisdiction.[21] As the statute prescribed, the regulations go on to state that the Center with primary jurisdiction may consult with other agency components.[22]

Although neither the statute nor the regulations explain what "primary jurisdiction" means, it seems clear that the FDA intends it to mean that the Center that has primary jurisdiction will review the combination product and ordinarily give it just one approval, that is, an NDA, PMA, or biologic license application (BLA) as appropriate. Section 3.4(b) makes it clear, however, that the FDA's designation of one agency component as having primary jurisdiction does not preclude, in appropriate cases, the requirement for separate applications, e.g., a 510(k) and a BLA. When separate applications are required, both can be reviewed by the lead Center, but "exceptional" cases may involve a second application to be reviewed by a different Center.[23] To facilitate this, the agency published new delegations giving officials in each of the three Centers the authority to clear devices and to approve devices, drugs, biologics, or any combination of two or more of them.[24]

Contemporaneous with publication of the new regulations, the FDA made public three new Intercenter Agreements between CDRH and CBER, CDRH and CDER, and CDER and CBER. They describe the allocations of responsibility for numerous categories of specific products, both combination and noncombination. According to the regulations, these intercenter agreements are not binding; they are intended to "provide useful guidance to the public,"[25] and, as a practical matter, to FDA staff as well.[26]

The Intercenter Agreements are a treasure trove of information. In addition to explicit guidance about which Center has the lead with respect to particular products and whether one Center or two will work on particular issues, they contain information and hints about whether the FDA believes it can regulate certain products at all, and if so, how.[27]

---

[21] *Id.* § 3.4(a)(1)-(3). Interestingly, the "primary mode of action" standard applies only to designation of an FDA Center for combination products. No standard is mandated for designating a Center for a noncombination product or for designating a kind of submission (e.g., NDA, PMA, or biologic license application (BLA)) for combination products. Although the legislative history suggests that Congress may have thought the kind of submission would also be governed by primary mode of action, the FDA apparently is free, within the confines of the statutes, to decide these questions on whatever basis it chooses. In Coyne Beahm, Inc. v. FDA, 1997 U.S. Dist. LEXIS 5453 (M.D.N.C. Apr. 25, 1997), the court determined that the FDA may designate the drug Center to regulate cigarettes, a combination drug-device product, using device legal authorities.

[22] 21 C.F.R. § 3.4(b).

[23] Preamble to Final Rule, 56 Fed. Reg. at 58,755.

[24] 21 C.F.R. § 5.33; Delegations of Authority and Organization; Center for Biologics Evaluation and Research, Center for Devices and Radiological Health, and Center for Drug Evaluation and Research, Final Rule, 56 Fed. Reg. 58,758 (Nov. 21, 1991).

[25] 21 C.F.R. § 3.5(a)(2).

[26] Although the Intercenter Agreements discuss certain combination products, they make no reference to the combination products amendments to the FDCA or to the implementing regulations announcing their availability; their focus, as the name Intercenter Agreements implies, is on how the Centers relate to each other, not on sponsors' need for information.

[27] Copies of the Intercenter Agreements are available from CDRH's Facts-on-Demand (800-899-0381) and the FDA's Dockets Management Branch, (HFA-305), Food and Drug Administration, 12420 Parklawn Drive, Rockville, MD 20857.

The regulations and Intercenter Agreements, however, do not answer every question, and the regulations recognize a role for the sponsor in cases of uncertainty. When the identity of the Center with primary jurisdiction is unclear or in dispute, or a sponsor believes its combination product is not covered by the Intercenter Agreements, a sponsor can request a designation from the FDA's product jurisdiction officer.[28] A sponsor "should" file a request for designation with the product jurisdiction officer before submitting its application for marketing approval or an investigational notice.[29] In practice, though, disputes or lack of clarity may not become evident until well into the review process, and it seems likely that the FDA would, if necessary, entertain requests for designation submitted at a later time.[30]

Section 3.7(c) of the regulations lists the information to be included in the request, all of which must fit on fifteen pages or less,[31] including the identity of the sponsor, detailed information on the product, where the developmental work stands, the product's known modes of action and its primary mode of action, and, importantly, the sponsor's recommendation for which Center should have primary jurisdiction and the reasons for the recommendation.[32]

The FDA promises to check the request for designation for completeness within five working days of receipt,[33] and to issue a letter of designation within sixty days of receipt of a complete request.[34] If the FDA does not meet the sixty-day time limit, then the sponsor's recommendation for the appropriate lead Center is honored.[35]

The agency's letter of designation can be changed only with the sponsor's written consent, or, if the sponsor does not consent, "to protect the public health or for other compelling reasons."[36] A sponsor must be given prior notice of any proposed nonconsensual change, and must be given an opportunity to object in writing and at a "timely" meeting with the product jurisdiction officer and appropriate Center officials.[37]

Has the product jurisdiction process solved the problems? Is there more consistency, and less duplication? These authors know of no surveys or studies that address these questions in any systematic fashion, and the FDA does not routinely publish or announce its decisions.[38] Even if some anomalies remain, however, Congress and the FDA have at least created a process that provides a forum for resolution of these issues.

---

[28] 21 C.F.R. §§ 3.5(b), 3.7(a). 21 C.F.R. § 3.6 designates the FDA Ombudsman as the product jurisdiction officer.

[29] *Id.* § 3.7(b).

[30] One disincentive for making designation requests after an application has been submitted is that filing or review by the product jurisdiction officer stays the review clock during the pendency of the review. *Id.* § 3.10.

[31] *Id.* § 3.7(c).

[32] *Id.* § 3.7(c)(1)-(3).

[33] *Id.* § 3.8(a).

[34] *Id.* § 3.8(b).

[35] *Id.* This provision is an intriguing example of a situation in which the FDA has created its own "hammer" provision, presumably to help the product jurisdiction officer capture the Centers' attention in a timely fashion.

[36] *Id.* § 3.9(b).

[37] *Id.*

[38] Requests for designation usually involve products that are, or are about to be, the subject of investigational notices (whether an investigational new drug (IND) or investigational device exemption (IDE)) or premarket approval applications (NDA, PMA, or BLA), and, consistent with the general rules for the release of information in these kinds of files, the FDA does not usually release information until the applications are processed. The FDA has not published a list of its decisions.

Authors' Note

As of this article's completion, the FDA has been sued by three companies whose ultrasound contrast agents are being regulated as drugs. The three companies have charged that the FDA's regulation of a fourth company's ultrasound contrast agent as a medical device, while continuing to treat the three companies' products as drugs, is unlawful. The plaintiffs obtained a preliminary injunction preventing the FDA from reviewing or approving any of the products until the agency resolves the disparity.[39] Whatever else might be said of this litigation, the fact that it occurred at all demonstrates that the FDA procedures discussed in this article are not adequate to resolve certain product jurisdiction issues.

---

[39] Bracco Diagnostics, Inc. v. Shalala, Civ. Nos. 97-0739, 97-0740, and 97-0742 (PLF) (D.D.C. 1997) (order of preliminary injunction).

chapter 10

Developments in Medical Device Regulation

Howard M. Holstein*
Edward C. Wilson**

Introduction

Until 1976, Congress had never enacted specific legislation governing the regulation of medical devices. Prior to that date, public protection from defective devices depended on the Food and Drug Administration's (FDA) enforcement of the limited provisions in the Federal Food, Drug, and Cosmetic Act of 1938 ("FDCA") and on judicial interpretations that extended the FDA's regulatory authority over drugs to devices. This combination of sources for the agency's authority proved cumbersome. By the mid-1970s, it had become clear that, due to significant and rapid scientific advances, and because some unsafe, ineffective, and even fraudulent devices, were occasionally marketed, an increase in federal regulation was needed. Since that time, Congress has enacted three pieces of legislation in an attempt to create a workable system to ensure the safety and effectiveness of medical devices.

Congress's first and most comprehensive legislative effort was the 1976 Medical Device Amendments, enacted on May 28, 1976,[1] which vastly expanded the FDA's statutory authority by creating a comprehensive regulatory scheme for devices. However, implementation of the 1976 Amendments proved more challenging and time consuming than anticipated. The 1976 law also contained what Congress perceived as significant regulatory gaps. Thus, in 1990, Congress further revised and expanded the FDA's regulatory authority over devices in the Safe Medical Devices Act of 1990 (SMDA).[2] Among other

---

*   Mr. Holstein is a Partner in the law firm of Hogan & Hartson L.L.P., Washington, D.C.

**   Mr. Wilson is an Associate in the law firm of Hogan & Hartson L.L.P., Washington, D.C. Special thanks are extended to Jonathan Kahan, Christopher Healey, Janice Hogan, Greta Oehlert, Debra Aleknavage, and Jeffrey Shapiro of Hogan & Hartson, and William Hare (formerly of Hogan & Hartson) for their valuable contributions to this chapter.

1   Medical Device Amendments of 1976, Pub. L. No. 94-295, 90 Stat. 539 (1976) (codified at 15 U.S.C. § 55 (1994) and 21 U.S.C. *passim* (1994)).

2   Safe Medical Devices Act of 1990, Pub. L. No. 101-629, 104 Stat. 4511 (1990) (codified at 21 U.S.C. § 301 *passim* and 42 U.S.C. §§ 263b-n (1994)) [hereinafter SMDA].

things, the SMDA provided the FDA with new enforcement authority, enabling the agency to seek civil penalties, device recalls, and temporary suspensions of premarket approval applications (PMAs). It also codified the FDA's interpretation of section 510(k) of the FDCA regarding device clearances and imposed time limits on the FDA's implementation of certain key provisions of the 1976 legislation, including decisions whether to downclassify or require PMAs for a number of class III devices. Finally, in the 1992 Medical Device Amendments, Congress "fine tuned" several provisions of the FDCA, specifically with respect to the medical device reporting, tracking, postmarket surveillance, and repair, replacement and refund provisions of the statute.[3]

This chapter sets forth the development of the legislation pursuant to which the FDA regulates medical devices. It also discusses several key implementing regulations and the areas that are likely to see change in the near future.

Major Legislative Events and Judicial Decisions Prior to the 1976 Medical Device Amendments, and the Need for Legislation

■ Development of Device Regulation

The Pure Food and Drugs Act of 1906[4] barred misbranded or adulterated foods and drugs from interstate commerce, but it did not provide for the regulation of medical devices. By the early 1930s, mounting abuses of medical devices, most clearly illustrated by the widespread distribution of quack devices, led to increased concern by the public and Congress.[5] Accordingly, when the 1938 Act was passed, medical devices were specifically included in the new law.[6]

Under the 1938 Act, the term "device" was defined as "instruments, apparatus, and contrivances, including their components, parts, and accessories, intended 1) for use in the diagnosis, cure, mitigation, treatment, or prevention of disease in man or other animals; or 2) to affect the structure or any function of the body of man or other animals."[7] The FDCA prohibited the shipment of misbranded devices in interstate commerce. Interstate shipment of adulterated devices, i.e., those composed of filthy, putrid, or decomposed substances; those prepared, packed, or held under unsanitary conditions; and those whose strength dif-

---

3   Medical Device Amendments of 1992, Pub. L. No. 102-300, 106 Stat. 238 (1992) (codified at 21 U.S.C. §§ 301 *passim* and 42 U.S.C. § 262.

4   Pub. L. No. 59-384, 34 Stat. 786 (1906) [hereinafter 1906 Act].

5   As support for the new law, the FDA released a collection from its "Chamber of Horrors," which contained examples of ineffective and dangerous devices that the agency was unable to regulate under the 1906 Act. Among the devices under attack were contraceptive devices, rejuvenators, nose straightness, height-stretching machines, and heated rubber applicators as cures for prostate gland disorders. *See* R. LAMB, AMERICAN CHAMBER of HORRORS (1936).

6   Pub. L. No. 75-717, 52 Stat. 1040 (1938) (codified as amended at 21 U.S.C. §§ 301-393).

7   *Id.* FDCA § 201(h), 21 U.S.C. § 321(h).

fered from or whose purity or quality fell below that which it purported or was represented to possess—also was prohibited.[8]

Nevertheless, because the 1938 Act did not give the FDA the authority to impose a system of advance approval for medical devices, the FDA again was left with "after-the-fact" regulation through enforcement actions in court. This state of affairs persisted until 1976. Despite this limitation, after 1938 the FDA did succeed in removing some grossly hazardous products from the market.[9] Other actions, including those involving unreliable thermometers and prophylactics, led to the development of voluntary industry standards to ensure quality.

Eliminating fraudulent devices was one of the FDA's major goals in the device area, but progress was slow. For example, under the 1938 Act, even after the FDA prevailed in a seizure action in one district court, a device manufacturer could continue to market a fraudulent device in other jurisdictions. This meant that the agency was required to bring multiple seizure actions to effectively remove the device from the market, which consumed substantial agency resources. Although injunctions and criminal prosecutions were available to the FDA, those measures generally were not used because they placed heavy demands on the FDA's limited resources.

Although the 1938 Act had given the FDA new, albeit limited, authority over devices, the FDA did not immediately initiate an energetic compliance program for devices. By the 1960s and early 1970s, however, evolving medical technology had created new regulatory problems in the device area. Sophisticated new products, including implanted devices, were entering the market without FDA premarket review of the safety or effectiveness of such products. These developments ultimately led to legislation in 1976 (described below) that strengthened the FDA's device authority. Before that development, however, the agency obtained some enhanced authority from the courts, which extended the agency's drug preclearance authority to certain types of devices.

■ Key Judicial Decisions Concerning Medical Devices

The first of the key cases involving medical devices was decided just before the enactment of the 1938 Act. In *United States v. 48 Dozen Packages... of Gauze Bandage...,*[10] the Second Circuit Court of Appeals found a medical device—a gauze bandage—to be a "drug" within the scope of the 1906 Act. The court reasoned that a bandage met the definition of "drug" because it was "a substance intended to be used for the cure, mitigation, or prevention of disease of either man or other animals...," and that the 1906 Act "should be given a fair and reasonable construction to attain its aim" [of preventing injury to the public health.].[11]

---

[8]   *Id.* FDCA § 501(a)(1), (a)(2), (b), 21 U.S.C. § 351 (a)(1), (a)(2),(b).

[9]   *See, e.g.,* United States v. 6 Devices, "Electreat Mechanical Heart," 38 F. Supp. 236, 238 (W.D. Mo. 1941) (the court stated that for individuals who used the device and suffered "from any disorder or ailment, use of the device" might and probably would be injurious).

[10] 94 F.2d 641 (2d Cir. 1938).

[11] *Id.* at 642.

During the 1960s, at the FDA's urging, the courts began expanding the 1938 Act's definition of "drug" to include a number of items that appeared to be devices, thereby bringing these products within the scope of the FDA's premarketing clearance authority. Again, the Second Circuit Court of Appeals took the lead. In *AMP, Inc. v. Gardner*,[12] the court held that a suture used to stitch blood vessels together during surgery was a "drug." In the court's view, the term "devices," as used in the 1938 Act, included relatively simple mechanical products, but the suture presented some of the same dangers as pharmaceutical products. Therefore, it was subjected to the regulatory requirements for drugs.

In the following year, 1969, in *United States v. An Article of Drug... Bacto-Unidisk*,[13] the Supreme Court addressed the question of whether a cardboard disc impregnated with various antibiotics and used to determine a patient's antibiotic sensitivity should be regulated as a device or a drug. In view of the legislative history of the 1938 Act, the Court believed it should "read the classification 'drug' broadly, and...confine the device exception as nearly as is possible to the types of items Congress suggested in the debates, such as electric belts [and] quack diagnostic scales...."[14] Moreover, the Court decided that the "device" definition was created primarily to avoid the "semantic incongruity of classifying as drugs 1) certain quack contraptions and 2) basic aids used in the routine operation of a hospital-items characterized more by their purely mechanical nature than by the fact that they are composed of complex chemical compounds or biological substances."[15]

Despite these favorable judicial rulings, the FDA was forced to resort to "after-the-fact" device regulation in the case of many devices that could not, even by broad court rulings, be brought within the definition of a drug. For example, it took eleven years to obtain full injunctive relief against the manufacturer of a heating device alleged to be ineffective as a cure for several diseases.[16] Court procedures provided many opportunities for defendants to engage in time consuming tactics. Moreover, the judicial decisions that expanded the definition of the term "drug" to include certain medical devices created as many questions as they resolved. The new authority could be exercised only on a device-by-device basis. Furthermore, manufacturers could always contend in court that particular articles classified by the FDA as drugs were devices under the statute. Litigation to remove fraudulent or harmful devices from the marketplace was costly and time consuming. In addition, the

---

[12]   389 F.2d 825 (2d. Cir. 1968).

[13]   United States v. An Article of Drug . . . Bacto-Unidisk, 394 U.S. 784 (1969).

[14]   *Id.* at 799-800 (footnote omitted).

[15]   *Id.* at 800. One can contrast a 1976 holding that a pregnancy detection kit is not a drug. A New Jersey district court justified this finding in United States v. An Article of Drug-OVA II, 414 F. Supp. 660 (D.N.J. 1975), *aff'd mem.*, 535 F.2d 1248 (3d Cir. 1976), on the ground that the test kit did not meet the "drug" definition of the Act. The kit was not listed in a compendium and the court did not regard it as being used for diagnosis of a disease, because pregnancy is not a disease. The court also found that the kit, which used an *in vitro* reagent, did not affect the structure or any function of the body. Thus, the court held that it was neither a drug nor a device. This anomalous result was remedied by the definition of device adopted in 1976, which included products intended to diagnose not just disease but also "conditions" such as pregnancy.

[16]   United States v. An Article of Device . . . Diapulse, 650 F.2d 908 (7th Cir. 1981); United States v. An Article of Device . . . Diapulse, No. 73 C 157-75 C 343 (N.D. Ill. Dec. 3, 1981); United States v. Diapulse Corp., 514 F.2d 1097 (2d Cir. 1975), *cert. denied*, 423 U.S. 838 (1975); Diapulse Corp. v. FDA, 500 F.2d 75 (2d Cir. 1974); United States v. Diapulse Corp., 365 F. Supp. 935 (E.D.N.Y. 1973), *aff'd mem.*, 485 F.2d 677 (2d Cir. 1973), *cert. denied*, 416 U.S. 938 (1974); United States v. Diapulse Corp., 457 F.2d 25 (2d Cir. 1972); United States v. Diapulse Mfg. Corp., 262 F. Supp. 728 (D. Conn. 1967), *aff'd*, 389 F.2d 612 (2d Cir. 1968), *cert. denied*, 392 U.S. 907 (1968); United States v. Diapulse Mfg. Corp., 269 F. Supp. 162 (D. Conn. 1967).

agency was unable to obtain increased funding to exert the full measure of its new author-ity, because reliance on expansive judicial interpretation of the "drug" definition left the scope of the FDA's authority undefined. Consumer representatives grew increasingly alarmed at the proliferation of new and sophisticated, but largely unregulated, medical devices. At the same time, the FDA saw the need for increased budgets, and industry sought consistency in government regulations. All the major interests turned to Congress for a solution.

■ Recognition of the Need for Greater Regulation

Interest in medical device legislation had, in fact, arisen before *AMP* and *Bacto-Unidisk*. Both the Johnson Administration[17] and the Nixon Administration[18] had sent device regu-lation bills to Congress, but no legislation had been enacted. In 1969, after *AMP* and *Bacto-Unidisk*, Secretary of Health, Education, and Welfare (HEW) Robert Finch appointed a medical device study group composed of HEW experts in medicine and tech-nology, and chaired by Theodore Cooper, M.D., then the Assistant Secretary for Health and Science Affairs. This group, later known as the Cooper Committee, was charged with developing a framework for medical device legislation.[19] The group collected data on device injuries and deaths, interviewed a variety of interested parties, and published a report in September 1970.[20]

Among the Committee's most significant conclusions were the following:

- The public deserves greater protection from unsafe and ineffective medical devices.

- Excessive government regulation could stifle research and development in biomedical technology and impede the introduction of new products.

- Nongovernmental peer review groups are essential to effective device regulation.

- The degree of regulation should be consistent with the risks posed by different types of devices.

Legislation reflecting these conclusions was eventually enacted in 1976.[21]

---

[17] The Medical Devices Safety Act of 1967 was introduced in the 90th Congress. *See* H.R. 10,726, 90th Cong., 1st Sess. (1967). Another Johnson Administration proposal was transmitted to Congress but never introduced. *See* Drug Information and Consumer Protection Amendment of 1969, Title 4, Medical Device Safety Act.

[18] Two separate bills were introduced under the Nixon Administration, each titled "Medical Device Safety Act." *See* H.R. 12,316, 92d Cong., 2d Sess. (1972) and H.R. 6073, 93d Cong., 1st Sess. (1973). S. 1446, 93d Cong., 1st Sess. (1973).

[19] The other members of the Comm. were: Charles Edwards, FDA Comm.; William Goodrich, FDA Chief Counsel; Seymour Kres Kober, M.D., D.D.S., Dir.r, Nat'l Inst. of Dental Research; S. Burroughs Hider, Deputy Dir., Nat'l Lab. of Med.; Robert Wringler, Ph.D., Deputy Dir., Nat'l Heart and Lung Inst.; Bruce Waxman, M.D., Dir., Health Care & Tech. Div., Health Services Mental Health Admin.; Arthur Wolf, Deputy Assistant Admin., Research and Dev., Consumer Protection and Envtl. Health Service; Constance Foshay, Office of Program Planning and Evalua-tion, Nat'l Heart & Lung Inst.; Mark Novitch, M.D., Special Assistant for Pharmaceutical Affairs, Office of Assis-tant Secretary for Health and Scientific Affairs.

[20] HEW STUDY GROUP ON MEDICAL DEVICES, MEDICAL DEVICES: A LEGISLATIVE PLAN (1970).

[21] *See* Pub. L. No. 94-295, 90 Stat. 540 (1976); *Medical Devices: Hearings on H.R. 6073, H.R. 9984 and H.R. 10061 Before the Subcomm. on Pub. Health & Environment of the House Comm. on Interstate and Foreign Commerce*, 93d Cong., 1st Sess. (1974).

Legislative Action to Regulate Medical Devices

■ The 1976 Medical Device Amendments

The Medical Device Amendments of 1976 is a complex law, negotiated primarily by lawyers for lawyers. The degree of detail in the Amendments is perhaps not surprising when one remembers the deterioration in the relationship between the executive and legislative branches that characterized the early 1970s and the resulting desire on the part of Congress to draw up specific guidelines for executive branch intervention. This inclination suited device manufacturers, because it favored use of extensive procedural safeguards before the FDA could exercise much of its authority.

Structure of the 1976 Amendments

In outline, the structure of the Amendments seems straightforward.[22] Devices available on the market on May 28, 1976, the day the law was passed (pre-amendments devices and devices similar to them, hereinafter "pre-amendments devices") were distinguished from devices introduced into commerce after that date. Pre-amendments devices were permitted to remain on the market, pending final classification or other action by the FDA, without any FDA review. The FDA was ordered to assign devices to one of three classes based on recommendations from advisory panels consisting of outside experts. Any device introduced after the enactment date was required to undergo one of several types of FDA review, depending primarily on the classification of the device.

For postamendments devices, the FDA review process is determined by whether the device is 1) a "new" device or 2) one that is substantially equivalent to a legally marketed class I or class II device, or to a class III device for which the FDA has not called for PMA's. (See *infra* note 214 and accompaning text.). "New" devices are automatically classified in class III, while substantially equivalent devices are classified into the same class as the device to which they are substantially equivalent (class I, II, or III). While "new" class III devices require FDA premarket approval before being introduced for sale in the United States, postamendments devices that are found substantially equivalent to a pre-amendments class III device can be marketed via a premarket notification (510(k)) until such time as the FDA, by regulation, calls for approval of a PMA for the pre-amendments class III device.

Congress also provided for a third group of devices, in addition to pre-amendments and postamendments devices; that are called "transitional devices" because they were regulated as drugs prior to enactment of the Medical Device Amendments. Transitional devices were automatically placed into class III, and were immediately subject to the FDA's PMA requirements. Examples of transitional devices include bone cements, contact lenses, absorbable sutures, and *in vitro* diagnostic tests for carcinoembryonic antigen.

---

[22]   The following textual explanation is merely an overview. Other sources summarizing the Amendments and discussing the legislative history in greater detail are available. *See, e.g.,* H.R. REP. No. 853, 94th Cong., 2d Sess. (1976) [hereinafter HOUSE REPORT]. *See also* THE FOOD & DRUG LAW INSTITUTE, AN ANALYTICAL LEGISLATIVE HISTORY OF THE MEDICAL DEVICE AMENDMENTS OF 1976 (1976); Health Indus. Mfrs. Ass'n (HIMA), Pharmaceutical Mfrs. Ass'n (PMA), Conference on The Medical Device Amendments of 1976, HIMA-PMA Report (1976).

Pre-amendments devices were assigned to one of the three classes based on the level of risk they presented, resulting in differing levels of regulatory control. If the safety and effectiveness of a device could reasonably be assured by what are known as "general controls" (described *infra*.), the Amendments provided that the device was to be assigned to class I.[23] If general controls were not considered adequate but would be adequate if combined with a performance standard, and if sufficient information existed about the device to guide the drafting of a requirement that the device meet a performance standard, the device was to be placed in class II. The FDA was to establish performance standards for devices in class II by defining specific requirements that a product must meet before and during marketing. If the combination of general controls and performance standards was inadequate to ensure safety and effectiveness, the device was assigned to class III, like all new devices developed after enactment, and thus subject to the more rigorous premarket approval requirements.

General controls are applicable to all devices, regardless of their class. The general controls for medical devices include requirements for facility registration and product listing with the FDA, premarket notification (unless specifically exempt), the maintenance of records and the filing of reports with respect to device marketing experience, adherence to good manufacturing practices (GMPs)—now called Quality System Regulation (QSReg) requirements,—and any distribution and use limitations the FDA may impose. In addition, the general controls provide the FDA with the authority to ban devices that present substantial deception or significant risks, and/or to detain devices that are alleged to violate the Amendments, pending legal action. Finally, the controls permit the FDA to require manufacturers to notify purchasers and users of devices that present unreasonable risks, and to impose corrective action in certain situations. These safeguards were intended to complement the adulteration and misbranding and general enforcement provisions of the 1938 Act.

After completing the final classification of pre-amendments devices, the FDA was authorized to set performance standards for class II devices and to require PMAs for class III products. To date, the FDA has been successful at finalizing only one performance standard.

Pre-amendments class III devices are allowed to remain on the market (without obtaining marketing clearance or approval) until the later of a) thirty months following final classification or b) ninety days following promulgation of a regulation specifically requiring a PMA for that type of device. Postamendments devices that are found to be "substantially equivalent" to pre-amendments class III devices may be marketed under a cleared 510(k) notice until the FDA requires PMAs for that category of device, at which time all pre-amendments and postamendments devices must be approved through the PMA process. Postamendments class III devices that are not substantially equivalent to a pre-amendments device must also obtain PMA approval prior to marketing. Congress provided a mechanism for changing the classification of a device if new information emerged regarding its safety and effectiveness. Reclassification of devices may be initiated by either the

---

[23]   A device may also be placed in class I when there is insufficient information to determine whether general controls are adequate to ensure its safety and effectiveness; but these devices are not to be used in life-supporting or life-threatening situations and must not pose unreasonable risks of illness or injury. FDCA § 513, 21 U.S.C. § 360(c).

agency or a manufacturer. As noted later, the SMDA included several provisions designed to change how the FDA treats class III pre-amendments devices.

■ Key Features of the 1976 Amendments

The first key element of the 1976 Amendments is a redefinition of the term "medical device."[24] This change was implemented in an attempt to make the term "medical device" exclusive of the term "drug," thus resolving the longstanding confusion about whether certain products should be classified and regulated as drugs or a devices. In general, products that accomplish their principal objectives by chemical action or by being metabolized by the body are drugs. Other products intended for health use are devices. Because regulatory jurisdiction over specific products, and over drug/device combinations continued to arise, however, this issue was revisited in the 1990 Act, as discussed below. [25]

Second, the Amendments significantly increased the FDA's ability to move rapidly against violative products. For example, the Amendments gave the agency new authority to ban devices;[26] to detain products administratively;[27] and to revoke an approved PMA in advance of any formal administrative hearing. [28]

Third, as noted above, the Amendments established a tiered system of regulation as recommended by the Cooper Committee. Under the statute, the extent of regulation to be applied to a device corresponds to the FDA's perceived risks associated with the use of the device, and the extent to which various controls will reduce that risk. By calibrating the level of regulation to the level of risk, Congress intended to make it possible for manufacturers of low risk products to remain in business without being subject to the same kinds of regulatory requirements imposed on drug manufacturers.

Fourth, the 1976 Amendments established the level of proof required to support a claim that a device is effective, which is somewhat less stringent than the requirements to substantiate drug efficacy. Two major types of evidence may be used to demonstrate safety and effectiveness: 1) the results of well controlled investigations,[29] and 2) other "valid scientific evidence... sufficient to determine the effectiveness of a device...."[30]

In addition to these four major changes, the 1976 Amendments affected a number of other important changes, including providing for the participation of outside experts at many points in the regulatory process;[31] establishing a presumption that violative medical devices have been shipped in interstate commerce, which is a threshold requirement for FDA jurisdiction;[32] limiting the agency's use of trade secrets submitted by a manufacturer to demonstrate safety and effectiveness to an evaluation of the manufacturer's own sub-

---

[24] *Id.* § 201(h), as amended 21 U.S.C. § 321(h).

[25] For a discussion of the issues surrounding the definition, *see infra* text accompanying notes 48-58.

[26] FDCA § 516(f), 21 U.S.C. § 360(f).

[27] *Id.* § 304(g), 21 U.S.C § 334(g).

[28] *Id.* § 515(e), 21 U.S.C. § 360(e).

[29] *Id.* § 513(a)(3)(A), 21 U.S.C. § 360c(a)(3)(A).

[30] *Id.* § 513(a)(3)(B), 21 U.S.C. § 360c(a)(3)(B).

[31] *See, e.g., id.* §§ 514, 515, 520(f)(3), 21 U.S.C. §§ 360d, 360e, 360j(f)(1)(B).

[32] *Id.* § 304(a)(1), 21 U.S.C. § 334(a)(1).

missions;[33] and establishing the procedural steps and preliminary determinations required before the agency is permitted to implement many of its final decisions.[34] While the 1976 Amendments provided the FDA with significantly expanded authority, Congress determined that further expansion and clarification were required and thus, device legislation was revised further in 1990.

■ The Safe Medical Devices Act of 1990

Developments Leading to Enactment of the 1990 Safe Medical Devices Act

From 1976 to 1990, the FDA was engaged in implementing a number of the provisions of the 1976 Medical Device Amendments. One of the most important developments during this period was the FDA's expanding use of the 510(k) provision, which permitted clearance of many devices via the 510(k) notification process rather than the more onerous PMA process.[35] Some argued that the FDA's interpretation of this provision was overly expansive, permitting too many products to be marketed via the more expedient 510(k) process rather than the PMA process. Others felt the 510(k) provision was never intend to be used for product clearance because it merely provided for a simple notification of intent to sell.

The FDA's implementation of the 1976 Amendments also was criticized for a number of other reasons. First, the agency had failed to establish any performance standards for class II devices. Second, the agency had not initiated reclassification of any pre-amendments class III devices or transitional devices, as authorized by the Amendments, in part because the statute imposed stringent requirements for the safety and efficacy evidence necessary to support reclassification. Third, the agency was slow to call for PMAs for most pre-amendments class III devices. Some in Congress also felt that these shortcomings in the FDA's implementation of the FDCA were exacerbated by some manufacturers' continuing failure to cooperate in conducting and reporting device recalls, to report adverse events, and to refrain from marketing modified devices until FDA approval or clearance was obtained.

Key Features of the 1990 Safe Medical Devices Act

In 1990 Congress enacted new legislation to ensure the FDA would more timely and effectively implement the device regulatory scheme, and to expand the FDA's authority to ensure manufacturers' compliance with the new regulatory requirements. The more salient provisions of the Safe Medical Devices Act (SMDA) are described below. Although many of the statutory provisions enacted under the 1990 Act have now been implemented through formal regulations, the substantive requirements imposed under these regulations are described later in this chapter.

---

[33] *Id.* § 520(c), 21 U.S.C. § 360j(c).

[34] 5 U.S.C. § 554 (1994).

[35] The agency's policy regarding use of the 510(k) notification process was, at that time, outlined in a memorandum written by Kshitij Mohan, Ph.D., who was the Director of the Office of Device Evaluation at that time, which became known as the "Mohan memorandum." *See* 510(k) Memorandum: Premarket Notification Program (June 30, 1986).

New Reporting and Monitoring Requirements. One of the key features of the 1990 Act was the establishment of a number of additional reporting requirements regarding device failures and adverse events. The SMDA requires device "user facilities," such as hospitals, nursing homes, and outpatient treatment centers, to report adverse events that led to the death of or serious bodily injury to their patients.[36] Events resulting in death must be reported to both the FDA and the manufacturer within ten work days after the facility becomes aware of the incident. Events that cause serious illness or injury must be reported within ten working days only to the manufacturer, rather than the FDA, unless the identity of the manufacturer is unknown. Certain device distributors are also required to submit medical device reports.[37]

On November 26, 1991, the FDA published a tentative final rule implementing the user and distributor provisions of the SMDA (and revising the reporting requirements for manufacturers).[38] Distributor reporting requirements became effective on May 28, 1992 when the provisions relating to distributor reporting in the November 1991 tentative final rule became final by operation of law.[39] The distributor reporting regulations require distributors to submit reports to the FDA and the manufacturer within ten working days of becoming aware of a death, serious illness, or serious injury involving a distributed device, and to submit reports to manufacturers regarding certain malfunctions of distributed devices.[40]

In 1995, the regulations governing manufacturer and user facility reporting were overhauled.[41] In that notice, the FDA stated that "in a future rulemaking, the FDA will propose in the *Federal Register* to revoke the distributor regulation that went into effect by operation of law and replace it with provisions based on notice and comment."[42] As discussed in detail below, the overhauled manufacturer and user facility reporting regulations were met with much resistance by industry and the FDA ultimately backed off of some of the more onerous requirements.[43]

In addition to expanded medical device reporting, as discussed above, the SMDA also requires manufacturers of certain types of "critical" devices to track their devices.[44] The types of devices that must be tracked, unless otherwise exempt, include permanently implantable and life sustaining or life supporting devices that could cause serious adverse health consequences in the event of failure. Although neither the proposed rule nor the final rule were published within the statutorily prescribed time frames, the final rule was published only ten months behind schedule.[45] Although the final rule listed examples of specific types of devices that are subject to tracking, and the agency has expanded the list since the publication of the final rule, the final rule stated that ultimately it is each manu-

---

[36]   FDCA § 519(b), 21 U.S.C. § 360i(b).

[37]   *Id.* § 519(a), 21 U.S.C. § 360i(a).

[38]   56 Fed. Reg. 60,024 (1991).

[39]   58 Fed. Reg. 46,514 (1993).

[40]   *See* 21 C.F.R. pt. 804 (1996).

[41]   60 Fed. Reg. 63,578 (1995).

[42]   *Id.* at 63,579.

[43]   *See* 61 Fed. Reg. 38,346 (1996); 61 Fed. Reg. 39,868 (1996).

[44]   FDCA § 519(e), 21 U.S.C. § 360i(e).

[45]   57 Fed. Reg. 22,966 (1992).

facturer's obligation to determine whether its devices meet the criteria for being subject to tracking regardless of whether they are included on the list of tracked devices.[46]

Furthermore, the SMDA also required manufacturers, importers, and distributors to promptly report certain device "removals or corrections."[47] The FDA promulgated a regulation on removals and corrections on May 19, 1997 that has an implementation date of November 17, 1997.[48] The regulation requires manufacturers, importers and distributors to report promptly to ten FDA any corrections or removals of a device undertaken to reduce a risk to health posed by the device or to remedy a violation of the FDCA caused by the device which may present a risk to health.[49] Parties who initiate a correction or removal of a device that is not required to be reported to the FDA under the regulation must maintain records of such removals and corrections.[50] The regulations do not apply to market withdrawals, routine serving, or stock recoveries.[51]

The final reporting/monitoring requirement imposed by the SMDA is the postmarket surveillance provision. Postmarket surveillance may only be required for permanently implantable, life supporting, or life sustaining devices that may lead to serious adverse health consequences in the event of failure, and for any other device that may cause death or other serious adverse health consequences. For these types of devices, the SMDA authorizes the FDA to require postmarket surveillance pursuant to an FDA approved protocol.[52]

Substantial Equivalence. In addition to the new reporting and monitoring requirements, the SMDA also effected four key changes regarding the issue of "substantial equivalence."[53] First, the SMDA in essence codified the FDA's policy, as outlined in the Mohan Memorandum,[54] defining "substantial equivalence" for purposes of determining which devices could be cleared via the 510(k) process. Second, the SMDA provided that when a manufacturer relies on substantial equivalence to a pre-amendments class III device for which the FDA has not called for PMAs, the manufacturer must certify in its 510(k) notice that it has searched for all available information on the device's safety and effectiveness, and must include citations to any adverse safety and effectiveness data.[55] Third, the FDA must issue a formal order finding a device to be substantially equivalent before it can be marketed.[56] Fourth, manufacturers are not limited to demonstrating substantial equivalence to those devices that were legally on the market prior to the enactment of the 1976 Amendments; instead, they can claim substantial equivalence to any "legally marketed device" that was either on the market prior to the 1976 Amendments or has been demonstrated to be substantially equivalent to such a device.[57]

---

[46] 57 Fed. Reg. 22,966 (1992) (codified at 21 C.F.R. pt. 821) (1997).

[47] FDCA § 519(f), 21 U.S.C. § 360i(f).

[48] 62 Fed. Reg. 27,183 (1997).

[49] *Id.*

[50] *Id.* at 27,192.

[51] *Id.* at 27,191.

[52] FDCA § 522, 21 U.S.C. § 360l.

[53] FDCA § 513(i)(1)(A), 21 U.S.C. § 360c(i)(1)(A).

[54] *See supra* note 35.

[55] FDCA § 513(i)(1)(A), 21 U.S.C. § 360c(i)(1)(A).

[56] *Id.*

[57] *Id.* § 513(i)(1)(A)(ii)(II), 21 U.S.C. § 360c(i)(1)(A)(ii)(II).

Enforcement Authority. The SMDA also provided the FDA with a number of new enforcement tools. In addition to the authority provided under the 1976 Amendments, the SMDA enabled the FDA to seek civil penalties against individuals and companies for certain violations of the FDCA, up to a limit of $15,000 per violation or an aggregate limit of $1,000,000.[58] In the seven years following enactment of the SMDA, the FDA has sought to impose civil penalties on only four occasions and came under fire from Congress when it did so. Representative Joe Barton (R-TX) wrote a pointed letter to the FDA questioning the circumstances in two cases where the agency sought civil penalties. It also criticized the agency for not having formal procedures in place for pursuing civil penalties before the civil penalty actions were initiated. In 1995, the FDA finalized procedures for providing notice and an opportunity for a hearing to those against whom the agency is pursuing civil money penalties.[59]

The SMDA also authorized the agency to order a recall of devices if the FDA determines that there is a reasonable probability that a device will cause death or other serious adverse health consequences.[60] In order to exercise this powerful new enforcement tool, the agency must first issue an order under which a company must stop shipment of the device and notify users and medical professionals of the order. After affording a prompt informal hearing on the order, if the agency determines that that a recall is warranted, the agency may proceed to recall the device, provided that recalls from users do not present greater risks than not recalling the device. In addition, the agency was also given authority to temporarily suspend PMAs if the agency determines that continued distribution would cause death or other serious adverse health consequences.[61]

Provisions to Streamline Device Reclassification. To address Congressional complaints regarding the FDA's delay in implementing certain provisions of the 1976 Amendments, the SMDA imposed deadlines on the agency for the completion of certain tasks, and reduced the obstacles to completion of other tasks. The SMDA required that by December 1, 1995, the FDA must downclassify to class I or class II any pre-amendments class III device for which the FDA had not published a regulation requiring the submission of a PMA. The SMDA also mandated that the FDA publish an order to require manufacturers of all pre-amendments class III devices for which PMAs have not yet been required, to submit any adverse information on their devices' safety and effectiveness.[62] However, as discussed later in this chapter, the FDA failed to downclassify or retain in class III within the statutory prescribed time frames most of the pre-amendments class III devices and, to date, has retained in class III or downclassified less than half of all the pre-amendments class III devices.

Prior to the enactment of the SMDA, Congress noted that excessive agency resources were expended to handle PMA applications for daily wear contact lenses. As a result, it passed legislation specifically aimed at ensuring the expeditious reclassification of these

---

[58]   FDCA § 303(g)(1)(A), 21 U.S.C. § 333(f)(1)(A).

[59]   60 Fed. Reg. 38,612 (1995).

[60]   FDCA § 518(e), 21 U.S.C. § 360h(e).

[61]   The final regulation implementing these provisions of the SMDA was issued in Nov., 1996. *See* 61 Fed. Reg. 59,004 (1996).

[62]   FDCA § 515(i), 21 U.S.C. § 360e(i).

class III devices.[63] The SMDA specifically required the FDA to downclassify daily wear soft or daily wear nonhydrophilic plastic contact lenses unless the agency determined that they meet the statutory criteria for class III devices.[64] The SMDA gave the FDA two years from the date of enactment to make the classification determination, but allowed the agency to extend this period one year.[65] Although the FDA availed itself of the one year extension, it failed to meet the statutory deadline for reclassification of the devices. In March 1994, four months after the statutory deadline for reclassifying contact lenses, the FDA published in the *Federal Register* a final rule downclassifying two types of contact lenses and suspended the review of all pending PMAs for the devices.[66]

Like the contact lens deadlines, the SMDA established a deadline for reclassification of transitional devices which are devices initially classified in class III because they had been previously regulated as drugs. By December 1, 1992, the agency was to issue a regulation for each transitional device that either reclassified it in class I or class II, or retained it in class III according to the criteria set forth in section 513(a) of the FDCA. As discussed later in this chapter, the FDA also failed to meet this deadline.

Expediting Establishment of Performance Standards. The SMDA also decreased the procedural complexity of promulgating performance standards. The FDA can now issue a performance standard via the ordinary notice and comment rulemaking process.[67] To provide the agency with added flexibility, the SMDA also permits the FDA to use other types of "special controls" in addition to formal performance standards, including postmarket surveillance, guidance documents, and other mechanisms the agency deems necessary.[68] To date, however, the agency has not taken advantage of the performance standards legislation and has only sparingly implemented special controls.

Combination Products. The SMDA also addressed ambiguities involving the drug/device definition and jurisdiction over combination products, by requiring the agency to designate areas of primary jurisdiction.[69] Subsequently, the agency has published intercenter agreements outlining each center's jurisdiction over specific categories of combination products.[70] The agency has also issued a regulation outlining a procedure for a manufacturer to request designation, in advance of any product submission, to identify which center will have jurisdiction over its product.[71]

Good Manufacturing Practices. Tucked away in a section of the SMDA entitled "Miscellaneous," Congress passed a provision relating to GMPs that arguably is one of the most important provisions of the law. In a one sentence provision, Congress granted the FDA the authority to regulate devices in the design phase. The SMDA permitted the FDA

---

[63] *Id.* § 520(l)(5), 21 U.S.C. § 360j(l)(5).

[64] *Id.*

[65] *Id.*

[66] 59 Fed. Reg. 10,283 (1994).

[67] FDCA § 514(b)(1)(A), 21 U.S.C. § 360d(b)(1)(A).

[68] FDCA § 513(a)(1)(B), 21 U.S.C. § 360c(a)(1)(B).

[69] FDCA § 503(g)(1), 21 U.S.C. § 353(g)(1).

[70] *See, e.g.,* Intercenter Agreement Between the Center for Drug Eval. and Research and the Ctr. for Devices and Radiological Health (1991).

[71] 21 C.F.R. § 3.7.

to establish regulations governing the "preproduction design phase" of device development and production.[72] Although the impact of this provision may not have been fully appreciated at the time it was enacted, it has a far reaching effect. As discussed more fully later in this chapter, the design control regulations that the FDA has implemented impose significant and burdensome requirements on most device manufacturers.

Other Provisions. In addition, the SMDA effected a number of other changes, including establishment of an Office of International Relations within the FDA to facilitate international regulatory harmonization;[73] creation of a Humanitarian Device Exemption (HDE) to promote development of devices that were intended for use in small patient populations;[74] and authorization of limited use of data in a PMA by other manufacturers one year after FDA approves the fourth device of a kind.[75]

■ The 1992 Medical Device Amendments

On June 16, 1992, Congress again enacted new medical device legislation.[76] While the 1992 amendments were not nearly as comprehensive as preceding legislation, several important changes were effected. Among other things, the 1992 Amendments made several changes to the manufacturer and user facility reporting requirements of the SMDA. The 1992 Amendments expanded the category of reportable events. While the SMDA required user facilities to report "information that reasonably suggests that there is a probability that a device has caused or contributed to" a reportable event, the 1992 Amendments eliminated the term "probability," requiring reporting if the facility received or became aware of "information that reasonably suggests that a device has or may have caused or contributed to" a reportable event.[77] This change was intended to make the user reporting requirements more consistent with the reporting requirements already imposed on manufacturers. The 1992 amendments altered the definitions of "serious illness" and "serious injury," to eliminate the requirement for reporting device related "temporary" impairments of a body function and "temporary" damage to a body structure.[78]

In addition, the 1992 Amendments imposed a new deadline, November 28, 1992, on the FDA for issuing a final device tracking regulation.[79] The 1992 Amendments also made it a prohibited act for a manufacturer to fail to submit a protocol for postmarket surveillance if required to do so by the FDA. Failure to submit the protocol would thus render the device misbranded.[80] Finally, the 1992 Amendments altered the "repair, replace, or refund" provision to permit the FDA to order any of these remedies if the device does not meet "state of

---

[72] FDCA § 520(f)(1)(A), 21 U.S.C. § 352 (f)(1)A). Although this provision of the SMDA expressly granted the FDA authority to regulate the preproduction design phase of device development, the FDA had argued that the agency had this authority even before passage of this SMDA provision.

[73] H.R. 3095, 101st Cong. § 15 (1990).

[74] FDCA § 520(m), 21 U.S.C. § 360j(m). 61 Fed. Reg. 33,232 (1996)

[75] FDCA § 520(h)(4)(A), 21 U.S.C. § 360j(h)(4)(A).

[76] Medical Device Amendments of 1992, Pub. L. No. 102-300, 106 Stat. 238 (1992) (codified at 21 U.S.C. §§ 301 *passim* and 42 U.S.C. § 262).

[77] Medical Device Amendments of 1992, § 5(a), 106 Stat. at 239.

[78] *Id.*

[79] *Id.* § 2(a), 106 Stat. at 238.

[80] *Id.* § 3(b), 106 Stat. at 239.

the art" with respect to either its design or its manufacture.[81] Previously, the FDA could only order these remedies if both the design and manufacture of the device were deficient.

Given the large body of legislation resulting from the 1976, 1990, and 1992 acts, it is not surprising that the FDA has yet to fully implement Congress's regulatory scheme. Despite these attempts to comprehensively define regulatory authority over medical devices, a number of provisions remain ambiguous, and may require further legislative clarification. The following section outlines the current system of regulations that has been implemented by the FDA, highlighting areas that remain incomplete or unresolved.

Post-1976 Regulatory and Judicial Developments

■ Is it a Device?

As a result of the SMDA, the FDCA now defines the term "device" as "an instrument, apparatus, implement, machine, contrivance, implant, *in vitro* reagent, or other similar or related article, including any component, part, or accessory, which is—1) recognized in the official *National Formulary*, or the *United States Pharmacopoeia*, or any supplement to them, 2) intended for use in the diagnosis of disease or other conditions, or in the cure, mitigation, treatment, or prevention of disease, in man or other animals, or 3) intended to affect the structure or any function of the body of man or other animals, and which does not achieve its primary intended purposes through chemical action within or on the body of man or other animals and which is not dependent upon being metabolized for the achievement of its primary intended purposes."[82] The House Report accompanying the version of the Amendments that was the basis for the law stated, somewhat optimistically, that "the proposed new definition of 'device' removes the gray area that exists under present definitions of 'drug' and 'device.'"[83] Thus far, the definition of "device"[84] has been liberally interpreted by the courts, even covering tape recordings used for hypnosis therapy for treatment of disease.[85] In other instances, however, the interpretation of the definition of "device" has been less clear.

Thus, several major definitional questions remain. Among them is whether particular products are drugs (and, if so, whether they are also biologics), devices, cosmetics, some combination thereof, or wholly outside the jurisdiction of the Act—and, regardless of the status of a particular product, which center in the FDA will regulate it. Similarly, in cases of doubt or controversy, what procedures should be employed by the FDA to resolve these questions also is a subject of great interest.

---

[81]　Medical Device Amendments of 1992, § 4, 106 Stat. at 239.

[82]　21 U.S.C. § 321(h). The definition was modified slightly by the Safe Medical Devices Act of 1990.

[83]　House Report, supra note 22, at 14.

[84]　FDCA § 201(h), 21 U.S.C. § 321(h).

[85]　United States v. Undetermined Quantities... Self-Hypnosis Tape Recordings, Med. Devices Rep. (CCH) ¶ 15,055 (W.D. MI. Nov. 22, 1982).

The drafters of the 1976 Amendments recognized it was important to decide whether particular products are "drugs" or "devices," and determined that, if a product's primary mode of action was mechanical, it should be treated as a device. Thus, if a health related product achieves its primary purpose by means not involving chemical reactions or metabolism, it is a device. [86] According to the FDA, however, the fact that a product is not metabolized and does not achieve its principal purpose by chemical action does not automatically make it a device.

This policy decision is exemplified by a letter the FDA wrote to the manufacturer of a product called Quick-Prep,[87] in response to its request for an the FDA opinion whether a saline solution was a drug or a device. The FDA ruled that it was a drug although it did not accomplish any of its primary purposes either by being metabolized or by chemical action on or within the body. This position is curious in light of the definition of "device." Similarly, products such as laxatives that work by mechanical action still may be considered drugs because they are "drug-like" substances. The FDA's countenance of this position increases the uncertainty about whether some products are drugs or devices.

In many cases, the various centers at the FDA resolve conflicts over regulation of specific products via a memorandum of understanding that spells out the jurisdictional reach of each Center. For example, an intercenter agreement between the Center for Devices and Radiological Health (CDRH) and the Center for Drug Evaluation and Research (CDER), which became effective on October 31, 1991, identifies which types of drug/device combination products are subject to regulation as devices and which are regulated as drugs.[88] The document is an attempt by the FDA to provide guidance to industry on the appropriate center to contact for drug/device combination products and to more clearly define the responsibilities of each center in reviewing submissions for combination products. To illustrate, the agreement states that CDRH has market approval authority for devices incorporating a drug component with the combination product having the primary intended purpose of fulfilling a device function. Examples include wound dressings with antimicrobial agents and dental devices with fluoride. Intercenter consultation for such combination product submissions is required if a drug or the chemical form of the drug has not been legally marketed in the United States as a human drug for the intended effect.

A number of questions remain, however, about the status of devices and drugs when used in combination. In general, the drug or device determination often rests on whether the primary purpose of these products is performed by the "drug or by the device" segment of the combination. Additionally, the greater the concern about the risks presented by a "drug-type" substance, the more likely it is that the agency will consider the combination a drug. The FDA's policies in this area are based upon the fact that drugs usually are regulated more stringently than devices.

---

[86] FDCA § 201(g),(h), 21 U.S.C. § 321(g),(h).

[87] Letter from William Randolph, Acting Associate Comm'r for Regulatory Affairs, FDA, to Lester J. Lifton, M.D.

[88] *See* Intercenter Agreement Between The Center for Drug Evaluation and Research and The Center for Devices and Radiological Health, (1991). Intercenter agreements also exist between CDRH and the Center for Biologics Evaluation and Research (CBER) and between CDER and CBER.

The FDA's product jurisdiction regulations[89] provide manufacturers with a mechanism for obtaining an official agency determination as to how a product will be primarily regulated. In general, manufacturers can prepare a request for designation (RFD) for submission to the FDA's ombudsman who is responsible for making product jurisdiction determinations. Under the regulations, RFDs are appropriate whenever the product jurisdiction is not covered by an intercenter agreement or when the product jurisdiction is in dispute. It is not uncommon for CDER and CDRH to have differing views over which center has primary jurisdiction over a product.

■ Classification and Reclassification

Device classification proceedings had begun even before passage of the Medical Device Amendments. With the sweeping new authorities contained in the 1976 Amendments, some observers expected that the FDA would promptly complete its classifications program. These expectations were not realized. It was not until 1988 that classification was substantially completed.

Although the FDCA provides five statutory bases for the reclassification of a device from class III to class II or class I, reclassification has not been a widely used mechanism. However, the FDA's reclassification efforts were more aggressive in the decade of the 1990s. For example, absorbable sutures were downclassified to class II in 1991,[90] magnetic resonance imaging devices were downclassified to class II in 1989,[91] and certain types of hip prostheses were downclassified to class II in 1989.[92] More recently, the FDA has published a proposed rule to downclassify to class II pedicle screw fixation systems for certain lumbar spine indications[93] and formally downclassified acupuncture needles to class II despite an historic institutional bias against acupuncture.[94] Additionally, in February of 1996 the FDA downclassified 111 class II devices to class I and at the same time exempted them from the 510(k) premarket notification requirements discussed below.[95]

It is likely that the FDA will continue its efforts to downclassify a number of class II devices to class I and to exempt many of them from 510(k) notification requirements. In June 1997, the FDA issued a policy document entitled *A New 510(k) Paradigm, Alternate Approaches to Demonstrating Substantial Equivalence in Premarket Notifications* in which the agency stated that CDRH was 1) evaluating 221 class I devices to determine which, if any, should be proposed for exemption from the 510(k) notification requirements and 2) examining class II devices to determine if any of those devices could be reclassified to class I and exempted from 510(k) notifications.[96] The draft guidance also states that pre-amendments class III devices for which general or special controls are sufficient to establish safety and effectiveness will be downclassified to either class I (and 510(k)

---

[89] 21 C.F.R. pt. 3.

[90] 56 Fed. Reg. 47,150 (1991).

[91] 54 Fed. Reg. 5077 (1989).

[92] 54 Fed. Reg. 48,238 (1989).

[93] 60 Fed. Reg. 51,946 (1995).

[94] 61 Fed. Reg. 64,616 (1996).

[95] 61 Fed. Reg. 1117 (1996).

[96] FOOD & DRUG ADMIN., A NEW 510(K) PARADIGM: ALTERNATE APPROACHES TO DEMONSTRATING SUBSTANTIAL EQUIVALENCE IN PREMARKET NOTIFICATIONS 3 (1997).

exempt) or class II status.[97] According to the FDA, the anticipated result of these down-classification efforts is to eventually reserve the 510(k) notification process to those devices that are in class II.[98] However, it remains unclear whether and to what extent the agency will be able to effect the changes discussed in the policy document.

■ Good Manufacturing Practices

The agency had begun drafting a device GMP regulation—probably the single most important device regulation applicable to devices of all classes—before the Amendments were enacted. The original GMP regulation became final on July 21, 1978,[99] and effective as of December 18, 1978. A GMP Advisory Committee, mandated by the Amendments,[100] devoted a substantial portion of its deliberations to successive versions of the GMP regulation. The regulation specified general requirements covering virtually all aspects of manufacturing. It was intended to ensure that regulated devices are consistently made according to written specifications. Failure to comply with the GMPs specified in the regulation renders a device violative of the FDCA.

Nearly twenty years after the original GMPs were promulgated, on October 7, 1996, the FDA published a final rule[101] to revise the GMP regulations for the purposes of 1) replacing quality assurance program requirements with quality *system* requirements that include design, purchasing, and servicing controls; 2) clarifying record keeping requirements for device failure and complaint investigations; 3) clarifying requirements for qualifying, verifying, and validating processes and specification changes; and 4) clarifying requirements for evaluating quality data and correcting quality problems. In addition, the new regulation is intended to better harmonize the FDA's GMP requirements for devices with the specifications for quality systems contained in ISO 9001 and other applicable international standards. The effective date of the new regulation was June 1, 1997.

The principal differences between the GMP regulations codified in 1978 and the new QSReg promulgated in October of 1996 are the following: 1) the elimination of the distinction between critical and noncritical devices and components; 2) the inclusion of requirements for design controls, purchasing controls, and servicing; 3) the inclusion of the requirement that manufacturers have a quality system (with management responsibility) as opposed to only a quality program or department; and 4) clarification of the FDA's requirements for validation, verification and the use of statistical techniques. Although the subject of extensive debate, manufacturers of device components, and third party servicers, still are not covered by the new QSReg.

There have been few judicial decisions involving the current device GMPs. A notable exception is the *in vitro* diagnostics industry. In a June 1987 decision regarding GMP procedures, *United States v. BioClinical Systems, Inc.*,[102] a court denied the FDA's informal

---

[97] *Id.*

[98] *Id.*

[99] 43 Fed. Reg. 31,508 (1978); 21 C.F.R. § 820.

[100] FDCA § 520(f)(3), 21 U.S.C. § 360j(f)(3).

[101] 61 Fed. Reg. 52,602 (1996).

[102] 2 MED. DEVICES REP. (CCH) ¶ 15,090 (D. Md. June 19, 1987).

attempt to establish a GMP requirement that manufacturers of plated culture media meet a 0.1 percent sterility assurance level. The FDA had adopted this position in a draft guideline without notice and comment. The court ruled that the FDA could not unilaterally make such a determination; rather, the agency had to follow the public review process set forth by the Administrative Procedure Act (APA).[103] On March 9, 1988, the court denied the FDA's request for a permanent injunction,[104] which the FDA had based on the company's alleged failure to meet the draft guideline, for the same reason. However, the QSReg, like the GMP regulations, is written broadly and is subject to different interpretations by industry and the FDA. The agency expects manufacturers to follow common industry standards and practices, even if they are not specifically spelled out in the regulations.

■ The Section 510(k) Process

Section 510(k) of the FDCA requires the filing of a premarket notification (510(k)) by a manufacturer prior to 1) initial marketing of a device; 2) making a change or modification to a cleared device that "could significantly affect the safety or effectiveness" of the device; or 3) making a major change or modification to the intended use of a cleared device.[105] The agency's use of the premarket notification requirements in section 510(k) of the FDCA is an excellent example of an administrative agency's deriving unexpected utility from a modest statutory provision.

Section 510(k) appears to be merely a housekeeping provision requiring notification to the agency of a manufacturer's intent to market a product. It was inserted late in the legislative process, and the legislative history indicates that the provision was included to enable the FDA to ensure that new devices subject to premarket approval would obtain that approval before commercial marketing.[106] The import of section 510(k) was that class I and class II devices (and pre-amendments class III devices until FDA required PMAs for them) can be marketed after a determination by the FDA that the device is substantially equivalent to one or more predicate devices, and that postamendments "new" class III devices can be marketed only after the FDA approval of a PMA.

By regulation, the FDA has given section 510(k) "teeth," although the provision appears to have been intended to afford mere surveillance authority. Now it is used by the FDA as a substantial mechanism to permit access to the market for new devices that are claimed to be similar to a legally marketed class I device, class II device, or class III device for which premarket approval is not required. This interpretation has raised many questions about how premarket notification fits into the statutory scheme in general and, in particular, how it meshes with the premarket approval provisions. It also has aroused congressional interest on more than one occasion.

---

[103] Pub L. No 79-404, 60 stat. 237 (1946) (codified at 5 U.S.C. § 551 et seq.).

[104] 14 MED. DEVICES, DIAGNOSTICS & INSTRUMENTATION, No. 12, at I&W 11-12 (1988).

[105] 21 C.F.R. § 807.81.

[106] Section 510(k) first appeared in a bill introduced in the House in March 1975. The House report accompanying the final version of the provision states: "This provision will enable the Secretary to assure that 'new' devices are not marketed until they comply with premarket approval requirements or are reclassified into cl assI or II."HOUSE REPORT, *supra* note 22, at 37. No other discussions of this provision appear in the legislative history.

The regulations promulgated pursuant to section 510(k) require manufacturers to submit to the FDA a 510(k) notification at least 90 days prior to the applicant's intended introduction into the market of a device that requires premarket clearance. However, a device that requires 510(k) clearance may not be marketed until the applicant receives an "order" from the FDA that states that the new device is substantially equivalent to a legally marketed predicate device. The FDA's regulations require manufacturers to include in the notification the classification status of the device and information such as proposed labeling and information (including nonclinical and, in some instances, clinical data) that demonstrates that the new device is substantially equivalent to a legally marketed predicate device.

Premarket notifications that include clinical information in order to demonstrate substantial equivalence are often referred to as "hybrid 510(k)s."[107] Usually, clinical information is collected to substantiate the safety and effectiveness of a product, not to establish its equivalence to another product. Some opponents of this practice have suggested that if the FDA insists on clinical trials to establish the substantial equivalence of a "new" device to a predicate device, the FDA should simply designate the product as a "not substantially equivalent" device and require premarket approval. Most companies, of course, are satisfied with present the FDA policy, because it enables them to avoid the onerous PMA process.

Initially, the agency required proof of equivalence to an actual pre-amendments device. However, section 513(i) of the FDCA (which was enacted with the passage of the Safe Medical Devices Act of 1990) makes it clear that a postamendments class I or class II device may be found substantially equivalent to any "legally marketed" class I or class II device or class III device for which the FDA has not yet called for PMAs. The predicate device, therefore, need not be a pre-amendments device, but it cannot be a device that was removed from the market by the FDA or determined to be misbranded or adulterated by judicial order.

The FDA responds to a 510(k) notification in one of three ways. The FDA can 1) decide that a device is substantially equivalent to a legally marketed device that does not require premarket approval; 2) decide that it is not substantially equivalent; or 3) notify the applicant that additional information is required in order to determine whether or not the device is, in fact, substantially equivalent. In the FDA's view, a finding that a device is not substantially equivalent to the predicate device means that it is a new class III device, which requires FDA approval of a PMA before being marketed.

Although the FDA's response to applications under section 510(k) establishes, for all practical purposes, whether a particular device can be marketed without a PMA, the FDA does not "approve" a premarket notification in the same way that it approves a PMA. The FDA's response to section 510(k) notifications makes clear that its findings under this provision extend only to whether a device is substantially equivalent to a predicate device and not whether if it is safe and effective for its intended use(s).

---

[107] If information concerning similarity to a predicate device must be obtained through a clinical trial, the trial is subject to the requirements of the IDE regulation, 21 C.F.R. § 812.2.

One of the most difficult decisions for 510(k) holders is when to submit a new premarket notification for changes that the 510(k) holder intends to make to a legally marketed device. As stated above, the FDA's regulations require that a new 510(k) notification be cleared by the FDA before the 510(k) holder makes a change or modification to the device that "could significantly affect the safety or effectiveness of the device, e.g., a significant change or modification in design, material, chemical composition, energy source, or manufacturing process"; or makes a major change or modification in the intended use of the device.[108]

Although the 510(k) holder is responsible for making the initial determination as to whether a change or modification *could significantly* affect safety or effectiveness, the FDA may second guess the company's decisions. If the FDA disagrees with the company's decision not to file a new 510(k) notification for a device modification or change, the agency may make the company file a 510(k) notification retrospectively and discontinue marketing the device while the 510(k) is pending. The agency may also take enforcement action against the company. As a practical matter, however, if the company has made a good faith effort to document the reasons that it did not submit a new 510(k) for the device change, if the reasons appear genuine, and there are no demonstrated safety problems with the modified device, the FDA may allow the company to continue marketing the device while the new 510(k) notification is pending.

Industry expressed concern that decisions whether to submit new 510(k)s for device changes are highly subjective and there is little agency guidance to assist companies in making these determinations. In response, the FDA issued a policy regarding the criteria that should be used in deciding whether a device modification or change requires a new 510(k) submission.[109] Though not binding on either industry or the FDA, the guidance provides a useful framework for making decisions about whether device changes require premarket clearance.

As stated above, on June 13, 1997, the FDA published a proposal for "A New 510(k) Paradigm."[110] Under this proposed scheme, class I devices would be exempt from the 510(k) notification requirement and manufacturers of class II devices would have the option of submitting: 1) a traditional 510(k) notification, 2) a Special 510(k): Device Modification, or 3) an Abbreviated 510(k) in order to market the device. Under the proposed Special 510(k): Device Modification option, a manufacturer who is intending to modify its own legally marketed class II device would conduct the necessary verification and validation activities to demonstrate that the design outputs of the modified device meet the design input requirements. The manufacturer would also have the option of using a third party to assess conformance with design controls. In this case, the Special 510(k) application would include both a conformance statement from the third party as well as a declaration of conformity signed by the manufacturer. The FDA proposed that Special 510(k)s will be processed by the Office of Device Evaluation (ODE) within 30 days of receipt. Modifications that affect the intended use or alter the basic fundamental scientific technology of the

---

[108] *Id.* § 807.81(a)(3)(i).

[109] OFFICE OF DEVICE EVALUATION, 510(K) MEMORANDUM: DECIDING WHEN TO SUBMIT A 510(K) FOR A CHANGE TO AN EXISTING DEVICE (Jan. 10, 1997).

[110] See *supra* note 96.

device would not be eligible for this alternate type of submission, but may be eligible for the proposed new Abbreviated 510(k) route as described below.

Under the proposed Abbreviated 510(k) option, device manufacturers would be permitted to submit Abbreviated 510(k)s for class II devices when a special controls guidance document (SCGD) exists or when the FDA has recognized an individual special control such as a relevant standard. These Abbreviated 510(k)s would include summary information that describes how special controls have been used to address the risks associated with the device type and a declaration of conformity with any relevant recognized standard(s), if applicable. In an Abbreviated 510(k), a manufacturer would also have the option of using a third party to assess conformance with the recognized standard. The FDA stated in the draft policy document what the agency anticipated that this new 510(k) paradigm, or selected aspects of it, could be implemented as early as the Fall of 1997. As noted previously, it is unclear at this time the extent to which changes to the 510(k) clearance process will be effected.

■ Registration, Listing, and Inspection

United States manufacturers, repackagers, relabelers, certain types of specification developers and initiators, and distributors of medical devices or components in commercial distribution must register their establishment and submit device listing information.[111] The initial establishment registration information is submitted to the FDA on form FD-2891 and the annual registration update is submitted on form FD-2891(a).[112] The device listing information required by the FDA is submitted to the agency on form FD-2892[113] and any changes are updated in June and December, or at the applicant's discretion.[114] The FDA does not currently charge any fees for registration and listing.

The FDA recently published regulations requiring that foreign manufacturers who export devices into the United States designate a person as their U.S.-designated agent.[115] The designated agent would be responsible for 1) submitting establishment registration information, 2) submitting device listing information, 3) submitting medical device reporting (MDR) reports, 4) submitting annual certifications, 5) acting as the official correspondent, and 6) submitting premarket notifications on behalf of the foreign entity. However, the regulation generated a great deal of controversy in the medical device industry primarily because foreign manufacturers were unable to find parties willing to act as U.S.-designated agents given legal implications of making false certifications. As a result, the FDA stayed the requirement indefinitely.[116]

The FDA uses the establishment registration and device listing information to maintain a data base of companies that are subject to FDA inspection as well as the types of products manufactured or distributed by each firm. The FDA uses this information to schedule

---

[111] 21 C.F.R. § 807.20.

[112] *Id.* § 807.25.

[113] *Id.*

[114] *Id.* § 807.30(b).

[115] 60 Fed. Reg. 63,606 (1995) (codified at 21 C.F.R. § 807.40).

[116] 61 Fed. Reg. 38,346 (1996).

inspections and to target mass mailings to segments of the medical device industry, or to the industry as a whole. The FDA conducts periodic inspections of registered facilities. The frequency of inspection is based on a number of factors including the level of risk of the devices manufactured by the firm; the date of the company's last inspection; whether major GMP violations were observed during previous inspections; whether the firm conducted a recalls recently, and whether the FDA has received consumer or competitor trade complaints. The manufacturing facilities of devices that are the subject of pending premarket approval applications (and, in some cases, PMA supplements) are typically inspected before the FDA approves the submission.

■ Investigational Devices

The investigational device exemption (IDE) regulation[117] was long in formulation, especially in view of the statutory requirement that regulations be issued 120 days after enactment of the Amendments.[118] The IDE rule was not published as a final regulation until 1980. Once again, a tiered system of regulation was adopted, this time based on a distinction between devices that present significant risk and those that do not. [119]

The provisions of the amendments concerning investigational devices were shaped by prior experience with the investigational new drug provisions. In many respects, the investigational device requirements are closely patterned after the drug provisions.[120] One significant difference, however, appears in the introductory clause to the investigational device provision, which specifically defines its purpose as encouraging the discovery and development of useful devices and maintenance of optimum freedom for scientific investigators. The IDE provisions expressly allow the FDA to vary the procedures and conditions of investigational exemptions in accordance with the extent and duration of testing, the number of subjects involved, and the need to make changes in the device during the course of the investigation.[121] The IDE and investigational drug provisions each provide for informed consent to study participants.[122]

The IDE regulations apply to most clinical investigations involving new products or new uses for existing products. For the following clinical investigations of medical devices, however, manufacturers need not comply with the IDE requirements:[123]

> (1) legally marketed devices that are being investigated (i) in the case of pre-amendments devices, in accordance with the indications in the labeling in effect at that time; or (ii) in the case of postamendments devices, in accordance with the labeling included in the cleared 510(k) notice.

---

[117] 21 C.F.R. pt. 812.

[118] FDCA § 520(g)(2)(A), 21 U.S.C. § 360j (g)(2)(A). The 120-day period expired on Sept. 27, 1976, and a notice of proposed rulemaking was published on Aug. 20, 1976. A final rule was not issued, however, until Jan. 18, 1980.

[119] 21 C.F.R. pt. 812.

[120] *Compare* FDCA § 520(g), 21 U.S.C. § 360j *with id.* § 505(i), 21 U.S.C. § 355(i). Note that some of the same regulations apply to both. *E.g.*, 21 C.F.R. § 50.

[121] FDCA § 520(g), 21 U.S.C. § 360j.

[122] *Compare id.* § 520 (g)(3)(D), 21 U.S.C. § 360j(3)(D) *with id.* § 505(i), 21 U.S.C. § 355(i).

[123] 45 Fed. Reg. 3732, 3751 (1980); 21 C.F.R. § 812.2(c).

(2)   investigations of diagnostic devices under certain conditions;

(3)   consumer preference testing;

(4)   investigations of devices intended solely for veterinary use; and

(5)   custom devices.

Investigations involving devices that present a "significant risk" are subject to more stringent application, approval and recordkeeping requirements than investigations that pose a nonsignifcant risk to subjects.[124] For example, nonsignificant risk device investigations need only be approved by institutional review boards, whereas significant risk device investigations must be approved by the institutional review boards of the proposed study sites, as well as by the FDA, before the study may begin.[125] Both types of investigations require the informed consent of subjects and close monitoring by sponsors and institutional review boards.

The FDA has become increasingly concerned about the size of some clinical investigations, the absence of proper follow-up procedures, and the length of some studies. The concerns are threefold. First, there is a question in some cases of the ethical justification for putting many subjects at risk. Second, agency officials suspect that some sponsors may be commercializing devices during the investigational phase. Third, in the agency's view, it may be difficult for a sponsor planning a large study to ensure adequate follow-up. The FDA has limited the number of patients and/or devices that may be included in investigations, pressed companies for adequate follow-up, and, in rare cases, terminated investigations.

The agency has written numerous warnings letters to companies for illegally promoting devices for unapproved uses. The FDA has also taken actions against companies and clinical investigators for violations identified during bioresearch monitoring inspections.[126]

■ Premarket Approval

In spite of the attention devoted throughout the legislative process to class III products, a final regulation specifying PMA procedures did not become effective until November 19, 1986.[127] This regulation outlines the expected contents of an original PMA and any supplements to that submission. It also sets forth the criteria to be used by the FDA for evaluating a PMA. The regulation covers postamendments class III devices distributed on or after May 28, 1976, pre-amendments devices placed in class III for which PMAs have been called for by the FDA, and transitional devices—devices which were considered new drugs or antibiotic drugs prior to the 1976 Amendments and are now regulated as class III devices.

PMAs are required for the following types of devices:

---

[124] 21 C.F.R. pt. 812.3(m).

[125] *Compare id.* § 812.2 *with id.* § 812.62-.66.

[126] *See* Letter from the FDA to Ace Medical (Aug. 11, 1993); Letter from the FDA to Fukuda Denshi America Corporation (Mar. 28, 1996), and Letter from the FDA to Albert Einstein Medical Center (Nov. 30, 1995).

[127] 45 Fed. Reg. 81,769 (July 22, 1986).

(1) devices on the market at the time of the 1976 Amendments that were subsequently classified or reclassified into class III (and devices that were found to be substantially equivalent to these pre-amendments devices before being classified into class III);

(2) devices on the market at the time of the 1976 Amendments that were then considered "new drugs," and devices substantially equivalent to these devices; and

(3) all devices developed after the 1976 Amendments that are not substantially equivalent to devices in class I or class II.

The FDA may require PMAs for products in the first category of medical devices, i.e., those pre-amendments devices placed in class III after review by one of the FDA's outside advisory panels, only after the agency publishes a regulation that establishes a timetable for their submission. Under section 515(i) of the FDCA, by December 1, 1995 (or December 1, 1996 after the FDA requested a one year extension), the FDA was required to down-classify any pre-amendments class III device for which the FDA had not published a final regulation requiring the submission of a PMA.

The FDA has been slow to call for PMA applications for pre-amendments class III devices and, consequently, missed the December 1, 1995 and December 1, 1996 deadlines for most pre-amendments class III devices. The FDA did develop a strategy document that placed a number of pre-amendments class III devices into one of three groups depending on the extent of use of the device and the likelihood of downclassification. Different schedules were established for evaluating the classification of the devices according to their groupings. In total, the strategy document addressed 117 pre-amendments class III devices.[128]

In an attempt to meet the schedules set forth in the strategy document, the FDA published orders in two August 14, 1995 *Federal Register* notices[129] that required manufacturers of certain devices falling into the second and third groupings to submit safety and effectiveness information to the FDA. Group 2 devices are those that the FDA believes have a high potential for being reclassified into class II and group 3 devices are those that the FDA believes are in current commercial distribution but are not likely candidates for reclassification.[130] The deadlines for submission of safety and effectiveness information for group 2 devices was either August 14, 1996 or August 14, 1997, depending on the device.[131] For group 3 devices the deadlines for submitting safety and effectiveness information were August 14, 1996 or August 14, 1997.[132] However, the FDA has since extended until August 14, 1998 the deadline for submission of safety and effectiveness information for certain group 3 devices.[133]

---

[128] 59 Fed. Reg. 23,731 (1994).

[129] 60 Fed. Reg. 41,984 (1995); 60 Fed. Reg. 41,986 (1995).

[130] 59 Fed. Reg. 23,731 (1994).

[131] 60 Fed. Reg. 41,984 (1995); 60 Fed. Reg. 41,986 (1995).

[132] 60 Fed. Reg. 41,986 (1995).

[133] 62 Fed. Reg. 32,352 (1997).

Group 1 devices are those that the FDA perceived as having fallen into disuse, but that present significant issues of safety and effectiveness. The FDA published a proposed rule in September 1995 to require submission of PMAs for all group 1 devices,[134] and published a final rule requiring the submission of PMAs one year later.[135] The final rule required the submission of a PMA on or before December 26, 1996 for each of the group 1 devices.[136]

Although the statutory requirements governing PMAs for devices and NDAs for drugs are similar in some respects, some significant differences exist between the two types of submissions. For example, NDAs must be supported by "substantial evidence," which is defined by the FDCA as evidence obtained through adequate and well controlled clinical investigations conducted by experts.[137] When reviewing the effectiveness of a device, however, the FDA is permitted to consider other valid scientific evidence as well. The House Report explains that the FDA can make use of data developed under procedures that are not as rigorous as those for drugs.[138] The language in section 515 of the FDCA clearly allows the FDA to rely on less formal evidence to demonstrate safety and effectiveness than the agency has prescribed for new pharmaceuticals. Nonetheless, in many cases, the FDA requires studies on medical devices that are designed like new drug trials (e.g., prospective, randomized controls). This requirement is based in part on the results of the report of the Committee for Clinical Review (also known as the Temple Report) in 1992. The Committee accepted the proposition that "the fundamental principles underlying evaluation of any therapeutic intervention, whether it is a drug, device, diet, or surgical procedure, are the same.

The 1976 Amendments also afford a device manufacturer choices about the type of administrative review it may seek if its application is not approved. The manufacturer may obtain review by a second outside scientific advisory panel or by an administrative law judge at a formal administrative hearing.[139] In contrast, a drug applicant has, as a matter of statutory right, only an opportunity for an FDA administrative hearing.[140] Regulations applicable to both, however, provide that the agency in its discretion may permit an applicant to waive its right to an administrative hearing and obtain a hearing before a public board of inquiry, a public advisory committee, or the Commissioner.[141]

In some situations, before the FDA can initiate proceedings to revoke a PMA, the agency must obtain advice on scientific matters from the relevant standing advisory panel.[142] In all cases, the FDA must afford an applicant the opportunity for an informal hearing prior to revocation.[143] In this respect, the revocation procedures for NDAs could be viewed as

---

[134] 60 Fed. Reg. 46,718 (1995).

[135] 61 Fed. Reg. 50,704 (1996).

[136] *Id.*

[137] FDCA § 505(d), 21 U.S.C. § 355(d).

[138] *See* HOUSE REPORT, *supra* note 22, at 40, 64. FDA regulations also permit the waiver of certain aspects of the requirements of adequate and well-controlled studies of drugs under certain circumstances. 21 C.F.R. § 314.126.

[139] FDCA § 515(g)(1), (2), 21 U.S.C. § 360e(g)(1),(2).

[140] *Id.* § 505 (j)(y)(c), 21 U.S.C. § 355(j)(y)(c).

[141] 21 C.F.R. pts. 13, 14, 15.

[142] FDCA § 515(e), (g)(2), 21 U.S.C. § 360e(e), (g)(2).

[143] *Id.* § 515(e)(1), 21 U.S.C. § 360e(e)(1).

more protective of the manufacturer since the new drug applicant has an opportunity for a full administrative hearing, in most circumstances,[144] before the FDA can revoke approval of an application.

In one area, the statute governing premarket approvals clearly grants more authority to the agency than does the statute governing new drug approvals—by permitting the FDA to require as a condition of approval that a device be marketed as a restricted device.[145] Among other possibilities, the FDA may impose restrictions on distribution channels and on who can prescribe or use the device. The only restriction specifically permitted in connection with drug approvals is a requirement that the drug be a prescription drug.[146] To date, only hearing aids and nicotine delivery systems (cigaettes) officially have been designated restricted devices by regulation.

Finally, the statute provides for an alternative to the PMA process, the product development protocol (PDP), but only with the agency's permission. The PDP is an attempt to join the investigational device exemption (IDE) with the premarket approval process. It was suggested initially as a procedure appropriate for complex, low volume electronic devices, and it was considered potentially useful for relatively small manufacturers. Despite these expectations, the PDP procedure laid dormant for nearly twenty years. However, in April 1997, the FDA issued a proposal to revamp and revive the PDP process.

The proposed PDP process is somewhat elaborate due to the industry-agency interaction. To initiate the process, the applicant must submit a Summary Outline of the proposed PDP and the FDA must make a determination that information in the PDP submission is sufficient. The FDA and the applicant then meet to discuss eligibility of the device for the PDP process. A "filing review" of the submission is then conducted and it is referred to an Advisory Panel for recommendations. After conducting its own complete review and taking into consideration the Advisory Panel recommendations, the FDA either issues an Approval Letter or provides feedback concerning the disapproval of the PDP, including any suggested modifications. Upon approval, the applicant develops preclinical data as outlined in the PDP. Once the preclinical data are complete, the applicant must meet with the appropriate Institutional Review Board to discuss preclinical results and determine whether clinical studies may begin. The applicant submits a Notice of Completion after the clinical data are developed and the FDA reviews it to see if all requirements are met. If so, the FDA declares the PDP complete at which point the device may legally go to market. The PDP procedure is optional for the sponsor; the FDA cannot require a sponsor to use a PDP.

The major distinguishing feature of a PDP from a PMA approach is the FDA's early involvement at the design or preclinical testing phase. Thus, the PDP approach involves a

---

[144] Note, however, that in circumstances where the Secretary determines "that there is an imminent hazard to the public health, he may suspend the approval of such application immediately . . . ." *Id.* § 505(e)(5), 21 U.S.C. § 355(e)(5).

[145] *Id.* § 520(e), 21 U.S.C. § 360j(e).

[146] The FDA has imposed limitations on the distribution and prescription of drugs marketed under approved NDAs. After the methadone case, American Pharmaceutical Ass'n v. Mathews, 530 F.2d 1054 (D.C. Cir. 1976), serious questions have been raised as to the FDA's authority to impose this type of restriction. Nevertheless, when a manufacturer is confronted with the option of accepting a restriction or appealing the denial of an NDA to the courts, it is not surprising that the restriction is usually accepted.

close relationship between the FDA and the sponsor in designing appropriate preclinical tests and clinical investigations to establish the safety and effectiveness of the device. Under a PDP, the FDA and the sponsor agree on how the device should be tested. Successful completion of the PDP constitutes the FDA approval of the device for marketing. However, the requirements for proof of safety and effectiveness are no less stringent under a PDP than they are under a PMA. The PDP offers little advantage if the device has already undergone considerable design investigation and evaluation. In practice, the PDP has proven to be rarely feasible for a manufacturer and overly demanding of the FDA's resources. However, the new proposal suggests that the PDP process may become a viable option in the future.

■ Medical Device Reporting Requirements

The FDA requires manufacturers, distributors, importers, and user facilities to report certain adverse events involving marketed devices in order to ensure that the agency is promptly informed of all serious problems or potentially serious problems associated with marketed devices. Manufacturers and user facilities are required to report under 21 C.F.R. part 803 and distributors and importers are required to report under 21 C.F.R. part 804.

The Medical Device Amendments of 1976 amended the FDCA by requiring that manufacturers, importers, and distributors maintain records and make reports necessary to assure that medical devices are not adulterated and misbranded and to otherwise assure the safety and effectiveness of medical devices.[147] In 1980, citing the authority granted by the Medical Device Amendments, the FDA proposed a medical device reporting regulation for manufacturers, distributors, and importers.[148] The FDA received, however, over 200 written comments in response to the proposed rule, most of them unfavorable, and, in 1981, the FDA placed the proposed rule in abeyance.[149] Two years later, the FDA finally reproposed a modified version of the rule[150] which became final with additional changes in 1984.[151]

The Safe Medical Devices Act of 1990 amended section 519 of the FDCA by 1) requiring user facility reporting; 2) directing the FDA to issue regulations implementing distributor reporting; and 3) requiring manufacturers and distributors to certify the number of reports submitted in a year or that no such reports were submitted to the FDA. A final regulation for distributor reporting was published in 1993.[152] For manufacturers, however, there was little change in reporting requirements between publication of the 1984 final rule and 1996, when a final rule affecting manufacturers and user facilities published in late 1995 became effective.[153] The FDA's effort to revise the MDR regulation generated controversy in the medical device industry. For example, the final rule had an annual certification requirement requiring that a company's CEO certify that the company had reported all

---

[147] FDCA § 519, 21 U.S.C. § 360i.

[148] 45 Fed. Reg. 76,183 (1980).

[149] 46 Fed. Reg. 57,568 (1981).

[150] 48 Fed. Reg. 24,014 (1983).

[151] 49 Fed. Reg. 36,326 (1984).

[152] 58 Fed. Reg. 46,514 (1993) (21 C.F.R. pt. 804).

[153] 60 Fed. Reg. 63,578 (1995) (final rule on revised manufacture and user facility reporting requirements).

reportable events. Because of the often subjective nature of the definitions, CEO's were concerned about potential criminal prosecutions if there was a disagreement whether a particular unreported event should have been reported. In response to industry's concerns, the agency revised the certification requirement to require certification only that 1) the individual certifying has read the MDR requirements under part 803; 2) the firm has established a system to implement medical device reporting; and 3) following the procedures of its medical device reporting system, the reporting site submitted the specified number of reports, or no reports, during the twelve month certification period.[154]

The final rule also required manufacturers to report certain baseline data and required foreign manufacturers to use U.S. designated agents to register, list, act as the official correspondent, submit annual certifications, submit 510(k) notices, and submit MDR reports.[155] Many in industry believed that the baseline data requested was confidential commercial information and that its collection would be unduly burdensome. The controversy over the provision led the FDA to stay the collection of certain baseline data until a pilot program testing the need for the data was completed.[156] The agency also put the U.S. designated agent requirement on hold indefinitely because of the difficulty foreign manufacturers had in finding willing agents.[157]

Currently, manufacturers must submit an MDR to the FDA within thirty days after receiving or otherwise becoming aware of information, from any source, that reasonably suggests that a device marketed by the manufacturer: 1) may have caused or contributed to a death or serious injury; or 2) has malfunctioned and such device or a similar device marketed by the manufacturer would be likely to cause or contribute to a death or serious injury, if the malfunction were to recur.[158] In addition, manufacturers must submit a five day report to the FDA within five working days after 1) becoming aware from any source, including trend analysis, that remedial action is necessary to prevent an unreasonable risk of substantial harm to the public health; or 2) becoming aware of an MDR reportable event for which the FDA has made a written request for the submission of a five day report.[159] Manufacturers also are required to submit baseline reports,[160] and supplemental reports.[161]

A user facility is required to report to the FDA and the manufacturer, if known, within ten working days whenever it receives or becomes aware of information, from any source, that reasonably suggests that a device has or may have caused or contributed to the death of a patient of the facility.[162] If there is a serious injury rather than a death, the user facility must report the incident within the working days to the manufacturer only.

---

[154] 61 Fed. Reg. 38,348 (1996).
[155] 60 Fed. Reg. 63,578 (1995)
[156] 61 Fed. Reg. 39,868 (1996)
[157] 61 Fed. Reg. 38,346 (1996)
[158] 21 C.F.R. § 803.50(a).
[159] *Id.* § 803.53.
[160] *Id.* § 803.55.
[161] *Id.* § 803.56.
[162] *Id.* § 803.30.

As explained earlier in this chapter, the distributor reporting regulations require distributors to submit reports to the FDA and the manufacturer within ten working days of becoming aware of a death, serious illness or serious injury involving a distributed device, and to submit reports to manufacturers within ten working days of receiving information about certain malfunctions of distributed devices.[163]

■ Humanitarian Device Exemption Regulation

On June 26, 1996, the FDA published regulations prescribing the procedures for submitting humanitarian device exemption (HDE) applications for humanitarian use devices ("HUD").[164] The new regulations implement section 520(m) of the FDCA, which was intended to create an incentive for the development of devices for use in the treatment or diagnosis of diseases or conditions affecting a small number of individuals. The regulations requires a manufacturer to show only that a device is safe and has a probable benefit to patients, but not a demonstration of effectiveness.

Section 520(m) authorizes the FDA to exempt a HUD from the effectiveness requirements of sections 514 (performance standards) and 515 (premarket approval) of the FDCA provided that 1) the device is to be used to treat or diagnose a disease or condition that affects fewer than 4,000 individuals in the United States; 2) the device would not be available to a person with such a disease or condition unless the exemption is granted; 3) no comparable device (other than a device that has been granted such an exemption) is available to treat or diagnose the disease or condition; and 4) the device will not expose patients to an unreasonable or significant risk of illness or injury, and the probable benefit to health from using the device outweighs the risk of injury or illness from its use, taking into account the probable risks and benefits of currently available devices or alternative forms of treatment. Exempting a HUD from the effectiveness requirements relieves manufacturers of a major disincentive to bringing devices for rare conditions to market—the great expense of conducting controlled clinical studies.

In accordance with the HUD regulations, there are two distinct steps necessary to obtain approval to market a HUD. First, the sponsor of a HUD must submit a request to the FDA's Office of Orphan Products Development (OOPD) seeking a determination that the disease or condition that the device is intended to treat or diagnose affects or is manifested in fewer than 4,000 individuals in the United States per year. The request for HUD designation should provide the following: 1) based upon current medical and scientific knowledge, the precisely defined proposed indication(s) for use; 2) a brief description of the device, including illustrations and a discussion of its principle of operation; and 3) documentation, with authoritative references appended, of the target population demonstrating that the rare disease or condition affects or is manifested in fewer than 4,000 people in the United States per year.

Second, if OOPD determines that the device is eligible for a HUD designation, an HDE application must be submitted to the FDA's Office of Device Evaluation. The HDE application is similar in both form and content to a PMA application; however, the HDE appli-

---

[163] *See* 21 C.F.R. pt. 804.
[164] 61 Fed. Reg. 33,232 (1996).

cation is not required to contain the results of scientifically valid clinical investigations demonstrating that the device is effective for its intended purpose.

The HDE application must include a summary of the indications for use of the device, significant physical and performance characteristics of the device, and any clinical and non-clinical data that are relevant to evaluating the safety and probable benefit of the device. The application must also contain sufficient information for the FDA to determine that the device does not pose an unreasonable risk of illness or injury to patients and that the probable benefit outweighs the risk of injury or illness from its use, taking into account the probable risks and benefits of currently available devices or alternative forms of treatment. The applicant is also required to include information regarding any clinical experience with the device, where available, and information which will enable the FDA to determine that the device would not otherwise be available unless an HDE were granted and that no comparable device (other than another HUD with an approved HDE or a device with an approved IDE) is available to treat or diagnose the disease or condition.

The application must also contain a report by an independent certified public accountant verifying that the amount charged does not exceed the costs of the device's research, development, fabrication, and distribution. Finally, the application must include an estimate of the number of patients who would be required to generate data to support a full PMA and an explanation of why such a study is not feasible or why the cost of conducting such a study could not reasonably be expected to be recovered. HDEs will be granted only during the five years following the regulation's effective date, and HDEs will be valid only for eighteen months. However, the applicant can receive eighteen month extensions and extensions can be granted after the initial five year period passes. The FDA's final HDE regulation became effective on January 22, 1997.

■ Restricted Devices

The 1938 Federal Food, Drug, and Cosmetic Act included a provision characterizing drugs and devices as misbranded if their labeling failed to give adequate directions for use.[165] The FDCA also permitted the FDA to exempt drugs and devices from that provision. The FDA interpreted the exemption provision as a grant of authority to limit the distribution of certain drugs (and later medical devices) to sale only on the prescription of a physician, and agency regulations to this effect were upheld by the courts.[166] It was the FDA's position that "adequate directions for use" meant adequate directions for lay use. Therefore, drugs and devices that could safely and effectively be used only under the supervision of a physician could not, as a matter of law, bear adequate directions for lay use. The FDA, by regulation, exempted such drugs and devices if they were labeled to be dispensed only by prescriptions.[167]

The 1976 Amendments expanded the FDA's authority to restrict the distribution and use of certain devices by enabling the FDA to characterize them as "restricted devices."

---

[165] FDCA § 502(f)(1), 21 U.S.C. § 352(f)(1).

[166] *See* United States v. Sullivan, 332 U.S. 689 (1948); United States v. El-O-Pathic Pharmacy, 192 F.2d 62 (9th Cir. 1951).

[167] FDCA § 503, 21 U.S.C. § 353.

Accordingly, the agency may impose stringent limitations on the sale, distribution, or use of devices when it believes that these limitations are needed and will provide reasonable assurance of safety and effectiveness.[168] Devices characterized as restricted under section 520(e) are automatically subject to additional FDA regulatory authority. For example, the FDA has jurisdiction over advertising for restricted devices, although advertising for non-restricted devices is regulated under less stringent rules by the Federal Trade Commission.[169] Finally, as previously noted, the manufacturers of restricted devices must give FDA inspectors access to virtually all of their manufacturing and distribution records.[170]

Becton, Dickinson & Co. v. FDA[171] grew out of a routine FDA inspection of the company's records regarding certain devices that the FDA maintained were restricted devices. The amendments give the FDA expanded inspection authority over restricted devices.[172] After initially admitting the inspectors, Becton, Dickinson refused to permit the inspection to proceed. The FDA obtained a search warrant. Becton, Dickinson challenged the warrant on the ground that the search was not authorized under the Amendments. Becton, Dickinson contended that, although the FDA had authority to restrict the sale, distribution, and use of a device by regulation, the agency had not promulgated a regulation pertaining to the device in question. The FDA countered that after enactment of the Amendments it published a *Federal Register*[173] notice setting forth its opinion that all prescription devices previously subject to the FDA's prescription device regulation were restricted devices.

Both the district court and the court of appeals rejected the FDA's contention that the *Federal Register* notice satisfied the statutory obligation to promulgate a specific regulation. Although the court of appeals viewed the issue as close, it held that the FDA was required to conduct a full rulemaking proceeding on restricted devices before it could impose any regulation. Moreover, in that rulemaking proceeding, the FDA would have to show that the potential risks from the device justified the restrictions. Even a liberal construction of the statute would not permit the court to sanction the FDA's failure to follow the procedures necessary to promulgate regulations of specific effect.[174] The court noted that if the FDA had begun its rulemaking proceeding after the amendments were enacted, it could have completed the process without resorting to the improper use of authority. A year later, the FDA's position on restricted device inspections also was rejected by the First Circuit Court of Appeals.[175] The result of these cases was to limit the FDA's authority to inspect and copy certain records that are not required to be kept under the GMP regulations, but which are subject to FDA inspectional authority over restricted devices.

---

[168] *Id.* § 520(e), 21 U.S.C. § 360j(e). The authority to restrict use of a device to certain categories of practitioners, however, is limited.

[169] *See id.* § 502(r), 21 U.S.C. § 352(r).

[170] *Id.* § 704, 21 U.S.C. § 374. The FDA's GMP regulation, 21 C.F.R. § 820, authorizes inspection of the majority of manufacturing and distribution records for all medical devices.

[171] 448 F. Supp. 776 (N.D.N.Y.), *aff'd*, 589 F.2d 1175 (2d Cir. 1978).

[172] FDCA § 520(e), 21 U.S.C. § 360j(e).

[173] 41 Fed. Reg. 22,620 (1976).

[174] *Becton, Dickinson & Co.,* 589 F.2d at 1181-82.

[175] *In re* Establishment Inspection of Portex, Inc., 595 F.2d 84 (1st Cir. 1979). Another case brought by the FDA over a restricted device inspection simply ended in 1981 without a decision.*See In re* Establishment Inspection of Sherwood Med. Indus., No. 77-065 (W.D. Mo. Apr. 6, 1977).

In October 1980, following the *Becton, Dickinson* and *Portex* decisions, the FDA published a proposed general rule that would have classified a great many devices as restricted devices.[176] The rule was later formally withdrawn.[177] Thus far, the implementation of restrictions on device has been primarily limited to restrictions contained in PMA approval letters. The restrictions generally have involved only a limitation on the use or sale of the device by prescription.

The FDA's final rule in 1996 to regulate the sale, distribution, and use of cigarettes and smokeless tobacco products has been the most politically charged use of the FDA's restricted device authority. The FDA's final rule[178] regulates nicotine containing cigarettes and smokeless tobacco products as restricted devices within the meaning of section 502(e) of the FDCA. Using that authority, the FDA has imposed restrictions on the advertising, sale, and distribution of such tobacco products to underage persons. The goal of the rule is to protect children and adolescents from the dangers of cigarettes containing nicotine and smokeless tobacco products. Such products will be misbranded if their advertising, sale, and distribution does not comply with the FDA's regulations.

In response to the FDA's final rule regarding the regulation of cigarettes and smokeless tobacco, the case of *Coyne Beahm, Inc. v. FDA*[179] was filed in U.S. district court. In that case, the plaintiff claimed that portions of the FDA's restrictions on cigarettes and smokeless tobacco are not authorized under the FDCA. The court found that the FDA may not restrict advertising and promotion of these products pursuant to section 520(e) of the FDCA.[180] The court concluded that "although the FDA has the authority under the FDCA to impose access restrictions and labeling requirements on tobacco products, the FDA lacks the authority to restrict their advertising and promotion."[181] It will be interesting to see how other courts interpret the FDA's rule restricting the advertising and promotion of tobacco products, when challenged, and whether the *Coyne Beahm* case will ultimately withstand appeals.

■ Custom Devices

During congressional consideration of the Medical Device Amendments, some legislators believed that there should be an exemption for custom devices, while others expressed the concern that such an exemption would be abused by manufacturers and practitioners. The result was section 520(b), which exempts custom devices from performance standards and premarket approval and clearance requirements but not from good manufacturing practice requirements or other provisions of the FDCA. [182]

---

[176] 45 Fed. Reg. 65,619 (1980).

[177] 46 Fed. Reg. 57,569 (1981).

[178] Regulations Restricting the Sale and Distribution of Cigarettes and Smokeless Tobacco Products To Protect Children and Adolescents, 61 Fed. Reg. 44,396 (1996).

[179] 1997 WL 200007 (M.D.N.C.)

[180] *Id.* at 200007, 21.

[181] *Id.*

[182] FDCA § 520(b), 21 U.S.C. § 360j(b).

What is a custom device? Section 520(b) defines the term as follows:

> [a device] intended for use by an individual patient named in [an] order by such physician, dentist (or other specially qualified person so designated) and is to be made in a specific form for such patient, or . . . intended to meet the special needs of such physician or dentist (or other specially qualified person so designated) in the course of [his] professional practice . . . .[183]

Emphasizing the narrowness of the provision, the House Report noted that "[i]t applies only to devices intended for use by a patient named by a particular physician, dentist, or other specially qualified person or a person under his professional supervision."[184]

In this spirit of narrow construction, the FDA has always taken the position that a custom device is unique and crafted specifically for an individual patient or physician, whereas a *customized* device is a recognized class of device that is widely disseminated but can be varied in size, shape or material on order of a physician to meet the needs of individual patients. The FDA's regulations effectively exclude *customized* devices from the definition a custom device and, therefore, customized devices are generally subject to the FDA's premarket approval or clearance requirements. A custom device is defined as one that—

(1) Necessarily deviates from devices generally available or from an applicable performance standard or premarket approval requirement in order to comply with the order of an individual physician or dentist;

(2) Is not generally available to, or generally used by, other physicians or dentists;

(3) Is not generally available in finished form for purchase or for dispensing upon prescription;

(4) Is not offered for commercial distribution through labeling or advertising; *and*

(5) Is intended for use by an individual patient named in the order of a physician or dentist, and is to be made in a specific form for that patient, or is intended to meet the special needs of the physician or dentist in the course of professional practice.[185]

The FDA believes that the "necessarily deviates" requirement means that the device is "sufficiently unique that clinical investigations would be impracticable."[186] For instance, the FDA has said that contact lenses ordered specifically for a named patient in a prescription do not satisfy the definition of a custom device because, among other things, clinical investigations of contact lenses are practicable.[187] Also, the FDA considers a prescription contact lens as "generally available" if it is merely a variation within a range of powers and anterior and posterior surface contours that other doctors could purchase for their

---

[183] *Id.*

[184] HOUSE REPORT, *supra* note 22, at 45.

[185] 21 C.F.R. § 812.3(b).

[186] 48 Fed. Reg. 56,778, 56,796 (Dec. 23, 1983).

[187] *Id.*

patients.[188] This interpretive approach coincides with the FDA's view that a customizable device is not a "custom device." A number of manufacturers who have called their devices "custom devices" have received warning letters indicating that their product does not meet the FDA's regulatory definition of a custom device. [189]

■ Exports

Sections 801 and 802 govern the export of unapproved devices. Under section 801(e)(1), a device that is 510(k)able may be exported without prior FDA approval of the export provided the device: 1) accords to the specifications of the manufacturer; 2) is not in conflict with the laws of the country to which it is intended for export; 3) is labeled on the outside of the shipping package that it is intended for export; and 4) is not sold or offered for sale in domestic commerce. Prior to the enactment of the FDA Export Reform and Enhancement Act on April 26, 1996,[190] devices that were not 510(k)able were required to meet the above requirements and as well as obtain FDA approval of their exportation, pursuant to section 801(e)(2).

The FDA Export Reform and Enhancement Act, which expedites the export of many class III devices, permits the export (for marketing) to anywhere in the world of a class III device that complies with the laws of that country and has marketing authorization in any country identified in section 802(b)(1)(A) of the FDCA. The countries listed in that section are Australia, Canada, Israel, Japan, New Zealand, Switzerland, South Africa, the countries in the European Union, and the countries in the European Free Trade Association. The exported device also must meet certain other regulatory requirements (e.g., the device must be manufactured, processed, packaged, and held in substantial conformity with current good manufacturing practice requirements or meet international standards as certified by an international standards organization recognized by the FDA). The exporting company must provide a "simple notification" to the FDA indicating that the company intends to export the device to countries listed in the Export Reform Act, or to other non-listed countries specified in the simple notification.

In addition, the Export Reform Act permits the export of a device intended for investigational use in certain listed countries in accordance with the laws of those countries *without* prior FDA approval of the export. If, however, the device is not 510(k)able, is not approved in any of the listed countries, and is intended to be exported to a nonlisted country for investigational purposes, the requirements of 801(e)(2) (including FDA approval of the export) must be met.

■ Federal Preemption

The 1976 Medical Device Amendments included a provision that preempted certain state

---

[188] *See* Contact Lens Mfrs. Ass'n v. FDA, 766 F.2d 592, 599 (D.C. Cir. 1985).

[189] *See, e.g.,* Warning Letter to Kremer Eye Associates (1995); Warning Letter to Pudenz-Schulte Medical (1995); Warning Letter to Respironics, Inc. (1994); Warning Letter to Medtronic Biomedicus (1994); Warning Letter to Geneva Lab., Inc. (1994); Warning Letter to Dental Health Products, Inc. (1994); Warning Letter to Med. Inc. (1993); Warning Letter to Orentreich Med. Group (1991).

[190] Pub. L. No. 104-134, 110 stat. 1321 (codified at 21 U.S.C. §§ 334, 381, 382; 42 U.S.C. § 262).

regulations of medical devices. Section 521 of the Amendments stated, in pertinent part, that—

(a)   Except as provided in subsection (b), no State or political subdivision of a State may establish or continue in effect with respect to a device intended for human use any *requirement*—

(1)   which is *different from, or in addition to, any requirement applicable under this Act* to the device, and

(2)   which relates to the safety or effectiveness of the device or to any other matter included in a requirement applicable to the device under this Act.[191]

In addition, section 521 authorized the FDA to grant exemptions from the preemption provision by regulation upon application by a state.[192] Before the agency promulgated its proposed regulations to implement section 521, California sought exemption for virtually its entire structure of medical device regulations.[193] While California's application was pending, however, the FDA issued final regulations that somewhat limited the extent of federal preemption.[194] In 1980, despite opposition from the manufacturing community, both at the hearing on California's application and in written comments on the proposed rule, the FDA approved part of California's application for exemption.[195]

Also, before the final regulations were issued, two cases addressing the federal device exemption provisions were decided. In *Kievlan v. Dahlberg Electronics,*[196] the California appellate court found that the state's prohibition on the advertising of hearing aids was not pre-empted by the federal statute and regulations. The California regulation was found not to be different from or additional to a federal requirement because no federal regulation on the subject existed.

The second case also dealt with hearing aids.[197] Florida enacted a statute requiring that a testing room be used for hearing tests, that purchasers of hearing aids be furnished with product brochures when they received their hearing aids, and that such purchasers be duly informed by labeling that a hearing aid can neither prevent further hearing loss nor restore normal hearing. The court upheld the Florida statute on the basis provided in section 521, that is, that none of the three requirements of the statute collided with federal requirements. According to the court, the areas of minimal procedures and equipment testing had not been addressed by federal statute, and provision of information mandated by the Florida statute merely supplemented existing federal requirements.[198] The requirement that information be distributed to each patient was seen as a general business requirement that

---

[191]   FDCA § 521(a), 21 U.S.C. § 360k(a) (emphasis added).

[192]   *Id.* § 521 (b), 21 U.S.C. § 360k(b). These exemptions may be granted only after notice and opportunity for a hearing. To qualify for exemption, the state requirements must be either more stringent than the federal requirements or compelled by local conditions, and they must not precipitate any violation of other applicable federal requirements.

[193]   42 Fed. Reg. 9186 (1977), corrected by 42 Fed. Reg. 12,442 (1977).

[194]   43 Fed. Reg. 18,661 (1978), corrected by 43 Fed. Reg. 22,010 (1978), amended by 46 Fed. Reg. 8454 (1981).

[195]   45 Fed. Reg. 67,321 (1980). The agency also responded to other state exemption applications at the same time.*See* 45 Fed. Reg. 67,325, 67,326 (1980).

[196]   78 Cal. App. 3d 951, 144 Cal. Rptr. 585 (1978), appeal dismissed, 440 U.S. 951(1979).

[197]   Smith v. Pingree, 651 F.2d 1021(5th Cir. 1981).

[198]   The federal hearing aid regulations are found at 21 C.F.R. § 801.420-421.

bore no direct relationship to the federal regulation under the amendments. Finally, the labeling requirement, although similar to a federal requirement, was distinguishable because it merely consisted of a reminder of rights under Florida law; it was not a prerequisite for complete instructional packaging.

On October 10, 1980, the FDA promulgated a final regulation addressing a number of state exemption applications relating to hearing aids. The FDA's most significant response was its finding that California's prohibition of all advertising for hearing aids burdened interstate commerce and imposed a additional requirement to existing federal requirements. The FDA did grant exemptions from preemption for state provisions that do not directly regulate hearing aids but merely control distribution or the means of distribution.

For devices other than hearing aids, however, the precise scope of this preemption provision remained ambiguous for nearly twenty years following its enactment. Federal circuits were divided on the meaning of the terms "requirement" and "different from, or in addition to."[199] Thus, for example, some circuits interpreted the provision to mean that clearance of a premarket notification for a device preempted some or all state common law claims,[200] while other circuits construed the provision to preserve all state common law claims.[201]

To resolve this split among the federal circuit courts, the Supreme Court granted certiorari in 1995 in *Medtronic v. Lohr.*[202] In *Medtronic,* Lora Lohr, who had received a pacemaker manufactured by Medtronic, and her spouse brought a state common law negligence and strict liability action against Medtronic for damages allegedly resulting from the device's failure. The Lohrs claimed that the Medtronic was negligent due to defective device design and failure to provide adequate instructions. The plaintiffs also presented a strict liability claim, alleging that the device was, at the time of sale, in a defective condition and unreasonably dangerous to foreseeable users. Medtronic counterargued that all of the plaintiffs' state law claims were preempted by the provision in section 521, quoted above.

The issue presented before the Supreme Court was the precise scope of the preemption provision. Because Medtronic's pacemaker had been cleared by the FDA through the 510(k) process, and was subject to continuing regulatory monitoring of its manufacture and labeling, Medtronic argued that the availability of state law remedies imposed a requirement "different from or in addition to" federal requirements, thus triggering the preemption provision.

The Court ultimately rejected Medtronic's argument, concluding that the 510(k) process does not preempt state law claims. Justice Stevens, writing for the Court, stated that—

> The company's defense exaggerates the importance of the § 510(k) process . . . . As the court below noted, "the 510(k) process is focused on equivalence, not

---

[199] *See, e.g.,* English v. Mentor Corp., 67 F.3d 477 (3d Cir. 1995) (510(k) clearance preempts state regulation); Feldt v. Mentor Corp., 61 F.3d 431 (5th Cir. 1995) (510(k) clearance does not preempt state regulation); Kennedy v. Collagen Corp., 67 F.3d 1453 (9th Cir. 1995) (state common law claims are not preempted by section 521 of Med. Device Amendments).

[200] *See, e.g.,* English v. Mentor Corp., 67 F.3d 477 (3d Cir. 1995).

[201] *See, e.g.,* Kennedy v. Collagen Corp., 67 F.3d 1453 (9th Cir. 1995).

[202] 116 S. Ct. 2240 (1996).

safety.". . . . As a result, "substantial equivalence determinations provide little protection to the public . . . ."[203]

While *Medtronic* appears to resolve the issue of the scope of the preemption provision for state law claims regarding products cleared through the 510(k) process, the opinion expressly leaves open the question of whether PMA approval would preempt state law claims. The FDA is considering revising its preemption regulation to provide further clarification.

■ Performance Standards and Special Controls

Immediately following enactment of the 1976 Medical Device Amendments, the FDA's authority to establish performance standards for medical devices initially generated some interest and a flurry of in-house activity. Nothing of substance, however, occurred in this area from 1976 until enactment of the SMDA in 1990.

Under the 1976 Amendments, section 514 of the FDCA[204] authorized the FDA to establish performance standards for class II devices[205] and set forth a complex process for the development of these standards. In addition, section 514 specified some of the features of devices that may be subjected to standards, and mentioned other organizations, including other federal agencies, that may be eligible to develop standards. Nevertheless, although a final procedural regulation for the development of standards was published on February 1, 1980,[206] not one section 514 performance standard was developed.

There were several reasons why the FDA did not issue any performance standards under section 514. First, the procedural burdens imposed by the statute were onerous unbearable. Second, no serious public health problems that could have been avoided by standards were identified with class II products. Third, voluntary standards groups emerged to provide a forum for discussion and actions on standards. Their activities, which often permit to participation by the FDA staff members, substantiated the view that writing standards is a laborious, time consuming, expensive process under the best of circumstances. Finally, in a period of scarce resources available for government regulation, using people and time for the drafting of device standards was not considered efficient.[207]

Recognizing that performance standards were difficult to prepare, FDA officials devoted considerable attention to other ways of addressing device problems, such as requesting voluntary action by manufacturers to resolve device problems; publicizing particular device problems; publishing educational and technical information for the users of

---

[203] *Id.* at 2254.

[204] 21 U.S.C. § 360d.

[205] Section 514 should be read as granting discretionary authority, since section 514(a)(1) does say "may." However, section 513(a)(1)(B) defines class II as consisting of those devices for which a performance standard is "necessary...to provide reasonable assurance of its safety and effectiveness." Another view is that the FDA is required to promulgate performance standards for all class II products. *See* Address by Allen Greenberg, FDA Medical Device Forum 3—A (Jan. 26, 1982).

[206] 45 Fed. Reg. 7474 (1980).

[207] There are divergent opinions concerning the impact of agency inaction on groups that develop voluntary standards. Some believe it gives these groups greater importance; others believe it reduces their role. The authors are of the latter view.

devices; encouraging agency participation in developing voluntary standards; developing guidelines for product testing and product labeling; and preparing and sending letters to companies notifying them of their violative conduct and requesting corrective action. Some of these alternatives, however, posed questions of procedural fairness, as well as questions about the rights and obligations of manufacturers and users. For example, publicizing alleged device defects before manufacturers were given an opportunity to explain these "defects" raised fairness questions. Product liability considerations also were involved. Association involvement in standard development raised antitrust questions. In *American Society of Mechanical Engineers, Inc. v. Hydrolevel Corporation,*[208] the Supreme Court held a trade association liable for the anticompetitive results of a standards related activity conducted for the association by an officer of a member company.

Congress recognized that, as written in the 1976 Medical Device Amendments, the procedures for establishing performance standards were unworkable. As a result, as discussed above, the SMDA attempted to decrease the procedural complexity of promulgating performance standards, permitting the FDA to issue standards via the ordinary notice and comment rulemaking process.[209] The SMDA also permitted the FDA to use other types of "special controls," such as postmarket surveillance, guidance documents, and other mechanisms, as an alternative to formal performance standards.[210]

Despite the liberalization of the procedures for developing performance standards, the agency has rarely utilized this tool. Since 1990, the agency has published only two proposed performance standards related to infant apnea monitors.[211] Only one has been finalized. While it appears likely that the FDA will continue to use a variety of voluntary controls rather than issuing formal performance standards in the future, one of the agency's proposals for legislative reform is to provide an easy mechanism to adopt performance standards in the device review process. Thus, in the future, there may be further legislative action regarding performance standards.

■ The FDA Guidance Philosophy

In addition to promulgation of significant regulations implementing the Medical Device Amendments of 1976, the FDA has developed important "guidance" documents for medical device manufacturers. The FDA chooses to follow the "guidance" route in part because guidelines are easier to promulgate than regulations, particularly under the past and present Administrations, which involve HHS and OMB in reviewing proposed FDA regulations. Since 1976 a large number of major guidelines have been formulated and disseminated on a wide range of topics. To ensure that a broad range of viewpoints relating to these guidelines was considered, many guidelines were distributed in draft to interested parties for comment. Guidance (or guideline) general topics include the content of 510(k), IDE, and PMA submissions for specific devices; GMP requirements; biocompatibility testing; and labeling for various devices.

---

[208] 456 U.S. 556 (1982).

[209] FDCA § 514(b)(1)(A), 21 U.S.C. § 360d(b)(1)(A).

[210] *Id.* § 513(a)(1)(B), 21 U.S.C. § 360c(a)(1)(B).

[211] 60 Fed. Reg. 9762 (1995) (infant apnea monitors); 60 Fed. Reg. 32,406 (1995) (electrode lead wires).

Guidelines represent practices, which, if followed by companies, the agency will consider acceptable to meet its regulatory requirements. A guideline has, however, no legal force; manufacturers are free to follow other practices as long as they meet the same ends of compliance with regulations. Guidelines do give companies some insight into the FDA's interpretation of various requirements, while providing manufacturers some freedom as to how to tailor their own processes to the requirements.

In practice, the FDA has placed a great deal more weight on practices recommended in guidance documents than is legally mandated. For example, in the *Bioclinical* [212] case, discussed previously, the FDA established GMP requirements via a draft guidance document, then took enforcement action against a company not in compliance with the requirements. The *Bioclinical* case points up the weaknesses of the guidance approach. Although the FDA may seek comments on the content of a guidance, the agency is not obligated to use the comments nor to provide a legal rationale for its position. Moreover, once the FDA has established its position in a guideline, FDA staff and field investigators are often reluctant to accept an alternative.

Although no one has suggested that the FDA cease using the guidance approach, there are many who question the agency's use of this mechanism in lieu of rulemaking. In fact, the FDA often has come under fire from industry for treating draft guidance documents as *de facto* regulations. In response to complaints from industry, in early 1997, the FDA developed guidelines for the agency's development, issuance and use of guidance documents. The guidelines, referred to as Good Guidance Practices (GGPs), set forth internal the FDA procedures for the development of guidance documents and prescribe the methods for implementing and disseminating new guidance documents. The GGPs also specifically state that guidance documents do not establish legally enforceable rights or responsibilities and are not legally binding on the public or the agency. It remains to be seen whether the GGPs will have any meaningful impact on the agency's approach to issuing guidance documents.

Prospects for FDA Reform

The 104th Congress expressed strong interest in "FDA Reform," with proposals ranging from modest efforts to reduce review times to broad attempts to eliminate the effectiveness requirement for medical devices. Although legislative ambitions regarding FDA reform have moderated somewhat, proposals for FDA reform will likely arise again in the foreseeable future. In light of increasing international regulatory harmonization, particularly in the European Union, the FDA is under considerable competitive pressure to achieve review times comparable to other international regulatory bodies. [213] Proposals for

---

[212] United States v. BioClinical Systems, Inc., 2 Med. Device Rep. (CCH) ¶ 15,090 (D. Md. June 19, 1987).

[213] The former FDA Comm'r, David Kessler, recently published an article in the *Journal of the American Medical Association* comparing the average approval times in the United States with approval times in Europe. The study concluded that FDA review times were generally shorter than European review times for corresponding product categories. David A. Kessler, et al., *Approval of New Drugs in the United States Comparison with the United Kingdom, Germany, and Japan*, 276 JAMA 1826 (1996).

greater international harmonization and/or third party review are likely to periodically resurface in an effort to expand the FDA's limited review resources.

To some extent, the FDA has averted comprehensive reform efforts by improving its efficiency in product review. The FDA has initiated a number of programs that are intended to expedite the product review process, such as the draft 510(k) Paradigm discussed in this chapter, and to offer alternatives to the traditional routes to market, such as the revitalization of the PDP program discussed above. It is yet to be seen how these initiatives will ultimately be received by industry and whether they will contribute to a decline in overall review times.

Conclusion

The FDA has made good progress in implementing the medical device legislation, although the agency is moving at a studied pace. In part, this pace has been dictated by the limited manpower and resources allocated to the agency. In recent years, FDA implementation has accelerated to some extent, particularly in the area of 510(k) review times and fulfilling export requests. Nonetheless, the FDA will likely face continuing pressure to accelerate review times, to coordinate its efforts with international regulatory bodies, to reduce obstacles to technological development, and to accomplish these goals without sacrificing its primary objective, consumer protection.

chapter 11

FDA and Radiological Health: Protecting the Public From Radiation Hazards

Alan R. Bennett*
Robert A. Dormer**

Background

■ Early History of Radiation Control

The first organized attempt to regulate radiation exposure came in 1929 with the formation of the Advisory Committee on X-Ray and Radiation Protection, an informal professional organization composed of industry representatives, which worked closely with the National Bureau of Standards. This organization later became known as the National Council on Radiation Protection and received a congressional charter in 1964.[1] It was a wholly private body, and its recommendations for controlling exposure to radiation were often adopted by states and provided for many years the basis for controlling use of radiation and radioactive materials by federal and state agencies and private users.

■ Congressional Involvement

Early Efforts to Control Radiation

Until 1946, almost all regulation of radioactive material took place at the state level. In that year, Congress passed the Atomic Energy Act,[2] giving the Atomic Energy Commission authority to regulate possession and use of certain artificial radioactive materials for the first time. The Atomic Energy Commission's jurisdiction, however, did not extend to radiation produced by machines, by most natural radioactive materials, or by artificial radioactive materials manufactured without the use of a nuclear reactor. Thus, neither con-

*   Mr. Bennett is a Partner in the law firm of Fox, Bennett & Turner, Washington, D.C.
** Mr. Dormer is a Partner in the law firm of Hyman, Phelps & McNamara, P.C., Washington, D.C.
    The authors would like to acknowledge the assistance of Steven L. Merouse, summer associate at Fox, Bennett & Turner, and Alexa Boonstra, summer associate at Hyman, Phelps & McNamara, P.C. on this project.
1   National Council on Radiation Protection and Measurements Act, Pub. L. No. 88-376, 78 Stat. 320 (1964).
2   Pub. L. 79-585, 60 Stat. 755 (1946).

sumer goods nor medical devices that emitted radiation were regulated by the federal government, and controls by the states were inconsistent and sometimes ineffective.

As the use of x-ray devices and other products of new medical technology increased sharply in the 1940s and thereafter, the need for uniform federal regulation became apparent.[3] In 1959, a document known as the Morgan Report recommended that primary responsibility for protecting the nation from radiation hazards be established in the U.S. Public Health Service (PHS).[4] Responding to this report, the Eisenhower Administration issued an Executive Order establishing the Federal Radiation Council (FRC).[5] This action was initially meant to alleviate public confusion and concern about fallout from testing of nuclear weapons and the absence of any single agency within the Executive Branch responsible for formulating radiation protection guidelines. The Council was composed of the heads of executive branch agencies and departments with an interest in radiation control, and was chaired by the Secretary of Health, Education, and Welfare (HEW). The Council, however, lacked the power to establish or to enforce standards. Its function was merely to serve as an advisory body to the President, who could then direct federal agencies to comply with the recommendations of the Council.

The Department of HEW began its involvement with radiation control through participation in the FRC. Shortly thereafter, the PHS instituted a program providing professional scientific advice and information to the states, which could promulgate their own regulations after consideration of the PHS' recommendations.[6] In response to the second Morgan Report, the PHS, on January 1, 1967, established the National Center for Radiological Health, predecessor of the Food and Drug Administration's (FDA's) former Bureau of Radiological Health (BRH), which is now the Center for Devices and Radiological Health (CDRH). At the time of its establishment, the Center continued the PHS' traditional role as a research body providing advice to the states, but it still lacked any enforcement authority.

Passage of the Radiation Control for Health and Safety Act

The inadequacy of federal regulation of radiation was brought into sharp focus during the first half of 1967. In May of that year, it was reported that between 90,000 and 100,000 color television sets manufactured by the General Electric Company between June 1966 and February 1967 were emitting radiation at levels up to 600 times greater than the stan-

---

[3]   A 1964 study by the Public Health Service revealed that 108 million Americans had some exposure to medical or dental x-rays in that year. This accounted for 90% of public exposure to x-rays. It was estimated that at least one-half of all medical x-rays exposed more of the patient's body to radiation than necessary for the size of the picture taken, that 25% of x-ray beam sizes were two or more times larger than the area of the x-ray film, and that at least 30% of the equipment used was ten or more years old. 113 CONG. REC. 36,232 (1967) (statement of Sen. Bartlett).

[4]   Three seminal reports were issued on the role of the federal government in radiation control. Two were issued in 1959 and 1966 by the National Advisory Committee on Radiation to the Surgeon General, chaired by Professor Russell H. Morgan of the Johns Hopkins Medical School. The third was a report on occupational exposure to radiation issued by the National Advisory Environmental Health Committee of the Surgeon General, under the chairmanship of Dr. Norton Nelson of New York University Medical School Sch. *Id.* at 36,230.

[5]   Exec. Order No. 10,831, 24 Fed. Reg. 6669 (Aug. 18, 1959), established the Federal Radiation Council. The Council later became a statutory body. *See* Pub. L. No. 86-373, § 274(h), 73 Stat. 688 (1959).

[6]   *See* 42 U.S.C. §§ 241, 246 (1994).

dard set by the National Council for Radiation Protection.[7] This revelation, concerning a product widely used by the public and occurring at a time when Congress was displaying heightened interest in product safety generally,[8] sparked immediate congressional attention. Within one month of the disclosure concerning television sets, Congressmen Paul G. Rogers and John Jarman introduced a bill that ultimately became the Radiation Control for Health and Safety Act of 1968 (RCHS Act).[9] Between June and August of 1967, seven bills were introduced in the House of Representatives, and two in the Senate, to address the issue of radiation control.

Initially, hearings on the bills focused on radiation emitted from television receivers, but soon the scope of the hearings grew to encompass consideration of other types of radiation-emitting products. During the course of the hearings, an accident at a Gulf Oil Corporation facility in Pennsylvania resulted in exposure of several workers to extremely high dosages of radiation from a defective Van deGraaf accelerator.[10] This incident demonstrated again the problems stemming from lack of federal regulation. For example, the federal government was not even notified of the accident until six days after it had occurred. This delay in turn delayed notice to other users of similar devices and created the possibility that other workers would be endangered.

During the hearings a considerable amount of testimony was also presented concerning overexposure to x-radiation arising from untrained radiological technicians and inadequate equipment. The National Center for Radiological Health estimated that about ten percent of the population was seriously overexposed to radiation from medical sources, and a 1967 survey indicated that two-thirds of the 112,000 x-ray devices surveyed were not in compliance with state recommendations or regulations.[11]

Finally, the Department of Defense conducted a survey of microwave ovens at Walter Reed Army Hospital and discovered that a substantial percentage of ovens did not comply with industry standards. Of the thirty ovens tested, only six were acceptable. The remainder had defects, including excessive leakage around the door and faulty door interlocks. One oven leaked radiation at levels that, according to Department of Defense personnel, were sufficient to cause eye cataracts.[12]

Given these findings, it is not surprising that the concept of federal regulation of radiation emissions from consumer products generated little controversy. Product manufac-

---

[7] Letter from V.G. Mackenzie, Assistant Surgeon General, to Rep. Paul G. Rogers, *reprinted* in 113 CONG. REC. 13,628 (1967). The letter is undated. It appears in the May 23, 1967 *Congressional Record* and refers to a May 18, 1967 letter. Therefore, the letter was written sometime between May 18 and May 23, 1967.

[8] *See, e.g.,* Joint Resolution to Establish a National Commission on Product Safety, H.R.J.RES. 280, 90th Cong., 1st Sess. (1967).

[9] *See infra* note 18 and accompanying text.

[10] *Hearings on H.R. 10790 Before the Subcomm. On Public Health and Welfare of the House Comm. On Interstate and Foreign Commerce,* 90th Cong., 1st Sess. 426 (1967) [hereinafter *Hearings on H.R.* 10790].

[11] S. REP. No. 1432, 90th Cong., 2nd Sess. 4 (1968). The problem was ultimately addressed by the Consumer - Patient Radiation Health and Safety Act of 1981 which set accreditation standards for radiological technician training programs and mandated the certification of operators of radiological equipment.

[12] Walter Reed Army Medical Center, Microwave Survey No. 42-13-86 (Sept. 7, 1967), *reprinted in Hearings in S. 2067, 3211, and H.R. 10790 Before the Senate Comm. On Commerce,* 96th Cong., 2d Sess. pt. 2, at 791 (1968) [hereinafter *1968 Hearings*].

turers generally supported the measure, although the issues of worker protection and standards for training radiological technicians generated much debate. Manufacturers strongly urged that the Secretary should promulgate performance rather than design standards.[13] Therefore, an advisory committee of qualified scientists and industry personnel was formed to advise the Secretary regarding appropriate standards, that standards be subject to judicial review, and that the federal government pre-empt state standards to avoid the possibility of inconsistent requirements.[14] Consumer groups were, of course, very supportive of the legislation.[15] They were particularly enthusiastic about government participation in setting standards, a function previously entrusted to private sector organizations such as the American College of Radiology and the American Dental Association.

The position of the executive branch was summarized by Surgeon General William Stewart: "In protecting man from radiation emission from electronic products we need clearly stated performance standards established, promulgated and enforced by competent authority concerned with health protection after free and full exchange of views and information among all parties concerned."[16]

Examination of the various bills disclosed several areas of sharp disagreement. Particularly controversial were whether the Secretary would have the power to seize products that did not meet performance standards and to inspect plants manufacturing radiation-emitting products. Another major dispute concerned whether workers who produce and test these products would be included within the scope of the bills.

When a bill emerged from the conference committee, it contained no provision authorizing government seizures or the promulgation of standards for protecting workers. A Senate provision that authorized the Secretary to conduct "such inspections as may be necessary to enforce" compliance had been eliminated, and the conferees had adopted instead a House amendment under which the Secretary could inspect plants only if he found "good cause" to do so. The more stringent regulatory provisions in the Senate version did prevail, however. These require manufacturers to repair, replace, or refund the price of electronic products that fail to comply with an applicable performance standard or contain a safety-related defect, and require dealers to keep records adequate to identify and trace ownership of defective and noncompliant products. The House bill, in contrast, would merely have directed the Secretary to work with the electronic products industry to establish a program for correcting defects and ensuring compliance with applicable standards.

Finally, the Senate agreed to remove from the performance-standards section of its bill a provision that would have authorized the Secretary to require attachment of accessories,

---

[13]   A design standard specifies how a device is to be constructed; a performance standard, in contrast, sets a permissible radiation emission level and permits the manufacturer to meet that level by any design it chooses.

[14]   *See, e.g., Hearings on H.R. 10790, supra* note 11, at 252 (statement of E. William Henry, Electronic Indus. Ass'n); *see also id.* at 173 (statement of James F. Young, Vice Pres., General Elec. Co.)

[15]   *See, e.g., 1968 Hearings, supra* note 14, at 735 (statement of Ralph Nader); *see also Hearings on H.R. 10,790, supra note* 11, at 434-35 (statement of American Pub. Health Ass'n).

[16]   *Hearings on S. 2067, Before the Senate Comm. on Commerce,* 90th Cong., 1st Sess. 87 (1967) (statement of William Stewart, Surgeon General of the United States).

such as shielding devices, to electronic products. This provision was unacceptable to some House members who believed the language might be interpreted to authorize issuance of design standards for electronic products. In exchange for the removal of this provision, House members agreed that the legislative history would state clearly that a broad construction of the term "performance standard" was intended.

On October 18, 1968, approximately seventeen months after the television set incident first led to its proposal, Congress enacted the Radiation Control for Health and Safety Act.[17]

Major Electronic Product Radiation Control Provisions

■ Purpose and Scope

The Electronic Product Radiation Control (EPRC) provisions direct the Secretary of Health and Human Services (DHHS) to establish and conduct a radiation control program. The EPRC provisions apply to all electronic products[18] capable of emitting radiation that are manufactured[19] in the United States or imported.[20] The CDRH is responsible for administering and enforcing the radiation control program,[21] which consists primarily of a set of performance standards designed to control and minimize product radiation.[22]

---

[17] In 1990, the Radiation Control for Health and Safety Act was recodified as part of the Federal Food, Drug, and Cosmetic Act (FDCA). The provisions of the latter act which incorporate the Radiation Control for Health and Safety Act, are now referred to as the Electronic Product Radiation Control (EPRC) provisions of the FDCA, and the new designation is used throughout this paper. Pub. L. No. 90-602, 82 Stat. 1173 (1968) (codified at 21 U.S.C. §§ 360hh-360ss (1994), formerly 42 U.S.C. §§ 263c-263n) (Pub. L. 101-629, § 19(a)(3), (4), 104 Stat. 4530 (1990) renumbered and moved 42 U.S.C. §§ 263c-263n to 21 U.S.C. §§ 360hh-360ss).

[18] An "electronic product" is any manufactured or assembled product which, when in operation, contains or is part of an electronic circuit, or any component or accessory of such product that emits or could emit radiation. FDCA § 531 (2), 21 U.S.C. § 360hh(2). Examples of electronic products subject to the EPRC provisions include x-ray machines used for diagnosis and treatment; x-ray machines used in research, education, or industrial application; electron microscopes; cathode ray tubes; high voltage vacuum tubes; microwave ovens; lasers; television receivers; ultraviolet lights; and infrared heaters and ultrasonic cleaners. S. REP. NO. 1432, *supra note* 12, at 6.

[19] The term "manufacturer" means any person engaged in the business of manufacturing, assembling, or importing electronic products. FDCA § 531 (3), 21 U.S.C. § 360hh(3).

[20] The EPRC provisions prohibit the importation into the United States of any electronic product that fails to comply with an established standard or that does not have affixed to it a certification label or tag. The statute authorizes the Secretary of the Treasury to destroy any electronic product refused admission into the United States, unless such product is exported within 90 days after refusal of admission. FDCA § 536 (a); 21 U.S.C. § 360mm(a).

[21] The Secretary's authority under the EPRC provisions has been delegated to the Comm'r of Food and Drugs., 21 C.F.R. § 5.10 (1997). That authority in turn, has been further delegated to the Director of CDRH. *Id.* § 5.86-5.92.

[22] The phrase "electronic product radiation" is defined as any ionizing or non-ionizing electromagnetic or particulate radiation, or any sonic, infrasonic, or ultrasonic wave emitted from an electronic product as the result of the operation of an electronic circuit in the product. FDCA § 531(1), 21 U.S.C. § 360hh(1).

■ Performance Standards

Performance standards promulgated by CDRH have been the key mechanism under the EPRC provisions for controlling electronic product radiation.[23] CDRH has published performance standards for fourteen categories of radiation-emitting products,[24] including television receivers,[25] diagnostic x-ray systems,[26] computed tomography (CT) equipment,[27] microwave ovens,[28] lasers,[29] sunlamps,[30] mercury vapor lamps,[31] ultrasonic therapy products,[32] and cabinet x-ray systems (including baggage inspection systems.)[33]

The performance standards generally prescribe, among other things, the maximum allowable radiation emission levels for electronic products, and include criteria for testing and measuring radiation emission levels. The EPRC provisions also provide that a performance standard may require use of warning labels and information on installation, operation, and use.[34] In addition, the EPRC provisions require a manufacturer of any electronic product subject to a performance standard to certify that the product conforms to the applicable standard by permanently affixing to the product a certification label or tag.[35]

The performance standards must be developed in consultation with the Technical Electronic Product Radiation Safety Standards Committee (TEPRSSC), a statutory advisory committee composed of fifteen representatives of industry, government, labor, and the general public. The Committee's function is to advise CDRH of the technical feasibility, reasonableness, and practicability of any proposal to establish or amend a performance standard.[36] Although CDRH is given broad discretion to promulgate performance standards through the use of either the informal or formal rulemaking procedures of the Administrative Procedure Act,[37] CDRH, before promulgating a performance standard, must: 1) consult with federal and state departments and agencies having related responsibilities or interest, and with appropriate professional organizations and interested parties; and 2) give consideration to a) the latest scientific and medical information on electronic product radiation, b) current relevant standards recommended by other agencies and expert groups,© the reasonableness and technical feasibility of a standard as applied to a particular product, and d) whether the standard meets the need for uniformity and reliabil-

---

[23] Even in the absence of a performance standard, the FDA has ample authority to protect the public from radiation-emitting products found to contain a safety-related defect. SeeFDCA § 535, 21 U.S.C. § 360ll.

[24] *See* 21 C.F.R. §§ 1020.10-1050.10.

[25] *Id.* § 1020.10.

[26] *Id.* § 1020.30.

[27] *Id.* § 1020.33.

[28] *Id.* § 1030.10.

[29] *Id.* § 1040.10-.11.

[30] *Id.* § 1040.20.

[31] *Id.* § 1040.30.

[32] *Id.* § 1050.10.

[33] *Id.* § 1020.40.

[34] FDCA § 543 (a)(1), 21 U.S.C. § 360kk(a)(1). *See also* 21 C.F.R. § 1010.3.

[35] *Id.* § 534 (h), 21 U.S.C. § 360kk(h); 21 C.F.R. § 1010.2.

[36] *Id.* § 534 (f), 21 U.S.C. § 360kk(f).

[37] *Id.* § 534 (b), 21 U.S.C. § 360kk(b). *See also* S. REP. NO. 1432, *supra* note 12, at 20.

ity of testing and measuring procedures and equipment.[38] Judicial review of a radiation emission standard issued under the EPRC provisions is available in a United States court of appeals if sought within sixty days of issuance of the standard.[39]

Several exemptions from performance standards are provided in the provisions. Electronic products intended for export are exempt, and CDRH is authorized to exempt from an applicable standard any product intended solely for use by a federal department or agency.[40] In addition, a variance from an applicable standard may be obtained by any manufacturer of an electronic product in certain prescribed circumstances.[41] CDRH will grant a variance when a deviation from a standard is so limited that it does not justify an amendment of the standard, or when insufficient time exists to permit amendment of the standard (and an amendment is warranted). The product manufactured under the variance must provide a degree of protection equal to or greater than that provided for under the standard.

■ Notification and the Duty to Repair, Replace, or Refund

CDRH has broad statutory authority to require a manufacturer to correct the radiation-related problems of a product. The provisions require a manufacturer to notify CDRH immediately of any radiation-related safety defect or failure of a product to comply with a performance standard.[42] CDRH may also determine, based on its own investigations, plant inspections and product report reviews, that a product has a defect or is not in compliance with FDA standards.

In addition to the duty to notify CDRH, a manufacturer must also notify purchasers of the defective or noncompliant product, and submit to CDRH for approval a corrective action plan in which the manufacturer explains how it will repair or replace the product or refund the purchase price.[43] Alternatively, if the manufacturer believes that the defect or failure to comply does not create a significant risk of injury (including genetic injury) to any person, the manufacturer may apply to CDRH for an exemption from the requirement to notify purchasers and submit a corrective action plan.[44]

---

[38] *Id.* § 534 (a)(1), 21 U.S.C. § 360kk(a)(1).

[39] *Id.* § 534 (d)(1), 21 U.S.C. § 360kk(d)(1).

[40] *Id.* § 534 (a)(3), (5), 21 U.S.C. § 360kk(a)(3), (5).

[41] *Id.* § 534 (a) (2), 21 C.F.R. § 1010.4; 21 U.S.C. § 360kk (a) (2).

[42] *Id.* § 535, 21 U.S.C. § 360ll(a)(1). *Compare* this requirement *with* the FDA's requirements to report adverse reactions associated with drugs, 21 C.F.R. § 314.80 (serious and unexpected adverse drug experiences required to be reported as soon as possible but in any event within fifteen working days of receipt of information about event)*and* medical devices, *id.* §§ 803.20, 802.53 (deaths or serious injuries associated with a device required to be reported by manufacturer within thirty days of becoming aware of information unless there is a risk of substantial harm to public health and then reporting must occur within five days of awareness of risk). If a manufacturer is required to report under both the EPRC provisions and part 803, the latter takes precedence, and the manufacturer is required to report *only* under part 803. *Id.* § 1003.10(c).

The regulations also contain a separate requirement for the reporting of accidental radiation occurrences. *Id.* § 1002.20. The concept of Medical Device Reports (MDRs), later applied to medical devices by part 803, was in part based on this provision.

[43] FDCA § 535 (f); 21 U.S.C. § 360ll(f).

[44] *Id.* § 535 (a)(2); 21 U.S.C. § 360ll(a)(2).

The manufacturer is entitled to a regulatory hearing before the FDA to determine whether the product is defective or fails to comply with the standard, and whether an exemption should be granted.[45] The Commissioner of Food and Drugs appoints a presiding officer who has not been involved in the investigation or action that is the subject of the hearing and who is "free from bias or prejudice."[46]

The hearing is intended to afford parties an opportunity to present evidence and cross-examine the government's witnesses. The procedure does not, however, provide for the full range of protections available to a litigant in a trial-type adversarial proceeding. For example, a manufacturer has no right to call agency staff as witnesses, even though they may have information helpful to the manufacturer's case. Because the Federal Rules of Evidence do not apply to these administrative proceedings, the authenticity and reliability of the documents introduced may not be subject to meaningful challenge. Despite the procedural infirmities in these hearings, however, they afford the manufacturer a means of contesting a CDRH determination that a product is defective or noncompliant, or of showing that an exemption from corrective action should be granted.

Once the FDA determines that an electronic product contains a defect or fails to comply with an applicable standard and that notification must be given to first purchasers, the EPRC provisions prescribe three alternative remedies. A manufacturer may be required to, 1) repair a product by making it conform to the applicable standard or correcting the defect without charge; 2) replace a product with an equivalent product that does comply with the applicable standard and contains no defect; or 3) refund the purchase price upon return of the product.[47] Regulations set forth in detail the requirements for remedying a defective or noncomplying product, including the procedure for obtaining CDRH approval of a manufacturer's "plan" for repair, replacement, or refund.[48]

■ Inspections, Records, and Reports

To ensure compliance by manufacturers with the EPRC provisions and the regulations established by CDRH, the FDA is authorized to inspect the facilities and procedures used by a manufacturer that relate to the radiation emissions of electronic products.[49] In addition, manufacturers are required to keep records, file reports with CDRH, and provide other information that may be required by CDRH.[50] The record keeping and reporting requirements vary with the nature of the electronic product. Generally they include a requirement that CDRH be notified prior to the marketing of an electronic product, and that a manufacturer retain records of quality control testing procedures and results, as they pertain to radiation emissions. CDRH has also promulgated regulations requiring dealers and distributors to supply manufacturers with the names and addresses of the initial purchasers of their products for use in the event that a manufacturer is required to give notice of a defective or violative product.[51]

---

[45]   *Id.* This hearing is held pursuant to the rules in 21 C.F.R. pt. 16.

[46]   21 C.F.R. § 16.42.

[47]   FDCA § 535 (f)(1)-(3), 21 U.S.C. § 360ll(f)(1)-(3).

[48]   21 C.F.R. § 1004.1-.6.

[49]   FDCA § 537 (a), 21 U.S.C. § 360nn(a).

[50]   *Id.* § 537(b), 21 U.S.C. § 360nn(b).

[51]   21 C.F.R. § 1002.40.

All of CDRH's regulations regarding record keeping and reports were substantially revised in 1995 to reduce the regulatory burden on manufacturers.[52] The revised regulations eliminated the need for some reports and reduced the amount of information required in other reports.

■ Prohibited Acts and Penalties

CDRH is authorized to seek injunctions (through the Department of Justice) against manufacturers to restrain violations of the requirements of the EPRC provisions.[53] CDRH may also seek injunctions against dealers or distributors to restrain them from selling or otherwise disposing of noncomplying electronic products.[54]

Noncompliance with any one of the requirements of the EPRC provisions regarding a performance standard; certification; notification; the duty to repair, replace, or refund; or the obligation to keep records or permit inspections is punishable by a judicially imposed civil penalty of not more than $1000 for each violation and product in question, not to exceed $300,000 for a series of related violations.[55] For the purpose of determining a manufacturer's maximum civil liability, each noncomplying or defective electronic product and each unlawful act or omission constitutes a separate violation of the provisions.[56] It is important to keep in mind that the EPRC Provisions contain no criminal penalties; while the FDA may use the criminal penalty provisions of the FDCA for violations regarding electronic products that are also medical devices, no such remedy exists for nonmedical electronic products.

Implementation of the EPRC Provisions

■ Judicial Enforcement

CDRH has seldom chosen to exercise its authority through litigation. Although the EPRC provisions became effective in 1968, the first lawsuit brought by CDRH to enforce the provisions did not occur until 1974. Between January 1, 1974, and January 1, 1996, approximately thirty-two judicial enforcement actions were filed by CDRH under the provisions.[57] Two were suits for an injunction, fourteen sought both a civil penalty and an

---

[52] 60 Fed. Reg. 48,374 (1995).

[53] FDCA § 539, 21 U.S.C. § 360pp.

[54] *Id.*

[55] FDCA §§ 538, 539 (b)(1), 21 U.S.C. §§ 360oo, 360pp(b)(1).

[56] *Id.* § 539 (b)(1), 21 U.S.C. § 360pp(b)(1).

[57] Summary of CDRH/FDA Completed Litigation (Jan. 1, 1982) and excerpts from Annual Reports to Congress on EPRC provisions.

injunction, and the remaining cases sought only a civil penalty.[58] All but three of these actions were settled before trial. The three litigated cases were *United States v. Hodges X-Ray, Inc.*,[59] *Throneberry v. United States Food and Drug Administration*,[60] and *United States v. DeHaven and Assoc., Inc.*[61]

In *Hodges* and *DeHaven*, the FDA sought civil penalties due to x-ray machine manfacturers' violations of the EPRC provisions. In both cases the defendants were unable to show they were not required to comply with the EPRC provisions or to provide any evidence to contradict the FDA. Accordingly, civil penalties were awarded in both cases.[62] In *Hodges*, the court of appeals also upheld the ruling that the district court, under the EPRC provisions, was not required to hold a separate hearing to determine the amount of civil penalties to be assessed.[63]

In *Throneberry*, plaintiffs sued the FDA for a declaration that the FDA's performance standard for sunlamp products did not apply to suntan booths that were manufactured and assembled before the effective date of the standard, but that were then disassembled and reassembled after that date. The FDA counterclaimed, charging various violations of the EPRC provisions. Although finding that the FDA had shown violations of the provisions, the court ruled that the installation of suntan booths, after the effective date of the performance standard, did not result in the "manufacture" of products.[64]

One reason for the paucity of lawsuits in this area is that the Bureau of Radiological Health had a non-adversarial relationship with manufacturers and utilized TEPRSSC, which included industry representatives, to develop performance standards. Now that there is no longer an identifiable center within the FDA exclusively dedicated to radiological health, it is likely that the amount of litigation concerning radiation control issues will be more comparable to the rest of the agency.

■ Administrative Proceedings

Manufacturers of electronic products have historically been very reluctant to challenge CDRH's compliance authority. From the enactment of the EPRC provisions in 1968, the

---

58 *See, e.g.,* U.S. DEPT. OF HEALTH AND HUMAN SERV., 1990 ANNUAL REPORT ON THE ADMINISTRATION OF THE RADIATION CONTROL FOR HEALTH AND SAFETY ACT OF 1968, PUBLIC LAW 90-602, at 28 ($24,000 civil penalty assessed against X-Ray Products, Inc. and Global X-Ray Products, Inc.) [reports in this series are hereinafter cited as ANNUAL REPORT]; 1987 ANNUAL REPORT sec.VIII ($18,000 civil penalty assessed against City X-Ray Company); 1986 ANNUAL REPORT, at 28 ($18,000 penalty assessed against Hodges X-Ray, Inc.; and a complaint requesting $90,000 for civil penalties filed against City X-Ray Co.); 1985 ANNUAL REPORT at 28-29 ($10,000 civil penalty assessed against CGR Medical Corporation (MA); $33,000 civil penalty assessed against CGR Medical Products (NY); $6900 civil penalty assessed against X-Ray of Greenville; $2000 civil penalty assessed against Shiring X-Ray Corp.; and $16,000 civil penalty assessed against General Electric Co.); 1984 ANNUAL REPORT 31 ($50,000 civil penalty assessed against CGR Med. Corp. (MD)); 1983 ANNUAL REPORT 23 ($15,000 civil penalty assessed against Rubinstein Dental Equipment Corp.; (in separate actions) $33,000 and $10,000 civil penalties assessed against CGR Med. Prods.); and personal correspondence with the FDA, Oct. 22, 1996 (approximately $70,000 assessed against Control Laser Corp.).

59 582 F. Supp. 35 (W.D. Ky. 1983), *rev'd in part*, 759 F.2d 557 (6th Cir. 1985).

60 Food Drug Cosm. L. Rep. (CCH) ¶ 15,065 (E.D. Tenn. Nov. 3, 1983).

61 Med. Device Rep. (CCH) ¶ 15,302 (E.D. La. Feb. 12, 1996).

62 In *DeHaven* the court also granted injunctive relief. *Id.* ¶ 15,660.

63 *Hodger*, 759 F.2d at 560.

64 *Throneberry*, Food Drug Cosm. L. Rep. (CCH) ¶ 14,430.

FDA has been required to participate in only two adversarial administrative proceedings, both of which occurred in the early years after enactment. Only once was a hearing conducted pursuant to the FDA's procedural regulations.[65]

The first administrative proceeding under the EPRC provisions resulted in the recall of more than 400,000 color television sets imported and sold by Matsushita Electric Corporation, J.C. Penney Company, and W.T. Grant Company.[66] All of these television sets were manufactured by the Matsushita Electric Industrial Company in Japan. CDRH charged that the sets did not comply with the performance standard for TV receivers because they were capable of emitting radiation in excess of the allowable exposure limit under certain conditions. CDRH asserted that, if a particular component in the television receiver were to fail, the voltage would rise on the picture tube, although the receiver would continue to display a picture, and the applicable emission limits would be exceeded.

All three firms applied for an exemption from corrective action on the ground that no significant risk of injury to users was presented. The companies attempted to prove that purchasers would not be exposed to excessive radiation because it was extremely unlikely that the components in question would fail. In support, they showed that there was no evidence that the components had ever failed in use. Nonetheless, the CDRH Director ruled that the manufacturers[67] had failed to meet the burden of proving that the components in question would not fail, and therefore did not establish that the television sets presented no significant risk of injury to any person.[68] The FDA, therefore, denied the exemption request, and the manufacturers were required to submit corrective action plans in which they agreed to repair noncompliant sets. The manufacturers chose not to seek judicial review.

In the second proceeding, the General Electric Company contested CDRH's determination that certain microwave ovens it had manufactured did not comply with the performance standard because some of the ovens leaked microwave radiation in excess of the standard.[69] The hearing officer held, in a decision approved by the Commissioner, that General Electric's microwave ovens did not comply with the federal performance standard.[70] General Electric then applied for an exemption from notification and corrective action. CDRH rejected this request because General Electric had failed to prove that no person would or could be injured from emissions in excess of the federal performance standard.[71] Ultimately, General Electric submitted a corrective action plan for the repair of 36,000 microwave ovens.

---

[65] Both proceedings were conducted before the regulations under 21 C.F.R. pt. 16 became final. The General Electric hearing, discussed *infra* notes 71-73, was conducted pursuant to part 16 by agreement of the parties. *See also* Ronald J. Greene, *Informal FDA Hearing*, 32 FOOD DRUG COSM. L.J. 354 (1977).

[66] For a report of the hearing and the surrounding events, see Walter Gundaker, *Getting the Picture on TV Recall*, FDA CONSUMER, Mar. 1975, at 9-13.

[67] Importers are included within the definition of "manufacturer." FDCA § 531 (3), 21 U.S.C. § 360hh(3).

[68] CDRH has the burden of proving that products are defective or violative. The manufacturer has the burden of demonstrating that an exemption should be granted. FDCA § 535 (a) (2), 21 U.S.C.§ 360ll(a)(2).

[69] *See* Ronald J. Greene, *supra* note 66.

[70] [1975-1977 Transfer Binder] Consumer Prod. Safety Guide (CCH) ¶ 43,238 (Jan. 1977).

[71] Letter from John C. Villforth, Dir., CDRH, to Ronald Greene, Counsel, General Electric Co. (Aug. 13, 1976).

These cases demonstrate that the FDA will interpret the statutory provision for exemptions from the applicable performance standard narrowly. Once an issue has progressed to the hearing stage, manufacturers of noncomplying or defective products face an almost insurmountable hurdle in attempting to prove that an exemption should be granted.[72] This is in large measure because they are faced with proving a negative—that no significant risk of injury, including genetic injury, exists for any person.

■ Unresolved Issues in Enforcement

From time to time, there have been discussions within CDRH, the FDA, and DHHS about whether the EPRC provisions were adequate to achieve their intended purposes or should be amended to give the agency additional regulatory authority. Currently, the FDA has the authority to regulate medical devices that use radiation under four different statutory regimes: The Medical Device Amendments of 1976 as amended by the SMDA of 1990, the EPRC provisions of the FDCA, the Consumer-Patient Radiation Health and Safety Act of 1981, and the Mammography Quality Standards Act of 1992.[73] Despite the breadth of the above laws, concerns about radiological dangers persist.

In 1993, Senator John Glenn held a hearing before the Committee on Governmental Affairs to examine federal regulation of medical radiation uses.[74] Senator Glenn convened the hearing after a serious accident occurred involving radiation therapy devices. During radiation therapy, the tip of a radioactive source wire broke off and was left inside the patient.[75] The patient died five days later after suffering extreme exposure to radiation.[76] Senator Glenn, fearing that similar accidents were possible, expressed concern that due to "the recent dramatic growth in medical radiation use over recent years, major questions have been raised as to whether Federal and state regulation provides an adequate margin of protection of public health and the rights of those who may be put at risk."[77]

The FDA, however, maintains that the regulation of medical uses of radiation therapy is adequate. In the preamble to a final rule amending performance standards for diagnostic x-ray systems, the FDA responded to similar concerns that its level of regulation was less than adequate.[78] The FDA maintained that in regulating equipment used for medical purposes, because the use produces a medical benefit, the FDA will weigh the benefit against the risk of exposure when the agency promulgates standards.[79] Indeed, the FDA has specifically recognized that it has additional flexibility in setting standards for medical devices which emit radiation, if the radiation is intended to be used to produce a medical benefit.[80]

---

[72] Many cases are disposed of prior to the hearing stage by the granting of an exemption where scientifically appropriate.

[73] Pub. L. No. 102-539, 106 Stat. 3547 (codified at 42 U.S.C. §§ 201 note, 263b, 263b note).

[74] *Federal Regulation of Medical Radiation Uses: Hearing Before the Comm. on Governmental Affairs*, 103d Cong., 1st Sess. (1993) [hereinafter *Radiation Hearing*].

[75] *FDA Seizes Omnitron 2000 Radiation Therapy Device*, RADIOLOGICAL HEALTH BULLETIN 2 Summer (1993).

[76] *Id.* The FDA and the Nuclear Regulatory Commission investigated the manufacturer following this incident and an unrelated incident. The FDA seized the high dose radiation devices and prohibited the company from distributing the devices until appropriate corrective actions were taken. *Id.*

[77] *Radiation Hearing, supra* note 75, at 4.

[78] 58 Fed. Reg. 26,386 (May 3, 1993).

[79] *Id.*

[80] *Id.* at 26,386-87.

However, despite the continued concern, it is generally agreed that CDRH has sufficient authority to protect the public from the dangers of excessive radiation emitted by electronic products.[81] This is particularly true for medical devices because the broad authority conferred on the FDA by the Medical Device Amendments and the SMDA supplements CDRH authority under the EPRC provisions.[82]

A number of unresolved questions about the applicability of the EPRC provisions and their implementation by CDRH remain. One major issue with which CDRH has wrestled on occasion, but left unanswered, is whether a manufacturer's obligation to repair or replace a defective or noncomplying product without charge or to refund the purchase price should extend for the entire life of the product. The EPRC provisions provide no guidance on this point.[83] The FDA has stated, however, that, if normal product wear results in radiation emissions in excess of the limit prescribed in a standard, the manufacturer may be cited for noncompliance because of its failure to design the product to maintain an acceptable level of radiation leakage throughout the product's useful life.[84] Industry sources argue that to hold a manufacturer liable for normal wear and tear runs counter to common commercial and regulatory practice, and imposes unnecessarily high costs. These costs are then passed on to consumers.

Furthermore, CDRH has never attempted to quantify what percentage of the total products produced that deviate from the standard it considers to present an unacceptable level of risk. If, for example, it could be shown that only one in 10,000 units of a particular electronic product might emit excess radiation, would that be sufficient to declare the entire product line defective or violative? To a great extent, this is an issue that can be intelligently addressed only on a case-by-case basis. CDRH must be able to evaluate not only the ratio of violative products to the total number of products produced, but also the degree of risk to a purchaser that would be caused by the potential emission. These two factors must be balanced against the cost to the manufacturer of corrective action. In the General Electric case, CDRH demonstrated that approximately two percent of the company's microwave ovens were noncomplying; General Electric argued that the rate of noncompliance was between one-half and one percent. The FDA held that the entire product line was noncomplying in part because the state-of-the-art in preventing radiation leakage was substantially better than that demonstrated by General Electric.

The section of the statute concerning civil penalties is somewhat unusual. As previously noted, the provisions give the U.S. district courts authority to impose civil penalties of up

---

[81] Conversation with Walter Gundaker, then Dir., Off. of Compliance, CDRH, FDA (Nov.12, 1988). Besides the 1993 hearing on federal regulation of medical radiation uses, there have been other congressional oversight hearings on radiation in the last several years: *The Effects of Traffic Radar Guns on Law Enforcement Officers, Hearing Before the Comm. on Governmental Affairs*, 102d Cong., 2d Sess. (1992). *Do Cellular and Other Wireless Devices Interfere With the Operation of Medical Equipment?*, *Hearing Before the Comm. on Gov't Operations Subcomm. on Information, Justice, Trans. and Agric.*, 103rd Cong. 2d sess. (1994). *Handheld Cellular Telephones and the Possible Health Risks Posed by Radio Frequency Radiation; Briefing Before the Comm. on Energy and Commerce Subcomm. on Telecommunications and Finance*, 103rd Cong. 1st Sess. (1993).

[82] Pub. L. No. 94-295, § 2, 90 Stat. 539, 552 (codified at 21 U.S.C. §§ 360e-360k).

[83] In contrast, the repair, replacement, and refund provision of the FDCA, FDCA § 518 (b)(2)(C), 21 U.S.C. § 360h(b)(2)(C), permits a manufacturer who elects to refund the purchase price of a medical device to deduct "a reasonable allowance for use if such device has been in the possession of the device user for one year or more . . . ."

[84] Compliance Policy Guide § 390.200 (Mar. 1995).

to $1000 per violation and not more than $300,000 for any related series of violations.[85] However, the provisions also provide that any civil penalty may be remitted or mitigated by the Secretary of DHHS,[86] thus permitting the Secretary to, in effect, modify a court decision. This differs from the scheme applicable to medical devices under the SMDA of 1990. There, the maximum penalty per violation is $15,000, or $1,000,000 per proceeding; the penalty may be assessed by an Administrative Law Judge after a hearing under part 16.[87] Those penalties are then appealable first within DHHS and then to federal court.[88]

CDRH has stated that it will seek civil penalties even without prior warning in cases of serious violations that could result in significant adverse health risks or that show intentional disregard of the law.[89] Serious violations of the provisions include, failure to notify CDRH of a product that contains a defect or fails to comply with an applicable performance standard, issuing a knowingly false certification, and refusal to initiate corrective action such as a recall when properly notified of the need for such action by CDRH.[90] In cases of violations that do not threaten serious adverse health consequences or do not demonstrate an intentional disregard of the law, CDRH will seek civil penalties only after prior warning.[91] For instance, before CDRH would seek civil penalties against a company that fails to carry out a recall adequately because of incomplete distribution records, CDRH will first issue a written notification of noncompliance.[92] Finally, for violations that present little or no risk of danger, CDRH will not normally consider civil penalties, but will consider other regulatory or administrative actions, such as requiring correction of future production to avoid false certification, as prohibited by section 360oo (a)(5).[93]

While there have been instances in which the agency's lack of seizure authority in the radiation area could have resulted in increased public health problems, the presence of seizure authority under the Medical Device Amendments has been an adequate alternative, at least as to medical products that emit radiation. For example, in *Hodges*, the FDA's investigation revealed that a particular type of x-ray machine emitted excess radiation, but, because the manufacturer was no longer in business, CDRH could not look to the company to repair or replace the products. Because the products concerned were also medical devices, however, FDA was able to utilize its authority under the Medical Device Amendments.[94] Ultimately, there are a small number of consumer products for which the FDA

---

85   FDCA § 539 (b)(1), 21 U.S.C. § 360pp(b)(l).

86   Under similar provisions of the Consumer Product Safety Act, 15 U.S.C. § 2069 (1994), the courts have held that the Commission lacks authority to assess civil penalties administratively and must proceed through the courts. Athlone Industries, Inc. v. CPSC, 707 F.2d 1485 (D.C. Cir. 1983); Advance Machine Co. v. CPSC, 666 F.2d 1166 (8th Cir. 1981). The *Hodges* decision makes clear that, if the FDA goes to court, the district court is not required to hold a separate hearing to determine the amount of civil penalties to assess for violations for the EPRC provisions. 759 F.2d at 565.

87   FDCA § 303 (f), 21 U.S.C. §333(f).

88   21 C.F.R. §§ 17.47, 17.51.

89   Compliance Policy Guide No. 7133.23 (Mar. 1, 1983).

90   *Id.*

91   *Id.*

92   *Id.*

93   *Id.* Minor violations include failing to attach a label to a product permanently or failing to adequately explain a testing program in a manufacturer report.

94   *See, e.g.,* Med. Devices Rep. (CCH) ¶ 14,672 (Dec. 19, 1979).

lacks seizure authority, but for these products the repair, replacement, or refund section of the EPRC provisions has generally been an adequate remedy.

In sum, it appears that in most cases, CDRH's statutory authority has been adequate. In the nearly thirty years the EPRC provisions have been in effect, FDA has rarely asked the courts to enforce them. This virtual absence of judicial intervention bespeaks CDRH's success in achieving compliance by manufacturers through careful development of standards and through reliance on the repair, replacement, or refund authority of the provisions.

Relation to Other Laws and Federal Agencies

The EPRC provisions are not the only federal legislation affecting manufacturers of electronic products. A number of other statutes, some enforced by other agencies, provide additional regulatory controls.

■ Medical Device Amendments of 1976,[95] the Safe Medical Devices Act of 1990,[96] and the Medical Device Amendments of 1992[97]

As mentioned above, radiation-emitting electronic products that are also medical devices[98] are regulated under the FDCA through the EPRC provisions and the Medical Device Amendments. These products include, but are not limited to, diagnostic x-ray equipment and ultrasonic therapy products. Other electronic products such as lasers are also regulated as medical devices under the Medical Device provisions of FDCA to the extent they are intended for use in the treatment or prevention of disease.[99] Regulation under the EPRC provisions, however, applies to all electronic radiation-emitting products regardless of their intended use.

Perhaps the major distinction between the Medical Device Amendments and the EPRC provisions is that, under the former, if a medical device is to be marketed, it must be safe and effective for its intended use. The purpose of the EPRC provisions, to protect the public from exposure to unnecessary emission of electronic product radiation, is a narrower regulatory mandate than that given under the medical device amendments to the FDCA. Arguably, an

---

[95] Pub. L. No. 94-295, § 2, 90 Stat. at 552.

[96] Pub. L. No. 101- 629, § 5, 104 Stat. at 4517-18.

[97] Pub. L. No. 102-300, § 6, 106 Stat. at 240.

[98] The term "device" is defined in part as an instrument, apparatus, implement, machine, contrivance, implant, in vitro reagent, or other similar or related article, including any component, part, or accessory, which is intended for use in the diagnosis of disease or other conditions, or in the cure, mitigation, treatment, or prevention of disease, in man or other animals, or intended to affect the structure or any function of the body of man or other animals. FDCA § 201 (h), 21 U.S.C. § 321(h).

[99] The legislative history of the Medical Device Amendments makes clear that, if a product is adequately regulated under another statute, including the EPRC provisions, the Medical Device Amendments were not intended to duplicate this regulation. H.R. REP. No. 853, 94th Cong., 2d Sess. 15 (1976). The FDA has attempted to adhere to congressional policy in this area.

x-ray machine that is ineffective because it fails to take x-rays of sufficient clarity to be diagnostically useful also would be defective or violative under the EPRC provisions because the machine would expose the patient to radiation without any offsetting benefit. CDRH has not, however, advanced this argument in any judicial or administrative proceeding.[100]

Following enactment of the Medical Device Amendments of 1976, the Bureau of Medical Devices was formed to develop and implement programs under the Medical Device Amendments. The BRH continued to be responsible for controlling electronic product radiation under the EPRC provisions,[101] even when the radiation was associated with a product that also qualified as a medical device.

In 1982, DHHS merged the Bureaus of Radiological Health and Medical Devices into a consolidated unit.[102] The notice that announced the merger stated that it was designed "to eliminate duplication of functions and [to] benefit the public through more efficient regulation based on sound science."[103] Although the two Bureaus had previously split their regulatory and enforcement responsibilities, all of these functions were consolidated into one unit within the reorganized CDRH. The responsibility for the enforcement of the EPRC provisions as with other statutes and laws rests with the Office of Compliance. Within that office, issues are currently referred to one of three respective enforcement divisions responsible for the product type. For example, diagnostic radiation devices and surgical lasers are entrusted to the Division of Enforcement I; ophthalmic lasers are entrusted to Division of Enforcement II; microwave ovens, non-medical lasers, and TVs are entrusted to Division of Enforcement III.

As previously noted, the overlap between the Medical Device Amendments and the EPRC provisions provides CDRH with additional methods of enforcement when an electronic product is also a medical device. Any medical device electronic product that is defective or noncompliant under the EPRC provisions also would probably be considered adulterated or misbranded under the FDCA. As a consequence, the FDA has the authority to institute a suit under the FDCA to seize the device.[104] Moreover, under this Act, the FDA has the authority to recommend that criminal proceedings be initiated against manufacturers of adulterated or misbranded devices.[105]

CDRH also may employ administrative remedies available under the Medical Device Amendments that are not found in the EPRC provisions. For example, the FDA administratively can detain a medical device that it believes to be adulterated or misbranded for up to twenty days to allow the Department of Justice time to file a seizure action.[106] Adminis-

---

[100] In the area of drugs, in contrast, courts have accepted the argument that drugs used to treat life-threatening conditions could not be "generally recognized as safe" unless they are both safe and effective. *See, e.g.,* Durovic v. Richardson, 479 F.2d 242 (7th Cir.), *cert. denied,* 414 U.S. 944 (1973).

[101] *See* 47 Fed. Reg. 15,412 (1982).

[102] Health and Human Serv., Press Release (July 12, 1982); 47 Fed. Reg. 44,614 (Oct. 8, 1982). Although the new unit was officially recognized in this notice as the Nat'l Ctr. for Devices and Radiological Health, the word "National" subsequently was removed from its title. 49 Fed. Reg. 10,166 (Mar. 19, 1984); 49 Fed. Reg. 14,931 (Apr. 16, 1984).

[103] 47 Fed. Reg. at 44,614 (1982).

[104] FDCA § 304, 21 U.S.C. § 334.

[105] *Id.* § 303, 21 U.S.C. § 333.

[106] The 20-day period may be extended for an additional ten days if necessary to accomplish a seizure. *Id.* § 304(g), 21 U.S.C. § 334(g).

trative detention is intended to eliminate the possibility that a product will disappear while the agency is reviewing evidence, obtaining internal approvals, and preparing the documents necessary for a seizure.

The SMDA of 1990 further expanded the FDA's regulatory authority over devices by adding civil penalties for violations of the FDCA relating to medical devices.[107] The SMDA also broadened the adverse incident reporting requirements to include user facilities and device distributors in addition to manufacturers.[108] Prior to the 1992 amendments to the SMDA, a "state-of-the-art" defense existed under the Medical Device Amendments that precluded the use of the repair, replace, or refund remedy for devices if they were manufactured according to the state-of-the-art. The existence of this defense made the EPRC provisions' "repair, replace, or refund" language easier to utilize. The 1992 amendments eliminated this defense, making the Medical Device Amendments section as easy to apply as the EPRC section,[109] although CDRH has still not relied upon this provision to any great extent in ordering medical device repairs, replacements, or refunds.

Prior to the SMDA, setting performance standards under the Medical Device Amendments of 1976 required the FDA to navigate a course through many procedural obstacles. The SMDA simplified the performance standard setting process for devices and made it more akin to the notice-and-comment rulemaking system under the EPRC provisions.[110] As of 1968, the FDA has promulgated fourteen performance standards under the EPRC provisions,[111] but has yet to promulgate a single performance standard under the Medical Device Amendments.[112]

Finally, 21 U.S.C. § 360ii (FDCA § 532) gives CDRH broad authority to conduct research in radiation control, to maintain a liaison with interested public and private groups, to disseminate educational material, and even to provide grants to promote studies in radiation control. This provision contrasts with the limited authority under the publicity provision of the FDCA,[113] which expressly authorizes the FDA to disseminate only information covering court decrees, imminent danger to health, or gross deception of the consumer.

CDRH officials believe that the two statutes have been administered in a manner that has minimized inconsistent and duplicative regulations. Because of the inclusion of an efficacy requirement, the Medical Device Amendments now essentially control the regulation of radiation-emitting medical products. Apparently, the only area of duplication that has raised some concern in the regulated industry is the interaction between the initial reports filed under the EPRC provisions for diagnostic x-ray equipment,[114] and the premarket

---

[107] *Id.* § 303(f), 21 U.S.C. § 333(f).

[108] *Id.* § 519(a), (b), 21 U.S.C. § 360i(a), (b).

[109] *Id.* § 518(b), 21 U.S.C.. § 360h(b).

[110] *See id.* § 514, 21 U.S.C. § 360d.

[111] 21 C.F.R. pts. 1010-1050. Center officials believe there will be few, if any, additional standards because technology is changing so rapidly that any standard would be obsolete before it is published.*See supra* note 103.

[112] As of the passage of the SMDA two performance standards have been proposed for medical devices. *See* 60 Fed. Reg. 32,406 (June 21, 1995) (proposed performance standard for electrode lead wires) and 60 Fed. Reg. 9762 (Feb. 21, 1995) (proposed performance standard for infant apnea monitors).

[113] FDCA § 705, 21 U.S.C. § 375.

[114] *Id.* § 537, 21 U.S.C. § 360nn; 21 C.F.R. § 1002.10. *See supra* note 103.

notifications filed under section 510(k) of the Medical Device Amendments.[115] CDRH officials do not believe, however, that this overlap is of major consequence because the submissions are quite different and have dissimilar purposes.

■ Mammography Quality Standards Act of 1992

In response to heightened awareness of breast cancer and the benefits of early detection, Congress passed the Mammography Quality Standards Act of 1992 (MQSA) to regulate the use of mammography equipment and the interpretation of mammograms and to establish standards for equipment used in conjunction with mammography, including radiological equipment.[116] The MQSA requires facilities that perform mammograms to meet quality standards and to be accredited by the FDA or an FDA approved inspection team.[117]

A mammogram can be an extremely difficult radiographic image to read due to the quality of the image or the training of the interpreter.[118] The MQSA is designed to improve detection by establishing national quality standards regulating the activities of the facility using mammography equipment.[119] These standards provide for the accreditation of facilities, on-site annual inspections of facilities, qualification standards for those who interpret the mammograms, and for related record keeping.[120] A facility must meet the standards in order to lawfully operate.[121]

To implement the MQSA, the Secretary of DHHS was required to promulgate regulations by October 1, 1994, establishing standards for accrediting bodies and the regulated facilities.[122] Recognizing that the FDA would not be able to meet the statutory deadline, Congress granted interim rulemaking authority to the FDA to address the immediate public health need until the standards are developed.[123] The FDA has twice used the interim rulemaking authority — December 21, 1993 and September 30, 1994.[124] The interim regulations have been used to provide facilities with a reasonable length of time to adapt to the increased regulation while balancing the need for improved mammography services.[125] However, at this time, the FDA still has not set comprehensive standards.[126] The FDA has stated that the final regulations are expected in 1997.[127]

---

[115] FDCA § 510(k), 21 U.S.C. § 360(k).

[116] In a related area, in 1985, the Health Resources and Service Administration of DHHS, in conjunction with CDRH, issued a final regulation that established minimum standards for the accreditation of radiological training programs and certification of equipment operators. The standards, which are voluntary for states and mandatory for federal agencies, were required by the Consumer-Patient Radiation Health and Safety Act of 1981, and were intended to reduce unnecessary exposure to radiation for medical and dental procedures.

[117] *Id.*

[118] 61 Fed. Reg. 14,856 (Apr. 3, 1996).

[119] *Id.*

[120] *Id.* at 14,857-58.

[121] *Id.* at 14,856.

[122] 38 Fed. Reg. 67,559 (Dec. 21, 1993) (codified at 21 C.F.R. §§ 900.1-900.7, 900.10-900.14, 900.18).

[123] 61 Fed. Reg. 14,857 (Apr. 3, 1996) (codified at 21 C.F.R. §§ 900.1-900.7, 900.10 - 900.15, 900.18).

[124] *Id.*

[125] *Id.*

[126] Due to the seriousness of breast cancer, there has been concern over the length of time the FDA has taken to finalize the rules. *See Lawmaker prods FDA to implement standards of mammography quality*, Washington Times, June 13, 1996.

[127] FDA Proposes Final Mammography Standards, FDA Talk Paper, (Mar. 29, 1996).

As of April 1996, the FDA estimated that of the more than 10,000 facilities providing mammography services, the majority had received full accreditation and certification under the interim regulations.[128] The FDA estimates that between October 1993 and October 1994, 427 mammography facilities closed for various reasons.[129] Those reasons include failure to apply for certification, voluntary closure, and failure to complete the accreditation and certification process.[130] By April 1995, another 340 facilities had closed.[131] The FDA had conducted 7,265 inspections of mammography facilities by February 1996.[132]

The MQSA provides for up to $10,000 in civil penalties for failure to comply with the act.[133] The MQSA also allows for the suspension or revocation of a certification where the facility has been involved in misrepresentation in obtaining a certificate, has failed to update the information required to receive a certificate, or fails to comply with government requests for more information or for permission to inspect a mammography facility.[134]

Although the MQSA establishes national standards for the use of mammography equipment, the MQSA does not preempt all state activity in the regulatory area.[135] However, a state law must be at least as stringent as the MQSA.[136] In addition to providing for state regulation of mammography standards, the MQSA also allows state involvement by permitting states to become certifying bodies.[137] As the accreditation body, the state will perform the accreditation inspection and then charge the mammography facility for the review.[138] The MQSA also allows states to carry out the annual inspections on behalf of the FDA and to seek reimbursement from the FDA.[139]

The FDA anticipates that the compliance cost to the facilities will reach $61.4 million annually.[140] It is estimated that the increase will raise the cost per screening by two to six percent.[141] If passed on to the consumer, the increased cost may reduce the demand for mammograms.[142] However, the FDA maintains that the improvement in the quality and the interpretation of the mammograms will more than offset the increased cost.[143]

---

[128] 61 Fed. Reg. 14,858.

[129] Id.

[130] Id.

[131] Id.

[132] Id.

[133] 42 U.S.C. § 263b(h).

[134] Id. § 263b(I).

[135] 61 Fed. Reg. 14, 858.

[136] Id.

[137] 42 U.S.C. § 263b(q).

[138] 61 Fed. Reg. 14,858.

[139] 42 U.S.C. § 263b(g).

[140] 61 Fed. Reg. 14,864.

[141] Id.

[142] Id.

[143] Id.

■ Consumer Product Safety Commission

CDRH also shares jurisdiction over some products with the Consumer Product Safety Commission (CPSC). The Consumer Product Safety Act (CPSA)[144] regulates consumer products, including those that emit radiation.[145] The definition of "consumer product," however, specifically excludes medical devices.[146] Therefore, products regulated under the Medical Device Amendments are exempt from regulation under the CPSA.[147]

Products that are subject to regulation under both the CPSA and the EPRC provisions include televisions and microwave ovens. Because the CPSA is patterned after the EPRC provisions, the methods of enforcing compliance available to the CPSC are essentially identical to those available to CDRH.

The CPSC is empowered to require a manufacturer to repair, replace, or refund the price of consumer products that fail to comply with a consumer product safety rule or that contain a defect creating a substantial risk of injury to the public.[148] Civil penalties may also be assessed for violations.[149] Unlike the EPRC provisions, the CPSA provides for imposition of criminal sanctions and for the seizure of noncompliant consumer products.[150] No seizure provision exists, however, for defective consumer products.[151]

In practice, the CPSC defers to CDRH on matters relating to the emission of radiation from consumer products. Indeed, in recent years, with the reduction of funding and staffing levels at the CPSC, this tendency has been reinforced. No memorandum of understanding encompasses this regulatory agreement. Rather, CDRH and the CPSC communicate informally to keep informed of matters of mutual interest.

■ Nuclear Regulatory Commission

CDRH and the Nuclear Regulatory Commission (NRC) have overlapping responsibility for regulating radiation therapy systems. These systems use radioactive materials, such as cobalt 60, in the diagnosis and treatment of medical conditions, especially cancer. Although the NRC has no authority to regulate medical products, it does have responsibil-

---

[144] 15 U.S.C. §§ 2051-2084.

[145] *Id.* § 2052(a)(l). A "consumer product" is "any article, or component part thereof, produced or distributed (i) for sale to a consumer for use in or around a permanent or temporary household or residence, a school, in recreation, or otherwise, or (ii) for the personal use, consumption or enjoyment of a consumer in or around a permanent or temporary household or residence, a school, in recreation, or otherwise. . . ." *Id.*

[146] *Id.* § 2052(a)(l)(H).

[147] Although medical devices are not regulated by the CPSC, the FDA and the CPSC have engaged in limited joint efforts to monitor medical devices that emit radiation. For a number of years, the FDA participated in the CPSC's National Electronic Injury Surveillance System (NEISS) to obtain voluntarily-supplied information from hospitals regarding a few medical devices and radiation-emitting products which caused injury. Under the terms of this interagency project, the CPSC was paid a fee for use of its Surveillance System. The partnership terminated in 1986, but the CPSC continues to collect data on medical devices. However, without a cost sharing arrangement with the FDA, the the CPSC cannot supply the FDA with the data. The FDA has expressed interest in reactivating its participation in the NEISS program in the future should additional funds become available.

[148] 15 U.S.C. § 2064(d).

[149] *Id.* § 2069.

[150] *Id.* §§ 2070, 2071.

[151] *See id.* § 2071(b).

ity to license physicians and hospitals or other facilities that use nuclear material for medical therapy.[152] Also, because radiation therapy systems are apparatuses used in the treatment of disease, they are medical devices and therefore subject to regulation under the FDCA.[153] Radiation therapy systems are not, however, ordinarily considered to be electronic products, and therefore CDRH does not regulate them under the EPRC provisions; rather, CDRH regulates their use under the Medical Device Amendments.

No formal agreement outlines the respective responsibilities of the NRC and CDRH in the area of electronic product radiation therapy. Rather, the two organizations exchange data on radiation hazards informally and share knowledge of incidents in which patients have been overexposed to radiation. If regulatory action is warranted because of radiation leakage or patient overexposure, the NRC typically defers to CDRH. It does so because CDRH has a wider choice of regulatory methods under the Medical Device Amendments than does the NRC under its statutory authority.[154] For nonradiation problems concerning radiation therapy systems, CDRH has sole responsibility for appropriate regulatory action because the NRC's authority is limited to radioactive materials.

While no formal arrangement exists between CDRH and the NRC regarding radiation-emitting electronics, in 1993 the FDA and the NRC signed a Memorandum of Understanding (MOU) to coordinate the regulatory programs of the two agencies as they relate to medical devices, drugs, and biological products which utilize byproduct, source, or special nuclear materials regulated by the Atomic Energy Act of 1954.[155] In the MOU the agencies agree to inform each other, through assigned contact persons, whenever either group receives a report on or becomes aware of a radiation public health problem. The agencies also agreed to coordinate investigations, upon request, and to exchange information with respect to investigations. Finally, the two agencies also agreed to exchange information about pending technologies for which regulations have yet to be developed and to allow inter-agency comment on special notifications to manufacturers, operators, licensees, or patients.

■ Environmental Protection Agency

The Administrator of the Environmental Protection Agency (EPA) is charged to "advise the President with respect to radiation matters, directly or indirectly affecting health, including guidance for all Federal agencies in the formulation of radiation standards and in the establishment and execution of programs of cooperation with States."[156] The EPA is, therefore, technically the lead federal agency in establishing federal policy on radiation.

---

[152] 42 U.S.C. § 2134. The NRC has published detailed regulations covering the medical use of radioactive by-product material. 10 C.F.R. pt. 35 (1997). The NRC has transferred its licensing authority to states that have agreed to assume responsibility for regulating certain radioactive materials within their borders. These states are known as "Agreement States."

[153] There is also considerable overlap between NRC's licensing authority over radioactive byproduct material and the FDA's authority to regulate drugs, including radiopharmaceuticals.

[154] NRC can obtain injunctive relief or civil penalties for violation of its licensing requirements, 10 C.F.R. § 35.990(a), (b), and criminal penalties for any willful violation, *id.* § 35.990(c). The FDA can, of course, detain and seize violative products, 21 U.S.C. § 334, in addition to obtaining injunctive relief, *id.* §332, and criminal penalties, *id.* § 333.

[155] 58 Fed. Reg. 47,300 (Sept. 8, 1993).

[156] Federal Radiation Council Authority, Pub. L. No. 86-373, 73 Stat. 688 (1959), transferred to EPA by Reorganization Plan No. 3 of 1970, as codified at 42 U.S.C. § 2021(h).

However, the EPA generally has not attempted to regulate medical devices or electronic products that are within CDRH's jurisdiction. For example, in 1986, the EPA proposed recommendations on limiting public exposure to radio frequency radiation.[157] Consumer products that emit radiation are typically regulated by CDRH through performance standards. The EPA recognized CDRH's statutory authority in this area and made the following statement, which typifies the EPA's deference to CDRH on regulatory matters in this field:

> [FDA] did not want any EPA Guidance to conflict with their responsibilities for developing product performance standards. EPA proposes, therefore, to exclude from consideration those exposures of the public resulting from electronic consumer products. Certain electronic consumer products may cause exposures that exceed the various limits discussed in this Notice, but any such exposures might be more readily controlled by product performance standards.[158]

Even though other agencies, such as the Federal Communications Commission, regulate radiation to a certain extent, CDRH is clearly the predominant agency in the field of radiological control concerning medical and consumer products.

Developments in Radiation Control

The need to ensure the safety of electronic products that emit radiation is a matter of ongoing concern to both regulators and legislators. Over the years, CDRH has revised the performance standards for microwave ovens,[159] laser products,[160] sunlamps,[161] and diagnostic x-ray systems, including fluoroscopic x-ray equipment.[162]

In recent years, CDRH has undertaken several initiatives involving the regulation of electronic products. These have included the following:

- An amendment to the performance standard for fluoroscopic equipment, in response to concerns that patients may be exposed to unnecessary and excessive radiation during fluoroscopically guided procedures.[163] The FDA was concerned about severe injuries during long periods of use, as well as injuries that might result from typical dosages,

---

[157] 51 Fed. Reg. 27,318 (July 30, 1986).

[158] *Id.* at 27,321. *See also* Med. Devices Rep. (CCH) ¶ 17,927 (Nov. 1986).

[159] 48 Fed. Reg. 57,481 (Dec. 30, 1983). The preamble to the 1983 amendments to the microwave oven standard shows that CDRH made a considerable effort to achieve agreement with the microwave industry on changes to the standard. *Id.* at 57,481-82.

[160] 50 Fed. Reg. 33,682 (Aug. 20, 1985). Among other things, the 1985 amendments to the laser products performance standard broadened the wavelength range that defines laser radiation and established a new "Class IIIa" laser product. The amendments also relaxed certain performance requirements relating to safety interlocks, viewing optics, remote control connectors, emission delay, key controls, and beam attenuators.

[161] 50 Fed. Reg. 36,548 (Sept. 6, 1985).

[162] 58 Fed. Reg. 26,386 (May 3, 1993); 59 Fed. Reg. 26,402 (May 19, 1994).

[163] 59 Fed. Red. 26,402 (May 19, 1994).

where inadequate protocols for patient treatment existed.[164] As part of this initiative, the agency sent letters to medical professional societies and hospitals warning of the dangers that could occur during these procedures and suggesting steps to minimize the risks.[165]

- Monitoring, in cooperation with the affected industries, the effects of electromagnetic radiation interference on medical equipment. Products that can emit electromagnetic interference (EMI) include cellular telephones, and various radio frequency and television transmitters. Between 1979 and 1993, more than 100 incidents of EMI were reported to the agency; these included incidents such as static on computer screens, a powered wheelchair that made quick and sudden movements, injuring the occupant, and a failed pacemaker.[166]

- Evaluating the risks of new technologies, such as cellular telephones, which were alleged to play a possible role in the development of brain cancer. After completing a review of the issue, tissue the FDA concluded that there was no conclusive evidence that cellular telephones contributed to adverse health effects.[167]

- Addressing new uses of existing technologies. For example, in recent years, diagnostic ultrasound equipment has been used to make "keepsake" videos of fetuses. The FDA has been unequivocal in its opposition to this practice, which it views as an unapproved use of a medical device which needlessly exposes a fetus to radiation for no therapeutic purpose. The FDA has also taken action to protect the air transportation community from visual impairment of pilots from exposure to laser light shows. As a result of more than fifty incidents that occurred in the Las Vegas area in a two-year period, a number of which were in critical or sensitive phases of flight, and ten of which resulted in visual impairment of pilots, the FDA, under its various procedures, declared a moratorium on outdoor laser displays in Clark County, Nevada.[168]

- Increasing vigilance over imported consumer products. In recent years, manufacturing sites for television receivers and microwave ovens have shifted in significant numbers to the Far East. Although less costly designs and manufacturing processes have saved money for consumers, there are serious questions about whether many of these products are manufactured with sufficient durability to meet the FDA standards over their useful life, or indeed, in the case of TV receivers, even meet them at the time of manufacture.[169]

---

[164] FDA Pub. Health Advisory: Avoidance of Serious X-Ray-Induced Skin Injuries to Patients During Fluoroscopically-Guided Procedures (Sept. 30, 1994).

[165] *Fluoroscopically Guided Procedures Have Potential for Skin Injury*, FDA QUARTERLY ACTIVITY REP., FOURTH QUARTER, FISCAL YEAR 1994, at 24.

[166] Rebecca D. Williams, *Keeping Medical Devices Safe From Electromagnetic Interference*, FDA CONSUMER, May 1995, at 13.

[167] RADIOLOGICAL HEALTH BULLETIN, Spring 1993. A recent epidemiological study further supports this conclusion. The study found no difference in mortality rates between customers who used portable, hand-held cellular telephones and those who used mobile, car-mounted phones. *Study Finds No Difference Between Hand-Held, Car-Mounted Cellular Phones*, BNA PRODUCT LIABILITY DAILY, Apr. 22, 1996.

[168] Letter from Philip J. Frappaolo, Deputy Dir., Office of Compliance, CDRH (Oct. 22, 1996).

[169] *Id.*

Conclusion

Because the FDA has considerably greater authority under the Medical Device Amendments than under the EPRC provisions to regulate electronic products that are also medical devices, it will probably use the Medical Device Amendments as a primary basis for both enforcement and standard-setting. It is highly unlikely that CDRH will issue any more performance standards under the EPRC provisions for electronic products that are also medical devices.

CDRH has already published standards for the most important radiation-emitting consumer products that are not medical devices, such as television receivers and microwave ovens. At the present time, there are no plans to issue additional standards. However, as new radiation-emitting technologies for consumer products, such as microwave driers, become available, CDRH may be compelled to issue new standards, revise existing ones, or refocus its enforcement efforts.[170]

At the time of their passage, the EPRC provisions were an important forerunner in the regulation of radiation-emitting products. During the early years of their existence, the EPRC provisions were the key method of regulating radiation-emitting products. Over time, however, their importance have lessened, at least in the case of medical devices, as reflected by the elimination of the Bureau of Radiological Health and the CDRH's decentralized enforcement of the EPRC provisions. Nonetheless, even with the advent of the Medical Device Amendments, and more recently the SMDA and MQSA, the EPRC provisions still fill an important niche for regulation of radiation-emitting nonmedical devices.

---

[170] One area where CDRH has been particularly active in enforcement is the commercial use of tanning beds and sunlamps. The American Medical Association (AMA) has advocated greater FDA involvement in the regulation of nonmedical uses of tanning equipment. In addition to working with physicians to promote state and local legislation regulating tanning facilities, the AMA "urges the FDA to take action that will ban the sale of and use of tanning equipment for non-medical purposes." POLICY COMPENDIUM (American Medical Ass'n 1996.)

chapter 12

Human Biological Drug Regulation: Evolution and Present Day Trends

Edward L. Korwek*

Introduction

The Center for Biologics Evaluation and Research (CBER) is in the throes of a regulatory and, more recently, a legislative revolution. Over the last couple of years the nature and scope of biologics regulation has changed in many ways—and probably more dramatically than in the last fifty years. While a number of recent reform initiatives seem directed at preempting legislative attempts to reinvent biologics regulation,[1] others began before the arrival of the anti-regulatory or deregulatory focus of the first Republican-controlled Congress in forty years.[2] Today, in light of administrative approaches that recently have been adopted to streamline or to harmonize with other drugs the oversight of biological drugs,[3] the replacement of the traditional scheme of biologics regulation with the mecha-

---

* Dr. Korwek is a Partner in the law firm of Hogan & Hartson, L.L.P., Washington, D.C. This article is based in substantial part on a paper by the author entitled *Human Biological Drug Regulation: Past, Present, and Beyond the Year 2000*, a special issue celebrating the *Food and Drug Law Journal's* 50th Anniversary. The author would like to express his appreciation to Robert P. Brady for his contribution on blood and blood products regulation.

1 *FDA Biologics Three-Tiered Manufacturing Changes Category System Being Adopted by Agency; FDA Reforms Touted by Clinton Administration in Pre-emptive Move*, F-D-C REP. ("The Pink Sheet"), Mar. 20, 1995, at 3. *See also* 60 Fed. Reg. 17,535 (1995) (guidance on changes to be reported for product and establishment applications).

2 *See* 59 Fed. Reg. 28,821 (1994); 59 Fed. Reg. 28,822 (announcing the Food and Drug Administration's (FDA's) review of general biologics and licensing regulations and regulations for blood establishment and blood products). *See also* 60 Fed. Reg. 2351 (1995) (notice of public meeting regarding same); *infra* note 100 and accompanying text.

3 *See, e.g.*, PRES. BILL CLINTON & VICE PRES. AL GORE, REINVENTING REGULATION OF DRUGS AND MEDICAL DEVICES, NATIONAL PERFORMANCE REVIEW. (1995); *FDA Announces Proposals to Streamline Medical Device and Drug Approvals*, GENETIC ENGINEERING NEWS, Apr. 1, 1995, at 3. *See also infra* notes 18, 89-92, and accompanying text; 60 Fed. Reg. 39,180 (1995) (FDA statement regarding drug effectiveness, probably in response to calls for changes in drug approval efficacy requirements); 60 Fed. Reg. 49,811 (1996) and 61 Fed Reg. 57,328 (1997) (proposed and final rules regarding prominence of name of distributor of biological products); 61 Fed. Reg. 40,153 (1996) (revocation of certain regulations, including additional standards for biologics). *See also* 62 Fed. Reg. 36,558 (1997) (announcement of revised Form FDA 356h, to market new drug biologic and antibiotic drugs); 62 Fed. Reg. 13,650 (draft guidance on providing clinical evidence of effectiveness of human drug and biological products); and 62 Fed. Reg. 37,925 (draft guidance on container closure systems for "drugs and biologics").

nism for the regulation of most other drugs seems inevitable for most biological drug products. Indeed, legislation has been passed by the House and Senate that would unify certain aspects of biological and other drug regulation.[4] This article identifies some of the many key events or developments that have helped to define biologics regulation, prior to the recent legislative changes, as it exists today under section 262 of the Public Health Service Act (PHS Act).[5] Regulatory trends also will be addressed where possible. Any review of this sort invariably will provoke a variety of different viewpoints and perhaps some disagreement. The long history of biologics regulation, beginning in 1902 with the Virus, Serum, and Antitoxin Act,[6] which predates the enactment of both the Pure Food and Drugs Act in 1906[7] and the Federal Food, Drug, and Cosmetic Act (FDCA) in 1938,[8] lends itself easily to differing viewpoints and interpretations. Moreover, such a ninety-year history cannot be easily reduced to a few pages of text.[9]

The discussion is organized into four broad categories: statutes or other enacted legislation that have been applied to enhance biologics regulation; the effects of AIDS; modern biotechnology developments that often have changed and challenged the scheme of biologics regulation; and blood and blood products oversight. Impacts of these topics are sometimes discussed in different sections. The legislative area primarily involves a review of the many older provisions of the FDCA that traditionally have been applied to human biological products because they are also drugs or devices. It also includes a brief mention of more recent laws amending the FDCA and a review of how—and sometimes why—biological drug regulation traditionally has differed from other drug regulation.

The AIDS topic primarily discusses: 1) the adoption of different approval criteria and of a fast track or priority system for biological drugs and other drugs to make some therapies available sooner, and 2) the important role of CBER in approving AIDS diagnostic tests. The "biotechnology" discussion involves a variety of modern or newer products,[10] such as

---

4 Food and Drug Administration Regulatory Modernization Act of 1997, H.R. 1411, 105th Cong. 1st Sess. (1997) and Food and Drug Administration Modernization and Accountability Act of 1997, S. 830, 105th Cong. 1st Sess. (1997).

5 Ch. 288, 37 Stat. 309 (1912) (codified at 42 U.S.C. §§ 201 et seq. (1988)). All textual references to sections of the PHS Act and of other statutes are to the law as codified.

6 Pub. L. No. 57-244, 32 Stat. 728 (1902).

7 Pub. L. No. 59-384, 34 Stat. 768 (1906) (codified at 21 U.S.C. §§ 1-15 (1934) (repealed in 1938 by 21 U.S.C. § 392(a) (1988)).

8 Pub. L. No. 75-717, 52 Stat. 1040 (1938), as amended at 21 U.S.C. §§ 301 et seq. (1994) [hereinafter FDCA].

9 For other discussions of biologics regulation, see generally William R. Pendergast, Biologic Drug Regulation, in 75TH ANNIVERSARY COMMEMORATIVE VOLUME OF FOOD AND DRUG LAW (FDLI 1984); PETER BARTON HUTT & RICHARD MERRILL, FOOD AND DRUG LAW, CASES & MATERIALS (2d ed. 1991) [hereinafter HUTT & MERRILL]; Eugene A. Timm, 75 Years of Compliance with Biological Product Regulations, 33 FOOD DRUG COSM. L.J. 225 (1978); Pittman, The Regulation of Biologic Products at NIH, 1902-1972, in NATIONAL INSTITUTE OF ALLERGY AND INFECTIOUS DISEASES, INTRAMURAL CONTRIBUTIONS, 1887-1987, at 61-70 (H.R. Greenwald, V.A. Harden eds. 1987); and Paul Buday, Fundamentals of United States Biological Product Regulations, 3 REG. AFF. 223 (1991). See also EDWARD L. KORWEK, U.S. BIOTECHNOLOGY REGULATIONS HANDBOOK (FDLI 1997).

10 The term "biotechnology" has been defined in a variety of ways. It has been described as processes using living organisms or part of organisms to make and modify products, to improve plants or animals, or to develop microorganisms for specific uses, OFFICE OF TECHNOLOGY ASSESSMENT, U.S. CONG., COMMERCIAL BIOTECHNOLOGY: AN INTERNATIONAL ANALYSIS 3 (1984); or as the "application of biological systems and organisms to technical and indus-

recombinant DNA-derived drugs,[11] monoclonal antibodies[12] for diagnostic and therapeutic use, and cell and gene therapy products.[13] It addresses not only some of the regulatory impacts of a whole new era of biological products, but also the Food and Drug Administration's (FDA's) initial efforts to accommodate them within the traditional biologics regulatory framework. More recent initiatives by the FDA to harmonize biological drug regulation with other drug regulation are also described. Blood and blood products remain one of the FDA's most intensively regulated areas. The reasons for that and the scope of FDA's activities are also addressed herein.

Interplay Between the Public Health Service Act and the Federal Food, Drug, and Cosmetic Act

Section 262 of the PHS Act today contains approximately fifteen provisions governing human biological therapeutic, prophylactic, and diagnostic products.[14] Nonhuman biological products are subject to similar provisions as part of the Virus, Serum, and Toxin Act of 1913,[15] which is patterned after the 1902 human biologics law.[16] These veterinary biological products are regulated by the Animal and Plant Health Inspection Service (APHIS) as part of the United States Department of Agriculture (USDA).[17] In light of the similar statutes involved, the subjects of human biologics and veterinary biologics regulation often are intertwined, despite the fact that jurisdiction over such products resides in two different statutes and departments of the federal government. Unfortunately, the statutory

---

trial processes." Office of Science and Technology Policy, Proposal for a Coordinated Framework in the Regulation of Biotechnology, 49 Fed. Reg. 50,856, 50,906 (1984). The term actually represents a collection of technologies, some old, others new. Plant and animal breeding are examples of traditional "old" biotechnological methods. Hybrid corn, foods such as bread, cheese, and yogurt, and medicines such as vaccines and hormones are well-known products of older biological methodologies. Modern or new biotechnology, which is the subject of this article, often involves a more precise ability to effect genetic changes and includes such newer techniques as recombinant DNA and cell fusion resulting in hybridomas that produce monoclonal antibodies. These methods sometimes are referred to as "genetic engineering." *See* Edward L. Korwek, *FDA Oversight of Biotechnology into the 21st Century*, THE BNA SPECIAL REPORT SERIES ON BIOTECHNOLOGY, Dec. 1989, at 49.

[11] "Recombinant DNA" has been defined as molecules developed outside living cells by joining natural or synthetic DNA segments to DNA that can replicate in a living cell. *See* National Institutes of Health (NIH), Guidelines for Recombinant DNA Research, 59 Fed. Reg. 34,496, 34,497 (1994).

[12] Monoclonal antibodies are antibodies that recognize a single, specific substance called an antigen and are produced by identical fused cells called hybridomas. For a basic discussion of hybridoma technology, see 1 OFFICE OF TECHNOLOGY ASSESSMENT, U.S. CONG., NEW DEVELOPMENTS IN BIOTECHNOLOGY, OWNERSHIP OF HUMAN TISSUES AND CELLS 35 (1987).

[13] *See infra* notes 234-58 and accompanying text.

[14] For a discussion of the history of the biologics law as it exists today, see Buday, *supra* note 9, at 225-27; HUTT & MERRILL, *supra* note 9, at 660-69; and Pendergast, *supra* note 9, at 293-300.

[15] Pub. L. No. 66-430, 31 Stat. 828 (1912) (codified at 21 U.S.C. §§ 151 et seq.).

[16] *See* Animal Health Institute v. USDA, 487 F. Supp. 376, 378 (D. Co. 1980).

[17] A list of licensed veterinary biological products is published regularly. U.S. DEP'T OF AGRIC., ANIMAL AND PLANT HEALTH INSPECTION SERV., VETERINARY BIOLOGICAL PRODUCTS (LICENSEES AND PERMITTEES) (1997).

similarities between human and other animal biologics have not always helped to clarify human biologics regulation.

The human biologics law contains provisions pertaining to licensing of both manufacturing facilities and products, sections 262(a) and 262(d)(1) which have since been reviewed or eliminated by new legislation.[18] Interestingly, the requirement of a product license under section 262(d)(1) is mentioned only obliquely in the context of an establishment license, which is the subject of a separate, more substantive provision, section 262(a). Specifically, the establishment license application (ELA) requirement of subparagraph (a) prohibits the "sale, barter, or exchange" of biological products unless they have been propagated, manufactured, and prepared at an establishment holding an unsuspended and unrevoked license. The product license application (PLA) provision in subparagraph (d)(1) requires the issuance of an establishment license only upon a showing that the establishment "and the products for which a license is desired" meet standards designed to ensure their safety, purity, and potency.

The remaining provisions not covering licensure deal with diverse topics. Misbranding prohibitions pertaining to false or misleading labeling are found in subparagraph (b).[19] Facility inspection authority is provided in subparagraph (c) and recall authority (including penalties) is in subparagraph (d)(2) (the latter upon a determination that a biological product presents an imminent or substantial hazard to public health).[20] General penalties for violations of the statute are covered in subparagraphs (d)(2)(B) and (f).[21] A separate approval requirement, in subparagraph (h), specifically covers partially processed biologicals, which was recently amended to allow the export of such products under less restrictive circumstances.[22]

How or why did such a simple and dated law passed in 1902 become so effective? Although the biologics statute has been amended several times, perhaps most notably in 1970 to include explicitly vaccines and blood and blood products,[23] the reason why section 262 has survived is as simple as the law itself: many of the provisions of the FDCA and other statutes have been applied to biological products to fill the statutory "gaps."

---

[18] *See infra* note 269 and accompanying text. *See also* 21 C.F.R. § 601.3(a) (establishment license), (b) (product license) (1997). These requirements recently have been amended to eliminate an establishment license for certain specified biotechnology and synthetic biological products. *See* 61 Fed. Reg. 24,227 (1996) (codified at, in relevant part, 21 C.F.R. § 601.2).

[19] Section 262(b) explicitly states that "no person shall falsely label or mark any package or container of any . . . product; nor alter any label or mark on any package or container of any . . . product . . . so as to falsify such label or mark."

[20] The recall provisions were enacted in 1986, Pub. L. No. 99-660, § 315, 100 Stat. 3751, 3783 (codified at 42 U.S.C. § 262(d)(2) (1994)), which explains why the penalties in the range of $100,000 for violations of recall orders are greater than other penalties under section 262. *See infra* note 21 and accompanying text.

[21] Under section 262(f), dating back to 1902, an individual who violates or aids in violating any provisions of section 262 commits a misdemeanor punishable by a fine of up to $500 or imprisonment of up to one year, or both. This monetary and term of imprisonment penalties are minimal compared to those in section 333 of the FDCA, which have been enhanced through 18 U.S.C. § 3571 (1994). *See generally* STEVEN M. KOWAL, FDA CRIMINAL ENFORCEMENT: HOW TO PREVENT AND DEFEND AGAINST LIABILITY (Wash. Legal Foundation 1992).

[22] For a discussion of exports of biological products, *see infra* notes 60-61 and 106, and accompanying text.

[23] Pub. L. No. 91-515, § 291, 84 Stat. 1297, 1308 (1970) (codified at 42 U.S.C. § 262(a)). Although interstate blood banks have been licensed under the biologic provisions since 1946, see 38 Fed. Reg. 2965, 2966 (1973), this amend-

■ Overlap of Section 262 and the Federal Food, Drug, and Cosmetic Act

Although some provisions of the FDCA (primarily those enacted in the last ten years) specifically refer to biologics,[24] the usual triggers for application of the FDCA to biological products have been the FDCA's definitions of a "drug" or a "device." Because these terms are defined, in relevant part, primarily in relation to the intended use of a product, such as in the diagnosis and prevention of disease or other conditions,[25] the jurisdictional boundaries of the FDCA are broad enough to cover biologics. This is because biological products are similarly defined under section 262 to be applicable to the "prevention, treatment, or cure of diseases or injuries of man."[26]

The definitional interplay between the FDCA and the biologics law was not recognized until the FDCA's passage in 1938.[27] For approximately thirty years no overlap had existed, and the legislative history of the 1938 Act seems to indicate that biologics were not to be subject to it.[28] Upon recodification of the biologics law in 1944, however, the interplay seems to have become recognized and intended.[29]

Most applications of the FDCA to biologics have occurred in the last twenty-five years, after the transfer of biologics regulation to the FDA in 1972.[30] At that time a different component of the FDA, the Bureau of Biologics, was established to handle separately biologics regulation.[31] Since then, the organizational responsibility within the FDA for biologics regulation has been merged with—and again separated from—the component of the FDA that handles other drug regulation.[32]

---

ment was the result of a 1968 decision by the Fifth Circuit Court of Appeals that citrated whole blood was not a biologic. Blank v. U.S., 400 F.2d 302 (5th Cir. 1968). This ruling conflicted with another decision in United States v. Steinschreiber, 219 F. Supp. 373 (S.D.N.Y.), aff'd, 326 F.2d 759 (2d Cir. 1963) (per curiam), cert. denied, 376 U.S. 962 (1964), that held that human plasma is subject to regulation as a biologic. For a discussion of the amendments to human biologics law and the subject court decisions involving blood products, see Pendergast, *supra* note 9, at 301.

[24] See, e.g., FDCA § 802; 21 U.S.C. §§ 382 (governing exports of drugs for commercial purposes, specifically refers to unapproved drugs "(including biologic products)"), id. § 735, 21 U.S.C. § 379g (pertaining to user fees, which refers to a "human drug application" as including "licensure of a biological product").

[25] Section 321(g) (FDCA § 201(g)) defines a "drug" to be articles intended for use in the diagnosis, cure, mitigation, treatment, or prevention of disease in man or other animals or articles (other than food) intended to affect the structure or any function of the body of man or other animals. Section 321(h) (FDCA § 201(h)) defines a device as an:

> instrument, apparatus, implement, machine, contrivance, implant, *in vitro* reagent, or other similarly related article which is intended for use in the diagnosis of disease or other conditions or in the cure, mitigation, treatment or prevention of disease in man or other animals or intended to affect the structure or any function of the body of man or other animals and which does not achieve any of its primary intended purposes through chemical reaction within or on the body of man or other animals and which is not dependent upon being metabolized for the achievement of any of its principal intended purposes.

[26] See 42 U.S.C. § 262(a); 21 C.F.R. § 600.3(h).

[27] Pendergast, *supra* note 9, at 298-99.

[28] Id.

[29] See HUTT & MERRILL, *supra* note 9, at 662-63. *But see* Pendergast, id. at 300, 303 (indicating that the 1944 recodification did not clarify the status of biologics under the FDCA).

[30] See 37 Fed. Reg. 12,865 (1972).

[31] Id.

[32] In 1982, the Bureau of Drugs and Bureau of Biologics were merged into what eventually became the Center for Drugs and Biologics. *See* 47 Fed. Reg. 26,913 (1982). Biological drug and other drug regulation was separated again in 1987.

Prior to the transfer of biologics to the FDA, they were regulated by the Division of Biological Standards of the National Institutes of Health (NIH).[33] The change in regulatory authority between NIH and the FDA is noteworthy, as is the controversy that led to the shift that involved the release by NIH of subpotent vaccines.[34] Biologics regulation today probably would be very different if the FDA were not directly involved.

Beyond the definitional interplay, the overlap of the two statutes also can be traced to similar provisions in both laws, appearing in section 262(g) of the PHS Act and section 392(c) of the FDCA. These sections state that nothing in either statute shall be construed in any way as "affecting, modifying, or repealing or superseding" the provisions of either act. The legislative history of the enactment of section 262(g) in 1944 arguably indicates that dual jurisdiction under both laws is legally appropriate, although debate exists on this topic.[35] Regardless of the appropriate construction of the two statutes, the interplay has gone largely unchallenged.[36] Moreover, from a regulatory standpoint, such dual jurisdiction seems desirable, if not necessary, given the shortcomings of section 262, as discussed below in part B.

The effect of section 392(c) of the FDCA on other statutes[37] has been the subject of extensive litigation for nonhuman (i.e., other animal) biological products regulated by APHIS. In 1981 a district and an appellate court held that a nonhuman animal biologic *is not* also simultaneously a veterinary "drug," despite the inclusive language of the term "drug" as defined in the FDCA.[38] These decisions, which were reversed on rehearing,[39] reflected the differences in the legislative history of the animal biologics law and the FDA's failure to implement the FDCA. They followed an earlier 1980 ruling that the biologics law did not reach intrastate veterinary biologics.[40] The 1913 law eventually was amended by the Food Security Act of 1985,[41] which made all animal biologics subject only to the jurisdiction of APHIS whether they were in intrastate or interstate commerce.

Despite the overlap of the FDCA and section 262, various products often have been called drugs, devices, or biologics. Although it appears that these classifications are mutually exclusive, they are not. Because human biological products are, by definition, simultaneously at least either drugs or devices, the more appropriate regulatory characterization

---

[33] For a discussion of organizational changes in the regulation of biologics, beginning with the Hygienic Laboratory as part of the Treasury Department in 1902 and its successor, NIH, in 1930, see HUTT & MERRILL, *supra* note 9, at 661, and Buday, *supra* note 9, at 225-26.

[34] *See generally* HUTT & MERRILL, *supra* note 9, at 665-68.

[35] *See supra* note 29 and accompanying text.

[36] Some debate has occurred about the application to biological drugs of various provisions of the FDCA as part of FDA administrative proceedings. *See, e.g.,* 38 Fed. Reg. 4319, 4319 (1973) (standards of safety and efficacy set forth in new drug provisions of section 355 of the FDCA applicable to biological products challenged as illegal). *See also* 38 Fed. Reg. 2965, 2965 (1973) (regulation requiring registration of blood banks is questioned as to whether it was the intent of Congress to classify blood as a drug).

[37] *Supra* note 35 and accompanying text.

[38] *See* Grand Laboratories v. Harris, 488 F. Supp. 618 (1980), *aff'd,* 644 F.2d 729 (8th Cir. 1981).

[39] *See* Grand Laboratories v. Harris, *rehearing en banc,* 660 F.2d 1288 (1981), *cert. denied,* 456 U.S. 927 (1982).

[40] *Animal Health Inst.,* 48 F. Supp. at 376.

[41] Pub. L. No. 99-198, § 1768(a), 99 Stat. 1354, 1654 (codified at 21 U.S.C. § 154a).

of such "combination" products is as "biological drugs or biological devices."[42] Put another way, the important regulatory determination is often whether a product that is a drug or device is also a biologic.

Examples of licensed biological drugs include various vaccines, such as the poliovirus vaccine, and more modern products, such as biological response modifiers, including various interferons.[43] Biological *in vitro* diagnostic devices include blood grouping reagents, and HIV and Hepatitis B and C test kits.[44] Many biological devices such as *in vitro* diagnostic kits are regulated as devices by the Center for Devices and Radiological Health (CDRH) instead of as biologics by CBER.[45] Approximately 300 monoclonal antibody *in vitro* diagnostic tests have been approved through the device premanufacture notification process. Consequently, the attention herein is often only on human biological drug regulation, although similar regulatory principles apply to the relatively few human biological devices that are licensed by CBER, such as diagnostic devices related to blood banking operations.

■ Provisions of the Federal Food, Drug, and Cosmetic Act Applied to Biologics

Approximately seventy different provisions of the FDCA are applicable to human biologics. The significant regulatory ramifications of this observation become apparent upon a summary review of a few of the relevant provisions. Biological drugs are not subject to new drug approval requirements, if they are licensed.[46]

Enforcement powers of the FDCA, such as seizure and injunction under sections 334 and 332, are also applied to biologics[47] since section 262 of the PHS Act has neither. Because section 262 also does not contain provisions regarding clinical testing, section 355(i) of the FDCA governing investigational drugs and implementing regulations also apply to biologics.[48] The requirement of an investigational new drug (IND) application for clinical studies on unapproved drugs is one of the earliest drug provisions applied to biological drugs.[49]

Although section 262 of the PHS Act requires that biological products be safe and potent, as well as pure, the FDA has applied the safety and efficacy requirements of the FDCA to

---

[42] *See, e.g.,* 21 C.F.R. §§ 310.4(a), 809.3(a).

[43] *See generally* FOOD & DRUG ADMIN., CENTER FOR BIOLOGICS EVALUATION AND RESEARCH, ESTABLISHMENT AND PRODUCTS LICENSED UNDER SECTION 351 OF THE PUBLIC HEALTH SERVICE ACT (1997).

[44] *Id.*

[45] *See generally infra* note 163.

[46] *See* 21 C.F.R. § 310.4(a).

[47] *See, e.g.,* United States v. Miami Serpentarium Laboratories, Inc., Food Drug Cosm. L.J. Rep. (CCH) ¶ 38,164 (S.D.Fla. 1982). The penalty provisions of 21 U.S.C. § 333, FDCA § 303, also are usually applied, given the relatively limited monetary and other penalties of section 262. *See supra* notes 20-21 and accompanying text.

[48] *See* 21 C.F.R. § 312.2 (stating that the requirement for an investigational new drug (IND) application for clinical investigations applies to products subject to 21 U.S.C. § 355, FDCA § 505 or to products subject to the licensing provisions of the PHS Act). *See also id.* § 312.3(b) (defining the term "investigational new drug" to mean a "new drug, antibiotic drug, or biological drug that is used in a clinical investigation").

[49] *See* 21 Fed. Reg. 5577 (1956).

biological drugs.[50] Biological drugs, therefore, are often said to be required to be "safe, pure, potent, and effective,"[51] criteria that reflect the literal requirements of both section 262 of the PHS Act and section 355 of the FDCA.[52]

The inclusion of efficacy with potency resulted because efficacy has been viewed at times as different from potency, which is not defined in section 262.[53] The two concepts are integrally related, however, because effective drugs usually must be potent. The FDA's definition of potency currently recognizes this interrelationship because it includes effectiveness.[54] Indeed, the 1902 biologics law (and therefore the current statute) has been viewed by some to include as part of the potency requirement at least some measure of "efficacy."[55] This requirement existed before the efficacy requirement was adopted as part of the Drug Amendments of 1962 for other human drugs.[56]

---

[50] *See generally* 21 C.F.R. § 601.25. *See also* 37 Fed. Reg. 16,679 (1972) (proposal to review safety, efficacy, and labeling of biological products); 38 Fed. Reg. 4319 (1973) (final regulation).

[51] *See, e.g.,* Dennis M. Donohue, *Blood and Blood Products: A Five Year Challenge,* 36 Food Drug Cosm. L.J. 27, 27 (1981) (speaking of safety, potency, and effectiveness requirements); 45 Fed. Reg. 73,922, 73,922 (1980) (stating that for a biological product to be licensed it must be "tested to ensure that it is safe, pure, potent, and effective").

[52] Section 262(d)(1) of the PHS Act states that licenses may be issued "only upon a showing that the establishment and the products for which a license is desired meet standards, designed to insure the continued safety, purity, and potency of such products...and licenses for new products may be issued only upon a showing that they meet such standards." 21 U.S.C. § 355(d)(5), FDCA § 505(d)(5) states that the FDA can disapprove a new drug application if there is a lack of substantial evidence that the drug is effective.

[53] An advisory panel charged with reviewing data and information concerning the safety, effectiveness, and labeling of bacterial vaccines and bacterial antigens with no U.S. standard of potency stated:

> [P]otency may be distinct from an ability to prevent, ameliorate, or modify in a beneficial way a disease state (effectiveness). For example, a given antigen may induce specific antibodies after a specified interval of time.... Whether such antibodies prevent or alter the course of disease is a separate problem. To illustrate, agglutinating antibody induced by the antigen may be found not to correlate with the prevention or modification of a given disease state.... Thus evidence that a substance is potent as an immunogen would be insufficient to support effectiveness, unless a previously established correlation existed.

42 Fed. Reg. 58,266, 58,273 (1977). *See also* William R. Pendergast, *Biologic Drugs, in* Food and Drug Law 311 (FDLI 1991) (saying that the efficacy provisions of the FDCA were "more precise" than the potency standard of the PHS Act).

[54] Potency is defined as "the specific ability or capacity of the product, as indicated by appropriate laboratory tests or by adequately controlled clinical data obtained through the administration of the product in the manner intended, to effect a given result." 21 C.F.R. § 600.3(s).

[55] *See, e.g.,* Pendergast, *supra* note 9, at 297, stating in the context of legislative changes to the biologics law in 1944 that:

> Congress recognized that not only should a drug be safe and "pure," but it should also be potent, i.e., effective. In recognizing these concepts, Congressional regulation of biologics under the Virus Act was far more advanced than regulation of other human drugs. Demonstration of efficacy...had been administratively required since 1902 and was legislatively imposed in 1944.

See also Timm, *supra* note 9, at 225-26 (stating that "such concern [for effectiveness] was built into the original 1902 Act for biologicals in its labeling dating requirements," referring to the fact that the 1902 Act required a label bearing an expiration date related to effectiveness). *See also* Pittman, *supra* note 9, at 64 (since an evaluation of potency had been complicated, the use of a certain test for typhoid vaccine finally confirmed the importance of a particular ingredient and therefore "that the relative potency of the vaccines reflected efficacy" [footnote omitted]) As a strict technical matter, however, a product could be potent by a particular laboratory test, but not necessarily effective clinically unless the potency assay has been correlated in a positive way with efficacy.

[56] Pub. L. No. 87-781, 76 Stat. 780 (1962) (codified at 21 U.S.C. §§ 321, 331-332, 348, 351-353, 355, 357-360, 372, 374, 376, 381).

The establishment registration and product listing requirements of section 360 of the FDCA also have been applied to biological drug products,[57] as have the drug advertising provisions of section 352(n).[58] The FDA approval of commercial exports of unapproved drugs (including biological drugs that are not "partially processed")[59] is governed by section 382 of the FDCA (adopted as part of the Drug Export Amendments of 1986 (DEA))[60] and recently amended by the FDA Export Reform and Enhancement Act of 1996.[61] User fees under the Prescription Drug User Fee Act of 1992 (PDUFA),[62] which is applicable to prescription biological and other drugs, are governed by section 379h. The PDUFA has reduced significantly the "drug lag,"[63] by reducing the traditional review period for approval applications for biological drugs and other drugs.[64] The salutary effects of the user fee legislation on approval times for biological drugs and other drugs have been recently outlined and, hence, its reauthorization seems imminent[65]

The Prescription Drug Marketing Act of 1987[66] and the Prescription Drug Amendments of 1992[67] amended the FDCA to prohibit prescription drug reimportation and the sale of prescription drug samples; to restrict sales of prescription drugs purchased by hospitals and other health care entities, and the distribution of prescription drug samples; and to provide for licensing of wholesale prescription drug distributors.[68] These provisions also apply to prescription biological drugs, except to blood and blood components intended for transfusion.[69]

---

[57] *See generally* 21 C.F.R. pts. 207, 607 (establishment registration and product listing for manufacturers of human blood and blood products). The FDA's initiative to require registration of blood banks and other entities collecting, manufacturing, preparing, or processing blood and blood products was controversial for a variety of reasons, including whether the FDA had the requisite legal authority, and whether registration was to be considered a prelude to product licensing. *See, e.g.,* 38 Fed. Reg. 2965 (1973).

[58] *See* 39 Fed. Reg. 43,654 (1974). Until recently, promotional labeling and advertising was handled by various components of CBER, not by a separate group as is the case with other drugs regulated by the Center for Drug Evaluation and Research (CDER). Now, much like other drug regulation, a separate biologics entity has been established called the Advertising and Promotional Labeling Staff that handles this area. *See* 58 Fed. Reg. 42,340 (1993); 59 Fed. Reg. 39,570 (1994).

[59] For a discussion of partially processed biologicals and their export requirements, see *infra* note 103 and accompanying text.

[60] Pub. L. No. 99-660, 100 Stat. 3743 (1986) (codified at 21 U.S.C. §§ 301 note, 333 note, 382; 42 U.S.C. §§ 241, 262).

[61] Pub. L. No. 104-134, §§ 2101-2104, 110 Stat. 1321-313 (1996) (to be codified at 21 U.S.C. §§ 301 note, 381, 382, 331, and 42 U.S.C. § 262).

[62] Pub. L. No. 102-571, 106 Stat. 4491 (1992) (codified at 21 U.S.C. §§ 321, 331, 342-343, 346a, 351-352, 360-362, 372, 376, 379c-h, 453, 601, 1033). The FDA has stated that under PDUFA the average review times have dropped more than 30% between 1992 and 1994, from 30 months to 20 months. 60 Fed. Reg. 59,559 (1995).

[63] The term "drug lag" refers to the slow rate by which drugs are approved and lack of new drug development in the United States. For a discussion of the topic, see generally Hutt & Merrill, *supra* note 9, at 580-83 and Mary Dunbar, *Shaking Up the Status Quo: How AIDS Activists Have Challenged Drug Development and Approval Procedures,* 46 Food Drug Cosm. L.J. 673, 686 (1991).

[64] For a general discussion of the performance goals for the FDA and other aspects of the PDUFA, see John F. Beary III, M.D., The FDA User Fee Program (Pharmaceutical Research and Mfrs. of Am. 1995) and Bruce N. Kuhlik, *Industry Funding of Improvements and the FDA's New Drug Approval Process: Prescription Drug User Fee Act of 1992,* 47 Food & Drug L.J. 483 (1992).

[65] *See, e.g.,* Food & Drug Admin., Fourth Annual Performance Report, Prescription Drug User Fee Act of 1992, Fiscal Year 1996 Report to Congress (1996). PDUFA expired at the end of Sep., 1997. S. 830, 105th Cong. Title VII (1997) and H.R. 1411, 105th Cong. § 101 (1997) would reauthorize PDUFA for five years.

[66] Pub. L. No. 100-293, 102 Stat. 95 (1987) (codified at 21 U.S.C. §§ 301 note, 331(t), 333(v), 353(c)-(e), 381).

[67] Pub. L. No. 102-353, 106 Stat. 941 (1992) (codified at 21 U.S.C. §§ 301 note, 333, 353, 353 note, 381).

[68] *See generally* 21 C.F.R. pt. 205 (guidelines for state licensing of wholesale prescription drug distributors). *See also* 59 Fed. Reg. 11,842 (1994) (proposed rules implementing the Prescription Drug Marketing Act and Prescription Drug Amendments of 1992).

[69] *See, e.g.,* 21 C.F.R. § 205.3(f)(8); 59 Fed. Reg. at 11,862 (to be codified at 21 C.F.R. § 203.1).

Other relevant provisions include those added to the FDCA as part of the Orphan Drug Act of 1983 (ODA);[70] section 353(g), adopted as part of the Safe Medical Devices Act of 1990 (SMDA),[71] governing combination product regulation; and sections 264[72] and 274e[73] of the PHS Act. The importance of section 264, which relates to the prevention of communicable disease transmission, is addressed below and in the section on AIDS. Section 274e, passed as part of the National Organ Transplant Act of 1984 (NOTA),[74] prohibits the selling and buying of organs and certain other transplants. The NOTA prohibition, certain provisions of the ODA, and section 353(g) are discussed in the biotechnology section of this article, primarily because of their importance to new biotechnologies.

Additional requirements that have been applied are based on a combination of statutory authorities. Current good manufacturing practice (GMP) regulations governing nonbiological and biological drug products,[75] in particular blood and blood components in intrastate commerce,[76] have been promulgated under a variety of provisions. Section 351(a)(2)(B) of the FDCA, pertaining, in relevant part, to the adulteration of drugs not manufactured in accordance with GMP requirements; section 264 of the PHS Act pertaining to the prevention of transmissible diseases such as hepatitis;[77] and section 262(d) of the PHS Act governing the conditions for licensure of establishments and products have been used to ensure that blood products (including blood) are prepared by proper manufacturing procedures and in compliance with relevant manufacturing regulations.[78] Adverse drug reporting requirements applicable to biologics[79] also are based on a variety of provisions, such as the misbranding sections 352(a) and 352(f)(2) of the FDCA and section 262(b) of the PHS Act, governing, respectively, misleading labeling of and inadequate warnings for drugs and the false labeling of biologics.[80]

■ Differences in Regulation Between Biological Drugs and Other Drugs

The previous review of how human biological drugs and other drugs are similarly regulated helps delineate the historical dissimilarities in regulation of the two classes of products. For example, biological products are subject to the mandatory recall provisions of section 262(d)(2)(A) if a substantial or imminent hazard exists, whereas nonbiological drugs are not. Until very recently perhaps the most significant difference is that many other drugs are

---

[70] Pub. L. No. 97-414, 96 Stat. 2049 (1983) (codified at 21 U.S.C. §§ 360aa et seq).

[71] Pub. L. No. 101-629, § 16, 104 Stat. 4511, 4526 (1990) (codified at 21 U.S.C. § 353(g)).

[72] Ch. 373, § 361, 58 Stat. 682, 703 (codified at 42 U.S.C. § 264) (authorizes the Dep't of Health and Human Serv. to make and enforce regulations to prevent the spread of communicable diseases). *See also* 21 C.F.R. pt. 1240 (implementing regulations).

[73] Pub. L. No. 98-507, § 301, 98 Stat. 2339, 2346 (1984), as amended at 42 U.S.C. § 274e.

[74] *Id.*, 98 Stat. at 2339, as amended at 42 U.S.C. §§ 273 et seq.

[75] *See* 21 C.F.R. § 210.2 (stating that the GMP regulations in pt. 211 and the biologics regulations are considered to supplement, not supersede each other).

[76] *Id.* pt. 606.

[77] *See* 39 Fed. Reg. 18,614, 18,614 (1974).

[78] The FDA's efforts to impose GMP requirements on intrastate blood banks, as well as interstate blood banking operations, were controversial. *See id.* at 18,614-15.

[79] *See* 21 C.F.R. subpt. D. These regulations were adopted in 1994. For a history of adverse experience reporting requirements pertaining to biologicals, see 59 Fed. Reg. 54,034, 54,034 (1994).

[80] *See, e.g.,* 55 Fed. Reg. 11,611, 11,613 (1990) (proposed rule on adverse experience reporting for licensed biological products).

subject to the new drug application (NDA) process, whereas human biologics were subject to both PLA and ELA requirements.[81] This distinction may seem inconsequential, particularly because manufacturing procedures are pervasively regulated as part of the NDA process. The ELA requirement has been deceptively problematic, however, for a variety of reasons discussed below. This ELA requirement and other differences have led to the conclusion that biological drugs historically have been regulated more pervasively than other drugs. Many recent changes in the biologics regulations now leave this maxim in doubt, at least with respect to certain biologic products that can be identified or characterized more rigorously, and particularly with the passage of new legislation.

To fully understand the significance of the ELA requirement and other traditional variations in biologics regulation, it is important to realize that conventional biologics, such as vaccines, often have been considered to be complex products that are difficult to characterize. They do not have a defined chemical structure that can be measured easily like chemically-synthesized drugs. Thus, biologics usually are defined in terms of their method(s) of manufacture. Changes in manufacturing methods, therefore, have been presumed always to affect the safety, purity, and potency (including efficacy) of a biological product.

These aspects of traditional biologics regulation involving the importance of manufacture have led to facility inspections usually being conducted by CBER rather than by FDA district personnel, as is done with other drugs, and to the requirement for one person, a "responsible head," to be in control of all matters pertaining to establishment operations.[82] Both of these aspects of biologics regulation are now in the process of changing.[83] Regulations have also prohibited almost any change in method of manufacture for biologics without first obtaining the approval of CBER.[84] Perhaps more importantly, however, is the fact that the FDA historically had interpreted the product and establishment license provisions of section 262 to mean that the *same* legal entity must hold both licenses. The product license had to "follow" the establishment license; thus, traditionally, only a licensed manufacturing entity could hold a product license.[85] Two companies, as different legal entities, could not "split" the dual license requirements: one company could not hold only a product license and another only an establishment license. The trend until very recently was to allow different types of manufacturing arrangements, whereby more than one entity could be involved in biologics manufacture.[86] "Split" licenses, however, were still not permitted. A company must have performed significant manufacturing steps to hold a product license.[87]

---

[81] Products that are licensed as biologics are not subject to NDA requirements. 21 C.F.R. § 310.4(a).

[82] *See id.* § 600.10(a) (responsible head requirement).

[83] *See Field Offices to Gain Role in Biologics Inspections*, WASH. DRUG LETTER, July 21, 1997, at 3, *and FDA ORA Responsibility for Biologics Pre-Licensing Inspections Being Considered; Team Biologics Plan Transfers Lead on Post-Approval Inspections to ORA*, F-D-C REP. ("The Pink Sheet"), Aug. 18, 1997, at 15; 62 Fed. Reg. 4221 (1997) (proposal to eliminate responsible head requirement).

[84] *See* 21 C.F.R. § 601.12. These regulations recently have been amended to allow more flexibility similar to that for other drugs. *See* 62 Fed. Reg. 39,890 (1997). *See also infra* note 92 and accompanying text.

[85] *See* 21 C.F.R. § 601.10(b). This interpretation of section 262 and the related restriction that a product and an establishment license cannot each be "split" between different legal entities seemed dubious. Section 262(d), which is the only section that mentions product licenses, albeit sometimes in the context of establishment licenses, does not require such licensing arrangements.

[86] *See infra* note 90 and accompanying text.

[87] *See* 57 Fed. Reg. at 55,545. For an in-depth discussion of manufacturing issues in the biologics area, see Gary E. Gamerman, *Regulation of Biologics Manufacturing: Questioning the Premise*, 49 FOOD & DRUG L.J. 213 (1994).

The traditional regulatory viewpoint that manufacturing changes presumptively affect the safety, purity, and potency (including efficacy) of biological drugs also has had significant competitive and other ramifications. For example, historically, no approved generic versions have existed for biological drug products. Thus, the Drug Price Competition and Patent Term Restoration Act of 1984,[88] governing abbreviated applications for generic drugs, has been interpreted not to apply to biological drugs.[89]

In response to complaints and the threat of new legislation concerning the extensive pre-approval requirements for manufacturing changes and to the viewpoint that many biologics today are more easily identified or characterized, often as a result of the use of modern biotechnology methods, the traditional approach to manufacturing arrangements[90] and changes[91] was altered significantly. Much more flexibility has now been also allowed, bringing biologics drug regulation more in line with other drug regulation.[92] Specifically, for example, FDA has changed the definition of a "manufacturer" to allow a license to be issued to an entity that does not perform any manufacturing operations.[93] Also, the ELA requirement—once viewed by the FDA to be the *sine qua non* of biologics regulation—now has been eliminated for certain categories of products that can be more easily characterized, such as monoclonal antibody products for *in vivo* use and for therapeutic recombinant DNA-derived products.[94] Legislation recently passed by the House and Senate eliminates the ELA requirement.[95]

Further, in response to advances in technology to characterize precisely the identity and structure of biological products, the FDA also recently announced the availability of a guidance document on demonstrating product comparability without the necessity of performing clinical trials when manufacturing changes are implemented.[96] Critics of this compara-

---

[88]   Pub. L. No. 98-417, 98 Stat. 1585 (1984) (codified at 15 U.S.C. §§ 68b-c, 70b (1994); 21 U.S.C. §§ 301 note, 360cc; 28 U.S.C. § 2201 (1994); 35 U.S.C. § 156, 271, 282 (1994)).

[89]   *See* 57 Fed. Reg. 17,950, 17,951 (1992).

[90]   *See* 57 Fed. Reg. 55,544 (1992) (FDA policy statement concerning cooperative manufacturing arrangements for licensed biologicals) *and infra* note 93 and accompanying text.

[91]   *See supra* note 84 *and infra* note 92.

[92]   *See* 60 Fed. Reg. 17,535 (1995) (guidance on changes to be reported for PLAs and ELAs); 60 Fed. Reg. 35,750 (1995) (FDA guidance document concerning use of pilot manufacturing facilities for development and manufacture of biological products); 61 Fed. Reg. 2739 (1996) (approved application changes reporting for biological and non-biological drugs); 61 Fed. Reg. 2749 (1996) (approved application changes reporting for biological drugs, guidance availability); 61 Fed. Reg. 2748 (1996) (announcing availability of draft guidance pertaining to changes to an approved application for well-characterized therapeutic recombinant DNA-derived and monoclonal antibody biotechnology products); 62 Fed. Reg. 39,904 (1997) (guidance availability for changes to an approved application for specified synthetic biological products); and *id.* (guidance availability for changes to an approved application for biological products). The new legislation also alters the way manufacturing changes are treated. *See* S. 830, 105th Cong. 1st Sess. § 614 (1997) and H.R. 1411, 105th Cong. 1st Sess. § 111 (1997).

[93]   61 Fed. Reg. 24,227 (1996) (codified at section 600.3(t)).

[94]   The FDA originally proposed to eliminate the establishment license application requirement for only well-characterized biotechnology products. *Id.* at 2733 (1996) (proposal). Because of the difficulty in defining precisely a "well-characterized" product, the FDA specified only certain categories of products to which the elimination of the ELA requirement would apply. *Id.* at 24,227.

[95]   *See* S. 830, 105th Cong. 1st Sess. § 610 (1997) *and* H.R. 1411, 105th Cong. 1st Sess. § 120 (1997).

[96]   *See* 61 Fed. Reg. 18,612 (1996) (announcing the availability of guidance document concerning demonstration of comparability of human biological products). *See also* FDA Guidance Concerning Demonstration of Comparability of Human Biological Products, Including Therapeutic Biotechnology-Derived Products, Center for Biologics Evaluation and Research, Center for Drug Evaluation and Research (Apr. 1996).

bility document have suggested that this guidance will now allow the approval of generic biological drugs, which have been predicted to be on the market in the next decade.[97] The process by which the FDA issued this guidance document was recently unsuccessfully challenged in court in the context of the FDA's approval of competitive orphan drug products.[98]

Biologics also have been subject to lot release requirements[99] since 1919,[100] although the precise statutory basis for this aspect of biologics regulation is unclear. Section 262 in its present form does not specifically authorize such practices. This requirement also appears to be a reflection of the practical consideration that product identity cannot be ensured through manufacturing controls. Thus, for example, lot release as a condition of licensure under section 262(d)(1) to ensure that a product is safe, potent, and pure seems to be justifiable. The FDA originally had proposed to modify its requirements for lot release, if there is sufficient evidence that a product can be manufactured to approved specifications.[101] More recently, however, the requirement was specifically eliminated for certain synthetic and modern biotechnology products, such as therapeutic recombinant DNA products and monoclonal antibodies.[102]

Other differences exist in the regulation of biologics, not directly related to manufacturing considerations. Although biologics are generally subject to IND requirements, certain biological devices are exempt if they are for *in vitro* diagnostic use that confirms a medically-established diagnostic product.[103] "Intermediate" or "partially processed" products subject to section 262 that are not in a form actually used for the treatment or prevention of disease, until recently, could not be exported legally for commercial purposes unless several fairly onerous conditions were met under section 262(h).[104] Such products usually need to be further processed before they can be used. Nonbiologic drug "intermediates," however, are not governed specifically by similar provisions. Therefore, they can be legally exported without meeting any particular FDA requirements.[105]

---

[97] *See Generic Biotech Drugs Likely to be on Market in Next Decade*, F-D-C- REP. ("The Pink Sheet"), May 13, 1996, Trade & Gov't Rep., at 9. A distinction between biologics and most other drug regulation that might encourage the development of biological generics is that drugs subject to NDAs often have trade secret protection of information in the NDA, whereas biological drugs do not. *See* 21 CFR §§ 601.51(e), 314.430(e)(2).

[98] *See* Berlex Laboratories, Inc. v. Food and Drug Administration, 942 F. Supp. 19 (D.D.C. 1996). The plaintiff argued, *inter alia*, that the guidance document was a substantive rule that required notice and opportunity for comment, which the court rejected. *See also infra* note 265.

[99] *See* 21 C.F.R. § 610.1-.2.

[100] Lot release requirements for biologics first appeared in 1919 in regulations implementing the 1902 biologics law. *See* Timm, *supra* note 9, at 227. The only other drugs for which lot release traditionally has been required are antibiotics and insulin. Antibiotic lot release (or batch certification requirements) were stopped in 1982. *See* 21 C.F.R. § 433.1. *See also* 47 Fed. Reg. 39,155 (1982). New legislation would repeal the separate satutory requirements for insulin and antibodics. H.R. 1411, 105th Cong. 1st Sess. § 122 (1997) (no comparable provision in S. 830).

[101] *See* 58 Fed. Reg. 38,771 (1993). Companies are not taking advantage of the lot release alternatives that have been proposed. *See FDA Seeks Biologics Rule Clarification Via Definition*, WASH. DRUG LETTER, July 31, 1995, at 2.

[102] *See, e.g.*, 60 Fed. Reg. 63,048 (1995); 61 Fed. Reg. 24,227 (1997). The FDA has advised that in light of the broader range of products that are not subject to ELA requirements, that it will revise its determination of which products will be exempt from lot-by-lot release requirements. 61 Fed. Reg. at 24,227.

[103] *See* 21 C.F.R. § 312.2(b)(2).

[104] Section 262(h)(1)(A) as amended in 1986 stated that the product can be exported only to specific countries; that it must be manufactured, processed, and packed in accordance with good manufacturing practice requirements; and must be labeled in certain ways, among other requirements. *See also infra* note 107.

[105] *See generally* 21 C.F.R. § 310.3(g) (defining the term "new drug substance" to exclude "intermediates").

The reason for this statutory anomaly is largely historical. The FDA viewed "intermediates" of biological drugs as subject to the traditional ban on the commercial export of unapproved biologics. "Intermediates" of all other drugs, however, are viewed not as "drugs" at all that are in most cases subject to the export ban. They need to be chemically reacted further and thus are not intended for uses subject to regulation as a drug under section 321(g)(1).

With the passage of the DEA in 1986, which for the first time allowed commercial export under specific circumstances, the inequality in exportation between biological drugs and most other nonbiological drugs was addressed. The 1986 amendments allowed export and therefore were viewed to permit a previously prohibited activity. In reality, however, the export provisions merely codified the previous regulatory position against export of "partially processed" biological drugs, because all other drug "intermediates" were then and are now still not usually subject to any export restrictions. Not surprisingly, the export provisions governing processed biologics as well as the various export prohibitions pertaining to most other drugs in general were recently changed.[106] Nonetheless, certain conditions must still be met to export partially processed biologics,[107] while other drug intermediates can still be exported freely.

Certain classes of biological products with similar characteristics, most notably, some vaccines and blood products, traditionally have been "standardized" in terms of safety, purity, or potency requirements. Some of these products, until recently, have been subject to requirements promulgated through specific standards regulations.[108] General standards exist for biological manufacturing facilities that are similar to drug GMP regulations,[109] as well as for many other biological requirements. Explicit authority exists for the promulgation of standards in section 262(d)(1).

Applicable biological standards must be met for a product to be licensed and for an establishment to maintain a valid product license.[110] This regulation of classes of biological products with similar properties through specific standards, which can be likened to monographs for over-the-counter drugs and antibiotics, has had some advantages and disadvantages. Uniform product standards are preferable to the imposition of individual, varying product requirements that can occur as part of the licensing process. Such standards, however, allow for much less flexibility to accommodate technological and other advancements; thus, they are often difficult to update and require extensive FDA resources to maintain. The promulgation by the FDA of product-specific standards therefore continues to wane, in favor of requirements imposed as conditions of product licensure. The imposition of requirements as conditions of licensure, instead of as product stan-

---

[106] *Supra* note 61.

[107] A partially processed biological can now be exported if it is (1) manufactured in accordance with GMPs or meets international manufacturing standards as certified by an international standards organization certified by the Secretary and (2) otherwise meets the requirements of 21 U.S.C. § 381(e)(1). Pub. L. No. 104-134, § 2104, 110 Stat. 1321-313 (1996) (codified at 42 U.S.C. § 262(h)).

[108] *See, e.g.,* 21 C.F.R. pts. 620 (bacterial product standards), 630 (viral vaccine standards), 640 (human blood and blood product standards), and 680 (miscellaneous product standards). These regulations have recently been removed or modified in an effort to streamline biologics regulation. *See* 61 Fed. Reg. 40,153 (1996).

[109] 21 C.F.R. subpt. B.

[110] *See id.* § 601.4.

dards adopted through notice and comment rulemaking, recently has been challenged in the context of allergenic products.[111]

Another one of the more important and unique aspects of biologics regulation is that many provisions of section 262 apply only to products in "interstate commerce." This language does not appear in the biologics provisions; the only terms utilized are "sell, barter, or exchange" and "send, carry, and bring for sale, barter, or exchange" from or into a state, possession, or foreign country. Nevertheless, products manufactured and distributed solely within a state (in intrastate commerce) are not subject to certain provisions of section 262, particularly the licensing provisions.[112] Intrastate blood banks and their blood products, for example, are not licensed by CBER.[113] The narrow reach of the "send, barter, or exchange" language of section 262, unlike the broad reach of the interstate commerce language of the FDCA, is based on the section's legislative history and the historical literal interpretation of various provisions of the statute.[114] Similarly, the 1913 veterinary biologics law has been interpreted as not applying to intrastate operations.[115]

Intrastate biologics facilities still are required to comply with certain other provisions of section 262 such as the misbranding provision of subsection (b), which applies regardless of whether or not interstate commerce exists. They also are subject to various sections of the FDCA that pertain to compliance with GMP regulations and the registration and listing requirements discussed previously. These requirements apply primarily because the FDCA, unlike section 262 of the PHS Act, has been interpreted broadly to apply even to products that are manufactured and sold solely intrastate, if they have components that move in "interstate commerce."[116]

Finally, no drugs other than certain biologics that are vaccines have been the subject of special legislation enacted to cover product liability claims. The National Swine Flu Immunization Act of 1976[117] and the National Childhood Vaccine Injury Act of 1986 (NCVIA)[118] provide federal compensation programs for victims of swine flu and certain common childhood vaccines. Both laws were enacted to encourage the development of certain vaccines important to public health, in exchange for at least some immunity from product liability claims.[119] As part of the compensation programs, the federal govern-

---

[111] Citizen Petition, Allergen Products Manufacturers Association (July 1, 1997) and Petition for Stay of Action, Allergen Products Manufacturers Association (July 1, 1997). *See also Citizen Petition Challenges FDA Use of Licenses in Place of Rulemaking,* INSIDE WASHINGTON'S FDA WEEK, Aug. 15, 1997, at 13.

[112] *See* FDA Talk Paper No. T82-14 (Mar. 2, 1982) (FDA warned that a certain therapy is unproven as safe and effective).

[113] *See* 38 Fed. Reg. at 2966 ("there currently is no statutory authority to license intrastate blood banking, . . .").

[114] *See Animal Health Inst.,* 487 F. Supp. at 379 (stating in the context of the veterinary biologics law that "the [human biologics] Act clearly excluded intrastate producers from its licensing requirement").

[115] *Id.* at 376. *See also supra* note 41 and accompanying text.

[116] *See, e.g.,* United States v. Dinnovin Pharmaceuticals, Inc., 475 F.2d 100 (2d Cir. 1973); Compliance Policy Guide 7153.11 (Aug. 3, 1988). *See also* 39 Fed. Reg. at 18,615 (the good manufacturing practices regulations and registration requirements are being imposed on intrastate facilities because Congress found that products of all drug manufacturing establishments "are likely to enter the channels of interstate commerce and directly affect such commerce").

[117] Pub. L. No. 94-380, § 317, 90 Stat. 1113, 1114 (1976) (codified at 42 U.S.C. §§ 247b et seq.).

[118] Pub. L. No. 99-660, 100 Stat. 3743 (1986) (codified at 42 U.S.C. §§ 300aa et seq.).

[119] *See* Evan Rosenfeld, *The Strict Products Liability Crisis and Beyond: Is There Hope For An AIDS Vaccine?,* 31 JURIMETRICS 187 (Winter 1991); HUTT & MERRILL, *supra* note 9, at 716-19.

ment defends against vaccine injury and death claims, and compensates victims. The source of funding for such compensation is different, however. Funds are appropriated to address claims pertaining to swine flu vaccines; in the case of childhood vaccines, claims are financed through a tax on manufacturers. Vaccines subject to the NCVIA also are governed by special statutory requirements pertaining to adverse experience reporting.[120]

The Impact of AIDS on Biologics Regulation

No discussion of any type of current drug regulation would be complete without the mention of AIDS. The early 1980s brought the recognition of a health crisis that may forever change the nature and scope of biological drug and biological device regulation. Nearly 350,000 people have died of AIDS.[121] In 1995, AIDS ranked eighth in the leading causes of death in all age groups.[122] Numerous articles, reports, and other commentary have been written on AIDS and FDA regulation.[123] One view is that the AIDS pandemic has led to the FDA's codification as part of its regulations of many of the informal practices of the past.[124] A different position is that AIDS has forced the FDA to adopt alternate approaches to regulation, even if some of the approaches are not always new.[125]

The precise effects of the AIDS crisis on the FDA and the regulatory process are still evolving and thus unclear. In 1993, the FDA published an interim rule[126] under section 262 of the PHS Act governing prevention of communicable diseases that required that certain testing, donor screening, and recordkeeping be performed to prevent the spread of AIDS and hepatitis from transplanted tissues (which usually have not been subject to FDA regulation). This rule was just recently finalized.[127] Roughly eight AIDS drugs were approved in 1996, thus totaling forty-two drugs approved for AIDS or AIDS-related conditions.[128] Of these total approvals, six are biological drugs.[129] One hundred and twenty-

---

[120] *See generally* 42 U.S.C. §§ 300aa-14, -25(b)(1), -28.

[121] PHARMACEUTICAL RESEARCH & MFRS. OF AM., NEW MEDICINES IN DEVELOPMENT FOR AIDS, GROUNDS FOR HOPE: 122 MEDICINES IN TESTING FOR AIDS 12 (1996) (survey).

[122] *Id.*

[123] *See, e.g.,* Dunbar, *supra* note 63. INSTITUTE OF MEDICINE, CONFERENCE SUMMARY, EXPANDING ACCESS TO INVESTIGATIONAL THERAPIES FOR HIV INFECTION AND AIDS (Nat'l Acad. Press 1991) [hereinafter IOM REPORT]; HUTT & MERRILL, *supra* note 9 at 689-92, 552-61; Jane E. Henney, *The Changing Approval Process,* 47 FOOD DRUG COSM. L.J. 505 (1992); John J. Smith, *Science, Politics, and Policy: The Tacrine Debate,* 47 FOOD DRUG COSM. L.J. 511 (1992); David A. Kessler, *Issues in Approving Drugs for AIDS Treatment,* 6 REG. AFF. 189 (1994).

[124] Smith, *supra* note 122, at 518.

[125] *See, e.g.,* Kessler, *supra* note 122, at 189.

[126] 58 Fed. Reg. 65,514 (1993) (codified at 21 C.F.R. pt. 1270).

[127] 62 Fed. Reg. 40,429 (1997). *See also* 62 Fed. Reg. 40,536 (announcing guidance on screening and testing of donors of human tissue).

[128] NEW MEDICINES IN DEVELOPMENT FOR AIDS, *supra* note 121, at 1, 14.

[129] *See id.* at 9-11.

two AIDS drugs are currently in testing;[130] about one quarter of these are biologics, such as cytokines, immunomodulators, and vaccines.[131]

Only time will tell whether the combination of these initiatives, approvals, and the development of new experimental therapies, in conjunction with the FDA's other efforts to adopt quicker routes to approval and to provide wider access to AIDS diagnostic agents and experimental therapies, will help stem the spread of the deadly disease. The future also will reveal whether the steps taken by the FDA to expedite approvals and provide wider access to experimental therapies compromise the safety and efficacy requirements of the FDCA and similar requirements of section 262 of the PHS Act.

■ Expanded Access: Treatment Uses, Sales, and Parallel Track Procedures

The relevance of the AIDS crisis to the drug approval process was recognized formally in 1987 with the finalization of the NDA Rewrite. This Rewrite officially began around 1982 and was intended to modernize and update new drug regulations.[132] A similar effort with respect to IND regulations, the IND Rewrite, began in 1983.[133] The IND Rewrite codified, for the first time, procedures authorizing the "treatment use" of investigational drugs, which generally includes the use of an investigational drug in patients as part of an uncontrolled and unblinded protocols. The FDA had allowed treatment uses under certain circumstances for some time, but it was not until the Rewrite that the IND regulations specifically authorized the practice.[134] In many respects the treatment use provisions that were adopted can be viewed as similar to the National Cancer Institute's "Group C" system for experimental cancer drugs.[135] This system, in operation since the mid-1970s, allows expanded access prior to approval of drugs in controlled clinical trials to cancer patients who are not part of such trials.[136]

Specific provisions governing the sale of investigational drugs, including biological drugs, were included as part of the 1983 treatment proposal. Although the sale of investigational drugs always was prohibited generally because it was considered to constitute the unlawful commercialization of unapproved drugs, investigational biological drugs needed explicit FDA approval for sale; other drugs did not.[137] Therefore, the FDA proposed to codify the requirement for the written approval for the sale of all investigational drugs.

The IND Rewrite proposal was controversial,[138] particularly the treatment and sale provisions. Comments raised issues about their legality, scope, and interpretation.[139] The debate about the treatment uses reflected the tension between allowing broader access to patients of

---

[130] *Id.* at 1.

[131] *See id.* at 2-10.

[132] *See* 47 Fed. Reg. 46,622 (1982) (proposed regulations); 50 Fed. Reg. 7452 (1985) (final regulations).

[133] *See* 48 Fed. Reg. 26,720 (1983) (proposed regulations); 52 Fed. Reg. 8798 (1987) (final regulations).

[134] 48 Fed. Reg. at 26,728, 26,729. *See also* Dunbar, *supra* note 63, at 683-86 (describing the FDA's early access procedures); IOM REPORT, *supra* note 122, at 8-9.

[135] 48 Fed. Reg. at 26,729.

[136] *See generally* 44 Fed. Reg. 25,510 (1979).

[137] *See* 48 Fed. Reg. at 26,734.

[138] *See generally* 52 Fed. Reg. at 8798.

[139] *See id.* at 8851-52.

investigational drugs in life-threatening or severely debilitating situations, and trying not to impede the collection of data that are necessary to obtain marketing approval. If treatment use of an investigational drug became widespread, patients and sponsors would be less likely to become involved in the approval process, thus inhibiting the approval of newer therapies. The provisions tried to strike an appropriate balance between allowing the increased availability for treatment use of promising new therapies and safeguarding the integrity of the approval process, including protecting the rights and safety of human subjects.[140]

Finalization of the IND Rewrite occurred four years later, at which time the FDA reproposed new regulations regarding treatment use and sale of investigational drugs. In the 1987 reproposal, the FDA for the first time specifically mentioned AIDS as a reason for the regulations.[141] It justified the sale provisions by saying that with the advent of biotechnology, sufficient incentives were needed to foster drug "and biological agent [ ]" development.[142] This was a reference to the fact that start-up biotechnology companies needed to recoup some of their costs of drug development, although traditionally the FDA has viewed the costs of drug development to be a normal part of doing business.

The newer provisions also allowed sale during treatment use, without the need for explicit prior approval,[143] if the FDA did not object within thirty days after receipt of notification of sale. Final treatment and sale use regulations issued two months later, substantially in the same form as they were proposed. The treatment regulations were modeled after the procedure utilized to provide expanded access to zidovudine (AZT), the first antiviral drug approved for the treatment of AIDS. The treatment IND for AZT was approved in five days.[144] Approximately forty treatment INDs have been allowed since 1987, mostly for nonbiological drugs; eleven treatment INDs involve sale.[145]

Perhaps the most important aspect of the treatment IND regulations is that they began or were part of a trend toward adoption of other regulatory procedures designed to speed the availability of new therapies. For example, the FDA also established a "1-AA" priority designation for the review of AIDS products.[146] The National Center for Drugs and Biologics, which was responsible for approval of biological drugs as well as other drugs, was split into the Center for Drug Evaluation and Research (CDER) and CBER.[147] Part of the reason for the re-establishment of biologics regulation as a separate component of the FDA was the view that a single center would provide better management of resources, focus on the development of AIDS vaccines and diagnostic tests, and coordinate other AIDS activities better.[148]

A significant step toward providing wider access to investigational drugs occurred in 1990, when the Public Health Service announced a proposed policy to make available

---

[140] *Id.* at 19,468-70.

[141] 52 Fed. Reg. at 8850.

[142] *Id.*

[143] *Id.*

[144] 53 Fed. Reg. 41,517 (1988).

[145] *See* FOOD & DRUG ADMIN., TREATMENT INVESTIGATIONAL NEW DRUGS (INDS) ALLOWED TO PROCEED (1997).

[146] *See* FOOD & DRUG ADMIN., STAFF MANUAL GUIDE 4820.3 (1992).

[147] *See* 52 Fed. Reg. 38,275 (1987).

[148] *Id.*

investigational drugs for AIDS and other HIV-related diseases under a "parallel track" protocol.[149] A final policy issued in 1992.[150] This policy makes available investigational drugs to people with AIDS and HIV-related diseases who have no therapeutic alternatives and cannot participate in controlled clinical trials. These patients would be treated in "parallel" with those in ongoing controlled clinical trials. The parallel track proposal is similar to the treatment IND concept, except that the investigational drug is available with less evidence of effectiveness than that needed for a treatment IND[151] and is only for patients with HIV-related diseases. Tens of thousands of patients with HIV infection have been treated through the parallel track mechanism.[152] This wide access has sometimes been controversial.[153]

■ Fast Track Approval Procedures

The FDA also established in 1988 an interim rule known as subpart E that provided for an expedited approval system for life-threatening or severely debilitating diseases.[154] This expedited approval is available particularly when no satisfactory alternative therapies exist. It does not apply to products for symptomatic relief, but only to those that impact survival or the progress of major disabilities. AZT, which was approved in a record 107 days,[155] also was used as the basis for the development of the new regulations.

On the same day that the FDA finalized its parallel track regulations, it proposed "subpart H" regulations governing accelerated approval.[156] These rules allow the approval of drugs for serious or life-threatening diseases where the products provide meaningful therapeutic benefits to patients beyond existing treatment. Dideoxyinosine (ddI), another antiviral agent, approved in October 1991, almost a year before the final regulations were published in 1992,[157] served as a model for the accelerated proposal.

The accelerated approval procedure is similar to the expedited approval process, but accelerated approval can be based on a surrogate endpoint that is reasonably likely to predict clinical benefit or is based on a clinical endpoint other than survival or morbidity. In exchange for granting drug sponsors early approval benefits, the FDA reserved authority to withdraw approval, and to impose postmarketing restrictions on distribution and dissemination of promotional materials.[158] Through 1994, five drugs were approved through the accelerated approval procedures, four (nonbiological) drugs for AIDS and AIDS-

---

[149] See 55 Fed. Reg. 20,856 (1990). See also Smith, supra note 122, at 516; Dunbar, supra note 63, at 697-700.

[150] 57 Fed. Reg. 13,250 (1992).

[151] 55 Fed. Reg. at 20,857.

[152] Kessler, supra note 122, at 191. Twenty-six thousand patients had received dideoxyinosine (ddI), another antiviral treatment for HIV, on parallel track. Id. at 193.

[153] See, e.g., IOM REPORT, supra note 122, at 30-32.

[154] See 53 Fed. Reg. 41,516 (1988) (codified at 21 C.F.R. § 312.80-.88). For a discussion of expedited approval procedures, see Dunbar, supra note 63, at 693-95, and Smith, supra note 122, at 515-16. New legislative actions, if signed by the president, will codify certain aspects of the fast track regulations. See supra note 4, § 613 and supra note 4, § 103.

[155] 53 Fed. Reg. at 41,517.

[156] See 57 Fed. Reg. 13,234 (1992). See also Smith, supra note 122, at 516-18.

[157] See 57 Fed. Reg. 58,942 (1992) (codified at 21 C.F.R. §§ 314.500-.560; 601.40-.46).

[158] See, e.g., 21 C.F.R. §§ 314.530, .560.

related conditions and one (biological) product for multiple sclerosis.[159] Interestingly, the accelerated approval rules were codified separately as part of the biologics regulations,[160] whereas the expedited approval provisions were not. More recently, in response to criticism of the FDA's focus on AIDS treatments, the agency announced a program of accelerated approval and expanded access specifically for cancer therapies.[161]

■ AIDS Diagnostic Testing

One of the other significant roles that CBER has played in the AIDS area relates to the approval of diagnostic tests. The first such AIDS test was approved in 1985. In January 1988, the FDA published a final rule requiring human blood and blood components intended for transfusion be tested and found negative by an approved HIV-1 antibody test.[162] Although federal health agencies such as the FDA sometimes have been criticized for their slow response to the transmission of AIDS through the blood supply,[163] the importance to the public health of the development of such tests and the significant role CBER has played in approving such tests cannot be overemphasized.

Generally, *in vitro* diagnostic tests for AIDS or any other disease or condition are medical devices. AIDS kits for screening or confirming HIV infection associated with blood banking operations, however, are licensed under section 262 of the PHS Act as biological devices.[164] Other tests intended for use in the detection of HIV and not associated with blood banking practices are "regulated" by CBER as biological devices.[165] Consequently, such products are subject to medical device requirements but are reviewed and approved by CBER. Examples of such devices regulated by CBER are urine and saliva collection kits for HIV testing. Because most of these tests involve blood or the presence of HIV antibodies, or both, and blood and antibodies normally are considered to be biologics, it seems reasonable, if not legally justifiable, that CBER review is involved. The continued need for CBER oversight of such medical devices sometimes has been questioned, resulting in some legislative proposals to switch jurisdiction to CDRH.

One of the significant roles that CBER continues to play in the AIDS testing area pertains to the approval of tests that are not intended to ensure the safety of the blood supply. These

---

[159] *See* Kessler, *supra* note 122, at 192. *See also* Sheila R. Shulman & Geffrey S. Brown, *The Food and Drug Administration's Early Access and Fast-Track Approval Initiatives: How Have They Worked?*, 50 FOOD & DRUG L.J. 503 (1995).

[160] *Compare supra* notes 153 and 156.

[161] *See, e.g.,* PRES. BILL CLINTON & VICE PRES. AL GORE, REINVENTING THE REGULATION OF CANCER DRUGS, NATIONAL PERFORMANCE REVIEW (1996). *See also* 62 Fed. Reg. 13,649 (1997) (guidance availability on approval of new cancer treatment uses for marketed drug and biological products); FDA BACKGROUNDER U.S. FOOD AND DRUG ADMINISTRATION, CANCER THERAPIES: ACCELERATING APPROVAL AND EXPANDING ACCESS, (Mar. 29, 1996); HHS FACT SHEET ACCELERATING APPROVAL AND EXPANDING ACCESS, CLINTON ADMINISTRATION INCREASES AVAILABILITY OF *Cancer Drugs* (Mar. 29, 1996); and *Expanded Access Protocols for Foreign-Approved Cancer Agents to be Proactively Solicited by FDA; Partial Response Will be Basis for Accelerated Approval,* F-D-C REP. ("The Pink Sheet"), Apr. 1, 1996, at 10.

[162] *See* 53 Fed. Reg. 116 (1988) (codified at 21 C.F.R. § 610.45).

[163] INSTITUTE OF MEDICINE, HIV AND THE BLOOD SUPPLY: AN ANALYSIS OF CRISIS DECISIONMAKING, COMMITTEE TO STUDY HIV TRANSMISSION THROUGH BLOOD AND BLOOD PRODUCTS (Nat'l Acad. Press 1995).

[164] Intercenter Agreement Between the Center for Biologics Evaluation and Research and the Center for Devices and Radiological Health pt. IV (1991).

[165] *Id.*

include home test kits designed to detect the presence of HIV infection and home speci-men collection kits. Both of these can involve nonblood samples, such as urine and saliva. Home test kits allow for a determination of HIV infection at home, similar to a home preg-nancy test kit. Home specimen collection kits provide instructions and equipment for sam-ple collection, packaging for shipment of the sample to a laboratory for HIV testing, and subsequent mechanisms for the individual to receive the results. Absent a significant change in AIDS demographics, the likelihood that CBER will approve AIDS home test kits in the near future seems remote. This is because CBER generally has taken a conser-vative posture regarding the approval of home collection kits.

In a series of *Federal Register* notices and public meetings that began in 1989, the agency has articulated fairly rigorous requirements for marketing home collection tests. In Febru-ary 1989, it stated that all blood collection kits labeled for HIV antibody testing were Class III medical devices subject to premarket application (PMA) approval under section 360e of the FDCA.[166] It also took the position that its approval was limited to marketing blood collection kits that were intended for "professional use only." This meant that such collection kits could not be labeled and marketed for home use, but for use only in a health care environment, such as hospitals, medical clinics, and other such testing facilities. Other aspects of obtaining approval for such collection kits included reporting test results directly to a professional health care provider for communication to the subject. The FDA also stated as part of the 1989 notice that a "kit" for testing at home for HIV antibodies was subject to licensing under the PHS Act.[167] This position seems to be contradicted by an intercenter agreement between CDRH and CBER later executed as a result of the pas-sage in 1990 of the SMDA. The agreement states that all such kits are regulated by CBER as medical devices.[168]

These and other requirements of the 1989 *Federal Register* notice were controversial for a variety of reasons. For specific product approvals that were being considered by the FDA, some AIDS activists and other advocacy groups felt the increased AIDS testing that would be allowed by home use collection kits would increase AIDS awareness, would allow for earlier access to AIDS treatment, and would change risky behavior.[169] Others raised issues regarding pre- and post-test counseling requirements; the possible loss of persons who might initially test positive for a screening test, but would not return for confirmatory test-ing; adequacy of the sample collection system; and broad societal issues, such as the use of the results for denial of health and life insurance, and for other purposes that effect dis-criminatory results.[170] Not surprisingly, a follow-up notice in July 1990 simply reiterated the five criteria enunciated in 1989 for approval of such collection kits, although it did indicate a willingness by the FDA to review applications for blood collection kits for HIV-1 testing for home use.[171]

---

[166] 54 Fed. Reg. 7279, 7280 (1989).

[167] *Id.* at 7280.

[168] *Supra* note 163.

[169] *See generally* Summary Minutes, 38th Meeting of the Blood Products Advisory Committee, Center for Biologics Evaluation & Research, Food & Drug Admin. (Dec. 17-18, 1992).

[170] *Id.*

[171] *See* 55 Fed. Reg. 30,982 (1990).

By late 1994, the FDA's regulatory mood had changed dramatically. After an additional public meeting widely supporting home collection kits and in light of "technological developments and the changing nature of the HIV epidemic," the FDA for the first time officially took the position in a *Federal Register* notice (published in 1995) that home specimen collection kits may be approvable.[172] It further provided information on the types of data that were necessary to obtain PMA approval. No changes were made in the FDA's position on home testing of specimens for evidence of HIV infection. To date, saliva- and urine-based HIV tests have been approved,[173] as well as home collection kits.[174]

The FDA's position on home specimen collection kits has been controversial in other respects. The view that collection containers labeled for HIV use are Class III medical devices was challenged in *Clinical Reference Laboratory, Inc. v. Sullivan*.[175] In this seizure action against devices intended for HIV use that did not have PMA approval, the district court ruled that urine and saliva specimen collection containers ultimately intended for use in HIV testing are medical devices subject to FDA jurisdiction.[176] It was argued that because the collection containers were used for insurance risk assessment purposes they were not devices used for medical diagnosis. The court also held that the "new" use of such containers for HIV testing renders the devices subject to Class III premarket approval requirements.[177] On appeal, the United States Court of Appeals for the Tenth Circuit affirmed the district court's decision that the specimen containers were medical devices.[178] It further held, however, that they were not Class III devices subject to PMA approval, because the containers were used mainly for specimen collection purposes and this use was not new.[179]

The implication of this decision is that specimen containers for bodily fluids such as blood, urine, and saliva, even if intended for use in HIV testing, are subject only to 510(k) premarket notification requirements, not the more onerous PMA provisions of the FDCA. The precise impact of the tenth circuit's decision on the FDA's regulation of specimen collection containers for HIV use remains unclear, particularly in light of the 1995 policy notice by the FDA reiterating PMA approval requirements for such devices.[180]

Blood and Blood Products

It is generally believed that the United States has one of the safest blood supplies in the world. This is due in large part to the development and implementation of standards for

---

[172] *See* 60 Fed. Reg. 10,087 (1995).

[173] *See* FDA Approves First Urine-Based HIV Test, FDA Talk Paper (Aug. 6, 1996); 61 Fed. Reg. 26,187 (1996) (announcement of approval in 1994 of HIV-1 oral specimen collection device).

[174] *See* FDA Approves First HIV Home Test System, Health and Human Serv. News, FDA (May 14, 1996); *see also* FDA Backgrounder, *Home-Use HIV Test Kits* (May 14, 1996).

[175] 791 F. Supp. 1499 (D. Kan. 1991).

[176] *Id.* at 1511.

[177] *Id.*

[178] United States v. An Undetermined Number of Unlabeled Cases, 21 F.3d 1026 (10th Cir. 1994).

[179] *Id.* at 1029.

[180] 60 Fed. Reg. 10,087 (1995).

donor suitability and product quality. Blood and blood products are among the oldest product categories regulated by CBER. They are also among those products granted the FDA's highest priorities with regard to product safety because of the risks of infectious disease transmissions and the agency's stated goal of ensuring that the nation's blood supply is as safe as possible.[181] As a result, blood and blood products have been, and will remain, one of the FDA's most intensively regulated product categories. Unlike other biological drug product categories, which as discussed herein have seen significant modifications in the applicable approval requirements and regulatory requirements, blood and blood products should expect to continue operating within the confines of a narrowly constructed regulatory system with no significant relaxation of requirements.

The broad term "blood and blood products" really encompasses three distinct product areas: blood,[182] blood components[183] and blood products.[184] Currently, the principal concern with regard to all of these products is, of course, the potential for viral contamination with AIDS and various forms of hepatitis. Traditionally, blood and blood products have required submission and approval of a PLA for each product and an ELA for the establishment where such product is propagated, manufactured and prepared.[185] Because, however, the "potency/efficacy" of blood and blood components has largely been established, the principal focus of the PLA/ELA submission is on the establishment and its ability to safely process, store and distribute these products. In contrast, most blood products continue to submit a more traditional PLA/ELA that focuses both on the potency/efficacy of the product and the establishment in which it is manufactured.

Establishments that manufacture blood and blood products must also register and list their products.[186] For blood establishments, there is an intense inspection process that focuses heavily on compliance with both the blood and drug GMPs[187] as well as with the general standards in the biologics regulations.[188] Special emphasis is placed on blood and plasma donor screening and testing.[189] Diagnostics for viral contaminants such as HIV and HBsAg intended to ensure blood donor and product safety are licensed pursuant to the PHS Act. Other diagnostics and devices utilized in blood banks are regulated as medical devices, some by CBER and some by CDRH.[190] In a limited number

---

[181] *See Hearing on FDA's Regulation of the Blood Industry Before the Subcomm. on Oversight and Investigations of the House Comm. on Energy & Commerce*, 103d Cong., 1st Sess. 20-91 (1993) (statement by FDA Comm'r David Kessler).

[182] 21 C.F.R. § 606.3(a). Blood is defined as "whole blood collected from a single donor and processed either for transfusion or further manufacturing."

[183] *Id.* § 606.3(c). A component is defined as "that part of a single-donor unit of blood separated by physical or mechanical means." Examples of such products are platelets and albumin.

[184] There are a wide array of blood products derived from blood and plasma including such products as Factor VIII and IX.

[185] 42 U.S.C. §§ 262(a), (d)(1).

[186] 21 C.F.R. §§ 207.7, 607.7.

[187] *See id.* pts. 606 (current GMPs for blood and blood components), 210-211 (current GMPs for drugs).

[188] *Id.* pts. 600, 601, 610.

[189] *Id.* pts. 610, 640.

[190] FDCA § 503 (g)(1), 21 U.S.C. § 353(g)(1), provides that combination product's primary mode of action will determine center jurisdiction.

of instances, such as pertaining to the use of minimally manipulated bone marrow, for example, the FDA has voluntarily refrained from exercising its authority under the PHS Act. Whether it is appropriate for the agency to refrain from exercising its regulatory authority in other situations, however, such as in the context of emerging new biological therapies, continues to be the subject of significant dispute. Thus, for example, the FDA's current initiatives to regulate placental/umbilical cord blood products and peripheral stem cell products intended for transplantation or further manufacture into injectable products have generated wide spread medical community, blood industry and congressional involvement. [191]

In the 1990s, there has been significant Congressional oversight of FDA's regulation of the blood supply.[192] The result of this oversight has been an increased compliance vigilance on the part of the FDA. In 1993, the Red Cross entered into a consent decree of permanent injunction agreeing to make substantial changes to its operations to ensure compliance with GMPs and other applicable standards.[193] Several other blood establishments subsequently have entered into similar decrees. In addition, the FDA has put a number of licensed blood establishments on notice that, unless substantial compliance was obtained, the agency would initiate a license revocation proceeding.[194] Two specific regulatory initiatives of note with regard to blood banks have been the development by CBER of quality assurance[195] and computer validation[196] guidelines. These guidelines communicate the FDA's firmly held belief that in order to ensure the continued safety to the nation's blood supply, it is essential that blood establishments implement effective control over manufacturing processes and systems.

In addition to its efforts to impose stringent parameters in the areas of quality assurance and computer software, in 1995, the FDA imposed the most sensitive blood test yet for

---

[191] *See, e.g.*, Comments submitted to FDA Docket No. 96N-0002 in response to publication of FDA's "Draft Document Concerning the Regulation of Placental/Umbilical Cord Blood Stem Cell Products Intended for Transplantation or Further Manufacture Into Injectable Products" 61 Fed. Reg. 7087 (1996).

[192] *See, e.g., Hearings on FDA's Regulation of the Blood Industry, supra* note 180; *Hearings on FDA's Regulation of the Blood Industry Before the Subcomm. on Oversight and Investigations of the House Comm. on Energy & Commerce*, 102d Cong., 2d Sess. (1991); IOM REPORT, *supra* note 122.

[193] United States v. American National Red Cross, Civ. No. 93-0949 (D.D.C. 1993).

[194] The FDA's primary enforcement tools against blood establishments are license suspensions and revocations. Revocation procedures generally begin with a Notice of Intent to Revoke which allows a certain period of time within which a licensee may demonstrate or achieve compliance with applicable standards. 21 C.F.R. § 601.5. Suspensions are limited to those situations where CBER has determined that grounds for revocation exist and that there is a danger to health which necessitates immediate cessation of all interstate shipments. Once the license is suspended, CBER must either issue a Notice of Intent to Revoke and provide an opportunity for an expedited hearing, or hold the revocation in abeyance while the licensee attempts to achieve compliance. *Id.* §§ 601.6, 601.7. The vast majority of license revocation procedures are resolved through issuance of a Notice of Intent to Revoke and subsequent compliance by the licensee.

[195] CBER Guideline for Quality Assurance in Blood Establishments (July 11, 1995).

[196] CBER, Draft Guideline for the Validation of Blood Establishment Computer Systems. (Sept. 28, 1993). On March 31, 1994, a letter was mailed to known blood bank software manufacturers. The letter advised the manufacturers that software products intended for use in the manufacture of blood and blood components, or for the maintenance of data that is used in making decisions regarding the suitability of donors, and/or the release of blood or blood components, are medical devices. Manufacturers of such software are subject to the device provisions of the FD&C Act and FDA's device regulations, including establishment registration, product listing, premarket notification or approval, cGMPs and adverse event reporting (MDRs).

HIV: the HIV-1 Antigen test.[197] More recently, in September 1996, the FDA and the Health Care Financing Administration finalized a look-back and notification rule applicable to all blood establishments and transfusion services that establishes quarantine procedures and imposes significant notification requirements to consignees and ultimately to any recipient of a unit of product distributed from a donor later determined to be HIV positive.[198] The development of such guidances specifically for blood establishments evidences the FDA's heightened concern for the safety of the blood supply in this country.

As the regulation of other therapeutic biologics moves inexorably towards harmonization with the way in which most other drugs are regulated by CDER, blood and blood products regulation should not change substantially from its present form given Congressional and FDA concern with regard to the safety of the blood supply. Undoubtedly CBER will work towards administrative efficiencies in the PLA/ELA and supplement approval process, but no major substantive changes are foreseeable.

The Modern Biotechnology Revolution and Biologics Regulation

Contemporaneous with the recognition of AIDS as a health crisis came the realization of the commercial potential of modern biotechnology. Before the advent of the newer biotechnologies, biological drug regulation was largely limited to two classes of products: vaccines and blood products (including blood). Modern biotechnology has both vitalized and challenged the nature and scope of biologics regulation.[199] Today, "biotechnology" and "biologics" are terms that have become inextricably linked. Many biologics, such as cytokines, immunomodulators, and vaccines, are derived from the use of modern biotechnology methods. Over twenty-three "biotechnology" drugs have been approved thus far.[200]

Biotechnology will likely continue to stimulate in the near future additional medical advances and pose further regulatory challenges.[201] Monoclonal antibodies and recom-

---

[197] Recommendations for Donor Screening with a Licensed Test for HIV-1 Antigen. (Aug. 8, 1995). Other protocols can be found in the following memoranda to blood establishments issued by CBER: Recommendations for the Management of Donors and Units that are Initially Reactive for Hepatitis B Surface Antigen (HBsAg) (Dec. 2, 1987); Revised Recommendations for the Prevention of Human Immunodeficiency Virus (HIV) Transmission by Blood and Blood Products (Apr. 23, 1992); Revised Recommendations for Testing Whole Blood, Blood Components, Source Plasma and Source Leukocytes for Antibody to Hepatitis C Virus Encoded Antigen (Anti-HCV) (Aug. 5, 1992).

[198] Final Rule, Current Good Manufacturing Practices for Blood and Blood Components: Notification of Consignees Receiving Blood and Blood Components at Increased Risk for Transmitting HIV Infection, 61 Fed. Reg. 47,413 (1996).

[199] *See, e.g.,* John C. Petricciani, *Will New Technologies Require Change in the Regulation of Biologics?,* 38 FOOD DRUG COSM. L.J. 131 (1983); Robert P. Brady & Daniel Kracov, *From Diphtheria Antitoxin to Cytokine Products: A Remarkable Scientific Journey/An Aging Regulatory Framework,* 3 REG. AFF. 105 (1991).

[200] *See* PHARMACEUTICAL RESEARCH & MFRS. OF AM., APPROVED BIOTECHNOLOGY DRUGS AND VACCINES (1995).

[201] *See* Shamel & Keough, *Sales of U.S. Biopharmaceutical Products Expected to Triple By 2004,* GENETIC ENGINEERING NEWS, Mar. 15, 1995, at 6.

binant DNA methods have led the way to second and third generations of newer products. Antisense compounds,[202] which can block certain chemicals in the body from causing diseases, and chemokines,[203] which may modulate HIV infection, are examples of more modern products being investigated. The use of transgenic animals that have had their genetic composition modified to produce pharmaceuticals also seems near at hand.[204]

A recent survey indicates that the number of biotechnology drugs in clinical tests grew twenty-one percent in the past year.[205] The majority of biotechnology drugs in development are in the monoclonal antibody and vaccine areas.[206] Other significant areas of development include gene therapy, interleukins, and human growth factors.[207] The fastest growing category is gene therapy,[208] a fact that brings into focus the importance of the human genome project. This is a government-funded effort to identify the approximately 100,000 genes in the twenty-three pairs of chromosomes present in human cells that are responsible for inherited characteristics, including certain diseases or conditions. It is predicted that the project will lead to the development of a wide range of new diagnostic agents for a variety of diseases and conditions, as well as biological and other therapies for their treatment.[209]

■ The Ambiguous Nature of Biologics

Biologics have become an amorphous, ill-defined group of products. Unless a drug is called a "vaccine" or "blood," or is derived from blood such as plasma or platelets, it often is difficult to decide whether it is a biological drug. The situation is confused further by the fact that some biologics are regulated as drugs and some drugs are regulated as biologics.[210] Similarly, veterinary biologics are a vague category of products where the distinction between biologics and other veterinary drugs is particularly important because two different federal agencies are involved in their regulation.

Section 262 of the PHS Act is not particularly useful in understanding the nature of "biologics." It does not define the term other than by reference to particular types of products. Specifically mentioned are a "virus, therapeutic serum, toxin, anti-toxin, vaccine, blood, blood component or derivative, allergenic product or analogous product, or arsphenemine

---

[202] *See* Korwek, *FDA Oversight, supra* note 10, at 49. *See also* Klausner, *Regulating Expression: Turning Off Unwanted Genes With Anti-RNA*, 9 BIO/TECHNOLOGY 763 (1985).

[203] *Chemokines Share Center Stage With Drug Therapies*, 273 SCI. 302 (1996).

[204] *See, e.g.*, Food & Drug Admin., Points to Consider in the Manufacture and Testing of Therapeutic Products for Human Use Derived from Transgenic Animals (1995); 60 Fed. Reg. 44,036 (1995) (announcing availability). *See also Transgenic Animals May Be Down on the Pharm*, 254 SCI. 35 (1991).

[205] *See* PHARMACEUTICAL RESEARCH & MFRS. OF AM., BIOTECHNOLOGY MEDICINES IN DEVELOPMENT (1996) (survey). *See also* Editorial, *Pharmaceuticals Based on Biotechnology*, 273 SCI. 719 (1996).

[206] *See* PHARMACEUTICAL RESEARCH & MFRS. OF AM., *supra* note 204, at 1.

[207] *Id.*

[208] *Id.*

[209] *See generally* Fox, *Directing the Genome Project*, 7 BIO/TECHNOLOGY 223 (1989). *See also* 270 SCI. 368 (1995) (genome issue). *See also From Genes to Genome Biology*, 272 SCI. 1736 (1996).

[210] *See* 21 C.F.R. § 310.4(b) (radiolabeled biologics are regulated by the NDA process); U.S. DEPT. OF HEALTH AND HUMAN SERVS., FDA, CDER, OFFICE OF MANAGEMENT, APPROVED DRUG PRODUCTS 3-329 (16th ed. 1997) (listing biological products approved under section 355 of the FDCA but handled by CBER).

or its derivatives." Many of these terms are difficult to understand or define, even from a scientific standpoint. The types of products that are subject to section 262 become almost impossible to comprehend because of the use of the language "analogous product." Depending on the limits or expansiveness of one's imagination, almost anything or virtually nothing can be viewed as "analogous" to another product as a legal or scientific matter. For example, some have suggested that transplanted organs and tissues (other than blood) could be regulated as biologics.[211]

The FDA's regulations do not help in identifying the types of products subject to section 262.[212] They often focus on the source of the product, such a therapeutic serum which is defined as the product obtained from blood by removing the clotting components and the blood cells.[213] One of the more significant aspects of the FDA's regulations pertains to the definition of a biological product that is "analogous to a toxin or anti-toxin." Such a product is a biologic if it is applicable to the prevention, treatment, or cure of disease or injuries of man through a "specific immune process," irrespective of its source.[214] What constitutes a "specific immune process" is difficult to ascertain. Bovine interferon has been classified by the FDA as a veterinary drug and not an animal biologic subject to APHIS jurisdiction because it does not act through a "specific immune process."[215]

This is an interesting characterization of bovine interferon. APHIS regulations that define a biologic do not currently mention this specific immune process language,[216] despite nearly identical provisions in the human and veterinary biologics statutes. Moreover, all interferons for human therapeutic uses are currently licensed as biological drugs. A petition has been submitted to clarify the veterinary biologics definition and the USDA's regulation of biologics.[217] APHIS' regulations defining a biological product recently have been amended to account for advancements in technology and for improved understanding of how veterinary biologics work.[218]

Despite the lack of clarity in the FDA's regulations, they do identify certain products that clearly are not biologics, such as hormones.[219] For example, hormones such as human insulin and human growth hormone, a few of the first "genetically engineered" products that have been commercialized, were approved as nonbiological drugs as part of the NDA process. Further, insulin has been specifically subject to approval under section 356 of the FDCA, which can imply that it is not a biologic subject to section 262 of the PHS Act. For the same reasons, antibiotics presumably also are not subject to the biologics provisions, because they has been specifically approved under a section 357 of the FDCA.

---

[211] *See generally Special Issue: The Regulation of Human Tissue and Organs*, 46 FOOD DRUG COSM. L.J. 1 (1991). *See also* HUTT & MERRILL, *supra* note 9, at 693-96 (citing legislative testimony of the FDA regarding its legal authority to regulate human transplants).

[212] *See* 21 C.F.R. § 600.3(h).

[213] *Id*. § 600.3(h)(2).

[214] *Id*. § 600.3(h)(5)(iii).

[215] The basis for this decision was that in 1982 the USDA and the FDA entered into a Memorandum of Understanding stating that veterinary biological products generally act through a specific immune process. 47 Fed. Reg. 26,458, 26,459 (1982). For commentary on this issue, see 51 Fed. Reg. 23,302, 23,346-47 (1986).

[216] *See* 9 C.F.R. § 101.2 (1997).

[217] *See* 62 Fed. Reg. 31,326 (1997) (to be codified at 9 C.F.R. pt. 101).

[218] *See* 61 Fed. Reg. 43,483 (1996).

[219] *See* 21 C.F.R. § 600.3(h)(5)(ii).

Because of the inherent ambiguities of the definition of a biological product, a variety of statements have been made about what products are biologics — sometimes incorrectly. Biologics often have been described in terms of their source, such as animal- or biotechnologically-derived, or obtained from living organisms.[220] They also have been described as proteins. As is the case with most other generalizations, these are inaccurate for a variety of reasons. Most notably, antibiotics and hormones can fall in some or all of these categories but they clearly are not biologics. No easy characterizations exist that will describe precisely all biologics.

■ Combination Products

Biological drugs and biological devices, as combination products, have caused intercenter jurisdictional problems, particularly with the advent of modern biotechnology. The development of new biotechnologies has led to a variety of products that are difficult to classify in terms of regulatory jurisdiction. Debate arose about which center(s) within the FDA would regulate the different, and sometimes novel, products.[221] This situation was addressed legislatively in 1990 with passage of the SMDA. A provision was added as section 353(g) to the FDCA to clarify which combination products are subject to regulation by CBER, CDER, or CDRH.

Section 353(g)(1) states that the center that will be assigned primary jurisdiction depends on the combination product's primary mode of action. If the primary mode of action is that of a biologic, then CBER has primary jurisdiction under section 353(g)(1)(c). If the primary mode of action is that of a drug "(other than a biological product)," then CDER has primary jurisdiction under section 353(g)(1)(A). Interestingly, there is no parallel parenthetical language for devices in section 353(g)(1)(B) as there is for drugs that excludes biologics.[222] This difference probably presents more of a technical drafting problem than a significant legal issue.

The "mechanism of action" test for determining primary jurisdiction is problematic for a couple of reasons. First, it can be difficult as a scientific matter to ascertain the precise mechanism of action of a particular product. Second, neither the FDCA nor section 262 of the PHS Act, nor the FDCA's implementing regulations, define drugs (including biological drugs) in terms of their mode of action. Sections 262(a) of the PHS Act and section 321(g)(1) of the FDCA are silent about how a biological or nonbiological drug must function. Except for devices,[223] therefore, no statutory standards exist indicating the modes of action of other products that are biological drugs or nonbiological drugs. Only the FDA's biologics regulations make a reference to products that act through a "specific immune mechanism," as mentioned previously. Even in this case, however, this description is one of the many possible characteristics of a biologic; this regulatory standard, therefore, is not dispositive of biologic status, either for a combination product or any other product.

---

[220] *See* Kevin L. Ropp, *Just What is a Biologic, Anyway?*, FDA CONSUMER, Apr. 1993, at 27 (stating biological products are made from living organisms).

[221] *See, e.g., Triage Team Seeks to Prevent Drugs/Biologics Turf Wars*, WASH. DRUG LETTER, Apr. 4, 1988, at 1-2.

[222] *See* FDCA § 503(g)(1)(B), 21 U.S.C. § 353(g)(1)(B).

[223] *See supra* note 25.

The FDA's regulations promulgated in 1991 pertaining to the process for designation of combination products and of other products where jurisdiction is in dispute do not clarify this matter.[224] In seeking information pertaining to the designation of the agency center with primary jurisdiction for the premarket review and other regulation of a combination product, however, the regulations take a broader approach than the narrow mechanism of action focus of the statute. A variety of types of information is sought pertaining to chemical, physical, or biological composition; manufacturing procedures; proposed use or indications; schedule and duration of use; dose; and route of administration.[225]

Presumably, these additional factors are used in deciding how and by which center particular combination products should be regulated. The precise legal basis for consideration of these other factors is unclear, although they are probably based on the agency's powers to promulgate regulations for efficient enforcement of the FDCA under section 371(a). Inter-center agreements also have been executed that provide more guidance as to the allocation of responsibility for regulation of product categories,[226] although, again, the precise statutory and other bases for the assignments are often unclear. Nevertheless, the agreements have helped to clarify the types of products that are subject to regulation as biologics. Thus far the product designation process seems to have worked well, despite the brevity and inadequacies of the implementing legislation.[227]

■ Biotechnology and Biologics

The vast array of modern biotechnology drug products continues to push the limits of the FDA's biologics definitions and require different approaches to regulation. In some cases, the traditional notion that the FDA does not regulate medical procedures or practices, often called the "practice of medicine,"[228] also is being challenged. A number of diverse regulatory events have been prompted by biotechnology developments.

In 1983, the FDA issued a *Federal Register* notice stating that all monoclonal products are subject to biologics' licensing requirements.[229] The widely-anticipated therapeutic effects of interferon also resulted in at least one court case involving a manufacturer trying to market interferon as a food,[230] and a notice in the *Federal Register* reminding manufacturers of the FDA's regulations pertaining to use of interferon labeled for animal testing.[231] The new biotechnologies also have been responsible in part for the reorganization of CBER into dis-

---

[224] *See* 56 Fed. Reg. 58,754 (1991) (codified at 21 C.F.R. pt. 3).

[225] 21 C.F.R. § 3.7.

[226] *See generally* 56 Fed. Reg. 58,760 (1991) (announcing the availability of intercenter agreements); *supra* note 163 (CBER/CDRH agreement).

[227] One significant failing of the process is that the FDA does not currently allow public access to designation decisions or their rationales. Thus, the agency is not only left as the sole repository of information, forcing others often to repeat the same or similar previous requests, but also is the only one able to adjudge the consistency of its decisions. S. 830, 105th Cong., 1st Sess. § 402 (1997) contains provisions governing product jurisdiction, whereas the comparable House bill, *supra* note 4, does not.

[228] *See, e.g.*, United States v. Evers, 453 F. Supp. 1141 (D. Ala. 1978), *aff'd*, 643 F.2d 1043 (5th Cir. 1981). *See also* 37 Fed. Reg. 16,503 (1972) (notice mentioning the legal status of prescribing for uses that are unapproved by the FDA).

[229] *See* 48 Fed. Reg. 50,795 (1983).

[230] *See, e.g.*, Biotics Research Corp. v. Schweiker, [1981-82 Transfer Binder] Food Drug Cosm. L. Rep. (CCH) ¶ 38,160 (D. Nev. 1982), *aff'd*, 710 F.2d 375 (9th Cir. 1983).

[231] *See* 48 Fed. Reg. 52,644 (1983).

crete review divisions oriented toward certain types of products. The Divisions of Cytokine Biology, Cellular and Gene Therapies, and Monoclonal Antibodies were established in early 1993 as part of a new Office of Therapeutics Research and Review.[232]

Biotechnology developments also prompted the FDA to initiate a new approach to providing guidance on data requirements. In 1983, the first "Points to Consider" (PTC) documents were issued to address and govern initially a variety of biotechnology topics such as the manufacturing and testing of monoclonal antibody products and interferon.[233] The PTC guidances often have provided useful guidance on subjects that involve rapid technological developments, although some have been concerned that the PTCs quickly become dated and are difficult to keep current. Over the past twelve years a variety of other topics have been the subject of PTC documents, such as recombinant DNA products and somatic cell and gene therapies.[234] Some of the reasons for these and other developments and the regulatory challenges that modern biotechnology presents can be best understood in the context of the new frontiers in medicine that cellular therapies and related products represent.[235] Cell therapy is the use of living cells usually for therapeutic purposes; the cells are implanted in the same patient or transplanted to a different patient. If the source of the cells is the same patient in which they are used, the cells are called autologous; if the cells are obtained from a person different from the person to be treated, the cells are said to be allogeneic; and if the cells are from a nonhuman animal species, such as pigs, the cells are described as xenogeneic.[236]

The cells usually utilized are somatic cells, i.e., cells that do not cause changes in the genetic make-up of the patient that are inherited by subsequent generations. In contrast, germ cell therapy is intended to cause changes that are passed on to descendants of a patient. Somatic and germ cells both may be "genetically engineered," often through recombinant DNA techniques. Usually this means that their genetic composition has been purposely altered to effect, for example, therapeutic results. The use of these types of genetically-altered somatic cells and of other technologies involving genes often have been referred to collectively as "gene therapy."[237]

---

[232] *See* 57 Fed. Reg. 54,241 (1992). *See also* Kathryn C. Zoon, *Initiatives and the New Structure at the Center for Biologics Evaluation and Research*, 6 REG. AFF. 201 (1994); *CBER Restructuring Proposal Would Create New Offices for Vaccines, Blood Products, And Licensing; Three Associate Center Directors To Be Added*, F-D-C REP. ("The Pink Sheet"), June 1, 1992, at 7.

[233] *See, e.g.*, 49 Fed. Reg. 1138 (1984) (announcing availability of four documents pertaining to monoclonal antibodies, recombinant DNA biological products, and interferon).

[234] *See generally* Congressional and Consumer Affairs Branch, Food & Drug Admin., Memoranda and Related Documents Pertaining to Human Blood and Blood Products, Center for Biologics Evaluation and Research, Points to Consider (PTC) (Aug. 1982 to present). *See also* 61 Fed. Reg. 5786 (announcing availability of addendum to the Points to Consider in Human Somatic Cell and Gene Therapy (issued in 1991).

[235] *See* Dutton, *Gene Therapy Techniques Advances Potential Treatments for Cancer*, GENETIC ENGINEERING NEWS, Mar. 1, 1995, at 8. *See also Gene Therapies Growing Pains*, 269 SCI. 1050 (1995); McCall, Weimer, Baldwin & Pierson, *Biotherapy: A New Dimension in Cancer Treatment*, 7 BIO/TECHNOLOGY 231 (1989); *Designer Tissues Take Hold*, 270 SCI. 230 (1995); W. Aliski, G. Castion & M. Osbond, *The Regulation of Living Cell Therapy (Biocare)*, 3 REG. AFF. 639 (1991).

[236] Xenotransplantation, the use in human beings of non-human animal materials such as organs, has been cautiously endorsed. *See* XENOTRANSPLANTATION: SCIENCE, ETHICS, AND PUBLIC POLICY (Inst. of Medicine, 1996). *See also infra* note 242.

[237] *See* 61 Fed. Reg. 18,749 (1996) (notice of public conference on gene therapy involving the development and evaluation of Phase I products and workshop on vector development). The clinical value of gene therapy has been questioned. *See* Report and Recommendations of the Panel to Assess the NIH Investment in Research in Gene Therapy (Dec. 7, 1995).

Somatic gene therapy experiments traditionally have been subject to NIH jurisdiction under the Guidelines for Research Involving Recombinant DNA Molecules.[238] This is because this type of experimental work is often government-funded and involves the use of recombinant DNA molecules. Gene therapy also has been subject to FDA biologics jurisdiction, because viral and cellular materials are used. Recently, the NIH Guidelines were amended to allow for a consolidated review by NIH and the FDA, in response to complaints that double review was required.[239]

The future role of NIH in the oversight of gene transfer work is unclear. The NIH Recombinant DNA Advisory Committee, which has been responsible for gene therapy experiment review, had been proposed to be discontinued and the responsibility for all gene transfer experiments has been proposed to be transferred to the FDA.[240] The FDA likely will be the only review within the Department of Health and Human Services that eventually will be required. CBER, for example, already has proposed a data bank to gather clinical data on gene therapy trials.[241] More than 600 patients thus far have been the subject of gene therapy.[242]

"Gene transfers" that possibly will be subject to at least FDA review and perhaps NIH oversight in the near future include xenotransplants[243] involving tissues or organs from other animals such as pigs or baboons that have been "humanized" by genetic alteration, and germ cell therapy involving attempts to correct heritable defects. While the concept of germ line alteration to correct metabolic deficiencies and other disorders once raised the specter of the brave new world of eugenics, it now seems likely that with the variety of somatic cell therapies currently in use, further work will be permitted eventually, albeit on a limited basis. Germ line therapy is likely to be controversial, much as somatic cell therapy was.[244]

Some of the complex definitional and other regulatory issues[245] represented by cellular and gene therapies can best be demonstrated by a commonly cited example of encapsulated pancreatic islet cells secreting insulin. If the cells are in an inert polymeric matrix to help prevent their rejection upon implantation, the matrix is clearly a device, the secreted insulin is a nonbiological drug, and islet cells are a biologic. This type of triple combination product and other similar products raise significant questions about the necessary

---

[238] *See supra* note 11.

[239] *See* 60 Fed. Reg. 20,726 (1995).

[240] *See* 61 Fed. Reg. 35,774 (1996). *See also RAC's Identity Crisis*, 269 Sci. 1054 (1995); *FDA Should Conduct Most Reviews of Gene Therapy Protocols, While RAC Should Continue as Policy Body-AD HOC Group; Database Development Supported*, F-D-C Rep. ("The Pink Sheet"), Sept. 4, 1995, at 5. The NIH has published a revised proposal to retain the RAC with different functions and membership. 61 Fed. Reg. 59,726 (1996).

[241] *See* Stone, *Gene Therapy Data Bank Stuck at Starting Gate*, 269 Sci. 467 (1995).

[242] *Id.*

[243] *See FDA Panel OKs Baboon Marrow Transplants*, 269 Sci. 293 (1995). Guidelines were recently issued by the Public Health Service on xenotransplantation. 61 Fed. Reg. 49,920 (1996).

[244] The first human gene therapy experiment was reviewed approximately 14 times before final approval was received, despite a lawsuit. *See NIH Expects to Conduct First Human Gene Therapy Studies Despite a Lawsuit by Rifkin*, Genetic Engineering News, Mar. 1989, at 1. *See also* President's Commission for the Study of Ethical Problems in Medicine and Biomedical and Behavioral Research, Splicing Life, A Report on the Social and Ethical Issues of Genetic Engineering With Human Beings (1982).

[245] *See, e.g.*, Epstein, *Regulatory Concerns in Human Gene Therapy*, 2 Human Gene Therapy 243 (1991).

approval(s), the regulatory mechanism(s) by which such approval(s) is (are) obtained, and the FDA status of materials that are used to prepare or develop such therapies.

A number of more subtle regulatory issues also are involved in this example, that relate primarily to the cellular component of the combination product. In light of the structural and functional interrelationships among cells, tissues, and organs, the dividing line as to the FDA's jurisdiction has been blurred by cellular and related therapies that often are developed by processing tissues and cells. With some notable exceptions, such as heart valve and dura matter allografts which are medical devices,[246] tissues, including their cellular components, and organs from which the tissues often are derived, typically are not regulated by the FDA, particularly as biologics. Moreover, if the cells are processed in ways that they can be used, sometimes only in a specific patient, and the cell or tissue processing is done by a physician, perhaps in or closely related to the operating theater, the activities that fall within the practice of medicine and those that are regulatable by the FDA are not always easily distinguishable. Further, the NOTA prohibition on the purchase or sale of certain human organs and subparts thereof could be construed to prevent the sale of such cellular therapies.[247] One of the key issues is, for example, whether FDA approval somehow negates or supersedes the requirements of NOTA, because approval under section 262 of the PHS Act clearly denotes commercialization.[248]

The scope and nature of the FDA's regulation of cellular and gene products was announced in a *Federal Register* notice published in October 1993.[249] Despite the wide publicity associated with the notice,[250] there does not yet seem to be full appreciation by the regulated community of its significance. Its broad scope, which covers the FDA status of tissue, cells, and materials used to process cells, suggests that it constitutes a substantive amendment to the FDA's definitions for biologics, among other regulations. Interestingly, the notice also fails to address practice of medicine or NOTA issues.

The document defines "somatic cell therapy" as the prevention, treatment, cure, diagnosis, or mitigation of disease or injuries in human beings by the administration of cells that have been manipulated or altered outside of the human body (i.e., *ex vivo*).[251] Cells subject to licensure as biologics include those manipulated in a way that changes the biological characteristics of the cell population, such as expansion, selection, encapsulation, activa-

---

[246] 58 Fed. Reg. 65,514, 65,514 (1993).

[247] Section 274e specifically states that "[i]t shall be unlawful for any person to knowingly acquire, receive, or otherwise transfer any human organ for valuable consideration for use in human transplantation . . . ." Valuable consideration is defined in section 274e(c)(2) not to include "reasonable payments associated with removal, transportation, implantation, processing, preservation, quality control, and storage of a human organ or the expense of travel, housing, and lost wages incurred by the donor of a human organ in connection with donation of the organ."

[248] *See* HUTT & MERRILL, *supra* note 9, at 696 (quoting legislative statement by the FDA concerning its legal authority to regulate human organ transplants and prohibit their sale saying that since the statutes the FDA administers are not intended to deal with ethical issues involved in the sale of therapeutic products, the FDA's regulation of human organs could not result in a ban on their sale for profit).

[249] *See* 58 Fed. Reg. 53,248 (1993).

[250] *See* Kessler, Siegel, Noguchi, Zoon, Feiden & Woodcock, *Regulation of Somatic-Cell Therapy and Gene Therapy By the Food and Drug Administration*, 329 N. ENG. J. MED. 1169 (1993).

[251] 58 Fed. Reg. at 53,250.

tion, or genetic modification.[252] Examples of somatic therapy listed by the FDA involve a wide range of cell types, including cultured cell lines.

The FDA also describes additional cells, tissues, and other materials subject to licensure that are used in the manufacture of somatic cell products, and ancillary products such as components of culture cell medium and substances used to activate or otherwise change the biological characteristics of cells. "Ancillary products," because they are intended to act on the cells and not to have an independent effect on the patient, are classified as medical devices.[253] Combination products in which the primary mode of action is that of the somatic cell therapy component, such as encapsulated pancreatic islet cells secreting insulin (which is specifically mentioned) are designated as biological products.[254]

The broad scope of this statement on somatic cell and gene therapy products has recently been addressed in the specific context of the regulatory status of autologous cells intended for implantation for structural repair and reconstruction. The agency recently announced a notice of public hearing to re-address the regulatory treatment of this special class of cellular products.[255]

The purpose of the hearing was to assess different regulatory approaches, other than by licensing, that may be appropriate for regulation of different types of autologous structural cells. Although this notice of hearing was thought to signal a trend toward further reconsideration of the type of regulation of such biological products, particularly as the FDA becomes more aware of the variety of new biotechnology products subject to the notice and of the enforcement and other resources that will be necessary to implement the notice, the agency resorted to the use of a traditional oversight mechanisms. After further discussion of the topic,[256] the FDA announced a licensure approach[257] to regulation, although some flexibility is allowed in clinical testing requirements.[258] More recently, the FDA announced a broad proposed approach to regulation of all cellular- and tissue-based products.[259]

---

[252] *Id.* For a regulatory review of cell and gene therapies, *see* Philip D. Noguchi, *From Jim to Gene and Beyond: An Odyssey of Biologics Regulation*, 51 FOOD & DRUG L.J. 367 (1996).

[253] 58 Fed. Reg. at 53,251. For a discussion of ancillary products regulation, see Richard S. Schifreen & Cynthia Louth, *Industry View on the Regulation of Ancillary Reagents*, 51 FOOD & DRUG L.J. 155 (1996).

[254] *Id.*

[255] *See* 60 Fed. Reg. 36,808 (1995).

[256] *See* 61 Fed. Reg. 9185 (1996) (announcing a round-table discussion of autologous cells manipulated *ex vivo* for structural repair).

[257] Guidance on Applications for Products Comprised of Living Autologous Cells Manipulated Ex Vivo and Intended for Structural Repair or Reconstruction 5 (May 1996). *See also* 61 Fed. Reg. 26,523 (1996) (announcing availability of this guidance).

[258] *Id.* at 4-5. The first approved cartilage product for autologous structural use was recently announced. FDA Grants Accelerated Approval to Help Repair Damaged Knee Cartilage, FDA Talk Paper No. T97-38 (Aug. 25, 1997); Draft guidelines also have been issued for autologous cells manipulated *ex vivo*. 62 Fed. Reg. 1460 (1997). *See also*, Draft, Quality Assurance Program for Establishments Manufacturing Autologous Cells Manipulated Ex Vivo (undated) *and* Outline for Draft CMC Section, Chemistry, Manufacturing and Controls Guidance for a Biologic Licensing Application for Autologous Cells Manipulated Ex Vivo for Structural Repair (undated).

[259] 62 Fed. Reg. 9721 (1997) (announcing availability of proposed approach). This initiative was part of another reinventing government initiative. *See* PRES. BILL CLINTON & VICE PRES. AL GORE, REINVENTING THE REGULATION OF HUMAN TISSUE, NATIONAL PERFORMANCE REVIEW (1997).

Finally, biological (and other) drugs also have caused significant problems with respect to implementation of the ODA.[260] Approximately 120 orphan drugs have been approved;[261] roughly twenty are biologics. The ODA currently provides, among other incentives, seven years of market exclusivity for drugs intended for rare diseases or conditions. This exclusivity generally means that if two drugs have the "same" structure and are to be used for the "same" purpose, usually only the first orphan drug to be approved is entitled to the several years of market exclusivity and that exclusivity will block marketing for seven years of the second competitive product.

Various issues regarding the ODA, such as the profitability of certain biological drugs and other nonbiological drugs (which in some cases have been derived by the use of genetic engineering techniques) have resulted not only in proposals for legislation to amend the ODA,[262] but also litigation.[263] This litigation has concerned what are the "same" or "different" drugs for purposes of applying the exclusivity provision. Some of these earlier problems associated with the ODA and its exclusivity provision stemmed from the FDA's lack of promulgation of implementing regulations for ten years after the law was enacted. This left orphan drug sponsors struggling, for example, to figure out the precise circumstances under which the market exclusivity provisions would be triggered with respect to competitive products.

Unfortunately, the FDA's regulations[264] are not likely to resolve some of these and the other problems, especially those posed by new biotechnology biological products. Indeed, a suit was recently decided involving two competitive orphan interferon products for the treatment of multiple sclerosis.[265] The market exclusivity provisions are especially problematic. For example, regulations defining what is the "same" drug apply different, sometimes inconsistent, standards for determining "sameness" depending on the type of product. They classify complex drugs (macromolecules) into four different categories: proteins, polysaccharides, polynucleotides, and a vague fourth category entitled "complex partly definable drugs," which includes vaccines.[266] Competitive protein drugs are the "same," even if some variation exists in chemical structure.[267] In contrast, nucleic acid drugs, which probably are biologics unless they are synthetically-derived, are the same

---

[260] *See* Marlene E. Haffner, *Orphan Products — Ten Years Later and Then Some*, 49 Food Drug Cosm. L.J. 593 (1994). *See also* Edward L. Korwek, *Orphan Drug Trial and Tribulations: Profitability, Patient Ceiling, Market Exclusivity, AIDS, and Biotechnology*, 3 Reg. Aff. 133 (1991).

[261] *See* Food & Drug Admin., Office of Orphan Products Development, List of Orphan Designations and Approvals (1997).

[262] *See* Korwek, *Orphan Drug Trial and Tribulations*, *supra* note 259, at 135-39.

[263] *See* Genentech v. Bowen, 676 F. Supp. 301 (D.D.C. 1987). *See also* Korwek, *Orphan Drug Trial and Tribulations*, *supra* note 259, at 142-51; Patricia J. Kenney, *The Orphan Drug Act — Is it a Barrier to Innovation? Does It Create Unintended Windfalls?*, 43 Food Drug Cosm. L.J. 667 (1988).

[264] *See generally* 21 C.F.R. pt. 316.

[265] *See* Berlex Laboratories, Inc. v. Food and Drug Administration, 942 F. Supp. 19 (D.D.C. 1996). This suit involved complex issues pertaining not only to the FDA's orphan drug regulations, but also to the FDA's criteria and procedures for approval of competitive biologic products. The court ruled in the FDA's favor in approving a competitive orphan product. *See also Berlex Sues FDA Claiming Biogen's Avonex Violates Betaseron Orphan Exclusivity; Files for Restraining Order Indicating Avonex Approval is Imminent*, F-D-C Rep. ("The Pink Sheet"), Apr. 29, 1996, at 15.

[266] 21 C.F.R. § 316.3(b)(13)(ii)(A)-(D).

[267] *See id.* § 316.3(b)(13)(ii)(A).

only if no variation exists.[268] Complex biological drugs, such as cell therapy products, which fall in the fourth category, are the same if they are "closely related" with similar therapeutic intent.[269] Cell therapies and other modern biotechnology products will likely pose additional, difficult challenges in defining the precise scope of the exclusivity and other orphan drug regulations.

Conclusion

Some may argue that the FDA, including CBER, which through its predecessors actually pre-dates the formation of the FDA in 1940, often has been and continues to be dragged into regulatory reform. Regardless of how or why CBER and its predecessors in the last fifty years have arrived at current-day approaches to biological products regulation, CBER has—as part of a federal regulatory agency often accused of being inflexible and paralyzed by bureaucracy and cautiousness—often responded well, perhaps even admirably so, to a variety of diverse events and developments, sometimes with important public health consequences.

One important recurrent issue that has persisted over the past few decades is whether any of the regulatory distinctions—some might say contradictions—that have endured for almost a century between biological drug products and most other drugs are still valid or appropriate. It is difficult to imagine, in this era of technological advances and extensive FDA regulatory authority over all aspects of drug (including biologics) production and marketing, the continued need for the regulation of both establishments and products by a license approval process, and for lot-by-lot release requirements.[270] The agency finally has recognized these types of considerations, having recently changed many of its policies and regulations regarding certain biologics, albeit often because of the threat of legislative action.

One could argue effectively today that unified drug regulation, the regulatory harmonization of biological drugs and most non-biological drugs via the NDA process, is suitable today for all biologics.[271] This seems particularly true because the FDA already has extensive control of manufacturing operations of all drugs through its GMP requirements and other regulations. For the future, however, one theme clearly emerges. Biologics regulation must continue to move toward newer, flexible approaches to accommodate a wide variety of technological advances and other developments that can significantly impact public health. The rigid mechanisms of the past must give way to "creative regulation" — once thought to be an oxymoron of biologics oversight. CBER's adherence to past

---

[268] *Id.* § 316.3(b)(13)(ii)(C).

[269] *Id.* § 316.3(b)(13)(ii)(D).

[270] The new legislation would also require FDA to minimize difference in the review and approval of products subject to NDAs and BLAs.

[271] As this text goes to press, the legislation passed by the House and Senate eliminated PLAs and ELAs and substituted biologics license application (BLAs) in their place.

approaches only will continue to underscore the continued need for legislative threats and remedies.

chapter 13

Advertising for Therapeutic Products

Caswell O. Hobbs, Esp.*

General Principles in Federal Trade Commission Consumer Protection Cases

The Federal Trade Commission (FTC's) "consumer protection" jurisdiction is based on that portion of section 5 that proscribes "unfair" and "deceptive" acts or practices.[1] The terms "unfair" and "deceptive," although frequently applicable to the same kinds of practices, are not synonymous. The legal standards relating to "deception" are relatively well established; the scope and limits of the legal standard of "unfairness" are still in a comparatively recent state of development. While this chapter focuses on the FTC's regulation of advertising, which is the FTC's predominant concern with therapeutic products, the same legal standards and analytical approach generally apply to the FTC's regulation of all other marketing practices.

■ General Legal Standards Applicable to Deception Cases

The legal standard governing proof of deception was updated by the FTC in 1984. For many years prior thereto, an accepted articulation of the deception standard was that any advertising representation that had the tendency and capacity to mislead or deceive a prospective purchaser was a deceptive practice in violation of the Federal Trade Commision Act (FTC Act).[2] In the 1984 *Cliffdale Associates, Inc.* proceeding,[3] however, the FTC stated that it found this definition

---

* Mr. Hobbs is a Partner in the law firm at Morgan, Lewis & Bockius, L.L.P., Washington, D.C.

[1] For parallel, but today essentially redundant, proscriptions pertaining specifically to false advertising of food, drugs, and cosmetics, see 15 U.S.C. §§ 12, 15, 52, 55(b)-(e) (1994) and discussion *infra* note at 152.

[2] *See* Chrysler Corp. v. FTC, 561 F.2d 357, 363 (D.C. Cir. 1977); *see generally* FTC v. Standard Educ. Soc'y, 302 U.S. 112 (1937); FTC v. Algoma Lumber Co., 291 U.S. 67 (1934); Charles of The Ritz Corp. v. FTC, 143 F.2d 676 (2d Cir. 1944).

[3] *In re* Cliffdale Assoc., Inc., 103 F.T.C. 110 (1984) (order).

to be circular and therefore inadequate to provide guidance on how a deception claim should be analyzed. Accordingly, we believe it appropriate for the Commission to articulate a clear and understandable standard for deception.

Consistent with its Policy Statement on Deception, issued on October 14, 1983, the Commission will find an act or practice deceptive if, first, there is a representation, omission, or practice that, second, is likely to mislead consumers acting reasonably under the circumstances, and, third, the representation, omission, or practice is material.[4]

The Commission's Policy Statement on Deception, which as adopted by and attached to the *Cliffdale* decision,[5] altered the analytical focus: 1) from advertising that has a "tendency and capacity to deceive" to advertising that is "likely to mislead"; 2) from conclusions drawn by "consumers" to those drawn by "consumers acting reasonably under the circumstances"; and 3) to include the "materiality" of the advertising representations including consideration of "detriment" or consumer "injury" caused by the advertising claims.[6] The FTC's Policy Statement on Deception, which remains the seminal document in FTC deception matters, is as follows:[7]

> Certain elements undergird all deception cases. First, there must be a representation, omission or practice that is likely to mislead the consumer. Practices that have been found misleading or deceptive in specific cases include false oral or written representations, misleading price claims, sales of hazardous or systematically defective products or services without adequate disclosures, failure to disclose information regarding pyramid sales, use of bait and switch techniques, failure to perform promised services, and failure to meet warranty obligations.
>
> Second, we examine the practice from the perspective of a consumer acting reasonably in the circumstances. If the representation or practice affects or is directed primarily to a particular group, the Commission examines reasonableness from the perspective of that group.
>
> Third, the representation, omission, or practice must be a 'material' one. The basic question is whether the act or practice is likely to affect the consumer's

---

4   *Id.* at 164-65. While the *Cliffdale Associates* decision represented the first adjudicatory application of the FTC's new deception standard, an earlier FTC policy statement described in detail the rationale for the Commission's formulation of this new deception standard. *See* Commission Enforcement Policy Statement on Deception, Letter from Chairman James C. Miller to Hon. John D. Dingell (Oct. 14, 1983). The policy statement in this letter was made part of the *Cliffdale Assoc.* decision. Cliffdale Associates, 103 F.T.C at 174-84. *See generally* Crawford, *Unfairness and Deception Policy at the FTC: Clarifying the Commission's Roles and Rules*, 54 ANTITRUST L.J. 303, 305-08 (1985).

5   The Cliffdale Associates standard was adopted by a three to two vote of the Commission, with two dissenting Commissioners arguing for retention of the existing deception standard. *Cliffdale Assoc.*, 103 F.T.C. at 184-98.

6   *Id.*; *In re* Thompson Medical Co., 104 F.T.C. 648, 788, 816-18 (1984) (order), *aff'd*, 791 F.2d 189 (D.C. Cir. 1986), *cert. denied*, 479 U.S. 1086 (1987).

7   *See, e.g.*, FTC v. Pantron I Corp., 33 F.3d 1088 (9th Cir. 1994), *cert. denied*, 115 S. Ct. 1794 (1995); Kraft, Inc. v. FTC, 970 F.2d 311 (7th Cir. 1992), *cert. denied*, 507 U.S. 909 (1993); FTC v. Silueta Distribution, Inc., 1995-1 Trade Cas. (CCH) ¶ 70,918 (N.D. Cal 1995); Stouffer Foods Corp., 5 Trade Reg. Rep. (CCH) ¶ 23,686 (1994) (final opinion).

conduct or decision with regard to a product or service. If so, the practice is material, and consumer injury is likely, because consumers are likely to have chosen differently but for the deception. In many instances, materiality, and hence injury, can be presumed from the nature of the practice. In other instances, evidence of materiality may be necessary.

Thus, the Commission will find deception if there is a representation, omission or practice that is likely to mislead the consumer acting reasonably in the circumstances, to the consumer's detriment.

***

The Commission will find an act or practice deceptive if there is a misrepresentation, omission, or other practice, that misleads the consumer acting reasonably in the circumstances, to the consumer's detriment. The Commission will not generally require extrinsic evidence concerning the representations understood by reasonable consumers or the materiality of a challenged claim, but in some instances extrinsic evidence will be necessary. (Footnotes omitted.)[8]

A practice can be found deceptive regardless of the advertiser's intent, and the absence of an intent to deceive is not a defense in an FTC proceeding.[9] The courts have confirmed that FTC can exercise its "expertise" to determine the meaning of an advertisement or sales representation and whether the representation has the capacity to deceive.[10] In recent years, however, the FTC has increasingly relied upon consumer surveys, premarket research conducted by advertisers, and other objective evidence for proof of deception; advertisers, of course, likewise introduce consumer survey evidence to attempt to demonstrate lack of consumer deception.[11] Representations directed to specific segments of the consumer population will be interpreted on the basis of their meaning to that particular group.[12] Advertising directed to children, for example, will be analyzed differently than advertising directed to more mature and knowledgeable audiences.[13]

An advertisement or other representation will be considered in its entirety, and the "net impression" of the representation will govern.[14] A representation may be made by

---

[8] *Cliffdale Assoc.*, 103 F.T.C. at, 175, 183, 192-93.

[9] *See, e.g.*, FTC v. Algoma Lumber Co., 291 U.S. 67 (1934); Porter & Dietsch, Inc. v. FTC, 605 F.2d 294 (7th Cir., 1979), *cert. denied*, 445 U.S. 950 (1980).

[10] *See, e.g.*, FTC v. Colgate-Palmolive Co., 380 U.S. 374 (1965); Kraft, Inc. v. FTC, 970 F.2d 311 (7th Cir. 1992), *cert. denied*, 507 U.S. 909 (1993); *cf.* Montgomery Ward & Co., Inc. v. FTC, 691 F.2d 1322, 1331 (9th Cir. 1982) ("While we do not disagree with the premise that the FTC has some expertise in consumer transactions, we would expect some indication of the source of the agency's knowledge").

[11] *See, e.g.*, Kraft, Inc. v. FTC, *aff'd*, 970 F.2d 311 (7th Cir. 1992), *cert. denied*, 507 U.S. 909 (1993); *In re* Thompson Medical Co., 104 F.T.C. 648 (1984) (order), *aff'd*, 791 F.2d 189 (D.C. Cir. 1986), *cert. denied*, 479 U.S. 1086 (1987); Stouffer Foods Corp., 5 Trade Reg. Rep. (CCH) ¶ 23,686 (1994) (final opinion).

[12] *See, e.g.*, ITT Continental Baking Co., Inc. v. FTC, 532 F.2d 207 (2d Cir. 1976); Wand Labs., Inc. v. FTC, 276 F.2d 952 (2d Cir.), *cert. denied*, 364 U.S. 827 (1960) (claims for baldness remedies judged by impact on bald men).

[13] *See, e.g.*, *In re* Topper Corp., 79 F.T.C. 681 (1971) (consent order) (meaning of advertisement judged by reference to the age group of children to whom advertisement is directed); *In re* of Lewis Galoob Toys, Inc., 114 F.T.C. 187 (1991) (consent order).

[14] *See, e.g.*, Aronberg v. FTC, 132 F.2d 165 (7th Cir. 1942); Removatron Int'l Corp., 111 F.T.C. 206, 292 (1988) (order), *aff'd*, 884 F.2d 1489 (1st Cir. 1984); *see also In re infra* note 75 and text accompanying; Porter & Dietsch, Inc., 90 F.T.C. 770 (1977) (order), *modified*, 605 F.2d 294 (7th Cir. 1979), *cert. denied*, 445 U.S. 950 (1980).

express or implied claims,[15] as well as by visual images.[16] Literal truth, hypertechnical construction, or inconspicuous disclaimers or disclosures will not save an advertising claim if it is misleading when the entire advertisement is considered as a whole.[17] Advertising that is capable of being interpreted in several ways, one of which may be misleading, will often be construed against the advertiser by the FTC. The FTC need not prove a willful, knowing, or deliberate act; intent to deceive is not an element of a violation.[18] The Commission has held that a consumer is not under any duty to make a reasonable inquiry into the truth of advertising, and that the FTC Act is violated if the advertising induces the first contact through deception, even though the purchaser later becomes fully informed before entering into the transaction.[19] A claim of product effectiveness is false if the product has no effect beyond its placebo effect.[20] Nor is a money-back guarantee a defense to a charge of deceptive advertising.[21] Reasoning that persons reading a print advertisement often will read only the headline, and thus will take their "net impression" of the advertisement from the headline, FTC cases have held that clarifying or contradictory disclosures in the text of an ad may not be sufficient to counteract the headline's impression upon consumers.[22] Although the FTC recognizes that "mere puffing" is not a violation of the FTC Act,[23] subjective opinions that can be disproved objectively are frequently deemed to be factual representations rather than puffery and thus evaluated pursuant to the "deception" standard.[24]

The failure of an advertisement to disclose material facts can also constitute a deceptive practice.[25] A "material" fact is one that is likely to affect a consumer's choice of or con-

---

15 *See e.g.*, Kraft, Inc. v. FTC, 970 F.2d 311 (7th Cir. 1992), *cert. denied,* 507 U.S. 909 (1993); Stouffer Foods Corp., 5 Trade Reg. Rep. (CCH) ¶ 23,686 (1994) (final opinion).

16 *See, e.g.*, Kraft, Inc. v. FTC, 970 F.2d 311 (7th Cir. 1992), *cert. denied*, 507 U.S. 909 (1993); St. Ives Lab., Inc., [1987-1993 Transfer Binder] Trade Reg. Rep. (CCH) ¶ 23,088 (1992) (consent order).

17 *See, e.g.*, American Home Prod. Corp. v. FTC, 695 F.2d 681 (3d Cir. 1982); P. Lorillard Co. v. FTC, 186 F.2d 52, 58 (4th Cir. 1950) ("To tell less than the whole truth is a well known method of deception; and he who deceives by resorting to such method cannot excuse the deception by relying upon the truthfulness *per se* of the partial truth by which it has been accomplished."); Bockensette v. FTC, 134 F.2d 369, 371 (10th Cir. 1943) ("Words and sentences may be literally and technically true and yet be framed in such a setting as to mislead or deceive.").

18 *See, e.g.*, Removatron Int'l Corp., 111 F.T.C. 206 (1988) (order), *aff'd*, 884 F.2d 1489 (1st Cir. 1984).

19 *See, e.g.*, Resort Car Rental Sys., Inc. v. FTC, 518 F.2d 962 (9th Cir.), *cert. denied*, 423 U.S. 827 (1975).

20 *See, e.g.*, FTC v. Pantron I Corp., 33 F.3d 1088 (9th Cir. 1994), *cert. denied*, 115 S. Ct. 1794 (1995).

21 *See, e.g.*, *id.*; *In re* Thompson Medical Co., 104 F.T.C. at 834 n.81.

22 *See e.g.*, *id. In re* Litton Indus., Inc., 97 F.T.C. 1, 70 n.5 (1981) (order); *In re* Giant Food, Inc., 61 F.T.C. 326, 348-49 (1962) (order), *aff'd*, 322 F.2d 977 (D.C. Cir. 1963), *cert. dismissed*, 376 U.S. 967 (1964).

23 *See, e.g.*, The Carlay Co. v. FTC, 153 F.2d 493 (7th Cir. 1946) (recognizing that such words as "easy," "perfect," "amazing," "prime," "wonderful," "excellent" are regarded in law as mere puffing); *In re* Pfizer, Inc., 81 F.T.C. 23, 64 (1972) (order); *In re* H.W. Kirchner, 63 F.T.C. 1283, 1290 (1963) (order) (advertising an inflatable swimming aid as "invisible" is "harmless hyperbole"); *In re* Bristol-Myers Co., 46 F.T.C. 162 (1949) (order), *aff'd on other grounds*, 185 F.2d 58 (4th Cir. 1959) ("beautify" and "whiten" teeth claims permitted as puffing).

24 *See, e.g.*, P. Lorillard Co. v. FTC, 186 F.2d 52 (4th Cir. 1950); *see generally Cliffdale Associates* , 103 F.T.C. 110 (1984) (order).

25 *See, e.g.*, *In re* J.B. Williams Co., Inc. 68 F.T.C. 481 (1966) (order), *aff'd and modified in part*, 381 F.2d 884 (6th Cir.), *modified*, 72 F.T.C. 865 (1967).

duct regarding a product or service.[26] Express claims and claims involving health or safety are presumed by the FTC to be material.[27] Material facts that the FTC has, following an administrative adjudicatory proceeding, ordered to be included as "affirmative disclosures" in a company's future advertising have included, for example, the ingredients of a product, and the nature of safety or medical risks involved in the use of a product.[28] The failure to disclose that physicians and health-care professionals who endorse products have a financial interest in the products can be deceptive.[29] When an affirmative disclosure is necessary to prevent consumers from being misled, the Commission requires that the disclosure be legible and understandable to ensure that the overall message communicated is accurate.[30]

An advertisement may also be found to be deceptive[31] as well as unfair[32] or both if the advertiser lacks adequate substantiation that demonstrates a reasonable basis exists to

---

[26] Information has been found "material" where it concerns its cost (*In re* MacMillan, Inc., 96 F.T.C. 208, 303-04 (1980) (initial decision)); the purpose of the product or service (*In re* Fedders Corp., 85 F.T.C. 38, 61 (1975) (initial decision), *aff'd*, 529 F.2d 1398 (2d Cir.), *cert. denied*, 429 U.S. 818 (1976)); its safety (In re Firestone Tire & Rubber Co., 81 F.T.C. 398, 456 (1972) (order); or its efficacy (*In re* J.B. Williams Co., 68 F.T.C. 481, 546 (1965) (order), *aff'd in part and modified in part*, 381 F.2d 884 (6th Cir.) modified, 72 F.T.C. 865 (1967)). Because the FTC also has adopted a "materiality" test in analyzing the deceptiveness of an implied advertising claim pursuant to the *Cliffdale Associates* criteria, it will be interesting to see whether these two standards of materiality are interpreted in an identical manner. In *Thompson Medical*, the Commission stated:

> In assessing the materiality of such implied claims, we are required to make our own evaluation of whether or not reasonable consumers would consider the information in the claims important. One aid to us in doing so for many claims is the fact that over the years our cases have established several categories of claims pertaining to the central characteristics of a product or service, such as those relaying to its purpose, safety, efficacy, or cost. We now presume that any implied claim in one of these categories is material.

In re Thompson Medical Co., 104 F.T.C. at, 816-17.

[27] *See Cliffdale Associates*, 103 F.T.C. at, 182-83.

[28] *See, e.g.*, Keele Hair & Scalp Specialists, Inc., 275 F.2d 18 (5th Cir. 1960); European Body Concepts, Inc., 5 Trade Reg. Rep. (CCH) ¶ 23,790 (1995) (consent order) (requiring disclosure that body wrapping treatments may be dangerous to persons suffering from certain physical ailments); Diet Center, Inc., 5 Trade Reg. Rep. (CCH) ¶ 23,466 (1993) (consent order) (weight loss center ordered to disclose that failure to follow diet program as recommended may put participants health at risk); Physicians Weight Loss Centers of America, Inc., et al., 5 Trade Reg. Rep. (CCH) ¶ 23,466 (1993) (consent order) (weight loss center ordered to disclose that very low calorie diet program required physician monitoring to minimize the potential for health risks); *In re* Thompson Medical Co., Inc., 104 F.T.C. at, 842 (prohibiting makers of topical analgesic from using the name Aspercreme unless its advertising and packaging made clear that it does not contain aspirin). In re American Home Prod. Corp., 98 F.T.C. 136, 368 (1981) (order), *aff'd*, 695 F.2d 681 (3d Cir. 1982), *modified*, 101 F.T.C. 698 (1983); *modified*, 103 F.T.C. 57 (1984), *modified*, 103 F.T.C. 528 (1984); *In re* Firestone Tire & Rubber Co., 81 F.T.C. 398, 456 (1972), *aff'd*, 481 F.2d 246 (6th Cir.), *cert. denied*, 414 U.S. 1112 (1972); S.S.S. Co. v. FTC., 416 F.2d 226 (6th Cir. 1969). *See generally* Commission's Enforcement Policy on Deception, *reprinted in Cliffdale Associates*, 103 F.T.C., at 182-83.

[29] *See, e.g.*, Body Wise Int'l, Inc., 5 Trade Reg. Rep. (CCH) ¶ 23,831 (1995) (consent order).

[30] *See, e.g.*, Spencer Gifts, Inc. v. FTC, 302 F.2d 267 (3d Cir. 1962) (printed words indicating products were colognes, not perfumes, were so faint and small that they could not be considered adequate notice that products were colognes); American Life and Accident Insurance Co. v. FTC, 255 F.2d 289 (8th Cir.), *cert. denied*, 358 U.S. 875 (1958) (disclosure of miniature insurance policy form did not cure false representations presented in easily read form letters). *See generally Cliffdale Associates*, 103 F.T.C., at 179-81 and cases cited therein.

[31] *See, e.g.*, Firestone Tire & Rubber Co. v. FTC, 481 F.2d 246, 250-51 (6th Cir.)*cert. denied*, 414 U.S. 1112 (1973); *In re* National Dynamics Corp., 82 F.T.C. 488 (1973) (order), *rev'd in part on other grounds*, 492 F.2d 1333 (2d Cir.), *cert. denied*, 419 U.S. 933 (1974), *reissued*, 85 F.T.C. 391 (1976) (modifying order).

[32] *See, e.g.*, *In re* Pfizer, Inc., 81 F.T.C. 23 (1972) (order).

demonstrate the truthfulness of the claim.[33] If the advertisement contains an express or implied reference to a specific type or quantity of substantiation, the advertiser will be expected to possess that specific level of support.[34] Absent a specific reference, however, the FTC assumes that the advertiser possesses a "reasonable basis" for the claim.[35] The Commission's determination of what constitutes a "reasonable basis" for a claim is based on a number of factors: 1) the type and specificity of the advertising claim; 2) the type of product involved; 3) the consequences of a false claim; 4) the benefits of a truthful claim; 5) the cost and benefits of developing additional substantiation for the claim; and 6) the amount of substantiation experts in the field believe is reasonable.[36] Higher levels of substantiation are frequently required for products or claims that relate to safety or efficacy, which cannot be easily evaluated by consumers (Food and Drug Administration (FDA)-regulated products frequently, if not always, fall in this category). This flexible approach to substantiation permits the FTC to balance the potential benefits to consumers resulting from dissemination of the advertisement if the information contained therein is true, against the potential harm that might result should such information be false.[37] It also permits the FTC to tailor the required substantiation standard to fit the particular type of claim presented by the advertisement.[38]

---

[33] See, e.g., FTC v. Removatron Int'l Corp., 111 F.T.C. 206 (1988) (order), aff'd, 884 F.2d 1489 (1st Cir. 1989). More specifically, the FTC interprets an objective claim as an implied representation to consumers that the advertiser possesses a "reasonable basis" to support the claim. See generally FTC Policy Statement Regarding Advertising Substantiation Program, 49 Fed. Reg. 30,999, 31,000 (1984), reprinted in In re Thompson Medical Co., 104 F.T.C. at 839.

[34] See, e.g., FTC Policy Statement Regarding Advertising Substantiation Program, 49 Fed. Reg. at 31,000. Occasionally referred to as "establishment claims," these types of claims may be made explicitly by words and phrases such as "established," "here's proof," and "medically proved." See, e.g., In re American Home Prod. Corp., 98 F.T.C. at 374. These claims also may be made implicitly through the use of language or visual aids such as scientific models or white-coated technicians, which can suggest that the claim is based upon scientific evidence. See, e.g., In re Bristol-Myers Co. 102 F.T.C. 21, 321 (1983) (order), aff'd, 738 F.2d 554 (2d Cir. 1984), cert. denied, 469 U.S. 1189 (1985); Standard Oil Co. of Cal., 84 F.T.C. 1401, 1472 (1974) (order), modified on other grounds, 577 F.2d 653 (9th Cir. 1978)). For example, use of the words "clinical" and "evidence," and reference to a "major hospital study," have been found to imply that the advertising claim is backed by a level of substantiation which would satisfy doctors. See Bristol-Myers Co., 102 F.T.C. at 330.

[35] See FTC Policy Statement Regarding Advertising Substantiation Program, supra note 33, at 31,000. Although the Commission will challenge only "reasonable" (according to the FTC) interpretations of advertising claims, it expects the advertiser to be aware of all such interpretations and to have prior substantiation for each representation. Id. Similarly, the FTC also expects advertisers to be aware of and maintain records of its consumer research data, including that which contrary to advertising claims based on other survey data. In re Amana Refrigeration, Inc., 102 F.T.C. 1262 (1983) (consent order) (requiring cessation of advertising claims based only on favorable portion of survey data without regard to conflicting survey results).

[36] In re Thompson Medical Co., 104 F.T.C., at 821; In re Pfizer, Inc., 81 F.T.C., at 64; see also FTC Policy Statement Regarding Advertising Substantiation Program, supra note 33, at 31,002.

[37] See, e.g., Comments of the Bureaus of Competition, Consumer Protection and Economics of the Federal Trade Commission to FDA Docket No. 85N-0061 in response to request for comments on proposed FDA regulations regarding public health messages on food labels and labeling (1987).

[38] Id. See also In re Porter & Dietsch, Inc., 90 F.T.C., at 885 (claims that any food, drug, or device can help a user achieve any result, such as weight loss, must be substantiated by "competent scientific or medical tests or studies"); Schering Corp., 5 Trade Reg. Rep. (CCH) ¶ 23,646 (1994) (consent order) (representations about the weight-loss benefits, nutritional content, or nutrition-related health benefits of Fiber trim, or any other food, food supplement, or drug must be based on competent and reliable scientific evidence; for certain specified appetite-suppressant or weight-related claims, the required scientific evidence must include at least two independent, adequate, and well-controlled double-blinded clinical studies).

Even though a "reasonable basis" may exist for a particular claim, if there is substantial inconsistency in, or controversy concerning, the evidence relevant to that claim, it may be necessary for a manufacturer to disclose the existence of the contrary evidence in order to ensure that consumers are not misled.[39] Thus, stated more generally, it may be necessary to qualify claims so that the limited nature of the substantiation is apparent to consumers and the advertisement does not imply to consumers that a higher level of substantiation exists.

A 1987 FTC consent agreement with a toothpaste manufacturer provides an illustration of the variability that can result from the FTC's flexible "reasonable basis" standard. The FTC required three separate and discrete levels of substantiation for different types of claims for the toothpaste in question: 1) at least one double-blind, well-controlled clinical trial was required to support claims relating to sensitivity to hot/cold substances or alleviation of symptoms of canker sores and cold sores; 2) at least two double-blind, well-controlled clinical trails were required to support claims relating to alleviation/cure of gum problems associated with gingivitis or peridontitis, or more effective reduction of plaque than other oral hygiene products; and 3) the FTC's basic substantiation requirement, (i.e., "test (s), analysis (es), research project (s), or study (ies) in which the evidence has been objectively obtained and evaluated by persons qualified to do so . . .",) was required to support general claims relating to the diagnosis, treatment, cure, or prevention of disease.[40]

Illustrative types of advertising, sales, and marketing practices frequently challenged as "deceptive acts or practices" violative of section 5 of the FTC Act include:

- Advertisements or sales representations that misrepresent the characteristics of products;[41]

- Deceptive price claims;[42]

---

[39] *See In re* National Comm'n on Egg Nutrition, 88 F.T.C. 89 (1976) (order),*aff'd*, 570 F.2d 157 (7th Cir. 1977), *cert. denied*, 439 U.S. 821 (1978); *compare In re* Bristol-Myers Co., 102 F.T.C. 21 (1983) (order) *aff'd*, 738 F.2d 554 (2d Cir. 1984), *cert. denied*, 469 U.S. 1189 (1985); *In re* Sterling Drug, Inc., 102 F.T.C. 395 (1983) (order), *aff'd*, 741 F.2d 1146 (9th Cir. 1984), *cert. denied*, 470 U.S. 1084 (1985).

[40] *In re* Jerome Milton, Inc., [1987-1993 Transfer Binder] Trade Reg. Rep. (CCH) ¶ 22,468 (1987) (consent order); *see also* FTC v. Pantron I Corp., 33 F.3d 1088 (9th Cir. 1994), *cert. denied*, 115 S. Ct. 1794 (1995).

[41] *See, e.g.*, FTC v. Algoma Lumber Co., 291 U.S. 67 (1934); Porter & Dietsch, Inc. v. FTC, 605 F.2d 294 (7th Cir. 1979), *cert. denied*, 445 U.S. 950 (1980); Kraft, Inc. v. FTC, 970 F.2d 311 (7th Cir. 1992), *cert. denied*, 507 U.S. 909 (1993). *See also* American Tobacco Co., 5 Trade Reg. Rep. (CCH) ¶ 23,683 (1994) (consent order) (prohibiting misrepresentations about the relative amount of tar and nicotine consumers will get by smoking various brands of cigarettes); Stouffer Foods Corp., 5 Trade Reg. Rep. (CCH) ¶ 23,686 (1994) (final opinion) (prohibiting corporation from misrepresenting the amount of sodium or any other ingredient in its frozen food products); North American Phillips Corp., 111 F.T.C. 139 (1988) (consent order) (proscribing claim that water filter would "help clean" tap water because, while the water filter may have removed some impurities, it added to the tap water a potentially hazardous chemical).

[42] *See, e.g.*, Spiegel, Inc. v. FTC, 411 F.2d 481 (7th Cir. 1969); Alamo Rent-A-Car, Inc., 111 F.T.C. 644 (1989) (order) (nondisclosure of mandatory fees and charges in response to consumer inquiries on toll free number); *In re* Encyclopedia Britannica, Inc., 100 F.T.C. 500 (1982) (modifying order) (discount from "regular" price claim may not be used unless "such price is an actual, bona fide price for which each such item has been openly and actively offered for sale in the recent and regular course of business for a reasonably substantial period of time"). *See generally* Guides Against Deceptive Pricing, 16 C.F.R. §§ 233.1 - 233.5 (1997); Guides Against Bait Advertising, 16 C.F.R. §§ 238.0 - 238.4; and Guide Concerning Use of the Word "Free" and Similar Representations, 16 C.F.R. §§ 251.1.

- Deceptive warranty representations;[43]
- Deceptive use of testimonials, endorsements, tests, surveys, demonstrations, mock-ups, etc.;[44]
- Failure to disclose health or safety considerations relevant to the use of the product, or other material facts about the product;[45]
- Failure to disclose existence of significant product defects;[46]
- Dissemination of advertising or sales representations without possessing a "reasonable basis" for verifying the truthfulness of the representations[47]

■ General Legal Standards Applicable to Unfairness Cases

Although acts or practices that are objectionable under section 5 of the FTC Act are often both unfair and deceptive, unfairness may be used as an independent basis for Commis-

---

[43] *See, e.g.*, Craftmatic/ Contour Organ Inc., [1983-1987 Transfer Binder] Trade Reg. Rep. (CCH) ¶ 22,220 (1985) (consent order) (deceptive failure to disclose that consumer must ship electric beds at their own expense to obtain warranty); *Peabody Barnes, Inc.*, 104 F.T.C. 503 (1984) (consent order) (failure to disclose information sufficient to determine the actual length of warranty coverage, if any); In re Montgomery Ward & Co. Inc., 97 F.T.C. 363 (1981) (order). *See also* Magnuson-Moss Warranty Act, *See generally* FTC Guides relating to the Deceptive Advertising of Guarantees, 16 C.F.R. §§ 239.1 - 239.5.

[44] *See, e.g.*, FTC v. Colgate-Palmolive Co., 380 U.S. 374 (1965); Volvo North America Corp., [1987-1993 Transfer Binder] Trade Reg. Rep. (CCH) ¶ 23,041 (1992) (consent order) (challenging TV advertisement showing an automobile withstanding the weight of a large truck being driven over it, without disclosing that the automobile had been structurally reinforced); In re National Media Corp., 5 Trade Reg. Rep. (CCH) ¶ 23,360 (1993) (consent order) (challenging, deceptive testimonial that use of crystals eliminated lumps in breasts or cured breast cancer; deceptive demonstration of performance of kitchen mixer; deceptive use of seal of approval); In re Kroger Co., 100 F.T.C. 573 (1982); (modifying order) (comparison survey of food product prices was deceptive when not performed in a "blind" fashion); In re Teledyne, Inc., 97 F.T.C. 320 (1981) (consent order) (cease claim of endorsement from major dental association); Cooga Mooga Inc., 92 F.T.C. 310 (1978) (consent order), *modified*, 98 F.T.C. 814 (1981) (celebrity endorsement misrepresented characteristics of acne remedy); In re Borden, Inc., 78 F.T.C. 686 (1971) (consent order) (misleading demonstration purporting to show quality of instant coffee); In re Campbell Soup Co., 77 F.T.C. 664 (1970) (consent order) (deceptive use of mock-ups in portraying contents of soup); *See also* FTC Guides for Use of Endorsements and Testimonials in Advertising, 16 C.F.R. §§ 255.0-255.5.

[45] *See, e.g.*, Porter & Dietsch, Inc. v. FTC, 605 F.2d 294 (7th Cir. 1979), *cert. denied*, 445 U.S. 950 (1980); In re American Home Prods. Corp., 98 F.T.C., at 385-86; In re Firestone Tire & Rubber Co., 81 F.T.C. 398 (1972) (order), *aff'd*, 481 F.2d 246 (6th Cir.), *cert. denied*, 414 U.S. 1112 (1973); In re Lorillard, 80 F.T.C. 455, 460-65 (1972) (consent order) (requiring six tobacco manufacturers to disclose health warnings in cigarette advertisements). *See also* Formu-3 Int'l, Inc., 5 Trade Reg. Rep. (CCH) ¶ 23,751 (1995) (consent order) (failure to warn customers about health risks associated with not following diet protocol); Campbell Soup Co., [1987-1993 Transfer Binder] Trade Reg. Rep. (CCH) ¶ 22,967 (1992) (consent order) (failure to disclose sodium contents of soups and resulting health risks in advertisement making health claims relating to heart disease); R.J. Reynolds Tobacco Co., [1987-1993 Transfer Binder] Trade Reg. Rep. (CCH) ¶ 22,736 (1990) (consent order) (failure to accurately disclose the results of a study of the health effects of smoking).

[46] *See, e.g.*, In re General Motors Corp., 102 F.T.C. 1741 (1983) (consent order) (failure to disclose the likelihood or an occurrence of a serious material defect in automobile); In re Chrysler Corp., 96 F.T.C. 134 (1980) (consent order) (failure to disclose premature rusting); *see also* In re International Harvester Co., 104 F.T.C. 949 (1984) (order).

[47] *See, e.g.*, In re Bristol-Myers Co., 102 F.T.C. 21 (1983) (order), *aff'd* 738 F.2d 554 (2d Cir. 1984), *cert. denied*, 469 U.S. 1189 (1985); In re National Dynamics Corp., 82 F.T.C. 488 (1973) (order), *rev'd in part on other grounds*, 492 F.2, 1333 (2d Cir.), *cert. denied*, 419 U.S. 993 (1974), *reissued*, 85 F.T.C. 391 (1976) (modifying order).

sion action even where deception has not been found.[48] In *FTC v. Sperry & Hutchinson Co.*,[49] the Supreme Court reaffirmed the FTC's authority to prohibit "unfair" practices that were neither deceptive nor anticompetitive. The Court held that the FTC can operate "like a court of equity" in considering "public values" to determine standards of fairness.[50] In 1980, the FTC issued a Policy Statement that "delineat[ed] the Commission's views of the boundaries of its consumer unfairness jurisdiction . . . ."[51] This policy statement was subsequently incorporated in the FTC's 1984 *International Harvester* decision, which is the Commission's current benchmark defining the scope of its unfairness powers,[52] and was codified for purposes of FTC rulemaking by statute in 1994.[53]

Illustrative categories of practices that have been found to be "unfair" to consumers include:

- Practices that exploit consumer weaknesses, expectations or vulnerabilities;[54]

- Practices that impose undue economic burdens on consumers;[55] and

---

[48] *See, e.g.*, FTC v. Sperry & Hutchinson Co., 405 U.S. 233 (1972); FTC v. R.F. Keppel & Bro., Inc., 291 U.S. 304 (1934); Wolf v. FTC, 135 F.2d 564 (7th Cir. 1943); *In re* International Harvester, Co., 104 F.T.C. 949 (1984) (order); *In re* Pfizer, Inc., 81 F.T.C. 23 (1972) (order); *In re* Chemway Corp., 77 F.T.C. 1250 (1971) (consent order); *In re* All-State Industries, 75 F.T.C. 465 (1969) (order), *aff'd*, 423 F.2d 423 (4th Cir. 1970), *cert. denied*, 400 U.S. 838 (1970); *In re* First Buckingham Community, Inc., 73 F.T.C. 938 (1968) (order).

[49] FTC v. Sperry & Hutchinson, 405 U.S. 233 (1972).

[50] *Id.* at 239. *See also* FTC v. Standard Educ. Soc'y., 302 U.S. 112, *reh'g denied*, 302 U.S. 779 (1937); Beneficial Corp. v. FTC, 542 F.2d 611 (3d Cir. 1976), *cert. denied*, 430 U.S. 983 (1977); Spiegel, Inc. v. FTC, 494 F.2d 59 (7th Cir.), *cert. denied*, 419 U.S. 869 (1974); *In re* Pfizer, Inc., 81 F.T.C. 23 (1972) (order).

[51] Commission Statement of Policy on the Scope of the Consumer Unfairness Jurisdiction, Letter from Chairman James C. Miller III to Senators Danforth and Ford (Dec. 17, 1980). These new unfairness standards were first applied in an adjudicatory proceeding in *In re* Horizon, Inc., 97 F.T.C. 464 (1981) (order).

[52] *In re* International Harvester, Co., 104 F.T.C. 949 (1984) (order). The *International Harvester* case also contains a useful discussion of the Commission's views as to the relationship between the FTC's deception and unfairness standards.

[53] Federal Trade Commission Act Amendments of 1994, Pub. L. No. 103-312, 108 Stat. 1691 (1994).

[54] *See, e.g.*, Beneficial Corp. v. FTC, 542 F.2d 611 (3d Cir. 1976), *cert. denied*, 430 U.S. 983 (1977) (unfair to use information obtained during tax preparation for purposes of soliciting loans); Arthur Murray Studio of Washington, Inc. v. FTC, 458 F.2d 622 (5th Cir. 1972) (unfair advantage taken of student's "deep seated" reasons for taking dance course). *In re* Travel King, Inc., 86 F.T.C. 715 (1975) (order) (unfair promotion of "psychic surgery" to desperate consumers with terminal illnesses). *See also* 16 C.F.R. § 429.1 (FTC rule providing a three day "cooling off" period for consumers to rescind door-to-door sales contracts which might have resulted from unfair advantage being taken of a lack of sales resistance).

[55] *See, e.g.*, Orkin Exterminating Co., Inc. v. FTC, 849 F.2d 1354 (11th Cir. 1988), *reh'g denied en banc*, 859 F.2d 928, *cert. denied*, 488 U.S. 1041 (1989); American Financial Serv. Ass'n v. FTC, 767 F.2d 957 (D.C. Cir. 1985), *cert. denied*, 475 U.S. 1011 (1986); Spiegel, Inc. v. FTC, 494 F.2d 59 (7th Cir.), *cert. denied*, 419 U.S. 896 (1974); Fone Telecommunications, [1987-1993 Transfer Binder] Trade Reg. Rep. (CCH) ¶ 23,348 (1993) (consent order) (unfair inducement to children to place telephone calls, and thereby incur a charge, without providing a reasonable means for those responsible for paying the charges to exercise control over the transaction); *In re* Amrep Corp., 102 F.T.C. 1362 (1983) (order), 768 F.2d 1171 (10th Cir. 1985), *cert. denied*, 475 U.S. 1034 (1986) (unfair provisions in consumer contracts); *In re* Australian Land Title, Ltd., 92 F.T.C. 362 (1982) (consent order) (unfair to sell undivided interests in land to numerous consumers); *In re* Bede Aircraft, Inc., 92 F.T.C. 449 (1978) (consent order) (unfair for company to refuse to invoke protection of Bankruptcy Act because such refusal prejudiced rights of customers); *In re* Carter Hawley Stores, Inc., 85 F.T.C. 1116 (1975) (consent order) (unfair write-off of consumers' unused department store credit balance); *In re* Pfizer, Inc., 81 F.T.C., at 62 ("Given the imbalance of knowledge and resources between a business enterprise and each of its customers, economically it is more rational and imposes far less cost on society to require a manufacturer to confirm his affirmative product claims rather than impose a burden upon each individual consumer to test, investigate, or experiment for himself").

- Practices that create risk of injury, particularly to children.[56]

For example, in *Pfizer, Inc.*,[57] the Commission concluded that it is an unfair practice for an advertiser to make an affirmative product claim without first possessing a "reasonable basis" for the claim. In *Beneficial Corp.*,[58] a determination of unfairness was grounded upon a violation of consumer expectations that tax information would be kept confidential. In *Uncle Ben's, Inc.*,[59] the FTC challenged as unfair TV advertising that showed an unsupervised child cooking on kitchen appliances, while in *General Foods Corp.*,[60] the FTC proscribed advertising showing an adult gathering and eating wild roots and berries, implying that children can safely do so. The Commission has also applied an unfairness analysis in rulemaking proceedings. The FTC's Care Labeling Rule, for example, requires laundering instructions for clothing to be disclosed because "it is unduly oppressive and unfair to consumers to withhold information essential to the ordinary use of products."[61] Similar reasoning underlies the FTC's rule that gasoline octane information be disclosed on gasoline pumps.[62]

The Commission's noteworthy decision in *International Harvester*[63] involved charges of both deception and unfairness arising from the respondent's failure to disclose a safety hazard associated with its farm tractors, which resulted in several deaths and injuries over a period of some years. The Commission found no deception, but upheld an unfairness finding based on an extended "cost-benefit analysis" balancing the injury from nondisclosure against the burden imposed by a disclosure requirement.[64] In the most recent federal court reaffirmation of the FTC's "unfairness" jurisdiction, the U.S. Court of Appeals for the Eleventh Circuit found that Orkin Exterminating Co. had acted unfairly by raising their fees to consumers whose contracts did not permit such fee increases.[65]

---

[56] *See, e.g., In re* International Harvester Co., 104 F.T.C. 949 (1984) (order); *In re* AMF Inc., 95 F.T.C. 310 (1980) (consent order) (bicycle advertisements depicting dangerous riding practices); *In re* Mego Int'l, Inc., 92 F.T.C. 186 (1978) (consent order) (children depicted using electrical toys/appliances near water without adult supervision); *In re* Hudson Pharmaceutical Corp., 89 F.T.C. 82 (1977) (consent order) (vitamin advertising directed to children); *In re* General Foods Corp., 86 F.T.C. 831 (1975) (consent order) (cereal advertisement depicting individual eating plants and berries in their raw and natural state); *In re* Philip Morris, Inc., 82 F.T.C. 16 (1973) (consent order) (distribution of razor blade samples in Sunday papers without adequate protective packaging).

[57] *In re* Pfizer, Inc., 81 F.T.C. 23 (1972) (order).

[58] *In re* Beneficial Corp., 86 F.T.C. 119 (1975) (order), *enforced in part, reversed in part on other grounds*, 542 F.2d 611 (3d Cir. 1975), *cert. denied*, 430 U.S. 983 (1977).

[59] *In re* Uncle Ben's, Inc., 89 F.T.C. 131 (1977) (consent order).

[60] *In re* General Foods Corp., 86 F.T.C. 831 (1975) (consent order).

[61] Trade Regulation Rule: Care Labeling of Textile Wearing Apparel, 36 Fed. Reg. 23,889 (1972); 16 C.F.R. §§ 423.1-423.10.

[62] Trade Regulation Rule Including A Statement of Its Basis and Purpose: Posting of Minimum Octane Numbers on Gasoline Dispensing Pumps, 36 Fed. Reg. 23,876, 23,880 (1972); 16 C.F.R. §§ 306.0-306.11.

[63] *In re* International Harverster, Inc. 104 F.T.C. 949 (1984) (order).

[64] *Id. at* 1062-67.

[65] Orkin Exterminating Co. v. FTC, 849 F.2d 1354 (11th Cir. 1988), *reh'g denied en banc*, 859 F.2d 928 (11th Cir. 1988), *cert. denied*, 488 U.S. 1041 (1989). *See also* California State Board of Optometry v. F.T.C., 910 F.2d 976 (D.C. Cir. 1990), *reh'g denied*, 924 F.2d 243 (restricting the FTC's right to promulgate unfairness rule as infringement on state sovereignty); FTC v. Indiana Fed'n of Dentists, 476 U.S. 447 (1986) (confirming the FTC's "unfairness" jurisdiction in antitrust proceedings).

■ Scope of Federal Trade Commission Remedies

As discussed previously, if the FTC determines, following an administrative adjudication, that a company's practices violate the FTC Act, the FTC issues a "cease and desist" order against the company. Such an order may also be entered pursuant to consent settlement procedures[66] and, in fact, most FTC proceedings are settled in this manner. The FTC has been afforded considerable discretion by the courts in its choice of remedies to be imposed by such orders,[67] and a company losing an FTC proceeding, or negotiating a consent agreement with the FTC, should anticipate the possibility of a far-reaching remedial order.

In addition to the company itself, the FTC's orders may also extend to corporate owners, officers or agents, and related individuals and organizations.[68] Advertising agencies, for example, have frequently been joined in proceedings challenging advertising that they prepared,[69] as well as paid endorsers of advertised products.[70] To enforce its orders, the FTC has the power to file civil penalty proceedings, to seek injunctions, and to seek monetary and other redress for consumers.[71]

If the FTC finds that an advertisement is misleading because of the failure to disclose a "material fact," the FTC can order that future advertising or oral sales presentations con-

---

[66] *See generally supra* note 15 and accompanying text.

[67] *See, e.g.,* Jacob Siegel Co. v. FTC, 327 U.S. 608, 611-13 (1946); Borg-Warner Corp. v. FTC, 746 F.2d 108 (2d Cir. 1984); Kraft, Inc. v. FTC, 970 F.2d 311 (7th Cir. 1992) *cert. denied,* 507 U.S. 909 (1993); Removatron Int'l Corp., 111 F.T.C., at 292; *cf.* TRW, Inc. v. FTC, 647 F.2d 942, 954 (9th Cir. 1981) (holding it an abuse of FTC discretion to issue an order where there exists no "cognizable danger" of recurrent violation).

[68] *See, e.g.,* FTC v. Standard Educ. Soc'y, 302 U.S. 112, *reh'g denied,* 302 U.S. 779 (1937); P.F. Collier & Son Corp. v. FTC, 427 F.2d 261 (6th Cir.), *cert. denied,* 400 U.S. 926 (1970). For the individual liability of owners or operating officials of businesses, see Southwest Sunsites, Inc. v. FTC, 785 F.2d 1431 (9th Cir.), *cert. denied,* 479 U.S. 828 (1986); FTC v. NCH, Inc., 1995-2 Trade Cas. (CCH) ¶ 71,114 (D. Nev. 1995); FTC v. Silueta Distribution, Inc., 1995-1 Trade Cas. (CCH) ¶ 70,918 (N.D. Cal 1995); FTC v. Safety Plus, Inc., 1993-2 Trade Cas. (CCH) ¶ 70,301 (D. Ky., 1993); United States v. Various Articles of Devices . . . which include Sporicidin Brand Disinfectant, 1992-1 Trade Cas. (CCH) ¶ 69,768 (D. Md. 1992); FTC v. Kitco of Nevada, Inc., 612 F. Supp. 1282 (D. Minn. 1985); Griffin Systems, Inc., 5 Trade Reg. Rep. (CCH) ¶ 23,603 (1994) (final opinion).

[69] *See, e.g.,* Doherty, Clifford, Steers & Shenfield, Inc. v. FTC, 392 F.2d 921 (6th Cir. 1968); Colgate-Palmolive Co. v. FTC, 310 F. 2d 89 (1st Cir. 1962); J. Walter Thompson USA, 5 Trade Reg. Rep. (CCH) ¶ 23,861 (1995) (consent order); *In re* Ogilvy & Mather Int'l, Inc. [1987-1993 Transfer Binder] Trade Reg. Rep. (CCH) ¶ 22,554 (1988) (modifying order); *In re* Bristol-Myers Co., 102 F.T.C. 21 (1983) (order).

[70] *See, e.g.,* Live Lee Productions, Inc., et al., 5 Trade Reg. Rep. (CCH) ¶ 23,842 (1995) (consent order); Numex Corp., 5 Trade Reg. Rep. (CCH) ¶ 23,402 (1993) (consent order); Synchronal Corp., et al., 5 Trade Reg. Rep. (CCH) ¶ 23,404 (1993) (consent order) (expert endorsers required to have competent and reliable scientific evidence to support any expert endorsement they provide, and to actually exercise their represented expertise by examining or testing the product).

[71] 15 U.S.C. §§ 45(1), 45(m), 57b(a)(2), 57b(b). *See, e.g.,* United States v. Johnson, 541 F.2d 710 (9th Cir. 1976), *cert. denied,* 429 U.S. 1093 (1977) (civil penalty action); United States v. Reader's Digest Ass'n., Inc., 494 F. Supp. 770 (D.C. Del. 1980), *aff'd,* 662 F.2d 955 (3d Cir. 1981), *cert. denied,* 455 U.S. 908 (1982) (injunctive action); FTC v. Glenn W. Turner Enter., Inc., 446 F. Supp. 1113 (D. Fla. 1978) (consumer redress action).

tain an "affirmative disclosure" of such facts.[72] Courts have upheld FTC affirmative disclosure orders when the FTC has made the threshold finding that consumers have been in the past, or would in the future, be deceived in the absence of such disclosures.[73] Affirmative disclosure orders generally have not been limited to specific time periods, because the theory of deception in such cases is that silence with regard to the product in question will always be deceptive.[74]

In addition to prohibiting the specific unlawful practices engaged in by the respondent, FTC cease-and-desist orders can also "fence-in" a company, i.e., can prohibit related unlawful practices not previously utilized by the company, or prohibit lawful activities that could be used the company to revive the illegal conduct.[75] Thus, the FTC's order can cover products or geographic areas other than those involved in the particular unlawful activities that were the subject of the FTC complaint.[76] For example, in the *Thompson Medical Co.* case, the FTC prohibited future comparative claims by the company for *any* analgesic product even though the unlawful claims related solely to the company's Aspercream analgesic product.[77]

---

[72] *See, e.g.,* Southwest Sunsites, Inc. v. FTC, 785 F.2d, at 1439; Amrep Corp. v. FTC, 768 F.2d 1171 (10th Cir. 1985), *cert. denied,* 475 U.S. 1034 (1986); Warner-Lambert Co. v. FTC, 562 F.2d 749, 759 (D.C. Cir. 1977), *cert. denied,* 435 U.S. 950 (1978); J.B. Williams Co. v. FTC, 381 F.2d 884 (6th Cir. 1967) (ordering maker of Geritol, an iron supplement, to disclose that Geritol relieves symptoms of fatigue only in those persons suffering from iron deficiency anemia, and that majority of people experiencing fatigue do not suffer from this anemia); Ward Lab., Inc. v. FTC, 276 F.2d 952 (2d Cir.), *cert. denied,* 364 U.S. 827 (1960) (ordering sellers of treatment for baldness to disclose that vast majority of cases of hair thinning and balding are attributable to heredity, age, and endocrine balance, and that treatment would have no effect on baldness caused by such factors). Recent consent orders illustrative of this principle include Taleigh Corp., 5 Trade Reg. Rep. (CCH) ¶ 23,783 (1995) (consent order); Third Option Lab., Inc. 5 Trade Reg. Rep. (CCH) ¶ 23,650 (1995) (consent order); Jason Pharm., Inc., [1987-1993 Transfer Binder] Trade Reg. Rep. (CCH) ¶ 23,073 (1992) (consent order); Sandoz Nutrition Corp., [1987-1993 Transfer Binder] Trade Reg. Rep. (CCH) ¶ 23,073 (1992) (consent order); National Center for Nutrition, [1987-1993 Transfer Binder] Trade Reg. Rep. (CCH) ¶ 23,073 (1992) (consent order); *In re* An-Mar Int'l Ltd., [1987-1993 Transfer Binder] Trade Reg. Rep. (CCH) ¶ 22,681 (1989) (consent order).

[73] *See, e.g.,* J.B. Williams Co. v. FTC, 68 F.T.C. 481 (1965) (order),*aff'd,* 381 F.2d 884 (6th Cir. 1967); Grolier, Inc. v. FTC, 699 F.2d 983 (9th Cir.), *cert. denied,* 464 U.S. 891(1983); *cf.* FTC v. Simeon Management Co., 532 F.2d 708 (9th Cir. 1976) (setting aside FTC order requiring affirmative disclosures due to absence of evidence in the record that consumers seeing advertisement would be deceived).

[74] The FTC, however, recently adopted a general "sunsetting" policy that automatically terminates (with only a few limited exceptions) all orders after a twenty-year period. Duration of Existing Competition and Consumer Protection Orders, 60 Fed. Reg. 58,514 (1995).

[75] *See, e.g.,* FTC v. Nat'l Lead Co., 352 U.S. 419 (1957); FTC v. Ruberoid Co., 343 U.S. 470 (1952); Jacob Siegel Co. v. FTC, 327 U.S. 608 (1946); Kraft, Inc. v. FTC, 970 F.2d 311 (7th Cir. 1992), *cert. denied,* 507 U.S. 909 (1983); Figgie Int'l Inc. v. FTC, 107 F.T.C. 313 (order), *aff'd in an opinion not for publication,* 1987-1 Trade Cas. (CCH) ¶ 67,546 (4th Cir. 1987); Borden, Inc. v. FTC, 674 F.2d 498 (6th Cir. 1981); Amrep Corp. v. FTC, 768 F.2d 1171 (10th cir. 1985), *cert. denied,* 475 U.S. 1034 (1986); Stouffer Foods Corp., 5 Trade Reg. Rep. (CCH) ¶ 23,686 (1994) (final opinion).

[76] *See, e.g.,* FTC v. Colgate-Palmolive Co., 380 U.S. 374 (1965); FTC v. Mandel Bros., 359 U.S. 385 (1959). For fencing-in provisions in FTC advertising cases, see, e.g., Bristol-Myers Co. v. FTC, 738 F.2d 554 (2d Cir. 1984), *cert. denied,* 469 U.S. 1189 (1985); Sears, Roebuck & Co. v. FTC, 676 F.2d 385 (9th Cir. 1982); Litton Indus. v. FTC, 676 F.2d 364 (9th Cir. 1982); Jay Norris, Inc. v. FTC, 598 F.2d 1244 (2d Cir.), *cert. denied,* 444 U.S. 980 (1979); Fedders Corp. v. FTC, 529 F.2d 1398 (2d Cir.), *cert. denied,* 429 U.S. 818 (1976); Scali, McCabe, Sloves, Inc. [1987-1993 Transfer Binder] Trade Reg. Rep. (CCH) ¶ 23,041 (1991) (consent order).

[77] *In re* Thompson Medical Co., 104 F.T.C., 837.

The Commission's cease-and-desist orders can also extend beyond simply a negative proscription of particular practices, and can require a company to undertake affirmative steps designed to eradicate or cure the effects of a violation.[78] For example, advertisers have been required to engage in "corrective advertising" designed to "correct" previous misrepresentations and thereby eradicate their lingering effects.[79] The FTC will order corrective advertising when it finds that: 1) the advertisements challenged by the Commission played a substantial role in creating or reinforcing a false belief in the public mind regarding the product; and 2) this belief is likely to remain even after the deceptive advertising ceases.[80] Following the Supreme Court's landmark 1976 and 1980 decisions in *Virginia State Board of Pharmacy v. Virginia Citizens Consumers Council*,[81] and *Central Hudson Gas & Electric Corp. v. Public Service Commission of New York*,[82] (holding that commercial speech,

---

[78] *See, e.g.*, Unocal, 5 Trade Reg. Rep. (CCH) ¶ 23,522 (1994) (consent order) (oil company charged with making unsubstantiated claims regarding the performance superiority of the company's higher octane gasolines required to send a corrective notice to some of its credit card customers, providing information about vehicle performance relative to the octane used); Eggland's Best, Inc., 5 Trade Reg. Rep. (CCH) ¶23,551 (1994) (Eggland required to include on its egg cartons, for one year, a corrective notice stating that no studies show that Eggland's eggs are different from other eggs in their effect on serum cholesterol). *See also* Nutri-System, Inc., 5 Trade Reg. Rep. (CCH) ¶ 23,466 (1994) (consent order); Diet Center, Inc., 5 Trade Reg. Rep. (CCH) ¶ 23,466 (1993) (consent order); Physicians Weight Loss Centers of America, 5 Trade Reg. Rep. (CCH) ¶ 23,466 (1993) (consent order); *In re* American Home Prod. Co., 98 F.T.C. 136 (1981) (order), *aff'd*, 695 F.2d 681 (3d Cir. 1982) *modified*, 101 F.T.C. 698 (1983); Sears, Roebuck & Co., 95 F.T.C. 406 (1980) (order), *aff'd*, 676 F.2d 385 (9th Cir. 1982); *In re* General Motors Corp., 86 F.T.C. 831 (1975) (consent order); *In re* Colgate-Palmolive Co., 59 F.T.C. 1452 (1961) (order).

[79] *See In re* Warner-Lambert Co., 86 F.T.C. 1398 (1975), *modified and enforced*, 562 F.2d 749 (D.C. Cir. 1977), *cert. denied*, 435 U.S. 950 (1978) (FTC did not exceed its authority in ordering corrective advertising to eliminate lingering effects caused by many years of deceptive advertising claims regarding medicinal powers of Listerine mouthwash); Eggland's Best Inc., 5 Trade Reg. Rep. (CCH) ¶ 23,551 (1994) (respondent ordered to label egg packages with a corrective notice stating that no studies show that Eggland's eggs are different from other eggs in their effect on serum cholesterol); *In re* BayleySuit, Inc., 102 F.T.C. 1285 (1983) (consent order) (respondent ordered to use best efforts to notify users about necessary safety modification until at least 80% of purchasers had been reached); *In re* Hair Extension of Beverly Hills, Inc., 95 F.T.C. 361 (1980) (consent order) (requiring at least $8000 worth of newspaper advertising that hair implants are unsafe); *In re* Hayoun Cosmetique, Inc., 95 F.T.C. 794 (1980) (consent order) (requiring six months' disclosure that no product can cure acne); *In re* Wasem's Inc. 84 F.T.C. 209 (1974) (consent order) (requiring company to run a designated number of corrective advertisements rather than merely to devote a certain percentage of total advertising time to such remedial advertising); *In re* ITT Continental Baking Co., 83 F.T.C. 865 (1973) (order), *modified*, 83 F.T.C. 1105 (1973), *enforced and modified in part*, 532 F.2d 207 (2d Cir. 1976), *modified*, 90 F.T.C. 181 (1977) (corrective advertising appropriate where record revealed that a substantial portion of the public continued to recall message contained in the deceptive advertising even after it had been discontinued); *In re* Amstar Corp., 83 F.T.C. 659 (1973) (consent order) (requiring specific wording in remedial advertisement, rather than a mere noting in the advertisement of the prior deception); *See generally* Note, *Federal Trade Commission Authority to Order Corrective Advertising*, 1978 WISC. L. REV. 605.

[80] *See, e.g.*, National Comm. on Egg Nutrition v. FTC, 570 F.2d at 165, *cert. denied*, 439 U.S. 821 (1978); Eggland's Best, Inc., 5 Trade Reg. Rep. (CCH) ¶ 23,551 (1994) (consent order); *In re* Bristol-Myers Co., 102 F.T.C. 21, 379 (1983) (order), *aff'd*, 738 F.2d 554 (2d Cir. 1984), *cert. denied*, 469 U.S. 1189 (1985).

[81] 425 U.S. 748 (1976).

[82] 447 U.S. 557 (1980).

while subject to some regulation, is protected by the First Amendment), however, the courts have more rigorously scrutinized FTC orders affecting advertising.[83]

The FTC can order companies to pay "consumer redress" for violations of the FTC Act.[84] In 1995 the FTC entered its first consumer redress award against a national grocery manufacturer and advertiser, requiring the Dannon Company to pay $150,000 for deceptive nutrition claims.[85] Other affirmative consumer protection remedies include mandatory arbitration of consumer disputes,[86] mandatory extension of "full" warranties to consumers,[87] construction of specified facilities and improvements on land sold to consumers,[88] and mandatory repair or replacement of, or monetary refund for, defective or unsafe products.[89] The Commission also has prohibited a merchant from entering into consumer contracts for more than a designated dollar amount, and has required a "cooling-off" period in consumer contracts during which the contract can be rescinded by the consumer.[90] Recently the FTC has ordered respondents to obtain a performance bond or

---

[83] *See, e.g.*, Beneficial Corp. v. FTC, 542 F.2d 611 (3d Cir. 1976),*cert. denied*, 430 U.S. 983 (1977); *cf.* United States v. Reader's Digest Ass'n, 662 F.2d 955, 965 (3d Cir. 1981), *cert. denied*, 455 U.S. 908 (1982) ("Any remedy formulated by the FTC that is reasonably necessary to the prevention of future violations does not impinge upon constitutionally protected commercial speech"). *See also* Kraft, Inc. v. FTC, 970 F.2d 311 (7th Cir. 1992), *cert. denied*, 507 U.S. 909 (1993); Grolier, Inc. v. FTC, 699 F.2d 983 (9th Cir.), *cert. denied*, 464 U.S. 891 (1983); Sears, Roebuck & Co. v. FTC, 676 F.2d 385 (9th Cir. 1982). In determining whether speech is commercial, the FTC and the courts consider: 1) whether the speech contains a message specifically promoting the demand for a product or service; 2) the means used to publish the speech; and 3) the speaker's economic or commercial motivation. *See, e.g.*, *In re* R.J. Reynolds Tobacco Co., Inc. [1987-1993 Transfer Binder] Trade Reg. Rep. (CCH) ¶ 22,522 (1988) (interlocutory order) (ALJ erred in finding that advertisement was not commercial speech subject to FTC jurisdiction. For a recent statement by the FTC on the First Amendment's impact on the regulation of commercial advertising, see Comments of the Federal Trade Commission before the FDA, in the Matter of Regulations Restricting the Sale and Distribution of Cigarettes (Jan. 1996).

[84] *See, e.g.*, FTC v. NCH, Inc., 1995-2 Trade Cas. (CCH) ¶ 71,114 (D. Nev. 1995) (consumer redress of $2.6 million awarded against corporation and officers); FTC v. Pacific Medical Clinics Management, 1992-1 Trade Cas. (CCH) ¶ 69,777 (S.D. Cal., 1992) (permanent injunction against a marketer of a low-calorie diet program and an award of $21.5 million in consumer redress).

[85] Dannon Co., Inc., 5 Trade Reg. Rep. (CCH) ¶ 23,932 (1995) (proposed consent order).

[86] *See, e.g.*, *In re* General Motors Corp. 87 F.T.C. 831 (1975) (order).

[87] *See, e.g.*, *In re* Kaufman and Broad, Inc., 93 F.T.C. 235 (1979) (consent order).

[88] *See, e.g.*, *In re* Flagg Indus., Inc., 90 F.T.C. 226 (1977) (consent order).

[89] *See, e.g.*, *In re* Saab-Scania of America, Inc., 107 F.T.C. 410 (1986) (consent order) (requiring Saab to make repairs or reimburse consumers for costs incurred due to paint problems with Saab cars);*In re* BayleySuit, Inc., 102 F.T.C. 1285 (1983) (consent order); *In re* Ford Motor Co, 96 F.T.C. 362 (1980) (consent order); *In re* Montgomery Ward & Co., Inc., 95 F.T.C. 265 (1980) (consent order). The courts have yet to ratify the Commission's authority to seek this form of remedy under the general provisions of section 5 of the FTC Act. *Cf.* Congoleum Indus., Inc. v. CPSC, 602 F.2d 220 (1979) (holding that the FTC Act does not contain authority for product recalls by the CPSC, which exercises FTC Act powers in enforcing the Flammable Fabrics Act); Heater v. FTC, 503 F.2d 321 (9th Cir. 1974); *see also* Amrep Corp. v. FTC, 475 U.S. 1034 (1986) (dissent to denial of Supreme Court review of scope of FTC remedial powers that were affirmed in 768 F. 2d 1171 (10th Cir. 1985)). The explicit inclusion of "consumer redress" power in the 1975 Magnuson-Moss Act, 15 U.S.C. § 57b01(b), however, has rendered this issue largely moot. *See* Sher, Norton, Hobbs, Pitofsky & Kramer, *Emerging Issues Under the Magnuson-Moss Warranty—Federal Trade Commission Improvement Act*, 45 Antitrust L.J. 72, 96-121 (1976). *See also* FTC v. Singer, 534 F. Supp. 24 (D. Cal.), *aff'd*, 668 F.2d 1107 (1981) (holding that the Commission was authorized to seek consumer redress for fraudulent scheme to sell business opportunities, and that the redress remedy is in addition to and not in lieu of any other remedy or right of action provided by state or federal law); FTC v. Glenn W. Turner Enters., Inc., 446 F. Supp. 1113 (D. Fla. 1978) (holding that FTC could obtain consumer redress under section 57b of FTC Act for act or practice that was specific subject of cease-and-desist order, even though act or practice may not have been repeated or continued in violation of order).

[90] *See, e.g*, Arthur Murray Studio of Washington, Inc. v. FTC, 458 F.2d 622 (5th Cir. 1972).

set up an escrow account before selling designated products in the future,[91] and to cease dealing with individuals who make representations proscribed by the FTC order.[92] The FTC has also ordered companies to stop using deceptive names or trademarks for products.[93] In the early 1990s the Commission initiated a series of cases against entities or individuals who "aided and abetted" in deceptive practices which violated section 5 of the FTC Act.[94]

As indicated previously, violation of a final FTC order can result in civil penalties. For example, in April 1994, General Nutrition, Inc., the largest retailer of nutritional supplements in the United States, agreed to pay a civil penalty of $2.4 million to settle charges that it violated the terms of two previousFTC orders.[95] This is one of the largest civil penalties ever obtained in a consumer protection matter by the Commission, and resolved allegations that General Nutrition failed to substantiate disease-reduction, weight-loss, muscle-building, and endurance claims for numerous products, made prohibited claims about certain amino acid products, and failed to make certain disclaimers when advertising the efficacy of "energy boosting" vitamin products.

FTC Regulation of Drug Advertising

■ Basic Legal Concepts[96]

As noted above, the FTC's authority to regulate drug[97] advertising is based upon the prohi-

---

91 *See, e.g.*, Original Marketing Inc., 5 Trade Reg. Rep. (CCH) ¶ 23,816 (1995) (consent order) (required to post $300,000 bond before marketing any weight loss product); Synchronal Corp., 5 Trade Reg. Rep. (CCH) ¶ 23,404 (1993) (consent order) (company ordered to pay $3.5 million in consumer redress, and to maintain a $500,000 escrow account prior to advertising similar products in the future).

92 *See, e.g.*, NuSkin Int'l, Inc., 5 Trade Reg. Rep. (CCH) ¶ 23,526 (1994) (consent order).

93 *See, e.g.*, Third Option Lab., 5 Trade Reg. Rep. (CCH) ¶ 23,799 (1995) (consent order); Metagenics, 5 Trade Reg. Rep. (CCH) ¶ 23,650 (1994) (proposed consent order) (marketer of calcium supplements ordered to discontinue the deceptive use of the "Bone Builder" name).

94 *See generally* Starek, Address Before the National Consumers League (Apr. 12, 1994); Steiger, Remarks Before the National Advertising Review Board (Dec. 9, 1992). *But see* Central Bank v. First Interstate Bank, 114 S. Ct. 1439 (1994) (private plaintiff may not maintain an aiding and abetting suite under § 10(b) of the Securities Exchange Act).

95 General Nutrition, Inc., 5 Trade Reg. Rep. (CCH) ¶ 23,600 (1994).

96 *See generally* Federal Trade Commission, Advertising for Over-The-Counter Drugs (May 1979) (final staff report and recommendations); Fedearl Trade Commission, Advertising for Over-The-Counter Antacids (Aug. 1983) (final staff report and recommendations).

97 Section 15 of the FTC Act defines the term "drug" to include "articles intended for use in the diagnosis, cure mitigation, treatment or prevention of disease in man or other animals," or "articles (other than food) intended to affect the structure or any function of the body of man or other animals." 15 U.S.C. § 55. "Therefore, although products such as skin creams[] [or] herbs . . . may not be considered 'drugs' . . . within the familiar meaning of the words, if advertised as providing health benefits, they may be considered drugs . . . under the act." Federal Trade Commission Report to Congress app., 33 n.110 (1995). *See also* FTC v. California Pac. Research Inc., 1991-2 Trade Cas. (CCH) ¶ 69,564, at 66,503 (D. Nev. 1991) ("Medical claims made for a product (i.e., claims that a product will affect the structure or function of the body) established such a product as a 'drug' under Section 15(c) of the FTC Act.").

bition, in section 5 of the FTC Act, of "deceptive acts or practices."[98] Section 12 of the FTC Act also contains a more specific, but essentially redundant,[99] prohibition against false and misleading drug advertisements.[100]

Prescription Drugs

The FTC drug precedents discussed in this chapter relate to over-the counter (OTC) drug products. This is a consequence of FTC's jurisdiction over OTC advertisements, and FDA policy and regulations that have restricted and discouraged direct-to-consumer (DTC) advertising of prescription drugs.[101] To date, theFTC has allowed the FDA to take the lead in dealing with prescription drug advertising directed to consumers and physicians and has not attempted to supplement the FDA's regulation of such advertising. The FTC, however, has not ceded its jurisdiction over such activities.[102]

The FDA called for a voluntary moratorium on the advertising of prescription drugs to consumers from 1982 to 1985 to consider the need for new regulations directly specifically to DTC advertising. The agency, however, withdrew its request for the moratorium and, rather than proposing regulations, issued a series of ad-hoc policy statements and warning letters to drug manufacturers concerning prohibited forms of advertising and promotion.[103]

---

[98] In 1962 Congress limited a portion of the FTC's authority over prescription drug advertising under section 12-17. Specifically, section 502(n) of the Federal Food, Drug, and Cosmetic Act, 21 U.S.C. § 352(n), precludes FTC jurisdiction under sections 12-17 of the FTC Act with respect to three items: drug name, formula, and summary of effectiveness and consequences of use.

[99] The distinction between sections 5 and 12 was originally in terms of remedy. In contrast to section 5, section 12 provided for injunctive relief for false, misleading, or deceptive advertising relating to food, drugs, devices, or cosmetics; see e.g., FTC v. Rhodes Pharm. Co., 191 F.2d 744 (7th Cir. 1951); In re The Great Atl. and Pac. Tea Co., 85 F.T.C. 601 (1975) (order). Section 408 of the Trans-Alaska Pipeline Authorization Act, Pub. L. No. 93-153, 87 Stat. 591 (1973) (codified in 15 U.S.C. §§ 45(1), 45(m), 53(b) & 53(c)), however, provided the Commission with general injunctive powers that have obviated the need for reliance on section 12. See generally 6 E. KITNER & W. KRATZKE, FEDERAL ANTITRUST LAW § 43.21, at 25 (1986).

[100] 15 U.S.C. §§ 52-56.

[101] See generally Withdrawal of Voluntary Moratorium on Direct-to-Consumer Advertising of Prescription Drugs, 50 Fed. Reg. 36, 677 (1985); 21 C.F.R. § 202.1 (1996) (prescription drug advertising). Notwithstanding the FDA's dislike of DTC advertising, the American Medical Association(AMA), in 1993, reversed its long-standing policy opposing DTC advertising, and stated it would accept such consumer advertising and that it would accept such advertisements for AMA publications and videos. See AMERICAN MED. ASS'N, GUIDELINES FOR DIRECT-TO-CONSUMER PRESCRIPTION DRUG ADVERTISING (1993).

[102] See generally Comments of the Staff of the Bureau of Consumer Protection and the Bureau of Economics of the Federal Trade Commission, Before the FDA in the Public Hearings on Direct-to-Consumer Promotion (Jan. 11, 1996). If the FTC does announce a regulatory policy for prescription drug advertising, it is likely that the FTC will utilize the warnings and indications of the prescription drug's new drug application (NDA) as the touchstone for evaluating the accuracy and adequacy of substantiation for prescription drug advertising. In the event that a DTC advertisement for a prescription drug prompted FTC scrutiny, the FTC's regulatory approach would probably be: 1) to analyze the ad for both explicit and implicit therapeutic or efficacy claims for the prescription drug product; 2) to evaluate the therapeutic claims in light of the data in that particular prescription drug's NDA to determine the truth and adequacy of substantiation for those claims; and 3) as to non-efficacy, or "effectiveness" claims, take a more flexible approach as to appropriate sources of substantiation. See generally Comments of the Staffs of the Bureaus of Economics and Consumer Protection of the Federal Trade Commission before the FDA in the Matter of Pharmaceutical Marketing and Information Exchange in Managed Care Environments (Jan. 16, 1996).

[103] See, e.g., Current Issues and Procedures, Division of Drug Marketing, Advertising and Communication (Apr. 1994); letter from Janet L. Rose, Dir., Division of Drug Marketing, Advertising, and Communications, to Randall L. Tobias, Chief Executive Officer, Eli Lilly and Company (July 19, 1994); letter from Cheryl Fossum Graham, Acting Dir., Division of Drug Marketing, Advertising, and Communications, to Fred Lyons, Chief Executive Officer, Marion Merrell Dow (Oct. 13, 1992.)

The recent and ongoing restructuring of the health care industry, and increased interest by consumers in managing their own health, has resulted in consumers and the health care industry demanding readily accessible information about prescription drugs. The pharmaceutical industry consequently has expanded significantly the amount of DTC advertising for prescription drugs. This more recent DTC advertising has included the use of video news released and related B-roll video tape for broadcast, computer networks, cable television networks, 800 telephone numbers, and general newspaper and magazine advertising.[104] These are all media that traditionally the FTC has regulated.

The FDA announced in August 1995[105] that it would conduct a public hearing on DTC promotion of prescription drugs through print, broadcast, and other types of media to determine whether modifications to its current policies necessary. If, as a result of the public hearings, the FDA adopts formal regulations on DTC advertising, the FTC at that time may express its views as to how the Commission may or may not exercise jurisdiction over such advertising.[106]

A proviso to the FTC Act, which has not had much relevance to OTC drug advertising but which may take on importance with increased prescription drug advertising, reads as follows:

No advertisement of a drug shall be deemed to be false if it is disseminated only to members of the medical profession, contains no false representation of a material fact, and includes, or is accompanied in each instance by truthful disclosure of, the formula showing quantitatively each ingredient of such drug.[107]

One of the few cases interpreting this language held that advertisements that fail to comply with each of the specified conditions do not come within the proviso. The advertisements in that case appeared in a medical journal that was sent primarily to members of the medical profession, but also reached lay persons.

Over-the-Counter Drugs

The "acts or practices" that the FTC has found deceptive in OTC drug advertising cases, as in other advertising cases, generally have taken one of four forms: 1) direct representations,[108] 2) representations which may reasonably be said to be implied by the advertis-

---

[104] Advertising spending on DTC advertising for prescription drugs increased 50% in 1994 to $240,000,000. *See* WALL ST. J., Sept. 14, 1995, at B-1.

[105] *See* 60 Fed. Reg. 42,581 (1995).

[106] It has been asserted by legal and economic experts that, unlike the FTC, the FDA does not have the appropriate expertise to review properly comparative cost-effectiveness and pharmacoeconomic claims now made by pharmaceutical manufacturers about prescription drug products for use by managed care entities and, indirectly, by physicians.

[107] 15 U.S.C. § 55(a)(1).

[108] *See e.g.*, FTC v. SlimAmerica, Inc., Civ. No. 97-6072 (D. Fla. 1997) (temporary restraining order issued to halt deceptive campaign claiming the diet product, Super-Formula, will "Blast up to 49 pounds off you in only 29 days"); Olsen Lab., 5 Trade Reg. Rep. (CCH) ¶ 23,717 (1994) (consent order) (false representation that external arthritis analgesic was a new or unique product in the treatment of arthritis pain); Synchronal Corp., 5 Trade Reg. Rep. (CCH) ¶ 23,541 (1994) (consent order) (false representation that cream was a baldness cure).

ing,[109] 3) failure to disclose material facts,[110] and 4) failure to possess adequate factual substantiation for an advertising claim.[111] The FTC Act specifies that a drug advertisement can be misleading and in violation of section 12 either because the representations in the advertising are deceptive or because the advertising fails to disclose material facts. The FTC Act further provides that,

> [I]n determining whether any advertisement is misleading, there shall be taken into account (among other things) not only representations made or suggested by statement, word, design, device, sound, or any combination thereof, but also the extent to which the advertisement fails to reveal facts material in the light of such representations or material with respect to consequences which may result from the use of the commodity to which the advertisement related under the conditions prescribed in said advertisement, or under such conditions as are customary or usual.[112]

As has been noted, deceptive representations can be implied as well as expressly stated. For example, in an early case involving American Medical Products,[113] the FTC held that advertisements that contained no express representation of safety, but that implied that most people could use the drug, thereby conveyed to consumers an unqualified claim of safety. Because the drug contained thyroid extract that was not safe for many people, the Commission found the advertising to be deceptive in violation of sections 5 and 12 of the FTC Act.[114] In this regard, it should be kept in mind that even if a drug label contains

---

[109] FTC v. Pantron I Corp. 33 F.3d 1088 (9th Cir. 1994) *cert. denied*, 115 S. Ct. 1794 (1994) (implied baldness cure); Sterling Drug, [1987-93 Transfer Binder] Trade Reg. Rep. (CCH) ¶ 22,837 (1990) (consent order) (implied that product relieves menstrual cramps); Adria Lab., [1983-87 Transfer Binder] Trade Reg. Rep. (CCH) ¶ 22,135 (1984) (consent order) (implied drug would not cause side effects associated with other pain relievers); In *re* American Home Prods. Corp., 98 F.T.C. at 373-76. (depiction of technical graphs and chemical formulas implied that the claims of superior pain relief were supported by scientific proof).

[110] FTC v. Pacific Med. Clinics Management Inc., 1992-1 Trade Cas., (CCH) ¶ 69,777 (S.D. Cal. 1992) (failure to disclose the absence of FDA approval of a drug used in weight loss program is false and deceptive under sections 5 and 12); Adria Lab., 1983-87 Transfer Binder, Trade Reg. Rep. (CCH) ¶ 22,135 (1984) (consent order) (complaint alleging failure to disclose that product, a non-aspirin pain reliever, may product side effects similar to aspirin).

[111] In the Matter of Jordon, McGrath, Case & Taylor, FTC Dkt. No. C-3684 (1996) (decision and order) (ordering manufacturer to cease and desist making claims that Doan's analgesic is more effective at relieving back pain than other OTC analgesics); Eton Derma Lab., 5 Trade Reg. Rep. (CCH) ¶ 23, 917 (1995) (complaint) (alleging an unsubstantiated claim for OTC acne remedy); Miles Inc., [1987-93 Transfer Binder] Trade Reg. Rep. (CCH) ¶ 22,896 (1991) (consent order) (alleging no substantiation for statement that vitamins would protect human lungs from effects of air pollution); PharmTech Research, [1983-1987 Transfer Binder] Trade Reg. Rep. (CCH) ¶ 22,055 (1983) (complaint) (alleging unsubstantiated ad claim that dietary supplement was associated with a reduction in cancer).

[112] 15 U.S.C. § 55.

[113] *In re* American Med. Prods., 32 F.T.C. 1376 (1941), *aff'd*, 136 F.2d 426 (9th Cir. 1943).

[114] *Accord* Carter Prod., Inc. v. FTC, 268 F.2d 461 (9th Cir.), *cert. denied*, 361 U.S. 884 (1959) ("liver" pills falsely implied to have effect on liver). *See also* Alva Lab. Inc., 66 F.T.C. 322 (1964) (order); *In re* Thompson Med. Co., 59 F.T.C. 287 (1961) (consent order); *In re* Positive Prod. Co. 33 F.T.C. 1327 (1941) (order); *In re* Glenn Lab. Inc., 25 F.T.C. 302 (1937) (order) (claim that a drug was "100% safe, taken as directed" was determined to be deceptive because it implied that the product could be safely taken by everyone when in fact the product should not be taken by certain classes of persons without consultation with a physician).

explicit warning information, inconsistent or misleading claims in advertising as to the product's safety can be found to negate the effect of the labeling information.[115]

The FTC also can challenge advertising for drugs based on the advertisement's failure to disclose "material facts." A "material fact" is one that would affect a significant number of consumers' determinations about whether or not to purchase a particular product.[116] Because health is a significant concern to most consumers, information about adverse effects that may be associated with the ordinary use of a drug product, or the use of the drug under the particular conditions represented in the advertisement, will usually be material to consumers.

> In *Porter & Dietsch, Inc.*,[117] for example, the Commission held that advertisements for an OTC diet aid were deceptive because they failed to make consumers aware that the drug could cause adverse effects for some users. The FTC's complaint did not allege that the ads made any affirmative representations of safety; it simply alleged that the omission of any reference to adverse effects constituted a material omission. The Commission required the following warning in all future advertisements for the product: "Warning: This product poses a serious health risk for some users. Read the label carefully before using."[118]

OTC drug advertisements also may be found deceptive where the statements are true only under a hyper technical construction for the advertisement,[119] or where the advertisement conveys more than one meaning, one of which is false.[120]

An advertisement can be found to be unfair or deceptive if the advertiser does not possess substantiation demonstrating that a reasonable basis exists for its advertising claims prior to the dissemination of such claims.[121] For example, in the seminal "ad substantiation" case, *Pfizer, Inc.*,[122] advertising for the company's Un-Burn product was challenged by the

---

[115] *In re* Jay Norris Corp., 91 F.T.C. 751 (1978) (order), *aff'd*, 598 F.2d 1244 (2d Cir. 1979),*cert. denied*, 444 U.S. 980 (1979) ("given [significant] hazards, it is clearly deceptive to make an unqualified representation of safety for this product. Respondents cannot simply advertise as 'safe' this noxious [product] and hope mail order consumers will read the label and use the product as directed").

[116] *See In re* Cliffdale Assoc., 103 F.T.C. 110 (1984) (order). *See generally* FTC v. Royal Milling Co., 288 U.S. 212, 216-17 (1933); Pep Boys - Manny, Moe & Jack, Inc. v. FTC, 122 F.2d 158, 161 (3d Cir. 1941);*In re* Simeon Management Co., 87 F.T.C. 1184, 1230 (1976) (order) , *aff'd* 579 F.2d 1137 (9th Cir. 1978).*See generally supra* notes 78 - 81 and accompanying text.

[117] *In re* Porter & Dietsch, Inc., 90 F.T.C. 770 (1977) (order), *modified*, 605 F.2d 294 (7th Cir. 1979), *cert. denied*, 445 U.S. 950 (1980).

[118] *Id.* at 886. The Seventh Circuit modified the warning to read as follows: "Warning: This product poses a serious health risk for users with high blood pressure, heart disease, diabetes, or thyroid disease. Read the label carefully before using." 605 F.2d at 307-08. *See also In re* W.K. Sterline, 33 F.T.C. 1412 (1942) (order); *In re* Pascal Co., 32 F.T.C. 1216 (1941)(order).

[119] *See, e.g., In re* Porter & Dietsch, Inc. 90 F.T.C. 770 (1977)*modified*, 605 F.2d 294 (7th Cir. 1979),*cert. denied*, 445 U.S. 950 (1980).

[120] *See, e.g.,* FTC v. Sterling Drug, 317 F.2d 669 (2d Cir. 1963).

[121] *See, e.g., In re* American Home Prods. Corp., 98 F.T.C. at 374; *In re* Bristol-Myers Co., 102 F.T.C. at 321; *In re* Pfizer, Inc., 81 F.T.C. at, 62; *In re* Revlon Inc. et al., [1987-1993 Transfer Binder] Trade Reg. Rep. (CCH) ¶ 22,728 (1989) (complaint). *See generally* FTC Policy Statement Regarding Advertising Substantiation Program, *supra* note 33 and accompanying text.

[122] *In re* Pfizer, Inc., 81 F.T.C. 23 (1972) (order).

FTC as unfair for lack of adequate substantiation.[123] The FTC found that Pfizer's advertising claims about the pain-relieving properties of Un-Burn were inadequately substantiated because Pfizer did not possess adequate and well-controlled scientific studies or tests that confirmed these claims *prior* to making such claims.[124] Advertisements lacking such a level of substantiation are unfair to consumers, whose ability to make an economically rational product choice is impaired, as well as to competitors, whose ability to compete fairly on the basis of price, quality, and service is impeded.[125]

In an action seeking permanent injunction against California Pacific Research, Inc., under section 13(b) of the FTC Act, the FTC sought to prevent false and misleading advertising relating to New Generation shampoo and conditioner products intended to prevent and restore hair loss.[126] The court found that the offending advertisements used techniques to enhance the credibility of the representations, for example, the use of testimonials, infomercials, and scientific approbation in order to appeal to the particularly vulnerable group of consumers (i.e., balding persons). In addition, the defendants could not produce adequate and well-controlled scientific tests to support its medical claims relating to hair loss, consistent with the requirements of the FDA's final rule on hair grower and hair loss prevention drug products.[127] One of the studies funded by the defendants demonstrated that the principal active ingredients in the shampoo was not effective in preventing hair loss. Consequently, the defendants were permanently enjoined from selling any New Generation products and the court ordered the defendants to pay $2,000,000 in equitable restitution. Reasonable substantiation also can be evaluated against testing methods and protocols established by the FDA through its OTC drug monograph review process.

In 1991, the FTC obtained a $375,000 civil penalty against Sterling Drug for violating an existing FTC cease-and-desist order prohibiting unsubstantiated claims. This case marks the first time the Commission obtained civil penalties arising out of an OTC advertising order for violations of the reasonable basis provision.

Health Foods/Homeopathic Products

In recent years the distinction between food and drugs has become increasingly blurred as advertisers have continued to advertise health benefits for food-based products. For purposes of FTC regulation of advertising, however, the distinction between foods and drugs has little significance. In these types of cases, the FTC generally challenges false advertising for a "food, drug, or nutritional supplement" without classifying the product in any one category.[128] Thus, many of the more recent cases discussed below pertain to health foods or homeopathic products.

---

[123] *Id.* at 23-25.

[124] *Id.* at 57.

[125] *Id.* at 62.

[126] FTC v. California Pac. Research, Inc., 1991-2 Trade Cas. ¶ 69,564 (D. Nev. 1991).

[127] 21 C.F.R. § 310.527.

[128] *See, e.g.*, In the Matter of Victoria Bie d/b/a Body Gold, FTC No. 942-3328 (1996) (settlement agreement) (challenging claims that chromium picolinate could promote long-term weight loss, reduce body fat, build muscle, increase metabolism, control appetite, reduce serum cholesterol, regulate blood sugar levels, increase energy and

■ Regulatory Coordination in Drug Matters Between the FDA and the FTC

As noted, the FDA and the FTC maintain close liaison in their regulatory activities to achieve a coordinated approach to the regulation for drug labeling and advertising. [129] For the first fifty years following the passage of the Pure Food and Drugs Act of 1906, [130] the FDA's regulation of drugs focused primarily on drug safety — adulteration, patent medicine abuses, misbranding, and the like. [131] Furthermore, the FDA's regulation of OTC drugs during this period was primarily court actions seeking to remove specific products from the marketplace. The 1962 amendments to the Federal Food, Drug, and Cosmetic Act, however, provided the FDA with the statutory power to adopt a comprehensive regulatory approach to ensure that OTC drugs were effective, as well as safe, prior to being offered for sale in the United States. [132]

Similarly, FTC activity relating to drugs through the 1960s involved the prosecution of false advertising cases against specific products, largely involving drug safety. [133] In the late 1960s, however, the FTC reoriented its regulatory activity to take cognizance of the FDA's new regulatory initiatives regarding drug efficacy, and focused particularly on the

---

stamina and even prevent diabetes); In the Matter of Nutrition 21, FTC No. 932-3282 (1996) (settlement agreement) (chromium picolinate); In the Matter of Universal Merchants, Inc., FTC No. 952-336 (1996) (settlement agreement) (chromium picolinate); In the Matter of Mutagenics, Inc. d/b/a Ethical Nutrients, FTC Dkt. No. 9267 (1996) (initial decision) (ordered manufacturer to cease and desist representing that Bone Builder, a calcium supplement, restores lost bone, restores bone strength, reduces or eliminates pain associated with bone ailments, is superior to and/or more effective than other forms of calcium in the prevention or treatment of bone ailments, or is more bioavailable, more absorbable of effectively utilized by the body than other forms of calcium); In the Matter of Abbot Labs., FTC No. 962-3069 (1996) (challenging claims that Ensure is doctor recommended as a meal supplement or replacement for healthy adults more than other nutritional supplements); Body Wise Int'l, Inc., 5 Trade Reg. Rep. (CCH) ¶ 23,831 (1995) (consent order) (weight loss and cholesterol reduction claims for niacin supplements).

[129] *See generally* FTC Overview, Ch.

[130] Pub. L. No. 59-384, 32 Stat. 632 (1906) (superseded by the Federal Food, Drug, and Cosmetic Act of 1938, Pub. L. No. 75-717, 52 Stat. 1040 (1938), as amended 21 U.S.C. §§ 301 et seq.

[131] *See, e.g.*, United States v. 3963 Bottles, More or Less ... Labeled Enerjol Double Strength, 172 F. Supp. 470 (D. Ill. 1958), *aff'd*, 265 F.2d 332 (7th Cir.), *cert. denied*, 360 U.S. 931 (1959) (drug product condemned as misbranded and a new drug introduced into interstate commerce without an effective new drug application establishing its safety); United States v. 9 Bottles, More or Less ... "Colusa Natural Oil," 78 F. Supp. 721 (D. Iowa 1947), *aff'd*, 176 F.2d 554, (8th Cir. 1948), *cert. denied*, 338 U.S. 911 (1950) (liquid and capsule products containing crude petroleum and labeled for treatment of psoriasis, eczema, athlete's foot, and leg ulcers constituted "misbranded" drugs); United States v. 5 One-Pint Bottles and 23 One-Gallon Bottles ..., 9 F. Supp. 990 (D. N.Y. 1934) (nonconforming drug sold under name recognized in *National Formulary* was adulterated).

[132] Drug Amendments of 1962, Pub. L. No. 87-781, 76 Stat. 780 (1962).

[133] *See, e.g.*, American Home Prods. Corp. v. FTC, 402 F.2d 232 (6th Cir. 1968) (upholding FTC finding that manufacturer falsely represented that its product, "Preparation H," would cure or remove hemorrhoids); Doherty, Clifford, Steers & Shenefield, Inc. v. FTC, 392 F.2d 921 (6th Cir. 1968) (upholding FTC finding that pharmaceutical company falsely advertised that its throat lozenge, "Sucrets," would kill germs contributing to existing throat infections and would provide more than temporary relief of sore throat pain); J.B. Williams Co. v. FTC, 381 F.2d 884 (6th Cir. 1967) (upholding FTC finding that company falsely implied that majority of persons experiencing fatigue, loss of strength, nervousness, and irritability were suffering from iron deficiency or iron deficiency anemia, and thus could seek relief by using company's products); Carter Prods. Inc. v. FTC, 268 F.2d 461 (9th Cir. 1959), *cert. denied*, 361 U.S. 884 (1959) (upholding FTC finding that company made misleading advertising claims by indicating that its laxative pills aided in digestion, promoted the production of liver bile, contained no strong medicines, and were perfectly safe to use).

FDA's "OTC Review Process."[134] The FDA's OTC Drug Review Process, and the FTC's proposed "OTC Drug Advertising Rule" constitute a noteworthy chapter in the federal regulation of drug advertising.

In 1975, the FTC initiated a rulemaking proceeding to consider the adoption of a "Trade Regulation Rule" that would have prohibited manufacturers of OTC drugs from making claims in drug advertising that were not permitted in FDA drug labeling.[135] After extensive hearings and deliberation, the FTC decided in 1981 to abandon this regulatory approach and to terminate the rulemaking proceeding. The Commission explained:

> The Commission has concluded that in advertising a drug for permissible (i.e., FDA-approved) purpose, advertisers should not always be limited (as they would have been under the original proposed rule) to the labeling language approved by FDA. . . . Despite its decision not to promulgate a rule, the Commission remains strongly committed to taking action on a case-by-case basis whenever necessary to insure the basis whenever necessary to insure the accuracy of OTC drug advertising and to avoid serious inconsistencies between advertising claims and FDA labeling determinations. Consequently, as FDA completes its expert analysis of the safety and effectiveness of each category of OTC drugs, the FTC will review the advertising for those drugs in order to determine whether any advertisement, taken as a whole, expressly or impliedly claims any purpose of use for which the drug in question has not been found to be safe and effective by the FDA. Commission action may also be taken, where appropriate, before a final FDA monograph is in place. In evaluating future OTC drug advertising, the Commission will consider factors such as the extent of dissemination of the advertising, weather the advertising is continuing, the nature of persuasiveness of the claims, the balance of risk to benefit, and other factors related to the injury consumers would be likely to suffer.[136]

Although the FTC has abandoned these rulemaking proceedings, the FDA's OTC Review Process remains highly relevant to the FTC's review of drug advertising. The FTC has accepted the conclusions and recommendations of the FDA's OTC Advisory Review Panels as evidence of adequate substantiation for performance claims for OTC drug products and, likewise, has held that FDA final monographs may be relied on to substantiate such claims.[137] In addition, the Commission has held that preliminary FDA rulemaking documents subject to future revision, such as tentative final monographs, are also presump-

---

[134] *See, e.g.*, Miles W. Kirkpatrick, *Regulating in the Public Interest*, 26 FOOD DRUG COSM. L.J. 593 (1971); Gerald J. Thain, *Drug Advertising and Drug Abuse — The Role of the FTC*, 26 FOOD DRUG COSM. L.J. 487 (1971); Mary G. Jones, *To Tell The Truth, The Whole Truth . . .*, 26 FOOD DRUG COSM. L.J. 173 (1971); Albert G. Seidman, *New FTC Approaches to Food, Drug and Cosmetic Problems*, 25 FOOD DRUG COSM. L.J. 172 (1970).

[135] FTC's Proposed OTC Drug Advertising Rulemaking, 40 Fed. Reg. 52,631 (1975).

[136] Termination of FTC's OTC Drug Advertising Rulemaking, 46 Fed. Reg. 24, 584 (1981). In a related proceeding, the Commission also terminated its antacid rulemaking proceeding, which would have required FDA-specified warning statements on antacid labeling to appear in all antacid advertising. The Commission concluded that the failure to include such warnings in advertising was not necessarily deceptive nor unfair. *Termination of FTC's OTC Antacid Drug Advertising Rulemaking*, 6 Trade Reg. Rep. (CCH) ¶¶ 38,003, 38, 044 (July 27, 1984).

[137] *In re* Thompson Med. Co., 104 F.T.C. 648 (1984) (order), *aff'd*, 791 F.2d 189 (D.C. Cir. 1986), *cert. denied*, 479 U.S. 1086 (1987); *In re* AHC Pharmacal, Inc., 101 F.T.C. 40 (1983) (modifying order).

tively reliable for substantiation purposes.[138] Conversely, an advisory panel or proposed FDA classification of a drug or ingredient as other than "generally recognized as safe and effective" results in a presumption by the FTC that advertising claims concerning the efficacy or safety of that product or ingredient may not be substantiated.[139] In these instances, the advertiser bears a heavy burden in persuading the FTC that, notwithstanding initial determinations by the FDA and/or its advisory panel, sufficient evidence exists to support its advertising claims.[140]

For example, in a proceeding involving Vaseline petroleum jelly,[141] the FTC found that the findings and conclusions of FDA Advisory Review Panels justified the use of certain claims prohibited under an older FTC order. Rather than confine Vaseline advertising to the findings of the FDA Review Panels, however, the FTC held that in the future either the findings and conclusions for the FDA Panels, or other competent and reliable scientific evidence, might be used by Vaseline as a reasonable basis to substantiate its advertising claims.[142]

The FTC proceeding against Simeon Management Corp.[143] illustrates a different form of interplay between FTC and FDA concerns and jurisdiction over drug efficacy advertising claims. Simeon advertised weight control treatments involving the use of the prescription drug, human chorionic gonadotropin (H.G.).[144] H.G. had not been approved by the FDA as effective in weight control, nor did the FDA regulations permit H.G. to be advertised as a treatment for obesity. Remarkably, the FDA did not challenge Simeon's advertising, however, the FTC determined that Simeon's advertisements implied that its weight control *treatments* were safe and effective. Thus, the advertisements were misleading to consumers because they failed to reveal that treatment involved using the drug H.G., which had not been approved by the FDA for use in weight reduction.[145] The FTC's complaint did not allege, however, that the *treatments* themselves were ineffective.

A third example of FTC and FDA regulatory coordination involves the agencies' joint approach to certain aspirin advertising. After meeting with FTC and FDA officials, ten U.S. aspirin manufacturers agreed to drop advertising claims that regular use of aspirin reduces the risk of a first heart attack in men.[146] FDA and FTC officials indicated to the aspirin manufacturers that the studies upon which such claims were based were, in their

---

[138] *E.g., In re* American Home Prods. Corp., 98 F.T.C. 136, 368 (1981) (order), *enforced as modified,* 695 F.2d 681 (3rd Cir. 1982), *modified,* 101 F.T.C. 698 (1983), *modified,* 103 F.T.C. 57 (1984), *modified,* 103 F.T.C. 528 (1984).

[139] *See, e.g., In re* Thompson Med. Co., 104 F.T.C. 648 (1984) (order), *aff'd,* 791 F.2d 189 (D.C. Cir. 1986), *cert. denied,* 479 U.S. 1086 (1987); *see also* FTC v. Pantron I Corp., 33 F.3d 1088 (9th Cir. 1994), *cert denied,* 115 S. Ct. 1794 (1995).

[140] Telephone interview with C. Lee Peeler, Assoc. Director for Advertising Practices, Bureau of Consumer Protection, Federal Trade Comm'n (Sept. 9, 1988).

[141] *In re* Chesebrough-Pond's Inc. 106 F.T.C. 567 (1985) (modifying order).

[142] *Id.* at 571.

[143] *In re* Simeon Management Corp., 87 F.T.C. 1184 (1976) (order), *aff'd,* 579 F.2d 1137 (9th Cir. 1978).

[144] *Id.* at 1227.

[145] *Id.* at 1229-31.

[146] *See, e.g., 10 Aspirin Make to Halt Ad Claim,* N.Y. TIMES, Mar. 2, 1988, at A26, Col. 1; *Aspirin Makers Agree to Drop Ad Claims That Use Can Prevent First Heart Attacks*, [Current Developments] Antitrust & Trade Reg. Rep. (BNA) No. 1357, at 44 (Mar. 17, 1988).

view, too preliminary to provide adequate substantiation for such advertising.[147] It is also noteworthy that the Texas and New York Attorneys General not only expressed similar concerns, but in addition obtained an agreement from Rorer Pharmaceutical Corp. whereby the company ceased promoting its Ascriptin brand of aspirin as "beneficial in the prevention of first-time heart attacks" until federal guidelines on aspirin advertising were promulgated.[148] Rorer also agreed to reimburse $30,000 of the investigating costs incurred by the Offices of the Attorneys General.[149]

■ Illustrative FTC Cases

Early OTC Drug Cases

In *Bristol-Myers Co.*[150] and *Sterling Drug, Inc.*,[151] the FTC completed a twelve-year proceeding involving a variety of efficacy and superiority claims for Bufferin, Excedrin, Excedrin PM, Bayer Aspirin, Bayer Children's Aspirin, Vanquish, Idol, and Cope. Most of the challenged claims for these products were found to be inadequately substantiated by the clinical, survey, and other evidence of record. The Commission also found deception in implications in advertising claims that a product contained a "special" or "unique" ingredient when that same ingredient was used in other products for the same purpose.[152] The third analgesic case involved American Home Products Corp.[153] in which the Commission held that even if an efficacy claim for an analgesic product were supported by a "reasonable basis," it was nonetheless deceptive to make that claim without affirmatively disclosing the existence of a "substantial question" as to its validity.[154] Subsequently the FTC reversed course and the "substantial question" theory was disavowed[155] in *Bristol-Myers* and *Sterling Drug*. The Commission also dropped portions of the *American Home Products* case to make it consistent with the latter two orders.[156]

---

[147] *Aspirin Makers Agree to Drop Ad Claims That Use Can Prevent First Heart Attacks*, *supra* note 146, at 448. FTC and FDA officials also objected to the claims due to the lack of affirmative disclosures regarding the necessity for prior consultation with one's physician and the risk of adverse reactions, i.e., cerebral hemorrhage. The FTC reported that it had been in contact with the FDA on the aspirin advertising and labeling health claims issue from the start, and had considered initiation of administrative or judicial enforcement action against the manufacturers should the advertisements continue. *Id.* For discussion of the scientific findings upon which the aspirin/heart attack claims were based, see *Preliminary Report: Findings From The Aspirin Component of the Ongoing Physicians Health Study*, 318 NEW ENG. J. MED. 262 (1988); *The Preliminary Report of the Findings of the Aspirin Component of the Ongoing Physician's Health Study*, 259 JAMA 3158 (1988).

[148] *See Rorer Group, Inc. — Aspirin Unit Agreed to Stop Using Ad on Heart Attacks*, WALL ST. J., July 13, 1988, at 28, col. 2.

[149] *Id.*

[150] *In re* Bristol-Myers Co., 102 F.T.C. 21 (1983) (order), *aff'd*, 738 F.2d 554 (2d Cir. 1984), *cert. denied*, 469 U.S. 1189 (1985).

[151] *In re* Sterling Drug, Inc., 102 F.T.C. 395 (1983) (order), *aff'd*, 741 F.2d 1146 (9th Cir. 1984), *cert. denied*, 470 U.S. 1084 (1985).

[152] *Id.* at 784-88; *In re* Bristol-Myers Co., 102 F.T.C. at 357-63.

[153] *In re* American Home Prods. Corp., 98 F.T.C. 136 (1981), *enforced as modified*, 695 F.2d 681 (3rd Cir. 1982), *modified*, 101 FTC. 698 (1983), *modified*, 103 F.T.C. 57 (1984), *modified*, 103 F.T.C. 528 (1984).

[154] *Id.* at 385-92.

[155] *In re* Bristol-Myers Co., 102 F.T.C. at 348-55; *In re* Sterling Drug, Inc. 102 F.T.C. at 776-77.

[156] *In re* American Home Prods. Corp., 77 F.T.C. 726 (1970), *modified*, 107 F.T.C. 427 (1986).

The FTC requires that express or implied advertising claims for the efficacy of an OTC drug product be substantiated by "competent and reliable scientific or medical" evidence, which is customarily further defined by the FTC as consisting of "tests, analyses, research, studies, or other evidence conducted and evaluated in an objective manner by persons qualified to do so, using procedures generally accepted in the profession or science to yield accurate and reliable results."[157] Upon completion of such studies, the data must permit a qualified expert to conclude that the product has the pharmaceutical qualities it is represented to have.[158] FTC decisions make it clear that, with respect to efficacy claims for OTC analgesic drug products, "competent and reliable scientific or medical evidence" should consist of at least two adequate and well-controlled, double-blinded clinical studies that conform to acceptable designs and protocols, and are conducted by different persons who are qualified by training and experience to conduct such studies, independently of each other.[159]

As noted previously, because the Commission believes that "advertisers of drug products subject to the joint jurisdiction of the FTC and the FDA will benefit from greater regulatory certainty if they can act with reasonable assurance that the two agencies will accept the same evidence to demonstrate the safety and efficacy of a particular ingredient,"[160] the FTC bases its substantiation requirements for OTC drug product claims on FDA determinations. If the FDA has published a monograph[161] that identifies conditions under which a product is safe and effective, then the advertiser may rely on the monograph, provided it substantiates the claim and has not been superseded.[162] The FTC also permits advertisers

---

[157] *See, e.g.,* Eton Derma Lab., Inc., 5 Trade Reg. Rep. (CCH) ¶ 23,917 (1995) (complaint); Revlon, 5 Trade Reg. Rep. (CCH) ¶ 23,449 (1993) (consent order); *In re* Adria Lab., Inc., 103 F.T.C. at 526; (consent order); *In re* Chesebrough-Pond's, Inc., 106 F.T.C. at 573 (modifying order).

[158] *See, e.g.,* Synchronal Corp., 5 Trade Reg. Rep. ¶ 23,404 (1993) (consent order); Patricia Wexler, M.D. [1987-1993 Transfer Binder] Trade Reg. Rep. ¶ 23,213 (1992) (proposed consent order); *In re* Biopractic Group, 104 F.T.C. 845 (1984); *In re* Thompson Med. Co., 104 F.T.C. at 821 n. 59; *In re* Sterling Drug, Inc. 102 F.T.C. 395 (1983) (order), *aff'd*, 741 F.2d 1146 (9th Cir. 1984), *cert. denied*, 470 U.S. 1081 (1985); *In re* Bristol-Myers Co., 102 F.T.C. 21 (1983) (order) *aff'd*, 738 F.2d 554 (2d Cir. 1984), *cert. denied*, 469 U.S. 1189 (1985).

[159] *See* Olsen Lab., Inc., 5 Trade Reg. Rep. (CCH) ¶ 23, 717 (1994) (consent order); *In re* Thompson Med. Co., 104 F.T.C. 648 (1984) (order), *aff'd*, 791 F.2d 189 (D.C. Cir. 1986), *cert. denied*, 479 U.S. 1086 (1987); *In re* Bristol-Myers Co., 102 F.T.C. 21 (1983), *aff'd*, 738 F.2d 554 (2d Cir. 1984), *cert. denied*, 469 U. S. 1189 (1985); *In re* Sterling Drug, Inc. 102 F.T.C. 395 (1983), *aff'd*, 741 F.2d 1146 (9th Cir. 1984), *cert. denied*, 470 U.S. 1084 (1985); *In re* American Home Prods. Corp. 77 F.T.C. 726 (1970), *modified*, 107 F.T.C. 427 (1986). *See also In re* Biopractic Group, 104 F.T.C. at 850. The FTC will require double blind studies for a variety of products that fall under the Federal Food, Drug, and Cosmetic Act. *See, e.g.,* Schering Corp., 5 Trade Reg. Rep. (CCH) ¶ 23,646 (1994) (consent order) (double blind studies required for claims about weight loss product and other drugs); Viral Response, Inc. [1987-1993 Transfer Binder] Trade Reg. Rep. (CCH) ¶ 23,135 (1992) (consent order) (double blind studies required for medical device that treats colds); Removatron Int'l., Inc., [1987-1993 Transfer Binder] Trade Reg. Rep. (CCH) ¶ 22,619 (1988) (order) (double blind studies required to substantiate claims about hair removal device).

[160] *In re* Thompson Med. Co., 104 F.T.C. 648 (1984) (order), *aff'd*, 791 F.2d 189 (D.C. Cir. 1986), *cert. denied*, 479 U.S. 1086 (1987) 104 F.T.C. at 826.

[161] *See, e.g., In re* Chesebrough-Pond's, Inc., 106 F.T.C. 567 (1985) (modifying order); *In re* Thompson Med. Co., 104 F.T.C. 648 (1984) (order), *aff'd*, 791 F.2d 189 (D.C. Cir. 1986), *cert. denied*, 479 U.S. 1086 (1987), 104 F.T.C. at 826; *In re* AHC Pharmacal, Inc., 101 F.T.C. 40, 41 (1983) (modifying order).

[162] *See, e.g., In re* Biopractic Group, 104 F.T.C. at 850; *In re* Thompson Med. Co., 104 F.T.C. 648 (1984) (order), *aff'd*, 791 F.2d 189 (D.C. Cir. 1986), *cert. denied*, 479 U.S. 1086 (1987); *In re* AHC Pharmacal, Inc., 101 F.T.C. 40, 41 (1983) (modifying order); *In re* American Home Prods. Corp., 77 F.T.C. 726 (1970), *modified*, 107 F.T.C. 427

to rely on findings and conclusions of FDA Advisory Review Panels[163] to substantiate OTC drug advertising claims. Although the Commission has indicated that "advertisers who comply with the FDA's requirement of well-controlled clinical tests to demonstrate efficacy [will] have adequate substantiation to make such claims in their advertisements," it also has acknowledged that it may be possible for drug advertisers to rely on other types of evidence, such as competent and reliable scientific tests, to comply with the FTC's substantiation requirement.[164] Should the FDA's views concerning safety or efficacy of a drug substance change over time, advertisers relying on FDA standards for the requisite level of substantiation must modify their advertisements accordingly.[165]

■ Thompson Medical

The FTC's reformulated deception standards (as announced in its 1984 *Cliffdale Associates* decision) were first used to analyze OTC drug advertising claims in the 1984 *Thompson Medical Co.* case.[166] The Commission found that Thompson deceptively represented to consumers that its OTC drug product, Aspercreme, was effective for the relief of arthritic pain; that such efficacy had been scientifically established; and that Aspercreme contained aspirin and was a newly discovered or developed product.[167] Seventeen different Aspercreme advertisements were reviewed by the FTC, as well as a great volume of consumer perception survey evidence, during the course of the agency's determination as to which of the ads conveyed the alleged implied claims.[168] Interestingly, the Commission held that an ad showing a woman holding two aspirin tablets and saying "Imagine being able to put the strong relief of aspirin right where you hurt most," implied that the product contained aspirin.[169] In contrast, however, the FTC declined to find any such implication in an ad with a headline reading "There's always been aspirin . . . Now there's Aspercreme," followed by the statement "An effective aspirin-like analgesic."[170] In identifying the express and implied claims conveyed by Thompson's advertisements, the Commission considered the "overall, net impression made" by the advertisement in order to "determine

---

(1986); *In re* Chesebrough-Pond's Inc., 106 F.T.C. at 568 (modifying order) A tentative final or final standard promulgated by the FDA that establishes that certain representations are supported by the scientific evidence acceptable to the FDA shall constitute, as long as it remains in effect, adequate substantiation for such representation. Revlon, Inc., 5 Trade Reg. Rep. (CCH) ¶ 23,449 (1993) (consent order). The FTC will not prohibit claims which meet standards promulgated by the FDA. Reg. Rep. (CCH) ¶ 23,814 (1995) (consent order); Olsen Lab., 5 Trade Reg. Rep. (CCH) ¶ 23,717 (1994) (consent order).

[163] *See, In re* Chesebrough-Pond's Inc., 106 F.T.C. at, 573.

[164] *In re* Thompson Med. Co., 104 F.T.C. at 826. In *Thompson Med. Co.,* the Commission nonetheless concluded that the evidence presented by Thompson did not suggest any rationale for requiring a different level of substantiation or efficacy claims in the Aspercreme advertisement than that level that the FDA was prepared to require for claims in the product's labeling. *Id* at 826-29. *See also Chesebrough-Pond's, Inc.,* 106 F.T.C. at 567 (modifying order).

[165] *See, e.g., In re* Thompson Med. Co., 104 F.T.C. at 829.

[166] *In re* Thompson, 104 F.T.C. 648 (1984), *aff'd,* 791 F.2d 189 (D.C. Cir. 1986) *cert. denied,* 479 U.S. 1086 (1987); *see also In re* Ogilvy & Mather Int'l, Inc., 5 Trade Reg. Rep. (CCH) ¶ 22,554 (1988) (modifying portions of 1983 consent order regarding advertising agency that developed advertising for Thompson Medical Co.'s Aspercreme product).

[167] *In re* Thompson Med. Co., 104 F.T.C. at 818-29.

[168] *Id.* at 788-818.

[169] *Id.* at 792-94.

[170] *Id.* at 800-01.

what message it reasonably [could] be interpreted as conveying to consumers."[171] The Commission emphasized that

> [I]f our initial review of evidence from the advertisement itself does not allow us to conclude with confidence that it is reasonable to read an advertisement as containing a particular implied message, we will not find the ad to make the implied claim unless extrinsic evidence allows us to conclude that such a reading of the ad is reasonable.[172]

In discussing the type and scope of the consumer interpretations to be drawn from an advertisement, the FTC stated that:

> [W]e do not require that all consumers reading or viewing [the advertisement] be sophisticated experts in interpreting the nuances of the English language. Absent reasons to conclude differently, we presume that advertisements are directed at ordinary members of the adult population who, as such, have a range of abilities. We look at how such individuals actually interpret the advertisements in real-life situations, not at how they would if they have sufficient time and incentives attentively to review the ads so as to come up with the most semantically correct interpretation of them.[173]

Based on consumer research showing consumer preference for aspirin-containing analgesics, as well as uncontradicted expert testimony that aspirin is considered the drug of choice for mild arthritic pain, the FTC determined that Thompson's implied aspirin content claim was important to reasonable consumers and thus material.[174] The Commission further concluded that Thompson's newness claims also were material because they implied product efficacy claims to arthritis sufferers.[175]

Of particular importance to drug advertisers is the FTC conclusion in *Thompson* that significant economic harm to the consumer can "result from the repeated purchase of an ineffective product by consumers who are unable to evaluate drug efficacy in an easy manner."[176] This rationale allows a finding of consumer injury under the FTC's new deception standards, even though no safety concerns relating to use of the product are present.

The FTC also found Thompson's efficacy claims to be deceptive because they lacked adequate substantiation.[177] The Commission ruled that Thompson should possess two well-controlled clinical tests in order to possess a reasonable basis for making its efficacy claims.[178] It required this relatively high level of substantiation because: 1) the product is a drug intended to improve the physical welfare of its users; 2) the drug efficacy claims are

---

[171] *Id.* at 820-21.

[172] *Id.* at 790.

[173] *Id.* at 789.

[174] *Id.* at 816.

[175] *Id.* at 817.

[176] *Id.* at 824.

[177] *Id.* at 821-29. *See generally In re* Pfizer, Inc. 81 F.T.C. 23 (1972) (order); *In re* National Dynamics Corp., 82 F.T.C. 488 (1973) (order), *rev'd in part on other grounds*, 492 F.2d 1333 (2d Cir.), *cert. denied*, 419 U.S. 993 (1974), *reissued*, 85 F.T.C. 391 (1976) (modifying order).

[178] *In re* Thompson Med. Co., 104 F.T.C. at 826.

the types of claims that cannot be readily verified by consumers; 3) although the cost of developing the required substantiation would be significant, the large potential market and likely high demand would not deter the development or advertising of such products; 4) while the health risk from using the product as advertised is uncertain and should be minimal if used as directed, significant economic harm to the consumer could result from repeated purchase of such a product, if ineffective; and 5) the substantiation standard generally applied by the scientific and medical community to claims for the efficacy of OTC analgesic drugs is that such claims must be based on at least two well-controlled clinical trials.[179] The FTC considered the inability of consumers to evaluate the analgesic effect by themselves in an uncontrolled environment a persuasive reason for consumers to expect, and the FTC to require, appropriate scientific testing before efficacy claims can be made.[180]

The Legacy of Thompson

The FTC has continued to devote a significant amount of its advertising enforcement resources to the OTC drug area.[181] For example, in a 1995 proceeding involving Taleigh Corporation, the Commission challenged advertising for diet pills and a stop-smoking patch, alleging that the false claims at issue were: 1) consumers can burn fat quickly and lose weight without diet or exercise, 2) there are no dangerous side effects, 3) the product is unique and has never before been sold without a prescription, 4) the product enables smokers to stop smoking quickly and easily, and 5) the advertiser possessed a reasonable basis for all claims and had scientific evidence to prove significant weight loss. The FTC also charged that the advertisers had failed to disclose that consumer endorsers had been compensated for their endorsements, and had falsely represented that consumer testimonials reflected the typical experience of a consumer using the product.[182]

Similarly, in another 1995 proceeding, the FTC alleged that Nu Skin International, Inc. deceptively advertised that: competent and reliable data showed that Nutriol stopped hair loss and stimulated hair growth, and that it was more effective than the prescription drug minoxidil in the treatment of hair loss; Face Life permanently removed facial wrinkles and was more effective than the prescription drug Retin-A; Celltrex promoted the healing of third degree burns; and using the three products resulted in physiological changes in the body, as well as cosmetic changes in appearance. To remedy these deceptive practices, the FTC's order included provisions that required Nu Skin to: 1) cease from advertising or selling any product that is represented as promoting hair growth or preventing hair loss, unless it is the subject of an approved new drug application for such purpose under the Federal Food, Drug, and Cosmetic Act; 2) cease from misrepresenting the performance, benefits, efficacy, or safety of any food, drug, device, or any other product or service, unless substantiated by reliable scientific evidence; 3) cease from dealing with anyone

---

[179] *Id.* at 821-26.

[180] *Id.* at 826.

[181] For other recent OTC drug cases, see, e.g., In the Matter of Jordan, McGrath, Case & Taylor, FTC Dkt. No. C-3684 (1996) (decision and order); Johnson & Johnson Consumer Prods., Inc., 5 Trade Reg. Rep. (CCH) ¶ 23,944 (1995) (proposed consent order); Olsen Lab., Inc., 5 Trade Reg. Rep. (CCH) ¶ 23,717 (1994) (consent order); FTC v. Pantron I. Corp., 33 F.3d 1088 (9th Cir. 1994), *cert. denied*, 115 S. Ct. 1794 (1995); St. Ives Lab., Inc., Sterling Drug, [1987-1993 Transfer Binder] Trade Reg. Rep. (CCH) ¶ 22,837 (1990) (consent order); Walgreen Co., 109 F.T.C. 156 (1987) (consent order).

[182] Taleigh Corp., 5 Trade Reg. Rep. (CCH) ¶ 23,783 (1995).

who makes any of the representations prohibited by the order; and 4) pay the FTC $1,000,000 to be used to provide redress to consumers.[183]

In *National Dietary Research, Inc.*, the FTC challenged deceptive advertising for "Food Source One," a compressed tablet made from plant fiber and other substances.[184] The Commission's order required National Dietary Research to cease: 1) making the representations challenged as false in the complaint unless they possessed scientific evidence substantiating the claims; 2) misrepresenting the contents or results of any test or study; 3) misrepresenting the fiber or nutrient contained in a product; 4) misrepresenting the nature of the research activities of National Dietary Research; 5) misrepresenting that any advertisement was not a paid advertisement if, in truth, it was; 6) representing that any testimonials are the typical experience of a consumer using the product, unless they are true and there was reliable evidence to substantiate the representations or disclose clearly in the advertisement that the representation is nontypical; 7) make only claims permitted in labeling by the FDA; and 8) pay $100,000 in consumer redress to the U.S. Treasury.

In *Third Option Laboratories, Inc.*, the FTC challenged advertising that "Jogging in a Jug" would cure or alleviate heart disease, arthritis, lethargy, dysentery, constipation, swelling of the legs and muscle spasms; lower serum cholesterol; break down calcium and other mineral deposits; improve the circulatory system; clean internal organs; prevent or reduce the risk of cancer, leukemia, heart disease, and arthritis; provide the same health benefits as jogging; stabilize blood sugar levels in diabetics; and aid in the recovery of viral infections. The Commission also alleged that Third Option Laboratories falsely represented that Jogging in a Jug was approved by the U.S. Department of Agriculture, and that the testimonials from consumers represented the typical experience of a consumer using the product. The Commission's order required Third Option Laboratories to, among other things: 1) cease from misrepresenting that any product had been tested or approved by any person, firm, or government agency; 2) make only representations permitted by the FDA, or under any new drug application approved by the FDA; 3) cease from using the name "Jogging in a Jug" or any name that communicated the same or similar meaning unless the material containing the name clearly contains the disclosure: "THERE IS NO SCIENTIFIC EVIDENCE THAT JOGGING IN A JUG PROVIDES ANY HEALTH BENEFITS;" 4) pay the FTC $480,000; and 5) notify past purchasers of Jogging in a Jug of the settlement and offer to refund their purchase price.[185]

In *Kingsbridge Media & Marketing, Inc.*,[186] the FTC obtained a temporary restraining order from a U.S. district court halting advertising for "Dream Away" and "Advanced Dream Away," which claimed that the diet pills caused weight loss while sleeping, in a short period of time, and without dieting or exercising.[187] The final consent settlement established a $1.1 million "consumer redress" fund for purchasers of "Dream Away"

---

[183] Nu Skin Int'l, Inc., 5 Trade Reg. Rep. (CCH) ¶ 23,526 (1994) (consent order).

[184] National Dietary Research, Inc., 5 Trade Reg. Rep. (CCH) ¶ 23,814 (1995) (consent order).

[185] Third Option Lab., Inc., 5 Trade Reg. Rep. (CCH) ¶ 23,799 (1995) (consent order).

[186] FTC v. Kingsbridge Media & Mktg., Inc., [1987-1993 Transfer Binder] Trade Reg. Rep. (CCH) ¶ 22,547 (1988) (final judgement and order). Another 1988 drug advertising case wherein the FTC obtained an order from district court is *In re* Sheldon Friedlich Mktg., Inc., 5 Trade Reg. Rep. (CCH) ¶ 22,526 (1988) (stipulated permanent injunction) (companies agreed not to misrepresent any products, including their "sex pills," sold through the mail).

[187] FTC v. Kingsbridge Media & Mktg., Inc., [1987-1993 Transfer Binder] Trade Reg. Rep. (CCH) ¶ 22,547 (1988).

weight loss products, and prohibited the marketers from misrepresenting or making unsubstantiated claims concerning the performance, efficacy, or safety of any food, drug, or device.[188] The order also required Kingsbridge Media to disclose in any future advertising for weight control or reduction products, programs or services that dieting and/or exercise is required in order to lose weight.[189]

In *FTC v. Pantron I Corp.*,[190] the FTC sought permanent injunction and monetary redress for false advertising of "Helsinki formula," a product that purportedly arrested hair loss and stimulated hair regrowth. The 9th Circuit Court affirmed the FTC's position that a claim of product effectiveness is false if the product has no efficacy beyond the placebo effect.

In *Adria Labs*,[191] the FTC charged that advertising claims that "Efficin is not Aspirin" falsely implied that Efficin was safer than aspirin in terms of possible side effects.[192] The consent order required the manufacturer to cease representing that any magnesium salicylate internal analgesic, including Efficin, contained no aspirin, and comparing the safety of any such product to any product containing aspirin, unless such representations are accompanied by prescribed disclosure warnings and substantiated by reliable and competent scientific evidence.[193]

FTC Regulation of Medical Device Advertising

The legal principles applicable to the FTC's regulation of advertising for medical device products are identical to those discussed in the preceding sections, as is the nature of the interaction between the FTC and the FDA.[194] The FTC's emphasis in reviewing advertis-

---

[188] *Id.* ¶22,230.

[189] *Id.*

[190] FTC v. Pantron I. Corp., 33 F.3d 1088 (9th Cir. 1994), *cert. denied*, 115 U.S. 1794 (1995).

[191] *In re* Adria Lab., Inc., 103 F.T.C. 512 (1984) (consent order).

[192] *Id.* at 513.

[193] *Id.* at 524-27.

[194] *See, e.g.* Carter Prod., Inc. v. F.T.C., 323 F.2d 523 (5th Cir. 1963) (claims implying permanent antiperspirant benefits prohibited); *In re* Spinal Health Serv., Inc., 102 F.T.C. 1319 (1983) (consent order) (requiring cessation of unsubstantiated claims that a "laser face lift" or a "biostimulation face lift" will provide a more youthful facial appearance, and that the benefits of such treatments will last as long as that of a surgical face life); *In re* Teledyne, Inc., 97 F.T.C. 320 (1981) (consent order) (requiring manufacturer of oral irrigating devices to cease, misrepresenting the content, results, or conclusions of any survey or opinion research; making unsubstantiated preventive or therapeutic claims about devices; and claiming that a professional body or any portion thereof has some brief, opinion, recommendation, endorsement, or follows some typical course of conduct unless and only to the extent such representation is true); *In re* Block Drug Co., 90 F.T.C. 893 (1977) (order) (finding efficacy claims for denture adhesives false, misleading, and unsubstantiated, and comparative performance claims for denture cleansers unsubstantiated); *In re* Colgate-Palmolive Co., 59 F.T.C. 1452 (1961) (order), *rev'd and remanded*, 310 F.2d 89 (1st Cir. 1962) (prohibiting advertiser from presenting a test, experiment, or demonstration as actual proof of a claim made for a product when it is not in fact a genuine test, demonstration, or experiment, and use of mock-ups, props, or substitutes is not disclosed).

ing and marketing practices focuses on medical device products that may involve potential risk to health and safety, and product efficacy claims.

Typical advertising claims for medical device products the FTC has challenged as false or misleading over the years include: claims concerning efficacy, comfort, composition, and safety of contact lens and eyeglass products;[195] claims regarding efficacy and physical characteristics of hearing aid devices;[196] claims conceding the effectiveness of hair-removal devices;[197] the use of diathermy devices;[198] claims relating to the health benefits of suntanning products or devices;[199] claims conceding therapeutic use of enuresis treatment devices;[200] claims relating to the use of electric muscle stimulation treatments as a substitute for exercise;[201] claims regarding efficacy and indications for use of hernia sup-

---

[195] *In re* Lens Craft Research & Dev. Co., 84 F.T.C. 355 (1974) (consent order) (seller of contact lenses ordered to cease mailing false adverting claims to run corrective advertisements); *In re* Leon A. Tashof trading as N.Y. Jewelry Co., 74 F.T.C. 1361 (1968) (order) (retailer required to cease using bait and switch and other false advertising practices, and failing to disclose details of credit charges); *In re* Rayex Corp., 65 F.T.C. 293 (1964) (modifying order) (assemblers of sunglasses ordered to cease misrepresenting the diopter curve of lenses, and falsely claiming conformance with Department of Defense standards and specifications); In re Riviera Trading Corp., 63 F.T.C. 114 (1963) (order) (requiring distributor of sunglasses to cease false representations concerning quality of lenses); *In re* The Plastic Contact Lens Co., 60 F.T.C. 158 (1962) (consent order) (distributor of contact lenses ordered to cease falsely representing safety and comfort of lens use); *In re* Bachmann Bros., Inc., 56 F.T.C. 1534 (1960) (order) (requiring distributor of sunglasses to cease false representations that imported sunglasses were manufactured in the United States and failing to mark cases of sunglasses with the country of origin).

[196] *See, e.g., In re* Beltone Elec. Corp., 88 F.T.C. 336 (1976) (consent order) (prohibiting hearing aid manufacturers from misrepresenting the uniqueness, benefits, characteristics, and efficacy of its products); *In re* Mather Hearing Aid Distrib., Inc., 78 F.T.C. 709 (1971) (order) (requiring manufactures of hearing aids to cease misrepresenting that their hearing aids involved a new scientific principle, and would be helpful regardless of the hearing disability and would prevent deafness); *In re* Sonotone Corp., 56 F.T.C. 1101 (1960) (consent order) (requiring manufacturer of hearing aids to cease false representations that its hearing aids were cordless, buttonless, and invisible).

[197] *See* Removatron Int'l Corp., 111 F.T.C. at 292.

[198] *See, e.g.,* Electro Thermal Co. v. FTC, 91 F.2d 477 (9th Cir. 1937) (ordering manufacturer to cease false and misleading claims for therapeutic effects of device to aid prostate gland problem).

[199] *See* In the Matter of Cal. Suncare, Inc., FTC Dkt. No. C-3715 (FTC 1997) (consent order) (ordering manufacturer of California Tan Heliotherapy Products for use in connection with tanning, to cease and desist from representing that the negative effects of sunlight exposure are caused only by over exposure and not by cumulative moderate exposure, that tanning is not harmful to the skin, misrepresenting that the use of their product prevents or minimizes the negative effects of sunlight exposure, or representing that sunlight exposure will reduce the risk of skin cancer. The manufacturer also must cease and desist making representations regarding any California Tan Heliotherapy product and its effect on cancer, blood pressure, serum cholesterol, Seasonal Affective Disorder, AIDS, the immune system, bone disorders, any health benefit, or similarity to exercise.)*In re* An-Mar Int'l, Ltd., [1987-1993 Transfer Binder] Trade Reg. Rep. (CCH) ¶ 22,681 (1989) (consent order).

[200] *See, e.g., In re* Paramedical Serv., Inc., 89 F.T.C. 99 (1977) (consent order) (requiring distributor and franchisee to cease misrepresenting that mechanical device used in treatment of bedwetting is unique and to give customers a written disclosure in advance of sale that the device is available elsewhere); *In re* Maurice J. Feil trading as The Enurtone Co., 56 F.T.C. 364 (1959) (order), *aff'd,* 285 F.2d 879 (9th Cir. 1960) (requiring distributors of trusses to cease making false representations in advertising).

[201] *See In re* Nutratone, Inc., [1987-1993 Transfer Binder] Trade Reg. Rep. (CCH) ¶ 22,682 (1989) (consent order).

port devices; and claims relating to the use of a device that emits electric sparks for the relief of pain.[202]

Illustrative of challenges to device claims, in recent cases against Ninzu, Inc., the FTC challenged advertising for an acupressure device that clips onto the ear. The Commission alleged that Ninzu, Inc., falsely represented that the device causes significant weight loss without the need to diet or exercise, controls appetite, and eliminates a person's craving for food. The Commission further alleged that Ninzu did not possess a reasonable basis for these claims, falsely represented that these claims were based on scientific evidence, and falsely represented that testimonials used to advertise the product reflect the "typical experience" of a consumer using the product.[203]

In *Lifestyle Fascination, Inc.*, the FTC took action against advertising for three devices: the Brain Tuner, a cranio-electric stimulation device; the Rhythm, an electronic acupuncture device; and the Aerobic Eye Exercise Glasses, a set of pinhole eyeglasses. The Commission alleged that Lifestyle falsely represented that: 1) the Brain Tuner would increase I.Q., increase energy levels, improve concentration, and reduce cravings for drugs and alcohol; 2) the Rhythm would relieve muscle, digestive, and nervous ailments; tone muscles; help the user lose weight; and relieve backaches, headaches, muscle pain, still shoulders, insomnia, and fatigue; and 3) the Aerobic Eye Exercise Glasses would result in long-term vision improvement, that they were an adequate substitute for prescription glasses or contact lenses, and that the advertisement testimonial reflected the experience of the typical consumer who has used the product.[204]

In *Haverhills*, the FTC took action against advertisements for Solar Gold Tanners, tanning devices that were promoted as a safe alternative to natural sun tanning because the devices did not pose a risk of harmful side effects ordinarily associated with sun tanning, did not increase the risk of skin cancer, and did not contribute to skin aging. Further, the FTC was concerned that there was no indication that protective eyewear was necessary when using the tanning device. In addition to prohibiting any further false and misleading representations concerning the safety of the devices, the FTC required that the ads either demonstrate through models or state the need for the use of protective eyewear, and that all future ads carry a statement that the user should read the mandatory FDA statement found on all tan-

---

[202] *See, e.g.,* In the Matter of Natural Innovations, Inc., FTC Dkt. No. C-3718 (1997) (consent order) (ordering manufacturer to cease and desist making representations that the device will relieve various types of pain, provides immediate or long term relief; the device is as or more effective than prescription or OTC medications, or physical therapy, chiropractic treatment, acupuncture or acupressure; or about the efficacy or relative efficacy of relieving pain from whatever source); *In re* R.C. Myrick trading as Carey Surgical Application Co., 60 F.T.C. 1621 (1962) (order) (requiring sellers of hernia trusses to cease disseminating false newspaper advertising claims concerning medical expertise of salesmen and comparative benefits, physical characteristics, and efficacy of trusses); *In re* Hoffmann Truss Corp., 59 F.T.C. 537 (1961) (consent order) (requiring distributors of trusses to cease making misrepresentations in advertising); *In re* Fred B. Miller trading as Miller Lab., Inc., 56 F.T.C. 1249 (1960) (consent order) (requiring distributors of trusses to cease making false representations that their trusses would bring permanent relief from ruptures and was more effective than competing products); *In re* Piper Brace Sales Corp., 54 F.T.C. 1778 (1958) (consent order) (requiring sellers of trusses to cease making misrepresentations and disparaging remarks concerning competitive products); *In re* Herbert B. Sykes trading as Sykes Hernia Control Serv., 52 F.T.C. 934 (1956) (order) (requiring seller to cease false representations that his "hernia control" device was radically different from the superior to a truss and that he conducts a clinic for hernia sufferers).

[203] Ninzu, Inc., 5 Trade Reg. Rep. (CCH) ¶ 23,752 (1995) (consent order).

[204] Lifestyle Fascination, Inc., 5 Trade Reg. Rep. (CCH) ¶ 23,606 (1994), 26,796 (1994) (consent order).

ning devices relating to eye injury, skin cancer, skin aging, and photosensitive reactions.[205]

In a 1994 enforcement proceeding, the FTC obtained civil penalties against Beltone Electronics Corp. for violating a 1976 FTC order prohibiting false and unsubstantiated performance claims for Beltone hearing aids.[206] The FTC settlement with Beltone stipulated that any representation about hearing aids that are approved by the FDA would constitute *prima facia* evidence that Beltone had substantiation of such representations. Interestingly, FTC Commissioner Mary Azcuenaga, in a concurring statement, indicated that she disagreed only with treating FDA approval of claims as merely *prima facia* evidence, and would have accepted FDA approval as *complete* substantiation.

In 1995, Dahlberg, Inc. sought to preclude FTC enforcement of a 1976 consent order concerning advertising claims made by Dahlberg about its hearing aids. Dahlberg argued that section 502(r) of the 1976 Medical Device Amendments[207] to the Federal Food, Drug, and Cosmetic Act transferred authority from the FTC to the FDA to regulate "intended use claims" made in device advertising. The court upheld the FTC's argument that it retained authority to regulate commercial advertising claims that do not rise to the level of intended use claims.[208]

In *Conair Corp.*, the FTC prohibited false and unsubstantiated claims of the "California Facial Skin Rejuvenation System," which included use of a hand-held sound wave medical device. The Commission's order required Conair to have competent and reliable scientific evidence to support any future representation it made that sound waves emitted (at any frequency) from any product it sells will firm or tone muscles, or improve the efficacy of a topically applied skin care product.[209]

In *Numex Corp.*, the FTC challenged claims for a hand-held mechanical roller device that Numex claimed would relieve various kinds of muscular pains including the pain of arthritis. The FTC challenged deceptive expert endorsements as well as deceptive consumer testimonials used in infomercials for Numex Corp.[210]

Johnson & Johnson settled an FTC proceeding in 1995, involving false claims as to condom failure rates in advertising promoting Johnson & Johnson's spermicidal lubricant as "condom insurance." The FTC charged that the company had made false and/or unsubstantiated representations concerning both the failure rate of condoms and the effectiveness of its product.[211]

---

[205] Haverhills, [1987-1993 Trade Reg. Rep.] (CCH) ¶ 22,903 (1991) (consent order).

[206] United States v. Beltone Elec. Corp., 5 Trade Reg. Rep. (CCH) ¶ 23,731 (N.D. Ill. 1994).

[207] Pub. L. No. 94-295, 90 Stat. 539.

[208] *In re* Dahlberg and the Fed. Trade Comm'n, 1995-1 Trade Cas. ¶ 70,963 (D. Minn. 1995).

[209] Conair Corp., 5 Trade Reg. Rep. (CCH) ¶ 23,352 (1993) (consent order).

[210] Numex Corp., 5 Trade Reg. Rep. (CCH) ¶ 23,402 (1993) (consent order).

[211] K-Y Plus Ad Campaign Disparaging Condom Effectiveness Based on Misrepresentation of Study results. (Oct. 11, 1995).

Self-Regulation and State Regulation

As a closing caveat, it should be noted that in addition to the FTC, several other entities, both public and private, also can have a significant impact on the advertising of drug and medical device products.

In the private sector the National Advertising Division (NAD) of the Council of Better Business Bureaus and its appellate body, the National Advertising Review Board (NARB) review, on a regular basis, the content of advertising and labeling for consumer products. NAD, the voluntary self-regulatory body sponsored by the advertising industry, reviews and issues nonbinding decisions concerning the validity of and substantiation for advertising claims. Although NAD has no power to compel advertisers to comply with its recommended advertising changes, most advertisers voluntarily either adopt NAD's recommendations or discontinue the advertising claims at issue. If an advertiser does not take sound action, NAD refers the matter to the FTC.[212] In addition, the broadcast networks routinely review all television and radio advertising, and decline to broadcast advertisements they consider to be deceptive or misleading as well as those not satisfying other specified network criteria, such as "good taste."[213] Finally, advertisers have turned to the federal courts to directly challenge competitors' allegedly unfair advertising practices by initiating civil actions and frequently seeking injunctive relief, pursuant to section 43(a) of the Lanham Act.[214] These cases frequently have been used

---

[212] *See, e.g.*, Lifestyle Fascination, Inc., NAD Case No. 3369 (1996) (challenging claims for Accutrim); Life Plus, NAD Case No. 3322 (1996) (challenging a number of claims regarding weight loss and weight management provided by Shape Plus and Endogen's affect on the body's ability to produce DHEA); McNeil Consumer Prods. Co., NAD Case No. 3313 (1996) (challenging claims for Extra Strength Tylenol); AST Research, NAD Case No. 3289 (1996) (challenging claims for Creatine Complex-5); Bausch & Lomb, Inc., NAD Case No. 3214 (1995) (challenging the continuing validity of exclusivity claims for eye drops); Bogdana Corp., NAD Case No. 3215 (1995) (challenged by infomercial marketing trade association against infomercial's claims that "Cholestaway" wafers provide substantial cholesterol reduction benefits); Gero Vita Int'l, NAD Case No. 3206 (1995) (investigating broad claims that the "GH3 Anti-Aging Pill" treats a variety of age-related ailments); Sonex Int'l Corp., NAD Case No. 3182 (1995) (addressing the breadth of, and substantiation for, comparative and efficacy claims for an UltraSonic toothbrush); Universal Merchants, Inc., NAD Case No. 3176 (1995) (NAD-instigated investigation into claims that "ChromaTrim-100 Weight Loss Chewing Gum" was clinically proven to burn fat, decrease appetite, and increase lean muscle tissue).

[213] *See generally*, 3 ROSDEN THE ADVERTISING LAW § 40.03 (1987).

[214] 15 U.S.C. § 1125. *See, e.g.*, Ortho Pharm. Corp. v. Cosprophar Inc., 32 F.3d 690 (2d Cir. 1994) (challenging comparison between drug product and cosmetic with alleged anti-wrinkle properties); Johnson & Johnson-Merck Consumer Pharmaceuticals Co. v. Rhone-Poulenc Rorer Pharm., Inc., 19 F.3d 125 (3d Cir. 1994) (challenging claims that defendant's product is "strongest antacid there is"); Mylan Lab., Inc. v. Matkari, 7 F.3d 1130 (4th Cir. 1993), *cert. denied*, 114 S. Ct. 1307 (1994) (challenging claims of bioequivalence between generic and innovator drug products); Johnson & Johnson-Merck Consumer Pharm. Co. v. SmithKline Beecham Corp., 960 F.2d 294 (2d Cir. 1992) (challenging advertising regarding antacid ingredients); McNeil-P.C.C., Inc. v. Bristol-Myers Squibb Co., 938 F.2d 1544 (2d Cir. 1991) (challenging comparative claims for the OTC analgesics); Sandoz Pharm. Corp. v. Richardson-Vicks, Inc., 902 F.2d 222 (3d Cir. 1990) (challenging claims of superiority and instant activity for cough syrup); SmithKline Beecham Consumer Healthcare v. Johnson & Johnson-Merck Consumer Pharm. Co., Inc., 1995-2 Trade Cas. (CCH) ¶ 71,172 (S.D.N.Y. 1995); American Home Prods. Corp. v. Procter & Gamble Co., 871 F. Supp. 739 (D.N.J. 1994) (challenging comparative claims regarding OTC analgesics); Energy Four, Inc. v. Dornier Med. Sys., Inc. 765 F. Supp. 724 (N.D. Ga. 1991) (challenging claims about the safety of lithotripsy electrodes); Genderm Corp. v. Biozone Lab., No. 92 C 2533, 1992 WL 220638 (N.D. Ill. Sept. 3, 1992) (challenging misrepresentations about the presence of an active ingredient).

by OTC drug marketers to challenge comparative advertising claims made by their competitors.[215]

In the public sphere, regulation at the state level also must be considered. State Attorneys General remain active in challenging, under state law, advertising by national advertisers.[216] Many state actions have taken a more expansive approach to the regulation of advertising and have brought actions that require advertisers to disclose facts that these states alleged are "material" to consumer purchase decisions even if there is no claim by the advertiser that specifically implicates these facts. For instance, an agreement with the Suzuki Motor Corporation requires Suzuki to include a warning on all Suzuki Samurai's that the sport utility vehicles handle differently from a typical passenger vehicle.[217] This warning was required despite the fact the Suzuki made no claims in its advertising as to the handling of its vehicle. Similarly, nine states negotiated jointly an Assurance of Discontinuance with Campbell Soup Company to stop Campbell's "Soup is Good Food" advertising campaign.[218] Unlike the FTC action, which alleged that Campbell made a health claim concerning heart disease that discloses only the health advantages and not the health disadvantages of its product relative to a particular health claim, the state action alleged that Campbell was blurring the advantages of the product with advantages of a healthy diet so that consumers would not understand the difference. This expansion of state regulation is thus an important consideration for advertisers in the development of advertising or other product information. In addition, private rights of action often are permitted under state "Little FTC Acts," which also may provide a source of challenges to drug or medical device advertising.[219]

---

[215] *See, e.g.*, Johnson & Johnson-Merck Consumer Pharm. Co. v. Rhone-Poulenc Rorer Pharm., Inc., 1994-1 Trade Cas., ¶ 70,537 (3d Cir. 1994); Sandoz Pharm. Corp. v. Richardson Vicks, Inc., 1993-2 Trade Cas. ¶ 70,463 (3d Cir. 1990); Pfizer, Inc. v. Miles, Inc., 1995 Trade Cas. ¶ 70,863 (D. Conn. 1994).

[216] *See, e.g.*, NATIONAL ASS'N ATTORNEYS GEN., Consumer Protection REPORT 12 (June 1995)(describing Texas attorney general's settlement with a company that allegedly made false claims that its dietary supplement was a drug); NATIONAL ASS'N ATTORNEYS GEN., Consumer Protection Report, 20 (Jan. 1993)(describing Minnesota and Wisconsin attorneys general's settlement with manufacture of diet pill who claimed that the pill could inhibit sugar absorption and would result in weight loss without dieting; CONSUMER PROTECTION REPORT, 7 (July 1993)(describing settlement with company that allegedly made "new and improved claim" for a product that was not new and improved); NATIONAL ASS'N ATTORNEYS GEN., Consumer Protection Report, 14 (Jan. 1992)(describing Massachusetts attorney general's settlement with toothpaste manufacturer who agreed to cease making claims that a product protects teeth "down to the root"); *See also* Stephen Paul Mahinka & Kathleen M. Sanzo, *Multistate Antitrust and Consumer Protection Investigations: Practical Concerns*, 63 ANTITRUST L.J. 213 (1994); Bruce Silverglade, *Business Gets a Headache: States Move to Fill FTC Role*, LEGAL TIMES, May 18, 1987, at 16; *Three-State Enforcers Demand Withdrawal of McDonald's Ads*, [Jan-June] Antitrust & Trade Reg. Rep. (BNA), No. 1296, at 932 (May 21, 1987); *Campbell Agrees to N.Y. State Restrictions on "Soup is Good Food" Ads*, FOOD CHEM. NEWS, Nov. 5, 1984, at 27.

[217] In the matter of American Suzuki Motor Corp., Agreement of Voluntary Compliance, California Attorney General *et al.* (Mar. 21, 1989). Signatories also included attorneys general from Massachusetts, Minnesota, Missouri, New York, Texas, and Washington.

[218] In the matter of Campbell Soup Co., Assurance of Discontinuance, Minnesota Attorney General (May 8, 1989). Signatories also included attorneys general from California, Illinois, Iowa, Massachusetts, Missouri, New York, Texas, and Wisconsin. *See also*, Stephen Paul Mahinka & Kathleen M. Sanzo, *supra* note 216.

[219] For a review of state "Little FTC Acts", see generally Marshall A. Leaffer & Michael H. Lipson, *Consumer Actions Against Unfair or Deceptive Acts or Practices: The Private Uses of Federal Trade Commission Jurisprudence*, 48 GEO. WASH. L. REV. 521 (1980); J. Shelton, *Unfair and Deceptive Acts and Practices* (National Consumer Law Center 1982); Annot., *Practices Forbidden by State Deceptive Trade Practice and Consumer Protection Acts*, 89 A.L.R. 3d 449 (1979) & (Supp. 1995).

Conclusion

The basic legal doctrines relating to FTC regulation of advertising seem likely to remain relatively stable. The steady pattern of evolution and refinement of these doctrines related to deception, unfairness, and advertising substantiation over the last twenty-five years suggest that radical changes or departures are unlikely. Nonetheless, because the FTC exercises considerable "prosecutorial discretion" in determining which advertising practices will be challenged in enforcement actions, and over time the Commission could become more aggressive in challenging advertising practices that, for reasons of policy, have not as yet been challenged by the Commission. Thus, risk-averse advertisers should seek the mainstream of FTC regulatory currents, rather than the boundaries because, in the time-lag between the formulation of an advertising claim and the ultimate resolution of an FTC challenge thereto, a modest shift in regulatory philosophy and/or prosecutorial discretion might well leave the advertiser vulnerable to unexpected legal consequences. For example, the legal "deception" standard that was ultimately applied to the advertising in *Thompson Medical Co.*[220] underwent a variety of subtle evolutions during the eight years that passed between initial dissemination of that advertising and the court's final decision in this case.

---

[220] *In re* Thompson Med. Co., 104 F.T.C. 648 (1984) (order), *aff'd*, 791 F.2d 189 (D.C. Cir. 1986), *cert. denied*, 479 U.S. 1086 (1987).

chapter 14

The Impact and Implications of Reimbursement, Fraud, and Abuse on Medical Devices, Drugs, and Biologics

Gordon B. Schatz, Esq.*
Joseph W. Metro, Esq.**

Introduction

The Federal Food, Drug, and Cosmetic Act (FDCA)[1] has been the primary focus of regulatory compliance, product development, and marketing for manufacturers of medical devices, drugs, and biologics. Technology companies must now look beyond the FDCA, however, to understand the significant impact and implications of reimbursement and fraud and abuse for product success. For example, many third-party payors once paid hospitals based on facilities' reasonable costs, which could vary depending on different products used to treat patients. Now, many insurers limit payment to certain fixed rates that do not vary to reflect different hospital costs. Thus, manufacturers may need to focus on improved health outcomes and the overall cost-effectiveness of their products when marketing to hospital customers. Similarly, where customers such as physicians are reimbursed on a fee-for-service basis for each use of a manufacturer's product, the availability of higher reimbursement levels for competing products or procedures can serve as a barrier to the acceptance of the manufacturer's product, even where that product offers clinical advantages. Further, the common means of meeting competition — discounts, value-added services, and the like — may implicate fraud and abuse standards or, in the case of prescription drugs, generate significant liability for Medicaid rebates.

* Mr. Schatz is a Partner in the law firm of Reed Smith Shaw & McClay LLP, Washington, D.C.
** Mr. Metro is a Partner in the health care group of the law firm of Reed Smith Shaw & McClay LLP, Washington, D.C.

[1] Pub. L. No. 75-717, 52 Stat. 1040 (1938) (codified as amended 21 U.S.C. §§ 301 et seq. (1994)).

This chapter presents an overview of the reimbursement and fraud and abuse issues that are important for technology manufacturers. Reimbursement and fraud and abuse principles derive from health insurance policies and programs. Although such policies and programs generally are contractual in nature, federal or state laws also may govern payment for items and services furnished to patients, particularly where the payor is a governmental entity. Because there are many different health insurance programs, reimbursement and fraud and abuse policies can vary widely, even for the same product. The primary categories of payors include: government payors (i.e., Medicare, Medicaid, the Department of Veterans Affairs (VA) and the Civilian Health and Medical Program of the Uniformed Services (CHAMPUS);[2] private nonprofit insurers (e.g., Blue Cross and Blue Shield plans);[3] commercial insurers; and managed care organizations (e.g., health maintenance organizations (HMOs)). This chapter will not attempt to address the wide diversity found in these many insurance programs, but rather will concentrate on Medicare and Medicaid. By virtue of their size, these programs often influence other insurers and therefore offer a good starting point for any reimbursement analysis.[4]

In a nutshell, technology manufacturers have learned to deal effectively with the Food and Drug Administration (FDA) to ensure product success. Likewise, manufacturers need to understand the unique data demands of payors, the regulatory barriers and opportunities in federal and state payment programs, and how best to position products to survive in a payment environment that will put increasing pressure on hospitals and doctors when they choose to use innovative medical products.

Basic Reimbursement Principles

To understand reimbursement, it is useful to distinguish coverage issues from payment issues. Questions of coverage raise the issue of whether *any* payment will be made for a product and under what circumstances. Payment questions deal with the amount or level of payment. Often, coverage and payment policies do not address specific devices, drugs, or biologics. Instead, the policies typically deal with the hospital or physician service or test provided to a patient who utilizes the product. In some circumstances, however, reimburse-

---

[2]   Medicare is a federally funded health insurance program for persons aged 65 or older who have end-stage renal disease or otherwise qualify by virtue of a disability. Medicaid is a joint federal-state welfare program that provides health services to the indigent. Medicare and Medicaid are administered by the Secretary of the Department of Health and Human Services (DHHS) through the Health Care Financing Administration (HCFA). The VA provides a variety of medical services to veterans both directly and through arrangements with private health care providers. The CHAMPUS program pays for care and services furnished to dependents of members of the armed forces.

[3]   These plans typically are organized under state law and operate in a single state or part of that state. Traditionally, Blue Cross plans pay for institutional care, while Blue Shield plans pay for physicians' services and outpatient care. Recently, a number of Blue Cross and Blue Shield plans have been converted to for-profit status.

[4]   During the 104th and 105th Congresses, numerous proposals to overhaul the Medicare and Medicaid programs were considered and adopted. These proposals featured elements designed to promote the use of managed care, payment reductions to providers under public programs, and expanded fraud and abuse remedies. Technology manufacturers should acknowledge the implications of these proposals for the marketing of their products, and should participate in the development of these policies.

ment policies focus directly on a particular drug, prosthetic device, or item of durable medical equipment. When policies are product-specific, they usually do not distinguish one manufacturer's product from another's, but rather cover and pay for the product regardless of which company manufactured it. Further, for many insurers, reimbursement for a product can vary depending on where the product is used (e.g., hospital inpatient or outpatient setting, ambulatory surgical center, physician's office, or patient's home).

Reimbursement for Medical Devices

■ Coverage for Medical Devices

Medicare

Medicare is the largest single health insurance program in the United States. Medicare reimbursement policies are significant both because of the potential volume of Medicare-related business and because of the influence its policies may have on other payors. The Medicare program is governed by federal statutes, regulations, and interpretative materials.

The Medicare program is divided into two parts (A and B), each of which covers a distinct set of services:[5] Part A includes hospital, skilled nursing facility, home health agency, renal dialysis, and hospice services; and Part B includes physician services, clinical laboratory and diagnostic tests provided outside the hospital, durable medical equipment, and other products provided to patients for use in the home.

Coverage Criteria. To analyze whether a product will be covered under Medicare, there are several authorities that typically need to be examined: the definitions of covered services; exclusions; and product- or procedure-specific policies.

Under the Medicare statute,[6] covered services include, among others:

- Inpatient hospital services;
- Inpatient psychiatric hospital services;
- Outpatient occupational therapy services;
- Extended care services;
- Home health services;
- Durable medical equipment;
- Physician services; and
- Medical and other health services, such as:
  — Supplies incident to a physician's services commonly furnished in the office, rendered without charge or included in the physician's bill;

---

[5] All Medicare beneficiaries are eligible for Part A services. Only those Medicare beneficiaries who pay a monthly premium are eligible for Medicare Part B. The overwhelming majority of Medicare beneficiaries pay the monthly Part B premium.

[6] 42 U.S.C. § 1395x et seq. (1994).

— outpatient hospital services;

— outpatient diagnostic services;

— outpatient physical therapy and occupational therapy;

— home dialysis supplies and equipment;

— Antigens prepared by a physician;

— Diagnostic x-ray tests;

— x-ray, radium, and radioactive isotope therapy, including materials and services of technicians;

— Surgical dressings, splints, casts, and other devices used for reduction of fractures and dislocations;

— Prosthetic devices (other than dental) that replace all or part of an internal body organ (including colostomy bags and supplies directly related to colostomy care), including replacement of such devices, and one pair of conventional eyeglasses or contact lenses furnished subsequent to each cataract surgery with insertion of an intraocular lens;

— Leg, arm, back, and neck braces, and artificial legs, arms, and eyes; and

— Screening mammography and pap smears.

For a product to be covered by Medicare, the product must fall within one of these statutorily-defined benefit categories. If a product cannot be so classified, the Health Care Financing Administration (HCFA) will not have the authority to cover the service. This is the case, for example, with home infusion therapy or disposable infusion pumps used in the home, because they do not qualify as durable medical equipment.

Even if a product is included in a covered benefit category, it may be excluded from coverage under the general authority that Medicare will not pay for any item or service that is "[n]ot reasonable or necessary for the diagnosis or treatment of illness or injury or to improve the functioning of a malformed body member."[7] Several cases have addressed the government's application of this concept and courts frequently have upheld the agency's exclusion of coverage.[8]

HCFA has proposed, but has not yet finalized, regulations setting forth four criteria that interpret this key requirement that services be "reasonable and necessary."[9] Specifically, under the proposed criteria, a device or procedure must be:

(1) safe and effective;

(2) not investigational or experimental;

(3) appropriate, in terms of the setting and type of personnel who administer the product or service; and

(4) cost effective.

Other HCFA policies historically have required that a device be approved by the FDA in order to be covered.

---

[7] *Id.* § 1395y(a)(1)(A).

[8] *See, e.g.,* Friedrich v. Bowen, 894 F.2d 829 (6th Cir. 1990); Wilkens v. Secretary of Health & Human Serv., 889 F.2d 135 (7th Cir. 1989); Goodman v. Sullivan, Civ. No. 88-4163 (S.D.N.Y. Apr. 17, 1989), *reprinted in* MEDICARE & MEDICAID GUIDE (CCH) ¶ 37,856; Pinneke v. Presser, 623 F.2d 546 (8th Cir. 1980).

[9] *See* 54 Fed. Reg. 4302 (Jan. 30, 1989).

Medical devices which have not been approved for marketing by the FDA are considered investigational by Medicare and are not reasonable and necessary for the diagnosis or the treatment of illness or injury, or to improve the functioning of a malformed body member. Program payment, therefore, may not be made for medical procedures or services performed using devices which have not been approved for marketing by the FDA.[10]

FDA-approved products that are used outside the scope of the FDA-approved labeling also may be covered if there is credible scientific evidence establishing safety and effectiveness of the use or the use is generally accepted within the medical community as safe and effective.[11] On the other hand, the mere fact of FDA approval may not be a sufficient basis for Medicare to cover a product. For example, HCFA denied coverage for a salivary stimulator that had received premarket approval, because there was insufficient data to establish the clinical utility of this electrostimulation, to evaluate its long-term effectiveness, and to identify those patients who would benefit from the procedure.[12]

In a notable recent regulation, HCFA clarified its prior policies to allow coverage for certain devices in an investigational stage, if underlying questions of safety and effectiveness already have been resolved.[13] Under the regulation, the FDA will categorize products furnished under an investigation device exemption (IDE) into the following categories:

Category A — Experimental/investigational. Innovative devices for which absolute risk has not been established and initial questions of safety and effectiveness have not been resolved, including Class III devices.

Category B — Nonexperimental/investigational. Devices in Class I, II, or III for which the incremental risk is the primary risk in question, so that underlying questions of safety and effectiveness of the device type have been resolved, or it is known that the device type can be safe and effective.

Medicare can cover a device under an IDE if the device is a Category B device. This offers manufacturers and technology users an important opportunity to obtain payment for devices or related services in advance of final premarket approval or 510(k) clearance. The device manufacturer can request re-evaluation of a categorization, and confidential commercial and trade secret information can be protected under the provisions of the new regulation.

Finally, coverage policies on specific procedures or technologies also may be found in the *Medicare Coverage Issues Manual* (CIM).[14] The CIM reports national Medicare policies on approximately 200 procedures or technologies. Some policies can be quite general, such as the policy for laser procedures, which states:

---

[10] MEDICARE HOSPITAL MANUAL, HCFA-Pub. 10, § 260.1(B); MEDICARE CARRIERS MANUAL, HCFA-Pub. 13-3, § 2303.1; MEDICARE INTERMEDIARY MANUAL, HCFA-Pub. 14-3, § 3151.1. As noted below, a recent HCFA regulation allows coverage of certain devices in an investigational stage.

[11] *See, e.g.,* 54 Fed. Reg. at 4306.

[12] 59 Fed. Reg. 26,653 (May 23, 1994).

[13] *See* 60 Fed. Reg. 48,417 (Sept. 19, 1995); 42 C.F.R. § 405.201 (1997).

[14] HCFA-Pub. 6.

Medicare recognizes the use of lasers for many medical indications. Procedures performed with lasers are sometimes used in place of more conventional techniques. In the absence of a specific noncoverage instruction, and where a laser has been approved for marketing by the Food and Drug Administration, contractor discretion may be used to determine whether a procedure performed with a laser is reasonable and necessary and, therefore, covered.[15]

Other Medicare coverage policies in the CIM can be quite detailed, defining specific patient conditions, limitations, and the length of time that products can be used and be covered.[16]

Procedures for Making Medicare Coverage Decisions. Although there are nearly 200 national coverage decisions, most decisions are made locally as a result of processing claims for most Medicare patients. Medicare contractors (fiscal intermediaries for Part A and carriers for Part B) review claims for services or products and determine coverage by applying national policies, if relevant policies exist, or making determinations based on general authority. Often, claims processing is the point of first contact between Medicare and a new technology. For durable medical equipment, prosthetics, orthotics, surgical dressings, and other products used in the patient's home, there are four durable medical equipment regional carriers. For physician and certain diagnostic services, there are approximately twenty-six local carriers. For hospital and nursing home services, there are approximately forty-five fiscal intermediaries.

The following is a diagram of the coverage process and key Medicare agencies involved with local, regional, or national decisions.

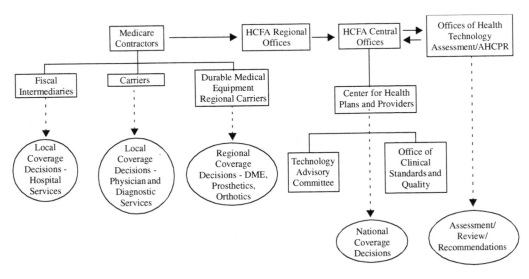

Manufacturers seeking coverage for a new technology should consider contacting contractors in the areas where claims will be processed to discuss coverage, especially if there is

---

[15]   *Id.* § 35-52.

[16]   *See, e.g., id.* §§ 50-13 (magnetic resonance imaging), 50-15 (electrocardiographic services), 60-14 (infusion pumps).

no national coverage policy. HCFA's central offices will undergo a restructuring over time, and decisionmaking on coverage may change.

Medicaid

The federal Medicaid statute gives states substantial latitude with respect to the mix of services they will cover.[17] While states are required to cover hospital and physicians' services, most states have adopted plans covering a broad variety of health care goods and services. Once a state elects to cover a particular service, it must furnish assistance of such "amount, duration, and scope" to reasonably achieve its purpose.[18] Under this standard, for example, one federal court ruled that a state must provide coverage for the drug AZT where the physician certifies its medical necessity.[19] Aside from these general federal standards, states have broad discretion to make coverage policies, and new technology will be assessed at the local, rather than the national, level. Nonetheless, states often adopt Medicaid coverage and reimbursement principles as part of their Medicaid state plan.

Blue Cross and Blue Shield Technical Evaluation Center

Another significant player in technology reimbursement is the Blue Cross and Blue Shield Association Technology Evaluation Center (TEC). This program, which includes participation by Kaiser Permanente, has established five criteria for examining coverage.

(1) The technology must have final approval from the appropriate government regulatory bodies.

(2) The scientific evidence must permit conclusions concerning the effect of the technology on health outcomes.

(3) The technology must improve the net health outcome.

(4) The technology must be as beneficial as any established alternatives.

(5) The improvement must be attainable outside the investigational settings.

The TEC criteria have articulated "outcomes" as a significant consideration in determining coverage, and often look beyond FDA proof of safety and effectiveness for documentation in the peer-reviewed medical literature of the clinical benefits of a new technology.

■ Payment for Medical Devices

Payment for medical devices will be determined based on the procedure utilizing the device and the setting in which the product is used. Payment methodologies can be complex and have changed significantly during the past fifteen years. This section provides an overview of the payment methods most significant for medical devices.[20]

---

[17] *See* 42 U.S.C. §§ 1396a(a)(10), 1396d(a); 42 C.F.R. pts. 440, 441.

[18] *See* 42 U.S.C. § 1396a(a)(10)(B); 42 C.F.R. § §440.200, 440.230.

[19] *See* Weaver v. Reagen, 886 F.2d 194 (8th Cir. 1989).

[20] Because of the diversity of payment methodologies, this chapter focuses on Medicare policies to illustrate these issues. As noted earlier, Medicaid and private insurers often are influenced by Medicare principles. Recent federal budget reform proposals would modify Medicare delivery and payment methodologies to reduce payments for virtually all types of items and services and to promote the use of managed care delivery systems.

Inpatient Hospital Services

Prior to 1983, Medicare paid hospitals on the basis of the reasonable costs incurred by hospitals in rendering care. This reasonable cost system was criticized, however, as lacking sufficient financial controls and contributing to inflationary medical costs. The Medicare prospective payment system (PPS) was implemented in 1983. Under PPS, when a device is used on a Medicare patient who is admitted to the hospital as an inpatient, most costs of the services rendered to the patient will be covered under a fixed payment determined by the diagnosis related group (DRG) into which the patient is classified. Therefore, payment to the hospital for services to a patient who receives procedures using, *inter alia* catheters, clinical laboratory or radiology equipment, orthopedic or cardiac implants, no longer directly reflects individual products or services rendered. Instead, payment for the device is part of the fixed amount a hospital receives to cover all items and services. For Medicare fiscal year 1997, there are 495 DRGs, each of which has been assigned a relative weight. Examples of this are shown in the following table:

DRG Number	Diagnosis related group	Relative Weight[a]	Estimated Payment[b]
1	Craniotomy	3.0486	$11,813
88	Chronic Obstructive Pulmonary Disease	0.9846	$3,815
106	Coronary Bypass with Cardiac Catheterization	5.5564	$21,531
107	Coronary Bypass without Cardiac Catheterization	4.0685	$15,765
112	Percutaneous Cariovascular Procedures	2.0946	$8,117
197	Cholecystectomy Except by Laparoscope	2.2679	$8,788
221	Knee Procedures with Complications and Comorbidities	1.8340	$7,107

a.   61 Fed. Reg. 46,165 (Aug. 31, 1996) (listing DRG weights for fiscal year 1997).

b.   Estimates based on an approximate national adjusted operating standardized amount of $3875, not reflecting geographic adjustment factors.

The DRGs are organized under twenty-five major diagnostic categories, generally based on an organ system (such as diseases and disorders of the nervous, respiratory, cardiac, digestive, endocrine, urinary, or reproductive systems).

The DRG payment covers primarily the hospital's operating costs, such as disposable supplies, hospital personnel, and the costs of many different types of equipment. Medicare pays hospitals separately for certain capital expenses, however. Historically, capital costs were reimbursed on a pass-through basis, but in 1991 HCFA began paying such costs under a prospective payment rate. Once phase-in of the prospective capital reimbursement system is completed, hospitals' capital payments will be based on a federal capital rate, adjusted by a DRG weight factor and a geographic adjustment factor.[21] Thus, for example, a patient receiving a test performed by magnetic resonance imaging would have the operating costs of the test paid under the DRG, but the capital-related costs of the MRI (depreciation, lease payments, interest, taxes) would be paid under the capital payment system.

---

21   *See* 42 C.F.R. § 412.300 et seq.

The DRG system is important for technology companies for several reasons. For products that are used in a hospital, the fixed nature of the payment may create financial disincentives to use products that add costs to an admission. Even a more clinically significant technological advance may not be accommodated within existing payment levels. Conversely, products that reduce overall costs of an admission or make the hospital more efficient can enable the hospital to realize financial advantages under the DRG payment.[22]

HCFA has been reluctant to create new DRGs or significantly refine existing DRGs to reflect new technologies such as automatic implantable cardioverter defibrillators and cochlear implants.[23] HCFA has asserted that generally even new technologies can fit within existing DRGs from the dual perspective of "clinical coherence" of all procedures classified into the DRG and the reasonableness of the payment level.

Hospital Outpatient Services

There are several methodologies HCFA uses to pay hospitals for outpatient services. As the DRG PPS is an attempt to control inpatient costs, outpatient payment methodologies similarly seek to control costs. For certain surgical procedures, which are covered by Medicare when performed in ambulatory surgery centers (ASCs), Medicare will pay the hospital an amount based on the lesser of a) the hospital's customary charges; b) the hospital's reasonable costs; or c) a blended amount, based partly on the hospital's costs and partly on the rate that would be paid if the procedure was performed in an ambulatory surgery center in the same area.[24]

For outpatient radiology services (including diagnostic and therapeutic radiology, nuclear medicine and CT scan procedures, magnetic resonance imaging, ultrasound and other imaging), payment to the hospital also is based on the lesser of the hospital's charges, costs, or a blended amount, but the blend for radiology services is weighted more heavily to the fee schedule amount.[25]

Congress has directed the Secretary of the Department of Health and Human Services (DHHS) to develop a prospective payment system for hospital outpatient services. On March 17, 1995, DHHS delivered a report to Congress proposing a system based on ambulatory patient groups. This APG system, now authorized to be implemented starting January 1, 1999, will replace the various methods now used to pay for hospital outpatient services.

Ambulatory Surgery Centers

HCFA has established a list of surgical procedures[26] that, when performed in a Medicare certified ASC, will be paid at a fixed rate. Covered surgical procedures are classified into one of the nine payment groups, illustrated in the following table:

---

[22] Similar incentives exist under managed care delivery systems, under which a fixed per capita amount is paid to cover all of a patient's health care services.

[23] *See, e.g.,* 60 Fed. Reg. 45,780, 45,789 (Sept. 1, 1995).

[24] 42 U.S.C. § 1395l(i). The blend is calculated based on: 58% of the hospital's costs and 42% of the ASC rate.

[25] The blend for radiology is based on: 50% of the fee schedule amount and 50% of the hospital's costs.

[26] *See* 60 Fed. Reg. 5185 (Jan. 16, 1995).

ASC Payment Group	Payment	Illustrative Procedure
1	$312	Biopsy, muscle, percutaneous needle
2	$419	Application of cranial tongs, caliper, or stereotatic frame
3	$479	Removal of implant — wire, pin, screw, metal band, nail, rod, or plate — deeply embedded
4	$591	Tendon transfer, four fingers
5	$674	Arthroplasty, radial head with implant
6	$785	Insertion of intraocular lens, not with cataract removal
7	$935	Arthroplasty with prosthetic replacement (total wrist)
8	$923	Cataract extraction with insertion of intraocular lens
9	$---	Extracorporeal shock wave lithotripsy

These payment rates cover the ASC's facility costs, including nursing and technician services, drugs, biologicals, surgical dressings, supplies, splints, casts, diagnostic services directly related to the surgery, and anesthesia materials.[27] Separate payment is available for physician services, lab or x-ray services (not directly related to the surgery), and prosthetic devices (except intraocular lenses are included in payment rates 6 and 8 (of the preceeding table).

Physician and Certain Diagnostic Services

Medicare pays for physician and certain diagnostic services (such as radiology, electrocardiograms, and ultrasound procedures) according to a resource-based relative value scale (RBRVS). This methodology is quite important for devices used in a physician's office because payment for the device may be included in payment for the physician service.

Payment is calculated according to the following summary formula:

$$\text{Relative Value Units} \times \text{Geographic Adjustment Factor} \times \text{Conversion Factor} = \text{Medicare Payment}$$

Relative value units (RVUs) have been calculated for nearly all physician procedures.[28] The RVUs are based on three components: 1) physician work, 2) practice expenses associated with staff and supplies in the physician's office, and 3) malpractice expenses. The conversion factors for 1997 are:

$40.9603	surgical services
$35.7671	primary care services
$33.8454	other nonsurgical services

---

[27] *See* 42 C.F.R. pt. 416.

[28] *See* 60 Fed. Reg. 63,124 (Dec. 8, 1995) (listing the RVUs for 1996); 61 Fed. Reg. 59,556 (Nov. 22, 1996) (listing the RVUs for 1997).

Generally, any supplies used in the physician's office will be paid as part of the RBRVS payment. Medicare will pay an additional modest amount for supplies used in the physician's office for a limited number of procedures, such as biopsies, endoscopies, colonoscopies, cystoscopies, and dilation and curettage.[29]

Clinical Laboratory Tests

When a clinical laboratory test is performed in the hospital outpatient setting, an independent clinical laboratory, or a physician's office, Medicare pays the lower of the actual charge for the test or the national limitation amount for the test. National limitation amounts, also known as fee caps, for a number of clinical laboratory tests were determined based on various percentages of the national median for the tests. As with many other components of Medicare, the U.S. Congress has considered reducing payment for laboratory tests. By 1996, Medicare payment was to be based on seventy-six percent of the national median.

Durable Medical Equipment, Prosthetics, Orthotics

Medicare covers and pays for various items of durable medical equipment, prosthetics and orthotics in accordance with federal laws and guidelines. Durable medical equipment is defined as equipment that:

- can withstand repeated use;
- is primarily and customarily used to serve a medical purpose;
- generally is not useful to a person in the absence of illness or injury; and
- is appropriate for use in the home.[30]

Payment for durable medical equipment, prosthetics, and orthotics generally is based on the lesser of the reasonable charge or the amount determined under a fee schedule. Congress established six classes of products paid under fee schedules, often referred to as the Six Point Plan.[31]

The six categories include:

- inexpensive or other routinely purchased durable medical equipment;
- items requiring frequent and substantial servicing, such as ventilators, nebulizers, aspirators, or intermittent positive pressure breathing machines;
- customized items;
- covered items other than durable medical equipment — e.g., prosthetic devices and orthotics;
- other items of durable medical equipment paid on the basis of a capped rental amount; and
- oxygen and oxygen equipment.

Congress also has established special payment rules for surgical dressings, ostomy products, transcutaneous electrical stimulators, and power wheelchairs.

---

[29] For a complete list of procedures allowing separate payment as of 1994 and 1995, see 58 Fed. Reg. 63,853, 63,853-54 (Dec. 2, 1993).

[30] 42 C.F.R. § 414.202.

[31] 42 U.S.C. § 1395m.

■ Coding for Medical Devices and Procedures

Codes are systems of numbers or alpha-numeric combinations that describe patient diseases, procedures, or products. These coding systems are essential for reimbursement. Codes describing patient conditions, services rendered, or products provided are placed by the hospital, physician, or supplier on the claim form submitted to the patient's insurer. The provider can submit the claim manually or electronically. In turn, the insurer processes the claim, reviews procedure or product codes, and makes coverage and payment decisions.

There are several major coding systems:

- International Classification of Diseases, Ninth Edition, Clinical Modification (ICD-9-CM);
- Current Procedural Terminology (CPT);
- HCFA Common Procedure Coding System (HCPCS); and
- American Hospital Association (AHA) Revenue Codes.

These coding systems are used with corresponding payment methodologies:

Coding System	Subject	Payment Method
ICD-9-CM	Patient diseases Inpatient hospital procedures	DRG
CPT	Physician and diagnostic procedures Clinical lab tests	RBRVS Fee schedule
HCPCS	CPT and alpha-numeric for products	Fee Schedule

Many new products can be described by existing codes; if so, coverage and payment levels already may be set based on prior products. Creating a new procedure or product code, however, may open an opportunity for changing a payment amount. At the same time, new codes may be disadvantageous if they enable insurers to pinpoint new products and deny coverage. The mere creation of a new code will not ensure coverage or payment at any particular level.

The agencies responsible for coding include:

Coding System	Responsible Agency
ICD-9-CM	ICD-9-CM Coordination and Maintenance Committee — HCFA and National Center for Health Statistics
CPT	American Medical Association CPT Editorial Panel
HCPCS	HCPCS Editorial Panel: HCFA, Blue Cross and Blue Shield Association and Health Insurance Association of America Statistical Analysis Durable Medical Equipment Regional Carriers

Manufacturers, physicians, or hospitals can submit requests to these agencies to create new or revised codes that will accurately describe new products or procedures as clinical practice evolves. Examples of new codes include:

ICD-9-CM	571.4	Chronic hepatitis
ICD-9-CM	81.00	Spinal fusion
CPT	52648	Contact laser vaporization with or without transurethral resection of prostate
HCPS	E0781	Ambulatory infusion pump

Reimbursement for Drugs and Biologics

■ Coverage

Medicare

As discussed earlier, Part A of the Medicare program generally provides reimbursement for institutional health care services (i.e., inpatient hospital, skilled nursing facility, home health, hospice, and dialysis services), while Part B generally relates to "outpatient" services (e.g., physicians' services, durable medical equipment, therapy, and laboratory services).

Under Part A, Medicare covers drugs ordinarily provided by hospitals and skilled nursing facilities for the care and treatment of inpatients.[32] Drug coverage usually is not provided for home health services (although coverage may be provided for home visits necessary to administer noncovered drugs). With respect to hospice care, Medicare covers drugs that are used primarily to relieve pain and symptoms of the patient's terminal illness.[33]

At present, Medicare Part B covers relatively few drugs for outpatient use.[34] Subject to the exceptions discussed below, Part B covers only prescription drugs that are furnished to a patient "incident to" a physician's services. This means that outpatient drugs are covered only if 1) they cannot be self-administered by the patient; 2) they are administered by a physician (or under a physician's supervision) on an outpatient basis; 3) they are reasonable and necessary for the treatment for which they are administered according to accepted standards of medical practice; and 4) they are furnished ordinarily in a

---

[32] *See* 42 C.F.R. § 409.13.

[33] *See* MEDICARE INTERMEDIARY MANUAL, HCFA-Pub. 13, § 3143.

[34] As part of the Medicare Catastrophic Coverage Act, Pub. L. No. 100-360, 102 Stat. 683 (1988), Congress added a comprehensive outpatient drug benefit to the Medicare program. A year later, in 1989, the benefit was repealed as part of the Medicare Catastrophic Coverage Repeal Act, Pub. L. No. 101-234, 103 Stat. 1979 (1989), due to concerns about potential added cost.

physician's office or clinic and represent a cost to the physician that is not charged separately in the physician's bill.[35] Further, most immunizations are not covered by Medicare.[36]

There are several exceptions to the general rule excluding self-administered drugs and preventative immunizations from coverage. Under specified circumstances, Medicare Part B covers antigens, pneumococcal pneumonia vaccine, Hepatitis B vaccine, blood clotting factors, immunosuppressive drugs, erythropoietin, drugs used to treat osteoporosis, and certain anticancer drugs.[37]

In some instances, drugs that are required for the effective use of durable medical equipment also may be covered under Part B. For example, Part B may cover tumor chemotherapy agents used with an infusion pump, or heparin used with a home dialysis system.[38] Other drugs similarly covered include respiratory medications used with nebulizers and certain pain management drugs administered through covered durable medical equipment.

Medicaid

Prescription drugs are among the "optional" categories of services that a state may cover under its Medicaid program.[39] If a state elects to cover prescription drugs, it must meet a number of specific provisions relating to coverage and utilization of outpatient prescription drugs adopted as part of the Omnibus Budget Reconciliation Act of 1990[40] and the Veterans Health Care Act of 1992 (CVHCA).[41]

Under those statutes, a drug manufacturer must enter into a series of agreements with the Secretaries of DHHS and the VA. These agreements generally require a manufacturer to provide rebates and discounts to specified purchasers, and are described in greater detail later.[42]

If a manufacturer enters into the required discount and pricing agreements, the Medicaid statute specifically limits the circumstances under which a state Medicaid program may otherwise exclude or restrict the manufacturer's drugs from coverage. First, the state may subject any drug to prior authorization requirements, provided that the state's prior authorization program furnishes a response within twenty-four hours and permits reimbursement for a seventy-two-hour supply of the drug in cases of emergency.[43] Second, a state may exclude or restrict coverage of drugs for uses other than those that are medically indicated.[44] Third, a state may exclude or restrict coverage of specifically enumerated classes

---

[35]   42 U.S.C. § 1395x(s)(2)(A).

[36]   *Id.* § 1395y(a)(7).

[37]   *Id.* §§ 1395x(s)(2)(G), (I), (J), (O)-(Q); 1395x(s)(10)(A)-(B).

[38]   *See* MEDICARE CARRIERS MANUAL, HCFA-Pub. 14, § 2100.5.

[39]   *See* 42 U.S.C. §§ 1396a(a)(10)(A), 1396d(a)(12).

[40]   Pub. L. No. 101-508, 104 Stat. 1388.

[41]   Pub. L. No. 102-585, 106 Stat. 4943.

[42]   42 U.S.C. § 1396r-8(a). *See infra* notes 63-81 and accompanying text.

[43]   42 U.S.C. § 1396r-8(d)(1)(A).

[44]   *Id.* § 1396r-8(d)(1)(B)(i).

of drugs.[45] Fourth, a state may exclude or restrict coverage of drugs pursuant to an agreement with the manufacturer.[46] Fifth, a state may provide limits on the quantity or number of refills for drugs if such limits are necessary to discourage waste.[47] Sixth, a state may restrict coverage of a drug pursuant to a formulary that meets various federal requirements.[48]

Regarding the last noted limitation on states, the formulary must 1) be developed by a committee of physicians, pharmacists, and "other appropriate individuals" appointed by the governor or the state's drug use review board; 2) include those drugs of a manufacturer that have not been excluded specifically or that are not otherwise subject to exclusion because they belong to one of the classes of drugs subject to exclusion or restriction; 3) exclude a drug from coverage with respect to a particular disease or condition for an identified population only if the drug "does not have a significant, clinically meaningful therapeutic advantage in terms of safety, effectiveness, or clinical outcome" over other drugs in the formulary; 4) not exclude drugs from coverage without a publicly available, written explanation; and 5) allow coverage for drugs excluded from the formulary under a prior authorization program.[49]

Coverage of Prescription Drugs Under Medicare and Medicaid Managed Care Programs

Historically, the Medicare and Medicaid programs have operated primarily on a fee-for-service basis, and the coverage rules described above have applied. Recently, however, managed care models have become increasingly important to these programs. Significantly, coverage standards for outpatient prescription drugs under Medicare and Medicaid are different in the managed care context.

HMOs furnishing Medicare-covered services reimbursed on a capitated basis generally may offer additional services that otherwise may not be covered by Medicare.[50] Moreover, to the extent such an HMO's reimbursement exceeds its costs by a statutorily defined amount, the HMO is *required* to use a portion of this "profit" either 1) to reduce beneficiaries, premiums, or out-of-pocket expenses, or 2) to provide additional health benefits other than Medicare coverage of prescription drugs to Medicare beneficiaries. Federal law does not regulate the scope of coverage under these circumstances.

With respect to Medicaid, drugs dispensed through HMOs are specifically exempt from the requirements relating to manufacturer rebate agreements, coverage limits, formulary standards, and the like.[51] In the Medicaid managed care context, an HMO with a managed care contract has significant latitude to employ restrictive formularies, prior autho-

---

[45] These classes include drugs for anorexia, weight loss or gain, fertility, cosmetic or hair growth purposes, symptomatic relief of coughs or colds, smoking cessation, as well as most prescription vitamins and minerals, nonprescription drugs, drugs that may be purchased only in connection with specified tests, barbiturates, and benzodiazepines. *Id.* § 1396r-8(d)(1)(B)(ii). In addition, the Secretary of DHHS is authorized to name additional classes of drugs subject to restriction because of clinical abuse or inappropriate use. *Id.* § 1396r-8(d)(3).

[46] *Id.* § 1396r-8(d)(1)(B)(iii).

[47] *Id.* § 1396r-8(d)(6).

[48] *Id.* § 1396r-8(d)(1)(B)(iv).

[49] *Id.* § 1396r-8(d)(4).

[50] *Id.* § 1395mm(c)(2).

[51] *See id.* § 1396r-8(j).

rization, or other coverage limits. Currently, more than one-third of the states have submitted requests to the federal government to provide comprehensive services to Medicaid beneficiaries through mandatory managed care arrangements on a statewide basis.

■ Payment

Medicare

Medicare payments for covered drugs vary according to the setting in which the drug is provided and whether the covered service falls under Medicare Part A or Part B.

Under Part A, payment for a drug depends on the service provider that furnishes the drug to the Medicare beneficiary. For hospital inpatients, payment for both prescription and nonprescription drugs is included in payments based on the patient's DRG.[52] Cost-based providers, like skilled nursing facilities and home health agencies, generally are reimbursed based on the lesser of the entity's "reasonable costs" of providing services (including pharmacy services), or its "customary charges" for such services.[53] For hospices, reimbursement is made using a cost-related prospective payment method, subject to a ceiling.[54]

To the extent that Medicare Part B currently covers drugs furnished "incident to" physician services, they are reimbursed separately from the physician's service. This method of reimbursing drug costs took effect on January 1, 1992, along with the introduction of the RBRVS system for physician services. Historically, Medicare reimbursed covered drugs that are incident to a physician's services at a rate equal to the lower of the estimated acquisition cost of the drug or the national average wholesale price of the drug.[55] Recent legislative amendments, however, require payment amounts equal to ninety-five percent of a drug's published average wholesale price.

Outpatient drugs that otherwise are covered by Medicare, but are not provided incident to a physician's services, are reimbursed under different methods depending on the drug in question. In general, reimbursement for such drugs is based on reasonable charges or payment levels set by the Secretary of DHHS. In one instance, however, reimbursement levels have been set by Congress. Medicare Parts A and B cover the provision of the drug erythropoietin when used in treating anemia induced by chronic renal failure or the use of the drug AZT. Payment for erythropoitin is set by statute at ten dollars per 1000 units, rounded to the nearest 100 units.[56]

Medicaid

The federal Medicaid statute does not prescribe specific standards for reimbursement of

---

[52] *See supra* notes 20-23 and accompanying text.

[53] *See id.* § 1395f(b).

[54] 42 C.F.R. § 418.302.

[55] *Id.* § 405.517. If a drug is manufactured by multiple sources, the median of national wholesale prices for equivalent generic drugs is used. Estimated acquisition costs are based on surveys of actual invoice prices to providers, and average wholesale prices are determined using published sources such as the "Red Book."

[56] *Id.* § 1395rr(b)(11).

prescription drugs and related pharmacy services.[57] Nonetheless, federal regulations provide some parameters for such reimbursement.

Specifically, the aggregate state payments for drugs may not exceed certain "upper limits."[58] HCFA establishes upper limits for multiple source drugs (except where a prescriber certifies a particular brand as medically necessary) where 1) at least three of the formulations of the drug approved by the FDA have been evaluated as therapeutically equivalent in the FDA's "Orange Book," and 2) at least three suppliers list the drug. For such drugs, the upper limit is established at 150% of the published price for the least costly therapeutic equivalent that can be purchased in quantities of at least 100, plus a reasonable dispensing fee.[59] For multiple source drugs certified as "brand medically necessary" and for other drugs, the state's aggregate payments may not exceed the lower of the estimated acquisition costs of the drug plus a reasonable dispensing fee, or the provider's usual and customary charge to the general public.[60]

Aside from these standards, states have wide latitude in establishing the method and amount of payments for drugs and pharmacy services. In most cases, states reimburse pharmacies an amount to cover drug costs as well as a separate dispensing fee. The amount to cover drug costs typically is expressed in terms of a percentage of published wholesale acquisition costs or average wholesale price, or a similar measure. A few states reimburse drug costs on the basis of the pharmacy's actual acquisition cost.

Recently, several states have implemented alternative pharmacy reimbursement that contain "most favored nation" features. Under "most favored nation" systems, the pharmacy agrees to accept from Medicaid the lowest level of reimbursement that it accepts from any other third-party payor. The Massachusetts Medicaid program, for example, has adopted a variation on this policy under which the pharmacy must agree to be reimbursed on a most favored nation basis, except third-party contracts that account for less than one percent of a pharmacy's prescription dollar volume are disregarded.[61]

Most favored nation policies are somewhat controversial, however, insofar as they have been viewed as anticompetitive in some circumstances. The U.S. Department of Justice has entered into antitrust consent decrees with three private health plans that employed most favored nation pricing in their provider contracts.[62] In each of these cases, the Justice Department emphasized that such clauses may have the effect of artificially discouraging deeper discounts to other plans, which ultimately may result in payment levels higher than

---

[57] The only statutory payment standard currently applicable to pharmacy services is the so-called "equal access" requirement of 42 U.S.C. § 1396a(a)(30)(A), which requires that state payments be "consistent with efficiency, economy, and quality of care and . . . sufficient to enlist enough providers so that care and services are available under the [state Medicaid] plan at least to the extent that such care and services are available to the general population in the geographic area." Several courts have ruled that health care providers (e.g., pharmacies) have a right-of-action to challenge inadequate payment levels under this provision. *See*, *e.g.*, Arkansas Medical Soc'y v. Reynolds, 6 F.3d 519 (8th Cir. 1993). In addition to the equal access requirement, Congress temporarily prohibited states from *reducing* pharmacy reimbursement as part of the Omnibus Budget Reconciliation Act of 1990. *See* 42 U.S.C. § 1396r-8(f). This moratorium on payment reductions expired on December 31, 1994. *Id.*

[58] 42 C.F.R. § 447.331(a).

[59] *Id.* § 447.332. For drugs that cannot be purchased in package sizes of at least 100, and for liquids, the commonly listed package size is used.

[60] *Id.* § 447.331(b).

[61] *See* MASSACHUSETTS MEDICAL ASSISTANCE PROGRAM, PHARMACY BULLETIN 50 (1995).

[62] *See* 60 Fed. Reg. 21,218 (May 1, 1995); 60 Fed. Reg. 5210 (Jan. 26, 1995); 59 Fed. Reg. 47,349 (Sept. 14, 1994).

what consumers would have to pay under full and open competition. Although the anti-trust laws generally do not apply to the states, state Medicaid programs employing most favored nation clauses can produce similar effects.

Federal Drug Pricing Legislation

In addition to regulating reimbursement to pharmacies for dispensing prescription drugs under Medicare and Medicaid, federal law mandates rebates and price reductions to certain purchasers from drug manufacturers. These laws can impact significantly the way in which a manufacturer may wish to market or distribute its products. For example, differential pricing, the use of wholesalers, and the provision of discounts all have implications under these statutes.

The Medicaid Drug Rebate Statute. In 1990, Congress enacted the Medicaid drug rebate statute,[63] which requires a drug manufacturer to agree to pay quarterly rebates for "covered outpatient drugs" that are dispensed and paid for under the Medicaid program's outpatient drug benefit, so that the manufacturer's products qualify for federal matching funds. The basic goal of the statute is to place state Medicaid programs on cost terms comparable to other large-volume purchasers of drugs.

Covered outpatient drugs subject to rebates include all FDA-approved drugs, biologics, and insulin. A product is not considered to be a "covered outpatient drug" for which a rebate is due, however, if it is furnished in connection with, *and its cost is covered as part of the reimbursement for*, certain other Medicaid-covered services.[64]

The amount of a rebate due from the manufacturer depends on whether the product is considered to be a single source, an innovator multiple source, or a noninnovator multiple source drug. A single source drug is a drug that is produced or distributed under an original new drug application (NDA).[65] An innovator multiple source drug is a drug that was originally marketed under an original NDA and for which there are two or more drug products marketed during a rebate period that are therapeutically equivalent and that are pharmaceutically equivalent and bioequivalent.[66] Noninnovator multiple source drugs include all other multiple source drugs.[67]

For single source drugs and innovator multiple source drugs, manufacturers must pay a "basic rebate" for each unit of a drug dispensed equal to the greater of: 1) the difference between the average manufacturer price (AMP) for the drug and the "best price" for the drug, or 2) the AMP times a statutory "rebate percentage."[68] For noninnovator multiple source drugs, the required rebate is equal to eleven percent of the AMP of the drug.[69]

AMP generally is defined by the statute as the "average price paid to the manufacturer for the drug in the United States by wholesalers for drugs distributed to the retail pharmacy

---

[63] 42 U.S.C. § 1396r-8.

[64] *Id.* § 1396r-8(k)(2)-(3) (emphasis added).

[65] *Id.* § 1396r-8(k)(7)(A)(iv).

[66] *Id.* § 1396r-8(k)(7)(A)(ii).

[67] *Id.* § 1396r-8(k)(7)(A)(iii).

[68] *Id.* § 1396r-8(c)(1)(A)-(B). The current rebate percentage is 15.1%.

[69] *Id.* § 1396r-8(c)(3).

class of trade."[70] Notably, HCFA's rebate agreement defines the term "wholesaler" broadly as "any entity (including a pharmacy or chain of pharmacies) to which the manufacturer sells the Covered Outpatient Drug, but that does not relabel or repackage the drug."[71] Thus, direct sales to providers are included in the AMP calculation.

"Best price," on the other hand, currently is defined as the "lowest price available from the manufacturer . . . to any wholesaler, retailer, provider, health maintenance organization, nonprofit entity, or governmental entity within the United States," excluding 1) prices charged to certain federal agencies, state veterans homes, and entities receiving funding under PHS grants; 2) prices under the Federal Supply Schedule; 3) prices under state pharmaceutical assistance programs; and 4) depot prices and single award contract prices. Nominal prices (i.e., prices less than ten percent of the AMP) also do not establish a best price.[72]

In addition to the basic rebate, a manufacturer must pay an "additional rebate" with respect to single source and innovator multiple source drugs. The additional rebate equals the amount by which the AMP for the drug exceeds the AMP in a "base period," after adjusting for inflation using the consumer price index.[73] The additional rebate is designed to provide a disincentive to drug price increases that exceed the rate of inflation.

Veterans Health Care Act Pricing to Federal Agencies. Section 602 of the VHCA establishes a separate manufacturer drug pricing program as an additional condition to federal Medicaid reimbursement or direct federal purchases by the Department of Defense, the VA, or the PHS.[74] While the Medicaid rebate statute requires retrospective rebates to Medicaid programs, the VHCA requires prospective discounts to certain federal purchasers. As explained below, these discounts are computed based on data entirely separate from that used under Medicaid.

The VHCA contains three basic requirements. First, the manufacturer must make each of its products available for procurement under the Federal Supply Schedule.[75] Notably, when negotiating Federal Supply Schedule contracts, the government's goal is to obtain pricing comparable to that of the vendor's most favored customer.[76]

---

[70] *Id.* § 1396r-8(k)(1). Manufacturers are required to calculate and report their AMP and best price to HCFA on a quarterly basis. HCFA recently published proposed regulations implementing the rebate statute. *See* 60 Fed. Reg. 48,442 (Sept. 19, 1995). HCFA also has interpreted the statute through the rebate agreement and informal "program releases" to manufacturers. These materials provide further guidance with respect to pricing calculation issues under the statute.

[71] *See* Medicaid Rebate Agreement ¶ I(ee).

[72] 42 U.S.C. § 1396r-8(c)(1)(C)(i). Further, best price is inclusive of cash discounts, free goods that are contingent on any purchase requirement, volume discounts, and rebates. *Id.* § 1396r-8(c)(1)(C)(ii).

[73] *Id.* § 1396r-8(c)(2).

[74] Pub. L. No. 102-585 § 602, 106 Stat. 4943 (1992).

[75] 38 U.S.C. § 8126(a)(1) (1994). The Federal Supply Schedule is a system under which a vendor enters into a government-wide, indefinite quantity contract, and is designed to enable the government to aggregate its volume when negotiating purchase prices. Individual federal agencies may then purchase supplies from the vendor at the contract price. The Federal Supply Schedule for drugs is administered by the VA.

[76] Under the Truth in Negotiations Act, federal contractors must disclose "current, accurate and complete" cost or pricing data for purposes of facilitating contract price negotiations. In one recent settlement under the False Claims Act, a drug manufacturer paid $7,000,000 to settle claims that it had not disclosed certain discounts to pharmacy chains when negotiating its federal contract price.

Second, the manufacturer must agree that the price it charges the Department of Defense, the VA, or the PHS for certain products may not exceed a "federal ceiling price." The federal ceiling price is equal to seventy-six percent of the AMP for the sales to nonfederal government purchasers plus an "additional discount."[77] The additional discount is comparable to the "additional rebate" under the Medicaid program, insofar as it penalizes manufacturers that increase their prices faster than the rate of inflation. To the extent that a manufacturer's federal ceiling price exceeds its most favored customer price, the government will continue to seek the lower price.

Third, manufacturers must agree to charge state veterans homes prices that do not exceed the Federal Supply Schedule price.[78]

Discounted Pricing to "Covered Entities." The VHCA also established an additional program under which manufacturers must make their products available at discounted prices to certain specified "covered entities."[79] Most of the classes of covered entities are clinics and similar programs receiving grants under the PHS Act, but certain hospitals serving a disproportionate share of indigent patients also are eligible for PHS discounts.[80] The amount of the PHS discount is equal to the AMP (as computed for purposes of the Medicaid rebate statute) times a "rebate percentage." The "rebate percentage" is equal to the average total rebate to Medicaid.[81]

Fraud and Abuse

The four principal bases for fraud and abuse enforcement activity relating to medical devices and pharmaceuticals are: the federal anti-kickback statute, state anti-kickback and professional practice statutes, false claims prohibitions, and state consumer protection statutes. FDA regulation also may become increasingly relevant in these areas in the future.

■ The Federal Anti-Kickback Statute

The federal anti-kickback statute[82] establishes criminal penalties with respect to any person who knowingly and willfully offers, pays, solicits, or receives any remuneration to induce or in return for 1) referring an individual to a person for the furnishing or arranging for the furnishing of any item or service payable in whole or in part under federal health care programs, or 2) purchasing, leasing, ordering, or arranging for or recommending pur-

---

[77] 38 U.S.C. § 8126(a)(2). In calculating the nonfederal average manufacturer price, the VA does not employ the same definitions or rules used by HCFA for calculating AMP under the Medicaid rebate agreement.

[78] *Id.* § 8126(a)(3).

[79] *See* 42 U.S.C. § 256b.

[80] *Id.* § 256b(a)(4).

[81] *Id.* § 256b(a)(2).

[82] *Id.* § 1320a-7b(b).

chasing, leasing, or ordering any good, facility, service, or item payable under federal health care programs.[83] In addition, the DHHS Office of Inspector General (OIG) may bring an administrative proceeding to exclude a provider from Medicare or Medicaid participation or to collect civil money penalties for anti-kickback violations, without having to obtain a criminal conviction under the statute. Judicial and administrative decisions have interpreted the statute broadly.[84]

Six statutory exceptions to the basic anti-kickback prohibition include: properly disclosed discounts or other reductions in price, payments to bona fide employees, payments to group purchasing organizations, waiver of coinsurance for Medicare Part B services for certain individuals who qualify for PHS programs, risk-sharing arrangements, and payment practices set forth in regulations defining conduct that will not be subject to enforcement.[85]

Pursuant to this last exception, the OIG's "safe harbor" regulations define payment practices that will not run afoul of the statute. The fact that a particular arrangement does not fall within a safe harbor does not mean that the arrangement is illegal. Rather, its facts and circumstances must be analyzed to determine whether the arrangement represents remuneration intended to induce prohibited referrals or recommendations. The safe harbors most pertinent to manufacturers of devices and drugs cover: equipment rental, personal services and management contracts, warranties, discounts, certain payments to group purchasing organizations, and compensation to employees.[86] As managed care delivery systems continue to expand in public programs, the recently enacted risk-sharing exception is likely to be significant for technology manufacturers. Regarding that exception, OIG will be issuing additional guidance through a negotiated rulemaking process.

Application to Medical Devices

Several applications of the anti-kickback statute to medical device marketing programs have been reported. In 1983, HCFA issued an intermediary letter notifying Medicare contractors that some manufacturers had been offering rebates, kickbacks, or "free goods" in return for the purchase of pacemakers or intraocular lenses.[87]

---

[83] Historically, the federal anti-kickback statute applied only to goods and services reimbursable under Medicare, Medicaid, or other state health care programs. The recent passage of the Health Insurance Portability and Accountability Act of 1996, however, expanded the statute to apply to all federally funded health care programs except the Federal Employees' Health Benefits Program. *See* Pub. L. No. 104-191, 110 Stat. 1936.

[84] *See* United States v. Greber, 760 F.2d 68 (3d Cir.), *cert. denied*, 474 U.S. 988 (1985) (payment for actual services rendered may violate statute if "one purpose" of the payment was to induce referrals); United States v. Bay State Ambulance & Hosp. Rental Serv., Inc., 874 F.2d 20 (1st Cir. 1989) (giving person an opportunity to earn money may constitute an improper inducement); Hanlester Network v. Shalala, 51 F.3d 1390 (9th Cir. 1995) (mandatory requirement of referrals in exchange for remuneration is unnecessary to violate the statute). Notably, however, in *Hanlester*, the Ninth Circuit ruled that a violation of the statute occurs only if an entity (i) knows that the statute prohibits remuneration intended to induce referrals and (ii) engages in prohibited conduct with the specific intent to disobey the law.

[85] 42 U.S.C. § 1320a-7b(b)(3). *See* 42 C.F.R. § 1001.952.

[86] To meet a safe harbor, every regulatory element must be satisfied. Although a detailed examination of those elements is beyond the scope of this work, this chapter will highlight some of the key requirements in various contexts. Nonetheless, the particular elements of a transaction must be compared with the applicable regulations when evaluating compliance.

[87] Medicare Part A Intermediary Letter No. 83-19, Part B Intermediary Letter No. 83-11 (Dec. 1983).

Questions about intraocular lense credit programs also were raised in a case that found that HCFA letters apparently permitting a sales practice negated the requisite criminal intent for violation of the anti-kickback statute.[88]

The OIG challenged manufacturers of blood glucose monitors for providing improper rebates to patients; these rebates had not been disclosed and thus contributed to the filing of false claims.[89]

Application to Prescription Drugs

Background and General Standards. Payments to physicians, other prescribers, pharmacists, pharmacy chains, and pharmacy benefits managers (PBMs) could be construed as payments to induce the purchase, order, or recommendation to purchase or order a particular drug.[90] On August 23, 1994, the OIG issued a "Special Fraud Alert" concerning prescription drug marketing practices that potentially run afoul of the anti-kickback statute.[91] The Special Fraud Alert described general conditions that might trigger scrutiny, and also identified a number of specific arrangements that OIG viewed as problematic if one purpose of the arrangements was to induce the provision of a specific prescription drug under Medicare or Medicaid. These programs included:

- "fee per switch" programs in which a manufacturer offered cash incentives to pharmacies each time the pharmacy persuaded the prescriber to change the prescription from a competitor's product to the manufacturer's product;
- in-kind bonuses (e.g., frequent flier miles) provided to physicians, suppliers, or managed care organizations in exchange for, or based on, prescribing particular products;
- bogus research grants for *de minimis* recordkeeping activities that have little scientific value and require little scientific pursuit; and
- payments for marketing functions in the guise of patient education and counseling programs that are within the scope of pharmacy practice.

Special Applications. The anti-kickback statute potentially has far-reaching implications with respect to a broad range of activities in the marketing of pharmaceuticals, including product supply arrangements, research grants, payments for pharmacy services, and educational subsidies. Several of these issues are described below.

With respect to product supply arrangements, manufacturers often provide discounts, rebates, and other incentives to purchasers of their products. The discount safe harbor may protect certain of these arrangements, depending on the nature of the price reduction and the method of reimbursement. Generally, in order to meet the safe harbor, the buyer must report the amount of the discount to the Medicare or Medicaid programs, while the seller

---

[88]   United States v. Levin, 973 F.2d 463 (6th Cir. 1992).

[89]   *See* OIG Report on blood glucose monitors (A-09-92-00834); letter from Richard Kusserow to Congressman J. Pickle (Mar. 13, 1992).

[90]   OIG focused its initial investigative efforts with respect to prescription drugs on promotional programs directed at physicians and other prescribers. *See* "Promotion of Prescription Drugs Through Payments and Gifts," OIG Report No. OEI-01-9000480 (1991). With respect to pharmacists and PBMs, the potential for a payment to be construed as an inducement arises out of the ability to substitute, or recommend the substitution of, one drug for another as part of the dispensing function.

[91]   *See* Medicare & Medicaid Guide (CCH) ¶ 42,609.

must provide the buyer with the information necessary to facilitate the reporting.[92] The discount safe harbor does not protect a discount on one product in exchange for an agreement to buy another product, discounts not offered to Medicare or Medicaid, or "discounts" in the form of retroactive rebates where the buyer is reimbursed other than on the basis of cost reports, as are most pharmacies.[93]

Many manufacturers seek to obtain data concerning their products and patients through pharmacist-patient contacts, and they also sponsor other research activities. Because such activities involve actual services, the personal services and management contracts safe harbor may provide protection for the transaction.[94] The most critical elements are whether the compensation is consistent with fair market value, is specified in advance, and is not tied to the volume or value of business generated. Some caution should be exercised, however, because OIG has scrutinized arrangements where manufacturers pay substantial sums for *de minimis* tasks with little scientific value, or where actual services are not performed. For example, in 1994 the government entered into a $161 million settlement with Caremark, Inc. in connection with a number of charges, including claims that Caremark allegedly paid bogus research grants to a physician for the marketing of a human growth hormone. Thus, additional relevant factors that should be considered when evaluating research grant programs include: 1) whether the researcher is selected because of special knowledge or previous dispensing history; 2) whether the data is sought by the manufacturer's research department or its marketing department; 3) whether bona fide scientific research is involved; and 4) whether the manufacturer actually collects and uses the data for some legitimate purpose.

Other manufacturers have sought to compensate pharmacists for "cognitive services" furnished to patients. Again, the personal services and management contracts safe harbor may offer some protection here. It is important to consider, however, whether the particular services for which compensation is being provided already are required by law. If so, the remuneration may be viewed as duplicative and therefore intended to induce referrals or product recommendations. For example, under federal law, pharmacists are required to offer a variety of patient counseling and recordkeeping services to Medicaid patients.[95] If payments are made for services within the scope of these requirements, they may be construed as duplicative and intended to induce referrals.

Manufacturers also may provide educational subsidies to prescribers and dispensers. Although there is no safe harbor to cover such activities, the level of risk should be reduced somewhat if such support complies with the FDA's policies on industry-supported research activities.[96]

Arrangements with Pharmacy Benefits Managers. The recent rise of PBMs and other managed care organizations presents new challenges for anti-kickback analysis because

---

[92] *See* 42 C.F.R. § 1001.952(h). Most state Medicaid programs, however, do not provide a mechanism on their claims forms by which pharmacies can report the amount of the discount.

[93] *Id.* § 1001.952(h).

[94] *See id.* § 1001.952(d).

[95] *See id.* § 456.705.

[96] *See* Draft Policy Statement on Industry-Supported Educational and Scientific Activities, 57 Fed. Reg. 56,412 (Nov. 27, 1992).

existing standards do not address the unique nature of these entities. Manufacturers may enter into a variety of arrangements with PBMs. Although some of these arrangements may be structured to fall within the new risk-sharing safe harbors or the personal services and management contracts safe harbor, other types of payments may require more careful analysis. Although there currently are no clear standards providing protection for PBM arrangements, and existing standards are not adequate for this purpose, a variety of factors suggest that current standards should be reexamined to take account of PBMs.

First, although the discount safe harbor may provide protection for certain price reductions to entities that actually purchase drugs, PBMs (which do not purchase drugs) often receive rebates in connection with the establishment of a formulary or based on volume or market share. These rebates usually are passed on, in whole or in part, to the third party payor or benefit plan with which the PBM has contracted. To the extent that a manufacturer provides a rebate to the payor (directly or through the PBM), the risk of fraud or overutilization should be reduced because the payor itself is, in effect, sponsoring the arrangement.[97]

Second, an existing safe harbor protects certain arrangements under which providers offer discounts to managed care organizations in order to become a member of the managed care organization's service network.[98] Although this safe harbor is not the same as manufacturer payments to PBMs to have the manufacturer's products listed on a formulary (because manufacturers do not qualify as providers), the offer of rebates to a PBM standing in the shoes of a payor is closely analogous to the conduct protected by the safe harbor.

Third, an existing safe harbor protects administrative fees paid by manufacturers to group purchasing organizations (GPOs).[99] GPOs are entities that negotiate prices on behalf of a number of purchasers in order to maximize the purchasers' buying power. A PBM, while not acting on behalf of actual purchasers of drugs, generally acts on behalf of a variety of health plans in negotiating rebates. Thus, administrative and similar fees paid to PBMs might be analogized to GPO fees, although the comparison here is somewhat more attenuated.

In short, although existing standards are not entirely adequate for addressing various types of arrangements with PBMs, they do suggest some analogies that may justify certain arrangements. It remains to be seen, however, whether OIG will modify its safe harbor regulations to account for the variety of arrangements with PBMs that already are present in the market.

■ State Anti-Kickback and Professional Practice Statutes

State anti-kickback laws often contain prohibitions that parallel those of the federal statute. Often these laws apply only to goods and services furnished under the state's Medicaid program, but a few apply broadly to all health care services and payors.[100] In addition, a large number of states have enacted professional practice statutes that prohibit kick-

---

[97] Indeed, the Medicaid rebate statute *mandates* such rebates to states in exchange for broad coverage of a manufacturer's products.

[98] *See* 42 C.F.R. § 1001.952(m).

[99] *Id.* § 1001.952(j).

[100] *See, e.g.*, MASS. GEN. LAWS ch. 175H, § 3 (Supp. 1996).

backs, fee-splitting, and other practices viewed as unprofessional conduct. Although these statutes may be interpreted as consistent with federal law, they need to be analyzed separately to determine the specific parties, programs, and conduct to which they apply. For example, many pharmacy practice standards preclude only the *payment* of kickbacks by pharmacists to prescribers.

■ False Claims Prohibitions

Federal statutes establish criminal, civil, and administrative penalties for false or fraudulent claims for reimbursement.[101] The definition of a false claim is generally broad, permitting prosecutors to make claims where there is no actual government payment. The statute also applies to corporate entities or other individuals who merely caused or conspired to cause a false claim to be filed. For example, in June 1995, a manufacturer of lymphedema pumps settled with the U.S. Department of Justice and paid $4.9 million to resolve questions over the manufacturer's recommendations to suppliers on which HCPCS billing codes to use. Further, the false claim need not be filed intentionally, but merely with "deliberate ignorance" or "reckless disregard" for the truth.

False claims prohibitions can be implicated where services were not medically necessary, where quantities are claimed in excess of what was dispensed, where reimbursement amounts were inflated, where incorrect codes are used in billing, or for other matters. Notably, the government has taken the position that kickbacks may form the basis for a civil false claim action; federal courts have split with respect to whether kickback allegations are a sufficient basis on which to bring such a lawsuit.[102]

Violations of false claims prohibitions can result in significant penalties, including criminal fines and imprisonment, treble damages, and civil penalties. Perhaps most significantly, the civil false claims statute authorizes "whistleblower" lawsuits, known as "qui tam" actions, whereby an individual (known as a "relator") may bring an action for false claims on behalf of the United States and receive a portion of any recovery.[103]

False claims prohibitions will be of principal concern to pharmacies, rather than manufacturers, because pharmacists actually submit reimbursement claims to governmental entities.[104] For example, the government recently has entered into settlements with pharmacies involving 1) failure to reflect discounts received by the pharmacies under an acquisition cost-based payment system, thereby resulting in the submission of inflated claims, and 2) improper identification of the drug package size from which prescriptions were dispensed, resulting in a claim for a higher "rate per unit" than otherwise would have been allowed. Nonetheless, false claims prohibitions have been applied to both device and drug manufacturers in their capacity as federal contractors.

---

[101] *See* 18 U.S.C. § 287 (1994); 31 U.S.C. § 3729 (1994); 42 U.S.C. § 1320a-7a(a).

[102] *Compare* United States *ex rel.* Roy v. Anthony, 1994 U.S. Dist. LEXIS 9768 (S.D. Ohio July 14, 1994) *with* United States *ex rel.* Pogue v. American Healthcorp, Inc., 1995 U.S. Dist. LEXIS 16710 (M.D. Tenn. Sept. 14, 1995).

[103] *See* 31 U.S.C. § 3730.

[104] As noted in the preceding section, however, manufacturers might be held liable for "causing" the submission of a false claim if they suggested improper billing codes or engaged in other conduct that resulted in the submission of a false claim.

■ State Consumer Protection Statutes

A number of states also have sought to regulate pharmaceutical promotion — and particularly manufacturer-sponsored incentives to promote the utilization of a particular drug — through their consumer protection statutes.[105] These statutes generally prohibit unfair, deceptive, and misleading trade practices. In general, the states have challenged programs under which a pharmacy receives a financial incentive to dispense a particular drug but does not disclose that incentive to the patient.

The states' concerns in this area include: the potential for pharmacy incentives to undermine the public trust in neutral professional decisionmaking, the potential health risk associated with switching prescriptions, undermining patients' ability to make informed decisions, invasion of consumers' privacy interests through disclosure of prescription information to the manufacturer, and anti-kickback concerns.

To address consumer protection issues, manufacturer-sponsored pharmacy incentive programs should provide for disclosure of relevant information to patients, consent from patients to the collection or dissemination of information, discount structures consistent with anti-kickback safe harbors, and assurances of validity of substantive promotional claims.

In addition, states have applied their consumer protection statutes to manufacturer-owned PBMs that implement pharmaceutical "switch" programs through communications with physicians and patients. Under these settlements, PBMs have been required to disclose their ownership affiliations as part of such communications, and have been required further to encourage their health plan clients to provide information to subscribers about PBM intervention programs. In addition, PBMs must be able to substantiate any pharmacoeconomic claims made during such communications.

■ The Future: The FDA's Role in Regulating Promotion

In addition to the various federal and state laws described above, manufacturers need to be aware that the FDA may become more active in the arena of marketing and promotion. Most notably, the FDA recently published notices of two public hearings to consider direct-to-consumer promotional activities and the marketing of pharmaceuticals in the managed care context.[106] While the FDA has had continuing involvement with respect to the latter issue, the public notice with respect to the former issue suggests that the agency may become directly involved in evaluating manufacturer-PBM relationships. Among other things, the agency seeks to examine:

- How, if at all, FDA regulations on pharmaceutical communication and promotion should be modified to account for the emergence of managed care?
- How should cost-effectiveness claims be monitored and substantiated?

---

[105] *See generally* David Woodward, *Recent Multistate Enforcement Initiatives: Prescription Drug Promotional Practices*, 50 FOOD & DRUG L.J. 295 (1995).

[106] *See* 60 Fed. Reg. 42,581 (Aug. 16, 1995); 60 Fed. Reg. 41,891 (Aug. 14, 1991). In addition, the FDA recently published a proposed rule that would require written "Medication Guides" to be produced by manufacturers and distributed by pharmacists in the event that current voluntary programs do not achieve certain "performance" goals in the coming years. *See* 60 Fed. Reg. 44,182 (Aug. 24, 1995).

- What types of comparative information are sought by managed care organizations and how do they use it?
- What assurances of independence from manufacturers are necessary to promote unbiased decisionmaking in formulary development?
- How should the FDA address substitution incentives sponsored by pharmaceutical manufacturers?
- What types of services do managed care organizations (including PBMs) request from manufacturers?

To the extent that the FDA becomes actively involved in the regulation of these issues, it may represent a further layer of regulatory review that will be necessary in connection with manufacturer-sponsored promotional programs.

Conclusion

With changes in Medicare and Medicaid payment, the shift to managed care, and heightened scrutiny of the costs of medical technology, manufacturers need to incorporate reimbursement strategies during the early stages of the product development process. Furthermore, manufacturers need to ensure that their promotional and marketing plans comply with federal and state fraud and abuse laws.

Manufacturers need to consider the following:

- expanded data-gathering, improved net health outcomes and cost-effectiveness;
- development of disease management protocols;
- support for peer-reviewed scientific articles;
- clarification of product and procedure coding;
- coordination with medical specialty societies; and
- regular communications with key insurers.

By understanding and working with customers and insurers on reimbursement issues, manufacturers can better direct the process of medical innovation and contribute to both quality and cost-effective care for patients.

chapter 15

The Food and Drug Administration's Regulation of Health Care Professionals

David G. Adams*

Introduction

One of the most persistent controversies facing the Food and Drug Administration (FDA over the years has been the agency's application of the provisions of the Federal Food, Drug, and Cosmetic Act (FDCA) to health care professionals such as medical practitioners[1] and pharmacists. While it is clear from the legislative history of the FDCA that Congress did not intend the statute as a mandate for federal regulation of these professions, its provisions do clearly affect, and in many instances restrict, the practices of health care professionals. Acknowledging this legislative history, the FDA has traditionally taken the position that it does not regulate the practice of medicine or pharmacy and has generally avoided regulatory actions that would directly restrict or interfere with professional service to patients. The agency has identified circumstances, however, in which it will seek to regulate the conduct of physicians, pharmacists, and other health-care professionals in the same manner that it regulates manufacturers and distributors of medical products. In the case of medical practitioners, the agency sought to regulate promotion and distribution of medical products, particularly when the products are suggested for "off-label use."[2] In the case of pharmacists, the agency has shown concern not only over promotion of products for off-label uses, but also over the nature and scale of pharmacists' compounding, promotion, and distribution of drugs. Although the FDA's policies affecting the practice of med-

---

* Mr. Adams is a Partner in the law firm of Olsson Frank, and Weeda, PC., Washington, D.C.

[1] The term "medical practitioners" as used herein is intended to include physicians, chiropractors, nurses, nurse practitioners, and others who use drugs or devices in the practice of the healing arts.

[2] "Off-label use" is a term of art that generally refers to the use of a drug or device in a manner that is outside of the product's labeling that is approved or authorized by FDA. *See* Washington Legal Foundation v. Kessler, 880 F. Supp 26, 28 n.1 (D.D.C. 1995). *See also* letter to the Honorable Joseph Barton, Chairman, Subcomm. on Oversight and Investigation, Comm. on Commerce, U.S. House of Rep., from Diane E. Thompson, Assoc. Comm'r for Legislative Aff., Food & Drug Admin. (Apr. 14, 1995).

icine and pharmacy are similar in certain respects, they have developed separately in numerous judicial enforcement actions and agency pronouncements.

Medical Practitioners

■ The "Practice of Medicine Exception"

Both the agency and the courts have recognized the many significant statements in the legislative history of the FDCA that the legislation was not intended to regulate the "practice of medicine" or, as it was later described, the "healing art."[3] Senator Royal Copeland, who introduced the legislation that was to become the FDCA, is commonly quoted in this regard:

> [T]he bill is not intended as a medical practices act and will not interfere with the practice of the healing art by chiropractors and others in the States where they are licensed by law to engage in such practice. It is not intended to permit the sale in interstate commerce or otherwise in Federal jurisdiction of adulterated or misbranded drugs or devices under the guise of the practice of a healing art. It is likewise not intended to permit the false advertising of drugs and devices under such guise.[4]

The references in the legislative history to the practice of medicine and of the healing art, however, do not define those phrases, and neither phrase is found in the FDCA itself.[5] Thus, while agreeing that the FDA does not or should not regulate the practice of medicine, the courts have not fashioned a general exemption to shield physicians from the adulteration, misbranding, and new drug provisions of the FDCA.[6] Nor have the courts found

---

[3]   References to the practice of the "healing art" were intended to clarify that Congress' concerns extended to chiropractors as well as medical doctors. S. REP. NO. 493, 73d Cong., 2d Sess. (1934), *reprinted in* C. DUNN, FEDERAL FOOD, DRUG AND COSMETIC ACT 111 (1938).

[4]   S. REP. NO. 361, 74th Cong., 1st Sess. (1935), *reprinted in* DUNN, *supra* note 3. Senator Copeland made this remark while explaining the significance of a qualification provided in the bill's definition of "drug." The definition stated at the outset that "[t]he term 'drug,' for the purposes of this Act and *not to regulate the practice of medicine*, includes...." S. 2800, 73d Cong., 2d Sess., § 2(b) (1934), *reprinted in* DUNN, *supra* note 3, at 72. (emphasis added). In the next draft of the bill, the phrase was changed slightly to "not to regulate the *legalized* practice of *the healing art.*" *Id.* at 93 (emphasis added). The qualification was dropped from the drug definition prior to passage because it was deemed unnecessary and possibly confusing. *See id.* at 403 (Senate debate); H.R. REP. NO. 2755, 74th Cong., 2d Sess. (1935), *reprinted in* Dunn at 554; *see also id.* at 578 (House debate).

[5]   The FDA has, in response to a congressional inquiry, defined the practice of medicine as "the examination, diagnosis, and treatment of individual patients based on judgments made by licensed health care professions...regulated by State Boards of Medicine, which license physicians." Letter to the Honorable Joseph Barton, *supra* note 2.

[6]   Although one court has stated that the legislative history "expressed a specific intent to prohibit FDA from regulating physicians' practice of medicine," it did so at the prodding of the FDA where a plaintiff requested the FDA intervene in a case involving capital punishment by lethal injection of approved drugs. Chaney v. Heckler, 718 F.2d 1174 (D.C. Cir. 1984), *rev'd*, 470 U.S. 821 (1985).

constitutional limitations on FDA's authority to regulate physicians.[7] Thus, the regulatory regimes for drugs and devices have been applied to medical practitioners and, unavoidably, to the practice of medicine itself.[8]

■ Regulation of Off-label Use of Approved or Authorized Products

Drugs

The FDA has formally recognized that certain medical practices are not subject to regulation under the FDCA. The most notable and longstanding exception is for off-label use of approved drugs in the practice of medicine.[9] The FDA's 1972 proposed rulemaking on off-label use[10] remains the most significant statement of agency policy on this issue.

The agency sought in the proposed rule to address the "widespread use of certain prescription drugs for conditions not named in the official labeling."[11] The agency proposed to address the issue not by regulating off-label use itself, but rather by imposing labeling and other requirements on manufacturers and distributors of drugs that are commonly used

---

[7] Although the Supreme Court stated in Linder v. United States, 268 U.S. 5, 18 (1925), that direct control of medical practice was beyond the reach of the federal government, lower courts have refused to limit the FDA's authority based on arguments that the practice of medicine must be left to the states. *See* United States v. Evers, 643 F.2d 1043, 1048-49 (5th Cir. 1981); Simeon Management Corp. v. FTC, 579 F.2d 1137, 1144 (9th Cir. 1978). The Supreme Court has generally held that doctors have no special constitutional rights other than those deriving from patient's rights. *See* Whalen v. Roe, 429 U.S. 589, 605 (1977) (confidentiality of medical records); Griswold v. Connecticut, 381 U.S. 479, 481 (1965) (right to contraceptives). Attempts to limit the FDA's authority based on assertions of patients' constitutional rights have not fared well. *See, e.g.*, United States v. Burzynski Cancer Research Inst., 819 F.2d 1301, 1313-14 (5th Cir. 1987) (cancer patients have no constitutional privacy right to obtain medical treatment when the treatment consisted of an unapproved drug) (citing United States v. Rutherford, 442 U.S. 544 (1979)).

[8] For an excellent discussion of the historical background of the FDCA and the FDA policy development related to the practice of medicine, *see* Peter Barton Hutt, *Regulation of the Practice of Medicine Under the Pure Food and Drug Laws*, FOOD & DRUG OFFICIALS OF THE U.S. Q. BULL. 3 (1969).

[9] *See* William L. Christopher, *Off Label Drug Prescription: Filling the Regulatory Vacuum*, 48 FOOD & DRUG L. J. 247, 247 n.6 (1993). The agency has followed a different policy with regard to animal drugs. Under the FDCA, new animal drugs are deemed adulterated if "used" outside of their approved labeling. *See* FDCA §§ 501(a)(5), 512(a) (1994), 21 U.S.C. §§ 351(a)(5), 360b(a). The FDCA also expressly precludes the administration of unapproved new drugs for animal use. FDCA § 512(a), 21 U.S.C. § 360b(a). This reflects a concern that harmful residues of such drugs could become present in food-producing animals. To allow more flexibility for veterinarians to legally administer approved drugs for unlabeled uses in non-food-producing animals, Congress recently amended this restriction. Codifying what was, for many years, the FDA enforcement policy, the Animal Medicinal Drug Use Clarification Act of 1994 amended the FDCA to allow, on the order of a veterinarian: 1) a new animal drug approved for one use to be used for a different purpose, and 2) a new drug approved for human use to be used in non-food producing animals. Animal Medicinal Drug Use Clarification Act of 1944, Pub. L. No. 103-396, 108 Stat. 4153 (1994) (to be codified at 21 U.S.C. § 360b(a)(4). The issue of drug compounding by veterinarians is addressed in an FDA policy statement. *See* Compliance Policy Guide § 7125.10 (Oct. 1, 1980), which states: "veterinarians may use in the compounding of prescriptions for their private practice whatever bulk drugs or other pharmaceuticals they may lawfully purchase. This falls under the general practice of veterinary medicine which is amenable to local or state laws with which the FDA has no desire to interfere." *Id.*

[10] 37 Fed. Reg. 16,503 (1972).

[11] *Id.*

off-label.[12] In declining to regulate actual off-label use, the agency acknowledged that package inserts often do not contain the most current information about new uses of drugs and that such new uses may sometimes be appropriate in the practice of medicine.[13] The agency stated unambiguously that such off-label uses would not violate the FDCA or its implementing regulations.[14]

While acknowledging the repeated statements in the legislative history that Congress did not intend the FDCA to interfere with or regulate medical practice, the agency concluded that "Congress clearly required the Food and Drug Administration to control the *availability* of drugs for prescribing by physicians."[15] The agency added:

> As the law now stands, therefore, the Food and Drug Administration is charged with the responsibility for judging the safety and effectiveness of drugs and the truthfulness of their labeling. The physician is then responsible for making the final judgment as to which, if any, of the available drugs his patient will receive in light of the information contained in their labeling and other adequate scientific data available to him.[16]

Although the proposed rule was never adopted, due in part to the strong opposition from the medical professionals,[17] the discussion of off-label use has remained an important statement of agency policy.[18] The policy is currently reflected in the FDA's investigational new drug (IND) regulations, which govern investigational use of unapproved new drugs. These regulations provide that no IND is required where the physician is prescribing an approved product for an unapproved (off-label) use in the practice of medicine.[19]

---

[12] The proposed rule authorized the following actions when "an unapproved use of a new drug may endanger patients or create a public health hazard, or provide a benefit to patients or to the public health": 1) requiring the manufacturer to revise the package insert to add the new use, 2) requiring contraindications, warnings, and similar information on labeling; 3) restricting refills; 4) requiring the manufacturer to substantiate the unapproved use; 5) restricting distribution, prescribing, dispensing, and administration (e.g., to physicians with specified qualifications); and 6) withdrawing approval of the product. *Id.* at 16, 504-05.

[13] *Id.*

[14] *Id.*

[15] *Id.* at 16,503-04 (emphasis added).

[16] *Id.* at 16,504.

[17] *See* Dep't Health, Education & Welfare, Review Panel on New Drug Regulation, Interim Report—Prescribing Drugs for Unapproved Uses 7-10 (1977).

[18] *See Use of Approved Drugs for Unlabeled Indications,* 12 FDA Drug Bull. 4-5 (Apr. 1982):

> Once a product has been approved for marketing, a physician may prescribe it for uses or in treatment regimens or patient populations that are not included in approved labeling...'[U]napproved' or, more precisely, 'unlabeled" uses may be appropriate and rational in certain circumstances, and may, in fact reflect approaches to drug therapy that have been extensively reported in medical literature.... Valid new uses for drugs already on the market are often first discovered through serendipitous observations and therapeutic innovations, subsequently confirmed by well-planned and executed clinical investigations.

> This policy was most recently confirmed by the agency in a notice requesting comments on the agency's policy in promotion of unapproved uses of approved drugs and devices. 59 Fed. Reg. 59,820 (1994).

> Although in 1991, the agency considered whether to withdraw the 1972 proposed rule, the agency ultimately declined to withdraw the proposed rule. The FDA noted, however, that it did not intend to proceed to a final rule at that time because it planned to assemble an "Unlabeled Use Task Force to examine the promotion and use of prescription drugs for indications not included on their approved labeling." Withdrawal of Certain Pre-1986 Proposed Rules; Final Action, 56 Fed. Reg. 67,440, 67,442 (1991).

[19] The FDA generally distinguishes clinical research from practice of medicine involving approved drugs. 21 C.F.R. § 312.2(b) (1997). *See also* David A. Kessler, *The Regulation of Investigational Drugs,* 320 N. Eng. J. Med. 281 (1989).

In applying this policy, the agency has drawn a critical distinction between off-label use in the practice of medicine and commercialization of off-label uses. The seminal case in this regard is United States v. Evers,[20] where the FDA challenged a physician's promotion and advertising of chelating drugs for a use that was not within the approved labeling.[21] Although the agency acknowledged that Dr. Evers could prescribe the drugs for an off-label use, it argued that Dr. Evers' commercial activities had misbranded the product under 21 U.S.C. § 352(f)(1) by creating a new intended use for which there were no "adequate directions" in the labeling.[22] The court of appeals rejected the agency's position, however, because Dr. Evers had distributed the drugs only to his own patients.[23] The court found that Dr. Evers had 1) no duty under the FDCA to provide adequate directions to other physicians since he had not distributed the drugs to other physicians; 2) no duty to provide adequate directions to his patients because the drug was a prescription drug,[24] and, 3) for obvious reasons, no duty to provide adequate directions to himself.[25]

Although Dr. Evers argued the broader proposition that the FDA had no jurisdiction over the practice of medicine, the court declined to reach the issue and appeared to accept the distinction drawn by the FDA in the preamble to the 1972 proposed regulation: "Of course, while the Act was not intended to regulated the *practice of medicine*, it was obviously intended to control the *availability of drugs* for prescribing by physicians." [26]

---

[20] 643 F.2d 1043 (5th Cir. 1981).

[21] *Id.* at 1045-46. Dr. Evers was using a chelating drug in the treatment of atherosclerosis, a use for which the drug was contraindicated. *Id.* at 1044-45. The agency had previously obtained relief against Dr. Evers in a case brought in Louisiana, where he was not licensed. United States v. An Article of Drug . . . Diso-Tate, No. 75-1790 (E.D. La. Sept. 28, 1976). Dr. Evers moved subsequently moved to Alabama where he was licensed, and resumed administering and promoting the drug. United States v. Evers, 453 F. Supp. 1141, 1142-43 (M.D. Ala. 1979).

[22] FDCA § 5029(f)(1), 21 U.S.C. § 352(f)(1). 643 F.2d at 1048-49. ("[T]he government agrees with Dr. Evers that the provisions of the Act and the regulations of the FDA that are now in force do not prevent him from prescribing for uses not approved by FDA drugs which have been approved by the FDA for some other purposes. The object of the government's case against Dr. Evers is not, therefore, his *prescription* of Calcium EDTA for use in the treatment of circulatory disorders. Instead, the government seeks to challenge Dr. Evers' *promotion* and *advertising* of chelating drugs for that use." *Id.*) (emphasis added).

[23] Although Dr. Evers' promoted the drug to other physicians, the court noted that such promotion did not constitute a violation of the FDCA because he did not sell or distribute the product to other physicians. *Id.* at 1053 n.16. The court emphasized in this regard that "the Act was intended to regulate the distribution of drugs in interstate commerce, not to restrain physicians from public advocacy of medical opinions not shared by the FDA." *Id.*

[24] 21 C.F.R. § 201.100 exempts prescription drugs from the requirement of adequate directions for use for patients where the product's labeling bears full disclosure labeling (the package insert) for the physician.

[25] United States v. Evers, 643 F.2d at 1044. The view of the *Evers* court may not be shared by other courts. In an earlier case involving a seizure of drugs held by physicians for their medical practice, the court appeared to reach a different result:

> It may be that physicians are not understood as holding for sale the drugs which they may administer or prescribe in connection with their treatment of patients. But the potentiality of harm to the public from misbranded drugs is not less because the intervening agency of distribution may be a physician rather than a layman...If forfeiture works any interference with claimants' practice of medicine it is a mere incident of their violation of the law in making representations concerning their drugs which the jury found were unwarranted, false or misleading.

United States v. 10 Cartons . . . Article of Drug Labeled in Part "Hoxey," 152 F. Supp. 360, 364 (W.D. Pa. 1957). *See also* United States v. Articles of Animal Drug Containing Diethylstilbestrol, 528 F. Supp. 202, 205 (D. Neb. 1981), in which the court held that, although prescription drugs are exempt from the requirement of adequate directions for use when dispensed to patients, FDCA § 503(b)(2), 21 U.S.C. § 353(b)(2) there is no such exemption while the drugs are held for sale prior to being dispensed. The court also noted that "an article of drug or device is 'held for sale' if it is used for any purpose other than personal consumption." *Id.*

[26] United States v. Evers, 643 F.2d at 1048 (emphasis added).

Medical devices

In the case of medical devices, the FDA and the courts have provided less flexibility for physicians than in the case of human drugs. The courts have shown a willingness to require adequate directions for use even for devices held by physicians for their own use,[27] and have enjoined physicians from using misbranded or adulterated devices and permitted seizures of devices in physicians offices.[28] Although the agency's regulatory approach to drugs and devices has, for the most part, appeared the same with regard to promotion, distribution, and off-label use,[29] the agency has reserved the right to regulate off-label use of devices. The agency has stated in response to a congressional inquiry that "[t]he Medical Device Amendments...give FDA authority to regulate the unapproved use of the medical devices,"[30] citing statutory provisions that provide "explicit authority over the use of devices."[31] The agency further states, however, that its "actions" have been the same for drugs and devices because of specific exemptions in the statute and regulations for the use of devices in the practice of medicine.[32] Although these exemptions include a provision allowing sale and use of a custom device that is not commercially available, the agency has not provided a general exemption from the requirement of an investigational device

---

[27] *See, e.g.,* United States v. Device Labeled "Cameron Spitler, Etc.,*" 261 F. Supp. 243, 246 (D. Neb. 1966). The court quoted United States v. Ellis Research Lab., 300 F.2d 550 (7th Cir.), *cert. denied,* 370 U.S. 918 (1962), in support of its position:

> Licensed practitioners are not exempt from the terms of the Act, and we see no reason why a device used solely by licensed practitioners should, for that reason alone, be exempt from that portion of the Act requiring the labeling to bear "adequate directions for use.

[28] *See, e.g.,* United States v. Diapulse Corp. of America, 514 F.2d 1097, 1098 (2d Cir.), *cert. denied,* 423 U.S. 838 (1975):

> The contention that the injunction [prohibiting interstate shipment of a misbranded device] was improperly extended to cover devices held by practitioners [was] also without merit. Such devices, used in the treatment of patients, may properly be considered "held for sale" within the meaning of the Food, Drug, and Cosmetic Act, 21 U.S.C. sec. 331(k).

See also Kordel v. United States , 335 U.S. 345 (1948); United States v. Kocmond, 200 F.2d 370 (7th Cir.), *cert. denied,* 345 U.S. 924 (1953); United States v. Device Labeled "Cameron Spitler, Etc.," 261 F. Supp. 243 (D. Neb. 1966); Drown v. United States, 198 F.2d 999 (9th Cir. 1952); United States v. 10 Cartons of Black Tablets, 152 F. Supp. 360 (W.D. Pa. 1957); United States v. Articles of Device Acuflex; Pro-Med, 426 F. Supp. 366 n.3 (W.D. Pa. 1977).

[29] In an informal notice dated February 1989, the agency stated:

> Good medical practice and patient interests require that physicians use commercially available drugs, devices, and biologics according to their best knowledge and judgment . . . Use of a product in this manner as part of the practice of medicine does not require the submission of an [IND] or an [IDE] . . . .

[30] See Letter to the Honorable Joseph Barton, *supra* note 2.

[31] *Id.,* citing 21 U.S.C. §§ 360, 360c, 360f, 360h, 360i, 360j, 360k (FDCA §§ 510, 513, 516, 518, 519, 520, 521). Agency personnel have suggested informally that the use of a device outside of authorization in the context of a device classification or finding of substantial equivalence will render the device a Class III device under FDCA § 513(f), 21 U.S.C. § 360c(f) requiring an approved premarket approval application (PMA), and that the use of a Class III device outside the labeling approved in a PMA will render it unapproved and, thus, adulterated under section 351(f) (FDCA § 501(f)). Although the agency has apparent authority to regulate physician use of restricted devices under 21 U.S.C. § 360j(e) (FDCA § 520(e)), ("sale, distribution, or *use*" outside of labeled restrictions) (emphasis added), there are few devices that qualify as restricted devices.

[32] The agency cites, in this regard, FDCA § 520(b), 21 U.S.C. 360j(b) (custom devices which are not generally commercially available and intended for use solely by individual patients); FDCA § 510(g)(2), 21 U.S.C. § 360(g)(2) (exemption from registration and listing); FDCA § 519(c), 21 U.S.C. 360i(c) (exemption from user reporting); FDCA § 520(g)(3)(D), 21 U.S.C. § 360j(g)(3)(D) (informed consent requirements for IDEs); 21 C.F. R. §807.65(d) (exemption from registration and listing); 21 C.F.R. 807.85(a) (exemption from premarket notification); 21 C.F.R. 808.1(d)(3) (exemption of state regulation of practice of medicine from pre-emptive effect of FDCA § 521, 21 U.S.C. § 360k.

exemption for the off-label use of an approved or authorized device in the practice of medicine. Moreover, the agency has, in another discussion of off-label use, suggested that under certain circumstances it may seek to regulate off-label use of devices.[33]

■ Regulation of Use and Distribution of Unapproved or Unauthorized Products

Drugs

Although the FDA generally does not attempt to intervene directly in the prescribing and administration of human drugs in the practice of medicine, the agency has in some cases sought to regulate the preparation and distribution of unapproved or otherwise illegal drugs by physicians. Shortly after its loss in the Evers case, the FDA successfully challenged the activities of another physician, Dr. Stanislaw R. Burzynski, under a different legal theory.[34] Unlike Dr. Evers, Dr. Burzynski was distributing an unapproved and controversial cancer treatment that he had himself manufactured. In Dr. Burzynski's case, the agency obtained injunctive relief under the new drug provisions of the FDCA, which prohibit introduction of unapproved new drugs into interstate commerce.[35] The agency's relief did not extend to intrastate sales by Dr. Burzynski in Texas because the FDCA does not prohibit holding unapproved new drugs for sale after shipment in interstate commerce.[36]

Medical devices

The agency's official pronouncements regarding off-label use of devices in the practice of medicine would apparently apply to devices that are customized to meet the needs of individual patients.[37] These statements would not clearly apply, however, to new devices invented for new uses. Thus, if a physician procures or develops a new device for a single patient, it may be protected as a custom device, while a device that may be used for more than one patient or is not in a specific form for an individual patient may subject the physician to liability under the FDCA.[38] A policy based on such distinctions poses obvious difficulties for physicians seeking to provide the best care for their patients.

---

[33] In a notice requesting comments on the agency's policy in promotion of unapproved uses of approved drugs and devices, states that it "does not intervene in unapproved use of devices *in the absence of a significant public health concern or significant risk to the patient*." 59 Fed. Reg. 59,820 n.3 (1994) (emphasis added).

[34] *See* United States v. Burzynski Cancer Research Inst., No. H-83-2069 (S.D. Tex. May 24, 1983); United States v. Burzynski Cancer Research Inst., 819 F.2d 1301, 1304 (5th Cir. 1987), *cert. denied sub nom,* Wolin v. United States, 484 U.S. 1065 (1988).

[35] FDCA § 201(d), 21 U.S.C. § 321(d).

[36] *See Burzynski Cancer Research Inst.,* 819 F.2d at 1305. *See also* Trustees of the Northwest Laundry & Dry Cleaners Health & Welfare Fund v. Burzynski, 27 F.3d 153, 155 & n.3 (5th Cir. 1994). Unlike the adulteration and misbranding provisions of the FDCA, the FDA's jurisdiction over unapproved new drugs is limited to introduction into interstate commerce. *See* FDCA § 301(d), 21 U.S.C. § 331(d). The adulteration or misbranding of the drugs in Texas would have resulted in a violation of FDCA § 201(k); 21 U.S.C. § 321(k) (held for sale after shipment in interstate commerce) if any of the drug's components came from out of state. The court in *Trustees of the Northwest Laundry* also noted that state laws may preclude intrastate marketing of an unapproved new drug. 27 F.3d at 155 & n.4.

[37] FDCA § 520(b), 21 U.S.C. § 360j(b).

[38] In United States v. Fulton, Food Drug Cosm. Law Rep. (CCH) ¶ 15,164 (C.D. Cal. July 29, 1992), a physician was enjoined from using unapproved liquid silicone in his medical practice. The physician was charged with violating 21 U.S.C. § 331(q) by "using a device which lacks pre-market approval, without an investigational device exemption, as required by 21 U.S.C. § 360j(g)." *Id.* The court held that the liquid silicone did not meet the requirements of the custom device exemption, 21 U.S.C. § 360j(b)(2)(A)(i), (ii). *Id.*

■ Restrictions on Availability to Practitioners

Drugs

As discussed above, the FDA and the courts have generally agreed that the FDCA is designed to restrict the availability of unapproved and otherwise illegal drugs to physicians. This includes availability of unapproved drugs intended for use in the practice of medicine. Such drugs are considered experimental under the agency's regulations and manufacturers cannot provide such drugs to physicians in the absence of an IND authorizing the physicians use of the product.[39] Drugs compounded by pharmacists pursuant to a physician's prescription are generally not subject to this requirement.[40] This vehicle for avoiding the IND requirements is circumscribed, however, by the agency's limitations on the availability of ingredients for use in compounding by pharmacists.[41]

These same limitations apply to the sale of prescription ingredients for use in compounding by physicians.[42] In cases involving restrictions on bulk drug ingredients intended for compounding by veterinarians,[43] courts have rejected arguments that the agency's regulation impermissibly interfered with the practice of medicine. The United States Court of Appeals for the Seventh Circuit upheld a seizure of bulk drug ingredients intended for use by veterinarians.[44] Disagreeing with the lower court's conclusion that the FDCA was not intended to "involve the agency in the practice of the healing arts,"[45] the appeals court stated:

> Congress gave the FDA comprehensive powers to license the manufacture of drugs and limit their sales. To regulate drugs is to be "involved" in the "practice of the healing arts." [46]

In a similar case involving bulk ingredients for veterinary compounding, the United States Court of Appeals for the Third Circuit distinguished the *Evers* decision as involving off-

---

[39]   21 C.F.R. § 312.3(a). The agency has promulgated treatment IND regulations to make possible the distribution of promising experimental drugs for patients with serious or immediately life-threatening diseases where there is no satisfactory alternative therapy, the drug is already the subject of a controlled trial under an IND, and the sponsor of the trial is actively pursuing agency approval. *Id.* § 312.34. The agency also authorizes emergency uses of investigational drugs where time does not allow the submission of an IND. *Id.* § 312.36.

[40]   *See* discussion *infra.*

[41]   *Id.*

[42]   21 C.F.R. § 201.120.

[43]   *See, e.g.,* United States v. Thomas, 840 F. Supp. 106 (D. Kan. 1993) (holding that there is no exemption from the adulteration and misbranding requirements of the FDCA for veterinarians); United States v. Rossoff, 806 F. Supp. 200 (C.D. Ill. 1992).

[44]   United States v. 9/1 Kg. Containers, More or Less of an Article of Drug for Veterinary Use, 854 F.2d 173 (7th Cir. 1988), *cert. denied,* 489 U.S. 1010 (1989, *reversing* 674 F. Supp. 1344 (1987). The drugs were seized from "middleman" companies bought the unblended ingredients from the manufacturer and shipped them in bulk to veterinarians who would compound them into combinations and doses suitable for their varied patients. *Id.* at 175. The bulk drug exemption in the FDA's regulations, 21 C.F.R. §201.122, required that the use of the bulk drug ingredients in the manufacture of a new animal drug be covered by an approved new animal drug application. *Id.* at 175, 178.

[45]   854 F.2d at 176, *quoting* 674 F. Supp. at 1348.

[46]   *Id.* The court went on to state:

> Phrases such as the one in the 1935 Senate Report (bill "not intended as a medical practices act and [would] not interfere with the practice of the healing art[s]") — not repeated in 1962 — never meant more than that medical licensure and discipline would continue to be the states' business; states, not the FDA, would decide whether (for example) physicians had

label use of a lawfully acquired drug as opposed to sale of unlawful bulk components intended for compounding unapproved new products.[47]

In the one notable case in which the agency attempted to impose controls on the availability of an *approved* drug, the agency was successfully challenged. In *American Pharmaceutical Association v. Weinberger*,[48] a federal district court held that the FDA had no authority to limit the distribution of methadone to certain hospitals for certain specific uses. Despite this holding, the FDA promulgated a regulation in 1992 that would authorize restrictions on distribution of drugs approved under special criteria, known as an accelerated approval process.[49] In response to comments that such restrictions would interfere with the practice of medicine, the agency asserted "broad authority...to issue regulations to help assure the safety and effectiveness of new drugs,"[50] and argued that, "rather than interfering with physician or pharmacy practice, the regulations permit, in exceptional cases, approval of drugs with restrictions so that the drugs may be available for prescribing or dispensing."[51]

Medical devices

The FDA's statutory authority over medical devices provides express authority to place restrictions on the availability of products for medical practitioners. The agency can establish through regulation or administrative order restrictions on the sale, distribution, or use of devices. Specifically, the FDA may promulgate regulations specifying that a device must be sold, distributed or used only upon the authorization of a practitioner licensed to administer or use the device.[52] The agency may confine the use of a device to persons with specific training or experience or to certain facilities where the restriction is required for the safe and effective use of the device.[53] The agency may also require that the label of a restricted device bear statements reflecting the restrictions that have been imposed.[54] The agency has, to date, used this authority very sparingly.

---

selected wisely from among methods of treatment. The full quotation, redacted by Schuyler and the district court, makes the point: the statute is "not intended as a medical practice act and [would] not interfere with the practice of the healing art *by chiropractors and others.*" So states set medical qualifications, and practitioners who do not use drugs (*i.e.*, chiropractors) may go on as before. Nothing in the history or structure of the Act permits drugs deemed ineffective or dangerous by the FDA to be available for use.

Id. at 176-77 (*citing* United States v. Rutherford, 442 U.S. 544 (1979) (emphasis in original).

[47] United States v. Algon Chemical, Inc., 879 F.2d 1154, 1162-63 (3d Cir. 1989).

[48] 377 F. Supp. 824 (D.D.C. 1974), *aff'd sub nom,* APhA v. Mathews, 530 F.2d 1054 (D.C. Cir. 1976).

[49] New Drug, Antibiotic, and Biological Drug Product Regulations; Accelerated Approval. 57 Fed. Reg. 58,942, 58,951 (Dec. 11, 1992). *See* 21 C.F.R. §§ 314.520, 601.42. Included in this rule are certain postmarketing regulations, under which the FDA may "(1) Restrict distribution to certain facilities or physicians with special training or experience, or (2) condition distribution on the performance of specified medical procedures." 57 Fed. Reg. at 58,943.

[50] *Id.* at 58,951.

[51] *Id.* at 58,952.

[52] FDCA § 520 (e)(1), 21 U.S.C. § 360j(e)(1). A person may not be excluded from using a device because he or she is not eligible for certification or has not been certified by the American Board of Medical Specialities. *Id.*

[53] *Id.*

[54] FDCA § 520(e)(2), 21 U.S.C. § 360j(e)(2).

Pharmacists

■ The "Practice of Pharmacy Exception"

As in the case of the practice of medicine, there is no general exemption in the FDCA for the practice of pharmacy. The act does, however, contain three specific, limited exemptions for pharmacy practice. Two of these exemptions apply expressly to "pharmacies" that dispense drugs "upon prescriptions of practitioners licensed to administer such drugs to patients under the care of such practitioners in the course of their professional practice, and which do not manufacture, prepare, propagate, compound, or process drugs or devices for sale other than in the regular course of their business of dispensing or selling drugs or devices at retail."[55] These pharmacies are exempted from the registration and drug listing provisions of the act[56] and from certain FDA inspection requirements.[57] The third exemption applies to any person authorized to dispense prescription drugs and exempts such drugs from most statutory labeling requirements, including the requirement of adequate directions for use.[58]

In the view of the agency, all statutory requirements outside these limited exemptions apply to pharmacists. Thus, the agency asserts that pharmacists are subject to statutory requirements such as 21 U.S.C. §§ 351(a)(2)(B) (current good manufacturing practice), 351(b) (USP standards), 351(c) (quality representations for non-USP drugs), 352(a) (false and misleading labeling), 352(f)(1) (adequate directions for use), 352(o) (failure to register as a manufacturer), 352(n) (failure to comply with regulations requiring brief summary of side effects and contraindications), and 355(a) (unapproved new drugs).[59] The agency also limits the availability of drug products and ingredients to pharmacists.[60]

---

[55] FDCA § 510(g)(1), 21 U.S.C. § 360(g)(1).

[56] *Id.*

[57] *Id.* § 704(a)(2)(A), 21 U.S.C. § 374(a)(2)(A).

[58] *Id.* § 503(b)(2),21 U.S.C. § 353(b)(2). This exemption is not limited to pharmacies, but applies to any person authorized to dispense prescription drugs. Under the exemption, dispensed drugs are required to comply only with the labeling requirements of 21 U.S.C. § 352(a), (l)(2), (3), (k), (l), FDCA § 502(a), (l)(2),(3),(k),(l), and with the packaging requirements of § 352(g), (h), (p) (FDCA § 502(g),(h),(p)). They are thus exempt from such requirements as adequate directions for use, *Id.* § 502(f)(1); 21 U.S.C. § 352(f)(1). The labeling for dispensed drugs is required to contain only minimal information, including the specific directions for use contained in the prescription. *Id.* § 503(b)(2), 21 U.S.C. § 353(b)(2).

[59] FDA, Compliance Policy Guide 7132.16 (1992). Because drugs dispensed by pharmacists are exempt from the requirement of adequate directions for use, § 352(f)(1) (FDCA § 502(f)(1)) would, presumably, apply only to drugs distributed by pharmacists to other commercial entities or drugs held for sale prior to dispensing. Pharmacists may also face regulation under the Prescription Drug Marketing Act (PDMA), Pub. L. No. 100-293, 102 Stat. 95 (1987); Pub. L. No. 102-353, 106 Stat. 941 (1992). The FDA has proposed a regulation that would require regulation of pharmacies as wholesalers of their pharmacy's sales to physicians exceeded five percent of their annual prescription drug sales. *See* 59 Fed. Reg. 11,842 (1994). Under the proposed regulation, pharmacies could engage in small-scale sales of drugs to physicians under a "practice of pharmacy" exemption. However, if pharmacies engaged in larger sales which approached wholesale distribution, they would be subject to the requirements of the PDMA. *Id.*

[60] As discussed in Part II, *supra*, the FDA interprets 21 U.S.C. § 352(f)(1) (FDCA § 502 (f)(1)) to require adequate directions for use for drug substances intended for compounding. The FDA regulations exempt components of prescription drugs from this requirement unless they are intended for use in compounding an unapproved new drug. 21 C.F.R. § 201.120. In United States v. Sene X Eleemosynary Corp., 479 F. Supp. 970 (S.D. Fla. 1979), the court upheld the FDA's authority to seize the bulk component intended for use by a pharmacists in compounding an unapproved new drug.

As with physicians, the FDA couples its claim of general jurisdiction over pharmacists with an assertion that the agency does not regulate the practice of pharmacy. The agency's position on the practice of pharmacy, however, is not based on general statements in the legislative history that the FDCA was not intended to regulate the practice of pharmacy. The policy is rather an extension of the three limited, statutory exemptions. The agency interprets these exemptions (for state-authorized dispensing and for pharmacies engaged "in the regular course of their business of dispensing or selling drugs or devices at retail"),[61] as extending only to "traditional" pharmacy practices. Outside these exemptions, the agency has adopted a policy of deference to traditional pharmacy practice. Thus, the agency historically has avoided regulation of traditional pharmacist compounding of unapproved drugs[62] and has encouraged pharmacists to provide patient information, including patient labeling and counseling, that may include information on off-label uses and fail to comply with misbranding provisions of the FDCA. The agency has also stated that its good manufacturing regulations do not apply to pharmacists engaged in the traditional practice of pharmacy. The preamble to the regulations explains that the regulations apply to "manufacturers," as distinguished from persons engaged in the traditional practice of pharmacy.[63]

Despite this stated deference to traditional pharmacy practice, the agency does, unquestionably, regulates pharmacists in certain aspects of their professional practices.[64] Moreover, because the practice of pharmacy necessarily involves preparation, handling, and dispensing of drugs, activities that are more closely related to the FDA's regulatory mission of ensuring safety, effectiveness, and proper labeling, the agency is more directly involved in regulating pharmacy than in regulating the practice of medicine. Where pharmacists have engaged in activities that the FDA regards as more analogous to manufacturing and commercial distribution than to the traditional practice of pharmacy, the agency has asserted jurisdiction and taken pharmacists to court. Although the courts have agreed in these cases that pharmacists are subject to regulation under the FDCA, the courts have not addressed the issue of whether the "practice of pharmacy" can be regulated under the FDCA because they have found that the pharmacists' actions were outside the traditional practice of pharmacy.[65]

■ Defining the "Traditional" Practice of Pharmacy

The agency's distinction between traditional practice of pharmacy and commercial manufacture and distribution, is key to its interpretation of the statutory exemptions for pharma-

---

[61] FDCA § 510(g)(1), 21 U.S.C. § 360(g)(1).

[62] Professionals and Patients for Customized Care v. Shalala, 56 F.3d 592, 593 n.3 (5th Cir. 1995), rev'g 847 F. Supp. 1359 (S.D. Tex. 1994). Compounding is a "process whereby a pharmacist combines ingredients pursuant to a physician's prescription to create a medication for an individual patient." Id. at 593.

[63] 43 Fed. Reg. 45,027 (1978). Although the agency does not apply its good manufacturing practice (GMP) regulations to the traditional practice of pharmacy, it maintains that the statutory requirement of GMPs is in 21 U.S.C.§ 342(a)(2)(B) (FDCA § 402 (a)(2)(B)) remains applicable.

[64] The potential liability of pharmacists under the FDCA was established early on in the agency's enforcement efforts. See United States v. Sullivan, 332 U.S. 689 (1948) (containers of sulfathiazole prepared by a retail druggist held misbranded).

[65] See Cedars North Towers Pharmacy, Inc., v. United States, Food Drug Cosm. Law Rep., (CCH) ¶ 38,200 (S.D. Fla. Aug. 20, 1978) (Civ. No 77-4695), reprinted in FEDERAL FOOD, DRUG, AND COSMETIC ACT: JUDICIAL RECORD 1978-1980, at 668-71; United States v. Sene X Eleemosynary Corp., 479 F. Supp. 970, 978 (S.D. Fla. 1979).

cists as well as to its enforcement policy regarding statutory requirements that remain applicable to pharmacists. Two district court cases from the late 1970s provide the earliest and most significant discussion of the distinction.

In the first case, *Cedars North Towers Pharmacy v. United States*,[66] the court identified six factors for consideration in distinguishing between manufacturing and the "regular course" of retail pharmacy practice: 1) whether the pharmacy engages in periodic compounding of different drugs as opposed to compounding particular drugs on a regular basis; 2) whether the pharmacy compounds drugs for individual patient prescriptions as opposed to orders contemplating larger amounts for office use; 3) whether distribution is limited to a particular geographic area as opposed to nationwide distribution; 4) whether the product is being advertised or promoted; 5) whether particular compounded drugs are offered at wholesale prices; and 6) the percentage of the pharmacy's gross income received from sales of particular compounded drugs.[67]

One year later, in *United States v. Sene X Eleemosynary Corp.*,[68] the court identified an additional concern that must be considered: The relationship between the pharmacist and patient. The court examined, among other things, whether there was a one-on-one relationship between the patient and the pharmacist or between the patient and the patient's agent dealing with the pharmacist.[69]

Although the agency has issued several policy statements related to certain aspects of its position on regulation of the practice of pharmacy,[70] the most coherent and far-reaching statement was issued in 1992 in the form of a compliance policy guide.[71] This document sets forth the agency's criteria for determining when a pharmacy's compounding activities exceed the bounds of traditional pharmacy practice and are subject to regulation as manufacturing or distribution. The guiding principle of the 1992 compliance policy guide (CPG) is the agency's stated concern over pharmacies whose "manufacturing, distribution, and marketing practices... are far more consistent with those of drug manufacturers and wholesalers than with retail pharmacies."[72]

---

[66] *Id.*

[67] *Id.*

[68] *Id.*

[69] *Id.* at 978-79.

[70] One of the earliest policy statements related to hospital pharmacies. Compliance Policy Guide § 7132.06 (1980). This compliance policy guide (CPG) provides that hospital pharmacies that compound and/or repackage drugs are not required to register under FDCA § 510; 21 U.S.C. § 360 unless they sell to other hospitals or drugstores. *Id.* The CPG also provides that such pharmacies may compound drugs in limited quantities prior to the receipt of prescriptions, provided that the pharmacy can document a historical demand for the quantities it compounds. *Id.* Another policy statement issued as a draft guideline in 1984 provided parameters in which the agency would not seek to regulate compounding of radiopharmaceuticals. Nuclear Pharmacy Guideline: Criteria for Determining When to Register as a Drug Establishment (May 1984). In 1991, the agency addressed the practice of pharmacy in another compliance policy guide related to processing and repacking of approved drugs. Compliance Policy Guide 7132c.06 (1991). The CPG provides that approved drugs subjected to further processing or repacking may be regulated as new drugs and provides an exception for "manipulations performed within the practice of pharmacy, *consistent with the approved labeling* of the product." *Id.* (emphasis added). The CPG does not clarify whether the agency will regard any manipulation outside of approved labeling as subject to regulatory action. Such an action would appear unlikely, at least where directed by a physician's prescription.

[71] Manufacture, Distribution, and Promotion of Adulterated, Misbranded or Unapproved New Drugs for Human Use by State-Licensed Pharmacies, Compliance Policy Guide 7132.16 (1992) [hereinafter 1992 CPG].

[72] *Id.* at 2.

While stating that the agency will continue to defer to state and local officials' regulation of the "day-to-day practice of retail pharmacy and related activities," the 1992 CPG lists nine factors the agency will consider in determining whether to bring a regulatory action against a pharmacy under the FDCA.[73] Seven of the agency's criteria reflect the concerns similar to those expressed in the *Ceders* and *Sene X* decisions over the physician-patient-pharmacist relationship and the similarity of the pharmacy operation to commercial manufacture and distribution: 1) soliciting orders to compound specific drugs; 2) compounding commercially-available products in large quantities or on a regular basis; 3) using commercial-scale equipment for compounding drug products; 4) compounding drugs in anticipation of receiving prescriptions rather than after receiving valid prescriptions; 5) offering compounded drugs at wholesale prices to practitioners or to retail entities for resale; 6) distributing a significant quantity of compounded products out-of-state; and 7) violating applicable state law regulating the practice of pharmacy.[74] Two of the agency's criteria relate only to product integrity: 1) receiving, storing, or using drug substances without obtaining written assurances that the drug substance was made in an FDA-approved facility; and 2) receiving, storing, or using drug components that are not guaranteed to meet official compendia requirements.[75]

The 1992 CPG provides that the FDA may consider other factors in determining whether activities by pharmacists should be regulated under new drug provisions of the FDCA, and the agency has done so in a recent proposal to regulate positron emission tomography (PET) radiopharmaceuticals as new drugs. Even though such products are prepared at the site of administration and administered the same day, the agency determined that PET centers should be regulated as manufacturers because the process itself was deemed outside the regular course of pharmacy.[76] Consistent with this reasoning, the agency stated that the drug good manufacturing practice (GMP) regulations apply to the compounding of PET products and proposed a rule that would amend the GMP regulations to allow PET compounding centers to apply for an exception or alternative to the particular requirements in those regulations.[77]

■ Required Patient Information

The FDA has asserted authority to require pharmacists to provide special patient labeling for prescription drugs they dispense. For certain prescription drug products, the agency currently requires that a patient package insert (PPI) be included at the time of dispensing to provide patients with important information on significant and, possibly, life-threatening risks of the products. The FDA has, for example, promulgated regulations requiring specifically-worded PPIs for oral contraceptives and conjugated estrogens.[78] The agency's

---

[73] *Id.* at 4-5.

[74] *Id.* at 5.

[75] *Id.*

[76] Notice of Positron Emission Tomography Radiopharmaceutical Drug Products; Guidance; Public Workshop, 60 Fed. Reg. 10,594, 10,595 (1995). The agency noted that the process involved irradiation of a target material in a cyclotron and chemical synthesis in a programmed, automated apparatus prior to preparation of the final solution. *Id.* at 10,595.

[77] Current Good Manufacturing Practices for Finished Pharmaceuticals; Positron Emission Tomography, 60 Fed. Reg. 10,517 (1995).

[78] 21 C.F.R. §§ 310.501, 310.515.

authority to require PPIs for conjugated estrogens was upheld in a judicial challenge brought by drug manufacturers.[79] The court found that, while drugs dispensed by pharmacists were exempt from the requirement of adequate directions for use, PPIs could be required under the agency's authority to ensure that labeling bears all material facts.[80]

More recently the FDA has proposed a regulation that would require pharmacists to dispense approved patient labeling for most or all prescription drugs.[81] According to the agency, the proposed regulation would enable pharmacists to provide patients with "high-quality and balanced information to take home," in addition to oral counseling. The agency states in the proposal, however, that it intends to delay implementation of such regulation to allow an opportunity for the goals of its proposal to be met through voluntary, private-sector initiatives.[82]

Conclusion

Although the FDA has been willing to exercise greater regulatory control over pharmacists than over medical practitioners, the agency has left regulation of both professions largely to the states. The greater degree of regulation of pharmacists results mainly from the similarities of their activities to those of pharmaceutical manufacturing and distribution entities. As the lines between pharmacy, drug manufacturing and distribution, and health care delivery become less certain in today's health care marketplace, the FDA's current policies and precedents suggest an even more intrusive regulatory posture. This trend will almost certainly be countered, however, by the need for greater flexibility and efficiency in the health care marketplace and the loss of the marketplace model for which the FDCA was designed.

---

[79]   Pharmaceutical Mfrs Ass'n v. FDA, 484 F.Supp. 1179 (D. Del.), *aff'd per curiam*, 634 F.2d 106 (1980).

[80]   *Id.* at 1183-86, citing 21 U.S.C. § 321(n) (FDCA § 201(n)). The court also rejected arguments that the patient package insert (PPI) requirement constituted an unconstitutional interference in the practice of medicine, noting that the practice of medicine is subject to federal regulation and that the constitutional rights of physicians are derivative of patients' rights and do not extend beyond those rights. 484 F. Supp. at 1187-89.

[81]   *See* 60 Fed. Reg. 44,182 (1995). This proposal is similar in many respects to a regulation proposed by the agency in 1979 that would have required phased in PPI requirements for broad classes of prescription drugs. 44 Fed. Reg. 40,016 (1979). After issuing a final regulation in 1980, 45 Fed. Reg. 60,754 (1980), and proposing to implement the PPI requirement for certain classes of drugs in 1980, 45 Fed. Reg. 78,516 (1980), and in 1981, 46 Fed. Reg. 160 (1981), the agency abruptly stayed the effective date of the rule pursuant to an executive order from the newly inaugurated President, 46 Fed. Reg. 23,739 (1981), and revoked the rule the following year, 47 Fed. Reg. 39,147 (1982).

[82]   60 Fed. Reg. at 44,183.

chapter 16

International Harmonization
of the Regulation of Drugs and
Biologics

Linda R. Horton*
Philip Chao**
Walla Dempsey***
Eric Flamm****

Introduction

This chapter surveys the vast array of international cooperation and harmonization initiatives in the area of pharmaceuticals (drugs and biologics) for human use, with an emphasis on the Food and Drug Administion's (FDA) involvement in these activities. The agency's international activities focus on those matters that have real public health impact and the potential to assist the FDA in carrying out its mission.

This chapter describes U.S. laws bearing on the FDA's international pharmaceutical regulatory issues and provides a historical overview of the agency's international involvement. It then presents information on the international organizations and efforts that are the most important in international cooperation and harmonization for pharmaceuticals. Without question, the centerpiece of the agency's harmonization initiatives for pharmaceuticals is a novel and effective program known as ICH: the International Conference on Harmonization of Technical Requirements for Registration of Pharmaceuticals for Human Use. Consequently, ICH is a prominent topic in this chapter. The World Health Organization (WHO) and other international organizations also are discussed.

---

* Ms. Horton is Director, International Policy, FDA.
* Mr. Chao is Associate Director, International Policy, FDA.
* Ms. Dempsey, is a Microbiologist, Center for Drug Evaluation and Research, FDA.
* Dr. Flamm is Associate Director for International Policy, FDA.

The chapter then discusses the basic elements found in many countries' regulatory systems (registration, nomenclature and terminology, product identity and quality issues, labeling and advertising controls, prescription controls, and adverse event reporting) and describes key international activities relating to each.

International activities relating to preclinical and clinical testing and approval receive separate treatment in this chapter because the complexity of these activities, and the resources they require, have resulted in relatively few countries undertaking them. After a discussion of the European Medicines Evaluation Agency (EMEA), a brief overview of several other countries' approval systems and related activities follows.

Next, the chapter reviews international activities involving such special product categories as vaccines, blood, tissues, orphan drugs, alternative medicine, generic drugs, counterfeit drugs, and tobacco. Furthermore, it includes a discussion on compliance-related international pharmaceutical activities: good manufacturing practice regulations (GMPs), inspections, compliance information sharing, agreements between the FDA and other countries, import activities, and export activities. Finally, although the FDA concentrates on the safety, effectiveness, and quality of pharmaceuticals, the need of the pharmaceutical industry to be attentive to a wide range of international and national programs affecting the economic aspects of pharmaceutical policies is discussed. The most important of these, price controls, trade agreements, intellectual property protection, controlled substances activities, population control, and environmental issues, are discussed briefly.

Principal U.S. Laws on International Drug Regulatory Issues

The discussion that follows supplements that in the chapter on International Harmonization, Enforcement, and Trade Policy. Additional discussions of U.S. legal authority are found later. on registration and listing by foreign firms. on agreements with other countries, and in the specialized discussions on intellectual property protection, controlled substances control, and other matters in this chapter.

■ The Federal Food, Drug, and Cosmetic Act of 1938

International harmonization in the United States is achieved by use of the same processes for rules and guidance documents as govern other agency policymaking. Therefore, one of the most important authorities for FDA harmonization initiatives is section 701(a) of the Federal Food, Drug, and Cosmetic Act (FDCA),[1] which, with other relevant provisions in that act and the Administrative Procedure Act,[2] governs the FDA's actions when the agency wishes to accept an international standard. In some instances, rulemaking is required, while in others, such as most ICH initiatives, the FDA has achieved harmonization through guidance documents. For example, the FDA publishes each ICH guideline as

---

[1]   21 U.S.C. § 371 (1994)

[2]   Pub. L. No. 79-404, 60 Stat. 237 (1946) (codified at 5 U.S.C. §§ 551-706 (1994)).

a draft guidance document for public comment[3] and a final ICH guidance document in the *Federal Register.*

■ The Public Health Service Act

The general authority described in the chapter on International Harmonization, Enforcement, and Trade Policy applies to international pharmaceutical activities. Furthermore, as with drugs, the FDA's authority over biologics[4] applies equally to domestic and foreign manufacturers that wish to market these products in the United States.

Historical Background

■ The Drug Importation Act of 1848[5]

The first broad federal law applicable to drugs generally[6] typifies several persistent themes in the FDA's international activities: protection of U.S. consumers against harmful imports, recognition of international standards, and need for enforcement.

Consumer protection was needed, at the national level because state controls were not equal to European, Middle Eastern, and Asian exporters, among others, who were exporting to the United States a wide variety of toxic, substandard, mislabeled, and counterfeit drugs,[7] to the detriment of its soldiers in the Mexican War.[8] With three-quarters of the nation's drug imports entering the country through the port of New York, prominent New York pharmacists and physicians came to believe a federal law was needed, and in 1846 they persuaded the Secretary of the Treasury to station a physician as drug inspector in the New York port.[9] Two years later he reported that "[m]ore than one-half of many of the most important chemical and medicinal preparations, together with large quantities of crude drugs, come to us so much adulterated, or otherwise deteriorated, as to render them

---

3   The FDA considers the comments independently and in conjunction with other ICH partners. For the FDA's policy on development, issuance, and use of guidance documents, see 62 Fed. Reg. 8961 (Feb. 27, 1997).

4   42 U.S.C. § 262 (1994).

5   Act of June 26, 1848, 9 Stat. 237.

6   The first federal pharmaceutical law was an 1813 law to ensure the availability of genuine smallpox vaccine rather than fake vaccine. 2 Stat. 806. After an outbreak of smallpox that was blamed on vaccine furnished under the law, it was repealed on the premise that the subject was best left to local authorities. 3 Stat. 677 (1822). The Biologic Act passed 80 years later established a broad system of federal control. 32 Stat. 728 (1902).

7   *See* James Harvey Young, Pure Food: Securing the Federal Food and Drugs Act of 1906, at 10, and sources cited therein (Princeton Univ. Press 1989).

8   *Id.* at 6-17. Doubts about commercially available drugs, imports or domestic, led the U.S. Navy to set up a small laboratory in Brooklyn to make its own drugs! Edward Squibb, a navy doctor, went from directing the lab to founding a drug company bearing his name. *Id.* at 17 and sources cited therein.

9   *Id.* at 10.

not only worthless as a medicine, but often dangerous;" also, counterfeiting of respectable European labels was rife.[10]

Because many European countries already enacted had and were enforcing laws forbidding adulterated drugs, "[t]his country [had] become the grand mart and receptacle of all the refuse merchandise . . . not only from European warehouses, but from the whole eastern world."[11] "Good enough for America" was the European descriptor for "articles reduced by decay or ingenuity to American price."[12] Products shipped to the United States from the East also were bad; for example, opium from Turkey or Asia nearly always was adulterated with cheaper material to the extent that the effectiveness of morphine made from it was compromised.[13]

In the resulting Drug Importation Act of 1848, which assigned to U.S. Customs the task of judging drug acceptability, international recognition was key. Customs' decisionmaking criterion was whether "drugs, medicines, medicinal preparations . . . are found, in the opinion of the examiner, to be so far adulterated, or in any manner deteriorated, as to render them inferior in strength and purity to the standard established by the United States, Edinburgh, London, French and German pharmacopoeias and dispensatories."[14]

This early "international harmonization provision" is understandable when one considers that in 1848 the United States Pharmacopeia (USP) was only twenty-eight years old.[15] The various European pharmacopeias needed to be cited both to provide for comprehensive coverage of medicinal preparations then in use and to avoid undue trade barriers against others' acceptable products — needs that also drive today's international pharmaceutical activities. Only the USP and the National Formulary (NF) were cited as a source of drug standards in the Food and Drugs Act of 1906.[16] By the twentieth century, the American drug standards collections had become sufficiently comprehensive and authoritative that Congress no longer believed resort to European texts was needed.

With regard to the enforcement aspects of the 1848 Act, first domestic drugs were omitted because it was believed that the force of public opinion and, if necessary, state laws could deal with them. This optimistic appraisal was not borne out by experience in the latter half

---

[10] *Id.* at 12 (quoting a 1848 House Report, *Imported Adulterated Drugs, Medicines, Etc.*).

[11] *Id.*

[12] Jacob Bell, a British pharmacy leader and member of Parliament, *quoted in* BOSTON NEWS-LETTER (Aug. 16, 1750). *See* JAMES HARVEY YOUNG, *supra* note 7, at 7 and sources cited therein.

[13] LEWIS C. BECK, ADULTERATION OF VARIOUS SUBSTANCES USED IN MEDICINE AND THE ARTS, WITH THE MEANS OF DETECTING THEM: INTENDED AS A MANUAL FOR THE PHYSICIAN, THE APOTHECARY, AND THE ARTISAN (1846).

[14] 9 Stat. at 238. As a measure of the antiquity of the Import Drug Act, the next law recorded in the *Statutes at Large* appropriates funds for Revolutionary War pensions. *Id.* at 239.

[15] The USP was founded when 11 physicians met in Washington, D.C., in 1820 to establish the first compendium of standard drugs in the United States FDA Backgrounder, Milestones in U.S. Food and Drug Law History (Feb. 1995). More limited pharmacopeia were published by state pharmacy societies, the first in 1778. Thomas V. DiBacco, *The Medicine Makers*, WASH. POST, Aug. 22, 1995, at 15.

[16] Pub. L. No. 59-384, 34 Stat. 768 (1906). The 1906 Act allowed the marketing of drugs that did not meet the USP or NF standard if the variant standard of strength, quality, or purity was stated plainly on the label. *Id.* § 7, 34 Stat. at 769. The FDCA, Pub. L. No. 75-717, 52 Stat. 1040 (1938), cited the USP, the NF, and the official *Homeopathic Pharmacopeia of the United States*.

of the nineteenth century. Second, the enforcement provisions crafted in 1848 to handle adulterated imports — condemnation, re-exportation, or destruction — are essentially identical to those found in the 1906 Act and in present section 801 of the 1938 Act.[17] As it is today, the importer could challenge the government's decision.[18]

During the latter half of the 19th century, customs chemists in six ports — New York, Boston, Philadelphia, Baltimore, Charleston, and New Orleans — reduced entry of adulterated drugs, and news of strict enforcement discouraged European exporters from sending bad drugs to the United States.[19] Later, the enforcement of the law became ineffectual due to political interference, ineffective drug standards or methods of analysis, unqualified or corrupt examiners, or reimportation of rejected goods at another U.S. port with a laxer examiner,[20] thus setting the stage for additional legislation.

■ The Food and Drug Imports Act of 1890

A food and drug import control law was passed in 1890 to prohibit the importation of any "adulterated or unwholesome food or drug or any vinous, spirituous or malt liquors, adulterated or mixed with any poisonous or noxious chemical drug or other ingredient injurious to health."[21] Because the violation was a misdemeanor available remedies were forfeiture and prosecution.[22]

While the 1848 Act was administered by the Customs Service, the 1890 Act was administered by the Bureau of Chemistry in the Department of Agriculture, the predecessor to the FDA. Thus, the 1890 law was a precursor to the broader Food and Drugs Act of 1906.

■ The Food and Drugs Act of 1906

After the enactment of the Food and Drugs Act of 1906, the Bureau of Chemistry moved aggressively against substandard drug imports. For example, during the years 1909 to 1912, there were 1350 rejections of a total of 1931 drug imports offered, or seventy percent.[23] By the 1930s, the compliance of drug imports with FDA's requirements had improved: 12,016 drug imports were detained of 49,402 offered between 1930 and 1939, or twenty-four percent.[24] During that period, as now, many bulk drug ingredients were

---

[17] 21 U.S.C. § 381.

[18] At its own expense, an importer could secure a reexamination by a competent analytical chemist chosen by the customs collector. Act of June 26, 1848, 9 Stat. 237.

[19] JAMES HARVEY YOUNG, *supra* note 7, at 14.

[20] *Id.* at 15.

[21] 26 Stat. 414, 415 (1890).

[22] *Id.* For adulterated food or drink imports, the Act provided an additional remedy of suspending imports by means of a Presidential proclamation, with the embargo applicable to articles from countries listed in the proclamation.

[23] James C. Munch, *A Half-Century of Drug Control*, 11 FOOD DRUG COSM. L.J. 305 (1956).

[24] *Id.* A general improvement in the "crude drugs" imported during 1928 was noted, as compared to past years. "The number of detentions on the ground of the presence of dirt, foreign material, or substitute material fell below those of other years." U.S. DEP'T OF AGRIC., ANNUAL REPORT 684 (1928).

imported.[25] Another recurrent issue that has spanned this century has been the offering of drugs, including import drugs, with unproven therapeutic claims.[26]

■ The Federal Food, Drug, and Cosmetic Act of 1938

Although international issues were generally not an important consideration in the lengthy congressional deliberations that preceded the enactment of the FDCA, it was the combination (by a small American firm) of a European wonder drug—sulfanilamide—with a toxic solvent (diethylene glycol) that led to the death of more than 100 children and congressional passage of the law.[27]

Over the course of the twentieth century, and particularly after World War II, the FDA came to be recognized world-wide as a preeminent authority on public health protection in the field of pharmaceuticals, due to the agency activities documented elsewhere in this volume. As the agency's domestic responsibilities and expertise increased, the FDA's international role grew, as well. As the U.S. government generally took on extraordinary responsibility in the post-World War II international institutions, the FDA in its areas of responsibility became an important leader. When the WHO, created in 1948, initiated standard-setting functions for pharmaceuticals, the U.S. health agencies became key players, particularly on vaccine standards.[28]

The thalidomide tragedy of the 1960s marked a change in the FDA's stature, internationally as well as domestically. That the FDA was able to prevent the marketing in the United States of a teratogenic drug that had been approved for marketing by European counterparts fostered an appreciation of the agency's leadership role as public guardian,[29] and led to new requirements under the Drug Amendments of 1962.[30]

The FDA's international activities intensified in the late 1960s, the 1970s, and the early 1980s. Regular meetings with counterparts became an important FDA international activity, beginning with the initiation in 1972 of "Tripartite meetings" of the FDA and its counterparts in Canada and the United Kingdom, "Bilateral meetings" in 1989 with the European Commission, and eventually "Trilateral meetings" with Mexico and Canada in 1993 (after several years of bilateral meetings with Mexico.).

During the 1970s and 1980s, international pharmaceutical issues took an unpleasant turn, as the U.S. domestic regulatory environment shifted from the 1960s to 1970s era of praise for the FDA's caution (typified by thalidomide) — and accompanying congressional criti-

---

[25]   U.S. DEP'T OF AGRIC., ANNUAL REPORT 704 (1929).

[26]   *See, e.g.,* U.S. DEP'T OF AGRIC., ANNUAL REPORT 669 (1927) (products detained due to unproven claims for cancer, tuberculosis, influenza, and diabetes); FOOD & DRUG ADMIN., ANNUAL REPORT (1950) 17 (1950) (topping the list were hair growers; a Canadian bear oil and a preparation labeled in four languages for syphilis, tumors, ringworms, abscesses, malaria, and rheumatism, and "any other impurity of the blood shown on the skin, liver, bladder, or kidneys").

[27]   GOVERNMENT AGENCIES 253 (Donald Whitney Ed., 1983).

[28]   FOOD AND DRUG ADMIN., REPORT OF THE FDA TASK FORCE ON INTERNATIONAL HARMONIZATION, app. E, at 1 (1992).

[29]   Dr. Frances Kelsey received the Presidential Award of Distinguished Federal Civilian Service from President John Kennedy. P. B. Hutt, *Investigations and Reports on the Food and Drug Administration, in* SEVENTY-FIFTH ANNIVERSARY COMMEMORATIVE VOLUME OF FOOD AND DRUG LAW 41 (FDLI 1984).

[30]   Pub. L. No. 87-781, 76 Stat. 780 (1962).

cism of what was viewed as insufficient caution on some drug approvals[31] — to strong criticism of the FDA for its role in "drug lag."[32] Compared with drug approvals in Great Britain and other countries, did the FDA's approvals take longer and occur later?

With the public's attention directed first to cancer deaths, and later to AIDS, the idea that useful therapy might be withheld due to bureaucratic delays seemed unacceptable. In 1979, the FDA acknowledged that some of its approvals took longer, but not for drugs that were therapeutic breakthroughs.[33] The agency experts also maintained that it made fewer mistakes in its approvals, in that fewer approved products in the United States later needed to be removed from the market.[34]

Whether a drug lag existed continued to be an issue in the mid-1990s. Early versions of various FDA reform bills introduced in the 104th Congress included "international hammer" provisions that if a sponsor who had filed a new drug application with the FDA and not received approval by the specified performance targets, but had met the marketing requirements of either the United Kingdom Medicines Control Agency or the European Union (EU), its drug would be deemed approved for the U.S. market unless the FDA, within thirty days, published a notice disapproving the application and setting forth the reasons for disapproval.[35] Commissioner Kessler, strongly opposed this provision as going too far.[36] Although the agency accepts foreign data and is working toward harmonizing data requirements the bill's provision to compel acceptance of approvals from the United Kingdom and the EU, with no counterpart provision that would compel the FDA to withdraw a drug withdrawn in the same countries, created concern.

At the end of 1995, the Commissioner made a presentation[37] that included statistics from two studies, one by the General Accounting Office (GAO)[38] and another by the FDA's

---

[31] Thomas Austern, *Drug Regulation and the Public Health: Side Effects and Contraindications of Congressional Committee Post Hoc Medical Judgments*, 19 FOOD DRUG COSM. L.J. 259 (1964); Peter Barton Hutt, *Balanced Government Regulation of Consumer Products*, 31 FOOD DRUG COSM. L.J. 592 (1976); Peter Barton Hutt, *Investigations and Reports on the Food and Drug Administration, in* SEVENTY-FIFTH ANNIVERSARY COMMEMORATIVE VOLUME, *supra* note 29, at 27.

[32] The term "drug lag" was coined by Dr. William Wardell in *The Drug Lag and American Therapeutics: An International Comparison*, a paper delivered before the Fifth International Congress of Pharmacology (July 26, 1972). For the voluminous literature on the subject, see HUTT & MERRILL, FOOD AND DRUG LAW CASES AND MATERIALS 583 (2d ed. 1991). *See generally* SEVENTY-FIFTH ANNIVERSARY COMMEMORATIVE VOLUME, *supra* note 27. One indicator of the dominance of the debate in FDA circles is that, in the 1984 predecessor to this volume, nearly half the references to international topics were on drug lag. Of 32 references to international issues — an amazingly small number considering the wealth of activities covered in the current chapter — some 14 concerned "drug lag." *Id.* at 51-64, 78, 256, 268, 270 (with multiple references on some pages). The other 18 international references involved imports, *id.* at 30, 32, 40; historical incidents, *id.* at 41, 73, 74, 75, 77, 79, 221, 222, 223, 228, 317; and drug abuse control, *id.* at 286, 287, 289, 291.

[33] *Compare* Donald Kennedy, *A Calm Look at "Drug Lag,"* 239 JAMA 423 (1978) *with* William Wardell, *A Close Inspection of the "Calm Look,"* 239 JAMA 2004 (1978).

[34] *Id.*

[35] S. 1477, 104th Cong., 1st Sess. § 4 (1995); H.R. 3199, 104th Cong, 1st Sess. § 4 (1995).

[36] *Revitalizing New Product Development From Clinical Trials Through FDA Review: Hearing on S. 1477 Before the Senate Comm. on Labor and Public Welfare,* 104th Cong., 2d Sess. 120 (1996).

[37] David A. Kessler, M.D., Comm'r of Food and Drugs, Remarks at the FDLI Annual Educational Conference, Washington, D.C. (Dec. 12, 1995).

[38] GENERAL ACCOUNTING OFFICE, FDA DRUG APPROVAL: REVIEW TIME HAS DECREASED IN RECENT YEARS, (1995) (Doc. No. GAO/PEMD-96-1).

staff[39] Both showed that the drug lag had been remedied. Commissioner Kessler presented additional statistics demonstrating that the FDA's approval times were competitive with those of the United Kingdom's Medicines Control Agency[40] and significantly faster than those of the EMEA and the Japanese Ministry of Health and Welfare.

Although some disputed the FDA's data,[41] the GAO's finding that approval processes in many industrialized nations may be converging, with approval times over the past ten years for France, Germany, Japan, the United Kingdom and the United States moving toward a similar review time, was not disputed.[42] As the end of the 104th Congress neared, congressional Committee staff dropped the "international hammer" provision from the bills.[43] By the end of 1996, Commissioner Kessler compiled more statistics and stated that additional approval figures showed that the FDA was ahead of other countries with regard to speedy as well as the sound and conservate, drug approval decisions.[44] By then attention had shifted to improving the efficiency of the drug development process, exemplified by a 1996 conference at Georgetown University.[45]

Organizations for Cooperation and Harmonization

■ The International Conference for the Harmonization of the Technical Requirements for Pharmaceuticals for Human Use[46]

ICH is a highly successful program that is an example of how the FDA has joined with

---

39   "Of the 58 new molecular entities that were approved in both the U.S. and the UK, 30 of them were first approved in the [U.S., which] . . . clearly shows we are not behind . . . . Of the 44 drugs approved in both the U.S. and Germany, we approved 31 of them first . . . . And in Japan, we first approved 10 of the 14 compounds eventually used in both countries. [As for] when these drugs became available to patients . . . the U.S. and the U.K. . . . were "pretty close" [while the U.S. is considerably faster than Germany and Japan with respect to these drugs.]" Remarks by Commissioner David A. Kessler, *supra* note 37, at 5-6.

40   The GAO found that in 1994 the approval times for new molecular entities actually were shorter in the United States than in the United Kingdom. GAO REPORT, *supra*, note 38, at 41. As is discussed in this chapter the GAO cautioned those who would compare the FDA and the Medicines Control Agency that the U.K. process is complex, with Agency review being only one part.

41   G. Mossinghoff, President, PhRMA, called the report "misleading" because "the key issue is 'total development time' for new drugs," and said reform is still necessary to reduce regulation of early clinical research. *Quoted in* J. Schwartz, *FDA Graded Highly on Relative Speed of Review Process*, WASH. POST, Nov. 8, 1995, at A15. Later, Mr. Mossinghoff said that the FDA's study looked at less than one half of the 126 new drugs approved between 1990 and 1994. Of the 126, 85 were first approved abroad. Of the 28 new chemical entities approved in 1995, 18 (or 64%) were first approved abroad. F-D-C REP. — ("The Pink Sheet"), Jan. 22, 1996, at 11.

42   GAO Report, *supra* note 38, at 41.

43   HOUSE OF REPRESENTATIVES, COMMERCE COMM. STAFF, THE DRUG AND BIOLOGICAL PRODUCTS REFORM ACT OF 1996: STAFF DISCUSSION DRAFT (1996).

44   David A. Kessler, Comm'r of Food and Drugs, Remarks at the FDLI Annual Educational Conference, Washington, D.C. (December 10, 1996).

45   *Symposium — Drug Development: Who Knows Where the Time Goes?* 52 FOOD & DRUG L.J. 141 (1997).

46   Sharon Smith Holston, *An Overview of International Harmonization*, 52 FOOD & DRUG L.J. 196 (1997); Paul M. Booth, *FDA Implantation of Standards Developed by the International Conference on Harmonization* , 52 FOOD &

counterparts in other countries to write harmonized guidelines that protect the public and benefit industry by reducing duplicative testing. Since 1989, the FDA has worked on ICH with the European Commission and Japan's Ministry of Health and Welfare.

The purposes of ICH are to: 1) provide a forum for dialogue between regulatory agencies and the pharmaceutical industry on differences in the technical requirements for product registration (i.e., requirements for product marketing) in the EU, Japan, and the United States; 2) identify areas where modifications in technical requirements or greater mutual acceptance of research and development procedures could lead to more efficient use of human, animal, and material resources without compromising safety, quality, or efficacy; and 3) make recommendations on practical ways to achieve greater harmonization in the interpretation and application of technical guidelines and requirements for registration.

From its inception, ICH has included participants not only from the three government agencies but also from industry. Manufacturers can help identify inconsistencies in testing or submission requirements. Industry participates through the principal trade association for the research oriented manufacturers in each of the regions, as discussed below. Also, the ICH Secretariat is administered in conjunction with the International Federation of Pharmaceutical Manufacturers Associations (IFPMA) in Geneva. The IFPMA is an non-governmental organization, founded in 1968, which has had an official voice in WHO on behalf of the pharmaceutical industry since 1971.[47] The Pharmaceutical Research and Manufacturers Association (PhRMA) is the U.S. member of the IFPMA.

ICH operates under the direction of the ICH Steering Committee, which is comprised of representatives from the FDA, the EU,[48] the Japanese Ministry of Health, PhRMA, the European Pharmaceutical Industry Association (EPIA), and the Japanese Pharmaceutical Manufacturers Association (JPMA). Official observer status has been given to WHO, the European Free Trade Area (EFTA), and the Health Protection Branch (HPB) of Canada (which adopts ICH guidelines as Canadian guidelines). WHO publicizes ICH's harmonized guidelines to WHO members.

ICH has carried out its activities not only through large public meetings marking ICH progress —ICH-1 in Brussels in 1991, ICH-2 in Orlando in 1993, ICH-3 in Yokohama in 1995, and ICH-4 in Brussels in 1997 — but also through an intense schedule of continu-

---

DRUG L.J. 203, 204-05 n. 11 (1997); Stephen A. Bent & Paul M. Booth, *ICH Sets Standards for Drug Developers; Convergence with the EU and Japan Seeks to Reduce Drug Approval Time,* Cost, NAT'L L.J., July 18, 1996, at C1; *Continuing Success for ICH,* HEALTH HORIZONS, Winter 1995/1996, at 14-15; Joseph Contrera, *Comment, The Food and Drug Administration and the International Conference on Harmonization: How Harmonious Will International Pharmaceutical Regulations Become?,* 8 ADMIN. L.J. AM. U. 927 (1995); David A. Kessler, *Harmonization,* PHARMACEUTICAL ENGINEERING, Jan./Feb. 1994, at 38-40; Peter O'Donnell, *GCPs in Europe on the Harmonization Agenda,* APPLIED CLINICAL TRIALS, Aug. 1993, at 20-23.

47 INTERNATIONAL FED'N OF PHARMACEUTICAL MFRS. ASS'N, LEGAL AND PRACTICAL REQUIREMENTS FOR THE REGISTRATION OF DRUGS (MEDICINAL PRODUCTS) FOR HUMAN USE, at ii (1980). The IFPMA also has consultative status with the World Intellectual Property Organization, the United Nations (U.N.) Industrial Development Organization (UNIDO), the U.N. Conference on Trade and Development (UNCTAD), and the Council of Europe. It is on the Roster of Non-Government Organizations of the U.N. Economic and Social Council. *Id.*

48 In 1997, the EU members were Austria, Belgium, Denmark, Finland, France, Germany, Greece, Ireland, Italy, Luxembourg, the Netherlands, Portugal, Spain, Sweden, and the United Kingdom. Applicants for accession to the EU, as of 1997, were Bulgaria, the Czech Republic, Estonia, Hungary, Latvia, Lithuania, Poland, Romania, Slovakia, and Slovenia. Other countries that have expressed interest in membership are Cyprus, Malta, and Turkey.

ous guideline-drafting by representatives of the six ICH members, with approximately fifty working groups (Expert Working Groups) that have met an average of four times each year.

The work products of ICH consist of a series of consensus guidance documents. These guidance documents, after successive ICH steps of review and acceptance including an opportunity for public review and comment in the respective jurisdictions, are forwarded to the regulatory agencies with the expectation that they will be formally adopted by the agencies. The ICH steps are:

- Step 1 Consensus sought — Technical experts sign.
- Step 2 Steering Committee signs, and public comment or consultation is sought at the national level by regulators.
- Step 3 Comments reviewed — drafts revised by technical experts.
- Step 4 Final draft endorsed by regulatory agency members of steering committee, and draft is prepared for adoption at the national level.
- Step 5 Final guideline adopted at national level by three regions.

The FDA in general adopts ICH guidelines as guidance documents rather than as rules. An example of when rulemaking was necessary was the agency's revision of its adverse experience reporting regulations for drugs and biologics to conform them to an ICH guideline.[49] Furthermore, the FDA employs a notice-and-comment process in adopting ICH guidelines merely as guidance, in accordance with the agency's good guidance practices policy.[50]

The table shows the ICH guidelines that have been published by the FDA at Step 2 for public comment, at Step 5, or both, as of July 1997:

Table 1

SAFETY (S)			
No.	Topic	Step 2	Step 5
S1A	Conditions Which Require Carcinogenicity Studies	8/21/95 60 FR 43,498	3/1/96 61 FR 8154
S1B	Carcinogenicity: Use of 2 Rodent Species	8/21/96 61 FR 43,298	
S1C	Dose Selections for Carcinogenicity Studies	3/1/94 59 FR 9752	3/1/95 60 FR 11,278

---

49   59 Fed.Reg. 54,046 (Oct. 27, 1994).

50   62 Fed. Reg. 8961 (Feb. 27, 1997).

Table 1 (con't)

S1C Adden.	Addendum to Dose Selection for Carcinogenicity Studies of Pharmaceuticals	4/2/97 62 FR 15,715	
S2A	Scientific Aspects of Genotoxicity Tests	9/22/94 59 FR 48,734	4/24/96 61 FR 18,198
S2B	Genotoxicity: Definition of Core Battery Tests	4/3/97 62 FR 16,026	
S3	Assessment of Systemic Exposure in Toxicity Studies	3/1/94 59 FR 9755	3/1/95 60 FR 11,274
S3B	Repeated Dose Tissue Distribution Studies	3/1/94 59 FR 9748	3/1/95 60 FR 11,274
S4	Single Dose and Repeat Dose Toxicity Tests	8/26/96 61 FR 43,934	
S5A	Detection of Toxicity to Reproduction for Medicinal Products	4/16/93 59 FR 21,074	9/22/94 60 FR 48,746
S5B	Detection of Toxicity to Reproduction; Addendum re: Male Fertility	8/21/95 60 FR 43,500	4/5/96 61 FR 15,360
S6	Safety Studies for Biotechnological Products	4/4/97 62 FR 16,438	

Table 2

EFFICACY (E)			
No.	Topic	Step 2	Step 5
E1A	Extent of Population Exposure Required to Assess Chemical Safety	3/1/94 59 FR 9746	3/1/95 60 FR 11,270

Table 2 (con't)

E2A	Clinical Safety Data Management: Definitions & Standards for Expedited Reporting	7/9/93 58 FR 37,408	3/1/95 60 FR 11,284
E2B	Clinical Safety Data Management: Forms of Reporting	10/1/96 61 FR 51,287	
E2C	Clinical Data Safety Management: Periodic Safety Updates	4/5/96 61 FR 15,352	7/17/96 61 FR 67,320
E3	Structure & Content of Clinical Study Reports	8/23/95 60 FR 43,910	7/17/96 61 FR 67,320
E4	Dose-Response Information to Support Drug Registration	7/9/93 58 FR 37,402	11/9/94 59 FR 55,972
E5	Ethnic Factors in Acceptability of Foreign Data		
E6	Good Clinical Practices	8/17/95 60 FR 42,948	5/9/97 62 FR 25,692
E6A, E6B	GCPs: Investigator's Brochure; Addenda on Essential Documents	8/9/94 59 FR 40,772	5/9/97 62 FR 25,692
E7	Studies in Support of Special Populations; Geriatrics	4/16/93 58 FR 21,082	8/2/94 59 FR 39,398
E8	General Guidelines/ Considerations for Clinical Trials	5/30/97 62 FR 29,540	
E9	Statistical Principles for Clinical Trials	5/9/97 62 FR 25,712	

Table 3

QUALITY (Q)			
Q1A	Stability Testing on New Drug Substances and Products	4/16/93 58 FR 21,087	9/22/94 59 FR 48,754
Q1B	Photostability Testing of New Drug Substances & Products	3/7/96 61 FR 9310	5/16/97 62 FR 27,116
Q1C	Stability Testing for New Dosage Forms	3/6/96 61 FR 9060	5/9/97 62 FR 25,634
Q2A	Validation of Analytical Procedures	3/1/94 59 FR 9750	3/1/95 60 FR 11,260
Q2B	Validation of Analytical Methods	3/7/96 61 FR 9316	5/19/97 62 FR 27,464
Q3A	Impurities in New Drug Substances	9/22/94 59 FR 48,740	1/4/96 61 FR 372
Q3B	Impurities; Extensions of Current Guideline	3/19/96 61 FR 11,268	5/19/97 62 FR 27,454
Q3C	Impurities; Residual Solvents	5/2/97 62 FR 24,302	
Q5A	Viral Safety Evaluation of Biotechnology Products Derived from Cell Lines of Human or Animal Origin	5/10/96 61 FR 21,882	
Q5B	Analysis of Expression of Construct in Cells for Production of r-DNA Derived Protein Products	8/21/95 60 FR 43,496	2/23/96 61 FR 7006
Q5C	Stability Testing of Biotech/Biological Products	8/21/95 60 FR 43,501	7/10/96 61 FR 35,466

Table 3 (con't)

Q5D	Biotech Products: Cell Substrates	5/2/97 62 FR 24,312	

Table 4

MEDICAL INFORMATION (M)			
M1	Medical information terminology		
M2	Electronic Standards for Transfer of Information of Data		
M3	Timing of Pre-clinical Studies in Relation to Clinical Trials	5/2/97 62 FR 24,320	

Building on past ICH successes, the participants have launched new topics on biotechnology, clinical trials, medical terminology, and electronic standards for the transfer of regulatory information. The latter topic was an exciting development as it involves a partnership between ICH and others having an interest in international standardization of safety-related terminology for pharmaceuticals: the Council for International Organizations for Medical Sciences (CIOMS), WHO, and the U.K. Medicines Control Agency.

To broaden participation in ICH, the FDA has taken steps to share information with, and obtain views from, generic trade associations and consumer organizations through meetings and other means.[51] In 1995 and 1996, the FDA began working with its ICH partners to involve generic industry representatives directly in meetings on draft guidelines that might affect them, i.e., drug quality topics. Generic industry representatives have achieved equitable status on expert working groups on topics that affect them, although some would still prefer the formal status of Steering Committee membership, as well.[52]

With the ICH IV meeting in Brussels in July 1997, ICH moved principally to a maintenance stage. Preceding the meeting, the ICH Steering Committee held numerous discussions concerning the future of ICH. FDA representatives attempted to persuade its ICH partners to move toward a Regulatory Forum in which an expanded group of regulatory agencies would form a core group, to be joined by industry representatives as needed. This proposal did not find support, although it was agreed that certain topics, e.g., GMPs or regulatory agency review practices, might be handled in cooperation with the broader

---

[51] *See, e.g.*, Discussion of Activities of the International Conference on Harmonization of Technical Requirements for the Registration of Pharmaceuticals for Human Use; Notice of Public Meeting, 59 Fed. Reg. 8648 (Feb. 23, 1994). For a criticism of ICH transparency, see Paul M. Booth, *FDA Implementation of Standards Developed by the International Conference on Harmonization, supra* note 46.

[52] ICH STEERING COMM., SUMMARY OF DECISIONS 1 (Mar. 5-6, 1997). This issue is discussed further in this chapter.

groups. The following was proposed by the IFPMA secretariat as a statement of principles:

> Where ICH actions on new issues, or on follow-up of existing guidelines, have implications for parties outside the direct membership of ICH, or where the consensus building process could benefit from input of specialist expertise, ICH will develop mechanisms to accommodate the need for broader access. These mechanisms may first focus on input at a regional level within the three ICH regions, but participation in Working Groups which are established by the Steering Committee may also be broadened appropriately.[53]

For example, if ICH takes on as a topic the harmonization of GMPs for bulk pharmaceuticals, it could broaden its participation in the working group so as to include participants in an effort already underway in the Pharmaceutical Inspection Cooperation Scheme.

■ The World Health Organization

WHO was founded as a result of a 1946 International Health Conference, chaired by the U.S. Surgeon General, and began operations in 1948.[54] The statutory aim of WHO is to attain the highest possible level of health for all people in the world. The WHO Constitution contains several provisions that bear on the organization's drug programs: Article 2 directs WHO to develop, establish, and promote international standards with respect to food, biological, pharmaceutical, and similar programs"; Article 23 empowers the Health Assembly to make recommendations on any matter within WHO's competence; and Article 21 gives the Assembly the authority to adopt regulations, namely "standards with respect to the safety, purity, and potency of biological, pharmaceutical, and similar products moving in international commerce" as well as "advertising and labelling of all biological, pharmaceutical and similar products moving in international commerce."[55] Because the United States subscribed to WHO by executive order, it does not have treaty status.[56] As WHO is an international organization, not a supranational organization, the resolutions of the World Health Assembly and the approved policies of the Organization are not binding on members. Also, Congress specifically stated that its permission for the President to accept membership in WHO did not empower WHO to enact legislation for the United States.[57] Therefore, any code or regulation issued by WHO requires domestic action such as legislation or rulemaking before it can have any legal effect in the United States.

As of 1997, 191 countries are members of WHO. Its headquarters is in Geneva and it has six regional offices. Its decisionmaking bodies are a World Health Assembly (representa-

---

[53] International Conference on Harmonization, The Future of ICH (1997).

[54] World Health Org., A Brief Overview of WHO's Activities in the Drug Field With Emphasis on PHA Activities (1993) (PHARM/84.23 Rev.5). This section of the chapter relies heavily on this WHO publication, which is updated regularly and available from WHO's Drug Regulatory Support Unit, WHO, 1211, Geneva 27, Switzerland.

[55] Allyn Lise Taylor, *Making the World Health Organization Work: A Legal Framework for Universal Access to the Conditions for Health,* 18 Am. J.L. & Med. 301 (Winter 1992).

[56] James R. Phelps, *The New International Economic Order and the Pharmaceutical Industry,* 37 Food Drug Cosm. L.J. 200 (1982).

[57] 22 U.S.C. § 290 (1994).

tives of all members countries), which meets once a year, and an Executive Board (thirty-one members), which meets twice a year.

Important WHO activities include:

- International harmonization of drug regulations. A 1992 resolution by the World Health Assembly noted the initiatives by regulatory agencies and the pharmaceutical industries in ICH and the International Conference of Drug Regulatory Authorities (ICDRA),[58] and urged member states to review and adopt, where appropriate, through national processes internationally accepted standards for testing and registering pharmaceuticals and biologicals.[59]
- Advice to countries on national drug regulatory authorities.[60] Advice covers laws and regulations, enforcement powers, technical competence, advisory bodies, independence of operation, licensing for products, manufacturers, and distributors, new drug assessments (which are discouraged for small regulatory authorities), and authorization for clinical trials.
- Advice to countries on developing national drug policies. Published in 1988,[61] an update was underway in 1996-1997 following a 1995 expert consultation.[62]

The Action Program on Essential Drugs aims at collaboration with members to ensure a regular supply at the lowest possible cost and rational use of a selected number of safe and effective drugs and vaccines of acceptable quality.[63] There is concern that the WHO "essential drugs" program is undermining global health due to production of antibiotic resistance from overuse of drugs listed as essential.[64] Also, U.S. pharmaceutical companies have been affected adversely by decisions of international and national institutions to treat the essential drugs list as a formulary, with the result that superior products from innovative companies may be discriminated against, as compared with lower-cost generics, and state-of-the-art therapy is not made available.

WHO has, begun work on a model formulary, to provide model general information and information on the prototype drug on the essential drugs list.[65] The formulary would be

---

[58] WHA 45.28, Harmonizing drug regulations, 45th World Health Assembly (May 1992). ICDRA is discussed in the next section of the chapter.

[59] World Health Org., 45th World Health Assembly Resolution, "Harmonizing Drug Regulations," Geneva, Switz. (May 11, 1992).

[60] *Guiding Principles for Small National Drug Regulatory Authorities*, 3 WHO DRUG INFORMATION 43 (1989); D.C. Jayasuriya, Medicinal Products Regulation in Developing countries: Concepts, Issues, and Approaches, WHO, Geneva (1995).

[61] World Health Org., Guidelines for developing national drug policies (1988). These guidelines had resulted from a request by the WHO Conference of Experts on the Rational Use of Drugs, a request that was repeated by the 39th World Health assembly in 1986 in a resolution on the rational use of drugs. WHA39.27.

[62] World Health Org., Report of the WHO Expert Committee on National Drug Policies, Geneva, Switz (June 19-23, 1995) (1996 draft). The 1996 draft seems to assume that the member countries to whom the report is directed operate highly centralized, planned economies, although most countries are moving to free market economies in which decisions about investment in drug manufacturing facilities are made in the private sector for economic reasons, rather than governmental preferences.

[63] Ursula Wasserman, *WHO: Essential Drugs for Developing Countries*, 16 J. WORLD TRADE L. 444 (1982).

[64] WORLD HEATH ASSEMBLY, IMPLEMENTATION OF WHO'S REVISED DRUG STRATEGY: SAFETY AND EFFICACY OF PHARMACEUTICAL PRODUCTS 4 (1992); W.E. Farrar, 152 J. INFECTIOUS DISEASES 1103 (1985).

[65] SCRIP, Oct. 1, 1996, at 17.

comprised of twenty-nine sections, and the first draft section on anesthetics confirmed industry's concerns that some products would be included, but not others.

Another restrictive policy is the WHO International Guidelines for Drug Donations, which states that "all donated drugs or their generic equivalents should be approved for use in the recipient country and appear on the national list of essential drugs, or if a national list is not available, on the WHO Model List of Essential Drugs unless specifically requested otherwise by the recipient." If the recipient country is in a highly chaotic or needy state, the requirements seem excessive in prescribing that the country approve the drug, add it to a national essential drugs list, or explicitly request it as a donation, even though it is not on a national or WHO drugs list.

WHO is a leading international organization in standard-setting for pharmaceuticals, particularly biological products.

■ International Conference of Drug Regulatory Authorities

In 1980, the FDA convened a meeting to which the agency invited the heads of the drug regulatory authorities from all around the world. Attendees found the meeting worthwhile, and ICDRA was born. ICDRA is comprised from representatives of more than 100 countries, meets biennially, and is viewed by WHO as its principal network of formally designated information officers.[66] A list of topics covered at the Eighth ICDRA, which met in Bahrain in November 1996, shows the wide range of topics covered and the unique role of this group as compared to the approval-oriented focus of ICH: an update on WHO activities and discussions of ICH guidelines (to promote acceptance by non-ICH countries), information exchange for small regulatory authorities, control of imports and exports through certificates, the role of a quality control laboratory, clinical trials, ethical drug promotion, pharmacovigilance, biotechnology, multisource (generic) drugs, medical use of controlled substances, herbal medicine, dietary supplements, counterfeit drugs, intellectual property protection, information technology, health care, and pharmacoeconomics.[67]

■ Council for International Organizations of Medical Sciences

Officials from both the Center of Biologics Evaluation and Research (CBER) and the Center for Drug Evaluation and Research (CDER) also participate in a consensus standard-setting activity sponsored by CIOMS that is aimed at standardizing medical definitions and adverse experience reporting.

■ The Organization for Economic Cooperation and Development

The Organization for Economic Cooperation and Development (OECD) the most advanced economies in the world. It has been a leader in harmonization of good laboratory practices (GLPs) and chemical testing guidelines for pesticides and toxic chemicals.

---

[66] FOOD & DRUG ADMIN., REPORT OF THE FDA TASK FORCE ON INTERNATIONAL HARMONIZATION app. G 1992 (letter from J. Dunne, Dir., World Health Org. Mar. 13, 1992.

[67] Roger Williams, FDA, Trip Report from ICDRA meeting, Bahrain (Nov. 10-13, 1996).

An OECD decision is binding on OECD members while a recommendation is merely advisory.[68] Before the FDA or a regulated firm can be bound, however, the FDA must employ notice-and-comment rulemaking.[69]

OECD has issued three decisions of particular interest to the FDA. First, a 1981 Decision on Mutual Acceptance of Data sets forth conditions under which data generated in the testing of chemicals in an OECD member country shall be accepted in other OECD countries for the purposes of assessment and other uses relating to the protection of man and the environment.[70] A 1989 Council Decision-Recommendation places more stringent requirements on countries to assure compliance with GMP requirements, as well as mechanisms to strengthen information exchange among OECD countries.[71] Finally, in 1997, OECD considered a Decision to allow non-OECD member countries to participate in OECD meetings relating to the 1981 and 1989 acts.[72] The applicability of these three decisions to pharmaceuticals was a topic of discussion in 1997.[73]

■ Scientific, Industry, and Consumer Organizations

A variety of nongovernmental organizations are active in the area of pharmaceuticals, including the IFPMA, the Commonwealth Pharmaceutical Association (CPA), the International Pharmacy Federation, the International Union of Pharmacology (IUHAR), the International Union of Pure and Applied Chemistry, and the World Federation of Proprietary Medicines Manufacturers. In addition, U.S. professional organizations such as the PDA (originally the Parenteral Drug Association) and the Drug Information Association have widened their international activities in recent years. For example, between 1989 and 1996, PDA expanded its field of interest beyond its original focus on parental drugs, established chapters in Canada and Japan, and signed cooperative agreements with similar organizations in Europe and Asia.[74]

■ Standards Organizations

The FDA is also involved in voluntary, consensus standards-development organizations such as the International Organization for Standardization (ISO), the American National Standards Institute, and the American Society for Testing and Materials. These activities

---

[68]　Organization for Economic Cooperation & Development, Rules of Procedure of the Organization, Rule 18, at 15 (June 1982).

[69]　Community Nutrition Institute v. Young, 818 F.2d 943 (D.C. Cir. 1987).

[70]　Decision of the Council concerning the Mutual Acceptance of Data in the Assessment of Chemicals, C (81) 30 (Final) (May 12, 1981).

[71]　Council Decision-Recommendation on Compliance with Principles of Good Laboratory Practice, C (89) 87 (Final) (Oct. 2, 1989).

[72]　Draft Council decision on adherence of non-member countries to the Council acts related to the mutual acceptance of data in the assessment of chemicals, ENV/EPOC/MIN (95) 7.

[73]　See infra text accompanying notes 134-36.

[74]　PDA, A Forum for Scientific Excellence 22-23 (Oct. 1996). Since 1994, "PDA" is the organization's official name, and its tagline is "An International Association for Pharmaceutical Science and Technology." Id. at 30.

are central to the program of the FDA's Center for Devices and Radiological Health. Several voluntary standards activities also are of interest to CBER and CDER.[75]

Basic Elements of Regulatory Systems

Not all countries make independent approval decisions on pharmaceuticals.[76] Many watch closely for approval decisions to first be made by respected counterparts, e.g., by demanding an export certificate or similar evidence of approval in the country of origin. Because of the complexity of the pharmaceutical decisionmaking process and the challenge of marshalling the expertise needed for decisionmaking, many countries rely heavily on decisions made by the United States, EU, and Japan.[77]

The ICH is contributing to the reduction of disparities in applications for marketing authorization because the specific criteria used in assessments of safety, efficacy, and quality for marketing approval continues to vary widely.

■ Registration and Listing

Most countries have some form of registration for pharmaceutical products. Some have contended multiple registration processes and requirements as a significant barrier to international pharmaceutical trade, claiming that many registration requirements favor local manufacturers.

Among countries, the definition of registration varies. In some countries, "registration" refers to the approval process; in others such as the United States, "registration" refers to a submission of information about each manufacturer along with a "listing" of its products.[78]

The requirements for registering products varies from country to country. In some countries, drug manufacturers, including foreign manufacturers, must register with the appropriate regulatory agency. In others, drug importers are required to register, or all registration must be handled by a locally incorporated company. Fees are collected by several countries.

■ Nomenclature and Terminology

Unique product names are important to avoid prescription errors and to aid in standardization activities. Similar product names for different approved drugs in different countries can be a problem, particularly among nations that have agreed to facilitate trade or com-

---

[75] *See infra* text accompanying notes 241 to 285.

[76] The International Federation of Pharmaceutical Manufacturers Associations (IFPMA) published a useful compilation of information on countries' regulatory sysems for pharmaceuticals.

[77] The U.S. EU, and Japan are fairly self-reliant in their drug approval decisionmaking.

[78] 21 U.S.C. § 360; 21 C.F.R. pt. 207.

merce between their countries. The converse — same names for different products — may also present, although this is less of a problem in countries with developed nomenclature systems.

Since 1953, WHO has maintained a program that provides for the selection and publication of International Nonproprietary Names (INN) of drug substances. WHO publishes cumulative lists of drug substances at regular intervals that cross references information to other nomenclature sources, including the national nonproprietary names and the ISO names. The lists also contain molecular formulas and Chemical Abstracts Service registry numbers, but they do not cover drug products that were well established in 1953, for example as morphine. Furthermore, INNs are for drug substances and not trademark names.

Medical Information Activities Prior to ICH.

There have been several attempts to harmonize the terminology used in adverse drug experience (ADE) reporting. Among the terminologies that have been developed are COSTART (FDA), WHO Adverse Reaction Terminology (WHO-ART), International Classification of Diseases, the Systematized Nomenclature of Medicine (SNOMED III), Unified Medical Language System (the NIH Library of Medicine, Japanese Adverse Reaction Terminology (JART), and the Medical Dictionary for Drug Regulatory Affairs (MEDDRA), of the Adverse Drug Reactions On-line Information Tracking System (ADROIT) (British Medicines Control Agency).[79]

Medical Information Activities Under ICH.

ICH has helped harmonize the presentation of safety and efficacy data from clinical studies. Similarly, ICH has recognized the need for standardization of medical terminology in several areas, including adverse drug experiance (ADE) reporting. Starting in 1992, ICH began work on a series of documents on the management of clinical safety data, and two years later "regulatory communications" was added as a topic area for consideration within ICH. Within this topic, the development of a single international medical terminology for regulatory purposes in product registration, documentation, and safety monitoring was given a high priority. Surprisingly little trouble was encountered in overcoming cultural differences to develop terms for the medical terminology, even in translating Eastern terms into Western languages.[80] By 1997 a set of terms was ready for initial distribution, but issues regarding copyright of the material as well as institutional arrangements for maintenance of the volume still needed to be resolved.

The ICH Steering Committee, in 1997, considered a proposal to establish a "legal entity," tentatively called the Association for International Cooperation on Harmonization.[81] The need to sing a contract with a maintenance organization for the international medical terminology led the Steering Committee to realize that ICH needed greater formality as an institution, in order to venture into areas of commercial law such as contracts, hiring, publication, and copyright. The legal entity would be formed under Swiss law and located in Geneva, and it would oversee the maintenance organization selected under the tender to

79   Food & Drug Admin., MEDDRA Alpha Testing Rep. (Mar. 13. 1995).

80   Europe Drug & Device Rep., Jan. 29, 1997, at 5.

81   Margaret Cone, Int'l Fed. of Pharm. Mfrs Ass'ns, Legal Entity for Administration of International Harmonization Initiatives [draft], Geneva (Feb. 1997).

maintain the ICH nomenclature (the ICH Medical Terminology Support Services Provider).[82] MCA maintains, however, that it has copyright interests in MEDDRA that cannot be relinquished without compensation under British copyright law; a majority of the ICH Steering Committee believes that the current compilation represents a collective effort of many players (and certainly FDA, PhRMA members, the Japanese government and industry) of which MEDDRA text is only one fraction.

■ Adverse Drug Experience Reporting

ADE reporting—also known as pharmacovigilance—is central to the development of a complete safety profile for a drug. In the United States, ADE reports are gathered during clinical trials and during post-marketing surveillance. The FDA requires reporting of foreign ADEs. For example, in 1990, the United States attorney in Newark announced the filing of criminal charges against Hoechst A.G. of Frankfurt, Germany, for failure to submit to the FDA timely reports of foreign ADEs occurring with a drug also marketed in the United States.[83]

Many countries have an ADE reporting system, which recommended by the WHO. Although the requirements for reporting have deviated widely among countries, ICH is expected to reduce international differences as to the types of events that must be reported and the speed with which the report is made. The hope is to make ADE reporting less complicated for multinational corporations, health care professionals, and ultimately for patients, and to maximize the production of valuable information from this data collection.

In 1968, after the thalidomide episode, the WHO developed an international ADE database. Currently, forty-five countries contribute information to that database, which is maintained at the WHO Collaborating Center for International Drug Marketing in Uppsala, Sweden.[84] The WHO reviews the database four times each year for suspected ADEs. If an ADE is suspected, the WHO conducts a literature search and, if no literature suggests that the drug caused the ADE, assigns experts to examine whether the ADE is attributable to the drug. The WHO then reports the results of these reviews and examinations to all member and associate member countries.[85]

In 1986, a CIOMS working group was formed to develop a uniform method and format for reporting of suspected ADEs. The goal was to create a system that utilized a standardized set of definitions, criteria and report form. The final report form design was similar to the FDA's 1639 form.[86] In 1989, a second CIOMS working group was convened to

---

[82]　*Id.*

[83]　Ellen J. Flannery, *Reporting Foreign ADRs and ADRs in Phase IV Studies, and the Significance of Causality Assessment*, 46 Food Drug Cosm. L.J. 43, 52 n.38 (1991): "The attorney commented that the charges 'mark the first time that a foreign drug manufacturer has been prosecuted for filing to provide the FDA with reports of adverse events occurring outside the United States.' See 52 F-D-C Rep. ("The Pink Sheet"), Dec. 17, 1990, at T&G 9. The NDA applicant was not Hoechst A. G., but its United States subsidiary."

[84]　See Fucik, H. & Edwards, I.R., *Impact and Credibility of the WHO Adverse Reaction System*, 30 Drug Info. J. 461 (1996).

[85]　*Id.* at 461.

[86]　*See* D.E Worden, *The Drive Toward Regulatory Harmonization: What is Harmonization and How Will it Impact the Global Development of New Drugs?* 29 Drug Info. J. 1663S (1995).

develop a standardized approach for regular safety updates on currently marketed products. A model, but complex, report form was developed, and the FDA, WHO, and EU met to discuss ways to reduce the complexity of this report procedure. Many of these efforts were later taken up by ICH.

ICH has adopted a harmonized guideline on "Clinical Safety Data Management: Definitions and Standards for Expedited Reporting" that has since been implemented by the regulatory agencies in the three ICH regions.[87] This guideline provides standard definitions and terminology for ADE reporting and outlines guidance for rapid reporting of ADEs during the clinical investigational phase of drug development. ICH has produced two additional documents that address the format of ADE reports and periodic safety updates for marketed products.

■ Labeling and Advertising

Patient Package Inserts

Patient package inserts are required in the EU,[88] a precedent that was cited by the FDA when it proposed to require Medication Guides for certain prescription drugs.[89] Australia also has a patient package insert requirement.[90]

Drug Advertising and Promotion

In 1988, the World Health Assembly adopted a resolution endorsing ethical criteria for drug promotion. The criteria, which were published by the WHO in 1988, are not binding on member nations. Instead, the ethical criteria represented "general principles" that members can adapt to fit their own political, economic, cultural, social, educational, scientific and technical situation.[91] The ethical criteria cover many topics, ranging from advertising to physicians, the general public, and medical representatives, to free samples, educational programs, post-marketing studies, and the promotion of exported drugs.

The IFPMA revised its Code of Pharmaceutical Marketing Practices in 1994. The revised IFPMA code was then considered at WHO and CIOMS meetings on improving the WHO ethical criteria. The IFPMA code was revised to devote more attention to medical representatives and their training, responsibilities, and remuneration, to expand the discussion of medical symposia and other verbal communication, to address hospitality and promotional items, to clarify the types of information that must appear in advertisements, and to

---

[87] See the table in section IV.A. of this chapter.

[88] Council Directive 92/27/EEC, Official J. of the European Communities; No. L113:8-12 (Mar. 31, 1992); Robert H. Vander Stichele & Marc G. Bogaert, *European Legislation and Research Projects Regarding Patient Education for Medication*, 29 DRUG INFO. J. 285 (1995).

[89] Food & Drug Admin., Prescription Drug Product Labeling; Medication Guide Requirements; Proposed Rule, 60 Fed. Reg. 44,182, 44,195 (Aug. 24, 1995).

[90] Kerry Bell, *Has Pharma Industry Policy Boomeranged in Australia?*, SCRIP MAG., Feb. 1996, at 16, 18.

[91] WORLD HEALTH ORG., ETHICAL CRITERIA FOR MEDICINAL DRUG PROMOTION, 4 (1988), endorsed by WHA 47.16, 47th World Health Assembly (May 11, 1994); Molinda Schoepe, *International Regulation of Pharmaceuticals: A WHO International Code of Conduct for the Marketing of Pharmaceuticals?*, 11 SYRACUSE J. OF INT'L L. & COM. 121 (1984).

include new text on communications to the public and audio-visual and computer-based promotional material.[92]

Yet, while such codes and resolutions represent an important change in labeling and promotional practices, and may have curbed some abuses, they are also largely unenforceable or have limited enforcement mechanisms.[93] Furthermore, firms that are not members of the associations may feel free to disregard these industry-developed resolutions.

Several European countries have vigorous enforcement programs on the advertising of pharmaceuticals to professionals, including France,[94] Sweden,[95] and the United Kingdom.[96] A frequent target is advertising of drugs for unapproved uses.

The EU is currently considering several directives involving pharmaceutical advertising, including one on telemarketing (including Internet promotion) of drugs. One issue is whether the directive should control only the advertising of prescription drugs, or whether it should apply to both prescription and over-the-counter (OTC) drugs.[97]

Much of the concern about pharmaceutical advertising and promotion however concerns developing countries, where the health care system is weak and prescription controls are lax.[98]

Controls Over Labeling and Advertising of U.S. Exports.

In the United States, the FDA Export Reform Act of 1996 has been described as providing the FDA with "new extraterritorial regulatory authority over the post-export marketing environment overseas":[99]

> [FDA] can now investigate alleged violations of labeling and promotional practices in foreign markets, and can ban further exports of a product whose labeling or promotion is found violative. The only constraint specifically imposed on FDA action in this regard is that, before taking final action, the agency must consult with the appropriate local public health official in the importing country where the violation is alleged. It appears that Congress intended such intervention by the FDA into the internal affairs of a sovereign

---

[92] *IFPMA Adopts Revised Marketing Code*, IAC NEWSLETTER DATABASE, Sept. 12, 1994.

[93] In 1994, complaints about the IFPMA code focused on the lack of effective enforcement mechanisms. The IFPMA code's principal sanction was adverse publicity. *See HAI Slams IFPMA Pharma Marketing Code*, IAC NEWSLETTER DATABASE, Nov. 14, 1994.

[94] SCRIP, Mar. 19, 1996, at 3; *Id.*, Feb. 20, 1996, at 3; *Id.*, (Dec. 15, 1995) (indicating that details of actions on pharmaceutical ads are published in the government's Journal Official).

[95] SCRIP, Aug. 16, 1996, at 5.

[96] SCRIP, July 9, 1996, at 3; *Id.*, Mar. 5, 1996, at 3.

[97] SCRIP, June 28, 1996, at 3; *Id.* June 14, 1996, at 3.

[98] See MILTON SILVERMAN, MIA LYDECKER & PHILIP LEE, BAD MEDICINE: THE PRESCRIPTION DRUG INDUSTRY IN THE THIRD WORLD 9-42 (Stanford Univ. Press 1992).

[99] Ansis Helmanis, *The FDA Export Reform and Enhancement Act of 1996, The FDA's New Extraterritorial Authority Over Labeling and Promotional Practices*, 51 FOOD & DRUG L.J. 631, 632 (1996).

foreign government to be. . ."interpreted as written only for those countries which are not . . . [developed] countries."[100]

As recently as 1987, as many as two-thirds of U.S. pharmaceuticals marketed in four developing countries lacked adequate directions for professional use.[101] The more serious problems today, however, concern the labeling and advertising practices of local firms in developing countries.[102]

Direct-to-Consumer Advertising

Direct-to-consumer (DTC) ads for prescription drugs are not allowed in the EU, although the arrival of the Internet greatly complicates the enforcement of this ban. The United Kingdom recently ordered a firm to stop advertising prescription drugs for sale on the Internet or face prosecution.[103] Recent changes in EU directives allow institutional advertising by pharmaceutical firms.[104]

The Pharmaceutical Manufacturers Association of Canada maintains an advertising code and has a Pharmaceutical Advertising Advisory Board that screens advertisements directed to professionals. As of 1996, Canada's Health Protection Branch was reviewing whether or not to permit DTC advertising in Canada, because the widespread availability of television broadcasts and print media from the United States, as well as the Internet, had meant that some two-thirds of Canadians had already seen DTC ads.[105]

Internet Issues

With the dramatic increases in the use of the Internet, manufacturers and distributors of FDA-regulated products have turned to the Internet as a medium for distributing information about their products. Even medical groups are providing on-line health information for consumers.[106]

The FDA currently is evaluating how its requirements and policies on labeling and advertising should be applied to product-related information on the Internet and whether additional regulations or guidance documents are needed, particularly as to drugs or devices not approved in the United States.[107]

---

[100] Remarks of Rep. Frederick S. Upton, 142 CONG. REC. H4095 (Apr. 25, 1996), quoted in Helmanis, *supra* note 99 at 632.

[101] U.S. CONGRESS, OFF. OF TECHNOLGY ASSESSMENT, DRUG LABELING IN DEVELOPING COUNTRIES (1993). Brazil, Kenya, Panama, and Thailand were the countries studied.

[102] SILVERMAN, LYDECKER, & LEE, *supra* note 98, at 42.

[103] EUROPE DRUG & DEVICE REPORT Nov. 1996, at 8.

[104] SCRIP, Feb. 23, 1996, at 4.

[105] SCRIP, June 25, 1996, at 19; Mar. 8, 1996, at 14.

[106] *Id.*, Mar. 22, 1997, at 19. For discussions on Internet issues *see* Reginald W. Rhein, *Law Enforcement and the Internet Superhighwaymen*, SCRIP MAG, Dec. 1996, at 18; Harry Rubin, Leigh Fraser, & Monica Smith, *US and International Law Aspects of the Internet: Fitting Square Pegs into Round Holes* 3 INT'L J.L. & INFO. TECH. 117 (1995).

[107] Food & Drug Admin., Promotion of FDA-Regulated Medical Products on the Internet, 61 Fed. Reg. 48,707 (Sept. 16, 1996) (announcing Oct. 16-17, 1996 public meeting). *See* Marc. J. Scheineson, *Legal Overview of Likely FDA Regulation of Internet Promotion*, 51 FOOD & DRUG L.J. 697 (1996).

The FDA's increasing use of the Internet as a place to post information on drug approvals, labeling, adverse event information, and advisory committee meetings was accelerated by an amendment to the Freedom of Information Act that required electronic access to federal agency dockets.[108]

Anti-Disparagement Laws and Comparative Advertising

Firms operating in the United States are sometimes startled to encounter other countries' advertising laws. For example, under anti-disparagement laws in the United Kingdom, pharmaceutical companies dare not run comparative advertisements lest they be required to pay damages to the firm whose product is the subject of a comparison.

Similarly, Philip Morris was sued by biscuit makers and fined for violating French laws barring comparative advertising, and advertising for cigarettes, after running ads claiming that the risk of eating a biscuit a day raised the chance of coronary heart disease in women by 49% whereas the increased risk of lung cancer from living with a smoker and his second-hand smoke was 19%.[109]

■ Prescription Versus Over-the-Counter Controls

The system for distinguishing between prescription and OTC drugs that is quite familiar to Americans does not exist in many countries. In countries lacking effective systems for limiting the use of drugs to dispensing by a pharmacist, upon an order by a physician, consumers can freely purchase drugs that in the United States are effectively limited to prescription.[110] In several European countries, fewer drugs have been available OTC,[111] while others in some countries a more complex system is in place in which there is a "third class of drugs" — between prescription and OTC — specially controlled by pharmacists.[112]

Many countries have traditionally limited the sale of prescription drugs, and sometimes OTC drugs as well (or certain OTC drugs), to apothecaries that frequently carry little else than medicines.[113] In these countries, the restrictions are often justified on the ground that allowing sales of medicines in, for example, supermarkets and convenience stores, would encourage over-medication. These restrictions have been breaking down, in part due to efforts to reduce health care costs by increasing the ability of consumers to self-treat

---

[108] Electronic Freedon of Information Act Amendments of 1996, Pub. L. No. 104-231, 110 Stat. 3048, *discussed in* F-D-C REP. ("The Pink Sheet"), Oct. 28, 1996, at 1-2.

[109] The fine was one million French francs ($195,000) for each time the ad had appeared in France. Syndicat National de la Biscuiterie Francaise v. Philip Morris, cited in *Big Tobacco Takes the Biscuit*, THE ECONOMIST, June 29, 1997. Philip Morris appealed the decision.

[110] *U.S. bans Rohypnol imports*, SCRIP, at Mar. 15, 1996, at 21.

[111] Bryan G. Reuben and Michael L. Burstall, *Pricing and Reimbursement Regulation in Europe: The Industry Perspective*, 29 DRUG INFO. J. 273, 278 (1995). By way of comparison, the percentage of drug sales made up by OTC drugs in several countries is as follows: Denmark, 14%; France 7%; Germany, 20%; Italy, 6%; Netherlands, 9%; UK, 17%; United States, 20-25%; and Japan, 15%.

[112] Philip Brown, *Overcoming the Pharmacy Barrier in the OTC Market*, SCRIP MAG., Feb. 1996, at 3; *Anti-emetics now in French pharmacies [not simply hospitals]*, SCRIP, Dec. 10, 1996, at 3.

[113] SCRIP, June 28, 1996, at 3.

minor ailments without the need to consult with a physician or pharmacist, and to pay for such self-treatment themselves rather than by the health care system.[114]

Within the EU, the lack of harmonization among member countries as to the legal status of products creates significant difficulties for OTC drug manufacturers in securing registration and undertaking EU-wide distribution efforts.[115] Solutions include improved implementation of a European directive that encourages switches to OTC drugs,[116] guidelines to clarify and narrow the prescription-only category, and establishment of more transparent switch procedures.[117] Another problem is that EU citizens traveling among EU countries encounter difficulties in having their prescriptions filled: A situation that is inconsistent with the notion of a free market for movement of goods and persons. The EU Health Ministers have called upon the Commission to create "Euroscripts," while at the same time guarding against the use of fraudulent or stolen prescription forms and ensuring that the pharmacist can correctly identify the prescription and avoid dispensing errors.[118]

Product Evaluation and Approval

If each country — or even a few dozen countries — devised its own peculiar regulatory system for pharmaceuticals, with its own unique testing and production requirements, industry costs would soar, and these costs would be conveyed to consumers or taxpayers (or both).[119] Furthermore, if each country were to prescribe a separate set of required product tests and a distinctive GMP approach, not only would health care costs increase, but the introduction of lifesaving products would be delayed. At the same time, regulatory costs would also be multiplied, as each country applied its own laws.

Although, in theory, user fees can assign these regulatory costs to manufacturers; in the end consumers or taxpayers pay. And if all countries that approve or register drugs charge more than nominal fees, the effect on innovation and health care costs would be catastrophic. Multinational corporations will become increasingly resistant to any significant user fees for repetitive testing or regulatory reviews beyond current charges viewed as yielding benefits exceeding costs (e.g., the FDA's Prescription Drug User Fee Act program.) The implementation of user fees by the FDA, the European Medicines Evaluation Agency, the British Medicines Control Agency, Canada's Health Protection Branch, and others will only increase pressure for harmonization, joint reviews of products, and deference to other countries' decisions.

---

[114] Philip Brown, *supra* note 112, at 3.

[115] *EU legal status by year-end?*, SCRIP, June 14, 1996, at 3.

[116] Council Directive 92/26/EEC; *Commission considering procedures to aid Rx-to-OTC switch*, EUR. DRUG & DEVICE REP., Feb. 5, 1996, at 1.

[117] *Id*. Transparent processes can take longer. *U.K. "consultation" can delay marketing authorizations*, SCRIP, Sept. 3, 1996, at 4.

[118] *EU Health Council moves in more detail*, SCRIP, Dec. 22/26, 1995.

[119] Linda. Horton, *Harmonization and Regulation: Where Do We Go From Here?*, PDA J. (1995).

The FDA is working within ICH and other fora so that a single set of core technical data, showing a drug safe, effective, and high quality will qualify for marketing approval all around the world. Even if a number of agencies, like the FDA, conduct independent reviews, at least the data requirements can be harmonized and regulatory reviews streamlined.[120] A number of countries, including Canada, Australia, and Sweden (before its accession to the European Union), participated in a cooperative activity known as the Pharmaceutical Evaluation Reports Scheme.[121]

Mutual recognition, i.e., reliance upon a decision, review, or inspection made by a foreign counterpart agency has received increased attention in recent years.[122] In situations where the FDA has domestic approval processes, e.g., its system for approving new drug applications (NDAs) or biologic product licenses, the agency is enthusiastic about harmonizing testing requirements and taking into account work done by counterparts, e.g., through joint reviews. However, the FDA has not been willing to entertain the notion of mutual recognition of approvals,[123] although joint reviews and sharing assessments are acceptable approaches. Rather, the FDA has confined its mutual recognition discussions to exchange of inspection reports measuring conformity with GMPs.

■ Choice of Countries for Research; Industrial Policy

Most developed countries wish to maintain an environment that fosters research and innovation—and that does not drive pivotal clinical trials needed for pharmaceutical marketing authorizations outside the country, because of unpredictable or excessive regulatory requirements. The choice of the relevant country in which to initiate clinical trials may be influenced by the nature of the product (e.g., biotechnology, new molecular entity, product under patent), the trial phase involved, the type of procedures required (notification versus approval), the contents of the dossier to be provided compared to the available data, the technical and scientific level of the investigators in the relevant field (as their reputation will influence how much recognition is given the results), the country's requirements, and the choice of the rapporteur country in the case of a European registration procedure.[124]

Interestingly, a United Nations' study found that the United States offered an unusually powerful attraction to foreign pharmaceutical companies deciding where to do preclinical and clinical trials:

---

[120] Moira Dower, *The Global Dossier and the Single Decision — Is It Just a Dream?*, SCRIP MAG, July/Aug. 1996, at 21; Ian Haydock, *On Course for a Global Dossier,* SCRIP MAG., Feb. 1996, at 10.

[121] SCRIP, Dec. 3, 1996, at 4.

[122] *See, e.g.,* the discussion of the Technical Barriers to Trade Agreement in the chapter on international harmonization, enforcement, and trade policy and on mutual recognition agreements in that chapter as well as the chapter on medical device harmonization in this volume.

[123] "With regard to the European Community, I believe that we should continue to standardize our requirements, but . . . it should be up to each country to decide in the end whether a drug should be approved or not." Statement by Commissioner Kessler, in *Revitalizing New Product Development From Clinical Trials Through FDA Review, Hearing on S. 1477 Before the Senate Committee on Labor and Public Welfare* 14(Feb. 21, 1996).

[124] C. Legrand, F. Cheix, H. Dumais & V. Laugel, *Clinical Trial Initiation Procedures in Europe: The Legal Framework and Practical Aspects,* 29 DRUG INFO. J. 201, 202 (1995). The rapporteur country is the one whose drug review authority takes responsibility for review of a manufacturer's submission and preparing a recommended decision for a committee comprised of member state representatives.

Research . . . is a task seldom performed in overseas subsidiaries [the main function of which ordinarily is distribution of drugs developed at research centers in the home country]. It tends to be highly centralized and carried out in only a few locations (usually in the country where the firm has its headquarters and one or two of its major markets). The only exception to this rule is the United States; in 1986, 26 foreign firms had research facilities in that country and by 1992 the number had risen to 75. Such a locational pattern would be unusual in other industries, though several considerations make it appealing to drug producers. First, the difficult job of coordinating research becomes more complicated if facilities were widely dispersed. Second, firms are traditionally very secretive about their research programmes and a highly centralized operation makes it easier to control information leaks. Finally, companies choose their research sites carefully to take advantage of research funding offered by host governments.[125]

Other commentators believe that the existence of what is perceived as a stringent regulatory environment can actually attract research (or production, or both) as companies seek the *cachet* that accompanies the declaration that research was done in a strict setting. At the same time, other research flows to countries where regulatory controls are lax, e.g., to the United Kingdom for early clinical trials because of the lack of controls over Phase I trials.[126]

Within the EU, there is considerable variation in how countries regulate research, with regard to the regulatory evaluation structures, the format of the dossier, and the time taken for review.[127] There is a high degree of harmonization as to ethical requirements and good clinical practices (GCPs), as discussed below, and most countries agree that the clinical trial submission must include a copy of the investigational protocol, chemical and pharmaceutical data, animal pharmacology data, and human data, mainly safety data.[128] As is discussed below, the ICH is helping to speed up the harmonization of clinical trial information.[129]

The issue of governmental role in pharmaceutical research is intriguing: there is a fundamental and probably unresolved issue of when it is justified for a government to influence market forces in order to stimulate the development of new drugs. Industrial policy consists of identifying sectors of the economy that the government wants to nurture (through subsidies) and protect (through barriers to imports and other competition). At different times, a number of countries, e.g., Japan, Korea, Taiwan, and Singapore, to name just a few, have adopted an industrial policy approach to some part of the drug or device sectors.[130]

---

[125] R. BALLANCE, UN INDUSTRIAL DEVELOPMENT ORGANIZATION, THE PHARMACEUTICAL INDUSTRY, MARKET AND STRUCTURE (Vienna, Austria 1995). Other factors might be availability of particular experts, resources in universities, intellectual property protection laws, and the availability of venture capital.

[126] Legrand, Cheix, Dumais, & Laugel, *supra* note 124, at 201, 202.

[127] *Id.* at 204, 206-07.

[128] *Id.* at 206.

[129] Yves Julliet, Gaby Danan, *Drug Safety: Legal Requirements in Europe and in the United States — A European Industry View*, 29 DRUG INFO. J. 291 (1995).

[130] U.S. CONGRESS, OFF. TECH. ASSESSMENT, BIOTECHNOLOGY IN A GLOBAL ECONOMY 155-55 (1991) (Doc. No. OTA-BA-494.

A recent report in the EU describes the "EU's new research strategy to help European firms catch up with the United States and Japan in the high-tech sectors of the future" with a focus "on the programs crucial to Europe's long-term innovation, competitiveness and prosperity," including biotechnology, vaccines, and antiviral medicines.[131]

In the United States, however, the federal government got involved in a number of different drug development programs not because of a perceived need to compete with other countries, but because of a view that more resources needed to be dedicated to the quest for therapies for specific diseases, and a belief that industry could not be expected to fill all these needs, e.g., reluctance to invest due to belief that the research in question would be expensive, slow, and risky.[132]

■ Preclinical Studies

The use of the term "preclinical studies" is a misnomer because it implies that all non-clinical testing of a product occurs prior to clinical testing. In fact, preclinical testing continues throughout most of the product development phase (both clinical and non-clinical) and in some cases may continue as post-marketing requirements dictate. Nonetheless, the term "preclinical" generally refers to the nonclinical analysis of product quality, safety, and activity.

Product Discovery Testing

The drug discovery phase of drug development[133] involves the isolation, selection, or synthesis of a test product, and is similar in most developed countries. By enabling assessment of product activity and mechanisms of action, these studies enable a decision breakpoint for the pharmaceutical company and provide useful information for clinical testing about dose selection and scheduling. Nonclinical studies designed to assess initial product activity or to establish general physical/chemical characteristics should follow solid scientific principles and be well controlled and well documented. The requirements for discovery and activity testing of products are generally dictated by scientific principles, not regulatory requirements, so that efforts to harmonize testing at this stage have not been necessary, or even desirable.

Toxicology Safety Testing

Determination of a drug's safety profile in animals as a prerequisite for clinical testing is a hallmark feature of most drug development plans, and a requirement by many regulatory agencies. The number, type, and duration of studies required often vary among countries. Harmonization of these requirements should reduce unnecessary testing, and allow phar-

---

[131] International Global Business Monitor, Bulletin #96-05, Jan. 31, 1996, at 1.

[132] GENERAL ACCOUNTING OFFICE, FEDERAL DRUG DEVELOPMENT PROGRAMS (July 17, 1981) (HRD-125 Doc. No, The best-known program was begun in 1955 to develop cancer drugs. Other targets of governmental drug development programs involved malaria (due to Army interest in 1963), vaccines (due to decline in number of manufacturers), viruses (lack of effective drugs, lack of industry interest in 1959 (interferon), epilepsy, contraceptives, and caries (cost of regulatory requirements), sickle cell anemia and Cooley's anemia (small patient populations), and narcotic abuse (stigma of ongoing patient use of methadone-like drugs in maintenance treatment).

[133] M. Scherer, *Pricing, profits and technological progress in the pharmaceutical industry,* 7 J. ECON. PERSP.

maceutical firms to focus on those studies necessary to assess a product's true toxicity profile.

Good Laboratory Practices. In the United States, non-clinical testing to assess product safety is required to be conducted in accordance with GLPs[134] to assure the quality and integrity of non-clinical safety data. Because safety data submitted for product evaluation may have been conducted in other countries, FDA has entered into memoranda of understanding (MOUs) with corresponding agencies in several countries regarding GLPs, including Canada, France, Germany, Italy, Japan, Netherlands, Sweden, and Switzerland.[135] Some of the MOUs have included mutual recognition of GLP inspections unless there is a serious concern about the data submitted or the inspections have not been completed within a specified timeframe. Other MOUs constitute a statement of intent to establish the uniformity of GLP standards and programs of inspections of GLP laboratories among countries.

For a number of years, OECD, a Paris-based international organization comprised of the developed countries of the world,[136] has undertaken an international harmonization activity on GLPs. The FDA has been active in this program.

International Conference on Harmonization. A major focus of ICH activities has been the development of harmonized guidelines for the assessment of toxicity of pharmaceutical products. Areas of harmonization activity[137] have included testing for carcinogenicity, genotoxicity, toxicokinetics and pharmacokinetics, and reproductive toxicity, as well as development of principles for the safety testing of biotechnology products. A guideline defining whether carcinogenicity studies are needed—based on intended use, duration of exposure and other risk factors—has reached consensus and is being implemented by ICH regions. Guidelines on the necessity of carcinogenicity studies in two species and dose selection criteria for those studies are under discussion. Guidelines on *in vitro* and *in vivo* tests for evaluation of genotoxicity and reproductive toxicity also have reached tripartite consensus and are being implemented. Two of the first documents adopted and implemented by the three ICH regions were a guideline on the test strategies and the rationale for integrating toxicokinetics into safety testing, and a guideline on the determination of a need to conduct repeat dose tissue distribution studies. Consensus on duration of repeat dose studies in rodents has been reached, but the duration of repeat dose studies in non-rodent species is under discussion.

■ **Clinical Testing**

Good Clinical Practices

The assessment of safety and efficacy of products during clinical studies depends upon the

---

[134] 21 C.F.R. pt. 58.

[135] FOOD & DRUG ADMIN., INTERNATIONAL COOPERATIVE AGREEMENTS MANUAL 55, 105, 121, 143, 153, 211, 333, 343 (Nov. 1996).

[136] As of 1997, OECD had 29 members, including Australia, Canada, the Czech Republic, Hungary, Iceland, Liechtenstein, Japan, Mexico, New Zealand, Norway, South Korea, Switzerland, Turkey, the United States, and the 15 European Union countries.

[137] *See* table in section IV.A. of this chapter for citations to the guidelines described in this paragraph.

quality of clinical trials and resulting data. ICH is producing harmonized guidelines on GCPs, an international ethical and scientific quality standard for designing, conducting, recording, and reporting trials that involve the participation of human subjects.[138] The resulting ICH guideline includes features of both FDA regulations and the European GCP requirements.[139] Clinical trials by design are expensive and challenging to implement in a manner that is both ethical and scientifically sound. The implementation of quality assurance standards, including audits of methods and results, is integral to the integrity of the data and the protection of human subjects. GCPs, although primarily motivated by concern about the protection of human subjects, also play a central role in the generation and correct interpretation of meaningful data from clinical trials and complement other guidance such as the ICH guideline under development in 1997 on "General Considerations for Clinical Trials."[140]

Many companies are entering into clinical studies in countries that have no established mechanism for the oversight of human research. Thus, it has been important to establish international standards for both the conduct and oversight of clinical trials. Harmonization of GCPs is now well underway, with an ICH guideline in place and many countries implementing similar standards. It remains to be seen whether other countries will be as strict as the FDA and the research integrity office of the Public Health Service in the enforcement of GCPs.

An additional issue is whether researchers should be required to disclose any interests they have in the research under review, e.g., in journal articles or in making presentations before governmental advisory committees. Although the FDA has proposed to require such disclosure, this view is not universally shared.

International agreements and declarations in the post-World War II era have shaped the conduct of biomedical research. Following the 1948 Nuremberg trials of Nazi scientists who conducted unethical, and sometimes grotesque, experiments upon concentration camp inmates, several countries, including the United States, agreed to issue the Nuremberg Code, a formal statement on medical ethics that led to present standards in the United States and elsewhere that protect human research subjects.[141] Its central feature is the right of a subject to be told about the benefits, risks, and purpose of the research, i.e., "informed consent."

Another key document is the Declaration of Helsinki,[142] the foundation of most current GCPs, including the FDA's regulations.[143] This declaration states that human subjects should be used in research only if the research is based upon scientific principles. All

---

[138] 60 Fed. Reg. 42,948 (Aug. 17, 1995) (ICH step 2 document).

[139] Good Clinical Practice of trials on medicinal products in the European Community. Doc. III 3976/88, in the rules for governing medicinal products in the European Community, Addendum to Vol. III, Brussels, European Commission 57-98 (July 1990).

[140] *See* table in section IV.A. of this chapter.

[141] R. Thompson, *Protecting "Human Guinea Pigs,"* in FOOD & DRUG ADMIN., NEW DRUG DEVELOPMENT IN THE UNITED STATES, at 18 (1990 ed.).

[142] Individual guidelines outline ethical considerations for research involving children, persons with mental or behavioral disorders, prisoners, subjects in underdeveloped communities, and pregnant or nursing women.

[143] 21 C.F.R. pt. 50, 312.

research utilizing human subjects should be preceded by adequate laboratory and animal experimentation, and a thorough review of the scientific literature should have been conducted to prevent unnecessary or ill-advised studies. In addition, clinical research should be conducted in accordance with a written protocol that has been reviewed by an independent committee. Research on human subjects should be conducted only by scientifically qualified persons under supervision of clinically competent medical personnel. All subjects should give informed consent while not under duress. Risk/benefit should be assessed in the trials in which confidentiality is maintained, and any publication of results should be scientifically accurate.

WHO developed, in 1993, two sets of guidelines designed to protect human subjects and ensure the quality of clinical trial data. The WHO/CIOMS International Ethical Guidelines for Biomedical Research Involving Human Subjects outlines information on informed consent and participation of special populations in clinical trials.[144] The WHO Guidelines for Good Clinical Practice for Trials of Pharmaceutical Products[145] discuss roles for clinical investigators, sponsors, and governmental authorities in the conduct and regulation of clinical trials to ensure protection of human subjects and integrity of the clinical data. According to the document, governmental regulation should provide the legal framework for conduct of clinical trials, and the governmental oversight bodies should be responsible for the review of clinical study protocols and protection of human safety. The oversight bodies should have the authority to require revisions in the protocol or termination of the study, if warranted, and they should be able to perform on-site inspections of clinical data.

ICH has drafted guidelines in several areas of clinical trial management. A consolidated GCP guideline[146] is scheduled to contain the consensus draft guidelines on the Content of Investigator's Brochure[147] and Addenda on Essential Documents. These guidelines have been adopted in the regulations or administrative procedures of the three ICH regulatory bodies. Another guideline is being developed by an ICH working group to address broad scientific issues in the conduct, performance and control of clinical trials; this guideline is not scheduled to be incorporated into the initial GCP guidelines.

■ FDA Acceptance of Foreign Data.[148]

The FDA routinely accepts data from foreign studies whether or not conducted under an investigational new drug (IND) exemptionin the assessment of product safety. Data from

---

[144] The guideline was approved the Expert Committee on the Use of Essential Drugs in November 1993, and was based on texts on good clinical practices in Australia, Canada, EU countries, Japan, Nordic countries, and the United States.

[145] The guideline outlines the standard for the design and conduct of scientifically sound and ethical clinical trials. It supports the acceptance of clinical data from other ICH regions by the ICH regulatory authorities (U.S., EU, and Japan).

[146] This ICH guideline outlines recommendations on the types of clinical and non-clinical information which should be included in the background material provided to investigators and others involved in the clinical trial.

[147] This document describes the information that must be provided to permit the evaluation of clinical trial conduct and resulting quality of the data.

[148] 21 C.F.R. § 312.120. *See* John J. Gorski, *An FDA-EEC Perspective on the International Acceptance of Foreign Clinical Data*, 21 CAL. W. INT'L L.J. 329 (Spring 1991).

foreign clinical studies are acceptable in support of marketing approval, provided the following criteria are met:

- The foreign studies are applicable to the U.S. population and U.S. medical practice;
- The studies have been performed by clinical investigators of recognized competence;
- The clinical data can be validated;
- All clinical study reports have statistical analysis performed;
- Foreign data supporting a drug's substantial evidence of safety and effectiveness has
- All case report forms are available;
- Case report data tabulated to U.S. standards;
- resulted from studies conducted in accordance with the Helsinki Declaration; and
- The foreign studies are adequate and well controlled.

■ FDA Acceptance of Foreign Experience

The issue of whether the FDA will consider foreign experience in deciding whether a drug is regarded as a new drug under U.S. law has affected several OTC drug monographs. The issue first arose in connection with a sunscreen containing ingredients that had not been in use in the United States before the initiation of the OTC drug review. Soon after, in preparing the OTC monographs for vaginal contraceptives, the FDA likewise received comments from affected firms arguing that a product that had been used to a material extent and to a material time in another country should be eligible for meeting legal requirements thorough compliance with a general class-type regulation rather than to have to submit a new drug application (NDA). Similar arguments were presented on behalf of European herbal product interests.

In 1996, the FDA published an Advance Notice of Proposed Rulemaking inviting public comment on these issues,[149] and particularly on whether drugs that have had significant marketing experience elsewhere ought to eligible for regulation under the OTC drug monograph system rather than through individual new drug applications.[150]

■ Cancer Drugs

In 1996, the President and Vice President announced a new the FDA initiative on Reinventing the Regulation of Cancer Drugs: Accelerating Approval and Expanding Access.[151] As one part of this program, the FDA noted that, while most new agents are available in the United States at about the same time as in other countries, if not earlier, there are occasional exceptions. The agency therefore provided for early expanded access to cancer treatments approved elsewhere in the world, based upon the data package submitted to the foreign regulatory authority. Therefore, whenever a cancer therapy for patients who are not curable or well-treated by currently available therapies is approved by a recognized foreign regulatory authority, the FDA intends to contact the U.S. sponsor and encourage the submission of an expanded access protocol, regardless of the length of

---

[149] 61 Fed. Reg. 51,625 (Oct. 3, 1996).

[150] *Id. See* Kenneth C. Baumgartner, *Getting a Grip on Material Time and Extent*, 49 Food & Drug L.J. 433 (1994).

[151] National Performance Review (Mar. 1996).

time that the product has been studied in the United States. A foreign regulatory authority is to be identified as having review practices, review standards, and access to specialized expertise in the evaluation of agents for use in cancer treatment that are sufficient to allow the FDA to conclude that a marketing approval action by that authority is likely to provide for an adequate basis for proper consideration of an expanded access protocol for U.S. patients.

■ Acquired Immune Deficiency Syndrome Drugs

The international interest in drugs for the prevention and treatment of AIDS, also known as Human Immunodeficiency Virus (HIV), has stimulated international cooperation on drug research and approval at the international,[152] regional,[153] and national levels.[154] The advent of protease inhibitors aggravated the stress fractures in the EU:

> AIDS activists . . . are fuming over the way [price controls] threaten to limit access to innovative AIDS medicines in countries such as Italy, Spain and the U.K . . . . Member countries already have shown that, when it comes to AIDS, any semblance of a single EU market in pharmaceuticals can unravel with dizzying speed. France already makes the new AIDS drugs available prior to formal regulatory approval in limited programs for patients who fail to respond to existing treatments. In Germany, once an AIDS drug is approved by the U.S. Food and Drug Administration, it becomes available in pharmacies—and the government reimburses the full cost to patients. In Holland, pressure from activists prompted an about-face by cost-conscious politicians, who had balked at picking up the tab for expensive new treatments, including protease inhibitors. New rules give Dutch patients access to FDA-approved treatments—or to drugs recommended for approval by the [EU export approval committee] . . . . Dutch officials are pushing to make their new rules on early access to AIDS drugs a Europe-wide policy.[155]

Other Countries' Approval Systems

■ European Union

Most countries in Western Europe have, for many years, had drug approval agencies and

---

[152] Jonathan Mann, *Worldwide strategies for HIV Control: WHO's Special Programme on AIDS*, 14 MED. & HEALTH CARE 290 (1986).

[153] A. David Brandling-Bennett, *The Impact of AIDS in the 19902, With Emphasis on the Region of the Americas*, 23 N.Y.U. J. INT'L L. & POL. 989 (1991).

[154] Julie C. Relihan, *Expediting FDA Approval of AIDS Drugs: An International Approach*, 13 B.U. INT'L L.J., 229 (1995)

[155] Stephen D. Moore & Shailagh Murray, *Merck Uses AIDS Drug To Target Wholesalers in the European Union*, WALL ST. J., Oct. 11-12, 1996, at 1, 7.

operated drug approval systems. Three of the best known are the Medicines Control Agency in the United Kingdom, the Agence du Medicament in France, and the BPRG in Germany.

Landmarks in the evolution of the EU system of pharmaceutical regulation were the issuance of the first harmonized directive in 1965,[156] the establishment of the Committee on Proprietary Medicinal Products (CPMP) in 1975,[157] the founding of ICH in 1989, and the establishment in London of the EMEA on January 1, 1995.[158] Over this thirty-year period, the countries in the EU made remarkable progress toward a harmonized system (at least with respect to drug safety, efficacy, and quality) in which the groundwork was laid for EU-wide approval decisions.

Inherent in the EU system is a certain amount of tension between centralization and decentralization. Most countries want to continue to play an important role in drug approval decisions, and each country's government is expected to retain responsibility for enforcement of pertinent directives such as the GMP directive. "Mixed competency" is the term used in the EU to describe a situation is which legal authority is divided, generally with EU institutions issuing legislation that is enforced by member countries, and often with the countries also maintaining authority to legislate in many areas. "Subsidiarity" is a related policy of favoring retention of governmental authority at the lowest level consistent with the rendering of effective service.[159]

The requirement to use the EMEA's centralized review is limited to biotechnology drugs. For other drugs, the sponsors may choose to use either the centralized procedure or seek local approval in a member country. The EMEA functions largely as a secretariat for a decentralized system that relies upon national regulatory and academic experts who carry out the drug evaluations, and receive a portion of the EMEA's user fee.[160] The EMEA continued and expanded upon the twenty-year old CPMP, a committee comprised of two experts from each country. Experts from two countries are assigned to serve as rapporteurs to review the dossier for a drug and to report their findings to the CPMP. The CPMP in turn makes a recommendation through the EMEA to the European Commission in Brussels as to whether the drug should be approved. At this point individual member countries are given the opportunity to raise objections to approval, and the Commission decides whether to grant a European marketing authorization. In addition, the legislation creating the EMEA allowed for the use of mutual recognition of a national approval, but only until 1998.

---

[156] Directive 65/65/EEC (OJ No L. 147, 9.6.75) 13 "laid down the principle . . . that [authorizations] for medicinal products in all Member States should be granted on scientific grounds of quality, safety, and efficacy, without regard to socio-economic considerations." EUROPEAN AGENCY FOR THE EVALUATION OF MEDICINAL PRODUCTS, FIRST GENERAL REPORT 8 (1995).

[157] Council Decision of May 20, 1975 setting up a pharmaceutical committee, 75/320/EEC (Official Journal of the European Communities No L 147/23 9.6.75) 207.

[158] Council Regulation No. 2309/93/EEC of July 22, 1993 (Official Journal of the European Communities No L214/1; *Euroagency for drug evaluation sets up shop in London's East End*, 371 NATURE 6 (1994); *FDA Reform and the European Medicines Evaluation Agency*, 108 HARV. L. REV. 2009 (June 1995); Richard F. Kingham et al., *The New European Medicines Agency*, 49 FOOD & DRUG L.J. 301 (1994); Eric M. Katz, *Europe's Centralized New Drug Procedures: Is the United States Prepared to Keep Pace?*, 48 FOOD & DRUG L. J. 577 (1993); GOVERNMENT ACCOUNTING OFFICE, EUROPEAN UNION DRUG APPROVAL: OVERVIEW OF NEW EUROPEAN MEDICINES EVALUATION AGENCY AND APPROVAL PROCESS (Apr. 1996) (Doc. No.GAO/HEHS-96-71).

[159] Philippe Meyer, *European Commission, The Future GMP Inspection System*, 28 DRUG INFO. J., 977 (1994).

[160] John P. Griffin, *The EMEA — Euromouse or White Elephant?*, SCRIP MAG. (1995).

In its first two years, the EMEA made solid progress for a new institution, although many problems remained relating to lack of mutual confidence among member states.[161] The EMEA faced a number of initial challenges. First, difficult discussions with the European parliament delayed the opening of the EMEA for a month.[162] The agency obtains funding through a combination of appropriations and user fees. For staffing, it also relies heavily upon cooperation with other EU institutions (especially the Commission) and the member countries.

Second, EMEA strived to establish credibility as a world-power drug approval body. The creation of the EMEA occurred at a time when the regulated industry was going through global consolidations,[163] when an extraordinary number of breakthrough drugs reached readiness for marketing authorization, when health care authorities on both sides of the Atlantic were applying enormous cost control pressures, and when the FDA had succeeded in slashing its review times due to the user fee legislation.

Third, EMEA needed to show it could function like an agency even though it had no approval authority of its own. Rather, it needed to obtain a recommendation from the CPMP, and then issue a recommendation for a drug approval that was in turn forwarded to the European Commission in Brussels for translation and issuance as a decision in the *Official Journal of the European Communities*.[164] The result was approval decisionmaking that looked slow compared to the FDA or the United Kingdom's Medicines Control Agency.[165]

Fourth, consumers pressed for greater transparency, prompting the EMEA to undertake a review of how to increase its openness to stakeholders.[166]

Fifth, many important aspects of the EU pharmaceutical system remained unharmonized, among them decisions on whether a drug is prescription or OTC as well as pricing and reimbursement systems.[167]

---

[161] SCRIP, Dec. 17, 1996, at 4.

[162] WORLD FOOD CHEM. NEWS, Feb. 22, 1995, at 33; SCRIP, Oct. 3, 1995, at 2.

[163] An expected effect of the downward pressure on costs, coupled with transnational mergers and the single market in the EU, is consolidation of manufacturing operations to reduce the rate of excess capacity in the industry. As profit margins fall, firms will abandon the practice of building a factory in each market as the economic penalties of underutilized factory capacity cannot be offset by the benefits of local presence, in the form of "a government's gratitude for local investment — expressed in the form of rapid product approval or the award of a favourable price." By the end of the 1990s, the world's larger drug companies would need only about 10 strategically located plants. R. BALLANCE. *Supra* note 125.

[164] *Streamlining EC approvals — Commission proposals*, SCRIP, Dec. 13, 1996; EU permission to continue, SCRIP, July 5, 1996, at 3; *Commission slow to decide*, SCRIP, Feb. 9, 1996, at 4.

[165] *EU review times*, SCRIP, Feb. 9, 1996, at 4; *GAO estimates European drug reviews of 298-448 days under new system*; *FDA Calls Report Evidence Against Six-Month Deadline in Agency Reform Legislation*, F-D-C REP. ("The Pink Sheet"), Apr. 15, 1996, at 9.

[166] National Consumer Council, Secrecy and Medicines in Europe (Sept. 1994); *More consumerist pressure on secrecy*, SCRIP, Sept. 30, 1994; Fernand Sauer, Executive Director, EMEA, Consultation on transparency and access to documents at the EMEA (Mar. 7, 1997).

[167] Christopher R. Smith, Note, *Pharmaceuticals, Intransigent Member States and a Single Market*, 18 B. C. INT'L & COMP. L. REV. 471 (1995); Leigh Hancher, *The European Pharmaceutical Market: Problems of Partial Harmonization*, 15 EUR. L. REV. 9 (Feb. 1990); EUR. DRUG & DEVICE REP., Feb. 5, 1996, at 3.

Sixth, efforts by the EMEA and the CPMP to spread rapporteur applications equitably among countries ran into objections on several fronts. Drug manufacturers had been able to select the rapporteur country when they used the CPMP process in pre-EMEA days; the CPMP relented and is allowing firms to name three or four preferences for rapporteur country.[168] The United Kingdom, which had served as rapporteur for thirteen of nineteen applications handled in the pre-EMEA process, was named rapporteur for the first new centralized application.[169] In the part of the European system in which approval is sought first at the national level, then generalized throughout the EU through mutual recognition, the MCA was responsible for eight of twenty-one successfully completed procedures. Other regulatory agencies in the EU that had not done so well in attracting applications expressed the view that the competition for work was a threat to their survival.[170]

Last but not least, there seemed to be a "revival of that lack of mutual confidence among the national regulatory authorities which had made the [former] procedures such an ordeal."[171] Awkward problems developed when a rapporteur country (Germany) requested additional data and the company simply withdrew the application rather than use the dispute resolution procedure.[172]

Comparisons are frequently drawn between the approval processes and approval times of the FDA and those of the United Kingdom's Medicines Control Agency. In a 1995 GAO study finding the FDA's approval times for new molecular entities to be faster than those of the Medicines Control Agency, GAO provided the following short summary of the Agency's process, presented here as a good snapshot of the Agency that, at century's end, comes closest to enjoying the international stature of the FDA:

> MCA's assessment is only the first step in a multistage process of drug review and approval. All applications for new active substances are also automatically referred to a government body called the Committee on the Safety of Medicines (CSM). CSM's expert subcommittees also assess the application, an these assessments, along with those from MCA, are provided to CSM. The CSM then provides advice to the Licensing Authority, which actually grants or denies the product license. However, the rate of rejection or requests for modifications or additional information is very high [99% in 1987-89] . . . a formal appeals process . . . may involve additional work...Thus the total time until the license is actually granted is considerably longer than the period of initial assessment by MCA. In contrast, the time FDA reports includes all the steps between an accepted NDA and the final decision on it.[173]

---

[168] *Choice of EU rapporteur not always possible*, SCRIP, Jan. 2/5, 1996, at 3; EUROPE DRUG & DEVICE LETT., Feb. 5, 1996, at 8.

[169] SCRIP, Aug. 2, 1996, at 3.

[170] *Id.* Nov. 8, 1996, at 3.

[171] *Contentious areas in mutual recognition, id*, Dec. 17, 1996, at 4.

[172] *Id.,* Dec. 17, 1996; *Id.,* Nov. 29, 1996, at 3; *Id.,* Aug.6, 1996; *Id.,* Jan. 16, 1996, at 6; *Id.,* Dec. 22/26, 1995, at 5.

[173] GENERAL ACCONTING OFFICE, FDA Drug Approval: Review Time Has Decreased in Recent Years, (Oct. 1995) 40 Doc. No. GAO/PEMD-96-1.

■ Switzerland and European Economic Area Countries

Switzerland, Liechtenstein, Norway, and Iceland remain outside the EU but work closely with the EU on pharmaceuticals. These four countries are members of the European Free Trade Agreement.[174] All but Switzerland are part of the European Economic Area, under which goods meeting EU requirements are allowed to flow freely.

■ Japan

The Pharmaceutical Affairs Bureau of the Japanese Ministry of Health and Welfare has the responsibility for regulation of pharmaceutical products in Japan.[175] Any person who intends to manufacture or import drugs in Japan must obtain the approval of the Ministry of an application for approval and license.[176] As in the United States, products are evaluated for safety, efficacy, and quality. A Japanese applicant submits the application to the prefectural (local) government, which then forwards it to the Ministry, while a foreign firm submits its application directly to the Ministry.[177] If the drug is identified as one requiring a consultation with the Central Pharmaceutical Affairs Council (CPAC), the application is forwarded to one of several committees consisting of members of the medical and scientific community, which evaluates the applications and makes recommendations to the CPAC, which in turn makes a recommendation to the Ministry respecting approval.[178]

In establishing its guidelines and requirements, Ministry paid special attention to international approaches and now accepts most foreign data if it meets Japanese standards.[179] This is a change from prior policy. Until 1986, foreign drug companies were required to conduct clinical trials in Japan, in Japanese people, and foreign companies could not apply directly to the Ministry for approval but were required to have a Japanese partner.[180] The changes made in 1986 to simplify and open the process were stimulated in part by the 1985 Market-Oriented Sector-Selective talks, which were bilateral trade negotiations between the United States and Japan aimed at simplifying market access and regulatory processes in Japan.[181] The resulting increase in competition in the Japanese market led Japanese firms to begin to think more globally, and cooperation with the United States and the EU in ICH has accelerated this trend.

---

[174] Linda R. Horton, et. al., *International Harmonization of Medical Device Regulation, in* 2 FUNDAMENTALS OF LAW AND REGULATION ch. 17 (FDLI 1997).

[175] PHARMACEUTICAL AFFAIRS BUREAU (PAB), MINISTRY OF HEALTH AND WELFARE (MHW), PHARMACEUTICAL ADMINISTRATION IN JAPAN, (9-13., Yakuji Nippo, 5th ed. 1991.

[176] *Id.* at 35.

[177] *Id.* at 39.

[178] For example, there is a Committee on Drugs (with numerous specialized committees to undertake initial reviews), a Committee on Antibiotic Products, and a Committee on Biologic Products. *Id.*

[179] *Id.* at 41.

[180] U.S. CONGRESS, OFF. TECHNOLOGY ASSESSMENT, BIOTECHNOLOGY IN A GLOBAL ECONOMY 86 (Oct. 1991) Doc. No. OTA-BA-494 (Oct. 1991).

[181] *Id.*

■ Canada

The HPB approves drugs for use in Canada[182] and cooperates closely with the FDA on a broad range of cooperative activities to assure prompt availability of safe and effective medical products. Importantly, the FDA and HPB have conducted several joint product reviews as a way to strengthen public health protection, through collaboration, while at the same time achieving harmonized approval decisions. For example, in the early 1990s, the FDA and Canada's HPB announced their joint review, and concurrent approval, of several AIDS drugs.[183] Future joint reviews will be facilitated by Canadian acceptance of ICH guidelines.

To facilitate further joint approvals, the FDA conducted a rulemaking to enable the agency to share safety and efficacy studies, which generally consist of confidential commercial information, with foreign officials. A second rulemaking, completed in 1995, allowed sharing of drafts and other predecisional documents with other countries' officials.[184]

■ Mexico

The Subsecretariat de Salud (SSA) in Mexico administers a drug approval program. Anyone wishing to sell pharmaceutical products in Mexico must register with SSA, submit an application, a fee, samples of the product for testing, copies of sanitary licenses, descriptions of the label and containers, and export certificates and product specifications issued by the country of origin.[185] In practice, SSA gives considerable weight to the fact that a drug has been approved by the FDA. In 1997, Mexico and the Pan American Health Organization (PAHO), the American branch of WHO, embarked on a program in which PAHO will assist Mexico in decisions on pharmaceuticals based on information provided by the sponsor and by the FDA.

SSA and the FDA have cooperated for many years, either on a bilateral basis or through the Trilateral annual meeting discussed previously in this chapter. In 1995, the three agencies signed an MOU that strengthens cooperation and harmonization activities.[186] The agreement puts in place a framework for a North American health protection agenda and builds upon many years of cooperation between the United States and its neighbors on food and drug control. The FDA regards this work a inspired by the North American Free Trade Agreement (NAFTA), supportive of NAFTA, and yet distinct from NAFTA in the opportunity for harmonization and other regulatory cooperation. Among trilateral cooperation topics are control of health fraud and promoting adherence to GMPs through a variety of joint training and joint inspection activities.

---

[182] Joel Lexchin, *Drug Makers and Drug Regulators, Too Close for Comfort: A Study of the Canadian Situation*, 31 Soc. Sci. Med. 1257 (1990).

[183] Food & Drug Admin., Report of the FDA Task Force on International Harmonization 50 (1992).

[184] Linda Horton, *The Food and Drug Administration's International Harmonization, Enforcement, and Trade Policy Activities, in* 2 Fundamentals of Law and Regulation ch. 5 (FDLI 1997).

[185] U.S. Dep't of Commerce, Registration Procedure for Pharmaceutical Products, NAFTA Facts, Doc. # 8406, Sept. 12, 1994, at 1. In January 1997, the fee was almost $60,000. Lars Noah, *NAFTA's Impact on the Trade in Pharmaceuticals*, 33 Hous. L. Rev. 1318 (1997).

[186] Food & Drug Admin., International Cooperative Agreements, Memorandum of Cooperation with Canada and Mexico on Cooperation in the Scientific and Regulatory Fields of Health 59 (Oct. 1995).

■ South America

With plans underway for a Free Trade Area of the Americas, and with ICH looking to the FDA to take steps to broaden the reach of ICH guidelines to the Americas region, cooperation among western hemisphere nations on pharmaceutical regulation is critical.

Most countries in the Americas maintain pharmaceutical approval systems with registration times of about six months — but varying from one to twenty-four months — not counting the time that it may take a firm to obtain an export certificate from the country of origin.[187] Almost all require information on whether a drug has FDA approval before making a decision on that drug for their citizenry; usually this information is in the form of an export certificate,[188] which suggests that some degree of recognition of U.S. approval is occurring in many cases.[189] In Argentina, Colombia, and Mexico, a typical regulatory review may be used along with, or in lieu of, requiring a certificate from the country of origin.[190] Local trials are looked on favorably, and several countries require medical journal articles (in english or translated into spanish) of clinical data.[191] Several countries require a certificate of analysis, and several require that the certificates be legalized by notaries or similar officials.[192]

The FDA has had a number of cooperative activities with the Brazilian Ministry of Health, particularly regarding vaccines. The FDA also maintains contacts with Argentina's Administracion de Medicamentos, Alimentos, y Tecnologia Medica (Drugs, Foods, and Medical Technology Administration).[193] PAHO coordinates and funds an array of technical cooperation and assistance activities in which the FDA is often a participant.

There is now a tendency toward forming regional bodies to issue harmonized regulations and, in some cases, to adopt a uniform approach toward harmonized approvals. The two best examples involve the countries of MERCOSUR,[194] discussed further in the general chapter on international harmonization earlier in this volume, and the Andean countries (Bolivia, Colombia, Ecuador, and Peru).

---

[187] W. Currie, Merck and Co., Inc., Registration in Central & South America (Dec. 1995). Not counting any additional time for an FDA export certificate, registration times were Argentina 6 months, Brazil 24 months, Costa Rica 6 months, Chile 12 to 24 months, El Salvador 4 months, Guatemala 3 months, Honduras 12 months, Mexico 10 to 15 months, Nicaragua 6 months, Panama 6 months, Peru 1 month, and Venezuela 6 months.

[188] *Id.*

[189] Argentina accepts an export certificate only from the United States., Japan, Switzerland, Sweden, Israel, Austria, Germany, France, United Kingdom, Netherlands, Belgium, Denmark, Spain, and Italy. Brazil accepts a certificate from any developed country, and Peru only from the United States. or an EU country. *Id.*

[190] *Id.*

[191] *Id.* Bolivia, Costa Rica, Ecuador, Guatemala, El Salvador, Honduras, Nicaragua, and Panama.

[192] *Id.* Allison Shurie, Intern; Food & Drug Admin., Legalization of Export Certificates (Aug. 1996).

[193] An FDA expert's report praised ANMAT and recommended strengthening its staff, improving the transparency of its decisionmaking, retaining jurisdiction over all food, drug, and medical device products in Argentina, strengthening its medical device program, and using publicity to protect the public health, and strengthening cooperation with counterparts in North America and Europe. M. Smith, FDA, An Evaluation of the Administracion Nacional de Medicamentos, Alimentos y Tecnologia Medica, Republic of Argentina 1-2 (May 25, 1995).

[194] Mercado Comun del Sur (MERCOSUR) is a free-trade area comprised of Argentina, Brazil, Paraguay, and Uruguay, with Bolivia and Chile joining in the near future.

The issue of intellectual property protection has been a source of conflict between the U.S. government and industry, on the one hand, and pharmaceutical companies in some South American countries.[195] Argentina has no patent law, and in Argentina and several other countries information produced by the innovative company benefits, facilitates, or shortens the approval process of a copied medicine or generic.[196] In some Latin American countries, health care procurement or reimbursement prices are set in a way that gives a preference or advantage to generic copies.[197] Lack of adequate intellectual property protection can undermine innovation, by discouraging development of indigenous industry and research into regional diseases, such as Chagus' Disease and leishmaniasis.[198]

In the absence of adequate intellectual property protection in another country, the FDA cannot undertake certain forms of technical cooperation, e.g., sharing confidential commercial information relevant to product approvals (such as internal FDA medical officers' memoranda on pending applications),[199] and its ability to cooperate on such matters as pharmaceutical GMPs is hindered because any joint inspections done must be done knowing that only the personal integrity of the other country's inspector, not the legislation of his or her country, assures the confidentiality of any trade secret processes observed during the inspection.

■ Australia

The Therapeutic Goods Administration (TGA) regulates pharmaceuticals as well as medical devices and cosmetics in Australia. The principal authority for these activities is the Therapeutic Goods Act of 1989, which centralized controls in a national government authority, rather than having authorities dispersed among Australia's states. TGA and the FDA cooperate on a wide variety of matters. TGA is keenly interested in the FDA's actions involving pharmaceuticals and therefore obtains information from the FDA about the pharmaceuticals through such means as personal visits, frequent use of the FDA's Website on the Internet, direct usage of an the FDA database concerning GMP compliance,[200] and the FDA's regulation on sharing information with foreign officials.[201]

■ Russia and New Independent States

The Russian Ministry of Health has the authority to approve drugs for use in the Russian Federation. In the mid-1990s, the U.S. government and the Russian government undertook a series of cooperative efforts aimed at helping to assure the availability of essential pharmaceuticals and other products and to curb the spread of communicable diseases, particularly diphtheria, that were a threat not only to the citizens of Russia, but to world

---

[195] W. Currie, Merck and Co., Inc., Registration in Central & South America (Dec. 1995).

[196] *Id.*

[197] *Id.*

[198] *Id.*

[199] 21 C.F.R. § 20.89 authorizes the FDA to share most non-public information with other countries without that information becoming public.

[200] *See infra* text accompanying notes 435 to 436.

[201] 21 C.F.R. § 21.89.

health generally. Among these activities were training for vaccines experts; joint seminars on a broad range of topics;[202] several MOUs aimed at strengthening cooperation and streamlining Russian importation of U.S. drugs, food, and medical devices;[203] and a similar MOU with Belarus.[204] The FDA also assisted the Russian Duma (lower house of parliament) in its drafting of pharmaceutical[205] and medical device legislation.[206] Seminars and cooperation also were undertaken with Ukraine.[207]

The disintegration of the former Union of Soviet Socialist Republics had led to a period of upheaval in the health care systems of that region and a redirection of U.S. foreign aid to the Russian Federation, Ukraine, and other new independent states. The U.S. Agency for International Development (AID) paid for the FDA's technical cooperation and assistance activities with Russia and Ukraine, and within the FDA these activities were led by the FDA's Deputy Commissioner/Senior Advisor.

The MOU signed by the FDA and its counterparts in the Russian government provides for the use of streamlined procedures in Russia for approval of FDA-approved products. This agreement helped to meet critical shortages of pharmaceuticals in Russia and also helped to reduce some of the red tape associated with shipments to Russia of U.S.-produced products.

China

China has a growing pharmaceutical industry and is extremely interested in how the FDA regulates pharmaceuticals. In fiscal year 1996 alone, the FDA had 389 visitors from China—Japan and Russia had 125 visitors each.[208] Approximately 278 of whom were interested in drug regulation.

■ Other Countries' Systems and Cooperation With the FDA

Israel's drug approval authority, as a matter of policy, follows and adopts the FDA's drug approval decisions. The FDA and its counterparts in Israel have been involved for many years in a variety of cooperative activities on medical products, including a seminar on regulation of research in 1995. In past years the FDA has also given technical assistance to Egypt and Saudi Arabia, under programs funded by AID.

India has a huge pharmaceutical industry, with 23,700 pharmaceutical manufacturing units providing products for the domestic market and for export.[209] The FDA gives only limited technical assistance to India in the pharmaceuticals area, because weak intellectual

---

[202] Linda R. Horton, Dir., Int'l Policy, FDA Trip Report, Trip to Moscow (May 1993).

[203] FOOD & DRUG ADMIN., INTERNATIONAL COOPERATIVE AGREEMENTS MANUAL 287, 295, 283, 325 (November 1996). The medical device agreement was simply a statement of intent with Russia on cooperation and information exchange on medical devices.

[204] *Id.* at 21.

[205] Linda R. Horton, Dir., Int'l Policy, FDA, Trip Report, Trip to Moscow (Mar. 1995).

[206] Linda R. Horton, Dir., Int'l Policy, FDA, Trip Report, Trip to Moscow (May 1997).

[207] Linda R. Horton, Dir., Int'l Policy, FDA, Trip Report, Trip to Ukraine (June 1995).

[208] Food & Drug Admin. International Visitors Program, Annual Report, at 6-10, 36 (1996).

[209] Indian production up 15%, SCRIP, Nov. 8, 1996, at 16.

property laws in that country could easily result in a situation where experts from the United States might unwittingly aid in the violation of intellectual property rights.

The FDA's technical assistance activities often mirror the foreign aid priorities of AID, because the FDA generally does not provide technical assistance unless either the problem being dealt with is presenting public health issues in the United States, e.g., violative imports, or the assistance is otherwise in the foreign policy interest of the United States, e.g., assistance to Middle East countries and Russia. In the latter case, the FDA's expenses are generally paid by AID, an international organization, or the country receiving the assistance. (More than half the U.S. foreign aid budget in recent years has been directed to Russia, Ukraine, and the Middle East, leaving relatively little for the neediest countries in Africa, the Americas, and Asia.)

Infectious Disease Control and Biologics

■ Emerging and Re-Emerging Diseases

Infectious diseases do not respect borders. Rather, with the vast numbers of tourists, business travelers, immigrants, and refugees that move around the globe, countries are increasingly interdependent in their disease control efforts.[210] The incubation periods for most infectious diseases are shorter than the duration of most jet plane flights, meaning that returning travelers or new arrivals have cleared Customs and proceeded to their destinations before symptoms have manifested themselves.[211]

According to the WHO, each year some 17,000,000 people succumb to pathogens, about a third of whom die.[212] Although the eradication of smallpox in 1977 was thought to mark the turning point in man's battle against infectious disease, by the end of the century even preventable diseases were far from under control and the emergence of pathogens resistant to known therapies complicated infection control efforts.[213]

---

[210] For a discussion of the international anxiety about travel by individuals with HIV in the early years after the disease was discovered, see Leonard J. Nelson III, *International Travel Restrictions and the AIDS Epidemic*, 81 Am. J. Int'l L. 230 (Jan. 1987).

[211] Dr. Joseph Losos, Dir. General, Laboratory Centre for Disease Control (LCDC), Health Protection Branch, Health Canada, Collaboration Between Canada, the United Kingdom, and the United States For Emerging Pathogens (Sept. 5, 1995) (proposing a quarterly consultation among Canada's LCDC, the U.S. Centers for Disease Control, and the U.K. Public Health Laboratory Service, until the WHO has completed its development of an international mechanism).

[212] *Curing the curable: Medicine can treat infectious diseases. To abolish them requires prosperity*, The Economist, May 25, 1996, at 17.

[213] *Id*. Culprits include laxity toward vaccination in many countries but particularly in Southern Asia and in Central and Eastern Europe; overuse of antibiotics, pesticides, and antimalarial drugs; and lack of economic development ("Europe was cured of cholera not by medicine but by the delivery of clean water to people's houses and the piping of sewage underground"). *Id*.

The outbreak of pneumonic plague in India in 1994 and the localized outbreak in 1995 of Ebola virus hemorrhagic fever in Zaire (renamed "the Congo" in 1997) were forceful reminders of how far the human race is from conquering infectious disease.[214] To respond to such crises, the WHO has announced plans to establish a strike force that can spring into action quickly to send international and national experts to the parts of the world experiencing a disease outbreak, and the World Bank is treating disease control as a high priority.[215] Developed countries are not spared: in 1996 there were 8400 reported cases of *E. coli* food poisoning in Japan[216] as well as eighteen deaths in Scotland.[217]

In the future, global climate change may markedly increase the range of many infectious diseases, especially those spread by insects (such as malaria, dengue, river blindness, sleeping sickness, and St. Louis encephalitis) or water (such as cholera).[218]

In late 1996, the United States and EU announced their plan to establish a global early warning network to alert doctors and governments about budding epidemics, focusing initially upon food-borne illnesses such as hepatitis and *E. coli* and extending to other diseases if the initial effort is successful.[219] Although the U.S. focal point for disease control is the Center for Disease Control, several of the measures announced to strengthen domestic and international surveillance, prevention, and response to such diseases[220] will involve the FDA:

- ensuring the availability of drugs, vaccines, and diagnostic tests needed to combat emerging and re-emerging infectious diseases;
- promoting public awareness of emerging and re-emerging infectious diseases through cooperation with nongovernment organizations and the private sector;
- strengthening research activities to improve diagnostics, treatment, and prevention, and improving the understanding of the biology of infectious diseases; and
- developing new approaches to detect and control emerging infectious diseases, with particular emphasis on combatting antimicrobial drug resistance.[221]

The U.S. government's plan is accomplish these goals through collaboration with the EU (U.S.-EU New Transatlantic Agenda), Japan (U.S.-Japan Common Agenda), Russia

---

[214] *Id.*

[215] DEAN T. JAMISON, W. HENRY MOSLEY, ANTHONY R. MEASHAM, JOSE LUIS BOBADILLA, DISEASE CONTROL PRIORITIES IN DEVELOPING COUNTRIES, (The World Bank, 1995).

[216] *Japan Jhuns Radishes after 'Possible Link' to E.Coli*, 382 NATURE 567 (Aug. 15, 1996).

[217] *World Health Organization Issues Warning on Increased Food Bacteria Risks*, WORLD FOOD CHEM. NEWS, Feb. 5, 1997, at 13.

[218] David Brown, *Infectious Disease May Rise as the World Gets Warmer*, WASH. POST, Jan. 17, 1996, *citing* Jonathan A. Patz, JAMA, Jan. 17, 1996.

[219] White House Briefing Room, Press Conference by President Clinton, President Santer of the European Commission, and Prime Minister Prodi of Italy (June 12, 1996). *Worldwide Network to Warn of Epidemics: Under Plan, U.S. and European Governments Will Take Lead in Reporting Outbreaks*, WASH. POST, Nov. 28, 1996, at A19.

[220] Presidential Decision Directive (June 12, 1996).

[221] L. Beaver, FDA Strategy for Responding to the Presidential Decision Directive on Emerging and Re-emerging Infectious Diseases (June 21, 1996).

(Gore-Chernomyrdin Health Committee), South Africa (Gore-Mbeki Commission), WHO, and other international partners.[222] Activities involve all of the FDA product areas (food, drugs, biologics, and diagnostic devices) and will include technical assistance, educational programs, training, workshops, advisory committee meetings, policy development and implementation, research and development, surveillance, reporting, liaison activities not only with other governments but also with academia, industry, and other non-government organizations.[223]

The WHO requires governments to report outbreaks of just three diseases, cholera, plague, and yellow fever, and thus omits such newer deadly diseases as Ebola. These well-publicized efforts help to combat the complacency about communicable disease that has resulted in delayed recognition of new emerging diseases (such as HIV in the 1980s).

■ Bovine Spongiform Encephalopathy[224]

In the late 1980s and the 1990s, traditional notions of how diseases are spread were shaken by bovine spongiform encephalopathy (BSE). Could oddly behaving proteins, known as prions, carry disease from one species to another through the food supply, transmitting an incurable, fatal neurological disease?[225] In March 1996, there was an announcement that ten Britons were believed to have acquired Cruetzfeldt-Jakob disease as a possible result of ingesting beef from cattle that had BSE.

The postulated association between consumption of beef from cows afflicted with BSE and the appearance of Creutzfeldt-Jakob disease raised serious issues not only about beef consumption and animal husbandry feeding practices, but also about a diverse array of bovine materials (e.g., gelatin and tallow) used in drug, biological, cosmetic, and medical device products.[226]

The BSE episode was a divisive in the EU.[227] Other countries in the EU were appalled to learn of the extent of British exports of cattle feed containing offal from possibly affected animals, and BSE began to be found in other European countries.[228] The United Kingdom promised to cull hundreds of thousands of cattle, then decided it would not do so, when the fiscal consequences were understood.[229] For a time the United Kingdom refused to cooperate on European decisionmaking until it was given assurances about its future abil-

---

[222] *Id.* The bilateral activities described in the text are regular — often bilateral — meetings held at the Presidential or Vice Presidential level to announce joint initiatives, with the FDA and other agencies playing a part when their activities are involved.

[223] *Id.*

[224] BSE is discussed in more detail in Linda R. Horton, *International Harmonization of Food and Veterinary Medicine Regulation, in* 1 FUNDAMENTALS OF LAW AND REGULATION ch. 13 (FDLI 1997).

[225] Gina Kolata, *Viruses or Prions: An Old Medical Debate Still Rages*, N.Y. TIMES, Oct. 4, 1994, at C1.

[226] Sue Green and Joanna McNamara, *BSE and the Pharmaceutical Industry*, REG. AFF. J. 728 (1996).

[227] *Cover-Up at the Commission?* EUROPEAN, Sept. 5-11, 1996, at 12.

[228] EU Parliament [Manuel Medina Ortega, rapporteur], Report on alleged contraventions or maladministration in the implementation of Community law in relation to BSE, Strasbourg (Feb. 25, 1997).

[229] *Id.* ¶ 12; *Cull 'Under Review,'* EUROPEAN, Sept. 12-18, 1996.

ity to export certain bovine products.[230] The BSE episode raised questions about the adequacy of the public health framework in the EU, the relationship among the member states and the European institutions, and the adequacy of the decisionmaking processes in the European Commission, European Council, and the United Kingdom.

Does Europe need an FDA?[231] If Europe had an FDA, would the BSE crisis have been prevented or mitigated? No one can answer that question, but 1996 and 1997 saw visits to the FDA by high-ranking French,[232] Irish,[233] and European[234] officials looking for a way to strengthen regulatory structures. Ironically, at the same time other countries were seeking to emulate the FDA, Congress was considering how to reform it or make it more like foreign drug approval agencies (concerning reliance on summaries, use of outside experts, and providing that approvals would not be delayed for time taken to conduct inspections).[235]

The BSE episode also produced a high degree of skittishness not only about the efficacy of measures to stop the practices thought to have led to the BSE crisis,[236] but also about the seemingly unrelated area of biotechnology.[237] EU officials were concerned about bovine materials from *outside* the EU: in early 1997, the EU published a directive that would exclude from cosmetics any ingredients derived from central nervous system tissue, i.e., eyes, spinal cords, and brains from cattle, sheep, or goat sources. The EU strictly interpreted this exclusion to apply to any ingredients that may include CNS tissue, from animals that may have had bovine, ovine, or caprine material in their feed stocks.[238] Further, the EU did not make a distinction between BSE countries and BSE-free countries in that they applied no legal definition of what constitutes a BSE-free country. Accordingly, the EU covered U.S. products in its directive. U.S. rendering processes for manufacturing tallow may include feed stock from CNS tissue. Therefore, the EU directive treated U.S. tallow as an ingredient prohibited by the directive. Officials in the EU (Directorate Gen-

---

[230] *Mad, Bad, and Dangerous: John Major's Policy of Non-Co-Operation with Europe is Part of a Worrisome Jingoistic Tendency in Britain*, THE ECONOMIST, May 25, 1996, at 16, 51-53.

[231] *Id.* II. Recommendations for the Future 3.7 ("It should be recommended that the EU equip itself with . . . a powerful Public Health Protection Unit, encompassing both human and animal health."). President Santer of the EU said that "he did not rule out the creation of an agency based on the model of the U.S. Food and Drug Administration," *Focus: European Union*, WORLD FOOD REG. REV., Mar. 1996, at 18.

[232] FOOD & DRUG ADMIN., INTERNATIONAL VISITORS PROGRAM ANNUAL REPORT, 14 (1996).

[233] Linda R. Horton, Dir. Int'l Policy, FDA, Meeting of Prime Minister John Bruton, Ireland, with Mary K. Pendergast, Deputy Commissioner/Senior Advisor to the Commissioner, Linda R. Horton, Janice Oliver, and John Vanderveen (Mar. 17, 1997).

[234] Paola Buonadonna, *Bonino grasps poisoned chalice*, THE EUROPEAN, Feb. 20, 1997, at 4.

[235] *See supra* note 35 and accompanying text.

[236] Concerns remained about the trustworthiness of industry interests in BSE countries. A British researcher told the European Parliament that Britain continues to export gelatin despite the EU ban, in FOOD CHEM. NEWS, Mar. 3, 1997, at 41. Richard Lacey, Professor, Leeds University, claimed that neither government nor industry knew from what animals the raw materials for gelatin were coming, that Britain exports 600,000 tons of gelatin a month, and that Britain is "exporting infectivity to the rest of the world, still." The British government denied the allegations and insisted that all raw materials used in the beef gelatin industry are imported. *Id.*

[237] Like the frowned-on practice of feeding ruminant offal to other ruminants, biotechnology was viewed as a departure from the traditional, time-tested agricultural methods.

[238] The information in this paragraph is based upon an internal FDA memorandum entitled Office of Executive Secretariat Weekly Information Update (Mar. 14, 1997).

eral XXIV) expressed concern about the possibility that BSE may exist in the United States even though no cases have been reported.[239] They also questioned whether the United States has adequate controls to assure that tallow was manufactured from healthy animals and that CNS tissue was excluded. Controls in the EU include veterinarian certification of animal health and restrictions on what parts of the animal may be introduced into the rendering process.

The directive would prohibit export of tallow to EU for incorporation in consumer products as well as finished products that contain tallow. Such a ban would have a significant impact on the U.S. tallow industry and cosmetic industry. Furthermore, the EU has considered extending the ban to gelatin and other pharmaceutical ingredients with bovine, sheep, or goat origin, causing such great alarm in pharmaceutical industry on both sides of the Atlantic that the European Commission acting on requests from the FDA and industry, delayed action.[240]

■ Vaccines and Other Biologics[241]

There has been active international standard-setting for biological product safety, efficacy, and quality for more than fifty years.[242] Officials from the FDA's Center for Biologics Evaluation and Research (CBER) have served as expert consultants to WHO, or as members of a variety of international committees that develop internationally accepted standards for control of biologics. In 1996, CBER formally requested designation as a WHO Collaborating Centre for Biological Standardization, to undertake collaborative studies to establish biological reference preparations, to undertake research and testing for improving the standardization and control of biological products for humans, to train laboratory personnel, and to provide scientific expertise in the development of WHO written requirements and recommendations.[243] The latter step was important because the FDA's regulations and guidance documents for biologics are highly influential internationally,[244] but (as is discussed below) in recent years there has been a trend in WHO toward increased use of European standards that, because of differences, exclude many U.S. products. Where the FDA has made a significant investment in the development of WHO standards, it has been able to use the standards when developing new regulations or amendments to existing regulations for the manufacture of certain biological products, e.g., typhoid vaccine, polio vaccine (live oral), and interferon alpha. For example, the FDA revised its regulations for polio virus vaccine (live oral) to bring them more in line with the WHO standards.[245] Although the FDA is revising or revoking many regulations imposing biologics standards,[246] as a part of the *Reinventing Government* activities for drugs and devices ini-

---

[239] Meeting between FDA officials and Emma Bonino, Commissioner, DG-XXIV (Mar. 26, 1997).

[240] WASH. POST, Apr. 8, 1997, at C5.

[241] John C. Petricciani, *International Expectations for Harmonization of Biological Standards*, 49 FOOD & DRUG L.J. 397 (1994).

[242] FOOD & DRUG ADMIN., REPORT OF THE FDA TASK FORCE ON INTERNATIONAL HARMONIZATION, app. E, at 1 (1992).

[243] Letter to Elwyn Griffiths, Chief, Biologicals Program, WHO, from Kathryn Zoon, Director, CBER, FDA (Nov. 19, 1996).

[244] FOOD & DRUG ADMIN, REPORT OF THE FDA TASK FORCE ON INTERNATIONAL HARMONIZATION, app. E, at 2 (1992).

[245] 56 Fed. Reg. 2148 (May 8, 1991).

[246] 60 Fed. Reg. 53,479 (October 13, 1995).

tiated in 1995 by President Clinton and Vice President Gore,[247] international and other standards will continue to be important in FDA decisions on individual product licensure.

WHO's efforts have been directed to many kinds of biological products, including vaccines, human blood and plasma products, blood testing reagents, and allergenic extracts, and have extended to biotechnology-derived growth factors, cytokines, and monoclonal antibody products. Of these, vaccine-related harmonization activities are the oldest and probably the most comprehensive. In addition to the WHO, other organizations active in standard-setting and harmonization for biologics include ICH and the Council of Europe, which administers the European Pharmacopeia.[248] Additionally, called the International Association of Biological Standardization also has done some work in this field.[249]

Many other international organizations, including UNICEF, the World Bank, and the U.S. AID, promote vaccination by funding purchases of vaccines that have prevented many childhood deaths.[250] These funding programs support vaccination programs such as the WHO Expanded Programme on Immunization, the Children's Vaccines Initiative,[251] and the Global Program on Vaccines, all of which aim to immunize all children against a number of different diseases and are on track to eliminate polio by the year 2000.[252]

WHO's endorsement since 1982[253] of use in immunization programs only of those vaccines that meet international standards was intended to deter countries from using vaccines that may be below minimum standards of safety, potency, and quality.[254] To meet the international standard, vaccines must be subject to control by the national control authority of the producing country, and that authority must supply a certificate stating that the vaccine meets these requirements.[255] And, to be considered a competent authority, the regulatory agency must meet the requirements of the Certification Scheme on the Quality of Pharmaceutical Products Moving in International Commerce.[256]

---

[247] NATIONAL PERFORMANCE REVIEW, REINVENTING DRUG AND DEVICE REGULATIONS, (Apr. 1995).

[248] FOOD & DRUG ADMIN., REPORT OF THE FDA TASK FORCE ON INTERNATIONAL HARMONIZATION app E., at 1 (1992).

[249] *Id*. app. G, letter from D. Magrath (Mar. 13, 1992). This group is a platform for a discussion and consensus on issues relating to biologicals, frequently as the basis for advice to WHO, that includes in its membership not only officials regulatory agencies but also of manufacturers, international health associations and academics. *Id*.

[250] Judy Mann, *There is Hope for the Children*, WASH. POST, Mar. 14, 1997, at E3, *quoting from* 1997 UNICEF report by Terry R. Peel.

[251] The Children's Vaccine Initiative was launched in 1990 at the meeting of the World Summit for Children in New York City. Its purpose was to harness new technologies to advance the immunization of children, e.g., a single dose, effective when given near birth, heat stable, containing multiple antigens, effective against diseases not currently targeted, and affordable. *See* INSTITUTE OF MEDICINE, THE CHILDREN'S VACCINE INITIATIVE: ACHIEVING THE VISION (Nat'l Academy Press, 1993); B.R. Bloom, *The United States Needs a National Vaccine Authority*, 265 SCIENCE 1378-80 (1994).

[252] WHA41.28 (May 1988); *Polio campaign in Asia immunizes 250 [million] infants*, 20 NATURE 670 (Feb. 20, 1997). *Polio gone by 2000, measles next*, SCRIP, Nov. 26, 1996, at 15.

[253] WHA 35/1982/REC/I. 25, WHA 35.31 (May 1982). Also, in setting the goal of global eradication of polio by the year 2000, the WHO called for universal use of polio vaccines meeting international requirements by the end of 1990. WHA 41.28 (May 1988). Plans for control of measles and elimination of neonatal tetanus also specify the use of vaccines meeting international standards. WHA 42 (May 1989).

[254] WHO A 45/8, Expanded Programme on Immunization and Vaccine Quality 17 (Apr. 1992).

[255] *Id*.

[256] WHA Resolution 41.18 (May 1988).

This elaborate and well-meaning scheme has had the unintended consequence of discriminating against U.S. products that meet FDA requirements — or FDA-approved company specifications — that do not meet precisely the international standards set by WHO but that result in products that are equivalent or even superior.[257] The discrimination is compounded when national or international procurements, or national laws on eligibility for marketing, base eligibility on compliance with WHO standards:

- Merck measles, mumps and rubella vaccine offers superior safety and efficacy but does not meet WHO standards for storage and transport that are met by inferior products.[258]
- A Wyeth Lederle diphtheria-tetanus-pertussis vaccine was barred from several procurements because it did not meet several scientifically irrelevant animal potency tests found in WHO standards.[259]
- In 1993 the government of Lithuania, using a World Bank loan, awarded a contract to a French firm for mumps vaccine even though, less than a year earlier, the same firm's vaccine had produced unacceptable levels of meningoencephalitis;[260] Merck's competing bid (for a vaccine that produces meningoencephalitis in only one of 2.5 million cases) was rejected on the basis that the price was too high.[261]
- Similarly, in 1995 the Hungarian government's procurement tender specified, for its measles-mumps-rubella vaccine, a strain of mumps vaccine that had caused such high rates of meningitis that the products had been pulled from the shelves in Canada, Japan, and the United Kingdom; because Merck's vaccine did not meet WHO standards, it was ineligible to bid.
- Assorted other problems vex WHO and other international organizations' handling of vaccines. For example, Even though South Korean Green Cross Hepatitis B vaccine lacked WHO approval, Green Cross beat out Merck in a November 1995 UNICEF tender for Pacific Island countries; UNICEF maintained that, although the Green Cross vaccine was not actually WHO approved, it is routinely used with WHO concurrence.[262] Another Korean vaccine that did have WHO approval, for Hepatitis B, had a 30% to 40% failure rate.[263]

---

[257] Linda Horton, Dir., Int'l Policy, FDA, notes from FDA meeting, Rockville, MD (July 11, 1996). U.S. vaccines that may not meet WHO standards may include those for pertussis (due to a stability test difference), measles, polio (due to a different upper limit for potency). *Id.* The difficulty U.S. firms experience in donating vaccines is illustrated by the decision of Wyeth Lederle to donate a million dollars in cash to the CVI rather than donating or selling vaccines as European manufacturers commonly do. Memorandum from Elaine Esber, Wyeth Donation to CVI (Dec. 10, 1996).

[258] M. Garenne, O. Leroy, J-P Beau, & I. Sene, *Child Mortality After High-Titer Measles Vaccines: Prospective Study in Senegal*, 338 THE LANCET 907-10 (1991); *Measles Battle Loses Potent Weapon*, 258 SCIENCE 546 (Oct. 23, 1992); 48 Weekly Epidemiological Record 357-61 (Nov. 27, 1992); R. Kambarami, K. Nathoo, F. Nkrumah, & D. Pirie, *Measles Epidemic in Harare, Zimbabwe, Despite High Measles Immunization Coverage Rates*, 69 Bulletin of the WHO 213-19 (1991).

[259] A. Capron, C. Locht & G.N. Fracchia, *Safety and Efficacy in New Generation Vaccines*, 12 VACCINES 667 (1994).

[260] SCRIP, Sept. 16, 1992.

[261] David Nalin, Measles, *Mumps and Rubella. Asia's Opportunity for Eradication*, MEDIMEDIA ASIA, MERCK SHARPE & DOHME, undated, at 3. The World Bank's procurement policies not only recommend that the contract be awarded to the lowest bidder but also that "a fast track registration process through which drugs of the lowest estimated bidder can be automatically registered." Standard Bidding Documents for Procurement of Pharmaceuticals and Vaccines, Trial Ed., (Sept. 1993), 27; DENIS BROUN, PROCUREMENT OF PHARMACEUTICALS IN WORLD BANK PROJECTS 16 (World Bank, Sept. 1993).

[262] UNICEF Australia, Pacific Regional, The Control of Hepatitis B Infection in Pacific Island Countries, Project Implementation Document 15 (Nov. 15, 1995).

[263] Letter from Merck Vaccine Division Hong Kong to Merck USA (May 21, 1996).

The role of WHO as clinical trials sponsor is also controversial: WHO pursued clinical trials of a possible malaria vaccine known as Spf66, the inventor of which has assigned to WHO an exclusive worldwide, royalty-free license, with production in Colombia.[264] Test results from refugee camps in Thailand found a slightly higher incidence of malaria among those injected with Spf66 than in a control group, and a trial in Gambia was equally disappointing.[265]

In 1989, WHO began promoting a vaccine for measles, intended to be less expensive than Western vaccines but, after field trials in Haiti, Togo, Senegal, and other developing countries, in 1992 withdrew the product due to higher mortality rates. In 1996, CDC made the shocking announcement that this same "WHO-approved vaccine was used in 1989 as one of two vaccines during a major measles epidemic in Los Angeles," and CDC had not disclosed to any of the parents that, in the United States, the vaccine was unlicensed and experimental.[266]

In order for a product to be certified as meeting WHO standards for vaccines and biologics, the manufacturer must undergo a detailed approval process — once — that includes a site visit by a WHO inspection team.[267] U.S. vaccine producers are reluctant to submit to the WHO-required joint inspection without assurance that WHO can protect the confidentiality of inspectional observations and documents submitted for review,[268] and because the lack of WHO safeguards to prevent conflict of interest among those individuals conducting inspections.[269] Unless WHO can address these fundamental concerns about confidentiality[270] and eliminate of conflicts of interest, or WHO is willing to allow the FDA inspections to substitute for its team inspections, U.S. vaccine manufacturers unwilling to take a chance on WHO inspections are likely to continue to have difficulty getting WHO approvals necessary for UNICEF and World Bank procurements. One solution favored by U.S. industry would be for WHO to allow conformity with the FDA's regulatory system generally to substitute for conformity to WHO standards. It would be difficult, however, for WHO to grant this form of recognition to the United States without opening the door to requests for similar status from many other countries.

Some industry officials believe that WHO holds the view that vaccines are products that can be produced under generic product monographs that prescribe the units of potency and

---

[264] WHO Task Force on Health Economics, WHO press release, Geneva (Nov. 1994).

[265] N.Y. TIMES, Sept. 15, 1996, *quoting from* THE LANCET (Sept. 1996).

[266] Marlene Cimons, *U.S. Measles Experiment Failed to Disclose Risk*, LOS ANGELES TIMES, *as reprinted in* WASH. POST, June 17, 1996.

[267] U.S. Commerce Dep't, Commercial Service Memorandum (Nov. 3, 1995).

[268] Linda Horton, Dir., Int'l Policy, FDA, Notes from meeting between FDA officials, PhRMA representatives, and scientists from Merck, Eli Lilly, and Wyeth Rockville, MD (July 19, 1996) [(referring to conversations with WHO inspection team prior to an intended inspection that, due to concerns about confidentiality and lack of conflict of interest safeguards, was not carried out)].

[269] The WHO inspection team for a hepatitis b vaccine approval included three people who had conflicts of interest: a current representative of a manufacturer from a country that does not respect intellectual property rights who was using his Pan American Health Organization credentials; a representative of a competitor; and a WHO official who at that time was working for another competitor from a country that does not adhere to intellectual property rights. Interview with a regulatory affairs specialist of a U.S. vaccine manufacturer (Sept. 10, 1996).

[270] Treaties assuring the privileges and immunities of international organizations such as WHO provide a legal basis for resisting subpoenas seeking the disclosure of materials in the files of international organizations.

the batch release tests to be done, and that need not require data on clinical performance or guidance on interpretation of the potency test.[271] This discussion illustrates how WHO sometimes functions as an international regulatory body with respect to international procurement of vaccine. It "generally rel[ies] on the application of *international requirements* by the competent national control authority" with WHO undertaking to certify vaccines to international standards "[o]nly in isolated cases, notably for smallpox, yellow fever, and BCG vaccines."[272] With respect to vaccines supplied by UNICEF, WHO staff and consultants actually review protocols and documentation, test random lots of vaccines for stability and potency, and conduct inspections of manufacturing sites.[273]

At times, excellent products can fail the WHO potency test while other producers' ineffective products pass; furthermore, some lots released that meet WHO standards can be superpotent.[274] Furthermore, while the FDA has moved from batch testing to emphasis on GMPs, process validation, and benchmarking, WHO continues to stress batch release based on tests of uneven scientific validity.[275]

One reason that the WHO vaccine standards often reflect neither the characteristics of U.S. products, nor FDA-imposed testing or GMP-type requirements, is that U.S. commercial interests do not play a significant role in the drafting of WHO standards, thus ensuring that the standards are written sufficiently broadly so as to cover their products—as well as European produced versions.[276] Increasingly, drafting for WHO is done by European Pharmacopeia experts, who almost always are European industry officials.[277] Although the USP allows foreign members, the European Pharmacopeia allows only European members. As noted earlier, the United States recently was granted observer status in the Council of Europe, which may facilitate future participation in European Pharmacopeia activities.

The U.S. industry fear is that European firms might be using WHO standards to block U.S. exports to key emerging markets—if those countries follow the WHO advice and enact laws that require adherence to WHO vaccine standards as a condition to marketing in that country.[278] Indeed, "the European industry is the main partner of the international organizations and supplies 67% of the vaccines purchased by UNICEF and PAHO."[279]

---

[271] Linda Horton, Dir., Int'l Policy, FDA, Notes from meeting between FDA officials, PhRMA representatives, and scientists from Merck, Eli Lilly, and Wyeth Rockville, MD (July 19, 1996). The U.S. view, on the other hand, is that, because vaccines are derived from biological materials, they are more difficult to identify and characterize (and sometimes present special issues of toxicity, infectivity, and consistency) that require *more* regulation than do most other pharmaceuticals. PETER BARTON HUTT AND RICHARD A. MERRILL, FOOD AND DRUG LAW: CASES AND MATERIALS 664-65 (2d ed., 1991). Many other countries, e.g., France, Canada, and Russia, likewise regulate vaccines in separate administrative subunits and sometimes under separate statutes.

[272] WHO A 45/8, Expanded Programme on Immunization and Vaccine Quality (April 1992) at 16.

[273] Author's notes from July 19, 1996, meeting, *supra* note 272.

[274] *Id.*

[275] *Id.*

[276] *Id.*

[277] *Id.*

[278] *Id.* Indeed, Merck reportedly was low bidder on a Brazilian procurement of vaccine but lost the contract because the vaccine met U.S., not WHO, standards. *Id.*

[279] Report, *Safety and Efficacy of New Generation Vaccines*, 12 VACCINE 687, 688 (1994); N. Baudrihaye, *European Vaccine Manufacturers: Present Status and Future Trends*, 10 VACCINE 893 (1992).

Furthermore, as part of EU industrial policy, vaccines and other products to combat viral diseases have been identified as a priority area for industrial development.[280]

U.S. industry concerns were heightened when, in 1996, the World Health Assembly came close to passing a Resolution offered during the meeting (without having undergone review by the WHO Executive Board, as is the usual procedure)[281] that called for member countries to "use only vaccines and other biological products of recognized and certified quality, safety, and efficacy and to adopt WHO requirements as part of their national regulations or to ensure by national regulations that products are at least as safe and as potent as those prepared in accordance with the requirements of WHO."[282]

When U.S. vaccine producers learned of this proposal and expressed concerns to the U.S. delegates at the meeting that the resolution may aggravate the difficulties U.S. vaccine producers faced already from WHO vaccine standards that excluded their products, the FDA representatives succeeded in persuading other countries' representatives that the Assembly should not adopt the resolution without first sending it to the WHO Executive Board via an expert ad hoc committee.[283] That gave the FDA time to produce, for the January 1997 Executive Board meeting, a redrafted version,[284] which was adopted by the Executive Board and forwarded to the Assembly, where it was adopted at its May 1997 meeting.[285] The redrafted version included provisions for a review of the WHO biologics standards program, a review of procedures for developing standards, and a retrospective review of existing WHO vaccine standards. The latter review provides an opportunity to eliminate obsolete and overly prescriptive features (or to relegate excessive detail to annexes that clearly are not to be accepted by countries as binding). Also, it is contemplated that this review will be conducted in a highly transparent manner, so that industry experts will have the opportunity to comment to their national delegates to identify provisions that have the effect of excluding safe, potent, and high-quality vaccines.

The proposed World Health Assembly resolution on use of WHO standards for biologicals brought to the fore a number of U.S. concerns regarding the relationship between WHO standards and the Agreement on Technical Barriers to Trade (TBT) of the World Trade Organization (WTO).

This is an opportune time for WHO to undertake a serious review of its procedures for developing standards and certifying products that would include consideration of how WHO will ensure that:

---

[280] European Commission, Task Force on Vaccines and Viral Diseases, First Report (Dec. 1995).

[281] U.S. mission, Geneva, unclassified cable, 49th World Health Assembly: Pharmaceutical and Biological Issues (May 31, 1996).

[282] 49th WHA, A49/A/Conf. Paper No. 2 (May 23, 1996). In 1992, a WHO report had recommended that health authorities use only vaccines meeting international standards, that countries producing vaccines assure that their vaccines meet the relevant international standards, and that national control authorities be sufficiently effective and competent. WHO A 45/8, Expanded Programme on Immunization and Vaccine Quality 17-18 (Apr. 1992).

[283] U.S. mission, Geneva, unclassified cable, 49th World Health Assembly: Pharmaceutical and Biological Issues, May 31, 1996; the World Health Assembly (May 1997).

[284] World Health Org., Quality of biological products moving in international commerce, EB 99.R22, Agenda item 16.5 (Jan. 21, 1997).

[285] U.S. mission, Geneva, unclassified cable, the WHO Executive Board (Feb. 1997).

- all Members have timely access to and the ability to comment on proposed standards, and that those comments are fully taken into account in the final adoption of standards;
- the development and adoption process for standards is fully transparent;
- any real or apparent conflicts of interest by expert consultants are revealed and taken into account;
- there is consistency in risk assessment and risk management approaches across all WHO biological standards development and certification activities; and
- the level of detail of WHO standards and certification requirements is, on the one hand, adequate to serve the needs of developing country Members relying on WHO standards and certifications as surrogate national approvals, and, on the other hand, is not unnecessarily detailed such that it precludes certification or acceptance of products that have been found by national authorities to meet the same or higher standards of safety, purity, potency and efficacy as those of WHO.

■ Blood

Special regulatory consideration is often given to those products derived from human blood or tissues because the risk of disease transmission is well documented. Maintaining the safety of the blood supply is an international goal. Among the groups that have been active in international harmonization of requirements for blood and blood products are WHO, the Council of Europe, the International Society for Blood Transfusion, and the Scientific and Standardization Committee of the International Society on Thrombosis and Haemostasis.[286]

During the late 1980s and the 1990s, blood safety scandals gripped the attention of health authorities in several countries, including Germany, France,[287] Canada, India,[288] and Japan:

> The president and two former presidents of Green Cross Corporation (Midori Juji), Japan's leading blood product manufacturer, were arrested last week in connection with the infection of thousands of Japanese through the use of non-heat-treated blood products in the 1980s. Further arrests are expected, possibly including a former official of the Ministry of Health and Welfare.... Prosecutors suspect that the three executives continued to promote the sale of non-heat-treated products in 1986, despite knowing [since 1984] the risk of HIV infection and the availability of safer heat-treated products . . . . The company [left] non-heat-treated products] on the market until 1988 — two years after the company had reported to the Ministry of Health and Welfare that withdrawal had been

---

[286] FOOD & DRUG ADMIN., REPORT OF THE FDA TASK FORCE ON INTERNATIONAL HARMONIZATION, app. E, at 1 (1992).

[287] *Ruling in French Blood Scandal*, WASH. POST, Mar. 12, 1997, at A24:

A French prosecutor investigating responsibility for a scandal over AIDS tainted blood transfusions has recommended clearing former prime minister Laurent Fabius . . . . In a report that outraged victims' families,[the prosecutor] also found no cause for prosecuting former health and social affairs ministers . . . . He said he did not rule out ministerial responsibility for the public health scandal but argued that theirs was political, not criminal, liability. The three, all Socialists, were in office when 1,250 hemophiliacs were infected by public health service blood products in 1985. The government delayed importing a U.S.-made AIDS blood-screener to give French laboratories time to develop their own. More than 400 of the infected hemophiliacs have since died.

[288] *Indian Supreme Court orders blood clean up*, SCRIP, Jan. 23, 1996, at 18.

completed . . . . Ministry officials face possible criminal charges for failing to order the withdrawal of non-heat-treated products.[289]

The family of one Japanese victim filed a charge of murder against both the president of Green Cross Corporation and the Ministry official who headed its biologics and antibiotics division from 1984 to 1986.[290]

Nor is blood the only tissue-derived biological product that has been involved in homicide cases: the distribution of human growth hormone extracted from cadavers, which led to cases of fatal Creutzfeldt-Jakob disease, led to the prosecution of five French physicians and health officials.[291] Two French governmental agencies, France Hypophyse (France pituitary) and the Paris Hospital Authority, continued to distribute cadaver-derived human growth hormone for ten years after the United States and the United Kingdom had banned this product.

Harmonization of regulatory requirements for blood products is particularly difficult because the health risks associated with infectious diseases. WHO has undertaken some activities in this area. For example, a 1991 WHO consultation on blood collection, processing, and quality control resulted in a series of recommendations (consistent with the U.S. approach).[292]

In 1991, the U.S. blood industry reacted with alarm when the European Commission[293] and the Council of Europe[294] proposed restrictions that were inconsistent with ones put in place by FDA in the early 1970s. The United States produces approximately half of the world's supply of plasma resource, for inclusion in products for therapeutic purposes (source plasma, albumin, coagulation concentrate products such as Factor VII and Factor IX, and immune globulin products).[295] When the United States-European controversy erupted, approximately 3,000,000 of the 7,000,000 liters of plasma produced in the United States were exported to Europe. The proposed restrictions also would have the effect of excluding U.S. plasma or forcing U.S. plasmapheresis facilities to make costly changes in their operations.[296] Also, use would be disallowed of plasma collected by plasmapheresis

---

[289] *Japan's HIV blood scandal broadens out*, 383 NATURE 291 (Sept. 26, 1996).

[290] *Id. Japanese firms face boycott*, SCRIP, Mar. 26, 1996, at 15; *Firms apologize in Japan blood affair*, id. Mar. 22, 1996, at 20; *Plot thickens in Japan blood affair*, *Id.*, Mar. 5, 1996, at 17.

[291] *French physicians charged over growth hormone 'poisoning,'* 385 NATURE 194 (Jan. 16, 1997).

[292] American Blood Resources Assoc'n FAX Letter 3 (Jan. 1992), reprinted in Food & Drug Admin., Report of the FDA Task Force on International Harmonization (1992), at Appendix G, as an attachment to letter from Robert W. Reilly, American Blood Resources Ass'n, April 27, 1992.

[293] Council Directive 89/381/EEC extending the scope of Directives 65/65/EEC and 75/319/EEC on the provisions laid down by law, regulation, or administrative action relating to proprietary medicinal products and laying down special provisions for medicinal products derived from human blood or human plasma, 181 OFFICIAL J. EUR. COMMUNITIES 44 (June 14, 1989).

[294] Council of Europe, European Health Committee (29th meeting), Committee of Experts on Blood Transfusion and Immunhaematology, Select Committee of Experts on Automation and Quality Assurance in Blood Transfusion Services, Guide on Preparation, Use, and Quality Assurance of Blood Components, Strasbourg (June 18-20, 1991).

[295] FOOD & DRUG ADMIN., REPORT OF THE FDA TASK FORCE ON INTERNATIONAL HARMONIZATION app. G., 1992, (letter from Robert W. Reilly, American Blood Resources Assoc'n, (Apr. 27, 1992).

[296] *Id.* For example, while the FDA allows a donor to undergo plasmapheresis twice a week, the Council of Europe limited the procedure to once a week. And while the FDA allows an individual to donate 50 to 60 liters of plasma a year (depending on body weight), the Council of Europe limited donations to a total of 15 liters a year.*Id.*

in countries allowing donors to donate quantities of plasma higher than was allowed by the Council of Europe.[297] A European trade association reportedly favored this restriction in order to exclude any non-European human plasma in any European plasma products and to force European self-sufficiency in blood and blood products.[298]

■ Human Tissues

The use of human tissues in medical treatment raises a broad array of medical and ethical issues that are resolved differently in various countries. In 1993, the FDA issued an interim rule on human tissue intended for transplantation, in part because of the agency's discovery that many tissues were being imported into the United States from sources that had not observed appropriate screening or aseptic precautions.[299]

Tissues also are being used in a wide range of legitimate applications.[300] In early 1997, the President and Vice President announced a new the FDA initiative establishing a comprehensive program for the regulation of human tissue.[301]

In the EU, the subject of tissue regulation was the subject of tremendous controversy in 1996 to 1997, when it was considered in conjunction with a medical devices directive dealing principally with *in vitro* diagnostic devices but including provisions on medical use of tissues.

Sensitive ethical and cultural issues are presented by the use of human tissues. For example, until 1997, organ transplants were virtually impossible in Japan because death was defined as the moment when the heart stops, after which other organs quickly become useless.[302] Almost every other country in the world treats death as occurring when electrical activity in the brain stops, even if the heart still beats.

Orphan Drugs

The U.S. orphan drug law[303] was enacted as a social policy initiative that combined government support with private research and development.[304] When the law was enacted in

---

[297] Swiss Serum and Vaccine Institute, Short Report, Council of Europe meeting (Sept. 24-26, 1991), reprinted in FOOD & DRUG ADMIN., REPORT OF THE FDA TASK FORCE ON INTERNATIONAL HARMONIZATION app. G. (1992), (attachment to letter from Robert W. Reilly, American Blood Resources Ass'n (Apr. 27, 1992).

[298] *Id.*

[299] 58 Fed. Reg. 65,514, 65,516 (Dec. 14, 1993).

[300] Biotechnology Biomaterials: A Global Regulatory Perspective for Tissue Engineered Products; a Workshop, Toronto, Canada (May 29, 1996).

[301] THE WHITE HOUSE NATIONAL PERFORMANCE REVIEW, REINVENTING HUMAN TISSUE REGULATION (Feb. 1997).

[302] W. Dawkins, *Hearts Rule Heads in Japanese Law*, FIN. TIMES, Jan. 6, 1997; K. Sullivan, *Japan Again Confronts Debate Over Transplants: Child on Way to U.S. Hopes for New Heart*, WASH. POST, Mar. 29, 1997 at A14.

[303] Pub. L. No. 97-414, 96 Stat. 2049 (1983); Pub. L. No. 98-551, 98 Stat. 2815 (1984); Pub. L. No. 99-91, 99 Stat. 387 (1985); Pub. L. No. 100-290, 102 Stat. 90 (1988). FDA regulations are found at 21 C.F.R. pt. 316.

[304] Paul Buday, *Hints on Preparing Successful Orphan Drug Designation Requests*, 51 FOOD & DRUG L.J. 75 (1996).

1983, no other country had a comparable statute in force, pending, or under consideration,[305] and only in the 1990s have other countries, e.g., Japan[306] and the EU,[307] begun to look to the U.S. program as an international model for similar legislation.[308] Within Europe, France has been particularly active in promoting EU orphan drug legislation and in 1994 included in its national law a provision for the accelerated use of orphan drugs prior to marketing approval.[309] Australia is considering recognizing FDA decisions as to orphan drug eligibility and streamlining approvals of such drugs by reliance upon FDA reviews of drug applications.[310]

Generic (Multi-Source) Drugs

> WHO has issued guidance on how countries should regulate "multi-source" drugs: "Multi-source pharmaceutical products are pharmaceutically equivalent products that may or may not be therapeutically equivalent. Multi-source pharmaceutical products that are therapeutically equivalent are interchangeable."[311]

The WHO document uses "multi-source pharmaceutical product" instead of "generic product" because the latter term has different meanings in different countries. In the WHO document had to the term "generic drug" means "a pharmaceutical product, usually intended to be interchangeable with the innovator product, which is usually manufactured without a license from the innovator company and marketed after expiry of patent or other exclusivity rights."[312]

Abbreviated applications for generic drugs are permitted in the United States,[313] Canada,[314] and the EU.[315] Within the EU, approvals are handled on a decentralized basis by

---

[305] *Id.*

[306] *Japan makes orphan designations four times a year*, SCRIP, Mar. 26, 1996, at 15.

[307] Draft Proposal for a European Parliament and Council Regulation on orphan medicinal products (Jan. 22, 1997). The European Commission heeded the FDA's suggestion that EU orphan drug status be available to products that had achieved such status in the United States or Japan. Letter to Patrick Deboyser, European Commission, from Marlene Haffner, FDA, on Draft Proposal dated Aug. 9, 1996 (Sept. 25, 1996). The European Medicines Evaluation Agency had already announced that orphan drugs would be eligible for a fee waiver or exemption, SCRIP, Dec. 15, 1995, at 5.

[308] J. Moran, *Towards an Orphan Drug Policy for Europe*, SCRIP MAG., Nov. 1996, at 25-27.

[309] *Id.* at 26.

[310] Meeting between Terry Slater, National Manager, Therapeutic Goods Administration, Australia, and Dr. Susan Alder, Director, Drug Safety and Evaluation Branch, with Marlene Haffner, Director of Orphan Products Development, FDA and Linda R. Horton, Director, Int'l Policy, FDA (Mar. 17, 1997).

[311] World Health Organization, Interchangeable Multi-Source Pharmaceutical Products: WHO Draft Guideline on Marketing Authorization Requirements 6 (Aug. 1994).

[312] *Id.* at 5.

[313] FDCA § 505(j); 21 U.S.C. § 355 (j).

[314] Health Canada, The Food and Drug Regulations, C.08.001.1 et. seq.

[315] Commission of the European Communities, CPMP Operational Working Party, Note for Guidance, Abridged Applications, 111/3879/90-EN, Draft 6 (Feb. 12, 1991).

the individual countries. Manufacturers have complained about inconsistent and nontransparent requirements, particularly as to bioequivalence and exclusivity periods, and have called for a harmonized approach or at least an EU list of reference products.[316] The EU Health Ministers have urged the Commission to examine existing rules on generic drugs, particularly those aimed at encouraging the prescribing of generic drugs and clarifying the technical requirements for their evaluation, registration, and approval.[317]

There is a trend among the health care systems in Europe and elsewhere to encourage physicians to prescribe generics. Among these countries are France,[318] Germany,[319] the United Kingdom,[320] Australia,[321] and Canada.[322] In those countries where pharmacists have not been allowed to substitute generics for prescribed brand-name drugs consideration is being given to allowing substitution.[323]

The low prices in Europe for brand-name drugs, due to tight governmental price controls or other reasons (in France, Italy, Portugal, Spain, and Sweden), as well as the availability of cheap parallel imports of brand-name drugs (in the United Kingdom, Denmark, Germany, and the Netherlands), undermine the ability of generic firms to gain a larger share in the EU market.[324]

An issue for the generic drug industry in the United States, and internationally, is participation in ICH. As was discussed previously in this chapter, initially industry participation in ICH was limited to representatives of the innovative firms, i.e., PhRMA, EFPIA, and JPMA. After complaints by the generic industry about the lack of opportunity to participate in the formulation of ICH guidelines, such as the quality topics, that would have an impact on generic producers as well as pioneer firms,[325] The FDA pressed for, and succeeded in obtaining, a larger role for generic firms in ICH. For example, generic representatives are allowed to participate in, and initial off on, drafts in the expert working groups for topics that will affect the generic drug industry.[326] Furthermore, any discussions in the Steering Committee of topics that might affect generic firms will be open to representatives of these firms. These steps secured full membership and participation in any working

---

[316] SCRIP, Feb. 2, 1996, at 3; *Id.*, Dec. 22/26, 1995, at 3.

[317] *Id.*, Dec. 22/26, 1995, at 7.

[318] *Id.,* Dec. 10, 1996, at 3; *Id.,* Jan. 30, 1996, at 3; *Id.,* Jan. 26., 1996, at 3.

[319] *Study says use generics and old drugs to cut German bill*, EUROPE DRUG & DEVICE REP., Sept. 30, 1996, at 7.

[320] SCRIP, Aug. 13, 1996, at 4. In the United Kingdom, 55% of prescriptions are written generically.

[321] SCRIP, July 12, 1996 at 15.

[322] During the 1970s, the Canadian provinces developed Pharmacare programs that provided drugs free of charge and, in order to make the program more affordable, generic substitution legislation was enacted in most provinces. B. Drinkwalter, Pres., Canadian Drug Manufacturers Ass'n, to the PDA/Ass'n Farmacia de Mexico, Mexico City 3 (June 7-9, 1995).

[323] As recently as 1993, substitution was not allowed in France, Italy, Spain, and Sweden. H.L. Timmer, Overview of Country-Specific Market Characteristics, Final Report of the Pan European Generics Project (Feb. 1993).

[324] *Id.*

[325] Letter to Kyozo Inari, Chairman of the ICH Steering Committee, from International Generic Pharmaceutical Alliance (Feb. 28, 1997); letter to David Kessler, FDA, from Robert A. Waspe, Generic Pharmaceutical Industry Ass'n (Sept. 24, 1996).

[326] Letter from Sharon Smith Holston and William Schultz, FDA, to Christina Sizemore, National Pharmaceutical Alliance (Feb. 13, 1997).

group but fell short of what the generics industry had requested, i.e., a full "seat at the table" as a full-fledged member of ICH, in the steering committee and otherwise. The steps taken were as far as the five ICH participants other than the FDA were willing to go. Therefore, order to have a more effective voice in ICH and other international fora, in 1997 several U.S., Canadian, and European trade associations formed the International Generic Pharmaceutical Alliance.

Governmental policy toward generic drugs is closely related to the issue of intellectual property protection for the discoveries of innovative firms. The World Trade Organization Agreement on Trade-Related Aspects of Intellectual Property Rights (TRIPS) brought into force an international norm of twenty years patent term for the innovator firm's products, including drugs.[327] TRIPS had the effect of delaying the FDA's approval of a number of pending abbreviated new drug applications (ANDAs) due to the extension of the patent life of several innovator drugs. Another issue, is whether a country's laws should allow the manufacturer of a generic drug to conduct bioequivalence studies comparing its product to the pioneer drug during the patent life of the pioneer.

The Canadian generic drug industry views harmonization of intellectual property laws, as driven by trade agreements, as undermining its competitive position both within Canada (in its competition with multinational brand-name producers) and in other countries. From 1923 to 1993, Canada had a compulsory licensing law that allowed generic manufacturers to import, make, use, or sell a patented medicine in return for royalty payments to the patent holder.[328] In response to pressure from the U.S. government and the multinational pharmaceutical industry, the Canadian government enacted legislation in 1987 and 1993 that brought its laws more in line with U.S. law. The 1987 law, referred to as Bill C-22, changed the patent term from seventeen years from the date of patent issue to twenty years from the date of patent application, guaranteed a ten-year exclusivity period for most new drugs, and fostered Canadian research and development by granting a full twenty years of patent protection to drugs invented and developed in Canada.[329] The 1993 law, Bill C-91, repealed compulsory licensing, restricted the export of generic pharmaceuticals until the Canadian patent expires, and tied the granting of federal approval of generic drugs to the patent expiry date.[330] This law was under review in 1997.[331]

The Canadian generic industry — and some health care professionals — believe that generic drugs should look like the drugs they copy, except for the manufacturer's imprint.[332] Under this approach, if a U.S. company manufacturing a product for Canada,

---

[327] Agreement on Trade-Related Aspects of Intellectual Property Rights (TRIPS), in World Trade Organization, The Results of the Uruguay Round of Multilateral Trade Negotiations: The Legal Texts, Geneva (1995), Annex 1C, 365-403.

[328] B. Drinkwalter, President, Canadian Drug Manufacturers Ass'n, to the PDA/Association Farmacia de Mexico, Mexico City 2-3 (June 7-9, 1995).

[329] *Id.* at 4-5.

[330] *Id.* at 6.

[331] Canadian Drug Mfrs. Asso'n (CDMA), Drug News & Views, (Summer 1997), at 1. CDMA favors repeal or revision of the 1993 law.

[332] *Id.* at 6.

has to manufacture a product that looks different from the one it markets in the United States and that is labelled bilingually (in English and French), thus reducing manufacturing efficiencies in a business where low cost production counts.[333]

Recent litigation in Canada has resulted in court decisions denying that the innovator firm to defend the unique appearance of a pharmaceutical as "trade dress" that is protectable under international and national trademark norms.[334] Therefore, generic companies are permitted to make generics that closely resemble the pioneer. Earlier, Eli Lilly had been granted an interim injunction preventing three generic drug manufacturers from marketing look-alike copies of the anti-depressant Prozac (fluoxetine),[335] but this approach was not followed when the matter was considered on the merits.

Alternative Medicine

In virtually every country, traditional medicines such as herbal medicines and other botanicals are widely used, as an alternative or complement to the kinds of pharmaceuticals typically approved by the FDA.[336] Indeed, many well-established drugs were discovered from botanical sources, e.g., vinblastine, taxol, quinine, pilocarpine, codeine, reserpine, and scopolamine,[337] and researchers are continually seeking new medicines from plant sources.[338]

WHO has defined "herbal medicines" as "finished, labelled medicinal products that contain as active ingredients aerial or underground parts of plants . . . whether in the crude state or as plant preparations."[339] According to WHO, herbal medicines may contain excipients, but if they are combined with chemically defined active ingredients they are not considered to be herbal medicines.

In Europe, most countries regulate phytomedicines as drugs.[340] The European Commission rejected the Parliament's call for a Traditional Medicines Evaluation Agency but is

---

[333] *Id.* at 19.

[334] CDMA, Drug News & Views, *supra* note 332, at 6, reporting an Apr. 25, 1997 federal court decision.

[335] SCRIP, Mar. 29, 1996, at 7. *Id.* The interim injunction followed the precedent set in two 1992 decisions by the Supreme Court of Canada (Ciba-Geigy Canada v. Apotex and Ciba-Geigy Canada v. Novopharm), which held that companies must avoid manufacturing and marketing look-alike drugs that create confusion among consumers. SCRIP, Mar. 22, 1996, at 13.

[336] WORLD HEALTH ORG. REGULATORY SITUATION OF TRADITIONAL HERBAL MEDICINES — A WORLDWIDE REVIEW (1996).

[337] Susan M. White, Proctor and Gamble, Selection of the Drug Route and Schedule, speech at Third DIA Sponsored Workshop on Botanicals (Jan. 27-28, 1997).

[338] MICHAEL J. BALICK, ELAINE ELISABETSKY & SARAH LAIRD, MEDICINAL RESOURCES OF THE TROPICAL FOREST: BIODIVERSITY AND ITS IMPORTANCE TO HUMAN HEALTH (Columbia Univ. Press, 1996; *SuperGen/Galencia anticancer tie-up* [to screen Peruvian plants for anticancer drugs], SCRIP, Dec. 6, 1996, at 11; *Phytopharm gears up for Zemaphyte launch* [eczema treatment based on Chinese herbal medicine], SCRIP, Nov. 8, 1996, at 13; *St. John's wort impresses in depression*, SCRIP, Aug. 13, 1996, at 17.

[339] WORLD HEALTH ORG., HERBAL MEDICINES (1991).

[340] Werner Busse, Schwabe Pharmaceuticals, How Can Lessons Learned (and Unlearned) From Non-U.S. Markets Be Applied to the U.S. Market?, speech at Third DIA Sponsored Workshop on Botanicals (Jan. 27-28, 1997). Dr. Busse's speech is the principal source for information presented in this paragraph.

trying to facilitate the registration of these products through additional guidelines on the core summary of product characteristics for these products.[341] Several countries including Belgium, Denmark, France, Germany, Spain, Sweden, and Switzerland have established specific national regulations on phytomedicines.[342] Quality standards for these products are published in European and national pharmacopeias, while Germany also uses monographs and France issues lists of plants traditionally used as drugs.[343] Canada regulates these products as drugs.[344]

Several Latin American countries, including Brazil and Mexico, have recently published national guidelines for the registration of phytomedicines. One of the main challenges in the regulation of these products is that their composition is complex, making it impossible to control all ingredients.[345] In this respect they are similar to other difficult-to-characterize pharmaceuticals, such as vaccines and allergenic extracts.

It is claimed that recent research in Europe on such standardized extracts as Ginkgo, Hawthorn, and Hypericum has shown them to be safe and effective in indications like dementia, heart failure, or depression.[346]

Chinese knowledge of botanical medicine dates back to the discovery of the herbal therapeutic Ma Huang around 3000 B.C.,[347] subsequently found to contain ephedrine, an effective but potentially deadly bronchodilator. Because ephedrine can cause heart attack stroke, seizures, psychosis, and death, the FDA has warned consumers not to purchase or consume dietary supplements containing natural sources of ephedrine.[348] In 1997, the FDA issued a proposed rule to ban dietary supplemenets containing more than eight milligrams of ephedrine per serving.[349]

Another Chinese product that came under the FDA scrutiny in 1997 was Cholestin, a red yeast product from China that was claimed to lower cholesterol levels; indeed, the product contains the same ingredient as a prescription anti-cholesterol drug, Mevacor.[350] Thousands of other Chinese medicine formulations are described in established books on Chinese medicines that are used not only in China but also in Japan and other Asian coun-

---

[341] Scrip, June 14, 1996, at 3; *Id.*, June 18, 1996, at 3.

[342] Konstantin Keller, *Herbal Medicinal Products in Germany and Europe: Experiences With National and European Assessment*, 30 Drug Info. J. 933 (1996).

[343] Joerg Gruenwald, Phytopharm Consulting, What Are the Implications of Considering a Botanical Product as a Single Therapeutic Entity? Speech at Third DIA Sponsored Workshop on Botanicals (Jan. 27-28, 1997).

[344] Mary Carman, *The State of Herbal Medicines in Canada*, 27 Drug Info. J. 155 (1993).

[345] An EU guideline states that, "The vegetable drug . . . in its entirety is regarded as the active ingredient."

[346] *Id.*

[347] M. Eric Gershwin, In Selection of Appropriate Therapeutic Uses 2, speech at Third DIA Sponsored Workshop on Botanicals (Jan. 27-28, 1997).

[348] Food & Drug Admin., Statement on Street Drugs Containing Botanical Ephedrine (Apr. 10, 1996).

[349] Food & Drug Admin., Dietary Supplements Containing Ephedrine Alkaloids, Proposed Rule, 62 Fed. Reg. 30,678 (June 4, 1997).

[350] Associated Press, *Is Cholestin a Drug?*, Wash. Post, Mar. 26, 1997, at A2.

tries.[351] Examples are aloe, toad venom, rhubarb, ipecac, and belladonna.[352] India and Ghana also have many plant-derived remedies, e.g., against asthma.[353]

Many countries have struggled to strike the right balance in arriving at a sound regulatory approach for these products. In the United States, interest in alternative medicine resulted in the creation of an Office of Complementary and Alternative Medicine in the National Institutes of Health. Also, the Dietary Supplement Health and Education Act[354] allowed certain products to be regulated as dietary supplements, rather than as drugs, even if their labeling made claims that they affect the structure or any function of the body.

Homeopathic drugs present related issues. Homeopathy originated in Germany more than two centuries ago with the writings of Samuel Hahnemann.[355] The homeopathic physician claims to analyze a constellation of physical, psychological, and emotional domains to devise an individualized treatment program that uses very diluted extracts of botanicals and other compounds. Homeopathy found its way to the United States, and the FDCA recognizes the *Homeopathic Pharmacopeia* as one of three official compendia.[356] The FDA has issued a Compliance Policy Guide that sets forth the agency's enforcement policy with respect to homeopathic drugs.

Homeopathic remedies remain popular in Germany, France, and Italy, but not in the Nordic countries or the United Kingdom. Implementing a 1992 EU directive, the European Commission recently completed a study in which it concluded that conventional placebo-controlled double-blind clinical trials may be used to evaluate the efficacy of homeopathic drugs.

In an era of international communication, through print and broadcast media as well as Internet and other electronic means, governments cannot easily control the accuracy of information presented to consumers about products. Furthermore, in the United States and many other countries, many subscribe to the view that there should be more "freedom of choice" with respect to the availability of products to consumers. At the same time, many consumers are quick to blame the government if a product reaches the market that is discovered to cause harm.

All of these factors put a premium on the availability to the public of unbiased information so that consumers confronted with the choice of whether to buy marketed products — particularly those that have not been subjected to scrutiny by the FDA or a similar body in another country — are sufficiently informed and skeptical. Although the FDA and its international counterparts can take a few actions each year against the most dangerous

---

[351] PHARMACEUTICAL ADMINISTRATION IN JAPAN 173 (5th ed., Editorial Supervision by the Pharmaceutical Affairs Bureau, Ministry of Health and Welfare, 1991).

[352] *Id.* at 181. Mary Jordan, *In Asia, Where It All Began, Herbal Medicine Makes a Recovery*, WASH. POST, July 8, 1996, at A11.

[353] M. Eric Gershwin, In Selection of Appropriate Therapeutic Uses speech at Third DIA Sponsored Workshop on Botanicals (Jan. 27-28, 1997).

[354] Pub. L. No. 103-417, 108 Stat. 4325 (1994) (codified at 21 U.S.C. § 301 note (1994)).

[355] *Support for scientific evaluation of homeopathy stirs controversy*, 383 NATURE 285 (Sept. 26, 1996). This article is the source of the information presented in the text.

[356] FDCA § 201(g), 21 U.S.C. § 321(g).

products, or those with the most egregious claims, the sheer volume of fraudulent activity prevents governments from taking effective enforcement action against every deceptive product or health care clinic. In sum, to combat health fraud, governments and others need to educate consumers to be wise in their decisions on products, and to be wary of outrageous claims.

As part of their ongoing cooperation on a wide range of topics of common interest, the FDA and its counterparts in Mexico and Canada meet regularly on the subject of health fraud and have developed a common action plan.

Tobacco Regulation

Tobacco smoking is considered by many to be the largest single avoidable cause of premature death internationally and the most important known carcinogen to which humans are exposed.[357] Many countries have imposed restrictions on tobacco.[358]

Even the FDA's tobacco regulations, which aim at protecting children from the risks of tobacco by regulating nicotine as a drug and cigarettes and smokeless tobacco as medical device-drug delivery systems, have international aspects.[359] A number of the measures that the agency has promulgated either are in place in other countries, or have been considered. In 1995, when the FDA published two *Federal Register* documents to initiate its control program for tobacco,[360] the agency cited experiences and control strategies in other countries and drew upon lessons learned elsewhere in constructing a regulatory approach.[361] Furthermore, as a result of the 1996 final rule,[362] many other countries have

---

[357] P. Boyle, Cancer, Cigarette Smoking and Premature Death in Europe, A review including the Recommendations of European Cancer Experts Consensus Meeting, Helsinki (Oct. 1996), for submission to *Lung Cancer* (Jan. 1997). Professor Boyle is Director, Division of Epidemiology and Biostatistics, European Institute of Oncology, Milan.

[358] *See, e.g.,* WORLD HEALTH ORG., LEGISLATIVE ACTION TO COMBAT THE WORLD TOBACCO EPIDEMIC (R. Roemer, ed., Geneva, 1993); Food & Drug Admin. Office of Policy, Tobacco Regulation Around the World (1996).

[359] King James I of England (VI of Scotland) condemned this import from the New World as, "A custom loathsome to the eye, hateful to the nose, harmful to the brain, dangerous to the lungs, and in the black stinking fume thereof, nearest resembling the horrible stygian smoke of the pit that is bottomless" in *A Counterblast to Tobacco,* quoted in THE ECONOMIST, Feb. 15, 1997.

[360] One was a *Federal Register* notice setting forth an analysis as to the agency's jurisdiction over nicotine as a drug and over cigarettes and smokeless tobacco as a drug delivery device. 60 Fed. Reg. 41,214 (Aug. 11, 1995). The other was a proposed rule in which the FDA proposed new requirements governing the sale and distribution of nicotine-containing products to children and adolescents in order to reduce their access to these products and to decrease the amount of positive imagery in advertising to which children are exposed. 60 Fed. Reg. 41,314 (1995). After a period for public comment in which the FDA received more than 700,000 comments, the agency considered the public comments and issued a final jurisdictional analysis and a final rule. 61 Fed. Reg 44,396 (Aug. 28, 1996).

[361] *Id. See, e.g.,* 60 Fed. Reg. at 41,324, 41,327, 41,332, 41,333.

[362] FDA, Regulations Restricting the Sale and Distribution of Cigarettes and Smokeless Tobacco Products to Protect Children and Adolescents, 60 Fed. Reg. 41,314 (August 11, 1995).

solicited information on the FDA's tobacco control measures and have considered patterning their youth tobacco control programs on some or all of the features of the FDA's rule.[363]

The Minister of Health of Canada has drafted new legislation for submission to its Parliament that would further restrict access by youth to tobacco products, establish the authority to regulate tobacco products' constituents and tobacco smoke emissions, strengthen health warnings, increase the amount of health information on packages, place limits on the marketing and promotion of tobacco products, and add new reporting requirements for tobacco manufacturers, distributors, and advertisers.[364] The new legislation contains many features similar to FDA's regulation[365] and is intended to overcome objections to the Canadian Tobacco Products Control Act that had been struck down by the Supreme Court of Canada in September 1995.

EU tobacco and health legislation has been under consideration for several years.[366] In late 1996, an expert committee issued a report to the European Commission recommending that measures to reduce tobacco consumption be the top health priority for the Commission and the European Parliament for the 1997–2001 period.[367] Recommendations included controls on additives in tobacco, limits on tar and nicotine, strengthened labeling (similar to the attention-getting warnings required in Australia), withdrawal of self-service displays and vending machines, restrictions on advertising, upward harmonization of tobacco product pricing through European tax policy, banning of smoking in public places, the workplace, and air flights, enhanced educational efforts, and an end to duty free sales of tobacco products within the EU.[368] For several years, the European Commission's efforts to enact a comprehensive tobacco regulatory program were stymied by the lack of sufficient votes in the European Council to overcome a "blocking minority" of countries opposed to stricter regulation.[369] In the absence of a harmonized approach, several member countries banned some or all tobacco advertising.[370] In 1991, the French Conseil constitutionnel[371] upheld the government's ban of direct and indirect advertising of tobacco products, in the face of industry contentions that the ban infringed freedom of enterprise as well as the property rights of tobacco manufacturers who were unable to

---

[363] For example, FDA Deputy Commissioner William B. Schultz was a speaker at the Smoke-Free Europe Conference in Helsinki (Oct. 2-3, 1996).

[364] Letter to Donna Shalala, Sec'ry Health and Human Serv. from David C. Dingwall, Minister of Health, Canada (Nov. 28, 1996).

[365] Howard Schneider, *Toronto Takes Tough Tack on Tobacco*, WASH. POST, Mar. 8, 1997, at A15.

[366] T. Patey, *Why Europe Can't Kick the Habit*, THE EUR., Oct. 17-23, 1996.

[367] High-Level Cancer Experts Committee, Europe Against Cancer: Recommendations on Tobacco, Helsinki (Oct. 1996). J. Wolf, *Flynn to Seek Tougher EU Rules on Tobacco*, WALL ST. J. EUR., Oct. 11-12, 1996.

[368] *Id.* at 4-8.

[369] J. Wolf, *supra* note 367. The European Commission's 1991 proposal to ban most cigarette advertising was blocked by several countries, including the United Kingdom, Germany, and the Netherlands.

[370] Finland has banned all advertising while France, Italy, and Portugal have banned most advertising. T. Patey, *supra* note 364, at 19; *Belgium to Ban Tobacco Ads*, THE EUR., Jan. 16-22, 1997.

[371] The French Conseil constitutionnel is a governmental body, created by the 1958 French Constitution, that reviews the exercise of legislative power by the parliament and the executive. J. BELL, FRENCH CONSTITUTIONAL LAW 1 (Oxford Univ. Press, 1992).

make use of their brand names to attract customers.[372] The Conseil considered the right to health a public interest justification for restricting these rights, so the legislation was not unconstitutional.

Several international organizations have been active in the field of tobacco and health, particularly the WHO, the UN Council for Trade and Development, and the International Agency for Research on Cancer.[373] In 1995, WHO began to consider the "the feasibility of initiating action to prepare and achieve an international convention on tobacco control to be adopted by the United Nations, taking into account existing international trade and other conventions and treaties,"[374] and in 1996 moved toward preparing a draft strategy for consideration by the World Health Assembly at its 1999 and 2000 meetings. The new strategy would take into account the views of public health experts, the support of the general public for tobacco controls, and research on what approaches have been used elsewhere, in other international conventions or in national tobacco laws, that would be useful features in a tobacco convention.[375] An initial planning meeting for the convention was held in Halifax in June 1997.

Another issue raised by tobacco is U.S. export policy for products that, while lawful, can cause harm.[376] U.S. tobacco companies have been accused of luring children all over the world into nicotine addiction.[377] The Reagan and Bush Administrations were criticized for adopting an aggressive stance involving not only discriminatory policies of countries such as Japan, Taiwan, South Korea, and Thailand[378] (that had policies favoring domestic brands or even domestic monopoly producers), but also these countries' regulations on health-related product labeling and advertising.[379]

---

[372] CC decision no. 90-283 DC of Jan. 8, 1991, AJDA 1991, 382. Article 11 of the 1789 Declaration of the Rights of Man and of the Citizen had declared that, "The free communication of thoughts and opinions is one of the most precious rights of man hence every citizen may speak, write and publish freely, save that he must answer for any abuse of such freedom in cases specified by law," in Bell, *supra* note 370, at 166. This right was carried over to the 1958 French Constitution, *id.* at 166-76, but is not interpreted as a constraint upon the ability of government to ban advertisements of tobacco.

[373] *See, e.g.,* IARC, Monographs on the Evaluation of Carcinogenic Risk to Humans, 38 Tobacco Smoking, Lyon (1986). Congress has authorized U.S. participation in IARC. Pub. L. No. 92-494 stat (Oct. 14, 1972) (codified at 22 U.S.C. § 290e-1).

[374] U.S. Mission Geneva, unclassified reporting cable, WHO Executive Board: Outcome of Annual Meeting; Tobacco Convention? (Feb. 1995).

[375] *World Health Organization Drafts Strategy for Tobacco Control,* 3 FDA WEEK, Jan. 24, 1997.

[376] U.S. GENERAL ACCOUNTING OFFICE, TRADE AND HEALTH ISSUES: DICHOTOMY BETWEEN U.S. EXPORT CONTROL POLICY AND ANTISMOKING INITIATIVES (May 1990) (GAO/NSTAD-90-190).

[377] J. MacKay, *U.S. Tobacco Export to the Third World,* J. NAT'L CANCER INSTITUTE, Monographs No. 12, 1992, at 25-28; G. Connolly and T. Chen, *International Health and Tobacco Use, in* TOBACCO USE: AN AMERICAN CRISIS, Jan. 9-12, 1993, at 72-74; *America's New Merchants of Death,* READER'S DIGEST, Apr. 1993; S. Sasser, *Opium War Redux,* THE NEW YORKER, Sept. 6, 1993, at 78-79; G. Frankel, *Big Tobacco's Global Reach* (4-part series), WASH. POST, Nov. 17, 1996, at A1, A24-25; WASH. POST, Nov. 18, 1996, at A1, A14-15; WASH. POST, Nov. 19, 1996, at A1, A18; *Id.,* Nov. 20, 1996, at A1, A22-23.

[378] Panel Report, Thailand, Restrictions on Impartation of and Internal Taxes on Cigarettes 287, 290-91 (Nov. 7, 1990).

[379] *Id.;* G. Frankel, *supra* note 377; T. Chen and Al Winder, *The Opium Wars Revisited as US Forces Tobacco Exports in Asia,* 80 AJPH 659-62 (June 1990); American Medical Ass'n Council on Scientific Affairs, *The Worldwide Smoking Epidemic: Tobacco Trade, Use, and Control,* 263 JAMA, 3312-18.

Anti-tobacco activists have been concerned about U.S. trade policy on tobacco because in 1989 the United States initiated a case against Thailand under the General Agreement on Tariffs and Trade (GATT), arguing that the combination of taxes and other restrictions resulted in such a disproportionate impact on imports as to act as a *de facto* ban on importation.[380] Thailand did not contest this argument but defended its exclusion of imports on public health grounds, i.e., that American cigarettes are so much better than Thai cigarettes that more women and children would start smoking them, particularly if the U.S. companies mounted their usual advertising campaigns:

> [W]hile competition had desirable effects on international trade in goods, this did not apply to cigarettes. Competition would lead to the use of better marketing techniques (including advertising), a wider availability of cigarettes, a possible reduction in their prices, and perhaps improvements in their quality. This might have the undesirable effect of leading to an increase in total consumption, especially among women and the young...once a market was opened, the United States cigarette industry would exert great efforts to force governments to accept terms and conditions which undermined public health and governments were left with no effective tool to carry out public health policies. Advertising bans were circumvented and modern marketing techniques were used to boost sales. Hence, Thailand was of the view that an import ban was the only measure which could protect public health. Any other measure which allowed imports in any amounts would not be effective . . . . The United States had made it clear that its objectives were not limited to market opening and national treatment . . . [but also, inter alia] the right for manufacturers of foreign cigarettes to advertise and conduct point-of-sale promotion even though such a right was denied to manufacturers of domestically-produced cigarettes. [Therefore] Thailand also sought from the Panel confirmation of its understanding that, in the event of its market for cigarettes being opened, its obligations with regard to the pricing, distribution, advertising, promotion, and labelling of cigarettes were limited to providing national treatment for foreign cigarettes.[381]

> A WHO submission agreed with Thailand's view that the very marketing of superior western brands could have adverse health consequences. Sophisticated manufacturing techniques and the milder taste of American blends were more dangerous than harsher, harder-to-smoke local brands and "these differences were of public health concern because they made smoking western cigarettes very easy for groups who might not otherwise smoke, such as women and adolescents, and create the false illusion among many smokers that these brands were safer than the native ones . . . ."[382]

The result was a finding by the GATT panel that Thailand's treatment of imported cigarettes violated the GATT and was not justified by public health considerations[383] but that advertising bans would be unobjectionable:

---

[380] Panel Report, Thailand, *supra* note 378, at 279-83.

[381] *Id.* at 287, 290-91.

[382] *Id.* at 296.

[383] *Id.* at 307.

A ban on the advertisement of cigarettes of both domestic and foreign origin would normally meet the requirements of the [GATT]. It might be argued that such a general ban on all cigarette advertising would create unequal competitive opportunities between the existing Thai supplier of cigarettes and new foreign suppliers . . . . Even if this argument were accepted, such an inconsistency would have to be regarded as unavoidable and therefore necessary within the meaning of [the GATT] because additional advertising rights would risk stimulating demand for cigarettes.[384]

In 1993, the Clinton Administration established an interagency group on tobacco and trade to consider whether to recommend a U.S. trade policy that would, among other things, set forth the Administration's approach of continuing to attack discriminatory practices in other countries while not attacking countries' public health regulatory approaches, such as labeling requirements or advertising bans.[385] The policy being considered included the principle that the United States will not contest actions by foreign governments to protect their own citizens by adopting legitimate health measures to reduce the consumption of cigarettes.[386]

The announcement in mid-1997 of a proposed settlement of pending state and class actions litigation involving tobacco-related deaths and injuries triggered a further review of U.S. policy in international tobacco trade and health.

Pharmacy, Pharmacopeial Harmonization, Product Standards, and Quality Testing

In this era in which most pharmacist activities consist of dispensing finished dosage form medicines in the same form in which they were received from the manufacturer, it is important to remember that the original purpose of a pharmacopeia was to guide in the compounding of drugs from raw materials. The first pharmacists date back to Egypt around 5000 B.C., and, beginning in that era a distinction was made between those who prepared remedies (the early pharmacists) and those who visited patients (the predecessors to today's physicians).[387]

---

[384] *Id.* at 224.

[385] White House, Talking Points on U.S. Cigarette Export Policy (Aug. 16, 1996).

[386] "We raise no objections to foreign countries imposing health-related restrictions on tobacco consumption. However, USTR has said that any restrictions imposed should apply equally to both domestic and foreign tobacco products...[U]nlike the Reagan and Bush Administrations, we have not pressed foreign governments to allow advertising by U.S. manufacturers, when advertising is prohibited for home country producers . . . . In the case of Korea, for example, we permitted a Korean ban on advertising to stand." The White House, Talking Points, U.S. Tobacco Exports, Nov. 19, 1996.

[387] Thomas V. DiBacco, *The Medicine Makers,* WASH. POST, Aug. 22, 1995, at Health Section P. 15. Pharmaceutical science goes back to the dawn of civilization, in ancient Egypt around 5000 B.C. *Id.*

Yesterday's pharmacist compounded drugs from a variety of materials, and the pharmacopeia governed ingredients and recipes. Today's pharmacist largely dispenses finished dosage form drugs, sometimes in prepackaged form. Seeking to make better use of pharmacists' training, while relieving an overload upon family physicians, the United Kingdom is considering allowing pharmacists to prescribe prescription drugs for patients.[388]

The first known pharmacopeia may have been the Ebers Papyrus, a sixty-six-foot long list of 811 drugs for various ailments as well as case histories, produced in Egypt around 1500 B.C.; drugs made from plants, animals, and minerals were important in this and other early compilations.[389] The famous first century A.D. manual on plant drugs, *De Materia Medica*, compiled by the Greek, Dioscorides continued in use until about 1600.[390] During the Middle Ages, Arab and Jewish cultures continued the publication of drug lists, established facilities such as the apothecary, and carried on the distinction between pharmacists and treating physicians that had begun with the Egyptians, Greeks, and Romans but had been discontinued in agrarian, medieval Europe.[391] During the seventheenth century, pharmacists were licensed and belonged to professional guilds, and the first English pharmacopeia was published.[392]

During the ninetheenth century, the successful extraction from plants and other raw materials of chemicals with drug properties inaugurated the modern age of analytical chemistry and strengthened the bonds between pharmacists and academic chemists.[393] The USP began in 1820, and the Drug Importation Act of 1848 recognized both the USP and a number of European pharmacopeias, an early form of international recognition.

Turning to modern international pharmacopeial ventures, the WHO's *International Pharmacopeia*, first published in 1953, is now a four-volume set that makes non-binding recommendations as to the purity and potency of essential drug substances, widely-used excipients, and related dosage forms.[394] ("These specifications should be adequate to assure the safety and efficacy of these products . . . but they should not be unnecessarily

---

[388] SCRIP, Dec. 17, 1996, at 7.

[389] *Id.*

[390] *Id.*

[391] *Id.*

[392] *Id.* The English physician Thomas Percival (1740-1804) developed a code of ethics for doctors, surgeons, and pharmacists. The latter were allowed to assist patients in minor instances in which they could render aid, but were expected to refer patients to physicians for more serious matters. A prescription from a physician became a binding order to the pharmacist.

[393] *Id.* In the middle of the 19th century, European scientists had begun to develop analytical chemistry techniques as part of their own defenses against drug adulteration, and American scientists took note of these achievements and extended them. See, *e.g.*, ERNST W. STIEF, DRUG ADULTERATION DETECTION AND CONTROL IN NINETEENTH-CENTURY BRITAIN (1966); ALEXANDRE A.B. BUSSY, TRAITE DES MOYENS DE RECONNOITRE LES FALSIFICATIONS DES DROGUES SIMPOLES ET COMPOSEES ET D'EN CONSTATER LE DEGRE DE PURETE (Paris 1829). The European influence is evident in American scientists' adoption and refinement as a part of early U.S. regulatory efforts. *See*, e.g., Edwin D. Faust, *Original and Select Observations on the Detection of Adulterations*, AM. J. SCI. & ARTS 19 (1831); LEWIS CALEB BECK, ADULTERATION OF VARIOUS SUBSTANCES USED IN MEDICINE AND THE ARTS (New York, 1846).

[394] World Health Org., A Brief Overview of WHO's Activities in the Drug Field, PHARM/84.23 Rev. 5, at 9 (May 1993).

stringent since this would increase the cost of the products.")[395] A related WHO activity is its development of simple basic tests for verification of the identity of drug substances, to aid countries in detecting counterfeit drugs.[396]

The European Pharmacopoeia was set up in 1964 and amended by a 1989 protocol so that the EU could join.[397] It has established legally enforceable specifications for over 800 medicinal substances in twenty-four nations.[398] Its pharmacopeial monographs have taken on added importance now that the EU's EMEA is using them.[399]

The USP has a wide variety of international activities, including:

- Mailing the *United States Pharmacopoeia Drug Information (USPDI)* to the director of each national drug authority;
- Having the USP translated into Spanish;
- Reaching an agreement with the Pharmaceutical Society of Australia that gives patients and health professionals access to the USP data base so that Australia, New Zealand, and other South Pacific countries may use U.S. monographs.[400]

In Europe, the Council of Europe,[401] which is comprised of thirty-eight countries, including the fifteen EU countries, publishes a *European Pharmacopeia*. In 1996, the United States was granted observer status in the Council of Europe,[402] which may facilitate cooperation on topics of interest to the FDA.

In September 1989, the pharmacopeial organizations in the United States, Japan, and Europe formed a voluntary association known as the Pharmacopeial Discussion Group (PDG).[403] In brief, the PDG sought to discuss and evaluate standards, test limits, and test methods and, where possible, to develop a consensus on test limits and test methods. The PDG recognized that pharmacopeial harmonization is both retrospective (dealing with established or published pharmacopeial monographs and methods) and prospective (inso-

---

[395] *Id.*

[396] *Id.* at 12-13.

[397] GLOBAL BUSINESS RELATIONS, INC., THE INTERNATIONAL ORGANIZATIONS REGULATORY GUIDEBOOK 186 (1995 ed.).

[398] *Id.* The 24 members, as of 1995, were the 15 countries of the EU plus the European Commission, Croatia, Cyprus, Iceland, Macedonia, Norway, Slovenia, Switzerland, Turkey. *Id.*

[399] *Id.*

[400] WASHINGTON DRUG LETTER, Dec. 4, 1995, at 6.

[401] The Council of Europe is an international organization, founded by treaty in 1949 and headquartered in Strasbourg, France, that promotes greater European unity by facilitating economic and social harmonization and promoting human rights and the principles of parliamentary democracy. THE INTERNATIONAL ORGANIZATIONS REGULATORY GUIDEBOOK, *supra* note 397, at 184. The Council of Europe should not be confused with the Council of Ministers of the European Communities, the principal lawmaking body of the EU, which holds semiannual meetings billed as the European Council. *Id.* at 193. As of 1995, the 32 members of the Council of Europe included all 15 EU countries plus Bulgaria, Cyprus, Czech Republic, Estonia, Hungary, Iceland, Liechtenstein, Lithuania, Malta, Norway, Poland, Romania, San Marino, Slovakia, Slovenia, Switzerland, and Turkey. Albania, Belarus, Croatia, Latvia, Macedonia, Moldova, Russia, and Ukraine enjoy "special guest" status and have applied for membership. *Id.*

[402] EUROPE DRUG & DEVICE REP. Feb. 5, 1996, at 8.

[403] *See* Z.T. Chowhan, *Pharmacopeial Harmonization: A Progress Report*, 30 DRUG INFO. J. 451 (1996).

far as new monographs and methods were concerned), with retrospective harmonization being more difficult given the binding nature of pharmacopeial standards and the number of marketed products that meet those standards.[404]

Good Manufacturing Practices, Inspections, and Other Compliance Issues

■ FDA, WHO, the Pharmaceutical Inspection Cooperation Scheme, and Other GMP Activities

GMPs refer to practices and procedures for manufacturing, processing, and packing drugs and drug products to ensure their identity, quality, and purity. In the United States, failure to comply with the FDA's GMPs[405] results in an adulterated product[406] and can result in FDA enforcement action, or voluntary action, that bars both domestic shipments, and even international shipments, of affected products.[407]

Internationally, the World Health Assembly, in 1969, endorsed GMP requirements for drugs consisting of "internationally recognized and respected standards" and has revised those requirements on several occasions.[408] The WHO GMPs were modeled on the FDA's drug GMPs. A recent FDA analysis confirmed this similarity as to written requirements, although the current priority is increasing harmonization as to compliance and enforcement.[409] Moreover, the FDA rulemaking to clarify the GMPs with respect to validation requirements[410] may necessitate a re-review as to whether WHO's GMPs — and those of the EU[411] and other U.S. trading partners — still are equivalent to the FDA's. Also, the EU does not apply the GMPs to bulk drugs.[412]

---

[404] *Id.* at 452.

[405] 21 C.F.R. pts. 210-211 (1996).

[406] *See* FDCA § 501(a); 21 U.S.C. § 351(a).

[407] See FDCA § 301(a); 21 U.S.C. § 331(a) (prohibiting the introduction or delivery for introduction into interstate commerce any adulterated or misbranded drug) and FDCA § 802(f)(1); 21 U.S.C. § 382(f)(1) (prohibiting exportation of a drug under section 802 of the act if the drug is not manufactured, processed, packaged, and held in substantial conformity with GMPs).

[408] *See* World Health Org., Annex 10 — Guidelines for Implementation of the WHO Certification Scheme on the Quality of Pharmaceutical Products Moving in International Commerce, WHO Technical Rep. Series No. 863, at 155 (1996).

[409] *PDA Interviews FDA's Stephanie Gray*, PDA NEWSLETTER, Sept. 1995, at 1, 3.

[410] 61 Fed. Reg. 20,104 (May 3, 1996).

[411] Commission Directive laying down principles and guidelines of good manufacturing practice for medicinal products for human use, Official Journal of the European Communities No L 193/30, at 83-86 (July 17, 1991).

[412] See discussion *infra*. D.E Worden, *The Drive Toward Regulatory Harmonization: What Is Harmonization and How Will It Impact the Global Development of New Drugs?*, 29 DRUG INFO. J. 1663S-1679S (1995).

The Pharmaceutical Inspection Cooperation Scheme PIC/S[413] is a cooperation program that originated as an international agreement, under the Convention for the Mutual Recognition of Inspection in Respect of the Manufacture of Pharmaceutical Products, commonly known as the Pharmaceutical Inspection Convention or (PIC). The eighteen members that signed the Convention were Australia, Austria, Belgium, Denmark, Finland, France, Germany, Hungary, Iceland, Ireland, Italy, Liechtenstein, Norway, Portugal, Romania, Sweden, Switzerland, and the United Kingdom.[414] The Netherlands has joined PIC/S, and the Czech Republic and Slovakia were expected to join in 1997.[415] The PIC/S would continue the program under the PIC for exchange of reports of inspections of pharmaceutical producers.

PIC became PIC/S to resolve a legal issue between the Commission and the member states. Because of the clear competence given to the Commission in the area of GMP legislation (although not enforcement), and the establishment of a genuine mutual recognition system for inspections within the community, the PIC convention may be viewed as inconsistent with the EU legislation.[416] European Commission officials apparently believed that membership by its member states in the PIC was inconsistent with the responsibility of the Commission for the harmonized GMP legislation. Because PIC serves effectively as a forum for regulatory authorities, including EU member state authorities, the participants decided to abandon the "convention label" but retain the activity as a cooperation program rather than a treaty.

■ Good Manufacturing Practices for Bulk Drugs

Bulk drug GMPs are a current harmonization priority.[417] Indeed, in the late 1990s, bulk drug GMP activities were underway in the FDA, WHO, PIC/S,[418] Asia-Pacific Economic Cooperation,[419] and the EU. Each had begun to consider the need for developing an international guidance document on bulk drug ingredients. Consolidation of these activities under the auspices of the PIC/S versus development in ICH of a new bulk drug guideline was the subject of discussion in 1997.

Underlying this interest is the recognition that, due to the increasing importation of bulk pharmaceutical chemicals for use in drug manufacturing, adequate attention to GMP controls by manufacturers and the government of the country of origin is essential to the qual-

---

[413] A list of PIC publications is available from the Secretariat of the Pharmaceutical Inspection Convention, 9-11 Rue de Varembe, 1202 Geneva 20, Switzerland.

[414] Karin Bredal Jensen, *Good Manufacturing Practice Inspection in Europe*, 29 DRUG INFO. J. 1211-16 (1995).

[415] *PIC/S harmonization progress*, SCRIP, Nov. 1, 1996, at 16.

[416] Karin Bredal Jensen, *supra* note 414.

[417] The U.S.-EU mutual recognition discussions were complicated by the lack of bulk drug GMPs in the EU, as many FDA inspections in the EU are of establishments manufacturing bulk drugs. Bulk drugs are sometimes called "starter materials," and generally the interest is in focusing attention upon active pharmaceutical ingredients (APIs). Manufacturers of inactive ingredients also favor increased harmonization activities.

[418] Therapeutic Goods Admin., Australia, Report of PIC/S Meeting on Active Pharmaceutical Ingredients, Canberra (Sept. 23-24, 1996).

[419] APEC is a governmental forum comprised of 18 Pacific Rim member economies: Australia, Brunei, Canada, Chile, Chinese Taipei, Hong Kong, Indonesia, Japan, Malaysia, Mexico, New Zealand, Papua-New Guinea, People's Republic of China, the Philippines, Singapore, South Korea, Thailand, and the United States.

ity of these substances. Current safeguards — finished dosage form manufacturers' checks of ingredients, the FDA's application to bulk drug manufacturers of those general GMP requirements that are applicable, and controls over the substances themselves such as the ICH guideline on drug impurities — are helpful but do not meet the need for a comprehensive approach. Because a number of bulk pharmaceutical chemicals increasingly are manufactured in developing countries such as China and India, the FDA and its counterparts undertook an activity, under the auspices of PIC/S, to draft harmonized GMPs applicable to the active pharmaceutical ingredients. A draft was expected by 1997. In 1997, consideration also was being given to a bulk drug GMP harmonization activity under ICH, but with the possibilty of including the members of the PIC/S effort in a new Expert Working Group.

■ Good Manufacturing Practices and ISO-9000

Another recent issue has been the relationship between drug GMPs and ISO 9000 quality systems, an international standard published by the ISO that sets forth a series of criteria for quality systems in a wide range of enterprises providing goods or services.[420] Questions about the relationship between ISO-9000 and FDA drug GMPs became more frequent following the FDA's decision to revise its device GMPs in conformity with ISO-9000.

Although the FDA has no plans to integrate, in any way, its drug GMP rules into ISO-9000, the agency did undertake a comparison of the two documents and established that the two paradigms are entirely consistent: "The principles and practices elucidated in the ISO standards are not in conflict with those provided by the CGMP regulations. Indeed, the voluntary ISO standards share common principles with FDA's CGMP requirements."[421]

Because U.S. pharmaceutical manufacturers that meet the FDA's GMP regulations have already essentially met the relevant quality system documentation needed for obtaining ISO 9000 "registration," a number of them have undertaken the necessary additional steps—documentation and audits—needed to obtain formal ISO-9000 registration. Their reasons for doing so have varied. Some do so for additional competitiveness in the marketplace because they see an outside conformity assessment as an imprimatur for their quality system. Manufacturers in developing countries sometimes see ISO-9000 registration as a way of reassuring customers of the quality of their products, as their use of independent third-party auditors may allay concerns about weaknesses in local regulatory authority infrastructure in assuring the quality of their products.

An ISO Committee, TC-198, has written a set of international standards on the sterilization of health care products by a variety of means (ethylene oxide, radiation, moist heat, and liquid chemicals) and on sterilization terminology, biological indicators, chemical

---

[420] THE ISO-9000 HANDBOOK (Robert W. Peach, ed., 2d. ed., CEEM Information Serv., 1994).

[421] "The principles and practices elucidated in the ISO standards are not in conflict with those provided by the CGMP regulations. Indeed, the voluntary ISO standards share common principles with FDA's CGMP requirements." Food & Drug Admin., Current Good Manufacturing Practice: Amendment of Certain Requirements for Finished Pharmaceuticals; Proposed Rule, 61 Fed. Reg. 20,105 (May 3, 1996).

indicators, microbiological methods, packaging, aseptic processing and sterilization resid-uals.[422] Although oriented pricipally to medical device sterilization, these standards also are used by pharmaceutical companies.

A separate ISO Committee, TC-209, is writing an international standard on cleanroom and associated controlled environments (for the electronic and aerospace industries as well as the pharmaceutical and medical device industries). Documents are being prepared in sepa-rate working groups on air cleanliness, specifications for testing, general principles/bio-contamination, evaluation and interpretation of data, and methodology for measuring the efficiency of process of cleaning.[423] The level of resources required to support these efforts, the risk of conflict with GMPs, and the risk of "harmonization downward" has led the FDA's three pharmaceutical centers (CBER, Centers for Drug Evaluation and Research, and the Centers for Veterinary Medicine) to minimize their participation in these activities.[424]

■ Inspections

Establishment inspections are the FDA's primary investigative technique.[425] The FDA has been an international leader in demonstrating the value of inspections to assure compli-ance with GMPs. In recent years, the FDA investigators have paid particular attention to process validation, laboratory operations, bulk pharmaceuticals, and microbial contamina-tion, and the agency emphasizes these concerns in its GMP work with other countries.[426]

Inspections are universally recognized as an essential component of a drug regulatory sys-tem by WHO, EU, and other countries. Within the EU, the legal basis for inspection is laid down in several laws and guidelines.[427] The European Commission is responsible for the harmonization of inspection procedures and technical matters, the EMEA is responsible for coordinating national inspections and pharmacovigilance, and the "supervisory author-ities" in the member states are responsible for conducting inspections of manufacturers located within their borders.[428] Inspection is ordinarily conducted by a qualified individual employed by the responsible agency in the country where the facility is located, but the inspection is on behalf of the EU as a whole, not simply that member state.[429] This divi-sion of responsibility is viewed as consistent with the principle of "subsidiarity," a pre-cept, discussed earlier, that only those matters are to be handled at a central level that can-

---

[422] PDA Letter, Mar. 1997, at 19; Melissa Moncavage, FDA, International Standards (1994).

[423] *Id.*

[424] Memorandum from Roger Williams, FDA, on ISO (Nov. 12, 1995).

[425] E. Pfeifer, *Enforcement, in* Seventh Fifth Anniversary Commemorative Volume of Food and Drug Law, 72, 91 (FDLI 1984). For an account of an FDA inspection, see *FDA ON Site, in* Food & Drug Admin., From Test Tube to Patient: New Drug Development in the United States 40-47 (1990 ed.).

[426] F-D-C Rep. ("The Pink Sheet"), Oct. 17, 1994, at T&G 10.

[427] Directive 75/319/EEC, as modified by Directive 89/341/EEC; Directive 91/356/EEC; Regulation 93/2309/EEC (Ju-ly 22, 1993); Compilation of Community Procedures on Administrative Collaboration and Harmonization of In-spections III/94/5698/EN (Jan. 1995).

[428] Karin Bredal Jensen, *supra* note 414.

[429] Philippe Meyer, *The Future GMP Inspection System*, 28 Drug Info. J. 977 (1994).

not be better handled at a lower or a decentralized level. For example, member states may decide whether to apply GMPs to investigational drugs.[430]

For imported drugs, batch testing by a qualified person in the member state where the product enters is contemplated, although foreign inspections can also be conducted when requested by a member state, the CPMP, or the Commission.[431] Three member states (the United Kingdom, Germany, and France) are able to conduct foreign inspections.[432]

The Commission's goal is to reach mutual recognition agreements (MRAs) with the United States, Japan, Canada, Australia, and New Zealand that will obviate both border batch testing and foreign inspections.

■ Sharing of Inspection Information with Other Countries

The FDA shares information with other firms through a variety of formal and informal arrangements. First, much information about FDA inspections is public and is shared with other countries upon request. Second, even non-public information can be shared, provided the requirements in FDA regulations are met.[433] Third, through Compliance Status Information System (COMSTAT), discussed below, certain countries have arranged for direct access to an the FDA computerized data base that includes information as to whether U.S. and foreign firms inspected by the FDA are in compliance with GMPs. Last but not least, as is discussed later in this chapter, the FDA enters the MOUs and MRAs with other countries in order to enhance cooperation and sharing of compliance information.

The general issue of increasing cooperation with other countries is discussed in a report on foreign inspections.[434]

■ Compliance Status Information System

COMSTAT, developed in the early 1970s as a computerized database on the current GMP status of pharmaceutical and medical device manufacturers, repackers, assemblers, contract sterilizers, and control testing laboratories, now includes information on some 20,000 firms that the FDA has inspected, in the United States and abroad.[435] Originally called the Government-Wide Quality Assurance Program, and aimed at providing timely information to U.S. procurement agencies about manufacturers' compliance status, COMSTAT has been broadened to assist FDA headquarters and other government agencies in assessing quickly the GMP compliance status of a firm. COMSTAT is a profile class-oriented system, not a product-specific system. In other words, in providing GMP compliance sta-

---

[430] John Turner, *The Monitoring of GMP Compliance in the Development of Medicinal Products in the United Kingdom*, 28 Drug Info. J. 983 (1994).

[431] Karin Bredal Jensen, *supra* note 414, at 1212-13.

[432] *Id.* at 1213.

[433] 21 C.F.R. § 20.89.

[434] Food & Drug Admin., Summary Report of the Foreign Inspection Working Group (June 1997).

[435] A document prepared for the FDA Foreign Inspection Working Group by Elaine Cole, FDA, summarizing COMSTAT (Jan. 1997), provided the information in this section.

tus information, COMSTAT does not provide information on each product that a manufacturer makes but rather categorizes pharmaceuticals and medical devices into broad categories, such as drug dosage forms, and provides compliance status information based on available inspection information.

In addition to U.S. government agencies, the drug approval authorities in Australia, Canada, and Denmark are able to directly access the COMSTAT database. They are able to obtain only publicly available information through this direct access, although follow-up inquiries can yield needed information not available to the public under the FDA's regulation on sharing non-public information with foreign officials.[436]

■ Foreign inspections[437]

The FDA began foreign inspections in 1955 when it conducted its first foreign antibiotic inspection; the first inspection of a non-antibiotic facility occurred in 1961.[438]

The FDCA applies equally to the products of domestic and foreign drug manufacturers. The FDA has authority to enter and inspect establishments where drugs are manufactured or held,[439] and the agency's authority to deny entry to imported products that "appear" to be adulterated or misbranded, or in violation of the new drug provisions[440] has been interpreted by the FDA as enabling the agency to deny entry to products produced in facilities that (or countries that) denied FDA investigators the right of inspection. Also, the registration and listing of foreign manufacturers are conditioned upon arrangements that allow the FDA to perform inspections "from time to time."[441]

The FDA presently inspects about 850 firms per year in up to sixty-two different countries.[442] Most inspections are in European countries, although a significant number occur in Japan. The FDA conducts these inspections in response to applications or submissions from or involving foreign firms and investigations of complaints or recalls, but also conducts routine and follow-up inspections.

The foreign firm is either the applicant or the source of the bulk drug identified in an application. The FDA conducts some inspections because a foreign firm has made a bid to supply products or is a supplier to the U.S. military. As in the case of domestic inspections, foreign inspections result in inspectional observations on the FDA-483 form, and feature discussions with the firms' management, responses to deficiencies, detailed written reports, and review by the FDA headquarters offices. Unlike domestic inspections, however foreign inspections occur only after the FDA has provided prior notice to the firm to be inspected.

---

[436] 21 C.F.R. § 20.89.

[437] QUALITY CONTROL REP. ("The Gold Sheet"), Sept. 1993, at 1-8.

[438] Food & Drug Admin., Foreign Inspection Working Group Report, *supra* note 435, at 9.

[439] FDCA § 704; 21 U.S.C. § 374.

[440] FDCA § 801; 21 U.S.C. § 381.

[441] FDCA § 510(i); 21 U.S.C. § 360 (i). Although registration is optional, listing is required, so the effect is to limit the entry into the United States to drugs from countries that allow FDA inspections.

[442] Food & Drug Admin., Foreign Inspection Working Group Report, *supra* note 435, at 11.

The FDA's foreign inspectors, in most cases, are senior investigators who are technically experienced and competent in their fields, able to work independently, capable of handling difficult situations, and diplomatic. The typical foreign inspection trip lasts three to four weeks, with two to five inspections per trip, and covers more than one country.

For drugs, a foreign inspection often involves one or more of the following areas: administrative information, raw materials (handling, storage, controls, etc.), production operations (standard operating procedures, validation, production records, packaging and labeling, facilities, equipment and maintenance), and product testing (procedures and methods). If any type of official FDA action results against the foreign firm, the action usually consists of automatic detention of the firm's products or disapproval of the relevant application or submission.

Drug inspections outnumber all other types of foreign inspections, except for those involving devices. In recent years, the number of foreign inspections involving drugs has increased significantly from 156 in fiscal year 1992, to 324 in fiscal year 1995. The increase in FDA resources devoted to foreign inspections, however, has not reduced the need for the FDA and its counterparts in foreign countries to harmonize regulatory requirements and to engage in cooperative regulatory activities. Although the FDA has engaged in several international discussions aimed at reaching agreements on exchanging inspectional results, the agency will continue to need to conduct foreign inspections in certain cases.

Because conducting foreign inspections is costly and difficult, the FDA seeks MOUs with other countries in order to enable it to rely upon inspections done by others. The FDA conducts inspections of foreign manufacturers as well as domestic firms.

■ Counterfeit Drugs

A worldwide problem, for developed and developing countries alike, is the trade in counterfeit drugs. WHO provides the following definition of a counterfeit drug:

> A counterfeit drug is one which is deliberately and fraudulently mislabelled with respect to identity and/or source. The term counterfeiting can apply to both branded and generic products and counterfeit products may include products with the correct ingredients, wrong ingredient, without active ingredients, with incorrect quantity of active ingredients or with fake packaging.[443]

A counterfeit product is one that is not made by or with the approval of the product license holder, but that is sold as if it were the genuine article.[444]

The problems caused by counterfeit drugs include: danger to the lives and health of patients, undermining the confidence of physicians and patients in the safety, efficacy and quality of drugs, defrauding health care providers and insurance companies, and damaging

---

[443] Philip Emafo, National Implementation Guidelines for Combating Counterfeit Drugs (draft), WHO at 1 (Aug. 2, 1996).

[444] Roger Cuff, *United Kingdom Guidelines on Counterfeit Drugs*, 29 DRUG INFO. J. 633, 634 (1995).

the business of the manufacturer whose products are copied, through loss of both revenue and confidence.[445]

In the Philippines in the early 1990s, several children died when inert substances were administered to children in the belief that they were active antibiotics.[446] Hundreds of people have died in Nigeria,[447] Bangladesh,[448] and other countries in recent years, because to counterfeit or substandard drugs.

Activities involving counterfeit drugs have been undertaken at the international level and by individual countries. WHO has issued a number of documents to assist countries in dealing with counterfeit drugs.[449] The advice is for countries to create or strengthen their national drug regulatory authorities, to strengthen laws and their enforcement, to maintain strict controls as to manufacture, importation, and distribution, to enact and enforce up-to-date intellectual property laws, and to increase public awareness.[450] Specific features to be included in national laws include defining counterfeit drugs and clearly distinguishing legal from illegal activities; requiring licensing or registration of manufacturers, importers, exporters, wholesalers, and distributors (with licenses suspended when the license-holder is convicted of an offense involving counterfeit drugs); providing for records that allow product tracking, dealing with reexports and drugs in duty-free zones; prescribing the administrative arrangements among responsible government agencies and law enforcement officials; and providing remedies stringent enough to deter wrongdoing, including seizure of products and closure of manufacturing facilities.[451]

Historically, there is little evidence of trade in counterfeits within and between countries where there are short, highly regulated distribution channels; therefore, keeping distribution channels short and highly regulated combats counterfeiting.[452] Other ways in which counterfeit drugs can be curbed involve control of routine bulk imports (including routine third-party testing), batch records accompanying products throughout the distribution chain, and a requirement applicable to pharmacists requiring the reporting of suspect goods.[453]

Cooperation among multinational and national pharmaceutical firms is also an important part of solving the counterfeit drug problem because the drug manufacturers of the drugs that are being copied are often the first to become aware of counterfeits, when they begin to receive complaints. Steps manufacturers can take include developing the capability to

---

[445] *Id.*

[446] *Id.* at 633.

[447] Alubo S. Ogoh, *Death for Sale: A Study of Drug Poisoning and Death in Nigeria*, 38 Soc. Sci. Med. 97 (1994); ten M. Ham, *Counterfeit Drugs: Implications for Health*, 11 Adverse Drug React Toxicology Rev. 59 (1992).

[448] *Diethylene Glycol: Yet Another Tragedy*, 6 WHO Drug Info. 169 (1992).

[449] National Implementation Guidelines, *supra*, note 443; World Health Org., Counterfeit Drugs: Report of a WHO/IFPMA Workshop, Geneva (Apr. 1-3, 1992),

[450] D.C. Jayasuriya, *Legislative Measures for Dealing With Counterfeit Drugs in Developing Countries*, 29 Drug Info. J. 623, 625 (1995).

[451] *Id.* at 626-27.

[452] Roger Cuff, *supra* note 443, 634.

[453] *Id.* at 634-35.

perform quick and accurate tests as to whether suspect products are counterfeit, maintaining a close and cooperative relationship with regulatory authorities on such matters as publicity and recalls, and maintaining information channels for the public and the medical profession to facilitate identification and return of counterfeit drugs.[454]

The EU has issued a Council Regulation to prohibit the free circulation, export, or transit of counterfeit and pirated goods.[455] Nigeria and China have enacted new legislative measures, and China has enforced the law with vigor, resulting in several sentences of life imprisonment for those responsible for manufacturing counterfeit drugs.[456]

The anti-counterfeit provisions of the FDCA[457] have been supplemented by the enactment of the Anticounterfeiting Consumer Protection Act of 1996, which provides the government with the authority to seize bogus products such as counterfeit infant formula, and to seek civil penalties and criminal prosecution.[458]

■ Parallel Imports

Controls on drug prices in twelve of fifteen EU countries, disparities among countries' prices, currency fluctuations, and other factors[459] have led to a situation in which exported drugs may be diverted from a low-price country to a high-price country where, as "parallel imports," they compete with drugs exported directly from the country of origin to the high-price country.[460] The resulting losses to manufacturers in both Europe and the United States — and the possibility that the movement of products to cash in on price differences may have detrimental effects upon their quality — have made the parallel imports problem a high priority for multinational drug companies.[461]

In the EU, rules on parallel imports are imposed nationally by the United Kingdom, the Netherlands, Denmark, and Germany, the high-price countries.[462] Within the EU, the low-price countries are Spain and Portugal, and to some extent France, and the disparity in prices between those countries and the high-price countries is sufficiently great that

---

[454] *Id.* at 635-36.

[455] Official Journal of the European Communities, no. C238/9 (Sept. 2, 1993).

[456] D.C. Jayasuriya, *supra* note 450, at 623, 626, citing CHINA NEWS, Oct. 18, 1993, at 3.

[457] FDCA §§ 301(i), 304(a)(2), 702(e), 21 U.S.C. §§ 331(i), 334(a)(2), 372(e).

[458] Pub. L. No. 104-153, 110 Stat. 1386 (July 2, 1996).

[459] SCRIP, Dec. 17, 1996, at 2.

[460] Richard M. Andrade, *The Parallel Importation of Unauthorized Genuine Goods: Analysis and Observations of the Gray Market*, 14 J. INT'L BUS. L. 409-36 (Fall 1993); James F. Baxley, *The Gray Market Controversy and the Court: An Analysis of Conflicting Court of Appeals on the Validity of Customs Regulations Permitting Unauthorized Third Party Importation of Trademarked Goods*, 18 SETON HALL REVIEW 55-99 (Winter 1988); Seth E. Lipner, *Gray Market Goulash: The Problem of At-the-Border Restrictions on Importation of Genuine Trademarked Goods*, TRADEMARK REP. Mar.-Apr. 1987, at 77-102; Robert Neuner, *Supreme Court Review of Parallel Imports*, N.Y.L.J., Feb. 10, 1987, at 1.

[461] SCRIP, Dec. 17, 1996, at 2.

[462] SCRIP, July 12, 1996, at 3.

demand for pharmaceutical products throughout the EU could be met by parallel imports from Spain and Portugal.[463]

In a number of instances, the European Commission and national governments took a series of positions that were viewed as undermining the position of the innovative companies of Europe and the United States.[464] Consequently, in 1995 and 1996, the issue of parallel imports in the EU topped the list of complaints by firms involved in the Transatlantic Business Dialogue, a forum for business to express views to government leaders in the European Commission and the U.S. government. The European Commission proposed to begin a consultation process in mid-1997 to try to find solutions to the problem.[465] An interim strategy attempted by one firm was to launch a breakthrough AIDS drug with a single EU-wide price denominated in the European Currency Units.[466]

International Cooperative Agreements

■ Authority

The FDA has the authority to enter into agreements with other countries in order to enhance consumer protection with respect to the products it regulates. The agency has explicit authority to enter into "arrangements" with other countries whose manufacturers export drugs to this country, and the agency is required to assure that these arrangements provide for the FDA to conduct inspections, "from time to time," of the foreign firm.[467] The FDA also has authority in the FDCA to assure that drugs are not adulterated, misbranded, or in violation of the new drug or other provisions,[468] to promulgate regulations for the efficient enforcement of the act (which the FDA believes extends to regulatory aspects of agreements),[469] and to assure that imports comply with the Act by examination of samples "or otherwise" (which the agency interprets to include agreements).[470] Finally, authority in the Public Health Service Act that has been delegated to the FDA provides explicit authority for cooperation with other countries.[471]

---

[463] Art. 379, Treaty of Accession of Spain and Portugal, discussed in Peter Lumley, *Parallel Imports from Spain — No Joy for the Research Industry*, SCRIP MAG. Mar. 1996, at 6-7.

[464] *Id.* SCRIP, Mar. 22, 1996, at 7; *Id.*, Jan. 16, 1996, at 8; *Id.*, Dec. 22/26, 1995. German health care law required the dispensing of parallel import drugs when the price was right. SCRIP, Mar. 15, 1996, at 5.

[465] SCRIP, Dec. 17, 1996, at 3.

[466] Stephen D. Moore and Shailagh Murray, *Merck Uses AIDS Drug to Target Wholesalers in the European Union*, WALL ST. J. EUR. Oct. 11-12, 1996, at 1, 7.

[467] FDCA § 510(i), 21 U.S.C. § 360(i).

[468] FDCA §§ 501, 502, 505, 21 U.S.C. §§ 351, 352, 355.

[469] *Id.* § 701, 21 U.S.C. § 371.

[470] *Id.* § 801, 21 U.S.C. § 381.

[471] *Id.* § 301, 21 U.S.C. § 331.

The FDA's agreements with other countries bear a variety of labels, MOU, Memorandum of Cooperation, and Exchange of Letters. In the United States, what is important is not the label or form of an agreement but rather its substance. All FDA international cooperative agreements other than the most innocuous exchanges of letters are cleared with the State Department under its Circular 175 clearance process, which enables that Department to fulfill a congressional reporting obligation under the Case-Zablocki Act.[472]

Although most FDA agreements with other countries are non-binding in character, the agency has the authority to enter binding agreements — consistent with its statutes — by going through notice-and-comment rulemaking on the aspects of the MOU that are binding. For example, if an article of the agency's MOU with its counterpart in the fictitious country of Slobovia states that, "FDA shall inform the Drugs Agency of Slobovia whenever the FDA withdraws a drug from the market," the FDA would need to conduct notice-and-comment rulemaking on that obligation.[473]

■ Memoranda of Understanding

The FDA MOUs on exchanging reports of drug inspections were signed with authorities in Switzerland in 1968,[474] Sweden in 1972,[475] and Canada in 1973.[476] In 1974, a year in which the agency sent inspectors to 121 manufacturers in twenty-four different countries, the FDA stated in its annual report that it "has a policy to recognize equivalent regulatory control by other nations through bilateral agreements."[477] In 1995, the FDA published a Compliance Policy Guide to set forth its priorities and procedures for MOUs and similar agreements.[478]

■ Mutual Recognition Agreement Negotiations with the European Union

In the mid-1990s, the focus of activity in the area of the FDA's agreements with other countries on drug GMPs was discussions with the European Commission, aimed at mutual reliance on one another's inspections. These discussions resulted in the 1997 initialling of an agreement,[479] subject to further ratification processes on each side of the Atlantic. The FDA agreements in drug GMPs and devices were part of broader mutual recognition agreement negotiations, led by the Office of the U.S. Trade Representative that also included telecommunications, electrical safety, and recreational craft. The Commission's

---

[472] 1 U.S.C.§ 112b, implemented at 22 C.F.R. pt. 181 and 11 Foreign Affairs Manual.

[473] Author's discussion with Margaret Porter, FDA Chief Counsel (Apr. 18, 1997).

[474] Letter from Secretary of State Dean Rusk, dated Oct. 28, 1968, in response to letter from Felix Schnyder, Ambassador of Switzerland, dated June 28, 1968, *in* FOOD & DRUG ADMIN., INTERNATIONAL COOPERATIVE AGREEMENTS MANUAL 341-42. (Nov. 1996)

[475] Memorandum of Understanding Between the Swedish National Board of Health and Welfare and FDA dated Oct. 17, 1972, *in id.*, at 337-39.

[476] Agreement of Cooperation Between the Canadian Department of National Health and Welfare [now Health Canada] and FDA dated Sept. 28, 1973, *in id.*, at 39-41.

[477] FOOD & DRUG ADMIN., ANNUAL REPORT 1015 (1974). In that year, the FDA took over the inspection of foreign drug manufacturers for Department of Defense procurements. *Id.*

[478] 60 Fed. Reg. 31,495 (June 15, 1995).

[479] Office of the USTR, Mutual Recognition Agreement Fact Sheet (June 20, 1997).

insistence on a "balanced package" meant that the EU would not agree to an MRA on telecommunications and recreational craft — viewed as more advantageous to the United States — unless there also were MRAs on pharmaceuticals — viewed as more advantageous to the EU.

There were several major issues in the drug negotiations:[480]

The first concerned the exchange of inspection reports. The FDA insisted that inspection reports should be exchanged routinely during the transition period — while the equivalence of regulatory systems is being established — and, thereafter, whenever a party needs such reports. The EU agreed to the exchange of inspection reports during the transition period, but balked at the idea that exchange of reports would be routine once the MRA became effective. It argued that, after the MRA reached its operational stage reports should be available only on an exceptional basis (i.e., for a reasoned purpose).

The second issue concerning differences among the abilities of EU member states. The FDA's view was that there cannot be mutual recognition without first determining the equivalence of each individual EU member state inspection authority.

Concerning preapproval inspections, the third issue the EU wanted all aspects of such inspections covered under the agreement, while the FDA initially insisted upon excluding preapproval inspections. After the 1996 Trans Atlantic Business Dialogue (TABD) meeting, the FDA agreed to phased-in coverage of preapproval inspections.

Fourth, are concerned coverage of bulk drug manufacturer inspections, the EU wanted to include these inspections, as they constitute a substantial proportion of FDA inspections in the EU. The FDA, however, was leery of including bulk drug inspections. The EU had no harmonized requirements for bulk drug GMPs, only three member countries regulated bulk drugs, and FDA's inspections of EU bulk drug manufacturers revealed a need for stricter controls for raw materials, analysis, and validation.[481] The negotiation focused on providing an transition period during which time the EU could establish a program of legislation and enforcement for bulk drug GMPs.

Even where a Member State had been found to be equivalent, the FDA insisted that it needed to reserve the right to inspect a manufacturing firm located in that Member State in order to fulfill both the requirements of the act for inspections "from time to time," as discussed above, and because of related regulatory policies. The FDA would always reserve the ability to inspect for any appropriate reason without a bureaucratic procedure set up that would have to be overcome if the agency believed it needed to inspect a firm. The EU wished to limit inspection rights to very extraordinary circumstances justifiable in a "safeguard" clause; however, inspections could conducted only pursuant to a reasoned request.

Finally, regarding the handling of inspection reports received under the MRA, the FDA insisted on the ability to treat inspection reports of foreign firms in accordance with the same disclosure policies that apply to domestic firms. Under 21 C.F.R. § 20.89, the FDA has the authority to treat another country's report as the other country's record (even

---

[480] Scrip, Oct. 10, 1995, at 16; Scrip, Nov. 8, 1996, at 15 (reporting on FDA public meeting held Oct. 30, 1996).

[481] Statement to author by Gerald Vince, FDA (Apr. 18, 1997).

though FDA has a copy of it) and therefore not subject to the U.S. Freedom of Information Act.)[482]

One of the reasons why the negotiations took four years (1993-1997) was the lack of harmonization as to how inspections are conducted, meaning that the transitional phase of the MRA will include an intense schedule of training and joint inspections aimed at assuring that EU inspections are done in a way that will meet the FDA's needs, and vice versa. There are differences in authority, funding, the EU's announced inspections versus the FDA's unannounced inspections, the EU's reliance on observation versus the FDA's attention to documents, the EU's reliance on end-product testing versus the FDA's greater attention to the GMP process, the EU's writing its inspection report in collaboration with the company versus the FDA's writing a much longer report without company involvement.[483]

The MRA negotiations took on a high profile in late 1996 and early 1997. Successful conclusion of these negotiations was endorsed by the TABD, a forum for "senior-level government and business leaders to identify and understand each other's priorities and to develop creative solutions to remaining barriers to transatlantic trade and investment."[484] At the first TABD meeting in Seville in 1995, pharmaceutical industry priorities had been parallel imports in the EU, restrictive pricing for drugs in the EU, rapid completion of ICH, and strengthening intellectual property protection.[485] By the second TABD meeting in Chicago in late 1996, the drug and device MRA issues topped the list of TABD issues. The business community as a whole expressed fervent interest in completing the pending MRAs — particularly telecommunications industry executives, who believed that the part of the MRA they were interested in was being held hostage to the FDA's conditions in the drug and device MRA negotiations.

The pharmaceutical manufacturers on both sides of the Atlantic banded together and, in cooperation with the FDA, crafted the broad outlines of a solution to the unresolved problems in the drug MRA negotiation.[486] First, the EU would concede the FDA's right to receive whatever inspection reports it needed and to do inspections for cause. Second, the FDA would include preapproval inspections in the MRA. TABD leaders named January 31, 1997 as the target date for signing the MRAs.

Support for completing the MRAs intensified when, at a semi-annual summit a few weeks later in December 1996, President Clinton and President Santer of the EU endorsed completion of the MRAs by the end of January 1997. This date was missed. On April 15, 1997, President Santer wrote to President Clinton urging that he personally intervene in the ongoing negotiations for an MRA, stating that "some US agencies remain very reluctant to apply the principles of mutual recognition that we both agreed should be implemented."[487] President Santer also expressed concern about the narrow scope of product

---

[482] U.S. Dep't of Justice v. Tax Analysts, 492 U.S. 136, 144 (1989); Tax Analysts v. U.S. Dep't of Justice, 913 F. Supp. 599 (D.D.C. 1996);

[483] *PDA Interviews FDA's Stephanie Gray*, PDA LETTER, Sept. 1995, at 1, 7.

[484] Alex Trotman, Chairman, Ford Motor Company, *in* TABD Background, Chicago (Nov. 8-9, 1996).

[485] SCRIP, Nov. 8, 1996, at 15.

[486] *Id.*, Nov. 26, 1996 and *Id.*, Nov. 22, 1996.

[487] Letter to Pres. Clinton from Pres. Santer (Apr. 15, 1997).

coverage proposed by the U.S. side for both drugs and devices. He closed by urging that both presidents join "in a decision to give clear instructions to our negotiators which will permit them to reach an early deal resulting in a mutual recognition agreement compatible with our industries' expectations, effective at the end of a transitional period not longer than three years and recognizing the systems in place on both sides without imposing new administrative hurdles" and that could be announced at the next U.S.-EU presidential sumit on May 28, 1997. Agreement was instead announced at the G-7 summit in Denver in June 1997.

A complicating factor that arose in 1997 was the FDA's effort to deal with the European Commission's insistence that all the "sectoral" MRAs be linked together with an umbrella agreement created a new set of issues, as the umbrella agreement contained a large number of provisions that were inconsistent with the drug and device agreements, the agency's authority, or both. The umbrella agreement was based on mutual recognition approaches applicable among member states of the EU.

The FDA recently has undertaken discussions on updated drug GMP agreements with counterparts in Canada[488] and Switzerland. As indicated above, the FDA has had MOUs with these countries that have aided international cooperation for more than a quarter of a century. Because Sweden is now a part of the EU, its cooperative activities with the FDA will be subsumed under the U.S.-EU MRA.

Import Activities

■ Section 801 of the Federal Food, Drug, and Cosmetic Act

General Overview

Section 801 of the FDCA addresses the importation of drugs, devices, and other FDA-regulated products.[489] In brief, upon the FDA's request, officials of the U.S. Customs Service are required to deliver samples of drugs and devices that are being imported or offered for import into the United States and to provide notice to the article's owner or consignee.[490] The owner or consignee then may appear before the FDA and introduce testimony.[491] The FDA, however, will provide an opportunity for a hearing only if the imported drug or

---

[488] Terms of Reference, Canada-United States Working Group on Pharmaceutical Good Manufacturing Practices Compliance Programmes (Apr. 1997).

[489] 21 U.S.C. § 381. The FDA has provided guidance on the agency's interpretation of section 801 in its Regulatory Procedures Manual, ch. 9, 337-85 (Aug. 1995).

[490] 21 U.S.C. § 381(a).

[491] *Id.*, "This proceeding...is not a conventional administrative law hearing. It is not an adversarial proceeding; FDA does not put in any evidence, but relies on its position as stated in the notice of the hearing. The importer can introduce testimony orally or in writing. No cross-examination occurs and no recording or transcript is normally made of the proceeding. Paul Hyman, *Legal Overview of FDA Authority Over Imports and Exports*, 42 FOOD DRUG COSM. L.J. 203, 205 (1987).

device may be refused admission into the United States.[492] There is no constitutional right to a hearing other than this informal process,[493] and the right to provide testimony may be satisfied by phone calls and correspondence even if no specific "hearing" was held.[494]

Additionally, the FDA is required to provide the Customs Service with a list of registered establishments, and if the imported drug of device is manufactured, prepared, propagated, compounded, or processed in an establishment that is not registered in the United States,[495] The FDA must request samples of such articles and provide notice to the drugs' owner or consignee, who may then appear before the agency and has the right to introduce testimony.[496]

Generally, the grounds for refusing admission of an imported drug into the United States are that it has been manufactured, processed, or packed under insanitary conditions, is forbidden or restricted from sale in the country in which it was produced or from which it is being exported, or appears[497] to be adulterated, misbranded, or in violation of the new drug provisions in section 505 of the FDCA; similar provisions apply to medical devices.[498] Until a decision on admitting a drug or device is made, however, the owner or consignee may execute a bond and secure delivery of the article.[499]

If the FDA refuses admission of the article because it is adulterated, misbranded, or violates the new drug provisions, but the drug can be brought into compliance, the owner or consignee may apply for authorization to relabel or to "perform other action to bring the article into compliance" with the act or "render it other than a food, drug, device or cosmetic."[500] The FDA may grant or deny authorization to relabel or recondition the article and may specify the procedures to be followed, the disposition of rejected articles or portions of such articles, time limits for compliance, and other conditions.[501]

It is important to note, however, that the owner or consignee does not have the right to reexport a refused article. Under section 304 of the Act,[502] the FDA may initiate seizure and condemnation proceedings against any drug that is adulterated or misbranded when

---

[492] 21 C.F.R. § 1.94(a).

[493] Bowman v. Retzlaff, 65 F. Supp. 265 (D. Md. 1946); Sugarman v. Forbragd, 405 F. 2d 1189 (9th Cir. 1968), *cert. denied*, 395 U.S. 960 (1969); Meserey v. United States, 447 F. Supp. 548 (D. Nev. 1977).

[494] Meserey v. United States, 447 F. Supp. 548 (D. Nev. 1977).

[495] Registration is required by section 510 of the FDCA (21 U.S.C. § 360).

[496] FDCA § 801(a); 21 U.S.C. § 381(a).

[497] The provision in section 801(a) enabling the FDA to refuse entry to any imported product that "appears" to be violative may be viewed as leveling the playing field between domestic and imported goods, for which establishment inspections are more difficult, Seabrook Int'l Foods, Inc. v. Harris, 501 F. Supp. 1086, 1091-92 D.D.C. 1980). Or this clause may be viewed as setting a more demanding standard for imports, *see* Paul Hyman, *supra* note 491, at 203, 206; William R. Pendergast, *Does, or Can, FDA Discriminate Against Foreign Origin Goods to the Advantage of Domestic Products?* 42 FooD DRUG COSM. L.J. 527 (1987).

[498] 21 U.S.C. § 381(a). Section 505(a) of the Act (*id.* § 355(a)) prohibits any person (including an importer) from introducing or delivering for introduction an unapproved new drug product into interstate commerce.

[499] *Id.* § 381(b).

[500] 21 C.F.R. § 1.95.

[501] *See* 21 CFR § 1.96(a)(1)-(a)(5).

[502] 21 U.S.C. § 334.

introduced into or while in interstate commerce or while held for sale after shipment into interstate commerce, or that cannot be introduced into interstate commerce under section 505 of the Act.[503] For devices, the agency has even broader seizure authority to seize adulterated or misbranded devices, as there is no requirement to show that a violative device is in interstate commerce.[504] The FDA also has successfully seized unapproved new drugs that were being transported "in bond" across the United States for shipment to a foreign country.[505] The cases have often involved questionable drugs or other products being transported to Mexico, and the FDA's concern may have been that the products ultimately would be offered again for entry into the U.S. market.[506]

If the drug or device is refused admission to the United States and the owner or consignee does not apply for permission to recondition the article or reexport it, it must be destroyed.[507]

Reimportation of Prescription Drugs

Some drugs that are offered for importation into the United States originally were manufactured in the United States and then exported. In 1988, as part of the Prescription Drug Marketing Act (PDMA),[508] section 801 of the FDCA was amended to prohibit the reimportation of prescription drugs that were originally manufactured in the United States and exported unless the drug's manufacturer imported the drug.[509] Congress took this action to protect U.S. citizens against subpotent and adulterated drugs and to prevent the importation into the United States of counterfeit drugs (as "reimported" U.S.-made drugs).[510]

The PDMA contains only two exceptions to the reimportation prohibition. A broad exception exists for drugs reimported into the United States by their manufacturers on the grounds that such reimportation is "necessary to avoid interference with usual and customary business practice . . . . "[511] A limited, case-by-case exception exists for medical emergencies.[512]

The "Personal Importation Policy"

Before April 26, 1996,[513] the general import requirements in section 801 of the act banned

---

[503] *See, e.g.,* United States v. Food, 2,998 Cases, 64 F.3d 984 (5th Cir. 1995). In this case, the court rejected the argument of the importer of certain adulterated and misbranded mushrooms that the FDA could invoke only the administrative remedies in section 801 of the act if an imported food was refused admission into the United States.

[504] 21 U.S.C. § 334(a).

[505] United States v. 197 Boxes K.H.3, 520 F. Supp. 467 (S.D. Tex. 1981); United States v. 300 Oz. Gerovital Lotion, 492 F. Supp. 114 (C.D. Cal. 1980).

[506] Paul Hyman, *supra* note 491, at 203, 210.

[507] 21 U.S.C. § 381(a).

[508] Pub. L. No. 100-293, 102 Stat. 95 (Apr. 22, 1988) (codified as amended in scattered sections of 21 U.S.C.); R. Angarola & J. Beach, *The Prescription Drug Marketing Act: A Solution in Search of a Problem?*, 51 Food & Drug L.J. 21 (1996).

[509] 21 U.S.C. § 381(d)(1).

[510] *See* S. Rep. 100-303, 100th Cong., 2d Sess. 2-3 (1988).

[511] *Id.* This exception is codified at 21 U.S.C. § 381(d)(1).

[512] *See* 21 U.S.C. § 381(d)(2).

[513] On this date, the FDA Export Reform and Enhancement Act (Pub. L. No. 104-134, 110 Stat. 134) became law. It was amended by Pub.L. No. 104-180, 110 Stat. 1321 (Aug. 6, 1996).

entry of all unapproved, imported drugs, regardless of whether those drugs were destined for sale in, or outside, the United States. Yet the FDA's enforcement of section 801 did allow for some unapproved drugs to be imported into the United States. For years, the agency has permitted individuals to import small quantities of unapproved drugs for their personal use, usually in situations where the drug was not available within the United States. As the number of AIDS cases grew in the United States, in July 1988 the FDA exercised its enforcement discretion and issued a more formal policy permitting persons suffering from AIDS, and from cancer, to import small doses of unapproved drugs for their personal use. This policy, which was originally known as the "mail import policy" (even though it included imports in personal luggage), was later expanded to cover drugs for all life-threatening or serious conditions and became known as the personal importation policy.

The policy instructed FDA personnel to exercise discretion in allowing personal shipments of drugs in the following situations:

> when the intended use is appropriately identified, such use is not for treatment of a serious condition, and the product is not known to represent a significant health risk; or when (1) the intended use is unapproved and for a serious condition for which effective treatment may not be available domestically either through commercial or clinical means; (2) there is no known commercialization or promotion to persons residing in the United States by those involved in the distribution of the product at issue; (3) the product is considered not to represent an unreasonable risk; and (4) the individual seeking to import the product affirms in writing that it is for the patient's own personal use (generally not more than three months supply) and provides the name and address of the doctor licensed in the U.S. responsible for his or her treatment with the product or provides evidence that the product is for the continuation of a treatment begun in a foreign country.[514]

This policy, however, excludes drugs covered under an import alert. After the FDA issued an import alert barring personal importation of RU-486, a medical abortifacient drug approved in Great Britain and France but not in the United States, the agency was involved in litigation with a pregnant woman who had filled a prescription for RU-486 in Britain and brought it back to the country, where it was seized at JFK airport.[515] The result was that the woman was not entitled to preliminary relief ordering return of the drug or barring enforcement on the ban on importation of the drug for personal use.

U.S. Customs, the FDA, and the Drug Enforcement Agency took action in 1996 to ban the personal importation of Rohypnol (flunitrazepam), the "date rape drug," following reports of growing abuse of the drug.[516] A 1994-1995 study of customs declaration forms col-

---

[514] Regulatory Procedures Manual 9-71-030(C). Customs agents are reportedly inconsistent in whether they allow medication for patients' own use to pass unimpeded into this country. Letter from Donald F. Klein, Pres., American Society of Clinical Psychopharmacology, to Michael F. Friedman, Lead Deputy Commissioner, FDA (Mar. 20, 1997).

[515] Benten v. Kessler, 505 U.S. 1084, 1085 (1992) (per curiam), rev'g 799 F. Supp. 281 (E.D.N.Y. 1992).

[516] Kathleen Day, *Countering Ill Effects of an Abused Drug: Firm Raises Awareness in Sex-Related Attacks*, WASH. POST, Nov. 2, 1996, at H1; Tim Friend, *'Monster' Drug Soon to Be on the Same List as LSD, Heroin*, USA TODAY, June 20, 1996, at 1A.

lected at the Mexico-Texas border crossing found that fourteen of the top fifteen products imported for personal use were controlled substances, including hypnotics, anti-anxiety drugs, stimulants, and narcotics, contradicting the assumption that the typical U.S. customer for cross-border purchases are elderly citizens buying prescription drugs OTC.[517]

Import-for-Export Provisions of 1996 Export Act

These exercises in the FDA's enforcement discretion did not help manufacturers seeking to import unapproved drugs or devices into the United States. Before April 26, 1996, a drug manufacturer could not import an unapproved drug or device or a component thereof (such as a bulk drug from a source other than the source listed in the manufacturer's marketing application) even if the manufacturer intended only to incorporate the unapproved drug, device, or component into a product destined for lawful export. This limitation as well as even louder complaints about the statute's higly restrictive export requirements, prompted Congress to enact the FDA Export Reform and Enhancement Act of 1996.[518] This law significantly changed section 801 of the act by permitting the importation of unapproved drug components, device components, parts, and accessories, food additives, color additives, and dietary supplements if the importer submitted a statement to the FDA at the time of the initial importation stating that the imported article is "intended to be further processed by the initial owner or consignee, or incorporated by the initial owner or consignee" into a product destined for export.[519] This provision, known as the "import-for-export" provision, also requires the importer to maintain records identifying how the imported article was used and, upon request, to submit a report to the FDA "that provides an accounting of the exportation or the disposition of the imported article, including portions that have been destroyed, and the manner in which such person complied" with the import requirements.[520] Any imported article that is not "further processed" or "incorporated" into a product destined for export must be destroyed or re-exported.[521]

The "import-for-export" provision does not apply to all FDA-regulated products in the same manner. The provision conditioned the importation of blood, blood components, source plasma, and source leukocytes (and their components, accessories, and parts) on compliance with the biologics provisions of the Public Health Service Act[522]— which require, among other things, that a biologic product be propagated or manufactured and prepared at a licensed establishment — or "under appropriate circumstances and conditions, as determined by the Secretary."[523]

Importation of tissues, tissue components, or tissue parts must comply with section 361 of the Public Health Service Act.[524] This provision authorizes the issuance of regulations to control communicable diseases.

---

[517] SCRIP, Mar. 15, 1996, at 21.

[518] Pub. L. No. 104-134, 110 Stat. 134, amended Aug. 6, 1996, Pub. L. No. 104-180.

[519] 21 U.S.C. § 381(d)(3)(A).

[520] *Id*. § 381(d)(3)(B).

[521] *Id*. § 381(d)(3)(C).

[522] Section 351(a), 42 U.S.C. § 262.

[523] 21 U.S.C. § 381(d)(4).

[524] 42 U.S.C. § 264.

The new "import-for-export" provision leaves critical terms undefined. For example, the terms "further processing" and "incorporated" are undefined, thereby giving the FDA and the industry no guidance as to the provision's intended scope. While importation of a bulk drug for incorporation into a finished drug product destined for export — or sterilization of a drug or device prior to reexportation — are practices that seem clearly to constitute either "incorporation,"or "further processing," it is less clear whether labeling a finished drug or device product represents "further processing," or whether storage of an unapproved, finished drug product destined for export constitutes "further processing." The FDA has adopted a broad interpretation of "further processing" and incorporation, to include almost all activities except for storage of an unapproved product; thus, in the examples given earlier, labeling activities conducted in the United States on an imported drug would be further processing, but mere storage of an imported article would not be treated as satisfying the "import-for-export" provision.

Additionally, an argument can be made that the FDA Export Reform and Enhancement Act will make it more difficult to enforce the reimportation prohibition in the PDMA. Given that the PDMA was supposed to prevent counterfeit drugs, falsely labeled as "American Goods Returned," from entering U.S. commerce, the "import-for-export" provision may inadvertently create the opportunity for counterfeit (or otherwise violative) drugs to enter U.S. commerce, when they have gained entry ostensibly for "further processing" or incorporation before being exported. Considering the FDA's scarce resources, there is reason for concern that such drugs would be able to enter the United States and be diverted into domestic commerce before the agency could detect them.

Import-for-export activities might be carried out in a foreign trade zone, which is a place within United States territory where products may be manufactured, or brought in and held, or further processed, for future import into the United States or for export to a foreign country, without tariffs and without officially entering commerce of the United States within the meaning of the customs laws.[525] The FDA successfully asserted jurisdiction over violative products in foreign trade zones in a case where the court enjoined the shipment of unapproved new drugs that were manufactured in a foreign trade zone using raw materials imported from Italy for export to Vietnam (at the request of the U.S. AID).[526]

■ Import Alerts

The FDA exercises administrative discretion to detain certain imported products.[527] These detentions are usually the result of information indicating that products imported from a particular firm or country may violate the act, and are implemented through documents known as "Import Alerts." The FDA's Division of Import Operations and Policy issues Import Alerts to FDA's district offices. The legal validity of an Import Alert is occasion-

---

[525] 19 U.S.C. § 81c. Paul Hyman, *supra* note 491, at 203, 210.

[526] United States v. Yaron Lab., Inc., 365 F. Supp. 917 (N.D. Cal. 1972).

[527] Section 801 does not contain explicit authority to detain an imported article, but the practice apparently results from the act's language giving importers the opportunity to bring an imported article into compliance with the act pending a decision on whether the article is to be admitted into the United States. *See* Paul M. Hyman, *Legal Overview of FDA Authority Over Imports,* FOOD & DRUG L.J. 525 (1994).

ally questioned. Courts have held certain Import Alerts to be regulations and have invalidated them due to their failure to adhere to the notice and comment rulemaking requirements in the Administrative Procedure Act.[528]

■ Registration and Listing by Foreign Firms

Section 510 of the FDCA[529] requires, among other things, that persons who own or operate any establishment engaged in the manufacture, preparation, propagation, compounding, or processing of a drug or drugs register all establishments with the FDA and list all drugs that are being manufactured, prepared, propagated, compounded, or processed for commercial distribution. This requirement applies only to establishments within the United States. For foreign manufacturers, section 510(i) permits, but does not require, establishment registration.[530] Drug listing is mandatory, however, for imported as well as domestic drugs.[531] Section 510(i) specifies that the registration is to occur pursuant to regulations promulgated by the FDA[532] and that the regulations include, among other things, provisions for the registration of any such establishment upon condition that adequate and effective means are available, by arrangement with the government of such foreign country or otherwise, to enable [FDA] to determine from time to time whether drugs...manufactured, prepared, propagated, compounded, or processed in such establishment, if imported or offered for import into the United States, shall be refused admission on any of the grounds set forth in section 801(a) of this Act."[533]

While section 510(i) of the act appears to give foreign firms the option whether to register their establishments, they as a practical matter *must* register due to other statutory provisions. First, as mentioned above, there is a requirement to list their products. Second, section 801(a) provides that, if an imported drug is manufactured, prepared, propagated, compounded, or processed in an establishment that is not registered in the United States, the FDA must request samples of such drugs and to provide notice to the drugs' owner or consignee who may then appear before the agency and has the right to introduce testimony.

Export Activities

The report of the President and Vice President on *Reinventing Drug and Device Regulation*, issued in April 1995, called for expansion of opportunities to export drugs and

---

[528] 5 U.S.C. § 553. *See, e.g.,* United States v. Articles of Drug, consisting of 203 Paper Bags, 634 F.Supp. 435 (N.D. Ill. 1986), *vacated as moot,* 818 F. 2d 569 (7th Cir. 1987); Bellarno Int'l Ltd. v. Food and Drug Admin., 678 F.Supp. 410 (E.D. N.Y. 1988); Benten v. Kessler, 799 F.Supp. 281 (E.D. N.Y. 1992), *rev'd,* 505 U.S. 1084 (1992).

[529] 21 U.S.C. § 360.

[530] *Id.* § 360(i).

[531] *Id.* § 360(j).

[532] These regulations are found at 21 C.F.R. pt. 207.

[533] 21 U.S.C. § 360(i).

devices.[534] This support, coupled with industry concerns and congressional interest, led to the enactment of the FDA Export Reform and Enhancement Act of 1996.[535]

■ Export Certificates for Pharmaceuticals Eligible for Commercial Distribution

International trade increasingly requires that products moving between nations be accompanied by documents attesting to the products' compliance with legal or regulatory requirements. These documents are known under various names, such as "export certificates," "certificates of free sale" (usually for products approved for domestic marketing in the exporting country), and "certificates to foreign governments."

Until enactment of the 1996 export reform amendment on April 26, 1996, the FDCA did not require the FDA to issue export certificates, although this was a legally permissible activity undertaken voluntarily by the agency. Each FDA center had its own program and procedures for issuing certificates, and the certificates themselves differed in name and format.[536] The enactment of the 1996 export reform law created an express legal basis for export certificates and led to an agency-wide effort among FDA's centers to reduce (but not eliminate) differences in their approaches. The 1996 law also added to U.S. law a category of export certificates that differed from its earlier pharmaceutical export certificate program, in that the FDA now must offer export certificates for certain products *not* eligible for "free sale" in the United States

FDA Export Certificate Program

For drug products, four different export certificates are now available. In November 1996, the FDA revised these certificates to reflect the provisions of the new law and setting fees, as authorized in the 1996 Act.[537] The new export law also permitted the agency to charge up to $175.00 for an export certificate provided that the agency issues the certificate within twenty days after receiving a request for a certificate.[538]

Two certificates, the "Certificates to Foreign Governments" and the "Certificates for Pharmaceutical Products," are for legally marketed drug products. To obtain a Certificate to Foreign Government, a firm must apply to the FDA and provide the following information: 1) the country of destination; 2) the drug's trade name or generic name; 3) the drug's active ingredient(s); 4) a copy of the container and package labeling; 5) a copy of the package insert; 6) the manufacturing facility's name and address; 7) a copy of the approval letter for the product or, if the product does not have an approval, the legal basis for permitting marketing of the drug product; and 8) a certification that the information in

---

[534] National Performance Review, Reinventing Drug and Device Regulation 5, 25-26 (Apr. 1995).

[535] Pub. L. No. 104-134, amended by Pub. L. No. 104-180. *See* Linda R. Horton, *Ethics and Trade: Exports of Unapproved Pharmaceuticals and Medical Devices*, 15 Med. & L. (Dec. 1996).

[536] *See* Murphy, G Emalee., *Certificates of Free Sale*, 49 Food & Drug L.J. 581 (1994).

[537] 61 Fed. Reg. 57,445 (Nov. 6, 1996). The fees differ between centers due to different operational procedures. For example, the Center for Drug Evaluation and Research (CDER) and the Center for Biologics Evaluation and Research (CBER) both charge the full $175 fee for the first certificate. For the second certificate, CDER charges $90, but CBER charges $175.

[538] 21 U.S.C. § 381 (e)(4)(B).

the application is true. For bulk drug substances, the firm must provide a sample container label for the bulk drug substance and the container label for the finished dosage form.

If the application for the certificate is satisfactory, the FDA prepares the Certificate to Foreign Government. The certificate provides the product's trade or generic name, its marketing application number (such as the product's NDA number), the drug's active ingredient, potency, dosage form, and package size. The certification, which is prepared before a notary public, also states that the product is being marketed in or may be legally exported from the United States and that the firm producing the drug is subject to periodic inspections and, at its last inspection, appeared to be in "substantial compliance" with GMPs.

The application process for a Certificate of a Pharmaceutical Product is similar to that for the Certificate to Foreign Government, except that the FDA requests three copies of the container labels and package inserts. The reason for this difference is that the Certificate of a Pharmaceutical Product represents the agency's effort to comply with the WHO export certification scheme. (The WHO scheme is described in more detail below). The Certificate of a Pharmaceutical Product contains the product's proprietary name and dosage form, its active ingredient(s) and amount per dose, and, if the product is approved for marketing in the United States, the name of the product license holder, the license status (whether the product remains approved), and the product license number and date of issue. Other information, such as whether an approved technical summary is attached and whether the manufacturing facility complies with GMPs (as recommended by the WHO), may also be included. If the product is not approved for marketing in the United States, the certificate explains why authorization is lacking. (For example, the FDA would state that approval was not required, has not been requested, is under consideration, or was refused.)

In 1996, the FDA created two other export certificates in response to a new provision in the FDA Export Reform and Enhancement Act that authorizes the agency, upon request, to certify that a drug to be exported meets the export requirements in section 801 or 802 of the Act even if the product has not met requirements for domestic marketing in the United States.[539] The FDA distinguishes these certificates from the Certificate to Foreign Government or the Certificate of a Pharmaceutical Product by referring to them as "Certificates of Exportability."

To obtain a Certificate of Exportability, a person must provide the following information: 1) country or countries of destination; if multiple countries are involved, the FDA will prepare a certificate for each country; 2) the drug's trade or generic name; 3) the drug's active ingredient(s); 4) the manufacturing facility's name and address; 5) a statement identifying the product to be exported and the provision of law (i.e., section 801 or 802 of the Act) permitting exportation, and a certification that the company and product to be exported complies with the applicable provisions in the act; and 6) a certification that the statements in the request for a certificate are true.

The new export law also permits the FDA to charge up to $175.00 for an export certificate provided that the agency issues the certificate within twenty days after receiving a request for a certificate.[540]

---

[539] *Id.* § 381(e)(4)(A)(ii).
[540] *Id.* § 381(e)(4)(B).

WHO Export Certificate Program

WHO has its own certification program for pharmaceuticals. Formally known as the WHO Certification Scheme on the Quality of Pharmaceutical Products Moving in International Commerce, the program originated with a 1969 World Health Assembly resolution,[541] which endorsed requirements for GMPs for drugs. Under the WHO scheme, each member nation, upon application by a "commercially interested party," must verify to the "competent authority" of another member nation that: a) a specific product is authorized to be marketed within its jurisdiction or explain why the product does not have marketing authorization; b) the plant which produces the product is subject to inspections to establish that the plant conforms to WHO's GMP standards; and c) all submitted information, including labeling, is authorized in the certifying country.[542] The certification scheme covers finished pharmaceutical products intended for human or animal use as well as, under a 1996 amendment, active ingredients.[543]

WHO member nations may decide whether to participate in the certification scheme and also whether to participate solely to control imports into their countries. Member nations who intend to use the WHO scheme to support pharmaceutical exports, however, must possess an "effective national licensing system" covering pharmaceutical products, manufacturers, and distributors, GMP requirements consistent with WHOs, effective controls to monitor drug product quality, the ability to conduct inspections to ensure that GMPs are observed, and the "administrative capacity to issue the required certificates, to institute inquiries in the case of complaint, and to notify expeditiously both WHO and the competent authority in any Member State known to have imported a specific product that is subsequently associated with a potentially serious quality defect or other hazard."[544] Each nation seeking to use the WHO scheme to support exports decides for itself whether it meets the listed WHO criteria.

The WHO scheme covers three types of certificates. A "Certificate of Pharmaceutical Product" is to be used when a product that is to be exported is under consideration for a product license that will authorize its importation and sale in the importing country, and the importing country has an administrative mechanism for renewing, extending, or reviewing product licenses. These certificates are issued by the government in the exporting country and, through a third party (such as the importer's agent or the product license holder) go to the competent authority in the importing country. These certificates contain the product's name and dosage form, the active ingredient's name and amount, the product license holder and/or manufacturing facility's name and address, the product's formula (including all excipients), and product information for health professionals and the public, as approved in the exporting country.[545]

A second certificate is the "Statement of Licensing Status of Pharmaceutical Product(s)," which states that a marketing license has been issued for a specific product or products in

---

[541] World Health Assembly Resolution WHA22.50.

[542] *See* World Health Organization Technical Report Series, No. 863, Guidelines for Implementation of the WHO Certification Scheme on the Quality of Pharmaceuticals Moving in International Commerce 1996, 156 (1996).

[543] *Id.*

[544] *Id.* at 156-57.

[545] *Id.* at 158-59.

the exporting country. This certificate has limited utility under the WHO scheme and is "intended for use by importing agents when considering bids made in response to an international tender" and "intended only to facilitate the screening and preparation of information."[546] More detailed information about a product is to be obtained through the "Certificate of Pharmaceutical Product."

The "Batch Certificate of a Pharmaceutical Product" exists primarily for vaccines, sera, and other biological products. Unlike the "Certificate of Pharmaceutical Product," manufacturers, rather than government authorities in the exporting country, normally prepare these certificates (although authorities in the exporting country can also prepare them) and provide them to the importing agent, who is usually the license holder in the importing country. These certificates are "intended to accompany and provide an attestation concerning the quality and expiry date of specific batch or consignment of a product that has already been licensed in the importing country."[547] It contains the final product's specifications at the time of batch release and analytical results.

The WHO certificate scheme also makes regulatory authorities responsible for various other duties, such as ensuring that a manufacturer applies identical GMPs to all pharmaceutical products (including those destined for export), ensuring that the manufacturer consents to the release of inspection results to authorities in an importing country, conducting inspections to satisfy the specific requirements of a requesting authority, and investigating product defects and complaints and notifying other countries.[548]

In late 1996, WHO began considering changes to its export scheme. These changes included making the WHO certification scheme mandatory for imported drugs so that the WHO-type product and batch certificates become part of the information that is submitted in the marketing application, encouraging regulatory authorities to contact their counterparts in an exporting country if a firm is unwilling to provide a WHO export certificate, and encouraging manufacturers and their associations to include WHO certificates in their applications in the importing country. In May 1997, the Fiftieth World Health Assembly adopted a resolution endorsing the guidelines for implementing the WHO certification scheme and urging member nations to implement the guidelines and to issue the WHO-type certificates beginning on January 1, 1998.[549]

It is unclear whether the WHO changes, as well as changes to the FDA's export certificates under the new export law, will result in significant differences between the two export certificate systems. It appears that the revised WHO export certificates will be considerably longer and more detailed than the certificates contemplated under section 802 of the FDCA.

---

[546] *Id.* at 159.

[547] *Id.* at 160.

[548] *Id.* at 161-62.

[549] Resolution of the Executive Board of the WHO, "Guidelines on the WHO Certification Scheme on the Quality of Pharmaceutical Products Moving in International Commerce," EB99.R21, dated Jan. 21, 1997.

■ Export Policy for Pharmaceuticals not Eligible for Commercial Distribution in the United States

The export provision in the FDCA had its origins in the Food and Drugs Act of 1906.[550] In brief, section 2 of the 1906 Act stated that:

> no article shall be deemed misbranded or adulterated within the provisions of this act when intended for export to any foreign country and prepared or packed according to the specifications or directions of the foreign purchaser when no substance is used in the preparation or packing thereof in conflict with the laws of the foreign country to which said article is intended to be shipped; but if said article shall be in fact sold or offered for sale for domestic use or consumption, then this proviso shall not exempt said article from the operation of any of the other provisions of this act.

This export provision remained essentially unchanged in the FDCA,[551] where it was codified as section 801(d). Section 801(d) of the 1938 Act stated that:

> A food, drug, device, or cosmetic intended for export shall not be deemed to be adulterated or misbranded under this Act if it (1) accords to the specifications of the foreign purchaser, (2) is not in conflict with the laws of the country to which it is intended for export, (3) is labeled on the outside of the shipping package that it is intended for export, and (4) is not sold or offered for sale in domestic commerce . . . .

The 1938 Act, however, also defined the term "new drug," and because unapproved new drugs were handled under separate prohibited act provisions,[552] rather than being deemed adulterated or misbranded, the FDA concluded that section 801(d) of the FDCA did not apply to new drugs.[553] As a result, the FDCA was interpreted as permitting the export of approved drugs, but not the export of unapproved new drugs. The pharmaceutical industry viewed the laws as impairing its ability to compete in international markets.[554]

To correct the situation, Congress enacted the Drug Export Amendments Act of 1986.[555] The 1986 Amendments added section 802 to the FDCA and established three different "tracks" for exporting unapproved drugs and unlicensed biological products. Under track 1, the FDA could approve the export of new human and animal drugs and biological products that were not approved in the United States, but the drug had to have the same active ingredient(s) as a product for which marketing approval in the United States was being sought. Exports under track 1 were confined to twenty-one specific countries listed in section 802 of the Act. Those countries were: Australia, Austria, Belgium, Canada, Denmark,

---

[550] Pub. L. No. 59-384, 34 Stat. 768.

[551] Pub. L. No. 75-717; 21 U.S.C. § 381(d).

[552] FDCA §§ 301(d), 505(a); 21 U.S.C. §§ 331(d), 355(a).

[553] *See, e.g.,* United States v. An Article of Drug, et c. . . . Ethionamide-INH, No. 67 C 288 (E.D. N.Y. Aug. 19, 1967); United States v. Yaron Lab., Inc., 365 F. Supp. 917, 919 (N.D. Cal. 1972); Compliance Policy Guide 7132c.01 (Oct. 1, 1980). "Intermediates," or drug ingredients, were allowed to be exported, as were drugs for investigational use under certain circumstances.

[554] *See* S. Rep. 99-225, 99th Cong., 2d Sess. 5-6 (1985).

[555] Pub. L. No. 99-660, 100 Stat. 3743.

the Federal Republic of Germany, Finland, France, Iceland, Ireland, Italy, Japan, Luxembourg, the Netherlands, New Zealand, Norway, Portugal, Spain, Sweden, Switzerland, and the United Kingdom.

Under track 2, the FDA could approve the export of drugs and biological products intended for the treatment of tropical diseases. Exports under this track were limited to countries in which the use of the drug or biological product had been determined by the agency to be safe and effective.

Track 3 applied to partially processed biological products and amended section 351 of the PHS act. The FDA was authorized to approve the export of partially processed human biological products intended for further manufacture in any of the twenty-one listed countries, but the product had to be approved or in the process of receiving approval from the foreign country.[556]

Additionally, in 1988 existing section 801(d) was renumbered as a new section 801(e)(1) of the Act.[557]

The 1986 Amendments, however, presented several problems and concerns. One significant problem was that the 1986 Amendments limited exports of unapproved drugs and biological products to twenty-one countries. Although the 1986 Amendments provided criteria for adding more countries to the list, it did not include any administrative mechanism for doing so, and the FDA interpreted the act as enabling only Congress to apply the criteria and add more countries to the list. Exports to countries that were not on the list were not permitted.

The requirement that the drug or biological product contain the same active ingredient as a drug or biological product for which marketing approval in the United States was being "actively pursued" also caused some concern among the industry. Questions arose concerning the degree to which the active ingredient had to be the same, whether the overseas intended use needed to be the same, and how actively the manufacturer had to be seeking FDA approval.

The very notion of requiring the FDA to approve a product's exportation generated increasing criticism and debate during the 1990s. The 1986 Amendments required a person, under track 1, to file an application to export a drug at least ninety days before the date on which the applicant proposed to export the drug; required the FDA to publish a notice in the *Federal Register* identifying the applicant, the drug to be exported, and the country to which the drug was being exported; and established requirements for the application as well as the agency's action on an application. For example, if the agency decided to disapprove an application, it had to provide a written statement to the applicant describing deficiencies that the applicant had to correct and giving the applicant sixty days to correct those deficiencies. Some firms charged that this approval process took too long; others questioned why the United States had any obligation to approve the exportation of a

---

[556] The 1986 Amendments did not alter the export requirements for insulin and antibiotics. These products remained subject to the basic export requirements that are now seen in section 801(e)(1) of the act, such that exports could occur without prior FDA approval.

[557] The Prescription Drug Marketing Act, Pub. L. No. 100-293, 102 Stat. 95 (Apr. 22, 1988).

product to a foreign country, particularly when the foreign country had its own public health authorities and had approved the product for marketing.

Congress addressed these export problems and concerns (as well as some others) through the FDA Export Reform and Enhancement Act of 1996.[558] For human drugs and biological products, the 1996 law:

- amended section 801 of the Act to make it easier to import unapproved components of drugs and biological products into the United States where those components are intended for incorporation or further processing by the initial owner or consignee into a drug or biological product that will be exported;

- amended section 801 of the Act to permit exportation of approved drugs to countries that have different or additional labeling requirements or conditions of use so long as the exported drug's labeling identifies those conditions for use that have not been approved in the United States;[559]

- replaced section 802 of the act entirely with a new section 802 of the Act that:

- eliminates the requirement for prior FDA approval for exports (except for those products intended to treat a tropical disease or to treat a disease that is "not of significant prevalence in the United States");

- eliminates the need for manufacturers to be seeking approval of the drug in the United States as a condition for exportation (in most cases, the manufacturer simply notifies the agency that it is exporting a particular product and identifies the country to which the product is being exported;

- significantly expands the list of countries to which products can be exported and provides that if the product has been approved by a listed country, it can be exported from the U.S. anywhere in the world, whether a listed country or not;

- provides an administrative mechanism for adding countries to the list and for exporting products to unlisted countries;

- authorizes exports of unapproved drugs and biological products intended for use in clinical investigations in any of countries identified in section 802(b) of the Act.[560] These countries are often referred to as the "listed countries;"

---

[558] Pub. L. No. 104-134, amended by Pub. L. No. 104-180. Industry dissatisfaction with the 1986 Amendments led to several attempts to persuade the FDA to modify its interpretation of the law, but some anomalies in the act could not be corrected through reinterpretations of the law. For example, the 1986 Amendments had neglected to include Greece, an EU member. This omission was corrected in the 1996 amendment, through a provision that refers to the European Union, thereby allowing automatic expansion of listed countries as countries join the EU.

[559] Before the enactment of the FDA Export Reform and Enhancement Act, neither section 801 nor section 802 of the act addressed exports of approved drugs to countries where the drugs would be used or labeled for unapproved uses. Generally, exports of approved drugs for approved uses are not subject to any export restrictions, but, until section 801 of the act was amended, exporting an approved drug for an unapproved use would have resulted in an unapproved drug and subjected the manufacturer to export approval under section 802.

[560] The countries identified in section 802(b)(1)(A)(I) of the act are Australia, Canada, Israel, Japan, New Zealand, Switzerland, South Africa, and the EU and EEA countries. At the time the FDA Export Reform and Enhancement Act became law, the EU countries were Austria, Belgium, Denmark, Germany, Greece, Finland, France, Ireland, Italy, Luxembourg, the Netherlands, Portugal, Spain, Sweden, and the United Kingdom. The EEA countries were the EU countries, Iceland, Liechtenstein, and Norway. Note that, because section 802(b)(1)(A)(I) of the act refers to the EU and EEA, rather than their individual members, the ranks of the "listed countries" will automatically expand as nations accede to the EU or join the EEA.

- authorizes the export of unapproved products to a listed country in anticipation of marketing approval in that country;
- authorizes the export of unapproved products intended to treat diseases that are "not of significant prevalence in the United States;" and
- eliminates the need for manufacturers to be seeking approval of the drug in the United States as a condition for exportation;
- eliminates the application and *Federal Register* notice requirements; and
- provides that the manufacturer simply notifies the FDA that it is exporting a particular product and identifies the country to which the product is being exported.

Exports under section 802 of the Act of drugs and devices not meeting U.S. approval requirements also must meet certain requirements. Under section 802(f) of the Act:

- the product must be manufactured, processed, packaged, and held in substantial conformity with GMP's or meet international standards as certified by an international standards organization recognized by the FDA;
- the product must not consist in whole or in part of any filthy, putrid, or decomposed substance and must not have been prepared, packed, or held under insanitary conditions whereby it may have been contaminated or made injurious to health;
- the container for the product must not be composed, in whole or in part, of any poisonous or deleterious substance which may render the contents injurious to health;
- the product must have the strength, purity, or quality that it is represented to possess;
- no substance may be mixed or packed with the drug that would reduce the drug's quality or strength or may substitute in whole or in part for another substance in the drug;
- the product must comply with the requirements in section 801(e)(1) of the Act[561] (statements on the outside of the shipping package, such as, "For export only," are often sufficient, and statements on the product's labeling, such as, "Not for sale in the United States," are often sufficient.
- the product cannot be the subject of a notice by the FDA determining that the probability of reimportation of the exported product would present an imminent hazard to the public health and safety of the United States, such that exportation must be prohibited;
- the product cannot present an imminent hazard to the public health of the country to which it would be exported; and
- the product must be labeled in accordance with the requirements and conditions of use in the listed country which authorized it for marketing and use the language and units of measurement used in or designated by the country to which the drug is being exported.

Additionally, a drug may not be exported if the drug is not promoted in accordance with the labeling requirements mentioned above.

Unfortunately, the legislative history for the FDA Export Reform and Enhancement Act is quite terse, thus making many issues ripe for debate or conflicting interpretations. For example, section 802(b) of the act states that an unapproved drug or biologic may be

---

[561] As stated earlier, section 801(e)(1) of the act requires that the drug or device to be exported: 1) accords to the specifications of the foreign purchaser, 2) does not conflict with the laws of the country to which it is intended for export, 3) be labeled on the outside of the shipping package that it is intended for export, and 4) not be sold or offered for sale in domestic commerce.

exported to any country if the drug or biologic complies with the laws of the importing country and "had valid marketing authorization by the appropriate authority" in any listed country. Neither the Act nor the legislative history defines or explains what constitutes "valid marketing authorization." Does a responsible government agency in a listed country have to affirmatively approve the drug for marketing? What if the government agency is silent and simply acquiesces to or permits the drug's marketing?

The inclusion of investigational drugs in the FDA Export Reform and Enhancement Act presents several unique problems as well. The 1986 Amendments did not address exports of investigational drugs, and which the FDA had regulated for years under its IND authority.[562] This export program is often called the "312 program" because the regulations governing exports of investigational drugs are at 21 C.F.R. § 312.110. Under the 312 program, any person who intends to export an unapproved new drug product for use in a clinical investigation must have an IND or must submit a written request to the FDA. The written request must provide sufficient information about the drug to satisfy the agency that the drug is appropriate for investigational use in humans, that the drug will be used for investigational purposes only, and that the drug may be legally used by the consignee in the importing country for the proposed investigational use. The regulations also required the request to specify the quantity of the drug to be shipped and the frequency of expected shipments. If the FDA authorized exportation of the drug, it would notify the government of the importing country.

The FDA had intended to revise the 312 program significantly by eliminating the written requests in favor of recordkeeping months before the FDA Export Reform and Enhancement Act became law, and had prepared a proposed rule to that effect. The enactment of the new export law, however, compelled the agency to stop work on the proposed rule as it was undergoing final clearance, partly because of the perception that Congress, in enacting section 802(c) of the Act, had established the boundaries on exporting investigational drugs so any different proposal from the FDA might be construed as acting contrary to congressional intent. As this book went to press, the FDA was striving to prepare a proposed rule that would reduce requirements for exports under the 312 program, while respecting the evident intent of Congress to maintainsome requirements for exports to unlisted countries.

■ Pros and Cons on Export Policy

United States policy regarding drug exports has varied considerably over the decades, and, as suggested in the preceding paragraphs, has adopted different approaches for different drugs. For example, approved drugs and biologics are not subject to any special requirements under the act whereas most unapproved drugs and biologics are subject to different requirements (depending on whether they are destined for or have received marketing authorization from a "listed country" under section 802 of the Act). Antibiotics are subject only to the export requirements in section 801(e) of the Act, but not those under section 802 of the Act, and therefore have never been subject to the export ban applicable to unapproved new drugs from 1938-1986 nor to the strict export approval requirements from

---

[562] The FDA issued regulations governing the exportation of unapproved new drugs for investigational use on Jan. 18, 1984 (49 Fed. Reg. 2095), with minor modifications since then.

1986-1996. Investigational drugs are also being handled in special ways, as described above. In short, U.S. law reflects different legislative values and goals, ranging from promoting free trade of drugs[563] to requiring the FDA to have a role in approving exports of unapproved drugs to countries lacking sophisticated regulatory systems.

Arguments in favor of regulating exports have included:

- The United States should not dump products of unknown safety and efficacy on foreign countries. The United States has an obligation to ensure that U.S. firms do not exploit citizens in foreign countries.
- Many countries lack adequate regulatory systems and need or rely on the FDA's expertise.
- Confidence in U.S. products may be undermined by lax export controls, ultimately harming U.S. competitiveness overseas.
- U.S. public health is threatened by exports of unproven and possibly ineffective drugs when foreign citizens who have used such products enter the United States and spread disease.
- The United States is a leader in protecting the public health, so lax export controls undermine the United States's leadership on international public health issues.
- Export controls have, on occasion, enabled the FDA to intercept problematic exports before they could cause a safety problem abroad.
- Conversely, arguments against export controls have stated:
- U.S. export controls do not account for the different needs or values in foreign countries, and foreign countries with developed regulatory systems can make their own decisions regarding U.S. exports. Moreover, U.S. export controls are a form of extraterritorial control that does not respect foreign sovereignty.
- Export controls result in shifting jobs overseas due to companies' needs to circumvent those controls.
- Reliance on the FDA's regulatory system creates a disincentive for foreign countries to develop their own regulatory infrastructure.
- Foreign public health may be threatened if U.S. export controls prevent a needed vaccine or drug from being imported.
- The FDA's scarce resources could be put to better use on domestic public health issues.
- Facilitating exports actually helps protect foreign citizens because U.S. manufacturers will no longer shift operations overseas and, therefore, will remain subject to FDA control.

Not surprisingly, as international trade has increased, the statutory controls placed on exports of unapproved drugs has decreased. Whether additional amendments to the act are to be made in order to further facilitate foreign trade remains to be seen.

---

[563] Indeed, according to a sponsor of the FDA Export Reform and Enhancement Act, "the export provisions are a trade issue first and foremost." 142 CONG. REC. H4046 (daily ed. Apr. 25, 1996) (statement of Rep. Upton). The sponsor added that, "I am sure that we will revisit this issue in the future. Frankly, if it were up to me, there would be almost no restrictions on the export of medical products which allow them for sale. In my mind, the job of the FDA is to protect the health and safety of the United States, and it is not to play health product policeman for the rest of the world." *Id.*

■ International Activities on Exports of Unapproved Products

Free Trade or Public Health?

Export of pharmaceutical products has had a checkered past. Most would readily agree that facilitating drug exports to needy foreign countries (particularly developing nations) benefits those nations and that multinational pharmaceutical firms deserve credit for developing drugs to treat major diseases — such a malaria, tuberculosis, syphilis, and typhoid fever — that are prevalent in developing nations. However, others would argue that pharmaceutical firms have also been responsible for questionable pricing and promotional practices that have led to irrational use of drugs, ill-advised drug prescribing or purchasing by health professionals or governments, and, ultimately, harm to foreign patients.[564]

These questionable practices often exacerbate problems in the developing country's health system. For example, unlike the United States where drugs are either available only by prescription or over-the-counter, a developing country may have little or no regulatory structure to control drug dispensing. The health professional in the developing country also may be inadequately trained, thus making him or her more reliant on information supplied by drug company salesperson that may be potentially misleading or inaccurate. Drugs may be over-prescribed (such as providing antibiotics for trivial maladies), prescribed for improper reasons (such as the drug being "new" or better because it is more expensive), or prescribed under cryptic names (to prevent the patient from purchasing the drug at lesser cost).[565]

In the mid-1970s, the pharmaceutical industry responded to stories of questionable practices by multinational pharmaceutical firms by adopting resolutions on drug labeling and on marketing practices. In the United States, the then-Pharmaceutical Manufacturers Association (now known as PhRMA) passed a resolution on labeling that was later adopted by IFPMA.[566] The resolution stated, *inter alia*, that pharmaceutical product labeling directed to health professionals should be consistent with the body of scientific and medical evidence for the product and that essential safety information, contraindications, and side effects should be communicated. In 1981, the IFPMA adopted a resolution on pharmaceutical marketing practices; the resolution acknowledged the industry's obligations:

- to ensure that all products it makes available for prescription purposes to the public are backed by the fullest technological service and have full regard to the needs of the public health;

---

[564] A description of the problems facing developing nations can be found in M. SILVERMAN, P. R. LEE, & M. LYDECKER, PRESCRIPTIONS FOR DEATH — THE DRUGGING OF THE THIRD WORLD (1982). The book describes practices as of 1982 such as promoting drugs without disclosing important adverse event or safety information, selling drugs that have been withdrawn from sale or never approved for use in the exporter's own country, exaggerated claims of efficacy, and bribing physicians and government officials to influence prescribing or purchasing decisions. By the time of publication of the author's second book, BAD MEDICINE, *supra* note 98, the principal abuses were by local producers, not U.S. or multinational firms.

[565] *Id.* at 87-94.

[566] *Id.* at 148-49.

- to produce pharmaceutical products under adequate procedures and strict quality assurance;
- to base the claims for substances and formulations on valid scientific evidence, thus determining the therapeutic indications and conditions of use;
- to provide scientific information with objectivity and good taste, with scrupulous regard for truth, and with clear statements with respect to indications, contraindications, tolerance and toxicity; and
- to use complete candor in dealings with public health officials, health care professionals, and the public.[567]

The discussion above in the section on drug advertising and promotion provides additional information on this issue.

United Nations Consolidated List

The United Nations publishes a Consolidated List of Products whose Consumption and/or Sale have been Banned, Withdrawn, Severely Restricted or Not Approved by Governments. The Consolidated List is "aimed at disseminating information internationally on products harmful to health and the environment" and "constitutes a tool which helps Governments to keep up-to-date with regulatory decisions taken by other Governments and assists them in considering the scope for eventual regulatory action."[568] Thus, government agencies that review applications for product registration can readily ascertain restrictive regulatory decisions made in other countries. The Consolidated List combines information produced by WHO's quarterly bulletin (WHO Drug Information and its Pharmaceuticals Newsletter) and by the International Register of Potentially Toxic Chemicals/United Nations Environment Program (UNEP/IRPTC)'s biennial Bulletin, Notification Scheme for Banned and Severely Restricted Chemicals, and computerized data bank.

The Consolidated List covers pharmaceutical, agricultural, industrial and consumer products. Although the information cannot be regarded as exhaustive, in terms of products or regulatory measures, it covers regulatory actions taken by a total of 92 governments on over 600 products.

The Consolidated List originated from a 1982 resolution by the UN General Assembly, "aware of the damage to health and the environment that the continued production and export of products that have been banned and/or permanently withdrawn on grounds of human health and safety - is causing in the importing countries", and "considering that many developing countries lack the necessary information and expertise to keep up with developments in this field"[569]

Subsequently, the General Assembly requested that an updated Consolidated List should be issued annually. Under a memorandum of collaboration between WHO and UNEP/IRPTC, WHO collects, screens and processes the information on measures by Govern-

---

[567] IFPMA Code of Pharmaceutical Marketing Practices, *reprinted in* M. SILVERMAN, P. R. LEE, AND M. LYDECKER, PRESCRIPTIONS FOR DEATH — THE DRUGGING OF THE THIRD WORLD 157-60 (1982).

[568] DEPARTMENT OF INT'L ECONOMIC & SOCIAL AFFAIRS, CONSOLIDATED LIST OF PRODUCTS WHOSE CONSUMPTION AND/OR SALE HAVE BEEN BANNED, WITHDRAWN, SEVERELY RESTRICTED OR NOT APPROVED BY GOVERNMENTS v-vi 4th ed. prepared in accordance with General Assembly resolutions 37/137, 38/149, 39/229 and 44/226.

[569] U.N. Res. 37/137.

ments on pharmaceutical products, and on health-related and environmental reasons for these measures. UNEP/IRPTC performs a similar function with regard to chemical products. The UN Secretariat coordinates these activities, ensures that relevant information is utilized for the List, and collects and reviews the commercial data. It also edits, translates, and publishes the Consolidated List.

Products are listed alphabetically; INN have been used whenever possible to identify pharmaceutical products, along with the effective date on which the regulation came into force; and a summary of regulatory measures taken by governments. Trade name data are included for most single ingredient pharmaceutical products; there are no trade name data for combination pharmaceuticals. For widely manufactured generic products, manufacturer data are not included.

The complexity of the UN consolidated List is indicated by its entry for thalidomide: five countries[570] have reported a total ban on the product while four others report that it is available only on a restricted basis for such purposes as leprosy.[571] The United States is not listed but would fall in the latter category.[572]

In its fourth edition, published in 1991, the UN reported that governments' interpretation of the criterion "severely restricted," in particular, continues to be applied very unevenly in reporting on national restrictive regulatory measures.

■ Export embargoes

The issue of when a country should employ export embargoes as an instrument of foreign policy can be highly controversial, particularly when an embargo covers medicine, medical supplies, and food.[573]

Economic Regulation

Drug regulatory systems cannot be compared in a vacuum without considering the country's health care system (and "the multitude of differences that exist . . . in political structures, cultural attitudes, historical settings, demographic distributions, hospital industries, medical professions, and legal systems"):[574] in some countries an approval by an FDA-type agency is followed by the real test of marketability, i.e., assuring that

---

[570] Denmark, Finland, Indonesia, Singapore, and Venezuela.

[571] Belgium, Canada, India, and New Zealand.

[572] *Thalidomide Protocols and Patient Brochures Designed by FDA*, 58 FOOD DRUG COSM. REP., Nov. 18, 1996, at T&G 4-5. Thalidomide is the subject of compassionate use INDs for leprosy. Also, AIDS buyers clubs have been distributing the drug for AIDS patients. *Id.*

[573] S. Rosenfeld, Cuba, *Food, Medicine: America Should Not Be in the Business of Inflicting Pain*, WASH. POST, Apr. 4, 1997, at A21, citing a report by American Ass'n for World Health (Mar. 1997).

[574] MARK A. HALL AND IRA MARK ELLMAN, HEALTH CARE LAW AND ETHICS IN A NUTSHELL, St. Paul, Minn., West Pub. Co (1990), at 41.

the product is eligible for purchase under the health care system and that the price is reasonable. The process of establishing a government reimbursement price between the drug manufacturer and the government pricing authorities can take months after the regulatory approval has been given, and the time it takes for pricing decision delays market entry and availability of products to patients. Mandatory generic substitution, use of formularies to steer physicians and patients to cheaper alternatives, and price controls have been quite controversial with multinational, research-oriented drug companies. A study by the GPO found that EU price controls may have a detrimental effect on European innovation and competitiveness suggesting that the United States should exercise care in considering adoption of pharmaceutical price controls as a way of controlling health care costs.[575]

Another adverse effect of price controls in the EU, along with divergences in prices charged, has been parallel imports, discussed previously in this chapter.

Trade Agreements and Implementing Laws

In addition to the globalization of public health and the industry, other forces that lead the United States international directions include increased trade, and trade agreements such as the WTO and NAFTA From 1990 to 1994, the FDA played a part in the negotiations and Congressional ratification of NAFTA and the WTO. The agency's participation helped to clarify that two agreements, the TBT[576] and on Sanitary and Phytosanitary Measures (SPS),[577] which includes food safety rules, would not undermine the ability of the United States and other countries to maintain their chosen level of consumer protection and to deviate from international standards when justified.[578]

The WTO and NAFTA agreements have been important for pharmaceutical trade — and health care.[579] First, effective January 1, 1995, many countries, including the United States, agreed to eliminate tariffs for pharmaceuticals and their ingredients.

---

[575] U.S. General Accounting Office, Prescription Drugs: Spending Controls in Four European Countries [France, Germany, Sweden, UK], 8, GAO/HEHS-94-30 (May 1994). GAO has issued several reports on drug price controls in other countries: Prescription Drugs: Companies Typically Charge More in the United States Than in Canada, GAO/HRD-92-110 (Sept. 1992); Prescription Drug Prices: Analysis of Canada's Patented Medicines Prices Review Board, GAO/HRD-93-51 (Feb. 1993); Prescription Drugs: Companies Typically Charge More in the United States Than in the United Kingdom, GAO/HRD-94-29 (Jan. 1994).

[576] John H. Jackson, William J. Davey & Alan O. Sykes, Jr., 1995 Documents Supplement to Legal Problems of International *Economic Relations* (3d ed., West Pub. Co. 1995). Chapter 9 of the NAFTA on Standards-Related Medicines corresponds to the TBT agreement.

[577] *Id.* at 121.

[578] Linda R. Horton, *GATT and NAFTA: The Technical Barriers to Trade Agrements and Pharmaceutical Harmonization*, 14 Pharmaceutical Engineering (May/June 1994).

[579] Lars Noah, *NAFTA's Impact on the Trade in Pharmaceuticals*, 33 Hous. L. Rev. 1293 (1997).

Second, the Agreement on Trade-Related Aspects of Intellectual Property Rights (TRIPS),[580] helped to strengthen and harmonize intellectual property protection on a global basis, as is discussed in further detail in the next section.

Third, the TBT agreement increases transparency as to standards and national regulations and provides a way for one country to challenge another country's regulations, in the WTO, on the basis that the regulations are more trade restrictive than necessary to fulfill a legitimate objective.[581] Nothing in any of these agreements, however, changes health protection regulations such as drug approval requirements or GMPs.

The TBT agreement covers three categories of measures: standards (non-mandatory documents, such as voluntary standards or FDA guidance documents), technical regulations, and conformity assessment procedures. For example, an ICH guideline is a standard, and an FDA regulation to make an ICH guideline mandatory, e.g., amending the adverse event reporting regulations to adjust criteria and timeframes to the ICH guide, is a technical regulation. The FDA's inspections and laboratory tests are conformity assessment procedures.

The TBT agreement states explicitly that each country may set its own level of protection.[582] As long as country treats its domestic pharmaceutical products and its imports in an equivalent manner, another country will have little prospect of success in challenging the regulatory system of another.[583] (There are additional requirements in the SPS Agreement on the application of sanitary and phytosanitary measures. A country must either base its measures on international standards or on a risk assessment.)

The TBT agreement strongly encourages countries to harmonize requirements to international standards,[584] participate in international standards activities,[585] and consider whether other countries have equivalent regulations.[586] At the same time, however, the TBT agreement allows countries to vary from international standards that "would be an ineffective or inappropriate means for the fulfilment of the legitimate objectives pursued"[587] and to find inequivalent the regulations of other countries that do not "adequately fulfil the objectives"[588] bearing in mind the ability of a country to set its own level of pro-

---

[580] Agreement on Trade-Related Aspects of Intellectual Property Rights (TRIPS), *in* World Trade Organization, The Results of the Uruguay Round of Multilateral Trade Negotiations: The Legal Texts, Geneva ann. 1C, 365-403 (1995).

[581] TBT Agreement, Art. 2.2.

[582] TBT agreement, preamble: "the members of the WTO [recognize] that no country should be prevented from taking measures . . . for the protection of human, animal or plant life or health, of the environment, or for the prevention of deceptive practices, at the levels it considers appropriate, subject to the requirement that they are not applied in a manner which would constitute a means of arbitrary or unjustifiable discrimination between countries where the same conditions prevail or a disguised restriction on international trade, or are otherwise in accordance with the provisions of this Agreement . . . "

[583] Horton, *GATT and NAFTA supra* note 578, at 33-42.

[584] TBT Agreement, Art. 2.4.

[585] TBT Agreement, Art. 2.6.

[586] TBT Agreement, Art. 2.7.

[587] TBT Art. 2.4.

[588] TBT Agreement, Art. 2.7.

tection.[589] In sum, the TBT Agreement acknowledges that there are good reasons why countries have requirements that are different, but it encourages movement toward international convergence of regulatory requirements.

By staying involved in the implementation phase, the agency believes that it can help make sure that the FDA's mandates, values, and expertise are factored into decisions. For example, the agency provided technical support to the U.S. Trade Representative (USTR) in its case involving the EU's refusal to accept beef from cattle treated with growth promoting hormones. Also, the FDA is active in several aspects of NAFTA implementation, particularly the Committee on Standards-Related Measures. In addition, the FDA has participated in the triennial review of the WTO, TBT, and SPS agreements, undertaken in 1997, and in new activities under the Asia Pacific Economic Cooperation program.[590] Furthermore, FDA now has a seat on two key committees under the USTR, the Trade Policy Staff Committee and the Trade Policy Review Group.[591]

The U.S. government administers a number of programs aimed at "unfair" export practices of other countries. If another country exports products to the United States at a price that is unfairly low due to "dumping" of underpriced goods, or certain subsidies to the industry involved, adversely affected U.S. firms can initiate an antidumping or countervailing duties case.[592] These cases sometimes involve pharmaceutical companies.

Intellectual Property Treaties and Statutes

Intellectual property protection includes general laws on patents, trademarks, tradenames, trade secrets, and confidential commercial information.[593] Many developed countries also have specialized laws governing products such as pharmaceuticals that require costly testing and governmental approval. Patent term extensions to account for the time needed to fulfill regulatory requirements are provided in Japan[594] and the EU,[595] as in the United States. Japanese law allows extension of up to five years, depending on the time lost dur-

---

[589] TBT Agreement, preamble.

[590] See Linda Horton, *The Food and Drug Administration's International Harmonization, Enforcement, and Trade Policy Activities, in* 2 FUNDAMENTALS OF LAW AND REGULATION ch. 5 (FDLI 1997).

[591] Linda R. Horton, *International Update*, 49 PDA J. PHARMACEUTICAL SCI. & TECH. 106 (May/June 1995).

[592] Michael A. Hertzberg and Jeffrey L. Snyder, *A Timely Review of the United States' International Trade Law for the Food and Drug Practitioner: The Need for Knowledge in a Period of Increased Internationalization*, 43 FOOD DRUG COSM. L.J. 123(1988) 123.

[593] For a homorous discussion of the topic, see Pobert Signore, *Juridic Park-Traps and Illusions of Harmonization*, 77 J. Pat. & TRADEMARK OFF. SOC'Y 699 (Sept. 1995)

[594] U.S. CONGRESS, OFFICE OF TECHNOLOGY ASSESSMENT, BIOTECHNOLOGY IN A GLOBAL ECONOMY, 93 (1991) (Doc. No. OTA-BA-494).

[595] *Id.* The EU provides for a Supplementary Protection Certificate (SPC) that provides effective protection for 16 years in almost all cases, by granting a supplementary certificate to holders of a basic European patent.

ing the approval process. The EU provides for a Supplementary Protection Certificate that provides effective protection for sixteen years in almost all cases, by granting a supplementary certificate to holders of a basic European patent.

■ Patents

The key treaty relevant to the pharmaceutical industry is the Paris Convention for the Protection of Industrial Property. This treaty and others are administered by a Geneva-based international organization known as the World Intellectual Property Organization. First adopted in 1883, and ratified by the United States in 1903, the Paris Convention is the major international agreement covering basic rights for protecting industrial property.[596] It covers patents, industrial designs, service marks, trade names, indications of source, and unfair competition. In all Paris Convention countries, the first step to gain worldwide protection for a patentable invention is to obtain a patent in the home country patent office. While most countries award patent priority to the first inventor to file for a patent, the United States awards patent priority to the first inventor to conceive, diligently reduce the practice, and claim the invention.[597]

The WTO Agreement on TRIPS[598] prescribed a patent period of twenty years counted from the filing date.[599] At the time the TRIPS agreement was signed, the U.S. patent period was seventeen years from the date the patent was granted, so the U.S. law needed to be changed. TRIPS also required all WTO members to become signers of the Paris Convention.[600] The WTO agreement was a package deal, i.e., all countries that wanted to be members of the WTO were required to sign onto all agreements, rather than to sign only those that interested them. Thus, even countries that had previously declined to become signatories to the Paris Convention are now under a WTO obligation to abide by this agreement.

■ Uruguay Round Agreements Act

The U.S. Congress, in enacting the Uruguay Round Agreements Act provisions implementing the TRIPS agreement, changed the U.S. law on patent term (replacing seventeen years from the date of grant with twenty years from the date of filing),[601] but nowhere discussed how the change was intended to affect the FDA's pending approvals of generic copies of innovator drugs whose patents were extended under the Uruguay Round Agreements

---

[596] U.S. Congress, Office of Technology Assessment, Biotechnology in a Global Economy, 206 (1991) (Doc. No. OTA-BA-494).

[597] *Id.* at 218.

[598] Agreement on Trade-Related Aspects of Intellectual Property Rights (TRIPS), *in* World Trade Organization, The Results of the Uruguay Round of Multilateral Trade Negotiations: The Legal Texts, Geneva (1995), Annex 1C, 365-403.

[599] TRIPS, Art. 33. In computing this time period, countries that do not have a system of original patent grant may rely upon the filing date in the system where the patent was originally granted. *Id.* fn. 8.

[600] TRIPS, Art. 2.

[601] Pub. L. No. 103-465 § 532 (Dec. 8, 1994). The relevant provision is found at 35 U.S.C. § 154(c)(1).

Act.[602] The FDA reluctantly concluded that the effect of the new law was to require delay in several pending generic approvals,[603] and a few manufacturers of pioneer drugs suddenly found themselves the beneficiaries of what may be viewed as "windfall" patent extensions.[604] For example, Glaxo's patent for Zantac was extended for twenty months, giving the firm additional net revenues of $6 million per day for each day that generic drugs were kept off the U.S. market,[605] or a total of $2.2 to 3.6 billion.[606] The agency's conclusion that it had no choice but to delay the applications for the generics, and the agency's adoption[607] of a method for determining new expiration dates of patents established by the Patent and Trademark Office[608] that was not as favorable to the innovator firms as the method originally proposed,[609] led to a flurry of litigation and legislative activity.

Congress considered, but did not adopt, legislation to reverse the effect of the Uruguay Round Agreements Act on ANDAs. On December 7, 1995, the U.S. Senate rejected, by a close vote, an effort to enact legislation to allow generic companies to market generic versions of drugs whose patents were extended under the WTO TRIPS agreement,[610] and the legislation was sent to the Judiciary Committee for a hearing.[611]

■ Bolar Provision

Another issue in which the interests of pioneer drug manufacturers differ from manufacturers of generic drugs is whether a country's laws should allow the manufacturer of a generic drug to conduct bioequivalence studies comparing its product to the pioneer drug during the patent life of the pioneer. In the United States, the so-called "Bolar" provision[612] allows this practice. Canada has a similar law.[613] In Europe, there is no counterpart to the Bolar provision, and the European Commission is adamantly opposed to amending

---

[602] Paul Kim, Special Commmittee on Aging, U.S. Senate, *Update on Emerging Regulatory Issues: GATT and Prescription Drugs*, *remarks at* FDLI Annual Educational Conference, Washington, DC. (Dec. 12, 1995). As was stated in a letter from FDA Deputy Commissioner William Schultz in a letter to Donald Beers, counsel for Glaxo (May 25, 1995):

> Here there were neither hearings nor a single word of debate on the floor of the House or Senate on the impact of the URAA on the [U.S. generic drug law]. Nor do the committee reports indicate that Congress understood that the URAA would both grant a patent term extension for certain pioneer products *and* block FDA from approving generic versions of those drugs until the extended patent terms have expired. Nonetheless, the language of the URAA directs that result.

[603] *Id.* 60 Fed. Reg. 30,309 (June 8, 1995).

[604] Submission of the Generic Pharmaceutical Industry Association in response to 60 Fed. Reg. 3398 (Jan. 17, 1995), at 6. Senator Hatch disputed the view that "there was an 'unintended' and 'technical oversight' which resulted in a 'windfall' to the innovator companies at the expense of consumers and the generic industry," stating that this view "is a vast over-simplification." F-D-C REP. ("The Pink Sheet"), Mar. 4, 1996, at 16.

[605] SCRIP, Dec. 15, 1995, at 15.

[606] K. Day and P. Blustein, *A Drug Maker's Unspoken Advocacy: Glaxo's Controversial Ad Part of a Billion-Dollar Fight Over Patent Law*, WASH. POST, Oct. 27, 1995, at F1.

[607] 60 Fed. Reg. 37,652 (July 21, 1995).

[608] 60 Fed. Reg. 30,069 (June 7, 1995).

[609] 60 Fed. Reg. 3398 (Jan. 17, 1995); 60 Fed. Reg. 15,748 (Mar. 27, 1995).

[610] *Id.*

[611] Hearing Before the Senate Committee on the Judiciary (Feb. 27, 1996).

[612] 35 U.S.C. § 271(e)(2). This provision states that it is not an act of infringement of a patent to use a patented drug for purposes related to obtaining regulatory approval of the product. It essentially overruled the court's decision in Roche Products, Inc. v. Bolar Pharmaceutical Co., 733 F.2d 858 (Fed. Cir. 1984),*cert. denied*, 469 U.S. 856 (1984).

EU law to add such a provision despite support for it from the European parliament and the generic industry.[614] Innovator drug companies in the United States and in Europe, on the other hand, would like to eliminate the Bolar provision from U.S. law.[615] Reflecting the activism of innovator firms, but not generic firms, in the TABD,[616] industry members of TABD had recommended the elimination from U.S. law of the Bolar provision. This industry recommendation did not constitute U.S. government policy. Nevertheless, the European and U.S. generic drugs trade associations have denounced TABD as "a one-sided dialogue [that] does not represent the view of the pharmaceutical industry as a whole" noting that the generic and bulk drug industries have not been invited to partici-pate.[617] In its participation in TABD, the FDA has attended discussions of FDA issues such as mutual recognition agreements for drug GMPs and devices, but not any discus-sions of whether Bolar should be repealed.[618]

■ The Challenge of International Harmonization of Intellectual Property Laws and the USTR's Role

Intellectual property protection laws in other countries have historically been a problem for the pharmaceutical industry. Many countries, particularly newly industrialized coun-tries such as India, Argentina, and other South American countries, do not provide patent protection for pharmaceuticals. Countries that resist enactment of strong intellectual prop-erty laws often wish to protect domestic industry from competition, to encourage domestic production without the need to pay hard currency royalties to other countries, and to reduce or control prices.[619]

During the 1980s and 1990s, considerable progress was made in strengthening intellectual property rights (IPR) around the world. Both Brazil and Canada increased patent protec-tion,[620] and the TRIPS agreement has broadened and deepened adherence to intellectual property protection norms.

Without question, the role of the USTR, aided by PhRMA, has been an important factor in identifying and tackling problem areas. U.S. trade law recognizes IPR as a high priority objective.[621] As required by this law, each year USTR goes through a "Special 301" pro-cess of identifying which countries deny adequate and effective protection for IPR or deny fair and adequate market access for persons that rely on intellectual property protection.[622] Countries that have the most onerous or egregious acts, policies, or practices and whose

---

[613] Bill C-91 (1993). Canadian Drug Manufacturers Ass'n, *International Generic Pharmaceutical Alliance Asks for Consistent Bolar Provisions*, DRUG NEWS & VIEWS, Summer 1997, at 7.

[614] SCRIP, Dec. 17, 1996, at 3; *Id*. Mar. 26, 1996, at 2.

[615] *GPIA expects Waxman-Hatch* "assault," *Id*. Nov. 29, 1996, at 15.

[616] Scrip No. 2190 (Dec. 17, 1996) 3.

[617] Scrip No. 2183 (Nov. 22, 1996) 16.

[618] Letter from Sharon Smith Holston to Alice Till, (April 1997).

[619] U.S. CONGRESS, OFFICE OF TECHNOLOGY ASSESSMENT, BIOTECHNOLOGY IN A GLOBAL ECONOMY, 92 (1991) (Doc. No. OTA-BA-494).

[620] *Id*. at 93.

[621] *See, e.g.*, 19 U.S.C. §§ 2242, 3581.

[622] *Id*. § 2411.

acts, policies, or practices have the greatest adverse impact (actual or potential) on the relevant U.S. products must be designated as priority foreign countries.[623] Priority countries may be subject to an investigation under the section 301 provisions of the Trade Act. USTR may not designate a country as a priority foreign country if it is entering into good faith negotiations or making significant progress in bilateral or multilateral negotiations to provide adequate and effective protection of IPR. USTR identifies priority countries each year, within thirty days after the issuance of the National Trade Estimate Report, and USTR at the same time indicates which countries deserve to be placed on a "priority watch list" or "watch list" due to particular problems with IPR that merit the focus of increased bilateral attention, with some countries indicated for "out-of-cycle" reviews so that their factual situation is assured review in less than one year. PhRMA is an active participant in this process.[624] (Indeed, the U.S. generic drug industry has questioned the extent to which USTR follows the advice given by PhRMA in aggressively seeking trade remedies against countries that do not enact intellectual property laws along the lines of those in the United States).[625]

The question of what kind of intellectual property laws should be enacted is a highly polarized, hotly debated topic in the hemisphere.[626] In earlier years, many countries's legal systems reflected hostility to intellectual property, due to a view that valuable health care discoveries should not be owned by private companies but should be a common good, available to all, and eligible for copying by others. Vestiges of this attitude are occasionally encountered, but more often today the chief impediment to enactment of modern intellectual property rights laws is the sheer economic interest of the national companies that wish to continue to ignore IPR and make generic copies of pioneer drugs.

The issue of intellectual property protection has been a source of conflict between the U.S. government and industry, on the one hand, and the domestic pharmaceutical industry, on the other, in some South American countries, and particularly Argentina. In recent years, the move to market economies, growing entrepreneurialism, and the completion of the WTO and its TRIPS Agreement have persuaded several governments in the Americas, most notably Brazil, to revise their legislation to match international approaches to patents, trademarks, and the like. The countries in the Andean Pact (Bolivia, Colombia, Ecuador, Peru, and Venezuela) recently agreed to a TRIPS-consistent decision giving each member country the right to strengthen its patent law.[627]

---

[623] OFFICE OF THE UNITED STATES TRADE REPRESENTATIVE, 1997 TRADE POLICY AGENDA AND 1996 ANNUAL REPORT OF THE PRESIDENT OF THE UNITED STATES ON THE TRADE AGREEMENTS PROGRAM, 124 (1997) (ISBN 0-16-048997-0).

[624] SCRIP, Mar. 1, 1996, at 15.

[625] SCRIP, Dec. 15, 1995, at 17. "There may be legitimate economic, social and health interests in a particular region at a particular state in a nation's development which justify differences in the level of intellectual property protection from what may be considered 'normal' in the U.S.," letter to USTR Mickey Kantor from Alfred Engelberg, patent counsel to the Generic Pharmaceutical Industry Association, *id.* He claimed that PhRMA had a "carefully orchestrated and well-financed effort to ensure an enduring framework of high drug prices and profits around the world." *Id.*

[626] SCRIP, June 18, 1996, at 13.

[627] SCRIP, Jan 9, 1996, at 16.

In 1997, Argentina was singled out by USTR for trade penalties,[628] in the form of withdrawal of preferential duties,[629] due to its continued failure to enact adequate IPR legislation, costing U.S. pharmaceutical companies an estimated half a billion dollars a year in lost sales.[630] The U.S. investigation of Argentina was closed in mid-1997.

In 1989, President Menem of Argentina had pledged to overcome resistance in the Argentine Congress and to enact a modern IPR law that would given pharmaceutical products immediate protection, provide a protection period of twenty years and protection for products currently in the research and development pipeline, and restrict the scope of compulsory licensing.[631] The law that was enacted in December 1995[632] fell considerably short of TRIPS-consistency, in the eyes of PhRMA and the USTR, in that it failed to provide for data exclusivity protection to assure that local firms could not launch generic versions of new original products early in the life of the original; was ambiguous and contradictory; included a ban on the transformation of pending process applications into product patents; restricted biotechnology; contained exceptions to patent rights and "open-ended" compulsory licensing provisions; had ambiguous language on exhaustion of rights; insufficiently protected health registration data; and provided ineffective enforcement procedures.[633] Cilfa, the Argentine Association of National Laboratories, disagreed with PhRMA's view and claimed that the 1995 law is TRIPS-consistent.[634]

Other parts of the world where intellectual property protection needs to be upgraded include Eastern Europe,[635] Turkey,[636] and India.[637] Based on PhRMA's contention that India "remains one of the world's worst offenders of patent rights," in 1996 the USTR initiated an investigation against India under section 302 of the Trade Act of 1974,[638] with respect to certain acts, policies, and practices of the Government of India that may result in the denial of patents and exclusive marketing rights to U.S. firms, due to the failure of the Indian government to provide a "mailbox" mechanism whereby companies can file patent applications before patent protection is provided.

It should be noted that the United States. is urging India to enact legislation not required by TRIPS, which did not require countries to provide a "mailbox" mechanism. The IFPMA has stated that this omission requires "urgent resolution" and also drew attention

---

[628] Harvey Bale, PhRMA's Senior VP-International, stated that Argentina is the drug industry's "number one global problem." F-D-C REPORTS ("The Pink Sheet"), May 5, 1997, at T&G-17.

[629] Among items losing duty-free treatment were chemicals, metals, manufactured products, and several agricultural items. 1995 imports from Argentina of these items totaled approximately $260 million. Office of the USTR, Press Release 97-31, USTR announces list of Argentine products to lose [General System of Preferences] benefits (Apr. 15, 1997).

[630] *Clinton removes half of Argentina's GSP benefits in patent fight*, INSIDE USTR, Jan. 17, 1997, at 4.

[631] SCRIP, Mar. 15, 1996, at 19;

[632] Nos. 24,481 and 24,572 of 1995; *Id.*, Dec. 22/26, 1995.

[633] *Id.*, Dec. 10, 1996, at 15

[634] *Id.*

[635] *Id.*, July 9, 1996, at 7; *Id.*, Feb. 9, 1996), at 3; *Id.*, Dec. 22/26, 1995, at 6.

[636] *Id.*, Mar. 1, 1996, at 15.

[637] *Id.*, Mar. 1, 1996, at 15.

[638] 19 U.S.C. § 2412. The results of the investigation will determine whether the USTR will proceed to the next step, an action against India under section 301 of the Trade Act. 19 U.S.C. § 2411.

to the transitional periods for TRIPS and the lack of provisions requiring that members allow which biotechnology to be patented.[639]

The TRIPS agreement permits member countries to exclude plants and animals other than micro-organisms from eligibility for patents.[640] In the EU, lack of intellectual property protection for biotechnology discoveries is believed to undermine European competitiveness.[641] Also, public concerns about the safety and environmental effects of biotechnology — and opposition on ethical grounds to the patenting of human genes and living plants and animals — are other factors that discourage research and development in Europe.[642] In early 1996, the European Commission announced its plan to spend $1.3 million in three years to improve public awareness and understanding of biotechnology.[643]

Controlled Substances Treaties

Three international treaties aim to control the international movement and use of narcotics and other drugs liable to abuse: the Single Convention on Narcotic Drugs (1961), the Convention on Psychotropic Substances (1971), and the UN Convention Against Illicit Narcotics Traffic. The first two treaties facilitate a uniform international policy on drug control policies on sale, distribution, manufacture, and medical utility of narcotics, psychostimulants, barbiturates, and other drugs with abuse potential. Each country that signs these agreements—and the United States and over 110 other countries have done so—is required to set manufacturing quotas, require import and export licenses, monitor the flow of controlled substances, and establish criminal penalties for illicit acts. Those developing countries that lack the infrastructure for establishing drug control policies are given mechanisms for ensuring the availability of needed drugs.

International enforcement activities to curb transborder shipments of narcotics and other drugs of abuse have exploded in recent years. Among the groups that are active in this area include Interpol, an international organization of national law enforcement.

In the United States, the Drug Enforcement Administration (DEA) is the principal agency at the federal level responsible for drug abuse control, including a heavy emphasis on international drug abuse control. DEA's decisions to schedule substances, after obtaining

---

[639] IFPMA, Implications of TRIPS on the Pharmaceutical Industry, Geneva (1995).

[640] TRIPS, Art. 27.3(b).

[641] SCRIP, Feb. 9, 1996, at 3. Earlier, the European industry had warned that biotechnology "is stagnating in Europe," compared with U.S. sales more than triple the EU level. EFPIA, The Pharmaceutical Industry in Figures (1995), quoted in SCRIP, Dec. 15, 1995, at 4.

[642] SCRIP, Mar. 26, 1996, at 2; *Morality Versus Progress — The Gene Patent Debate*, SCRIP MAG., Feb. 1996, at 38-40; George Poste, *A lead from the U.K. id.*, at 42-43. In 1995, the European Parliament rejected a draft directive to permit patenting of lifeforms. Tom Wilkie, *The question of morality, id.*, at 45-48. For additional discussion of patents for lifeforms, see Linda R. Horton, *International Harmonization of Food and Veterinary Medicine Regulation, in* 1 FUNDAMENTALS OF LAW AND REGULATION, ch. 13 (FDLI 1997).

[643] SCRIP, Jan. 30, 1996.

a binding FDA recommendation as to the medical uses of the drug, are relied upon in many other counties.[644] Much of DEA's enforcement work is in the Western Hemisphere, due to an elaborate system of drug production, distribution, and money laundering involving Colombia, Mexico, and other Latin American countries.[645]

In the EU, the combination of lack of harmonization of laws on consumption and trafficking in illegal drugs, and lack of consensus that harmonization is a sufficient priority to justify expanding EU jurisdiction into an area traditionally left to member states, complicates cooperative law enforcement efforts.[646] Debate continues as to whether liberal, permissive attitudes or repressive approaches to the drug abuse problem are the best deterrent: some member states — including France, Greece, Ireland, and Sweden — seek stronger laws and enforcement while others, such as the Netherlands and Spain, have a more tolerant approach.[647] The Netherlands is Europe's biggest maker of Ecstacy, identified by the UN International Narcotics Control Board in Vienna as the most urgent drug abuse problem in Western Europe.[648] The difficulty of controlling flows of illicit drugs from the Netherlands and other "soft" countries into France and other "tough" countries is one of several enforcement in Europe.[649]

Another area of differences among countries involves approaches to the treatment of addicts and substance abusers.[650]

Population Control

Overpopulation in a number of countries threatens to overwhelm available resources with dire consequences for public health and peace.[651] Regulatory policies governing contraceptive products are therefore important. Most women in developing countries want to delay or avoid having another child, yet for millions contraceptive services are still difficult to obtain, unaffordable, or of poor quality.[652] In 1994, international donors contrib-

---

[644] Kathleen Day, *Countering Ill Effects of an Abused Drug*, WASH. POST, Nov. 2, 1996, at H1.

[645] *Drug Lords' Profits Find Haven in Mexico*, WASH. POST, July 8,1996, at A1-9.

[646] Victor Smart and Saskia Sissons, *Dublin's War on Crime Tests Partners' Unity*, THE EUR., July 4-10, 1996, at 1.

[647] Saskia Sissons, *Haven Fights Drug Menace*, THE EUR. (June 20-26, 1996), 10; *Detectives Ran Drugs in Name of the Law: A Dutch Police Operation's Cover Was So Deep That It Ended Up Bankrolling International Crime Syndicates, id.* (May 23-30, 1996).

[648] Saskia Sissons, *Ecstasy Abuse is Europe's Biggest Drugs Problem*, THE EUR., Mar. 6-12, 1997, at 1.The active ingredient in Ecstasy is ephedrine, the subject of an FDA proposed rule. 62 Fed. Reg. 30,678 (June 4, 1997).

[649] Tony Snape, *Customs Fraud Unit to Plug EU Gaps*, THE EUR., Feb. 27-Mar. 5, 1997, at 1; *Front line in the fight against fraud, id.*, Oct. 24-30, 1996, at 28.

[650] *See, e.g.,* Lane Porter, William J. Curran & Awni Arif, *Comparative Review of Reporting and Registration Legislation for Treatment of Drug and Alcohol Dependent Persons*, 8 INT'L J.L. & PSYCHIATRY 217 (Spring 1986).

[651] *In the Family Way*, WASH. POST, Mar. 1, 1997, at A18 (reporting data from Population Reference Bureau, Macro International, Population Action International, Alan Guttmacher Institute).

[652] *Id.*

uted more than one billion dollars toward family planning assistance, with the United States as the largest contributor.[653]

The FDA's role as a premier drug approval authority — coupled with the overall U.S. role as a major donor in international population control activities — has, at times, raised difficult policy questions. Should the U.S. government pay for a drug or device for contraception that is not allowed to be used by U.S. citizens (or allowed only as a strictly controlled investigational drug)? For example, at a time when the injectable contraceptive drug DepoProvera was not approved for use in the United States, the U.S. AID procured the drug from foreign sources and distributed it for use in what were supposed to be controlled clinical trials intended to show safety and effectiveness of the drug. This program was very controversial among U.S. consumer organizations who were certain that the U.S. government was "drugging the Third World."

The advent of HIV infection, as well as increases in other forms of sexually transmitted diseases, has led international population control advocates to emphasize barrier methods of birth control — condoms or diaphragms, coupled with contraceptive foam — due to the need to control spread of disease as well as unwanted births.

At the same time, the highly personal and elective nature of birth control (and the even more highly charged, related issue of abortion) has caused controversy to erupt in international settings, as well as national ones, about the extent to which one government should impose its values on others. For example, the issue overshadowed two international conferences in the mid-1990s, the UN Conference on Population in Cairo and the UN Conference on Women in Beijing.

The "freedom of choice" argument frequently heard in discussions of drugs for cancer, HIV, and other life-threatening illness also is heard in the case of contraceptives, abortion, and abortifacient drugs such as RU-486. As was discussed previously in this chapter, the availability of RU-486 in other countries but not in the United States[654] has been controversial in the United States.

Environmental Issues

■ The Montreal Protocol on Substances that Deplete the Ozone Layer[655]

This agreement controls the production, trade, and use of chlorofluorocarbons, or CFCs, which are believed to contribute to the depletion of the ozone layer of the world's atmosphere. Depletion of the ozone layer is believed to pose grave danger to humans due to

---

[653] *Id.* U.S. contributions (in millions) were $548 in 1995, $356 in 1996, and $385 for 1997. *Id.*

[654] Foreign pharmaceutical companies feared that filing a new drug application would lead to retaliation by U.S. anti-choice groups.

[655] 26 I.L.M. 1541 (Sept. 16, 1987).

increased human exposure to ultraviolet radiation and therefore to increased risk of melanoma, other forms of skin cancer, and cataracts.[656]

In 1979, the FDA issued regulations restricting use of CFCs in FDA-regulated products to essential uses. At that time, use of CFCs was deemed essential in certain aerosol medications such as metered-dose-inhalers for asthma. With the implementation of the Montreal Protocol, however, even such valuable uses of CFCs are being phased out, because the seriousness of the risk to human health posed by depletion of the ozone layer and due to the advent of alternatives to drugs containing these products.[657] In September 1996 the FDA approved the first alternative propellant metered-dose inhaler.[658]

In early 1997, the FDA published an advance notice of proposed rulemaking asking for comment on a suggested approach for withdrawing "essential use" status for products using CFC propellants in light of the increasing availability of alternatives.[659] Under the proposed strategy for the transition from CFC-based products to alternative aerosol delivery products, the agency would require post-marketing data proving safety, efficacy, and patient acceptance before a non-CFC based product could be considered to be an acceptable alternative. The challenge is to strike an appropriate balance between the availability of adequate treatment alternatives and the need to protect human health from dangers from ozone-depleting substances.

■ International Programs for Chemical Safety

International Hazard Classification Systems

In early 1997, the U.S. Department of State published a notice in the *Federal Register* describing the activities of several U.S. agencies concerning international harmonization of chemical safety and health information.[660] The activities described had begun, or accelerated, with the 1992 United Nations Conference on Environment and Development (UNCED) in Rio de Janeiro. UNCED had announced a bold new action plan for the environment known as Agenda 21.[661] A program initiative resulting from the conference entitled "Environmentally Sound Management of Toxic Chemicals Including Prevention of Illegal International Traffic in Toxic and Dangerous Products" called for 1) harmonization of procedures for international assessment of chemical risks, 2) harmonization of chemical hazard classification and labeling rules, 3) information exchange on toxic chemicals and chemical risk, 4) risk reduction programs, 5) strengthening capabilities for managing chemicals, and 6) prevention of illegal traffic in toxic products.

---

[656] D. Brack, International Trade and the Montreal Protocol, Royal Institute of International Affairs 39-63 (1996). The Montreal Protocol elaborated on a 1985 treaty known as the Vienna Convention and was, in turn, amended at meetings in London in 1990 and Copenhagen in 1992. UNEP, Status of Ratification/Accession/Acceptance/Approval of the Vienna Convention for the Protection of the Ozone Layer (July 31, 1995) (UNEP/OzL./Rat.46).

[657] *CFC-Free Asthma Drugs*, 122 U.S. NEWS & WORLD REP., Jan. 13, 1997, at 63.

[658] *Id.*

[659] 62 Fed. Reg. 10,242 (Mar. 6, 1997).

[660] Dep't of State, Bureau of Oceans and International Environmental and Scientific Affairs; International Harmonization of Chemical Safety and Health Information, 62 Fed. Reg. 15,951 (Apr. 3, 1997).

[661] *Rio Review to Rejuvenate Green Initiatives*, 385 NATURE 188 (Jan. 16, 1997).

Although the harmonization effort had not attracted much attention from the FDA and FDA-regulated industries, as it appeared to focus initially on pesticides and other toxic and dangerous chemicals, by the time the State Department published its notice the intent to include pharmaceuticals and food additives in the harmonization of criteria for hazard classification and for data sheets, at least for purposes of worker safety, transportation, and environmental controls, was made clear.[662] The prospect of covering even environmental, occupational, and transport hazards of pharmaceuticals and food ingredients was strongly opposed by the regulated industry[663] and led Senator Jesse Helms to write to Secretary of State Madeleine Albright urging that the scope of the Intergovernmental Forum on Chemical Safety exclude pharmaceuticals and food substances.[664]

The part of the UNCED program that involved development of testing guidelines by the OECD caused serious concern in the pharmaceutical industry, for several reasons. Applicability to drugs of the proposed testing method for the international hazard classification scheme could involve test methods that do not take into account the ICH harmonized testing guidelines for safety testing of pharmaceuticals. Moreover, national regulatory authorities, such as the FDA, administer their own animal and human testing requirements that are more scientifically relevant to these products than are OECD methods..

In April 1997, OECD provided reassurance that there is no intent to require pharmaceutical firms to use OECD test methods rather than an ICH guideline or other suitable approach.[665] The purpose of the OECD effort is to reduce duplication, not impose redundant or duplicative test requirements, generate results of little value, disrupt drug development, and, because the various test methods differ, lead to different or conflicting results.[666]

Prior Informed Consent

In November 1994, international efforts towards a mandatory "prior informed consent" procedure for certain hazardous chemicals began when several UN organizations took up the recommendation of the 1992 Rio conference and proceeded with the preparation of a mandatory prior informed consent convention. These efforts represented an extension and a continuation of a voluntary system (often known as the London guidelines) adopted in 1987 by the UN Food and Agriculture Organization (FAO) and the UN Environment Programme (UNEP) and later amended in 1989. The London guidelines exempted pharmaceuticals and food additives.

Under a mandatory PIC procedure, a country that exports certain dangerous or toxic chemicals would be obligated to notify the government of the importing country of the impending exportation of the chemical. The importing country, in turn, would be able to

---

[662] *See* Pharmaceutical Research and Mfrs. of America, International Harmonization Efforts Re: Chemical Safety Management — Implications for Pharmaceuticals, 1 Jan. 9, 1997.

[663] Letter to Rafe Pomerance, Dep't of State, from PhRMA (Jan. 17, 1997) and from the Animal Health Institute, *cited in* Food Chem. News, Mar. 3, 1997.

[664] Letter dated Feb. 7, 1997, described in Food Chem. News, Mar. 3, 1997, at 4.

[665] Amy Rispin, EPA, Newsletter (Apr. 1997).

[666] *Id.* 2-3. *See U.S. to Attend Global Chemical Talks Before Solving Dispute on Drugs, Inside Washington's FDA*, Jan. 24, 1997, at 3.

decide whether to consent to the chemical's importation, to not consent to its importation, or to impose conditions on the importation.[667]

The Governing Council of UNEP, in May 1995, authorized its Executive Director to work with the FAO to prepare a legally binding procedure. Negotiations towards that end began in March 1996, and in September 1996, the negotiators had agreed to extend the PIC procedure to a broad range of chemicals and hazardous pesticides.

While the voluntary process had applied, since 1987, to pesticides and hazardous chemicals, but not to pharmaceuticals and food additives, its possible application to FDA-regulated products represented a problem to the U.S. pharmaceutical industry. The industry viewed a mandatory PIC process as reinserting some governmental action and delay before exports could occur, thereby negating the elimination of prior FDA approval for virtually all drug exports under the 1996 export law. As of May 1997, the likely outcome of this controversy was for the U.S. government to oppose strongly at least the inclusion of pharmaceuticals in a binding PIC procedure.

Other Chemicals Discussions

In 1997, work was underway to negotiate a global legally binding instrument on persistent organic pesticides aimed at establishing a Montreal Protocol-type system for such chemicals as DDT, aldrin, dieldrin, endrin, heptachlor, hexachlorobenzene, mirex, toxaphene, PCBs, dioxin, and furans, and another new area of concerns was endocrine disrupters.[668]

■ The Convention on International Trade in Endangered Species of Wild Fauna and Flora

This treaty is aimed at controlling the import and export of products made from endangered species.[669] Trade that contravenes Convention on International Trade in Endangered Species of Wild Fauna and Flora (CITES) is now one of the world's biggest illegal businesses, perhaps ranking behind only arms, narcotics and prostitution.[670] This treaty can affect pharmaceuticals, e.g., by limiting trade in rhinoceros horns, tiger parts, and bear bile in pharmaceuticals popular in many parts of Asia. In 1993, the parties to CITES criticized the steps take by China and Taipei to control illegal trade in rhinoceros horn and tiger specimens and urged prohibition of trade in these species.[671]

■ International Environmental Management Standards

ISO is developing standards to promote common approaches to systems for management of environmental effects during production, distribution, use of products, disposal, and

---

[667] *See* UNEP, Report of the Intergovernmental Negotiating Committee for an International Legally Binding Instrument for the Application of the Prior Informed Consent Procedure for Certain Hazardous Chemicals and Pesticides in International Trade on the Work of its Second Session, UNEP/FAO/PIC/INC.2/7, at 21 (1995).

[668] *See* Horton, *supra* note 634, for a discussion of this issue.

[669] 12 I.L.M. 1085 (Mar. 3, 1973).

[670] *Trade in Animals: Bear-faced Gall*, THE ECONOMIST, Nov. 9, 1996, at 44. China has 481 bear farms, with over 7500 animals producing 7 tons a year of bear bile, used for cancer, hemorrhoids, conjunctivitis, and sinusitis. *Id.*

[671] Decisions of the Standing Committee on Trade in Rhinoceros Horn and Tiger Specimens, Brussels, Sept. 6-8, 1993.

recycling; environmental audits; standards for environmental performance evaluation; life-cycle analysis; and eco-labeling.[672] U.S. pharmaceutical firms are participating in this endeavor.[673] The importance of pollution control for pharmaceuticals companies, to avoid liability exposure, is demonstrated by the huge sums of money paid by Japanese chemicals companies to people who had consumed fish that became mercury-contaminated due to the companies' emissions.[674]

■ National Environmental Policy Act

National Environmental Policy Act (NEPA) requires environmental impact statements for "major Federal actions significantly affecting the quality of the human environment."[675] In 1992, U.S. public interest organizations were unsuccessful in their effort to obtain a judicial declaration that the Office of the U.S. Trade Representative was required by NEPA to prepare environmental impact statements applicable to its negotiation of trade agreements such as NAFTA and the Uruguay Round agreements. The court of appeals held that the organizations had failed to identify any "final agency action" judicially reviewable under applicable U.S. law.[676] The USTR decided, nevertheless, to prepare an environmental impact assessment on NAFTA.

Conclusion

Global pharmaceutical international activities exemplify a wide array of models of international cooperation, ranging from information sharing, parallel activities, joint activities, harmonization, mutual recognition, and even supranationalism in the EU.[677]

From these various models for international activities, the FDA has made international harmonization of requirements for pharmaceuticals — both drugs and biologics — a top priority,[678] a goal that is shared by the agency's counterparts in other countries as well as

---

[672] N. Roht-Arriaza, *Shifting the Point of Regulation: The International Organization for Standardization and Global Lawmaking on Trade and the Environment*, 22 ECOLOGY L.Q. 479, 501 (1995).

[673] Dorothy Bowers, Vice President, Merck, presentation to FDA Standards Policy Committee, Rockville, MD (1996).

[674] *Slow Justice*, ECONOMIST, May 25, 1996, at 43; the firm Chisso paid $234,000,000 for mercury victims in the town of Minamata, with some money going to a medical facility and some going to 4400 individuals ($24,300 in a lump sum payment and @220/month. In 1996 Swowa Denko, another chemical company, compensated an additional 7000 people in Niigata, another town.

[675] 42 U.S.C. § 4332.

[676] Public Citizen v. Office of the United States Trade Representative, 970 F. 2d 916 (D.C. Cir. 1992), *aff'g* 782 F. Supp. 139 (D.D.C. 1992).

[677] Supranationalism occurs when a sovereign country yields all, or a part, of its sovereignty to another body. For example, the European Community, or European Union (EU), rests upon the notion that member countries have agreed to give up their lawmaking powers over goods, persons, services, and capital to the European lawmaking bodies, the European Commission, Council, and Parliament, once these institutions have put in place a harmonized directive.

[678] *See, e.g.*, NATIONAL PERFORMANCE REVIEW, REINVENTING DRUG AND DEVICE REGULATIONS 5, 30-31 (Apr. 1995). The chapter earlier in this volume on FDA's International Harmonization, Enforcement, and Trade Policy Activities has additional information on FDA harmonization initiatives.

the worldwide pharmaceutical industry. Creating a harmonized international standard is ordinarily done in one of three ways, each of which is resource intensive: developing a standard domestically and taking it to an international forum for adoption at the international level; taking an already existing international standard and bringing it to the domestic level for acceptance in a rule, guidance document,[679] or other domestic process; and working in an international forum with counterparts from other countries to develop a new international standard "from scratch."

The priority accorded to international harmonization reflects the globalization of public health: as people and goods move freely across borders, no regulatory agency or company can afford to think any longer of its challenges or its opportunities solely in national terms.[680] Also, the industries that the FDA regulates increasingly are multinational in their operations.[681] Multinational corporations developing products for global marketing have had to negotiate through a labyrinth of multiple regulatory systems, a process that is being streamlined by ICH and other activities.

The globalization of public health — and of the health product industries[682] — presents a chance to *advance* public health through harmonization. Fostering pharmaceutical development is just one example. Companies increasingly develop, test, and seek marketing approval for new products on a worldwide basis. Internationally harmonized standards for testing, quality, and manufacturing make product development more efficient and speed the worldwide availability of new therapies. Harmonization of regulatory requirements or methods, where possible, reduces paperwork requirements and communication errors as well as product development time. In addition, counterparts in other countries can help FDA assure the safety, effectiveness, and quality of products offered for importation into the United States, particularly through regulatory oversight of compliance with GMPs.

In sum, harmonization benefits all. It benefits industry by replacing many different standards with one international standard that industry must meet. It brings cost savings to industry, enhanced opportunities for export and decreased time to bring new products to market.

---

[679] The Food and Drug Administration's Development, Issuance, and Use of Guidance Documents, 62 Fed.Reg. 8961 (Feb. 27, 1997).

[680] *See, e.g.,* TB Groups at Risk, WHO Report on the Tuberculosis Epidemic (1996); *Transmission of Multidrug-Resistant Mycobacterium Tuberculosis During a Long Airplane Flight,* 334 New Eng. J. Med. 933 (1996).

[681] A recent report considered by the Industry Committee of the Organisation for Economic Co-operation and Development's Directorate for Science, Technology and Industry described the challenge of developing effective regulatory policies in an age of globalization:

[C]onsideration must be given to the following: i) that technological developments and innovations create new markets that fall outside the scope of existing regulations; ii) since markets have become more international, that it is becoming increasingly difficult for domestic regulatory authorities to control the behavior of their national private sector 'actors;' iii) the extent to which regulatory regimes affect the attractiveness of a given country as a location for investment by global firms; iv) the indirect effects of regulation and their impact on input prices, since in global markets firms can engage in regulatory arbitrage by moving their business or capital to the country with the most favourable regulations; and v) to establish the extent to which the effectiveness of regulations is affected by the new forms of interrelationships (e.g. networked firms) that are developing.

Regulation and Industrial Competitiveness: A Perspective for Regulatory Reform, DSTI/IND(97) 1, at 6 (Feb.11, 1997).

[682] Mergers during the 1980s and 1990s have produced a relatively small number of innovative firms, many of them multinational in character.

Harmonization also benefits regulatory agencies by enabling them to make more efficient use of their resources, as other countries share the workload of developing new standards. A large up-front investment of FDA resources, however, is needed to reach harmonization. Because of to severe resource constraints, the agency must focus attention on the highest priorities, and strive to make participation in those activities very effective.

Last, but not least, harmonization benefits patients by bringing them the latest therapies, and at reduced costs. Given the current pressure around the world to control health care costs, regulatory officials are looking for ways to make their requirements more uniform so that drugs are affordable for consumers and duplicative regulatory burdens do not discourage important research needed to bring therapies to market. International harmonization serves these goals.

chapter 17

International Harmonization of Medical Device Regulations

Linda R. Horton*
Michelle Hoyte**
Naomi Kawin***

Introduction

Efforts to achieve harmonization of medical device regulation made significant progress in the 1990s, with activities ranging from medical device quality systems, to adverse event reporting, to product standards, to clinical evaluation. In each of these areas there have been significant steps toward convergence of regulatory systems, in the space of a few short years. These efforts have been led by officials from the United States, the European Commission, European Member States, Japan, Canada, and Australia. The impetus toward international harmonization has come from both the private as well as the public sector. As international interest in medical device production and regulation has mushroomed in other countries, particularly countries that sometimes are characterized as emerging markets (e.g., Argentina, China, Malaysia, Singapore, South Korea, and Taiwan), the increasingly global medical device industry has made international harmonization a high priority.[1]

The U.S. government has embraced harmonization of the Food and Drug Administration's (FDA's) regulatory requirements and guidelines with those of other countries as a part of the President's and Vice President's National Performance Review.[2] The private sector has encouraged international harmonization both as a means of increasing U.S. industry's

* Ms. Horton is the Director of International Policy, Office of Policy, Food and Drug Administration

** Ms. Hoyte was, at the time this article was written, Acting Director, International Relations and External Affairs Staff, Center for Devices and Radiological Health, Food and Drug Administration. She has since taken a position
*** as Director of International Regulatory Affairs, American Red Cross Biomedical Services.

Ms. Kawin is the Associate Director for International Policy, Office of Policy, Food and Drug Administration.

The views expressed are those of the authors and not necessarily those of the Food and Drug Administration.

1 *See, e.g.*, William George, Chairman, Medtronics, Presentation at FDLI's Annual Educational Conference, Washington, D.C. (Dec. 10, 1996); Robert G. Britain, National Electrical Manufacturers Association, *Coping With International Issues* (Dec. 1990) (presentation).

2 NATIONAL PERFORMANCE REVIEW, REINVENTING DRUG AND DEVICE REGULATIONS 5, 30-31 (1995).

access to foreign markets, and for the opportunity it offers to incorporate selected foreign-regulatory practices into the U.S. system. Matching device requirements with those of other countries can expedite worldwide marketing of new products by reducing duplicative or conflicting controls.

This chapter describes FDA's authority to undertake international activities involving medical devices; an overview of the major device regulatory systems other than that of the United States (principally the European Union (EU),[3] Canada, and Japan); FDA's agreements with other regulatory bodies and particularly the 1997 EU-U.S. mutual recognition agreement (MRA); harmonization activities in the Global Harmonization Task Force (GHTF) and other organizations; specific harmonization activities involving standards, good manufacturing practices (GMPs), and other subjects; export-related activities; problems of developing countries; health care economic regulation of medical devices; and international influences on proposals to change the U.S. system.

U.S. Laws on International Medical Device Issues

■ An International Mandate

A unique aspect of the FDA's international program for medical devices is that the agency has an explicit international mandate. By the time the Safe Medical Devices Act of 1990 (SMDA)[4] was enacted, the global interests of the U.S. medical device industry were quite evident. While international considerations had played no significant role in the congressional deliberations leading to the enactment of the two earlier U.S. medical device laws, the Federal Food, Drug, and Cosmetic Act (FDCA) of 1938[5] and the Medical Device Amendments of 1976,[6] they were important in 1990.

The SMDA added a new section 803[7] to the FDCA:

OFFICE OF INTERNATIONAL RELATIONS

SEC. 803. (a) There is established in the Department of Health and Human Services an Office of International Relations.[8]

---

[3] The term "European Union" took precedence over "European Community" or the earlier "European Economic Community," at least as to external relations with "third countries" such as the United States, with the signing of the Treaty on European Union [Maastricht Treaty], *reprinted in* EUROPE AGENCE INTERNATIONALE, D'INFORMATION POUR LA PRESSE, Doc. No. 1759 (Feb. 7, 1992).

[4] Pub. L. No. 101-629, 104 Stat. 4511.

[5] Pub. L. No. 75-717, 52 Stat. 1040 (1938) (codified as amended at 21 U.S.C. §§ 301 et seq. (1994)).

[6] Pub. L. No. 94-295, 90 Stat. 539. Export policy was the one exception, in that the issue of whether to relax export policy for drugs was briefly a subject of controversy in the congressional consideration of the device law.

[7] 21 U.S.C. § 383.

[8] In 1992, the FDA established an International Relations Staff in its Center for Devices and Radiological Health (CDRH), 57 Fed. Reg. 14,584 (Apr. 22, 1992). This staff is now located in CDRH's Division of Small Manufacturers Assistance in its Office of Health and Industry Programs, and standards management (another internationally oriented activity) is handled by its Office of Science and Technology (effective May 1, 1995).

(b) In carrying out the functions of the office under subsection (a), the Secretary may enter into agreements with foreign countries to facilitate commerce in devices between the United States and such countries consistent with the requirements of this Act. In such agreements, the Secretary shall encourage the mutual recognition of —

(1) good manufacturing practice regulations promulgated under section 520(f), and

(2) other regulations and testing protocols as the Secretary determines to be appropriate.

As is evident, the FDA's international authority includes authority to enter into agreements with other countries, an activity discussed further in this chapter.

■ Standards Authority

Three principal laws govern the FDA's international device standards activities. First, the FDCA contains detailed provisions for device standards,[9] which have been part of the law since the Medical Device Amendments of 1976, and which were greatly simplified by the SMDA. In streamlining the procedures for mandatory performance standards for devices, Congress ensured that the FDA would consider certain international impacts. First, the FDA is required, to the maximum extent practicable, to consult with nationally and internationally recognized standard-setting entities as well as with other federal agencies.[10] Second, in setting an effective date for a standard, the FDA must establish the date "so as to minimize, consistent with the public health and safety, economic loss to, and disruption or dislocation of, domestic and international trade."[11] Third, whereas the 1976 Act called for mandatory performance standards for the vast array of devices in the large intermediate category (Class II), the SMDA provided for greater flexibility in that a range of "special controls" could be implemented for Class II devices, including "development and dissemination of guidelines, recommendations, and other appropriate actions as the Secretary deems necessary to provide [reasonable assurance of the safety and effectiveness of the device]."[12]

Under this amended provision, the FDA can issue rules or guidance documents in which the agency incorporates appropriate aspects of international standards or U.S. voluntary consensus standards. For example, the FDA has announced its intention to increase use of international standards.[13] Also, the FDA plans to incorporate, in relevant guidance documents, references to the leading international standard governing medical device electrical safety.

Second, the Trade Agreements Act, the general U.S. statute that implements the World Trade Organization (WTO) Agreement on Technical Barriers to Trade, instructs federal agencies to use international standards, as appropriate, as the basis for technical regula-

---

[9]   FDCA § 514, 21 U.S.C. § 360d.

[10]   *Id.* § 514(a)(4)(B), 21 U.S.C. § 360d(a)(4)(B).

[11]   *Id.* § 514(b)(3)(B), 21 U.S.C. § 360d(b)(3)(B).

[12]   *Id.* § 513(a)(1)(B), 21 U.S.C. § 360c(a)(1)(B).

[13]   60 Fed. Reg. 53,078 (Oct. 11, 1995).

tions.[14] To elaborate on this requirement, the Office of Management and Budget (OMB) has issued a guide known as Circular A-119[15] that guides and directs federal activities in the area of standards.

Finally, the National Technology Transfer and Advancement Act,[16] enacted in 1996, has been described as making the OMB circular part of the law.[17] It requires federal agencies to use voluntary consensus standards in their activities:

(d)   Utilization of Consensus Technical Standards by Federal Agencies; Reports

(1)   In general. — Except as provided in paragraph (3) of this subsection, all Federal agencies and departments shall use technical standards that are developed or adopted by voluntary consensus standards bodies, using such technical standards as a means to carry out policy objectives or activities determined by the agencies and departments.

(2)   Consultation; participation. — In carrying out paragraph (1) of this subsection, Federal agencies and departments shall consult with voluntary, private sector, consensus standards bodies and shall, when such participation is in the public interest and is compatible with agency and departmental missions, authorities, priorities, and budget resources, participate with such bodies in the development of technical standards.

(3)   Exception. — If compliance with paragraph (1) of this subsection is inconsistent with applicable law or otherwise impractical, a Federal agency or department may elect to use technical standards that are not developed or adopted by voluntary consensus standards bodies if the head of each such agency or department transmits to the Office of Management and Budget an explanation of the reasons for using such standards. Each year, beginning with fiscal year 1997, the Office of Management and Budget shall transmit to congress and its committees a report summarizing all explanations received in the preceding year under this paragraph.

(4)   Definition of technical standards. — As used in this subsection, the term "technical standards" means performance-based or design-specific technical specifications and related management systems practices.

The Technology Act also expanded the authority of the National Institute for Standards and Technology (NIST) of the U.S. Department of Commerce to "coordinate the use by Federal agencies of private sector standards emphasizing where possible the use of standards developed by private, consensus organizations,"[18] and "to coordinate Federal, State, and local technical standards activities and conformity assessment activities, with the goal

---

14   19 U.S.C. §§ 2531-2582 (1994). This provision has been law since the enactment of the Trade Agreements Act of 1979 and was amended by the Uruguay Round Agreements Act, Pub. L. No. 103-465, 108 Stat. 4809 (1994). See*The Food and Drug Administration's International Harmonization, Enforcement, and Trade Policy Activities*, elsewhere in this text, for a more complete discussion of the WTO and the WTO Agreement on Technical Barriers to Trade.

15   58 Fed. Reg. 57,643 (Oct. 26, 1993); 61 Fed. Reg. 68,312 (Dec. 27, 1996) (proposed revision).

16   Pub. L. No. 104-113, 110 Stat. 775 (1996) (codified at 15 U.S.C. § 272 (1994)).

17   Kathleen Kono, *OMB Circular A-119 Becomes Law*, ASTM STANDARDIZATION NEWS, May 1996, at 40-42.

18   15 U.S.C. § 272(b)(3).

of eliminating unnecessary duplication and complexity in the development and promulgation of conformity assessment requirements and measures."[19]

In 1997, the FDA and other federal agencies were initiating activities to comply with the requirements of this law. One of the challenges presented to agencies has been to achieve the appropriate balance between the obligation to base standards on international standards set forth in the Trade Agreements Act, with the obligation in the Technology Act to "use technical standards that are developed or adopted by voluntary consensus standards bodies" in their activities.[20]

■ Imports

U.S. law applies identical substantive requirements to domestically-produced and imported medical devices. U.S. consumers must be protected from the same health risks, regardless of the geographical source of the devices. Furthermore, to comply with the General Agreement on Tariffs and Trade of the WTO agreements, a country's laws must be no less favorable to imports than to domestic products.[21]

Special procedures for imports are found in the FDCA[22] and the Radiation Control for Health and Safety Act of 1968[23] (which became part of the FDCA due to provisions in the 1990 SMDA). Foreign device processors who wish to export devices to the United States must follow GMPs,[24] shall be permitted to register their establishments,[25] and are required to list their devices with the FDA.[26]

Congress made clear its intent that no foreign firm be allowed to ship devices into the United States without the FDA's having "adequate and effective means" to ensure compliance.[27] Adding to language in the drug registration provisions of the Drug Amendments of 1962,[28] the 1976 Device Amendments assured that the regulations for registration of any foreign device establishment were to be

> upon condition that adequate and effective means are available, by arrangement with the government of [the] foreign country or otherwise, to enable [the Commissioner of Food and Drugs] to determine from time to time whether drugs or devices manufactured, prepared, propagated, compounded, or processed in such establishment, if imported or offered for import into the United States, shall

---

[19] *Id.* § 272(b)(13).

[20] *Id.*

[21] General Agreement on Tariffs and Trade, Oct. 30, 1947, 55 U.N.T.S. 187 [GATT 1947], art. III.

[22] FDCA § 801(a), 21 U.S.C. § 381(a). For a more detailed discussion of import controls, see chapters in this text on *The Food and Drug Administration's International Harmonization, Enforcement, and Trade Policy Activities* and *International Harmonization of the Regulation of Drugs and Biologics.*

[23] Pub. L. No. 90-602, 82 Stat. 1173 (codified at 42 U.S.C. §§ 263b-n).

[24] FDCA § 801(a), 21 U.S.C. § 381(a).

[25] *Id.* § 510(i), 21 U.S.C. § 360(i). Domestic firms are required to register, but the practical distinction in treatment is blurred due to the requirement for all firms, domestic and foreign, to comply with the requirement to submit product lists to the FDA.

[26] *Id.*

[27] *Id.*

[28] Pub. L. No. 82-781, 76 Stat. 780 (1962).

be refused admission on any of the grounds set forth in section 801(a) of [the] Act [i.e., adulteration, including lack of required premarket approval or clearance and noncompliance with GMPs, or misbranding].[29]

For domestic firms, a biennial inspection requirement was made applicable to registered establishments that manufacture Class II and Class III devices.[30]

■ Export Law

While U.S. medical device law is focused primarily on protecting the health of U.S. consumers, provisions were included in the FDCA on medical device exports that allowed export of noncompliant devices provided that certain requirements were met. As authority over medical devices expanded, statutory provisions on device export have become more complex, due to changes made by the 1976 Medical Device Amendments and the 1996 FDA Export Reform and Enhancement Act.[31]

Elements of Medical Device Regulatory Systems[32]

Many countries have some regulatory controls over medical devices, or particular types of devices, and yet there are relatively few countries that have put in place a comprehensive system of control for medical devices.[33] This situation may be contrasted with food and drug regulation, where virtually all countries have a regulatory program. Medical device technology generally is newer, and many countries only recently have begun to see the need for regulating medical devices. Countries have tended to pick and choose among the potential elements of a medical device system according to their needs. For example, countries that import a high proportion of medical devices place priority on registration and postmarket surveillance.[34] In deciding what devices should be allowed on the market, many countries that primarily import devices have chosen to follow the lead of other countries, particularly the United States, in making assessments as to whether a device is safe and effective. For example, the 2,188 requests for FDA export

---

[29] FDCA § 510(i), 21 U.S.C. § 360(i).

[30] *Id.* § 510(h), 21 U.S.C. § 360(h).

[31] Pub. L. No. 104-134, 110 Stat. 1321 (1996) (codified at 21 U.S.C. §§ 334, 381, 382; 42 U.S.C. § 262. Current law on exports of medical devices, found in sections 801 and 802 of the FDCA, 21 U.S.C. §§ 381, 382, is discussed further in this chapter.

[32] See FOOD & DRUG ADMIN., LEGISLATIVE CONCEPTS FOR THE REGULATION OF MEDICAL DEVICES (1997). In 1996, Robert Eccleston, FDA, prepared a report for the World Health Organization that is relevant to the development of international and national systems for device regulation. As this chapter went to press, however, the report had not yet been made public.

[33] Kathleen Hastings, FDA, Regulating Medical Devices: A Comparison of U.S. and Foreign Systems and Advantages of the U.S. System Over Others 6 (1996).

[34] J. Nobel, *The Universe of Medical Devices, in* C.W.D. VAN GRUTING, MEDICAL DEVICES: INTERNATIONAL PERSPECTIVES ON HEALTH AND SAFETY 7,18 (Elsevier Science B.V. 1994).

certificates for devices that the FDA received in fiscal year 1996 show the value of the FDA imprimatur.

Given the challenge and costliness of building a regulatory program like the FDA's that includes an independent review of products by experts in the diverse array of medical devices on the market, many countries have elected to rely heavily on the FDA's decisions on medical devices (evidenced in export certificates or otherwise), looked to the EU model described below, or attempted to craft a system that makes use of both FDA and EU approaches or decisions.

The fact that so many devices are produced in or for the FDA-regulated U.S. market probably has had the effect, globally, of establishing and maintaining a higher level of safety and effectiveness than would exist if there was no FDA system.[35] In the debate about the effects of FDA regulation on U.S. competitiveness, what is overlooked sometimes is the public health contribution that FDA regulation of medical devices has made beyond U.S. borders, and the value internationally of an FDA approval to the exporting firm. The FDA is widely viewed as the gold standard,[36] as other countries rely heavily on the FDA's decisions in their product marketing authorizations; thus companies that have complied with its requirements find the path to market easier elsewhere.[37]

The next section of the chapter reviews several of the medical device regulatory systems around the world that are fairly comprehensive, although none comes close to the U.S. system in breadth, depth, sheer complexity, and consumer protectiveness. As discussed in detail in other chapters in this text, the U.S. system includes the following elements:

- categories of control;
- methods for identifying manufacturers and products (registration, nomenclature, and terminology);
- adverse event reporting and investigation;
- product removal authority;
- GMPs, inspections, and compliance;
- product evaluation and standards; and
- clinical evaluation.

These are not listed in order of importance, but rather in some rough approximation of order of complexity, from lowest to highest. In the discussion that follows, how these elements are incorporated into the principal regulatory systems in the world and in emerging systems will be reviewed.

The table below summarizes five other medical device regulatory systems. The European Economic Area (EEA) comprises the fifteen EU members (Austria, Belgium, Denmark, Finland, France, Germany, Greece, Ireland, Italy, Luxembourg, the Netherlands, Portugal, Spain, Sweden, and the United Kingdom), and three remaining members of the European

---

[35] Linda R. Horton, Harmonization and MRAs, Presentation at Reg. Aff. Prof. Soc'y Conference, Cannes, France (Apr. 29, 1997); letter to Larry G. Kessler from Joel J. Noble, ECRI (Jan. 25, 1996).

[36] Regulating Medical Devices, *supra* note 34.

[37] For example, Canada, Australia, Israel, Argentina, China, and Taiwan closely follow FDA decisions on products, and some of these countries apply streamlined marketing requirements for FDA-approved imports.

Free Trade Area (EFTA) (Iceland, Liechtenstein, and Norway). Switzerland is a member of EFTA but not of the EEA, but nevertheless applies the EU directives.[38]

Other Countries' Regulatory Systems for Medical Devices

Country	Clinical Trials Required Approval?	GMPs Required?	Mandatory Event Reports?	A Process for Product Withdrawal?	Labeling Control?
Australia	Yes for 9 devices	Yes	Yes	Yes	Yes
Canada	Yes for 4 devices	No, but proposed	No, only voluntary	Yes	Yes
EEA and Switzerland	Yes for active implantables and Class III devices	Yes, if approval is based on quality systems, not type test[41]	Yes. Still being implemented in some countries	Yes	Yes
Japan	Yes for new device types	Yes	Yes	Yes	Yes

■ The European Union[41]

Pre-Harmonization Requirements

In the EU, legislative attention to medical device regulation got a slightly earlier start than in the United States, but was interrupted by war. In 1927 Italy had enacted a law that provided a framework on which device regulation could be based.[42] Later the United Kingdom's Department of Health set specifications for certain products such as blood sets and surgeon's gloves bought by the National Health Service, and eventually moved to a "quality systems" approach in which emphasis was placed upon manufacturers' adherence to quality control in product production.[43] In several countries, but notably Germany and France, national standards bodies were active in establishing standards for medical

---

38   Dr. Jean-Bernard Ramelet, statement at the Global Harmonization Task Force Meeting, Lisbon, Portugal (Oct. 9, 1996) (reporting that as of April 1, 1996, his country had transposed the EU Medical Device Directives).

39   Memorandum from Joseph Levitt, Deputy Director, Center for Devices and Radiological Health, Food and Drug Admin., to Linda Horton, Dir., Int'l Policy, Food & Drug Admin. (May 20, 1994) (regulatory requirements in foreign countries (May 20, 1994)).

40   A "type test" is the conduct of testing of one or more samples of a product to ascertain conformity with either a product standard, or the manufacturer's or the customer's specifications.

41   See the chapter in this text on *The Food and Drug Administration's International Harmonization, Enforcement, and Trade Policy Activities. See also* Linda R. Horton, *Medical Device Regulation in the European Union*, 50 FOOD & DRUG L.J. 461 (1995); Michelle Hoyte, EU, speech to Center for Devices and Radiological Health officials (1995); Richard F. Kingham, *Regulation of Medical Devices in the European Community*, 47 FOOD & DRUG L.J. 563 (1992).

42   M. Carlisle, *Medical Devices Directive: industry's perspective, in* C.W.D. VAN GRUTING, *supra* note 35, at 223.

43   *Id.*

devices that were, in theory, voluntary, but that were functionally mandatory when conformity with standards was made a condition for government health care reimbursement.[44]

Although these national requirements impeded the free movement of goods, European Community harmonization activities for medical devices began quite late compared to the work done on European harmonization of food, drugs, and cosmetics in the 1960s and 1970s. No work was done in the Community lawmaking institutions until Member States, inspired by developments in the United States, began to enact medical device laws:

> The [U.S. 1976 Medical] Device Amendments were like a stone thrown into a pond. The ripples began to reach Europe in the 1980s . . . . national governments [in the European Community] began to introduce new or develop existing medical device laws. Holland introduced a pre-market notification system. Norway and Sweden introduced GMP regulations and product registration. Italy introduced a decree under the 1927 framework law subjecting a large number of devices to premarket registration. Spain introduced a bewildering number of laws on different device products. Belgium strengthened the registration requirements for sterile devices. West Germany treated devices as "fictitious drugs" under its Medicines Act, while France introduced a homologation law which originally affected only certain electromedical devices but has since been expanded to cover a wide range of active and non-active devices . . . . The result was that national device legislation led to a partitioning of the European market place by technical barriers to trade.[45]

In 1979, European industry, frustrated at the regulatory fragmentation of the European market, formed a confederation of European medical device trade associations called the European Confederation of Medical Devices Association (EUCOMED).[46] This group was successful in preparing guidance documents on labeling, sterilization, packaging, and GMPs, but was unsuccessful in persuading Member States to refrain from regulation. EUCOMED turned to the European Commission, persuaded it to include medical devices in its 1992 single-market program, and in 1987 prepared a report on what the European medical device legislation should include.[47] At the time that the European Commission began to develop harmonizing directives for medical devices, the Member States with the broadest medical device regulatory programs were the United Kingdom and Germany.[48] The Commission sought a way to incorporate features of these existing systems to increase the acceptability of the new legislation on a Community-wide basis, a process aided by the development within the jurisprudence of the European Court of Justice of what Americans call preemption, that is, if a product meets the European Community's essential requirements and a Member State's additional requirements exceeded that which was necessary to meet the goals of the legislation, these additional requirements could not

---

[44] *Regulation of Medical Devices, supra* note 42, at 564.

[45] M. Carlisle, *supra* note 43 at 224.

[46] EUROPEAN COMMISSION DIRECTORATE-GENERAL III-INDUSTRY, MEDICAL DEVICES IN EUROPE: REFERENCE DOCUMENTS; CONTACT POINTS 41 (1996). This publication lists other European trade associations as well. *Id.* at 33-64.

[47] M. Carlisle, *supra* note 43, at 224-25.

[48] C.W.D.van Gruting, *Medical devices and public policy: the pharmaceuticals analogy, in* C.W.D. VAN GRUTING, *supra* note 35, at 203, 208.

be enforced.[49] Based on these new legal developments, as well as the frustration with the slow pace of harmonization in many areas, the European Commission developed a novel legal approach (known as the "new approach") and applied it to a wide variety of products,[50] including medical devices.

The New Approach to Regulation

In the EU foods and drugs are regulated in basically the same way that they are regulated in the United States, under highly specific directives (now known as "old approach" directives) detailing and defining the technical requirements for a product.[51] An example in the medical devices area is a 1984 directive on electrical medical device safety, which remains in effect.[52] The newer EU medical devices are subject to a quite different, "new approach" regulatory philosophy.[53] The new approach includes four key elements: 1) "essential requirements"; 2) presumption of conformity, if the product complies with voluntary standards that have been the subject of notice in the *Official Journal*; 3) mutual recognition, in that Member States of the EU must accept products that are lawfully manufactured in any other Member State if the products meet the EU essential requirements; and 4) a "modular" approach to conformity assessment, in which manufacturers are given a degree of flexibility in selecting which regulatory approach will govern their products, e.g., type testing of the product for conformity with a standard versus compliance of the manufacturing facility with quality systems requirements (which may include a review for adherence to relevant standards).[54]

Market entry is based on a manufacturer's declaration of conformity with the directives, based in some cases on self-declaration only and, in others, on third-party review by "notified bodies."[55] Notified bodies are conformity assessment bodies that have been designated by the "competent authority" of that Member State (i.e., a regulatory agency)[56] to carry out product certification, or quality systems registration, in accordance with the requirements of specified EU directives. The term "notified" derives from the requirement for each competent authority to notify the Commission as to which bodies on its territory are considered capable of performing specific evaluations in each directive. In most EU countries, notified bodies are in the private sector, while for a few (e.g., France and Ireland), these bodies are part of the government.

---

[49]   Case 120/78, Rewe-Zentral AG v. Bundesmonopolverwaltung fur Branntwein, 1979-2 E.C.R. 649 (1979) (Cassis de Dijon); Case 178/84, Commission v. Germany, 1987-3 E.C.R.1227 (1987) (German beer case).

[50]   *E.g.*, pressure vessels, toys, construction products, electromagnet compatibility, machinery, and personal protective equipment. *See* L. Horton, *supra* note 42.

[51]   THE ISO-9000 HANDBOOK 350-54 (2nd ed. 1994) (available from CEEM Information Services, Fairfax, Virginia). The European Commission also has published a large volume of literature on the new approach directives. *See, e.g.,* EUROPEAN COMMISSION, GUIDE TO THE IMPLEMENTATION OF COMMUNITY HARMONIZATION DIRECTIVES BASED ON THE NEW APPROACH AND THE GLOBAL APPROACH (1994).

[52]   Council Directive 84/539/EEC on electromedical equipment used in human or veterinary medicine, 1984 O.J. (L 300).

[53]   Council Resolution of 7 May 1985, 1985 O.J. (C 136) 01.

[54]   Council Directive 90/683 concerning the modules for the various phases of the conformity assessment procedures that are intended to be used in the technical harmonization directives, O.J. (L 380), amended by Council Decision 93/465/EEC, 1993 O.J. (L 220).

[55]   EUROPEAN COMMISSION DIRECTORATE-GENERAL III-INDUSTRY, *supra* note 47, at 21-28 (list of notified bodies).

[56]   *Id.* at 15-16 (list of contacts in competent authorities).

A manufacturer that has complied with the requirements of the relevant directives is permitted to affix to the product a CE mark.[57] The CE mark — French for "Conformite Europeene" — is required in order to sell any product manufactured or distributed in the EU under the new approach directives.[58] It is the final result of the product certification process, and signifies proof that a product meets the essential requirements of the directives.

EU Device Legislation

The three principal EU medical device directives that have been enacted are the Active Implantable Medical Device Directive,[59] and the Medical Devices Directive.[60] The European Commission has proposed a directive on *in vitro* diagnostic products. The European Commission also has prepared guidance documents on medical device vigilance, classification, auditing, and borderline issues with other directives.[61] Furthermore, as discussed later, the European Commission has adopted the many harmonized standards,[62] conformity with which serves as a "safe harbor" showing compliance also with the directive. For example, one of these standards adopts ISO-9001 as applied to medical devices.[63]

The Active Implantable Medical Devices Directive became effective in 1993, and compliance with it was required for all devices in 1995.[64] Active implantable medical devices are a special category of devices that are a subset of U.S. Class III devices. During the transition period between the date when a directive is effective and the date when compliance with it is required, manufacturers have the option of complying with the medical device laws of each Member State or complying with the directives.

The Medical Devices Directive became effective on January 1, 1995, and compliance with it is required for all medical devices on June 14, 1998.

Classification

The Medical Devices Directive includes a section on classification. There are four classes of medical devices — Class I, Class IIA, Class IIB, and Class III:

- Class I devices enter the marketplace with only a manufacturer's self-declaration of conformity.[65]

---

[57] Council Directive 93/68/EEC (July 22, 1993) amending directives 88/378/EEC, 89/106/EEC, 89/336/EEC, 89/392/EEC, 89/686/EEC, 90/384/EEC, 90/385/EEC, 90/396/EEC, 91/263/EEC, 92/42/EEC, 73/23/EEC, 1993 O.J. (L 220) (relating to the CE marking).

[58] THE ISO-9000 HANDBOOK, *supra* note 52, at 354-55.

[59] Council Directive 90/385 on the approximation of the laws of the Member States relating to active implantable devices, 1990 O.J. (L 189) 17; amended by Council Directive 93/42/EEC, 1993 O.J. (L 169); Council Directive 93/68/EEC, 1993 O.J. (L 220).

[60] Council Directive 93/42 concerning medical devices, 1990 O.J. (L 169) 17.

[61] EUROPEAN COMMISSION DIRECTORATE-GENERAL III-INDUSTRY, *supra* note 47, at 5.

[62] *Id.* at 9-11 (list of harmonized standards).

[63] CEN standard, EN 46001, Quality systems — medical devices — particular requirements for the application of EN 29001, Commission communication in the framework of the implementation of Council [Directives on active implantable medical devices and medical devices], Publication of titles and references of European harmonized standards under the Directives, 1994 O.J. (C 277) 6.

[64] Council Directive 90/385 on the approximation of the laws of the Member States relating to active implantable devices, 1990 O.J. (L 189) 17, amended by Council Directive 93/42/EEC, 1993 O.J. (L 169); Council Directive 93/68/EEC, 1993 O.J. (L 220).

[65] Special provisions govern Class I devices that have additional attributes, such as sterility or a measurement function.

- Class IIA devices are subject to production quality system control registration by a third-party body.
- Class IIB and Class III devices are subject to quality system control for both production and design.
- Furthermore, Class III devices that are critical devices undergo a clinical evaluation by the manufacturer, and the conformity of the device's design must be considered separately by a notified body before the device is placed on the market.

A manufacturer determines the classification of the device based on the rules in the Directive; the Commission also has developed guidance in this area.[66] Manufacturers consult with the notified bodies in making this decision. The Commission has stated that classification is based on intended use.[67]

Modular Conformity Assessment

A device's classification determines the conformity assessment procedure that can be used. The "global approach" encompasses the EU's mix-and-match rules for testing and certification of product safety. It provides various options by which manufacturers can certify product conformance with requirements. The range of possible procedures available to a manufacturer to assess conformity of a product depends in large part on the level and nature of the risks associated with the product. The lowest risk products enter the market simply on a manufacturer's self-declaration of conformity to requirements, including quality system norms. The highest risk products (Class III) require a review by a notified body. Examples of Class III devices are: surgically invasive devices for transient use to diagnose or control heart or central nervous system defects, or to monitor/correct heart or circulatory system defects; surgically invasive devices for long-term use (implantable, absorbable, or with a biological effect, or used in direct contact with heart or central circulatory/nervous system, or undergo chemical change in the body or administer medicine; implantable or long-term invasive contraceptives, and devices for prevention of sexually transmitted diseases).

The Directives state that modules can be used for a particular class of devices; the manufacturer can select the desired module, within the limits put in place in the Directive. For example, the Medical Devices Directive states that a manufacturer must follow procedures for full quality assurance (module H) or product type examination (module B), coupled with either EC verification (module D) or product quality assurance (module F).[68]

Standards are the key to EU regulation.[69] The Directives permit manufacturers to identify which standards are to be used in assessing compliance with the essential requirements. Although a manufacturer will find it easiest to satisfy a notified body of the compliance of its device with the applicable directive if there is a pertinent European Committee for Standardization (CEN) or European Committee for Electrotechnical Standardizations

---

[66] The European Commission has prepared guidance documents on medical device vigilance, classification, auditing, and borderline issues with other directives. EUROPEAN COMMISSION DIRECTORATE-GENERAL III-INDUSTRY, *supra* note 47, at 5.

[67] *Id.*

[68] Council Directive 93/42 concerning medical devices, 1993 O.J. (L 169) 17.

[69] Christa Altenstetter, City Univ. of New York, Regulating healthcare technologies and medical supplies: a comparative overview, presentation at the Fourth Biennial International Conference of the European Community Studies Association, Charleston, N.C. 12 (May 11-14, 1995).

(CENELEC) standard (see the discussion later), the manufacturer remains free to identify other standards such as international standards, national standards, or company specifications, that the manufacturer believes are the appropriate measure of the device's compliance. CEN and CENELEC are generating a broad range of medical device standards to maximize the availability of European standards, and to reduce the need to resort to Member States' national standards or manufacturers' specifications.

Manufacturers can select a notified body within the EEA as long as it has been deemed technically qualified by a national authority for the required tasks. In the contractual arrangements between the manufacturer and the notified body, the parties agree on the time limits for completion of the verification operation and the assessment.[70]

Central Obligations and Essential Requirements

The central obligations of the Medical Devices Directive are set forth in articles 2 and 3.[71] Article 2 requires Member States to "take all necessary steps to ensure that devices are placed on the market and put into service only if they do not compromise the safety and health of patients, users and, where applicable, other persons when properly installed, maintained and used in accordance with their intended purpose."[72] Article 3 requires devices to meet the essential requirements set out in annex I that apply to them.[73] Annex I elaborates on both general requirements and requirements for design and construction (for example, chemical, physical, and biological properties; infection and microbial contamination; construction and environmental properties; measuring functions; protection against radiation; and energy sources).[74]

In both the Implantable Medical Device Directive and the Medical Devices Directive, an annex lists essential requirements, e.g., biocompatibility, sterility, electrical safety, and labeling.

Member States' Role: Principally Post-Market

As is evident from the above discussion, the European system is quite unlike the U.S. system in that, rather than contemplating a single regulatory body with nationwide scope similar to the FDA, the EU system is multifaceted and contemplates roles for the European Commission, the fifteen Member States' competent authorities (and sometimes local governments, as well), the notified bodies, and more than a dozen standards organizations.

The competent authorities are responsible for implementation of the Directives, which are not self-executing, but rather must be "transposed" into each Member State's national law. Other responsibilities of the competent authorities are overseeing clinical investigations, reviewing decisions on classification (essentially made by manufacturers with input by notified bodies), medical device adverse event reporting and other surveillance, and enforcement. A competent authority's decision is valid only within the territory of that

---

[70] Council Directive 93/42/EEC, 1990 O.J. (L 169) art. 16(4).

[71] *Id*. arts. 2, 3.

[72] *Id*. art. 2.

[73] *Id*. art. 3.

[74] *Id*. ann. I.

Member State, while the decisions of both the European Commission and the notified bodies are applicable throughout the EEA.

Safeguard Clause

When a Member State ascertains that devices otherwise eligible for free marketing may compromise the health or safety of patients, users, or other persons, it shall take all appropriate interim measures to withdraw the product from the market, or prohibit it from being placed on the market.[75] The Commission and other Member States must be notified of the decision, whereupon the Commission will review it to determine if the interim measures are justified. If they are, the Commission will initiate a process intended to result in each Member State taking uniform action concerning the product. If the Commission finds the measures unjustified, it informs the Member State and manufacturer, and could bring an infringement action against a Member State that retains the interim measures.

Difficulties in Transposing the Directives

Difficulties in transposing the EU Directives into national law have been encountered, including delays in transposition, incomplete transposition, and Member States enacting additional requirements.[76]

When an initial draft directive on *in vitro* diagnostic devices (IVDs) was presented to the European Parliament in March 1997, the Commission received an extraordinary number of comments and amendments.[77] In general, the Parliament advocated two major changes: first, that common means of controls be established that Member States could implement individually or jointly as a means to evaluate the safety and performance of IVDs, including those currently on the market; and, second, that a database be constructed to identify or "register" IVD products by generic category (e.g., HIV test kits). How broadly the controls should be applied was an issue; for example, there was uncertainty about whether to apply control measures to such products as genetic tests and tumor markers. There was also disagreement as to whether certain groups of products (e.g., blood grouping products like HIV and hepatitis tests) should be subjected to batch testing given their impact on health if inaccurate test results are provided. The issue of batch testing was further complicated by differing policies among Member States regarding the frequency of batch testing. In France, for example, batch testing was required for every blood grouping product, whereas Germany required only sample batch testing for the same products. In light of Parliament's suggested revisions and the sensitive issues requiring resolution, the EU's original target date of 1998 for the IVD Directive to be effective was postponed. At the time this book went to press, the EU's work on the IVD Directive was still underway.

The enactment of the Directive has been fraught with other controversy: concerns about the narrow scope of Class III in the legislation;[78] the relinquishment of government approval authority over products, regulated by some members as drugs, to private sector

---

[75] *Id.* art. 8.

[76] L. Horton, *supra* note 42, at 461, 474-76.

[77] Michelle Hoyte, Report of Meeting Concerning Remarks by Norbert Anselmann, European Commission, at Global Harmonization Task Force meeting, Lisbon (Oct. 1996).

[78] *Commission rejects third-party certification for many IVDs*, 7 DRUG & DEVICE REP. Feb. 17, 1997, at 3.

bodies;[79] and the inclusion of coverage of devices (not just *in vitro* devices) made from human tissue.[80] Also, the Parliament had proposed to add provisions to the legislation to require the use of all eleven official EU languages,[81] but the European Commission insisted on its original approach of requiring labeling in a language likely to be understood, but with the ability of the individual Member State to require labeling in the local language.[82]

France has been particularly dissatisfied with the European approach to medical device legislation. It has invoked the safeguard clause several times (in its desire to have stricter regulations over breast implants, condoms, and products containing bovine materials).[83] The Commission regarded the French action as an unconventional use of the safeguard clause, in that the actions have challenged whether the European Directives are appropriate for handling high risk products, rather than showing how products failed to meet the applicable Directive, or that the standards were not appropriate or appropriately applied.

Also, industry has complained about continuing national differences in regulation among Member State systems, although these national differences are not viewed by the Commission as major problems since they remain within a recognized framework of acceptable interpretations.[84]

Harmonized Standards

CEN and CENELEC need to be viewed as part of the EU system because of their key role in developing voluntary, EU-wide standards that help to articulate how manufacturers can meet the essential requirements of the Directives. CEN and CENELEC have as their members the national standards organizations of the EU and EFTA countries, which are voting members of CEN and CENELEC with a number of affiliates as observers.[85]

All fifteen Member States in the EU have standards organizations, which play a key role not only in CEN and CENELEC standards development activities, but also in International Standards Organization (ISO) and International Electrotechnical Commission (IEC) activities. Examples of national standards bodies are the British Standards Institute, the Association Francoaise de Normalisation (French Standardization Association), and the Deutsches Institut fur Normung (German Standards Institute).[86]

CEN and CENELEC generate a broad array of standards. In January 1992, for example, CEN's workload included 6550 matters spread among 245 active technical committees

---

[79] *Parliament committee wants premarket approval for IVDs,* 6 EUR. DRUG & DEVICE REP., Feb. 5, 1996, at 1; *[European Parliament] Committee votes for national IVD registration,* EUR. DRUG & DEVICE REP., Feb. 19, 1996, at 4.

[80] *Parliament committees split over human tissue devices,* 6 EUR. DRUG & DEVICE REP., Feb. 5, 1996, at 3; *Commission still pushing human tissue regulation,* 7 EUR. DRUG & DEVICE REP., Feb. 17, 1997, at 1.

[81] *Amendment would allow national device language labeling,* 6 EUR. DRUG & DEVICE LETTER, Feb. 19, 1996, at 4-5.

[82] *Commission rejects mandatory IVD local language requirement,* 7 EUR. DRUG & DEVICE REP., Feb. 17, 1997, at 3.

[83] *French provoke unexpected use of safeguard clause,* CLINICA, Apr. 21, 1997.

[84] *Shell-shocked industry must accept national differences,* CLINICA, Apr. 21, 1997.

[85] Bulgaria, Cyprus, the Czech Republic, Hungary, Poland, Romania, Slovakia, and Turkey are affiliates of CEN. The Czech Republic, Hungary, Poland, and Turkey are also affiliates of CENELEC.

[86] EUROPEAN COMMISSION DIRECTORATE-GENERAL III-INDUSTRY, *supra* note 47, at 29.

and more than a 1000 working groups; CENELEC had 64 active technical committees.[87]

Both CEN and CENELEC have active medical device standards activities, some of them supported by the European Commission as a key element in the EU medical device program. As of May 1992, CEN had sixteen technical committees in the health care area[88] working on 345 active approved projects, CENELEC/Technical Committee 62 on electrical medical devices had sixty-five such projects, and CEN/CENELEC shared working groups on quality systems and active implantable medical devices.[89]

The Vienna Agreement[90] reduces duplication of effort among international and European standards bodies.[91] It covers standards activities of the ISO and CEN. A similar agreement assures coordination between the work of the IEC and CENELEC. Therefore, for example, as prescribed in the Vienna agreement, CEN tries to emphasize horizontal standards on essential requirements and avoiding laying down overly prescriptive rules that would exclude promising new materials, while ISO has issued standards for the composition of materials that have been found satisfactory in clinical use.[92]

In 1996, European participants in an ISO committee that was rewriting both the ISO standard (ISO 4074) and the CEN standard (EN 6000) for latex condoms announced that they intended to cease participating in the ISO committee and instead develop a standard for these products in a CEN committee.[93] FDA and American National Standards Institute (ANSI) officials protested this, and European officials agreed to return to the ISO committee provided that the committee could provide assurance of timely progress toward an adequately protective standard; that assurance was provided.[94]

The United Kingdom's Medical Device Agency

The Medical Device Agency (MDA) is an Executive Agency of the United Kingdom's Department of Health. An Executive Agency is expected to support its activities wholly or in part through user fees, and often possesses more authority over its decisions (both substantive decisions and such matters as personnel hiring and firing, compensation levels, and acquisition of property) than a traditional entity in a ministry in a parliamentary country normally does.

---

[87] R. Moore, *An overview of European standardization in the health care sector, in* C.W.D. VAN GRUTING, *supra* note 35, at 237.

[88] The groups deal with dentistry; sterilizers for medical purposes; *in vitro* diagnostic systems; ophthalmic optics, sterilization; non-active medical devices; biocompatibility of medical and dental materials and devices; respiratory and anaesthetic equipment; chemical disinfectants and antiseptics; rescue systems; medical informatics; terminology, symbols and information provided with medical devices; clinical investigation of medical devices; medical alarms and signals; non-active surgical implants; and technical aids for the disabled. *Id.* at 238.

[89] *Id.*

[90] The Vienna Agreement of June 27, 1991, on technical cooperation between ISO and CEN replaced the Lisbon Agreement of September 13, 1989, on exchange of technical information between ISO and CEN.

[91] International Standards Org. and European Comm. for Standardization, Guidelines for TC/SC Chairmen and Secretariats for implementation of the Agreement on technical cooperation between ISO and CEN (Vienna Agreement) (1997).

[92] W.H. Wheble, *Design validation through clinical testing, in* C.W.D. VAN GRUTING, *supra* note 35, at 53, 62.

[93] *ISO not CEN to revise Europe and world condom standards,* 6 EUR. DRUG & DEVICE REP., Nov. 25, 1996, at 1.

[94] *Id.*

As was mentioned earlier, the United Kingdom's medical device program traditionally has had a strong focus on quality systems GMP requirements, although prior to the European directives the program was strictly a voluntary adjunct to the United Kingdom's health care system's procurement program.[95]

The MDA is by far the largest competent authority in the EU, and the largest contributor of personnel to activities in both the Commission and the Global Harmonization Task Force. The MDA has published a number of useful guidance documents on a range of subjects, including medical device vigilance, clinical investigations, and biocompatibility assessment.[96]

■ Japan

An Evolving Medical Device System[97]

Medical devices have been regulated under the Japanese Pharmaceutical Affairs Laws since 1960.[98] In recent years, Japanese medical device requirements have undergone significant revisions, based on a review by a medical device panel created by the Japanese Ministry of Health and Welfare (MHW) Pharmaceutical Affairs Board (PAB) to evaluate Japan's medical device laws, regulations, and policies.[99]

At each stage of the review, the MHW held hearings and sought input from foreign governments as well as domestic and international trade organizations.[100] As a result of recommendations from this panel, the Japanese government published revised laws and regulations governing medical devices in June 1994, and began implementing them on July 1, 1995. The revisions include a risk-based classification system, new quality system requirements aligned with international standards, enhanced post-market surveillance, and an improved application review process.

Components of the System

These revised regulations cover classification, licensing of the manufacturing facility, premarket review, clinical trials, adverse event reporting, and labeling.

---

[95] Gordon Higson, *Developments in the United Kingdom, in* C.W.D. VAN GRUTING, *supra* note 35, at 391, 391-92.

[96] Medical Device Agency, The Medical Devices Vigilance System, Guidance Notes for Manufacturers on Clinical Investigations to be Carried out in the UK, Information for Clinical Investigators, Pre-clinical Assessment Guidance for Assessors, and Guidance on Biocompatibility Assessment (1996).

[97] The requirements that cover the regulation of medical devices in Japan can be found in the Pharmaceutical Affairs Law. Law No. 145 of 1960, revised by Law No. 50 of 1994; Enforcement Ordinance of the Pharmaceutical Affairs Law, MHW Ordinance No. 11 (1961) (revised by MHW Ordinance No. 22 (1995)); Enforcement Regulations of the Pharmaceutical Affairs Law, MHW Ordinance No. 1 (1961).

[98] JAPAN FED'N OF MEDICAL DEVICES ASS'N, PHARMACEUTICAL AFFAIRS LAW, EXTRACTS OF PARTS AFFECTING MEDICAL DEVICES (1996).

[99] Yukio Matsutani, New Regulations for Medical Devices in Japan, Address Before the Sixth Global Medical Device Conference sponsored by the Health Indus. Mfrs. Ass'n, Vancouver, Canada (June 1995).

[100] At one time, the product approval process was slow and included requirements for clinical trials in Japan. Philip Agress, *Problems Encountered in Marketing U.S. Devices in Japan: Discussions between the Two Governments Aimed at Easing Difficulties*, 38 FOOD DRUG COSM. L.J. 43 (1983). Although U.S. firms no longer regard MHW regulatory delays to be a serious problem, extremely strict health care financing reimbursement is a major industry concern.

Medical devices in Japan are classified into Class I (lowest risk), Class II, and Class III (highest risk). Also, there are separate categories for devices for home use and new medical devices. The class or category of the medical device determines the product approval process it must undergo.

- Class I medical devices, which are listed in the regulation,[101] are defined as having a low degree of risk for the human body, and include such products as *in vitro* diagnostic equipment and X-ray film.
- Class II medical devices are products that have a high degree of risk for the human body and are equivalent to products currently on the market.
- Class III medical devices are products that are implanted in the body and are directly life sustaining, such as vascular grafts and cardiac valve prosthesis.

New medical devices are devices whose structure, usage, or effectiveness/efficacy are different from those of existing, approved devices, as designated by the MHW.[102] Medical devices for home use are evaluated as a separate category from medical devices for professional use.

Licensing of Manufacturing Facility

For any medical device that is to be sold in Japan, a manufacturer must obtain a *kyoka* (license) by submitting an application to the prefectural governor or, in the case of imports, to the MHW.[103] This license is applicable to the business premises, including the importer's office or the manufacturing facility of a manufacturer. In the past, the examination for the *kyoka* was based simply on the material conditions, such as buildings and facilities for the manufacture of medical devices, and the personnel involved, including the technical director in charge of manufacturing. Under the 1994 revised requirements, manufacturers also must meet Japanese GMP requirements,[104] which are harmonized with the ISO 9000 series of quality system standards.[105]

Once a license is issued, the prefectural governor or the MHW keeps a register of the licenses for the manufacture of medical devices. The licenses are valid for five years, except that for manufacturers involved in the repair of medical devices, the license is valid for three years.

Product Approval Process

Manufacturers also must obtain *shonin* (approval) for most products intended for manufacture or import and sale in Japan. As discussed earlier, the classification of the device determines the process for product approval.

Class I products are exempt from the approval process and can proceed to market once the manufacturer has obtained the *kyoka*.

---

[101] Enforcement Regulations, *supra* note 99, art. 18

[102] *Id.* art. 21-2-2.

[103] In Japan, prefectures are local government units, analogous to states in the United States. The governor is the highest official of the prefecture.

[104] Kenichi Matsumoto, The Evolving Health Care and Regulatory Environment and its Impact on Industry Competitiveness, Address Before the Sixth Global Medical Device Conference, Vancouver, Can. (June 1995).

[105] As is discussed *infra*, the ISO has issued a series of voluntary standards entitled "governing quality systems."

Class II devices, sometimes referred to as "me too" products, are a category of products that are "substantially equivalent" to products already on the market with certain exclusions as described in the law.[106] For these products, the MHW can require a designated investigation organization (DIO) to conduct the evaluations of these equivalent products. While these DIOs are essentially third-party reviewers who conduct conformity assessments on behalf of the MHW, the final approval letter is issued by the MHW. At this time, the Japan Association for the Advancement of Medical Equipment is the only DIO that has been selected by the MHW.

For Class III medical devices, evaluations are conducted and approvals are issued by the MHW. In addition, manufacturers and importers or distributors of these devices are required to maintain a tracking system for these products, which should include pertinent records related to the use of the device, such as name and address of the patient, the user, and the medical facility. Medical devices for use in the home also must be evaluated by the MHW.

Any new medical device must be evaluated by the MHW for approval prior to marketing, and must later undergo a re-examination based on the results of the use of the device following its introduction to the market.[107] The application for re-examination should include documented results of clinical trials, and any studies or reports with respect to efficacy and usefulness of the product. The term for submitting an application for the re-examination review varies as follows:

- for medical devices having an obviously new structure, the term is four years after the product is placed on the market;
- for medical devices designated by the enforcement ordinance, devices that obviously have new effectiveness/efficacy and devices having new usage, the term is designated by the MHW and is less than four years; or
- for orphan products, the term is designated by the MHW and is between four and seven years.

Products that already have been approved may be re-evaluated due to advances in science and technology. Re-evaluations are conducted for a range of products designated and publicly announced by the MHW.[108]

In order to obtain *shonin*, the sponsor must submit the following information in support of an application for approval:

- data concerning the origin of the medical device;
- data concerning the biochemical properties, standards, and test methods;
- data concerning stability;
- data concerning electrical, biological, and radiation safety;
- data concerning performance; and
- data concerning the results of clinical trials.

---

[106] Enforcement Ordinance, *supra* note 99, art. 1-5-2.

[107] *See supra* note 2.

[108] Pharmaceutical Affairs Law, *supra* note 99, art. 14-5.

The application is reviewed by the MHW (or the DIO) and the approval letter is issued by the MHW. The MHW or the prefectural government must keep a register of approvals,[109] which includes the approval number and date of approval, name and address of the recipient, name of the item approved, structure of approved item, properties or effects of approved item, the directions for use of approved item, and standards and test methods for approved items.

Marketing Medical Devices in Japan

Manufacturers located in Japan submit the applications for licensing and for approval to the prefectural government (where the manufacturing facility is located), which forwards it to the MHW. Within the MHW, the application is reviewed in the Medical Devices Division within the PAB.[110] Licensing and approval decisions are issued from the MHW through the prefectural government to the manufacturer.

Foreign medical device manufacturers can either establish an office in Japan and sell products using their sales force or a Japanese distributor, or they can export products to Japan and arrange for a Japanese distributor to sell them. If the foreign manufacturer does not maintain an office in Japan, then the local distributor who files the *shonin* essentially will own them. Although the *shonin* can be transferred if the manufacturer changes distributor, transfer is not automatic.

An alternative to using a distributor is the in-country caretaker system, which would allow foreign manufacturers to acquire the approvals in their names.[111] The in-country caretaker, unlike the local distributor, acts as a liaison between the MHW and the manufacturer. This person is responsible for preparing the documentation submitted to the MHW, ensuring the ongoing safety and efficacy of imported products, and acting as negotiator on the foreign manufacturers behalf during the registration process. In-country caretakers must meet the requirements set forth in the medical device laws and regulations.

■ Canada[112]

Proposed Medical Device Regulations of 1997

In 1997, the Canadian Health Protection Branch (HPB) proposed a significant revision of its medical device regulatory system.[113] The proposed revisions are intriguing to those interested in international harmonization of medical device regulatory requirements, because HPB officials examined and evaluated various regulatory systems, especially

---

[109] Enforcement Regulations, *supra* note 99, art. 20.

[110] According to the *Global Medical Technology Update*, published by the Health Indus. Mfrs. Ass'n, the MHW has decided to dismantle the PAB as of July 1997. The PAB traditionally has been the MHW Bureau responsible for product approval for both drugs and medical devices, and through a separate office, industry promotion. It was decided to separate these offices after a public outcry in 1996 as a result of Japan's HIV scandal. After July 1997, medical devices will be registered with a new "Pharmaceutical Safety Bureau."

[111] Ames Gross & Tricia Hwang, *Changing Regulatory Environment in Japan's Medical Device Industry Opens New Opportunities for American Companies*, MEDICAL DEVICE & DIAGNOSTIC INDUS., Jan. 1995.

[112] The Minister of National Health and Welfare publishes a quarterly newsletter, *The Medical Devices Bulletin*, that includes news about the Canadian program. Subscription inquiries can be directed to Medical Devices Bureau, Health Protection Branch, Postal Locator 0301H1, Tunney's Pasture, Ottawa, Ontario K1A OL2.

[113] *Medical Devices Regulations Part I*, CANADA GAZETTE, Feb. 15, 1997, at 410-44.

those of the United States and the EU, to develop a system they believed would raise the level of regulatory scrutiny for products sold in Canada. At the same time, they recognized that the revised regulations should be harmonious with those of other countries, in order to facilitate meaningful negotiations toward MRAs. These new regulations would represent a compromise between the United States and the EU systems, and thus might serve as a model for many countries for medical device regulatory controls.

Medical Device Regulations of 1978

The medical device regulations were established under the authority of the Canadian Food and Drugs Act,[114] and applied to all medical devices sold or advertised in Canada. The regulations included provisions for labeling, product testing, and importation and recall or correction of a device. Device manufacturers were required to furnish the Canadian government, within ten days of first sale of the medical device in Canada, a notification containing specified information relating to the identity of the device, the name and address of the Canadian distributors, a copy of the labeling, and a statement of the intended use. Although the regulations allowed the Canadian government to request further information, there was no premarket scrutiny of the product prior to sale, for a majority of the medical devices distributed in Canada.

The premarket review process was limited to products listed in the table of part V of the regulations, which represented approximately five percent of the annual notifications received by the Canadian government: contact lenses designed or represented for prolonged wear, menstrual tampons, any device designed to be implanted into the tissues or body cavities of a person for thirty days or more, and test kits for the detection of serological markers indicative of infection by AIDS associated with retro viruses.

With respect to any product listed in this table that is a new device, it may be sold or advertised for sale only if the manufacturer has submitted evidence of device safety and effectiveness, and receives a notice of compliance from the government. In order for such a device to be regarded as a new device, it must not have been sold previously in Canada by a specific manufacturer; is different from any device sold previously in Canada by that manufacturer; or is identical with a device sold previously in Canada by the manufacturer that has been recalled or withdrawn previously from the market, or that the manufacturer has ceased to sell or manufacture.

The Review That Preceded the Canadian Proposals

As part of a continuing review of Canadian federal regulatory programs, and in recognition of the increased volume and complexity of new medical devices, the HPB established the Medical Device Review Committee in 1991 to formulate recommendations concerning the regulation of medical device and associated activities.[115] These recommendations, included in a report published in 1992, focused on harmonization with other regulatory systems in order to facilitate the negotiation of MRAs.[116] The HPB committee developed many of its 1992 recommendations using U.S. medical device requirements as a model. At

---

[114] Medical Device Regulations, C.R.C. 1978, c. 871.

[115] HEALTH PROTECTION BRANCH, DIRECTION FOR CHANGE: REPORT OF THE MEDICAL DEVICES REVIEW COMMITTEE (1992).

[116] Id.

that time, the European medical directives were still in the formative stages. The European directives influenced subsequent revisions of the draft Canadian regulations.

In 1993, an implementation plan was published to act on the Committee's recommendations.[117] Under this plan, working groups were formed to classify medical devices based on a risk-based classification system and to develop proposals on which new regulations would be based. The new regulations' working groups generated sixteen proposals for new regulatory requirements. These proposals, made public in March 1995,[118] were based on two principles identified by the Medical Device Review Committee. First, the level of scrutiny afforded a device would be dependent on the risk the device presents. Second, the safety and efficacy of medical devices would best be assessed through a balance of quality systems, premarket scrutiny, and postmarket surveillance.

In developing these proposals, Canadian officials reviewed requirements in both the United States and the EU, adopting aspects of each program that seemed appropriate for their regulatory system. HPB also reviewed and rejected certain alternatives to the proposed regulations, which included maintaining the status quo and establishing a voluntary program, because the previous regulations did not include a quality system requirement and the need to harmonize with mandatory regulatory systems of other countries.

Contents of the 1997 Canadian Proposals

The 1997 proposed regulations were published with an opportunity for further review and comment. Once these regulations are published in final form in the *Canada Gazette,* they will have the force and effect of law. Although the new regulations are scheduled to take effect in February 1998, certain requirements related to establishment registration, quality systems, and device registration will be phased in over a longer time period.

Under these proposals, the level of review of medical devices will be based on a risk-based classification system that divides devices into the four categories: Class I (lowest risk), Class II, Class III, and Class IV (highest risk). Contrasted with the previous requirements, which required some form of premarket scrutiny for an estimated five percent of devices marketed in Canada, the new requirements are expected to require approximately fifty percent of medical devices to undergo some form of premarket scrutiny before they can be marketed in Canada. A significant proportion of this premarket scrutiny, however, will be in the area of quality system audits.

Devices sold in Canada under the proposed requirements will be required to meet eleven fundamental safety and effectiveness requirements that are comparable to the requirements in the European medical device directives. Further, manufacturers will be required to provide evidence that their devices are manufactured in accordance with a certified quality system. Class I products are exempt from this quality system requirement, unless they are sterile or provide a measuring function that must be validated. The quality system audits will be conducted on behalf of the government by a third-party auditing program, similar to the European system's use of notified bodies to conduct audits on behalf of the EU competent authorities.

---

[117] HEALTH PROTECTION BRANCH, DEVELOPMENT OF AN IMPROVED MEDICAL DEVICES REGULATORY PROGRAM (1993).

[118] HEALTH PROTECTION BRANCH, PROPOSED REGULATORY REQUIREMENTS FOR MEDICAL DEVICES SOLD IN CANADA: REPORT OF WORKING GROUP #4 (1995).

The proposed requirements have a number of post-market surveillance requirements, including tracking implanted devices and an adverse event reporting system. The Canadian government has indicated it will develop interpretive guideline documents upon finalization of the regulatory proposals, and will perform a benefits and cost study with respect to the regulations. Additionally, the government plans to publish a new user fee regulation, which will be based on the requirements included in the final rule.

Canada-European Union Mutual Recognition Agreements

Like the United States, Canada has reached an MRA with the EU and Australia as well as a partnership arrangement with the United States. These arrangements will be facilitated by the adoption of a new system that is predicated on proven features of other national device regulatory systems, notably the U.S. and the EU systems.

■ Mexico, "Trilateral" Activities, and Latin America

Production of most medical devices in Latin America is found in Mexico, Brazil, and Argentina. These countries also import a large percentage of the medical devices used, which means that the design and application of a regulatory control system must take into account the need for border controls for imports.

Mexico's medical device program includes the following.[119]

First, four procedures for importing devices into Mexico are available, all of which are expedited by a U.S. export certificate. If the device is a U.S. Class I or Class II device, it can enter Mexico with a Mexican Registration number; or by an Advisor application stating what is being imported, and the amount and date of importation.[120] If the device is one that will need to be tracked (e.g., pacemakers and defibrillators), it must be registered and the proposed importation is reviewed by the Mexican government (registration is expedited when the applicant attaches an FDA export certificate indicating that the product is eligible for free sale in the United States).

An Import Authorization Permit for certain devices (e.g., radiation sources including x-rays and ultrasound devices, surgical products, implants, contact lenses, and hearing aids) requires 1) an Advisor application, 2) either an advisory notice that serves as an application to import or a sanitary license if the firm is one that has been in business for a long time,[121] and 3) either a Mexican registration or an FDA certificate.

Second, the requirements outlined above apply to domestic firms and their products as well as imports. There are approximately 2000 registered firms in Mexico. They manufacture surgical devices, gloves, cardiac filters, catheters, and syringes.

---

[119] Collin Figueroa, Food & Drug Admin., Trip Report, Meetings with the Mexican Ministry of Health, Mexico City (Jan. 29-Feb. 6, 1996). Unless otherwise stated, this report is the source of the information in the discussion in the text of Mexican medical device regulation.

[120] The Advisor is an individual who represents the firm before the Subsecretariat de Salud (SSA), must complete the advisor application, and must be a professional, e.g., physician or a chemist or engineer, preferably Ph.D.

[121] Mexico has dismantled the sanitary license requirement but treats it as substitute for the less burdensome advisory notice with respect to those firms that had obtained a sanitary license under the previous regulatory scheme.

The Mexican Ministry of Health has issued a non-mandatory guide on GMPs, applicable to both sterile and nonsterile products.[122] Prior notice of verifications (formerly called inspections) must be given by the verifier (formerly called the investigator). If a firm is not in compliance with the regulations, the Subsecretariat de Salud (SSA) issues a letter of warning notifying the firm of its noncompliant status. If no correction is made, a second warning is issued, which could be followed by shutting the facility down or arresting the manager (these actions are apparently infrequent).

Mexico's medical device program is small and in need of additional resources. Many verifiers work out of their homes due to lack of adequate office space, and few staff members have access to computers. The Mexican government is putting additional resources into the program and, subject to available resources, the FDA strives to include Mexican verifiers in its GMP training programs as part of its broad program of technical cooperation with the SSA on device GMPs.

The regulatory agencies of the three North American Free Trade Agreement countries have several collective activities. First, a longstanding cooperative activity is a health fraud program between the FDA and its Mexican counterparts that, since 1994, has included Canada's HPB as well. Second, an annual bilateral meeting between the FDA and the SSA included HPB observers in 1993, and was dubbed the "Trilateral" in 1994. Finally, a semi-annual compliance and policy forum between the FDA and HPB now includes Mexico as a full-fledged member; this group is known as the Canada-United States-Mexico Compliance Information Group.

Argentina's Administracion Nacional de Medicamentos, Alimentos, y Tecnologia Medica (ANMAT) (Drug, Food, and Medical Technology Administration) administers a new medical device regulatory program.[123] All devices must be registered with ANMAT prior to marketing or importation; having a certificate of free sale for products made in the United States or Western Europe simplifies the registration process.[124] Argentina supplies approximately twenty-five to thirty percent of devices used through local production, and imports the rest.[125] The Argentine medical device market is viewed as attractive to U.S. and European firms, due to increased spending on health care.[126]

In South America, the Mercado Comun del Sur's (MERCOSUR's) harmonization activities are being undertaken by the governments of Argentina, Brazil, Paraguay, and Uruguay. The Mercado Comun del Sur (MERCOSUR in Spanish and MERCOSUL in Portuguese) is a free trade area. Harmonized model regulations have been drafted on medical device quality systems, an audit guide for auditors, and other topics for adoption by national regulatory agencies.

The planned formation, during the first decade of the 21st century of a Free Trade Area of the Americas may facilitate links between North and South American harmonization

---

[122] Secretary de Salud (SSA) Guia para las buenas practicas de manufactura de los dispositivos medicos (1995).

[123] Resolution 256 (effective Jan. 1997).

[124] *Argentina shows healthy medtech growth*, CLINICA, Apr. 21, 1997.

[125] *Id.*

[126] *Id.*

efforts under MERCOSUR, the three North America Free Trade Agreement partners, and other subregional groups.

■ China and Other Asian Countries

Asian countries have expanded production of medical devices, and many of them are regarded as important markets for the sale of medical devices. The U.S. Health Industry Manufacturers Association (HIMA) and EUCOMED consider the two biggest challenges facing device manufacturers in every major and emerging market to be health care cost containment and proliferation of regulation.[127] "Despite their tremendous growth rates, many governments are beginning to promote increased device regulation, restrictive reimbursement policies, and special protection for local producers."[128] In 1995, HIMA opened an office in Asia and initiated a number of activities to persuade Asian countries that they should adopt requirements that are harmonious with international approaches.[129]

As of 1996 and 1997, China was moving rapidly to establish comprehensive medical device legislation. The State Pharmaceutical Administration of China (SPAC) is responsible for much of China's regulation of medical devices, while the Ministry of Health is responsible for regulating devices used in government-run hospitals.[130] The documentation to be required for imports likely will include proof of product approval from the exporting government; quality assurance certification for certain high-risk devices, and a list of technical service organizations to be used for maintenance of electromedical devices and other advanced equipment.[131] Features favored by industry also may be included — regulation of *in vitro* diagnostics as devices not drugs, reliance on international standards and third-party bodies for review of quality systems, and self certification in lieu of premarket approval for low-risk devices.[132]

In 1995 the Republic of Korea put into effect a device law that requires local product testing of every shipment of eleven categories of device products (an estimated forty percent of all imports)[133] by one of its eight product-specific testing agencies.[134] Other countries do not demand local testing of each shipment of imports, nor is there scientific justification for such a requirement. After heavy pressure by U.S. industry and the U.S. Department of Commerce to adopt a more internationally acceptable approach,[135] the Korean Ministry of Health and Welfare agreed to propose changes in the law.[136] Korean officials agreed to eliminate all local testing requirements for each shipment. Instead, Korea would

---

[127] Health Indus. Mfrs. Ass'n, *Cost and regulation emerging problems in emerging markets*, IN BRIEF, Apr. 1995, at 2a.

[128] *Id.*, (statement by Ulrich Nafe, Chairman, EUCOMED).

[129] Health Indus. Mfrs. Ass'n, *New Asia office works for change in Thai, Korean rules*, IN BRIEF, Apr. 17, 1995, at 4.

[130] Health Indus. Mfrs. Ass'n, *Chinese regulatory officials touring U.S. device companies*, IN BRIEF, Jan. 17, 1995, at 4.

[131] Health Indus. Mfrs. Ass'n, *China to issue device regulations this year*, IN BRIEF, Feb. 23, 1995, at 4.

[132] Health Indus. Mfrs. Ass'n, *Magazine represents HIMA in U.S. government medical mission to China*, IN BRIEF, May 1, 1995, at 1.

[133] Health Indus. Mfrs. Ass'n, *New Asia office works for change in Thai, Korean rules*, IN BRIEF, Apr. 17, 1995, at 4.

[134] *Korean device regulation proposed revisions eliminate in-country testing* , 21 M-D-D-I REP. ("The Gray Sheet"), Dec. 11, 1995, at I & W-5.

[135] Health Indus. Mfrs. Ass'n, *HIMA seeks major changes in Korean device law*, IN BRIEF, Jan. 17, 1995, at 4.

[136] *Korean device regulation proposed revisions eliminate in-country testing*, *supra* note 136.

follow a three-tiered, risk-based system similar to that of the United States, including ISO-9000 quality system controls, a postmarket surveillance system, and product recall authority.[137] Safety and effectiveness requirements would be required only for Class III devices such as pacemakers, heart valves, and artificial tissue.

Australia and New Zealand

Australia imports approximately eighty-five percent of the devices used by its population.[138] The quality, safety, and efficacy of devices are assessed and monitored under the authority of the Therapeutic Goods Act of 1989 by the Therapeutic Goods Agency (TGA); the health care system does not impose any significant additional controls.[139]

Components of the Therapeutic Devices Program includes device evaluation, import and export controls, production requirements, and controls on distribution of devices. Also, TGA maintains controls on clinical trials, administers a problem reporting and information dissemination scheme, undertakes standards development and testing for compliance, and inspects for compliance with GMPs.[140]

Australia employs a two-tiered system. The most stringently regulated tier must be the subject of premarket evaluation by TGA for quality, safety, and efficacy required of goods subject to the Australian Register of Therapeutic Goods. Australia has required premarket evaluation of only nine categories of devices: implantable intraocular lenses; intraocular visco-elastic fluids; intrauterine contraceptives; implantable pacemakers; defibrillators and cardioverters, and their accessories; prosthetic heart valves; powered drug infusion systems; implants of human or animal origin; and implantable breast prostheses containing other than water or saline solution. Other devices may be subject to lesser requirements such as compliance with standards that are listed on the register.

Australia is revising its regulatory system to be more like that of the EU, in order to facilitate the signing of an MRA that already has been "initialed" with the intent of future signing.[141] Australia now embraces the concept of third parties (in EU parlance, notified bodies) to perform conformity assessments for device companies with verification by TGA. Additional efforts are ongoing to further harmonize the TGA device regulatory system with that of the EU, in complementary administrative and legislative actions. As this volume went to press, however, the MRA had not been finalized because the EU did not want to conclude an agreement without a list of the notified bodies eligible to participate, and because an agreement had not yet been reached concerning participants.

In New Zealand, legislation was developed in 1996 to establish a system that is conceptually equivalent to the EU system, with provision for collection of minimal product license fees, use of third-party entities to review manufacturers' quality systems, and a post-market surveillance program.[142]

---

[137] *Id.*

[138] Derrick Beech, *Developments in Australia*, *in* C.W.D. VAN GRUTING, *supra* note 35, at 353.

[139] *Id.* at 355.

[140] *Id.* at 357.

[141] Statement by John Cable, TGA, at the Global Harmonization Task Force Meeting, Lisbon, Portugal (Oct. 7, 1996).

[142] Report by Sheriff Vallance, at the Global Harmonization Task Force Meeting, Lisbon, Portugal (Oct. 9, 1996).

The FDA's Third-Party Pilot Program for 510(k)s and for Inspections

The President's and Vice President's National Performance Review, *Reinventing Drug and Device Regulation*, issued in April 1995, included the development of a pilot program for review of low-risk medical devices by outside review organizations to determine if such a system could be developed permanently.[143] Included were initial reviews of low and medium risk devices, i.e., devices in Class I as well as certain Class II devices for which clinical data are not required as part of the premarket notification under section 510(k). The FDA would continue to make the final decision on whether the device met the statutory requirement for "substantial equivalence."[144]

Examples of devices eligible for the program are thermometers, surgical gloves, and tampons. Although few manufacturers took advantage of the program, reportedly because the devices eligible for it were ones for which the premarket notification procedure was regarded as nonproblematic, the FDA's initial assessment of its usefulness was generally favorable. The FDA's principal interest in undertaking this pilot program was coping with added workload with diminishing resources. The FDA also was interested, however, in the EU's use of third-party review entities (notified bodies) in its medical device approval processes.

The devices eligible for this two-year pilot study represent those whose reviews are in the intermediate range of complexity. They are not the lowest risk devices exempted from 510(k)s, nor are they the devices that, due to novelty, risk, need for clinical data, or similar factors, must be the subject of premarket approval applications or FDA-reviewed 510(k)s.

Memoranda of Understanding and Mutual Recognition Agreements

■ FDA Policy

The FDA sees value in entering into agreements with other countries to enhance public health protection, and facilitate commerce in safe and quality foods, drugs, and medical devices consistent with public health protection and the requirements of the law. The FDA's overall policy for initiating, developing, and monitoring memoranda of understanding (MOUs) was set forth in a 1995 FDA guide.[145]

---

[143] REINVENTING DRUG AND DEVICE REGULATIONS, *supra* note 2, at 5, 20-21; 61 Fed. Reg. 14,789 (Apr. 3, 1996). This is a domestic policy initiative of interest internationally due to EU reliance on private sector review bodies for devices generally.

[144] 21 U.S.C. §§ 351(f), 360(k).

[145] 60 Fed. Reg. 31,485 (June 15, 1995).

■ Mutual Recognition Agreements: A Variable Concept

The term "MRA" has become popular among those involved in regulations, trade, standards, and conformity assessment discussions, and yet those who use it do not always stop and make sure they are using a common definition. An MRA might be viewed as the most advanced form of agreement, a reciprocal agreement reached after a finding that the partner's system is sufficiently trustworthy that one country can safely reduce coverage of products from the other country.

The term "MRAs" generally means either reliance on one another's conformity assessment system or, where such reliance is not practicable, exchange of the results of conformity assessments.

The FDA MRA authority is provided for explicitly in the FDCA[146] and requires that device MRAs be in accordance with agency legal requirements.[147] This authority enables the agency to enter into international cooperative agreements with other countries. Some of these agreements are known as MOUs, Memoranda of Cooperation, or other names.

The European definition of MRA was influenced heavily by its internal market harmonization activities as aided by a European Court of Justice interpretation of the Treaty of Rome. Mutual exchange of conformity assessment results was a key part of the 1985 European Council Resolution on the New Approach, which was the ideological basis for EU medical device regulation. Reference is made to "the mutual recognition of the results of tests," and interpretive documents elaborate that "[t]o further promote international trade in regulated products, mutual recognition agreements for test reports or conformity certificates may be concluded on a case by case basis between the Community and the non-Community partners concerned."[148]

The U.S. Trade Agreements Act gives the U.S. Trade Representative the "responsibility for coordinating United States discussions and negotiations with foreign countries for the purpose of establishing mutual agreements with respect to standard-related activities."[149] This coordinating responsibility in no way derogates from FDA responsibility.

---

[146] The FDA may "enter into agreements with foreign countries to facilitate commerce in devices between the United States and such countries consistent with the requirements of this," and in such agreements the FDA "shall encourage the mutual recognition of . . . good manufacturing practice regulations . . . and other regulations and testing protocols as the [Commissioner] determines to be appropriate." FDCA § 803, 21 U.S.C. § 383 (as amended by the Safe Medical Devices Act, Pub. L. No. 101-629, 104 Stat. 4511).

[147] The FDCA permits foreign firms to register their establishments, requires them to list their products with the FDA, and states that:

> [FDA's implementing regulations] shall include provisions for registration of any such establishment upon condition that adequate and effective means are available, by *arrangement with the government of the foreign country* or otherwise, to enable the [Commissioner] to determine from time to time whether drugs or devices manufactured, prepared, propagated, compounded, or processed in such establishment, if imported or offered for import into the United States, shall be refused admission . . . .

21 U.S.C.§ 360(I).

[148] E. Jongen, The creation of an internal market for industrial goods in Europe through technical harmonization, standardization, certification and mutual recognition (1991).

[149] 19 U.S.C. § 2541 (1994); the Trade Agreements Act of 1979, Pub. L. No. 96-39, 93 Stat. 144, as amended by the Uruguay Round Agreements Act, Pub. L. No. 103-465, 108 Stat. 4809.

MRAs among conformity assessment bodies are becoming increasingly common, as public and private sector entities such as laboratory accreditation bodies enter MRAs with one another on conformity assessment practices, often to facilitate the exchange of reports from testing or audits. These MRAs make an important contribution to commerce, but do not bind governments unless governments agree to be bound.

For all these various MRA approaches, a fundamental question is, "whose requirements are being met?" Private testing bodies, such as Underwriters Laboratories, for example, test to the requirements of the customer. The international analogue is that the conformity assessment is done in accordance with the laws of the importing country. Businesses, however, often prefer that MRAs would address the laws of the exporting country. Statements have been made at the Transatlantic Business Dialogue meetings in Seville and Chicago that included the popular credo of "tested once, accepted everywhere" (or "approved once, accepted everywhere").

Of necessity, there must be equivalence (although not necessarily total harmonization) for an exporting country's regulatory measures to be sufficient for the importing country. Even after an equivalent level of protection is achieved in the written legal requirements, an uneven playing field may develop if there is inequivalent harmonization in how laws are applied. For the FDA, an MRA contemplates a finding that the other country has a regulatory system that is equivalent to the FDA's in its application as well as its wording. In addition, equivalence is called for in the WTO agreements.

◼ The FDA-EU Mutual Recognition Agreement for Medical Devices

History of Discussions

Since April 1994 the United States has been engaged in negotiations with the EU to conclude MRAs on conformity assessment in several areas, including medical devices. In June 1997, agreement was reached. These negotiations were coordinated by the U.S. Trade Representative's office. The EU had undertaken similar discussions with several other countries, including Switzerland, Canada, Australia, New Zealand, and Japan.

In an early session of the negotiations, the FDA proposed the use of a building block approach, which would start with mutual recognition of a component of the regulatory process and then build toward full mutual recognition as both parties gained confidence in each other's conformity systems. The FDA proposed that the initial emphasis be on exchange of inspection reports (known in the EU as audit reports), because the FDA and the EU had achieved harmonization of their approaches to quality systems, or GMPs.

The EU rejected the building block approach to MRAs as failing to provide for "total market access." This phrase connotes a situation where the exporting party is able to conduct the relevant control procedures on its territory to satisfy the requirements of the importing country, without additional procedures.

An early problem area was the EU's request that the FDA "delegate" authority to bodies within the EU to make a final decision about approval for products that would be offered for marketing in the United States. Because the FDCA requires U.S. government review of medical device premarket applications,[150] the FDA could not delegate authority to EU bodies. Furthermore, the FDA held that the current law was based on solid public policy, and declined to seek statutory change.

Breakthrough

The FDA agreed to extend the MRA beyond exchange of inspection reports to exchange of initial reviews of premarket submissions, with the FDA making the final decision, as to low- to medium-risk devices. The EU agreed that the scope of the discussions on premarket elements could be limited to such products. For these devices, the Commission offered that the notified bodies in the EU evaluate EU-made devices for the U.S. market in accordance with applicable FDA criteria. These reviews would be reviewed by the FDA.

Concurrently, U.S. bodies would review U.S.-made devices for the EU market in accordance with the applicable EU criteria in the appropriate directive. These reviews could be done by the FDA or by accredited third parties in the United States.

In 1997, the FDA agreed to include in the MRA an expanded version of its third-party pilot program for review of low- to medium-risk premarket notifications. The EU agreed to relinquish its objective of receiving a delegation of authority from the FDA enabling its bodies to make final approval decisions for the United States, provided that a sufficiently broad scope of coverage of the agreement could be achieved. Much of the final work on the MRA consisted of efforts by the parties to identify devices that were good candidates for the review (not too novel or high-risk), and for which there was guidance available to help ensure that the EU bodies carried out a successful initial evaluation that met U.S. requirements.

Elements of the Mutual Recognition Agreement

The MRA will cover routine and premarket inspection reports. All medical devices — high-, medium-, and low-risk — are covered as to quality system inspections if the devices are marketed in the EU and the United States, are subject to audit requirements, and have been inspected by a participating body. EU manufacturers will rely on participating EU bodies to provide reports to the FDA. The FDA expects to seek only abbreviated reports for routine inspections from EU bodies (full reports will be provided on request). It is anticipated that the FDA generally will endorse quality assessment inspection reports provided by the EU, as agreed to under the MRA, and that it will not reassess those reports except for specifically agreed circumstances. The transition period under the MRA is three years.

The result, after the transition or equivalency assessment, will be a substantial drop in the number of FDA-led inspections in the EU. The benefit will be fewer delays and less duplication between EU audits and U.S. inspections.

It is expected that the European Commission will nominate EU bodies, and the FDA will assess them, and that the two parties will jointly list participating bodies. In nominating bodies the Commission will strive to ensure sufficient coverage for EU manufacturers. The MRA also will provide that the FDA or U.S. conformity assessment bodies designated by the FDA in the United States will provide inspection reports to the EU to meet EU requirements.

---

[150] FDCA § 515, 21 U.S.C. § 360e.

The EU notified body would conduct premarket reviews for the identified products and conduct quality system audits at EU plant sites. These reviews and reports would be submitted to the FDA for its consideration. The FDA would reserve the right to make a final decision on marketing, just as it maintains the right of re-inspection.

The agency plans to prepare guidance documents that will include more Class II/tier 2 products in the pilot program over a three-year transition period, based on the validation of products nominated by the EU. The FDA would accept nominations from the EU for product category inclusion, so that maximum benefits and application coverage could be realized.

The FDA would agree to assess the equivalency of additional EU notified bodies for inclusion in the third-party program. The FDA anticipates it generally would endorse the results provided by the EU under the MRA, following the extensive confidence building period inherent in the equivalency determination and the preparation of guides, for the existing third-party pilot program.

Furthermore, within three years of transition, the FDA would agree to develop means for third parties to provide certification in the United States and the EU to appropriate and applicable standards, such as the electrical safety standards in IEC 601, as a part of market applications. This approach will reduce the cost and delays to market by manufacturers, and helps increase convergence between the U.S. system and the EU standards-based system.

Also, under the MRA, within a year, the FDA would agree to analyze a report from EU notified bodies, based on experience in the EU, on the validity of using quality assessment inspections of facilities that have implemented design controls as a route to market authorization, in lieu of 510(k)s, where the concerns about the device are in such areas as design modification. This approach, when found valid, also could reduce significantly the number of 510(k) reports submitted by manufacturers. The importance of this "design control" proposal is that the FDA regulatory intention is to make quality assessment inspections with the introduction of "design controls" into a new and expanded route to market, which then would be used as an alternative to 510(k)s in designated cases.

■ The FDA-MDA Memorandum of Understanding

In 1986 the FDA and the United Kingdom's MDA signed an MOU that provided for cooperation and sharing of inspection results.[151] The MOU had a built-in sunset of five years, and cannot be renegotiated because the European Commission has the exclusive mandate to negotiate agreements with other countries on medical devices.

■ Agreements with Canada and Mexico

A Trilateral MOU was signed in 1995 by officials of the FDA and its counterparts in Canada and Mexico.[152] The MOU contemplates increased harmonization and cooperation, particularly the exchange of information on a broad range of activities, including medical device regulation.

---

[151] FOOD & DRUG ADMIN., INTERNATIONAL COOPERATIVE AGREEMENTS MANUAL 353 (1996).

[152] Id. at 59.

The FDA and the HPB are developing a partnership agreement that will include a pilot program of joint review activities involving specific ear, nose, and throat devices, including cochlear implants, tympanotomy tubes, and ossicular prostheses, as well as orthopedic devices.[153] The purpose of this effort is to improve understanding of the regulatory procedures of the two jurisdictions, and to identify more efficient ways to handle reviews. A formal protocol for sharing confidential information without public disclosure has been developed.[154]

The FDA and the HPB also have an MOU, signed in 1974, on cooperation in the area of radiological health, addressing the control of radiation emission of electronic products.[155]

In 1995, the Canadian General Standards Board proposed establishing an agreement with the FDA on condoms and medical gloves. This Board, which is part of the Canadian government's Department of Supply and Services, conducts facility assessments and product testing for other Canadian agencies, including the HPB.

■ FDA-TGA Exchange of Letters

The FDA has informal arrangements with Australia's TGA, memorialized in an exchange of letters.[156] The two agencies have made use of employee exchange programs in order to promote cooperation, understanding, and common approaches.

■ The Russian Federation

In 1996, the FDA and representatives of the Ministry of Health and Medical Industry of the Russian Federation signed a memorandum of intent to conclude a memorandum of understanding concerning cooperation and information exchange on medical devices.[157] As of 1997, the agreement had not been signed, although the FDA and officials of the Russian parliament and Ministry of Health have held two consultations on Russian medical device legislation.[158]

■ Japan

In 1996, the FDA held discussions with Japan's MHW about reaching an agreement to facilitate exchange of inspection results.[159] The agreement would resemble those that the FDA has entered with the MDA and the TGA.

---

[153] 3 MEDICAL DEVICES BULL., 8 (Spring 1997).

[154] This protocol is based on the FDA's 1995 revision in its regulation, 21 C.F.R. § 20.89, on sharing information with foreign officials.

[155] INTERNATIONAL COOPERATIVE AGREEMENTS MANUAL, *supra* note 153, at 43.

[156] *Id.* at 353.

[157] *Id.* at 325.

[158] Linda Horton, Trip Reports, Meetings With Russian Officials on Medical Device Legislation, Copenhagen, Denmark (Jan. 1997) and Moscow, Russian Federation (May 1997).

[159] CENTER FOR MEDICAL DEVICES & RADIOLOGICAL HEALTH, INTERNATIONAL ACTIVITIES REPORT 5 (1996).

Organizations for Cooperation and Harmonization

■ Global Harmonization Task Force[160]

The GHTF, an international forum focused on medical device regulation, has embarked on several activities that will move the participating countries closer to harmonization, and even mutual recognition, of regulatory processes.

Formed in 1992, the GHTF is comprised of government and industry representatives from North America, Europe, Asia, and Australia, as well as observers from other countries including the Republic of Korea, China, Brazil, Argentina, Poland, the World Health Organization (WHO), ISO, and CEN. The GHTF consists of a main task force (which meets once a year), and study groups that concentrate on a particular aspect of medical device regulation and meet three or four times a year. The Task Force meeting includes reports from each study group as to the status of pending projects, presentations from delegates of member and observer nations about important developments in their medical device regulatory systems, assignments to leadership positions in the GHTF and its study groups, and new work that should be taken up by the GHTF and its groups.

The terms of reference for the GHTF were initially narrow. They focused primarily on the quality systems harmonization, because the EU was establishing new requirements and the FDA was preparing to revise its 1978 GMP rule. Also, work had progressed significantly on an international quality systems standard. After the GHTF was able to celebrate its first major achievement, the harmonization of quality system requirements in the United States, Canada, Japan, and the EU as well as the development of a guidance document on the application of these requirements, the GHTF committed itself to undertaking several new assignments within the four study groups.

At its 1995 meeting, the GHTF decided to expand the scope of GHTF activities beyond the quality system area. First, it was agreed that the current requirements for adverse incident reporting and post-market surveillance are sufficiently similar to develop internationally harmonized rules. Second, it was agreed that Study Group 1 would have a new mandate, to focus on the development of premarket approval packages that would be generally acceptable.

Study Group 1 (Regulatory Systems)[161]

This group seeks to harmonize medical device regulatory requirements pertaining to premarket evaluation. Its main focus at the 1996 GHTF meeting was existing requirements in Australia, Canada, the EU, Japan, and the United States, although representatives from other nations and world regions, as well as from WHO, monitored the meetings.

---

[160] Michelle Hoyte, *Moving Countries Closer to Mutual Recognition: Global Harmonization Task Force's New Initiatives*, REG. AFF. FOCUS, Feb. 1996.

[161] Except as otherwise noted, the discussions of the Global Harmonization Task Force study group activities that follow are based upon a report by Michelle Hoyte, Food & Drug Admin., of the Global Harmonization Task Force Meeting in Lisbon, Portugal (Oct. 1996).

The Study Group is conducting ground-breaking efforts to converge the format and content of manufacturer premarket submissions, which are either reviewed by national authorities such as the FDA, reviewed by notified bodies, or relied on by medical device companies for self-certification and maintained in their files for future audits by national authorities. Discussions at the 1996 meeting concentrated on a planned multi-national activity involving the development and pilot-testing of harmonized premarket review standards for three types of devices: patient monitors, cardiac pacemakers, and hip stem implants. The long-term impact of this pilot effort is not totally clear, because the volume of medical devices in use around the world seems to preclude the development of standardized review criteria on a product-by-product basis. One distinct possibility is the production of generalizable requirements for devices arrayed by category, e.g., orthopedic implants or some subcategory of orthopedic implants.

An ongoing problem for the Group is reconciling different, legislatively-directed regulatory approaches for evaluating new products before they enter the marketplace. The principal difference lies with the scope of premarket reviews. In the United States, for example, the FDA evaluates both safety and effectiveness of devices, as opposed to the EU's review of safety and product performance characteristics. The Study Group, however, has indicated that these differences will not be an impediment to harmonizing premarket submission formats and requirements for most devices. The Group's mandate also includes labeling (a decision made after a standards technical committee — ISO TC 210 — meeting concurrently with the GHTF meeting offered to prepare a standard on labeling requirements).[162]

Study Group 2 (Post-Market Vigilance)

This group, created as a result of a decision at the 1995 meeting to broaden GHTF's scope, has undertaken an ambitious agenda of activities on adverse incident reporting. The FDA has offered to provide a convener for the new study group.

The main thrust of the group is reaching a general accord among the four principal Task Force member nations and the EU on the criteria for reporting device-related incidents (i.e., death, serious injuries, and devices performing out of specifications) that should be reported to national authorities by manufacturers, as well as the nature and format for such reports.

A draft document, prepared a delegate from Norway, has outlined the basic principles of reporting device incidents to national competent authorities, regardless of whether they are single events or a series of events. In addressing the draft, the Study Group has agreed that the obligation to report device-related adverse events rests with manufacturers, and that the means by which to make such reports rests with national competent authorities.

Based on this understanding, the Study Group has enunciated two major goals for an internationally harmonized reporting system:

• national authorities must receive from manufacturers reports relating to adverse events arising from the use of medical devices; and

---

[162] Michelle Hoyte, FDA Report from the Global Harmonization Task Force Meeting, Vancouver, Canada (June 1995).

- national authorities should share, to the maximum extent feasible, report information in order to prevent similar events from occurring elsewhere.

With respect to the timing of reports, the Study Group has agreed on an approach that is based on two scenarios: one in which the cause of the event (a death or serious injury) is known and the other in which the cause of the event is not known. In the latter case, the device manufacturer should report the event to the responsible national health authority no later than thirty days after the event, regardless of the stage of investigation. The Study Group also agreed that this reporting scheme is appropriate for all devices except life-sustaining devices (e.g., ventilators, dialysis equipment) because they are most commonly used on seriously-ill patients making attribution of an event to the performance of a device problematic.

In addition to the document on reporting criteria, both government and industry members of the Group have developed a number of draft documents, including a model reporting form, a proposal for harmonizing reporting requirements, a draft set of reporting "rules" with case scenario examples, and an initial data element matrix. The completed work on the individual documents eventually will be consolidated into a single guideline.

The Study Group also has discussed sharing information regarding devices and events that pose an unreasonable risk of public harm despite a lack of definitive information as to the cause of an event, however, confidentiality, particularly as it relates to sharing of event reports among national health authorities, may be problematic. Several members of the Group were apprehensive about sharing information in cases when an investigation is ongoing and aimed at ascertaining and confirming causality. In addition, the need to protect such information from public disclosure, which could lead to speculative news stories, reactive actions by health professionals, and possible tort liability, has been a concern to the Study Group 2 members. Regardless of whether reports are disseminated electronically or in hard copy, some countries (especially the United States because of its Freedom of Information and congressional access laws) could have difficulty in protecting reports of a preliminary nature. The FDA can, however, withhold reports of pending investigations from public disclosure.[163]

The Study Group initiated work on the issue of electronic data interchange, to develop definitions for terms used in each of the documents, and to consider whether to expand the focus to include manufacturer's reporting of information concerning events to health professionals and device users in general in the near future.

Study Group 3 (Quality Systems)

After achieving success in the harmonization of a quality systems standard, Study Group 3 has devised a guidance document relating to quality control validation. The guidance also comments on countries' quality system regulations and guidelines.

Study Group 4 (Auditing)

This group has prepared a GHTF guidance document on regulatory auditing of quality systems of medical device manufacturers that is expected to be in final form in early 1998. Several issues, however, have arisen about publication of the final guidance documents,

---

[163] 5 U.S.C. § 552(b)(7).

their global availability, and their enforceability. Although no decisions have been made, the Group has agreed generally on:

- the need for a mechanism to disseminate the materials to national health authorities, either via the World Wide Web and/or in hard copy form;
- the necessity for periodic updating to ensure the material in the documents remains fresh, relevant, and usable; and
- the possibility of making the documents administratively enforceable, which would require "credentialing" by the full GHTF as well as the governments involved.

Another issue being confronted by the GHTF is how to continue to perform in an effective manner with the enlarged number of Task Force meeting participants. The difficulties facing the Task force have been recognition of the value of allowing nations with an interest in establishing device regulatory programs to learn and profit from experiences of countries with mature systems, on the one hand, and the management of GHTF and the attendance at Study Group meetings becoming hampered by the exponential rise in the number of meeting participants, on the other. Also, sporadic attendance by some participants has made the environment in which the Study Groups operate less conducive to productive discussion and work progress.

In response to these concerns, at the 1996 meeting Task Force members have suggested allowing single representatives from regional or subregional groupings (e.g., Southeast Asia) to attend GHTF sessions. Alternately, more time could be reserved for progress updates by the Task Force Study Groups because most work is produced by these groups, and then Task Force materials and reports of proceedings could be circulated to all interested countries.

The Task Force has formed a work group to assess the procedural issues and make recommendations to the full Task Force. Industry and regulatory representatives from each of the four nations and the EU were appointed to serve on this group. Invitations also were extended to all of the participants to offer relevant comments, ideas, and suggestions in writing to the Task Force.

■ Standards Organizations

International Groups

The principal international bodies active in developing standards for medical devices are the ISO and the IEC. These organizations are referred to in annexes to the Agreement on Technical Barriers to Trade of the new WTO agreements.[164] The U.S. member body to the ISO and the IEC is ANSI.[165] The ISO works through technical committees. To organize its participation in a technical committee, a country's national standards body often estab-

---

[164] Technical Barrier to Trade Agreement, ann. 1 (Terms and Their Definitions for the Purpose of This Agreement), ann. 3 (Code of Good Practice for the Preparation, Adoption and Application of Standards).

[165] ANSI does not develop standards but coordinates most U.S. nontreaty international and national standards activities. ANSI is a nonprofit private-sector entity that collaborates with the government through inclusion of government members (including an FDA representative) on its Board of Directors and committees, and, recently, through an MOU with the NIST. (The MOU was signed on July 24, 1995.)

lishes a Technical Advisory Group to formulate a national position to be taken to the technical committee by a named national delegate.

U.S. National Organizations

Among the U.S. national standards development organizations that develop standards for medical devices are the American Society for Testing and Materials, the Association for the Advancement of Medical Instrumentation (AAMI),[166] and the National Committee for Clinical Laboratory Standards for diagnostic products. These bodies coordinate the development of both national and international standards.

In 1995, ISO created a new committee, TC-210, on "Quality management and corresponding general aspects for medical devices." ISO assigned AAMI to administer this committee. TC-210 is intended to facilitate resolution of cross-cutting issues on medical device standardization.

As a standards organization that follows the procedural requirements of ISO, ANSI, and AAMI, TC-210 is open to participation by any country (including any individual EU member country) that is a member of ISO. Industry and device users, as well as government officials, participate. In contrast, because GHTF operates less formally and with working groups of a manageable size, it may be possible for GHTF to make more progress in producing harmonization documents than can a larger, broader, more formal forum such as an ISO committee.

ISO's TC-210 is addressing four areas:

- documentation on quality systems, which will consist of technical procedures for implementing the ISO-9000 standards series relating to quality systems for medical devices followed a year later by a formal standard;
- guidance for countries pursuing regulations on quality systems regarding the process for drafting the rules so as to promote coherent standards from nation to nation;
- organizing symbols, nomenclature, and labeling requirements to better ensure uniformity among nations; and
- a joint ISO/IEC venture aimed at producing guidance on how to conduct risk analysis and risk management programs.

■ World Health Organization

WHO's priorities in the area of medical devices are international collaboration, information exchange, and strengthened national capacities for decisionmaking through training and other forms of technology transfer. WHO has focused on providing guidance on selection and use of essential equipment for health facilities, such as basic radiological, sterilization, and laboratory equipment. For example, the WHO Global Action Plan on Management, Maintenance and Repair of Health Care Equipment was launched in 1987,[167] accompanied by a worldwide network of United Nation agencies, nongovernmental orga-

---

[166] Michael J. Miller, *U.S. International Standards Strategies*, 46 FOOD DRUG COSM. L.J. 311 (1991).

[167] World Health Org., Background Document for the WHO Programme on Maintenance and Repair of Hospital and Medical Equipment, Doc. No. SHS/86.5 (1986).

nizations, bilateral donors, and many other institutions from both industrialized and developing countries.

In 1996, at the request of WHO, the FDA provided an expert consultant who studied the global situation involving medical devices — regulatory, health care availability, and device repair issues — from the standpoint of developing as well as developed countries. As of July 1997, this report had not been made public.

WHO cooperates not only with national governments, but also with several collaborating centers for health care technology that WHO has designated around the world.

ECRI

ECRI is an independent nonprofit institution in Pennsylvania that engages in product evaluation and testing, problem investigation, publications and information services, consultation services, and forensic engineering.[168] ECRI publishes, on WHO's behalf, a newsletter entitled *Health Equipment Management*, which is circulated to WHO member countries to increase knowledge and competence on regulation, procurement, service, and user training. Other ECRI activities on behalf of WHO are described in this chapter.

Other WHO Collaborating Centers

These centers include the Netherlands Organization for Applied Scientific Research, the United Kingdom's Department of Health, the Swedish Testing Institute for Medical Supplies, and the Center for Biomedical Engineering of the State University of Campinas in Brazil.[169]

Details about Harmonization Activities in Specific Areas

■ Categories of Control

Because of the diversity of existing medical devices and the continual introduction of new devices, countries have had difficulty identifying which devices need which controls. In the United States and the EU, this identification was made through a statutory creation of classes (three in the United States and four in the EU) with an effort to sort devices into each category either by the government directly, in the United States, or by manufacturers, in the EU (with a potential for government intervention in the event of an error). Australia's Register of Therapeutic Goods also includes a classification system for devices to achieve appropriate levels of control.[170]

---

[168] ECRI, established in 1955, was previously known as the Emergency Care Research Institute. It now uses its acronym as its name. J.Nobel, *Role of ECRI, in* NORMAN F. ESTRIN, THE MEDICAL DEVICE INDUSTRY 177.

[169] B.Wang, *Developments in Brazil and other major Latin American countries, in* C.W.D. VAN GRUTING, *supra* note 35, at 339, 349.

[170] Derrick Beech, *supra* note 140, at 357.

Canada classifies devices and has been a leader in promoting the redirection of regulatory review processes from a device category approach to a risk-based approach.[171] In order to assist in determining the degree of regulatory control for a device, Canada is developing a framework for assessing the risk profile of medical device technologies, with the assistance of computer-based decision support systems.[172]

■ Identifying Manufacturers and Products

Registration and Listing

A registration system of manufacturers and importers of medical devices, and of the products themselves is a basic feature of regulatory systems. Registration systems should be based on a recognized nomenclature system so that a country's regulators can communicate effectively with companies, hospitals, users, and other governments about the devices in question.

The EU currently is in the process of establishing a European data base on: 1) manufacturers, authorized representatives, and medical devices; 2) certificates granted, refused, or withdrawn; and 3) vigilance.[173] Access to the data collected will be restricted to competent authorities and, where justified, notified bodies. This initiative responds to criticisms by both Member States[174] and the European Parliament[175] that the lack of a comprehensive collection of information about products lawfully on the market in the EU undermined the single market, while the lack of a registry of shared information about products removed from the market due to safety problems exposed European patients to threats.

Nomenclature

The Universal Medical Device Nomenclature and Coding System. This system is the most commonly used system of nomenclature for medical devices, and was developed by ECRI to facilitate international communication and exchange of information on health care technology.[176] Its purpose is to facilitate identifying, processing, filing, storing, retrieving, transferring, and communicating information about medical devices. Use of the system ranges from hospital inventory controls to regulatory systems. To overcome language barriers, ECRI's nomenclature has been translated from English into Chinese, Dutch, French, German, Italian, Norwegian, Portuguese, Russian, Spanish, and Turkish. ECRI's five-digit computer code for each device also permits data exchange based on numerical identifiers.[177]

Nomenclature Developed by Standards Organizations. Other nomenclature span a range of activities such as promoting standard terms in the health care industry (for exam-

---

[171] E.G. Letourneau & P.D. Neufeld, *Models for medical device regulations, in* C.W.D. VAN GRUTING, *supra* note 35, at 151, 159

[172] *Id.* at 156.

[173] Norbert Anselmann, Presentation to Regulatory Aff. Prof. Soc'y, Cannes, France (Apr. 28, 1997).

[174] *Spain plans to introduce strict device notification rules,* 6 DRUG & DEVICE REP., Feb. 5, 1996 at 7.

[175] 7 DRUG & DEVICE REP., Feb. 17, 1996 at 4.

[176] J. Nobel, *supra* note 170, at 190; J. Nobel, *supra* note 35 at 14.

[177] J. Nobel, *supra* note 170, at 192.

ple, the codes used for various diseases and conditions on health insurance claim forms). In the United States, many of these activities are coordinated by ANSI.

Adverse Event Reporting. The value of adverse effects reporting in countries with comprehensive medical device systems is widely recognized. The EU is putting into place a mandatory device vigilance program that parallels its pharmacovigilance programs for adverse effects related to drugs. Sweden and Norway have had systems for some time. Canada has had a voluntary system since 1975, and Australia and the United Kingdom both have operated voluntary systems.[178]

One of the functions played by ECRI as a WHO collaborating center is to serve as the worldwide focal point for gathering and disseminating information on problems and hazards with medical devices.[179] Both the FDA and the EU have announced their intention to use the ECRI system in their national systems and in harmonization activities under the GHTF.

ECRI has identified nine causes of device-related adverse events, a categorization scheme that may serve as a basis for countries to categorize and share information on adverse events: device failure, device interaction, user error, maintenance error, packaging error, tampering, support system failure, environmental factor, and idiosyncratic patient reaction.[180] Device failure may be broken down into design error, labeling error, manufacturing error, software deficiency, component failure, power source failure, and failure of accessory.

■ Conformity Assessment

Technical Barriers to Trade Agreement; International Standards Organization's Guides and Standards

As is discussed in the chapter on International Harmonization, Enforcement, and Trade Policy Activities, the WTO Technical Barriers to Trade Agreement covers standards, technical regulations, and conformity assessment.[181] The latter phrase refers to inspections, audits, laboratory testing, and other measures to ensure that products or systems conform to applicable voluntary standards or technical regulations. Conformity assessment can be a private sector activity, e.g., the familiar "UL" symbol on electrical cords, or public sector, e.g., FDA inspections of medical device manufacturers.

International standards organizations, and particularly the ISO and the IEC, have recognized a need to articulate common principles and approaches applicable to a wide range of conformity assessment activities. Accordingly, a series of guides has been prepared on a variety of conformity assessment activities, such as laboratory proficiency and accreditation processes, that are referred to in national and international discussions of

---

[178] J. Nobel, *Adverse effects reporting*, *in* C.W.D. VAN GRUTING, *supra* note 35, at 275, 279.

[179] J. Nobel, *supra* note 170, at 190.

[180] M.E. Bruley, *Accident and forensic investigation*, *in* C.W.D. VAN GRUTING, *supra* note 35, at 127, 129.

[181] NATIONAL RES. COUNCIL, STANDARDS, CONFORMITY ASSESSMENT AND TRADE IN THE 21ST CENTURY, (Nat'l Academy Press 1995).

conformity assessment issues.[182] The ISO/IEC Guides that are often referred to include:[183]

- Guide 2 — General terms and definitions concerning standardization and related activities.
- Guide 7 — Requirements for standards suitable for product certification.
- Guide 22 — Information on manufacturer's declaration of conformity with standards or other technical specifications.
- Guide 23 — Methods of indicating conformity with standards for third-party certification systems.
- Guide 38 — General requirements for the acceptance of testing laboratories.
- Guide 39 — General requirements for the acceptance of inspection bodies.
- Guide 40 — General requirements for the acceptance of certification bodies.

As this volume went to press, these guides were in the process of being converted into ISO or IEC standards, so that the numbers given will become obsolete. Nevertheless, a few are mentioned so that the reader can be cognizant of international activity in this area. Some of these guides originally were prepared for one purpose (e.g., metrology labs) and while they are useful in some areas, in others for which there have been discussions of their use, they are too general, e.g., the EU's 1997 proposal to use ISO guides in lieu of good laboratory practice rules for tests for carcinogenicity on laboratory animals.

Good Manufacturing Practices and ISO-9001[184]

All countries with firms that manufacture medical devices need to promulgate GMP regulations, and enforce them through inspections and compliance activities.[185] Indeed, due to the substantial progress made in harmonizing the GMP/product quality systems requirements area, the FDA believes that this area provides the foundation for the broadest possible international harmonization in the near term.

The international standard for quality systems known as ISO 9001, as adapted by the EU and the FDA,[186] is becoming widely recognized by medical device regulatory authorities worldwide. In view of the role of GMPs in the production of high quality devices and the harmony between the EU and the FDA on the substantive standard, GMPs based on ISO-9001 are a high priority for any country with manufacturers of medical devices.

---

[182] ISO/IEC GUIDES COMPENDIUM, CONFORMITY ASSESSMENT (3rd ed. 1995). *See also* ISO 9000 HANDBOOK, *supra* note 52, at 383.

[183] *Id.*

[184] *See generally,* ISO 9000 HANDBOOK, *supra* note 52. W. Schwemer, *ISO 9000 Standards*, 5 REG. AFF. 1 (1993)

[185] Many countries, encouraged by economic considerations and WHO policies, are developing indigenous industries to produce simple, inexpensive devices. Candidates for local manufacture, for which the development challenge is relatively modest, are devices for which compliance with GMPs is relatively easy (such as hospital beds and wheelchairs). Local production of disposable devices used in large quantities in health care can help stem the outflow of foreign currency for imports of such high volume products. Thus, good candidates for local manufacture are devices such as syringes, needles, catheters, IV infusion sets, and surgical instruments. These devices are relatively simple in design, but do require continuous attention to GMPs.

[186] 61 Fed. Reg. 52,602 (Oct. 7, 1996).

The FDA's new final rule on device GMPs[187] is central to the device program and an example of how the FDA can accept a voluntary standard as the foundation for a mandatory technical regulation. It also demonstrates how the process of harmonizing regulatory requirements is facilitated by using an international standard as a basis.

The 1996 rule replaced the FDA's 1978 medical device GMP regulations and strengthened requirements for controls on device designs. Furthermore, it reflected an agency decision to strive for compatibility with ISO-9000.

ISO-9000 is actually a set of five standards. It contains a general guidance for the selection and use of the remaining four. ISO 9001 is the most comprehensive, and includes design development and servicing capabilities in addition to the elements contained in ISO 9002. ISO 9002 includes the basic elements of quality assurance, such as management responsibility, control systems review, and training, as well as the quality control elements contained in ISO 9003. ISO 9003 relates to finished product quality control, and includes detection and control of defective product during final inspection and testing. ISO 9004 contains guidance for producers to develop quality management systems, and addresses, among other things, product liability and safety issues. Each of these documents is self contained: it can be used alone, or it can be used in combination with one or more of the others.

Quality system specifications contained in ISO 9001 have been adapted, on an international basis, to medical devices. The FDA, which has published a proposed rule[188] to revise its medical device GMP regulations to ensure compatibility with quality systems specifications contained in ISO 9001, has begun looking at how the ISO 9000 Standard Series can make a useful contribution in other product areas regulated by the agency. A meeting of FDA officials was held on December 5, 1994, with invited speakers from the Registrar Accreditation Board, ANSI, and the U.S. Technical Advisory Group to ISO Technical Committee 176.[189] As stated above, the European Commission has adopted the CEN standard, EN 46000, that adapts ISO-9001 to medical devices.

Inspections, Quality System Audits, and Compliance

It is important that industry implementation of GMPs be monitored to ensure compliance. Essential elements of a monitoring program include written inspectional programs, an appropriate infrastructure, established inspectional cycles, appropriate training of inspectors, proper inspectional and support equipment, and adequate resources. Inspection reports that contain adequate information to make possible a determination of appropriate follow-up action also are crucial.

These activities may be carried out either by government inspectors, by qualified "third party" (private sector) inspectors, or a combination of the two. In the EU, a system is in

---

[187] *Id*. The FDA published the proposed rule in the *Federal Register* on November 23, 1993 (58 Fed. Reg. 61,952) and a working draft of the final rule on July 24, 1995 (60 Fed. Reg. 37,856). The agency also held both a public meeting and an advisory committee meeting on the draft to provide additional opportunities for public input.

[188] 61 Fed. Reg. 52,601, (Oct. 7, 1996).

[189] An article that discusses the ISO 9000 Standards, their use globally, the FDA's enforcement of quality system/control requirements, and the compatibility of the FDA's requirements with the requirements of the ISO 9000 Standard Series was published in 5 Reg. Aff. 1 (1993).

place that extensively uses third-party auditors. Other nations are interested in the EU "Conformity-assessment"[190] approach because it can be implemented without the same investment in infrastructure that traditional food and drug systems have required. (At this early stage in implementation of the EU Directives, it is unknown whether this approach will be successful, with the greatest controversy surrounding high-risk products.)

In the United States, GMP inspectors historically have been government employees, with no private sector involvement. The FDA, however, currently is considering whether companies with good inspectional records could be audited by private-sector third parties in lieu of routine FDA inspections.[191]

Third-party auditors are active in the United States in auditing companies' ISO-9001 activities. Because U.S. device GMPs now incorporate the features of ISO-9001, these private-sector auditors, although not accredited by the FDA, in effect have become a supplement to FDA's inspection system. It is important, therefore, to promote an understanding of what FDA inspectors look for, so that ISO quality system auditors can look for compliance with the FDA's GMP requirements. The goal is to reduce the incidence of situations where an establishment in ISO compliance is found out-of-compliance with FDA requirements, by enhancing the ability of ISO registrars to look for violations.

Despite the increasingly broad reach of ISO 9000-based GMPs, there remains a wide divergence in how different regulatory systems approach not only inspections or audits to oversee compliance with these requirements, but also the needed followup. In the last several years, the FDA has had an active program of inspections and enforcement actions to ensure compliance with its existing GMP requirements.[192] Few, if any, national regulators bring as many enforcement actions against domestic firms or detain imports from foreign firms due to failure to follow GMPs or other requirements as does the FDA.

■ Product Removal Authority

All countries should have mechanisms for removing problematic products from the market.[193]

■ Product Evaluation

Another important area concerns harmonization of testing requirements by means of collaboration on testing guidelines between EU experts (Commission and Member State representatives), and their counterparts in the FDA and other developed countries. The princi-

---

[190] "Conformity assessment" is a European term that is creeping into general usage. The term encompasses not only testing and inspections by government inspectors, but also tests and audits done by various third-party "regulators," i.e., testing laboratories, certification and laboratory accreditation bodies, and quality system registrars.

[191] This is an outgrowth of the FDA's new effort to define required qualifications, as part of a new inspector certification program.

[192] A highly publicized example is an FDA enforcement action in 1994 resulting in a consent decree of permanent injunction against Siemens, a German-based multinational company that is the second-largest medical device manufacturer in the world. In the consent decree, the company agreed to comply in the future with all GMP, adverse experience reporting, and premarket notification requirements. United States v. Siemens Medical Sys., Civ. No. 94-912 (D.N.J. 1994) (consent decree of permanent injunction entered Mar. 23, 1994).

[193] *See* LEGISLATIVE CONCEPTS, *supra* note 33.

pal fora for such collaboration are the GHTF; an ISO committee on medical devices (TC-210); and various other standards committees under the auspices of the ISO, CEN, and ANSI and standards development groups.

■ Product Standards

Voluntary standards — which increasingly are international standards — play an important role in medical device harmonization. The FDA's overall standards policy, published in 1995,[194] includes a brief summary of the FDA's standards activities.

For more detailed information on standards activities, the following sources are particularly recommended: for device standards activities, the Center for Devices and Radiological Health publishes an annual report on its standards activities, including names of committees, what standards they are developing, and FDA participants.[195] Reports of annual meetings of AAMI are an excellent source of "inside information" on the workings of particular committees.[196] ANSI is the principal source for copies of standards in the United States, and provides a diverse array of information, training, and assistance to manufacturers, government agencies, and others interested in standards. Finally, the NIST publishes many useful compilations in this area,[197] and provides services to those in search of information about standards.

Private sector efforts to voluntarily standardize certain aspects of their products, and to provide a contractual basis for suppliers to assure purchasers a safe and quality product, increasingly are adopted by governments as regulatory standards. Accordingly, many private sector efforts may now form a basis for a certain degree of governmental standardization. In the United States, for example, the SMDA[198] paved the way for the incorporation of voluntary standards into FDA regulations and guidance documents by allowing special controls other than mandatory performance standards to address safety and effectiveness concerns about Class II devices. As was discussed above, the EU also has enacted legislation that relies on voluntary standards, and other countries are following suit.

The FDA has had extensive involvement with standards in its regulation of medical devices, as well as electronic products that emit radiation. Voluntary standards committees are an excellent example of industry-government partnership that enhances public protection. The investment that the agency makes in standards work — by sending its experts to play an active role in a few hundred activities — pays dividends in improved public protection.

---

[194] 60 Fed. Reg. 53,078 (Oct. 11, 1995).

[195] *See, e.g.*, FOOD & DRUG ADMIN., CENTER FOR DEVICES & RADIOLOGICAL HEALTH, STANDARDS ANNUAL REPORT (1995).

[196] *See, e.g.*, Association for the Advancement of Medical Instrumentation, 1994 International Standards Conference on Medical Devices: International Standards and Regulatory Harmonization Conference Report, Arlington, VA (1994).

[197] *See, e.g.*, NATIONAL INST. OF STANDARDS & TECH., STANDARDS ACTIVITIES OF ORGANIZATIONS IN THE UNITED STATES, SPECIAL PUB. 806 (1996).

[198] Pub. L. No. 101-629, 104 Stat. 4511.

These activities bring together the best minds in industry, academia, clinical practice, and government from all over the world. FDA experts and U.S. private-sector experts are full players. Setting a voluntary standard benefits industry through reduced inconsistency in public and private requirements. The interaction that frequently occurs between the Center for Devices and Radiological Health officials and members of the manufacturing and health care communities during the standards development process, provides knowledge and insight into the use of products, problems, and the effectiveness of solutions. Frequently, public discussion of a problem that occurs in the consensus-building process results in manufacturers and users of a medical device implementing the solution before a standard is formally completed.

In an April 1995 program review, the Center reported that in 1994, 192 Center staff members served as primary and alternate liaison representatives on 440 committees and subcommittees in 38 standards developing organizations (domestic and foreign). The Center has reviewed 286 draft standards; of these, 134 were being developed by nine international standards organizations.

The Center has encouraged participation in the development of standards as a useful adjunct to regulatory controls. Some standards used by the agency are useful to the industry and to FDA reviewers in the review of premarket approval applications, some complement GMPs in such areas as sterility control, and others concern measurement or test methods.

■ Clinical Evaluation

The FDA is a world leader in approval decisions on medical devices. In many countries, the most important factor in a nation's decision on whether to admit a medical device to market is whether the FDA has approved the product. The table earlier in this chapter shows how a number of other countries require testing of selected products.

As discussed above, the GHTF recently began an initiative on harmonizing format for submission of device testing requirements. This activity will facilitate efforts to increase harmonization of device testing requirements in a manner similar to the International Conference for the Technical Requirements for the Registration of Pharmaceuticals for Human Use.

To date, international and national voluntary standards organizations have been the international vehicles for harmonizing nonclinical and clinical testing requirements for medical devices, and for standardizing recurring product characteristics.

Biocompatibility is an important issue for medical devices. Since the 1970s, ISO/Technical Committee 150 on Surgical Implants has been issuing standards on metallic, plastic, and ceramic materials. Standards have been issued on biological evaluation of medical devices/guidance for selection of tests; tests for genotoxicity, carcinogenicity, and reproductive toxicity; selection of tests for interactions with blood; tests for cytotoxicity/*in vitro* methods; tests for local effects after implantation; and degradation of materials related to biological testing.[199] One of the criteria for acceptance of the Technical Com-

---

[199] ISO 10993-1, 3, 4, 5, 6, 9.

mittee 150 standards is that there have been no reported instances of serious biocompatibility problems.[200]

One area of controversy is that in the relevant CEN technical committees, some members have proposed that for new materials there should be requirements that such materials have been rigorously tested in accordance with new biocompatibility tests laid down by ISO/Technical Committee 194. The Technical Committee 150 standard materials, however, were not all submitted to such tests. Materials that through long use in humans are believed to be adequately biocompatible, but have had untoward reactions have led to many changes in the composition of materials listed in this standard.

Among CEN committees active in topics related to clinical evaluation are CEN 206 dealing with biocompatibility, CEN 258 that produced a standard on clinical investigations, and CEN 285 on surgical implants.

The FDA uses the workproduct of voluntary standards groups by referring to them in guidance documents that the agency makes available to the public on permissible (but nonmandatory) approaches to the development and testing of medical devices. There are more than 300 references to completed consensus standards (and selected sections of additional draft standards that are not yet complete), in 195 FDA guidance documents for applications for conducting clinical trials with investigational devices and for permitting devices to be marketed.[201] These guidance documents are widely disseminated by the Center for Devices and Radiological Health to all interested parties.

The agency also can adopt voluntary standards in regulations, such as the agency's 1997 performance standard for electrode lead wires and patient cables, which adopted the IEC 601 standard with respect to this aspect of device safety.[202]

Challenges in Harmonization and Mutual Recognition Agreements

Considering the dissimilarities between the U.S. and the EU systems, and the requirement in section 803 of the FDCA that agreements reached be consistent with the Act's requirements[203] a full MRA for medical devices is not possible at this time. Therefore, the MRA between the United States and the EU that was initialed in June 1997 focused on areas where an MRA was achievable, i.e., reliance on one another's quality systems inspections and initial assessments of premarket notifications (510(k)s). The first three years will consist of confidence-building steps that generally are considered to be an essential component of a bilateral agreement of this type. The medical device area presents unique challenges due to the fundamental differences between U.S. and EU medical device regu-

---

[200] V.H. Wheble, *supra* note 95, at 62.

[201] J. McCue, Food & Drug Admin., July 2, 1997.

[202] 62 Fed. Reg. 25,477 (May 9, 1997).

[203] 21 U.S.C. § 383.

lation. These differences make it difficult to go further than what is contemplated in the currrent MRA.

■ Type Testing Products Versus Clinically Meaningful Results

The European system looks at testing the device for conformance to a standard, whereas the United States looks for "effectiveness," understood as clinically meaningful results gauged through clinical trials involving the device. For the European system, "[n]o judgement on efficacy or effectiveness shall be carried out by the Notified Body. Once the device is found to perform as indicated, it is up to the professional judgement of the clinician to choose the right device for the patient."[204]

■ The Role of Government

A large challenge in achieving harmonization between the EU and the United States concerns the limited government involvement in Europe in decisions as to whether a product may be placed on the market. Governmental control authorities play no direct role in such decisionmaking.

The issue of mutual acceptance of inspection results also is challenging to the United States, because European inspections of manufacturers are conducted by private notified bodies selected by each manufacturer. These notified bodies also review test results.

■ A Race to the Bottom?

An unresolved question is whether the marketplace competition among notified bodies to attract dossiers for European device marketing authorizations will result in a race to the top or a race to the bottom. Will manufacturers seek out strong ("gold standard") or weak bodies for reviews? Could increased workload or market competition press tougher reviewers into letting devices go on the market after insufficient scrutiny?

■ Conflict of Interest

Conflicts of interest need to be addressed because the FDA's rules are stricter than those of the EU, and EU notified bodies sometimes perform other services such as consulting.

■ Medical Device Reporting

The success of mutual recognition will depend on a high quality system for collection of adverse event information, an essential element of a system in which premarket approval authority is as diffused as it is in Europe. Although several Member States have passed laws for mandatory or voluntary reporting, a comprehensive EU-wide adverse event reporting system is still being implemented.

---

[204] D. Pirovano, *Developments in the European Community, in* C.W.D. VAN GRUTING, *supra* note 35, at 218 (referring to the Active Implantable Medical Device Directive).

■ Enforcement Differences

Despite the substantial harmony between the EU's quality system standard, EN 46000, and the FDA's final rule for device GMPs,[205] there is considerable difference in the regulatory approaches of the United States and the EU for inspections or audits to oversee compliance with these requirements and response to findings of noncompliance.

■ The Desirability of Harmonization

The current concept of an MRA is an agreement that enables parties with nonharmonized systems to carry out, on behalf of the other, a review of a product in accordance with the other's requirements. This idea of reciprocal commitments avoids some problems, but creates others. For example, the desire to save resources by minimizing duplicative testing requirements will not be met if there is not an effort to harmonize testing requirements.

■ Concern about Unequal Benefit

EU negotiators have been concerned that European industry would not benefit from an MRA focused on exchange of quality systems audit results as much as U.S. industry would, because the FDA would continue to require additional premarket review (beyond the quality certification) for a larger group of devices than would the EU. For example, FDA authorization for medical devices certifies product quality, safety, and efficacy. The EU-wide medical device authorization certifies only quality and safety.

■ FDA Concern That Pilot Program Is Only a Pilot

FDA negotiators insisted that the agreement do nothing to impede its ability to terminate the third-party pilot program for 510(k) reviews, if the program did not meet expectations.[206]

Export-Related Activities

■ Policy

Export law governing FDA-regulated products has involved a balancing of two goals: 1) ensuring that U.S. manufacturers do not market unsafe products in foreign countries, and 2) promoting U.S. exports and maintaining U.S. competitiveness in the international mar-

---

[205] 61 Fed. Reg. 52,602 (Oct. 7, 1996).

[206] Letter to the Honorable Leon Brittan, European Comm., from Stuart Eizenstat, Undersecretary of Commerce (June 14, 1997).

ketplace. The issue of exports of devices not allowed to be used in the United States has been less contentious than the issue of exports of unapproved drugs.[207]

■ Statutory Provisions

Compliant Products

A food, drug, device, or cosmetic that fully meets FDA requirements may be exported with no additional controls.[208] This remains the law in all cases although the requirements of the importing country must be met.

Basic Scheme

In general, according to the basic scheme in the 1938 Act,[209] a food, drug, device, or cosmetic that does not meet FDA requirements may be exported if all of the following requirements are met:

(1) it accords to the specifications of the foreign purchaser,

(2) it is not in conflict with the laws of the country to which it is intended for export,

(3) it is labeled on the outside of the shipping package that it is intended for export, and

(4) it is not sold or offered for sale in domestic commerce.[210]

Medical Device Amendments and Section 801(e)

Under provisions added by the 1976 Medical Device Amendments,[211] still found in present law, devices that must undergo premarket approval for U.S. marketing, but that lack such approval, are eligible for export if, in addition to the four general requirements described above, "the [Commissioner] has determined that the exportation of the device is not contrary to the public health and safety[212] and has the approval of the country to which

---

[207] The Senate-passed version (S. 510, 120 CONG. REC. 1798 (1974)) of the Medical Device Amendments included a "sleeper" provision that would have relaxed the ban then in effect on export of unapproved new drugs to conform it to the proposed approach for medical devices (the provision now found in section 801(e)). S. 510, 93d Cong., 2d Sess. 120 CONG. REC. 1798 (1974). After a consumer organization discovered the drafted provision, it persuaded the House and Senate conferees to delete the drug export provisions but did not object to the same policy being applied to devices. The conference report explained that the bill was medical device legislation, not drug legislation. H.R. REP. NO. 1090, 94th Cong., 2d Sess. (1976). Ten years passed before Congress enacted legislation to allow exports of unapproved drugs to certain listed countries, Drug Export Amendments Act of 1986, Pub. L. No. 99-660, 100 Stat. 3743 (codified at 21 U.S.C. § 382; 42 U.S.C. §§ 241, 262). Further export liberalization was achieved for both drugs and devices, in the FDA Export Reform and Enhancement Act of 1996, Pub. L. No. 104-134, 110 Stat. 1321 (codified at 21 U.S.C. §§ 334, 381, 382; 42 U.S.C. § 262).

[208] *See* Lesley R. Frank, Gregory H. Levine & William W. Vodra, *Exportation of Medical Devices, in* BASIC OUTLINES ON MEDICAL DEVICE LAW AND REGULATION (FDLI 1997).

[209] 21 U.S.C. § 381(d) (now 21 U.S.C. § 381(e)).

[210] *Id.* § 381(e)(1).

[211] Pub. L. No. 94-295, 90 Stat. 539 (1976).

[212] The issue arose immediately whether the "public health" was that of the United States or that of the receiving country. Michael F. Cole, *Import and Export of Medical Devices,* 34 FOOD DRUG COSM. L.J. 140, 141 (1979). The FDA concluded that U.S. public health was what was intended.

it is intended for export."[213] The FDA requires a letter from the receiving country and basic safety data on the device (either in an investigational device permit or in the export request).

FDA Export Reform and Enhancement Act

In 1996, Congress amended U.S. medical device law regarding export of drugs and medical devices. For devices that may not be sold in the United States, the 1996 FDA Export Reform and Enhancement Act:[214]

(1) amended section 801 of the Act to make it easier to import component parts, accessories, or other articles of a device, if those component parts, accessories, or other articles are intended for incorporation or further processing by the initial owner or consignee into a device that will be exported under section 801(e) or section 802 of the Act, or section 351(h) of the PHS Act;

(2) amended section 801 of the Act to permit export of devices under section 801(e) of the Act or under section 802 of the Act; and

(3) replaced section 802 of the Act in its entirety with a new section 802 of the Act that:

— eliminated the requirement for prior FDA approval for exports with respect to devices approved in a listed country, no matter where in the world the devices were destined for export;

— eliminated the requirement for prior FDA approval for exports (for devices destined for clinical investigations in a listed country);

— created an administrative mechanism for the addition of countries to the list or for the FDA to approve exports of specific products to unlisted countries;

— authorized exports of unapproved devices intended for use in clinical investigations in any of twenty-five countries identified in section 802;

— authorized the export of unapproved devices to a listed country in anticipation of marketing approval in that country;

— created a simple notification process for exported devices (as opposed to the application process under section 801(e)(2) of the Act) (notification is not required for devices exported for investigational use to a listed country or devices exported in anticipation of marketing authorization in the listed country); and

— authorized the FDA to permit the export of unapproved devices intended to treat tropical diseases or other diseases that are "not of significant prevalence in the United States."

---

[213] 21 U.S.C. § 381(e)(2). This provision also applies to export of devices that do not comply with applicable requirements of performance standards under section 360d, that are banned devices under section 360f, or that are investigational devices under section 360j(g).

[214] Pub. L. No. 104-134, 110 Stat. 1321 (1996), as amended by Pub. L. No. 104-180, 110 Stat. 1594 (1996).

■ Export Certificates

Firms exporting medical devices often ask the FDA to supply an export certificate (sometimes called a certificate of free sale) for use in obtaining marketing authorizations in other countries. A 1994 FDA Compliance Policy Guide[215] and Center for Devices and Radiological Health guidance documents describe the procedure for requesting these certificates. The FDA Export Reform and Enhancement Act has provided for user fees for export certificates for drugs and devices, provided that the FDA issues them within twenty days.[216]

■ Administrative Streamlining of Exports

Even before the 1996 Export Act, the FDA undertook several initiatives in response to industry concerns about timely export clearances:

- The average turnaround time was decreased from sixty-five days to ten days.[217]
- In the Administration's 1995 *Report on Reinventing Drug and Device Regulation*, the FDA announced its interest in both administrative and legislative streamlining of the export requirements.[218]
- In 1995, the FDA published a proposed rule that would deregulate exports of unapproved devices to countries having a regulatory system.[219] After the enactment of the 1996 Export Act, the FDA determined that the rulemaking was no longer needed and withdrew the proposal.

■ Trade Activities

The FDA has been involved in U.S. Trade Representative and Commerce Department discussions with several countries, including Japan, Korea, and Taiwan, about the scientific or other testing requirements that these countries have proposed or adopted.Government-led regional initiatives such as the Asia Pacific Economic Forum (APEC) are delving into medical device issues. APEC's Committee on Investment has a Subcommittee on Standards and Conformance (SCSC) that has planned seminars in Singapore in 1996 on electromagnetic capability, a subject of interest to device manufacturers and users. In 1997, the SCSC considered undertaking activities on medical devices.

Problems of Developing Countries

Distribution of medical device technology is starkly a world of haves and have-nots. In 1991, the annual per capita expenditure for medical equipment, in U.S. dollars, was $118

---

[215] 59 Fed. Reg. 46,257 (Sept. 7, 1994).

[216] The FDA published two notices to implement the export certificate provisions of the 1996 Export Act. 61 Fed. Reg. 57,444 (Nov. 6, 1996); 61 Fed. Reg. 57,555 (Nov. 6, 1996).

[217] *FDA moves to streamline device exportation rules*, 22 DEVICES & DIAGNOSTICS LETTER, Nov. 3, 1995, at 4.

[218] NATIONAL PERFORMANCE REVIEW, REINVENTING DRUG AND DEVICE REGULATION, 5, 25-26 (1995).

[219] 60 Fed. Reg. 58,308 (Nov. 27, 1995).

in the United States, $53 in the European Union, $12 in Asia, and less than $1 in Subsaharan Africa.[220] Production and consumption are concentrated in a few countries. In 1992 the United States produced 47% and consumed 42% of the total ($70.9 billion), EU countries produced 26% and consumed 26%, Japan produced 18% and consumed 17%, Canada produced 2% and consumed 3%, Australia produced 1% and consumed 1%, and all remaining countries produced 6% and consumed 10%.[221] Developed countries, which account for approximately 23% of the world's population, consume 90% of its medical devices.[222]

At the request of the WHO, in 1996 an FDA expert prepared a report on a global approach to medical devices with particular attention to the problems of developing countries. International discussions of medical devices are dominated by a few affluent countries, while others face confounding choices in selecting medical devices from the many available. Although meaningful evaluation by health agencies in those countries might begin with a determination of the device's approval status, other factors such as the appropriateness of the device are also important:

> The rapid growth of technology markets has led in some countries to a certain degree of misuse. Low-volume, high-cost health technology often absorbs an unduly large proportion of health resources and, consequently, other health programmes of a higher priority suffer. In many countries, indiscriminate use of high technology means sophisticated medicine for the few and poor quality or no care for the great majority.[223]

A related factor is that the U.S. regulatory system separates certain health care product decisions in ways that many other countries do not.

Health Care Economic Regulation of Medical Devices

Health care system regulation of medical devices consists of a set of issues on the periphery of the FDA's responsibility, and yet are as crucial to medical device utilization as regulatory agency decisions.[224] Of particular interest to manufacturers is whether health care system reimbursement or purchase of the device will be allowed, and whether its use will be reimbursed. Health care management institutions (government agencies, hospitals, and other health providers) want to know whether the device is cost effective, including the costs for purchase, operation, and maintenance.

---

[220] A. Issakov, *Health care equipment: a WHO perspective*, in C.W.D. VAN GRUTING, *supra* note 35, at 3.

[221] U.S. Industrial Outlook 1992, Med. Dental Instrum. Supplies 1992; 45: 1-10.

[222] A. Issakov, *Service and maintenance in developing countries*, in C.W.D. VAN GRUTING, *supra* note 35, at 21.

[223] *Id.*

[224] Christa Altenstetter, City University of New York, Regulating healthcare technologies and medical supplies: a comparative overview, presented at the Fourth Biennial International Conference of the European Community Studies Association, Charleston, N.C. (May 11-14, 1995).

Despite their contribution to health care, some devices' complexity and cost force difficult choices in *all* countries, not only as to whether safety, effectiveness, and quality warrant market entry, but also as to whether they have a place in a country's health care system. Even in the highly decentralized and heterogeneous health care system in the United States, reimbursement decisions of the Health Care Financing Administration and private health care providers can make or break a product, almost as effectively as a decision against approval by an FDA-type agency. For example, the FDA may approve a device that is safe and effective but that costs much more than an already marketed device. In the absence of clear evidence that the newly approved device is markedly superior to the older product, the procurement and reimbursement agencies and insurance companies might pay for the device, refuse to pay, or set the reimbursable amount at the cost of the cheaper device, as the "reasonable and necessary" cost. Decisionmaking on medical technology payment issues has become increasingly contentious in the United States, and debates over health care policy have taken note of the fact that the United States leads the world not only in medical device production and consumption but also in per capita health care costs.

In public policy toward medical devices, the U.S. system draws distinctions that many other countries do not draw among regulatory decisions; health care delivery, procurement, and utilization issues; and industrial development and trade matters. Other countries more closely coordinate public health regulatory issues with health care delivery, so that marketing authorization is linked to reimbursement authorization. Other countries also have industrial policies that nurture health technology. Japan is the most widely known example.

For developing countries and middle income countries, the most important decisions on medical devices might be described best as "health care cost-effectiveness decisionmaking" as opposed to FDA-style risk-benefit decisionmaking. In today's world marketplace, it is often quite easy for hospitals, attracted to the latest technology, to order devices with no government intervention, by making direct contacts with company representatives (local or in the manufacturing country). Some of these sales undoubtedly have resulted in rapid diffusion of the latest health care innovations and have saved lives. Others, however, have strapped the purchasers with ongoing maintenance costs that cause reallocation of scarce health care resources from other areas of greater need.[225]

> The pressing problem now seen in almost every developing country is not merely the substantial burden of equipment that is inappropriate to the country's health priorities, but the even greater amount of equipment that is appropriate and could contribute to the country's health goals but lies idle due to the inappropriate management of its introduction to the country. In many developing countries, the most obvious symptom is not the lack of medical equipment but the presence of equipment, sometimes more than 50%, that is not usable or not used.[226]

In response to the rapid diffusion of high technology devices without corresponding consideration of how they fit into the health care environment, the concept of "appropriateness" evolved. After the controversy associated with its essential drugs list, (discussed in the chapter on drug international harmonization), the WHO has not established an "essen-

---

[225] *See generally,* A. Issakov, *supra* note 224.
[226] *Id.* at 4.

tial devices list" but has taken many other steps to improve the information available to national decisionmakers about the selection of health care technology.

The term "appropriate technology" has come to acquire a certain meaning in international discussions of medical device issues:

> [A]ppropriate technology is health care technology that is appropriate to use in a specific-use environment and that considers that nation's or region's predominating diseases and public health and economic priorities. Classically, this term carried the implication of indiscriminate transplantation of sophisticated Western medical technology to relatively poor developing nations that had very different health priorities.[227]

International Influence on U.S. Congressional Deliberations

In the mid-1990s, reform of U.S. medical device regulation became the subject of heated debate, with many administrative and legislative ideas under active review as this volume went to press. Proposals for change based upon European models should be mentioned. Many U.S. manufacturers are supporters of the EU approach to device regulation,[228] and the EU medical device system initially attracted the attention of some U.S. lawmakers as a possible approach for the United States.

In the executive branch, the President's and Vice President's National Performance Review *Reinventing Drug and Device Regulation*, issued in April 1995, included the development of a pilot program for review of low-risk medical devices by outside review organizations to determine if such a system could be developed permanently.[229]

In Congress, initiatives have ranged from non-controversial provisions to streamline acceptance of international device standards, to provisions compelling use of third-party reviewers even for high-risk products (in some versions without FDA review of third-party decisions), to "hammer provisions" that would require the FDA, if a device is marketed in the EU or the United Kingdom, to allow its marketing in the United States unless it published a notice by a specified time. In 1995-1996, strong Administration opposition to the compelled use of third-party reviewers and to the hammer caused support to wane for these ideas. In addition, a report from the General Accounting Office found that it is too soon to determine the possible value in the United States of the EU approach to medical devices.[230]

---

[227] J. Nobel, *supra* note 35, at 9.

[228] *See, e.g.*, Robert G. Britain, *Which Way FDA? Looking to Europe: FDA Could Benefit from Europe's Device Review Model*, 17 MEDICAL DEVICE & DIAGNOSTIC INDUS., Nov. 1995, at 24.

[229] *Id.* at 5, 20-21. This is a domestic policy initiative of interest internationally due to EU reliance upon private sector review bodies for devices generally.

[230] U.S. GENERAL ACC'G OFF., REPORT MEDICAL DEVICE REGULATION: TOO EARLY TO ASSESS EUROPEAN SYSTEM'S VALUE AS MODEL FOR FDA (1996).

Conclusion

One might think that because medical device regulation is a fairly new phenomenon, it would lend itself more easily to harmonization than would food and drug regulation with their longstanding legal practices and national traditions.[231] Yet, that is not the case. In fact, in no other field under the FDA's purview is there such a wide divergence among international regulatory models as in the medical device field. Although the FDA's pioneering medical device regulatory system has been influential internationally in many respects — classification, limitation of approval requirements to high-risk products, attention to GMPs and other fundamentals such as biomaterials, and treating *in vitro* diagnostics as devices rather than as drugs — many other countries have found it too ambitious and costly to emulate the U.S. system in the way that they have copied the FDA's food and drug regulatory systems.

Although resource constraints prevent many countries from adopting an FDA approach to devices, their leaders nevertheless hold that the FDA's medical device regulatory system is the most respected in the world. The status of a product in the United States matters to officials in other countries. In addition, when other countries have developed a useful solution to a problem, the FDA derives a benefit from learning about alternative approaches, e.g., the third-party pilot program.

For all of the above reasons, the FDA's international activities in the area of medical devices probably will intensify in coming years, and will lead to further consideration of successful global approaches to ensuring the safety and effectiveness of medical devices.

---

[231] While medical device regulation is a 20th century phenomenon, food regulation is as old as recorded history and drug regulation dates back to at least the Middle Ages.

Index

■ H